All too often people miss out on good movies simply be̶... ...em by black and white photography, subtitles or a glut of special effects. The **BLOOMSBURY GOOD MOVIE GUIDE** offers directions and suggestions to ensure cinema-goers and TV and video watchers alike can enjoy and better understand the best in world cinema. It assesses thousands of movies, providing a fresh look at old favourites, as well as springing some surprises, and gives profiles of hundreds of influential film people from both sides of the camera. Extensive cross-referencing and a comprehensive index complement the suggestions for further watching (*View Ons*) from the individual entries and the 20 diagrammatic networks that take you from a key film to a wide range of connected films – *Marie Antoinette* starring Norma Shearer, for example, leads to *Gone With The Wind*, *Some Like It Hot*, *Annie Hall* and *sex, lies and videotape*.

This up-to-date and authoritative guide is completed by over 80 movie 'menus' listing films linked by subject and theme.

With an unrivalled combination of English and foreign-language pictures, and details and concise summaries of over 5,000 films, each rated according to the quality of direction, acting, script, cinematography, score or special effects, the **BLOOMSBURY GOOD MOVIE GUIDE** offers an excellent introduction to international cinema and plenty to stimulate the film buff.

David Parkinson is 29 and watches more films than are good for him.

To Peter,

Happy Christmas 1991

love

Annie xx

David Parkinson

Bloomsbury
Good Movie Guide

B L O O M S B U R Y

First published in Great Britain 1990
This paperback edition published 1991

Copyright © David Parkinson 1990
Bloomsbury Publishing Limited, 2 Soho Square, London W1V 5DE

The moral right of the author has been asserted

British Library Cataloguing in Publication Data

A CIP catalogue record for this book
is available from the British Library

ISBN 0 7475 0968 9

1 3 5 7 9 10 8 6 4 2

Designed by Malcolm Smythe

Typeset by Discript, London

Printed in Great Britain by Clays Ltd, St Ives plc

For everyone who has sat through a movie with me

Contents

Introduction   ix

Entries A–Z   1
including special viewing 'skeins'

An American in Paris   12
The Big Heat   42
The Birth of a Nation   46
Fantasia   116
The Freshman   128
The Harder They Fall   152
In the Heat of the Night   172
Krakatoa, East of Java   192
Man Made Monster/The Electric Man   218
Marie Antoinette   222
My Darling Clementine   240
Oh What a Lovely War   254
Raiders of the Lost Ark   302
She Done Him Wrong   330
Star Wars   344
Tom Jones   364
Umberto D   376
The Wicked Lady   398
Yankee Doodle Dandy   406
Zéro de Conduite   410

Title index   413

Name and theme index   449

Everyone likes a good movie.

This book is intended to help the casual viewer make the best choice when deciding what to watch on TV or hire from the local video shop and guide film buffs to some of the interesting features that do the rounds of film clubs and arts cinemas.

The films themselves are the important thing and it has been my aim throughout to be brief, using one-line summaries to whet the appetite. There is little or no film trivia included – what there is has been ruthlessly rounded up and confined to this box:

- Humphrey Bogart and John Wayne wore toupées

- Two alternative endings were filmed for *Casablanca*, which was originally to have starred Ronald Reagan and Ann Sheridan

- Clark Gable was recorded as a girl on his birth certificate, and his eating a carrot in *It Happened One Night* inspired cartoonist Bob Clampett to create Bugs Bunny

- Gable was on Goering's 'Most Wanted' list, but Greta Garbo was Hitler's favourite actress

- Vivien Leigh's estate, Tara, is destroyed by fire in *Gone with the Wind*, but the set that was burned came from *King Kong*, the finale of which was originally set in Grand Central Station as opposed to atop the Empire State

- Howard Hawks was US Junior Tennis Champion in 1914, Katharine Hepburn won the Connecticut State Golf Championship at the age of 16, and Michael Curtiz fenced for Hungary at the 1912 Olympics

- Master of suspense Alfred Hitchcock was knighted

- Emil Jannings only won the inaugural Best Actor Oscar after the Academy decided not to award it to canine superstar Rin Tin Tin, who had polled the most votes

- Marilyn Monroe was the model for Tinkerbell in Disney's *Peter Pan*

- James Stewart keeps all the hats he wears in his films

- Billy Wilder wanted to open *Sunset Boulevard* with a tracking shot along a row of corpses in a morgue, one of which, William Holden, would sit up and explain what he is doing there

The rest is simply essential information about essential viewing.

EXPLANATORY NOTES

Inclusion of movies
There are over 6,000 films included in this book. They have been selected simply because they are worth watching – 150 of them are particularly recommended, either because they are accepted classics, or because they are personal favourites – or both. This selectivity ensures the exclusion of the pulp that clutters up more encyclopaedic tomes. An arrow (>) in front of a film title indicates that the film has its own main entry.

Dating from Georges Méliès' 1902 *A Trip to the Moon* to those on general release in December 1989, and drawn from all over the world, the movies range from slapstick comedies to surrealist experiments, European art films to Hollywood musicals.

Arrangement of movies
They have been arranged:

- in 'menus' which deal with films according to subject or theme

- in 'skeins', which can best be described as film family trees

- within the individual entries on actors, actresses, or directors

- in 'View ons' – which lead on from the themes or action of one of the 150 classic films or which list a selection of other noteworthy films made by the subject of an entry, thus enabling Viewers to follow up movies which have especially interested them.

All films have, at the very least, a one-line synopsis, giving details of plot, stars, awards won, or other pertinent facts; are listed in the Index and cross-referenced either by title, director or subject matter to give the fullest breadth of precise, relevant information. Seemingly many casual Viewers are put off a movie because it was filmed in black and white, runs for over 90 mintues or is in a foreign language. Consequently details of running times, film stock and country/studio of of origin have been largely excluded from the general entries, thus freeing the movies from popular prejudices and allowing them to stand on their own merit.

How to find a film

While most guides simply list films alphabetically, leaving them in rather inglorious isolation, the aim of this unique book is to show the relationship of films of every nationality and collect them according to subject and key personnel.

Consequently, the first place to look for a movie is in the Index – each page reference leading the Viewer to a new aspect of the plot or a fresh fact about the film.

Should someone be overcome with a desire to discover all the book has to tell about, for example, *The Best Years of Our Lives*, a glance at the Index will take them to an entry on the film itself, to entries on two of its stars Myrna Loy and Fredric March, its director William Wyler, its theme of 'picking up the pieces' and on its performance at the 1946 Oscar Ceremony.

Titles

Where movies have more than one title, the one currently used in the UK is listed as the main entry, while alternatives (usually the titles by which they were known in the UK or the US at the time of their release) are given in brackets. Similarly, foreign language films are included according to the title by which they are known in the UK, with original foreign titles, US and other alternatives (aka) listed in subsequent brackets.

Ratings

Movies are reviewed according to the quality of their:

- ☞ – direction
- ☆ – acting
- ✍ – screenplay
- ▨ – cinematography
- ♫ – soundtrack
- ✳ – special effects

Any of these symbols may appear in brackets after a film title and indicate that this is what is particularly recommended about the film.

Abbreviations

The following abbreviations are used:

- AA – Academy Award
- AAN – Academy Award nomination
- d – director
- m – music
- ph – cinematographer
- w – screenwriter

Film folk

The 150+ directors, actors and actresses included as main entries in the text have been chosen because of their influence on international cinema. If at all possible, examples of their work are represented in the 150 'reviewed' films. There are many personalities, such as Ettore Scola, Claudette Colbert and David Niven who had a strong case for inclusion – maybe next time – but I have had to be strict and while indulging my love of Laurel & Hardy, William Powell and Myrna Loy, I resisted an entry on such personal favourites as Nathalie Baye, even though she stars in one of the featured films, *The Return of Martin Guerre*. An arrow (>) in front of someone's name indicates that he or she is featured as a main entry.

Acknowledgements

My thanks to everyone who has helped and encouraged me during the writing of this book, particularly Kathy Rooney, Sian Facer and Kate Newman at Bloomsbury and Robyn Karney and Nancy Duin for their suggestions at the editorial stage.

My special thanks, however, go to all those who made these marvellous movies.

David Parkinson

À Bout de Souffle (Breathless)

☞ ☆ ▦

France • SNC • 1960 • 90 mins • b/w
**wd >Jean-Luc Godard　ph Raoul
Coutard　m Martial Solal
>Jean-Paul Belmondo, Jean Seberg**

This masterpiece of young *Cahiers du Cinéma* critic Jean-Luc Godard heralded the arrival of the *Nouvelle Vague* (New Wave) in French cinema. Directors such as >François Truffaut, >Claude Chabrol, >Alain Resnais and Godard, heavily influenced by the Golden Age of Jean Vigo and >Jean Renoir and the Hollywood of >Alfred Hitchcock and >Howard Hawks, experimented with narrative and editing techniques to produce fast-moving tales such as this one of Michel Poiccard (Belmondo), a >Bogart devotee, who kills a policeman and is betrayed to the authorities by Patricia (Seberg), his arty American girlfriend. Jumpcutting throughout scenes to emphasize the vigour of their youth and keeping us in a constant state of uncertainty and anticipation, Godard depicted the immense excitement of 1960 Parisian life and made it respectable to be a drifter.

. Godard's film was inspired by the American 'B' movie
•*Gun Crazy* (Joseph H. Lewis 1950) (♫), while the re-make
•*Breathless* (Jim McBride 1983) has Richard Gere as a Las Vegas car thief fleeing to the coast.
•>Bogart plays the rebel in *Bullets or Ballots* (William Keighley 1936) (☆), in which cop >Edward G. Robinson infiltrates Bogie's gang.
•A revolutionary is betrayed by his homosexual lover of one night in *The Kiss of the Spiderwoman* (Hector Babenco 1985) (☆ ☞ ▦).
•Betty and Zorg are a similarly tragic offbeat couple in >*Betty Blue* (*37°2 Le Matin*) (Jean-Jacques Beineix France 1986) (☞ ☆ ▦ ♫♫).

ACADEMICS

Above Suspicion (Richard Thorpe 1943) ☆
Oxford don Fred MacMurray and wife >Joan Crawford spend their honeymoon spy-hunting.
The Decline of the American Empire (*Le Déclin de l'Empire Americain*) (Denys Arcand, Canada 1986) ☆
Highbrow discussion of French-Canadian is-

sues at a dinner party unleashes sexual revelations and political attitudes.

***Educating Rita* (Lewis Gilbert 1983)** ☆ ✍♫
Attempting to better herself through further education, Julie Walters befriends drunken academic >Michael Caine.

***Friends and Husbands* (*Heller Wahn*)
(>Margarethe Von Trotta, West Germany 1982)** ☞ ☆
Academic >Hanna Schygulla and artist Angela Winkler's domestic crises disrupt their careers.

***Half Moon Street* (Bob Swaim 1987)**
American academic Sigourney Weaver has a dangerous liaison with politician >Michael Caine.

***The Male Animal* (Elliott Nugent 1942)** ✍ ☆
Meek college professor >Henry Fonda comes out of his shell when wife >Olivia de Havilland's eye begins to roam.

***Sweet Liberty* (Alan Alda 1986)** ☆
Bob Hoskins scripts and >Michael Caine stars in a film based on historian Alda's treatise on the American Revolution.

***>Wild Strawberries* (*Smultronstället*)
(>Ingmar Bergman, Sweden 1957)** ☞ ☆ ■ ✍
Dreams and encounters transform the life of old professor Victor Sjöström.

ACADEMY AWARDS

> Oscars

ACCIDENTAL DEATH

***>A Bout de Souffle* (*Breathless*) (>Jean-Luc Godard, France 1960)** ☞ ☆ ■

***Black Orpheus* (*Orfeu Negro*) (Marcel Camus, France 1958)** ■ ♫
Tram driver seeks his girlfriend in Hell after killing her at Rio carnival.

***Death of a Cyclist* (aka *Age of Infidelity*) (*Muerte de un Ciclista*) (Juan Antonio Bardem, Spain 1955)**
A hit-and-run accident opens a sequence of tragedies for an adulterous couple.

***Hallelujah!* (>King Vidor 1929)** ☞
A black cotton worker's remorse after he commits manslaughter turns him to religion.

***The Love of Jeanne Ney* (aka *Lusts of the Flesh*) (*Die Liebe der Jeanne Ney*) (>G.W. Pabst, Germany 1927)** ☞
A German girl flees the Crimea after her Bolshevik lover shoots her diplomat father.

***Madame X* (Sam Wood 1937)** ✍
Destitute woman is unknowingly defended for murder by her son.

***Mr Denning Drives North* (Anthony Kimmins 1951)** ☆
John Mills' accidental victim's body mysteriously disappears.

***>Rebecca* (>Alfred Hitchcock 1940)** ☞ ☆ ■ ✍♫

***The Reckless Moment* (>Max Ophüls 1949)** ☞ ✍
Joan Bennett is blackmailed for accidentally killing her daughter's roguish lover.

***Smilin' Through* (Sidney Franklin 1932)** ☆
Norma Shearer, >Fredric March and >Leslie Howard suffer three generations of melodrama after a wedding-day killing.

***Twenty-One Days* (Basil Dean 1937)** ✍ ☆
>Graham Greene screenplay has lawyer >Laurence Olivier passing blame for his brother's crime on to an old eccentric.

***The Woman in the Window* (>Fritz Lang 1944)** ☆ ☞ ✍
>Edward G. Robinson covers his tracks when an unknown girl embroils him in a murder.

ACTORS AND ACTRESSES

***The Bit Part* (Brendan Maher, Australia 1987)** ☆ ✍
Australian teacher packs it in to tread the boards.

***The Dresser* (Peter Yates 1983)** ☆ ✍ ☞
Camp dresser Tom Courtenay gets tyrannical actor Albert Finney to the stage on time.

***The Goodbye Girl* (Herbert Ross 1977)** ☆ ✍♫
Single-parent Marsha Mason finds love with aspiring actor Richard Dreyfuss.

***The Great Garrick* (James Whale 1937)** ☞ ■
Brian Aherne's Garrick crosses pranks with the Comédie Française company.

The Incredible Sarah (Richard Fleischer 1976) 🖋 ☆
Glenda Jackson plays the great, ultimately one-legged, Sarah Bernhardt.
Mephisto (István Szabó, Hungary 1981) ☆ ☞ 🖋 ■
Ruthless actor Klaus Maria Brandauer spies for the Nazis to further his career.
Nobody's Fool (Evelyn Purcell 1987) ■
Rosanna Arquette's romance with Eric Roberts gives her the confidence to act.
The Rite (Riten) (>Ingmar Bergman, Sweden 1969) 🖋 ☆ ☞
Acting troupe is mercilessly pilloried during an obscenity trial.
The Royal Family Of Broadway (>George Cukor/Cyril Gardner 1930) ☞ ☆
>Fredric March got an AAN for his role in this story of a theatrical family not unlike the Barrymores.
Salut l'Artiste (Yves Robert, France 1973) ☆
Seedy sex and family lives of bit-part actor >Marcello Mastroianni.
Shakespeare Wallah (James Ivory 1965) 🖋 ■
Inter-racial love hamstrings a Shakespearian company's Indian tour.
Simon And Laura (Muriel Box 1965) ☆ 🖋
Ideal TV couple Peter Finch and Kay Kendall detest each other in real life.
Story of the Late Chrysanthemums (Zangiku Monogatari) (>Kenji Mizoguchi, Japan 1939) ☞ ■
A Kabuki actor suffers for his ineptitude marginally less than his audiences, until he finds love.

Adam's Rib 🖋 ☆ ☞ ♫
USA • MGM • 1949 • 101 mins • b/w
d >George Cukor w Ruth Gordon/Garson Kanin   ph George J. Folsey m Miklos Rozsa
>Katharine Hepburn, >Spencer Tracy, David Wayne, Tom Ewell, Judy Holliday, Jean Hagen

The combination of a Kanin/Gordon script, an all-star cast and Cukor's direction, which makes this battle of the sexes so slick, was forged because Hollywood was becoming sufficiently nervous about the coming of TV to feel the need of a sure-fire box-office hit. Adding sophistication to the Screwball Comedy and the Woman's Picture, this tale of courtroom rivalry and marital difficulty ruffled feathers with its promotion of career women and reversal of sexual stereotypes. When lawyer Amanda (Hepburn) gets an acquittal for Doris Attinger (Holliday) for shooting at her adulterous husband (Ewell), her own marriage to stubborn, sexist DA, Adam Bonner (Tracy), is jeopardized. Tears and a new hat guaranteed the reconciliation required in 1949, which seems rather unsatisfactory in slightly more enlightened times.

 •Cher plays another battling female lawyer in Suspect (Peter Yates 1987) (🖋 ☆), and Debra Winger fights her case in league with Robert Redford in Legal Eagles (Ivan Reitman 1986).
•The battle of the sexes sees Fred MacMurray and Rosalind Russell's roles reversed in Take a Letter, Darling (UK: Green-Eyed Woman) (Mitchell Leisen 1942) (☞ 🖋).
•Lawyer John Cleese is tempted off the straight and narrow in A Fish Called Wanda (Charles Crichton 1988) (☆ 🖋 ☞).
•>Meryl Streep is a female victim of the courts as the 'Dingo Baby' mother Lindy Chamberlain in A Cry in the Dark (Fred Schepisi 1988) (☆).
•Parisian doctor Maurice Chevalier's philanderings prompt a musical comedy of marriage in One Hour with You (>George Cukor/>Ernst Lubitsch 1932) (☞ ☆).

ADULTERY

All This and Heaven Too (Anatole Litvak 1940) ☆ ■
French governess >Bette Davis' love for Charles Boyer leads him to murder his wife.
The Baker's Wife (La Femme du Boulanger) (Marcel Pagnol, France 1938) 🖋 ☞ ☆
Villagers break a bread strike caused by the baker's sulk at his wife's adultery.
Betrayal (David Jones 1983) 🖋 ☆
Jeremy Irons and Patricia Hodge cuckold Ben

Kingsley in Harold Pinter's screen adaptation of his stage play.

Le Bonheur (Happiness) **(Agnès Varda, France 1965)** ✍

Man promises wife that a mistress will enrich their marriage. He is wrong and the wife drowns herself.

Cynara **(>King Vidor 1933)** ☆ ☞

Ronald Colman's affair with a young girl ends in more than just tears.

The Face of Another (Tanin No Kao) **(Hiroshi Teshigahara, Japan 1966)** ☞

A seriously disfigured scientist is accused of adultery with his own wife.

Infidelity **(aka** *The Five Day Lover***)** *(L'Amant de Cinq Jours)* **(Philippe De Broca, France 1961)** ☆

Jean Seberg has an affair with her best friend's lodger.

To Joy (Till Glädje) **(>Ingmar Bergman, 1949)** ✍ ■

Ménage among musicians causes discord in Victor Sjöström's orchestra.

ADVERTISING

Artists and Models **(>Raoul Walsh 1937)**

Ida Lupino ends Jack Benny's search for a model for his silverware promotion.

Bright Lights, Big City **(James Bridges 1988)**

Yuppiedom proves too much for Michael J. Fox (and the audience).

Hard to Handle **(>Mervyn Le Roy 1933)** ☆ ☞

>James Cagney wheels and deals in this lowlife advertising comedy.

How to Get Ahead in Advertising **(Bruce Robinson 1989)** ☆

Richard E. Grant discovers the hard knocks of the hard sell in this Dr Jekyll and Mr Boil fable.

The Hucksters **(Jack Conway 1947)** ☆ ☞

War veteran >Clark Gable struggles to satisfy the demands of his clients and his women.

Lover Come Back **(Delbert Mann 1961)** ☆

Doris Day and Rock Hudson as ad execs fighting a chaste battle of the sexes.

The Rise and Rise of Michael Rimmer **(Kevin Billington 1970)** ✍ ☆

Pythonesque British satire of the banality of publicity.

The African Queen ☆ ☞ ✍ ■

GB • IFD/Romulus-Horizon • 1951 • 103 mins • col

d >John Huston   w James Agee   ph Jack Cardiff   m Allan Gray
>Humphrey Bogart, >Katharine Hepburn

As Katharine Hepburn explains in her book *The Making of the African Queen*, John Huston's insistence on realistic locations inflicted many of the trials and tribulations faced by Rose Sayer and Charlie Allnutt in C. S. Forester's novel on herself and Humphrey Bogart. With marked similarities to *The Vessel Of Wrath* (Erich Pommer 1938), (remade as *The Beachcomber*, Muriel Box 1954), this gentle, almost effortless tale of a river journey that brings a prim missionary and a sleazy drunk through natural and wartime perils to late-in-life love was seemingly made for its stars. However, Huston initially had to coax out Bogart's Oscar-winning steamer captain and Hepburn's starchy Eleanor Roosevelt-like maid, performances that make this animosity-to-love relationship one of the screen's most charming and gripping romances.

•Another prim-and-grim romance occurs when nun Deborah Kerr falls for Robert Mitchum in *Heaven Knows Mr Allison* (>John Huston 1957) (☞ ☆).

•A great eccentric journeys down the Amazon in search of an opera venue in *Fitzcarraldo* (>Werner Herzog, West Germany 1982) (☞ ✍).

•Love comes from the adversities faced by a musical family in occupied Austria in *The Sound of Music* (Robert Wise 1965) (♫).

•>Michael Douglas and >Kathleen Turner go on a romantic adventure in *Romancing the Stone* (Robert Zemeckis 1984) (☆).

•A small sailing craft provides a delightful floating honeymoon in *L'Atalante* (Jean Vigo 1934) (☞ ■ ☆).

L'Âge d'Or (The Golden Age)
(☞ ■ ✍)
France • Vicomte de Noailles • 1930 • 63 mins • b/w

d >Luis Buñuel w Luis Buñuel/Salvador Dali ph Albert Dubergen
Gaston Modot, Lya Lys, Max Ernst, Pierre Prévert, Jacques Brunius

While the visual element of the first Buñuel/Dali collaboration *Un Chien Andalou* (*The Andalusian Dog*) (including slicing an eyeball and spiders emerging from a hole in a hand) aimed to shock, the moral content of this second exercise in surrealist cinema succeeded, as it was banned worldwide. The Establishment is mercilessly attacked throughout: the ruling classes who continue partying as a maid burns to death; a civil servant who ruthlessly pursues then neglects power; corrupt and incompetent police; and, naturally, the relic-worshipping Catholic Church. The surrealism is both erotic and hilarious, ranging from the heroine Lys sucking a statue's toes to the hero Modot pulling a cow from a bed and later throwing burning trees, giraffes and bishops from an upstairs window. As they say in book reviews, 'wickedly funny'.

 •The anti-clerical theme recurs in *El* (*This Strange Passion*) (>Luis Buñuel, Mexico 1952) (☞) in which a man's sexual jealousy drives him into a monastery.
•Surrealism and celibacy dominate *The Seashell and the Clergyman* (*La Coquille et le Clergyman*) by pioneer feminist director Germaine Dulac (France 1928) (☞).
•The Marquis de Sade's fictional perversities are translated to Mussolini's Italy in *Salo: The 120 Days of Sodom* (*Salo O Le Centiventi Giornate di Sodoma*) (>Pier Paolo Pasolini, Italy 1975) (■ ☞).
•Liberated women challenge masculinity and morality in *Wish You Were Here* (David Leland 1987) (☆) and *A Nos Amours* (*To Our Loves*) (Maurice Pialat, France 1983) (✍).
•Surrealism rears in *Head* (Bob Rafaelson 1968) (♫ ☆), starring The Monkees and co-written by the director and >Jack Nicholson and in *>Drowning By Numbers* (Peter Greenaway 1988) (✍ ☞ ☆ ♫ ■).

AGE GAP

Bachelor Knight (US: *The Bachelor and the Bobbysoxer*) (Irving Reis 1947) ☆ ✍
>Myrna Loy's young sister Shirley Temple falls for the former's boyfriend >Cary Grant.
Blanche (Walerian Borowczyk, France 1971) ■
A medieval noble fails startlingly to impose fidelity on his young wife.
Claudia (Edmund Goulding 1943) ☆ ✍
Teenage wife Dorothy McGuire grows up with the help of Robert Young.
The Company of Wolves (Neil Jordan 1984) ♫ ■
A grandmother guides a girl through werewolf nightmares and sexual awakenings.
Dodes'kaden (>Akira Kurosawa, Japan 1970) ✍ ☞
A boy and an old man shelter from extreme poverty in an imaginary house.
Girl with Green Eyes (Desmond Davis 1963) ✍ ☆
Edna O'Brien story of a Dublin girl's love for menopausal author Peter Finch.
Lovers and Other Strangers (Cy Howard 1969) ♫ ✍ ☆
Sharp adult comedy in which lovers discover that their parents have sexual hang-ups.
Paper Moon (Peter Bogdanovich 1973) ✍ ☆ ■ ☞ ♫
Ryan O'Neal uses daughter Tatum's cuteness to sell Bibles in Depressed Midwest.
Tokyo Story (*Tokyo Monogatari*) (Yasujiro Ozu, Japan 1953) ☆ ☞
Couple despair at the relentlessness of ageing after visiting their married children.

AGENTS AND DOUBLE AGENTS

Against the Wind (Charles Crichton 1947) ✍ ☞
There is a traitor in the midst of a class of trainee saboteurs.

The Four Feathers **(Lothar Mendes and others 1929)** ☆
A supposed coward restores his reputation as a secret agent.
Funeral in Berlin **(Guy Hamilton 1967)** ✍ ☆
>Michael Caine as Len Deighton's agent Harry Palmer in this Berlin defection thriller.
The Prize **(Mark Robson 1963)** ☆ ✍
>Paul Newman discovers the drawbacks of winning the Nobel Prize in a tolerable >Hitchcock homage.
The Silent One **(US:** *Escape to Nowhere***)** (*Le Silencieux*) **(Claude Pinoteau, France 1973)** ☆
Bewildering but watchable blend of ambush, kidnap and double identity.
The Spy Who Came in from the Cold **(Martin Ritt 1966)** ☆ ✍
>Richard Burton as disillusioned spy in adaptation of the John Le Carré novel.
They Got Me Covered **(David Butler 1943)** ☆ ☞
Journalist Bob Hope stumbles across espionage in the Pentagon.
The Thirty-Nine Steps **(>Alfred Hitchcock 1935)** ✍ ☞ ☆ ■
>Robert Donat is John Buchan's murder suspect Richard Hannay tracking down clues to a secret formula.
Thunderball **(Terence Young 1965)** ☆ ✍
>Sean Connery's Bond tidies up after someone carelessly allows SPECTRE to steal atom bombs.

Ai No Corrida (The Empire of the Senses (aka In the Realm of the Senses) ☞ ■ ☆ ✍

Japan • Argos/Oshima/Shibata • 1976 • 105 mins • col
wd Nagisa Oshima   ph Hideo Ito
m Minoru Miki
Tatsuya Fuji, Eiko Matsuda, Aoi Nakajima, Meika Seri

Based on a notorious murder case which scandalized society as Japan prepared to invade China in 1936, *Ai No Corrida* is as much about role reversal as >*Adam's Rib*, with Sada Abe (Matsuda) increasingly using her lover Kichizo

(Fuji) for her own pleasure; and as much about oppression as *1984* (Michael Radford 1984). However, its reputation derives from the violent pornographic scenes, which culminate in Kichizo's castration. The sensationalism should not be allowed to overshadow the beauty of the film's copious historical and cultural images. *Last Tango in Paris* (>Bernardo Bertolucci 1972) and *9½ Weeks* (Adrian Lyne 1986) might have had trouble with censors and moral crusaders, but they are family entertainment compared with Nagisa Oshima's study of sexual and political extremes. Fascinating throughout, but not one for the squeamish.

 •Oshima continued the theme in *Empire Of Passion* (aka *Phantom Love*) (*Ai No Borei*) (Japan 1978), when an old man's ghost returns to haunt the wife who killed him.
•Alan Alda is destroyed by his lust for aide >Meryl Streep in *The Seduction of Joe Tynan* (Jerry Schatzberg 1979) (☆ ✍).
•Sex relieves political tension for Daniel Day Lewis, Juliette Binoche and Lena Olin, this time in 1968 Czechoslovakia in *The Unbearable Lightness of Being* (Philip Kaufman 1988) (☆ ☞ ■ ✍).
•Jeanne Moreau is the dominant woman in *The Lovers* (*Les Amants*) (>Louis Malle, France 1958) (☞ ☆ ■).
•Another cast persuaded that 'It's art, not porn' appears in *I Am Curious – Yellow* (*Jag Ar Nyfiken Gul*) (Vilgot Sjöman, Sweden 1967).
•The Sino-Japanese War brings Pu Yi to the throne of Manchukuo as *The Last Emperor* (>Bernardo Bertolucci 1987) (■ ☞).

Alexander Nevsky ■ ☞ ♫

USSR • Mosfilm • 1938 • 112 mins • b/w
d >Sergei Eisenstein   w Pyotr Pavlenko/Sergei Eisenstein   ph Edouard Tissé   m Sergei Prokofiev
Nikolai Cherkassov, Nikolai Okhlopov, Andrei Abrikosov, Dmitri Orlov

This epic of the 13th-century prince, whose humanity and humour inspires his army to repel Swedish and German invaders, was an unashamed piece of propaganda designed to flatter Stalin and encourage the Russian people on the eve of another Teutonic invasion, but it has survived its political purpose to become one of cinema's visual splendours. There is more chance of discovering a lost >Laurel and Hardy psychological thriller than there is of finding an Eisenstein comedy, but here he is closer to portraying believable human beings than elsewhere in his *oeuvre*. The highlight is the magnificent battle on the ice, but the combination of historical finery, close-up and landscape and Prokofiev's score make this one of the most colourful black-and-white films ever made.

 •Wartime resurrected another inspiring leader in the visually stunning *Henry V* (>Laurence Olivier 1944) (✍ ☆ ■ ☞).
•The most famous of all sisters-in-arms is played by >Ingrid Bergman in *Joan of Arc* (Victor Fleming 1948) (☆).
•To >Michael Caine's dismay, >Sean Connery rises to power from humble beginnings in an adaptation of Rudyard Kipling's *The Man Who Would Be King* (>John Huston 1975) (☆ ☞ ✍).
•The political, rather than the military, war leader (ie Churchill) was glorified in *Young Mr Pitt* (>Carol Reed 1942) (☆ ☞ ✍).

All About Eve ☆ ✍ ☞
USA • Twentieth Century Fox • 1950 • 138 mins • b/w
wd >Joseph L. Mankiewicz   **ph** Milton Krasner   **m** Alfred Newman
>Bette Davis, George Sanders, Anne Baxter, Gary Merrill, Celeste Holm, >Marilyn Monroe

The winner of six Oscars in 1950, including Best Picture as well as Best Direction for Joseph L. Mankiewicz, *All About Eve* uses the decline of a *grande dame* of the theatre and the rise of a brash newcomer to examine the theme shared with another 1950 movie, >*Sunset Boulevard* (>Billy Wilder): the eclipse of Hollywood. Having recently been sacked by Warners, Bette Davis, as Margo Channing, confirmed her position as the most venomous screen bitch, spitting out the bitterness as she fights the ambitiously ruthless Eve Harrington (Baxter) and counters the doubts of New York producers. Although the machine-gun dialogue occasionally lapses into soapspeak, it is a goldmine of usable insults. The film is also culpable for inflicting the fatal 'dumb blonde' persona on Marilyn Monroe.

 •Ballerina Claire Bloom tries to revive the flagging career of Chaplin's clown Calvero in *Limelight* (>Charles Chaplin 1952) (✍ ☆), but nothing can prevent the collapse of >Laurence Olivier's stand-up comic Archie Rice in John Osborne's *The Entertainer* (Tony Richardson 1960) (☆ ✍).
•The star of a film festival falls prey to the demands of a celebrity in *Stardust Memories* (>Woody Allen 1980) (☞ ■).
•The glamour of the movies is totally stripped away in *Beware of a Holy Whore* (*Warnung Vor einer Heiligen Nutte*) (>Rainer Werner Fassbinder, West Germany 1970) (☞).
•Another Tinsel Town starlet is born in *The Goddess* (John Cromwell 1958), while young actress >Katharine Hepburn's ruthless ambition attracts the attention of Adolphe Menjou and Douglas Fairbanks Jr in *Morning Glory* (Lowell Sherman 1933) (☆).
•Despite having >Paul Newman as a lover, another ageing siren, Geraldine Page bites the dust in Tennessee Williams' *Sweet Bird of Youth* (Richard Brooks 1962).
•An elderly actress loses her daughter as well as her fame in *Applause* (Rouben Mamoulian 1929).

ALL BOYS TOGETHER

The Bachelor Party (Delbert Mann 1957) ✍
New York book-keepers float rather than drown their sorrows on a stag night.
The Boys in the Band (William Friedkin 1970) ☞
Home truths fly as a straight accidentally attends a gays-only party.
Diner (Barry Levinson 1982) ☞ ☆ ✍
Mickey Rourke and Steve Guttenberg amongst

students realizing childhood doesn't last forever.

Husbands (John Cassavetes 1970) ☆

Peter Falk, Ben Gazzara and director indulge in menopausal fling.

The Last Detail (Hal Ashby 1973) ☆ ☞ ✍

Sailors >Jack Nicholson and Otis Young take Randy Quaid on a last binge before jail.

The Long Voyage Home (>John Ford 1940) ■ ☞ ✍ ☆

Craft with drunken captain smuggles weapons from West Indies before crew head off on Scandinavian shoreleave.

Three Comrades (Frank Borzage 1938) ■ ✍

Trio all love the same tubercular girl in F. Scott Fitzgerald screenplay set in Weimar Germany.

The Time of Your Life (H. C. Potter 1948) ☆ ■

>James Cagney and cronies put the world to rights in a California bar.

The Way Ahead (US: *Immortal Battalion*) (>Carol Reed 1944) ☞ ✍ ☆

David Niven boosts morale while training a troublesome batch of recruits.

All girls together

Bachelor Girls (UK: *The Bachelor's Daughters*) (Andrew Stone 1946) ☆

Adolpe Menjou acts as father to four shop girls to help them win rich husbands.

Caged (John Cromwell 1950) ☆

Teenage thief terrorized in brutal women's prison.

Club de Femmes (Jacques Deval 1936) ☆

Sexual, Capra-corn and *noir*esque awakenings of various girls in a boarding house for young ladies.

The Future is Woman (*Il Futuro è Donna*) (Marco Ferreri, Italy 1984) ☆

>Hanna Schygulla befriends pregnant Ornella Muti and threatens her own marriage.

A Girl Must Live (>Carol Reed 1939) ☞

Runaway teenager Margaret Lockwood joins gold-digging chorus line.

The Group (>Sidney Lumet 1966) ☞ ■ ✍

Episodic look at subsequent lives and careers of four college contemporaries.

Moscow Distrusts Tears (US: *Moscow Does Not Believe In Tears*) (*Moskava Slezam ne Verit*) (Vladimir Menshov, USSR 1979) ☆

How three factory girls make out in the big wide world.

Seven Women (John Ford 1966) ☞ ☆

Missionaries show fortitude in 1935 in the face of Chinese bandits.

Stage Door (Gregory La Cava 1937) ☆ ✍ ■

>Katharine Hepburn and >Ginger Rogers seek stardom from a women-only theatrical boarding house.

The Women (>George Cukor 1939) ☆ ☞ ■

Norma Shearer and all-star female cast in high-society divorce comedy.

All Quiet on the Western Front
☞ ✍ ■ ☆

USA • Universal • 1930 • varies between 105 & 140 mins • b/w

d Lewis Milestone w Lewis Milestone/Maxwell Anderson/Del Andrews/George Abbott ph Arthur Edeson m David Broekman

Lew Ayres, Louis Wolheim, Slim Summerville, John Wray

Lewis Milestone's adaptation of Erich Maria Remarque's novel realistically exposes the true horror and folly of the war machine from recruitment to death. Reckless heroism and jingoistic bombast are confined to the Home Front, while in the trenches, everyone is scared, no one wants to die and yet men do, in their millions. Nine years after *All Quiet* was released, the world was again at war and national propaganda movies were being churned out to support the war effort. It was a cruel misuse of this anti-war film, when, on its reissue in 1939, it was accompanied by an anti-Nazi message. Similar projects following the Second World and Vietnam wars have yet to match the emotion and authenticity of this classic, which just shades *The Big Parade* (>King Vidor 1925) as the most important pacifist statement ever committed to film.

•World War I and the blind patriotism of people back home was examined in *Westfront 1918* (aka *Comrades of 1918*) (>G.W. Pabst, Germany 1930) (☞ ✍), while the trenches, with their hero-worship and cowardice, were the subject of *Journey's End* (James Whale 1930) (✍), an adaptation of R.C. Sheriff's stage success.

•Popular songs provide a caustic commentary on events in *Oh, What a Lovely War!* (>Richard Attenborough 1969) (♫ ☞ ■ ☆).

•The duplicity of governments conducting wars is studied in *Les Carabiniers* (*The Soldiers*) (US: *The Riflemen*) (>Jean-Luc Godard 1963) (☞ ✍).

•Lewis Milestone captured the brutality and futility of the Salerno landings of 1943 in *A Walk in the Sun* (✍ ☞ ■) (1946).

Allen, Woody
(Allen Konigsberg) American
actor/writer/director (b 1935)

TV gag writing, stand-up cabaret and a deep love of radio and film lie at the root of Woody Allen's cinema. Early acting and writing credits – *What's New Pussycat?* (Clive Donner 1965) (✍) (Peter Sellers is less interested in his fashion creations than in the models), *What's Up, Tiger Lily?* (co-d with Senkichi Taniguchi 1966) (✍) (Allen spoof dialogue dubbed onto poor Japanese spy thriller) and *Casino Royale* (>John Huston/Ken Hughes/Val Guest/Robert Parrish/Joe McGrath/Richard Talmadge 1967) (☆ ☞ ♫) (David Niven as ageing 007 with Allen as incompetent nephew) were followed by two stage hits. He returned to the cinema with what he called, in the >Fellini inspired *Stardust Memories* (1980) (■ ☆ ☞) (Allen as a director seeking escape from film festival and domestic problems) 'the early funny ones'. These include the spoof documentary *Take the Money and Run* (1969) (✍ ☆) (Allen outstanding as an inept small-time crook), *Sleeper* (1973) (☆) (Allen as a frozen specimen who falls for >Diane Keaton some time in the future), and the Tolstoy parody *Love And Death* (1975) (☆ ✍) (Allen and >Diane Keaton thwart the Napoleonic invasion of Russia). The neurotic, sexually preoccupied underdog that became the Allen acting trademark came of age

in the Oscar-winning >*Annie Hall* (1977) (✍ ☆ ☞) and >*Manhattan* (1979) (✍ ☆ ■ ☞ ♫). Although Allen appeared in cameo in *Hannah And Her Sisters* (1986) (☆ ☞) (the lives and loves of three New York sisters), his other recent ventures have been more diverse: >Ingmar Bergman was imitated in *Interiors* (1978) (■) (three sisters argue over their lives and the fate of their depressed mother) and in *A Midsummer Night's Sex Comedy* (1982) (☞) (three couples grow restless with their relationships during country weekend); newsreel was parodied in >*Zelig* (1983) (✍ ☞ ☆ ✳ ■ ♫); and nostalgia dominated the action of *Broadway Danny Rose* (1984) (■ ✍) (Mia Farrow complicates life for Allen's talentless talent-spotting agent), *The Purple Rose of Cairo* (✍ ☆) (1985) (ultimate homage to the romance of the movies has a film star stepping through the screen to brighten up Mia Farrow's Depression life) and *Radio Days* (✍ ☞) (1987) (radio and romance dominate family life in 1940s' New York). Currently preferring a writer/director role, the latest from the prolific Allen is always eagerly awaited.

 •*Bananas* (1971): Allen leads a military coup in South America.
•*Everything You Always Wanted to Know about Sex* (1972) (✍ ☆): sketches of varying quality from foreplay to ejaculation.
•*The Front* (Martin Ritt 1975) (☆ ✍): Allen sells scripts for HUAC blacklisted writers.
•*September* (1988): relationships crumble and Mia Farrow cries a lot.
•*Another Woman* (1989) (✍ ☆ ☞): Gena Rowlands rents a room to write in and subsequent events and eavesdroppings cause her to re-evaluate her life.

Altman, Robert
American writer/director (b 1925)

A World War II pilot turned TV director, Altman first tasted success with the Oscar-nominated study of a Korean War field-hospital, *M*A*S*H* (1970) (✍ ☞). Homages to the Western – *McCabe and Mrs Miller* (1971) (gunfighter Warren Beatty and Julie Christie set up a chain of brothels) – and *film noir* – *The Long Goodbye* (1973) (☞ ✍) (Philip Marlowe investigates the murder of a friend's wife) and *Thieves Like Us* (1974) (☞) (youngest of trio of escapees falls in love) – pre-dated a sequence of sundries which, for all their quality, lacked a unifying identity: chauvinist gamblers in *California Split* (1974) (☆) (no matter what cards are dealt, Elliott Gould and George Segal come up smiling), country and western music in *Nashville* (1975) (♫ ☞) (a political boss organizes a concert to win an election), feminism in *Three Women* (1977) (☆) (Shelly Duvall and Sissy Spacek exchange roles as teacher and student of life after latter's hospitalization) and cartoon heroes in *Popeye* (1980) (☆ ☞) (Robin Williams as the sailor who finds his strength in spinach). Not only the pursuit of esoteric projects has provoked controversy: in 1976 he refused the Berlin Golden Bear for big-budget flop *Buffalo Bill And The Indians* or *Sitting Bull's History Lesson* (1976) (☞ ☆) (>Paul Newman as Cody talking over his reputation).

•*The James Dean Story* (with George W. George 1957) (■): the Dean fascination early evident in this suitably moody, sharply filmed homage.
•*That Cold Day in the Park* (1969) (☞): spinster Sandy Dennis fails to heed *Boudu Saved from Drowning* and invites a Canadian tramp to her home.
•*Brewster McCloud* (1970) (✍): an eccentric believes he can fly.
•*A Wedding* (1978) (☆ ☞): a family squabble and scandal at a tense reception.
•*Health* (1979) (☆): a health food conference proves hard to swallow for all the delegates and hosts.
•*A Perfect Couple* (1979) (☞ ✍): an antique dealer and a Los Angeles pop singer meet through a dating agency.
•*Come Back to the Five and Dime, Jimmy Dean, Jimmy Dean* (1982) (✍ ☆): James Dean fans commemorate his making *Giant* near their town.
•*Streamers* (1983): raw recruits argue a lot in their dormitory.
•*Secret Honor* (1984) (☆): a student production has Richard Nixon reflecting on Watergate and US power politics.
•*Beyond Therapy* (1988) (☞ ☆): various pro-

fessionals seek a solution to middle age in psychiatry.
•*Fool For Love* (1988) (☆): Sam Shepherd and half-sister Kim Basinger shout at each other in a motel room.
•*The Dumb Waiter* (1989) (✍): John Travolta stars in Harold Pinter's adaptation of his own play.

Amadeus ☞ ■ ☆ ♫ ✍
USA • Saul Zaentz • 1985 • 159 mins • col
d >Miloš Forman w Peter Shaffer
ph Miroslav Ondricek m Mozart & Salieri
F. Murray Abraham, Tom Hulce, Elizabeth Berridge, Jeffrey Jones, Simon Callow, Roy Dotrice

Peter Shaffer's play merited a movie treatment, but few would have anticipated the humour, colour and sinister verve that Miloš Forman instilled into the story of the destruction of Wolfgang Amadeus Mozart (Hulce) by Antonio Salieri (Abraham), let alone that it would sweep the Academy Awards. From the moment Mozart *père* loses control, (in almost Frankenstein fashion), of his creation, his son is prey as much to his own eccentricity and genius as to the envious designs of Joseph II's Italian court composer. A superb costume drama, *Amadeus* catches the period perfectly, and stages the classical pieces with an enthusiasm and inspiration that constantly retains lay interest.

•Another creative genius to enjoy royal patronage was *Molière* (Ariane Mnouchkine, France 1978) (■ ☞).
•Away from the etiquette of the Hapsburg court there was eighteenth-century English bawdiness in *Tom Jones* (Tony Richardson 1962) (■ ✍ ☞).
•Ray Milland uses indirect means to do away with Grace Kelly in *Dial M for Murder* (>Alfred Hitchcock 1954) (☞ ☆ ✍).
•Staged operatic excerpts also abound in *The Story of Gilbert and Sullivan* (US: *The Great Gilbert and Sullivan*) (Sidney Gilliat 1953) (♫).
•Ronald Colman becomes obsessed with de-

stroying soap king Vincent Price in *Champagne for Caesar* (Richard Whorf 1950) (🖉 ☆).
•Tchaikovsky is the tortured composer in *The Music Lovers* (Ken Russell 1970) (☆).

AMERICANIZATION

The Americanization of Emily (**Arthur Hiller 1964**) 🖉
James Garner introduces Julie Andrews to more than chewing gum.

Bagdad Café (**Percy Adlon 1988**) 🖉 ☆
A fat German woman and her magic kit revive the fortunes of sleepy American café.

Chan is Missing (**Wayne Wang 1982**) ☞
A San Franciscan Chinese cabby goes missing with his colleague's cash.

Dim Sum (**Wayne Wang 1985**) ☆
A woman seeks an identity outside the strict limits of her Chinese family.

Four Friends (**UK: *Georgia's Friends*)
(Arthur Penn 1981**) ☞
A Yugoslavian boy experiences an Indiana childhood.

The Lonely Passion of Judith Hearne (**Jack Clayton 1988**) ☆ 🖉
A drunken Irish piano teacher (>Maggie Smith) mistakes returned American emigrant Bob Hoskins' friendship for romance.

Moonstruck (**Norman Jewison 1987**) ☆ ♫
Cher won an AA for falling for fellow Italian-American Nicholas Cage.

Popi (**Arthur Hiller 1969**) ☆
New York poverty and racism fail to bother a Puerto Rican family.

'68 (**Steven Kovacs 1988**) ☞
The lives and loves of a Hungarian restaurant family from 1956 to 1968.

AMNESIA

The Blue Dahlia (**George Marshall 1946**) 🖉
Raymond Chandler story of a war vet unable to recall the circumstances of his wife's death.

The Clay Pigeon (**Richard Fleischer 1949**) 🖉 ☞ ☆
A sailor on trial for treason eventually recalls the real traitor.

Crack Up (**Irving Reis 1946**) 🖉
A forgery expert implicates himself when he fails accurately to recall recent events.

Hangover Square (**John Brahm 1944**) 🖉 ♫ ☞
An Edwardian composer kills London women in fits of blind rage.

Love Letters (>**William Dieterle 1945**) ☞
Joseph Cotten menaces war-shocked Jennifer Jones.

The Morning After (>**Sidney Lumet 1986**) ☆
If >Jane Fonda didn't kill the man in bed with her, who did?

Random Harvest (>**Mervyn Le Roy 1942**) ☞ ☆ 🖉
Ronald Colman is enjoying life until he remembers his miserable existence as an aristocrat.

So Long at the Fair (**Terence Fisher 1950**) ☆
Jean Simmons searches Paris for her missing brother, aided by Dirk Bogarde.

Someone Behind the Door (**aka Two Minds for Murder**) (**Nicolas Gessner 1971**)
Anthony Perkins manipulates killer Charles Bronson's amnesia.

ANCIENT WORLD

Alexander the Great (**Robert Rossen 1956**) ■
>Richard Burton as Philip of Macedon's eldest boy.

Carry On Cleo (**Gerald Thomas 1963**) ☆ 🖉
Kenneth Williams delivers immortal line 'Infamy, infamy, they've all got it in for me.'

Cleopatra (**Cecil B. De Mille 1934**) ■ ☆
Claudette Colbert is the only thing not OTT in this Egypt epic, unlike >Joseph L. Mankiewicz's 1963 version with Elizabeth Taylor where everything is OTT.

Demetrius and the Gladiators (**Delmer Daves 1954**) ☆
Victor Mature gets thumbs up at Colosseum matinées.

The Fall of the Roman Empire (**Anthony Mann 1964**) ☆
Not bad, but hardly a rival to Gibbon's *Decline*.

AN AMERICAN IN PARIS
(Vincente Minnelli 1951) ♫ ☞

THE GERSHWIN BROTHERS

COVER GIRL
(Charles Vidor 1943) ☆ ♫
(lyricist Ira teamed with Jerome Kern for this tale of Rita Hayworth's rise to modelling fame)

A DAMSEL IN DISTRESS
(>George Stevens 1937) ✍ ♫
(George and Ira's songs and P. G. Wodehouse's story have >Fred Astaire dancing into >Joan Fontaine's heart)

DELICIOUS
(David Butler 1931) ♫
(Janet Gaynor's Irish rose marries into wealth in New York to the accompaniment of the Gershwin's songs)

KISS ME STUPID
(>Billy Wilder 1964) ♫ ☞
(singer Dean Martin falls for small town songwriter's wife Kim Novak)

LADY BE GOOD
(Norman Z. McLeod 1941) ♫
(the Gershwins among the tunesmiths represented in the show penned in the film by husband and wife team Eleanor Powell and Robert Young)

PORGY AND BESS
(Otto Preminger 1959) ✍ ♫
(George's music enlivens Du Bose and Dorothy Heyward's play about slum girl Dorothy Dandridge's love for cripple Sidney Poitier)

RHAPSODY IN BLUE
(Irving Rapper 1945) ♫
(biopic of the brothers with Robert Alda as George and Herbert Rudley as Ira)

RICHARD RODGERS

EVERGREEN
(Victor Saville 1934) ♫
(aspiring Jessie Matthews takes her mother's place and finds stardom)

STATE FAIR
(Walter Lang 1945) ♫
(family win pig prizes and hearts at fair)

OKLAHOMA!
(>Fred Zinnemann 1955) ♫ ✍
(cowboy Gordon Macrae woos Shirley Jones from evil rival Rod Steiger)

CAROUSEL
(Henry King 1956) ♫ ✍
(dead rogue Gordon Macrae returns to earth to help his family)

THE KING AND I
(Walter Lang 1956) ☆ ♫ ✍
(governess Deborah Kerr charms irascible Siamese king Yul Brynner)

PAL JOEY
(George Sidney 1957) ☆ ♫
(nightclub owner Frank Sinatra mistreats Rita Hayworth and Kim Novak)

SOUTH PACIFIC
(Joshua Logan 1958) ♫ ✍
(James A. Michener stories of romance and heroism during Pacific war)

COLE PORTER

ANYTHING GOES
(Lewis Milestone 1936) ✍
(liner passengers find romance in P. G. Wodehouse/Guy Bolton script)

KISS ME KATE
(George Sidney 1953) ✍ ♫
(cast of The Taming of the Shrew fall in love off-stage)

ROSALIE
(W. S. Van Dyke 1938) ☞ ♫
(American football player Nelson Eddy falls for princess Eleanor Powell)

SOMETHING TO SHOUT ABOUT
(Gregory Ratoff 1943) ✍
(PR man Don Ameche clashes with show star Janet Blair)

HIGH SOCIETY
(Charles Walters 1956) ☆ ♫
(musical remake of >The Philadelphia Story [>George Cukor 1940] (☆ ✍ ☞))

CAN CAN
(Walter Lang 1960) ♫
(Shirley MacLaine dances and Frank Sinatra is sued)

> ## Artist >Gene Kelly finds love amongst rags not riches in this George and Ira Gershwin musical

IRVING BERLIN

FOLLOW THE FLEET
(Mark Sandrich 1936) ♫
(shore leave sailor >Fred Astaire woos singer >Ginger Rogers)

ON THE AVENUE
(Roy Del Ruth 1937) ♫
(lampooned heiress Madeleine Carroll comes to love satirist Dick Powell)

THIS IS THE ARMY
(>Michael Curtiz 1943) ♫
(the composer himself and Ronald Reagan are among Warner promo cast)

BLUE SKIES
(Stuart Heisler 1946) ♫ ☆
(showgirl is beloved of dancer >Fred Astaire and club owner Bing Crosby)

EASTER PARADE
(Charles Walters 1948) ♫ ☆
(dance team >Fred Astaire and Judy Garland love, lose, then love each other)

ANNIE GET YOUR GUN
(George Sidney 1950) ♫ ☆
(romance and rivalry between sharpshooters Betty Hutton and Howard Keel)

CALL ME MADAM
(Walter Lang 1953) ♫
(ambassador Ethel Merman livens up dowdy imaginary state)

THERE'S NO BUSINESS LIKE SHOW BUSINESS
(Walter Lang 1954) ☆ ♫
(>Marilyn Monroe is member of a vaudeville family experiencing highs and lows)

JEROME KERN

CENTENNIAL SUMMER
(Otto Preminger 1946) ♫ ✍
(a family enters the spirit of the 1876 Great Exposition celebrating the 100th anniversary of the War of Independence)

CAN'T HELP SINGING
(Frank Ryan 1944) ♫
(Kern's music and E. Y. Harburg's lyrics accompany Deanna Durbin as she risks the wildest parts of the west to join her army beau)

ROBERTA
(William A. Seiter 1934) ☆ ♫
(>Fred Astaire and >Ginger Rogers help Irene Dunne run her Paris fashion house)

SHOWBOAT
(James Whale 1936) ☞ ♫/
(George Sidney 1951) ♫
(Kern teamed up with Oscar Hammerstein II for the songs sung by the cast of a floating revue)

SWING TIME
(>George Stevens 1936) ☞ ♫
(>Fred Astaire loses >Ginger Rogers as he feels responsible for the girl next door)

TILL CLOUDS ROLL BY
(Richard Whorf 1946) ♫
(Robert Walker as Kern; Judy Garland, Lena Horne, Frank Sinatra, June Allyson, Van Heflin and Van Johnson co-star)

MODERN MUSICALS

OLIVER!
(>Carol Reed 1968) ☞ ✍ ▪
(low life and innocence in >Dickensian London)

SWEET CHARITY
(Bob Fosse 1969) ♫
(Shirley MacLaine as misued taxi dancer with heart of gold)

FIDDLER ON THE ROOF
(Norman Jewison 1971) ☆ ♫
(Topol's family of Russian Jews work the land and seek marriage)

CABARET
(Bob Fosse 1972) ☆ ♫
(Liza Minnelli experiences Berlin during Nazi rise)

JESUS CHRIST SUPERSTAR
(Norman Jewison 1973) ♫
(students re-enact the events of Holy Week)

ROCKY HORROR PICTURE SHOW
(Jim Sharman 1975) ♫ ☆ ✍
(transvestite vampire Tim Curry shelters Susan Sarandon and Barry Bostwick)

ANNIE
(>John Huston 1982) ☞ ♫
(orphan de-Scrooges hermit millionaire Albert Finney)

A CHORUS LINE
(>Richard Attenborough 1985) ☆ ♫
(auditioners try to impress Broadway producer >Michael Douglas)

Fiddlers Three (**Harry Watt 1944**) ✍
Three tars transported back to Rome by a lightning bolt.

A Funny Thing Happened on the Way to the Forum (**Richard Lester 1966**) ☞ ■ ♫
Stephen Sondheim musical of Plautus' tale of a scheming slave.

Land of the Pharoahs (**>Howard Hawks 1955**) ☞ ☆
Egyptian ruler has problems with builders during the erection of his pyramid.

The Last Days of Pompeii (**Merion C. Cooper/Ernest Schoedsack 1935**) ■
Preston Foster witnesses the Crucifixion before perishing when Vesuvius erupts.

Roman Scandals (**Frank Tuttle 1933**) ■ ☆
Eddie Cantor goes to sleep and wakes up in ancient Rome.

The Sign of the Cross (**Cecil B. De Mille 1932**) ☆ ☞ ■
>Fredric March gets religion during the reign of >Charles Laughton's Nero.

The 300 Spartans (**Rudolph Maté 1962**) ■
Spartan soldiers are entrusted with leading Greece in a spot of Persian bashing.

Andersson, Harriet
Swedish actress (b 1932)

Not to be confused with another of >Ingmar Bergman's stalwarts Bibi Andersson, Harriet first shone as the selfish seductress in *Summer With Monika* (US: *Monika*) (*Sommaren Med Monika*) (1953) (☞ ■), in which a teenage girl abandons her baby to the father after a holiday romance. She came to typify Bergman's sensual woman, first as Anne in *Sawdust and Tinsel* (aka *The Naked Night*) (*Gycklarnas Afton*) (1953) (☞ ■ ☆), in which a circus owner's reconciliation with his wife is diverted when his mistress (Andersson) is seduced; then as the maid Petra in *Smiles of a Summer's Night* (*Sommarnattens Leende*) (1955)(✍ ☞ ■ ☆) (a lawyer's family plays sexual musical chairs during a country weekend); Karin in *Through a Glass Darkly* (*Såsom I En Spegel*) (1961) (☞ ☆) (Andersson accompanies novelist Gunnar Björnstrand and their eccentric family to a remote island); Agnes in *Cries and Whispers* (*Viskingar Och Rop*) (1973) (☞ ■

☆), whose cancer agony is alleviated by her sisters and a servant; and another maid, Justina, in >*Fanny and Alexander* (*Fanny och Alexander*)(1982) (☞ ■ ✍ ☆). Work with Finnish director husband Jörn Donner includes *Adventure Starts Here* (*Här Börjar Äventyret*) (1965) (✍) (love across Finnish, Swedish, and German language barriers), and with Mai Zetterling, *The Girls* (*Flickorna*) (1968) (✍ ☆) (actresses in Aristophanes' *Lysistrata* improve their lives through the play's influence).

•*A Lesson in Love* (*En Lektion I Karlek*) (>Ingmar Bergman 1954) (✍ ☞): Harriet is prominent in the problems faced by married couple Gunnar Björnstrand and Eva Dahlbeck in this rare Bergman comedy.

•*Journey into Autumn* (aka *Dreams*) (*Kvinnodröm*) (>Ingmar Bergman 1955) (☞ ☆): female photographer Eva Dahlbeck and model Andersson are frustrated by love affairs.

•*A Sunday in September* (*En Söndag I September*) (Jörn Donner 1962) (☆): dissection of a 'too young to be married' affair.

•*Now About These Women* (US: *All These Women*) (*För Att Inte Tala Om Alla Dessa Kvinnor*) (>Ingmar Bergman 1964) (■ ✍): biographer's research into a cellist's career is hampered by tales of sexual prowess.

•*Loving Couples* (*Älskande Pär*) (Mai Zetterling 1964) (✍ ☆): expectant women discuss their paths to pregnancy.

ANGELS

The Angel Who Pawned Her Harp (**Alan Bromly 1954**) ✍
Diane Cilento spreads a little happiness in Islington.

>*The Bishop's Wife* (**Henry Koster 1947**) ☆ ✍ ■ ☞

Cabin in the Sky (**>Vincente Minnelli 1943**) ☞ ♫
Black musical in which angels and devils argue over the destiny of man's soul.

For Heaven's Sake (**George Seaton 1950**) ☆
Clifton Webb and Edmund Gwenn patch up a showbiz marriage.

Heaven Can Wait (**Warren Beatty 1978**) ☆
Beatty seeks life extension from angel James Mason to woo Julie Christie in this remake of *Here Comes Mr Jordan*.

Here Comes Mr Jordan (**Alexander Hall 1941**) ✍ ☆ ☞
Comic search of dead-before-time Robert Montgomery for new body after his is cremated.

The Horn Blows at Midnight (**>Raoul Walsh 1945**) ☆ ☞
Jack Benny comes to destroy earth with the Angel Gabriel's horn.

I Married an Angel (**W. S. Van Dyke 1942**) ✍
Anita Loos script has angel Jeanette MacDonald catching Nelson Eddy's roving eye.

>*It's a Wonderful Life* (**>Frank Capra 1946**) ☆ ☞ ✍

Wings of Desire (**>Wim Wenders 1987**) ■ ☞
Angel Bruno Ganz is tempted to do more than merely watch over Berlin.

ANIMALS

Balthazar (*Au Hasard Balthazar*) (**>Robert Bresson 1966**) ✍ ■
Simple and delightful telling of the life and death of a donkey.

The Bears and I (**Bernard McEveety 1974**) ■
Patrick Wayne befriends three bear cubs.

Born Free (**James Hill 1965**)
The friendship between Joy and George Adamson (Virginia McKenna and Bill Travers) and Elsa the lioness.

The Brave One (**Irving Rapper 1956**) ✍
A small boy's pet bull is threatened with death in the ring.

Dr Dolittle (**Richard Fleischer 1967**) ♫ ☆
Hugh Lofting's hero talks to the animals and they talk to him.

The Great Adventure (**Arne Sucksdorff 1953**) ■
Farm boys raise a stolen otter.

Never Take No for an Answer (**Maurice Cloche 1951**) ✍
Paul Gallico tale of a boy and a sick donkey searching for the pope and a miracle.

The Yearling (**Clarence Brown 1946**) ☞ ■
Boy keeps a pet deer despite his father Gregory Peck's opposition.

Annie Hall ✍ ☆ ☞
USA • United Artists • 1977 • 93 mins • col
d >Woody Allen   w Woody Allen/Marshall Brickman   ph Gordon Willis   m Various
>Woody Allen, >Diane Keaton, Tony Roberts, Paul Simon, Shelly Duvall

Woody Allen came of age as a moviemaker with this story of the brief affair of neurotic comedian Alvy Singer (Allen) and Annie Hall (Keaton), an equally insecure singer. Raiding the store of nostalgia that was to fuel *The Purple Rose of Cairo* and *Radio Days*, Allen uses an innovative narrative technique that comments on and directly includes the audience in the action, while allowing him scope for slapstick in addition to the celebrated one-liners that had been the staple of his previous ventures. The precise balance of wit, realism and pathos makes this a constant joy and the Best Picture, Screenplay, Director and Actress Oscars that it won were fully merited.

•True love simply can't find a way in *A Man and a Woman* (*Un Homme et une Femme*) (Claude Lelouch, France 1966) (☞ ☆).
•Liv Ullmann's neurosis-induced dumbness is passed on to her nurse Bibi Andersson in *Persona* (>Ingmar Bergman, Sweden 1966) (☆ ☞ ■ ✍).
•>Dustin Hoffman and Mia Farrow waver over an affair following a one-night stand in *John and Mary* (Peter Yates 1969) (☆).
•Steve McQueen and Natalie Wood are another odd couple falling in love in *Love with the Proper Stranger* (Robert Mulligan 1964) (☆ ■ ☞ ✍).
•Neil Simon's New York childhood is recalled in *Brighton Beach Memoirs* (Gene Saks 1986) (✍).

Another Country ☆ ■ ♫ ☞ ✍

GB • Twentieth-Century Fox/Virgin/Goldcrest
• 1984 • 90 mins • col

d Marek Kanievska **w** Julian Mitchell
ph Peter Biziou **m** Michael Storey

Rupert Everett, Colin Firth

There have been numerous films about brutality and homosexuality in public schools, ranging from the classic *Tom Brown's Schooldays* (both Robert Stevenson's 1940 version and Gordon Perry's in 1951) to the satirical *If...?* (Lindsay Anderson 1968). Even though the events that formed the psychological motive for the defection of a barely fictitious Guy Burgess are here only just sufficiently well-told to steer them away from cliché and the cobbling together of Oxford and stately home settings barely create a credible school environment, there is something special about this almost perfect portrayal of a period of transition and suspicion. The entire cast perform superbly, notably Everett as Guy and Firth as Judd, enhancing the pervading atmosphere of arrogant vulnerability that characterized the generation helplessly trapped between world wars. A captivating film.

 •Housemaster's wife Deborah Kerr takes pity on an unhappy boy in *Tea and Sympathy* (>Vincente Minnelli 1956) (☆).

•A gay film student falls for the schoolboy subject of a documentary on parental brutality in *Abuse* (Arthur J. Brennan 1983).

•From Burgess' schooldays to a school for spies – *From Russia with Love* (Terence Young 1963) (✍ ☆).

•Despite their differences two more boys sustain a close friendship in *Friends for Life* (*Amici per la Pelle*) (Franco Rossi, Italy 1955) (☆ ✍).

ANTHOLOGIES

***The Big Parade of Comedy (aka MGM's Big Parade of Comedy)* (1964)**

An unusual blend of slapstick, screwball and satire.

***The Crazy World of >Laurel and Hardy* (1964)**

The greatest hits of two 'funny gentlemen and two funny, gentle men'.

***Days of Thrills and Laughter* (1961)**

Classic cuts from horror, melodrama, adventure and comedy silents.

***The Golden Age of > Buster Keaton* (1975)**

Synchronized stunts and sight gags from his shorts and features.

***The Golden Age of Comedy* (Robert Youngson 1957) ☆ ✍**

>Laurel and Hardy, Ben Turpin and Harry Langdon are amongst those on display.

***Harold Lloyd's Funny Side of Life* (1963)**

The best moments from Lloyd's two-reel silents.

***Harold Lloyd's World of Comedy* (1962)**

Highlights of a career in which high places were pre-eminent.

***>Laurel and Hardy's Laughing Twenties* (1965)**

Excerpts from the shorts of Stan and Ollie and their rivals.

***The Love Goddesses* (1965)**

Chauvinistic parade of screen sirens.

***That's Entertainment* (1974)**

Compilation of magic MGM moments stolen by Donald O'Connor's 'Make 'Em Laugh'.

***That's Entertainment Part Two* (1976)**

>Fred Astaire and >Gene Kelly slap backs in cash-in sequel to above.

***When Comedy Was King* (1959)**

Selection of silents from Keystone Cop slapstick to Keaton stone face.

ANTI-HEROES

***Aguirre, Wrath of God (Aguirre, der Zorn Gottes)* (>Werner Herzog, West Germany 1972) ■ ☞**

Klaus Kinski as conquistador seeking El Dorado in 16th-century Peru.

***The Bank Dick* (UK: *The Bank Detective*) (Eddie Cline 1940) ☆**

>W.C. Fields stars as the security detective and wrote script as 'Mahatma Kane Jeeves'.

***Being There* (Hal Ashby 1979) ☆**

Peter Sellers as a simpleton taken for a sage by US media and government.

Father Goose **(Ralph Nelson 1964)** ☆ ✍
>Cary Grant as a coward protecting Leslie Caron and her young female charges from Japanese invaders.

Hail the Conquering Hero **(>Preston Sturges 1944)** ✍ ☞
Man unfit for war service is presumed a hero by hometown folks.

A Handful of Dust **(Charles Sturridge 1988)** ✍ ☆ ▣
Evelyn Waugh tale of a fogeyish aristocrat stranded in Brazil after a smart society cuckolding.

The History of Mr Polly **(Anthony Pelissier 1949)** ☆ ✍
John Mills as H.G. Wells' draper's assistant fleeing his drab life.

Malcolm **(Nadia Tass 1986)** ☆
Backward man devises brilliant, robot-conducted robberies.

Roxanne **(Fred Schepisi 1987)** ☆ ✍
Steve Martin as a big-nosed fireman in an updating of *Cyrano de Bergerac*.

Antonioni, Michelangelo
Italian director (b 1912)

A graduate of the University of Bologna, Antonioni progressed from film criticism in the 1940s through screenwriting to direction in 1950 with *Chronicle of a Love* (aka *Story of a Love Affair*) (*Cronaca di un Amore*) (lovers Lucia Bosé and Massimo Giroth plan to kill her husband and are haunted by guilt when he dies naturally). His world is inhabited by creative people who find inter-communication virtually impossible, and narrative has been progressively ousted by image and technical set-piece. Following studies of creative women – *The Lady Without Camellias* (aka *Camille Without Camellias*) (*La Signora Senza Camelie*) (1953) (☞ ☆) (the rapid rise and fall of a movie starlet) and *The Girl Friends* (*Le Amiche*) (1955)(☞ ☆) (a fashion designer's pre-occupation with her friends' troubles harms her career) – he concentrated on social misfit couples: >*L'Avventura* (1960) (☞ ▣ ✍ ☆), *La Notte* (*The Night*) (1961) (▣ ☞), which depicts a day in the life of novelist >Marcello Mastroianni and wife Jeanne Moreau; and *The*

Eclipse (*L'Eclisse*) (1962) (☞ ▣), in which Monica Vitti opts out of a ménage with Alain Delon and Francisco Rabal. *Blow Up* (1966) (☞ ✍), in which elusive evidence frustrates photographer David Hemmings' murder investigation and the audience's patience, and *Zabriskie Point* (1970), in which a wastrel student steals a plane, formed a short English-language diversion. Since *The Passenger* (1975) – >Jack Nicholson's change of identity lands him in fatal gun-running escapade – Antonioni has veered so far towards the self-indulgent as to be unintelligible.

 •*The Cry* (US: *The Outcry*) (*Il Grido*) (1957) (▣): a sugar worker and his daughter search for their wife/mother.

•*The Red Desert* (*Il Deserto Rosso*) (1964) (▣): a woman's affair fails to alleviate her depression at her industrial surroundings.

•*The Oberwald Mystery* (*Il Mistero di Oberwald*) (1979) (▣ ☆): a queen falls for the lookalike of her dead husband in this reworking of Jean Cocteau's *The Eagle Has Two Heads*.

•*Identification of a Woman* (*Identificazione di una Donna*) (1982): a director searches for the ideal leading lady for his next film.

Apocalypse Now ☆ ☞ ▣ ✍ ♫
USA • Omni Zoetrope • 1979 • 153 mins • col
d >Francis Ford Coppola w John Milius/Francis Ford Coppola ph Vittorio Storaro m Carmine Coppola/Francis Ford Coppola
Martin Sheen, >Marlon Brando, Robert Duvall, Frederic Forrest, Dennis Hopper

This story of a government assassin with orders to liquidate a renegade army officer in Vietnam promises much. The fact that this up-dating of Joseph Conrad's *Heart of Darkness* largely delivers, won Francis Ford Coppola the 1976–79 >*African Queen* Memorial Award for a Production Fraught with Difficulties. Shooting time was extended and financial difficulties were exacerbated by the coronary and dietary problems of stars Martin Sheen and Marlon Brando, and it is to the director's credit that he was still able to produce such a tense thriller. Outstanding is the Wagner-accompanied bombing of a beach, simply to allow a soldier to surf, surely cinema's most appalling revelation of man's potential for inhumanity.

 •Spanish conquistadors endure the dangers of the Peruvian jungle in *El Dorado* (Carlos Saura 1989) (■).

•Moving through jungle proved less of a problem for Christoper Lambert in *Greystoke: The Legend of Tarzan, Lord of the Apes* (Hugh Hudson 1984) (☆).

•Mercenaries >Gary Cooper, David Niven and Broderick Crawford crush terrorism in 1906 Philippines in *The Real Glory* (Henry Hathaway 1939) (☆).

•Martin Sheen's son Charlie re-echoes the anti-Nam sentiments in *Platoon* (Oliver Stone 1987).

•The horror of war is still perceived as glamour in some movies, notably *Rambo II* (Sylvester Stallone 1985).

The Apu Trilogy ☞ ✍ ■ ☆
wd >Satyajit Ray>   ph Subrata Mitra
m Ravi Shankar

Pather Panchali (Little Song of the Road)
India • The Government of West Bengal • 1955 • 115 mins • b/w
Kanu Bannerjee, Karuna Bannerjee, Subir Bannerjee

Aparajito (The Unvanquished)
India • Epic Films • 1957 • 108 mins • b/w
Kanu Bannerjee, Karuna Bannerjee, Sumiran Ghosjal, Subodh Ganguly

Apur Sansar (The World of Apu)
India • Satyajit Ray/The Government of West Bengal • 1959 • 103 mins • b/w
Soumitra Chatterjee, Sharmila Tagore, Alok Chakravarty, Dhiresh Mazumaer

The Indian cinema industry is the busiest in the world, annually producing in excess of 700 films. Although films set in India, particularly the Raj era, are popular in the West, strict content control has meant that few Indian films enjoy worldwide repute. Satyajit Ray's Bengali trilogy is a notable exception. *Pather Panchali*, beginning the series in 1955, is a wistful view of village life, abject poverty and family ties, seen through the eyes of a small boy, Apu. Having examined the father/son relationship in *Pather*, *Aparajito* takes Apu through teenage struggles in the company of his mother, and *Apur Sansar* completes the cycle with Apu's reconciliation with his own son, showing that he has learned the secrets of family life through his hardships. The sensitive photography and the gentle wisdom behind the laughter and tears of the narrative make *Apu* a fascinating and rewarding experience.

 •The evolution of generations rather than an individual is portrayed in the remarkable epic *Heimat (Homeland)* (Edgar Reitz. West Germany 1983) (☞ ✍ ☆).

•A small boy runs away from his village and encounters the exploitation and degradation of Indian urban poverty in *Salaam Bombay!* (Nira Nair 1988) (■).

•A Chinese family man travels to Taiwan to seek work in *The Time to Live and the Time to Die (Tongnian Wangshi)* (Hou Hsaio-hsien, Taiwan 1985) (☞ ✍).

•Another journey of a life, this time a cynical, fallible Bolshevik is told in *The Maxim Trilogy* (Grigori Kozintsev/Leonid Trauberg): (*The Youth of Maxim*) (*Yunost Maksima*) (1935), *The Return of Maxim* (*Vozurashcheniye Maksima*) (1937) and *The Vyborg Side* (*Vyborgskaya Storona*) (1939) (✍).

ARABIAN NIGHTS

Algiers (John Cromwell 1938) ☆ ☞
Charles Boyer's Casbah crime career is sidetracked by Hedy Lamarr.

Ali Baba and the Forty Thieves (Arthur Lubin 1944) ✍
A prince poses as an outlaw to avenge his usurpation.

The Arabian Nights (aka *A Thousand and One Nights*) (*Il Fiore delle Mille e una Notte*) (>Pier Paolo Pasolini 1974) ■ ☞
Ten tales told around a prince's search for a kidnapped servant girl.

Carry On Up the Khyber **(Gerald Thomas 1966)** ☆

Kenneth Williams' Khasi of Kalabar leads Afghan revolt against the British Governor Sid James.

Lost in a Harem **(Charles Reisner 1944)** ☆ ✍

Abbott and Costello fall foul of a hypnotic sultan.

The Mask of Dimitrios **(Jean Negulesco 1944)** ☆ ☞

This screen version of the Eric Ambler novel pits writer >Peter Lorre against villain Sidney Greenstreet.

Pépé le Moko **(Julien Duvivier 1936)** ☆ ☞

Paris gangster >Jean Gabin blows his Casbah cover when he falls in love.

Road to Morocco **(David Butler 1942)** ☆

Anthony Quinn menaces Bob Hope, Bing Crosby and Dorothy Lamour.

The Thief of Bagdad **(>Michael Powell/ Ludwig Berger/Tim Whelan 1940)** ■ ☞ ✍

Sabu helps an elderly king regain his throne from the evil Conrad Veidt.

Army life

Biloxi Blues **(>Mike Nichols 1988)** ☆

Matthew Broderick stars in the second part of Neil Simon's movie autobiography.

From Here to Eternity **(>Fred Zinnemann 1953)** ☞ ☆

Burt Lancaster takes time off from things military to roll in the surf with Deborah Kerr.

The Life and Death of Colonel Blimp **(>Michael Powell/Emeric Pressburger 1943)** ☞ ✍ ☆

Roger Livesey serves queen, two kings and country against the Mahdi, Kruger and Kaiser.

An Officer and a Gentleman **(Taylor Hackford 1982)**

Debra Winger helps Richard Gere survive Lou Gossett, Jr's tough training regime.

Private Benjamin **(Howard Zieff 1980)** ☆

Goldie Hawn joins the army to forget and instantly regrets her decision.

Private's Progress **(John Boulting 1956)** ✍ ☆

Ian Carmichael flukes heroism to Terry-Thomas' disgust and Dennis Price and >Richard Attenborough's profit.

Tire-au-Flanc **(>Jean Renoir 1928)** ☆ ✍

Georges Pomiés as a timid poet comically unsuited to trench life.

Tunes of Glory **(Ronald Neame 1960)** ☆ ✍

Upper-class commander John Mills clashes with Scottish RSM >Alec Guinness.

The Virgin Soldiers **(John Dexter 1969)** ✍

Screen version of the Leslie Thomas novel about raw recruits in 1950s Malaysia.

The Way Ahead **(US: *Immortal Batallion*) (>Carol Reed 1944)** ☞ ✍ ☆

Eric Ambler and Peter Ustinov propaganda pic about troop training.

Art and artists

Aloïse **(Liliane de Kermadec, France 1975)** ☆

Isabelle Huppert as a primitivist committed to an asylum because of her conscientious objection to World War I.

Caravaggio **(Derek Jarman 1984)** ■ ☞

Beautifully filmed prologue to the death of the 16th-century perfectionist.

Edvard Munch **(Peter Watkins 1974)** ☆ ☞

The young manhood of the Norwegian Expressionist and his rebellion against upbringing.

Holy Matrimony **(John Stahl 1943)** ☆

Famous artist Monty Woolley takes advantage of his supposed death to live quietly with Gracie Fields.

The Light that Failed **(>William Wellman 1939)** ☆

Ronald Colman in Kipling's tale of an artist steadily losing his sight.

Mikael **(US: *Chained*) (Carl Dreyer, Germany 1924)** ☞

An ageing artist's model is stolen from him by an arrogant aristocrat.

A Month in the Country **(Pat O'Connor 1988)** ■ ☆ ✍

Colin Firth and Kenneth Branagh spend an idyllic summer restoring and excavating in the village church.

The Moon and Sixpence (Albert Lewin 1943) ☆ ✍

Adaptation of the W. Somerset Maugham novel inspired by the life of Paul Gauguin.

Moulin Rouge (>John Huston 1952) ■

Jose Ferrer as Henri Toulouse-Lautrec in the Montmartre of the 1890s.

Rembrandt (Alexander Korda 1936) ☆ ■

>Charles Laughton outstanding as the Dutch 17th-century painter.

Savage Messiah (Ken Russell 1972) ■

The brief, pre-First World War love of teenage painter Gaudier and older woman Sophie Brzeska (Dorothy Tutin).

The Wolf at the Door (Henning Carlsen 1987) ☆

Donald Sutherland as Gauguin on his painting expeditions to Tahiti.

Ashes and Diamonds (Popiol I Diament) ☞ ☆ ✍

Poland • Film Polski • 1958 • 104 mins • b/w

d >Andrej Wajda   w Andrej Wajda/Jerzy Andrzejewski   ph Jerzy Wojcik   m Various

Zbigniew Cybulski, Ewa Krzyzanowska, Adam Pawlikowski

Set in devastated Warsaw at the end of World War II, Andrej Wajda's film deals with the ambiguous relief felt by the Poles on being liberated from the Nazis by the Soviet army. Maciek Chelmicki (Cybulski) realizes that a nationalist plot to murder the Communist district secretary, Szczuka has failed and tracks him down to his hotel to assassinate him. In the course of his one-night stay, he flirts with Krystyna (Krzyzanowska), the hotel barmaid, and considers abandoning the cause and acquiescing to the new system. Killed in a stunning, firework-accompanied shootout on a rubbish dump, Cybulski, with his leather jacket and pale green glasses (showing black in monochrome), became a rebel hero on a par with James Dean, although there are times when you expect him to break into a Roy Orbison number.

 •Members of the Polish Resistance are trapped in the sewers of Warsaw in *Kanal* (US: *They Loved Life*) (aka *Sewer*) (>Andrej Wajda 1957) (✍ ☞).
•A chink appears in >Humphrey Bogart's armour when >Edward G. Robinson holds guests hostage at Lionel Barrymore's hotel in *Key Largo* (>John Huston 1948) (☆ ☞); while the comings and the goings of the clientele, including >Greta Garbo provide the interest in *Grand Hotel* (Edmund Goulding 1932) (☆ ✍).
•Edward Fox is the assassin on the trail of Charles de Gaulle in Frederick Forsyth's *The Day of the Jackal* (>Fred Zinnemann 1973) (✍ ☆ ☞).
•*Rebel without a Cause* (>Nicholas Ray 1955) (☆ ☞) gave the world the ultimate teen idol, James Dean.

ASPIRING STARS

Because of Him (Richard Wallace 1945) ☆

>Charles Laughton and Franchot Tone set Deanna Durbin on her way.

Born to Dance (Roy Del Ruth 1936) ☆

Eleanor Parker persuades >James Stewart to put on his dancing shoes.

A Chorus Line (>Richard Attenborough 1985) ☆ ♫

>Michael Douglas selects a cast by forcing them to act naturally.

Dance Girl Dance (Dorothy Arzner 1940) ☞

Dancing girls find that life has a habit of intruding on ambition.

Forty-Second Street (Lloyd Bacon 1933) ☆ ♫ ✍

The ultimate 'It'll be all right on the night' backstage drama.

Hearts of the West (UK: Hollywood Cowboy) (Howard Zieff 1975) ☆

Likeable Jeff Bridges nearly blunders into early talkie fame.

Hollywood Shuffle (Robert Townsend 1987) ✍ ☆

Townsend exposes the racism of star-making in the modern entertainment industry.

Next Stop Greenwich Village (Paul Mazursky 1975) ☆

Autobiographical account of a Jewish stand-up comic learning his trade.

Asquith, Anthony
British director (1902–1968)

Son of Liberal Prime Minister H. H. Asquith, Oxford graduate Asquith entered films in 1925 at the invitation of >Douglas Fairbanks and Mary Pickford. His silent *Cottage on Dartmoor* (aka *Escaped from Dartmoor*) (1929), in which a jailbreaker is harboured by his mistress, passed unnoticed, and the co-directed (with Alexander Korda) *Moscow Nights* (1935) (Bolshevik >Laurence Olivier is spared execution by his girlfriend's sacrifice) fluttered few pulses. Adaptations of stage plays and realistic war adventures were to prove his forte. He avoided overt staginess in >George Bernard Shaw's *Pygmalion* (1938) (☆ ✍ ☞)(>Leslie Howard, who co-directed, makes a lady of Cockney Wendy Hiller), *The Doctor's Dilemma* (1959) (☆) (>Alastair Sim among the doctors trying to cure Dirk Bogarde's TB) and *The Millionairess* (1960) (☆) (well goodness gracious me, Sophia Loren's heart goes boom diddy boom when she meets Indian doctor Peter Sellers) and in Terence Rattigan's *French without Tears* (1939) (✍) (younger sister breaks hearts of language students, including that of Ray Milland), *While the Sun Shines* (1946) (a soldier and a French girl redirect the path of true love to a mutual friend), *The Winslow Boy* (1948) (☆ ✍ ☞) (after a petty theft, a young sailor's career is salvaged by devoted father Cedric Hardwicke) and *The Browning Version* (1950) (☞ ✍) (few are sorry to see Latin master Michael Redgrave retire). He successfully captured a stiff upper-lip heroism intended to inspire the nation in *Tell England* (US: *The Battle of Gallipolli*) (1931) (friends die senselessly during ill-fated 1915 raid on Gallipolli), *We Dive at Dawn* (1943) (☞) (John Mills risks his crew's lives and his sub in a reckless pursuit of a Nazi warship) and *The Way to the Stars* (US: *Johnny in the Clouds*) (1945) (☞ ☆ ✍) (a warm-hearted drama around a B&B's proximity to RAF airfield and its guests' concern for the fly boys). Later all-starrers – *The VIPs* (1962) (☆) (>Richard Burton, Elizabeth Taylor, and Margaret Rutherford among those fogged in at an airport) and *The Yellow Rolls Royce* (1964) (stories about the undeserving owners of a luxury car, including >Ingrid Berg-

man) – meant that Asquith sadly went out as he came in.

•*Quiet Wedding* (1940) (✍ ☞ ☆): Rattigan play about snobbery impeding bourgeois wedding arrangements.

•*Cottage to Let* (US: *Bombsight Stolen*) (1941) (☞ ☆): Nazi spy John Mills tries to kidnap inventor >Alastair Sim.

•*The Demi-Paradise* (US: *Adventure for Two*) (1943) (☆): Soviet >Laurence Olivier's study of British life is coloured by dotty Margaret Rutherford.

•*Fanny by Gaslight* (US: *Man of Evil*) (1944): wicked peer James Mason's attempted seduction of Phyllis Calvert is thwarted by Stewart Granger.

•*The Importance of Being Earnest* (1952) (✍ ☆ ☞): classic Oscar Wilde play made glorious by Dame Edith Evans' delivery of exclamation, 'A handbag!'.

•*The Final Test* (1953) (☆): Jack Warner, like Don Bradman before him, finishes his cricket career with a duck.

ASSASSINATION

The American Friend **(>Wim Wenders 1977)**
Based on Patricia Highsmith's *Ripley's Game*, a dying man kills to leave his widow money.

Assassin for Hire **(Michael McCarthy 1951)** ✍
A successful killer is finally arrested for a job he did not do.

The Conformist **(*Il Conformista*) (>Bernardo Bertolucci, Italy 1969)** ☞ ☆ ✍
Powerless against the rise of Mussolini, Jean-Louis Trintignant throws in his lot with the Fascists, who order him to kill his former professor.

The Day of the Jackal **(>Fred Zinnemann 1973)** ☆ ✍ ☞
Anglo-French cop cooperation to prevent sniper killing de Gaulle.

The Manchurian Candidate **(John Frankenheimer 1962)** ☆ ☞
Frank Sinatra realizes that Angela Lansbury is manipulating shell-shocked Laurence Harvey to kill liberal politician.

The Mission (*Ferestadeh*) (Parviz Sayyad, West Germany/USA 1983) ✍
A hit-man for the Islamic Revolution is loathe to waste his target.

A Pain in the A** (*L'Emmerdeur*) (Edouard Molinaro 1973) ✍
A political assassin is hampered by a hapless suicide in the neighbouring hotel room; the film was the model for *Buddy Buddy*.

The Parallax View (Alan J. Pakula 1974) ✍
Murder witnesses die under Warren Beatty's watchful eye.

The Sixth of July (*Shestoe Iulya*) (Yuli Karasik, USSR 1968) ✍
Factual account of a 1918 coup against Lenin sparked by the murder of the German ambassador.

Three Days of the Condor (Sydney Pollack 1975) ☆ ✍ ☞
Robert Redford becomes the target of warring CIA departments.

Astaire, Fred
(Frederick Austerlitz) American actor (1899–1987)

Astaire developed his light comic and song-and-dance skills during his vaudeville partnership with his sister Adele. The man who reputedly taught Edward VIII to dance gained this verdict after a 1932 screen test: 'Can't act. Can't sing. Slightly bald. Can dance a little.' The 1933 *Dancing Lady* (Robert Z. Leonard) (☆) (>Joan Crawford is indecisive over millionaire >Clark Gable and stage manager Astaire) was the prelude to the series of classics he made with >Ginger Rogers, the most outstanding being: *Flying Down to Rio* (Thornton Freeland 1933) (✻) (a Brazilian musical capped with a dance number on the wings of an airborne plane); *The Gay Divorcee* (Mark Sandrich 1934) (☆ ☞) (Ginger mistakes Fred for the co-respondant hired to gain her her divorce); >*Top Hat* (Mark Sandrich 1935) (☆ ☞ ✍♪); *Swing Time* (>George Stevens 1936) (☞ ☆) (Fred's loyalty to the girl next door keeps him from Ginger); *Follow The Fleet* (Mark Sandrich 1936) (☆) (sailor Fred meets singer Ginger on shore leave); and *Shall We Dance?* (Mark Sandrich 1937) (♪ ☆) (dancers pretend-

ing they are married for publicity purposes are blessed with a brilliant George and Ira Gershwin score). Astaire the perfectionist, able to dance anything majestically, proved hard to match. The following were tried with mixed results: Eleanor Powell in *Broadway Melody of 1940* (Norman Taurog 1939) (☆) (even if the dance pairing is not familiar, its route to stardom is); Rita Hayworth in *You'll Never Get Rich* (Sidney Lanfield 1941) (a dancer sees marriage as the best way off the chorus line); Judy Garland in *Easter Parade* (Charles Walters 1948) (♪ ☆) (tetchy dancer Fred finally gets along with new partner, aided by several Irving Berlin classics); Vera-Ellen in *The Belle of New York* (Charles Walters 1952) (♪) (a sugar daddy romances a Salvation Army singer); and Cyd Charisse in *The Band Wagon* (>Vincente Minnelli 1953) (✍ ☆ ♪) (a past prime dancer aims for a final bow in the spotlight). The retirement announced after *Blue Skies* (Stuart Heisler 1946) (♪ ☆) (Fred and Bing Crosby play tug-of-war over the same girl) in 1946, was quickly broken, although he now preferred more dramatic roles, such as in *The Towering Inferno* (John Guillerman/Irwin Allen 1974) (☞ ■ ✻) (an all-star guest list is caught in a blazing skyscraper). A genuine movie star.

 WITH >GINGER ROGERS: •*Roberta* (William A. Seiter 1935) (♪ ☆): Fred, Ginger and a Jerome Kern score help Irene Dunne run a Parisian fashion house.

•*Carefree* (Mark Sandrich 1938) (♪): a girl falls in love with her psychiatrist to Irving Berlin serenades.

•*The Story of Vernon and Irene Castle* (H.C. Potter 1939) (☆ ♪): biopic of dancing team split up by First World War.

•*The Barkleys of Broadway* (Charles Walters 1949) (☆): a comedy actress's success with 'serious drama' imperils her marriage.

WITH OTHERS: •*A Damsel in Distress* (>George Stevens 1938) (✍ ☆): dancer Fred woos aristocrat >Joan Fontaine in this P. G. Wodehouse musical.

•*You Were Never Lovelier* (William A. Seiter

1941) (♫): hotelier Adolphe Menjou schemes to marry off his daughter Rita Hayworth.

•*Holiday Inn* (Mark Sandrich 1942) (♫ ☞): Fred and Bing Crosby are after same girl again, but at least Bing gets to croon 'White Christmas'.

•*Yolanda and the Thief* (>Vincente Minnelli 1945): Fred is, for once, the baddie, with designs on heiress Lucille Bremer's fortune.

•*Ziegfeld Follies* (>Vincente Minnelli 1946) (☆ ☞ ■): Fred interprets deceased impressario >William Powell's plot for new show.

•*Three Little Words* (Richard Thorpe 1950): Fred and Red Skelton in a biopic of songsmiths Bert Kalmar and Harry Ruby.

•*Royal Wedding* (UK: *Wedding Bells*) (>Stanley Donen 1951): in London for a show, Fred falls in love with his aspiring co-star.

Attenborough, Sir Richard
British actor/producer/director (b 1923)
A baby face ushered Attenborough into a number of late-juvenile parts: *In Which We Serve* (Noël Coward/>David Lean 1942) (⚞ ☆ ☞) (episodes from the lives and battles of sub wreck survivors); *Brighton Rock* (US: *Young Scarface*) (John Boulting 1947) (⚞ ☆) (Dickie as Pinkie, >Graham Greene's teenage gangster who marries a naïve murder witness to prevent her testifying); *The Guinea Pig* (US: *The Outsider*) (Roy Boulting 1949) (☆ ⚞) (a bright poor boy is hauled over class coals at an exclusive public school); and *Morning Departure* (US: *Operation Disaster*) (Roy Baker 1950) (☆) (a sub is doomed and only eight men can escape, but which ones?). He formed a partnership with director Bryan Forbes in the late 1950s, producing *Whistle Down the Wind* (1961) (⚞ ☞) (Hayley Mills believes killer Alan Bates is Christ) *The L-Shaped Room* (1962) (⚞ ☆ ♫) (Lynne Reid Banks story of Leslie Caron holing up in a seedy guest house prior to having an abortion) and *Séance on a Wet Afternoon* (1964) (⚞) (a psychic and her spouse kidnap a child to publicize her powers at a staged seance). Meanwhile, Attenborough developed his character acting talent, demonstrating it in such films as *Guns at Batasi* (John Guillermin 1964) (☆) (lips stiffen as African rebels attack a British base), *Conduct Unbe-*

coming (Michael Anderson 1975) (⚞) (high jinks in a Raj mess get out of hand and Susannah York is assaulted) and *The Chess Players* (>Satyajit Ray 1977) (☆ ☞) (Sanjeev Kumar and Saeed Jaffrey would rather play chess than contemplate the advent of Dickie's red coats), and in roles as varied as Albert Blossom in *Doctor Dolittle* (Richard Fleischer 1967) (♫ ☆) (with David Attenborough for a brother, Sir Richard finds talking to the animals no problem) and as Christie in >*Ten Rillington Place* (Richard Fleischer 1971) (☆ ⚞ ☞). He is now perhaps more renowned for his cast-of-thousands directorial projects: *Oh What a Lovely War!* (1969) (♫ ☞ ■ ☆) (World War I told through the popular songs of the time), *A Bridge Too Far* (1977) (☞ ☆ ⚞ ■) (all-star Allied regiments narrowly fail to capture the bridgehead at Arnhem), >*Gandhi* (1982) (☞ ☆ ⚞ ■) and >*Cry Freedom* (1987) (☞ ☆ ⚞ ■ ♫).

 AS ACTOR: •*Private's Progress* (John Boulting 1956) (⚞ ☆):Dickie and Dennis Price pick up the valuable pieces of art in the wake of the Allied advance.
•*The Angry Silence* (Guy Green 1960) (☆): shades of >*I'm All Right, Jack* as Dickie alone blacklegs a strike.
•*Only Two Can Play* (Sidney Gilliat 1961) (☆): Kingsley Amis tale of the social-climbing affairs of randy Welsh librarian Peter Sellers.
•*The Dock Brief* (US: *Trial and Error*) (James Hill 1962) (☆ ⚞): Peter Sellers as a hack lawyer defending Dickie in John Mortimer screenplay).
AS DIRECTOR: •*Young Winston* (1972) (☞ ■ ☆): Boer War press career of Churchill (Simon Ward).
•*Magic* (1978) (☆): Anthony Hopkins as a ventriloquist driven to kill by his dummy.
•*A Chorus Line* (1985) (☆ ♫): Broadway producer >Michael Douglas delves into the lives of auditioners, almost turning a casting into a whodunnit.

Audran, Stéphane
(Colette Dacheville) French actress (b 1932)
Apart from >*The Discreet Charm of the Bourgeoisie* (*Le Charme Discret de la Bourgeoisie*) (>Luis Buñuel, France 1972), *Clean Slate*

(*Coup de Torchon*) (Bertrand Tavernier, France 1981) (☆ ☞ ✍) (colonial cop >Philippe Noiret eliminates his life's complications, including his wife Audran and his mistress Isabelle Huppert) and >*Babette's Feast* (*Babettes Gaestebud*) (Gabriel Axel, Denmark 1988) (☆ ■ ☞ ✍), Audran's best work has been done in conjunction with her second husband, >Claude Chabrol. Stunningly beautiful in a >Dietrich kind of way, Audran portrays respectable women, frequently called 'Hélène', caught up in adultery and murder. First appearing as an ingenue – in *Les Bonnes Femmes* (*The Girls*) (1960) (☆ ☞) (four bored shop assistants seek excitement, but mediocrity won't let go), *The Third Lover* (*L'Oeil du Malin*) (1962) (☞ ■ ☆) (a hack journalist ruins the marriage of a bestselling novelist and his wife) and *The Champagne Murders* (*Le Scandale*) (1967) (☆) (a nasty ménage of gold-diggers try to pin murder on a millionaire) – she graduated to playing sexually frustrated women in *The Unfaithful Wife* (*La Femme Infidèle*) (1969) (✍ ☆ ☞) (Audran's marriage to Michel Bouquet is saved when he murders her lover), *The Butcher* (*Le Boucher*) (☞ ☆) (coy school teacher Audran is courted by a shy butcher who proves to be a brutal sex killer) and *La Rupture* (*The Breakup*) (1970) (☞ ✍ ☆) (a detective spies on Audran to obtain damning evidence in a child-custody case), and ultimately sexually aware women in *Les Biches* (*The Does*) (1968) (☆ ☞ ✍) (Audran won the Berlin Best Actress Award as one half of a lesbian affair broken by Jean-Louis Trintignant), *Just Before Nightfall* (*Juste Avant la Nuit*) (1971) (■ ☞) (a wife and a cuckold take the news of her husband's murder of his mistress like adults) and *Blood Wedding* (aka *Wedding In Blood*) (*Les Noces Rouges*) (1973) (☞) (a mayor uses his deputy's affair with his wife to corrupt advantage). In 1981, she appeared as Carla in the TV adaptation of Evelyn Waugh's *Brideshead Revisited*. She has more recently opted for minor roles in Chabrol's pictures, notably in *Violette Nozière* (*Violette*) (1978) (✍ ☆ ☞) (wild teenager Isabelle Huppert poisons her mother Audran, and regrets failing to kill her) and *Cop au Vin* (*Poulet au Vinaigre*)(1985) (☞ ☆) (Inspector Lavardin (Jean Poiret) investigates small town property deal murder).

•*Landru* (>Claude Chabrol 1962) (☆ ☞): true story of a suave murderer of trusting women.

•*La Ligne de Démarcation* (*The Line of Demarcation*) (>Claude Chabrol 1966) (☞ ☆ ✍): provincials keep spies and Allied pilots from the Gestapo.

•*A Murder is a Murder...Is a Murder* (*Un Meurte est un Meurte*) (Etienne Perier 1972) (✍ ☆): a stranger demands payment for Audran's murder from her husband, who is the murder suspect and dependent on sister-in-law (also Audran) and railway inspector >Claude Chabrol for an alibi.

•*Dead Pigeon on Beethoven Street* (Samuel Fuller 1972): a private eye is killed by German protection gang.

•*And Then There Were None* (Peter Collinson 1974) (✍): guests on a remote island disappear one by one in >Agatha Christie remake.

•*Vincent, François, Paul and the Others* (*Vincent, François, Paul...et les Autres*) (Claude Sautet 1974) (■ ☆): a frustrated writer, a doctor and a tool-hire owner (>Yves Montand) rely on the lives of others to alleviate their mid-life crises.

L'Avventura ☞ ■ ✍ ☆
Italy/France • Cino del Duca/PCE/Lyre • 1960 • 145 mins • b/w
d >Michelangelo Antonioni
w Michelangelo Antonioni/Elio Bartolini/ Tonino Guerra   ph Aldo Scavarda
m Giovanni Fusco
Monica Vitti, Lea Massari, Gabriele Ferzetti, Dominique Blanchar

At a time when most other Italian directors were still exploring the poverty of postwar Italy, Antonioni discovered Neo-Realism among the materially opulent and morally bankrupt. *L'Avventura* is populated by the same helpless, idle rich that inhabit the realms of *Brideshead*, enjoying nothing, easily bored and callously disloyal to even their nearest and dearest. Anna (Massari) disappears following a row during an island picnic. As her lover Sandro (Ferzetti) and friend Claudia (Vitti) fall in love with each other during their nationwide search, you get the feeling that Anna is well out of this shallow world, but not for one moment do you wonder where she's gone, such is the allure of even the most unpleasant aristos. The stuff of tinsel soaps, but requires a touch more concentration.

 •The disappearance of some Australian schoolgirls in 1900 is recalled in *Picnic at Hanging Rock* (Peter Weir 1975) (■).

•>John Wayne is on the trail of the Indians who killed his brother and sister-in-law and kidnapped his niece in *The Searchers* (>John Ford 1956) (☞ ■).

•There is little paradise on the island inhabited by the warring boys in William Golding's *Lord of the Flies* (Peter Brook 1963) (■ ✍).

•Dispassionate love among the idle classes is also the subject of *The Prince and the Showgirl* (1957) (■) starring director >Laurence Olivier and >Marilyn Monroe.

Babette's Feast (Babettes Gaestebud) ☆ ▦ ☞ ✍

Denmark Panorama Film International/ Nordisk Film/Danish Film Institute • *1987* • *103 mins* • *col*

wd Gabriel Axel   ph Henning Kristiansen   m Per Norgaard

>Stéphane Audran, Jean-Philippe Lafont, Gudmar Wivesson, Bibi Andersson

La Grande Bouffe (Marco Ferreri 1973) (☞) and *Dim Sum* (Wayne Wang 1986) examined eating as, respectively, a mode of death and a necessity of life, but the magnificent *Babette's Feast*, based on Karen Blixen's novella, treats the preparation and consumption of food as a rare and pure pleasure. Stéphane Audran, the quietly determined Babette, is a French cook who repays the charity of the daughters of a tyrannical Danish pastor with a splendid banquet. As she collects the delicious ingredients, we learn the backgrounds of her guests, so that a loose end is tied and a new discovery revealed with every course served. The contrast between the diners' gentility as well as the succulent delicacies and the windswept remoteness of the village holds us spellbound as the action sweeps from prayer meeting to barrack, café to court. An unusual but mouthwatering treat.

 •James Joyce's short story of an eventful Dublin dinner party is told in *The Dead* (>John Huston 1988) (☞ ✍ ☆ ▦).

•The return of an uninvited dinner guest involves teacher Vanessa Redgrave in tragedy in *Wetherby* (David Hare 1985) (✍ ☆ ▦).

•Scottish soldiers of fortune rob the daughter of a 16th-century Danish pastor in *Sir Arne's Treasure* (aka *The Three who Were Doomed*) (*Herr Arnes Pengar*) (Mauritz Stiller 1919) (☞ ▦ ✍).

•Devotion of a sexual kind unites Scandinavian sisters Ingrid Thulin and Gunnel Lindblom in *The Silence* (*Tystnaden*) (>Ingmar Bergman 1963) (☆ ☞).

•A trucker transforms a transport café into a *haute cuisine* restaurant in *Tampopo* (Juzo Itami, Japan 1986) (✍ ☆).

BABIES

Baby Boom (Charles Shyer 1987) ☆
Yuppy mother >Diane Keaton takes the baby food market by storm.

Bachelor Mother (Garson Kanin 1939)
☆ ☞ ✍

Shopgirl >Ginger Rogers finds an abandoned baby and the boss's son David Niven is presumed to be the father.

A Bedtime Story (Norman Taurog 1933)
Maurice Chevalier postpones philandering for baby-sitting.

Boy Meets Girl (Lloyd Bacon 1938) ☆ ✍
Screenwriters >James Cagney and Pat O'Brien make a film star of an unborn baby.

Don't Bother to Knock (Roy Baker 1952) ☆
>Marilyn Monroe as a crazed babysitter threatening to kill a child.

Father's Little Dividend (>Vincente Minnelli 1951)
>Spencer Tracy finds it hard to whip up enthusiasm for his grandchild.

The Great Lie (Edmund Goulding 1941)
☆ ✍

>Bette Davis cares for the baby abandoned by Mary Astor.

Rosemary's Baby (>Roman Polanski 1968)
✍ ☆ ☞

Mia Farrow gives birth to the devil's child.

Three Men and a Cradle (Trois Hommes et un Couffin) (Coline Serreau, France 1985)
✍ ☆

Flat-sharers learn to cope with the baby found on their doorstep.

Three Men and a Baby (Leonard Nimoy 1987) ☆

Hollywood re-make of the above film with Tom Selleck, Steve Guttenberg and Ted Danson.

BAFTA:
British Academy of Film and Television Arts Awards for Best Film
Until 1969, awards were given to British films only

1948
***Odd Man Out* (US: *Gang War*) (>Carol Reed)** ☞ ☆ ■
James Mason as an injured IRA assassin on the run.
1949
***The Fallen Idol* (US: *The Lost Illusion*) (>Carol Reed)** ☆
>Graham Greene story of butler Ralph Richardson, who is hero-worshipped by the son of the house.
1950
>*The Third Man* (>Carol Reed) ☆ ☞ ♫ ✍ ■
1951
***The Blue Lamp* (Basil Deardon)** ✍ ☆
Jack Warner is killed by Dirk Bogarde but lives on in 'Dixon of Dock Green'.
1952
***The Lavender Hill Mob* (Charles Crichton)** ✍ ☆ ☞
Stanley Holloway, Sid James and Alfie Bass abet >Alec Guinness in a bullion heist.

1953
***The Sound Barrier* (US: *Breaking the Sound Barrier*) (>David Lean)** ☞
Ralph Richardson sacrifices lives to fly one of his planes faster than the speed of sound.
1954
>*Genevieve* (Henry Cornelius) ✍ ☆ ♫ ☞
1955
***Hobson's Choice* (>David Lean)** ☆ ✍ ☞
Worm John Mills turns against >Charles Laughton's tyrannical cobbler.
1956
***Richard III* (>Laurence Olivier)** ✍ ☆ ■ ☞ ♫
The director is brilliant as Shakespeare's hunchbacked usurper.
1957
***Reach for the Sky* (Lewis Gilbert)** ☆
Kenneth More in a biopic of artificial leg pilot Douglas Bader.

1958

The Bridge on the River Kwai (>David Lean) ✍ ☆ ☞
>Alec Guinness commands PoWs force-labouring on the Burma railroad.

1959

Room at the Top (Jack Clayton) ■ ☆
Mercenary clerk Joe Lampton (Laurence Harvey) progresses oblivious of the death of his lover Simone Signoret.

1960

Sapphire (Basil Dearden) ☆
London plain clothes bobbies investigate a racial killing.

1961

Saturday Night and Sunday Morning (Karel Reisz) ☆ ✍ ☞
Factory worker Albert Finney finds rebellion too problematic and embraces convention.

1962

>*A Taste of Honey* (Tony Richardson) ✍ ☞ ☆

1963

Lawrence of Arabia (>David Lean) ■ ☞ ♫
Peter O'Toole in a biopic of First World War hero T. E. Lawrence.

1964

Tom Jones (Tony Richardson) ✍ ■ ☆
Henry Fielding's bawdy 18th-century tale of greed, sloth and lust.

1965

>*Dr Strangelove; or, How I Learned to Stop Worrying and Love the Bomb* (>Stanley Kubrick) ✍ ☞ ☆ ■

1966

The Ipcress File (Sidney J. Furie) ☆ ✍
>Michael Caine as Len Deighton's spy Harry Palmer discovering insider treason.

1967

The Spy Who Came in from the Cold (Martin Ritt) ■ ☆
>Richard Burton as John Le Carré's disillusioned secret agent.

1968

A Man for All Seasons (>Fred Zinnemann) ☆ ✍ ■ ☞
Paul Scofield excels as Sir Thomas More opposing Henry VIII's divorce.

1969

>*The Graduate* (>Mike Nichols) ☆ ☞ ♫ ✍

1970

Midnight Cowboy (>John Schlesinger) ♫ ☆
>Dustin Hoffman pimps for novice gigolo Jon Voight.

1971

Butch Cassidy and the Sundance Kid (George Roy Hill) ☆ ♫ ✍
>Paul Newman and Robert Redford as loveable Wild West rogues.

1972

Sunday Bloody Sunday (>John Schlesinger) ☆ ☞
Murray Head sleeps with both Glenda Jackson and Peter Finch.

1973

Cabaret (Bob Fosse) ♫ ✍
Life in Weimar Berlin based on Christopher Isherwood's autobiographical novels.

1974

Day for Night (*La Nuit Americaine*) (>François Truffaut) ☞ ✍
Tempers fray during the filming of a love story in Nice.

1975

Lacombe, Lucien (>Louis Malle) ✍ ☞ ☆
Teenager collaborating with Nazis pays for the victimization of a family.

1976

Alice Doesn't Live Here Anymore (>Martin Scorsese) ☞ ☆
Widow Ellen Burstyn tries her luck as a singer.

1977
>One Flew Over the Cuckoo's Nest
(>Miloš Forman) ☆ ✍ ☞
1978
>Annie Hall (>Woody Allen) ✍ ☆ ☞
1979
>Julia (>Fred Zinnemann) ☆ ✍ ☞ ▓
1980
>Manhattan (>Woody Allen)
✍ ☆ ▓ ☞ ♪
1981
The Elephant Man (David Lynch)
▓ ☆ ✍ ☞ ✳

John Hurt as Victorian John Merrick who, suffering from a rare deforming disease, is exploited as a freak.
1982
Chariots of Fire (Hugh Hudson) ♪ ✍
British runners from privileged and Presbyterian backgrounds win medals at 1924 Paris Olympics.
1983
>Gandhi (>Richard Attenborough)
☞ ☆ ✍
1984
Educating Rita (Lewis Gilbert) ☆ ✍ ♪
Julie Walters rekindles drunken tutor >Michael Caine's interest in life and literature.

1985
The Killing Fields (Roland Joffe) ☆ ♪
Newspaper cameraman witnesses full horror of war in Cambodia.
1986
The Purple Rose of Cairo (>Woody Allen)
Jeff Daniels walks off the screen and enlivens Mia Farrow's drab life.
1987
>A Room With a View (James Ivory)
☆ ▓ ☞ ✍
1988
>Jean de Florette (Claude Berri) ☆ ✍
☞ ▓
1989
The Last Emperor (>Bernardo Bertolucci) ☞ ▓ ✍
Pu Yi (John Lone) is deposed as Emperor of China and later installed as Japanese puppet ruler of Manchukuo.
1990
Dead Poets Society (>Peter Weir 1989) ☆ ☞
English teacher Robin Williams' inspiring poetry lessons tragically conflict with a student's strict upbringing.

Banks

American Madness (>Frank Capra 1932) ☞
Anthem for the Depression times as small investors save a failing bank.

The Bank Dick (UK: *The Bank Detective*)
(Eddie Cline 1940) ☆
>W. C. Fields as a security guard who hates his life and work.

Cash on Demand (Quentin Lawrence 1963) ☆
Timid, pedantic manager Peter Cushing outwits robbers.

Dog Day Afternoon (>Sidney Lumet 1975) ☞ ☆
Al Pacino and his lover John Cazale exchange banter with hostages until their demands are met.

Perfect Friday (Peter Hall 1970)
Stanley Baker as the manager who robs his own bank and is cheated by Ursula Andress.

The Steel Trap (Andrew Stone 1952) ☞ ☆
Joseph Cotten has more trouble returning cash than stealing it when his conscience is pricked.

Take the Money and Run (>Woody Allen 1968) ✍ ☆
Dud crook's raid fails when the teller can't decipher his stand-and-deliver note.

Barrault, Jean-Louis
French actor (b 1910)
Primarily a stage actor, Barrault's film appearances have been limited, but of a uniformly

high standard. His Baptiste Debureau in >*Les Enfants Du Paradis* (*Children of Paradise*) (1945) – a second collaboration with >Marcel Carné and Jacques Prévert following *Drôle de Drame* (*Bizarre, Bizarre*) (1937) (✍ ☆ ☞) (a face-saving lie comes back to haunt a writer) – was a superb demonstration of the mime technique he developed under Etienne Decroux and ranks among the great performances of French cinema. >Max Ophüls' 1950 *La Ronde* (☞ ✍ ☆) (an unending circle of lovers begins and ends with a prostitute) and >Jean Renoir's 1959 *Testament of Dr Cordelier* (US: *Experiment in Evil*) (*Le Testament du Dr Cordelier*) (☆ ☞) (a re-working of *Dr Jekyll and Mr Hyde*), briefly lured him away from prestigious theatre directorships. A 13-year absence from cinema ended in 1981 with *The Night of Varennes* (*La Nuit de Varennes*) (Ettore Scola) (■ ☞ ☆), in which a star cast follow the intercepted flight of Louis XVI and Marie Antoinette from revolutionary Paris.

 •*The Puritan* (*Le Puritain*) (Jeff Musso 1937) (☆ ✍): Liam O'Flaherty story of a killer driven by excessive morality.

•*The Pearls of the Crown* (*Les Perles de la Couronne*) (Sacha Guitry/Christian-Jaque 1937) (☆ ✍): Barrault as Napoleon in through-the-ages ownership tale of three pearls from a Tudor necklace.

•*Symphonie Fantastique* (Christian-Jaque 1942) (☆ ♫): the life and times of Hector Berlioz.

•*The Longest Day* (Andrew Marton/Ken Annakin/Bernhard Wicki 1962) (■ ☆): vast cast of stars 'fight them on the beaches'.

The Battleship Potemkin (US: Potemkin) (Bronenosets Potemkin) ☞ ■ ✍

USSR • Goskino • 1925 • 75 mins • b/w

wd >Sergei Eisenstein ph Edouard Tissé/V. Popov

A. Antonov, Grigori Alexandrov, Vladimir Barski, Levshin

The events during and following the mutiny on board the Russian warship *Potemkin* as it lay

at anchor outside Odessa in 1905, and even the glorification of the workers struggling valiantly against the imperialist oppressors, are largely beside the point in Eisenstein's silent masterpiece. It is as an exercise in pure filmmaking that has been so consistently influential, that the scene of the pram catapulting down the steps was imitated as recently as 1986 in Brian De Palma's *The Untouchables* (☆) (Kevin Costner and >Sean Connery pursue >Robert De Niro's Al Capone). The rapid cross-cutting gives the impression of an animated photographic collage, conveying with harrowing conviction the despair, cruelty, degradation and horror experienced by all who were caught up in this thwarted revolt. The film is 75 minutes packed with reasons why silent films are still worth watching.

 •The 1905 revolution failed, but the antics of Rasputin, as depicted in *Agony* (*Agonia*) (Elem Klimov 1975) (☞ ■ ☆), helped discredit the monarchy prior to 1917.

•The mental decline of >Humphrey Bogart's Captain Queeg precipitates *The Caine Mutiny* (Edward Dmytryk 1954) (☆).

•In *Arsenal* (>Alexander Dovzhenko 1929) (☞ ■) more Ukrainians further the workers' cause.

•Charlton Heston's resistance to oppression is brutally punished on the *Planet of the Apes* (Franklin Schaffner 1968) (✳ ✍).

BED AND BOARD

The Bed Sitting Room (Richard Lester 1969) ☆
Spike Milligan/John Antrobus view of the British reaction to nuclear holocaust.

The L-Shaped Room (Bryan Forbes 1962) ✍ ☆ ♫
Eccentric tenants help Leslie Caron through an abortion trauma.

The Lodger (US: The Phantom Fiend) (Maurice Elvey 1932/John Brahm 1944) ✍
A man who keeps to himself is suspected of being Jack the Ripper.

London Belongs to Me (US: Dulcimer Street)
(Sidney Gilliat 1948) ☆ ☞
>Alastair Sim leads tenants in defence of accused murderer >Richard Attenborough.
The Passing of the Third Floor Back
(Berthold Viertel 1935) ✍ ☆
Jerome K. Jerome tale of a Christ-figure (Conrad Veidt) transforming co-habitants' lives.
Rising Damp (Joe McGrath 1980) ☆
Leonard Rossiter is splendid as seedy landlord Rigsby in this TV tie-in.
Separate Tables (Delbert Mann 1958) ✍ ☆
Wendy Hiller pities David Niven when his boasts are exposed in this screen version of Terence Rattigan's play.
The Sidewalks of New York (Jules White/
Zion Myers 1931) ☆
Owner >Buster Keaton falls in love with slumdweller Anita Page.
Strange Boarders (Herbert Mason 1938) ✍
One of the guests in a B&B is a spy; a flatfoot postpones his honeymoon to discover which.
>*Turtle Diary* (John Irvin 1985)) ☆ ✍ ☞ ■

Belle de Jour ☞ ☆ ✍ ■
France/Italy Paris Film/Five Film 1967 100
mins col
d >Luis Bu9uel w Luis
Bu9uel/Jean-Claude Carri/re ph Sacha
Vierny
>Catherine Deneuve, Jean Sorel, Michel
Piccoli, Genevi/ve Page

After Emma Bovary and then Catherine Deneuve in this film, there must have been uncomfortable suspicions in the mind of every male doctor in France. But while Madame Bovary was content simply to vent her sexual frustration with one lover, Jean Sorel's bedroom timidity drives his wife to work in a Parisian brothel. Here she discovers her true sexual self, and saves her marriage through indulging in sado-masochistic fantasies shared with clients ranging from the raunchy to the repulsive. Bu9uel's study of Freudian hang-ups is hugely erotic, but is not simply a titillating sex romp. It laments the lack of communication within marriage, condemns bourgeois conventionality and argues convincingly for monogamy.

Danny Kaye also spends his life daydreaming in *The Secret Life of Walter Mitty* (Norman Z. McLeod 1947) (☆).
Another doctor's wife is >Greta Garbo in *The Painted Veil* (Richard Boleslawski 1934) (☆), but she helps George Brent cure Chinese sick. Aribert Mog is the timid husband of child bride Hedy Lamarr in *Ecstasy* (*Extase*) (Gustav Machaty 1933), whose nude scenes caused it to be banned or censored worldwide.
Julie Walters is the Cynthia Payne-like madame of a suburban brothel in *Personal Services* (Terry Jones 1988).
The starker realities of prostitution are explored in *Working Girls* (Lizzie Borden 1987) (☆).
A couple devoid of sexual hang-ups are exploited by an opportunist restaurateur in *Eating Raoul* (Paul Bartel 1982).
Another housewife with a secret is Jeanne Moreau in *The Lovers* (*Les Amants*) (>Louis Malle 1958) (☞ ♫ ☆).
However, there are also some unfaithful doctors, one being Maurice Chevalier in *One Hour with You* (>George Cukor/>Ernst Lubitsch 1932) (☞ ♫).

The Belly of an Architect
■ ☞ ☆ ✍ ♫
UK 1987 118 mins col
wd Peter Greenaway ph Sacha Vierny
m Wim Mertens
Brian Dennehy, Chloe Webb, Lambert
Wilson, Sergio Fantoni

Stourley Kracklite (Dennehy) arrives in Rome for a commemoration of the architect Boull)e and promptly loses control of his destiny. Bureaucratic snags disrupt his exhibition, while he attributes the pain of his cancer to his adulterous wife's (Webb) poisoning him. As his grasp on reality slips away and the agony in his guts becomes unbearable, he develops an obsession with his paunch and the classical anatomies of ancient statues, which drives him to enlarge a photocopy of Augustus's abdomen and secure it beneath his own shirt. Peter Greenaway's hypnotic yet accessible play on *I Claudius* and the seductive photography showing the lesser-known beauties of the Eternal City add up to a leisurely but uncomfortable stroll through a gallery of unpleasantly pretentious rogues.

 •>Spencer Tracy believes >Katharine Hepburn to have been responsible for the death of her hero husband in *Keeper of the Flame* (>George Cukor 1942) (☆).

•Brigitte Bardot mocks scriptwriter husband Michel Piccoli's attempts to set-up filming of *The Odyssey* for director >Fritz Lang in *Contempt* (*Le Mépris*) (>Jean-Luc Godard 1963) (☆ ✍).

•Mervyn Johns is an architect whose recurrent dreams drive him to murder his shrink Roland Culver in *Dead of Night* (Alberto Cavalcanti/Basil Dearden/Robert Hamer/Charles Crichton 1945) (☞ ☆ ♫).

•Greenaway also wrote and directed *The Draughtsman's Contract* (1982) (■ ☞ ✍), in which an 18th-century draughtsman discovers that his commission involves much more than sketching a stately home.

Belmondo, Jean-Paul
French actor (b 1933)

Belmondo abandoned a brief boxing career for acting in 1950, and nine years of stage and screen work honed the character and anti-heroic comedy technique, complemented by his unprepossessing looks, that was to place him in great demand among New Wave French directors. For >Jean-Luc Godard he made >*À Bout de Souffle* (*Breathless*) (1960) (☞ ☆ ✍), *A Woman is a Woman* (*Une Femme est une Femme*) (1961)(☞ ✍ ☆) (Anna Karina won the Cannes Best Actress Award as a stripper hoping that Belmondo is Mr Right) and *Pierrot Le Fou* (1965) (✍) (bored Belmondo has crime adventures across France with accomplice Anna Karina). For >Claude Chabrol he appeared in *Web of Passion* (*Leda*) (1959) (☆) (a vintner's mistress is murdered and members of his household, including slovenly Hungarian son-in-law Belmondo, are suspected) and *Docteur Popaul* (*High Heels*) (aka *Scoundrels in White*) (1972) (☆) (Belmondo dates plain women, in-

cluding Mia Farrow, for their minds). He was also directed by >Louis Malle in *The Thief of Paris* (*Le Voleur*) (1967) (☆ ✍ ☞) (defrauded of his inheritance Belmondo learns crime from a priest (Julien Guiomar) to finance his affair with Geneviève Bujold); by >François Truffaut, *The Mississippi Mermaid* (*La Sirène du Mississippi*) (1969) (✍ ☞ ☆) (tobacco planter Belmondo discovers that his arranged marriage to >Catherine Deneuve might be a fatal mistake); and by>Alain Resnais in *Stavisky* (1973) (exposure of Jewish financier Belmondo implicates prominent Establishment figures and undermines the 1934 French government).

 •*Moderato Cantabile* (Peter Brook 1960) (☆ ✍): Jeanne Moreau won the Cannes Best Actress Award for gleaning clues in a café murder case from customer Belmondo.

•*That Man from Rio* (*L'Homme de Rio*) (Philippe De Broca 1964) (☆): a pilot and his girlfriend go in hot pursuit of some valuable statues.

•*Is Paris Burning*? (René Clément 1965) (✍): Belmondo, >Orson Welles, >Yves Montand and Charles Boyer are among those involved in >Francis Ford Coppola and Gore Vidal telling of the 1944 liberation of Paris.

•*Borsalino* (Jacques Deray 1970) (☆): lowlifers Belmondo and Alain Delon use force to corner the Marseilles meat market.

•*The Scoundrel* (*Les Mariés de l'An Deux*) (Jean-Paul Rappeneau 1971) (■ ✍): Belmondo, having fled the French Revolution, returns to be re-united with his wife and gain a position at Napoleon's court.

Ben-Hur ☆ ☞ ✍ ■
USA • MGM • 1959 • 217 mins • col
d >William Wyler/Andrew Marton
w Karl Tunberg   ph Robert L. Surtees
m Miklos Rozsa
Charlton Heston, Haya Harareet, Jack Hawkins, Stephen Boyd, Hugh Griffith

Initially a silent classic, the epic story of the Jewish noble whose revolutionary exploits against the might of Rome condemn him to a life of slavery was resurrected by William Wyler in 1959, and it went on to trawl an unprecedented 12 Oscars. As in the 1926 version, the sea battle and the chariot race live longest in the memory, for as Ben-Hur (Heston) takes his revenge on the ruthless Messala (Boyd) for betraying him to the authorities and then seeks solace in an emerging Christianity, it all gets tackily devout. The producer Sam Zimbalist must have been relieved that he had failed to land Rock Hudson or >Marlon Brando for the lead, as only Charlton Heston's conviction sustains interest. However, there is much else to applaud in Hollywood's most impressive epic, particularly Surtees' splendid cinematography and Rozsa's stirring score.

•Another Roman spectator sport is the subject of *Demetrius and the Gladiators* (Delmer Daves 1954) (☆).

•Life is hell on wheels for drivers James Garner and >Yves Montand in *Grand Prix* (John Frankenheimer 1966).

•The brutality of serfdom is to the fore in the chilling *Sansho the Bailiff* (*Sansho Dayu*) (>Kenji Mizoguchi 1954) (☞■ ☆).

•>Kirk Douglas plays another slave troubling the Roman Empire in *Spartacus* (>Stanley Kubrick 1960) (☞ ☆), while Peter Ustinov's Nero proves that damage can be equally easily done from the top in *Quo Vadis?* (>Mervyn Le Roy 1951) (☆ ☞).

Bergman, Ingmar
Swedish writer/director (b 1918)

Son of a chaplain to the Swedish Royal family and perhaps the most personal director of all, Bergman has concentrated his highly individual and influential style and the efforts of his ensemble (variously including Max Von Sydow, Bibi Andersson, >Harriet Andersson and Liv Ullmann) on three main areas. THE INCONSTANCY OF LOVE: *Summer Interlude* (aka *Illicit Interlude*) (*Sommarlek*) (1951) (■ ☞): ballerina's recollections of an adolescent romance that ends in tragedy; *Summer with Monika* (US: *Monika*) (*Sommaren Med Monika*) (1952) (☞■): reckless teenage girl fails to see why her life should be ruined by an unwanted baby; *Sawdust and Tinsel* (aka *The Naked Night*)

(*Gycklarnas Afton*) (1953) (☞ ■ ☆): reconciliation and adultery at the circus; *Smiles of a Summer's Night* (*Sommarnattens Leende*) (1955) (✍ ☞ ■ ☆): country weekend flirtations that inspired >Woody Allen's *A Midsummer Night's Sex Comedy*; >*Wild Strawberries* (*Smultronstället*) (1957) (☞ ☆ ■ ✍). THE DISCOMFORT OF RELIGION AND THE DUPLICITY OF THE CHURCH: >*The Seventh Seal* (*Det Sjunde Inseglet*) (1957) (■ ☞ ☆ ✍); *The Face* (US: *The Magician*) (*Ansiktet*) (1958) (☆ ☞): magician Max Von Sydow is refused entry to Stockholm to prevent him conning citizens; *The Virgin Spring* (*Jungfrukällan*) (1960) (✍ ☆ ■): Best Foreign Film Oscar winner tells of martyrdom of and subsequent miracle connected with a 14th-century girl; *Through a Glass Darkly* (*Såsom i em Spegel*) (1961) (☞ ☆): novelist with a son who hates women, a daughter who is going mad and a son-in-law who is a nervous wreck sweeps them all off to a remote island; and *Winter Light* (*The Communicants*) (*Nattvardsgasterna*) (1962) (☞ ☆): a pastor enduring a crisis of faith seriously disturbs his congregation. THE CHARACTER AND THE INTERREACTION OF MODERN WOMEN: *So Close to Life* (US: *Brink of Life*) (*Nara Livet*) (1958) (☆): Ingrid Thulin, Eva Dahlbeck, and Bibi Andersson discuss their pregnancies in a maternity ward; *The Silence* (*Tystnaden*) (1963) (☆ ☞): Ingrid Thulin is keen to show more than sisterly affection to Gunnel Lindblom; *Persona* (1966) (☆ ☞): actress Liv Ullmann and nurse Bibi Andersson assimilate each other's personalities; *The Touch* (*Beröringen*) (1971) (■): a doctor's bored wife falls for an archaeologist; *Cries and Whispers* (*Viskingar Och Rop*) (1973) (☞■ ☆): >Harriet Andersson is nursed through her cancer by her sisters and a loyal servant; *Face to Face* (*Ansikte mot Ansikte*) (1976) (☆): Liv Ullmann as a psychiatrist falling prey to nervous tension; and *Autumn Sonata* (1978) (☆): >Ingrid Bergman's lover dies so she visits her long-lost daughter Liv Ullmann. Bergman retired after his childhood autobiography >*Fanny And Alexander* (*Fanny Och Alexander*) (☞ ■ ✍ ☆) in 1982.

•*Prison* (US: *The Devil's Wanton*) (*Fängelse*) (1948) (■): a mother regrets giving away her child, can't get it back and loses her lovers in this dream-sequenced metaphor for Hell.

•*Thirst* (US: *Three Strange Loves*) (*Törst*) (1949) (☆ ☞): a man's present wife and his ex-wives are miserable and unable to escape their claustrophic situations.

•*Waiting Women* (US: *Secrets of Women*) (*Kvinnors Väntan*) (1952) (☞ ☆ ✍): three women tell stories, two of potential affairs and one of the weakness of her husband.

•*The Devil's Eye* (*Djävulens Öga*) (1960) (☆): the Devil sends Don Juan to corrupt pastor Nils Poppe's daughter Bibi Andersson.

•*Now About These Women* (US: *All These Women*) (*För Att Inte Tala Om Alla Dessa Kvinnor*) (1964) (■ ✍): biographer Jarl Kulle discovers his cellist subject paid more attention to his women than his music.

•*Hour of the Wolf* (*Vargtimmen*) (1967) (☆ ☞): artist Max Von Sydow is tormented by daydreams and nightmares.

•*The Shame* (*Skammen*) (1968) (☆ ✍ ☞): Liv Ullmann and her gentle giant husband Max Von Sydow's unwilling participation in a civil war corrupts their comfortable relationship.

•*Scenes from a Marriage* (*Scener ur ett Aktenskap*) (1973) (☞ ☆): confrontations lead to acceptance as Liv Ullmann becomes accustomed to Erland Josephson's mistress Bibi Andersson.

•*The Serpent's Egg* (*Das Schlangenei*) (1977) (✍): a trapeze artist is a victim of and an eyewitness to Hitler's rise to power.

Bergman, Ingrid
Swedish actress (1915–1982)

Audiences demanded demure victims. Bergman misguidedly envisaged herself as a serious artist, and consequently she enjoyed a somewhat patchy career. Her appearances in *Pa Solsidan* (*On the Sunny Side*) and *Intermezzo: A Love Story* (both Gustaf Molander 1936) (Ingrid falls in love with violinist Gosta Ekman, the father of her piano student) invited Hollywood offers, although the re-make of the second film, with Bergman opposite >Leslie Howard was delayed until 1939. Beginning

with *Dr Jekyll and Mr Hyde* (Victor Fleming 1941) (✍ ☆) (Spencer Tracy as the scientist whose evil alter ego terrorizes Bergman's prostitute), the 1940s were a golden era for Bergman. >*Casablanca* (>Michael Curtiz 1942) (☆ ☞ ✍♫■); *For Whom the Bell Tolls* (AAN; Sam Wood 1943) (☞ ☆) (>Gary Cooper's aid for Bergman's band of Spanish Civil War partisans costs him his life); *Gaslight* (UK: *The Murder in Thornton Square*) (AA; >George Cukor 1944) (☞ ☆ ■) (suffering from a split personality Charles Boyer inflicts mental cruelty on Bergman when she discovers his murderous past); *The Bells of St. Mary's* (AAN: >Leo McCarey 1945) (☆ ✍) (*Going My Way* Father O'Malley (Bing Crosby) doesn't always see eye to eye with Bergman's schoolteaching Sister Benedict) and >*Notorious* (>Alfred Hitchcock 1946) (☞ ☆ ✍ ■) show her at her dependable best. However, a fourth Oscar nomination for her role in *Joan of Arc* (Victor Fleming 1948) (■) (the Maid of Orleans is burned as a heretic for claiming that heavenly voices inspired her military victories) kindled those 'serious actress' pretentions that were not fully doused until her disastrous collaboration with >Roberto Rossellini, the man she married after an adulterous affair that outraged the 'moral majority', ended in 1956. *Anastasia* (Anatole Litvak 1957) (☆) (Bergman persuades Yul Brynner's Russian exiles that she is the murdered Tsar's daughter) brought public reconciliation and a second Oscar, but after *Indiscreet* (>Stanley Donen 1958) (☆ ✍) (Bergman loves >Cary Grant when she believes he is already married, but plots revenge when she discovers that he is only a confirmed bachelor), she only glimmered fleetingly in *Murder on the Orient Express* (AA; >Sidney Lumet 1974) (✍ ☆) (Albert Finney's Hercule Poirot discovers that all murder suspects have motives) and *Autumn Sonata* (AAN; >Ingmar Bergman 1978) (☆) (bereaved Bergman seeks solace in her sorrow with alienated daughter Liv Ullmann).

•*Walpurgis Night* (*Valborgsmassoafton*) (Gustaf Edgren 1935) (☆): secretary Bergman has the boss's child.

•*June Night* (*Juninatten*) (aka *A Night in June*) (Per Lindberg 1940) (☆): Bergman is unable to live down the shooting that is the skeleton in her cupboard.

•*Adam Had Four Sons* (Gregory Ratoff 1941) (☆): Bergman as a governess raising Warner Baxter's brood in star-making tear-jerker.

•*Saratoga Trunk* (Sam Wood 1945) (☆ ☞): scarlet woman Bergman scandalizes New Orleans by encouraging >Gary Cooper to overcome the saboteurs of railway he is building.

•*Spellbound* (>Alfred Hitchcock 1945) (☞ ☆): psychiatrist Bergman helps amnesiac imposter Gregory Peck find the man he has replaced and why he has disappeared.

•*Arch of Triumph* (Lewis Milestone 1948) (✍): Czech refugee Charles Boyer's search for SS war criminal >Charles Laughton is punctuated by a romance with Bergman's flighty Italian girl.

•*Under Capricorn* (>Alfred Hitchcock 1949) (☞): Joseph Cotten arrives in 1830s Australia to discover cousin Ingrid has become an alcoholic through the strain of her intolerable marriage.

•*Eléna et les Hommes* (US: *Paris Does Strange Things*) (>Jean Renoir 1956) (☆ ☞): Polish princess Bergman has to select a husband from a trio of boot tycoon, dashing soldier and idle noble.

•*Inn of the Sixth Happiness* (Mark Robson 1958) (☆ ■): biopic of missionary Gladys Aylward, helped and hindered by >Robert Donat and Curt Jurgens.
>**Rossellini, Roberto**

BERLIN

Berlin: Symphony of a Great City (*Berlin: Die Sinfonie einer Gross-Stadt*) (**Walter Ruttmann 1927**) ■ ☞
Fly-on-the-wall record of Berlin on a spring day.

Cabaret (**Bob Fosse 1972**) ☆ ♫
Kit Kat Klub singer Liza Minnelli shares Michael York with gay aristocrat during the rise of Nazism.

A Foreign Affair (>**Billy Wilder 1948**) ☆ ✍
>Marlene Dietrich as a former Nazi collaborator competing for US soldier John Lund with visiting congresswoman Jean Arthur.

Germany, Year Zero (*Germania, Anno Zero*) (>**Roberto Rossellini 1947**) ☞ ☆ ■
Semi-documentary tale, with non-professional cast, of a 12-year-old boy forced into feeding family amid the ruins of the bombed city.

The Man Between (>**Carol Reed 1953**) ☞ ☆
James Mason as a racketeer whose amours are bad for business.

The Murderers Are Among Us (US: *Murderers Among Us*) (*Die Mörder Sind Unter Uns*) (**Wolfgang Staudte 1946**) ✍ ☆
A concentration camp doctor agonizes over denouncing an SS captain to the authorities.

One, Two, Three (>**Billy Wilder 1961**) ☆ ☞ ✍
Hustler >James Cagney sets out to market Coca-Cola in Cold War Berlin.

Wings of Desire (>**Wim Wenders 1987**) ■ ☞
An angel Bruno Ganz is sent to watch over the city but falls in love with a trapeze artist.

Berlin Film Festival
The Golden Bear, introduced in 1955, is awarded to the Best Film

1951
Cinderella **(Wilfred Jackson/Hamilton Luske/Clyde Geronomi)**
Disney telling of the fairy tale: voted Best at the Festival by audience acclamation.

1952
One Summer of Happiness **(aka *She Danced for the Summer*) (*Hon dansade en Sommer*) (Arne Mattson)** ■
A student attending his girlfriend's funeral reminisces about their romance.

1953
The Wages of Fear **(*La Salaire de la Peur*) (Henri-Georges Clouzot)** ✍ ☞ ■ ☆
>Yves Montand and his poverty-stricken partners drive lorries of nitro-glycerine along pot-holed roads.

1954
Hobson's Choice **(>David Lean)** ☆ ✍ ☞
Brenda De Banzie persuades John Mills to stand up to his father-in-law >Charles Laughton.

1955
The Rats **(*Die Ratten*) (Robert Siodmak)** ☆ ☞ ■
Refugee Maria Schell gives her baby away to Heidemarie Hatheyer, then fights to re-gain the child.

1956
Invitation to the Dance **(>Gene Kelly)** ☆
Three dance stories: 'Circus', 'Ring Around The Rosy' and 'The Magic Lamp'.

1957
>*Twelve Angry Men* **(>Sidney Lumet)** ☆ ☞ ✍

1958
>*Wild Strawberries* **(*Smultronstället*) (>Ingmar Bergman)** ☞ ☆ ■ ✍ ♫

1959
The Cousins **(*Les Cousins*) (>Claude Chabrol)** ☞ ■
Country cousin Gérard Blain is outdone in labour and love at the Sorbonne by townie Jean-Claude Brialy.

1960
Lazarillo **(Cesar Ardavin)** ■ ✍
A boy learns how to survive in the company of 17th-century Castilian down-and-outs.

1961
La Notte **(*The Night*) (>Michelangelo Antonioni)** ■ ☞
How 24 hours affects the marriage of novelist >Marcello Mastroianni and Jeanne Moreau.

1962
A Kind of Loving **(>John Schlesinger)** ☞ ☆ ✍
Film adaptation of Stan Barstow's novel has Alan Bates enduring his mother-in-law Thora Hird's interference in his marriage to June Ritchie.

1963
Bushido **(aka *Oath of Obedience*) (aka *Cruel Tales of Bushido* (*Bushido Zankiku Monogatari*) (Tadashi Imai)** ☞
The influence of the samurai mentality affects a Japanese family from the 17th century to the end of the Second World War.
Shared with **The Devil** (US: *To Bed...or Not to Bed*) (*Il Diavolo*) **(Gian Luigi Polidoro, Italy)** ✍ ☆
Alberto Sordi's sexual hopes for a trip to Sweden are comically disappointed.

1964
Waterless Summer **(aka *I Had My Brother's Wife*) (US: *Dry Summer*) (*Susuz Yaz*) (Ismail Metin)** ✍
During a drought, Turkish brothers feud over the water supply and the younger one's wife.

1965
Alphaville **(*Alphaville, Une Etrange Aventure de Lemmy Caution*) (>Jean-Luc Godard)** ☞ ■
Private eye Eddie Constantine travels

through space to a planet where conformity is law and love illegal.

1966

Cul de Sac (>**Roman Polanski**)

Fleeing gangsters find uneasy sanctuary in an odd couple's island castle.

1967

Le Départ (**Jerzy Skolimowski, Belgium**) ■

A hairdressing Billy Liar dreams of winning a rally in his boss's fast car.

1968

Who Saw Him Die? (aka *Eeny Meeny Miny Moe*) (*Ole Dole Doff*) (**Jan Troell**) ■

Timid teacher Per Oscarsson is tormented by rowdy pupils and his impatient wife.

1969

Early Works (*Early Years*) (**Zelimir Zilnik**) ☆

The attempts of four Yugoslav youths to bring Marxism to the peasants result in a violent clash with the police.

1970

No award

1971

The Garden of the Finzi-Continis (*Il Giardino dei Finzi-Continis*) (>**Vittorio De Sica**) ☞ ■ ☆ ✍

Wealthy Italian Jews lower the class barriers as Fascist persecution increases and the authorities close in.

1972

The Canterbury Tales (*Il Racconti di Canterbury*) (>**Pier Paolo Pasolini**) ■ ☞ ✍

The director as Chaucer persuading pilgrims to tell tales en route from Southwark.

1973

Distant Thunder (*Ashanti Sanchez*) (>**Satyajit Ray**) ☞ ✍

The effects of famine on a Bengali village shown in distressing detail.

1974

The Apprenticeship of Duddy Kravitz (**Ted Kotcheff**) ☆

Pushy careerist Jew (Richard Dreyfuss) learns to temper his exuberance.

1975

Adoption (*Örökbefogadás*) (**Márta Mészáros**) ■

Deprived of a child, a middle-aged widow develops a part-maternal, part-sexual relationship with a teenage girl.

1976

Buffalo Bill and the Indians, or *Sitting Bull's History Lesson* (>**Robert Altman**) (☞ ☆) (**Award refused**)

Legendary Western hero discusses the merits of his reputation.

1977

The Ascent (*Voskhozhdenie*) (**Larisa Shepitko**) ■ ☞

Soviet freedom fighters escaping invading Nazis across snow are threatened by starvation and treason.

1978

The Trouts (**Jose Luis Garcia Sanhex**) ✍

A fishing club's annual dinner is disrupted by the effects of the main course – trout caught in a sewer.

Shared with **Ascensar** (*The Lift*) (**Tomas Munoz**) ✍

Four people's dislike of each other grows as they wait for a mischievous child to free them from a broken-down lift.

and **What Max Said** (aka *The Words of Max*) (aka *Max's Words*) (**Emilio Martinez Lazaro**) ☞

A man, unhappy at the prospect of middle age, attempts to reconstruct his life.

1979

David (**Peter Lilienthal**)

The adventures of a rabbi's son en route to Israel following Nazi persecution.

1980

Heartland (**Richard Pearce**) ☞ ■

Conchata Ferrell has enough on her hands with her small daughters let alone miserable cowboy Rip Torn.

Shared with **Palermo or Wolfsburg**
(Werner Schroeter) (☆)
A Sicilian goes to work in Germany and
kills the two men who mock him.
1981
Deprisa, Deprisa (*Fast, Fast*) **(Carlos**
Saura) ☆ ☞
A waitress joins a tearaway gang, and their
fortunes take a violent turn for the worse.
1982
Veronika Voss **(>Rainer Werner**
Fassbinder) ■ ☞
>*Sunset Boulevard* echoes as a journalist
delves into the drug-addicted life of faded
UFA Studio actress.
1983
Ascendancy **(Edward Bennett) ☆**
The violence brought by World War I and
the Irish civil war unhinges a Belfast girl,
Julie Covington.
Shared with **The Beehive** (*La Colmena*)
(Mario Camus) (✍)
The ramifications of the Spanish Civil War
for ordinary people are studied in this adap-
tation of Camilo Jose Cela's novel.
1984
Love Streams **(John Cassavetes) ☆**
When Gena Rowlands' marriage disinte-
grates, she turns to her worthless brother
Cassavetes for support.
1985
Wetherby **(David Hare) ✍ ☆ ■**
A lonely policeman (Stuart Wilson) inves-
tigating a suicide falls for equally lonely
witness Vanessa Redgrave.

Shared with **The Woman and the**
Stranger (*Die Frau und der Fremde*)
(Rainer Simon, East Germany) ✍
An escaped German First World War PoW
heads for the home town of the friend
whose identity he has assumed.
1986
Stammheim **(Reinhard Hauff) ☆**
Recreation of the 1975–77 terrorist trial
and the suspicious deaths of the group's
leaders Andreas Bader and Ulrike Meinhof.
1987
The Theme (*Tema*) **(Gleb Panfilov,**
USSR) ☆ ☞
A successful writer goes home and loses the
love of his painter girlfriend because he has
sold out to fame and the politically easy life
while she had remained true to her art.
1988
Red Sorghum (*Hong Gaoliang*) **(Zhang**
Yimou) ■
A woman and her abductor join peasants in
resisting the Japanese invaders.
1989
Rain Man **(Barry Levinson) ☆ ☞ ✍**
Car dealer Tom Cruise kidnaps his TV-ob-
sessed autistic *savant* half-brother >Dustin
Hoffman to inherit from their father's will.
1990
Larks on a String (*Skrivanci Na Nitih*)
(Jirí Menzel 1989) ☞
Shared with **The Music Box** **(Constantin**
Costa-Gavras 1989) ☞

Bertolucci, Bernardo
Italian writer/director (b 1940)

Despite assistant-directing >Pasolini's *Accatone* (1961), Bertolucci's prize-winning 1962
book *In Cerca del Mistero* (*In Search of Mystery*) suggested a future as a poet. Cinema was
ultimately to benefit from his talent, but there
is undoubted poetry in even his most political
films. *The Grim Reaper* (*La Commare Secca*)
(1962) (■) (friends of a prostitute talk about
their meetings with her on the day she is murdered) showed a facility for delineating character, but *Before the Revolution* (*Prima della
Rivoluzione*) (1964) (☞) (a Parma youth de-
liberates between sexual and political rebellion
or his father's wishes), which dealt with radical
politics and deviant sexuality, gave a clearer
indication of his predilections. *The Conformist*
(*Il Conformista*) (1970) (☞ ■ ☆) (Jean-Louis
Trintignant seeks to come to terms with his
troubled childhood by undertaking a Fascist-
inspired assassination), *Last Tango in Paris*

(1972) (☆ ☞) (>Marlon Brando's overbearing sexual demands destroy Maria Schneider), >*1900* (1976) (✍ ☆ ■ ☞), *La Luna* (1979) (■ ☆) (opera singer Jill Clayburgh commits incest with her teenage son) and *The Tragedy of a Ridiculous Man* (*La Tragedia di un Uomo Ridicolo*) (1981) (☆ ☞) (left-wing son of a factory owner is suspected of involvement in his own kidnapping), developed these themes as well as his command of technique, a mastery showcased in the luxuriant Oscar-winning *The Last Emperor* (1988) (☞ ■ ✍) (the life and troubled times of the boy ruler of China who is exploited by Japanese invaders).

•*Once Upon a Time in the West* (Sergio Leone 1967) (☆ ✍): Claudia Cardinale is menaced by >Henry Fonda and his band of baddies in this film co-written by the spaghetti western-specialist director Sergio Leone and Bertolucci.
•*Partner* (1968) (☞): based on >Dostoevsky's *The Double*, a humiliated shy man develops an aggressive alternative persona.

The Best Years of Our Lives
☆ ☞ ✍ ■

USA • Samuel Goldwyn • 1946 • 182 mins • b/w

d >William Wyler w Robert Sherwood ph Gregg Toland m Hugo Friedhofer

>Fredric March, >Myrna Loy, Teresa Wright, Dana Andrews, Virginia Mayo, Hoagy Carmichael, Harold Russell, Cathy O'Donnell

After spending the war years pumping out shameless propaganda extolling the virtues of reckless heroism and domestic frugality, Hollywood could be accused of jumping on the pacifist band wagon for producing such a stark condemnation of war as *The Best Years of Our Lives*. However, the poignant, often bitter observations and real situations confound any cynicism, especially as cinematographer Toland and Oscar-winning Best Supporting Actor Russell had seen action themselves, the latter having actually lost his hands. Dominating the 1946 Oscars, *Best Years* brought the best out

of director Wyler and his superb cast of couples, Andrews and Mayo, O'Donnell and Russell, and March and the impeccable Myrna Loy, leaving even present day audiences feeling part of every awkward moment and painful rediscovery. And yet still the lessons went unlearned.

•Not all wives waited patiently for returning men; factory worker Goldie Hawn, for example, had an affair with Kurt Russell in *Swing Shift* (Jonathan Demme 1984) (☆).
•There is so little of Timothy Bottoms left in 1918 that he demands to die in *Johnny Got His Gun* (Dalton Trumbo 1971) (✍).
•The effects of World War II on the defeated peoples of the Axis are studied in *Two Pennyworth of Hope* (US: *Two Cents Worth Of Hope*) (*Due Soldi di Speranza*) (Renato Castellani, Italy 1952) (☆ ✍).
•Flying instructor Dan Dailey finds himself hailed as a hero in *When Willie Comes Marching Home* (>John Ford 1949) (☆ ✍).
•Deprived of a sympathetic welcome, some veterans were driven to crime, but did Robert Young, Robert Mitchum or Robert Ryan murder a Jew in *Crossfire* (Edward Dmytryk 1947) (☞ ✍ ☆)?
•Japan's recovery from the atomic bomb is considered in *Children of Hiroshima* (*Genbaku No Ko*) (Kaneto Shindo 1952) (■).

BETRAYAL

Against the Wind **(Charles Crichton 1947)** ✍ ☆
A saboteurs' training school is infiltrated by a Nazi sympathizer.
Cry of the City **(Robert Siodmak 1948)** ■ ☞
Gangster Richard Conte is turned in by his childhood friend, cop Victor Mature.
I Walk Alone **(Byron Haskin 1948)** ☆
Burt Lancaster leaves prison intent on avenging himself on the man who informed on him, >Kirk Douglas.
The Informer **(>John Ford 1935)** ☆
Screen version of a Liam O'Flaherty novel telling of a cowardly informer Victor McLaglen pursued by the IRA for betraying a leader.

Kiss of Death (Henry Hathaway 1947) ☆
Victor Mature betrays his own gang so Brian
Donlevy hires assassin Richard Widmark to
teach him a lesson.

Masquerade (Basil Dearden 1965) ☞
An Arab prince is kidnapped, but the abductors
have a quisling in their ranks.

The Samurai (Jean-Pierre Melville 1967) ☆
Alain Delon as an assassin whose alibi is under-
mined by his girlfriend.

Betty Blue (37°2 Le Matin)
☞ ♫ ☆ ☞ ✍
*France • Claudie Ossard-Jean-Jacques Beineix
• 1987 • 121 mins • col*
**wd Jean-Jacques Beineix
ph Jean-François Robin　m Gabriel Yared
Béatrice Dalle, Jean-Hugues Anglade**

Betty (Dalle) and Zorg (Anglade) are simply
happy to enjoy themselves, loafing and loving
their way through life, until she discovers the
manuscript of his brilliant novel. Her love for
him becomes confused with ambition, and the
inevitable incursion of her own manic depression condemns the couple to a choice between
uncertain success and their penurious, but
carefree existence. Jean-Jacques Beineix's
study of apathetic genius and misplaced confidence leaps between extreme joys and
tragedies with an honesty and insight that
leaves you willing the pair to redemption as if
they were your closest friends. The fleeting
emotions are wonderfully captured in Yared's
haunting soundtrack.

 •>Woody Allen and >Diane Keaton's offbeat romance is the subject
of >*Annie Hall* (Woody Allen 1978)
(✍ ☆ ☞).

•Isabelle Adjani and Jacques Dutronc have
nothing in common until they discover shoplifting in *Violette et François* (Jacques Ruffio
1977) (☆ ✍); while in *The Moon in the Gutter*
(*La Luna dans le Caniveau*) (Jean-Jacques Beineix 1983) (☆), >Gérard Depardieu is only
interested in Nastassja Kinski because he suspects her brother of raping his sister.

•André Téchiné was awarded Best Director at
Cannes in 1985 for *Rendez-Vous* (☆), a tale of
an actress suffering under creative and romantic strain.

•Apathetic poet Tom Conti has more fun ruf-
fling the feathers of literary *poseurs* than fur-
thering his career in *Reuben, Reuben* (Robert
Ellis Miller 1984) (☆ ✍).

Bicycle Thieves (US:The Bicycle Thief) (Ladri di Biciclette)
☞ ☆ ✍ ■
Italy • PDS/ENIC • 1948 • 90 mins • b/w
**d >Vittorio De Sica　w Vittorio De
Sica/Cesare Zavattini/Oreste
Biancoli/Suso Cecchi d'Amico/Adolfo
Franci　ph Carlo Montuori　m Alessandro
Cicognini
Lamberto Maggiorani, Enzo Staiola**

As the film adaptation of Giovanni Guareschi's
Little World of Don Camillo (filmed as *Il Piccolo Mondo di Don Camillo* by Julien Duvivier
in 1952) showed, postwar Italians, disillusioned with Fascism, had to seek political and
social answers in either the traditional doc-
trines of the Catholic Church or the radical
optimism of Communism. Vittorio De Sica's
moving film concentrates on one of the many
proud individuals whose slender means and
will to survive warded off the hunger and humiliation of poverty. Antonio Ricci (non-actor
Maggiorani) will lose a rare offer of employment as a bill sticker unless he can find his
stolen bicycle. As he traipses the streets with
his worshipping son, Bruno (Staiola), he gradually loses his hope, dignity and the boy's respect. Their understanding is only restored
when son consoles father, desolate at his own
resort to theft. An unusual cinematic moment
– an intelligent weepie.

 •Odd character Pee Wee Herman
has his treasured red bicycle stolen
by a rich, fat rival in *Pee Wee's Big
Adventure* (Tim Burton 1988).

•One brother makes bikes, another steals them
in Alexei Sayle's Thatcherite Britain version of
Bicycle Thieves – Didn't You Kill My Brother?
(Bob Spiers 1987) (✍ ☆).

• In *Naked Hearts* (Edouard Luntz 1966) (☞ ■) two prisoners vow to go straight, but feeling the pinch of Parisian poverty one becomes a thief.

• > Jack Lemmon searches for his disappeared son in Chile with the help of the boy's wife Sissy Spacek in *Missing* (Constantin Costa-Gavras 1982) (☆ ✍).

• Realizing that a boy's hero-worship of him is damaging the homelife of Van Heflin and Jean Arthur, gunfighter Alan Ladd affects clay feet in *Shane* (>George Stevens 1953) (☞ ☆).

BIG BUSINESS

As Young as You Feel (Harmon Jones 1951) ☆ ✍
Monty Woolley saves the company that has forcibly retired him by impersonating its chairman.

Executive Suite (Robert Wise 1954) ☆ ✍
>Fredric March, >Barbara Stanwyck and William Holden are among the board members manoeuvring for company control.

The Fountainhead (>King Vidor 1949) ☞
>Gary Cooper as an architect who refuses to be dictated to by tycoon Raymond Massey.

How to Succeed in Business without Really Trying (David Swift 1967) ☆ ✍
Window cleaner Robert Morse finds it appallingly easy to assume control of a corporation in this witty musical.

Just Tell Me What You Want (>Sidney Lumet 1980)
Ali McGraw seeks >Myrna Loy's help in seeking to loosen a tycoon's possessive grip.

Patterns of Power (US: Patterns) (Fielder Cook 1956) ☞ ✍
Company boss Van Heflin uses flyer Everett Sloane to force time-server Ed Begley to resign.

A Time for Revenge (Tiempo de Revancha) (Adolfo Aristarain 1981) ✍
Argentinian demolition expert enters a company under an assumed name, but his days as a union official are not easily forgotten.

The Toast of New York (Rowland V. Lee 1937) ☆
>Cary Grant helps Edward Arnold become astoundingly rich in this biopic of Jim Fisk.

Woman's World (Jean Negulesco 1954) ☞ ☆
Salesmen and wives are put through their paces to assess their suitability for promotion.

The Big Sleep ☆ ✍ ☞ ■
USA • Warner Brothers • 1946 • 114 mins • b/w

d >Howard Hawks   w William Faulkner/Leigh Brackett/Jules Furthman ph Sid Hickox   m Max Steiner
>Humphrey Bogart, Lauren Bacall, Martha Vickers, John Ridgely, Dorothy Malone

Having breathed life into Dashiel Hammett's Sam Spade in *The Maltese Falcon* (>John Huston 1941) (☞ ☆ ■ ✍) (Spade gets to a valuable statue ahead of >Peter Lorre and Sidney Greenstreet), Bogart here perfected the art of screen private eye in his portrayal of Philip Marlowe in Hawks' confusing, crackling treatment of Raymond Chandler's novel. This is less a whodunnit than a how-to-solve-it and even the writers fail to name the chauffeur's killer. As the blackmail of General Sternwood's daughter becomes a case of murder, we wade with Marlowe through every clue and red herring, Bogart himself being the only gauge as to whether we are on the right trail. He dominates the action, outsmarting the baddies and getting the girl, Lauren Bacall, just as he did in *To Have and Have Not* (>Howard Hawks 1945) (☆ ☞ ✍) (Ernest Hemingway novel of a boat captain Bogart resisting the Nazis in the French West Indies) and in real life. Because Marlowe isn't a Holmes or a Poirot and has fumbled his way through, we are not only able to identify with him, but feel less foolish for guessing so hopelessly wrong.

• *The Big Sleep* was remade by Michael Winner in 1978 with Robert Mitchum as Marlow and James Stewart as General Sternwood.

• Richard Dreyfuss falls for a woman whom he and Emilio Estevez have under surveillance in *Stakeout* (John Badham 1987) (☆).

• General Sternwood's children may have

THE BIG HEAT
(>Fritz Lang 1953) ☞ ☆

CORRUPTION NOIR

THE BEAST OF THE CITY
(Charles Brabin 1932) ☆
(>Jean Harlow as moll of gangster pursued by cop Walter Huston)

THE GLASS KEY
(Stuart Heisler 1942) ✍ ☆
(minder Alan Ladd saves politician Brian Donlevy from ruin)

ALL THE KING'S MEN
(Robert Rossen 1949) ☞ ✍ ☆
(power corrupts Broderick Crawford and destroys his political career)

ROGUE COP
(Roy Rowland 1954) ■
(local gangster bribes cop into co-operation)

SWEET SMELL OF SUCCESS
(Alexander Mackendrick 1957)
☆ ☞
(press agent helps break up columnist's sister's marriage)

PRISON

>I AM A FUGITIVE FROM A CHAIN GANG
(>Mervyn Le Roy 1932) ☞ ☆ ✍
(brutal life on rockpile ends in escape)

FURY
(>Fritz Lang 1936) ☞ ☆ ■
(murder suspect >Spencer Tracy is not even safe in jail)

CANON CITY
(Crane Wilbur 1948) ☆
(semi-documentary study of a jail-break)

CONVICTED
(Henry Levin 1950) ☆
(Glenn Ford witnesses Broderick Crawford's murder of a prison informer)

GANGSTERS

THE PETRIFIED FOREST
(Archie Mayo 1936) ☆ ✍
(>Bette Davis and >Leslie Howard among hostages taken by >Humphrey Bogart)

HIGH SIERRA
(>Raoul Walsh 1941) ☞ ☆
(one-for-the-road raid proves gangster >Humphrey Bogart's downfall)

THE KILLERS
(Robert Siodmak 1946) ☞ ✍
(background justification to a gangster's murder)

KISS OF DEATH
(Henry Hathaway 1947) ☆
(gangster sends psychopathic assassin Richard Widmark to kill informer Victor Mature)

CRY OF THE CITY
(Robert Siodmak 1948) ☞ ☆
(childhood friends now on opposite sides of the law)

NIGHT AND THE CITY
(>Jules Dassin 1950) ✍
(crooked wrestling bouts arranged by underworld)

> ### Bereaved cop Glenn Ford
> ### crusades against corruption

FEMMES FATALES

THE LETTER
(>William Wyler 1940) ☞ ☆ ✍
(murderess >Bette Davis' self-defence plea is confounded by a letter)

LAURA
(Otto Preminger 1944) ✍ ☞ ☆
(detective on a murder case without a death)

BUILD MY GALLOWS HIGH (US: *OUT OF THE PAST*)
(Jacques Tourneur 1947) ☆
(private eye Robert Mitchum falls for the girl he is trailing for gangster >Kirk Douglas)

WOMAN ON THE BEACH
(>Jean Renoir 1947) ☞
(a beauty manipulates coastguard and brutal husband)

THE LADY FROM SHANGHAI
(>Orson Welles 1948) ☞ ☆ ✍
(mysterious Rita Hayworth implicates naïve Welles in crime)

DEADLIER THAN THE MALE
(Ralph Thomas 1967) ✍
(Bulldog Drummond on trail of evil genius using *fatale femme* hit squad)

COP AU NOIR

SO DARK THE NIGHT
(Joseph H. Lewis 1946) ☆ ✍
(French cop solves crime in holiday hotel)

THE MAN WHO CHEATED HIMSELF
(Felix Feist 1950) ☆
(brothers torn between family and professional duty)

ON DANGEROUS GROUND
(>Nicholas Ray 1951) ☞
(Robert Ryan falls for blind sister of a murder suspect)

THE RACKET
(John Cromwell 1951) ☞
(police put gangster out of business)

KANSAS CITY CONFIDENTIAL (UK: *THE SECRET FOUR*)
(Phil Karlson 1952) ✍
(cheated by retirement, cop plans robbery)

proved problematic, but they are angels next to the brother and sister portrayed in Jean Cocteau's *Les Enfants Terrible* (US: *The Strange One*) (Jean-Pierre Melville 1950) (✍ ▓).

•Marlowe's search for a missing girl is re-enacted in *Farewell, My Lovely* by Dick Powell in Edward Dmytryk's 1944 version (✍ ☆ ▓) and by Robert Mitchum in the 1975 adaptation (Dick Richards) (aka *Murder My Sweet*) (☆ ☞), aided by alternately Claire Trevor and Charlotte Rampling.

•Marlowe was spoofed by >Robert Altman in *The Long Goodbye* (1973) (✍) with Elliott Gould in the lead.

BIGAMY

The Bigamist (Ida Lupino 1953) ☞
Travelling salesman Edmond O'Brien is married to both >Joan Fontaine and the director.

The Bigamist (Il Bigamo) (Luciano Emmer 1956) ✍
>Vittorio De Sica cross-examines >Marcello Mastroianni during a bigamy trial.

The Captain's Paradise (Anthony Kimmins 1953) ☆
Skipper >Alec Guinness has mousy Celia Johnson in Gibraltar and vibrant Yvonne De Carlo in Tangier.

A Cat and Two Women (Neko to Shozo to Futari no Onna) (Shiro Toyoda, Japan 1956) ✍ ☆
Hisaya Morishige has two wives but still prefers his cat's company.

The Constant Husband (Sidney Gilliat 1954) ☆
Rex Harrison regains his memory to discover that he is married to Kay Kendall and four others.

Monsieur Verdoux (>Charles Chaplin 1947) ✍ ☞
Chaplin marries and murders various women to afford little luxuries for his invalid wife.

My Favourite Wife (Garson Kanin 1940) ☆ ✍
Shipwrecked wife Irene Dunne returns unexpectedly to find that >Cary Grant has remarried.

Suzy (George Fitzmaurice 1936) ☆
>Jean Harlow isn't a war widow after all, but is both Mrs >Cary Grant and Mrs Franchot Tone.

Too Many Husbands (GB: My Two Husbands) (Wesley Ruggles 1940) ☆
Jean Arthur in another variation of shipwreck survival bigamy with Melvyn Douglas and Fred MacMurray.

The Bishop's Wife ☆ ✍ ▓ ☞
USA • Samuel Goldwyn • 1947 • 108 mins • b/w

d Henry Koster   w Robert E. Sherwood/Leonardo Bercovici   ph Gregg Toland   m Hugo Friedhofer

>Cary Grant, Loretta Young, David Niven, Monty Woolley, Gladys Cooper, Elsa Lanchester

Quite simply one of the most joyous films ever made. David Niven is a harassed bishop whose pre-occupation with repairing his cathedral causes him to neglect his congregation and his loyal but strained wife Loretta Young. An angel with a mission, Dudley (Grant) teaches her to enjoy herself once more, restoring her radiance and provoking the jealousy that re-kindles Niven's love. Although it was nominated for Best Picture in 1947, the critics panned it as corny moralizing, but it is all done so well that you couldn't care less. Niven's Henry Brougham is so straight-laced that you want to poke him with a sharpened crozier; Young's beauty grows as she sheds her timidity; and Grant plays the angel with a devilish glee that borders on the sinful. All this and Toland's stunning photography, too.

•Scottish teacher Tom Conti's claim to be able to work miracles is doubted by colleagues and clergy in *Heavenly Pursuits* (US: *Gospel According to Vic*) (Charles Gormley 1987) (☆).

•>James Stewart's despair is appeased when guardian angel Henry Travers shows him how he has enriched the life of his town in >*It's a Wonderful Life* (>Frank Capra 1946) (☆ ☞ ✍).

•William Holden is the stranger in town causing havoc among the inhabitants and with Kim

Novak's pulse rate in *Picnic* (Joshua Logan 1956) (☆).

•Montgomery Clift is the cleric in crisis, reluctantly guarding his housekeeper's confessional murder admission in *I Confess* (>Alfred Hitchcock 1953) (✍ ☞ ☆); while Robert Duvall's priest is disturbed by the business methods employed by his brother >Robert De Niro in *True Confessions* (Ulu Grosbard 1981) (☆).

BLACKMAIL

Alibi (Pierre Chenal 1937) ☆
A nightclub dancing partner blackmailed by killer >Erich Von Stroheim falls for undercover cop.

The Big Knife (Robert Aldrich 1955) ☆
Fading film star Jack Palance signs a detrimental contract under duress.

Blackmail (>Alfred Hitchcock 1929) ☞
Scotland Yard man keeps his girlfriend out of a murder case but lays himself open to accusation and extortion.

Blackmailed (Marc Allégret 1950) ✍
A blackmailer's victims discover safety in numbers and kill him.

The Brides of Fu Manchu (Don Sharp 1966)
Christopher Lee blackmails influential men by threatening to kill their kidnapped girlfriends.

Crossroads (Jack Conway 1942) ☆
>Basil Rathbone blackmails amnesiac envoy >William Powell by convincing him that he has a criminal past.

The Naked Truth (US: *Your Past is Showing*) (Mario Zampi 1957) ☆
Terry-Thomas is among the TV stars anxious to prevent Peter Sellers revealing their peccadilloes.

The Suspect (Robert Siodmak 1944) ☆
No sooner is >Charles Laughton free of his shrewish wife than he has a blackmail burden to shoulder.

BLINDNESS

Butterflies Are Free (Milton Katselas 1972) ☆
Goldie Hawn's love for a blind man is hampered by his over-protective mother.

City for Conquest (Anatole Litvak 1940) ☆ ☞
Boxer >James Cagney loses his sight in the ring.

Dark Angel (Sidney Franklin 1935) ■ ☆
War-blinded >Fredric March urges his fiancée Merle Oberon to marry Herbert Marshall.

Magnificent Obsession (John M. Stahl 1935) ☞ ☆/**(Douglas Sirk 1954)**
Having accidentally caused Irene Dunne/Jane Wyman's blindness, Robert Taylor/Rock Hudson cures it.

The Miracle Worker (Arthur Penn 1962) ☆
The story of the education of Helen Keller (Patty Duke) under the tutelage of Annie Sullivan (Anne Bancroft).

Mr Skeffington (Vincent Sherman 1944) ☞ ✍
Claude Rains' blindness prevents him seeing >Bette Davis's infidelities and fading looks.

A Patch of Blue (Jerry Goldsmith 1965) ☆
A blind girl raises hackles in a racist tenement by falling for Sidney Poitier, unaware that he is black.

Tommy (Ken Russell 1975) ♫ ☞
Roger Daltrey as the deaf, dumb and blind pinball wizard who becomes a rock star.

Twenty-Three Paces to Baker Street (Henry Hathaway 1956) ☆ ✍
Van Johnson recognizes a killer by his overheard voice in a London pub.

Wait until Dark (Terence Young 1967) ✍ ☞ ☆
Alan Arkin's baddies terrorize Audrey Hepburn while searching her house for a doll full of heroin.

THE BLITZ

The Bells Go Down (Basil Dearden 1943) ■
The unlikely pairing of James Mason and Tommy Trinder as heroic firemen.

Blitz on Britain (Harry Booth 1960) ■
Documentary retrospective narrated by Alistair Cooke.

Hanover Street (Peter Hyams 1979)
>Harrison Ford rather regrets rescuing his lover Lesley-Anne Down's husband Christopher Plummer from the debris.

THE BIRTH OF A NATION
(>D. W. Griffith 1915) ☞ ☆ ■

SILENT HOLLYWOOD

BROKEN BLOSSOMS
(>D. W. Griffith 1919) ☆ ☞
(Chinese man driven to New York slum murder when >Lillian Gish is killed)

THE FOUR HORSEMEN OF THE APOCALYPSE
(Rex Ingram 1921) ☆
(Rudolph Valentino as Argentinian fighting First World War for France)

THE SHEIK
(George Melford 1921) ☆
(desert romance of English heiress Agnes Ayres and Rudolph Valentino)

THE COVERED WAGON
(James Cruze 1923) ☞
(trekkers search for new life out West)

BEN-HUR
(Fred Niblo 1925) ☞ ■ ✍
(career of Jewish slave in ancient Rome who becomes a Christian)

FLESH AND THE DEVIL
(Clarence Brown 1926) ☆ ☞
(>Greta Garbo as vamp taunting three lovers)

WINGS
(>William Wellman 1927) ☞ ■
(World War I fliers in tragic accident)

MEDITERRANEAN SILENTS

THE ASSASSINATION OF THE DUKE OF GUISE
(L'ASSASSINATION DE DUC DE GUISE)
(Charles Le Bargy 1908) ☆
(Henry III of France plans political murder)

QUO VADIS?
(Enrico Guazzoni 1912) ■
(Christians are persecuted in reign of Nero)

THE LOVES OF QUEEN ELIZABETH (L'AMOURS DE LA REINE ELIZABETH)
(Louis Mercanton/Henri Despontaines 1912) ☆
(tangled love affairs of Sarah Bernhardt at the Tudor court)

CABIRIA
(Giovanni Pastrone 1914) ☞
(slave dreams of Cinderella transformation)

JUDEX
(Louis Feuillade 1916) ✍
(12-part serial of crusading crime-fighter)

THE LATE MATHIAS PASCAL (L'HOMME DE NULLE PART)
(Marcel L'Herbier 1924 –6) ☞
(banker assumes new identity in Rome)

SCANDINAVIAN SILENTS

THOMAS GRAAL'S BEST FILM (THOMAS GRAALS BÄSTA FILM)
(Mauritz Stiller 1917) ☞ ✍
(screenwriter bases film on his beloved secretary)

SIR ARNE'S TREASURE (aka THE THREE WHO WERE DOOMED) (HERR ARNES PENGAR)
(Mauritz Stiller 1919) ☞ ■ ✍
(pastor's daughter loves then betrays an outlaw)

EROTIKON
(Mauritz Stiller 1920) ☞ ■
(academic shuns snobbery for simple true love)

THE PHANTOM CARRIAGE (aka THY SOUL SHALL BEAR WITNESS) (aka THE STROKE OF MIDNIGHT) (KÖRKALEN)
(Victor Sjöström 1921) ☞ ☆
(a drunkard re-experiences sobriety and reforms)

WITCHCRAFT THROUGH THE AGES (HÄXAN)
(Benjamin Christensen 1922) ☞ ■ ✍
(as the title suggests using etchings and short plays)

THE MASTER OF THE HOUSE (aka THOU SHALT HONOUR THY WIFE) (DU SKAL AERE DIN HUSTRU)
(Carl Dreyer 1925) ☞ ✍ ☆
(in almost horror movie fashion, an aged nanny reforms a tyrannical family man)

THE PASSION OF JOAN OF ARC (LA PASSION DE JEANNE D'ARC)
(Carl Dreyer 1928) ☞
(last day of the Maid of Orleans' trial)

US recovers
from Civil War

GERMAN SILENTS

>THE CABINET OF DR CALIGARI (DAS KABINETT DES DR CALIGARI)
(Robert Wiene 1919) ☞ ■ ✍ ☆
(madman dreams a doctor is a fairground murder menace)

DR MABUSE, THE GAMBLER (DR MABUSE, DER SPIELER)
(>Fritz Lang 1922) ☞ ■
(master criminal Rudolph Klein-Rogge rigs big business and casinos)

WARNING SHADOWS (SCHATTEN)
(Arthur Robison 1923) ■ ☞
(hypnotist liberates staid bourgeois couples)

THE LAST LAUGH (DER LETZTE WALZER)
(>F. W. Murnau 1934) ☆ ☞
(pompous hotel doorman >Emil Jannings is taught humility)

PANDORA'S BOX (aka LULU) (DIE BÜCHSE DER PANDORA)
(>G. W. Pabst 1929) ☞ ☆ ■
(vamp Louise Brooks causes sexual havoc in high society)

SOVIET SILENTS

>THE BATTLESHIP POTEMKIN (US: POTEMKIN)
(BRONENOSETS POTEMKIN)
(>Sergei Eisenstein 1925) ☞ ■ ✍
(mutiny and revolution in Odessa in 1905)

MOTHER (MAT)
(>V. I. Pudovkin 1926) ☞ ■
(after her son is killed, a mother leads revolution)

STORM OVER ASIA (aka THE HEIR OF GENGHIS KHAN) (POTOMO CHINGIS-KHANA)
(>V. I. Pudovkin 1928) ☞ ■
(tenuous heir of Genghis Khan leads revolt in 1918)

THE NEW BABYLON (NOVYI VAVILON)
(Leonid Trauberg/Grigori Kozintsev 1929) ☞
(effects of 1871 Commune on Parisian life)

THE GENERAL LINE (aka THE OLD AND THE NEW) (GENERALNAYA LINYA) (aka STAROYE I NOVOYE)
(>Sergei Eisenstein 1929) ☞ ■
(peasants discover industrialization)

Hope and Glory (John Boorman 1986) ☆ ✍
Young boy's bomb-site adventures are curtailed by evacuation exile to his grouchy grandfather's house on the Thames.

I Was a Fireman (aka *Fires Were Started*)
(Humphrey Jennings 1942) ☞ ■
Tense documentary following London fire unit's fighting of a bomb blaze.

Journey for Margaret (W. S. Van Dyke 1942) ☆
Journalist Robert Young rescues orphan Margaret O'Brien and adopts her.

London Can Take It (Harry Watt 1940)
A documentary short that aimed to prove to the US that Britain was not about to succumb to air raids.

Millions Like Us (Frank Launder/Sidney Gilliat 1943) ✍
An ordinary family do their bit, despite bombing and bereavement.

To Each His Own (Mitchell Leisen 1946) ☆ ☞ ✍
>Olivia De Havilland discovers the soldier son that she thought she'd never see again.

The Blue Angel (Der Blaue Engel) ☆ ☞ ✍ ■ ♫
Germany • *UFA* • *1930* • *98 mins* • *b/w*
d >Josef Von Sternberg w Robert Liebmann/Karl Zückmayer/Karl Vollmüller ph Günter Rittau/Hans Schneeberger m Friedrich Holländer
>Emil Jannings, >Marlene Dietrich

The destructiveness of love and the helpless willingness of its victims has never been so depressingly or hauntingly examined on screen as in Josef Von Sternberg's adaptation of Heinrich Mann's novel *Professor Unrath*. Abandoning his career, the elderly, respected academic marries the bewitching nightclub singer, Lola Lola, and ekes out a humiliating existence as a music-hall clown, before drinking himself to death. *The Blue Angel* is perhaps *the* most famous German film ever made. It is its director's masterpiece and displayed its stars Jannings and Dietrich at the top of their form, for although both enjoyed subsequent success, neither truly recaptured the power of these performances. The real highlight is not Dietrich's 'Falling in Love Again', but Jannings' pathetic slapstick routine.

 VIEW ON ►

•Nightclub vamps are the central characters in *Lola* (Jacques Demy 1960) (☞ ☆): Anouk Aimée is torn between three persistent suitors; and in *Pandora's Box* (aka *Lulu*) (>G. W. Pabst 1929) (☞ ☆ ■): Lulu (Louise Brooks) is desired by a doctor, his son and a lesbian countess before Jack the Ripper steps in.
•In a variation on >*Snow White and the Seven Dwarfs* and the director's own 1942 film *Ball of Fire* (☆ ☞ ■) (>Barbara Stanwyck blows the dust off lexicographer >Gary Cooper), music professor Danny Kaye is led astray by gangster's moll Virginia Mayo in *A Song is Born* (>Howard Hawks 1948) (■ ☞).
•A German school, boasting young Peter Ustinov and Charles Hawtrey among its Hitler Youth, is infiltrated by teacher spy Will Hay in *The Goose Steps Out* (Will Hay/Basil Dearden 1942) (☆ ✍).
•Robert Duvall beats the booze to resume his country-and-western career in *Tender Mercies* (Bruce Beresford 1983) (☆); but singer Bing Crosby's alcohol-free comeback is hijacked by the emergence of his wife Grace Kelly in *The Country Girl* (George Seaton 1954) (☆ ✍).

Body Heat ☆ ✍ ☞ ■
USA • *Warner Brothers* • *1981* • *113 mins* • *col*
wd Lawrence Kasdan ph Richard H. Kline m John Barry
>William Hurt, >Kathleen Turner, Ted Danson

There have been few such stunning movie debuts as Kathleen Turner's Matty Walker in Lawrence Kasdan's 1981 interpretation of the *film noir* classic, *Double Indemnity* (>Billy Wilder 1944) (☞ ☆ ✍). She oozes much more than perspiration during the steamy summer when she persuades incompetent lawyer Ned Racine (an impeccable William Hurt) to kill her husband for a share of her bed and the new life that her inheritance will provide. As the icy Matty coolly betrays him, and with the heat now really on, Racine sweats more and more with every scene. A wonderful evocation of physical and mental discomfort, and although you feel for him in his trap, you have to admire her scheming genius.

•An open fridge and a subway grating cool >Marilyn Monroe, but who is to stop licentious neighbour Tom Ewell getting hot under the collar in *The Seven Year Itch* (>Billy Wilder 1955) (☞ ☆)?
•Chauffeur Robert Mitchum is the stool pigeon for Jean Simmons' murderous schemes in *Angel Face* (Otto Preminger 1952) (■).
•Journalist Debra Winger investigates Theresa Russell's growing list of late husbands in *Black Widow* (Bob Rafaelson 1987) (☆).
•Isabelle Adjani is the *femme fatale* prepared to use any means to avenge her mother's rape in *One Deadly Summer* (*L'Été Meurtier*) (Jean Becker 1983) (☆ ☞).
•>Jean Gabin and Simone Simon plan to kill her husband in >Emile Zola's novel of murder on the railway *La Bête Humaine* (*The Human Beast*) (>Jean Renoir 1938) (☞ ✍ ☆).
•Richard Dreyfuss is the slack lawyer in *Nuts* (Martin Ritt 1987) (✍ ☆), whose reluctance to prove Barbra Streisand's sanity changes into a romance-inspired conviction.
•Kathleen Turner lives to 'enjoy' the fruits of her crime, but the murderer of a taxi driver pays the full penalty in *A Short Film About Killing* (*Krótki Film o Zabijaniu*) (Krzysztov Kieslowski 1989) (☞ ■).

Bogart, Humphrey
American actor (1899–1957)
Naval action in World War I and a 16-year stage apprenticeship fashioned the physical and professional Bogart style. His portrayal of Duke Mantee in *The Petrified Forest* (Archie Mayo 1936) (☆ ✍) (gangster Bogart hijacks travellers including >Leslie Howard and >Bette Davis) started a seemingly interminable sequence of gangster roles including: *Bullets or Ballots* (William Keighley 1936) (☆) (Bogie's gang is infiltrated by undercover cop >Edward G. Robinson); *San Quentin* (Lloyd Bacon 1937) (☆) (jailbird Bogart's sister Ann Sheridan is in

love with warden Pat O'Brien); *Dead End* (>William Wyler 1937) (☆ ☞ ■) (superb Gregg Toland photography captures gangster Bogart terrorizing luxury flats); *Racket Busters* (Lloyd Bacon 1938) (mobster Bogart's trucking business take-over bid is challenged by government agent George Brent); and *King of the Underworld* (Lewis Seiler 1939) (☆) (doctor Kay Francis attempts a vigilante round-up of Bogart's gang after they kill her husband). Bogart's career started to be rejuvenated with roles in >Raoul Walsh's *They Drive by Night* (UK: *The Road to Frisco*) (1940) (☞ ■) (George Raft and Bogart as truckers seeking a better life, only to be implicated in Ann Sheridan's deadly plans) and *High Sierra* (1941) (☞ ☆) (Bogart blows his farewell heist as his mind is elsewhere – ie on Ida Lupino and Joan Leslie). However, it was >John Huston who placed Bogie in his milieu in: *The Maltese Falcon* (1941) (☞ ☆ ■ ✍) (Bogie as Sam Spade hot on the trail of the title statue), *Across the Pacific* (1942) (☆ ☞) (Mary Astor and Sidney Greenstreet are among those whom Bogart suspects of being Japanese sympathizers), *The Treasure of the Sierra Madre* (1948) (☆ ☞ ♫) (gold prospectors Bogart, Walter Huston and Tim Holt fall prey to their own greed and the gun-toting baddies), *Key Largo* (1948) (☆ ✍) (Bogart's nerve is questioned by hideaway villain >Edward G. Robinson) >*The African Queen* (AA; 1952) (☆ ☞ ✍ ■) and *Beat the Devil* (1953) (☆ ✍) (Bogart, Jennifer Jones, Gina Lollobrigida and >Peter Lorre are among those in a shipboard competition for a uranium mine). Without Walsh and Huston, it is unlikely that there would ever have been the myth or the other film classics: >*Casablanca* (>Michael Curtiz 1942) (☆ ☞ ✍ ♫ ■); *Passage to Marseilles* (>Michael Curtiz 1944) (☆) (resistance fighter Bogart's prison past is revealed and excused by Claude Rains); *To Have and Have Not* (>Howard Hawks 1945) (☆ ☞ ✍) (the Nazis may have taken Martinique, but they will never lay hands on Bogie's fishing boat); >*The Big Sleep* (>Howard Hawks 1947) (☆ ✍ ☞ ■); and *The Caine Mutiny* (Edward Dmytryk 1954) (☆) (Bogart accuses his crew of mutiny, but the real events emerge at the trial).

•Angels with Dirty Faces (>Michael Curtiz 1938) (☆ ☞ ✍): die-hard gangster Bogart mocks >James Cagney's inclination towards decency.
•*Dark Victory* (Edmund Goulding 1939) (☆): Bogie as stable manager to tumour victim >Bette Davis.
•*The Roaring Twenties* (>Raoul Walsh/Anatole Litvak 1939) (☞ ☆): war hero >James Cagney makes it big in bootlegging under Bogart's tutelage.
•*Dead Reckoning* (John Cromwell 1947) (☞ ☆): Bogie postpones medal ceremony to look for disappeared buddy with Lizabeth Scott.
•*The Two Mrs Carrolls* (Peter Godfrey 1947) (☆): >Barbara Stanwyck inspires artist Bogart, but faces death when his Muse deserts him.
•*Dark Passage* (Delmer Daves 1947) (☞ ☆): Lauren Bacall shelters escaped convict Bogart while he hunts the real murderer.
•*Knock on any Door* (>Nicholas Ray 1949) (☆): lawyer Bogart defends tearaway although all concerned are convinced of the latter's guilt.
•*In a Lonely Place* (>Nicholas Ray 1950): screenwriter Bogart's temper lands him in the dock for murder and loses him Gloria Grahame.
•*The Enforcer* (UK: *Murder Inc.*) (Bretaigne Windust 1951) (☆ ☞): DA Bogart crusades to bust Everett Sloane's assassination bureau.
•*The Desperate Hours* (>William Wyler 1955) (☆): >Fredric March's family refuse to be intimidated when Bogart's band of escaped convicts seizes their house.
•*The Harder They Fall* (Mark Robson 1956) (☆): in his last film, Bogie exposes Rod Steiger's rigging of boxing bouts.

Born Yesterday ☆ ✍ ☞
USA • Columbia • 1950 • 103 mins • b/w
d >George Cukor w Albert Mannheimer ph Joseph Walker
m Frederick Hollander
Judy Holliday, Broderick Crawford, William Holden, Howard St John

Like >Frank Capra, George Cukor occasionally found it difficult to resist extolling the 'virtues' of the American Way. As a result this film version of Garson Kanin's play was liberally seasoned with nauseous patriotic tirades, but mercifully they are diluted by Judy Holliday's hilarious, Oscar-winning performance as Billie Dawn, whose *faux pas* before an influential senator convince her shady, scrap king lover (Crawford) to hire a journalist (Holden) to carry out a Pygmalion transformation. She learns quickly and not only exposes Crawford's corruption, but also takes a handsome cut for herself. Some stinging dialogue and a superb supporting cast.

 •Rex Harrison sets out to educate flower girl Audrey Hepburn in *My Fair Lady* (>George Cukor 1964) (♫ ☞ ✍).
•George Bancroft's gangster gets caught and sees the error of his ways in *Thunderbolt* (>Josef Von Sternberg 1929) (☞ ☆).
•>Carole Lombard turns on her manipulative Svengali John Barrymore in *Twentieth Century* (>Howard Hawks 1934) (☞ ✍ ☆).
•Sarah Miles avenges her rejection by teacher >Laurence Olivier in *Term of Trial* (Peter Glenville 1962) (☆).
•>Paul Newman and Robert Redford keep the ill-gotten gains won from Robert Shaw in an elaborate gambling con in *The Sting* (George Roy Hill 1973) (♫ ✍ ☆).

Brando, Marlon
American actor (b 1924)
Cinema's foremost disciple of Method acting, Brando was nominated for four consecutive Best Actor Oscars for his performances in: *A Streetcar Named Desire* (>Elia Kazan 1951) (✍ ☞ ☆) (Tennesee Williams' play in which Brando physically and mentally assaults sister-in-law >Vivien Leigh); *Viva Zapata!* (>Elia Kazan 1952) (☞ ☆) (John Steinbeck screenplay of historical betrayal of the Mexican revolutionary); *Julius Caesar* (>Joseph L. Mankiewicz 1953) (✍ ☆ ☞) (John Gielgud and James Mason as Cassius and Brutus act Brando's Mark Antony off the screen in Shakespeare's Ides of March murder); and >*On the Waterfront* (>Elia Kazan 1954) (☞ ☆ ■ ✍). He finally won the Oscar for the last. The versatility at his command – whether Napoleon in

Desirée (Henry Koster 1954) (■) (Jean Simmons as Bonaparte's fiancée who goes on to become Queen of Sweden) or Fletcher Christian in *Mutiny on the Bounty* (Lewis Milestone 1962) (■) (Brando heads for Tahiti, having set Trevor Howard adrift in an open boat), whether a Japanese in *The Teahouse of the August Moon* (Daniel Mann 1956) (☆) (Brando exploits GIs despite Glenn Ford's opposition) or a German in *The Young Lions* (Edward Dmytryk 1958) (✍) (Brando teams up in a war adventure with Montgomery Clift and Dean Martin), whether in a musical such as *Guys and Dolls* (>Joseph L. Mankiewicz 1955) (♫ ☆) (Frank Sinatra wagers gangster Brando that the latter can't seduce Salvation Army girl Jean Simmons) or a comedy such as *The Countess from Hong Kong* (>Charles Chaplin 1967) (Brando as a diplomat pursued by his Russian lover Sophia Loren) – has hamstrung rather than advanced his career. With the notable exceptions of >*The Godfather* (>Francis Ford Coppola 1972) (✍ ☞ ■ ♫ ☆) and *Last Tango in Paris* (>Bernardo Bertolucci 1972) (☞ ☆) (Brando and Maria Schneider discover 101 uses for butter), he has since found refuge in big bucks for minimum screen time, witness *Superman* (Richard Donner 1978) (the baby that Brando and Susannah York send from Krypton becomes mild-mannered Clark Kent aka Christopher Reeve) and >*Apocalypse Now* (>Francis Ford Coppola 1979) (☆ ☞ ■ ✍ ♫).

 •*The Men* (>Fred Zinnemann 1950) (☆ ☞): Teresa Wright helps Brando overcome war disability.

•*The Wild One* (Laslo Benedek 1954) (☞): bikers Brando and Lee Marvin rev engines and raise hell in a small US town.

•*The Saboteur – Code Name Morituri* (Bernhard Wicki 1965) (☞): Brando as a Nazi agent posing as a pacifist on Yul Brynner's warship.

•*Reflections in a Golden Eye* (>John Huston 1967) (☞): murder brews as Deep South soldier Brando's simmering marriage to flirtatious Elizabeth Taylor reaches boiling point.

•*Queimada!* (*Burn*) (Gillo Pontecorvo 1970) (■): Brando becomes involved with revolutionaries opposing Portuguese big business on a Caribbean island.

•*The Missouri Breaks* (Arthur Penn 1976): Brando and Jack Nicholson play ranchers and rustlers in the great American West.

Bresson, Robert
French director (b 1907)

An erstwhile painter, Bresson brought to his cinema his eye for detail and ability to define character deftly. Following *Les Anges du Péché* (*Angels of the Streets*) (1943) (✍ ☞ ☆) (novice nun Renée Fauré is victimized by her mother superior for trying to convert a delinquent girl) and *Les Dames du Bois de Boulogne* (*Ladies of the Park*) (1945) (☞ ✍) (a Diderot fable in which an ex-lover tricks her man into marrying a whore he believes is a virgin), his penchant for using non-actors and voice-over narrative was matched only by his painstaking approach, which restricted him to only 11 films over the next 38 years. However, the meticulousness yielded superb pictures: *The Diary of a Country Priest* (*Journal d'un Curé de Campagne*) (1950) (☞ ☆) (a curé dies of cancer realizing he has offered his congregation little pastoral comfort), *A Man Escaped*, or *The Wind Bloweth Where It Listeth* (*Un Condamné à Mort s'est Echappé, ou Le Vent Souffle où il Vent*) (1956) (■ ☞) (a Resistance fighter plans to escape from the Nazis with a teenage accomplice), *Pickpocket* (1959) (☞) (inspired by >Dostoyevsky's *Crime and Punishment* and containing some superb pocket picking routines, a thief vows to improve his skills after an arrest, but is reformed through love), *The Trial of Joan Of Arc* (*Procès de Jeanne d'Arc*) (1962) (✍ ☞) (historical testimony is used in this reconstruction of the Maid of Orleans' trial and burning), and the beautiful life and times of a donkey, *Balthazar* (*Au Hasard Balthazar*) (1966) (✍ ☞). Subsequently, only *Four Nights of a Dreamer* (*Quatre Nuits d'un Reveur*) (1971) (■ ☞) (artist Guillaume Des Fortês dissuades Isabelle Weingarten from suicide, but she abandons him when her lover returns) has recaptured that originality and lyricism.

 •*Mouchette* (1967) (■ ☞): a young teenager Nadine Nortier is driven to suicide by her hopeless, loveless family life.

•*A Gentle Creature* (*Une Femme Douce*) (1969) (☞ ✍): >Dostoyevsky story flashbacks through the marriage of a couple at once perfectly and ill-matched that results in her suicide.

•*Lancelot of the Lake* (aka *The Grail*) (*Lancelot du Lac*) (aka *Le Graal*) (1974) (■ ☞ ☆): having failed to find the Holy Grail, Lancelot seduces King Arthur's queen, Guinevere.

•*Money* (*L'Argent*) (1983) (☞): Tolstoy story sees the innocent bearer of a forged bank note driven to violent murder.

Bringing Up Baby ✍ ☞ ☆
USA • RKO • 1938 • 102 mins • b/w
d >Howard Hawks   w Dudley Nichols/Hagar Wilde   ph Russell Metty   m Roy Webb
>Katharine Hepburn, >Cary Grant, May Robson, Charles Ruggles, Walter Catlett, Fritz Feld, Barry Fitzgerald

The screwball comedy is one of cinema's most endearing and enduring inventions, and this, with its outrageous exaggerations, perfectly timed gags and role-reversal satire, is the fastest and funniest. Museum palaeontologist David Huxley (Grant) lost his sense of fun at about the time his precious dinosaurs became extinct. But from the moment heiress Susan Vance (an electrifying Hepburn) hits his ball on the golf course to attract his attention, he is unwillingly enrolled on a crash course in coping with and loving a walking disaster area. Although Baby, a leopard, takes title billing, the real animal star is Susan's dog, George (later to enjoy deserved fame as the >*Thin Man* dog, Asta), for burying a priceless dinosaur bone in a field.

•Life becomes a catalogue of disasters for musicologist Ryan O'Neal when Barbra Streisand sets her cap at him in *What's Up, Doc?* (Peter Bogdanovich 1972) (☆ ☞ ✍).

•A fur coat thrown from a window lands on Jean Arthur leading her to a romance with Ray Milland in the >Preston Sturges scripted *Easy Living* (Mitchell Leisen 1937) (✍ ☆ ☞).

•A chimp was the animal upstaging the human cast of Ronald Reagan and Diana Lynn in *Bedtime for Bonzo* (Frederick De Cordova 1951) (☆).

•Singer >Ginger Rogers is disapproved of by botanist >James Stewart's folks in *Vivacious Lady* (>George Stevens 1938) (☆ ✍).

•Palaeontologist >Gérard Depardieu believes Sigourney Weaver is solely interested in his research in *A Woman or Two* (*Une Femme ou Deux*) (Daniel Vigne 1985).

•Poor little rich girl >Olivia De Havilland torments fortune-seeking Montgomery Clift in *The Heiress*, an adaptation of >Henry James's *Washington Square* (>William Wyler 1949) (☆ ☞).

BRITISH EMPIRE

Guns at Batasi (John Guillermin 1964) ☆
>Richard Attenborough organizes backs-to-the-wall resistance during an African uprising.

The Heart of the Matter (George More O'Ferrall 1953) ✍ ☆
>Graham Greene inflicts adultery and career boredom on colonial cop Trevor Howard in Sierra Leone.

Khartoum (Basil Dearden 1966) ■
General Gordon (Charlton Heston) disobeys PM Gladstone (Michael Hordern) and is besieged by the Mahdi (>Laurence Olivier).

The Kitchen Toto (Harry Hook 1988) ☆ ✍
A serving boy is terrorized into participating in a Mau-Mau attack in Kenya.

Ohm Krüger (Hans Steinhoff 1941) ☆
Paul Krüger (>Emil Jannings) leads the Boers against the British during the 1899–1902 South African war in this Nazi propaganda film.

Under Capricorn (>Alfred Hitchcock 1949) ☞
Marital misery and life in 1830s Australia drive >Ingrid Bergman to drink.

White Mischief (Michael Radford 1988) ■
Kenyan society is scandalized when Greta Scacchi's cuckold husband Joss Ackland shoots Charles Dance.

Zulu (Cy Endfield 1964) ✍
>Michael Caine and Stanley Baker are among

the troops defending Rorke's Drift in 1879 Zulu Wars.
>The Raj

BROTHELS

The Best House in London (Philip Savile 1968) ✍
David Hemmings seeks MP George Sanders' support for a state-funded brothel.
The Cheyenne Social Club (>Gene Kelly 1970) ☆
>James Stewart and >Henry Fonda as ageing cowboy heirs to Shirley Jones' establishment.
Love and Anarchy (*Film d'Amore e d'Anarchia*) (Lina Wertmüller, Italy 1973) ☞ ■ ☆
Giancarlo Giannini resides in a brothel while on a mission to assassinate Mussolini.
Paint Your Wagon (Joshua Logan 1969) ♫ ☆ ✍
A brothel is kept busy as Lee Marvin and >Clint Eastwood among others dig for Californian gold.
Pretty Baby (>Louis Malle 1978) ☞ ☆
Madame Susan Sarandon sells virgin Brooke Shields to the highest bidder, Keith Carradine.
Sandakan-8 (*Sandakan Hachiban Shokan: Bokyo*) (Kei Kumai, Japan 1975) ☆ ☞ ✍
Berlin Film Festival Best Actress winner Kinuyo Tanaka works in a Borneo brothel to support her family back in Japan.
Walk on the Wild Side (Edward Dmytryk 1962) ☆
Laurence Harvey discovers that the love of his life >Jane Fonda was once on the staff at >Barbara Stanwyck's brothel.
Working Girls (Lizzie Borden 1987) ☆
Prostitutes talk about their clients and their lives between tricks.
> Prostitution

BROTHERS

And God Created Woman (aka *And Woman Was Created*) (*Et Dieu Créa La Femme*) (Roger Vadim 1956)
Brigitte Bardot prefers brother-in-law Christian Marquand to husband Jean-Louis Trintignant.

The Birch Wood (*Brzezina*) (>Andrej Wajda 1970) ☞ ■
A forester is unable to disclose his love to a village girl and loses her to his tubercular brother.
The Brothers (David Macdonald 1947) ☆ ■
Orphan Patricia Roc divides the menfolk of a Skye fishing port.
The Crowd Roars (>Howard Hawks 1932) ☞ ☆
Racing driver >James Cagney tries and fails to dissuade his brother from following the same career.
A Duel in the Sun (>King Vidor & others 1946) ☆ ☞
Lionel Barrymore and >Lillian Gish are unable to prevent Gregory Peck and Joseph Cotten's sibling rivalry over Jennifer Jones.
A Hole in the Head (>Frank Capra 1959) ✍
Frank Sinatra looks to brother >Edward G. Robinson to bail out his struggling hotel.
Rocco and His Brothers (*Rocco e i Suoi Fratelli*) (>Luchino Visconti 1960) ☞
Alain Delon and family find poverty just as uncompromising in Milan as in southern Italy.
True Confessions (Ulu Grosbard 1981) ☆
Priest Robert Duvall is indecisive about revealing brother >Robert De Niro's criminal activities.

Buñuel, Luis
Spanish writer/director (1900–1983)
A remarkable director with a most distinctive style, Buñuel's *œuvre* shunned the logic of progression and often of content, but unceasingly fascinates and amuses. His Surrealist work – *Un Chien Andalou* (*The Andalusian Dog*) (1928) (✍ ■) (a series of shocking and anti-clerical images financed by Buñuel's mother) and >*L'Age D'Or* (*The Golden Age*) (1930) (☞ ■ ✍), both with Salvador Dali – and *Land without Bread* (*Las Hurdes*) (1932) (a documentary on the abject poverty of the Spanish region of Las Hurdes) attracted international attention, but wanderlust and political involvement prevented worthwhile creativity. His Communist sympathies mitigated against a Hollywood career and he settled in Mexico in 1947, where *The Young and the*

Damned (aka *The Forgotten*) (*Las Olvidados*) (1950) (☆ ☞) (a naïve boy learns the ways of the street to survive in the Mexico City slums), *Susana* (US: *The Devil and the Flesh*) (*Demonio y Carne*) (1950) (✍ ☞) (a girl offends a rich Catholic family with her promiscuity), *The Adventures of Robinson Crusoe* (*Las Aventuras de Robinson Crusoe*) (1952) (☞) (Daniel Defoe's castaway endures desert island solitude), *El* (US: *This Strange Passion*) (1952) (☞ ☆) (unable to trust his young bride, a middle-aged man is driven to attempted murder and a monastic exile), and *Nazarin* (1958) (☞ ✍ ☆) (a devout priest is mocked for his Christ-like existence by all but a prostitute) stand out amid a number of sub-standard melodramas. Shuttling between Mexico and Europe, the quality of his later output was phenomenal, particularly: *Viridiana* (1961) (✍ ☞) (novice nun Silvia Pinal shelters society's outcasts in the home of an uncle who has maltreated her), *The Exterminating Angel* (*El Angel Exterminador*) (1962) (✍ ☞ ☆) (trapped in a single room, sophisticated party guests resort to the law of the jungle), *Simon of the Desert* (*Simon del Desierto*) (1965) (☞ ■) (Claudio Brook's St Simon Stylites prays for the world atop a column in the wilderness), >*Belle de Jour* (1966) (☞ ☆ ✍ ■), *Tristana* (1970) (☞ ☆) (trusting >Catherine Deneuve becomes the victim of her guardian Fernando Rey's developing chauvinism), >*The Discreet Charm of the Bourgeoisie* (*Le Charme Discret de la Bourgeoisie*) (1972) (☞ ☆ ■ ✍) and *That Obscure Object of Desire* (*Cet Obscur Objet de Désir*) (1977) (☞ ☆ ✍) (businessman Fernando Rey ruins himself in the hope of sleeping with his maid Conchita, played by both Carole Bouquet and Angela Molina). A film-maker who entertains because he challenges.

VIEW ON ▶ MEXICAN FILMS: •*A Mexican Bus Ride* (aka *Ascent to Heaven*) (*Subida al Cielo*) (1951) (✍): brothers endure an eventful journey on the way home to see their dying mother.
•*Wuthering Heights* (*Abismos de Pasión*) (1953) (■): Emily Brontë's novel of doomed love adapted to the Mexican desert.
•*The Criminal Life of Archibaldo de la Cruz*

(aka *Rehearsal for a Crime*) (*Ensayo de un Crimen*) (1955) (☞): driven by childhood trauma, a would-be Jack the Ripper is unceasingly thwarted in his attempts to murder women. FRENCH FILMS: •*Cela S'Appelle L'Aurore* (1955) (☞): a Corsican doctor becomes embroiled in adultery and murder while his wife is away on holiday.
•*Diary of a Chambermaid* (*Journal d'une Femme de Chambre*) (1963) (✍ ☞ ☆): Jeanne Moreau in the Octave Mirbeau tale of a maid who brings sexual liberation to a stuffy bourgeois household.
•*The Milky Way* (*La Voie Lactée*) (1969) (☞): tramps on a pilgrimage to the Spanish Marian shrine of Santiago De Compostela discuss Catholicism with fellow travellers.
•*The Phantom of Liberty* (*Le Fantôme de la Liberté*) (1974) (☞): characters mistake self-interest for liberty in episodes ranging from the brutal liberation of a town in Napoleonic Spain to a discussion in modern Paris.

Burton, Richard
(Richard Jenkins) British actor (1925–84)
A Welsh miner's son, educated in true *How Green Was My Valley* fashion, Burton's acclaimed theatre work led to *My Cousin Rachel* (AAN: Henry Koster 1952) (✍) (>Daphne Du Maurier tale of a man's growing love for his foster father's mysterious widow >Olivia De Havilland). Epics such as *The Robe* (AAN: Henry Koster 1953) (☆ ■) (Burton, Jean Simmons and Victor Mature are among the early Christians seeking Christ's Crucifixion garment), *Alexander the Great* (Robert Rossen 1956) (■) (Burton as the all-conquering yet short-lived Greek soldier) and *Cleopatra* (>Joseph L. Mankiewicz and others 1963) (■) (Burton as Mark Antony, Rex Harrison as Julius Caesar and Elizabeth Taylor in the title role) showcased the looks and tones but suffocated the talent seen in *Look Back in Anger* (Tony Richardson 1959) (✍ ☆) (the original angry young man, Burton's dissatisfaction with life is not appeased by affair with wife Mary Ure's best friend Claire Bloom). Rowing offstage with on-off wife Elizabeth Taylor, he was cynical and irksome in *The Spy Who Came in From the Cold* (Martin Ritt 1965) (☆ ✍) (Bur-

ton as a spy no longer interested in the purpose or etiquette of espionage) and *Who's Afraid Of Virginia Woolf?* (AAN: >Mike Nichols 1966) (☆ ☞) (academic Burton and wife Taylor perpetuate a blazing row throughout George Segal and Sandy Dennis' visit). Ill-served by stardom and alcohol, Burton preferred the stage in his later career, but still turned in fine performances in *Anne of the Thousand Days* (AAN: Charles Jarrott 1969) (✍ ☆ ■) (Burton as Henry VIII courting then cursing Geneviève Bujold as Anne Boleyn), *Equus* (AAN: >Sidney Lumet 1977) (☆ ☞) (psychiatrist Burton in the Peter Shaffer play investigating Peter Firth's repeated blinding of horses) and *1984* (Michael Radford 1984) (☆) (screen version of the George Orwell novel in which Burton brainwashes John Hurt's Winston Smith into loving Big Brother).

•*Becket* (AAN: Peter Glenville 1964) (☆ ■): Burton as the Archbishop of Canterbury whose preference for ecclesiastical duty over loyalty to friend and king Henry II (Peter O'Toole) leads to his murder.
•*The Night of the Iguana* (>John Huston 1964) (☞ ☆): Tennessee Williams' play has Burton as an ex-priest desired by Deborah Kerr, Ava Gardner and Sue Lyon.
•*The Taming of the Shrew* (Franco Zeffirelli 1966) (✍ ☆ ☞): Shakespeare play in which Burton's Petruchio tames Elizabeth Taylor's Kate.
•*Where Eagles Dare* (Brian G. Hutton 1968) (✍): Burton and >Clint Eastwood in Alistair MacLean adventure rescuing a PoW from a Nazi-held castle.
•*Under Milk Wood* (Andrew Sinclair 1971) (☆ ✍ ■): Burton studies Elizabeth Taylor and Peter O'Toole among the other inhabitants of Dylan Thomas's Welsh village, Llareggub.
•*The Assassination of Trotsky* (>Joseph Losey 1972) (■): Stalinist Alain Delon kills Leon Trotsky (Burton) with an ice-pick in Mexico City.

BUTLERS

The Admirable Crichton (US: *Paradise Lagoon*) (Lewis Gilbert 1957) ☆
Kenneth More organizes employer Cecil Parker's household on a desert island.

By Candlelight (James Whale 1933) ☞ ☆
Paul Lukas exploits his being mistaken for his prince master.

Candleshoe (Norman Tokar 1977) ☆
Disney tale in which David Niven prevents an inheritance fraud.

The Chiltern Hundreds (US: *The Amazing Mr Beecham*) (John Paddy Carstairs 1949) ✍ ☆
Butler Cecil Parker stands against the earl's son David Tomlinson in parliamentary election.

Fancy Pants (George Marshall 1950) ☆
Actor Bob Hope is conned into butlering for a cowboy family in this *Ruggles of Red Gap* remake.

If You Could Only Cook (William A. Seiter 1935) ☆
Millionaire Herbert Marshall and waif Jean Arthur work as butler and cook.

My Man Godfrey (Gregory La Cava 1936) ☆
>Carole Lombard mistakes millionaire >William Powell for a tramp, but love persuades him to accept a post as her butler.

Ruggles of Red Gap (>Leo McCarey 1935) ☆ ☞ ✍
>Charles Laughton as a typical English butler serving a Wild West family.

Thank You, Jeeves (Arthur Greville Collins 1935) ✍ ☆
Arthur Treacher as the ice-cool P. G. Wodehouse butler keeping David Niven's Bertie Wooster out of gun trouble.

The Cabinet of Dr Caligari

Germany • Decla-Bioscop • 1919 • 90 mins • b/w

d Robert Wiene   **w** Carl Meyer/Hans Janowitz   **ph** Willy Hameister

Werner Krauss, Conrad Veidt, Lil Dagover, Friedrich Feher

Modern horror makers would do well to study this early Expressionist venture into psychological horror, for its terror is based on continuously disconcerting our perceptions, not cheap screams gained from expensive effects. Our narrator, Francis, takes us to a world of optical illusion, kidnap and murder, where the predictions of Cesare, a fairground fortune teller controlled by the evil Dr Caligari, coincide with a spate of local deaths. When his own girl Jane disappears, Francis tracks her to an asylum, where Caligari performs zombie experiments. But just before the groans of 'predictable happy ending' ring out, the twist: we are shown another institution, again Caligari's, but at which he is a caring doctor and Francis is a seriously disturbed patient. The ultimate tale of the unexpected.

 •An evil hypnotist and man of 1000 faces plans world domination in *Dr Mabuse, the Gambler* (*Doktor Mabuse, der Spieler*) (>Fritz Lang 1922) (☞ ■).

•In the Edgar Allan Poe mystery a >Bela Lugosi-trained killer ape perpetrates *The Murders in the Rue Morgue* (Robert Florey 1932) (☆ ☞).

•A vaudeville memory man alone can clear >Robert Donat of murder and resolve John Buchan's espionage mystery *The Thirty Nine Steps* (>Alfred Hitchcock 1935) (☎ ☞ ☆).

•Mad scientist Steve Martin sees lobotomy as the only treatment for >Kathleen Turner's temper in *The Man with Two Brains* (Carl Reiner 1983) (☆).

•A corpse in a coffin is at the centre of brothers John Mills and Ralph Richardson's dispute over a tontine in *The Wrong Box* (Bryan Forbes 1966) (☎ ☆).

Cagney, James
American actor (1899–1986)

A chorus dancer and female impersonator in vaudeville, Cagney only had to slap a grapefruit into Mae Clarke's face in *The Public Enemy* (UK: *Enemies of the Public*) (>William Wellman 1931) (☞ ☆ ✍) (streetkid Cagney rises to bootlegging baron only to die in a gang war) to become a tough guy legend. Numerous dirty rats, often with soft hearts, enhanced the celebrity: *G Men* (William Keighley 1935) (☆ ✍) (Cagney becomes an FBI agent and finds that the killer of his best friend is also a pal); *Angels with Dirty Faces* (>Michael Curtiz 1938) (☆ ☞ ✍) (priest Pat O'Brien begs Cagney to act scared before his electrocution to disillusion hero-worshipping youths); *The Roaring Twenties* (>Raoul Walsh/Anatole Litvak 1939) (☞ ☆) (discovering that 1920s America is not a land fit for heroes, Cagney smuggles liquor); and *White Heat* (>Raoul Walsh 1949) (☞ ☆ ✍) (Cagney as a gangster tied to his mother Margaret Wycherly's apron strings). Punchy drama provided the bulk of his work: *Footlight Parade* (Lloyd Bacon 1933) (☆ ■ ♪) (Busby Berkeley production numbers enliven Cagney's struggles to compete with the movies); *The Fighting 69th* (William Keighley 1940) (☆) (arrogant Cagney irritates his trench platoon, but has the stuff of heroes); and *The Time of Your Life* (H.C. Potter 1948) (☆ ■) (Cagney's drinking partners can right the world, but not their own domestic difficulties). However, energetic comedies provided the highlights of Cagney's career: *Hard to Handle* (>Mervyn Le Roy 1933) (✍ ☆) (PR man Cagney makes fast bucks out of the latest crazes, whether they be dance marathons or wonder diets); *Boy Meets Girl* (Lloyd Bacon 1938) (☆ ✍) (filmwriters Cagney and Pat O'Brien turn an unborn baby into a movie star); *The Strawberry Blonde* (>Raoul Walsh 1941) (☆ ✍) (Cagney can't decide whether to stroll down the avenue with >Olivia De Havilland or Rita Hayworth); *One, Two, Three* (>Billy Wilder 1961) (☆ ☞ ✍) (Cagney as a bustling businessman intent on marketing Coca-Cola in East Berlin); and especially the flag-waving biopic *Yankee Doodle Dandy* (AA: >Michael Curtiz 1942) (♪ ☆) (the showbiz career of George M. Cohan from family act to Broadway songsmith and dance man).

VIEW ON ▶ •*Winner Take All* (Roy Del Ruth 1932) (☆): Cagney as a heart-of-gold boxer helping a sick child.
•*Jimmy the Gent* (>Michael Curtiz 1934) (☆):

>Bette Davis falls for Cagney, a conman who drums up fake heirs for unclaimed inheritances.
•*Here Comes the Navy* (Lloyd Bacon 1934) (☆): sailor Cagney finds it hard to forget that officer Pat O'Brien is a close friend.
•*Ceiling Zero* (>Howard Hawks 1935) (☞ ☆): Cagney's romantic entanglements jeopardize Pat O'Brien's dangerous flying mail mission.
•*A Midsummer Night's Dream* (Max Reinhardt/>William Dieterle 1935) (✍ ☆ ☞ ■): Cagney as Bottom, the weaver transformed into an ass during the feud between the King and Queen of the fairies.
•*Captains of the Clouds* (>Michael Curtiz 1942) (☆): arrogant Cagney irritates fellow pilots, but proves to have the stuff of heroes.
•*Johnny Come Lately* (*Johnny Vagabond*) (William K. Howard 1944) (☆): a journalist jailed for vagrancy exposes the corruption of the men who sentenced him.
•*Kiss Tomorrow Goodbye* (Gordon Douglas 1950) (☆): spitting flames, gangster Cagney takes brutal revenge on the partner who betrayed him then plans a major heist.
•*Love Me or Leave Me* (AAN: Charles Vidor 1955) (☆ ♪): Doris Day as singer Ruth Etting made and then destroyed by gangster Cagney.
•*Mister Roberts* (>John Ford/>Mervyn Le Roy 1955) (☆): Captain Cagney prevents sailors >Henry Fonda, >William Powell and >Jack Lemmon from seeing World War Two action.
•*Man of a Thousand Faces* (Joseph Peveney 1957) (✍): the early career of silent horror star Lon Chaney, Sr.
•*Ragtime* (>Miloš Forman 1981) (☆ ■): Cagney as a shirking police chief unaffected by simmering racism during a museum hostage siege.

Caine, Michael
(Maurice Micklewhite) British actor (b 1933)
Since playing Harry Palmer in the Len Deighton series – *The Ipcress File* (Sidney J. Furie 1965) (Palmer discovers that MI5 chiefs are involved in the kidnap of a top scientist), *Funeral in Berlin* (Guy Hamilton 1966) (✍ ☆) (Caine assesses senior Soviet soldier Oscar Homolka's wish to defect) and *Billion Dollar Brain* (Ken Russell 1967) (Caine, retired from

the Secret Service thwarts Oscar Homolka's world domination plans) – and then *Alfie* (AAN: Lewis Gilbert 1966) (☆ ✍) (fast-talking Cockney Romeo Caine might marry Julia Foster, but his eye continues to roam), Caine's workaholism has meant that he has had to survive more career-killing pulp than any other current star. His performances in the excellent >*Sleuth* (Joseph L. Mankiewicz 1972) (✍ ☆ ☞) and *The Man Who Would Be King* (>John Huston 1975) (☆ ☞ ✍) (soldier >Sean Connery is mistaken for tribal god but refuses to heed Caine's warnings against megalomania and endangers them both) won him further Oscar nominations, but failed to induce increased selectivity. However, as proved by his work in *The Italian Job* (Peter Collinson 1969) (☆ ✍ ■) (Caine executes Noël Coward's perfect Turin traffic-jam crime), *Dressed to Kill* (Brian De Palma 1980) (☞) (transvestite Caine stalks witness to his mental home murder Angie Dickinson) and *Mona Lisa* (Neil Jordan 1986) (☆ ✍) (Bob Hoskins chauffeurs and minds Caine's top call-girl Cathy Tyson), he rarely turns in a poor performance. This trend continued throughout the 1980s, deadpan comedy providing the high points: *Educating Rita* (AAN; Lewis Gilbert 1983) (☆ ✍♫) (Caine as a frustrated poet and drunken academic rejuvenated by further education student Julie Walters), *Hannah and Her Sisters* (AA; >Woody Allen 1986) (☆ ☞) (Caine admits that his wife Mia Farrow is wonderful, but can't control his crush on her sister Barbara Hershey), *Surrender* (Jerry Belson 1987) (☆ ✍) (Caine as a wealthy novelist resisting an affair with Sally Field, believing that she loves his money and not him) and *Dirty Rotten Scoundrels* (Frank Oz 1988) (☆ ✍) (Caine and Steve Martin as conmen competing for easy touches on the French Riviera).

VIEW ON ▶ •*Pulp* (Mike Hodges 1972) (☆): penny dreadful writer Caine lands in a gangster situation straight out of one of his books.
•*Black Windmill* (Don Siegel 1974) (☆): Caine risks danger rather than stump up the ransom for his kidnapped son.
•*California Suite* (Herbert Ross 1978) (☆ ✍):

Caine reassures nominee >Maggie Smith as they dress for the Oscar ceremony.
•*Escape to Victory* (US: *Victory*) (>John Huston 1982) (☞ ✍): Caine as an ex-professional footballer leading a PoW escape after playing a Nazi team in Paris.
•*Deathtrap* (>Sidney Lumet 1982) (☆ ✍ ☞): novelist Caine plans an ingenious murder of his own to free his writer's block.
•*Blame it on Rio* (>Stanley Donen 1984) (☆): menopausal Caine has an affair with the teenage daughter of his best friend.
•*Water* (Dick Clement 1986) (♫): guerilla Billy Connolly leads the resistance group against the marketing of mineral water found on the Caribbean island where Caine lives.
•*Half Moon Street* (Bob Swaim 1987): screen version of the Paul Theroux novel about academic Sigourney Weaver endangered by an affair with a mysterious politician (Caine).
•*Without a Clue* (Thom Eberhardt 1989) (✍ ☆): crime-solver Dr Watson (Ben Kingsley), forced to find a Sherlock Holmes when his fame spreads, hires actor Caine for the part.

Camille

USA • MGM • 1936 • 108 mins • b/w

d >George Cukor   w Frances Marion, James Hilton/Zoë Akins   ph William Daniels   m Herbert Stothart

>Greta Garbo, Robert Taylor, Lionel Barrymore, Henry Daniell

Garbo's Marguerite Gautier is one of the most legendary tragic performances given by any actress on screen. As the Parisian coquette who abandons the love of her life, Armand Duval (Taylor), because his father Barrymore has threatened his inheritance, she displays enough human weakness and indecision to fuel a hundred Hamlets and yet radiates such beauty and potential for living that we mourn her death as if she were a personal friend. However, Irving G. Thalberg and George Cukor deserve credit for the sumptuous backgrounds and restrained direction that prevented the classic love story of Alexandre Dumas *fils* from slipping into sticky melodrama.

•In the life story of the Second Empire courtesan on whom Dumas based his novel – *The Lady of the Camélias* (*La Dame aux Camélias*) (Mauro Bolognini 1981) (☆ ■) – Alphonsine Duplessis is played by Isabelle Huppert.

•Ali McGraw's fatal illness intrudes into her affair with Ryan O'Neal in *Love Story* (Arthur Hiller 1970) (✍).

•Alain Delon plays both the outlaw and his twin carrying on a crusade against Louis XVI's government in another Dumas classic *The Black Tulip* (*La Tulipe Noir*) (Christian-Jaque 1963) (✍).

•The life of the idle rich in Tsarist Russia is explored in *Several Days in the Life of I.I. Oblomov* (aka *Oblomov*) (*Neskolko Dnei Iz Zhizni I.I. Oblomov*) (Nikita Mikhalkov 1979) (■ ☆).

•Tolstoy's tale of a stifling marriage like that Garbo is warned against by Lionel Barrymore drives Oleg Yankovsky to violence and remorse in *The Kreutzer Sonata* (*Kreitzerova Sonata*) (Mikhail Schweitzer/Sofia Milkina 1987) (☆ ✍).

Cannes Film Festival
Palme d'Or for Best Film

1946
The Battle of the Rails (*La Bataille du Rail*) (René Clément) ☞ ■
Semi-documentary tale of the sabotage of the French rail network under the Vichy government that also won Clément Best Director.

1947
Antoine and Antoinette (Jacques Becker) ☆ ✍
A humdrum couple win a lottery, but what's happened to the ticket?

1948
No festival

1949
>*The Third Man* (>Carol Reed) ☆ ☞ ♫ ✍ ■

1950
No festival

1951
Miracle in Milan (*Miracolo a Milano*) (>Vittorio De Sica) ☞ ■
A cabbage-patch foundling helps Milanese homeless with the help of a magic dove.
Shared with Miss Julie (*Fröken Julie*) (Alf Sjöberg, Sweden) ✍ ☆
An adaptation of the August Strindberg play about a bored daughter shocking her dour family by tempting the butler.

1952
Othello (>Orson Welles)
Welles as the Moor induced into suffocating his wife by a vengeful courtier.
Shared with Two Penny Worth of Hope (US: *Two Cents Worth of Hope*) (*Due Soldi di Speranza*) (Renato Castellani, Italy) ☆ ✍
Villagers debate whether to support Rome or Moscow while a war veteran tries to ingratiate himself with his demanding farmer father-in-law.

1953
The Wages of Fear (*Le Salaire de la Peur*) (Henri-Georges Clouzot) ✍ ☞ ■ ☆
Desperate for money, South American drivers, one of whom, Charles Vanel, received the Best Actor award, transport explosives across treacherous country.

1954
Gate of Hell (*Jigokumon*) (Teinosuke Kinugasa) ☆ ■
A medieval warlord atones for driving a woman to suicide because of his lust by entering a monastery.

1955
Marty (Delbert Mann) ☆
Ernest Borgnine's last chance for love is

jeopardized by the conventions of New York's Little Italy.

1956

The Silent World (*Le Monde du Silence*) (Jacques-Yves Cousteau/>Louis Malle) ■

The silent, fascinating beauty of the ocean bed as captured by the famous diver.

1957

Friendly Persuasion (>William Wyler) ☞ ⚏

>Gary Cooper and a Quaker community debate joining the Unionist cause in the US Civil War.

1958

The Cranes Are Flying (*Letyat Zhuravli*) (Mikhail Kalatozov) ■ ☆

Although never doubting her man has survived the war, a hospital ancillary contracts a loveless marriage.

1959

Black Orpheus (*Orfeu Negro*) (Marcel Camus) ■

A Rio tram driver goes to Hell to find the girlfriend that he has accidentally killed.

1960

>*La Dolce Vita* (*The Sweet Life*) (>Federico Fellini) ☞ ☆ ■ ⚏ ♫

1961

Viridiana (>Luis Buñuel) ⚏ ☞

Abused by her uncle and cousin, a novice nun turns their house into a refuge for the destitute.

Shared with **The Long Absence** (*Une Aussi Longue Absence*) (Henri Colpi, France) ☆ ⚏

A café owner meets a tramp whom she believes to be her husband supposedly killed in a Nazi prison camp.

1962

The Given Word (*O Pagador de Promessas*) (Anselmo Duarte) ☆ ⚏

A priest refuses to accept a crucifix that a Brazilian farmer had promised at a voodoo ceremony in thanks for the recovery of his donkey.

1963

The Leopard (*Il Gattopardo*) (>Luchino Visconti) ■ ☞ ⚏

In 1860s Italy, petty prince Burt Lancaster despairs of his family's future as his nephew Alain Delon marries beneath him.

1964

The Umbrellas of Cherbourg (*Les Parapluies de Cherbourg*) (Jacques Demy) ♫ ■

All-sung-dialogue story telling of pregnant >Catherine Deneuve's marriage of convenience.

1965

The Knack...And How to Get it (Richard Lester) ☆ ☞

The pace of timid teacher Michael Crawford's life is increased by renting rooms to Lothario Ray Brooks and naïve Rita Tushingham.

1966

A Man and a Woman (*Un Homme et une Femme*) (Claude Lelouch) ☞ ☆

Jean-Louis Trintignant and Anouk Aimée dally over committing themselves to an affair.

Shared with **The Birds, the Bees and the Italians** (*Signori e Signore*) (Pietro Germi) ⚏

Sex trilogy: a man feigns impotence to get away with adultery; a tired husband moves in with a barmaid; and men flock round the village Lolita.

1967

Blow Up (>Michelangelo Antonioni)

A photographer is unable to find proof that he has witnessed a murder.

1968

No awards

1969

If... (Lindsay Anderson) ☞ ⚏ ☆

Malcolm McDowell leads public school boys in revolt against the staff.

1970

*M*A*S*H* (>Robert Altman) ⚏ ☞

Infighting and heroics of the cynical staff of a Korean War field hospital.

1971

The Go-Between (>Joseph Losey)
✍ ☞ ☆
L. P. Hartley tale of a small boy carrying *billets doux* between tenant farmer Alan Bates and the well-born Julie Christie.

1972

The Working Class Goes to Heaven (*US: Lulu the Tool*) (*La Classe Operaia va in Paradiso*) (Elio Petri) ☆ ✍
Temporary unemployment transforms a Stakhanovite into a union activist.
Shared with The Mattei Affair (*Il Caso Mattei*) (Francesco Rosi/Tonino Guerra)
Semi-documentary reconstruction of the sinister death of oil man Enrico Mattei.

1973

Scarecrow (Jerry Schatzberg) ☆
Hoboes Gene Hackman and Al Pacino hitch-hike their way across the USA, but see little of the wild side.
Shared with The Hireling (Alan Bridges) ✍
L. P. Hartley story concerning chauffeur Robert Shaw falling for his mistress Sarah Miles.

1974

The Conversation (>Francis Ford Coppola)
Bugging professional Gene Hackman finds himself a victim of his own handiwork.

1975

Chronicle of the Burning Years (aka *Chronicle of the Years of the Brazier*) (aka *Chronicle of the Years of Embers*) (*Ahdat Sanawouach el-Djamr*) (*Chronique des Années de Braise*) (Mohammed Lakhdar-Hamina, Morocco) ☆ ☞
The Algerian revolt against the French is seen through the eyes of poor villagers.

1976

Taxi Driver (>Martin Scorsese) ☆
Vietnam vet >Robert De Niro loses control after his rejection by Cybill Shepherd.

1977

Padre Padrone (*Father, Master*) (Paolo & Vittorio Taviani) ☞ ■
A bullying father consigns his small son to the isolation of a shepherd's life.

1978

The Tree of Wooden Clogs (*Albero degli Zoccoli*) (Ermanno Olmi) ☞ ■ ☆
The lives and characters of four Lombard peasant families co-habiting in a farm-house.

1979

The Tin Drum (*Die Blechtrommel*) >Volker Schlöndorff ☞ ☆
A temperamental boy refuses to grow and his intransigence shames Danzigers in the face of the invading Nazis.
Shared with >Apocalypse Now (>Francis Ford Coppola) ☆ ☞ ■ ✍ ♫

1980

All That Jazz (Bob Fosse)
Fast-living director Roy Scheider's heart can't keep pace with him.
Shared with >Kagemusha (>Akira Kurosawa) ☞ ■ ✍ ☆

1981

Man of Iron (>Andrej Wajda) ☞
A journalist reporting on the Solidarity strike meets the son of a past labour leader, considered in Wajda's earlier *Man Of Marble*.

1982

Missing (Constantin Costa-Gavras) ☆ ✍
Jack Lemmon's search for his son is frustrated by the Chilean authorities.
Shared with Yol (Serif Gören) ✍
Five Turkish parolees return home to a variety of disappointments and disasters.

1983

The Ballad of Narayama (*Narayama-Bushi-Ko*) (Shohei Imamura) ■ ☆
An old woman prepares to honour a village custom demanding that 70 year-olds be abandoned on a mountain top.

1984

Paris, Texas (>Wim Wenders) ☞
Itinerant Harry Dean Stanton is reunited with his lost bride Nastassja Kinski.

1985

When Father Was Away on Business (Otac na Sluzsobtbenom Putu) (Emir Kusturica) ☆ ■ ✍
A small boy's recollection of his father's betrayal to the Yugoslav authorities by his mistress.

1986

>*The Mission* (Roland Joffé) ✍ ■ ☆ ☞ ♫

1987

Pelle the Conqueror (*Pelle Erobereren*) (Bille August, Denmark) ☆ ✍
Despairing of cowherd father Max Von Sydow's abject condition, son Pelle Hvenegaard aims to conquer the world.

1988

Under Satan's Sun (*Sous le Soleil de Satan*) (Maurice Pialat) ☆
>Gérard Depardieu is revered as a saint after a rebellious girl commits suicide.

1989

sex, lies and videotape (Steven Soderbergh)
A love triangle is disrupted by an impotent video voyeur.

Capra, Frank
Sicilian-born American director (b 1897)

Directing early Harry Langdon features – *The Strong Man* (1926) (☆) (war vet searches for his penfriend) and *Long Pants* (1927) (☆) (a country mouse eventually gets the better of his town cousins) – gave Capra a liking for comedy, witness >*It Happened One Night* (1934) (✍ ☆ ☞), *You Can't Take it With You* (☆ ✍ ☞) (1938) (eccentric Jean Arthur's love for >James Stewart is opposed by his rich father Lionel Barrymore), both Best Picture/Director winners, and *Arsenic and Old Lace* (made 1942, released 1944) (✍ ☞ ☆) (>Cary Grant's discovery that his dotty aunts murder male visitors with homemade wine is compounded by his brother Raymond Massey's arrival with his own haul of victims). Indeed humour alone prevented these panegyrics on the American Way, (which had made him), from lapsing into completely unpalatable, patriotic propaganda. The public lapped up such pre-war 'Capracorn' as *Mr Deeds Goes to Town* (AA: 1936) (☞ ☆) (Jean Arthur is attracted by poet >Gary Cooper's decency amid New York rogues), *Mr Smith Goes to Washington* (AAN: 1939) (☆ ☞ ✍) (senator >James Stewart is backed by his wife Jean Arthur in a crusade against the corrupt Claude Rains) and *Meet John Doe* (1941) (✍ ☆ ☞) (>Barbara Stanwyck succeeds in convincing politically exploited tramp >Gary Cooper that life is still worth living) and although Major Capra's *Why We Fight* series (1942–1945) (☞ ■) (seven propaganda documentaries on the course of the conflict) boosted the war effort, only >*It's a Wonderful Life* (1946) (☆ ☞ ✍) and *State of the Union* (UK: *The World and his Wife*) (1948) (☆ ☞) (>Katharine Hepburn buries the marital hatchet to help >Spencer Tracy become President) were applauded by more politically aware audiences. Despite this, Capra's canon has retained its popularity because of the quality performances he enticed out of such stars as >Clark Gable, >Gary Cooper, >James Stewart, Claudette Colbert and Jean Arthur.

•*Tramp, Tramp, Tramp* (Harry Edwards 1926) (☆): the Capra script has Harry Langdon hoping to impress >Joan Crawford in a walking race.
•*The Miracle Woman* (1931) (☆): >Barbara Stanwyck abandons the Bible for a life of crime.
•*Dirigible* (1931) (✳ ☞): when one airship pilot dies in the Arctic, his buddy consoles his colleague's wife.
•*Platinum Blonde* (1931) (☆ ☞ ✍): journalist Robert Williams trades banter with colleague Loretta Young and the eponymous heiress >Jean Harlow.
•*American Madness* (1932) (☞): Walter Huston and Pat O'Brien lead the small investors

intent on bailing out a bankrupt bank.

•*The Bitter Tea of General Yen* (1932) (☆): missionary >Barbara Stanwyck falls for Chinese kidnapper Nils Asther.

•*Lady for a Day* (1932) (☆ ✍): gangsters help old lady May Robson convince her daughter that she is wealthy.

•*Lost Horizon* (1938) (☞ ☆): the film version of James Hilton's novel sees Ronald Colman enjoying the idyllic society of Shangri-La in the Tibetan mountains.

•*Here Comes the Groom* (1951) (☆): unless Jane Wyman sees sense, abandons Franchot Tone and marries Bing Crosby, two orphans will be deported.

Carné, Marcel
French writer/director (b 1909)

Assisting >René Clair on *Sous Les Toits de Paris* (*Under the Roofs of Paris*) (1930) (☞) (the trials and loves of a Parisian street-singer) heralded a 15-year collaboration with surrealist poet Jacques Prévert that produced several unquestioned classics of French cinema. The absurdist comedy *Drôle de Drame* (*Bizarre, Bizarre*) (1937) (✍ ☆ ☞) (a thriller writer's lie to a bishop has repercussions throughout Edwardian London) was followed by the intense romantic dramas *Quai des Brumes* (*Port of Shadows*) (1938) (☆ ▪) (guardian Michel Simon thwarts Michèle Morgan and killer >Jean Gabin's elopement) and >*Le Jour se Lève* (*Daybreak*) (1939) (☆ ☞ ✍ ▪), styled and scripted in a way that demonstrated a complete understanding of cinematic technique and their stars' needs. However, their master work >*Les Enfants du Paradis* (*Children of Paradise*) (1945) (☞ ▪ ☆ ✍) also proved to be their swan song, the partnership ending after the coolly received *Gates of the Night* (*Les Portes de la Nuit*) (1946) (▪) (>Yves Montand is among those unable to celebrate liberation because of broken love affairs). Despite being only 36, Carné was unable to assimilate postwar trends, and although he directed a further thirteen films his work went out of vogue following the attack of the *Cahiers* critics.

•*Jenny* (1936) (☆): hunchback >Jean-Louis Barrault is hired by a club owner to end the manager's affair with gangster Albert Préjean.

•*Hôtel du Nord* (1938) (✍): among the couples registered there are suicide-pact lovers and a killer and his moll on the run.

•*Les Visiteurs du Soir* (*The Devil's Envoys*) (1942) (✍ ☆): Devil Jules Berry sends disguised minstrels Arletty and Alain Cuny to sew disaster at a medieval wedding.

•*Thérèse Raquin* (*Therese*) (*The Adulteress*) (1953) (✍ ☆): updated >Emile Zola story of the murder and blackmail that follow bored housewife Simone Signoret's affair with Italian lorry driver Raf Vallone.

•*The Young Wolves* (*Les Jeunes Loups*) (1968) (✍): handsome good-for-nothing Christian Hay exploits older women and misuses his loyal girlfriend Haydée Politoff to further his own ends.

CARS

The Cars that Ate Paris (Peter Weir 1975) ☞

Scrap dealers arrange accidents to tide them over a slack time.

Chitty Chitty Bang Bang (Ken Hughes 1968) ♫ ☆

Eccentric inventor Dick Van Dyke takes two children and his girlfriend on adventures in a flying car.

The Fast Lady (Ken Annakin 1962) ☆

Stanley Baxter's roadhog heroics win him the admiration of Julie Christie.

>Genevieve (Henry Cornelius 1954) ✍ ☆ ♫ ☞

The Great Race (Blake Edwards 1965) ☆ ☞ ▪

>Jack Lemmon and Tony Curtis employ foul means to win the inaugural New York-Paris car race.

Le Mans (Lee H. Katzin 1971) ▪

Steve McQueen as an ungracious competitor in the famous 24-hour race.

The Love Bug (Robert Stevenson 1968) ✍

A Volkswagen with a mind of its own outwits thieves in this classic Disney actioner.

Two Lane Black Top (Monte Hellman 1971)
James Taylor and Warren Oates race custom
cars around the countryside.
Winning (James Goldstone 1969) ■
Race ace >Paul Newman's ambition drives him
and Joanna Woodward apart.

Casablanca ☆ ☞ ✍ ♫ ■

USA • *Warner Brothers* • 1943 • 102 mins •
b/w

d >Michael Curtiz   w Julius J. & Philip G.
Epstein/Howard Koch   ph Arthur
Edeson   m Max Steiner
>Humphrey Bogart, >Ingrid Bergman,
Claude Rains, Paul Henreid, S. Z. Sakall,
Sydney Greenstreet, >Peter Lorre, Dooley
Wilson, Marcel Dalio, Leonid Kinskey

This legendary story of Nazi-occupied French
Morocco and the ill-fated romance of Ilsa Lund
(Bergman) and streetwise nightclub owner,
Rick Blaine (Bogart) is one of Hollywood's
most popular and most durable mainstream
movies. There are more oft (and occasionally
erroneously) quoted screen gems here than
elsewhere; Dooley Wilson's rendering of the
recurrent 'As Time Goes By' conjures up the
entire film after just a couple of bars; and the
ensemble performances, especially those of
Rains, Henreid, Lorre and Greenstreet, are of
a uniquely high standard. If castaways could
select Desert Island Movies, the scenes of the
Paris affair and the misty airstrip would undoubtedly put this among the most requested.

•Bogie took on Hitler again, this
time off the West Indies in *To Have
and Have Not* (>Howard Hawks
1945) (☆ ☞ ✍).
•Teacher >Charles Laughton unwillingly
defies the Nazis in *This Land is Mine* (>Jean
Renoir 1943) (☆ ✍).
•Night clubs of the seedier kind are central to
the action of *No Surrender* (Peter Smith 1986)
(✍), in which the Alan Bleasdale script sends
Liverpudlian Unionist and Republican Irish to
the same club on New Year's Eve, and to
Stormy Monday (Mike Figgis 1988) (☆ ✍), in
which cleaner Sean Bean and moll Melanie

Griffith uncover gangster Tommy Lee Jones's
contract on Newcastle club owner Sting.
•Casablanca was spoofed, by the >Marx Brothers in *A Night in Casablanca* (Archie Mayo
1946) (☆) and by >Woody Allen in *Play it
Again, Sam* (Herbert Ross 1972) (✍).

CASTING DOUBT

Christmas Holiday (Robert Siodmak 1944)
☞
Deanna Durbin grows suspicious about >Gene
Kelly's long absences.

Indiscreet (>Stanley Donen 1958) ☆ ✍
>Ingrid Bergman begins to suspect >Cary
Grant is not married at all, but a confirmed
bachelor.

The October Man (Roy Baker 1947) ☆
Amnesiac John Mills might or might not be the
killer in Eric Ambler's story.

**The Paradine Case (>Alfred Hitchcock
1947)** ☞ ☆ ✍
Gregory Peck's court battle with >Charles
Laughton is hindered by his love for suspect
Alida Valli.

The Prowler (>Joseph Losey 1951) ☞ ✍
Is Evelyn Keyes really safe from protective cop
Van Heflin?

The Secret (*Le Secret*) (Robert Enrico 1974)
✍ ☆
>Philippe Noiret believes that escapee Jean-
Louis Trintignant has been persecuted in
prison; his wife Marlène Jobert doesn't. Who is
right?

**Shadow of a Doubt (>Alfred Hitchcock
1943)** ☞ ✍
Joseph Cotten might be a hero to his niece, but
to widows he is a menace.

Suspicion (>Alfred Hitchcock 1941)
☞ ☆ ✍ ■
Following Nigel Bruce's death, >Joan Fontaine
becomes convinced that >Cary Grant is up to
no good.

Unfaithfully Yours (>Preston Sturges 1948)
✍ ☞
Conductor Rex Harrison believes his wife
Linda Darnell is having an affair.

Chabrol, Claude
French writer/director (b 1930)

Cahiers du Cinéma critic and Twentieth-Century Fox publicist Chabrol, as befits a biographer (with >Erich Rohmer) of >Alfred Hitchcock, excels at the psychological thriller. These are usually slow, detached tales of dangerous triangles in which married Charles and Hélènes (the latter usually played by his wife >Stéphane Audran) scheme against each other on account of amorous Pauls: *Les Biches* (*The Does*) (1968) (☆ ☞ ✍) (Audran's lesbian affair is shattered when Jean-Louis Trintignant steals Jacqueline Sassard); *The Unfaithful Wife* (*La Femme Infidèle*) (1969) (✍ ☆ ☞) (Michel Bouquet's covered-up crime of passion saves his marriage to Audran); *The Butcher* (*Le Boucher*) (1970) (☞ ☆) (timid butcher Jean Yanne reveals himself to be the killer threatening a village school); *La Rupture* (*The Break-up*) (1970) (☞ ✍ ☆) (Michel Bouquet hires a private eye to gather custody evidence against his daughter-in-law Audran); *Just Before Nightfall* (*Juste avant la Nuit*) (1971) (■ ☞) (Michel Bouquet murders his mistress and confesses to his wife Audran and her husband François Périer); and *Blood Wedding* (US: *Wedding in Blood*) (aka *Red Wedding*) (*Les Noces Rouges*) (1973) (☞) (Mayor Claude Piéplu blackmails his deputy Michel Piccoli into fronting his corrupt dealings). Lacking critical and commercial consistency in the late 1970s, Chabrol has only recently returned to form with *Cop au Vin* (*Poulet au Vinaigre*) (1984) (☞ ☆) (a police inspector investigates the death of a bullying property developer) and its sequel *Inspecteur Lavardin* (1986) (☞ ☆) (a detective is troubled by a seemingly incomprehensible murder case and an old flame).

 •*Le Beau Serge* (*Bitter Reunion*) (1958) (☞): a dying student is reunited with an old friend who has abandoned his pregnant wife and turned to drink.
•*The Cousins* (*Les Cousins*) (1959) (☞ ■): idle Jean-Claude Brialy enjoys the success in love and study deserved by his country cousin Gérard Blain.
•*A Web of Passion* (*Leda*) (1959) (☆): a wine merchant is murdered and the unsavoury members of his household are suspected.
•*The Third Lover* (*L'Oeil du Malin*) (1962) (☞ ■ ☆): a hack journalist inflicts his bitterness and mediocrity on a successful writer and his wife.
•*The Line of Demarcation* (*La Ligne de Démarcation*) (1966) (☞ ☆ ✍): citizens of an occupied town attempt to lead Allied agents and airmen across France to safety from the Nazis.
•*The Champagne Murders* (1967) (☆): female champagne boss, her secretary and a former lover seek to remove a rival from a takeover bid by having him committed for murder.
•*Nada* (1974) (✍ ☞): kidnapping terrorists discover that no one uses violence more ruthlessly than the Establishment.
•*Killer!* (*This Man Must Die*) (*Que la bête meure*) (1969) (☞ ✍): out to avenge the death of his son, Michel Duchaussoy takes the blame when the murderer's own son pips him to the post.
•*Une Partie de Plaisir* (*Love Match*) (aka *Pleasure Party*) (1975) (☞ ✍): a husband orders his mousy wife to take a lover; she does and enjoys it.
•*Violette Nozière* (1978) (✍ ☆ ☞): Stéphane Audran survives her daughter Isabelle Huppert's poison plot to wreak her revenge.
•*The Proud Ones* (*Le Cheval d'Orgeuil*) (1981) (☞): while World War I blazes away, simple life goes on as usual for the peasants of Brittany.
•*Hatter's Ghosts* (*Les Fantômes du Chapelier*) (1982) (☞): Simenon tale about respectable Michel Serrault murdering small town women.

Chaplin, Sir Charles ('Charlie')
British actor/writer/director (1889–1977)

Initiated in slapstick by Fred Karno, Chaplin left the troupe in 1913 to join Mack Sennett's Keystone studio, devising the Tramp character in his second film *Kid Auto Races at Venice* (Henry Lehrman 1914). Directing after acting in only 11 shorts, his universal popularity enabled him to dictate terms to the studio heads at Essanay, where he made *The Tramp* (1915) (✍) (Chaplin loses Edna Purviance when her lover returns) and at Mutual, where he made

The Rink (1916) (☆) (incompetent waiter Charlie poses as a baronet), *Easy Street* (1917) (☆ ☞) (Chaplin beats poverty by becoming a cop and ridding the slums of villain Eric Campbell), *The Cure* (1917) (☆) (guests at a health spa over-indulge in liquor-laced mineral water), *The Immigrant* (✍ ☞ ☆) (1917) (Chaplin meets Edna Purviance on a boat, treats her to a meal and persuades her to marry him) and *The Adventurer* (1917) (☆) (Charlie as an escapee who hides out in Eric Campbell's mansion). In 1919, along with >Douglas Fairbanks, Mary Pickford and >D.W. Griffith, he founded United Artists and, by blending slapstick and satire, began to explore the psychological make up of Charlie and those who confront and comfort him: *The Kid* (1921) (✍ ☞) (Edna Purviance abandons Jackie Coogan but returns for him and rewards Charlie for his fostering); >*The Gold Rush* (1925) (☆ ✍ ☞ ■); *City Lights* (1931) (☞ ☆ ✍) (Charlie takes up boxing and odd jobs to fund cure for flower girl Virginia Cherrill's blindness) and >*Modern Times* (1936)(☆ ✍ ☞ ■). The painstakingly made spoof, *The Great Dictator* (1940) (Chaplin as Hitler lookalike Adenoid Hynkel), the bigamist melodrama, *Monsieur Verdoux* (1947) (Chaplin marries and murders women to provide for his invalid wife) and the autobiographical *Limelight* (1952) (☆ ☞ ✍ ♫) (Chaplin as the clown Calvero who loses his touch just as ballerina prodigy Claire Bloom finds fame) virtually closed his career. Personal problems and political rejection by the US reduced *A King in New York* (1957) (deposed king Chaplin finds that monarchy and the American dream make uncomfortable bedfellows) and The *Countess from Hong Kong* (1967) (diplomat >Marlon Brando can't escape the attentions of Russian noblewoman Sophia Loren) to embarrassing disasters.

⏵VIEW ON▶ •*The Floorwalker* (1916) (☆): swapping places with a lookalike, Charlie falls down an escalator a lot, somehow making it funny each time.
•*The Pawnshop* (1916): slapstick with a ladder and cheating customers precede Chaplin foiling a robbery.
•*A Dog's Life* (1918) (☆ ✍): a stray finds a wallet, which helps Charlie set up a farm with Edna Purviance.
•*Shoulder Arms* (1918) (☆): Chaplin leaves his flooded trench, and disguised as a tree gets behind enemy lines to win the war and Edna Purviance.
•*The Idle Class* (1921) (■): Charlie is mistaken for Edna Purviance's rich husband; filmed, as ever, by Rollie Totheroh.
•*A Day's Pleasure* (1921) (☆): the Chaplin family picnic is hamstrung by a traffic jam and an unsteady river boat.
•*Pay Day* (1922) (☆): having caught bricks in the most dexterous way, Charlie spends his pay on a drunken night.
•*A Woman of Paris* (1923) (☆): Edna Purviance abandons her artist lover for Adolphe Menjou's wealth but atones by adopting orphans.
•*The Pilgrim* (1923) (☆): escapee Charlie masquerades as a clergyman, botches the service and is recognized by an old lag.

CHILDHOOD

Forbidden Games (*The Secret Game*) (*Jeux Interdits*) (René Clément 1952) ✍ ☞ ☆
A five-year-old girl and a peasant boy build an animal cemetery during the Nazi occupation.

The Horse Without a Head (Don Chaffey 1963) ✍
Crooks Leo McKern and Herbert Lom stash loot in a rocking horse.

Hue and Cry (Charles Crichton 1946) ☆ ✍
East End crook turns boys' newspaper into a blag rag.

My Life as a Dog (Lasse Hallström, Sweden 1985) ☆ ■
An orphan learns about football, boxing and girls while staying with his country grandparents.

The Red Balloon (*Le Ballon Rouge*) (Albert Lamorisse 1956) ■ ☞
On his way to school in Paris a small boy finds a balloon that momentarily brings him joy and hope.

Somewhere in Europe (US: *It Happened Somewhere in Europe*) (*Valahol Európában*) (Géza Radványi 1947) ✍

Penniless Hungarian children find a wonderland in the castle of a reclusive composer.

Village of the Damned (Wolf Rilla 1960)
✍ ■

Screen version of John Wyndham's *The Midwich Cuckoos*, in which a village's children prove to be beings from another planet.

Whistle Down the Wind (Bryan Forbes 1961) ✍ ☞
Hayley Mills befriends stranger Alan Bates, believing this killer to be Christ.

CHILDREN'S LITERARY CLASSICS

The Adventures of Tom Sawyer (Norman Taurog 1938) ✍ ☆
The classic Mark Twain tale in which Tom clears Muff Potter by proving that Injun Joe is the Mississippi murderer.

Emil and the Detectives (Gerhard Lamprecht 1931) ✍
Erich Kastner classic of the thief trapped by Berlin's children, scripted by >Billy Wilder.

Heidi (Allan Dwan 1937) ✍
Johanna Spyri story of the orphan (Shirley Temple) who improves the lives of her grandfather, a goatherd and a rich cripple.

Huckleberry Finn (>Michael Curtiz 1939) ☞ ☆
Tobacco-chewing unruly rascal Mickey Rooney and a runaway slave have adventures on a raft on the Mississippi.

Kidnapped (Alfred L. Werker 1938/Robert Stevenson 1959/Delbert Mann 1971) ✍
Scottish Highland boy is sold as a slave and becomes involved with the outlaw Alan Breck in Robert Louis Stevenson's Jacobite adventure.

King Solomon's Mines (Robert Stevenson 1937/Compton Bennett 1950/J. Lee Thompson 1985) ✍
H. Rider Haggard's story sends explorers on a quest for African diamond mine.

Little Lord Fauntleroy (John Cromwell 1936) ✍ ☆
American boy Freddie Bartholomew charms his English grandfather C. Aubrey Smith in this Frances Hodgson Burnett story.

Little Women (>George Cukor 1933) ✍ ☆
>Katharine Hepburn as Jo in this Louisa M. Alcott melodrama about the four March sisters.

The Secret Garden (Fred M. Wilcox 1949) ☆
Screen version of Frances Hodgson Burnett novel has Margaret O'Brien bringing a little light and happiness to Herbert Marshall's household.

Swallows and Amazons (Claude Whatham 1974) ✍ ■
During a 1920s holiday, children have sailing races and capture villains in this Arthur Ransome classic.

Treasure Island (Victor Fleming 1934) ☆
✍/(Byron Haskin 1950) ☆
Robert Louis Stevenson tale of the pirate Long John Silver, played respectively by Wallace Beery and Robert Newton.

CHINESE CINEMA

The Big Parade (Da Yuebing) (Chen Kaige 1986) ■
Teenage soldiers have aspirations of appearing in National Day Parade on Tienanmen Square, Beijing.

The Black Cannon Incident (Hei Pao Shi Jian) (Huang Jianxin 1985) ✍ ■
An interpreter is sacked from a Sino-German building project when the authorities take his message about a missing chess piece for industrial espionage.

Bus Number Three (Xiaozi Bei) (Wang Jiayi/Luo Tai 1980) ✍ ☆
Life on a bus carrying people of all professions to work.

Crows and Sparrows (Wuya Yu Maque) (Zheng Junli 1949) ✍ ☆
Tenants are threatened with vagrancy as a corrupt landlord plans to flee to Taiwan to escape the People's Army.

A Great Wall (Peter Wang 1986) ✍ ☆
The amorous and cultural adventures of a US teenager staying with his roguish uncle in Beijing.

The Horse Thief (Daoma Zei) (Tian Zhuangzhuang 1986) ■
Stunningly filmed story of a man, driven to rustling to feed his family, who is exiled after breaking his repentance oath.

In the Wild Mountains (Ye Shan) **(Yan Xueshu 1986)** ✍
An industrious brother and an idle one come to realize that life would improve if they swapped wives.

Red Sorghum **(Zhang Yimou 1988)** ■
The atrocities that villagers in North-West China perpetrate on themselves pale beside those of the Japanese razing the land for a military road.

Spring River Flows East (Yijiang Chunshui Xiang Dong Liu)
(Cai Chusheng/Zheng Junli 1947)
A teacher abandons his family to help the Red Cross tend wounded of the 1931 war, but then abandons his principles for bourgeois bigamy and comfort.

Yellow Earth (Huang Tudi) **(Chen Kaige 1984)** ■ ✍
A folk historian lodges with a conservative family and tries to modernize them.

CHRISTIE, AGATHA

Alibi **(Leslie Hiscott 1931)** ✍
Hercule Poirot (Austin Trevor) proves that a suicide was, in fact, a nigh perfect murder, in this screen version of *The Murder of Roger Ackroyd*.

And Then There Were None **(UK: Ten Little Niggers) (>René Clair 1945)** ✍ ☆ ☞
Guests with criminal pasts are invited to a remote island and are killed one by one.

Death on the Nile **(John Guillermin 1978)** ✍ ■ ☆
Peter Ustinov as Poirot refusing to believe the obvious during an Egyptian sight-seeing cruise.

Endless Night **(Sidney Gilliat 1971)**
Hywel Bennett appears to detest Britt Ekland, the best friend of his rich wife Hayley Mills.

Lord Edgware Dies **(Henry Edwards 1934)** ✍
Austin Trevor's Poirot clears a peer's young wife of murder.

Love from a Stranger **(Rowland V. Lee 1937)** ☆ ✍ ♪
Ann Harding suspects that her husband >Basil Rathbone is a killer, in the film version of the short story 'Philomel Cottage'.

The Mirror Crack'd **(Guy Hamilton 1980)** ✍
Angela Lansbury's Miss Marple identifies the source of actress Elizabeth Taylor's death threats.

Murder Ahoy **(George Pollock 1964)** ☆
Margaret Rutherford's Marple is anything but all at sea on Lionel Jeffries' training ship.

Murder at the Gallop **(George Pollock 1963)** ✍ ☆
Margaret Rutherford reveals that an old man's fear of cats was not the cause of his death, in this film version of *After the Funeral*.

Murder Most Foul **(George Pollock 1964)** ☆ ✍
Juror Margaret Rutherford unearths new evidence by watching Ron Moody's theatre group from the wings, in the celluloid adaptation of *Mrs McGinty's Dead*.

Murder on the Orient Express **(>Sidney Lumet 1974)** ✍ ☆
Poirot (Albert Finney) discovers that the victim was party to a child killing and that star passengers have a common link.

Murder She Said **(George Pollock 1961)**
Only Margaret Rutherford believes that she has witnessed a killing through a train window, from Christie's *4.50 from Paddington*.

Witness for the Prosecution **(>Billy Wilder 1957)** ✍ ☆ ☞
Tetchy lawyer >Charles Laughton is suspicious of >Marlene Dietrich's evidence at husband Tyrone Power's trial.

CHRISTMAS

Christmas Eve **(Edwin L. Marin 1947)** ☆
A Yuletide reunion is enlivened by sons saving their mother from embezzlement.

Christmas in Connecticut **(UK: Indiscretion) (Peter Godfrey 1945)** ☆
Agony aunt >Barbara Stanwyck has to invent a happy family life for a Christmas publicity stunt.

Holiday Inn **(Mark Sandrich 1942)** ♪ ☞
Bing Crosby sets up a club that opens on holidays when he falls out with his partner >Fred Astaire.

Miracle on 34th Street (UK: *The Big Heart*) **(George Seaton 1947)** ☆ ✍
Edmund Gwenn goes to court to prove that he is the real Father Christmas to, among others, a young Natalie Wood.

One Magic Christmas **(Philip Borsos 1983)**
Angel Harry Dean Stanton grants Mary Steenburgen's daughter's wish for a family Christmas.

Santa Claus – The Movie **(Jeannot Szwarc 1985)** ✳
An elf (Dudley Moore) sells the secret for a magical sweet to tycoon John Lithgow.

Scrooge **(Brian Desmond Hurst 1951)** ✍ ☆
>Alastair Sim as >Charles Dickens' miser reformed by ghosts of Christmas Past, Present and Future.

White Christmas **(>Michael Curtiz 1954)** ♫
Bing Crosby and Danny Kaye organize an army reunion for a retired general.

CINDERELLA

Ask Any Girl **(Charles Walters 1959)** ☆
Receptionist Shirley MacLaine wins playboy David Niven.

The Bride Wore Red **(Dorothy Arzner 1937)** ☆
Robert Young and Franchot Tone vie for chorus girl >Joan Crawford in Tyrolean re-telling.

Cinderella **(Wilfred Jackson/Hamilton Luske/Clyde Geronomi 1950)**
Disney telling complete with cute mice, Ugly Sisters and Prince Charming.

The Farmer's Daughter **(H. C. Potter 1947)** ☆ ✍
Congressman Joseph Cotten's Swedish maid Loretta Young becomes a prominent politician herself.

The Gay Deception **(>William Wyler 1935)** ☞
Posing as a doorman, a prince courts the hotel's secretary.

The Glass Slipper **(Charles Walters 1954)** ■
Tomboy Leslie Caron goes to Michael Wilding's ball thanks to fairy godmother Estelle Winwood.

The Slipper and the Rose **(Bryan Forbes 1976)** ■
Silky modern production with Richard Chamberlain charming hard-up Gemma Craven.

Spring Parade **(Henry Koster 1940)** ☆
Baker's helper Deanna Durbin is swept out of the kitchen by prince Robert Cummings.

CIRCUSES

Annie Get Your Gun **(George Sidney 1950)** ♫
Betty Hutton as Annie Oakley shooting out Wild West show hegemony with Howard Keel.

The Big Circus **(Joseph Newman 1959)** ☆
Victor Mature and a cast including >Peter Lorre and Vincent Price, ensure that a bankrupt show goes on.

The Circus **(Charles Chaplin 1928)** ☆
Chaplin as a prop man helping a clown to woo a circus ballerina.

The Clowns (*Il Clowns*) **(>Federico Fellini 1970)** ✍ ☆
Record of some of the great clowns' memoirs and routines.

The Greatest Show on Earth **(Cecil B. De Mille 1952)** ■
>James Stewart and Charlton Heston are among the artistes involved in this big top melodrama (winner of the Best Picture Oscar).

Lili **(Charles Walters 1952)**
Paul Gallico tale of teenage Leslie Caron enamoured of a carnival magician.

Lola Montès **(>Max Ophüls 1955)** ✍ ☆
Ringmaster Peter Ustinov tells the story of the courtesan's affair with the mad king Ludwig of Bavaria.

Sally of the Sawdust **(>D.W. Griffith 1925)** ☆
Somewhere between the adventures and schemes of >W.C. Fields's dodgy juggler Eustace McGargle, Carole Dempster finds love.

Street Angel **(Frank Borzage 1928)** ☆
Janet Gaynor received an AAN as the whore who finds a better life under the big top.

Trapeze **(>Carol Reed 1956)** ☆ ☞
Burt Lancaster and Tony Curtis's daring young men flying at each other as rivals for Gina Lollobrigida.

Citizen Kane ☞ ☆ ▓ ✍ ♫

USA • RKO • 1941 • 119 mins • b/w

d >Orson Welles   w Orson
Welles/Herman J. Mankiewicz   ph Gregg
Toland   m Bernard Herrmann

Orson Welles, Joseph Cotten, Dorothy
Comingore, Everett Sloane, Paul Stewart,
Ray Collins, Agnes Moorehead

Rather than discovering the meaning of Charles Foster Kane's dying word, 'Rosebud', newsreel reporter Jerry Thompson's interviews with those who knew the newspaper magnate succeed only in deepening the mysteries shrouding Kane's professional, political and personal life. In many ways, 'Rosebud' symbolizes a repentance of a lifetime of material and mental corruption that has secured wealth but not happiness, but flashbacks suggest that Kane has been equally sinned against as sinning. Eerily photographed and scored by, respectively, Toland and Herrmann and superbly played by a cast that was to become almost Welles' rep company, *Kane* is remembered for Welles' exceptional directorial debut, even though he is towering in the title role. Only a minor box office hit on account of William Randolph Hearst's vendetta against what he saw rightly as a personal indictment, it is justifiably many critics' all-time great.

•Barge skipper Jean Dasté has an equally strong possession obsession in *L'Atalante* (Jean Vigo 1934) (☞ ▓ ☆), while the possession of a white horse inspires Polish cavalry officers charging Nazi Panzers in *Lotna* (>Andrej Wajda 1964) (☞ ✍).
•TV personality Jose Ferrer's notorious past is exposed in a 'This Is Your Life'-like retrospective in *The Great Man* (Jose Ferrer 1956) (☆ ✍).
•Self-made man >Spencer Tracy is destroyed by megalomania in >Preston Sturges's script *The Power and the Glory* (William K. Howard 1933) (☆ ✍).
•A variety of witnesses and acquaintances reveal what they know of a female drop-out after she is found dead in a ditch in *Vagabonde* (aka *Sans Toit Ni Loi*) (Agnès Varda 1985) (☞ ✍).

Clair, René

*(René-Lucien Chomette) French
writer/director (1898–1981)*

Invalided out of World War I, Clair went on retreat at a Dominican monastery before entering cinema through journalism. The silent surrealism of *Entr'acte* (1924) (☞ ✍) (odd balls race around Paris after a runaway hearse) and farce of >*The Italian Straw Hat* (*Un Chapeau de paille d'Italie*) (1927) (☞ ✍ ▓), identified Clair with an effervescent wit that was (and still is) lamentably disdained by academics, who demanded unadulterated intellectualism in French cinema, although Hollywood's comic élite were hugely influenced by his *Sous Les Toits de Paris* (*Under the Roofs of Paris*) (1930) (☞) (street entertainer Albert Préjean risks jail to protect a girl from her evil lover Gaston Modot), *Le Million* (☞ ✍) (a painter searches Paris for his lost lottery ticket) and *A Nous La Liberté* (*Freedom for Us*) (1931) (☞ ♫) (popular songs abound as an ex-con's gramophone business goes to the wall and he cheerfully hits the road with his old cellmate). Wounded by domestic criticism, this elegant and much maligned director went to Britain to make *The Ghost Goes West* (1935) (☞ ✍ ☆) (Scottish castle is transported to the US, resident ghost >Robert Donat and all) and to the US for *I Married a Witch* (1942) (☞ ☆) (Veronica Lake curbs her father's desire to avenge their Salem witchcraft trial execution at the hands of her husband >Fredric March's ancestor) and *It Happened Tomorrow* (1944) (☞ ✍) (reporter Dick Powell enjoys friendship with an unfailing headline clairvoyant until the scoop is his own death). Following his return to France in 1947, he found his studio-bound style labelled by the New Wave as '*cinéma du papa*' and he was only able to produce a handful of inferior pictures.

•*Crazy Ray* (*Paris qui Dort*) (1923) (☞ ☆): a mad inventor's stun gun enables him to play pranks on the paralysed population of Paris.
•*Le Fantôme du Moulin Rouge* (1925) (☞ ☆): surrealism again, as Albert Préjean leaves his body to play pranks on the this time animated population of Paris.

•*Les Deux Timides* (1928) (☞ ✍): having lost a court case through fear of a mouse, a lawyer fights to keep his girl.

•*The Fourteenth of July* (*Quatorze Juillet*) (1932) (☞ ✍): romance is in the air for a flower seller and a taxi driver on Bastille Day.

•*The Last Millionaire* (*Le Dernier Milliardaire*) (1934) (☞): an exiled millionaire's return to bail his country out of depression is inspired as much by love for the princess as by patriotism.

•*The Flame of New Orleans* (1941) (☞): gold-digger >Marlene Dietrich passes herself off as a European countess.

•*And Then There Were None* (UK: *Ten Little Niggers*) (1945) (✍ ☆ ☞): >Agatha Christie whodunnit based on the nursery rhyme 'Ten Little Indians'.

•*Silence is Golden* (US: *Man about Town*) (*Le Silence est d'Or*) (1947): director Maurice Chevalier teaches an actor to seduce, but both love the same girl.

•*Beauty and the Devil* (*La Beauté du Diable*) (1949): >Faust (Michel Simon) sells his soul to Devil Gérard Philipe in return for the latter's good looks so that he can woo Simone Valère.

•*Night Beauties* (US: *Beauties of the Night*) (*Les Belles-de-Nuit*) (1952) (☞ ✍): Gérard Philipe travels the centuries in his dreams and meets his dream women.

•*Summer Manoeuvres* (US: *The Grand Maneuver*) (*Les Grandes Manoeuvres*) (1955) (☆): suave soldier Gérard Philipe wagers that he can bed Michèle Morgan.

•*Gates of Paris* (US: *Gates of Lilacs*) (*Porte des Lilas*) (1957) (☞ ■): a drifter shelters a gangster only to kill him when he alienates his girlfriend's affection.

Clairvoyance

Blithe Spirit (>David Lean 1945) ✍ ☆
Margaret Rutherford as Noël Coward's medium summoning up the ghost of Rex Harrison's teasing first wife.

The Clairvoyant (Maurice Elvey 1934) ☆
Fraud Claude Rains' disaster warnings are fatally ignored.

The Crystal Ball (Elliott Nugent 1943) ✍
Paulette Goddard foretells that no good will come of Ray Milland's crooked schemes.

Family Plot (>Alfred Hitchcock 1976) ☞
Barbara Harris invents a missing heir and stumbles into a missing body and jewel theft mystery.

Hanussen (István Szabó 1988) ☞ ☆ ✍
Klaus Maria Brandauer predicts the coming of Hitler and is persecuted by the Austrian authorities as a Nazi.

Juliet of the Spirits (*Giulietta degli Spiriti*) (>Federico Fellini 1965) ☆
Wronged wife Giulietta Masina seeks comfort in spirit voices from her past and future.

Night of the Demon (US: *Curse of the Demon*) (Jacques Tourneur 1957) ☞ ✍
Dana Andrews treats vengeful wizard Niall MacGinnis' threats with cynicism, but the arrival of a medieval demon sparks off genuine terror.

Palmy Days (A. Edward Sutherland 1932) ■
The Gregg Toland cinematography and Busby Berkeley choreography enliven this Eddie Cantor fake medium hokum.

Séance on a Wet Afternoon (Bryan Forbes 1964) ✍
A psychic and her unscrupulous husband kidnap a child in order to publicize her powers.

Cold War

The Big Lift (George Seaton 1950) ✍
Montgomery Clift as an airman involved in supplying Berlin during the 1947 Soviet blockade.

The Day the Earth Stood Still (Robert Wise 1951) ✍
An alien and a robot come to warn earth about the dangers of superpower confrontation.

Iron Curtain (>William Wellman 1948) ☞
Biopic of disillusioned Soviet Igor Gouzenko who exposed a spy ring.

The Kremlin Letter (>John Huston 1970) ☆
US spies are sent to Moscow to retrieve an erroneously signed treaty.

The Russians Are Coming, the Russians Are Coming (Norman Jewison 1966) ☆
A Soviet sub washes up on a US beach and the crew are just as scared as the residents.

Topaz (>Alfred Hitchcock 1969) ☞
Screen version of the Leon Uris novel about a

French spy called in to help flailing US intelligence.

Torn Curtain (>Alfred Hitchcock 1966) ☞ ☆

Paul Newman's faked defection mission is placed under threat by Julie Andrews' bid to save their love affair.

Yesterday Girl (*Abschied von Gestern*) (Alexander Kluge 1966) ✐

A wild East German girl finds life just as restrictive on the other side of the Wall.

Colonel Redl

Hungary/West Germany/Austria • Mafilm Studio • Objectiv/Mokep/Film Und Fersehen/ZDF/ORF • 1984 • 149 mins col

d István Szabó w István Szabó/Peter Dobai ph Lajos Koltai m Various

Klaus Maria Brandauer, Hans-Christian Blech, Armin Müller-Stahl, Eva Szabó

Basing the film, the winner of the Special Jury Prize at Cannes, on actual events and various literary sources (chiefly John Osborne's *A Patriot for Me*) István Szabó uses the isolation and betrayal of a poor Galician Jew, who rose through army ranks to the position of Imperial spymaster, to highlight the reasons for the decline and fall of the Austro-Hungarian Empire. Surrounded by those he will destroy and who will destroy him, Redl, torn between his facility for deceit and devotion to honour, is blackmailed into treachery and ultimate suicide to prevent the shaming revelation of his bisexuality. The implied involvement of Archduke Franz Ferdinand, the heir to the Hapsburg throne, whose assassination sparked World War I, suggests an intriguing cover-up. Klaus Maria Brandauer is magnificent in the title role.

•Farley Granger is the Austrian soldier betrayed in *Senso (The Wanton Contessa)* (>Luchino Visconti 1954) (☞ ■ ✐) by jilted quisling Alida Valli in the last days of Austrian rule in Venetia.
•Napoleon dishes out yet more punishment to Austrian military prestige in 1806 in *Austerlitz*

(The Battle of Austerlitz) (Abel Gance 1959) (☞ ■).
•The Hapsburg dynasty is rocked by Crown Prince Rudolph (Charles Boyer)'s tragic adultery with teenage Marie Vetsera (Danielle Darrieux) recounted in *Mayerling* (Anatole Litvak 1935) (☞ ☆ ■).
•>Erich Von Stroheim is the Hapsburg prince forced to abandon peasant girl Fay Wray for crippled princess Zasu Pitts in *The Wedding March* (>Erich Von Stroheim 1928) (☞ ✐).
•Franz Ferdinand's unhappy marriage and assassination, is chronicled in *Sarajevo (Mayerling to Sarajevo)* (>Max Ophüls 1940) (☞).
•Heroic devotion to the cause is shown by a Red Army officer fighting in the Civil War in 1919 in *Chapayev* (Georgi Vasiliev/Sergei Vasiliev 1934) (☞).
•Ambitious actor Klaus Maria Brandauer collaborates with the Nazis to further his career, in *Mephisto* (István Szabó 1981) (☞ ☆ ■), while treachery as depicted by Hollywood is spoofed mercilessly in *Top Secret!* (Jim Abrahams/David Zucker/Jerry Zucker 1984) (✐ ☆).

COMPOSERS

>*Amadeus* (>Miloš Forman 1984) ☞ ■ ☆ ♪ ✐

Wolfgang Amadeus Mozart.

The Chronicle of Anna Magdalena Bach (*Chronik der Anna Magdalena Bach*) (Jean-Marie Straub, West Germany 1967) ■ ♪

Johann Sebastian Bach's life and works seen through the eyes of his second wife.

The Great Mr Handel (Norman Walker 1942) ☆ ♪

How Wilfred Lawson sat right down and wrote himself *The Messiah*.

The Great Waltz (Julien Duvivier 1938) ♪ ■

Fernand Gravet as Johann Strauss giving the waltz to Vienna.

The Magnificent Rebel (Georg Tressler 1960) ✐

Disney vision of the young Beethoven's scrapes in late 18th-century Vienna.

Mahler **(Ken Russell 1974)** ☞ ■ ♫
Robert Powell as the Jewish composer and
conductor.

Song of Love **(Clarence Brown 1947)** ☆
The friendship of >Katharine Hepburn and
Paul Henreid's Clara and Robert Schumann
and Robert Walker's Brahms.

A Song to Remember **(Charles Vidor 1945)**
☆
Frederick Chopin (Cornel Wilde)'s love for
French novelist George Sand (Merle Oberon).

Symphonie Fantastique **(Christian-Jaque**
1947) ☆ ♫
>Jean-Louis Barrault as the 19th-century
French composer Hector Berlioz.

Testimony **(Tony Palmer 1988)** ☆
Ben Kingsley as Dmitri Shostakovitch seeking
artistic expression within Stalinist Russia.

Tchaikovsky **(Igor Talankin 1970)** ♫
Watch in conjunction with Ken Russell's *The
Music Lovers* (1970), as they balance each
other's excesses and omissions.

CONFIDENCE TRICKSTERS

Always a Bride **(Ralph Smart 1953)** ✍ ☆
Peggy Cummins plays on hotel guests' soft
hearts by pretending to have been left at the
altar.

Blonde Crazy **(UK:** *Larceny Lane***) (Roy Del**
Ruth 1931) ☆ ✍
Bellhop >James Cagney and hotel maid Joan
Blondell supplement their wages by swindling
residents.

Boy **(***Shonen***) (Nagisa Oshima, Japan**
1969) ✍
Parents extort from motorists who 'run into'
the son they have trained to feign injury.

The Confessions of Felix Krull **(***Der*
*Bekenntnisse des Felix Krull***) (Kurt**
Hoffmann, West Germany 1957) ✍
A con man fleeces a series of male and female
lovers in the film version of Thomas Mann's
last novel.

Every Day's a Holiday **(A. Edward**
Sutherland 1937) ☆ ✍
Mae West sells Brooklyn Bridge to anyone
stupid enough to buy it.

Fashions of 1934 **(>William Dieterle 1934)**
☆
>Bette Davis acting as his conscience, >Wil-
liam Powell cons his way to fashion fame.

Kind Lady **(George B. Seitz 1935)** ☆
>Basil Rathbone's gang plan to soak an old
woman but prove to have a golden streak
through their black hearts.

Connery, Sean
(Thomas Connery) British actor (b 1930)

After enlisting in the Royal Navy at 15 and then
taking jobs as varied as model and assistant
undertaker, Connery's undistinguished early
acting career was resurrected by the Bond
series of which the best were, >*Dr No* (Terence
Young 1962) (☆ ✍ ☞ ♫), *From Russia with
Love* (1963)(☆ ✍) (Connery and a decoding
device are the target of Soviet baddie Robert
Shaw), *Goldfinger* (Guy Hamilton 1964) (☆ ✍)
(gold thief sets his sights on Fort Knox) and
Thunderball (Terence Young 1964) (☆)
(SPECTRE agent Adolfo Celi threatens Miami
with atom bombs). Shedding the suave persona and the toupee of 007, Connery has ma-
tured into a dependable actor, his distinctive
Scottish tones never detracting from the credibility of his performances: Robin Hood in
Robin and Marian (Richard Lester 1976) (■)
(Sherwood Forest's favourite son is not as
young as of old, but Audrey Hepburn still loves
him); King Agamemnon in *Time Bandits*
(Terry Gilliam 1981) (✍ ☞ ✳) (a young boy
travels through time with thieving dwarfs
seeking a treasure map), a Turkish janissary in
Highlander (Russell Mulcahy 1986) (☆ ✳)
(Christopher Lambert as a medieval soldier
advised by Connery in an immortality showdown with a vicious rival), a medieval monk in
The Name of the Rose (Jean-Jacques Annaud
1987) (☆ ■ ✍) (set to solve monastic murders
before an ecclesiastical congress, Connery
finds himself suspected by an old enemy, Inquisitor F. Murray Abraham); and an Irish-
American cop in *The Untouchables* (AA: Brian
De Palma 1987) (☆) (Kevin Costner's Elliot
Ness and a hand-picked team risk life and limb
to bring >Robert De Niro's Al Capone to justice).

•*Marnie* (>Alfred Hitchcock 1964) (☞): Connery has shoplifting and sexual problems with Tippi Hedren.

•*The Hill* (>Sidney Lumet 1965): Connery mutinies against the military police during the North African campaign against Rommel.

•*A Fine Madness* (Irvin Kershner 1966) (☆): Jean Seberg is unable to tame poet Connery during his violent bouts.

•*The Man Who Would Be King* (>John Huston 1975) (☆ ☞ ✍): surviving an arrow wound Connery is hailed as a god, but fails to heed >Michael Caine and proves all too human.

•*Five Days One Summer* (>Fred Zinnemann 1982) (■ ☞ ☆): doctor Connery's romantic Alpine holiday is spoiled by the loss of his girl to a guide.

•*Never Say Never Again* (Irvin Kershner 1983) (☆): back to Bond to thwart SPECTRE bigwigs Blofeld (Max Von Sydow) and Largo (Klaus Maria Brandauer)'s nuclear threat and woo Kim Basinger.

•*The Presidio* (Peter Hyams 1988) (☆): cop Connery is forced to chase diamond crooks with his daughter's disapproved-of lover as his partner.

•*Indiana Jones and the Last Crusade* (>Steven Spielberg 1989) (☆): Connery as >Harrison Ford's old man helping him reach the Holy Grail before the Nazis.

CONVENT LIFE

The Nun's Story (>Fred Zinnemann 1959)
☞ ☆ ✍

Doctor Peter Finch guides Audrey Hepburn through the trials of her novitiate and deliberations on her future.

La Religieuse (aka Suzanne Simonin, la religieuse de Diderot) (US: The Nun) (Jacques Rivette 1965) ✍

Screen version of Diderot's novel has a nun subjected to sexual advances from a Mother Superior and a priest.

The Singing Nun (Henry Koster 1966) ☆

Debbie Reynolds as the nun who hit the charts with 'Dominique'.

The Sound of Music (Robert Wise 1965)
♫ ☆ ✍

A nun's chorus wonder how to solve a problem like Julie Andrews.

Thérèse (Alain Cavalier, France 1986)
■ ☞ ☆

Catherine Mouchet as the consumptive contemplative who was canonized for her devout life.

Viridiana (>Luis Buñuel 1961) ✍ ☞

Novice Sylvia Pinal opens to the poor the house of an uncle who maltreated her.

Cooper, Gary

(Frank Cooper) American actor (1901–1961)
Romantic hero in a voluminous silent career, Cooper demonstrated a quiet virility in a series of thoughtful adventures: as a legionnaire in *Morocco* (>Josef Von Sternberg 1930) (☆ ☞) (Cooper and Adolphe Menjou compete for cabaret star >Marlene Dietrich) and in *Beau Geste* (>William Wellman 1939) (☆ ☞) (P. C. Wren tale of three English brothers suspecting each other of theft, surviving a martinet commandant and resisting an Arab revolt); as a lawman, *The Westerner* (>William Wyler 1940) (☆) (Cooper keeps outlawed judge Roy Bean from falling for famed Edwardian beauty Lily Langtry) and in >*High Noon* (AA: >Fred Zinnemann 1952) (☆ ☞ ✍♫); and as a soldier in *A Farewell to Arms* (Frank Borzage 1932) (☆ ☞) (war wounded Cooper falls for nurse Helen Hayes in Ernest Hemingway's World War I tale) and in *The Lives of a Bengal Lancer* (Henry Hathaway 1934) (Cooper and Franchot Tone guarding the North West Frontier against marauding Afghans). His best roles, however, comprised morally upright men engaged in often lone fights against injustice: *Mr Deeds Goes to Town* (AAN: >Frank Capra 1936) (☞ ☆) (poet Cooper clings to his principles amid the temptations of New York); *Sergeant York* (AA: >Howard Hawks 1941) (☆ ☞) (Cooper as a gentle giant from hicksville roused to heroics in the trenches); *The Pride of the Yankees* (AAN: Sam Wood 1942) (✍ ☞ ☆) (Paul Gallico-scripted biopic of dead-before-time baseball hero Lou Gehrig) and *For Whom the Bell Tolls* (AAN: Sam Wood 1943) (☞ ☆) (Hemingway

adventure in which Cooper courts >Ingrid Bergman and death helping Spanish Civil War partisans to blow a bridge).

 •*Desire* (Frank Borzage 1936) (☆ ☞): Cooper is lured by a Spanish jewel thief >Marlene Dietrich in an >Ernst Lubitsch-produced comedy.

•*The General Died at Dawn* (Lewis Milestone 1936): mercenary Cooper resists the tyranny of Chinese warlord Akim Tamiroff.

•*Bluebeard's Eighth Wife* (>Ernst Lubitsch 1938) (☞ ✍):>Wilder/Brackett script has impoverished noble's daughter Claudette Colbert cure Cooper of marriage mania.

•*Blowing Wild* (Hugo Fregonese 1953) (☆): Cooper is caught up with jealous fellow oil man Anthony Quinn and his manic wife >Barbara Stanwyck.

•*The Court-Martial of Billy Mitchell* (UK: *One Man Mutiny*) (Otto Preminger 1955) (☆): true story of the fate of a US air corps general (Cooper) after he sued the army following a flying disaster.

•*Love in the Afternoon* (>Billy Wilder 1957) (☆): Audrey Hepburn keeps Cooper abreast of jealous husband Maurice Chevalier's vengeful movements around Paris.

•*Man of the West* (Anthony Mann 1958): gunslinger Cooper is talked into a swan song stick-up.

•*The Naked Edge* (Michael Anderson 1961): Deborah Kerr begins to suspect that her tycoon husband (Cooper) framed Peter Cushing for a murder he himself committed.

Coppola, Francis Ford
American writer/director (b 1939)
Son of Carmine Coppola the composer, Francis Coppola has come a long way since his early 1960s pornography shorts and technical involvement in Roger Corman's cult horror movies. He is acclaimed for both his scriptwriting – *Patton* (UK: *Patton – Lust for Glory*) (co-authored with Edmund H. North) (AA: Franklin Schaffner 1970) (☆ ✍ ☞) (George C. Scott as the uncompromising WWII American general who led the Anzio landings); *The Great Gatsby* (Jack Clayton 1974) (✍ ☆) (F. Scott Fitzgerald story of mysterious reclusive millionaire

Robert Redford and careless driver Mia Farrow); and both >*Godfathers* (1972 & 1974) (✍ ☞ ■ ♫ ☆) which he co-wrote with Mario Puzo – and producing – *THX 1138* (George Lucas 1971) (Robert Duvall rebels against the restrictions of a future cloned society); *American Graffiti* (George Lucas 1973) (☆ ♫) (college-bound Richard Dreyfuss leads teenage friends on last-night revels) and *Hammett* (>Wim Wenders 1982) (✍ ☞) (Frederic Forrest as the crime writer Dashiel Hammett finding novel material as well as a missing Chinese girl) – as well as directing *You're a Big Boy Now* (1967) (☞) (naïve librarian's rites of passage) and *Finian's Rainbow* (1968) (■) (>Fred Astaire tries to lay his hands on leprechaun Tommy Steele's crock of gold) – and combinations of all three: >*Apocalypse Now* (1979) (☆ ☞ ■ ✍ ♫); *One from the Heart* (1981) (■) (Paradise Travel Agency girl Teri Garr and Reality Wrecking driver Frederic Forrest waste the 4th of July arguing); and *Gardens of Stone* (1988) (☞ ☆ ✍) (Arlington Cemetery officer James Caan helps a young man fulfil his cherished ambition to fight in >Vietnam). In short he is among the most influential and unpredictable of modern directors.

 •*Dementia 13* (UK: *The Haunted and the Hunted*) (1963) (✍): an Irish castle, stormy weather and a family reunion: all we need now is an axe killer…

•*The Rain People* (1969) (☆): bored housewife Shirley Knight ponders a future of marriage and pregnancy in company of mentally-retarded hitch-hiker James Caan.

•*The Conversation* (1974) (☆ ✍): phone tapper Gene Hackman is driven to paranoia by his work.

•*Rumble Fish* (1983) (■): Mickey Rourke and Matt Dillon as biker brothers in this screen version of S. E. Hinton's teen novel.

•*The Cotton Club* (1984) (♫): the story of the famous speakeasy is enlivened by Gregory Hines' dancing.

•*Peggy Sue Got Married* (1986) (☆ ✍): >Kathleen Turner goes back to teenage and wonders whether to still love husband Nicholas Cage, given hindsight.

•*Tucker: The Man and His Dreams* (1988) (☆): Jeff Bridges's obsession with his flash but ultra-safe car lands him in court for fraud.

CORRUPTION

All the King's Men (Robert Rossen 1949)
☞ ✍ ☆

Rising politician Broderick Crawford discovers that it is not just absolute power that corrupts absolutely.

Another Part of the Forest (Michael Gordon 1948) ✍ ☆

Lillian Hellman shows how the nasty sisters in her play *The Little Foxes* learned their trade from unprincipled father >Fredric March.

The Big Easy (Jim McBride 1987) ☆

Cop Dennis Quaid fights to expose corrupt New Orleans cops with the help of Ellen Barkin.

The Glass Key (Stuart Heisler 1942) ✍ ☆

Dashiell Hammett tale of how petty politician Brian Donlevy is saved from ruin by his partner Alan Ladd.

The Great McGinty (UK: Down Went McGinty) (>Preston Sturges 1940) ☞ ✍ ☆

AA-winning script tells of tramp Brian Donlevy and villain Akim Tamiroff slithering up the greasy pole of politics.

The Lion is in the Streets (>Raoul Walsh 1953) ☆

Con man >James Cagney is turned from protector to persecutor by power.

Mr Smith Goes to Washington (>Frank Capra 1939) ☆ ☞ ✍

>James Stewart shuns personal opportunity in order to perform his public duty.

Repentance (Pokjaniy, Monanieba) (Tengiz Abuladze, USSR 1984) ✍ ☆

Anti-Stalin tale of a woman who desecrates the grave and the reputation of a lately dead monstrous mayor.

Short Encounters (aka Short Meetings) (aka Brief Encounters) (Korotkie Vstrechi) (Kira Muratova 1967) ☆

Petty corruption on a Soviet housing committee punctuates a bisexual ménage.

Solid Gold Cadillac (Richard Quine 1956) ☆ ✍

Unworldly shareholder Judy Holliday's ques-tions show up the fraudulence of the executives.

COSTUME DRAMA

Allonsanfan (Paulo & Vittorio Taviani 1974) ■ ☆

Noble >Marcello Mastroianni's disenchantment with Louis XVIII's restoration fails to prevent him betraying a revolutionary.

Anthony Adverse (>Mervyn Le Roy 1936) ✍

While >Fredric March fights Napoleon, his wife >Olivia De Havilland becomes an operatic star.

The Betrayer (Vanina Vanini) (>Roberto Rossellini 1961) ☞ ■

A princess's love for a 19th-century Italian revolutionary causes his death.

Carnival in Flanders (La Kermesse Héroïque) (Jacques Feyder 1935) ☞ ■ ☆

Cowardly 16th-century townsmen flee the invading Spaniards, leaving their wives to deal with the foe.

Harakiri (Seppuku) (Masaki Kobayashi 1962) ■ ☞

A Samurai seeks employment at the close of a 17th-century Japanese civil war.

The House of Rothschild (Alfred Werker 1934) ☆

George Arliss leads the rise of an eminent Jewish banking family.

If I Were King (Frank Lloyd 1938) ☆

Ronald Colman as the poet François Villon leading a revolt against Louis XI of France (>Basil Rathbone).

The Leopard (Il Gattopardo) (>Luchino Visconti 1963) ■ ☞ ✍

Burt Lancaster views the Risorgimento and his son's marriage in the same way – disasters.

The Man in Grey (Leslie Arliss 1943) ☆

Regency bitch Margaret Lockwood fails to steal Stewart Granger from Phyllis Calvert, getting brutal James Mason instead.

The Marquise of O (Die Marquise von O) (>Erich Rohmer 1976) ☞ ✍

A pregnant Italian noblewoman insists that the Russian officer who raped her marries her to give the child a name.

The Pearls of the Crown (*Les Perles de la Couronne*) (Sacha Guitry/Christian-Jaque 1937) ✍

Pearls given to historical celebrities, such as >Jean-Louis Barrault's Napoleon are sought by a group of collectors.
>**Dickens, Charles, French Revolution, monarchy, Napoleonic Wars**

COURTROOM DRAMA

The Accused (>William Dieterle 1948) ☆ ☞
Robert Cummings is entrusted with proving that academic Loretta Young killed in self-defence.

Anatomy of a Murder (Otto Preminger 1959) ■
>James Stewart dislikes accused murderer Ben Gazzara, defending him only out of interest in his wife Lee Remick.

Carrington VC (US: *Court Martial*) (>Anthony Asquith 1954) ☆ ☞
Army hero-turned-swindler David Niven throws himself on the mercy of a military court.

The Dock Brief (James Hill 1962) ☆ ✍
>Richard Attenborough's best defence is the incompetence of his lawyer Peter Sellers.

J'Accuse (*I Accuse*) (Abel Gance 1919) ☞ ✍
A pacifist summons the war dead to testify to the human race's belligerence.

Jagged Edge (Richard Marquand 1985) ✍ ☆ ☞
Glenn Close's defence of lover/client Jeff Bridges depends on one key of a missing typewriter.

Kramer versus Kramer (Robert Benton 1979) ☆
>Dustin Hoffman and >Meryl Streep wound each other during a harrowing child custody case.

The Trials of Oscar Wilde (US: *The Man with the Green Carnation*) (Ken Hughes 1960) ☆ ✍
Peter Finch is magnificent as the 19th-century Irish playwright whose libel suit implicates him in homosexual activity.

The Verdict (>Sidney Lumet 1983) ☆ ✍
Has-been lawyer >Paul Newman battles it out with James Mason in a hospital malpractice trial.

Witness for the Prosecution (>Billy Wilder 1957) ✍ ☆ ☞
>Agatha Christie play concerning lawyer >Charles Laughton's belief in his infallible eye for a truthful witness being tested by >Marlene Dietrich.

COVER-UPS

All the President's Men (Alan J. Pakula 1976) ☆ ✍
>Dustin Hoffman and Robert Redford as journalists digging up the facts of the Watergate scandal.

Defence of the Realm (David Drury 1986) ✍ ☆
Denholm Elliott and Gabriel Byrne penetrate a nuclear near-miss obfuscation.

Maskerade (*Masquerade in Vienna*) (Willi Forst, Austria 1934) ✍ ■ ☆
Anton Walbrook paints a Vienna society wife as a masked nude and passes off common girl Paula Wessely as the model.

No Way Out (Roger Donaldson 1987) ✍
Kevin Costner closes in on Gene Hackman's involvement with a call girl and a Russian agent.

The Reckless Moment (>Max Ophüls 1949) ☞ ☆
James Mason threatens to expose Joan Bennett's crime of passion.

A Song for Europe (John Goldschmidt 1984) ✍
A naïve businessman discovers that there is far more to Switzerland than chocolate and cuckoo clocks.

The Whistle Blower (Simon Langton 1987) ✍
>Michael Caine refuses to believe his top secret communications expert son Nigel Havers' death was an accident.

COWARDICE

Airplane! (Jim Abrahams/David Zucker/Jerry Zucker 1980) ✍ ☆
Robert Hays hasn't flown since nightmare raid in 'Nam, but called on to land crippled plane in hilarious disaster spoof.

Attack **(Robert Aldrich 1956)** ☆
Coward Jack Palance leads troops in the liberation of Belgium.

Caught in the Draft **(David Butler 1941)** ☆ ✍
Wimp actor Bob Hope finds that the army draft board and colonel's daughter Dorothy Lamour are more than a match.

The Court Jester **(Norman Panama/Melvin Frank 1955)** ☆
Knock-kneed rebel Danny Kaye puts on the motley to overthrow wicked king >Basil Rathbone.

The Four Feathers **(Zoltan Korda 1939)** ✍ ☆
Branded coward for not volunteering for war service in the Sudan, John Clements undertakes covert operations.

Paths of Glory **(>Stanley Kubrick 1957)** ☆ ☞ ▉
Adolphe Menjou's fitness for command in the First World War is challenged by >Kirk Douglas' defence of a trio of cowards.

Crawford, Joan
(Lucille Le Sueur) American actress
(1904–1977)
Crawford's harsh glamour and aggressive androgyny addled her private life and caused her professional image to veer from 'movie star' to 'box office poison'. Her roles comprised four types: RUTHLESS SCHEMER: *Paid* (US: *Court Martial*) (Sam Wood 1930) (☆) (Crawford plots vengeance on those who had her jailed), *Rain* (Lewis Milestone 1932) (▉) (Crawford as the ambitious whore Sadie Thompson in a W. Somerset Maugham tale) and *Dancing Lady* (Robert Z. Leonard 1933) (☆) (Joan ponders the most advantageous match – dance partner >Fred Astaire or playboy >Clark Gable); ULTIMATE 'WOMAN'S PICTURE' HEROINE: *Strange Cargo* (Frank Borzage 1940) (☆) (the Second Coming appears to hamstring >Clark Gable's Joan-aided escape from Devil's Island), *A Woman's Face* (>George Cukor 1941) (☆) (Joan's liaison with sinister Conrad Veidt ends when Melvyn Douglas operates on her disfigured cheek) and *Mildred Pierce* (AA: >Michael Curtiz 1945) (☆ ☞) (Joan's rebellion against slaving over a hot stove leads to a restaurant business and mur-

der); MENOPAUSE BITCH: *Humoresque* (Jean Negulesco 1946) (☆ ✍) (Crawford's interest in violinist John Garfield has little to do with musical appreciation), *Possessed* (AAN: Curtis Bernhardt 1947) (☆) (nurse Joan marries her employer Raymond Massey, still harbouring hopes of a torrid affair with Van Heflin) and *The Damned Don't Cry* (Vincent Sherman 1950) (☆) (Joan gambles on the grass being greener on the other side of her dull marriage; it isn't); and AGEING AND DESPERATE WOMEN: *Sudden Fear* (AAN: David Miller 1952) (✍ ☞) (*noir* tale of worthless gold-digger Jack Palance plotting to kill heiress wife Crawford), *Johnny Guitar* (>Nicholas Ray 1954) (☆) (gambling hostess Crawford and banker Mercedes McCambridge feud over a little piece of Arizona), *Autumn Leaves* (Robert Aldrich 1956) (✍) (Crawford's toyboy husband Cliff Robertson proves to be a homicidal maniac with her next on the chopping list) and *Whatever Happened to Baby Jane?* (Robert Aldrich 1962) (☆) (>Bette Davis, a child star whose career plunged at puberty tires of nursing crippled sister Joan). Her struggle for identity and consistency of performance was well captured by Faye Dunaway in *Mommie Dearest* (Frank Perry 1981) (☆), although that film's other theme, that of Crawford as monstrous mother currently tends to overshadow her screen achievements.

 •*Tramp, Tramp, Tramp* (Harry Edwards 1926) (☆): Harry Langdon hopes his heel-toe technique will win walking race and Crawford.

•*Dance, Fools, Dance* (Harry Beaumont 1931) (☆): riches to rags Joan as a reporter exposing Chicago gangster >Clark Gable.

•*The Last of Mrs Cheyney* (Richard Boleslawski 1937): Crawford as a con woman whose upper-class victims include >William Powell and Robert Montgomery.

•*They All Kissed the Bride* (AAN: Alexander Hall 1942) (☆): Joan falls for Melvyn Douglas, the journalist busily exposing her company's shortcomings.

•*Above Suspicion* (Richard Thorpe 1943) (☆): academic Fred MacMurray and Joan spend their honeymoon hunting spies.

•*Torch Song* (Charles Walters 1953) (▉): club

singer Crawford spends her time throwing tantrums and catching blind pianist Michael Wilding.

•*The Female on the Beach* (Joseph Pevney 1955): during a sentimental journey to her late husband's beach house, Joan is stalked by neighbour Jeff Chandler.

Cry Freedom ☞ ☆ ✍ ■ ♪
GB • UIP/Universal • 1987 • 158 mins • col
d >Richard Attenborough   w John Briley
ph Ronnie Taylor   m George
Fenton/Jonas Gwangangwa
Kevin Kline, Denzel Washington,
Penelope Wilton, John Thaw

Richard Attenborough made *Cry Freedom* in the hope that all who saw it would be moved to, at the very least, recognize the evils of apartheid in South Africa. The story of newspaper editor Donald Woods' friendship with Steve Biko, Biko's murder in police custody and Woods' subsequent banning and flight is a harrowing experience, but one that achieves most of its director's ambitious targets because it manages to entertain and enthral as much as it exposes and castigates. Even reduced to basics, the political content of Biko's message might elude some, but few could ignore the brutality and corruption that attended his murder or the vindictive repression and reprisal faced by the Woods family. Kevin Kline is superb as the quietly determined journalist.

 •Another white sympathizer persecuted by the South African authorities, Ruth First (Barbara Hershey), is recalled in *A World Apart* (Chris Menges 1988) (☆).
•The harsh reality of life in the township of Soweto is depicted in the story of a minor gangster in *Mapantsula* (Oliver Schmitz 1988) (✍).
•Journalist Jutta Lampe is roused to action by the labelling of her Bader Meinhof sister Barbara Sukowa's hunger strike death as suicide in *The German Sisters* (>Margarethe Von Trotta 1981).
•A Rome policeman acts as a law unto himself,

in the Best Foreign Film Oscar-winning *Investigation of a Citizen Above Suspicion* (*Indagine su un Cittadino al di Sopra di Ogni Sospetto*) (Elio Petri 1970), when he taunts his own force with clues following the murder of his girlfriend.
•Kurt Russell leads time-bombed president Donald Pleasance from the pursuing forces of future world oppression in *Escape from New York* (John Carpenter 1981) (✍).

Cukor, George
American director (1899–1983)
From dialogue director on >*All Quiet on the Western Front* (Lewis Milestone 1930) (☞ ✍ ☆ ■) to Hollywood's oldest-ever director (82) of *Rich And Famous* (1981) (glitzy adventures of college friends turned writers Jacqueline Bisset and Candice Bergen), Cukor owed his longevity to a shrewd choice of material, careful handling of his casts and a consistently accessible technique. An interpreter rather than innovator, Cukor specialized in LITERARY AND STAGE CLASSICS: *Little Women* (AAN: 1933) (✍ ☆) (Louisa May Alcott tale of four mid-19th-century poorish sisters and their sensible mother), *David Copperfield* (1934) (☞ ☆ ✍) (>Charles Dickens' epic of boy loathed by stepfather >Basil Rathbone and befriended by kindly family man >W. C. Fields prior to a happy-ever-after marriage), *Sylvia Scarlett* (☞ ☆) (>Katharine Hepburn as androgynous con partner of >Cary Grant in Compton Mackenzie novel), *Romeo And Juliet* (1936) (■ ☞) (Norma Shearer and >Leslie Howard as >Shakespeare's doomed Veronese lovers), >*Camille* (1937) (☆ ✍ ☞ ■) and *Travels with My Aunt* (1972) (✍ ☞) (>Graham Greene tale of accountant's life enlivened by trans-European scrapes with aunt >Maggie Smith); SHOW PEOPLE: *What Price Hollywood?* (1932) (☞ ✍) (waitress Constance Bennett watches the man who made her a star drink himself to death), *A Double Life* (1947) (✍ ☞ ☆) (Ronald Colman is so obsessed with playing Othello that he lives the role off-stage to Shelley Winters' detriment) and *A Star Is Born* (1954) (☞ ✍ ☆) (reworking of *What Price Hollywood?* with Judy Garland witnessing the demise of fallen screen idol James Mason); THE BATTLE OF THE

SEXES: *Holiday* (UK: *Free to Live*) (aka *Unconventional Linda*) (1938) (rich girl >Katharine Hepburn steals sister Doris Nolan's fiancé >Cary Grant), >*The Philadelphia Story* (1940) (☆ ✍ ☞), >*Adam's Rib* (1949) (✍ ☆ ☞ ♫), >*Born Yesterday* (1950) (☆ ✍ ☞) and *Pat and Mike* (1952) (☆ ☞) (sports entrepreneur >Spencer Tracy's competitive streak is sparked by multi-talented >Katharine Hepburn's belittling of his life); and DIRECTING WOMEN: >Katharine Hepburn in *A Bill of Divorcement* (1932) (☆) (John Barrymore comes out of the asylum to discover that his daughter has a mind of her own), Norma Shearer as the subject of gossip in *The Women* (1939) (☆ ✍ ☞) (Anita Loos/Jane Murtin script from the Claire Booth hit play of bitching among bored socialites), >Joan Crawford in *A Woman's Face* (1941) (☆) (surgeon Melvyn Douglas rebuilds Crawford's face and life away from crime), >Greta Garbo in *Two-Faced Woman* (1941) (☆) (in her last film, ski-instructor Greta poses as her own twin to keep her husband Melvyn Douglas), >Ingrid Bergman in *Gaslight* (UK: *The Murder of Thornton Square*) (1944) (☞ ☆ ✍) (Charles Boyer as the schizophrenic husband prepared to kill Ingrid to keep his deadly past shrouded), and >Marilyn Monroe in *Let's Make Love* (1960) (millionaire >Yves Montand joins a show cast when he discovers that he is to be the subject of their jokes).

⬛VIEW ON▶ •*Dinner at Eight* (1933) (☞ ☆): the trials and tribulations of guests dressing for and attending a dinner party.

•*Susan and God* (UK: *The Gay Mrs Trexel*) (1940) (✍ ☞): >Fredric March hits the bottle because of >Joan Crawford's dose of only-in-spirit religion.

•*Her Cardboard Lover* (1942) (☆): Norma Shearer hires Robert Taylor to test the reflexes of George Sanders' jealousy.

•*Keeper of the Flame* (1943) (☞ ☆): journalist >Spencer Tracy investigates the death of >Katharine Hepburn's youth leader husband.

•*The Marrying Kind* (1952) (☞ ☆): as Judy Holliday and Aldo Ray scream out their divorce case, they decide to forget all about it.

•*The Actress* (1953) (☞ ☆): Jean Simmons defies her father >Spencer Tracy's wishes in this telling of actress/writer Ruth Gordon's early career.

•*It Should Happen to You* (1954) (☆ ☞): film-maker >Jack Lemmon falls for Judy Holliday as she blows her savings in the hope of TV stardom.

•*Les Girls* (1957) (☞): Dancers take out an injunction against the publication of the memoirs of their trio's antics by the third member Kay Kendall.

•*The Chapman Report* (1962): a sexologist conducts a study of the suburb sack life of a group of women, including >Jane Fonda.

•*My Fair Lady* (AA: 1964) (♫ ☞ ✍): musical version of >George Bernard Shaw's *Pygmalion*.

The Curse of the Cat People
USA • RKO • 1944 • 70 mins • b/w
d Robert Wise/Gunther Fritsch   w De Witt Bodeen   ph Nicholas Musuraca
m Roy Webb
Kent Smith, Simone Simon, Jane Randolph, Julia Dean, Ann Carter, Elizabeth Russell

Although the film marks the return of the cursed Irena of *Cat People* (Jacques Tourneur 1942) (■ ✍ ☞) (Simone Simon kills friends when she turns into a panther) producer Val Lewton's first choice of 'Aimée and Her Friend' as the title for this insightful adaptation of a Robert Louis Stevenson story of child psychology might have been more apt than the one that eventually graced the billboards. Lonely Aimée creates an idolized invisible friend from the photograph of the tragic Irena which she finds in her father's belongings. Through a curious mixture of callous manipulation of events and caring betrayal of the girl's trust, Irena leads Aimée into the danger from which her father rescues her and rediscovers his love for her. In this, the most charming horror film ever made, brilliantly brooding lighting heightens the chilling suspense as we falsely anticipate terror.

•A politician is cursed with impotence, but this proves the least of his problems in >*Xala* (aka *The Curse*) (Ousmane Sembène 1974) (☆ ⌔ ☞ ■).
•The horror is equally restrained in *The Haunting* (Robert Wise 1963) (■ ☞) when sceptics spend a weekend in a dark old house.
•A young girl has angel Harry Dean Stanton as an invisible friend ensuring a good time is had by all in *One Magic Christmas* (Philip Borsos 1985).
•A lonely girl, obsessed with >Karloff's >Frankenstein befriends a stranger believing him to be the spirit of the Monster in *The Spirit of the Beehives* (*El Espiritu de la Colmene*) (Victor Erice, Spain 1973) (☞ ■ ☆).
•An alien and a small boy find mutual consolation in isolation in >*E.T. – The Extra-Terrestrial* (>Steven Spielberg 1983) (✳ ⌔ ■ ☆ ☞).

Curtiz, Michael
(Mihaly Kertész) Hungarian director
(1888–1962)

Leaving Hungary in 1918, Curtiz's extensive and neglected trans-European films prefaced his early Warners' talkie *Tenderloin* (1928) (gangsters pursue a fortune-seeking dancer) and the first colour feature *The Mystery of the Wax Museum* (1933) (☞ ■ ⌔ ☆) (disfigured sculptor Lionel Atwill rebuilds his melted wax museum with human models). Averaging four films a year between 1930 and 1942, Curtiz, a tyrant on the set, displayed almost unrivalled versatility. HOODLUMS: *Jimmy the Gent* (1934) (☆) (tough gangster >James Cagney helps invalid child), *Kid Galahad* (1937) (☞ ☆) (boxer >Edward G. Robinson's training to be 'a contender' is endangered by jealous cornerman and >Bette Davis's qualms) and *Angels with Dirty Faces* (1938) (☞ ☆ ⌔) (fearless >James Cagney prevents the development of a hero cult through his death-day cowardice); COSTUME ADVENTURES: *Captain Blood* (1935) (☞ ☆) (fleeing from >Basil Rathbone's Judge Jeffreys Errol Flynn terrorizes the seas and wins >Olivia De Havilland), *The Adventures of Robin Hood* (co-directed with William Keighley 1938) (☞ ☆ ■) (Claude Rains as Prince John joins the cast of *Blood* who play Guy of Gisbourne, Robin and Marian respectively), *The*

Private Lives of Elizabeth and Essex (1939) (☞ ☆) (Good Queen >Bette (Davis) puts national security before her love for Errol Flynn) and *The Sea Hawk* (1940) (⌔ ☆ ☞) (privateer Errol Flynn confounds Spaniard Claude Rains for Flora Robson's Elizabeth I); WESTERNS: *Dodge City* (1939) (>Olivia De Havilland stands by her man Errol Flynn as he makes rail travel safer for Wild West commuters), *Virginia City* (1940) (☞) (dancer Miriam Hopkins tries to steal Unionist gold from Errol Flynn) and *Santa Fé Trail* (1940) (Errol Flynn's capture of rebel John Brown (Raymond Massey) is complicated by his love for Brown's daughter >Olivia De Havilland); BIOPICS: *Yankee Doodle Dandy* (1942) (♫ ☆) (>James Cagney as the patriotic showman George M. Cohan) and *Night and Day* (1946) (♫ ☞ ☆) (>Cary Grant as songwriter Cole Porter). In addition, there was a pot-pourri including: *Black Fury* (1935) (☞) (Paul Muni battles against both mining bosses and unions), *Four Daughters* (AAN: 1938) (☞ ☆) (a slice of Claude Rains' family's small-town life ends in the death of son John Garfield), *Captains of the Clouds* (1942) (☆) (talkative Canadian pilot >James Cagney silences his critics with some air heroics), *Mildred Pierce* (1945) (☆ ☞) (>Joan Crawford spreads her wings only to get them singed in a murder case) and *Life with Father* (1947) (☆ ☞ ⌔) (Irene Dunne is appalled by her proper husband >William Powell's confession that he is unbaptized). Oh, yes, and >*Casablanca* (1942) (☆ ☞ ⌔ ♫ ■).

•*Noah's Ark* (1929) (☞): >Myrna Loy among a cast contrasting the Old Testament flood with the First World War.

•*20,000 Years in Sing Sing* (1932) (☞ ☆): >Bette Davis kills a man helping >Spencer Tracy escape, but he takes the rap.

•*Passage to Marseilles* (1944) (☆): Devil's Island escapee >Humphrey Bogart later plays a part in foiling Nazis.

•*Flamingo Road* (1949) (☞): carnival dancer >Joan Crawford is persecuted by prosecuting sheriff Sydney Greenstreet.

•*White Christmas* (1954) (♫): Bing Crosby and

Danny Kaye set up a sentimental reunion for their hard-up general.

•*We're No Angels* (1955) (☞ ☆): escaped convicts >Humphrey Bogart, Peter Ustinov and Aldo Ray teach scheming >Basil Rathbone a lesson.

•*The Best Things in Life Are Free* (1956) (♫ ☞): biopic sees Gordon MacRae, Dan Dailey and Ernest Borgnine play songwriters Buddy De-Sylva, Ray Henderson and Lew Brown.

DANCE AND DANCERS

Bolero **(Wesley Ruggles 1934)** ☆ ☞
>Carole Lombard watches George Raft lured away from his career by nightclubs.

Break the News **(>René Clair 1938)** ☞ ✍
Jack Buchanan's publicity stunt death of partner Maurice Chevalier goes wrong when the latter disappears.

Carmen **(Carlos Saura; Spain 1983)** ▨ ☞
Captivating Spanish flamenco version of Bizet's opera.

Dirty Dancing **(Emile Ardolino 1987)** ♫
Jennifer Gray is taught a lot more than dancing by holiday camp partner Patrick Swayze.

Fame **(Alan Parker 1980)** ☞
Students run the gamut of starlet emotions at New York's High School for the Performing Arts.

Invitation to the Dance **(>Gene Kelly 1954)** ☆
Kelly's toes twinkle in a trio of dance fables.

The Red Shoes **(>Michael Powell/Emeric Pressburger 1948)** ▨
Ballerina Moira Shearer kills herself when Anton Walbrook insists she choose between him and her career.

St Martin's Lane **(US:*Sidewalks of London*) (Tim Whelan 1938)** ☆
Street entertainer >Charles Laughton forlornly loves rising star >Vivien Leigh.

Saturday Night Fever **(John Badham 1978)** ♫
John Travolta lives for the bright lights of the disco.

Tales of Beatrix Potter **(US:*Peter Rabbit and the Tales of Beatrix Potter*) (Reginald Mills 1971)** ☆
Balletic interpretations of the famous animal fables.

They Shoot Horses, Don't They? **(Sidney Pollack 1969)** ✍ ☆
>Jane Fonda and Susannah York are among those involved in a Depression dance marathon.

The Turning Point **(Herbert Ross 1977)** ☆ ▨
This tale of ballerina Shirley MacLaine visiting retired colleague Anne Bancroft was showered with AANs.

The Unfinished Dance **(Henry Koster 1947)** ☆
Margaret O'Brien's jealousy of Cyd Charisse's talent leads to a crippling accident.
>Astaire, Fred, Kelly, Gene, Rogers, Ginger

Dassin, Jules
American writer/director (b 1911)

Never the most artistic of directors, even Dassin hungered for more than the diet of froth he was permitted at MGM – *Reunion in France* (UK: *Mademoiselle France*) (1942) (☞) (fashion designer >Joan Crawford helps >John Wayne fight the Nazis) and *The Canterville Ghost* (1944) (☆) (Oscar Wilde tale of 17th-century ghost >Charles Laughton desirous of quitting the haunting business). A pioneer in the use of downtown location filming, he was a leading light in postwar shadowy thrillers known as *film noir*: *Brute Force* (1947) (☞) (Burt Lancaster leads a prison revolt against monstrous governor Hume Cronyn), *The Naked City* (1948) (☞) (semi-documentary police procedural with New York cop Barry Fitzgerald on the trail of a killer) and *Thieves' Highway* (1949) (☞) (a trucker carries on a vendetta against the men who injured his father). In 1951, the testimony to the House Un-American Activities Committee of film director Edward Dmytryk (who identified him as a Communist) drove Dassin to prolonged European unemployment, which ended with *Rififi* (1955) (☞ ✍) (Jean Servais' gang come to bloody blows during a loot share out), a stylish thriller notable for its c. 28-minute silent jewel theft, and *Never on Sunday* (*Pote Tin Kyriaki*) (AAN for direction: 1960) (☞) (Dassin himself as an academic playing Pygmalion to Melina Mercouri, his real-life Greek wife). Since *Topkapi* (1964) (☆) (Eric Ambler tale of a raid on a Turkish museum), Mercouri's career as Greek Minister of Culture has proved the more significant.

 •*Two Smart People* (1946): Lucille Ball traipses across New Orleans after her missing loot.
•*Night and the City* (1949) (✍): wrestling promoter Herbert Lom is among those cheated by fast bucker Richard Widmark.
•*Circle of Two* (1979) (☆): art teacher >Richard Burton becomes enamoured of student Tatum O'Neal.

Davis, Bette
American actress (1908–1989)

Through the mediocrities that she was contracted to do, which provoked a protracted feud with Warners, Davis developed the dual screen nature that made her the most important American film actress of the Golden Age – the prize bitch and the abused heroine. Combining both in *20,000 Years in Sing Sing* (>Michael Curtiz 1933) (☞ ☆) (Bette helps >Spencer Tracy escape, but kills a man in the process), she followed a discernable pattern of machination and tribulation. Withering with a glance, she schemed her way through *Bordertown* (Archie Mayo 1935) (☆) (Mexican lawyer Paul Muni fancies his chances with bored wife Davis), *Jezebel* (AA: >William Wyler 1938) (☆ ☞ ✍ ■) (bitchy belle Davis' red dress makes her an outcast, but her stirring plague nursing paves the way for >Henry Fonda's proposal), *The Letter* (AAN: >William Wyler 1940) (☞ ☆ ✍) (Herbert Marshall finds evidence to prove that Bette's involvement with the death of his friend was more than an accident), *The Little Foxes* (AAN >William Wyler 1941) (☆ ✍ ☞) (Bette is the pick of the pack as a post-US Civil War family tear each other to shreds with their schemes), *Old Acquaintance* (Vincent Sherman 1943) (☆ ✍) (novelists Davis and Miriam Hopkins go to extremes to bitch up each other's lives), and >*All About Eve* (>Joseph L. Mankiewicz 1950) (☆ ✍ ☞), in which she revived the spoiled stage star of *Dangerous* (AA: Alfred E. Green 1935) (☆) (Franchot Tone keeps actress Bette out of the cocktail cabinet, ensuring a tearful comeback). She lent dignity to pathos with her suffering in such films as *Dark Victory* (AAN: Edmund Goulding 1939) (☆) (Davis's hectic social life with friends, including George Brent and Ronald Reagan is ended by a brain tumour), *The Great Lie* (AAN: Edmund Goulding) (1941) (☆ ✍) (Bette cares for lover George Brent's child when Mary Astor abandons it) and *Now Voyager* (AAN: Irving Rapper 1942) (☆ ✍) (psychiatrist Claude Rains encourages Bette to live a full life and she transforms the life of the wallflower daughter of forbidden lover Paul Henreid). Wrinkling rapidly, Davis fell victim to more sinister torment in *Whatever Happened to Baby Jane?*

(AAN: Robert Aldrich 1962) (☆) (crippled >Joan Crawford is terrorized by embittered child actress sister Davis) and some inferior TV movies, before luxuriating in the role of *grande dame* with >Lillian Gish in *The Whales of August* (Lindsay Anderson 1988) (☆) (a gentle tale of elderly sisters taking to extremes a disagreement over the installation of a window on to the bay).

 •*Of Human Bondage* (John Cromwell 1934) (☆ ✍): W. Somerset Maugham tale in which >Leslie Howard has his life ruined by his affair with waitress Davis.

•*Front Page Woman* (>Michael Curtiz 1935) (☞ ☆): reporters Davis and George Brent squabble over murder mystery scoops.

•*The Petrified Forest* (Archie Mayo 1936) (☆ ✍): Davis and >Leslie Howard are among the travellers held hostage by >Humphrey Bogart.

•*It's Love I'm After* (Archie Mayo 1937) (☆ ✍): ideal stage couple Bette and >Leslie Howard make the fur fly in real life.

•*The Sisters* (Anatole Litvak 1939) (☆): Davis survives her marriage to drunkard Errol Flynn, the San Francisco earthquake and a spell in a brothel.

•*The Old Maid* (Edmund Goulding 1939) (☞ ☆):US Civil War drama has Bette abandoning her daughter to cousin Miriam Hopkins and later regretting it.

•*Juarez* (>William Dieterle 1939) (☆ ☞): >John Huston script has Bette as the Empress Carlotta driven insane by Mexican revolt against her husband, the Emperor Maximilian (Brian Aherne).

•*The Private Lives of Elizabeth and Essex* (>Michael Curtiz 1939) (☞ ☆): Errol Flynn's political and romantic treason with >Olivia De Havilland, leads to Davis signing his death warrant.

•*All This and Heaven Too* (Anatole Litvak 1940) (☆ ✍): Charles Boyer murders his unstable wife to further his affair with governess Davis.

•*The Man Who Came to Dinner* (William Keighley 1941) (✍ ☆ ☞): radio celebrity Monty Woolley breaks his hip and insists that his hosts must accommodate him and his secretary, Davis.

•*Watch on the Rhine* (Herman Shumlin 1943) (✍ ☆): Dashiell Hammett's script of Lillian Hellman's play sees Paul Lukas and Davis chased to Washington by Nazi agents.

•*Mr Skeffington* (Vincent Sherman 1944) (☞ ✍): ageing Davis repays her blind husband Claude Rains' trust in her with infidelity.

•*A Stolen Life* (Curtis Bernhardt 1946) (☆): Davis cheats on husband Glenn Ford by assuming the identity of her twin sister.

• *Deception* (Irving Rapper 1946) (☆ ✍): composer Claude Rains avenges Davis's return to her cellist lover Paul Henreid by trying to ruin their relationship.

•*The Star* (AAN: Stuart Heisler 1952) (☆): fallen idol Davis is bailed out and cared for by former co-star Sterling Hayden.

•*Madame Sin* (David Greene 1972) (☆): Denholm Elliott sidekicks for Davis's splendidly outrageous villain as she plots a submarine hi-jack.

DEEP SOUTH, USA

Attack of the Giant Leeches (Bernard Kowalski 1959)
Leeches drag human take-aways back to their swamp.

Deliverance (John Boorman 1972) ☞ ■
A quartet on a canoeing holiday become a maniac's moving target.

The Heart is a Lonely Hunter (Robert Ellis Miller 1968)
Deaf mute Alan Arkin receives a mixture of scorn and sympathy in a small town.

In the Heat of the Night (Norman Jewison 1967) ☆ ✍
Bigot cop Rod Steiger comes to respect black superior Sidney Poitier.

Reap the Wild Wind (Cecil B. De Mille 1942) ☞ ☆
>John Wayne and Ray Milland are distracted from salvaging wrecks to court belle Paulette Goddard.

The Reivers (Mark Rydell 1970)
An estate worker, a black groom and the family's youngest son drive from the Mississippi to Memphis.

The Sound and the Fury (Martin Ritt 1959) ■

William Faulkner tale sees Yul Brynner attempting to revive the dwindling fortunes of his family.

De Havilland, Olivia

American actress (b 1916)

From being the romantic motivation for Errol Flynn's derring-do – *Captain Blood* (>Michael Curtiz 1935) (☞ ☆) (Flynn's exploits on the high seas are inspired by a hatred of >Basil Rathbone and love for the 19-year-old Olivia), *The Adventures of Robin Hood* (>Michael Curtiz/William Keighley 1938) (☞ ☆ ■) (Lincoln greened outlaw Errol's exploits are inspired by a hatred of >Basil Rathbone and love for Olivia) and in *Dodge City* (>Michael Curtiz 1939) (Flynn runs the railway wreckers out of town out of love for Olivia), De Havilland developed the character she played as Melanie Hamilton in >*Gone with the Wind* (Victor Fleming 1939) (☆ ■ ✍ ☞ ♫), whose unsuspected strength emerges in adversity: *Hold Back the Dawn* (AAN: Mitchell Leisen 1941) (☆ ☞) (Charles Boyer contracts a loveless marriage with Olivia to side-step US immigration), *To Each His Own* (Mitchell Leisen 1946) (☆ ☞ ✍) (Olivia meets long-lost son John Lund during the Blitz), *The Snake Pit* (AAN: Anatole Litvak 1948) (☆ ☞) (Psychiatrist Leo Genn leads amnesiac Olivia through mental hospital hell to recovery) and *The Heiress* (AA: >William Wyler 1949) (☞ ☆ ✍) (>Henry James's story *Washington Square* in which De Havilland takes her revenge on her gold-digging young lover Montgomery Clift). Her few comedies were entertaining enough: *It's Love I'm After* (Archie Mayo 1937) (☆ ✍) (Olivia as flighty heiress complicating the flimsy marriage of >Bette Davis and >Leslie Howard) and *Four's a Crowd* (>Michael Curtiz 1938) (☆) (Publicity man Errol Flynn falls for tetchy millionaire's daughter De Havilland), but there was also a sinister streak: *The Dark Mirror* (Robert Siodmak 1946) (☆ ☞) (Lew Ayres is never certain whether he is with twee Olivia or her unstable twin) and *Hush, Hush, Sweet Charlotte* (Robert Aldrich 1964) (☆) (Joseph Cotten and Olivia's torment of sister >Bette Davis recalls the night she believes she murdered her man).

 •*The Charge of the Light Brigade* (>Michael Curtiz 1936) (☞ ☆): volunteering for the Crimean War to forget Olivia, Errol Flynn leads the suicide charge.

•*The Strawberry Blonde* (>Raoul Walsh 1941) (☆ ✍): Olivia and Rita Hayworth are rivals for the love of dentist >James Cagney.

• *They Died with Their Boots On* (>Raoul Walsh 1941) (☞ ☆): Olivia is the girl left behind as Erroll Flynn's General Custer meets Sitting Bull.

•*The Well Groomed Bride* (Sidney Lanfield 1946) (✍): Olivia helps Ray Milland find the bottle of champagne required to launch a naval ship.

•*Devotion* (Curtis Bernhardt 1943) (☆ ☞ ✍): Ida Lupino, Olivia and Nancy Coleman as the Brontë sisters Emily, Charlotte and Anne.

•*My Cousin Rachel* (Henry Koster 1952) (✍): >Richard Burton unveils Olivia's mysterious past in >Daphne Du Maurier melodrama.

•*Libel* (>Anthony Asquith 1959) (☆): (Olivia accuses Dirk Bogarde of impersonating an aristocrat.

Deneuve, Catherine

(Catherine Dorléac) French actress (b 1943)

Wrongly relegated behind Bardot as the personification of French beauty, Deneuve's allure has enabled her to play a number of types, with equal efficiency: FEMMES FATALES: *Repulsion* (>Roman Polanski 1965) (☞ ☆) (Terrified of sex, Deneuve kills men who come too close), *The Last Metro* (*Le Dernier Metro*) (>François Truffaut 1980) (☞ ☆ ✍) (Deneuve keeps the show on in occupied Paris, while hiding Maquis man >Gérard Depardieu and a gay director in her Jewish husband's theatre) and *The Hunger* (Tony Scott 1984) (☆ ■) (Deneuve as a bisexual vampire preferring Susan Sarandon to David Bowie); ADULTERESSES: >*Belle de Jour* (>Luis Buñuel 1967) (☞ ☆ ✍ ■) and *Mayerling* (Terence Young 1968) (☆ ■) (Omar Sharif as Rudolph, heir to the Hapsburg throne who commits suicide with his lover Deneuve after his annulment plea is dismissed); and

HEROINES: *The Umbrellas of Cherbourg* (*Les Parapluies de Cherbourg*) (Jacques Demy 1964) (♫ ☞) (pregnant Deneuve decides she can't wait until her lover returns from the army and marries a jeweller for well-heeled convenience), *The Magic Donkey* (US:*Donkey Skin*) (*Peau d'Âne*) (Jacques Demy 1970) (☆ ✍) (fairytale king Jean Marais can only marry a woman as beautiful as his dead wife – unfortunately this is his daughter Deneuve) and *Tristana* (>Luis Buñuel 1970) (☞ ☆) (trusting ward Deneuve is victimized by increasingly chauvinistic guardian Fernando Rey).

 Benjamin or The Diary of an Innocent Young Man (*Benjamin ou les Mémoires d'un Puceau*) (Michel Deville 1968) (■): Deneuve is one of the women from whom an 18th-century orphan learns about sex.

• *See Here My Love* (*Écoute Voir...*) (Hugo Santiago 1978) (♫ ☆): bisexual private eye Deneuve uncovers a Fascist radio-wave brainwashing plot.

• *The Mississippi Mermaid* (*La Sirène du Mississippi*) (>François Truffaut 1969) (✍ ☞ ☆): Deneuve substitutes herself for >Jean-Paul Belmondo's mail-order bride, intent on mayhem.

• *Dirty Money* (US: *A Very Curious Girl*) (*La Fiancée du Pirate*) (Jean-Pierre Melville 1972) (✍): cop Alain Delon falls for gangster Richard Crenna's moll Deneuve while on his trail.

• *Let's Hope It's a Girl* (*Speriamo che sia Femmina*) (Mario Monicelli 1985) (☆ ☞): when impoverished noble >Philippe Noiret dies, the family affairs are left in the hands of Deneuve and Liv Ullmann.

De Niro, Robert
American actor (b 1943)

Through a dedication to his art demanding immense mental and physical discipline, De Niro has become one of the greatest screen actors of his generation. His genius for 'social anger' was first harnessed in *Mean Streets* (>Martin Scorsese 1973) (☞ ☆ ♫) (Harvey Keitel's bid for life away from Little Italy crime is hamstrung by family responsibility to De Niro). It was repeated in *Taxi Driver* (>Martin

Scorsese 1976) (☆) (disturbed by war and rejection, De Niro attempts a political assassination and the salvation of child whore Jodie Foster), *The Deer Hunter* (AAN: Michael Cimino 1978) (■♫ ☆) (De Niro and his buddies find their hunting experience inadequate when playing Russian roulette in Vietnam) and *Raging Bull* (AA: >Martin Scorsese 1980) (☆ ☞ ■) (biopic of Jake La Motta, the boxer who became a stand-up comic following a prison stretch). His ability to totally assimilate character won him acclaim in >*The Godfather II* (AA: >Francis Ford Coppola 1974) (✍ ☞ ■ ♫ ☆), >*1900* (*Novocento*) (Bernardo Bertolucci 1976) (✍ ☆ ■ ☞) and >*Once Upon a Time in America* (Sergio Leone 1984) (✍ ☆ ☞ ♫). An uncomfortable romantic lead – eg, *Falling in Love* (Ulu Grosbard 1984) (☆) (a chance bookshop encounter leads to De Niro's long-distance adultery with >Meryl Streep) – he has developed a comic touch, exhibited in *New York, New York* (>Martin Scorsese 1977) (☞ ☆) (saxophonist De Niro abandons Liza Minnelli to concentrate on his career only for her to find stardom) and *The King of Comedy* (>Martin Scorsese 1982) (☆ ☞ ✍) (De Niro kidnaps comic idol Jerry Lewis and issues a ransom demand of his own TV chat show), in *Brazil* (Terry Gilliam 1984) (☞ ✳) (a victim of an omnipresent future state is rescued by terrorist De Niro posing as a State heating engineer) and *Midnight Run* (Martin Brest 1988) (☆ ✍) (De Niro as a bountyhunter avoiding rivals, cops and Mafia assassins to bring bent bookie Charles Grodin to book). He also revelled in extravagant cameos in *Angel Heart* (Alan Parker 1987) (✍) (Devil De Niro sends Mickey Rourke to look for a missing person who turns out to be himself) and *The Untouchables* (Brian De Palma 1987) (☆) (De Niro's Al Capone avoids arrest by federal agents Kevin Costner and >Sean Connery).

 • *Bang the Drum Slowly* (John Hancock 1973): a baseball star discovers he's been struck out with leukaemia.

• *The Last Tycoon* (>Elia Kazan 1976) (☞ ☆): Harold Pinter screenplay of F. Scott Fitzgerald

novel about movie mogul De Niro's inability to get over his wife's death.

•*True Confessions* (Ulu Grosbard 1981) (☆): De Niro's methods of business are disapproved of by his priest brother Robert Duvall.

•>*The Mission* (Roland Joffe 1987) (✍ ■ ☆ ☞ ♫).

•*Jacknife* (David Jones 1989) (☆): De Niro tries to bring 'Nam-affected Ed Harris into the 1980s.

Depardieu, Gérard
French actor (b 1948)

Despite teenage years of crime and his imposing bulk, Depardieu comes over as an everyday, likeable guy with the enthusiastic devilment of an overgrown child. If not quite a blank canvas, his flexibility has ensured his appearance in seemingly just about every worthwhile French movie since 1974. ON EITHER SIDE OF THE LAW: *Making It* (US: *Going Places*) (*Les Valseuses*) (Bertrand Blier 1973) (♫ ☆) (petty thieves Depardieu and Patrick Dewaere have equal disregard for people's property and women's rights); *Les Chiens* (Alain Jessua 1979) (☆) (Depardieu, whose guard dog school booms during a rape spate, becomes the target of a corrupt politician seeking election popularity); *Police* (Maurice Pialat 1985) (☆ ☞) (unprincipled cop Depardieu falls for Sophie Marceau, the brains behind a Marseilles drug ring); and *Tenue de Soirée* (*Evening Dress*) (Bertrand Blier 1987) (☆) (gay crook Depardieu seduces married Michel Blanc into becoming a partner in crime and in bed). IN HISTORICAL ROLES: from medieval peasant >*The Return of Martin Guerre* (*Le Retour de Martin Guerre*) (Daniel Vigne 1981) (☆ ✍ ■ ☞) to the French Revolutionary leader, *Danton* (>Andrej Wajda 1982) (☆ ☞ ■) (popular with the *sans culottes*, but not with Convention colleagues, Depardieu is tried for corruption); from Italian peasant in >*1900* (*Novecento*) (Bernardo Bertolucci; 1976) (✍ ☆ ■ ☞) to Maquis fighter in occupied Paris in *The Last Metro* (*Le Dernier Metro*) (>François Truffaut 1980) (☞ ☆ ✍) (>Catherine Deneuve runs her Jewish husband's theatre, hiding company members Depardieu and a gay director in the process). IN MODERN DRAMAS: *The Last Woman* (*L'Ultima Donna*) (*La Dernière*

Femme) (Marco Ferreri 1975) (☆) (Depardieu's feminist wife Zouzou deserts him and he meets unliberated Ornella Muti, only for the women to unite in taking his son); *Get Out Your Handkerchiefs* (*Préparez vos Mouchoirs*) (Bertrand Blier 1978) (✍ ☆) (Foreign Film AA winner in which Depardieu hires lovers to thaw his unresponsive wife Carole Laure) and *The Woman Next Door* (*La Femme d'á Côté*) (>François Truffaut 1981) (☆) (Depardieu renews his affair with his old flame Fanny Ardant when she becomes his new neighbour in a Grenoble suburb). Depardieu is eminently watchable.

•*This Sweet Sickness* (*Dîtes-lui Que Je L'Aime*) (Claude Miller 1977) (☆ ✍): Patricia Highsmith story has Depardieu building a home for a sweetheart who has no intention of leaving her husband.

•*Buffet Froid* (*Cold Cuts*) (Bertrand Blier 1979) (☆): Depardieu is suspected of mass murder.

•*My American Uncle* (*Mon Oncle Amérique*) (>Alain Resnais 1980) (☞): an animal behaviourist studies the humdrum lives of a trio, including factory owner Depardieu.

•*Loulou* (Maurice Pialat 1980) (☆ ✍): Isabelle Huppert leaves her secure marriage for a fling with sex-crazed slob Depardieu.

•*The Moon in the Gutter* (*La Lune dans le Caniveau*) (Jean-Jacques Beineix 1982) (☆): Depardieu keeps tabs on the rapist of his sister by taking up with the suspect's sister Nastassja Kinski.

•>*Jean de Florette* (Claude Berri 1987) (☆ ✍ ☞ ■).

•*Under Satan's Sun* (*Sous le Soleil de Satan*) (Maurice Pialat 1988) (☆): priest Depardieu fails to reform a wild girl, but is revered as a saint by villagers when she kills herself.

•*Camille Claudel* (Bruno Nuytten 1989) (☆ ■): Isabelle Adjani won Berlin Festival Best Actress Award as the student/lover of sculptor Auguste Rodin (Depardieu) who is forced to leave him to pursue her own career.

DESERTS

The Flight of the Phoenix **(Robert Aldrich 1965)** ☆
>James Stewart and >Richard Attenborough are among marooned plane crew squabbling over ways of escape.

Ice Cold in Alex **(US:*Desert Attack*) (J. Lee-Thompson 1958)** ☆ ■
Ambulance driver John Mills, with Nazis in pursuit, drives across North Africa to buy his staff a drink.

The Immortal Sergeant **(John Stahl 1943)** ☆
Veteran soldier Thomas Mitchell bolsters the courage of recruits, including >Henry Fonda.

Lawrence of Arabia **(>David Lean 1962)**
■ ☞ ♫
Peter O'Toole as T.E. Lawrence who rallied the Arabs against the Turks during the First World War.

The Lost Patrol **(>John Ford 1934)** ☞ ■ ☆
Victor McLaglen and >Boris Karloff as members of a patrol under attack in Mesopotamia.

Sahara **(Zoltan Korda 1943)** ☆ ■
>Humphrey Bogart races the Nazis to an oasis.

Woman of the Dunes **(US:*Woman in the Dunes*) (*Suna no Onna*) (Hiroshi Teshigahara, 1964)** ■
A scientist seeking rare insects is imprisoned by a woman living in a sand pit and is forced to dig deep to keep them both alive.

De Sica, Vittorio
Italian actor/writer/director (1902–1974)
Debuting in 1918, De Sica acted in over 150 films, progressing from 1930s idol to comic policeman in *Bread, Love and Dreams* (*Pane, Amore, e Fantasia*) (Luigi Comencini 1953) (☆) (De Sica pursues nurse Marisa Merlini and tart Gina Lollobrigida hoping to marry whichever'll have him) and *Bread, Love and Jealousy* (*Pane, Amore, et Gelosia*) (Luigi Comencini 1954) (☆ ✍) (De Sica is engaged to the nurse, Lollobrigida to his deputy Roberto Risso, but who will marry whom?) and military imposter in *General della Rovere* (>Roberto Rossellini 1959) (☞ ☆ ✍) (Nazi stooge De Sica is supposed to smoke out Italian partisans but joins their cause). From the mid-1940s, he often took roles to finance his collaborations with screenwriter Cesare Zavattini. Depicting without sentiment the poverty and desperation of postwar Italy, they largely set the criteria for Neo-Realist cinema in films such as *Shoeshine* (*Sciuscia*) (1946) (☞ ☆ ✍) (semi-documentary and honorary Oscar-winning film of young black marketeers whose dreams of buying a horse are shattered by their arrest), >*Bicycle Thieves* (US: *The Bicycle Thief*) (*Ladri de Biciclette*) (1948) (☞ ☆ ✍ ■) and *Umberto D* (1952) (☞ ☆ ■) (proud evicted pensioner Carlo Battisti is forced to beg to keep his faithful dog and pregnant maid). Aside from the notable dramas *Two Women* (*La Ciociara*) (☞ ☆) (1960) (the trials and humiliations of Cannes and AA-winning Sophia Loren and her daughter in flight from the Nazis, Allies and partisans in 1943 Italy) and *The Garden of the Finzi-Continis* (*Il Giardino dei Finzi-Contini*) (1970) (☞ ■ ☆ ✍) (AA and Berlin Festival-winning tale of wealthy Jews turning their house into a sanctuary against Fascist genocide), De Sica progressively succumbed to directing the kind of acute comedies in which he appeared: *Gold of Naples* (*L'Oro di Napoli*) (1955) (☞ ☆ ✍) (quartet of stories: a worm turns against a racketeer; Sophia Loren loses her wedding ring on an assignation; De Sica gambles away the family fortune and a wife cures mental illness with sex therapy), *The Roof* (*Il Tetto*) (1957) (☞ ✍) (a brick layer has one night to construct a shack knowing eviction is illegal once a building has a roof), and *Yesterday, Today and Tomorrow* (*Ieri, Oggi, Domani*) (1963) (☞) (Foreign Film Oscar-winning trilogy, including the tale of Sophia Loren avoiding jail by continuously getting pregnant by >Marcello Mastroianni).

•*Miracle in Milan* (*Miracolo a Milano*) (1950) (☞ ■): a cabbage-patch foundling improves the lives of the poor through the powers of a magic dove.
•*The Indiscretion of an American Wife* (1953) (☞): Montgomery Clift and Jennifer Jones resolve their love affair in a night on Rome railway station.
•*Like Father, Like Son* (US: *The Tailor's Son*) (*Padri e Figli*) (Mario Monicelli 1957) (☆): the

lives and marriages of five inter-related families, including those of De Sica and >Marcello Mastroianni.

•*The Condemned of Altona* (1962) (☆): >Fredric March mediates between the feuding members of his family to die with peace of mind.

•*Marriage, Italian Style* (*Matrimonio all'Italiana*) (1964) (☞): Sophia Loren feigns a fatal illness to prevent long-time lover >Marcello Mastroianni marrying a young girl.

DETECTIVES

The Adventures of Sherlock Holmes (US:*Sherlock Holmes*) (Alfred Werker 1939) ☆ ✍
>Basil Rathbone and Nigel Bruce as Holmes and Dr Watson prevent the theft of the Crown Jewels.
For the remainder of the series >Basil Rathbone.
For a selection of other Holmes films >*The Hound of the Baskervilles*.

Appointment with Death (Michael Winner 1988)
Peter Ustinov's Hercule Poirot solves a matricide in the heat of Palestine.
>**Agatha Christie.**

Charlie Chan at the Opera (H. Bruce Humberstone 1936) ✍
Warner Oland as the Oriental detective tracking the killer of the opera >Boris Karloff.
SERIES: with Warner Oland: 1931: *Charlie Chan Carries On*; *The Black Camel*; 1932: *Charlie Chan's Chance*; 1933: *Charlie Chan's Greatest Case*; 1934: *Charlie Chan's Courage*; *Charlie Chan in London*; 1935: *Charlie Chan in Paris*; *Charlie Chan in Egypt*; *Charlie Chan in Shanghai*; 1936: *Charlie Chan's Secret*; *Charlie Chan at the Circus*; *Charlie Chan at the Race Track*; 1937: *Charlie Chan at the Olympics*; *Charlie Chan on Broadway*; *Charlie Chan at Monte Carlo* – later series with Sidney Toler and Roland Winters were of less than noteworthy quality.

The Falcon Strikes Back (Edward Dmytryk 1943) ☆
Tom Conway is suspected of murder but still solves a bond fraud.

SERIES: with George Sanders: 1941: *The Gay Falcon*; *A Date with the Falcon*; 1942: *The Falcon Takes Over*; *The Falcon's Brother*; with Tom Conway: 1943: *The Falcon and the Co-Eds*; *The Falcon in Danger*; 1944: *The Falcon in Hollywood*; *The Falcon in Mexico*; *The Falcon Out West*; 1945: *The Falcon in San Francisco*; 1946: *The Falcon's Alibi*; *The Falcon's Adventure*; with John Calvert: 1948: *The Devil's Cargo*; *Appointment with Murder*; *Reach for Danger*.

Father Brown (US: *The Detective*) (Robert Hamer 1954) ✍ ☆
>Alec Guinness as G. K. Chesterton's priest thwarting Peter Finch's theft of a church crucifix.

Maigret Sets a Trap (*Maigret Tend un Piege*) (Jean Delannoy, 1957) ✍ ☆
>Jean Gabin as Georges Simenon's inspector, whose staged arrest provokes rivalry between the suspect's mother and wife.
For other Maigret films >Jean Gabin and >Charles Laughton.

Mr Moto's Gamble (Norman Foster 1937) ☆
>Peter Lorre as J. P. Marquand's Japanese detective solving a smuggling mystery during a boat trip between Honolulu and Shanghai.
SERIES: 1937: *Think Fast Mr Moto*; *Thank You Mr Moto*; 1938: *Mr Moto's Gamble*; *Mr Moto Takes a Chance*; *Mysterious Mr Moto*; 1939: *Mr Moto's Last Warning*; *Mr Moto in Danger Island*; *Mr Moto Takes a Vacation*.

The Saint Takes Over (Jack Hively 1940)
George Sanders as Leslie Charteris's rogue-turned-crusader, once more on the police's prime suspect list.
SERIES: with George Sanders: 1939: *The Saint Strikes Back*; *The Saint in London*; 1940: *The Saint's Double Trouble*; *The Saint Takes Over*; 1941: *The Saint in Palm Springs*; with Louis Hayward: 1938: *The Saint in New York*; with Hugh Sinclair: 1941: *The Saint's Vacation*; *The Saint Meets the Tiger*.

Sexton Blake and the Hooded Terror (George King 1938)
Tod Slaughter as the all-action amateur crime-fighter unmasking villainous millionaires. With David Farrar: 1943: *Meet Sexton Blake*; *The Echo Murders*.

THE DEVIL

Alias Nick Beal (UK:*The Contact Man*) (John Farrow 1949) ☆ ☞ ■
Ray Milland's offer of power to politician Thomas Mitchell becomes a matter of life and death.

All That Money Can Buy (aka*The Devil and Daniel Webster*) (aka *Daniel Webster and the Devil*) (aka *Here is a Man*) (>William Dieterle 1941) ☞ ☆ ♫
A farmer keeps his soul courtesy of Edward Arnold's pleading at his trial in this adaptation of Stephen Vincent Benét's play *The Devil and Daniel Webster*.

Angel On My Shoulder (Archie Mayo 1946) ☆ ✍
Satan Claude Rains grants gangster Paul Muni a new lease of life in the body of a judge providing he perverts the course of justice.

Bedazzled (>Stanley Donen 1967) ☆
Peter Cook purchases Dudley Moore's soul for a crack at the seven deadly sins.

The Devils (Ken Russell 1970) ☞ ☆
Vanessa Redgrave leads the possessed nuns of Loudun in executing priest Oliver Reed in adaptation of Aldous Huxley's novel.

The Devil's Eye (*Djävulens Öga*) (>Ingmar Bergman, 1960) ☆
Irritated by Bibi Andersson's virginity, the devil sends Don Juan to seduce her.

The Masque of the Red Death (Roger Corman 1964) ☆ ■
Medieval Satanist Vincent Price can't prevent the plague gatecrashing his masked ball.

To the Devil a Daughter (Peter Sykes 1975) ☆
Dennis Wheatley tale of priest Christopher Lee seeking Satanic offspring Nastassja Kinski.

Les Visiteurs du Soir (*The Devil's Envoys*) (>Marcel Carné 1942) ✍ ☆
Disguised minstrels' role in the Devil's plan to cause mayhem in a medieval castle is distracted by romance.

The Devil Rides Out (US:The Devil's Bride) ☆ ✍ ☞
GB • Hammer • 1967 • 95 mins • col
d Terence Fisher w Richard Matheson
ph Arthur Grant m James Bernard
Christopher Lee, Charles Gray, Leon Greene, Patrick Mower, Gwen Ffrangcon Davies

Packed with every devil-worshipping cliché and acting excess (no wonder the studio was called Hammer), this all-expense-spared hokum none the less provides non-stop entertainment. Why Christopher Lee, seemingly the epitome of an English aristocrat, with a niece living a comfortably upper middle-class life in the country, should be called the Duc de Richelieu is never explained, but why pry too deeply when this man's knowledge of demonic ritual can alone prevent evil coven master Charles Gray adding to his collection of souls. The exorcism scene inside the circle is truly terrifying, draining the energy you had conserved to blast the appallingly tacky ending. If cult film means laughing helplessly even without a long night's drinking, this Dennis Wheatley adaptation is cult par excellence.

 •Bob Hope and Paulette Goddard's demon-dashing methods rely more on luck than judgement in *The Ghost Breakers* (George Marshall 1940) (☆).
•>Robert De Niro as Louis Cypher lures detective Mickey Rourke into Hell in search of a missing singer who, through a transmutation of souls is Rourke himself, in*Angel Heart* (Alan Parker 1987) (✍).
•Mia Farrow is helped in the rearing of the anti-Christ by husband John Cassavetes and neighbours Ruth Gordon and Sidney Blackmer in *Rosemary's Baby* (>Roman Polanski 1968) (✍ ☆ ☞).
•US Ambassador Gregory Peck and wife Lee Remick are to be the unhappy parents of a devilish tot in *The Omen* (Richard Donner 1976) (✍).
•Stefanie Powers is held captive by the religious maniac inhabiting Tallulah Bankhead's

English country house, in *Fanatic* (US: *Die! Die! My Darling*) (Silvio Narizzano 1965).

DICKENS, CHARLES

David Copperfield (>George Cukor 1935) ☞ ☆ ✍

Mistreated by stepfather Murdstone and befriended by eccentric Mr Micawber, our orphaned hero grows up to become a writer and, as a widower marries his long-time sweetheart.
Great Expectations (>David Lean 1946) ☞ ■ ✍ ☆

Pip (John Mills) is repaid for his kindness to convict Finlay Currie and marries childhood love Jean Simmons.
Hard Times (*Tempos Dificeis*) (*Este Tempo*) (Joao Botelho, 1989) ✍

The iniquities and tragedies of the factory system are explored in this Portuguese telling.
>Little Dorrit (Christine Edzard 1987) ✍ ☞ ☆ ■

The Mystery of Edwin Drood (Stuart Walker 1935) ☞ ✍

An ending is supplied to the unfinished novel about addicted chorister Claude Rains's pursuit of Heather Angel.
Nicholas Nickleby (Alberto Cavalcanti 1947) ✍ ☆

An evil headmaster and a troupe of ham actors mar and make Derek Bond's life of righting wrongs and looking for love.
The Old Curiosity Shop (Thomas Bentley 1934) ✍

A hunchbacked moneylender has designs on an antique shop and its owner's granddaughter.
Oliver Twist (>David Lean 1948) ✍ ☞ ☆

An orphan in a tug of war between a kindly man and underworld villains, led by >Alec Guinness's pickpocket king Fagin.
The Pickwick Papers (Noel Langley 1952) ✍ ☆

A middle-aged innocent learns about life through picaresque adventures and a breach of promise case.
Rich Man's Folly (John Cromwell 1931)

Wealthy George Bancroft learns the skills of fatherhood in adaptation of *Dombey and Son*.

A Tale of Two Cities (Jack Conway 1935/Ralph Thomas 1958) ✍ ☆

Respectively, Ronald Colman and Dirk Bogarde as the lawyer who gives his life to rescue the husband of his loved one from the French Revolutionary guillotine.

Dieterle, William

(Wilhelm Dieterle) German-born actor/director (1893–1972)

An actor of some note in German silents, his direction of *Ludwig II: King of Bavaria* (*Ludwig der Zweite, König von Bayern*) (1929) served notice of his partiality for biopics, which were sandwiched between an impressive range of diverse and successfully executed projects. *The Last Flight* (1931) (☞ ☆) (a quartet of pilots try to rebuild their lives in postwar Paris) and *Fog over Frisco* (1934) (☆ ☞) (fast-living socialite >Bette Davis's murder is investigated by hack journalist Donald Woods) demonstrated a faculty for human drama and the action thriller. His flair for literary adaptation was shown in *A Midsummer Night's Dream* (co-director Max Reinhardt 1935) (✍ ☆ ☞ ■) (Oberon, King of the Fairies, taunts Queen Titania with love-at-first-sight potion) and *The Hunchback of Notre Dame* (1939) (☞ ■ ☆) (>Charles Laughton as bellringer Quasimodo who protects the gypsy Esmeralda (Maureen O'Hara) in the Victor Hugo classic). However, the substance of his work was provided by filmed biographies: *The Story of Louis Pasteur* (1936) (☞ ✍) (Paul Muni as the scientist who finds a cure for anthrax in sheep), *The Life of Emile Zola* (1937) (☞ ☆) (Paul Muni's novelist fights the anti-Semitism and injustice of the notorious Dreyfus Case), *Juarez* (1938) (☆) (Austrian archduke Brian Aherne and wife >Bette Davis are abandoned by Napoleon III to face the wrath of Paul Muni's Mexican revolutionaries), *Dr Ehrlich's Magic Bullet* (1940) (☞ ☆ ✍) (>Edward G. Robinson finds a a cure for venereal disease) and *A Despatch From Reuters* (UK: *This Man Reuter*) (1940) (☞ ☆) (>Edward G. Robinson guides the worldwide news-gathering agency through its early days). *Kismet* (1944) (☞ ☆) (magician Ronald Colman defeats a wicked Arab ruler and wins

>Marlene Dietrich), *Duel in the Sun* (co-directing with >King Vidor and others 1946) (☆ ☞) (brothers Gregory Peck and Joseph Cotten's love for half-breed Jennifer Jones causes a family rift) and *Portrait of Jennie* (UK: *Jennie*) (1948) (☞ ♫ ■) (artist Joseph Cotten falls for ghost Jennifer Jones in a reversal of *The Picture of Dorian Gray*) preceded Dieterle's victimization by the House Un-American Activities Committee and a resumption of his theatre career in Germany.

 •*The Firebird* (1934) (☞): suspicion is cast over a theatre troupe when a ladies'-man actor is murdered.

•*Dr Socrates* (1935) (☞ ☆): doctor Paul Muni is caught up in crime after treating a wounded gangster.

•*All That Money Can Buy* (aka *The Devil and Daniel Webster*) (aka *Daniel Webster and the Devil*) (aka *Here is a Man*) (1941) (☞ ☆ ♫): Daniel Webster (Edward Arnold) battles with devil Walter Huston for a farmer's soul.

•*Tennessee Johnson* (UK: *The Man on America's Conscience*) (1942) (☞): Van Heflin stars in a biopic of the USA's 17th President Andrew Johnson.

•*The Searching Wind* (1946) (☞ ✍ ☆): Robert Young and Sylvia Sidney are berated for ignoring the significance of events in Europe from the rise of Mussolini onwards in this adaptation of Lillian Hellman's play.

•*Love Letters* (1945) (☞ ♫): Joseph Cotten helps shell-shocked Jennifer Jones recover her memory.

•*The Turning Point* (1952): an organized crime case will make or break lawyer William Holden's career.

Dietrich, Marlene

(Maria Magdalena Von Losch) German actress (b 1901)

An enigmatic screen siren, only >Josef Von Sternberg appeared to appreciate the optimum deployment of Dietrich's smouldering, economic talent, hence her post-1935 inconsistency. An unspectacular German career culminated in >*The Blue Angel* (*Der Blaue Engel*) (1930) (☆ ☞ ✍ ■ ♫). Subsequently,

Von Sternberg's adoration encapsulated her in roles depicting her as a professional or social whore with allure: *Morocco* (1930) (☆ ☞) (cabaret singer Marlene teases >Gary Cooper and Adolphe Menjou); *Shanghai Express* (1932) (☆ ☞) (Clive Brook protects Marlene on a train besieged by Warner Oland's Chinese bandits); *Blonde Venus* (1932) (☞) (singer Dietrich is tempted away from marriage to chemist Herbert Marshall by >Cary Grant) and *The Devil is a Woman* (1935) (☞) (Lionel Atwill loses with good grace when Cesar Romero wins dancer Dietrich). Post Von Sternberg, she supplemented her considerable cabaret income with films of various types: COMEDIES: *Desire* (Frank Borzage 1936) (☆ ☞) (>Gary Cooper falls for jewel thief Marlene in a sparkling >Ernst Lubitschesque comedy) and *Angel* (>Ernst Lubitsch 1937) (☞ ☆ ✍) (diplomat Herbert Marshall neglects Marlene into the arms of his best friend Melvyn Douglas); LOW-LIFE: *Destry Rides Again* (George Marshall 1939) (☆ ✍) (Marlene as bar singer Frenchy helping timid sheriff >James Stewart tame baddie Brian Donlevy); and THRILLERS: *A Touch of Evil* (>Orson Welles 1958) (☆ ✍ ☆) (Marlene as the Madame of a brothel in the town where corrupt cop Welles and Charlton Heston are feuding over a murder inquiry); *Stage Fright* (>Alfred Hitchcock 1950) (☞ ✍) (Dietrich as the theatre star whom Richard Todd claims is guilty of the murder for which he is hunted) and *Witness for the Prosecution* (>Billy Wilder 1958) (✍ ☆ ☞) (Marlene resorts to perjury to fool >Charles Laughton into clearing Tyrone Power).

 •*A Modern Dubarry* (*Eine Dubarry von Heute*) (Alexander Korda, Germany 1927): Marlene as one of the many hoping for the high life in the tale of a model who becomes a king's mistress.

•*Dishonoured* (>Josef Von Sternberg 1931) (☞ ☆): a war-widowed whore serves the Kaiser as spy X-27 before love with Victor McLaglen leads to defection.

•*The Scarlet Empress* (>Josef Von Sternberg 1934) (☞ ☆): Catherine the Great (Marlene)'s human lovers are recalled in historical fic pic.

•*The Garden of Allah* (Richard Boleslawski

1936) (☆ ■): monk Charles Boyer comes out of the desert cloisters to woo seen-it-all socialite Marlene.

•*The Flame of New Orleans* (>René Clair 1941) (☞): Marlene poses as an exiled countess in order to marry a fortune.

•*Manpower* (>Raoul Walsh 1941) (☆): no sooner has >Edward G. Robinson plucked Marlene from dance hall degradation than she is off with factory worker George Raft.

•*Golden Earrings* (Mitchell Leisen 1947) (☆ ☞): gypsy Dietrich smuggles Ray Milland and a secret formula out of Nazi Germany.

•*Martin Roumagnac* (US: *The Room Upstairs*) (Georges Lacombe, 1947) (☆): classy whore Marlene is murdered by her builder >Jean Gabin.

•*A Foreign Affair* (>Billy Wilder 1948) (☆ ✍): soldier John Lund protects Nazi moll Marlene from the authorities until he falls for visiting congresswoman Jean Arthur.

•*No Highway in the Sky* (UK: *No Highway*) (Henry Koster 1951) (✍ ☆): Nevil Shute tale places Marlene and >James Stewart in a plane that he predicts is about to crash.

•*Rancho Notorious* (>Fritz Lang 1952) (☆): a cowboy masquerades as a badman hiding at Marlene's hostel for outlaws to find his fiancée's killer.

•*Black Fox* (Louis Clyde Stouman 1962) (■): Dietrich narrates this documentary on the rise of Hitler.

•*Just a Gigolo* (David Hemmings 1978): Marlene as the elderly patron of struggling Berlin gigolo David Bowie.

The Discreet Charm of the Bourgeoisie (Le Charme Discret de la Bourgeoisie) ☞ ☆ ■ ✍

France/Spain/Italy • Greenwich • 1972 • 105 mins • col

d >Luis Buñuel   w Luis Buñuel/Jean-Claude Carrière   ph Edmond Richmond, Fernando Rey, >Stéphane Audran, Delphine Seyrig, Bulle Ogier

Luis Buñuel spent his career condemning middle-class predilections for conformity and social respectability. In this late masterpiece,

winner of the Best Foreign Film Oscar, he finds a discreet charm in a group of diners' insistence on playing by the rules as they relentlessly search for a meal, despite such drawbacks as a dead patron, a restaurant without food, finding themselves seated on a stage without knowing their lines and the gunning-down of a gangster, while the irresistible temptation of sex in the garden demonstrates their child-like delight in breaking with convention. The biting barbs, presented in a bewildering blend of dream and bizarre reality, are almost fondly gentle, as if they are a thank you to his prey for 43 years of exceptional material.

 •Bourgeois ideology is more savagely attacked by a Maoist commune in *La Chinoise* (*The Chinese Girl*) (>Jean-Luc Godard 1967) (☞).

•The pointless lives of small town people are attacked in *The Firemen's Ball* (*Horí, Má Panenko*) (>Miloš Forman 1967) (☞ ✍).

•The naïveté of intellectuals >Alastair Sim and Roland Culver is exposed during question time on an army base in *Folly to Be Wise* (Frank Launder 1952) (☆).

•The revolutionary motivation of eight diverse characters is depicted in the frantic collage of ideas in *Jonah Who Will Be 25 in the Year 2000* (*Jonas Qui aura 25 ans en l'an 2000*) (Alain Tanner (☆ ■).

DIVORCE

The Awful Truth (>Leo McCarey 1937) ☆ ☞ ✍

This screwball comedy has >Cary Grant and Irene Dunne remarry – each other.

Background (US:*Edge of Divorce*) (Daniel Birt 1953) ☆

Valerie Hobson and Philip Friend stick it out for the children's sake.

Divorce American Style (Bud Yorkin 1967) ☆

Dick Van Dyke and Debbie Reynolds find they just can't live without the perpetual domestic duelling.

Divorce Italian Style (Divorzio All'Italiana)
(Pietro Germi 1961) ☆
>Marcello Mastroianni's method of divorce involves seduction and a crime of passion.
Faces **(John Cassavetes 1968)** ☆
Businessman John Marley resists divorcing Gena Rowlands because he is afraid of a lonely old age.
Gertrud **(Carl Dreyer, Denmark 1964)**
☞ ■ ✍
Having left her husband for a musician, Rena Pens Rode still fails to find the love she cherishes.
Love Crazy **(Jack Cummings 1941)** ☆
>William Powell feigns madness to prevent >Myrna Loy divorcing him, and is institutionalized to teach him a lesson.
Une Partie De Plaisir (aka Love Match) **(US: Pleasure Party)** **(>Claude Chabrol 1975)**
☞ ✍
A bullying husband demands his wife takes a lover; when she does he divorces her.
Shoot the Moon **(Alan Parker 1982)** ✍ ☆
Albert Finney and >Diane Keaton try to remain friends despite new partners.

Dr No ☆ ✍ ☞ ♫
GB • United Artists/EON • 1962 • 111 mins • col
d Terence Young w Richard Maibaum/Johanna Harwood/Berkely Mather ph Ted Moore m Monty Norman
>Sean Connery, Ursula Andress, Bernard Lee, Lois Maxwell

The film that introduced the watching world to Ian Fleming's 007 and made stars of Connery and Andress was an amusing, exciting spy thriller as opposed to the glitzy, gadget-ridden escapism that became synonymous with the subsequent series. Bond is sent to a Caribbean island to rout the world domination schemes of master criminal and SPECTRE agent, Dr No. Bond so obviously enjoyed completing his mission – wise-cracking double entendres, surviving Heath Robinson death plots, killing at will and seducing every available woman – that he has, with Dr Who-like rejuvenation,

avoided the suggested dotage of *Casino Royale* and insisted on repeating the formula.

• Moore Bond, this time with Roger swapping secrets with Barbara Bach in *The Spy Who Loved Me* (Lewis Gilbert 1977) (✍ ♫).
• Timothy Dalton's tougher Bond is sacked from the Secret Service and heads for South America to save CIA buddy Felix Leiter in *A Licence to Kill* (John Glen 1989).
• George C. Scott discovers that dolphins are being trained to assassinate the US President in >Mike Nichols' tale of underwater espionage *The Day of the Dolphin* (1973) (☞).
• James Mason delves into a Foreign Office suicide and uncovers spying in high places, in *The Deadly Affair* (>Sidney Lumet 1966) (☞ ☆ ✍), an adaptation of John Le Carré's *Call for the Dead*.
• Gene Hackman is Master Criminal Lex Luthor pitting his wits against Christopher Reeve's kryptonian strength in *Superman* (Richard Donner 1978) (✳).

Doctor Strangelove; or How I Learned to Stop Worrying and Love the Bomb ✍ ☞ ☆ ■
GB • Columbia • 1963 • 93 mins • b/w
d >Stanley Kubrick w Stanley Kubrick/Terry Southern/Peter George ph Gilbert Taylor m Laurie Johnson
Peter Sellers, George C. Scott, Sterling Hayden, Slim Pickens

Slim Pickens rodeoing his way to infinity on a nuclear warhead might have become the movie moment, but there are many other memorable images in Kubrick's disturbing nuclear black comedy. A large number of them are phallic because a Soviet water-poisoning plot imagined by General Jack D. Ripper has caused him to lose his sexual potency and it is his thirst for revenge that has placed the world on the verge of holocaust. It is bad enough that the planet's fate is in the hands of such macho hooligans, but when salvation depends on a semi-robotic lunatic, Strangelove (one of three marvellous Sellers portrayals), then laughter alone prevents despair. Fortunately it's not in short supply. The pay-phone/Coca-Cola machine sequence is poetic and I personally would have loved Kubrick to have slipped the proposed slapstick pie fight into the finale background.

•An accidental holocaust seems inevitable when a rogue bomber holds course for Moscow and US President >Henry Fonda prepares to doom New York for the sake of world peace in *Fail Safe* (>Sidney Lumet 1964) (✍ ☞ ☆).

•In *Seven Days in May* (John Frankenheimer 1964) (☞ ✍ ☆) disillusioned soldier Burt Lancaster threatens to detonate a stolen bomb unless President Richard Widmark reveals his corruption.

•The survivors of the big blast fall victim to their prejudices in *Five* (Arch Oboler 1951).

•Nuclear testing in Nevada places extra strain on war-disturbed Jon Voight and his family in *Desert Bloom* (Eugene Corr 1986) (☆).

•Private eye Mike Hammer (Ralph Meeker) prevents the theft of radio-active material in *Kiss Me Deadly* (Robert Aldrich 1955) (✍).

•Time is also running out for cop Nick Nolte and crook Eddie Murphy in *48 Hrs* (Walter Hill 1982) (✍).

DOCTORS

Black Friday (Arthur Lubin 1940) ☆ ✍
Surgeon >Boris Karloff gives academic >Bela Lugosi a dead mobster's brain to find hidden loot.

The Citadel (>King Vidor 1938) ☆ ☞
>Robert Donat as A. J. Cronin's GP who leaves Welsh mining ailments for Harley Street hypochondria.

Corridors of Blood (Robert Day 1958) ☆ ✍
The subjects for >Boris Karloff's anaesthesia experiments are supplied by grave-robber Christopher Lee.

Doctor in the House (Ralph Thomas 1954) ☆
Dirk Bogarde, Kenneth More and Donald Sinden stumble through medical school.
SERIES: all directed by Ralph Thomas; with Dirk Bogarde: *Doctor at Sea* (1955); *Doctor at Large*

(1957); *Doctor in Distress* (1963); with Michael Craig: *Doctor in Love* (1960); with Leslie Phillips: *Doctor in Clover* (1966); *Doctor in Trouble* (1970).

Dr Kildare's Wedding Day (UK:Mary Names the Day) (Harold S. Bucquet 1942)
Lew Ayres's fateful day sees tragedy come to Blair General Hospital and Lionel Barrymore's grouchy Dr Gillespie squeeze out a little sympathy.
SERIES: with Lew Ayres and Lionel Barrymore: 1938: *Young Dr Kildare*; 1939: *Calling Dr Kildare*; *The Secret of Dr Kildare*; 1940: *Dr Kildare's Strange Case*; *Dr Kildare Goes Home*; *Dr Kildare's Crisis*; 1941: *The People Vs Dr Kildare*; 1942: *Dr Kildare's Victory*; with Barrymore alone: 1942: *Calling Dr Gillespie*; *Dr Gillespie's New Assistant*; 1943: *Dr Gillespie's Criminal Case*; 1944: *Three Men in White*; *Between Two Women*; 1947: *Dark Delusion*.

Dr X (>Michael Curtiz 1932) ☞ ☆
Will journalist Lee Tracy discover the hospital killer and save Fay Wray before the next full moon?

The Ex-Mrs Bradford (Stephen Roberts 1936) ☆ ✍
Doctor >William Powell's ex-wife Jean Arthur embroils them both in a murder mystery.

House Calls (Howard Zieff 1978) ☆
Walter Matthau finds handling hospital bureaucracy only slightly more difficult than seducing Glenda Jackson.

Not as a Stranger (Stanley Kramer 1955) ☆ ☞
Robert Mitchum juggles his career and a romance with >Olivia De Havilland.

A Silent Duel) (Shizuka Naru Ketto) (>Akira Kurosawa 1947) ☆ ☞
A country doctor who becomes an army surgeon abandons his fiancée out of honour when a cut while operating gives him syphillis.

DOCUMENTARY

The Animals Film (Victor Schonfeld 1981) ☞ ✍
Julie Christie narrates this study of man's inhumanity to beast.

À Propos de Nice (Jean Vigo 1930) ☞ ■
Satirical comparison of the rich and poor on the French Riviera.
The Back of Beyond (John & Janet Heyer/Roland Robinson 1953) ■
A delivery man's 330-mile journey along the Birdsville Track between two Australian outback towns.
Cuba Si! (Chris Marker 1961) ☞ ■
The Cuban Revolution from Fidel Castro's coup in 1959 to the Bay of Pigs invasion of 1961.
Danish Blue (Gabriel Axel 1968)
Semi-spoof examination of the pornographic industry in Denmark.
A Diary for Timothy (Humphrey Jennings 1946) ☞
A father promises a Blitz baby that he will be brought up in a free world.
Don't Look Back (D. A. Pennyhacker 1967) ♫ ■
An arty, lively look at Bob Dylan's 1965 British tour.
Drifters (John Grierson 1929)
The life, work and danger of a North Sea trawling fleet.
Every Day Except Sunday (Lindsay Anderson 1957) ☞ ■
Life with the porters and stall-holders at the Covent Garden Flower Market.
The Fall of the Romanov Dynasty (*Padenye Dinastii Romanovykh*) (Esfir Shub 1927) ☞
The Russian Revolution told through newsreel footage edited into a narrative by a pioneering female director.
Farrebique (George Rouquier 1947) ☞ ■
A French peasant family's busiest time of year is marred by death.
The Great Road (*Veliky Put'*) (Esfir Shub 1927) ☞
Newsreels and reconstructions celebrate a decade of progress under Bolshevism.
The Hour of the Furnaces (*La Hora de los Hornos*) (Fernando E Solanas 1968) ☞
Interviews, newsreel footage and song trace the evolution of Argentina.
Housing Problems (Edgar Anstey/Arthur Elton 1935) ■
A study of the cramped and dilapidated houses in London's East End.

I Was a Fireman (aka *Fires Were Started*) (Humphrey Jennings 1943) ☞ ■
A London fire unit is called out to deal with a blaze during the Blitz.

Dogs

The Bar Sinister (US:*It's a Dog's Life*) (Herman Hoffman 1955) ✍
The autobiography of a bull terrier in the New York slums.
Benji (Joe Camp 1974)
An unwanted mongrel wins itself owners by rescuing their kidnapped children.
Digby: The Biggest Dog in the World (Joseph McGrath 1973) ✍
This Disney caper has Jim Dale and Spike Milligan on the trail of a dog enlarged by a vegetable growth chemical.
The Fox and the Hound (Art Stevens/Ted Berman/Richard Rich 1981) ✍ ■
An adorable Disney tale of animals brought up together who find themselves on opposite sides of a hunt.
Goodbye My Lady (>William Wellman 1956) ☞
A Mississippi boy befriends a dog, but, on discovering its value, can't decide whether to return it.
Greyfriars Bobby (Don Chaffey 1960) ✍
The touching story of an Edinburgh dog who remains faithful to his tramp master, even after death.
Lassie Come Home (Fred M. Wilcox 1943) ✍
The movies' most memorable mutt has adventures returning to Elizabeth Taylor after her folks can't afford to keep the dog.
Old Yeller (Robert Stevenson 1957) ✍
This Disney weepie has a young country boy's dog remain faithful through thick and thin.
One Hundred and One Dalmatians (Wolfgang Reitherman/Hamilton S. Luske/Clyde Geronimi 1961) ✍ ■
The Disney classic of valuable dogs fleeing the clutches of the wicked Cruella De Ville.
Owd Bob (US:*To the Victor*) (Robert Stevenson 1938) ✍
An obedient Lake District sheepdog is accused of brutal attacks on sheep.

Storm in a Teacup (Ian Dalrymple/Victor Saville 1937) ☆ ✍
>Vivien Leigh finds nationwide support for an old lady who has refused to buy a dog licence.

DOING TIME

The Ghost That Never Returns (*Prividenie, Kotoroe ne Vozvrashchaetsya*) (Abram Room, USSR 1929) ■
An imprisoned striker's life is endangered during his day's remission from a South American jail.
The Jackal of Nahueltoro (*El Chacal de Nahueltoro*) (Miguel Littín 1969) ☞ ✍ ☆
Mass murderer Nelson Villagra is re-educated in a Chilean jail and then shot.
Midnight Express (Alan Parker 1978) ☆ ☞ ✍ ♩
Drug smugglers Brad Davis and John Hurt endure the hardships of a Turkish prison.
Pardon Us (aka *Jailbirds*) (James Parrott 1931) ☆ ✍
>Laurel and Hardy disrupt prison teacher James Finlayson's lesson and then lead a jailbreak.
Republic of Sin (*La Fievre Monte a el Pao*) (>Luis Buñuel 1960) ☞ ☆
Idealist Gérard Philipe is forced to abandon his principles to keep order in a riotous island penitentiary.
Two Way Stretch (Robert Day 1960) ☆ ✍
Peter Sellers and vicar impersonator Wilfrid Hyde White plan their robbery during visiting time at Lionel Jeffries's jail.

La Dolce Vita (The Sweet Life)
☞ ☆ ■ ✍ ♩
Italy/France • Riama/Pathé • 1960 • 173 mins • b/w
d >Federico Fellini **w** Federico Fellini/Tullio Pinelli/Ennio Flaiano/Brunello Rondi **ph** Otello Martelli **m** Nino Rota
>Marcello Mastroianni, Anouk Aimée, Anita Ekberg, Alain Cuny

Coveting the intellectual reputation of a serious writer and the decadent delights of the idle rich, journalist Marcello Rubini (Mastroianni) jostles with the *paparazzi* after movie stars, flying statues of Christ and society celebrities by day and suffocates in an unsatisfactory relationship by night. When his role model, Steiner, kills his children and himself, Marcello realizes the implications of his cul-de-sac situation and plunges into a prolonged 'Lost Weekend' full of the excesses and degradations only Fellini could concoct. Bewitched, then destroyed by what lies on the other side of the fence, Marcello's plight was the director's fascinating Dantesque warning that Italy was still politically and socially prone to the false expectations that had resulted in Fascism.

•A poor little rich girl seeks a life away from her father's wishes in *Champagne* (>Alfred Hitchcock 1928) (☞).
•Tommy Steele's amorous adventures in high society lead to his humiliation in *Half-a-Sixpence* (George Sidney 1967) (✍♩), the musical version of H. G. Wells' novel *Kipps*.
•Idleness declines into decadence in ancient Rome in *Fellini Satyricon* (>Federico Fellini 1969) (■ ☞).
•Robert Redford tries to take the blame for bright young thing Mia Farrow's fatal road accident in the 1974 adaptation of F. Scott Fitzgerald classic *The Great Gatsby* (Jack Clayton) (✍ ☆), while Alan Ladd does the same for Betty Field in the lacklustre 1949 version (Elliott Nugent).

Donat, Robert
British actor (1905–1958)
Given elocution lessons to lose a Lancashire-accented stammer, the handsome Donat's asthma limited opportunities to build on the fame he found in some of the best British films of the period: >*The Private Life of Henry VIII* (Alexander Korda 1933) (☆ ✍ ☞ ■); *The Thirty-Nine Steps* (>Alfred Hitchcock 1935) (✍ ☞ ☆ ■) (a memory man holds the key to the murder for which Donat is the chief suspect); *The Ghost Goes West* (>René Clair 1936) (☞ ✍ ☆) (Donat as a Scottish ghost suffering homesickness when his castle is moved to the USA); *The Citadel* (>King Vidor 1938) (☆ ☞)

(doctor Donat suffers qualms of conscience having left the exhausting demands made by the Welsh valleys for Harley Street luxury) and >*Goodbye Mr Chips* (AA: Sam Wood 1939) (☆ ☞ ✍ ■). Other films were made in the brief postwar breaks in his debilitating illness – *The Winslow Boy* (>Anthony Asquith 1948) (Donat's lawyer defends the young naval recruit who has been abandoned by all but his father Cedric Hardwicke during his trial for petty theft) and *Lease of Life* (Charles Frend 1951) (☆ ✍) (vicar Donat spends the last year of his life solving the problems of his parishioners).

 •*The Count of Monte Cristo* (Rowland V. Lee 1934) (☞ ☆): the Alexandre Dumas adventure has Donat as an escaped nobleman out to pay back the man who framed him, Louis Calhern.

•*Knight without Armour* (Jacques Feyder 1937) (☆): James Hilton tale of a Russian countess >Marlene Dietrich avoiding the Red Army through the help of translator Donat.

•*Young Mr Pitt* (>Carol Reed 1942) (☆ ☞ ✍): the conduct of the Napoleonic Wars and an addiction to port ushers Britain's youngest Prime Minister (Donat) to an early grave.

•*Perfect Strangers* (US: *Vacation from Marriage*) (Alexander Korda 1945) (☆ ✍): weak-willed couple Donat and Deborah Kerr learn to stand up for themselves on active service.

•*The Magic Box* (John Boulting 1951): Donat heads the British star cast in this biopic of the pioneer film-maker William Friese-Greene.

•*The Inn of the Sixth Happiness* (Mark Robson 1958) (☆ ■): Chinese mandarin Donat helps missionary >Ingrid Bergman lead children across the mountains away from war danger and Curt Jurgens.

Donen, Stanley
American director (b 1924)

Arriving in Hollywood as a choreographer, Donen worked with >Gene Kelly on *Anchors Aweigh* (George Sidney 1945) (☆ ♫) (sailors Kelly and Frank Sinatra meet a small boy who wants to go to sea and fall for his auntie), *Take Me Out to the Ball Game* (UK: *Everybody's Cheering*) (Busby Berkeley 1949) (✍ ☞) (Kelly

rebels against Esther Williams managing his baseball team: Sinatra aims to become coach's pet), >*On the Town* (1949) (♫ ☆ ☞ ✍) and >*Singin' in the Rain* (1952) (♫ ☆ ✍ ☞ ■) (the latter being two Donen/Kelly co-directed) and with Fred Astaire on *Funny Face* (1957) (☆ ☞) (fashion photographer Fred turns gauche bookseller Audrey Hepburn into a cover girl). Subsequently, Donen has attempted, with much distinctive style but mixed success, stage adaptations – *Seven Brides for Seven Brothers* (1954) (♫) (Howard Keel's brothers raid a village for wives in a film beloved in its day but now surely unforgivable) and *The Pajama Game* (1957) (☞ ☆) (rag trade rep Doris Day prefers canoodling to negotiating with boss's rep) – as well as the >Hitchcock-inspired thrillers, *Charade* (1963) (☆ ☞ ✍) (in search of her husband's fortune, Audrey Hepburn is uncertain whether to trust Walter Matthau or >Cary Grant) and *Arabesque* (1964) (☞) (academic Gregory Peck's mission to decipher an ancient manuscript is threatened by violent vested interests) and romantic comedies such as *Indiscreet* (1958) (☆ ✍) (>Ingrid Bergman decides to teach >Cary Grant a lesson for avoiding marriage), *The Grass is Greener* (1960) (☞ ☆) (aristocrat >Cary Grant's fuddiness drives Deborah Kerr into the arms of stately home tourist Robert Mitchum) and *Two for the Road* (1967) (☞ ✍) (Frederic Raphael's script has Albert Finney and Audrey Hepburn reviewing their marriage on a French motoring tour).

 •*Royal Wedding* (UK: *Wedding Bells*) (1951): while putting on a show in London >Fred Astaire falls in love.

•*Give a Girl a Break* (1953): another 'just-one-audition-from-stardom' chance for three aspiring girls.

•*Deep in My Heart* (1954) (☆): Jose Ferrer as songwriter Sigmund Romberg is helped to fame by Paul Henreid and Merle Oberon.

•*It's Always Fair Weather* (co-directed with >Gene Kelly 1955) (☞ ✍): Kelly's army colleagues are reunited for a soppy TV show and by the end of the night have settled their differences.

•*Damn Yankees* (UK: *What Lola Wants*) (1958) (☞): a baseball fan sells his soul to get results for his team.

•*Bedazzled* (1967) (☆): Devil Peter Cook allows Dudley Moore to sample the deadly sins in return for his soul.

•*Staircase* (1969): gay hairdressers >Richard Burton and Rex Harrison bemoan their lot and missed opportunities.

•*Blame it On Rio* (1984) (☆): afflicted by holiday menopause blues, >Michael Caine can't resist the advances of his best friend's teenage daughter.

DOOMED LOVE

An Affair to Remember (>Leo McCarey 1957) ☆ ☞
Deborah Kerr fails to keep her rendezvous with shipboard lover >Cary Grant.

Elvira Madigan (Bo Widerberg 1967) ☞ ✍
A circus performer and an army officer's adultery is so frowned upon by 19th-century Swedish society that they are driven to suicide.

Escape Me Never (Paul Czinner 1935) ☞ ☆
Single mother Elisabeth Bergner loses her beloved composer to Penelope Dudley Ward.

The Forty First (Sorok Pervyi) (Yakov Protazanov 1927) ☆
A Red Army heroine is caught between duty and her love for a White Army prisoner.

Les Jeux Sont Faits (The Chips Are Down) (Jean Delannoy 1947) ✍
Jean-Paul Sartre's script gives dead lovers a day to make love in order to regain life.

The Lacemaker (La Dentellière) (Claude Goretta 1977) ☆ ✍
Hairdresser Isabelle Huppert has too little in common with her rich student lover.

Lady Jane (Trevor Nunn 1987) ☆ ■ ✍
Helena Bonham Carter and Cary Elwes as Lady Jane Grey and Guildford Dudley, political pawns against Mary Tudor.

My Way Home (Igy Jottem) (Miklos Jansco 1964) ☆
After nomadic misadventures at the close of WWII, a Hungarian befriends a wounded Russian soldier who has been forced into cowherding.

Sid and Nancy (Alex Cox 1986) ♫ ☆
Gary Oldman and Chloe Webb as punk rocker Sid Vicious and his addict girlfriend Nancy Spungen.

Summer with Monika (US:Monika) (Sommaren Med Monika) (>Ingmar Bergman 1952) ☞ ■
A naïve boy's love for a tearaway girl results in his becoming a single father.

The Way We Were (Sydney Pollack 1973) ☆ ✍
Robert Redford and Barbra Streisand's career ambitions outgrow their romance.

DOSTOYEVSKY, FYODOR

The Brothers Karamazov (Richard Brooks 1958) ✍ ☞

The Brothers Karamazov (aka The Murder of Dmitri Karamazov) (Bratya Karamazovy) (Ivan Pyriev 1968) ☞ ■
One of the three brothers is guilty of patricide, but the wrong one is tried.

Crime and Punishment (>Josef Von Sternberg 1935 ☞ ☆/Pierre Chenal 1935 ☆/Georges Lampin 1956) ☆
Respectively >Peter Lorre, Pierre Blanchar (Best Actor Venice) and Robert Hossein as the impoverished student Raskolnikov, conscience stricken after murdering a pawnbroker.

The Eternal Husband (L'Homme au Chapeau Rond) (Pierre Billon 1946) ☆ ✍
Embittered widower Trusotsky (Raimu) detests his wife's lover and their love child.

Four Nights of a Dreamer (Quatre Nuits d'un Reveur) (>Robert Bresson 1971) ■ ☞
A variation of *White Nights*: an artist helps a woman over her desertion, but loses her himself when her lover returns.

The Gambler (Karel Reisz 1975) ☆
James Caan as a Russian literature teacher driven by Dostoyevsky's story of a compulsive gambler.

The Great Sinner (Robert Siodmak 1949) ✍
Gregory Peck's potential as a novelist is dissipated by his love of the tables.

The Idiot (Georges Lampin 1946) (*L'Idiot*) ☞/(Ivan Pyriev 1957) (*Nastasia Filipovna*) ✍

Charitable noble Prince Mishkin's interest in Nastasia Filipovna is misinterpreted by her guardian and her lover.

White Nights (>Luchino Visconti 1957) (*Le Notti Bianche*) ☞ ☆ /(Ivan Pyriev 1959) (*Beliye Nochi*) ☞

>Marcello Mastroianni and Oleg Strizhenov respectively dream of chivalry towards a girl who dreams of her lover's return.

Douglas, Kirk

(Issur Danielovitch [later Demsky]) American actor (b 1916)

Waiting tables and wrestling to fund his degree, Douglas' honest style was showcased in a number of tough guy roles, where aims are achieved through ruthless manipulation: *Champion* (AAN: Mark Robson 1949) (☆ ✍) (single-minded boxer Douglas dies alone in the ring); *Ace in the Hole* (aka *The Big Carnival*) (>Billy Wilder 1951) (☞ ✍ ☆) (journalist Douglas manipulates the rescue of a man in an abandoned mine to his paper's advantage); *The Bad and the Beautiful* (AAN: >Vincente Minnelli 1953) (☆ ☞) (the film people he has abused talk about their experience of ruthless producer, Kirk) and *Two Weeks in Another Town* (>Vincente Minnelli 1962) (>Edward G. Robinson gives drunk director Kirk one more chance, but old habits die hard). More than capable of sensitive characterizations – *A Letter to Three Wives* (>Joseph L. Mankiewicz 1949) (✍ ☞ ☆) (Kirk as one of three husbands suspected of fooling around with the local spitfire), *Lust for Life* (>Vincente Minnelli 1956) (☆ ☞) (Douglas as the mentally unstable artist Vincent Van Gogh) and *Strangers When We Meet* (Richard Quine 1960) (Douglas's Beverly Hills architect has an affair with Kim Novak) – he was more usually a rugged hero in Westerns such as *The Big Sky* (>Howard Hawks 1952) (■) (pioneers following the Missouri river are attacked by Indians), *Gunfight at the OK Corral* (John Sturges 1957) (☆) (Kirk as drunken Doc Holliday to Burt Lancaster's sheriff Wyatt Earp) and *Lonely Are the Brave* (David Miller

1962) (☆) (Douglas's Wild West badman is run out of town by a flying posse); in epics such as *The Vikings* (Richard Fleischer 1958) (☆ ☞ ■) (one-eyed Kirk and Tony Curtis in a power struggle for Northumbria and Janet Leigh) and *Spartacus* (>Stanley Kubrick 1960) (☞ ☆) (Kirk as the slave who led a revolt against the might of the Roman Empire); and war stories, *Paths of Glory* (>Stanley Kubrick 1957) (☆ ☞ ■) (Douglas defends three World War I soldiers at their court martial before Adolphe Menjou), *Seven Days in May* (John Frankenheimer 1964) (☞ ✍ ☆) (Kirk discovers mad military man Burt Lancaster's coup plot against >Fredric March) and *Is Paris Burning?* (René Clément 1966) (✍) (Kirk as General George Patton in a re-creation of the liberation of Paris).

 • *The Strange Love of Martha Ivers* (Lewis Milestone 1946) (✍ ☆): >Barbara Stanwyck is concerned that her husband Van Heflin will discover her murderous past when old beau Kirk hits town.

• *Young Man With a Horn* (UK: *Young Man of Music*) (>Michael Curtiz 1949) (♫ ☆): factional re-creation of the life of Bix Beiderbecke.

• *Along the Great Divide* (>Raoul Walsh 1951) (✍): Kirk saves Walter Brennan from the gallows in this Western whodunnit.

• *Detective Story* (>William Wyler 1951) (☞ ☆ ✍): Kirk is so furious that his wife Eleanor Parker once slept with a gangster that he can barely concentrate on beating up crooks.

• *The List of Adrian Messinger* (>John Huston 1963) (☞ ☆ ✍): Kirk involved in a whodunnit that also offers a game of whoisit as disguised stars Robert Mitchum, Frank Sinatra, Burt Lancaster and Tony Curtis fool cop George C. Scott.

• *Cast a Giant Shadow* (Melville Shavelson 1966): disappointed that World War II was over so soon, Kirk goes to Palestine to help the Israeli cause.

• *There Was a Crooked Man* (>Joseph L. Mankiewicz 1970) (☆): Kirk wants to recover his loot and enjoy it, but >Henry Fonda's lawman keeps getting in the way.

• *The Fury* (Brian De Palma 1978) (✍): Kirk

tries to rescue his ESP son whom John Cassavetes hopes to use for evil political gain.

Douglas, Michael
American actor/producer (b 1945)

Failing to make an impression in Disney's 'one boy and his lion' adventure *Napoleon and Samantha* (Bernard McEveety 1972) (when Douglas's grandpa dies, he runs away from home), Douglas preferred a TV role in *The Streets of San Francisco* to cinema acting, although he won a Best Picture Oscar producing >*One Flew Over the Cuckoo's Nest* (>Miloš Forman 1975) (☆ ✍ ☞). He was rehabilitated to movie screens in *Coma* (Michael Crichton 1978) (Geneviève Bujold and Douglas uncover the fact that Richard Widmark comatoses patients and uses them for transplants) and *The China Syndrome* (James Bridges 1979) (TV news crew Douglas and >Jane Fonda question the safety of >Jack Lemmon's nuclear plant), and he won fame in *Romancing the Stone* (Robert Zemeckis 1984) (☆ ✍) (>Kathleen Turner's romantic novelist is rescued in South America by ungallant adventurer Douglas) and *Jewel of the Nile* (Lewis Teague 1985) (☆) (this time Turner is rescued in the Middle East by Douglas). *Fatal Attraction* (Adrian Lyne 1987) (Douglas's fling with Glenn Close haunts him and wife Anne Archer) made him a superstar, and *Wall Street* (AA: Oliver Stone 1987) (☆) (Douglas proves to ambitious stockbroker Charlie Sheen that nice guys get nowhere) put him 2–0 up on his father, with time on his side.

•*Summertree* (Anthony Newley 1971) (☆): student Douglas goes to Vietnam.

•*The Star Chamber* (Peter Hyams 1982): Douglas as a member of a secret court of judges punishing injustice, until his conscience pricks him.

•*A Chorus Line* (>Richard Attenborough 1985) (☆♫): Broadway producer Douglas casts his show by relaxing the auditioners into playing their true selves.

•*Black Rain* (Ridley Scott 1989): Douglas as a tough cop in Japan paying more than just a nod to *House of Bamboo* (Samuel Fuller 1955).

Dovzhenko, Alexander
Soviet director (1894–1956)

Bathing the Soviet countryside in soft light, Dovzhenko's classic films – *Arsenal* (1929) (☞) (events on the home and battle fronts inspire revolution in the Ukraine), *Earth* (*Zemlya*) (1930) (☞ ■) (Ukrainian kulaks are panicked into murder when progressive peasants plan to buy a tractor) and *Ivan* (1932) (☞) (working on a dam has different effects on three labourers called Ivan) – painted romantic pictures of rural life, rather than propagandizing the progress of collectivization, although Dovzhenko's films do have political content, particularly *Shors* (*Shchors*) (1939) (in a film made at Stalin's own request, a Ukrainian academic liberates Kiev and educates his soldiers), a study of revolutionary intellectualism. During World War II, he made documentaries such as the snappily titled *Victory in Right-Bank Ukraine and the Expulsion of the Germans from the Boundaries of the Ukrainian Soviet Earth* (*Pobeda Na Pravoberezhnoi Ukraine Tiznanie Nemetskikh Zakhvatchikov Za Predeli Ukrainskikh Sovetskikh Zemel*) (1945).

•*Zvenigora* (1928): poetically filmed semi-documentary on the lives of rural peasants.

•*Aerograd* (*Frontier*) (1935) (☞): Japanese agents attempt to destroy a new airbase town in Siberia.

•*Michurin* (1948): biopic of a leading Soviet horticulturalist.

Dracula (☞ ☆ ■ ✍)
USA • Universal • 1931 • 84 mins • b/w

d Tod Browning   w Garrett Fort   ph Karl Freund   m Tchaikovsky
>Bela Lugosi, Helen Chandler, Dwight Frye, Edward Van Sloan

Imitated numerous times but never bettered, this is the seminal corruption of Bram Stoker's novel, although *Count Dracula* (*El Conde Dracula*) (Jesus Franco 1970) can boast the only authentic, moustachioed Count. Bela Lugosi's Hungarian accent, sinister elegance and hypnotic eyes make him the perfect, irresistibly charming vampire, whose Transylvanian title gains him access to the homes of Whitby's socially ambitious. The scenes at Castle Dracula may be clumsy reproductions of those in >F. W. Murnau's *Nosferatu* (1922) (☞ ■ ☆) and Renfield's lust for flies is more comic than demonic, but the overall effect is still frightening and there is genuinely evil menace in Lugosi's slow, seductive conquests.

•The colour of blood adds to Hammer's gory version of *Dracula* (US: *Horror of Dracula*) (Terence Fisher 1958) (☆) with Christopher Lee as the Count and Peter Cushing as Van Helsing.
•Female fangs get to work, largely on female victims in *The Hunger* (Tony Scott 1983) (☆ ■)when >Catherine Deneuve fights off ageing by feeding off the blood of David Bowie and Susan Sarandon and in *The Vampire Lovers* (Roy Ward Baker 1970) (✍), in which Peter Cushing seeks to stake out Ingrid Pitt's Carmilla Karnstein, the heroine of Sheridan Le Fanu's prototype vampire novel *Carmilla*.
•The legend was spoofed in *Blacula* (William Crain 1972), in which African prince William Marshall revives 150 years after he first realized Dracula was a pain in the neck and in *Love at First Bite* (Stan Dragoti 1979), which has George Hamilton as a modern Count whose idea of night life includes something in a lighter vein than bloodsucking.
•Barbara Steele's wicked witch resurrects to torment her executors in an adaptation of Nikolai Gogol's story of the living dead *Black Sunday* (Mario Bava 1960).

DREAMS AND DREAMERS

Billy Liar (>John Schlesinger 1963) ☞ ☆ ✍ ■
Tom Courtenay daydreams through work at a funeral parlour, two engagements, a family death and a proposal from Julie Christie.

Dead of Night (Alberto Cavalcanti/Charles Crichton/Robert Hamer/Basil Dearden 1945) ☞ ☆ ✍
Nightmares trouble an architect during psy-

chotherapy; he cures them by killing the psychiatrist.
Give My Regards to Broad Street (Peter Webb 1986) ♫
Paul McCartney searches for album tapes apparently stolen by a reformed crook, sings some excellent songs and wakes to find. . .
Hour of the Wolf (Vargtimmen) (>Ingmar Bergman 1967) ☆ ☞
Liv Ullmann tends artist Max Von Sydow during a bout of hallucinations.
I've Heard the Mermaids Singing (Patricia Rozema 1987) ☆ ☞ ✍
A gallery assistant's heroine-worship daydreams are shattered as she proves to be a sham.
Night Beauties (US:Beauties of the Night) (Les Belles de Nuit) (>René Clair 1952) ☞
A shy musician dreams of deeds of chivalry throughout the ages.
The Secret Life of Walter Mitty (Norman Z. McLeod 1947) ☆
Danny Kaye enjoys dreaming of brave deeds more than he does performing them following >Boris Karloff's robbery.
White Nights (Le Notti Bianche) (>Luchino Visconti 1957) ☞ ☆
Inspired by dreams of heroism, a young man saves a girl from suicide, but there is no happy ending.

DROP OUTS

All Night Long (Toute une Nuit) (Jean-Claude Tramont 1981) ☆
A couple drift into a one-night stand and drift away again.
Bartleby (Anthony Friedman 1970) ✍
Paul Scofield attempts to discern why John McEnery has retired into his shell.
Charles, Dead or Alive (Charles Mort ou Vif) (Alain Tanner, 1969) ☆
A Swiss watchmaker drops out and becomes so apathetic that he consents to being committed to an asylum.
Easy Rider (Dennis Hopper 1969) ☆
Biking their way across the USA, Hopper and Peter Fonda introduce crook lawyer >Jack Nicholson to wacky baccy.

Ferris Bueller's Day Off (John Hughes 1986)
Arrogant schoolboy Matthew Broderick doesn't let the fact that he knows no one in any of the right places spoil his day.

The History of Mr Polly (**Anthony Pelissier 1949**) ☆ ✍
Tired of his humdrum marriage, draper John Mills enjoys pottering around in a country pub.

I Love You, Alice B. Toklas (**Hy Averback 1968**) ☆
Peter Sellers packs in the law and wears a flower in his hair.

Lost in America (**Albert Brooks 1985**)
Middle-class Brooks and Julie Haggerty set off on their *Easy Rider*-inspired jaunt in a luxury-camper.

The Rain People (**>Francis Ford Coppola 1969**) ☆
Pregnant housewife Shirley Knight absconds to decide whether she wants her child or its father.

Sullivan's Travels (**>Preston Sturges 1941**) ☞ ✍ ☆
Film-maker Joel McCrea is tired of comedy and, disguised as a tramp, seeks the serious side of life.

Travelling North (**Carl Schultz 1988**) ☆ ☞
Leo McKern retires to remote northern Australia to the disgust of his townie daughter.

Drowning By Numbers
✍ ☞ ☆ ♫ ▓

GB • Film Four International/Elsevier Vendex Film • 1988 • 118 mins • col
wd Peter Greenaway   ph Sasha Verney
m Michael Nyman
Joan Plowright, Juliet Stevenson, Joely Richardson, Bernard Hill, Jason Edwards

Take John Lennon's advice from *Tomorrow Never Knows* and 'Turn off your mind, relax and float downstream', for if you try to analyse this gorgeous film too closely, you could do yourself brain damage. Three women (Plowright, Stevenson and Richardson), all called Cissy Colpitt, murder their husbands and blackmail idle coroner Majid (Hill) into passing unincriminating verdicts, much to the delight of his ghoulish son Smut who collects deaths.

There are more number games here than in a lifetime of *Sesame Street*, some chokingly funny sight gags and a bewildering array of images, all so softly photographed that we believe ourselves to be witnessing an Arcadia, not a flagrant disregard for the law or a series of cruel crimes. If Peter Greenaway wants to take over where >Buñuel left off, that's fine by me.

• More small children obsessed with death are the two who build an animal cemetery in occupied France in *Forbidden Games* (aka *The Secret Game*) (*Jeux Interdits*) (René Clément 1952) (✍ ☞ ☆).

• Another lonely child faced with the disintegration of the family home is Luciano De Ambrosis in *The Children Are Watching Us* (*I Bambini ci Guardano*) (>Vittorio De Sica 1943) (☞ ☆).

• It's only when Burt Lancaster gets out of the swimming pools of his rich neighbours that he finds it tough to stay afloat in *The Swimmer* (Frank Perry/Sydney Pollack 1968) (✍ ▉).

• Swimming also made the names of the Australian Annette Kellerman and Esther Williams the latter playing the former in the factional biopic *Million Dollar Mermaid* (UK: *The One-Piece Bathing Suit*) (>Mervyn Le Roy 1952).

• Jean-Pierre Léaud is obsessed with three women, one sexually and two politically in *Masculine-Feminine* (*Masculin-Feminin*) (>Jean-Luc Godard 1966) (☞).

• Three women from different ages and backgrounds – 1895 aristocratic; 1932 bourgeois and 1969 worker – but with the same name are the subject of *Lucia* (Humberto Solas 1969) (✍).

• Winona Ryder and Christian Slater attempt to break the high school hegemony of three identically named teen-bitches, in *Heathers* (Michael Lehmann 1989) (✍ ☆).

DRUGS

Blue Velvet (**David Lynch 1986**) ☆
Pusher Dennis Hopper makes club singer Isabella Rossellini pay for her fixes in brutal sex.

Christiane F. (Ulrich Edel 1981) ☞
A teenage Berliner, unable to endure cold turkey, turns to prostitution to finance her habit.

The Connection (Shirley Clarke 1961)
A series of 'Beat' improvisations keep addicts amused until fix-time.

The Courier (Joe Lee/Frank Deasy 1988) ☆
Ian Bannen pursues drug baron Gabriel Byrne across Dublin.

The French Connection (William Friedkin 1971) ☆ ✍
Gene Hackman as cop Popeye Doyle on to a drugs ring in Marseilles.

Jeanne Eagels (George Sidney 1957) ☆
Kim Novak in the biopic title role of a Broadway dance star unable to quit a fatal addiction.

The Lineup (Don Siegel 1958) ☞
Semi-documentary policier depicts the San Francisco drug squad in action.

The Man with the Golden Arm (Otto Preminger 1956) ☞ ☆
Frank Sinatra as a card sharp who begins to lose his touch through his heroin addiction.

Who'll Stop the Rain? (UK: *Dog Soldiers*) (Karel Reisz 1978)
Nick Nolte smuggles drugs on his return from Vietnam, but the gangsters he sold it to want more.

Drunks

Barfly (Barbet Schroeder 1987)
Mickey Rourke and Faye Dunaway would get more drinking in if they shouted less in this portrait of poet Charles Bukowski.

Come Back Little Sheba (Daniel Mann 1952) ☆ ☞
Shirley Booth (AA) is more concerned about her missing dog than about Burt Lancaster's attempts to quit drinking.

Come Fill the Cup (Gordon Douglas 1951) ☆
Alcoholism surrounds journalist >James Cagney; he beats the bottle, but it involves his boss's son Gig Young with gangster Raymond Massey.

The Country Girl (George Seaton 1954) ☆ ✍
Bing Crosby's back on the booze as his sobered up comeback is hijacked by William Holden's interest in his wife Grace Kelly.

The Cure (>Charles Chaplin 1917) ☆
Guests at a health hotel are enlivened when Charlie drops liquor into the spa.

Days of Wine and Roses (Blake Edwards 1962) ☆
>Jack Lemmon drives Lee Remick to drink, but when he dries out, she is left high and dry.

Le Feu Follet (US: *The Fire Within*) (aka *Will O'the Wisp*) (aka *A Time To Live and a Time To Die*) (>Louis Malle 1963) ☆ ☞
A drunken writer gives his friends the chance to prevent his suicide, an offer they choose to refuse.

Herr Puntila and His Servant Matti (*Herr Puntila und Sein Knecht Matti*) (Alberto Cavalcanti, Austria 1955)
A millionaire is benevolent drunk and tyrannical sober, in this Bertolt Brecht play based on a character in >Chaplin's *City Lights*.

I'll Cry Tomorrow (Daniel Mann 1955) ☆
Susan Hayward pulls out all the stops as well as the corks in this biopic of 1930s star Lillian Roth.

The Lost Weekend (>Billy Wilder 1945) ☞ ✍ ☆
Ray Milland as the depressed writer who can only see the future through the bottom of a glass while on a weekend bender.

Duck Soup ☆ ☞ ✍
USA • Paramount • 1933 • 68 mins • b/w
d >Leo McCarey w Bert Kalmar/Harry Ruby/Arthur Sheekman/Nat Perrin
  ph Henry Sharp m/ly Bert Kalmar/Harry Ruby
>The Marx Brothers (Groucho, Chico, Harpo, Zeppo), Margaret Dumont, Louis Calhern, Edgar Kennedy

Just as *A Night at the Opera* (Sam Wood 1935) (✍ ☆) (the brothers cause mayhem while working for an opera company) is too thin to be a genuine satire of artistic pretention, *Duck Soup* can't really claim that its political content is anything other than an excuse for a series of dazzling visual jokes and acerbic verbal cracks. But here profound statement would have been an unwelcome intrusion. Groucho's elevation to power in Freedonia confounds the maxim that absolute power corrupts absolutely, because he is already a Grade A charlatan and proud of it. While Harpo and Chico work for and against the state, Groucho – whose dialogue is a catalogue of wish-I'd-said-that insults – rules with hilarious tyranny, for example refusing an armistice because the battlefield rent was paid in advance. Exhausting fun.

 •Peter Sellers finds himself in all departments of state as another imaginary nation goes to war in *The Mouse That Roared* (Jack Arnold 1959) (☆).
•Cinema owner Oskar Homolka is the enemy within London in *Sabotage* (US: *A Woman Alone*) (>Alfred Hitchcock 1936) (☞ ✍).
•Temporary tyranny afflicts Max Dearly, the millionaire who has saved his state from bankruptcy in *The Last Millionaire* (*La Dernière Milliardaire*) (>René Clair 1934) (☞).
•The relationship between the Fascist dictators Hitler (Adenoid Hynkel, Dictator of Ptomania) and Mussolini (Benzini Napaloni, Dictator of Bacteria) is lampooned in *The Great Dictator* (>Charles Chaplin 1940).

DU MAURIER, DAPHNE

The Birds (>Alfred Hitchcock 1963) ☞ ▓
Birds exhibit inexplicably violent behaviour in a small coastal town.

Don't Look Now (Nicolas Roeg 1973) ☞ ☆ ▓
Donald Sutherland and Julie Christie go to Venice to try and forget their recently drowned daughter.

Frenchman's Creek (Mitchell Leisen 1944) ✍ ☆
>Basil Rathbone drives >Joan Fontaine into the arms of a French pirate in 17th-century Cornwall.

Hungry Hill (Brian Desmond Hurst 1946) ✍
Jean Simmons, Margaret Lockwood and Dennis Price are among those prolonging an Irish feud over three generations, in this Du Maurier script.

Jamaica Inn (>Alfred Hitchcock 1939) ✍ ☆ ☞
Orphan Maureen O'Hara is adopted by smuggler >Charles Laughton in Regency Cornwall.

My Cousin Rachel (Henry Koster 1952) ✍
>Olivia De Havilland as the mysterious woman who turns >Richard Burton's suspicions into adoration.

>Rebecca (>Alfred Hitchcock 1940) ☞ ☆ ▓ ✍ ♫

The Scapegoat (Robert Hamer 1959) ✍
>Alec Guinness finds himself guilty of a murder that his aristocratic lookalike has committed.

The Years Between (Compton Bennett 1946) ✍ ☆
An adaptation of the Du Maurier play in which Michael Redgrave returns from war to find that wife Valerie Hobson now holds his seat in Parliament.

EARLY FILMS

The Conquest of the Pole (La Conquête du Pôle) (Georges Méliès 1912) ☞

A spaceship, a balloon and a car race to the frozen wastes only to be eaten by a giant, fall into the ice or freeze.

The Dream of a Rarebit Fiend (Edwin S. Porter 1906) ☞ ✳

A man pays the price for eating too close to bedtime.

The Great Train Robbery (Edwin S. Porter 1903)

Boarding at a telegraph office, baddies rob the train only to perish in a desert shoot out.

The Life of an American Fireman (Edwin S. Porter 1903) ☞

A fireman, dreaming of his wife and child, is forced to rescue them from a blaze

Rescued From an Eagle's Nest (Edwin S. Porter 1907)

Lumberjack >D.W. Griffith rescues a baby from an eyrie.

A Skater's Debut (Max Linder 1905) ☆

Famous French comic film-maker has trouble finding his feet on the ice.

The Trip To The Moon (Le Voyage dans la Lune) (Georges Méliès 1902)

Elderly explorers have adventures on the moon having landed in its eye.

Uncle Tom's Cabin (Edwin S. Porter 1903)

Spirited version of Harriet Beecher Stowe's anti-slavery novel.

EASTERN EUROPE

Eroica (Heroism) (Andrzej Munk, Poland 1957) ✍

Two stories: a petty crook finds his role within the Resistance; and POWs taunt Nazis into believing that there's been an escape.

Closely Observed Trains (US: Closely Watched Trains) (Ostre Sledované Vlaky) (Jiří Menzel, Czechoslovakia 1966) ☞ ✍

A young train driver on a lonely branch line tries to lose his virginity.

Knife in the Water (Noz w Wodzie) (>Roman Polanski Poland 1962) ☞ ☆

A husband has to compete for his wife's affections with a stranger they invite on their sailing holiday.

The Lost Forest (aka *The Forest of the Hanged*) (aka *Forest of Hanged Men*) (Liviu Ciulei, Rumania 1965) ☞ ✍

The director won the best direction award at Cannes for this story of the refusal of a soldier in the Austro-Hungarian army to kill his countrymen.

The Party and the Guests (US: *A Report on the Party and the Guests*) (*O Slavnosti a Hostech*) (Jan Nemec, Czechoslovakia 1966) ✍

When guests at a party discover that one man isn't enjoying it, they hunt him with vicious dogs.

The Red and the White (*Csillagosok, Katonák*) (Miklós Jancsó, Hungary/USSR 1968) ✍

A band of Hungarians fight for the Red Army against the Tsarist forces.

Stars (*Sterne*) (Konrad Wolf, East Germany/Bulgaria 1959) ✍ ☆

A Nazi death camp guard attempts to save the girl he has fallen for.

Stone Wedding (*Nunta de Pietra*) (Mircea Veroiu/Dan Pita, Rumania 1973) ✍

Two tales: a poor woman saves to bury her daughter in a wedding gown; and a fiddler runs off with the bride.

Stronger Than the Night (*Stärker als die Nacht*) (Slatan Dudow, East Germany 1954) ✍

A Communist suffers at the hands of the Nazis and the German partisans.

The Switchboard Operator (aka *The Tragedy of a Switchboard Operator*) (US: *Love Affair*) (aka *The Case of the Missing Switchboard Operator*) (aka *An Affair of the Heart*) (*Ljubavni Slueaj*) (*Tragedija Sluzbenice P.T.T.*) (Dušan Makavejev, Yugoslavia 1967)

A telephonist is accidentally killed by her Turkish lover during a row over the postman.

The Thistles of Baragan (*Ciulinii Baraganului*) (Louis Daquin, Rumania 1957 ✍)

A true tale of the brutal repression of a 1907 peasant rebellion.

Those Wonderful Movie Cranks (Jirí Menzel, Czechoslovakia 1978)

An itinerant Czech projectionist establishes Prague's first cinema.

WR – Mysteries of the Organism (*WR – Misterije Organizma*) (Dušan Makavejev, Yugoslavia 1971)

Semi-documentary study of the sexual theories of Wilhelm Reich.

Eastwood, Clint
American actor/director (b 1930)

Lumberjack, swimming instructor and undistinguished bit-part player before TV's *Rawhide* (1958–1965), Eastwood made his name as 'The Man with No Name' in Sergio Leone's spaghetti western trilogy *A Fistful of Dollars* (1964) (☞ ☆), *For A Few Dollars More* (1965) (☆) and *The Good, the Bad and the Ugly* (1966) (♫ ☆). Subsequently, his selection of films evoked a wrier, more politically astute >John Wayne: WESTERNS: *High Plains Drifter* (also directed 1973) (Hiring man-with-no-name Clint to protect a town proves akin to putting a fox in a chicken coop), *The Outlaw Josey Wales* (also directed 1976) (Clint exacts a brutal revenge on the rapists of his wife) and *Pale Rider* (also directed 1985) (an angel with no name protects a town against a ruthless mining company); TOUGH COPS: *Dirty Harry* (Don Siegel 1971) (☆) (Clint as Harry Callahan is directed across San Francisco by an extorting sniper), *Magnum Force* (Ted Post 1973) (Harry's reluctantly accepted partner is shot and then seeks the killers with an axe to grind), *The Enforcer* (James Fargo 1976) (Harry tracks down an assassination gang), *Sudden Impact* (also directed 1984) (Sondra Locke picks off her rapists and Harry is loathe to stop her), *The Dead Pool* (Buddy Van Horn 1989) (Liam Neeson is Harry's prime suspect when a 'just-for-fun' celebrity death list becomes a reality); ADVENTURE: *Where Eagles Dare* (Brian G. Hutton 1969) (Clint and >Richard Burton are sent to rescue an officer from an impenetrable Nazi castle), *The Eiger Sanction* (also directed 1975) (Clint as a CIA hit man after a spy on a mountaineering expedition) and *Firefox* (also directed 1982) (>Vietnam vet Clint on Moscow mission to steal plane). To pursue the John Wayne analogy, the musical *Paint Your Wagon* (Joshua Logan 1969) (♫ ☆ ✍) (Clint and Lee Marvin scandalize a mining town by setting up home with Jean Seberg) was his >*Quiet Man*, while *Heartbreak Ridge* (1986) (ageing soldier Clint takes raw recruits into Grenada) was disturbingly close to a *Green Berets*. Usually his own director since *Play Misty For Me* (1971) (✍) (DJ Clint is attacked by a listener who thinks he is neglecting her), his biopic of Charlie Parker – *Bird* (1988) (♫ ☆ ☞) was an impressive venture solely behind the lens.

 •*Hang 'Em High* (Ted Post 1967): Clint works his way through the men who were going to hang him.
•*Coogan's Bluff* (Don Siegel 1968) (☆) A hick sheriff recaptures an escapee in the grand old cowboy manner.
•*Two Mules for Sister Sara* (Don Siegel 1970) (☆): Clint rescues Shirley MacLaine from molestation, believing her to be a nun; in fact, she is a Mexican revolutionary.
•*Thunderbolt and Lightfoot* (Michael Cimino 1974) (☆): disguised as a preacher, escapee Clint has to figure out how to recover his loot after someone's put a building on top of it.
•*Every Which Way But Loose* (James Fargo 1978): battling trucker Clint and his orangutan track down country singer Sondra Locke.

ECCENTRICS

Champagne for Caesar (Richard Whorf 1950) ☆ ✍
Ronald Colman tries to bankrupt Vincent Price's soap company by winning its radio promo quiz prize.
Don Quixote (aka Adventures of Don Quixote) (Don Quichotte) (>G.W. Pabst 1933) ✍ ☞
A musical version of Cervantes' novel of the would-be knight and his squire Sancho Panza.
Fitzcarraldo (>Werner Herzog 1982)
Klaus Kinski cruises down Peruvian jungle waters in search of a site for an opera house.
Housekeeping (Bill Forsyth 1987) ☆ ☞
Eccentric aunt Christine Lahti liberates and irritates both of her nieces.

The Jerk (Carl Reiner 1979)
Raised by a black family, naïve Steve Martin wins and loses a fortune.
The Madwoman of Chaillot (Bryan Forbes 1969) ☆
>Katharine Hepburn spends her life in Paris re-living her tortuous past with the help of an all-star cast.
Mon Oncle (Jacques Tati 1956) ☞ ☆ ✍ ■
Monsieur Hulot artlessly undermines the technology of his sister's 'house of the future' and charms his lonely nephew.
Sitting Pretty (Walter Lang 1948) ☆
Clifton Webb as genius babysitter taming Robert Young and Maureen O'Hara's unruly children.
Withnail & I (Bruce Robinson 1987) ✍ ☆ ☞ ♫
It's 1969 and while Paul McGann is seeking theatre work, Richard E. Grant suggests a break in a ramshackle cottage.

8½ (Otto e Mezzo) ☞ ☆ ✍ ■
Italy • Cineriz • 1963 • 138 mins • b/w
d >Federico Fellini w Federico Fellini/Ennio Flaiano/Tullio Pinelli/Brunello Rondi   ph Gianni Di Venanzo m Nino Rota
>Marcello Mastroianni, Claudia Cardinale, Anouk Aimée, Barbara Steele

This Best Foreign Film Oscar winner is Federico Fellini's admission that having made 7½ films (one-and-a-half being made up by acting in *L'Amore* (*Woman*) (aka *Ways of Love*)) (>Roberto Rossellini 1948) and an episode in *Boccaccio 70* (Federico Fellini/>Luchino Visconti/>Vittorio De Sica 1962) (☞)), he was now suffering from director's block, for *8½* is about the struggle to make *8½* . Guido Anselmi (Mastroianni) is a film-maker lacking a plot and a leading lady for his next picture, his frustration symbolized by a snarled traffic jam. Rummaging through the inhabitants and influences of his past for inspiration proves fruitless, but he rediscovers his creativity during a swirling dance at a reception for the film, when he realizes that art is life and that he must live fully in order to create credibly. Seen as a metaphor for the history of Italian cinema, *8½* is dizzying, but ceaselessly watchable.

 •The problems of making films are not eased when the cast is selected, especially when they prove susceptible to love, stage fright and reckless driving as *Day For Night* (*La Nuit Américaine*) (>François Truffaut 1973) (☞ ✍) proves.

•*Directed By Andrei Tarkovsky* (Michal Leszczylowski 1988) is a study of the director at work on his last film *The Sacrifice*.

•A student director finds her investigation into a 1950s bricklayer obfuscated by the authorities in *Man of Marble* (Andrej Wajda 1972) (☞).

•A professor (Victor Sjöström) becomes aware of his faults and rediscovers how to live in >*Wild Strawberries* (*Smultronstället*) (>Ingmar Bergman 1957) (☞ ✍ ■ ☆).

•Creative block is the problem facing a writer in *My Dinner With André* (>Louis Malle 1981) (☆).

•The film style of *8½* is parodied in the episode about Louise Lasser's inability to make love without the risk of detection from *Everything You Wanted to Know About Sex* (>Woody Allen 1972) (✍ ☆).

Eisenstein, Sergei
Soviet writer/director (1898–1948)

Eisenstein brought a sense of rhythm, derived from his knowledge of Japanese ideographs, to the Kino Eye theories and montage influences of Vertov and Kuleshov, introducing art and accessibility to post-Revolution Soviet cinema. Portraying the masses as hero, he shunned traditional narrative, expressing himself and his Marxism through rapid cutting to and from human close-up and the environment. In *Strike* (*Stachka*) (1925) (☞ ■) (after a sacked comrade commits suicide, the workers go on strike only to be repressed by cavalry), and >*The Battleship Potemkin* (US: *Potemkin*) (*Bronenosets Potemkin*) (1925) (☞ ☆ ✍) and *October* (aka *Ten Days That Shook the World*) (*Oktyabr*) (1928) (☞ ■) (the 10 world shaking days when the Bolsheviks overthrew Alexander Kerensky), he chronicled the liberation of the proletariat and in *The General Line* (aka *The Old and the New*) (*Generalnaya Linya*) (1929) (☞ ■) (having been wowed by a mechanized milking machine, the peasants fall over themselves to be collectivized) he celebrated the advent of Party-sponsored progress. Accusations of promoting art over dialectic led to a frustrated assignment in Mexico, the result of which, *Thunder Over Mexico* (1933), he disowned. The historical epics >*Alexander Nevsky* (1938) (■ ☞ ♫) and >*Ivan the Terrible* (*Ivan Groznyi*) (Part I 1944, Part II 1946) (☞ ■ ☆ ♫ ✍), with their dual contemporary commentary, in part restored his Soviet standing, although his international fame has never tarnished.

 •*Romance Sentimentale* (co-directed with Grigori Alexandrov; 1930) (☞ ■): a beautiful opening sequence of crashing waves and rustling leaves gives way to the love affair of a female pianist.

•*Bezhin Meadow* (1966): a reconstruction of the surviving stills of a proposed epic telling of a father's shooting of his son for supporting the collectivization of their village.

ELECTIONS

The Best Man **(Franklin Schaffner 1964)** ✍ ☆
>Henry Fonda and Cliff Robertson seek President Lee Tracy's personal recommendation at the party convention.

Boy's Town **(Norman Taurog 1938)** ☆ ✍ ☞
Brash bully Mickey Rooney stands for the presidency of >Spencer Tracy's reform school.

The Candidate **(Michael Ritchie 1972)** ☆
Come polling day, Robert Redford has forgotten his principles and his family.

Don Camillo's Last Round **(*Don Camillo e l'Onorevole Peppone*) (Carmine Gallone 1955)** ✍
Giovanni Guareschi's belligerent priest schemes to defeat the communist Peppone in the mayoral elections.

The Great Man Votes **(Garson Kanin 1939)** ☆
Interested parties court dipsomaniac Professor John Barrymore to secure his casting vote.

Hold That Co-Ed (UK: *Hold That Girl*)
(George Marshall 1938) ☆
Joan Davis kicks the college football team and
candidate John Barrymore to victory.
The Last Hurrah (>John Ford 1958) ☆ ☞
>Spencer Tracy seeks one last term of office.
Left, Right and Centre (Sidney Gilliat 1959)
☆
>Alastair Sim manages TV celebrity Ian Car-
michael's campaign.
Nasty Habits (Michael Lindsay-Hogg
1976) ⚏
Nun Glenda Jackson runs a ruthless convent
campaign in this screen version of Muriel
Spark's Watergate-inspired novel *The Abbess
of Crewe*.
The Phantom President (Norman Taurog
1932) ☆
A dull candidate is replaced on public occasions
for extrovert lookalike George M. Cohan.
State of the Union (UK:*The World and His
Wife*) (>Frank Capra 1948) ☆ ☞
Feuding >Katharine Hepburn and >Spencer
Tracy patch things up for the polls.

END OF THE WORLD

The Bed-Sitting Room (Richard Lester
1969) ☆
A manic Spike Milligan/John Antrobus comedy
of life on a holocaust bomb site.
The Bedford Incident (James B. Harris
1965) ⚏ ☆
Richard Widmark's routine surveillance of a
Soviet sub leads to atomic attack.
The Day the Earth Caught Fire (Val Guest
1961) ⚏
They tried to keep it quiet but it's true, the
nuclear tests have knocked the earth off its axis
and on to a collision course with the sun.
Five (Arch Oboler 1951)
Sexual and racial tensions dissipate the few
survivors of the bomb.
Letters from a Dead Man (*Pisma Myortvovo
Cheloveka*) (Konstantin Lopushansky
1986) ■ ☞
An academic victim of error bombing describes
his wife's radiation death to his missing son by
letter.

Nostalgia (*Nostalghia*) (>Andrei Tarkovsky
1983) ☞ ■
A Soviet writer must successfully carry a candle
across a sulphur pit to prevent the end.
On The Beach (Stanley Kramer 1959) ☆
Gregory Peck, >Fred Astaire and Ava Gardner
await the return of a submarine searching for
life after the event.
When the Wind Blows (Jimmy M. Murkami
1987) ■
Animated version of Raymond Briggs' story of
pensioner victims of government belligerence
and inadequate information dying of radiation
sickness.
When Worlds Collide (Rudolph Maté 1951)
■
One spaceship will escape the inter-planetary
collision, but who will occupy the seats?
Whoops Apocalypse (Tom Bussman 1987)
⚏ ☆
The kidnapping of a British royal, Princess
Wendy, prompts a sub skipper to blow the
world away.

Les Enfants du Paradis (Children Of Paradise) ☞ ■ ☆ ⚏
France • Pathé • 1945 • 195 mins • b/w
**d >Marcel Carné   w Jacques Prévert
ph Roger Hubert   m Maurice
Thiriet/Joseph Kosma/G. Moque
Arletty, >Jean-Louis Barrault, Pierre
Brasseur, Marcel Herrand, Maria Casarès,
Pierre Renoir**

The most elegant obscene gesture in the history of cinema, Carné and Prévert's beautiful
re-creation of Parisian theatrical lowlife in the
1840s is, in its own right, a remarkable statement of the defiance of occupied France, but
the fact that it was shot over a period of two
years right under the Gestapo's nose makes it
even more deliciously daring. Captivating actress Garance (Arletty), uncrowned queen of
the untamed, the spirit of Free France and of
liberated Woman, resists the attempts of all to
possess her, whether they are scurrilous
rogues, celebrated actors or bashful mimes.
Always haloed in golden light, she even retains
her allure after breaking the heart of Baptiste

Debureau (Barrault), the doleful mime, who has won us with his charming routines. An enchanted world you only leave with great reluctance.

 •John Hurt is exploited in the sinister sideshows of Victorian London in *The Elephant Man* (David Lynch 1980) (■ ☆ ✍ ☞ ✳), while those of Paris are more joyously captured in *Eléna Et Les Hommes* (US: *Paris Does Strange Things*) (>Jean Renoir 1956) (☆ ☞) in which >Ingrid Bergman's marital options are limited to three uninspiring men.

•Carnival barker Tyrone Power finds feigning supernatural powers more profitable in a no holds barred study of lowlife *Nightmare Alley* (Edmund Goulding 1947) (☆ ✍).

•Jacques Tati's long-time assistant Pierre Etaix was also a magnificent mime as he demonstrated in *Yoyo* (1965) (☆); (a child clown grows up to restore his millionaire father's crumbling chateau).

•The busy street life of Paris provides the setting for another love triangle, here between a street singer, a Rumanian emigrée and her cruel protector in *Sous les Toits de Paris* (*Under the Roofs of Paris*) (>René Clair 1929) (☞).

•The story of a Soweto gangster *Mapantsula* (Oliver Schmitz 1988) (✍) was also made under the noses of the authorities, this time the South African police.

E.T. – The Extra Terrestrial
✳ ✍ ■ ☆ ☞

USA • Universal • 1982 • 115 mins • col

d >Steven Spielberg w Melissa Mathison ph Allen Daviau m John Williams

Henry Thomas, Peter Coyote, Drew Barrymore, Dee Wallace

Steven Spielberg, that self-styled Peter Pan, has been called the modern Disney, and he certainly comes close to the magical formula here, with a little help from Carlo Rimbaldi's irresistible little creature from outer space. E.T., abandoned on earth by a retreating space-

ship, is befriended and protected from the authorities by a small boy, Elliott (Thomas), but even he cannot forestall the homesickness that threatens to kill the alien. An inducer of tears of all varieties and an indictment of the adult world's inability to find reality in fantasy, the best of the big budget blockbusters is nonetheless regrettably guilty of racist stereotyping and sexist patronization.

 •Alien David Bowie's waning powers leave him prone to earthly pressures and vices in *The Man Who Fell to Earth* (Nicolas Roeg 1976) (☞).

•Joe Morton, despite a talent for video games, has to contend with being black, poor and alien in *Brother from Another Planet* (John Sayles 1984) (☆).

•Tom Hanks's romance with mermaid Daryl Hannah is subjected to interference from frightened, uncomprehending people, in *Splash!* (Ron Howard 1984) (☆ ✍), while the alien warning of the dangers of war is greeted with hostility in *The Day the Earth Stood Still* (Robert Wise 1951);

•A mysteriously uncommunicative boy who frightens the citizens of 19th-century Nuremberg into violence in *The Enigma of Kaspar Hauser* (US: *Every Man for Himself and God Against All*) (aka *The Mystery of Kaspar Hauser*) (*Jeder für Sich und Gott Gegen Alle*) (>Werner Herzog 1974) (☞ ✍) and a mentally retarded Cliff Robertson whose operation results in temporary genius in *Charly* (Ralph Nelson 1968) (☆ ✍) are both examples of human aliens, while Judy Garland has to get home in >*The Wizard of Oz* (Victor Fleming 1939) (☆ ■ ♫ ✍ ☞)

EXPLORERS

***The Adventures of Marco Polo* (Archie Mayo 1938)** ☆

>Gary Cooper as the Italian on trading travels to China meets up with >Basil Rathbone and Sigrid Gurie.

***Call Me Bwana* (Gordon Douglas 1962)**

Bob Hope disguises himself as jungle explorer to trace a space probe.

Christopher Columbus **(David MacDonald 1949)** ☆

>Fredric March's voyage to the New World is financed by Ferdinand of Aragon and Isabella of Castile.

The Far Horizons **(Rudolph Maté 1955)** ☆

Fred MacMurray and Charlton Heston as the early 19th-century explorers of the Louisiana Purchase territory, Meriwether Lewis and William Clark.

Hudson's Bay **(Irving Pichel 1940)** ☞ ☆

Biopic expert Paul Muni as French Canadian trapper Pierre Radisson.

The Royal Hunt of the Sun **(Irving Lerner 1969)** ✍ ☆

Robert Shaw as *conquistador* Francisco Pizzaro slaughtering the Incas of Peru.

Scott of the Antarctic **(Charles Frend 1948)** ☆ ■

John Mills leads the ill-fated British attempt to beat Norwegian Roald Amundsen to the Pole.

Stanley and Livingstone **(Henry King 1939)** ☆ ☞

>Spencer Tracy as the American journalist sent to discover the whereabouts of Scottish missionary Cedric Hardwicke.

Fairbanks, Douglas

(Douglas Ulman) American actor (1883–1939)

Anita Loos satires and bustling burlesques brought the former Wall Street clerk and soap company executive the capital that co-financed United Artists and launched the swashbuckling career for which he is fondly remembered. In films that he often co-scripted under the name Elton Thomas, such as *The Mark of Zorro* (Fred Niblo 1920) (☆) (chubby Doug as acrobatic Mexican outlaw taunting the imperialist Spanish authorities) and *Robin Hood* (Allan Dwan 1922) (☆) (a boisterous, fun-loving Robin keeps order in Sherwood for Lionheart Wallace Beery), he created unremittingly cheerful American heroes from Hispanic and English folk outlaws, reprising the lovable rogue in *The Thief of Bagdad* (>Raoul Walsh 1924) (☆ ☞ ■) (Casbah thief Doug smiles throughout his magic duel with a tyrannical caliph). Dumas' cavalier D'Artagnan quit clowning long enough to foil scheming ministers in *The Three Musketeers* (Fred Niblo 1921) (☆ ■) and *The Iron Mask* (Allan Dwan 1929) (☆), but while his style epitomized 'Motion Picture', the Fairbanks' formula did not easily translate into

Talkies such as *The Private Life Of Don Juan* (Alexander Korda 1934) (the great lover announces his death in order to ease his seduction of Merle Oberon).

 •*Flirting With Fate* (Christy Cabanne 1916): the comic picaresque adventures of touring variety act.
•*The Mollycoddle* (Victor Fleming 1920) (☆ ☞): Teddy Roosevelt-figure Doug shows great fortitude in the unfamiliar surroundings of the wilds.
•*Don Q, Son of Zorro* (Donald Crisp 1925) (☆): this classic swashbuckling adventure has Yankee Doug returning to dad's stamping ground to win Mary Astor.
•*The Black Pirate* (Albert Parker 1926): avenging his father, Doug brings fair raiding practices to the high seas.
•*The Gaucho* (Dick Jones 1928): Doug as Mexican Robin Hood defending Marian shrine against invaders.
•*The Taming of the Shrew* (Sam Taylor 1929): Doug and Mary Pickford in >Shakespeare's tale of the wooing of a sharp-tongued woman.

FALLEN IDOLS

Beau Brummell **(Curtis Bernhardt 1954)** ☆
Stewart Granger is banished from court for insulting Prince Regent Peter Ustinov.

>*Bicycle Thieves* **(US:** *The Bicycle Thief***)** **(***Ladri di Biciclette***) (>Vittorio De Sica 1948)** ☞ ☆ ✍ ■

The Fallen Idol **(US:** *The Lost Illusion***)** **(>Carol Reed 1948)** ✍ ☆
A small boy is witness to the accidental death of butler Ralph Richardson's wife in this screen version of >Graham Greene's novella.

The Goddess **(John Cromwell 1958)** ☆
Kim Stanley's glamorous film fame is short, and not sweet.

Jeanne Eagels **(George Sidney 1957)** ☆
Kim Novak in biopic of Broadway dance star brought down by drugs.

Network **(>Sidney Lumet 1976)** ☆ ✍ ☞
TV pundit Peter Finch becomes a cult for speaking his mind, but William Holden is determined to silence him.

Shoot the Pianist **(US:** *Shoot the Piano Player***) (***Tirez sur le Pianiste***) (>François Truffaut 1960)** ☞ ☆
Reduced to tinkling ivories in sleazy bar, pianist Charles Aznavour helps his crooked brothers escape from gangsters.

Tender Mercies **(Bruce Beresford 1983)** ☆
Singing his own compositions, Robert Duvall's country star halts his drunken decline.

The World of Henry Orient **(George Roy Hill 1965)** ☆
Two teenage New York girls become disillusioned with the pianist they had hero-worshipped.

Fanny and Alexander (Fanny och Alexander) ☞ ■ ✍ ☆

Sweden • Filminstituten/Swedish TV One/ Gaumont • 1982 • 188 mins • col

wd >Ingmar Bergman   ph Sven Nykvist m Daniel Bell
Gunn Wallgren, Börje Ahlstedt, Christina Schollin, Bertil Guve, Pernilla Alwin, >Harriet Andersson

If your knowledge of Ingmar Bergman is based on >Woody Allen's homages *Interiors* (1978) (☞) (sisters relive old family squabbles before their depressive mother Geraldine Page can take no more) and *September* (1988) (Mia Farrow cries a lot because her parents have new partners, and her friends love in vicious circle), you would be convinced this, his final film which flits the full gamut of cinematic emotions, was made by someone else. There *are* moments of brooding psychology and intense solemnity, notably when Alexander is brutalized by his dour pastor stepfather, but the story of the Ekdahls is largely a joyous, optimistic celebration of a childhood and family life. The Christmas festivities are everything we believe a traditional Christmas should be. Whose long winter evenings would not fly by if they too had an uncle with such a range of petomanic party pieces? The meandering narrative is so involving it creates a nostalgia for an era few could recall and gives Sven Nykvist the opportunity to produce some of colour cinematography's most eloquent work.

 •The Generation Game is played over 80 years by a bourgeois Italian family, within one room redecorated to denote period, in *The Family* (Ettore Scola 1988) (■).

•A Victorian nursery is filled with the stories and the fussings of a traditional nanny in *Biddy* (Christine Edzard 1983) (■).

•The strict regime of a Liverpudlian father shapes the lives of his son, daughters and hardworking wife in *Distant Voices, Still Lives* (Terence Davies 1988) (♫ ✍ ☆ ☞).

•Cursed by a witch, a dour 17th-century Danish pastor is the victim of his adulterous wife in *Day of Wrath* (*Vredens Dag*) (Carl Dreyer 1943) (☞ ✍ ■).

•Another relationship spoiled by an uncontrollable temper is scriptwriter >Humphrey Bogart and Gloria Grahame's in *In a Lonely Place* (>Nicholas Ray 1950).

•Childhood discoveries abound for a boy and his small sister when their mother's illness forces them to spend *A Summer at Grandpa's* (*Dongdong de Jiaqui*) (Hou Hsiao-hsien 1984) (☞ ☆ ■).

FANTASIA
(Ben Sharpsteen 1940) ♫ ☞ ■

CLASSIC DISNEY

>*SNOW WHITE AND THE SEVEN DWARFS*
(David Hand 1937) ☞ ■ ✍ ♫
(dwarfs' housekeeper finds her handsome prince)

PINOCCHIO
(Ben Sharpsteen/Hamilton Luske 1940) ✍ ☞ ■ ♫
(puppet comes to life and learns about living)

DUMBO
(Ben Sharpsteen 1941) ✍ ☞ ■ ♫
(huge-eared elephant learns to fly)

BAMBI
(David Hand 1942) ☞ ✍ ■
(the joys and fears of a wild deer)

ALICE IN WONDERLAND
(Clyde Geronomi/Hamilton Luske/Wilfred Jackson 1951) ☞ ■ ✍
(Lewis Carroll's heroine in her dream land)

DISNEY SECOND WAVE

PETER PAN
(Wilfred Jackson/Clyde Geronomi/Hamilton Luske 1953) ♫ ✍ ☞
(J. M. Barrie's unageing hero in Never Never Land)

LADY AND THE TRAMP
(Hamilton Luske/Clyde Geronomi/Wilfred Jackson 1955) ✍ ☞
(expensive pedigree dog bow wooed by street mongrel)

101 DALMATIANS
(Wolfgang Reitherman/Hamilton Luske/Clyde Geronomi 1961) ☞ ✍
(adventures of dog family on the run)

THE SWORD IN THE STONE
(Wolfgang Reitherman 1963) ✍
(T. H. White's *The Once and Future King* sees King Arthur trained by magician Merlin)

WINNIE THE POOH AND THE HONEY TREE
(Wolfgang Reitherman 1966) ✍ ♫
(A. A. Milne tales culminate in Pooh Bear getting stuck in Rabbit's front door)

THE JUNGLE BOOK
(Wolfgang Reitherman 1967) ✍ ♫ ☞
(Rudyard Kipling's tale of boy raised by jungle animals)

NON-DISNEY

RACE FOR YOUR LIFE, CHARLIE BROWN
(Bill Melendez 1977) ✍
(*Peanuts* characters at summer camp)

THE LORD OF THE RINGS
(Ralph Bakshi 1978)
(books 1 & 2 of J. R. R. Tolkien's fantasy epic)

WATERSHIP DOWN
(Martin Rosen 1978) ✍ ♫ ☞
(Richard Adams' tale of repression resisted in rabbit warren)

AN AMERICAN TAIL
(Don Bluth 1986) ☞ ♫
(lost Russian mouse seeks his immigrant family)

THE PIED PIPER
(Jirí Barta 1986) ☞
(rat charmer punishes ungrateful citizens of Hamelin by stealing their children)

ASTERIX IN BRITAIN
(Pino Van Lamsweerde 1988) ✍ ☞
(indomitable Gauls aid Britons against Roman Empire)

Animated interpretations of classical music pieces

LIFE/ANIMATION

VICTORY THROUGH AIR POWER
(H. C. Potter 1943) ✍
(Disney World War II propaganda exercise)

SONG OF THE SOUTH
(Harve Foster 1947) ☞ ■
(plantation morality tales of Brer Rabbit)

MARY POPPINS
(Robert Stevenson 1964) ☆ ☞
♫ ✳
(governess Julie Andrews [AA] improves lives of lonely London children)

BEDKNOBS AND BROOMSTICKS
(Robert Stevenson 1971) ☞ ■
(flying bed leads to wonderland adventures)

>WHO FRAMED ROGER RABBIT?
(Robert Zemeckis 1988) ☞ ■ ☆
✍
(detective Bob Hoskins clears name of rabbit in murder case)

MOONWALKER
(Jerry Kramer/Colin Chilvers 1988) ■ ✳ ♫
(Michael Jackson collage of music, dance and sketches)

ADULT ANIMATION

ANIMAL FARM
(John Halas/Joy Batchelor 1955) ✍ ☞ ■
(George Orwell's fable of Fascism and Communism)

YELLOW SUBMARINE
(George Dunning 1968) ♫ ☞ ✍
■
(The Beatles crush Blue Meanies to restore music to Pepperland)

FRITZ THE CAT
(Ralph Bakshi 1971) ☞
(alley cat tastes New York lowlife)

HEAVY TRAFFIC
(Ralph Bakshi 1973) ■
(cartoonist thirsts after lewd experiences)

WHEN THE WIND BLOWS
(Jimmy T. Murakami 1987) ■
(naïve pensioners perish at the end of the world)

NEW WAVE DISNEY

THE ARISTOCATS
(Wolfgang Reitherman 1970) ✍
♫
(alley tom saves a prize cat and her kittens from kidnap)

ROBIN HOOD
(Wolfgang Reitherman 1973)
☞ ■
(a fox outlaw outwits lion Prince John and his snake sidekick)

THE RESCUERS
(Wolfgang Reitherman/John Lounsbery/Art Stevens 1977) ☞
■ ✍
(heroic mice bring a girl back to her parents from a treacherous swamp)

THE FOX AND THE HOUND
(Art Stevens/Ted Berman/ Richard Rich 1981) ✍
(puppy and a cub meet again during a fox hunt)

BASIL, THE GREAT MOUSE DETECTIVE (US: THE GREAT MOUSE DETECTIVE)
(John Musker/Ron Clements/ Dave Michener/Burny Mattinson 1986) ☞ ✍
(Baker Street mouse crosses swords with a sewer rat)

OLIVER AND COMPANY
(George Scribner 1989) ✍
(this retelling of >Charles Dickens' tale of lowlife crime pits an orphaned kitten against crooked canines)

FARMERS

Blockade (>William Dieterle 1938) ☆ ☞ ✍
Meek >Henry Fonda leaves the farm to fight in the >Spanish Civil War.

Come Next Spring (R.G. Springsteen 1955) ☆
A prodigal son returns to the farm and impresses all with his change for the better.

Country (Richard Pearce 1985) ☆
Jessica Lange and Sam Shepard survive the threat of a bank foreclosing and the family farm being lost.

Earth (Zemlya) (>Alexander Dovzhenko 1930) ☞ ■
Rich kulaks fearing collectivization unite against the purchase of a tractor.

Field of Dreams (Phil Alden Robinson 1989) ✍ ☆ ☞
Kevin Costner risks losing his farm as he insists on following a ghostly voice's order to build a baseball field.

Farrebique (Georges Rouquier 1947) ☞ ■
A French farming family adhere to age-old routine despite dramatic events at close of the war.

Gold Is Where You Find It (>Michael Curtiz 1938) ☞ ☆
Failed prospectors George Brent and Claude Rains turn to tilling and aiding >Olivia De Havilland.

>Jean De Florette (Claude Berri 1986) ☆ ✍ ☞ ■

>Out Of Africa (Sidney Pollack 1985) ☆ ☞ ✍ ■ ♫

Places in the Heart (Robert Benton 1984) ☆
Widowed Sally Field ploughs on to spite unpleasant neighbours, with the help of blindman John Malkovich and drifter Danny Glover.

Red Psalm (Még Kér a Nép) (Miklós Jancsó 1971) ☞ ✍
Late 19th-century farmhands' dispute resolved by violent means.

The Tree of Wooden Clogs (Albero degli Zoccoli) (Ermanno Olmi 1978) ☞ ■ ☆
Late 19th-century Lombard co-tenants share such experiences as a traditional wedding and the tension over the illness of their cow.

Fassbinder, Reiner Werner
German actor/writer/director (1946–1982)

Combining the narrative structure of Hollywood *film noir*, particularly Douglas Sirk and >Max Ophüls, and the claustrophobic sets of Expressionism, Fassbinder, a luminary of New German Cinema, specialized in ironical allegories of the sexual, social and economic preoccupation of the third estate: *Why Does Herr R Run Amok? (Warum Läuft Herr R Amok)* (1969) (☞ ☆) (middle-class mediocrity Kurt Raub's realization that he is going nowhere fast leads to sudden and tragic outburst of violence); *The Merchant of the Four Seasons (Der Händler der Vier Jahreszeiten)* (1972) (☞) (Hans Hirschmüller is one of life's failures, but he is good at drinking, so he does it to excess); *>Fear Eats The Soul* (US: *Ali: Fear Eats the Soul*) (aka *Ali*) (*Angst Essen Seele Auf*) (1973) (☞ ☆ ✍) *Mother Kusters Goes to Heaven (Mutter Küsters Fahrt zum Himmel)* (1975) (☆) (Brigitte Mira's response to her husband's killing of a factory boss is to join a Marxist terrorist group); and the parasitic: *The Bitter Tears of Petra Von Kant (Die Bitteren Tränen der Petra Von Kant)* (1972) (☞ ☆) (Margit Carstensen abandons Irm Hermann for the more passionate >Hanna Schygulla); *Effi Briest (Fontane Effi Briest)* (1974) (✍ ☞ ☆) (Theodor Fontane's *belle époque* novel has elderly aristocrat duelling with >Hanna Schygulla's lover); and *Fox* (US: *Fox and His Friends*) (*Faustrecht der Freiheit*) (1975) (☞) (Fassbinder as fairground barker embezzled of his lottery fortune by rich gay lover); *Satan's Brew (Satansbraten)* (1976) (✍) (murderous poet Kurt Raab adopts the lifestyle and works of symbolist writer Stefan George); and *Chinese Roulette (Chinesisches Roulette)* (1976) (✍ ☞) (parents and their lovers have their lives dissected by crippled daughter on country weekend). His best efforts, however, came when he relaxed his extreme left-wing pose: *The Marriage of Maria Braun (Die Ehe der Maria Braun)* (1979) (☆ ☞) (>Hanna Schygulla enjoys life, with a black GI and then a rich businessman, either side of her jealous husband's return from the war) and 13-episode/975-minute TV adaptation of Alfred Döblin's epic novel *Berlin-Alexanderplatz*

(1980) (☞ ✍ ☆ ■) (ex-con Gunter Lamprecht tries to go straight in Weimar Germany, but is prisoner of his violent emotions).

 •*Martha* (1973) (☞): a bourgeois 1940s couple's relationship from love at first sight to happy ever after.

•*The American Soldier* (*Der Amerikanische Soldat*) (1970) (☞): a Vietnam vet becomes a Munich police assassin).

•*Beware of a Holy Whore* (*Warnung vor Einer Heiligen Nutte*) (1970): a film crew and cast wait around while the fate of their film is discussed by financiers.

FATAL ILLNESS

The American Friend (*Der Amerikanische Freund*) (>Wim Wenders 1977)
A dying man sets up pension fund from proceeds of assassinations.

>*Camille* (>George Cukor 1936) ☆ ✍ ☞

Cleo from Five to Seven (*Cléo de 5 à 7*) (Agnès Varda 1961) ☞ ☆
Corinne Marchand awaits the results of medical tests.

DOA (aka *Dead on Arrival*) (Rocky Morton/Annabel Jankl 1989) ✍
Dennis Quaid has been poisoned and Meg Ryan helps him find out who is responsible.

Eighty Thousand Suspects (Val Guest 1963) ✍
Bath is plagued by smallpox.

The Honey Pot (>Joseph L. Mankiewicz 1966) ☞ ✍
Volpone inspires Rex Harrison to tease mistresses, but when Susan Hayward dies, >Maggie Smith suspects Rex.

Living (aka *Doomed*) (US:*To Live*) (*Ikiru*) (>Akira Kurosawa 1952) ☞ ✍
A cancer-afflicted civil servant rouses himself from lethargy to get a slum playground built.

The Shootist (Don Siegel 1976) ☆
Gunfighter >John Wayne makes his farewells to >James Stewart and Lauren Bacall.

Terms of Endearment (James L. Brooks 1983) ☆
Debra Winger's illness brings more pain to unlucky-in-love mother Shirley MacLaine.

FATHERS AND SONS

Adalen 31 (aka The Adalen Riots) (Bo Widerberg 1969) ■ ☞
Cannes Special Jury prize-winning story of son witnessing father's fatal involvement in 1931 pulp mill strike.

All My Sons (Irving Reis 1948) ✍
This Arthur Miller play adaptation has Burt Lancaster uncovering >Edward G. Robinson's dodgy war dealings.

Any Number Can Play (>Mervyn Le Roy 1949) ☞
>Clark Gable quits gambling to spend more time at home.

Bellman and True (Richard Loncraine 1988) ✍
Computer expert Bernard Hill and his son are kidnapped by crooks planning a daring crime.

Family Business (Constantin Costa-Gavras 1987) ☞
Johnny Halliday is blackmailed into teaching his son safe-cracking; then the son betrays him.

Father (*Apa*) (István Szabó, Hungary 1966) ☞ ✍
Father was a pro-Jewish war hero, but his son comes to doubt his reputation and motives for fighting.

A House of Strangers (>Joseph L. Mankiewicz 1949) ☆ ☞
Martinet father >Edward G. Robinson loses control of family after jail term.

Nothing in Common (Garry Marshall 1986) ☆
Tom Hanks sacrifices his advertising career to care for dying Jackie Gleason.

There Was a Father (*Chichi Ariki*) (Yasujiro Ozu 1942) ☞ ✍
A widower and his son remain best of friends even though his education keeps them far apart.

The Watchmaker of St Paul (*L'Horloger de St Paul*) (Bertrand Tavernier 1973) ☆
>Philippe Noiret's life disintegrates when his son is suspected of murder.

When Father Was Away on Business (Otac na Sluzsobtbenom Putu) **(Emir Kusturica 1983)** ☆ ☞ ✍

A boy's impressions of his philandering father's denunciation as a Stalinist in Tito's Yugoslavia.

FAUST

Beauty and the Devil (Beauté du Diable) **(>René Clair 1949)** ☞

A plain man sells soul for good looks to win a woman who doesn't know he's alive.

Faust **(>F.W. Murnau 1926)** ☞ ■

Mephistopheles >Emil Jannings gives professor Gösta Ekman a new lease of life.

The Queen of Spades **(Thorold Dickinson 1948)** ✍ ☆ ☞

The Pushkin story of soldier (Anton Walbrook) who loses his soul to attain the secret of card playing from Edith Evans.

The Sacrifice (Offret) **(Andrei Tarkovsky, Sweden 1986)** ☞ ■ ☆

Erland Josephson bargains to prevent a nuclear holocaust.

>*The Seventh Seal (Det Sjunde Inseglet)* **(>Ingmar Bergman 1957)** ■ ☞ ☆✍

The Student of Prague (Der Student von Prag) **(Henrik Galeen 1926)** ☞ ✍

To pay off his debts, Conrad Veidt loses his reflection, which haunts him to death.

Fear Eats the Soul (US: Ali: Fear Eats the Soul) (aka Ali) (Angst Essen Seele Auf) ☞ ☆ ✍

West Germany • Tango Film • 1973 • 92 mins • col

wd >Rainer Werner Fassbinder ph Jürgen Jürges

Brigitte Mira, El Hedi Ben Salem, Barbara Valentin, Irm Hermann, Rainer Werner Fassbinder

Derived from Douglas Sirk's *All That Heaven Allows*, >Rainer Werner Fassbinder's best film sets a cross-cultural, age gap romance in modern Munich to study prejudice, peer pressure and permanence in love. Emmi (Mira), a widowed cleaning woman marries Ali, a handsome young Moroccan (Salem), and is promptly scorned by family and friends. Such animosity serves only to draw the couple closer together, their mutual affection gradually earning their neighbours' respect. However, this belated acceptance corrodes the determination to survive forged in adversity. While a sharply observed attack on bigotry, this is also a touching, if unconventional, love story.

 •A youth with funeral fixation has an age gap love affair with an 80-year old in *Harold and Maude* (Hal Ashby 1971) (☆).

•>Katharine Hepburn finds it easier to accept daughter Katharine Houghton's love for Sidney Poitier than >Spencer Tracy in the cross race love study *Guess Who's Coming to Dinner?* (Stanley Kramer 1967) (☆ ☞ ✍).

•Robert Taylor and Rock Hudson respectively atone for blinding Irene Dunne and Jane Wyman by becoming surgeons in the against-all-odds romance *Magnificent Obsession* (John M. Stahl 1935 (☞ ☆)/Douglas Sirk 1954).

•A clutching mother doesn't want her son to leave home and his father doesn't want him marrying his own mistress, in Jean Cocteau's disapproval of marriage comedy *Les Parents Terribles (The Storm Within)* (1948) (✍ ☞ ☆).

Fellini, Federico
Italian writer/director (b 1920)

A cartoonist whose cinema career began as a gag writer, Fellini co-scripted the significant neo-realist films *Rome, Open City (Open City) (Roma, Città Aperta)* (>Roberto Rossellini 1945) (a Resistance fighter brings death to all who offer him sanctuary) and *Paisà (Paisan)* (>Roberto Rossellini 1946) (the episodic progress of the Allies from Anzio to Florence). Following the classic studies of abused woman he constructed around his wife Giulietta Masina, *La Strada (The Road)* (☆ ☞ ✍ ■) (1954) (Foreign Film AA winner has Masina humiliated by circus strongman Anthony Quinn) and >*Nights of Cabiria (Le Notti di Cabiria)* (1957) (☆ ☞ ✍ ■) – his work became increasingly autobiographical; >*8½ (Otto e Mezzo)* (1963) (☞ ☆ ✍ ■), *Juliet of the Spirits (Giulietta degli Spiriti)* (1965) (☆) (Masina seeks solace from her miserable life in a clairvoyant), and *Amar-*

cord (1974) (☞ ✍) (another Foreign Oscar for autobiographical tale of teenage sexual awakening in Fascist Rimini), while the fascination with decadence manifested in >*La Dolce Vita* (*The Sweet Life*) (1960) (☞ ☆ ■ ✍ ♫) re-emerged in the sumptuous, but disappointing *Fellini Satyricon* (1969) (■ ☞) (the immorality of your choice in ancient Rome) and *Fellini's Roma* (1972) (☞ ■) (the contrasts between seedy Rome of his early manhood and the fashionable city of today). *Ginger and Fred* (*Ginger e Fred*) (1986) (☞ ☆) (Astaire and Rogers impersonators >Marcello Mastroianni and Giulietta Masina re-unite for TV show), combining hilarious satire and touching nostalgia, raises hopes of more in the same vein.

 •*The White Sheik* (*Lo Sceicco Bianco*) (1952) (☞): a bride spends honeymoon night with her pin-up idol.

•*I Vitelloni* (*The Young and the Passionate*) (1953) (☞ ✍): a layabout tires of the macho life and seeks a career.

•*The Swindlers* (aka *The Swindle*) (*Il Bidone*) (1955) (☆): Broderick Crawford leads trio of crooks disguising themselves as priests to con the poor.

•*The Clowns* (*Il Clowns*) (1970) (✍ ☆): a documentary captures performances of some of Europe's great clowns.

•*Alex in Wonderland* (Paul Mazursky 1970): Fellini gives a dispirited arty director (Donald Sutherland) a few tips on surviving the critics' sticks and stones.

•*Casanova* (aka *Fellini's Casanova*) (1976) (☞ ☆): Donald Sutherland's great womanizer's conquests not always up to the standards his reputation demands.

•*City of Women* (*La Città delle Donne*) (1980) (☞ ☆): >Marcello Mastroianni lives all his female phobias in a dream world ruled by women.

•*And The Ship Sails On* (*E la Nave Va*) (1983) (■ ☞): celebrities accompany a singer's ashes on voyage to island burial in the last days before World War I.

•*Intervista* (1983) (☆): Fellini's celebration of his career includes interviews from Japanese TV and snippets with >Marcello Mastroianni.

Fields, W.C.
(William Dukenfield) American actor (1879–1946)

A juggler and vaudevillian who performed at Buckingham Palace in 1905, Fields appeared in numerous shorts, including *The Dentist* (Leslie Pearce 1932) (☆) (impatient Fields tortures his nervous patients) and *The Fatal Glass of Beer* (Clyde Bruckman 1933) (a prodigal son story set in the Alaskan wastes), but rarely did he do his comic range justice prior to the celebrated Mr Micawber in *David Copperfield* (>George Cukor 1935) (☞ ☆ ✍) (an eccentric family man shelters a boy ejected by cruel stepfather >Basil Rathbone). Then his portrayal of idle shopkeepers in *It's a Gift* (☆ ✍) (Norman Z. McLeod 1934) (W.C. packs family into a jalopy and after a hilarious picnic sets up as orange grower) and *Man on the Flying Trapeze* (UK: *The Memory Expert*) (Clyde Bruckman 1935) (☆) (Fields is allowed to stay in employment because of his memory) and deflated know-it-alls in *Poppy* (A. Edward Sutherland 1936) (☆) (medicine man Eustace McGargle knows best when daughter has crush on mayor's son), *You Can't Cheat An Honest Man* (George Marshall 1939) (Fields as circus owner on verge of blowing his top) and *My Little Chickadee* (Edward Cline 1939) (☆ ✍) (cardsharp Fields and Mae West team up to outwit Western town baddy) fulfilled the potential of the misogynistic child-hater, bulbous of nose and bibulous of speech, trapped in a domestic abyss.

 •*Her Majesty, Love* (>William Dieterle 1931) (☞): slob Fields's behaviour jeopardizes his daughter's marriage-above-her-station.

•*Tillie and Gus* (Francis Martin 1933) (☆): W.C. and Alison Skipworth as card cons helping relations inherit their due.

•*Alice in Wonderland*) (Norman Z. McLeod 1933) (☆ ✍): W.C.'s Humpty Dumpty gives Charlotte Henry's Alice the benefit of his advice from his wall.

•*The Old Fashioned Way* (William Beaudine 1934) (✍): an actor manager keeps his troupe one step ahead of the debt collectors.

•*Six of a Kind* (>Leo McCarey) (1935) (☞ ☆):

Fields's sheriff catches a couple harbouring stolen cash in their car.

•*The Bank Dick* (UK: *The Bank Detective*) (Eddie Cline 1940) (☆): W.C. as bank security guard who hates his life and his job.

•*Never Give a Sucker an Even Break* (UK: *What a Man*) (Eddie Cline 1941): Fields in series of sketches ranging from impersonating a Russian to trying to sell a movie script.

FILMS À CLEF (FACT MADE FICTION)

The Actress (>George Cukor 1953) ☞ ☆
Jean Simmons defies father >Spencer Tracy and goes on the stage; Ruth Gordon's early career.

The Carpetbaggers (Edward Dmytryk 1964) ☆
Aeroplane tycoon seeks excitement in Hollywood; George Peppard as Howard Hughes-like character.

>*Citizen Kane* (>Orson Welles 1941) (☞ ☆ ■ ✍ ♫)
Fictional career of newspaper baron William Randolph Hearst.

The Comic (Carl Reiner 1969) ☆
Dick Van Dyke as silent comedian finished by the Talkies *à la* >Buster Keaton.

Fame is the Spur (Roy Boulting 1947) ☆
Michael Redgrave as worker, whose rise to political power resembles that of first Labour PM Ramsey MacDonald.

Heartburn (>Mike Nichols 1986) ☆ ☞
>Meryl Streep and >Jack Nicholson in adultery drama based on Nora Ephron's split from Watergate journalist Carl Bernstein.

Little Caesar (>Mervyn Le Roy 1930) ☞ ☆
>Edward G. Robinson as Al Caponesque gangster in the bootlegging business.

The Moon and Sixpence (Albert Lewin 1943) ☆ ✍
George Sanders as stockbroker taking a leaf out of Paul Gauguin's book and becoming an artist.

My Favourite Year (Richard Benjamin 1982) ☆
Recollections of a hopeful's encounters with a drunken Hollywood star (Peter O'Toole) who could be mistaken for Errol Flynn.

Personal Services (Terry Jones 1987) ☞
Julie Walters as suburban madam not dissimilar to Cynthia Payne.

Young Cassidy (Jack Cardiff/>John Ford 1964)
Rod Taylor has amorous and theatrical adventures that Sean O'Casey might have had.

FILM-MAKING

Abbott and Costello in Hollywood (S. Sylvan Simon 1945)
Unsuccessful agents have adventures with stars on the MGM lot.

Blonde Bombshell (US: *Bombshell*) (Victor Fleming 1933) ☆
>Jean Harlow is wooed on the sound stage by Franchot Tone.

The Cameraman (Edward Sedgwick 1928)
>Buster Keaton becomes a cinematographer to get closer to actress Marceline Day.

Day for Night (*La Nuit Américaine*) (>François Truffaut 1973) ☞ ✍
Truffaut as a director having problems with a cast that includes Jacqueline Bisset and Jean-Pierre Léaud.

>*8¹/2* (*Otto e Mezzo*) (>Federico Fellini 1963) (☞ ☆ ✍ ■)

Hellzapoppin' (H.C. Potter 1941) ✍
Vaudeville comics Ole Olsen and Chic Johnson turn their act into a movie.

Lady Killer (Roy Del Ruth 1933) ☆ ☞
>James Cagney feels usheretting isn't true involvement in the movies and heads for Hollywood.

Merton of the Movies (Robert Alton 1947) ✍ ☆
Red Skelton's attempts to make it as a serious actor reveal a slapstick comic genius.

My Favourite Year (Richard Benjamin 1982) ☆
Recollections of a hopeful's encounters with drunken stuntman Peter O'Toole.

>*Singin' in the Rain* (>Gene Kelly/>Stanley Donen 1952) (♫ ☆ ✍ ☞ ■)

Fonda, Henry
American actor (1905–1982)
Notwithstanding a long career totalling over

85 acting roles, Fonda's unquestioned reputation as a fine screen actor is largely dependent on a limited number of restrained performances as decent, common men. >John Ford moulded the architypal Fonda persona in *Young Mr Lincoln* (1939)(☆ ☞ ■) (Abe as young lawyer combatting prejudice and meeting Mary Todd) and *Drums Along the Mowhawk* (1939) (☞ ☆) (Fonda and Claudette Colbert resist Indians during the War of Independence), >*The Grapes of Wrath* (AAN: 1940) (☞ ■ ☆ ✍) and *My Darling Clementine* (1946) (☞ ☆♫) (Fonda's Wyatt Earp rids Tombstone of baddies with Victor Mature's help), which he revisited in *The Ox-Bow Incident* (UK: *Strange Incident*) (William Wellman 1943) (☆ ✍ ☞) (Fonda can't prevent innocent men being lynched) and >*Twelve Angry Men* (>Sidney Lumet 1957) (☆ ☞ ✍), although >Fritz Lang used him as sympathetic lawbreaker in *You Only Live Once* (1937) (☞ ☆) (framed Fonda flees for the border with wife Sylvia Sidney) and *The Return of Frank James* (1940) (☆ ☞ ■) (Fonda avenges the death of brother Tyrone Power witnessed in *Jesse James* (Henry King 1938) (☞ ☆)) and Sergio Leone employed him as a black knight in *Once Upon a Time in the West* (1969) (Fonda's desperadoes terrorize Claudia Cardinale). A desire to work, prompted somewhat by an unsatisfactory private life, induced him into an excess of commonplacers, although *On Golden Pond* (Mark Rydell 1981) (☆ ■) (pensioners Fonda and >Katharine Hepburn make lifestyle even more idyllic by settling score with daughter >Jane Fonda) brought the overdue Oscar.

VIEW ON ▶
•*The Trail of the Lonesome Pine* (Henry Hathaway 1936) (☞): Fonda disapproves of city slicker Fred MacMurray smartening up sister Sylvia Sidney.
•*The Wings of the Morning* (Harold Schuster 1937) (☆ ■): Irish peer Fonda and gypsy Arabella repeating the romance of their 19th-century ancestors.
•*The Story of Alexander Graham Bell* (UK: *The Modern Miracle*) (Irving Cummings 1939) (☆): Fonda as Don Ameche's lab assistant and best man at wedding to Loretta Young.

•*The Lady Eve* (>Preston Sturges 1941) (✍ ☞ ☆): >Barbara Stanwyck schemes to pay back Fonda for foiling her liner card con.
•*The Fugitive* (>John Ford 1947) (✍ ☞ ☆): Fonda as the whiskey priest fleeing anti-clerical troops in >Graham Greene's *The Power and the Glory*.
•*Fort Apache* (>John Ford 1948) (☞ ☆ ■): commander Fonda has trouble with his number one >John Wayne and romancing daughter Shirley Temple.
•*War and Peace* (>King Vidor/Mario Soldati 1956) (☞ ■ ✍ ☆): Fonda as Pierre Bezukhov, head of one of three noble families facing Napoleon's invasion of 1812.
•*The Wrong Man* (>Alfred Hitchcock 1957) (☞ ☆): musician Fonda is unable to prove his innocence because of his resemblance to a hold-up crook.
•*My Name is Nobody* (Tonino Valerii 1973) (♫ ☞ ☆): ageing gunfighter Fonda is persuaded out of retirement and into a showdown by a young devotee.

Fonda, Jane
American actress (b 1937)

If her father represented Liberal America, Jane Fonda's views on >Vietnam *F.T.A.* (aka *Fuck the Army*) (aka *Free the Army*) (Francine Parker 1972) (Fonda and Donald Sutherland star in an anti-war revue); and *Coming Home* (AA: Hal Ashby 1978) (crippled vet Jon Voight first wins Fonda's sympathy then her heart); nuclear power, *The China Syndrome* (James Bridges 1979) (☆ ✍) (TV journalist Fonda and cameraman >Michael Douglas film >Jack Lemmon panic at suspected plant leak), and modern woman >*Julia* (AAN: >Fred Zinnemann 1977) (☆ ✍ ☞ ■) and *Nine To Five* (Colin Higgins 1980) (☆) (Fonda, Dolly Parton and Lily Tomlin humiliate their chauvinistic boss), have earned her a radical tag. Excellent comedienne in *Cat Ballou* (Eliot Silverstein 1965) (☆ ✍♫) (Fonda as teacher turned outlaw keeping gunfighter Lee Marvin sober enough to avenge her father) and *Barefoot in the Park* (Gene Saks 1967) (✍ ☆) (poor newlyweds Fonda and Robert Redford marry her mother Mildred Natwick to mystery neighbour Charles Boyer), she has subsequently favoured films with a social conscience, *They Shoot Horses Don't They?* (AAN: Sydney Pollack 1969) (✍ ☆) (Fonda at a dance marathon that ends in death) and *Klute* (AA: Alan J. Pakula 1971) (☆ ✍) (Donald Sutherland, investigating the death of a scientist, is doubly interested in whore Fonda, who last saw him alive) and melodramatic weight, *On Golden Pond* (Mark Rydell 1981) (☆ ■) (Fonda opens up an old feud with parents >Henry Fonda and >Katharine Hepburn while picking up her stepson from her parents' summer home) and *The Morning After* (>Sidney Lumet 1987) (☆) (waking from a bender, Fonda finds herself in bed with a dead man, but did she kill him?).

 •*Walk on the Wild Side* (Edward Dmytryk 1962) (☆): news of Fonda's career at >Barbara Stanwyck's brothel leaks out.

•*The Chapman Report* (>George Cukor 1962): Fonda as one of the women whose sex life is investigated in scientific survey.

•*Barbarella* (Roger Vadim 1968) (■): Jane has outer space adventures in AD 4000 on the trail of death ray.

•*Fun with Dick and Jane* (Ted Kotcheff 1977) (☞ ☆): sacked businessman George Segal and wife Jane maintain appearances through crime.

•*Agnes of God* (Norman Jewison 1984) (☆ ✍): nun Meg Tilly's deadly secret is kept from journalist Fonda by mother superior Anne Bancroft.

Fontaine, Joan

(Joan De Beauvoir De Havilland
Japanese-born British actress (b 1917)

>Olivia De Havilland's younger sister, using names as awful as Joan St John, struggled in her early leading roles *Damsel In Distress* (>George Stevens 1937) (✍ ☆) (aristocrat Joan falls for dancer >Fred Astaire) and *Gunga Din* (>George Stevens 1939) (☞ ☆) (Joan is >Cary Grant's romantic inspiration in North-West frontier adventure romp), before *The Women* (>George Cukor 1939) (☆ ✍ ☞) (Joan as one of cast of 135 women fascinated by wife Norma Shearer and shopgirl >Joan Crawford's tug-of-war for rich man) put her in touch with

the timid, devoted waif of >*Rebecca* (>Alfred Hitchcock 1940) (☞ ☆ ■ ✍ ♫), *Suspicion* (>Alfred Hitchcock 1941) (☞ ☆ ✍ ■) (Joan marries >Cary Grant without knowing his background and comes to suspect he is a murderer), *Jane Eyre* (Robert Stevenson 1943) (☆ ☞ ✍) (governess Joan is devoted to >Orson Welles, but he is keeping a secret from her in a room upstairs) and *Letter from an Unknown Woman* (>Max Ophüls 1948) (☞ ☆ ■) (Joan tolerates philandering pianist Louis Jourdan's amours in 19th-century Vienna). Attempts to shake the persona met with disapproval, although she could be a quite convincing screen bitch: *Frenchman's Creek* (Mitchell Leisen 1944) (✍ ☆) (Joan takes up with a 17th-century French pirate after he shelters in her Cornish parlour), *Ivy* (Sam Wood 1947) (☞ ■) (Joan poisons one rich patron too many) and *Serenade* (Anthony Mann 1956) (☞) (Joan and Sarita Montiel clamour over opera star Mario Lanza).

 •*The Constant Nymph* (Edmund Goulding 1943) (☆): composer Charles Boyer leaves wife for ailing teenager Joan.

•*The Affairs of Susan* (Willliam A. Seiter 1945) (☆ ✍): Fontaine has four lovers each with a different personality.

•*The Emperor Waltz* (>Billy Wilder 1948) (☞ ☆): Bing Crosby can't interest Franz Joseph of Austria in a gramophone, but can sell himself to royal niece Joan.

•*Born to be Bad* (>Nicholas Ray 1950) (☆ ☞): Joan's dual love with millionaire Zachary Scott and novelist Robert Ryan is exposed.

•*Ivanhoe* (Richard Thorpe 1952) (✍ ■): Joan as Lady Rowena in Sir Walter Scott's novel of bold knights.

•*Casanova's Big Night* (Norman Z. McLeod 1954) (✍ ☆): Bob Hope masks as the great lover and duels with >Basil Rathbone.

•*Beyond a Reasonable Doubt* (>Fritz Lang 1956) (☞ ☆): Joan crusades to free pressman Dana Andrews from murder he has framed himself for to prove dangers of circumstantial evidence.

Ford, Harrison

American actor (b 1942)

Very much associated with the roles of Han Solo in George Lucas's blockbusting *Star Wars* trilogy *Star Wars* (1977) (☆ ✳), *The Empire Strikes Back* (1980) (✳) and *The Return of the Jedi* (1983) (✳) – and Indiana Jones in >Steven Spielberg's escapist Raiders trio (*Raiders of the Lost Ark* (1981) (☆ ☞), *Indiana Jones and the Temple of Doom* (1984) (☆) and *Indiana Jones and the Last Crusade* (1989) (☆) – Ford has struggled to discover the ideal milieu for his impassive style. His excursions are, however, always watchable: his cynical futuristic detective Rick Deckard in *Blade Runner* (Ridley Scott 1982) (✳ ☆) and anti-corruption cop John Book, investigating a murder amidst the pacifist Amish in *Witness* (Peter Weir 1985) (✍ ☞ ☆), superior to the priggish professor in *The Mosquito Coast* (Peter Weir 1985) (☆) (Paul Theroux story of trials Ford puts Helen Mirren and children through while taking ice machine to South America) and romantic comedian in *Working Girl* (>Mike Nichols 1988) (☆ ☞) (secretary Melanie Griffith benefits from boss Sigourney Weaver's injury to show her worth and seduce businessman Ford).

•*The Conversation* (>Francis Ford Coppola 1974) (☆ ✍): Ford as bugging expert Gene Hackman's contact.

•*Force Ten from Navarone* (Guy Hamilton 1978): Ford joins Robert Shaw and Edward Fox in blowing up a Yugoslavian bridge.

•*Hanover Street* (Peter Hyams 1979): USAAF pilot Ford's love for nurse Lesley-Anne Down hampered by his rescuing her husband Christopher Plummer from Blitz.

•*Frantic* (>Roman Polanski 1988) (☆): doctor Ford stumbles into a Parisian murder mystery when his wife is kidnapped from their hotel room.

Ford, John

(Sean O'Feeney) American director (1895–1973)

Intrinsically linked with the Western, John Ford's conviction in the absolute rectitude of the hierarchical structure of American political, military and social life is the mainstay of all his films. His canon is a screen history of the USA from Independence, (*Drums Along the Mowhawk* (1939) (☞ ☆) (>Henry Fonda and Claudette Colbert keep marauding Indians off their land) to *Young Mr Lincoln* (1939) (☆ ☞ ■) (>Henry Fonda defends a foregone law case and wins a reputation for honesty), the Civil War (*The Horse Soldiers*) (1959) (☞) (>John Wayne and William Holden blow up a Confederate rail line), the Wild West (*My Darling Clementine*) (1949) (☞ ☆ ♫) (>Henry Fonda's Wyatt Earp and Victor Mature's Doc Holliday clean up Tombstone), the pioneering West (*The Iron Horse*) (1924) (☞) (overcoming natural and man-made difficulties determined labourers complete the cross-continental rail link), the Indian wars (*Fort Apache*) (1948) (☞ ☆ ■) (soldier >John Wayne and daughter Shirley Temple are insubordinate to >Henry Fonda), Mexican wars (*Rio Grande*) (1950) (☞) (>John Wayne has Indian problems on the Mexico border), the Great War (*Pilgrimage*) (1933) (☞) (mother relives relationship with her son while visiting his war grave), the Depression (>*The Grapes of Wrath*) (1940) (☞ ■ ☆ ✍) (☞ ■ ☆ ✍), the Second World War, (*They Were Expendable*) (1945) (>John Wayne and Robert Montgomery bicker over tactics and women in Pacific war), the Korean War (*This is Korea*) (1951) and *Vietnam, Vietnam* (exec. prod. 1971). A man of his age, he freely and regrettably discriminated against women and non-Aryans and is, consequently, the link between the right-wing cinema of >Griffith and Stallone.

THE WESTERNS:

•>*Stagecoach* (1939) (☞ ☆ ■ ✍)

•*She Wore A Yellow Ribbon* (1949) (☞ ☆): Little Big Horn veteran >John Wayne goes on one last mission before retirement.

•*Wagonmaster* (1950) (☞): Mormons face the dangers of the trail en route to Utah.

•*The Searchers* (1956) (☞ ■ ☆): >John Wayne's family are kidnapped by Indians and he sets out to find them.

•*Sergeant Rutledge* (1960) (☞ ✍): black soldier jumps rape trial, but returns to help accusers against Indians.

•*Two Rode Together* (1961) (☞ ☆): >James Stewart and Richard Widmark row on their way to pow-wow with the Comanches.

•*The Man Who Shot Liberty Valance* (1962) (☞ ☆ ✍): >James Stewart is lionized for shooting Lee Marvin but >John Wayne's finger had been on the trigger.

•*Cheyenne Autumn* (1964) (☞): Indians reject their reservation and have various clashes returning to homelands.

WAR MOVIES:

•*The Lost Patrol* (1934) (☞ ■ ☆): Victor McLaglen and >Boris Karloff in rearguard fight in Mesopotamian desert.

•*The Long Voyage Home* (1940) (■ ☞ ✍ ☆): a heart-broken, drink-sodden skipper guides a small boat full of weapons across the dangerous Atlantic.

OTHERS:

•*Arrowsmith* (1931) (☞): Ronald Colman as selfless doctor in adaptation of Sinclair Lewis novel.

•*The Informer* (1935) (☆): IRA man Victor McLaglen sells leader for £20 and is pursued for his treachery.

•*The Prisoner of Shark Island* (1936) (☆ ☞ ✍): Warner Baxter as Dr Samuel Mudd who is unjustly accused of Lincoln's assassination but proves himself a hero during a prison epidemic.

•*Wee Willie Winkie* (1937): Rudyard Kipling tale has Shirley Temple acting as mascot to Raj regiment.

•*Tobacco Road* (1941) (☞ ■): poor whites in Georgia dread the thought of eviction, but soon make plans for their new land.

•*How Green Was My Valley?* (1941): Roddy McDowall's childhood in Welsh mining village.

•*The Three Godfathers* (1948) (☆): an on the run trio led by >John Wayne saves a baby abandoned in the desert.

•>*The Quiet Man* (1952)(✍ ☞ ☆ ■ ♫).

•*Mogambo* (1953): >Clark Gable takes Ava Gardner (AAN) and Grace Kelly on a Kenyan gorilla shoot.

•*The Sun Shines Bright* (1953) (☞ ✍): repeated and further episodes in the life of the small town post-Civil War judge first seen in Ford's 1934 film *Judge Priest* (☞ ☆).

Forman, Miloš
Czech-born American director (b 1932)

An international reputation for gentle satire and keen observation forged in the radical Czech films *Peter and Pavla* (US: *Black Peter*) (*Cerny Petr*) (1964) (☞) (a trainee store detective has relationship problems), *A Blonde In Love* (US: *Loves of a Blonde* (*Lásky Jedné Plavovlásky*) (1965) (☞) (a factory girl is disapproved of by Prague pianist's parents) and *The Fireman's Ball* (*Horí, Má Panenko*) (1967) (☞ ✍) (a charity ball is blighted by disasters and disrupted by a fire call), Forman defected during the Soviet repression of 1968. Although Hollywood afforded teen rebellion movie *Taking Off* (1970) (☞) (parents seeking daughter in hippy commune let their own hair down) a cool welcome, his standing has been restored through Best Picture and Best Direction Oscar winners >*One Flew Over the Cuckoo's Nest* (1975) (☆ ✍ ☞) and >*Amadeus* (1984) (☞ ■ ☆ ♫ ✍).

•*Hair* (1978) (☞ ♫): musical sees a >Vietnam volunteer turn on, tune in and drop out in the recruiting office.

•*Ragtime* (1981) (☞ ☆): having received no justice through the usual channels, a victimized black pianist turns to explosives.

Frankenstein ☆ ☞ ✍ ✳ ■
USA • Universal • 1931 • 71 mins • b/w
d James Whale **w** Garrett Fort/Francis Edward Faragoh/John L. Balderston
ph Arthur Edeson **m** David Broekman
>Boris Karloff, Colin Clive, Mae Clarke, Edward Van Sloan, Frederick Kerr, Dwight Frye

The fact that Mary Shelley survived let alone drew inspiration for her story of man playing God from the manic visit to Byron described in the Ken Russell film *Gothic* (1987) excuses her skimping on descriptive details of mad scientist Baron Frankenstein's creation. Fortunately make-up man Jack Pierce was more diligent and it is his vision that has sustained the genre, right through to Hermann Munster of 1960s TV fame. Karloff's almost child-like monster, particularly when confronted with fire and a little girl playing, is a supreme blend of horror and pathos, remotely matched only by Lon Chaney Jr's *Man Made Monster* (UK: *The Electric Man*) (George Waggner 1940) (☆), while the Baron's lab – Expressionist shades of >*Metropolis* – was not bettered until >Alec Guinness's in *The Man in the White Suit* (Alexander Mackendrick 1951). More a tear than a fearjerker.

•A Jew constructs a monster out of clay to protect the Prague ghetto in *The Golem* (Paul Wegener/Carl Boese 1920) (☞ ■)/Julien Duvivier 1936) (☞).
•The transplanted brain of a top scientist malfunctions unleashing *The Colossus of New York* (Eugene Lourie 1958) (✳).
•Andy Griffith is the country boy who is turned into a monster by media over-exposure in *A Face in the Crowd* (>Elia Kazan 1957) (☞ ✍ ☆).
•There are gentle giants on the loose in *Big Foot and the Hendersons* (US: *Harry and the Hendersons*) (William Dear 1987) (✳) (John Lithgow's holidaying family meet a country park yeti) and *Of Mice and Men* (Lewis Milestone 1939) (☆ ☞ ✍) (Lon Chaney Jr's strength forces him and partner Burgess Meredith away from their farm job in an adaptation of >John Steinbeck's novel).
•There is an evil doctor on the loose in Fay Wray's hospital in *Dr X* (>Michael Curtiz 1932) (☞ ☆).
•A surgeon rebuilds his daughter's face from the skin of his victims in *Eyes Without a Face* (US: *The Horror Chamber of Doctor Faustus*) (*Les Yeux sans Visage*) (Georges Franju 1959) (☞ ✍).
•Elizabeth Taylor's cosmetic surgery gives her the confidence to ditch dour husband >Henry Fonda in *Ash Wednesday* (Larry Peerce 1973) (☆).

FRENCH REVOLUTION

Carry On Don't Lose Your Head (Gerald Thomas 1969) ☆ ✍
Black Fingernail Sid James rescues the Duc de Pommesfrites (Charles Hawtrey) from Citizen Camembert (Kenneth Williams)'s guillotine.
Danton (>Andrej Wajda 1982) ☆ ☞ ■
Extremists within the Convention, jealous of >Gérard Depardieu's popularity, arrest him on trumped up corruption charges.
Lafayette (Jean Dréville 1961) ■
French troops help the American colonists defeat the British, learning revolutionary ideals in the process.
La Marseillaise (>Jean Renoir 1937) ☞ ✍ ♪
Troops from Marseilles spread the anthem on their way to fight the invading Prussians in 1792.
The Night of Varennes (*La Nuit de Varennes*) (Ettore Scola 1982) ■ ☆
The coach carrying Restif De Bretonne (>Jean-Louis Barrault), Casanova (>Marcello Mastroianni) and countess >Hanna Schygulla follows the fleeing royal family.
Orphans of the Storm (>D. W. Griffith 1921) ☞ ☆ ■
>Lillian and Dorothy Gish witness the storming of the Bastille and survive the guillotine.
The Scarlet Pimpernel (Harold Young 1934) ☆ ✍
Mild-mannered English aristo >Leslie Howard rescues Merle Oberon from Raymond Massey, in the screen version of Baroness Orczy's swashbuckling novel.
A Tale of Two Cities (Jack Conway 1935) ☆ ✍/(Ralph Thomas 1958) ✍ ☆
Ronald Colman and Dirk Bogarde respectively as >Charles Dickens' heroic lawyer Sidney Carton.

The Frog Prince ☆ ✍ ■
GB · Goldcrest · 1985 · 90 mins · col
d Brian Gilbert   w Posy Simmonds
ph Clive Tickner
Jane Snowden, Alexandre Sterling, Diana Blackburn, Oystein Wiik

Continuing where *French without Tears*

THE FRESHMAN
(Sam Taylor/Fred Newmeyer 1925) ☆

HAROLD LLOYD

GRANDMA'S BOY
(Fred Newmeyer 1922)
(country cousin Lloyd becomes a hero through a magic potion in this, his personal favourite film)

SAFETY LAST
(Fred Newmeyer/Sam Taylor 1923) ☆ ☞
(having failed to become a success in the city, Lloyd climbs a building to draw attention to himself)

WHY WORRY?
(Fred Newmeyer/Sam Taylor 1923) ☆
(hypochondriac Lloyd's South American rest cure coincides with a revolution)

GIRL SHY
(Fred Newmeyer/Sam Taylor 1924) ☆
(Lloyd's stuttering bestselling writer on love prevents a girl from marrying the wrong man)

HIGH AND DIZZY
(Fred Newmeyer/Sam Taylor 1924) ☆
(drunken Lloyd tries to rescue sleepwalking Mildred Davis from high rise peril)

FOR HEAVEN'S SAKE
(Sam Taylor 1926) ☆
(millionaire Lloyd gets a bunch of drunks to a church on time)

THE KID BROTHER
(Lewis Milestone/Ted Wilde 1927) ☆
(by catching the baddies and getting the girl, Lloyd proves his worth to his sheriff brother)

HARRY LANGDON

TRAMP TRAMP TRAMP
(Harry Edwards 1926) ☆
(Harry hopes to walk into >Joan Crawford's good books in this >Frank Capra/Arthur Ripley script)

THE STRONG MAN
(>Frank Capra 1926) ☆ ☞
(Belgian soldier Harry falls for the Red Cross volunteer who has been writing letters to him)

LONG PANTS
(>Frank Capra 1926) ☆
(Harry defies his mother's dictate that keeps him in short trousers and sets out to emulate his hero – Don Juan)

HIS FIRST FLAME
(Harry Edwards 1927) ☆
(Harry loves a gold-digger, but her good-natured sister saves our naïve hero in this >Capra-scripted comedy)

THE CHASER
(Harry Langdon 1928) ✍
(a judge refuses Harry's wife a divorce, but insists he assumes her role as a housewife for thirty days or go to jail)

Clumsy student Lloyd
becomes football hero

MACK SENNETT – Scriptwriter/Producer

THE MASQUERADER
(>Charles Chaplin 1916) ✍
(Fatty Arbuckle's life is not all that it seems)

FATTY AND MABEL ADRIFT
(Roscoe Arbuckle 1916) ☆ ✳
(Fatty Arbuckle and Mabel Normand's beach-house is
put to sea by vengeful villains)

MICKEY
(Richard Jones 1917) ✍
(poor girl Mabel Normand's role in high society depends on her winning a horse race)

THE EXTRA GIRL
(Richard Jones 1923) ✍
(down-on-her-luck actress Mabel Normand continues
to tread the boards like a real trooper)

THE SHRIEK OF ARABY
(Richard Jones 1923) ✍ ☆
(Ben Turpin stars in this spoof of Valentino's classic
The Sheik)

HAL ROACH – Producer

IT'S A GIFT
(Fred Guiol 1923) ✳
(inventor Snub Pollard's ingenious devices are often
more trouble than they are worth)

BIG MOMENTS FROM LITTLE PICTURES
(Fred Guiol 1924) ✍
(Will Rogers spoofs such movie luminaries as Valenti-
no, >Douglas Fairbanks and the Keystone Cops)

CALL OF THE CUCKOO
(Fred Guiol 1927) ☆
(>Laurel & Hardy and Charley Chase have cameo roles
in this tale of a badly built house where nothing works
properly)

PUTTING PANTS ON PHILIP
(Clyde Brookman/>Leo McCarey 1927) ☆
(embarrassed Oliver Hardy tries to cover up what Scottish Stan Laurel keeps beneath his kilt)

HATS OFF
(Hal Yates/>Leo McCarey 1927) ☆ ☞
(Laurel and Hardy have to get a washing machine to
the top of a flight of steps in this forerunner to *The
Music Box*)

THE FINISHING TOUCH
(Clyde Bruckman 1928) ☆
(builders Laurel & Hardy's true vocation lies in demolition)

YOU'RE DARN TOOTIN'
(Edgar Kennedy/>Leo McCarey 1928) ☆
(musicians Stan and Ollie infuriate a conductor with
their ineptitude)

(>Anthony Asquith 1939) () left off, Posy Simmonds's autobiographical screenplay was one of the few joyful moments in the troubled history of the British film company Goldcrest. It's too early for the 1960s to be swinging uncontrollably when Jenny (Snowden), an English student at the Sorbonne, falls in love with undergraduate Jean-Philippe (Sterling). Before she commits herself, she wants assurance that his motives go deeper than his polished veneer of charm. When he refuses her request to learn the Balcony Scene from *Romeo and Juliet*, the kind of task knights of old would have given their eye teeth for, it seems that true love will founder, but we have reckoned without a Metro romance finale that comfortably pre-dates *Crocodile Dundee* (Peter Faiman 1986) (☆). Beautifully capturing Paris, this wistful romantic comedy is worth a tear or two.

•Imogen Stubbs' French romance in the industrial north is far grittier and ultimately doomed in *Nanou* (Conny Templeman 1987) (☆).

•A Marxist is faced with a difficult choice between her politics and her society photographer boyfriend, in *Rouge Baiser* (Vera Belmont 1985) (☞).

•>Alastair Sim and Margaret Rutherford are the elderly ingenues lost in France in *Innocents in Paris* (Gordon Parry 1953) (☆ ✍).

•The fortunes of town and country cousins at the Sorbonne inform *Les Cousins* (*The Cousins*) (>Claude Chabrol 1959) (☞ ■).

•The French satirize an Englishman's view of the French in >Preston Sturges's *The French They Are a Funny Race* (1957) (☞).

•Liverpudlian Alexandra Pigg fights to join sailor Peter Firth in the Soviet Union in the cross-culture love story *Letter to Brezhnev* (Chris Bernard 1986) (✍ ☆).

•An arrogant male's refusal to contemplate any sex that does not have him in the dominant position causes the rows that pepper *The End of the World in Our Usual Bed in a Night Full of Rain* (Lina Wertmüller 1978) (☞).

FUTURE SOCIETY

Alphaville (*Alphaville, Une Étrange Aventure de Lemmy Caution*) (>Jean-Luc Godard 1965) ☞ ■

Private eye Eddie Constantine investigates on a planet where conformity is law and love illegal.

Blade Runner (Ridley Scott 1982) ☆ ✳

>Harrison Ford hunts down androids seeking life extensions from their scientist creator in the Los Angeles of 2019.

Brazil (Terry Gilliam 1985) ☞ ✳

In a totalitarian Britain, things break down, people disappear and the saviour is a terrorist heating engineer >Robert De Niro.

A Clockwork Orange (>Stanley Kubrick 1971) ☞ ■

Brainwashed thug Malcolm McDowell discovers the brave new world is a violent one, in this adaptation of Anthony Burgess's novel.

Forbidden Planet (Fred M. Wilcox 1956) ✳

Adaptation of *The Tempest* sees an expedition land on a planet to discover that Walter Pidgeon and daughter Anne Francis are the only survivors of the earth colony.

Logan's Run (Michael Anderson 1976) ✍

Michael York takes Jenny Agutter on his escape from a society where euthenasia is compulsory at 30.

Memoirs of a Survivor (David Gladwell 1981) ☆ ✍

Julie Christie retreats from the decline of humanity to an old house in this Doris Lessing tale.

1984 (Michael Anderson 1955) ✍

Michael Redgrave as Winston Smith who is watched by Big Brother in the Fascist state of Oceania.

Things to Come (William Cameron 1936) ✳ ■ ♫

As the Blitz hits London, Raymond Massey gets a preview of the glass domed future as predicted in H. G. Wells's novel.

Gabin, Jean

(Jean-Alexis Moncorgé) French actor (1904–1976)

The films of Jean Gabin act as a barometer of French self-opinion in the half century following the Treaty of Versailles. As 'Collective Security' began to crumble, his decent proletarian, victim of society and love, reflected the incipient pessimism: *Pépé Le Moko* (Jean Duvivier 1936) (☆ ☞) (Casbah gangster Gabin is caught when love forces him into the open); >*La Grande Illusion* (*Grand Illusion*) (Jean Renoir 1937) (☆ ☞ ✍ ■); *Quai des Brumes* (*Port of Shadows*) (>Marcel Carné 1938) (☆ ☞) (killer deserter Gabin's elopement with Michèle Morgan is foiled by her guardian); *La Bête Humaine* (*The Human Beast*) (>Jean Renoir 1938) (☞ ✍ ☆) (train driver Gabin plots with lover Simone Simon to kill her husband and his colleague); and >*Le Jour se Lève* (*Daybreak*) (Marcel Carné 1939) (☆ ☞ ✍ ■). Elevated to the bourgeoisie, he foretold of postwar recovery: *Love is My Profession* (*En Cas de Malheur*) (Claude Autant-Lara 1958) (☆) (lawyer Gabin leaves his dull marriage for client Brigitte Bardot in this Simenon tale) and *Les Grandes Familles* (*The Possessors*) (Denys De La Patellière 1958) (Gabin fights off rivals to ensure that his weak son inherits a booming business). Then he testified to France's new prosperity and security in roles that encompassed sagacity – *Maigret Sets a Trap* (US: *Inspector Maigret*) (*Maigret Tend un Piège*) (Jean Delannoy 1957) (✍ ☞) (Gabin as Simenon's detective using a decoy to tempt a killer into an indiscretion) and *Maigret Sees Red* (*Maigret Voit Rouge*) (Gilles Grangier 1963) – and comedy: *Le Vieux de la Veille* (Gilles Grangier 1960) (☆) (Gabin leads a revolt in an old people's home) and *Le Président* (Henri Verneuil 1961) (☆) (Gabin as a politician who has fun exercising power).

•*Zouzou* (Marc Allégret 1934) (☆): Gabin as a ladies' man sailor accompanying Josephine Baker on her fame-seeking trip to Paris.

•*La Belle Équipe* (*They Were Five*) (Julien Duvivier 1936) (☆ ✍): Gabin and his fellow lottery winners buy a riverside inn, only to fall out over flirtatious Viviane Romance.

•*The Lower Depths* (*Les Bas Fonds*) (>Jean Renoir 1936) (☆ ☞): thief Gabin and impoverished noble Louis Jouvet live in a poor house in this adaptation of Maxim Gorky's play.

•*The Walls of Malapaga* (*Au delà des Grilles*) (aka *Le Mura di Malapaga*) (René Clément 1949) (☆ ☞): murderous stowaway Gabin falls for Genoan waitress Isa Miranda in a film that won the Best Actress and Director awards at Cannes.

•*Grisbi* (US: *Honour Among Thieves*) (*Touchez pas le Grisbi*) (Jacques Becker 1953) (☆): Gabin won the Best Actor award at Venice as one of the bank robbers coming to blows over the proceeds.

•*French Cancan* (US: *Only The French Can*) (>Jean Renoir 1955) (☆ ☞): Gabin as owner of the Moulin Rouge caught between a dancer and a spitfire mistress.

•*Les Misérables* (Jean-Paul Le Chanois 1957) (☆ ■ ✍): Gabin as Victor Hugo's Jean Valjean, whose life is blighted by a murder he did not commit.

•*Archimède the Tramp* (US: *The Magnificent Tramp*) (*Archimède le Clochard*) (Gilles Grangier 1958) (☆ ✍): (Gabin took the Best Actor award at Berlin for his performance as a grumpy old hobo with a taste for confrontation and comfort.

•*Maigret et L'Affaire Saint-Fiacre* (Jean Delannoy 1958): as Simenon's pipe-smoking detective insisting on solving a crime his own way.

•*A Monkey in Winter* (*Un Singe en Hiver*) (Henri Verneuil 1962) (☆): Gabin, a hotelier and novelist >Jean-Paul Belmondo discuss cherished dreams of adventure, but lack the nerve to undertake them.

•*The Big Snatch* (US: *Any Number Can Win*) (*Mélodie en Sous-Sol*) (Henri Verneuil 1963) (☆ ☞): Gabin has doubts about including impetuous Alain Delon on his farewell robbery.

•*Verdict* (US: *Jury of One*) (*Le Testament*) (André Cayatte 1974) (☆): Sophia Loren tries to clear her rapist son by kidnapping judge Gabin's sick wife.

Gable, Clark
American actor (1901–1960)

In 1931, James Cagney discovered grapefruit in *Public Enemy* (UK: *Enemies of the Public*), Gable slapped Norma Shearer in *A Free Soul* (Clarence Brown 1931) (lawyer Lionel Barrymore tries to keep his daughter away from

mobster Gable) and both became stars. While Cagney gradually shrugged off the gangster image, Gable continued to play slight variations on the theme of charming, fast-talking rascals, hitting all the right notes in >*It Happened One Night* (AAN: >Frank Capra 1934) (✍ ☆ ☞), *San Francisco* (W. S. Van Dyke 1936) (☆ ☞ ✳) (on the eve of the 1906 earthquake, club owner Gable's affair with Jeanette MacDonald is refereed by priest >Spencer Tracy), *Saratoga* (Jack Conway 1937) (☆) (the Anita Loos co-written script has bookie Gable wooing horse breeder's daughter >Jean Harlow) and of course, >*Gone with the Wind* (AAN: Victor Fleming 1939) (☆ ■ ✍ ☞ ♫). Two years in the Army Air Corps followed the death of his wife >Carole Lombard, but the ensuing depression failed to lift and his career declined sadly; of his later films, the only ones worthy of mention are: *Mogambo* (>John Ford 1954) (☞ ☆) (Gable escorts Ava Gardner and Grace Kelly on safari; *Teacher's Pet* (George Seaton 1957) (☆) (editor Gable falls for journalism professor Doris Day); and his final film *The Misfits* (>John Huston 1961) (☞ ☆) (ageing cowhand Gable falls for >Marilyn Monroe, in an Arthur Miller script).

 •*Red Dust* (Victor Fleming 1932) (☞ ☆): rubber planter Gable is vamped by Mary Astor but prefers prostitute >Jean Harlow.

•*Chained* (Clarence Brown 1934) (☆ ☞): >Joan Crawford leaves married man Otto Kruger for Gable after a shipboard romance.

•*Mutiny on the Bounty* (AAN: Frank Lloyd 1935) (☆ ☞ ✍): Gable's Fletcher Christian rebels against >Charles Laughton's tyrannical Captain Bligh.

•*Test Pilot* (Victor Fleming 1938) (☆ ☞): >Myrna Loy and >Spencer Tracy keep unruly pilot Gable on the rails.

•*Too Hot to Handle* (Jack Conway 1938) (☆): cameraman Gable helps aviatrix >Myrna Loy find her lost brother in South America.

•*Strange Cargo* (Frank Borzage 1940) (☆): >Joan Crawford helps convicts, including Gable and >Peter Lorre flee, Devil's Island.

•*Honky Tonk* (Jack Conway 1941) (☆): (con

man Gable fails to put one over judge's daughter Lana Turner.

GAMBLERS

Atlantic City, USA (>Louis Malle 1980) ☞ ☆
Burt Lancaster and Susan Sarandon both received AANs for their roles in this tale of a casino con.
Bay of Angels (La Baie des Anges) (Jacques Demy 1962) ☞ ☆
Lucky beginner Claude Mann is fleeced by compulsive Jeanne Moreau.
The Cincinnati Kid (Norman Jewison 1965) ☆
>Edward G. Robinson and Steve McQueen dispute stud poker supremacy.
Gambling Lady (Archie Mayo 1934) ☆
>Barbara Stanwyck fails to learn the lesson of her father's debt suicide and gambles her way into a murder mystery.
Gilda (Charles Vidor 1946) ■ ☆ ☞
Gambler Glenn Ford hopes that Rita Hayworth's jealous husband doesn't rumble their affair.
The Hustler (Robert Rossen 1961) ☆ ⚄
>Paul Newman makes a fast buck and learns about life while playing pool.
The Lady Eve (>Preston Sturges 1941) ⚄ ☞ ☆
>Barbara Stanwyck and Charles Coburn set out to repay >Henry Fonda for escaping their shipboard card con.
Mississippi Gambler (Rudolph Maté 1953) ☞
Tyrone Power finds Piper Laurie amid the tables of a river boat.

Gandhi ☞ ☆ ⚄ ■

GB • Columbia/Goldcrest • 1981 • 188 mins • col
d >Richard Attenborough w John Briley ph Billy Williams/Ronnie Taylor m George Fenton
Ben Kingsley, Candice Bergen, Edward Fox, John Mills, John Gielgud, Trevor Howard

Just managing to stay the right side of hagio-graphy, Richard Attenborough's long-cherished dream is a monumental tribute to the lawyer whose policy of passive resistance earned him the respect of diametrically opposed religious factions and India its independence. As the film elevates him from South African obscurity to worldwide renown, Ben Kingsley's Mahatma superbly conveys the courageously determined humility that made Gandhi such an inspiring leader and difficult political adversary, while Attenborough's understanding of just where to prick the contemporary conscience and his disciplined handling of a vast cast of extras, suggests that he is to be the 20th-century's foremost cinematic historian.

•Adolf Hitler is shown to be a leader of great charisma in *Triumph of the Will (Triumph des Willens)* (Leni Riefenstahl 1935) (☞ ■).
•Peter Sellers is the English actor impersonating an Indian and causing chaos at *The Party* (Blake Edwards 1968) (☆).
•Julie Christie parallels her great aunt Greta Scacchi's affair with Raj prince Shashi Kapoor, in the screen version of Ruth Prawer Jhabvala's Booker Prize-winning *Heat And Dust* (James Ivory 1982) (⚄ ■ ☞ ☆).
•Hero to some (>Marlon Brando), villain to others (John Gielgud and James Mason), Louis Calhern's *Julius Caesar* was assassinated in >Joseph L. Mankiewicz's 1953 adaptation of >Shakespeare's Roman tragedy (⚄ ☆ ☞ ■).

GANGSTERS

Al Capone (Richard Wilson 1959) ☆
Rod Steiger as the Underworld King of Chicago.
The Amazing Dr Clitterhouse (Anatole Litvak 1938) ☆
Crime specialist >Edward G. Robinson studies and then joins >Humphrey Bogart's gang.
Baby Face Nelson (Don Siegel 1957) ☆
Mickey Rooney goes from being hailed as Public Enemy No. 1 to a hail of FBI bullets.
The Big Combo (Joseph H. Lewis 1955) ☞ ⚄
Cop Cornel Wilde and hood Richard Conte fall

out over women and their interpretations of the law.

Force of Evil (Abraham Polonsky 1948) ☆
Thomas Gomez kills his lawyer John Garfield's brother.

G Men (William Keighley 1935) ☆ ✍
Gangster killer of >James Cagney's best friend is also a childhood buddy.

Guys and Dolls (>Joseph L. Mankiewicz 1955) ♫ ☆
Frank Sinatra avoids marriage, organizes crap games and bets that gangster >Marlon Brando can't seduce Salvation Army girl Jean Simmons.

Little Caesar (>Mervyn Le Roy 1930) ☆ ☞
>Edward G. Robinson as an Al Capone-like gangster experiencing highs and lows.

Garbo, Greta
(Greta Gustafsson) Swedish-born actress (1905–1990)

The 'sophisticated, scornful and superior' woman that Mauritz Stiller created in *The Atonement of Gösta Berling* (US: *The Legend of Gösta Berling*) (*Gösta Berlings Saga*) (1924) (☞ ☆) (Garbo as an Italian countess encountering depraved defrocked priest Lars Hanson) was the Garbo of her splendid silents: *Joyless Street* (US: *The Street of Sorrow*) (aka *Street of Sorrow*) (*Die Freudlose Gasse*) (>G.W. Pabst 1925) (☞ ☆) (impoverished Greta is forced to enter a Viennese brothel); *The Temptress* (Mauritz Stiller/Fred Niblo 1926) (☆ ✍) (Garbo drives besotted men to ruin and Lionel Barrymore to murder); *Flesh and the Devil* (Clarence Brown 1926) (☆ ☞) (Greta endures a brace of marriages, but really loves John Gilbert); and *Wild Orchids* (Sidney Franklin 1929) (☆) (Garbo is caught up in a Java love triangle). However, from *Anna Christie* (AAN: Clarence Brown 1930) (☆ ☞) (Garbo talks in the title role playing >Eugene O'Neill's drunken waterfront whore in love with sailor Charles Bickford), the MGM alliance of an androgynous appearance and a capacity for suffering provided the persona for her roles in: *Mata Hari* (George Fitzmaurice 1931) (☆) (Garbo as the First World War spy ruined by falling for target Ramon Novarro); *Grand Hotel* (Edmund Goulding 1932) (✍) (ballerina Garbo wants to be alone while the rest of those in the hotel are involved in murder and romance); *Anna Karenina* (Clarence Brown 1935) (☆ ✍ ☞) (aristocrat >Basil Rathbone's wife Greta has a doomed, exiled affair with army officer Vronsky [>Fredric March] in this adaptation of the Leo Tolstoy novel); >*Camille* (>George Cukor 1936) (☆ ☞ ✍); *Marie Walewska* (US: *Conquest*) (Clarence Brown 1937) (☆ ☞ ✍) (Garbo as the Polish countess who bears Charles Boyer's Napoleon a son and visits him in exile); and >*Ninotchka* (AAN: >Ernst Lubitsch 1939) (✍ ☞ ☆ ■). In the majestic finale of *Queen Christina* (Rouben Mamoulian 1933) (☆ ☞) (17th-century Swedish queen abdicates and goes into exile when marriage to Spanish ambassador John Gilbert is opposed), where she impassively watches the receding Swedish coastline, we are challenged to interpret her feelings for ourselves. The brevity of her career and the totality of her solitude means we must do the same with the real Garbo.

 •*Love* (Edmund Goulding 1927): a silent dress rehearsal for *Anna Karenina* with John Gilbert as Vronsky.

•*The Kiss* (Jacques Feyder 1929) (☆): Greta is tried for her husband's murder after a kiss from Lew Ayres in the last MGM silent.

•*Romance* (AAN: Clarence Brown 1930) (☆ ☞): Greta as an opera singer torn between a rich patron and a devoted admirer.

•*Susan Lenox: Her Fall and Rise* (UK: *The Rise of Helga*) (Robert Z. Leonard 1931) (☆): Garbo is unlucky in love with all but >Clark Gable, but they are fated to remain apart.

•*As You Desire Me* (George Fitzmaurice 1932) (☆): Greta forgets she is married to Melvyn Douglas and has fling with writer >Erich Von Stroheim.

•*The Painted Veil* (Richard Boleslawksi 1934) (☆): Greta in W. Somerset Maugham story, is torn between two lovers: husband Herbert Marshall and paramour George Brent.

•*Two-Faced Woman* (>George Cukor 1941) (☆): believing husband Melvyn Douglas is two-timing her, Greta poses as her own twin sister.

The General ☆ ✍ ☞ ■
USA • United Artists • 1926 • 80 mins • b/w
d >Buster Keaton/Clyde Bruckman   w Al
Boasberg/Charles Smith   ph J. Devereux
Jennings/Bert Haines
Buster Keaton, Marion Mack, Glen
Cavander

The relationship between Buster Keaton's
Confederate locomotive driver Johnny Gray
and Southern beauty Annabelle Lee (Mack) is
based on such pinball repartee that it might be
called a silent screwball comedy. In the train
chase that launched a thousand car chases, she
helps and hinders the man rejected from military service to become a hero as he lures the
Unionists, who stole his *General*, behind the
lines – but not without a struggle and some of
the most precise and athletic gags ever performed before a camera. While celebrating the
power of the machine in almost >Eisensteinian
fashion, Keaton's conquest of the truculent
steam engine demonstrates that man's
pugnacity can still overcome his frailty. The
most complete silent comedy.

•If *Go West* (Edward Buzzell 1940)
(☆) looks familiar, it is because it
is the >Marx Brothers' tribute/pa-
rody, while *The Great Locomotive Chase*
(Francis D. Lyon 1956) (✍) is the Disney version.
•Local rail enthusiasts keep a branch line open
by running it themselves, in the Ealing comedy
The Titfield Thunderbolt (Charles Crichton
1952) (✍ ☞).
•Another war, the Second World War, saw
another train chase with Frank Sinatra on the
footplate of *Von Ryan's Express* (Mark Robson
1965) (✍ ☆).
•Stunning stunts abound in Harold Lloyd's
Safety Last (Sam Taylor/Fred Newmeyer 1923)
(☆ ■) (a clock face saves Lloyd on a climb up
a department store) and in *Our Hospitality*
(Buster Keaton/Jack Blystone 1923) (☆ ■),
including one on a waterfall.

Genevieve ✍ ☆ ♫ ☞
GB • GFD/Sirius • 1954 • 86 mins • col
d Henry Cornelius   w William Rose
ph Christopher Challis   m Larry Adler
Kenneth More, John Gregson, Dinah
Sheridan, Kay Kendall

What was intended, and has been loved by
millions as a good-natured British comedy
about two vintage cars racing between London
and Brighton, can now be seen as a damning
condemnation of the chauvinistic, win-at-all-
costs competitive streak that drives so many
enthusiasts and brings interminable hardship
to their partners. The calamities that mar the
progress of a cast that became a national institution become so predictable after just ten
miles outside the capital that their banality
irritates, but the reactions they induce, to the
accompaniment of Larry Adler's famous har-
monica theme, are ceaselessly amusing and
revealing. It is regrettable that the film reflects
its time by permitting the male ego to be ultimately soothed by a cooing female, but it still
creeps beneath the principles whenever it's
shown.

•Male aggression dominates life in
an Australian town in *Outback*
(Ted Kotcheff 1970) and in Robert
Redford's career as a daredevil flier in *The
Great Waldo Pepper* (George Roy Hill 1975) (☆
■).
•A flying vintage car carries Dick Van Dyke's
family on adventures in a child-hating country,
in *Chitty Chitty Bang Bang* (Ken Hughes
1968) (☆ ✳).
•Emilio Estevez's car obsession brings more
danger than pleasure in *Repo Man* (Alex Cox
1984) (☆ ✳).
•Richard Pryor is among those at the *Car Wash*
(Michael Schultz 1976) (♫), although car care
is the last thing on most of their minds.

GHOSTS

The Amazing Mr Blunden (Lionel Jeffries
1972) ☞ ☆
Benign ghost Laurence Naismith takes two

children back a century to settle unfinished business.

The Bespoke Overcoat (Jack Clayton 1956) ✍ ☆

Nikolai Gogol tale of a ghost urging a tailor to steal the coat he needs to survive.

Dona Flor and Her Two Husbands (Dona Flor e Seus Dois Maridos) (Bruno Barreto, Brazil 1976) ✍

On the anniversary of his death, a man returns to discover his wife has remarried.

Don't Take It to Heart (Jeffrey Dell 1944) ✍
The Blitz awakens a match-marring ghost.

Kwaidan (Masaki Kobayashi 1964) ☞ ▣
Four Western tales given Japanese settings and awarded an AAN and a Special Jury Prize at Cannes.

Miracle in the Rain (Rudolph Maté 1954) ✍ ☞

The Ben Hecht story of soldier Van Johnson keeping a rendezvous with Jane Wyman despite being killed in action.

The Portrait of Jennie (UK: Jennie) (>William Dieterle 1948) ☞ ☆ ♫

Artist Joseph Cotten sees the subject of a painting (Jennifer Jones) return to life and increase in beauty.

The Scoundrel (Ben Hecht/Charles MacArthur 1935)

Deceased writer Noël Coward returns to trade witticisms with Alexander Woolcott and find the meaning of life.

Sylvia and the Ghost (US: Sylvia and the Phantom) (Sylvie et le Fantôme) (Claude Autant-Lara 1944) ✍

The ghost of a castle portrait comes to meet its teenage admirer.

Topper (Norman Z. McLeod 1937) ☆ ✍
>Cary Grant and Constance Bennett as the ghostly Kirbys who spice up banker Roland Young's drab life.

Topper Returns (Roy Del Ruth 1941) ☆
Joan Blondell and Roland Young combine to point a finger at her killer.

>**Haunted Houses**

Girls' schools

The Belles of St Trinian's (Frank Launder 1954) ☆ ✍
>Alastair Sim as headmistress Miss Fritton and her bookie brother Clarence who is after a racehorse that is hidden in the riotous school.

Blue Murder at St Trinian's (Frank Launder 1957) ☆ ✍
The ghoulish girls beat up Italian students and a jewel thief on a Unesco educational visit to Rome.

Brides of Dracula (Terence Fisher 1960) ☆ ☞ ✍
The Count's descendant causes havoc in a boarding school, until Peter Cushing arrives with the garlic and stake.

Claudine (Serge De Poligny 1939) ✍
An adaptation of Colette's saucy schoolday recollections.

Mädchen in Uniform (Girls in Uniform) (aka Children in Uniform) (Leontine Sagan 1931)/(Geza Radvanyi 1958) ✍
A nervous girl becomes accustomed to school through the comfort of a female teacher.

Olivia (Jacqueline Audry 1950) ✍
Dorothy Bussy's autobiographical tale of an English girl's involvement in a bitter dispute at a French school.

The Prime of Miss Jean Brodie (Ronald Neame 1969) ☆ ✍
>Maggie Smith as Muriel Spark's Edinburgh teacher worshipped by her girls and two teachers.

Suspiria (Dario Argento 1976) ✍
Jessica Harper is kept on her toes by a series of murders at a dance school.

Gish, Lillian
American actress (b 1896)

Acting from the age of five, Gish was introduced to mentor >D. W. Griffith by 'America's sweetheart' Mary Pickford. As a waif with courage, she was the heroine of his *The Birth of a Nation* (1915) (☞ ☆ ▣) (the lives and loves of two families during the US Civil War), *Broken Blossoms* (1919) (☆ ☞) (Gish is murdered by her father who in turn is killed by her Chinese lover) and *Way Down East* (1920) (☆ ☞ ✍)

(Richard Barthelmess rescues Gish from a life of misfortune and abuse). Griffith and Gish parted over money and as MGM head Irving Thalberg favoured flappers to sufferers, Gish faded, although she has always been well-received in character roles: *Duel in the Sun* (AAN: >King Vidor and others 1942) (☆ ☞) (Gish and husband Lionel Barrymore mediate between feuding sons Gregory Peck and Joseph Cotten); *The Comedians* (Peter Glenville 1967) (✍ ☆) (Gish joins >Richard Burton and >Alec Guinness under threat, in >Graham Greene's Haitian adventure); *A Wedding* (>Robert Altman 1978) (☆ ☞) (Gish as the bed-ridden matriarch unimpressed by ceremony feuding); and *The Whales of August* (Lindsay Anderson 1988) (☆) (sisters Gish and >Bette Davis squabble through old age with friends Vincent Price and Ann Sothern).

•*Hearts of the World* (>D. W. Griffith 1918) (☆ ☞): stories of how Lillian, sister Dorothy Gish, >Erich Von Stroheim and Noël Coward are affected by First World War events.
•*True Heart Susie* (>D. W. Griffith 1919) (☆): Gish sells a cow to pay for her ungrateful boyfriend's education.
•*Orphans of the Storm* (D. W. Griffith 1921) (☞ ☆ ■): the Gish sisters survive the French Revolution.
•*The Scarlet Letter* (Victor Sjöström 1927) (☆ ☞): Gish as a woman accused of adultery in Nathaniel Hawthorne's tale of puritanical Boston.
•*The Wind* (Victor Sjöström 1927) (☆ ☞ ■): As the wind batters her remote shack, Gish endures a loveless marriage and defends herself against a rapist.
•*Night of the Hunter* (>Charles Laughton 1955): Gish tries to protect two children from whom fake preacher (Robert Mitchum) is trying to get loot location details.

Godard, Jean-Luc
French-born Swiss actor/writer/director
(b 1930)
An idle Sorbonne undergraduate and prolific *Cahiers du Cinéma* critic, Godard's immeasurably influential debut feature >*A Bout de Souffle* (*Breathless*) (1960) (☞ ☆ ■) disturbed the traditions of film-making. However the rapid cuts incorporated in that film were nothing compared to his use of negative footage in *A Married Woman* (US: *The Married Woman*) (*Une Femme Mariée*) (1964) (☞ ✍) (Macha Meril has her life dictated by her lovers and advertisements), a fading soundtrack in *Two or Three Things I Know About Her* (*Deux ou Trois Choses que Je Sais d'Elle*) (1967) (☞ ✍) (housewife Marina Vlady keeps up with the Joneses through part-time prostitution), including the clapperboard in *La Chinoise* (*The Chinese Girl*) (1967) (☞) (young people set up a Maoist commune, but principles tumble as living together becomes more difficult) and showing simultaneous action in opposite quarters of the screen in the experimental video *Numéro Deux* (1975) (☞ ■) (a 'home movie of family life' showing the frustrations and disappointments of ordinary people). He reused the premise of accidental death first used in *A Bout de Souffle* in *It's My Life* (US: *My Life to Live*) (*Vivre Sa Vie*) (1962) (☞) (a semi-documentary telling of a girl's drift into prostitution) and *Masculine-Feminine* (*Masculin-Féminin*) (1966) (☞ ☆) (Jean-Pierre Léaud won the Berlin Best Actor award as an ex-soldier torn between politics and women) and examined more off-beat criminals in *The Outsiders* (aka *Band of Outsiders*) (*Bande à Part*) (1964) (☞ ✍) (✍) (Anna Karina plans a robbery at the house where she works, but it goes wrong) and *Pierrot le Fou* (1965) (bored >Jean-Paul Belmondo has crime adventures across France with accomplice Anna Karina). Godard's Communism – shrouded in allegory in *Les Carabiniers* (*The Soldiers*) (aka *The Riflemen*) (1963) (☞ ✍) (youths volunteer for a war but are betrayed by a secret peace treaty), *Alphaville* (*Alphaville, une Étrange Aventure de Lenny Caution*) (1965) (☞ ✍) (a *film noir* private investigator solves a crime on a tyrannized planet) and *Le Weekend* (1967) (☞ ■) (an ordinary weekend disintegrates into a mêlée of traffic jams, violence and cannibalism) – was more overtly demonstrated in the 1969–1972 non-commercial collaborations with the Dziga Vertov Group. Subsequently, only *Tout Va Bien* (1972) (☞ ☆) (TV reporter >Jane Fonda and

film-director >Yves Montand are held hostage by strikers) has matched originality with restraint.

 •*The Little Soldier* (*Le Petit Soldat*) (1960) (✍): a French agent finds himself pursued by both sides in Geneva.

•*A Woman is a Woman* (*Une Femme est une Femme*) (1961) (☞ ✍ ☆): Cannes Best Actress winner Anna Karina wants a baby and turns to >Jean-Paul Belmondo to do the fathering.

•*Le Gai Savoir* (1969): Jean-Pierre Léaud and Juliette Berto sit in TV studio and discuss education.

•*First Name Carmen* (*Prénom Carmen*) (1983) (☞): a corruption of Prosper Mérimée's story has a kidnap plot masked by the making of a film.

•*Hail Mary* (*Je Vous Salue, Marie*) (1984): this controversial nativity story makes Joseph a cab driver and no one believes in immaculate conceptions.

•*Detective* (1985) (☆):Nathalie Baye and Jean-Pierre Léaud are among the hotel guests under the scrutiny of a *flic* investigating a long-unsolved murder.

•*King Lear* (1988): Burgess Meredith and Molly Ringwald as Lear and Cordelia in tenuous 20th-century version of >Shakespeare's story of a father's mistreatment by his daughters.

The Godfather Parts I & II
✍ ☞ ■ ♫ ☆
PART I
USA • Paramount • 1972 • 175 mins • col
d >Francis Ford Coppola w Francis Ford Coppola/Mario Puzo ph Gordon Willis m Nino Rota
>Marlon Brando, Al Pacino, Robert Duvall, James Caan, John Cazale, Talia Shire, >Diane Keaton

PART II
USA • Paramount • 1974 • 200 mins • col
d >Francis Ford Coppola w Francis Ford Coppola/Mario Puzo ph Gordon Willis m Nino Rota

Al Pacino, >Robert De Niro, >Diane Keaton, Robert Duvall, John Cazale

A single epic, which can not only boast Best Picture Oscars for each episode, but also the longest intermission in screen history – two years. Brando might have won the Oscar for his vibrant Don Vito Corleone in 1972 and the 1974 sequel might have been stolen by De Niro's portrait of the mobster as a young man, but the predominant theme is the Faust-without-the-Devil decline of Michael Corleone, a startlingly inconsistent performance by Pacino. At his sister's wedding, he's a uniformed war hero, with his non-Italian girlfriend, Kay (Keaton), appearing to have less in common with the Family than the tamed senators and movie stars among the guests. But when Vito is gunned down and his brothers – the hot-headed Sonny (Caan) and the timid Fredo (Cazale) – botch up the simplest acts of extortion and murder, Michael can't refuse the offer to step into the Don's spats. Having sold his soul to further the family business, he ironically destroys his family life, and as the flashbacks in *Part II* relentlessly show, he lacks the restraint and sense of honour to invite 'father like son' comparisons. At once romantic and brutal, packed with memorable moments, such as the horse's head in bed and the restaurant assassination scenes, *The Godfather* challenges the idea that the Family that slays together, stays together.

 PART I. •Cher won the Best Actress Oscar for being in love with one brother and betrothed to another in another Italian family saga *Moonstruck* (Norman Jewison 1987) (☆ ✍♫).
•>Jean Gabin tries to ensure his inheritance will even survive his weak son, in *Les Grandes Familles* (*The Possessors*) (Denys De La Patellière 1958).
•>Kathleen Turner and >Jack Nicholson are Mafia assassins in love and with contracts on each other, in *Prizzi's Honor* (☆ ☞ ✍) (>John Huston 1986).
•Walter Matthau lands himself in a jam when he steals Mafia money, in *Charley Varrick* (Don Siegel 1973) (☆ ✍).

PART II.•Francesco Rosi won Best Director at Berlin for his true story of a Sicilian Mafioso *Salvatore Giuliano* (1961) (☞ ■).

•Editor Jack Hawkins also loses out when he puts duty before family in *Front Page Story* (Gordon Parry 1953) (☆).

•Famous through the scripts of the black-listed writers he is helping, >Woody Allen is almost spoiled by success in *The Front* (Martin Ritt 1976) (☆ ✍), just as Barbra Streisand, winner of the Best Actress Oscar, lost her husband through her Broadway fame, in *Funny Girl* (>William Wyler 1968) (☆ ☞♫).

•Charlie Sheen is ruined because others, notably >Michael Douglas, are more ruthless and experienced than he is, in *Wall Street* (Oliver Stone 1987) (☆).

GOLD DIGGERS

Black Widow (Bob Rafelson 1987) ☆
Theresa Russell bumps off rich men until journalist Debra Winger gets on her case.

Breakfast at Tiffany's (Blake Edwards 1961) ☆ ✍
Audrey Hepburn's antics keep writer neighbour George Peppard topped up with material, in this Truman Capote story.

The Flame of New Orleans (>René Clair 1941) ☞
>Marlene Dietrich extorts a proposal out of rich man Roland Young, but fails to reach the altar.

Gold Diggers of 1933 (>Mervyn Le Roy 1933) ☞♫
1933 and a trio of showgirls seek to land rich husbands – couldn't be much else really, could it?

Gold Diggers of 1935 (Busby Berkeley 1935) ☞♫
Impresario Adolphe Menjou puts on a show in a country mansion, the hit of which is 'The Lullaby of Broadway'.

How to Marry a Millionaire (Jean Negulesco 1953) ☆ ✍
Lauren Bacall, >Marilyn Monroe and Betty Grable take a flat to court such wealthy men as >William Powell.

Laughter (Harry D'Abbadie D'Arrast 1930) ✍ ☞ ☆
Nancy Carroll marries Frank Morgan for his money, but still loves painter >Fredric March.

Of Human Bondage (John Cromwell 1934) ☆ ✍
Upper-bracket >Leslie Howard is ruined through his liaison with waitress >Bette Davis.

> **Millionaires**

The Gold Rush ☆ ✍ ☞ ■
USA • United Artists • 1925 (sound version 1942) • 72 mins • b/w

wdm >Charles Chaplin   ph Rollie Totheroh/Jack Wilson

Charlie Chaplin, Georgia Hale, Mack Swain

Chaplin was never simply a silent clown, but *The Gold Rush* is the last of what >Woody Allen's fans in *Stardust Memories* would call the 'early funny ones'. An outsider among the outcasts, The Tramp's undaunted humanity brings love and compassion to the selfish society of the prospectors, where only greed and ambition keep out the cold and frustration. Having survived the slights of the girl he loves and boiled his boot to feed a starving rival (cinema's funniest and most dignified meal), Charlie deservedly finds gold and romance, but even though we know he is nobody's fool, there is more than a slight suspicion that his overwhelming generosity will lead to his wealth being as shamelessly exploited as his poverty.

 •>Humphrey Bogart, Walter Huston and Tim Holt are the gold hunters in *The Treasure of the Sierra Madre* (>John Huston 1948) (☆ ☞♫).

•Avidity is graphically discussed in >*Greed* (>Erich Von Stroheim 1923) (☞ ■ ☆).

•George Formby's family fortune is stashed in one of six chairs in *Keep Your Seats Please* (Monty Banks 1936) (☆).

•Daryl Hannah loves large-nosed, outcast fireman Steve Martin in *Roxanne* (Fred Schepisi 1987) (☆ ✍), an update of *Cyrano de Bergerac*.

•A small boy's virtue is rewarded by Gene

Wilder in Roald Dahl's *Willy Wonka and the Chocolate Factory* (Mel Stuart 1971) (✍ ☆ ■).

Gone with the Wind ☆ ■ ✍ ☞ ♫
USA • MGM • 1939 • 220 mins • col

d Victor Fleming w Sidney Howard & others ph Ernest Haller/Ray Rennahan m Max Steiner

>Clark Gable, >Vivien Leigh, >Leslie Howard, >Olivia De Havilland, Hattie McDaniel

Pre-occupying the entire US film industry while in production and enthralling audiences ever since, Margaret Mitchell's sprawling Civil War story of female fortitude and folly is the Technicolor jewel in Hollywood's crown. The sets (many painted onto the film stock) may vary from the woefully plastic to the majestically real, but that is the only criticism that can be levelled against the 220 minutes that gave David O. Selznick victory in the Battle of the Producers over 'boy wonder' Irving Thalberg, who had derided the scheme in 1936. Steiner's score, Walter Plunkett's costumes and Fleming's direction (with a little help from friends >George Cukor and Sam Wood) are impeccable, but the life and loves of the skittish Southern belle, who learns little from her mistakes other than how to endure their consequent hardship, is predominantly a triumph for the art of screen acting. However, McDaniel's Mammie, Howard's Ashley Wilkes, De Havilland's Melanie, Gable's Rhett Butler and Leigh's Scarlett O'Hara were such perfect personifications that all subsequently suffered somewhat from typecasting.

 •>Joan Crawford and Sally Field battle against adversity respectively in *Mildred Pierce* (>Michael Curtiz 1945) (☆ ☞) and *Norma Rae* (Martin Ritt 1979) (☆).
•Teenager Megan Follows keeps the farm going when her mother Christine Lahti leaves her crippled father Ray Baker in *Stacking* (Martin Rosen 1987) (☆).
•Another husband who quite frankly couldn't give a damn is Raimu in >Dostoyevsky's *The Eternal Husband* (*L'Homme au Chapeau Rond*) (Pierre Billon 1946) (☆ ✍).
•Milkman Topol won't let troubles break up his family or get him down, in *Fiddler on the Roof* (Norman Jewison 1971) (♫ ☆).

Goodbye Mr Chips ☆ ☞ ✍ ■
GB • MGM • 1939 • 114 mins • b/w

d Sam Wood w R. C. Sherriff/Claudine West/Eric Maschwitz ph Frederick A. Young m Richard Addinsell

>Robert Donat, Greer Garson, Paul Henreid, John Mills

Sam Wood, whose best films to date had been the >Marx Brothers' comedies, *A Night at the Opera* and *A Day at the Races*, might have appeared an eccentric choice to direct an adaptation of James Hilton's rather idealized tale of public schoolmastering, but the end result fully justified the selection. He coaxed an Oscar-winning performance from Robert Donat as Mr Chipping, no mean achievement considering he pipped >Clark Gable's Rhett Butler. Wood lost out himself only to Victor Fleming (for >*Gone with the Wind*) in the Best Direction category, in the process persuading the moguls that this was the man for such classics as *Kitty Foyle* (1940) (☞ ☆) (>Ginger Rogers suffers a series of love crises before realizing she doesn't need men), *King's Row* (1941) (☞ ■ ☆) (the phobias, foibles and peccadilloes of an unpleasant small town) and *For Whom The Bell Tolls* (1943) (☞ ☆) (>Gary Cooper and >Ingrid Bergman fall in love and fight in the >Spanish Civil War). However, Wood was at his most impressive in his telling of Chipping's evolution from gauche novice to respected headmaster, perfectly capturing the public school spirit and a dying Empire's view of itself and its world position. Unashamedly sentimental, but enormously watchable.

•Peter O'Toole and Petula Clark found themselves in the musical *Goodbye Mr Chips* (Herbert Ross 1969).
•>Alastair Sim and Margaret Rutherford are heads of schools forced to share premises in

The Happiest Days of Your Life (Frank Launder 1950) (☆ ✐).
•The effects, during World War II, on a French school of harbouring a Jewish boy are examined in *Au Revoir les Enfants* (>Louis Malle 1988) (☞ ✐ ■).
•The body of the headmaster that Simone Signoret and Vera Clouzot have murdered pops up all over the school in *Les Diaboliques* (*The Fiends*) (US: *Diabolique*) (Henri-Georges Clouzot 1954) (☆ ☞ ✐).

The Graduate ☆ ☞ ♫ ✐
USA • United Artists/Embassy • 1967 • 105 mins • col
d >Mike Nichols w Calder Willingham/Buck Henry ph Robert Surtees m Paul Simon/Dave Grushin
>Dustin Hoffman, Anne Bancroft, Katharine Ross

Returning to a welcome more befitting a 'Nam veteran than a college graduate, Ben's education is completed when he is seduced by family friend Mrs Robinson. But as he sickens of her sexual exploitation of him, he seeks solace in her daughter Elaine. With a fury not quite as hell-like as Alex Forrest's in *Fatal Attraction* (Adrian Lyne 1987) (Glenn Close resorts to terror when >Michael Douglas ignores their fling), the scorned Mrs Robinson threatens exposure to stop her lover becoming her son-in-law. A popular theme of the student demonstrations of 1968, this daring discussion of sexuality, parental expectation and the age gap is made all the more entertaining by the Simon and Garfunkel classics that comprise the soundtrack.

•Young men simply look and don't touch in the sharp satire on male ogling *The Lizards* (*I Basilischi*) (Lina Wertmüller 1963) (☞).
•By taking up with Ali McGraw, Jewish librarian Richard Benjamin loves above his station in *Goodbye Columbus* (Larry Peerce 1969) (☆ ✐).
•Tom Berenger is educated in love by Karen Black among others in *In Praise of Older Women* (George Kaczender 1977) (✐).

•Bob Hope bungles all his affairs until, disguised as the fabled lover, he meets >Joan Fontaine in *Casanova's Big Night* (Norman Z. McLeod 1954) (✐ ☆).

La Grande Illusion (Grande Illusion) ☆ ☞ ✐ ■
France • Cinedis • 1937 • 117 mins • b/w
d >Jean Renoir w Jean Renoir/Charles Spaak ph Christian Matras/Claude Renoir m Joseph Kosma
>Jean Gabin, >Erich Von Stroheim, Pierre Fresnay, Marcel Dalio

German flying ace Von Rauffenstein (Von Stroheim) shoots down a plane carrying three French soldiers – a noble (Fresnay), a bourgeois (Dalio) and a worker (Gabin) – who survive only to be taken prisoner. Repeated escape attempts result in their detention in the maximum security PoW camp that Von Rauffenstein has commanded since he was cripplingly wounded. Ostensibly a pacifist statement, Renoir uses the idea that 'in war, all are prisoners' to examine such critical themes of the day as the folly of duty, the out-moded chivalry of an antiquated aristocracy, the rise of the proletariat and the dangerous rivalries promoted by nationalism. The hope that such a film would convert an increasingly militaristic world regrettably proved to be a grand delusion.

•The relations between French and Germans following the collapse of a mine shaft are explored in *Kameradschaft* (*La Tragédie de la Mine*) (>G.W. Pabst 1931) (☞ ✐ ■).
•Three other French soldiers in World War I, defended by >Kirk Douglas, face court martial before Adolphe Menjou, in *Paths of Glory* (>Stanley Kubrick 1957) (☆ ☞ ■).
•Ryuichi Sakamoto plays the gay Japanese commandant who falls in love with PoW David Bowie in Laurens Van Der Post's *The Sower and the Seed – Merry Christmas, Mr Lawrence* (Nagisa Oshima 1983) (♫).
•Although not quite as incapacitated as Von Rauffenstein, petty thief >Marcello Mastroianni is hampered by an arm in a splint in

Persons Unknown (US: *Big Deal on Madonna Street*) (aka *The Usual Unidentified Thieves*) (Il Soliti Ignoti) (Mario Monicelli 1958) (☆ ✍).
•Tension mounts among the PoWs of *Stalag 17* (>Billy Wilder 1953) (☛ ☆ ✍ ■) as they suspect William Holden of betraying escape plans.
•The civility shown by Von Rauffenstein is a far cry from the hostility dealt out in the Chinese gulag depicted in *The Last Day of Winter* (*Zuihou Yige Dongri*) (Wu Ziniu 1986) (☆ ■).

Grant, Cary
(Alexander Archibald Leach) British actor (1904–1986)

The most dependable and watchable actor in Hollywood history, Grant rose to fame alongside >Marlene Dietrich in *Blonde Venus* (>Josef Von Sternberg 1932) (☛) (Grant hopes to lure Marlene away from her secure marriage with Herbert Marshall), the first of many legendary co-stars. Among the others were: Mae West, *She Done Him Wrong* (Lowell Sherman 1933) (☛ ☆) (nightclub singer Mae seduces Grant who is working out of the neighbouring mission aiming to save fallen women) and *I'm No Angel* (Wesley Ruggles 1933) (☆ ✍) (lion-tamer Mae sues millionaire Grant for breach of promise); >Katharine Hepburn, *Sylvia Scarlett* (>George Cukor 1936) (☛ ☆) (Cary and Kate as cons in Victorian England fleecing Brian Aherne until she falls for him), >*Bringing Up Baby* (>Howard Hawks 1938) (✍ ☛ ☆), *Holiday* (>George Cukor 1938) (☛ ☆) (Kate steals Cary away from his engagement to Doris Nolan) and >*The Philadelphia Story* (>George Cukor 1940) (☆ ✍ ☛); Irene Dunne, *The Awful Truth* (>Leo McCarey 1937) (☆ ☛ ✍) (Irene and Cary divorce and discover they can't live without each other), *My Favourite Wife* (Garson Kanin 1940) (☆ ✍) (shipwrecked Irene comes home to find Cary has married again) and *Penny Serenade* (AAN: >George Stevens 1941) (☆ ✍) (the happy courtship leads to a troubled marriage made worse by the death of their children); and Jean Arthur, *Only Angels Have Wings* (>Howard Hawks 1939) (☆ ☛) (Jean comes between cargo plane boss Grant and Richard Barthelmess) and *The Talk of the Town* (>George Stevens 1942) (☆ ☛ ✍)

(Cary appeals to lawyer Ronald Colman to defend him against false arson accusations; he simply appeals to Jean). Grant was an excellent comedian: *Topper* (Norman Z. McLeod 1937) (☆ ✍) (ghosts Cary and Constance Bennett tease banker Roland Young into life); >*His Girl Friday* (Howard Hawks 1940) (✍ ☛ ☆); *Arsenic and Old Lace* (>Frank Capra 1944) (✍ ☛ ☆) (Cary's dotty aunts have corpses in every nook and there are more to come when Raymond Massey and >Peter Lorre turn up); and *Monkey Business* (>Howard Hawks 1952) (☆ ☛) (a chimp invents a youth potion and Cary and >Ginger Rogers regress to childhood size). He could also combine humour with toughness: *Gunga Din* (>George Stevens 1939) (☛ ☆) (Grant joins Victor McLaglen and Douglas Fairbanks Jr for adventures on the North-West Frontier); *Mr Lucky* (H. C. Potter 1942) (☆) (Grant as a reformed crook who organizes jumble sales for the war effort); *None but the Lonely Heart* (AAN: Clifford Odets 1944) (☆ ■) (Cary finds a purpose in life after his mother Ethel Barrymore [AA] dies of cancer); and *Houseboat* (Melville Shavelson 1958) (Sophia Loren, maid to widower Cary's children, is a rich woman disillusioned with wealth). And he was equally at home with debonair duplicity: *Suspicion* (>Alfred Hitchcock 1941) (☛ ☆ ✍ ■) (>Joan Fontaine believes Grant murdered his friend Nigel Bruce and now is after her), >*Notorious* Alfred Hitchcock 1946) (☛ ☆ ✍ ■); *To Catch a Thief* (>Alfred Hitchcock 1955) (☛ ☆) (with Grace Kelly's help, retired jewel thief Cary discovers who is carrying out copycat crimes on the Riviera); *North by Northwest* (>Alfred Hitchcock 1959) (☛ ☆ ✍ ■ ♫) (mistaken for a spy, Grant becomes a target on Mount Rushmore and of a crop plane after he tumbles to what James Mason is up to) and *Charade* (>Stanley Donen 1964) (☆ ✍ ☛) (does Audrey Hepburn trust Grant or Walter Matthau in the search for a missing fortune?).

 •*Alice in Wonderland* (Norman Z. McLeod 1933) (☆ ✍): Cary as the Mock Turtle teaches Charlotte Henry the Lobster Quadrille.
•*Night and Day* (>Michael Curtiz 1946) (☆ ☛ ♫): factitious biopic of songwriter Cole Porter.

•>*The Bishop's Wife* (Henry Koster 1947) (☆ ✍ ■ ☞).

•*Bachelor Knight* (US: *The Bachelor and the Bobbysoxer*) (Irving Reis 1947) (☆ ✍): Cary is the subject of judge >Myrna Loy and young sister Shirley Temple's affections.

•*Mr Blandings Builds His Dream House* (H. C. Potter 1948) (☆ ✍ ☞): idle workmen and capricious carpentry conspire against Cary and >Myrna Loy's move to the country.

•*I Was a Male War Bride* (UK: *You Can't Sleep Here*) (>Howard Hawks 1949) (☆ ☞ ✍): Ann Sheridan smuggles husband Cary home disguised as a WAC.

•*The Pride and the Passion* (Stanley Kramer 1957) (✍): Grant, Frank Sinatra and Sophia Loren combat the Napoleonic occupation of Spain in the screen version of C. S. Forester's novel *The Gun*.

•*An Affair to Remember* (>Leo McCarey 1957) (☆ ☞): Deborah Kerr and Cary agree to follow up a shipboard romance, but she stays away after a crippling car accident.

•*Indiscreet* (>Stanley Donen 1958) (☆ ☞): Cary invents a wife to avoid marriage to >Ingrid Bergman.

•*The Grass is Greener* (>Stanley Donen 1960) (☆ ☞): indifferent aristo Cary is roused into saving his marriage when Deborah Kerr has a fling with tourist Robert Mitchum.

•*That Touch of Mink* (Delbert Mann 1962) (☆): wealthy Cary is for once resisted, but it is by secretary Doris Day, whose cinema duty it was to resist everyone.

•*Father Goose* (Ralph Nelson 1964) (☆ ✍): drifter Cary is given the responsibility of spotting Japanese planes and a gaggle of schoolgirls on a Pacific island.

The Grapes of Wrath ☞ ■ ☆ ✍
USA • Twentieth Century Fox • 1940 • 128 mins • b/w

d >John Ford   w Nunnally Johnson
ph Gregg Toland   m Alfred Newman
>Henry Fonda, Jane Darwell, John Carradine, Charley Grapewin

It is perhaps ironic that cinema's greatest apologist for traditionalism and the methods of the Wild West pioneers should win the Best Director Oscar for this enlightened attack on the brutal tyrannies of Depression feudalism. But John Ford's conviction in the themes of family solidarity and the will to survive manages to amplify the power of John Steinbeck's epic narrative of the Joads' tragic trek from Oklahoma to California and subsequent struggles against the inhumanities and injustices of the ruling classes. He is ably abetted by a fine cast led by a faultless Fonda, and by Toland's remarkable cinematography, which elevates barren scrub to holiday brochure status.

 •Woody Guthrie was told California was the place he ought to be, so he loaded up his guitar and moved there in *Bound for Glory* (Hal Ashby 1976) (☞ ♫).

•Wealthy medieval families had their fair share of problems as Peter O'Toole's Henry II and >Katharine Hepburn's Eleanor of Aquitaine (which won her an AA) prove when deciding the succession in *The Lion in Winter* (Anthony Harvey 1968) (☆ ✍ ■).

•Bob Hoskins finds work as a chauffeur to call girl Cathy Tyson after leaving prison in *Mona Lisa* (Neil Jordan 1986) (☆ ✍).

•Farmers are faced with eviction from their traditional lands in *Tobacco Road* (>John Ford 1941) (☞ ■).

•City slickers Fred MacMurray and Claudette Colbert learn the ropes of country life from Ma and Pa Kettle (Marjorie Main and Percy Kilbride) in *The Egg and I* (Chester Erskine 1947) (☆ ✍).

GREAT LOVERS

The Adventures of Don Juan (UK: *The New Adventures of Don Juan*) (Vincent Sherman 1949) ☆ ■

Errol Flynn adds action to amours as he fights the tyranny of Philip III's minister the Duc De Lorca.

Alfie (Lewis Gilbert 1966) ☆ ✍

>Michael Caine as the London Lothario whose adventures eventually teach him responsibility.

Casanova (aka *Fellini's Casanova*)
(>**Federico Fellini 1976**) ☞
Donald Sutherland as the legendary 18th-century Italian who will make love to everyone and anything.
Casanova's Big Night (**Norman Z. McLeod 1954**) ☆ ✍
Bob Hope disguises himself as the Great Man to test >Joan Fontaine's virtue for suitor >Basil Rathbone.
Darling (>**John Schlesinger 1965**) ☆ ☞
Julie Christie has various sexual and flashy career adventures in search for elusive happiness.
I'm No Angel (**Wesley Ruggles 1933**) ☆ ✍
Lion tamer turned socialite Mae West wins a breach of promise case and >Cary Grant.
The Knack ... and How to Get It (**Richard Lester 1965**) ☆ ☞
Womanizer Ray Brooks teaches naïve teacher Michael Crawford about women.
The Sheik (**George Melford 1921**) ☆
Heiress Agnes Ayres is the subject of Rudolph Valentino's affections.
Shampoo (**Hal Ashby 1975**) ☆
Hairdresser Warren Beatty pampers clients Lee Grant and Julie Christie on more than a professional basis.
She's Gotta Have It (**Spike Lee 1986**) ☞ ■ ✍
Three men are exploited by a liberated black woman.

Greed

USA • Metro-Goldwyn • 1923 • 110 mins • b/w
wd >Erich Von Stroheim   ph Ben Reynolds/William Daniels/Ernest B. Schoedsack
Gibson Gowland, Zasu Pitts, Jean Hersholt

McTeague (Gowland), a quack dentist, seduces Trina (Pitts) and they seem set for life when she wins a lottery. However, the coins are there only to be caressed, not spent, and the couple slide into squalor and violence, perishing at the hands of Marcus Schouler (Hersholt), the man who introduced them. A long-cherished project that produced a long, condemned picture. Von Stroheim's ten-hour transliteration of

Frank Norris' novel *McTeague* was, at the insistence of Irving Thalberg, twice cut, the second more accurately a mauling, seriously impairing the logic of the narrative, but retaining several scenes of cinematic greatness, especially the shambolic wedding and the grotesque close-ups of human gluttony.

 •Burgess Meredith has to think for two as Lon Chaney Jr has more brawn than brain, in *Of Mice and Men* (Lewis Milestone 1939) (✍ ☆).
•The concept of 'man as animal' is explored in *A Clockwork Orange* (>Stanley Kubrick 1971) (☞ ✍) when Malcolm McDowell resorts to violence to survive, and in *The Lost Weekend* (>Billy Wilder 1945) (☞ ✍ ☆) in which Ray Milland's surrender to alcohol dehumanizes him.
•Dentists abound in *The Man Who Knew Too Much* (>Alfred Hitchcock 1956) (☞ ☆) in which dentist >James Stewart searches for his kidnapped son in the Casbah, in *The Paleface* (Norman Z. McLeod 1948) (☆ ✍) which sends dentist Bob Hope into the West to rout the baddies in the manner of his lawman father, and in *Marathon Man* (>John Schlesinger 1976) (☆ ☞) in which Nazi dentist >Laurence Olivier tortures >Dustin Hoffman to discover the whereabouts of some diamonds.
•Two friends love the same woman in >*Jules Et Jim* (>François Truffaut 1961) (☞ ☆ ✍).
•Cascading coins are central to the coronation scene of *Ivan the Terrible* (*Part I*) (*Ivan Groznyi*) (>Sergei Eisenstein 1942) (☞ ☆ ■ ♫).

GREENE, GRAHAM

Across the Bridge (**Ken Annakin 1957**) ✍
Killer financier Rod Steiger lies low on the Mexican border.
Brighton Rock (**US:** *Young Scarface*) (**John Boulting 1947**) ✍ ☆
>Richard Attenborough kills a petty crook at the races and marries a witness to keep her silent.
The Comedians (**Peter Glenville 1967**) ✍ ☆
>Richard Burton is driven from Port-au-Prince by Haitian dictator Papa Doc Duvalier's Ton-Tons Macoute henchmen.

Confidential Agent (Herman Shumlin 1945) ✍ ☆

On a munitions mission to Britain, Spanish partisan Charles Boyer falls for mine owner's daughter Lauren Bacall.

Day for Night (*La Nuit Américaine*) (>François Truffaut 1973) ☞ ✍

Greene himself makes a fleeting appearance as an insurance representative watching the rushes of Truffaut's troubled film.

The End of the Affair (Edward Dmytryk 1954) ✍

Deborah Kerr has an affair with writer Van Johnson but is racked with guilt for betraying husband Peter Cushing.

England Made Me (Peter Duffell 1972) ✍ ☆

Naïve Michael York is caught up in the dodgy dealings of German financier Peter Finch.

The Fallen Idol (US: *The Lost Illusion*) (>Carol Reed 1948) ✍ ☆

An adoring boy loses faith in butler Ralph Richardson when he sees the accidental death of his wife.

The Fugitive (>John Ford 1947) ✍ ☞ ☆

>Henry Fonda as the whiskey priest of *The Power and the Glory* running from anti-clerical Mexicans.

The Heart of the Matter (George More O'Ferrall 1953) ✍ ☆

Trevor Howard as the Sierra Leone cop bored with his wife, doubting his faith and in love with shipwreck survivor Maria Schell.

The Honorary Consul (US: *Beyond the Limit*) (John MacKenzie 1984) ✍ ♫

Doctor Richard Gere is embroiled in the Argentinian kidnap of dipso diplomat >Michael Caine.

The Human Factor (Otto Preminger 1979) ✍ ☆

>Richard Attenborough investigates a secrets leak at the Foreign Office.

Loser Takes All (Ken Annakin 1956) ✍

Playing the tables at Monte Carlo destroys the life of a cautious accountant.

The Ministry of Fear (>Fritz Lang 1944) ☞ ✍ ☆

Asylum releasee Ray Milland wins a cake containing a Nazi microfilm.

Our Man in Havana (>Carol Reed 1959) ✍ ☆

Noël Coward believes that the diagrams of >Alec Guinness's vacuum cleaners are Soviet missiles.

The Quiet American (>Joseph L. Mankiewicz 1957) ✍ ☞

Journalist Michael Redgrave betrays lifesaving pacifist Audie Murphy to the Vietnamese Communists.

A Shocking Accident (James Scott 1982) ✍ ☆

Rupert Everett tells his girlfriend how his father was accidentally killed by a falling pig.

The Stranger's Hand (Mario Soldati 1953) ✍ ☆

Trevor Howard rescues his son from kidnappers in Venice.

>The Third Man (>Carol Reed 1949) ☆ ☞ ♫ ✍ ■

This Gun for Hire (Frank Tuttle 1942) ✍ ☆

Veronica Lake helps assassin Alan Ladd uncover Nazi agents in this adaptation of Greene's novel *A Gun for Sale*.

Travels with My Aunt (>George Cukor 1972) ✍ ☞

Accountant Alec McCowen's European trip is enlivened by his aunt >Maggie Smith's adventures.

Went the Day Well? (US: *Forty-Eight Hours*) (Alberto Cavalcanti 1942) ✍ ☞ ☆

Leslie Banks leads villagers in resisting a Nazi invasion and revealing the enemy within.

Gregory's Girl ✍ ☞ ☆ ■

GB • Lake/NFFC/STV • 1980 • 91 mins • col
wd Bill Forsyth ph Michael Coulter
m Colin Tully
John Gordon Sinclair, Dee Hepburn, Claire Grogan, Chic Murray

Gangling teenager Gregory's schooldays at a Scottish comprehensive have been dominated by frustrated attempts to score in front of goal and girls. When pretty classmate Dorothy succeeds him as striker for the school football team, she appears the perfect match, but meeting her for a date is another ball game altogether. Blending the role reversal of screwball comedy, the contemporary comment of social realism and the male *naïveté* of >Laurel and Hardy, Bill Forsyth's film is a wistful, yet incisive study of obsession, competition and cooperation and the respective maturity levels of teenage boys and girls. Nigh on perfection.

•Football provides PoWs >Michael Caine and Sylvester Stallone with an escape route during a game in Paris with a Nazi XI, in *Escape to Victory* (US: *Victory*) (>John Huston 1981) (☞ ☆).

•Olympic athlete Mariel Hemingway is torn between improving her performance in the locker room and on the track in *Personal Best* (Robert Towne 1982) (☆).

•Kindly teacher Jean-François Stevenin guides his charges through the pitfalls of growing up, in *Small Change* (*L'Argent de Poche*) (>François Truffaut 1976) (☞ ☆).

•A timid boy, bullied by his Latin master, finds consolation in the arms of prostitute Mai Zetterling, in the >Ingmar Bergman-scripted *Frenzy* (US: *Torment*) (*Hets*) (Alf Sjöberg 1944) (✍ ☆).

•>Humphrey Bogart persuades Audrey Hepburn that she loves him, not his brother William Holden, in *Sabrina* (UK: *Sabrina Fair*) (>Billy Wilder 1954) (✍ ☞ ☆).

Griffith, D. W.
(David Wark Griffith) American screenwriter/director (1875–1948)
Initially acting in such movies as *Rescued from an Eagle's Nest* (Edwin S. Porter 1907) (lumberjack D.W. rescues a baby from an eyrie) to gain theatre bookings, Griffith, often working with cameraman Billy Bitzer and screenwriter Anita Loos, made in excess of 480 silent shorts for Biograph between 1908 and 1913, including *The Musketeers of Pig Alley* (1912) (☞) (>Lillian Gish battles against Bowery poverty), *The Lonedale Operator* (1911) (☞) (a raid on a railway telegraph office culminates in a chase across the desert), and *The Battle of Elderbush Gulch* (1913) (a fast-moving cowboy shootout), developing cross-cutting, backlighting and narrative techniques in the process. Only the quantity of output declined after he pro-

gressed to features. Nowadays his social stance is unacceptable, but the epic scale of his vision of history – >*Intolerance* (1916) (☞ ■ ☆) (Babylon and 16th-century France), *Orphans of the Storm* (1921) (☞ ☆ ■) (the Gish sisters are rescued from the guillotine during the French Revolution), *America* (1924) (wicked Red Coat Lionel Barrymore gets his comeuppance at Lexington during the Revolutionary War) and *The Birth of a Nation* (1915) (☞ ☆ ■) (how ordinary people like >Lillian Gish played their part in the Union's victory in the US Civil War) – and grasp of contemporary life – *Broken Blossoms* (1919) (☆ ☞) (when >Lillian Gish is murdered by her brutal father Donald Crisp, her Chinese lover Richard Barthelmess avenges her) and *Way Down East* (1921) (☆ ☞ ✍) (seduced by a dandy, then enslaved by a farming family, >Lillian Gish is saved from icy waters by Richard Barthelmess) – made him the most influential American director of his generation and, some would claim, of all time.

•*Hearts of the World* (1918) (☆ ☞): the Gish sisters, >Erich Von Stroheim and Noël Coward are wrapped up in World War I experiences.

•*Dream Street* (1921) (☞): gypsy dancer Carole Dempster is rescued from ardent pursuers by a street preacher.

•*One Exciting Night* (1922) (☞ ✍): everyone is a suspect as guests search a spooky house for hidden loot.

•*Abraham Lincoln* (1930) (☞ ☆): Walter Huston progresses through this biopic from law career, through Gettysburg Address to theatre assassination.

•*The Struggle* (1932): based on >Émile Zola's story 'The Drunkard', it tells of a wife's struggle to dry out an alcoholic mill worker.

Guinness, Alec
British actor (b 1914)
Distracted by advertising copywriting and interrupted by naval war service, Guinness's stage apprenticeship with John Gielgud eventually led to >Dickensian debut roles in *Great Expectations* (>David Lean 1948) (☞ ■ ✍ ☆) (as Herbert Pocket to John Mills's Pip) and

Oliver Twist (>David Lean 1949) (✍ ☞ ☆) (as a controversially anti-Semitic Fagin). His Ealing comedies – >*Kind Hearts and Coronets* (Robert Hamer 1949) (✍ ☆ ☞ ■), *The Lavender Hill Mob* (Charles Crichton 1951) (✍ ☆ ☞) (security clerk Guinness smuggles bullion in the shape of Eiffel Towers) and *The Ladykillers* (Alexander Mackendrick 1955) (☆ ☞ ✍ ♫) (Guinness's gang, pretending to be a string quartet, are captured by landlady Katie Johnson) – demonstrated his flexibility. His reputation was confirmed by his Oscar-winning performance in *The Bridge on the River Kwai* (>David Lean 1957) (✍ ☆ ☞) (Guinness stands up for PoW's rights while forced-labouring on the Burma railroad). Other solid character performances followed: *The Horse's Mouth* (Ronald Neame 1958) (☆ ✍) (Guinness, who also scripted the film, as Joyce Cary's troublesome artist Gulley Jimson): *Our Man in Havana* (>Carol Reed 1959) (✍ ☆) (vacuum salesman Guinness stumbles on to real secrets while peddling fake ones to the British government) and *Tunes of Glory* (Ronald Neame 1960) (☆ ✍) (regimental new broom John Mills clashes with experienced Scottish Sergeant Major Guinness). Then came a disappointingly thin period, filled only by diverse cameos: *Lawrence of Arabia* (>David Lean 1962) (■ ☞ ♫) (Guinness as the untrustworthy Arab leader Prince Faisal); *Doctor Zhivago* (>David Lean 1965) (☞ ☆ ♫) (Guinness as the Red Army officer who gets the story of Julie Christie and Omar Sharif's love affair out of Rita Tushingham); and *Cromwell* (Ken Hughes 1970) (☆ ✍) (Guinness as a dignified Charles I opposing Richard Harris's ranting MP for Huntingdon). His role as Obi-Wan Kenobi in *Star Wars* (George Lucas 1980) (☆ ✳) and its sequels sparked a revival, leading to parts in *A Passage to India* (>David Lean 1977) (☞ ☆ ■) (as the Indian mystic Professor Godbole), >*Little Dorrit* (Christine Edzard 1987) (✍ ☞ ☆ ■) and *A Handful of Dust* (Charles Sturridge 1988) (✍ ☞ ☆) (Guinness as the lunatic Mr Todd who imprisons cuckolded squire James Wilby in the Brazilian jungle so that he will read him >Dickens).

•*The Mudlark* (Jean Negulesco 1951) (☆ ✍): an urchin meets Disraeli (Guinness) and Queen Victoria (Irene Dunne) while burgling Windsor Castle.

•*The Man in the White Suit* (Alexander Mackendrick 1951) (✍ ☆): Guinness invents an indestructable suit, but hasn't quite got the formula right.

•*The Card* (US: *The Promoter*) (Ronald Neame 1952) (☆ ☞ ✍): potteries clerk Guinness wheedles his way to wealth in an adaptation of the Arnold Bennett novel.

•*Father Brown* (US: *The Detective*) (Robert Hamer 1954) (✍ ☆): Guinness as G. K. Chesterton's priest detective investigates the theft of a priceless crucifix.

•*To Paris With Love* (Robert Hamer 1954) (☆): Guinness and his son matchmake for each other.

•*The Prisoner* (Peter Glenville 1955) (☆): Guinness as a Cardinal brainwashed by Jack Hawkins in a Fascist state.

•*Hitler – The Last Ten Days* (Ennio De Concini 1973) (☆): Guinness and Eva Braun (Doris Kunstmann) debate the future as the Allies approach.

GUNFIGHTERS AND SAMURAI

Antonio das Mortes (Dragão da Maldade contra o Santo Guerreiro) (Glauber Rocha 1969) ☞ ✍

The Brazilian director was voted 'Best' at Cannes for this tale of a hitman joining the peasants he is supposed to terrorize.

***Backlash* (John Sturges 1956)** ☞

Richard Widmark discovers that his father betrayed his partners for Indian gold.

***Cat Ballou* (Eliot Silverstein 1965)** ☆ ✍ ♫

Lee Marvin as both the drunken gunfighter helping >Jane Fonda and the man he is supposed to kill.

***The Gunfighter* (Henry King 1950)** ☞ ☆

Gregory Peck's reputation precedes him and spoils his chance of a new life.

***The Magnificent Seven* (John Sturges 1960)** ☆ ☞ ♫

Yul Brynner leads the gang hired to defend a

Mexican village in the Western adaptation of *The Seven Samurai.*

The Seven Samurai (*Shichinin No Samurai*) (>Akira Kurosawa 1954) ☞ ■

Leader Takishi Shimura and dashing Toshiro Mifune dispute the best way of ridding a 16th-century Japanese village of bandits.

Shane (>George Stevens 1953) ☞ ☆

Alan Ladd rids Van Heflin and Jean Arthur of villains, but harms their home life.

This Gun for Hire (Frank Tuttle 1942) ✍ ☆

In this >Graham Greene story assassin Alan Ladd and Veronica Lake uncover fifth columnists.

Yojimbo (>Akira Kurosawa 1961) ☞ ☆ ✍

Samurai Toshiro Mifune rids a town of feuding factions by tricking them into self-destruction.

GYPSIES

Alex and the Gypsy (John Korty 1976) ☆

>Jack Lemmon abandons escorting James Woods to court to court gypsy Geneviève Bujold.

Golden Earrings (Mitchell Leisen 1947) ☆ ☞

>Marlene Dietrich helps Ray Milland smuggle a poison gas formula out of Nazi Germany.

Happy Gypsies (aka *I Even Met a Happy Gypsy*) (*Sreo Sam Cak I Srecne Cigane*) (aka *Skulpjaci Perja*) Alexander Petrović, Yugoslavia 1967) ■ ✍

A feather-selling gypsy kills the father of a girl he hopes to seduce and hits the road with his family.

The Hunchback of Notre Dame (Wallace Worsley 1923) ☆

Lon Chaney, Sr. as Victor Hugo's bellringer offering sanctuary to Patsy Ruth Miller's gypsy Esmeralda.

The Little Minister (Richard Wallace 1934) ☆ ■

This J. M. Barrie play has vicar John Beal believing that noble's daughter >Katharine Hepburn is a heathen gypsy.

The Raggedy Rawney (Bob Hoskins 1989) ☞ ✍

An army deserter disguised as a woman is taken for a lucky mascot by gypsies until their lives take a turn for the worse.

Robin Hood (Wolfgang Reitherman 1973) ☞ ■

The Disney cartoon Robin disguises himself as a gypsy fortune teller to pickpocket Prince John.

The Squall (Alexander Korda 1929) ☆

Gypsy >Myrna Loy upsets Loretta Young and Zasu Pitts by flirting with their farming men.

The Virgin and the Gypsy (Christopher Miles 1970) ☆ ■

Vicar's daughter Joanna Shimkus falls for fortune teller Franco Nero.

Wings of the Morning (Harold Schuster 1937) ☆ ■

Irish peer >Henry Fonda and gypsy Arabella repeat the romance of their 19th-century ancestors.

Hamlet ☆ ✍ ☞ ■ ♫
GB • Rank/Two Cities • 1948 • 142 mins • b/w
d >Laurence Olivier w William Shakespeare ph Roger Furse m William Walton
Laurence Olivier, Eileen Herlie, Basil Sydney, Jean Simmons, Felix Aylmer, Stanley Holloway

The second, and sole black-and-white, segment of Olivier's great Shakespearian trio. Informed by his father's ghost that his uncle, now his stepfather, is a regicide, the Danish student prince allows his indecision and incipient madness to destroy those around him and delay the day of his vengeance. The gloomy atmosphere and haunting shadows bring the 1948 Best Picture Oscar-winner close to Bard *noir*, but despite the severe, some might say savage, cutting, it remains true to the themes that have fascinated generations of theatregoers and gave the eponymous hero his familiar page-boy appearance.

•Other versions of the play include a translation by Boris Pasternak (Grigori Kozintsev 1964) (☞) and Tony Richardson's 1969 production (☆ ☞) with a bearded Nicol Williamson, Marianne Faithfull as Ophelia, Anthony Hopkins as Claudius, and Gordon Jackson as Horatio.
•A farmer is roused by a ghost to oppose the diversion of a river away from his land in *The Milagro Beanfield War* (Robert Redford 1988) (■ ☞).
•Opera singer Jill Clayburgh has an incestuous affair with her son in *La Luna* (>Bernardo Bertolucci 1979) (■ ☆).
•An industrialist's son sees Olivier's *Hamlet* and vows to avenge his mother's rapid remarriage, in *Ophelia* (>Claude Chabrol 1962) (☞ ✍).

HAPPY FAMILIES

Cavalcade (Frank Lloyd 1933) ✍ ☞
The Noël Coward play traces a family history from the Boer War to the First World War.

Centennial Summer (Otto Preminger 1946) ♫ ✍

A family does its bit to make the 1876 Philadelphia Great Exposition a credit to the USA.

Dear Octopus (US: *The Randolph Family*) (Harold French 1943) ☆ ✍

Michael Wilding and Celia Johnson are among the toffs gathering for a family reunion.

Here Come the Huggetts (Ken Annakin 1948) ☆

Jack Warner and Kathleen Harrison head the working-class London family disrupted by niece Diana Dors.

Life with Father (>Michael Curtiz 1947) ☆ ☞ ✍ ♫

Irene Dunne balances the books and their three sons to suit stickler father >William Powell, in this film adaptation of Clarence Day's stories.

Meet Me in St Louis (>Vincente Minnelli 1943) ♫ ☆

Judy Garland's family prepare for the St Louis World Fair in the story that inspired *Centennial Summer*.

Numéro Deux (>Jean-Luc Godard 1975) ☞ ■

This family are contented simply because they have chosen to accept the mediocrity of their lot.

State Fair (Henry King 1933) ☞ ☆/(Walter Lang 1945) ☆

While respective fathers Will Rogers and Charles Winninger exhibit their prize pigs, their siblings seek romance.

This Happy Breed (>David Lean 1944) ✍ ☞

This Noël Coward play chronicles the fortunes of an everyday London family headed by father Robert Newton.

A Tree Grows in Brooklyn (>Elia Kazan 1945) ☆ ☞

Drunken father James Dunn tries to improve the lot of his New York Irish family, but can't beat the bottle.

A Hard Day's Night ♫ ☆ ✍ ☞
GB • United Artists • 1964 • 85 mins • b/w
d Richard Lester **w** Alun Owen
ph Gilbert Taylor **m** Lennon/McCartney

John Lennon, Paul McCartney, George Harrison, Ringo Starr, Wilfred Bramble, Norman Rossington, John Junkin, Victor Spinetti

The marketing of Elvis Presley and Cliff Richard decreed that rock stars spin off into films as intrinsically nice clean cuts. The Beatles broke the mould, embodying the irreverence of their rock'n'roll and shunning the sentiment of their ballads, as they ad libbed their way through a familiar 24 hours of banal questions, petty regulation and screaming adoration. Dick Lester's skilled direction presents limitless opportunity for The Fabs to mock authority and shirk duty, without allowing their evident anti-establishment independence to detract from the working-class respectability of the Mop Top image. Titler of the film, Ringo, has the most 'acting' to do; Paul's characteristic willingness is mercifully balanced by the shady schemes of his grandfather (Bramble) and John and George deliver their wisecracks with natural deadpan timing honed at 1001 press conferences. Oh yeah, the music is brilliant too.

 •Beatlemania took the USA by storm in 1964 and the hysteria is recalled, in *I Wanna Hold Your Hand* (Robert Zemeckis 1978) (✍ ♫).

•Michael Crawford and Oliver Reed steal the Crown Jewels from the Tower of Swinging London, in *The Jokers* (Michael Winner 1967) (✍).

•Mel Smith watches helplessly as his fellow aliens are manipulated into the rock business by Gryff Rhys Jones, in *Morons from Outer Space* (Mike Hodges 1985) (☆).

•Liverpool wit is tinged with Irish prejudice when Orangemen and Republicans book into the same club for New Year, in *No Surrender* (Peter Smith 1986) (✍ ☆).

•More Beatles: Ringo has a sacrificial ring wedged on his finger and is pursued by Leo McKern and Eleanor Bron, in *Help!* (Richard Lester 1965) (♫ ☆), while the working band is captured rehearsing an album in *Let It Be* (Michael Lindsay-Hogg 1970) (♫ ■).

Harlow, Jean

*(Harlean Carpenter) American actress
(1911–1937)*

Beginning as a support in >Laurel and Hardy's *Double Whoopee* (Lewis R. Foster 1929) (☆ ✍) (Stan and Ollie as inept doormen in a >Leo McCarey co-authored script) and an extra in Chaplin's *City Lights* (>Charles Chaplin 1931) (☞ ☆ ✍) (Charlie boxes and carries out odd jobs to finance an operation for flowergirl Virginia Cherrill's blindness), Harlow rarely departed from comedy during her tragically brief career: *The Public Enemy* (>William Wellman 1931) (Jean as the girl who tempts >James Cagney away from Mae Clarke); *China Seas* (Tay Garnett 1935) (☞ ☆) (>Clark Gable and Harlow tussle with Chinese pirates); and *Riff Raff* (Robert Z. Leonard 1935) (Harlow and >Spencer Tracy hurl insults and pull cons on the fish docks). In the footsteps of Clara Bow, Harlow combined glamour and humour in *The Platinum Blonde* (>Frank Capra 1931) (☆ ☞ ✍) (heiress Harlow suspects her journalist husband Robert Williams of canoodling with Loretta Young), *Red Headed Woman* (Jack Conway 1932) (☆) (shopgirl Jean marries the boss, but his snobby friends make life uncomfortable for her), *Dinner at Eight* (>George Cukor 1933) (☞ ☆) (Harlow and her crooked husband Wallace Beery are one of the couples having heated discussions prior to eating out), *Reckless* (Victor Fleming 1935) (☆) (agent >William Powell helps star Harlow cope after her husband's suicide in this rather tactless use of an episode from Harlow's own life) and *Libeled Lady* (Jack Conway 1936) (☆ ☞ ✍) (>Spencer Tracy hopes to get >Myrna Loy to drop a lawsuit by making journalist >William Powell woo her, but he is engaged to Harlow and she uncovers the plot). Thrice married and, like >Marilyn Monroe after her, much manipulated, Harlow died of cerebral oedema during the shooting of *Saratoga* (Jack Conway 1937) (daughter of horse breeder Lionel Barrymore, Jean is swept off her feet by bookie >Clark Gable), and the film had to be completed with her double (silent and only seen from the back).

•*Hell's Angels* (Howard Hughes 1930) (☞ ☆): Oxford flyboys Ben Lyon and James Hall fight the Kaiser and each other over Jean.

•*Red Dust* (Victor Fleming 1932) (☞ ☆): rubber planter >Clark Gable prefers whore Harlow to rich Mary Astor.

•*Blonde Bombshell* (US: *Bombshell*) (Victor Fleming 1933) (☆ ☞): in a story that must have seemed all too familiar, Harlow is a movie star wanting to change her dumb blonde image.

•*Hold Your Man* (Sam Wood 1933) (☆ ☞): moll Harlow and gangster >Clark Gable trade rapid fire, but only verbally.

•*The Girl from Missouri* (Jack Conway 1934) (☆): chorus girl Harlow wants to make sure she has the right millionaire, either Franchot Tone or Lionel Barrymore.

•*Wife Versus Secretary* (Clarence Brown 1936) (☆ ☞ ✍): >Myrna Loy's mother-in-law convinces her that Jean is more than just a secretary to publisher >Clark Gable.

Harvey ☆ ✍ ☞

USA • U-I • 1950 • 104 mins • b/w

d Henry Koster **w** Mary Chase
ph William Daniels **m** Frank Skinner

>James Stewart, Josephine Hull, Victoria Horne, Cecil Kellaway, Jesse White, Peggy Dow

Elwood P. Dowd is an amiable inebriate, who has drifted happily through life to middle age. But when domestic friction follows his insistence that his sole companion is a Pookah, a benevolent Irish spirit that manifests itself as a six-foot rabbit visible only to himself, his concerned sister begins proceedings to have him certified. However, with the innate sense of reasonableness and self-preservation characteristic of the disturbed, Elwood eludes the legal and medical authorities and his sister is the one to become an inmate of the private clinic. Mary Chase's Pulitzer Prize-winning play was tailor-made for Stewart, ably supported by a Broadway cast whose roles seem second nature, particularly 1950 Best Supporting Actress winner, Josephine Hull.

THE HARDER THEY FALL
(Mark Robson 1956) ☆

FIGHT GAME

GENTLEMAN JIM
(>Raoul Walsh 1942) ☞ ☆
(Errol Flynn as late 19th-century
champion Jim Corbett)

BODY AND SOUL
(Robert Rossen 1947) ☆ ☞
(John Garfield fights to save sick
sister)

THE SET-UP
(Robert Wise 1949) ☆
(honest ageing boxer Robert Ryan
beaten by racketeers)

FAT CITY
(>John Huston 1972) ☞ ☆
(Stacey Keach finds life tough out-
side the ring)

RAGING BULL
(>Martin Scorsese 1980) ☆ ☞ ▣
(>Robert De Niro [AA] in biopic of
Jake La Motta)

HOMEBOY
(Michael Seresin 1988) ♫
(Mickey Rourke in a kind of
>Rocky >On the Waterfront)

US SPORT

KNUTE ROCKNE, ALL AMERICAN
(Lloyd Bacon 1940) ☆
(Pat O'Brien and Ronald Reagan in
biopic of college football coach)

THE BABE RUTH STORY
(Roy Del Ruth 1948)
(William Bendix in biopic of base-
ball legend)

THE BAD NEWS BEARS
(Michael Ritchie 1976) ☆ ✍
(Walter Matthau revives fortunes
of kids' lousy baseball team)

SLAP SHOT
(George Roy Hill 1977) ☆
(>Paul Newman caught up in the
vendettas and violence in ice hockey)

NORTH DALLAS FORTY
(Ted Kotcheff 1979) ☆
(Nick Nolte experiences the trials
of being a retired pro-football
player)

THE NATURAL
(Barry Levinson 1984) ☆ ☞
(brilliant batter Robert Redford
suspected of being just too good)

BULL DURHAM
(Ron Shelton 1989) ☆ ✍
(baseball groupie Susan Sarandon
makes a pitch for Kevin Costner)

MAJOR LEAGUE
(David Ward 1989) ✍
(woman coach wants to end a winning streak to take baseball team to
new stadium)

THE OLYMPICS

>OLYMPISCHE SPIELE 1936
(OLYMPIAD) (US: OLYMPIA)
(Leni Riefenstahl 1938) ☞ ▣ ♫
(Jesse Owens steals Hitler's
thunder at Berlin games of 1936)

MILLION DOLLAR MERMAID
**(UK: THE ONE PIECE BATHING
SUIT)**
(>Mervyn Le Roy 1952) ☞
(Esther Williams as Australian
swimmer Annette Kellerman
trained by Victor Mature)

GEORDIE
(Frank Launder 1955) ☆
(Highlander Bill Travers trained by
>Alastair Sim for Olympic ham-
mer-throwing event)

THIRTEEN DAYS IN FRANCE
**(Claude Lelouch/François Rei-
chenbach 1968)** ▣ ☞
(official film of Grenoble Winter
Games)

DOWNHILL RACER
(Michael Ritchie 1969) ▣
(dedication of an Olympic skier
Robert Redford)

THE GAMES
(Michael Winner 1970)
(four men prepare for the Rome
marathon in 1960)

CHARIOTS OF FIRE
(Hugh Hudson 1981) ♫ ✍ ☆
(Cambridge man and Scottish
missionary compete in 1924
Games)

Journalist >Humphrey Bogart
exposes rigged boxing bouts

HORSE POWER

GRAND PRIX
(John Frankenheimer 1966) ☆
(>Yves Montand is among those lapping up the fast cars and fast lifestyles on Formula 1 circuit)

LE MANS
(Lee H. Katzin 1971) ■
(drama surrounding the famous 24-hour race)

THE LAST AMERICAN HERO
(Lamont Johnson 1973) ☆
(adventures of wild stock car driver Jeff Bridges)

KENTUCKY
(David Butler 1938) ☞
(rearing thoroughbreds destroys lives of breeders)

NATIONAL VELVET
(Clarence Brown 1944) ✍
(Grand National glory for Elizabeth Taylor and Mickey Rooney in steeplechase classic)

CHAMPIONS
(John Irvin 1983) ♫
(jockey John Hurt's fight against cancer has triumphant outcome)

WORLDWIDE SPORT

THE ARSENAL STADIUM MYSTERY
(Thorold Dickinson 1939)
(murder disrupts big soccer cup match)

HARD, FAST AND BEAUTIFUL
(Ida Lupino 1951) ✍ ☞
(pushy parent dominates tennis star's career)

THE FINAL TEST
(>Anthony Asquith 1953) ☆
(traumas of cricketer Jack Warner preparing for last innings)

THE MOMENT OF TRUTH (IL MOMENTO DELLA VERITÀ)
(Francesco Rosi 1964) ☞ ■
(candid view of bullfighting)

THE CLUB
(Bruce Beresford 1980) ✍ ☆
(boardroom squabbles distract Aussie Rules football team)

THE COLOR OF MONEY
(>Martin Scorsese 1986)
(pool room hustlers >Paul Newman and Tom Cruise enter important tournament)

•>Gary Cooper is the eccentric poet whose disdain of money impresses Jean Arthur, in *Mr Deeds Goes to Town* (>Frank Capra 1936) (☞ ☆), while Treasury official Cecil Parker is equally hopeless with private income, in *Dear Mr Prohack* (Thornton Freeland 1949) (✍ ☆).

•Vanessa Redgrave wants to leave artist husband David Warner because of his gorilla fixation in *Morgan – A Suitable Case for Treatment* (Karel Reisz 1966) (☆ ✍).

•A Soviet saddlemaker finds it impossible to find a bride for his slow-witted adopted son, so he is given the choice of three prostitutes in *A Slap in the Face* (*Poshchyochina*) (Genrikh Malyan 1980) (✍ ☞).

•Another huge beast, this time visible, is the result of a sheepdog swallowing a wonder vegetable growth potion in Disney's *Digby, the Biggest Dog in the World* (Joseph McGrath 1973) (✍).

•New doctor Robert Powell hears four terrible case histories when he joins the staff of a remote *Asylum* (Roy Ward Baker 1972) (✍ ☆), while >Oliver Hardy visits shell-shocked >Stan Laurel in a sanitarium, in *Blockheads* (John G. Blystone 1938) (☆ ✍).

HAUNTED HOUSES

The Amityville Horror (Stuart Rosenberg 1979)
James Brolin and Margot Kidder are terrorized by the cast of a brutal murder.

Beetlejuice (Tim Burton 1988) ✍ ✳ ☆
Ghosts Alec Baldwin and Geena Davis change their minds about Michael Keaton exorcising their house of people.

The Cat and the Canary (Elliott Nugent 1939) ✍ ☆
Bob Hope and Paulette Goddard search for hidden loot in an old dark house.

Celine and Julie Go Boating (*Céline et Julie Vont en Bateau*) (Jacques Rivette 1974) ☞ ■ ✍
Magician Juliet Berto and librarian Dominique Labourier interfere with the course of a habitual haunting.

Fright Night (Tom Holland 1985) ✍
TV ghost hunter Roddy McDowall baulks at shooing real vampire Christopher Sarandon.

The Ghost and Mrs Muir (>Joseph L.Mankiewicz 1947) ☞ ✍
Gene Tierney falls for ghostly sea captain Rex Harrison.

The Haunting (Robert Wise 1963) ☞ ✍
A variety of scientists and sceptics agree to spend the night in an old Boston mansion.

High Spirits (Neil Jordan 1988) ✍ ✳
Steve Guttenburg revives 18th-century murder victim Daryl Hannah in Peter O'Toole's supposedly unhaunted Irish castle.

A Quiet Place in the Country (*Un Tranquillo Posto di Campagna*) (Elio Petri 1969) ✍ ☞
Berlin Special Jury film of a ghost-obsessed writer who is driven to believing he has killed his mistress Vanessa Redgrave.

Return to Glennascaul (>Orson Welles 1951) ✍ ☆ ☞
A short film of a man entertained at a house which next day appears long deserted.

The Spiral Staircase (Robert Siodmak 1945) ☞ ✍ ■
Mute Dorothy McGuire guesses wrongly which of Ethel Barrymore's sons is killing deformed girls.

Thark (Tom Walls 1932) ✍
Ben Travers' farce has a millionaire wagering he can spend a night in his eerie mansion.

The Uninvited (Lewis Allen 1944) ✍ ☞ ☆
Gail Russell's dead mother's ghost takes possession of Ray Milland and Ruth Hussey's home.

> ghosts

Hawks, Howard
American director (1896–1977)
Cornell engineering graduate and speed sports enthusiast, Hawks reflected his admiration for professional achievement and fast action in the people he employed (writers Ben Hecht, William Faulkner and Charles Lederer and a host o͡f ͡⅃ the subjects examined in his highly diversified canon. ACTIONERS: *The Dawn Patrol* (1930) (☞ ■) (Richard Barthelmess and Douglas Fairbanks Jr are among the fly boys awaiting World War I missions); *The Crowd*

Roars (1932) (☞ ☆) (>James Cagney tries to talk brother Eric Linden out of joining him on the race track); *Tiger Shark* (1932) (accustomed to the taste of fisherman >Edward G. Robinson, having eaten his hand, a shark polishes him off, leaving his wife free to join her lover); *Only Angels Have Wings* (1939) (☆ ☞) (Jean Arthur causes a feud between cargo pilots >Cary Grant and Richard Barthelmess); and *To Have and Have Not* (1944) (☆ ☞ ✍) (>Humphrey Bogart and Lauren Bacall resist the Nazis in the French West Indies). GANGSTER FILMS: *The Criminal Code* (1931) (☞ ✍) (framed for one murder, an innocent man is caught up in a prison killing), and *Scarface* (1932) (☞ ☆) (Paul Muni in an incestuous fantasy based on Al Capone). WESTERNS: *Red River* (1948) (☞ ☆) (>John Wayne and Montgomery Clift pioneer a cattle trail); *The Big Sky* (1952) (☞) (>Kirk Douglas leads pioneers through Indian territory); *Rio Bravo* (1959) (☞ ☆) (>John Wayne helps tipsy lawman Dean Martin fight off baddy allcomers); and *Rio Lobo* (1970) (☞) (US Civil War colonel >John Wayne foils a Confederate gold heist). While all these matched the best in their respective genres, Hawks' particular forte was confronting men with strong women: *Twentieth Century* (1934) (☞ ✍ ☆) (actress >Carole Lombard hits the top and has enough of >Svengali Lionel Barrymore); >*Bringing Up Baby* (1938) (✍ ☞ ☆); >*His Girl Friday* (1940) (✍ ☞ ☆); >*The Big Sleep* (1946) (☆ ✍ ☞ ■) and *I Was a Male War Bride* (US: *You Can't Sleep Here*) (1949) (☆ ☞ ✍) (Ann Sheridan gets >Cary Grant out of liberated Europe by dressing him as a WAC). Restrained narrative and sparse technique make Hawks the most accessible of directors.

•*A Girl in Every Port* (1928) (☞ ☆): rough and ready sailor Victor McLaglen wins the heart of the elegant Louise Brooks.

•*Today We Live* (1933) (☞ ☆): the trench adventures of >Joan Crawford and admirers >Gary Cooper, Franchot Tone and Robert Young.

•*Barbary Coast* (1935) (☞ ☆): >Edward G. Robinson makes Miriam Hopkins his star turn, but can't turn her head.

•*The Road to Glory* (1936) (☞ ■ ☆): the trench adventures of >Fredric March and Lionel Barrymore's platoon.

•*Come and Get It* (1936): the life of a 19th-century lumberman, co-directed with >William Wyler and photographed, as many of Hawks' films were, by Gregg Toland.

•*Ball of Fire* (1936) (☞ ☆ ■): >Gary Cooper as one of the seven lexicographers wowed by stripteaser >Barbara Stanwyck.

•*A Song is Born* (1947) (■ ☞): moll Virginia Mayo seduces music professor Danny Kaye in a remake of the previous film.

•*Sergeant York* (AAN: 1941) (☆ ☞): >Gary Cooper as the gentle farmer who is infuriated into trench heroics.

•*The Thing* (UK: *The Thing from Another World*) (1951) (☞ ✍): Hawks and >Orson Welles offering a little help to director Christian Nyby in this tale of an alien thawing out in the Arctic.

•*Monkey Business* (1952) (☆ ☞): >Cary Grant and >Ginger Rogers regress to childhood courtesy of a chimp-manufactured potion.

•*Gentlemen Prefer Blondes* (1953) (☞ ☆): >Marilyn Monroe and Jane Russell descend on Paris in search of millionaires, because diamonds are a girl's best friend.

•*Hatari!* (1962): >John Wayne as a big game hunter in Tanzania.

•*Man's Favourite Sport* (1963) (☞ ☆ ✍): Rock Hudson is helped to win a fishing competition by Paula Prentiss.

•*El Dorado* (1966): shootist >John Wayne and wino lawman Robert Mitchum tame cattle baron James Caan.

HEIRESSES

Can't Help Singing (Frank Ryan 1944) ☆
Deanna Durbin leaves luxury to camp-follow her soldier boyfriend.

Chase a Crooked Shadow (Michael Anderson 1957) ✍
Richard Todd pretends to be Anne Baxter's brother, hoping to make a killing.

The Gay Desperado (Rouben Mamoulian 1936) ☞ ☆
Ida Lupino falls in love with her kidnapper Nino Martini.

Goin' to Town (Alexander Hall 1935) ☆
Singer-turned-oil heiress Mae West moves into society for respectability and love.

The Heiress (>William Wyler 1949) ☞ ☆ ✍
>Olivia De Havilland punishes Montgomery Clift for his designs on her fortune.

>*It Happened One Night* (>Frank Capra 1934) ✍ ☆ ☞

Love is News (Tay Garnett 1937) ✍
Loretta Young marries scandal sheet journalist Tyrone Power to see how much he enjoys the prying.

Love on the Run (W. S. Van Dyke 1936) ☞ ☆

Pressman >Clark Gable helps >Joan Crawford avoid an arranged marriage and discover a spy ring in a stately home.

My Name is Julia Ross (Joseph H. Lewis 1945) ✍
A young girl is kidnapped because of her likeness to an exploitable heiress.

>*The Philadelphia Story* (>George Cukor 1940) ☆ ✍ ☞

Hepburn, Katharine
American actress (b 1907)

Famous for her mettle on and off screen, Hepburn has won a unique place in the artistic and social history of a male-dominated industry – as an exceptional actress and assertive feminist. In dramas, she played ambitious career women: *Christopher Strong* (Dorothy Arzner 1933) (☆) (aviatrix Hepburn commits adultery with Colin Clive and suicide when she gets pregnant); *Morning Glory* (AA: Lowell Sherman 1933) (☆) (aspiring actress Kate impresses Adolphe Menjou and Douglas Fairbanks Jr); *Little Women* (>George Cukor 1933) (✍ ☆) (Kate as Jo, the artistic one of the four March sisters who falls for writer Paul Lukas); *Alice Adams* (AAN: >George Stevens 1935) (this screen version of the Booth Tarkington novel has humble Kate winning wealthy Fred MacMurray despite prejudice from both sides of the tracks); *Sylvia Scarlett* (>George Cukor 1936) (☞ ☆) (Kate's androgynous heroine joins >Cary Grant in conning Brian Aherne); *Mary of Scotland* (>John Ford 1936) (☆ ☞) (>Fredric March helps Queen of Scots

Kate resist rebels and invaders, but does not defeat them); *A Woman Rebels* (Mark Sandrich 1936) (☆) (Hepburn defies Victorian convention and has an illegitimate child with Herbert Marshall). She added humour to her repertoire in the many battle-of-the-sexes comedies she did with >Spencer Tracy: *Woman of the Year* (AAN: >George Stevens 1942) (☆ ☞) (sportswriter Tracy has his masculine pride dented by Kate's celebrity as an upholder of worthy causes); *State of the Union* (UK: *The World and his Wife*) (>Frank Capra 1948) (☆ ☞) (Kate postpones her divorce to help politician husband Tracy secure his re-election); >*Adam's Rib* (>George Cukor 1949) (✍ ☆ ☞♪); and *Pat and Mike* (>George Cukor 1952) (☆ ☞) (gruff sports entrepreneur Tracy becomes all-round athlete Kate's promoter and they fall in love – eventually). And she found a lot of laughs in her roles as an heiress with >Cary Grant in >*Bringing up Baby* (>Howard Hawks 1938) (✍ ☞ ☆) and >*The Philadelphia Story* (AAN: >George Cukor 1940) (☆ ✍ ☞). She received other Academy nominations for >*The African Queen* (>John Huston 1951) (☆ ☞ ✍ ■), *Summertime* (UK: *Summer Madness*) (>David Lean 1955) (☆ ☞) (spinster Kate holidays in Venice and is charmed by Rossano Brazzi), *The Rainmaker* (Joseph Anthony 1956) (☆) (con man Burt Lancaster wakes Kate's heart, but she refuses to abandon her ungrateful father and brothers), *Suddenly Last Summer* (>Joseph L. Mankiewicz 1959) (☆ ✍) (Kate is so ashamed of her gay son's death at the hands of pretty Arab beach boys, she tries to have Elizabeth Taylor committed to prevent the tale leaking out) and *Long Day's Journey into Night* (>Sidney Lumet 1962) (☆ ☞) (it is 1912; Ralph Richardson is a faded actor and Hepburn is his drug-addicted wife, but their sons have the real problems). Oscars were also received for *Guess Who's Coming to Dinner* (Stanley Kramer 1967) (☆ ☞ ✍) (Kate persuades >Spencer Tracy to accept their daughter's love for Sidney Poitier), *The Lion in Winter* (Anthony Harvey 1968) (☆ ✍ ☞) (Kate as Eleanor of Aquitaine feuding over the royal succession with Peter O'Toole as Henry II) and *On Golden Pond* (Mark Rydell 1981) (☆ ■) (pensioners

Kate and >Henry Fonda bicker affectionately in their dream retirement cottage).

 •*A Bill of Divorcement* (>George Cukor 1932) (☆): by the time John Barrymore emerges from an asylum, his malleable daughter Kate is a determined young woman.
•*The Little Minister* (Richard Wallace 1934) (☆ ■): a Scottish vicar believes that earl's daughter Kate is a fallen gypsy.
•*Stage Door* (Gregory La Cava 1937) (☆ ☞ ∠): Kate is among the aspiring actresses staying at a theatrical boarding house.
•*Keeper of the Flame* (>George Cukor 1942) (☞ ☆): journalist >Spencer Tracy investigates Kate's involvement in the accidental death of her youth leader husband.
•*Desk Set* (UK: *His Other Woman*) (Walter Lang 1957) (☆): Kate and Joan Blondell enjoy life in a radio station library until >Spencer Tracy implements an efficiency scheme.
•*The Madwoman of Chaillot* (Bryan Forbes 1969) (☆): Kate hosts a salon in Paris, but her eccentricity is simply a mask for her regret at the passing of her life.
•*A Delicate Balance* (Tony Richardson 1974) (☆ ∠☞): Edward Albee's adaptation of his own play has Paul Scofield, Joseph Cotten and Lee Remick resenting Hepburn's matriarchal power over their family.
•*Rooster Cogburn* (Stuart Millar 1975) (☆): Kate replays her role as the tough preacher woman of >*The African Queen* to help >John Wayne outwit some outlaws.

Herzog, Werner
(Werner Stipetic) German writer/director (b 1942)
As a documentary maker, primarily concerned with man's conflicts within himself, (eg the blind mute in *Land of Silence and Darkness* (*Land des Schweigens und der Dunkelheit*) [1971] ☞) and with Nature – *The Flying Doctors of East Africa* (*Die Fliegenden Ärzte von Ostafrika*) (1970) (☞) and a threatened volcanic eruption in *La Soufrière* (1974) (☞ ■) – Herzog has brought a unique talent for portraying character and the power of natural beauty to his fictional works: *Signs of Life*

(*Lebenszeichen*) (1968) (☞ ☆) (left to guard an unused ammo dump on Kos, Nazi soldier Peter Brogle goes mad with boredom), *Aguirre, Wrath of God* (*Aguirre, der Zorn Gottes*) (1974) (■ ☞) (Klaus Kinski as a blustering *conquistador* seeking El Dorado in 16th-century Peru); *Stroszek* (1977) (☞ ☆) (a trio of ne'er-do-wells emigrate to the USA and bungle a robbery); *Woyzeck* (1978) (☞ ☆) (Georg Büchner's play has Klaus Kinski as a simple soldier toiling to keep his mistress, until her infidelity prompts a violent reaction); *Fitzcarraldo* (1982) (☆ ☞) (Klaus Kinski as an eccentric cruising down the Amazon in search of a site for his opera house); and *Cobra Verde* (1988) (☞ ■) (Klaus Kinski as a trader negotiating for slaves with the King of Dahomey).

 •*Even Dwarfs Started Small* (*Auch Zwerge haben klein angefangen*) (1970): an examination of people's obsession with possession.
•*Fata Morgana* (1971) (☞ ■): the evils of poverty and colonialism are analysed in a desert setting.
•*The Enigma of Kaspar Hauser* (US: *Every Man for Himself and God Against All* (aka *The Mystery of Kaspar Hauser*) (*Jeder für Sich und Gott Gegen Alle*) (1974) (☞ ■): this Special Jury winner at Berlin tells of the impact on Nuremberg of a man who has no experience of human beings.
•*The Great Ecstasy of Woodcarver Steiner* (*Die Grosse Ekstase des Bildschnitzers Steiner*) (1975) (☞): a revealing short documentary on the character and achievements of a ski-jumper.
•*Heart of Glass* (*Herz aus Glas*) (1976) (☞): a shepherd reveals the formula for a special glass that will bring prosperity to a Bavarian village.
•*Nosferatu the Vampire* (*Nosferatu: Phantom der Nacht*) (1979) (☞ ■ ☆): Klaus Kinski as Dracula lured to his daybreak death by Isabelle Adjani's Lucy Harker.

HIDE AND SEEK

The Bandits of Orgosolo (*Banditi a Orgosolo*) (>**Vittorio De Sica** 1961) ☞ ■
A shepherd is wrongly accused and returns to

his sheep to lay low, but when they die, he resorts to crime.

Fires on the Plain (*Nobi*) **(Kon Ichikawa 1959) ☞ ☆**

Fearing the Americans, a Japanese soldier retreats into the jungle where worse terrors await.

The Fruit Machine **(Philip Savile 1988)** ✍ ☆

Gay teenagers hide out in Brighton having witnessed the Liverpool nightclub killing of transvestite Robbie Coltrane.

Gates of Paris (US: *Gate of Lilacs*) (*Portes des Lilacs*) **(>René Clair 1957) ☞ ■**

A drifter shelters a gangster only to kill him when he makes a play for his girlfriend.

It Always Rains on Sundays **(Robert Hamer 1947)** ☆ ✍

Escapee John McCallum stays with mistress Googie Withers hoping husband Jack Warner doesn't detect him.

>*Le Jour se Lève* (US: *Daybreak*) (**>Marcel Carné 1939)** ☆ ☞ ✍ ■

The Small Voice (US: *Hideout*) **(Fergus McDonell 1948)** ✍

Gangsters hole up in Howard Keel and Valerie Hobson's pretty cottage.

Such a Pretty Little Beach (US: *Riptide*) (*Une si Jolie Petite Plage*) **(Yves Allégret 1949)** ☞ ■ ✍

A man hides out in the hotel where he met the singer he is now suspected of killing.

>The Third Man (**>Carol Reed 1949)** ☆ ☞ ♫ ✍ ■

High Noon ☆ ☞ ✍ ♫

USA • United Artists • 1952 • 85 mins • b/w
d >Fred Zinnemann w Carl Foreman
ph Floyd Crosby m Dmitri Tiomkin
>Gary Cooper, Grace Kelly, Thomas Mitchell, Lloyd Bridges, Lon Chaney Jr

Will Kane (Cooper)'s decision to forsake his darling (Kelly) on their wedding day, resume his badge of office and, having been abandoned by all and sundry, do what a man's gotta do and shoot it out with the desperados who have vowed to repay him for jailing them is an archetypal screen example of upholding the law through true grit. Exhausted, ill and begin-

ning to mistrust the movie-made Western myth, Cooper was still sufficiently the all-American hero to merit the Best Actor Oscar. Yet, ironically, Foreman's screenplay is not, in fact, a celebration of courage, but a parable exposing the fair-weather friend mentality that poisoned professional and personal relationships in Hollywood during the McCarthyite witch hunts of the 1950s. Foreman was blacklisted for his pains and 'good all-American, bullet-headed, Saxon mothers' sons' continued to win the West.

•>Kirk Douglas plays the personification of Greek courage, in *Ulysses* (Mario Camerini 1954) (☆ ■).

•>Marlon Brando is the baddy who causes trouble in >Jane Fonda and Robert Redford's town, in *The Chase* (Arthur Penn 1966) (☆).

•>Henry Fonda is the decent lawman guarding the citizens of Tombstone against the Clanton gang, in *My Darling Clementine* (>John Ford 1946) (☞ ☆ ♫).

•Nobuko Miyamoto is also prepared to put up with abuse to do her job, checking up on petty tax evasions in *A Taxing Woman* (*Marusa no Onna*) (Juzo Itami 1987) (☆ ✍) and chasing evaders owing millions in *A Taxing Woman II* (Juzo Itami 1988) (☞ ☆).

•In *Man of the West* (Anthony Mann 1958) (☆ ☞), Gary Cooper stands alone again, this time as an ex-outlaw resisting peer pressure to return to crime.

•USAF pilots are trained to be the new breed of hero – astronauts – in *The Right Stuff* (Philip Kaufman 1983) (☆).

His Girl Friday ✍ ☞ ☆

USA • Columbia • 1940 • 92 mins • b/w
d >Howard Hawks w Charles Lederer
ph Joseph Walker m Sydney Cutner
>Cary Grant, Rosalind Russell, Ralph Bellamy, Clarence Kolb, Frank Jenks, Billy Gilbert, Ernest Truex, Roscoe Karns

The shortage of a male dinner guest during a reading of Ben Hecht and Charles MacArthur's play *The Front Page* inspired Howard Hawks to introduce a romantic twist to this classic story of journalistic morality. Hildy Johnson (Russell) is still an ace reporter but also now, the ex-wife of ruthless editor Walter Burns (Grant) and on the verge of resigning to marry weakling Bruce Baldwin (Bellamy). Always devious but never dislikable, Burns is aided in delaying her departure by the irresistible scoop opportunity that arises when corrupt city bosses botch the execution of an innocent man. The breakneck comedy ultimately fails to provide a pro-feminist finale, but Cary Grant (cracking Archie Leach jokes 48 years before John Cleese in *A Fish Called Wanda*) and Rosalind Russell are dazzling.

 •A TV station re-make has Burt Reynolds and >Kathleen Turner in the Burns and Johnson roles and Christopher Reeve as the man trying to lure her away from reporting, in *Switching Channels* (Ted Kotcheff 1988) (☆ ✍).
•>Kirk Douglas is a desperate journalist protecting the scoop when a man is trapped in a disused mine, in *Ace in the Hole* (US: *The Big Carnival*) (>Billy Wilder 1951) (☞ ✍ ☆).
•Vincent Price sets his journalists Dana Andrews, George Sanders and Ida Lupino in competition to scoop a murder case and fill the vacant editor's chair, in *While the City Sleeps* (>Fritz Lang 1956) (☞ ✍ ☆).
•Joel McCrea is caught up in a pre-war spy chase that takes him across Europe in *Foreign Correspondent* (>Alfred Hitchcock 1940) (☞ ✍).
•Jeff Goldblum and Lindsay Crouse are amongst the staff of a 1960s underground paper in *Between the Lines* (Joan Micklin Silver 1977) (☞ ☆ ✍).

Hitchcock, Alfred
British director (1899–1980)
Developing the influences of German Expressionism and Soviet montage into his distinctive suspense style during his British period (to 1939), Hitchcock produced the interesting, but nowadays creaky *Blackmail* (1929) (☞) (a Scotland Yard man is blackmailed for diverting murder suspicion from his girlfriend), *Murder* (1930) (☞ ☆) (juror Herbert Marshall finds the evidence to clear Nora Baring of murder) and

Number 17 (1932) (☞) (jewel thief Anne Grey leads the police to the house where her old gang used to meet). Subsequently, his classic thrillers were populated by: INNOCENTS CLEARING THEIR NAMES: *The Man Who Knew Too Much* (1934) (☞ ✍) and (1955) (☞ ☆) (respectively, Leslie Banks and >James Stewart play dentists whose sons are kidnapped by spies to prevent exposure), *The Thirty-Nine Steps* (1935) (✍ ☞ ☆ ■) (>Robert Donat, suspected of murder and espionage, heads to Scotland for clues to clear himself), *Saboteur* (1942) (☞ ✍ ☆) (Robert Cummings is chased across the country for detonating a munitions factory, but he is on the trail of the real traitor), *Spellbound* (1944) (☞ ☆) (psychiatrist >Ingrid Bergman helps amnesiac imposter Gregory Peck find the doctor he has replaced and discover why he has disappeared), *Strangers on a Train* (1951) (☞ ✍) (crackpot Robert Walker tries to coax tennis star Farley Granger into carrying out each other's murders to avoid detection), *The Wrong Man* (1957) (☞ ☆) (>Henry Fonda is committed for a murder because it is in the witnesses' interests to frame him), and *North by Northwest* (1959) (☞ ☆ ✍ ■ ♫) (Cary Grant is mistaken for a spy, and he and Eva Marie Saint are pursued when he realizes the extent of the real spies' plan); THE UNTRUSTWORTHY: >*Rebecca* (1940) (☞ ☆ ■ ✍ ♫) *Suspicion* (1941) (☞ ☆ ✍ ■) (newlywed >Joan Fontaine suspects husband >Cary Grant is up to no good when she discovers he does not spend all day at work as he claims), >*Notorious* (1946) (☞ ☆ ✍ ■) and *Marnie* (1964) (☞) (>Sean Connery has sexual and shoplifting problems with mysterious Tippi Hedren); and KILLERS: *The Lodger* (1926) (☞) (secretive lodger Ivor Novello is suspected of being >Jack the Ripper), *Shadow of a Doubt* (1943) (☞ ✍) (widow killer Joseph Cotten tries to kill his favourite niece Teresa Wright when she suspects him), *Rope* (1948) (☞ ☆ ✍ ■) (bored little rich boys strangle a friend, hiding him in a trunk that is centre stage throughout a party, but their former teacher >James Stewart discovers the 'joke'), >*Rear Window* (AAN: 1954) (☆ ☞ ✍ ■), >*Psycho* (AAN: 1960) (☞ ♫ ☆ ✍ ■) and *Frenzy* (1972) (Barry Foster is the London 'necktie killer' who allows the blame to fall on old friend Jon Finch). Crackling with wit and sexual as well as psychological tension, a Hitchcock film, complete with a 'spot the director' challenge, is readily recognizable and always enjoyable.

 •*Easy Virtue* (1927) (☞): a young woman's artist lover commits suicide and her drunken husband divorces her after the scandal.

•*The Farmer's Wife* (1928) (☞): widowed farmer Jameson Thomas clumsily tries to find a new wife.

•*Rich and Strange* (US: *East of Shanghai*) (1931) (☞): a young couple spend their inheritance travelling.

•*Secret Agent* (1936) (☞ ☆): an adaptation of the Somerset Maugham story 'Ashenden' has reluctant spy John Gielgud contracted to kill >Peter Lorre.

•*Young and Innocent* (US: *A Girl was Young*) (1937) (☞): suspects flee police attention in this screen version of the Josephine Tey novel *A Shilling for Candles*.

•*The Lady Vanishes* (1938) (☞ ✍ ☆): Michael Redgrave and Margaret Lockwood stumble on to a spy plot when Dame May Whitty goes missing.

•*Foreign Correspondent* (1940) (☞ ✍): journalist Joel McCrea's pursuit of a spy scoop lands him in increasing danger in pre-war Europe.

•*Lifeboat* (AAN: 1944) (☞ ✍ ☆): a Nazi U-boat captain is among the survivors of a sea battle, but can he be trusted?

•*The Paradine Case* (1947) (☞ ☆ ✍): Gregory Peck's court duel with >Charles Laughton is hindered by his love for suspect Alida Valli.

•*Stage Fright* (1950) (☞ ✍): Richard Todd blames actress >Marlene Dietrich for the murder with which he is being connected.

•*I Confess* (1953) (☞ ✍ ☆): priest Montgomery Clift is prevented from revealing the name of a murderer by his confessional vow and becomes a suspect himself.

•*Dial M for Murder* (1954) (☞ ☆ ✍): Ray Milland arranges his wife Grace Kelly's death, but when she kills the assassin in the struggle, a love letter appears to be her motive for murder.

•*To Catch a Thief* (1954) (☞ ☆): retired jewel thief >Cary Grant is assisted by Grace Kelly to discover who is copying his style.

•>*The Trouble with Harry* (1954) (■ ☞ ☆ ✍).

•*Vertigo* (1958) (☞ ☆ ✍): James Stewart witnesses Kim Novak's bell tower death, or does he?

•*The Birds* (1963) (☞ ■): inexplicably the birds in a small port attack *en masse* and wreak havoc, until just as inexplicably they become calm.

•*Torn Curtain* (1966) (☞ ☆): >Paul Newman's faked defection is jeopardized by his lover Julie Andrews following him.

Hoffman, Dustin
American actor (b 1937)

Jettisoned into fame by >*The Graduate* (>Mike Nichols 1967) (☆ ☞ ♫ ■), as a 30-year-old playing someone of 20 who refuses to trust anyone older than 30, Hoffman's mastery of naturalistic acting has subsequently kept him at the forefront of his profession. Vulnerability, occasioned somewhat by his diminutive stature, has landed him in a number of situations over which he has no control: *Midnight Cowboy* (AAN: >John Schlesinger 1969) (♫ ☆ ☞) (Hoffman as the crippled Ratso Rizzo who tries to pimp for gigolo Jon Voight); *Marathon Man* (>John Schlesinger 1976) (☆ ☞) (runner Dustin becomes involved in Nazi dentist >Laurence Olivier's search for diamonds); *Kramer versus Kramer* (AA: Robert Benton 1979) (☆) (Hoffman and >Meryl Streep battle for the custody for their young son); *Tootsie* (AAN: Sydney Pollack 1982) (☆) (out-of-work actor Dustin turns transvestite to land a part in a TV soap opera, but risks losing Jessica Lange); and *Death of a Salesman* (>Volker Schlöndorff 1985) (☆ ☞) (Hoffman as Arthur Miller's failure whose expectations for his son and himself have fallen far short). However, there have also been aggressors: *Straw Dogs* (Sam Peckinpah 1971) (mild academic Hoffman lashes out when Cornish locals assault him and his wife Susan George); *Lenny* (AAN: Bob Fosse 1973) (biopic of the controversial comedian Lenny Bruce); *All the President's Men* (Alan J. Pakula 1976) (☆ ✍) (*Washington Post* journalists Hoffman and Robert Redford break the Watergate scandal);

and *Agatha* (Michael Apted 1978) (☆) (American journalist Hoffman disregards husband Timothy Dalton to discover Vanessa Redgrave, the missing crime writer >Agatha Christie in a Harrogate hotel). An Oscar-winning performance in *Rain Man* (☆ ☞ ⚐) (Barry Levinson 1988) (autistic savant Hoffman is manipulated then loved by his opportunist half-brother Tom Cruise) seems to confirm that his participation in the dire *Ishtar* (Elaine May 1987) (Dustin and Warren Beatty as talentless songwriters caught up in the Middle East with Isabelle Adjani) was merely a favour for a friend.

•*John and Mary* (Peter Yates 1969) (☆): Dustin and Mia Farrow waver over an affair after a one-night stand.

•*Little Big Man* (Arthur Penn 1970) (✳ ☆): the causes and course of Custer's Last Stand told by lone surviving eye witness Hoffman.

•*Papillon* (Franklin Schaffner 1973) (☆): a memoir of Devil's Island based on Henri Charrière's book.

•*Straight Time* (Ulu Grosbard 1977) (☆): finding going straight impossible, former petty crook Hoffman returns to crime as an armed robber.

•*Family Business* (>Sidney Lumet 1989) (☆ ☞): Hoffman, >Sean Connery and Matthew Broderick as three generations of New York baddies joining forces on a robbery.

HOMOSEXUALITY

The Boys in the Band (William Friedkin 1970) ☞
Home truths fly as a straight arrives at a party, unaware it is gays only.

La Cage aux Folles (Edouard Molinaro 1978) ⚐ ☆
A gay club owner tries to shroud the background of his son from his prospective in-laws.

The Fourth Man (Die Vierde Man) (Paul Verhoeven, 1983) ⚐ ☞
A gay Dutch novelist warns a religious visionary against an affair with a mysterious widow.

Maurice (James Ivory 1988) ☞ ■ ☆
James Wilby as E. M. Forster's repressed upper-class homosexual, exposed for his affair with gardener Rupert Graves.

My Beautiful Laundrette (Stephen Frears 1985) ☞ ☆
Neo-Nazi thug Daniel Day Lewis helps Asian Gordon Warnecke run his uncle Saeed Jaffrey's London launderette.

Parting Glances (Bill Sherwood 1986) ⚐
Lovers are faced with the news that one of their ex-partners has AIDS.

Prick Up Your Ears (Stephen Frears 1987) ☆ ☞ ⚐
Gary Oldman and Alfred Molina excel as 1960s playwright Joe Orton and his lover Kenneth Halliwell.

Querelle (>Rainer Werner Fassbinder 1982) ☞ ⚐
Sea captain Franco Nero and whore Jeanne Moreau are addicted to drug-smuggler Brad Davis in a screen adaptation of Jean Genet's novel.

Sunday Bloody Sunday (>John Schlesinger 1971) ☆ ☞
Murray Head sleeps with both Jewish doctor Peter Finch and businesswoman Glenda Jackson.

Torch Song Trilogy (Peter Bogart 1989) ☆ ⚐
Jewish mother Anne Bancroft finds it hard to accept drag queen Harvey Fierstein's relationship with Matthew Broderick.

Victim (Basil Dearden 1961) ☆ ■ ☞
Lawyer Dirk Bogarde tries to help numerous respectable closet gays who are being blackmailed.

HORSES

Black Beauty (James Hill 1971) ⚐
Anna Sewell's tale of a mistreated cab horse who is cared for in retirement.

The Black Stallion (Carroll Ballard 1979) ⚐
A boy and his horse survive a shipwreck to win a big flat race under Mickey Rooney's training.

The Bride Wore Boots (Irving Pichel 1946) ☆
>Barbara Stanwyck's marriage to Robert Cummings is threatened by her passion for and his hatred of horses.

Broadway Bill (UK: *Strictly Confidential*) (>Frank Capra 1934) ☞ ☆

Trainer Warner Baxter turns >Myrna Loy's horse into a champion.

Come On George (Anthony Kimmins 1939) ☆

George Formby brings the best out of a temperamental race horse.

Francis (Arthur Lubin 1950) ✍

No one believes Donald O'Connor's claim that his war-heroics are due to the advice of a donkey.

The Galloping Major (Henry Cornelius 1951) ☆

Basil Radford heads a syndicate that buys what seems to be a useless horse.

The Miracle of the White Stallions (UK: *The Flight of the White Stallions*) (Arthur Hiller 1962) ☆

This Disney adventure has Robert Taylor preventing the Nazis taking the Lippizaner horses from the Spanish Riding School in Vienna.

National Velvet (Clarence Brown 1944) ✍

Mickey Rooney and Elizabeth Taylor train their horse to win the Grand National.

Phar Lap (Simon Wincer 1985) ✍

Famous Australian race horse of the Depression is struck down by a mystery disease.

The Red Pony (Lewis Milestone 1949) ☆ ✍

>Myrna Loy's son blames hired hand Robert Mitchum for the death of his pet.

Sing You Sinners (Wesley Ruggles 1938) ☆ ✍

Gambler Bing Crosby and brothers Fred MacMurray and Donald O'Connor club together to buy a nag.

HOSPITALS

Behind the Mask (Brian Desmond Hurst 1958) ☆

Michael Redgrave holds the white coats while an administrative board squabble over policy.

Britannia Hospital (Lindsay Anderson 1982) ☆

Administrator Leonard Rossiter's 500th anniversary jamboree is disrupted by striking staff and mad surgeons.

Carry on Nurse (Gerald Thomas 1958) ✍

The traditional recipe of lecherous males, incompetent professionals, innuendo and stern women moulded to the hospital environment.

A Farewell to Arms (Frank Borzage 1932) ☆ ☞

War wounded >Gary Cooper falls for nurse Helen Hayes at a World War I field hospital.

Green for Danger (Sidney Gilliat 1946) ☆ ✍

>Alastair Sim as Cockrill of the Yard in an operating-table-murder comedy whodunnit.

The Hospital (Arthur Hiller 1971) ✍

Writer Paddy Chayevsky won an Oscar for this tale in which a series of deaths can't be explained by natural causes.

The Interns (David Swift 1962) ☆

Tragedies come thick and fast in this 'realistic' look at hospital life.

M*A*S*H (>Robert Altman 1970) ✍ ☞

Donald Sutherland and Elliott Gould as surgeons at a Korean War mobile army surgical hospital.

The National Health (Jack Gold 1973) ☆

Male patients led by orderly Jim Dale cause trouble on the ward.

People Will Talk (>Joseph L. Mankiewicz 1951) ☆ ☞

Hume Cronyn so disapproves of Dr >Cary Grant's unorthodox style and successful bedside manner that he tries to have him struck off.

War Requiem (Derek Jarman 1988) ■

>Laurence Olivier as an old vet, recalling First World War poet Wilfred Owen's memories of a field hospital.

Young Dr Kildare (Harold S. Bucquet 1938) ☆ ✍

Intern Lew Ayres is taken up by chief surgeon Lionel Barrymore.

HOTELS

California Suite (Herbert Ross 1978) ☆ ✍

Comic studies of guests, spoiled by >Jane Fonda and Alan Alda's over-talkative marriage breakdown.

Grand Hotel (Edmund Goulding 1932) ✍

Murder and romance catch up with guests including >Joan Crawford and John and Lionel Barrymore, but >Greta Garbo prefers to be alone.

Hotel Paradiso (Peter Glanville 1966) ☆ ✍
>Alec Guinness leads the farce on a bed-hopping evening at a seedy Parisian hotel.

Hotel Reserve (Victor Hanbury/Lance Comfort 1944) ✍ ☆
Austrian refugee James Mason will be allowed to stay in France if he can expose the spy among the guests.

Hotel Sahara (Ken Annakin 1951) ☆
Hotelier Peter Ustinov changes allegiance according to the fortunes of the Second World War desert campaign.

Plaza Suite (Arthur Hiller 1971) ✍ ☆
Stories highlighted by Walter Matthau coaxing his nervous daughter out of the bathroom and up the aisle.

>*Psycho* (>Alfred Hitchcock 1960) ☞ ♫ ☆ ✍ ■

The Shining (>Stanley Kubrick 1980) ☆ ☞
Blocked writer >Jack Nicholson goes berserk at a haunted hotel.

Sweet Lorraine (Steve Gomer 1987) ☆
Maureen Stapleton's unfashionable hotel enjoys its last summer before closure.

The Hound of the Baskervilles
USA • Twentieth-Century Fox • 1939 • 80 mins • b/w
d Sidney Lanfield   w Ernest Pascal
ph Peverell Marley   m Cyril Mockridge
>Basil Rathbone, Nigel Bruce, Lionel Atwill, Morton Lowry, Wendy Barrie

Rathbone and Bruce's Holmes and Watson pictures form the greatest 'B' movie series ever made, and this, the first, set the highest standards. Pressing business in London prevents Holmes travelling to the Dartmoor home of the cursed Baskerville family, but he is sufficiently concerned for the endangered heir that he sends the good doctor to stand guard. While Watson endures the delights and dangers of rural hospitality, the disguised master sleuth installs himself in a cave and passes the time unravelling the mystery of the flashlight messages, shattering the legend of the hound and exposing the murderer. The slightly makeshift sets are more than made up for by the supreme portrayal of the leads.

•OTHER HOLMESES:
•Clive Brook in *Sherlock Holmes* (William K. Howard 1932) (☆): Professor Moriarty imports gangsters, but Holmes remains unruffled.
•Arthur Wontner in *The Missing Rembrandt* (Leslie Hiscott 1932): a blackmailer is uncovered and a painting recovered.
•Christopher Lee in *Sherlock Holmes and the Deadly Necklace* (Terence Fisher 1962) (☆): a German film that has Holmes on the trail of vicious jewel thieves.
•Robert Stephens in *The Private Life of Sherlock Holmes* (>Billy Wilder 1970) (☞): elder brother Mycroft (Christopher Lee) involves Sherlock in a German sub mystery in the Scottish Highlands.
•Nicol Williamson in *The Seven Per Cent Solution* (Herbert Ross 1976) (✍): Watson (Robert Duvall) hopes that Sigmund Freud (Alan Arkin) can cure Holmes's drug addiction.
•Nicholas Rowe in *Young Sherlock Holmes and the Pyramid of Fear* (US: *Young Sherlock Holmes*) (Barry Levinson 1985) (✍): a schoolboy Holmes and Watson stumble onto an evil Eastern cult in the East End.
•Christopher Plummer in *Murder by Decree* (Bob Clark 1978) (✍): >Jack the Ripper clues lead to some of the highest in the land.
•>Michael Caine in *Without a Clue* (Thom Eberhardt 1989) (✍ ☆): Holmes is a figment of the imagination of supersleuth Watson (Ben Kingsley), who has to hire an actor to play him.
OTHER FILMS:
•Soumitra Chaterjee is the Indian Holmes tracing a gold statuette, in *The Elephant God* (*Joi Baba Felunath*) (>Satyajit Ray 1972) (☞ ✍).
•>Boris Karloff plays two brothers suffering from a family curse, in *The Black Room* (Roy William Neill 1935) (☆ ✍).
•A cinema projectionist dreams of sleuthing, in *Sherlock Junior* (>Buster Keaton 1924) (☆ ✍).
•Disney's *Basil, The Great Mouse Detective* (US: *The Great Mouse Detective*) (John Musker/Ron Clements/Dave Michener/Burny Mattinson 1986) (☞ ✍) is set in the underworld of the London sewers.
•Baker Street's other sleuth is played by

George Curzon in *Sexton Blake and the Hooded Terror* (George King 1938).
> **detectives, Rathbone, Basil**

House of Games
USA • Orion/Rank • 1987 • 102 mins • col
wd David Mamet   ph Juan Ruiz Anchia
m Alaric Jans
Lindsay Crouse, Joe Mantegna, Mike Nussbaum

Seattle psychiatrist Margaret Ford (Crouse), bored by the stability that success has brought, envies the excitement her patients seem to enjoy through their eccentricities. When a reforming gambler offers to introduce her to Mike (Mantegna), a master of ingenious fraud, her penchant for exposing duplicity and unravelling tangled skeins leads her into a dangerous world where she finds herself surprisingly at home. Like *The Mousetrap* or >*Sleuth* (Joseph L Mankiewicz 1972) (🖎 ☆ 🖙), the best way to view Mamet's mesmerizing directorial debut is simply to suspend disbelief and wallow in the deception, as the sleight of hand is undetectable.

 •>Paul Newman and Robert Redford stage an elaborate betting con to fleece Robert Shaw, in *The Sting* (George Roy Hill 1973) (🖎 ☆).
•Love and luck make the world go round in *The Pick Up Artist* (James Toback 1986) (🖎).
•Bookie Charlton Heston discovers the dangers of gambling when he and Lizabeth Scott are pursued by a vengeful better, in *Dark City* (>William Dieterle 1950) (🖙).
•John Qualen's money-making method in *Angels Over Broadway* (Ben Hecht 1940) (🖎) involves playing against cardsharps and leaving before the hustle; but he gets hooked.
•William L. Petersen captures crooks by understanding the psychology of their crime in *Manhunter* (Michael Mann 1986) (🖎 ☆).

HOW THE OTHER HALF LIVES

I'm No Angel **(Wesley Ruggles 1933)** ☆ 🖎
Lion tamer Mae West sues wealthy >Cary Grant for breach of promise.

Kipps **(US: *The Remarkable Mr Kipps*) (>Carol Reed 1941)** 🖎 🖙 ☆
Draper's assistant Michael Redgrave is drawn into Phyllis Calvert's higher society in the screen version of H. G. Wells' novel.
Ladies of Leisure **(>Frank Capra 1930)** 🖙 ☆
Gold digger >Barbara Stanwyck develops scruples about fleecing a millionaire.
Midnight **(Mitchell Leisen 1939)** ☆ 🖙 🖎
Parisian aristo John Barrymore hires Claudette Colbert to lure Don Ameche away from his wife Mary Astor.
A Nest of Gentlefolk **(*Dvorianskoe Gnezdo*) (Andrei Mikhalkov-Konchalovsky 1969)** 🖎
The Ivan Turgenev tale of a bored noble's love for his neighbour's daughter.
Our Betters **(>George Cukor 1933)** 🖙 🖎
This Somerset Maugham play has Constance Bennett causing scandals in London society to shame her philandering husband.
Remember Last Night? **(James Whale 1936)** 🖎

Robert Young and Constance Cummings wake up to discover that there was a murder at their party.
The Swimmer **(Frank Perry/Sydney Pollack 1968)** ☆
Burt Lancaster discovers the shallowness of his rich neighbours as he swims home via their pools.

Howard, Leslie
(Leslie Stainer) British actor/director (1893–1943)
Dignified, creative men who acted decently towards their lovers were Leslie Howard's stock in trade: *Of Human Bondage* (John Cromwell 1934) (☆ 🖎) (Howard takes it on the chin as waitress >Bette Davis destroys his life); *Romeo and Juliet* (>George Cukor 1936) (■ 🖙) (Howard is forced apart from Norma Shearer when he is exiled for killing her brother Tybalt [>Basil Rathbone]); *Intermezzo: A Love Story* (UK: *Escape to Happiness* (Gregory Ratoff 1939) (☆) (violinist Leslie falls for his daughter's piano tutor >Ingrid Bergman); and >*Gone with the Wind* (Victor Fleming 1939) (☆ ■ 🖎 🖙 ♫). He also excelled in roles in which applied brains triumphed over

evil brawn: *The Scarlet Pimpernel* (Harold Young 1934) (☆ ✍) (aristo Howard rescues nobles threatened with execution from the French Revolutionary committees); *Pimpernell Smith* (US: *Mister V; The Fighting Pimpernel* (1941) (✍ ☆) (Howard directs himself in this tale of an archaeology professor rescuing refugees from under the nose of the Nazis); and *Forty Ninth Parallel* (US: *The Invaders*) (>Michael Powell 1941) (☆ ☞ ✍) (Howard and >Laurence Olivier are among those trying to prevent U-boat men washed up in Canada from reaching the neutral USA). A great patriot – he directed and starred in *The First of the Few* (US: *Spitfire*) (1942) (☆ ✍) (a biopic of the inventor of the Spitfire, R. J. Mitchell) and directed *The Gentle Sex* (1943) (☞) (episodes from the lives of women who volunteer for war work from the armed forces to the land girls) – he was killed in 1943 when his plane was shot down, supposedly in the belief that Churchill was a passenger.

•*Berkeley Square* (AAN: Frank Lloyd 1933) (☆ ✍): Leslie journeys to the 18th century and lives the life of his ancestor in the family home.
•*British Agent* (>Michael Curtiz 1934) (☆ ☞): diplomat Howard falls for Bolshevik spy Kay Francis despite the danger.
•*The Petrified Forest* (Archie Mayo 1936) (☆ ✍): Howard (repeating his Broadway success) and >Bette Davis are among the hostages held in the desert by >Humphrey Bogart (also fresh from the stage hit).
•*Stand-In* (Tay Garnett 1937) (☆ ✍): maths genius Howard attempts to revive the fortunes of a film studio, in spite of temperamental actress Joan Blondell and drunken producer >Humphrey Bogart.
•*Pygmalion* (>Anthony Asquith 1938) (☆ ✍ ☞): Leslie makes a lady out of cockney flower girl Wendy Hiller.

Hurt, William
American actor (b 1950)
Debuting in Ken Russell's outlandish cult study of sensory deprivation *Altered States* (1979) (☆ ☞ ✱), Hurt is in constant demand to play essentially decent men – *Gorky Park*

(Michael Apted 1983) (☆ ✍) (Hurt as a Moscow cop on the trail of Lee Marvin's sable-smuggling operation) and *Children of a Lesser God* (AAN: Randa Raines 1986) (☆ ✍) (Hurt as an unorthodox special needs teacher who falls for deaf-and-dumb cleaner Marlee Matlin) – who remain sympathetic even when swaggering, as in *The Big Chill* (Lawrence Kasdan 1983) (☆ ☞ ✍) (Hurt, Glenn Close, and Kevin Kline are among those reliving their student days at a friend's funeral) and *Broadcast News* (James L. Brooks 1987) (☆ ☞ ✍) (feisty TV news editor Holly Hunter is loved by anchor man Hurt and ace reporter Albert Brooks), or led astray, as in >*Body Heat* (Lawrence Kasdan 1981) (☆ ✍ ☞ ■) and *The Kiss of the Spiderwoman* (Hector Babenco 1985) (☆ ☞ ■) (gay Hurt is put in a cell with revolutionary Raoul Julia to induce him to betray colleagues).

•*The Janitor* (US: *Eyewitness*) (Peter Yates 1980) (☆): caretaker Hurt is coaxed by his favourite TV celebrity Sigourney Weaver into giving details of a murder he hasn't witnessed.
•*The Accidental Tourist* (Lawrence Kasdan 1988) (☆ ☞ ✍): travel writer Hurt is torn between beautiful wife >Kathleen Turner and a wacky dog walker Geena Davis.

Huston, John
American-born Irish actor/writer/director
(1906–88)
Ex-boxer and former Mexican cavalryman, Huston began his film career as a scriptwriter (usually as a co-author): *Jezebel* (>William Wyler 1938) (☆ ☞ ✍ ■) (bitchy belle >Bette Davis is rehabilitated by >Henry Fonda); *Dr Ehrlich's Magic Bullet* (AAN: >William Dieterle 1940) (☞ ☆ ✍) (the story of the discovery of a cure for syphilis); *Sergeant York* (AAN: >Howard Hawks 1941) (☆ ☞) (country hick >Gary Cooper becomes a trench hero); and *High Sierra* (>Raoul Walsh 1941) (☞ ☆) (>Humphrey Bogart makes a fatal slip on his last robbery when he is torn between two lovers). It was during the making of this last film that Huston met Bogie, whose career he was to affect dramatically. Combining short story-telling and artistic skills as a director (and often

screenwriter), Huston explored the interaction of: QUESTING PEOPLE: *The Maltese Falcon* (1941) (☞ ☆ ■ ✍) (Bogart's Sam Spade on the trail of a statuette also desired by >Peter Lorre and Sidney Greenstreet), *The Treasure of the Sierra Madre* (AA: 1948) (Bogie and the director's AA-winning father Walter Huston go prospecting in the California hills), *The Asphalt Jungle* (AAN: 1950) (✍ ☞ ■ ☆) (hugely influential thriller, in which ex-prison inmate Sterling Hayden plans a swansong heist), *Beat the Devil* (1954) (☆ ✍) (Bogart and rivals in a shipboard war of words over the future of a uranium mine), *Moby Dick* (1956) (☞ ☆ ✍) (Gregory Peck as Captain Ahab after Herman Melville's great white whale), *The Misfits* (1961) (☞ ☆) (ageing cowhand >Clark Gable teaches Montgomery Clift how to lasso and falls for >Marilyn Monroe), and *The Night of the Iguana* (1964) (☞ ☆) (ex-priest >Richard Burton is torn between bawdy hotelier Ava Gardner, demure tourist Deborah Kerr and nymphet Sue Lyon); and ODD COUPLES: *The Red Badge of Courage* (1951) (☞ ✍) (Audie Murphy and Bill Mauldin are innocents thrown into US Civil War action), >*The African Queen* (1951) (☆ ☞ ✍ ■), *Heaven Knows Mr Allison* (1957) (☞ ☆) (nun Deborah Kerr becomes accustomed to Robert Mitchum's rough-and-ready ways on a desert island), *The Barbarian and the Geisha* (1958) (☞ ☆) (America's first diplomat to Japan, >John Wayne, depends on Eiko Ando to pave his way) and *The Man Who Would Be King* (1975) (☆ ☞ ✍) (soldier >Sean Connery is taken for a god, but power goes to his head in spite of >Michael Caine's caution). These themes were repeated in the best of his later films: *Prizzi's Honour* (1986) (☆ ☞ ✍) (Mafia assassins >Kathleen Turner and >Jack Nicholson find love across the contracts); and his tribute to his adopted land, *The Dead* (1988) (☞ ✍ ☆ ■) (James Joyce short story of a Dublin coterie's Christmas get-together).

VIEW ON ▶ •*Key Largo* (1948) (☆ ✍): >Humphrey Bogart's courage appears to fail him as >Edward G. Robinson shelters from a storm in Lionel Barrymore's hotel.

•*Moulin Rouge* (1953) (■): Jose Ferrer as the crippled artist Henri Toulouse-Lautrec.
•*Freud* (1963) (☞): Montgomery Clift as the Viennese doctor discovering the Oedipus complex.
•*The List of Adrian Messinger* (1963) (☞ ☆ ✍): a war hero detective pursues a mass murderer who is also a master of disguise.
•*The Kremlin Letter* (1970) (☆): a treaty is signed in error and has to be retrieved.
•*Fat City* (1972) (☞): Stacy Keach as a small-time boxer getting too old for the ring.
•*The Life and Times of Judge Roy Bean* (1972): >Paul Newman as the legendary outlaw judge torn between Ava Gardner and Jacqueline Bisset.
•*The Mackintosh Man* (1973) (☞ ☆): imprisoned to gain credibility, agent >Paul Newman trails British spies to Ireland.
•*Chinatown* (>Roman Polanski 1974) (☆ ☞ ✍): Huston (here as actor) plays an incestuous villain hunted by private eye >Jack Nicholson.
•*Hollywood on Trial* (David Helpern Jr 1976): Huston narrates an account of the effects of the House UnAmerican Activities Committee on the film industry.
•*Escape to Victory* (US: *Victory*) (1981) (☞ ✍): PoW >Michael Caine and assorted soccer stars escape after a match against Nazis.
•*Annie* (1982) (☞ ♫): an orphan melts the heart of millionaire Albert Finney in this adaptation of the stage smash.

HYPNOSIS

The Climax (George Waggner 1944) ☆
>Boris Karloff manipulates an opera singer.
Condemned to Death (Walter Forde 1932) ✍
A killer hypnotizes the judge who sentenced him so that he kills too.
Dr Mabuse, the Gambler (*Doktor Mabuse, der Spieler*) (>Fritz Lang 1922) ☞ ■
The man of a thousand faces and piercing eyes plans to rule the world.
The Face of Dr Fu Manchu (Don Sharp 1968) ☆
Christopher Lee as the evil criminal who ensures complicity with a stare.

Fear in the Night (Maxwell Shane 1947) ✍
A hypnotee clicks back to reality to discover he might be a murderer.

The Mask of Dijon (Lew Landers 1946) ☆
>Erich Von Stroheim as the scorned magician murdering hypnotized critics.

Nightmare (Maxwell Shane 1956) ☞ ✍ -
>Edward G. Robinson helps his musician brother Kevin McCarthy to clear his name of murder while hypnotized; a remake of *Fear in the Night*.

Road to Rio (Norman Z. McLeod 1947) ✍ ☆
Bob Hope and Bing Crosby rescue Dorothy Lamour from evil-eye aunt Gale Sondergaard.

Whirlpool (Otto Preminger 1950) ✍
Gene Tierney is blamed for the murder committed by hypnotist Jose Ferrer.

I Am a Fugitive from a Chain Gang ☞ ☆ ✍

USA • Warner Brothers • 1932 • 90 mins • b/w

d >Mervyn Le Roy   w Sheridan Gibney/ Brown Holmes/Robert E. Burns   ph Sol Polito

Paul Muni, Glenda Farrell, Preston Foster, Allen Jenkins, Helen Vinson

In Robert E. Burns' autobiographical vindication of the 'injured by injustice' theme central to Victor Hugo's *Les Misérables*, James Allen (Muni) returns from the trenches determined to test the United States' reputation as the land of opportunity, but a false accusation results in hard labour. Even though he escapes and makes good, he remains a prisoner of his past, being forced to marry a woman who has discovered his identity and who betrays him when he loves elsewhere. Apart from exposing the fallibility and brutality of the legal and penal systems, *Chain Gang* questions the validity of the American Dream as encroaching worldwide Depression became a reality.

 •Woody Allen is comically tied to a chain gang, in *Take the Money and Run* (>Woody Allen 1969) (✍ ☆), while Tony Curtis and Sidney Poitier have race rows escaping, bound together, in *The Defiant Ones* (Stanley Kramer 1958) (☞ ☆).

•British PoWs are forced to labour on the Burma railroad, in *The Bridge on the River Kwai* (>David Lean 1957) (✍ ☆ ☞).

•>Spencer Tracy is the wronged man bent on avenging his persecution in a small town, in *Fury* (>Fritz Lang 1936) (☞ ☆ ■).

•Paul Muni found the USA a land unfit for heroes again in *Scarface* (>Howard Hawks 1932) (☞ ☆), a romanticized biopic of Al Capone.

•Prison life was parodied by >Laurel and Hardy, in *Pardon Us* (James Parrott 1945) (☆ ✍).

•A Christ-like priest delights in his poverty and works of charity in *Nazarín* (>Luis Buñuel 1958) (☞ ✍ ☆).

IMAGINARY STATES

>*Duck Soup* (>Leo McCarey 1933) ☆ ☞ ✍
The Eagle Has Two Heads (US: *Eagle With Two Heads*) (*L'Aigle a Deux Têtes*) (Jean Cocteau 1948) ☆ ☞
Jean Marais, an anarchist and lookalike of the dead king fails in an assassination bid on the queen because he falls in love with her.
The King's Vacation (John Adolfi 1933) ✍
George Arliss abandons the throne to meet his subjects.
Lost Horizon (>Frank Capra 1937) ☞ ☆
Ronald Colman discovers Shangri-La in the Himalayan mountains.
The Merry Widow (>Ernst Lubitsch 1934) ☞ ✍ ☆
Broke king Edward Everett Horton despatches Maurice Chevalier to woo wealthy American widow Jeanette MacDonald.
The Mouse That Roared (Jack Arnold 1959) ☆
Peter Sellers as queen, prime minister and commander-in-chief of a small state declaring war on the USA in the hope of receiving massive aid when it loses.
The Oberwald Mystery (*Il Mistero di Oberwald*) (>Michelangelo Antonioni 1980) ■ ☆
Remake of *The Eagle Has Two Heads*.
The Prisoner Of Zenda (John Cromwell 1937) ☆ ✍ ■ ☞
Ronald Colman saves Ruritania from tyranny by substituting himself for lookalike kidnapped king.

I'm All Right, Jack ☆ ✍ ☞
GB · British Lion · 1959 · 104 mins · b/w
d John Boulting w Frank Harvey/John Boulting ph Max Greene m Ken Hare
Peter Sellers, Ian Carmichael, Terry-Thomas, Irene Handl, >Richard Attenborough, Dennis Price, Liz Fraser, John Le Mesurier, Margaret Rutherford

Following the fortunes of the characters introduced in the Boulting Brothers' satire of National Service, *Private's Progress* (1956) (✍ ☆) (incompetent recruit Carmichael's war is followed from square bashing to battle winning) this biting British comedy of industrial manners further develops the themes of embezzlement and the supremacy of individual over institution. Ian Carmichael's guileless graduate and Dennis Price and Richard Attenborough's corrupt capitalists are wonderful creations, but the show is comprehensively stolen by Peter Sellers' factory union leader, Fred Kite. A rulebook martinet who pompously spouts half-digested dialectic from propaganda pamphlets, Kite, despite hopelessly mishandling the resulting strike, never entirely loses our sympathy, and there is something endearing about a conviction in the Soviet solution that can be summed up by dreams of 'all them cornfields and ballet in the evenings'.

•Unionization and theft hit a car factory in *Blue Collar* (Paul Schraeder 1978) (☞).

•Michael Redgrave is the working-class hero who rises from pit to Parliament in A. J. Cronin's *The Stars Look Down* (>Carol Reed 1939) (☞ ☆).

•True life labour struggle and how US big business used terror and corruption to avoid unionization is the subject of the documentary *Native Land* (Leo Hurwitz/Paul Strand 1942) (☞ ■).

•A family finds itself on either side of the argument when Siberian peasants are to be highrise housed, in *Farewell* (*Proshchanie*) (Elem Klimov 1981) (✍ ☞).

•>Greta Garbo and her attachés are the spoofed communists in >*Ninotchka* (>Ernst Lubitsch 1939) (✍ ☆ ☞).

•>Richard Attenborough's participation in a strike is used by the Communist Party for propaganda purposes, in *The Angry Silence* (Guy Green 1960) (☆ ✍).

IMMIGRANTS

America, America (UK: *The Anatolian Smile*) (>Elia Kazan 1963) ☞
A Greek dreams of leaving repression in Turkey and comes to the USA.

Black Joy (Anthony Simmons 1977) ☆
Inter-island rivalry between Caribbean immigrants in Brixton.

Days of Heaven (Terrence Malick 1978) ■
A trio of immigrants abandon tough Chicago for the midwest.

The Dolly Sisters (Irving Cummings 1945) ✍
Betty Grable and June Haver as a Hungarian vaudeville act.

The Emigrants (Utvandrarna) (Jan Troell 1970) ✍
A Swedish family endures an appalling sea crossing to settle in Minnesota.

Gateway (Alfred Werker 1938) ☆
Irish emigrant Arleen Whelan has a shipboard romance with journalist Don Ameche.

Hold Back the Dawn (Mitchell Leisen 1941) ☆ ☞
This >Billy Wilder and Charlie Brackett script has Charles Boyer marrying >Olivia De Havilland to gain US citizenship.

The Immigrant (>Charles Chaplin 1917) ✍ ☞ ☆
Charlie helps Edna Purviance on the voyage and in poverty in New York.

A Lady without a Passport (Joseph H. Lewis 1950) ☞
Immigration official John Hodiak bends the rules to help Hedy Lamarr leave Cuba.

The New Land (Nybyggarna) (Jan Troell 1972) ☆ ✍
The sequel to *The Emigrants* with Max Von Sydow and Liv Ullmann struggling to get their farm going.

Soursweet (Mike Newell 1988) ✍
An Ian McEwan script of Timothy Mo's novel of Hong Kong gang warfare in London.

The Swissmakers (Die Schweizermacher) (Rolf Lyssy 1978) ✍
An immigration assessor rejects an Italian baker and a German doctor in favour of a Yugoslav ballerina, because he fancies her.

IMPERSONATION

The Doctor Takes a Wife (Alexander Hall 1940) ☆
Loretta Young talks doctor Ray Milland into posing as her husband at high-class functions.

Folies Bergère (UK: The Man from the Folies Bergère) (Roy Del Ruth 1935) ☆ ✍
Professional mimic Maurice Chevalier pretends to be a banker and lands the real financier in trouble with wife Merle Oberon and mistress Ann Sothern.

The Great Impersonation (Alan Crosland 1935) ✍
A German passes himself off as the noble he has killed in the First World War.

The Great Imposter (Robert Mulligan 1961) ☆
Tony Curtis as Ferdinand Waldo Demara who impersonated people to fulfil his dreams and exercise his sense of fun.

Lancer Spy (Gregory Ratoff 1937) ☆
George Sanders is sent to Germany as his spy double.

Mad about Music (Norman Taurog 1938) ☆
Schoolgirl Deanna Durbin adopts Herbert Marshall as her father to end teasing.

The Masquerader (Richard Wallace 1933) ☆
Ronald Colman is called up to stand in for his drug-addicted politician cousin.

No Man of Her Own (Mitchell Leisen 1949) ☆ ☞
Pregnant >Barbara Stanwyck persuades a family that she was newlywed to their son who died in the train crash she survived.

The Whole Town's Talking (UK: Passport to Fame) (>John Ford 1935) ☆ ☞
Gangster >Edward G. Robinson lays low by posing as his doppelganger, a bank clerk, but Jean Arthur is suspicious.

INCEST

Alpine Fire (Hohenfeuer) (Fredi Murer 1985) ■ ☆
The mountain air fuels a Swiss teenager's affair with her deaf and dumb brother.

Country Dance (aka Brotherly Love) (J. Lee-Thompson 1969) ■
Scottish noble Peter O'Toole has designs on sister Susannah York.

Chinatown (>Roman Polanski 1974) ☆ ☞ ✍
Detective >Jack Nicholson discovers that

>John Huston has a daughter by his daughter Faye Dunaway.

Dearest Love (US:*Murmur of the Heart*) (*Le Souffle au Coeur*) (>Louis Malle 1971) ☞
A son's illness and a mother's broken love affair bring them closer together.

La Luna (>Bernardo Bertolucci 1979) ■
Opera star Jill Clayburgh sleeps with her temperamental son.

Mourning Becomes Electra (Dudley Nichols 1947) ⌂
Michael Redgrave heads a family wracked by guilt at incest, cowardice and murder following the US Civil War.

Of a Thousand Delights (US:*Sandra*) (*Vaghe Stelle dell'Orsa*) (>Luchino Visconti 1965) ☆ ☞
Claudia Cardinale is blamed by her mother for her Jewish father's murder during the war, but adored by her lustful brother.

Injustice

Call Northside 777 (Henry Hathaway 1948) ☆ ⌂
Pressman >James Stewart proves that a slum boy is innocent of copicide.

City Streets (Rouben Mamoulian 1931) ☆
>Gary Cooper prevents Sylvia Sidney being framed a second time, in Dashiell Hammett's screenplay.

The Confession (*L'Aveu*) (Constantin Costa-Gavras 1970) ☆ ☞
>Yves Montand as Artur London, the Czech foreign minister who was a victim of a purge in 1951.

Dark Passage (Delmer Daves 1947) ☞ ☆
Lauren Bacall shelters >Humphrey Bogart while he finds out who committed the murder he has done time for.

Les Misérables (Richard Boleslawski 1935) ☞ ☆ ⌂ ■/(Lewis Milestone 1952) ☆ ⌂
Victor Hugo's tale of a wronged man who builds a new life after imprisonment, only for the past to catch up with him.

A Place of Weeping (Darrell Roodt 1986) ⌂
A white South African farmer is discharged for the murder of a black man, but the latter's wife keeps fighting.

A Place in the Sun (>George Stevens 1951) ☆ ⌂ ☞
Montgomery Clift's false conviction for murdering pregnant Shelley Winters robs him of marriage to rich Elizabeth Taylor.

Insanity

David and Lisa (Frank Perry 1963) ☞
A couple in a special needs school fall in love.

Frances (Graeme Clifford 1984) ☆
The tragic mental decline of actress Frances Farmer (Jessica Lange).

I Never Promised You a Rose Garden (Anthony Page 1977)
A teenager's suicidal tendencies lead to her confinement.

In This Our Life (>John Huston 1942) ☆ ☞ ⌂
Neurotic >Bette Davis ruins the lives of her family, particularly those of her sister >Olivia De Havilland and her husband George Brent.

Inadmissible Evidence (Anthony Page 1968) ☆
Private and professional problems slowly drive lawyer Nicol Williamson to breakdown.

King's Row (Sam Wood 1941) ☞ ■ ⌂
A powerful study of the fears and phobias of a small American town.

Mine Own Executioner (Anthony Kimmins 1947) ☆ ☞ ⌂
A shell-shocked war veteran kills the wife of the psychiatrist who is counselling him.

Signs of Life (*Lebenszeichen*) (>Werner Herzog 1968) ☞ ☆
Guarding an outpost on a Greek island, a Nazi soldier goes crazy with loneliness.

The Snake Pit (Anatole Litvak 1948) ☆ ☞
Psychiatrist Leo Genn helps >Olivia De Havilland through the torments of recovering her mind and memory.

Splendor in the Grass (>Elia Kazan 1961) ☞ ☆ ⌂
Prevented from romancing Warren Beatty, Natalie Wood goes insane, in this AA-winning script by William Inge.

IN THE HEAT OF THE NIGHT
(Norman Jewison 1967) ☆ ✍

US REALISM

SALT OF THE EARTH
(Herbert Biberman 1954) ☞
(bitter dispute at a New Mexico zinc mine)

MARTY
(Delbert Mann 1955) ☆ ☞ ✍
(troubled romance of a backward butcher Ernest Borgnine [AA])

THE YOUNG STRANGER
(John Frankenheimer 1957) ☆
(son of successful film mogul falls foul of the law)

A COLD WIND IN AUGUST
(Alexander Singer 1960) ☆
(a teenager's love affair with a middle-aged stripper ends when he sees her perform)

SLAVES OF NEW YORK
(James Ivory 1989) ☞ ▣
(Tama Janowitz's view of life in the yuppie US of the 1980s)

JAPANESE CHIVALRY AND REALISM

THE LOYAL 47 RONIN (GENROKU CHUSHINGURA)
(>Kenji Mizoguchi 1941–2) ☞ ✍
(samurai avenge the death of their warlord)

JUDO SAGA (SANSHIRO SUGATA)
(aka SUGATA SANSHIRO)
(>Akira Kurosumoto 1943) ☞ ▣
(late-19th-century martial artist invents judo)

FLOATING CLOUDS (UKIGUMO)
(Mikio Naruse 1959) ☞ ✍
(a nurse drifts into prostitution when a soldier won't leave his invalid wife)

PANDEMONIUM (SHURA)
(Toshio Matsumoto 1970) ☞
(samurai frustrated in love goes on killing spree)

THE CEREMONY (GISHIKI)
(Nagisa Oshima 1971) ☞ ✍ ☆
(the history of one family since the Second World War)

INDIAN REALISM

THE FOREST (KAADU)
(Girish Karnad 1973) ☞ ✍
(young boy witnesses brutal crimes in dense woods)

THE SEEDLING (ANKUR)
(Shyam Benegal 1974) ✍
(landlord's son persecutes deaf mute farmer's family)

THE CHURNING (MANTHAN)
(Shyam Benegal 1976) ☞ ▣
(villagers resist the march of progress)

THE ROYAL HUNT (MRIGAYA)
(Mrinel Sen 1976) ☞
(government duty comes before friendship)

THE OUTSIDERS (OKA OORIE KATHA)
(Mrinal Sen 1977) ☞ ▣
(the dispute between a man's lazy father and industrious wife ends in tragedy)

HALF-TRUTH (ARDH SATYA)
(Govind Nihalani 1983) ✍
(policeman driven to despair by corruption)

> Racist policeman Rod Steiger resists help
> of coloured superior Sidney Poitier

EMERGING AFRICA

SOLEIL O (aka OH, SUN)
(Med Hondo 1970) ☞
(this Mauretanian film is a study of racism and religion in an unnamed French colony)

THE LION HAS SEVEN HEADS (DER LEONE HAVE SEPT CABECAS)
(Glauber Rocha 1970) ☞ ■
(characters symbolize the Congo's past)

HARVEST: 3000 YEARS (MIRT SOST SHI AMIT)
(Haile Gerima 1975) ☞ ✍
(Ethiopian farmers resort to arms when the land proves too unrelenting)

REED DOLLS (POUPÉES DE ROSEAU)
(Jillali Ferhati 1981) ☞
(a Moroccan teenager is left to fend for herself when husband dies)

AN EGYPTIAN STORY (HADDUTA MISRIYA)
(Youssef Chahine 1982) ☞
(while a film director is in hospital, he reminisces on his life)

SARRAOUNIA
(Med Hondo 1986) ■ ☞
(tribal queen in Burkino Faso leads revolt against imperialist forces)

SOUTH AMERICAN REVOLUTIONARY

THE GUNS (OS FUZIS)
(Ruy Guerra 1963) ☞
(violence and superstition provide no solutions for starving Brazilian peasants)

THE DEATH OF A BUREAUCRAT (LA MUERTE DE UN BUROCRATA)
(Tomas Gutierrez Alea 1966) ☞ ✍
(Cuban widow fights petty regulations to claim pension)

BLOOD OF THE CONDOR (YAWAR MALLKU)
(Jorge Sanjines 1969) ✍
(sterility and sterilization provoke tribal violence in Bolivia)

ALSINO AND THE CONDOR
(Miguel Littin 1982) ☞
(a Nicaraguan peasant boy is transfixed by guerrilla helicopters)

CAMILA
(Maria Luisa Bemberg 1984) ✍ ☞ ☆
(a priest and his lover run away from the Argentinian authorities)

ASIAN AND MIDDLE EASTERN REALISM

A TOUCH OF ZEN (HSIA NU)
(King Hu 1969) ☞
(in this Taiwanese film, an academic and a young woman drive away soldiers by creating the illusion that a fort is haunted)

THE CRUEL SEA (BAS YA BAHAR)
(Khalid Siddik 1971) ☞
(Kuwaiti pearl fisherman sets his heart on a rich girl)

THE CYCLE (DAYEREH MINA)
(Daryush Mehrjui 1974) ✍
(an Iranian country boy is corrupted by Tehran while raising money to pay for a cure for his sick father)

MANDALA
(Lim Kwon-Taek 1982) ■
(a controversial South Korean study of the lifestyle of Buddhist monks)

JAGUAR
(Lino Brocka 1980) ☆
(Filipino thug falls for gangster's film star moll)

Intimate Lighting (Intimní Osvtleni) ♫ ☞ ☆ ■

Czechoslovakia • Ceskoslovensky Film Barrandov • 1965 • 72 mins • b/w

d Ivan Passer w Ivan Passer/Jaroslav Papoušek/Václav Šašek

ph Miroslav Ondrícek/Jan Strecha m Oldrich Korte

Zdnek Bezušek, Jan Vostrcil, Vera Kresadlová, Karel Blazek, Jaroslava Stredá

A city cellist (Bezušek), basking in his petty celebrity, comes to a small rural town to give a concert as a favour to a former conservatoire colleague (Vostrcil) who, through his lack of ambition, is now principal of the music school. Ivan Passer's film has no more plot than this, the remainder being occupied with the cultural and character clashes, reminiscences and musical unity of the two men and their women: a condescending sophisticate (Kresadlová) and a homely mother of three (Streda). A gentle film that sends viewers out, if not whistling catchy tunes, then certainly charmed and relaxed.

•Having sold his mansion, Chabi Biswas spends his last rupees on a classical concert in *The Music Room (Jalsaghar)* (>Satyajit Ray 1958) (☞ ■).
•>Alastair Sim leads the protest against the closing down of the village hall where concerts are held, in *Let the People Sing* (John Baxter 1942) (✍ ☆).
•The dialogue is sung throughout in the story of >Catherine Deneuve's decision to marry for convenience, *The Umbrellas of Cherbourg (Les Parapluies de Cherbourg)* (Jacques Demy 1964) (♫ ☞).
•Dexter Gordon is a saxophonist destroying his career and himself through his drinking, in *Round Midnight* (Bertrand Tavernier 1986) (☆ ♫ ☞ ✍).
•Songs are a critical part of family life in good and bad times in the Liverpool of the 1950s, in *Distant Voices, Still Lives* (Terence Davies 1988) (♫ ✍ ☞).
•A visiting celebrity, a bishop on a river cruise, is the backdrop for the Gabriel Garcia Marquez novel of avenging honour and enduring love *Chronicle of a Death Foretold* (Francesco Rosi 1987) (■ ✍ ☆).

Intolerance ☞ ■ ☆

USA • D. W. Griffith • 1916 • 115 mins • b/w

wd >D.W. Griffith ph Billy Bitzer

Mae Marsh, >Lillian Gish, Constance Talmadge, Robert Harron

Such were the values of his age that D. W. Griffith was unable to equate the pro-Ku Klux Klan scenes in *The Birth of a Nation* (1915) (☞ ☆ ■) (how a family gets involved in and survives the US Civil War) with the title of his next film. However, the 'four stories in search of a theme' that populate this remarkable achievement display a greater awareness. The fall of Babylon, Christ's Passion, the Huguenot persecution and the victimization of a modern tenement dweller are not noteworthy in themselves, but the monumental sets (particularly Belshazzar's banqueting hall, in spite of the fact the decoration boasts every style *except* Babylonian) are awesome, and the cutting and montage techniques Griffith employed were an important influence on the Soviet agit-prop and narrative cinema of, among others, >Eisenstein and >Pudovkin.

•Italian building brothers come to America and work on the sets of *Intolerance*, in *Good Morning Babylon (Good Morning Babilonia)* (Paulo & Vittorio Taviani 1987) (■ ☞ ✍).
•A vision of Christ ends the war between two imaginary states, in *Civilization* (Thomas Ince 1916) (☞ ■ ✍).
•Four tales by W. Somerset Maugham were adapted for the screen by R. C. Sherriff in *Quartet* (Ralph Smart/Harold French/Arthur Crabtree/Ken Annakin 1948) (✍ ☆ ☞).
•The evolution of man from ape to outer space is studied, in *2001 – A Space Odyssey* (>Stanley Kubrick 1968) (☞ ✍ ♫).
•>Buster Keaton starred in and directed a spoof of *Intolerance – The Three Ages* (1923) (☆ ✍).

INVENTORS AND PIONEERS

A Dispatch from Reuters (UK:*That Man Reuter*) (>**William Dieterle 1940**) ☞ ☆
>Edward G. Robinson heads the pioneer news-gathering agency.

Dr Erlich's Magic Bullet (>**William Dieterle 1940**) ☞ ☆ ✍
>Edward G. Robinson discovers the cure for syphilis.

Edison The Man (**Clarence Brown 1940**) ☆
>Spencer Tracy's impoverished lifestyle pays dividends when he invents the light bulb.

The First of the Few (US: *Spitfire*) (>**Leslie Howard 1942**) ☆ ✍
The director stars as R. J. Mitchell, designer of the Spitfire.

The Great Moment (>**Preston Sturges 1944**) ☞
Joel McCrea as W. T. G. Morgan discovers anaesthetics.

Lloyd's of London (**Henry King 1936**) ✍
Tyrone Power founds the insurance company in the City of the 18th-century.

Madame Curie (>**Mervyn Le Roy 1943**) ☞ ☆
Greer Garson and Walter Pidgeon as Polish scientists Marie and Pierre Curie discovering radium.

The Magic Box (**John Boulting 1951**) ☆
>Robert Donat as William Friese-Greene, Britain's moving picture pioneer.

The Spirit of St Louis (>**Billy Wilder 1957**) ☆ ☞
>James Stewart as Charles Lindbergh, the first man to fly the Atlantic.

The Story of Alexander Graham Bell (UK:*The Modern Miracle*) (**Irving Cummings 1939**) ☆
Don Ameche confounds the cynics to patent the telephone.

The Story of Louis Pasteur (>**William Dieterle 1936**) ☞ ✍
Paul Muni as the French chemist who cured rabies by building up immunity through injections of the bacteria.

Young Tom Edison (**Norman Taurog 1940**)
Mickey Rooney as the wonder boy risking clips around the ear to perform his experiments.

THE IRISH

Cal (**Pat O'Connor 1984**) ✍ ♫
A Catholic terrorist falls for a Protestant widow, in the screen version of Bernard MacLaverty's Ulster novel.

Captain Boycott (**Frank Launder 1947**) ☆
Peasant Stewart Granger and priest Alastair Sim lead a revolt against an extortionist landlord.

Da (**Matt Clark 1988**) ☆ ✍
Martin Sheen returns to Ireland for his bigoted father's funeral and is taunted by his memory.

The Dead (>**John Huston 1987**) ☞ ✍ ☆ ♫
Two elderly music teachers and their friends gather for a Christmas dinner.

Eat the Peach (**Peter Ormrod 1986**) ✍
An unemployed pair try to beat poverty and boredom by setting up a wall of death.

Happy Ever After (US: *Tonight's the Night*) (**Mario Zampi 1954**) ☆ ✍
Tenants queue up for the honour of bumping off unpopular new landlord David Niven.

Juno and the Paycock (>**Alfred Hitchcock 1930**) ✍ ☞
The prospect of inheriting a fortune brings trouble to a poor Dublin family.

The Plough and Stars (>**John Ford 1936**) ✍ ☞ ☆
The Sean O'Casey play has >Barbara Stanwyck rowing with Preston Foster over his use of political violence.

>*The Quiet Man* (>**John Ford 1952**) ✍ ☞ ☆ ■ ♫

The Rising of the Moon (>**John Ford 1957**) ☞ ✍
A trio of stories by Frank O'Connor, Malcolm J. McHugh and Lady Gregory.

Ulysses (**Joseph Strick 1967**) ☆ ✍
James Joyce's epic of a day in the life of a poet and a Jewish journalist.

Irma La Douce ✍ ☞ ☆
USA • United Artists • 1963 • 146 mins • col
d >Billy Wilder w Billy Wilder/I. A. L. Diamond ph Joseph La Shelle
m André Previn
Shirley MacLaine, >Jack Lemmon, Lou Jacobi

A box office and TV hit, Wilder and Diamond's non-musical adaptation of Monnot and Breffort's stage show was, amazingly, considered a critical calamity. Reunited, the stars of *The Apartment* (>Billy Wilder 1960) (☞ ☆ ✍) (Lemmon sees red when boss Fred MacMurray rents his flat to seduce adored co-worker MacLaine), MacLaine and Lemmon, are excellent as Irma the prostitute and Nestor the gendarme who abandons his beat on Casanova Street to become her pimp, only to be tormented by the thought of Irma with her clients. Disguised as a lord, Nestor corners the Douce market, but when the complexities of his double life drive him to 'drown' the apocryphal aristocrat, he is arrested for murder. OK, so it's occasionally sentimental and stereotyped, but the snowball of snobbish slating the film has received misses the simple point that it's enjoyable.

•Bob Hoskins has to balance a demanding boss (>Michael Caine) with helping whore Cathy Tyson find her lost girlfriend, in *Mona Lisa* (Neil Jordan 1986) (☆ ✍).

•Nathalie Baye is a prostitute helping the police with their inquiries, in *La Balance* (Bob Swaim 1982) (☆ ✍).

•Four villagers are convinced they have committed a murder, but have they? Answers in >*The Trouble with Harry* (>Alfred Hitchcock 1955) (■ ☞ ☆ ✍).

•Sophia Loren is the wicked lady escaping jail by pregnancy, in *Yesterday, Today and Tomorrow* (*Ieri, Oggi, Domani*) (>Vittorio De Sica 1963) (☞).

ISLANDS

The Adventures of Robinson Crusoe (>Luis Buñuel 1953) ☞
Daniel Defoe's castaway survives isolation and the elements before rescue.

The Blue Lagoon (Frank Launder 1949) ✍
Jean Simmons and Donald Houston as kids surviving a shipwreck, having a kid and sailing away again.

Castaway (Nicolas Roeg 1987) ☞ ☆ ■
In this screen version of Lucy Irving's autobiography, Amanda Donahoe agrees to endure island isolation with stranger Oliver Reed, but they don't get on.

Ebb Tide (James Hogan 1937) ✍
Castaways Ray Milland, Oscar Homolka and Barry Fitzgerald compete for pearls with religious maniac Lloyd Nolan.

The Hurricane (>John Ford/Stuart Heisler 1937) ☞ ✍
An island's political and volcanic situation can only be described as unstable.

The Island (*Hadaka no Shima*) (Kaneto Shindo, Japan 1961) ■
A family's annual trek to the mainland to fetch its water.

Island in the Sky (>William Wellman 1953) ☞ ☆
>John Wayne and his comrades show *sang froid* while abandoned in Greenland.

Island in the Sun (Robert Rossen 1957) ☆
Racist James Mason has trouble relating to his wife >Joan Fontaine and Harry Belafonte.

The Swiss Family Robinson (Ken Annakin 1960)
>John Mills heads the castaway family in this Disney telling of the Johann Wyss children's classic.

It Happened One Night ✍ ☆ ☞
USA • Columbia • 1934 • 105 mins • b/w
d >Frank Capra w Robert Riskin
ph Joseph Walker m Louis Silvers
>Clark Gable, Claudette Colbert, Walter Connolly

The film Columbia didn't want to make, Claudette Colbert hated and in which MGM forced Gable to star as a punishment gave birth to screwball comedy, was the first to win the 'Big Four' Oscars and, courtesy of Gable's bared chest in the motel room scene, caused annual undershirt sales to drop by 50 per cent. So what was all the fuss about? Ellie Andrews (Colbert) is a runaway heiress en route to marry a wastrel playboy. Peter Warne (Gable) is a journalist out to regain his job by getting a scoop in discovering her whereabouts. They should hate each other – and do. Gamma-ray dialogue abounds as they hitch, bus and feud across America to the final, but by no means inevitable, realization that each has met a match. Lucky stars thanked Mr Capra for insisting that the picture be made.

 •Crime novelist >Agatha Christie (Vanessa Redgrave) went missing when husband Timothy Dalton was unfaithful, in *Agatha* (Michael Apted 1978) (☆).

•>Marilyn Monroe steps off the Greyhound and into a rodeo romance with unreliable cowboy Don Murray, in *Bus Stop* (Joshua Logan 1956) (☆).

•Nastassja Kinski is the runaway found in a peepshow by drifter husband Harry Dean Stanton, in *Paris, Texas* (>Wim Wenders 1984) (☞).

•Rutger Hauer's thumbing a ride spells trouble for Tom Howells in *The Hitcher* (Robert Harmon 1986) (✍).

The Italian Straw Hat (Un Chapeau de Paille d'Italie) ☞ ✍ ■ France • Albatross • 1927 • 74 mins • b/w

wd >René Clair   ph Maurice Desfassiaux/Nicolas Roudakoff

Albert Préjean, Olga Tschechowa, Marise Maia, Alice Tissot

Silent comedy is often regarded as the sole preserve of Hollywood, but with *Entr'acte* (1924) (☞ ✍) (a runaway hearse is pursued across Paris) and *The Italian Straw Hat*, René Clair demonstrated the blooming health of the French comic tradition. Driving to his wedding, a bridegroom's horse eats a woman's hat. A simple replacement is out of the question as not only was the hat a gift from her jealous husband, but she is also out with a secret admirer. Our hero now has to combine his wedding with finding a replica bonnet, a labour that leads the guests on a frantic slapstick chase through the town, culminating in the jailhouse. A wonderful lampoon of the middle class and the ludicrous rigidity of wedding etiquette.

 •A man's long-cherished ambition to host a mystery tour goes comically wrong, in the Jacques Prévert script *Voyage Surprise* (Pierre Prévert 1946) (✍ ☆).

•>Oliver Hardy decides to elope, but foolishly relies on >Stan Laurel to get him down the ladder on time, in *Our Wife* (James W. Horne 1931) (☆ ✍).

•The family feud and the bride disappears with another man at an eventful reception after *A Wedding* (>Robert Altman 1978) (☆ ☞).

•Pierre Etaix would simply settle for a girl to love him in *The Suitor* (*Le Soupirant*) (Pierre Etaix, 1962) (☆ ☞).

•>Spencer Tracy leads the merry dance when news breaks of a buried cache, in *It's a Mad, Mad, Mad, Mad World* (Stanley Kramer 1963) (☆ ☞ ✍).

•An incriminating garment threatens Dennis O'Keefe's marriages, in both *Up in Mabel's Room* (Allan Dwan 1944) (✍) and *Getting Gertie's Garter* (Allan Dwan 1945) (✍ ☆).

It's a Wonderful Life ☆ ☞ ✍ USA • RKO • 1946 • 129 mins • b/w

d >Frank Capra   w Frances Goodrich/Albert Hackett/Frank Capra ph Joseph Walker/Joseph Biroc   m Dmitri Tiomkin

>James Stewart, Henry Travers, Donna Reed, Lionel Barrymore, Beulah Bondi, Gloria Grahame

George Bailey (Stewart) has sacrificed his fulfillable ambitions to administer the savings and loan office on which the citizens of his small town depend. However, when the books don't balance (through no fault of his own) and accusations fly, George, regretting his unsung loyalty, contemplates suicide. It is then that guardian angel Clarence (Travers) intervenes, rejuvenating George by taking him on a tour of how the town would have developed had he never lived to improve it. Made for the Liberty production company co-owned with >William Wyler, >George Stevens and Sam Briskin, this classic 'Capra corn' cleverly uses its savings bank setting to proffer the independent advice that the wisest investment is in other people.

•>Kathleen Turner goes back to high school and is given the chance to alter her fate, in *Peggy Sue Got Married* (>Francis Ford Coppola 1986) (☆ ✍).

•A professor (Victor Sjöström) is *en route* to receive an honorary degree when various happenings force him to reflect on his life, in >*Wild Strawberries* (*Smultronstället*) (>Ingmar Bergman 1957) (☞ ☆ ■ ✍).

•Bored gods have some fun with earth by giving timid clerk Roland Young magical powers, but he is unable to control them, in H. G. Wells' story *The Man Who Could Work Miracles* (Lothar Mendes 1936) (☆ ☞ ✍ ■).

•>Alec Guinness loses his inhibitions and enjoys romance and playing at being a business tycoon with guest house residents on his *Last Holiday* (Henry Cass 1950) (☆ ✍).

•Commercial artist George Segal has reached a career and sexual crisis in *Loving* (Irvin Kershner 1970) (☞ ☆).

Ivan the Terrible (Ivan Groznyi) (Parts I & II)
Part I ☞ ■ ☆ ♫ ✍
USSR • Mosfilm • 1944 • 99 mins • b/w
Part II (aka *The Boyars' Plot*) ☞ ■
☆ ✍ ♫
USSR • Mosfilm • 1946 • 88 mins • b/w (col sequence)
wd >Sergei Eisenstein ph Edouard Tissé
m Sergei Prokofiev
Nikolai Cherkassov, Ludmila Tselikovskaya, Serafima Birman, Pavel Kadochnikov, Mikhail Nazvanov,
>Vsevolod Pudovkin

Stalin was so pleased with how the first part (of what Eisenstein intended to be a trilogy) paralleled his achievements – forging a nation out of the ruling class's corrupt ambition and the ignorant masses' intransigence and defending

the Motherland from Teutonic barbarians – with those of the medieval founder of Russia, that he awarded the film-maker the Stalin Prize. The sequel, *The Boyars' Plot*, which intimated a waning of powers in later life, found less favour, however, remaining unscreened until 1958, when both Eisenstein and Stalin were long dead. Filmed with a theatricality suggesting opera or tableau (a staginess reinforced by the Old Russian blank verse dialogue), there are many memorable moments, including Part I's coronation, with its coin shower and Brueghelesque close-ups and Part II's colour dream sequence. Part III – *Ivan's Struggles* remained unfinished at Eisenstein's death.

 •>Marlene Dietrich is another Russian ruler, Catherine II, in this fantasy of her love life, *The Scarlet Empress* (>Josef Von Sternberg 1934) (☞ ☆).

•Events in contemporary England revolved around a Protestant plot to usurp the Catholic succession of Mary Tudor (Jane Lapotaire) in favour of her cousin Jane Grey (Helena Bonham-Carter), in *Lady Jane* (Trevor Nunn 1986) (☆ ■ ✍).

•A trapper claiming descendancy from Genghis Khan is used by British volunteers fighting for the White Army to aid the invasion of Mongolia, in *Storm over Asia* (aka *The Heir to Genghis Khan*) (*Potomok Chingis-Khana*) (>V. I. Pudovkin 1928) (☞ ✍ ■).

•Slum dweller Anna Magnani is the ambitious mother trying to get movie stardom for her daughter in *Bellissima* (>Luchino Visconti 1951) (☞ ✍).

•Ivan (Conrad Veidt), Haroun-al-Raschid (>Emil Jannings) and >Jack The Ripper (>William Dieterle) have their stories told during a tour around the *Waxworks* (*Das Wachsfigurenkabinett*) (Paul Leni 1924) (☆ ☞).

JACK THE RIPPER

***Hands of the Ripper* (Peter Sasdy 1971)** ☆
Jack's daughter witnesses his murder of her
mother and it continues to haunt her.

***Jack the Ripper* (Robert S. Baker 1958)** ✍
The prostitute killings are traced to a surgeon.

***The Lodger* (US: *The Phantom Fiend*)
Maurice Elvey 1932)** ☞
Ivor Novello is the mysterious man on the top
landing suspected of being the Ripper; a Talkie
remake of >Hitchcock's 1926 silent version.

***The Man in the Attic* (Hugo Fregonese
1953)**
Jack Palance as the lodger whose comings and
goings coincide with murder.

***Murder by Decree* (Bob Clark 1978)** ✍
Christopher Plummer's Sherlock Holmes
traces the killings to the guarded doors of
Buckingham Palace.

***Pandora's Box* (aka *Lulu*) (*Die Büchse der
Pandora*) (>G. W. Pabst 1929)** ☞ ☆ ■
Louise Brooks taunts a doctor and his son and
a lesbian countess before succumbing to Jack.

***A Study in Terror* (James Hill 1965)** ✍
Holmes (John Neville) and Watson (Donald

Huston) brave the fog of Whitechapel to trap
the Ripper.

JAMES, HENRY

***Aspern* (Eduardo di Gregorio, Portugal
1981)** ☆ ✍
Jean Sorel seeks a poet's *billets doux* in the
household of Boule Ogier and Alida Valli in this
version of 'The Aspern Papers'.

***The Bostonians* (James Ivory 1984)** ✍ ☞ ☆
Christopher Reeve is attracted to both suffra-
gette Vanessa Redgrave and protégé Madeleine
Potter.

***Daisy Miller* (Peter Bogdanovich 1974)** ✍
☞
Cybill Shepherd as the captivating American
who dies touring Europe.

***The Europeans* (James Ivory 1979)** ■ ✍ ☞
Countess Lee Remick comes to 19th-century
Boston to find herself a rich husband.

***The Heiress* (>William Wyler 1949)** ☞ ☆ ✍
>Olivia De Havilland persecutes a gold-digging
lover in an adaptation of *Washington Square*.

***The Innocents* (Jack Clayton 1961)** ✍ ☞
'The Turn of the Screw' sees governess Debo-

rah Kerr's pupils possessed by the malicious spirits of the household's dead servants.

The Lost Moment (Martin Gabel 1947) ✍

Agnes Moorehead owns a poet's letters now sought by publisher Robert Cummings in this adaptation of 'The Aspern Papers'.

Jannings, Emil
(Theodor Janez) Swiss-born Austrian actor (1884–1950)

A ship's cook before turning to films, Jannings was a favourite star of >Ernst Lubitsch - *The Eyes of the Mummy* (*Die Augen der Mummie Ma*) (1918) (☞ ☆) (mummy Jannings pursues his prisoner Pola Negri to London) and *Madame Dubarry* (US: *Passion*) (1919) (☞ ☆) (adventuress Pola Negri comes to the court of Jannings' Louis XV and becomes his ennobled mistress) - and >F. W. Murnau: *The Last Laugh* (*Der Letzte Mann*) (1924) (☆ ☞) (the decline and humiliation of a pompous hotel doorman), *Tartuffe* (*Tartüff*) (1925) (☞ ☆) (schemer Jannings takes over the life and lover of his patron, in Molière's play) and *Faust* (1926) (☞ ■) (Gösta Ekman sells his soul to Jannings' Devil). Moving to Hollywood, he made *The Way of All Flesh* (AA: Victor Fleming 1927) (☆ ✍) (seduced and robbed by a blonde on a train, bank clerk Jannings is too ashamed to come home and so becomes a tramp) and *The Last Command* (AA: >Josef Von Sternberg 1928) (☞ ☆) (tsarist officer Jannings flees to Hollywood where he becomes a victim of sadistic director >William Powell). Then, unable to perform English-language talkies, he returned to Germany, where he gave his legendary performance as Professor Unrath in >*The Blue Angel* (*Der Blaue Engel*) (>Josef Von Sternberg 1930) (☆ ☞ ✍ ■ ♪). With the rise of Hitler, Jannings' Nazi sympathies and collaboration irretrievably tarnished his acting reputation.

•*Anna Boleyn* (US: *Deception*) (>Ernst Lubitsch 1920) (☞ ☆): Henry VIII (Jannings) has his second wife Henny Porten executed for failing to provide a male heir.

•*The Wife of Pharaoh* (aka *The Loves of Pharaoh*) (*Das Weib des Pharaos*) (>Ernst Lubitsch 1921) (☞ ☆): pharaoh Jannings insults his intended Ethiopian princess by seducing her servant.

•*Waxworks* (*Der Wachsfigurenkabinett*) (Paul Leni 1924) (☆ ☞): Jannings as a waxwork of the evil ruler of Baghdad Haroun-al-Raschid.

•*Variety* (US: *Vaudeville*) (*Variété*) (E. A. Dupont 1925): ageing man on the trapeze Jannings is driven to murder by the athletic and sexual prowess of his new partner.

•*The Patriot* (*Die Patriotin*) (>Ernst Lubitsch 1928) (☞ ☆): Jannings as the insane turn-of-19th-century Tsar Paul, murdered by chief minister Lewis Stone.

JAZZ

All Night Long (Basil Dearden 1961) ✍

Trumpeter Patrick McGoohan is provoked, Othello style, into assaulting his wife by >Richard Attenborough.

Begone Dull Care (Norman McLaren 1953) ♪

The Oscar Peterson Trio accompany this vibrant animated short.

The Benny Goodman Story (Valentine Davies 1955) ♪

Steve Allen as the clarinettist struggling to perfect and gain acceptance for his 'new sound'.

Bird (>Clint Eastwood 1988) ♪ ☆ ☞

DeForrest Kelly as legendary saxophonist Charlie 'Bird' Parker.

Blues in the Night (Anatole Litvak 1941)

The adventures of a touring jazz band, notable for >Elia Kazan as a clarinettist.

The Glenn Miller Story (Anthony Mann 1954) ♪ ☆ ☞ ✍

>James Stewart as the inventor of swing and June Allyson as the wife waiting for news of his plane.

Jazz on a Summer's Day (Aram Avakian 1960) ♪

Louis Armstrong and Thelonius Monk top the bill at the 1958 Newport Jazz Festival.

Orchestra Wives (Archie Mayo 1942) ♪

A naïve girl attunes to the competitive world of showbiz when she marries a trumpeter.

Paris Blues (Martin Ritt 1961)

Musicians >Paul Newman and Sidney Poitier

find Joanne Woodward and Diahann Carroll, thus keeping them away from Louis Armstrong.

Round Midnight (Bertrand Tavernier 1986) ☆ ♫ ☞ ✍
Dexter Gordon received AAN for his portrayal of the saxophonist with his finger on self-destruct.

Satchmo the Great (Edward Murrow/Fred Friendly 1956) ♫
Footage of Louis Armstrong on tour in Europe and Africa.

Jean de Florette ☆ ✍ ☞ ■
France • Renn Productions/ Films A2/RA12/DD • 1986 • 121 mins • col
d Claude Berri   w Claude Berri/Gérard Brach   ph Bruno Nuytten   m Jean-Claude Petit
>Yves Montand, >Gérard Depardieu, Daniel Auteuil, Elisabeth Depardieu

It is the mid-1920s and Ugolin Soubeyran (Auteuil) returns to Les Romarins in Provence, hoping to make his fortune growing carnations. The scheme seems set to flounder when the secret subterranean source of water he needs for irrigation passes to townie hunchback Jean Cadoret (Gérard Depardieu), himself intent on rural riches. Ugolin's uncle César (Montand), hoping immediate failure will break Jean's spirit, recommends damming the spring and denying its existence. Hauling water across the hills, Jean's family, assisted by an increasingly guilt-ridden Ugolin, remain undaunted until severe drought drives Jean to drink and he dies blasting bedrock in a desperate attempt to build a well. But as the roguish Soubeyrans celebrate their victory, Jean's daughter Manon sees them unclogging the spring and swears vengeance. This beautifully filmed version of Marcel Pagnol's fable leaves you longing for *>Manon des Sources*.

•A concealed spring is the salvation of another farmer in *The Milagro Beanfield War* (Robert Redford 1988) (✍ ☞).
•Idle shopkeeper >W. C. Fields reckons his future lies in an orange farm, in *It's a Gift* (Norman Z. McLeod 1934) (☆ ✍).
•Victor Hugo's hunchback Quasimodo is played to perfection by >Charles Laughton, in *The Hunchback of Notre Dame* (>William Dieterle 1939) (☞ ■ ☆).
•Bourvil is the father, son and cousin refusing to sell land to >Philippe Noiret because of a health spring, in *All the Gold in the World* (*Tout L'Or du Monde*) (>René Clair 1961) (☞ ☆ ✍).

JEKYLL AND HYDE

All of Me (Carl Reiner 1984) ☆
Lily Tomlin and Steve Martin compete for the control of his body after an experiment goes wrong.

Altered States (Ken Russell 1980) ☆ ☞ ✳
Sensory deprivation experiments have their effect on >William Hurt.

Dr Jekyll and Mr Hyde (Rouben Mamoulian 1931) ☆ ☞ ■/(Victor Fleming 1941) ☆ ✍
>Fredric March and >Spencer Tracy, respectively, change through a potion to terrorize prostitutes Miriam Hopkins and >Ingrid Bergman.

Dr Jekyll and Sister Hyde (Roy Ward Baker 1971) ✍
Ralph Bates still swallows the formula and kills prostitutes, but now he transforms into a woman.

The Fly (Kurt Neumann 1958) ☆/ (David Cronenberg 1986) ✳ ☆
David Hedison and Jeff Goldblum, respectively, turn into a fly when an insect disrupts a teleportation experiment.

The Nutty Professor (Jerry Lewis 1963)
Jerry Lewis swigs his potion and becomes a pop star.

The Picture of Dorian Gray (Albert Lewin 1945) ☆ ✍
George Sanders discovers his friend Hurd Hatfield allows his portrait to bear his age in this screen version of Oscar Wilde's novel.

JEWEL THIEVES

The Adventures of Arsène Lupin (***Les Aventures d'Arsène Lupin***) **(Jacques Becker 1956)** 🖉

Parisian thief Robert Lamoureux is kidnapped by Kaiser Wilhelm II.

Algiers **(John Cromwell 1938)** ☆ 🖙

Charles Boyer's spectacular career hiccups when he falls for Hedy Lamarr and is caught.

11 Harrowhouse **(Aram Avakian 1974)** 🖉 ☆

James Mason and Charles Grodin steal diamonds from John Gielgud's vault via a giant vacuum cleaner.

Fantômas **(Louis Feuillade 1913)** 🖙 🖉

Thief *extraordinaire* keeps one step ahead of a pursuing policeman and journalist.

The Hot Rock **(UK: *How to Steal a Diamond In Four Uneasy Lessons*) (Peter Yates 1972)** ☆ 🖉

Robert Redford and George Segal steal a diamond from a New York museum.

Raffles **(Sam Wood 1939)** ☆ 🖉

Cricketing cracksman David Niven keeps secret his life from >Olivia De Havilland and himself out of the clutches of flatfoot Dudley Digges.

The Return of The Pink Panther **(Blake Edwards 1974)** ☆ 🖉

Peter Sellers's Inspector Clouseau and jewel thief Christopher Plummer both investigate a copycat snatch from a museum.

The Threepenny Opera (***Die Dreigroschenoper***) **(>G.W. Pabst 1931)** 🖙 🖉

Bertolt Brecht and Kurt Weill's adaptation (moved forward a century) of John Gay's tale of 18th-century London theft *The Beggar's Opera*.

>*To Catch a Thief* **(>Alfred Hitchcock 1955)** 🖙 ☆

Grace Kelly assists >Cary Grant in search of the copycat who is trying to frame him.

Topkapi **(>Jules Dassin 1964)** ☆

The security system in a Turkish museum proves inadequate.

>*Trouble in Paradise* **(>Ernst Lubitsch 1932)** 🖙 🖉 ☆ ■

Le Jour se Lève (US: Daybreak)

☆ 🖙 🖉 ■

France • 1939 • 95 mins • b/w

d >Marcel Carné w Jacques Viot/Jacques Prévert ph Curt Courant/Philippe Agostini/André Bac m Maurice Jaubert
>Jean Gabin, Arletty, Jules Berry, Jacqueline Laurent

A study of inevitability, especially coupled with the ease with which the decent can be provoked to evil, sounds like >Fritz Lang's Hollywood territory, but as war clouds gathered over Europe, the depressing fatalism that pervades *Le Jour se Lève* could only have come from frightened France. Carné and Prévert's 'poetic realism' script chronicles the sordid events that led François (Gabin) to shoot animal trainer Valentin (Berry) and take refuge in the tenement room of Clara (Arletty), one of the two women the pair were involved with. Such compelling depictions of helpless adversity were popularized by the shadowy *film noir* melodramas of Cold War America, when pessimism was once more the predominant political mood.

 •The Hollywood remake, *The Long Night* (Anatole Litvak 1947) (☆ 🖉) has >Henry Fonda, Barbara Bel Geddes and Vincent Price in the leads.

•Mild-mannered >Richard Attenborough suddenly turns violent and barricades himself in a room, in *The Man Upstairs* (Don Chaffey 1958) (☆).

•Screenwriter >Humphrey Bogart's temper earns him a murder rap and loses him Gloria Grahame, in *In a Lonely Place* (>Nicholas Ray 1950) (☆).

•A frightened boy seeks consolation in love with a woman whose husband is in the trenches, in *Devil in the Flesh* (*Le Diable au Corps*) (Claude Autant-Lara 1947) (🖙 🖉).

JOURNALISM

Absence of Malice **(Sydney Pollack 1981)** 🖉

Journalist Sally Field wrongly implicates >Paul Newman in the disappearance of a dock union official.

After Office Hours (**Robert Z. Leonard 1935**) ☆ ✍
Editor >Clark Gable and his love-hate reporter Constance Bennett solve a society murder mystery.

All the President's Men (**Alan J. Pakula 1976**) ☆ ✍
>Dustin Hoffman and Robert Redford delve beneath the Watergate cover-up.

Arise My Love (**Mitchell Leisen 1940**) ☆ ✍
Reporter Claudette Colbert becomes involved in pilot Ray Milland's war exploits in this Charles Brackett/>Billy Wilder script.

Between the Lines (**Joan Micklin Silver 1974**) ☞ ☆ ✍
A satirical look at life on a 1960s protest paper.

Blessed Event (**Roy Del Ruth 1932**) ☆
Gossip columnist Lee Tracy given the job of boosting circulation with well-chosen exaggerations.

Five Star Final (**>Mervyn Le Roy 1931**) ☆ ✍ ☞
Editor >Edward G. Robinson is ordered by the newspaper's owner to drag up a 20-year-old murder case, no matter who gets hurt.

The Front Page (**Lewis Milestone 1931**) ☆ ✍ ☞/(**>Billy Wilder 1974**) ☞ ☆ ✍
Adolphe Menjou and Walter Matthau, respectively, strain during escaped killer story, to keep ace reporter Pat O'Brien and >Jack Lemmon on the job.

Judaism

The Apprenticeship of Duddy Kravitz (**Ted Kotcheff 1974**) ☆
Pushy Jewish lawyer Richard Dreyfuss learns that nice guys finish first.

Gentleman's Agreement (**>Elia Kazan 1947**) ☆ ☞ ✍
Writer Gregory Peck poses as a Jew to better his knowledge of anti-semitism.

The Heartbreak Kid (**Elaine May 1972**) ✍
Hating his marriage, Charles Grodin attempts to win Cybill Shepherd.

Hester Street (**Joan Micklin Silver 1974**) ☆ ■
Carol Kane as a late-19th-century immigrant learning to cope with New York and her husband's adultery.

The Jazz Singer (**Alan Crosland 1927**) ☆/(**Richard Fleischer 1980**) ☆ ♫
Al Jolson and Neil Diamond, respectively, are estranged then reunited with their cantor fathers Warner Oland and >Laurence Olivier over their singing careers.

Jew Suss (**US:** *Power*) (**Lothar Mendes 1934**) ■/(**Veit Harlan 1940**)
In the first, a philanthropic Württemberg Jew discovers that he is actually a Gentile, but in the second, an offensive Nazi propaganda piece, he behaves like a barbarian.

Make Me an Offer (**Cyril Frankel 1954**) ☆
Antique dealer Peter Finch covets a famous vase.

Next Stop, Greenwich Village (**Paul Mazursky 1975**) ☞
Slum boy Lenny Baker nurses fame-and-fortune dreams.

>Shoah (**Claude Lanzmann 1985**) ✍ ☞

Yentl (**Barbra Streisand 1983**) ☆
An Isaac Bashevis Singer tale of a Jewish girl dressing as a boy to fulfill her ambitions.

Jules et Jim ☞ ☆ ✍

France • Film Du Carrosse/SEDIF • 1961 • 105 mins • b/w
d >François Truffaut w François Truffaut/Jean Gruault ph Raoul Coutard m Georges Delerue
Jeanne Moreau, Oskar Werner, Henri Serre

La belle époque Paris, and two inseparable students – an Austrian, Jules (Werner), and a Frenchman, Jim (Serre) – are captivated by the vivacious Catherine (Moreau). Their innocent *ménage*, filled with some of the freshest and most charming moments of friendship captured on film, culminates in Jules successfully proposing on the eve of the First World War. The embodiment of the complex contradictions of modern womanhood, Catherine, discontented with domesticity, persuades Jim to come to Austria in the hope of re-creating the past, but succeeds only in causing heartache. Hopelessly smitten and immune to her selfishness, the two men readily respond to her caprice, but never having attempted to understand her motives and insecurities, they fail to detect the incipient despair that will cost Catherine and Jim their lives. In a virtuoso technical performance, Truffaut variously uses an undercranked, travelling and distorted camera, stills, slow motion, newsreel and freeze-frame footage to supremely capture era and emotion in this adaptation of the Henri-Pierre Roché novel. Truly the masterpiece of a genius.

•>Fredric March, >Gary Cooper and Miriam Hopkins also solve their triangle by all living together, in *Design for Living* (>Ernst Lubitsch 1933) (☞ ✍ ☆).

•A complicated relationship, this time between a brother and a sister, leads to tragedy in Jean Cocteau's classic story *Les Enfants Terribles* (aka *The Strange Ones*) (Jean-Pierre Melville 1950) (✍ ☞ ▓ ♫).

•Director >François Truffaut reworked another Henri-Pierre Roché novel by setting it in Wales, in *Anne and Muriel* (US: *Two English Girls*) (*Les Deux Anglaises et le Continent*) (1971) (☞).

•Just as *Jules et Jim* is a perfect evocation of 1890s France, post-World War I England is beautifully portrayed, in *A Month in the Country* (Pat O'Connor 1988) (▓ ☆ ✍), as Colin Firth restores a church fresco and Kenneth Branagh searches for Saxon remains.

Julia ☆ ✍ ☞ ▓

USA • Twentieth-Century Fox • 1977 • 117 mins • col

d >Fred Zinnemann   w Alvin Sargent
ph Douglas Slocombe   m Georges Delerue
>Jane Fonda, Vanessa Redgrave, Jason Robards Jr, Maximilian Schell

Drawing on playwright Lillian Hellman's autobiography, *Pentimento*, Alvin Sargent's Oscar-winning script follows the friendship of two women with divergent ambitions but a unifying loyalty, from childhood, through an idyllic Oxford to post-Anschluss Vienna. Though parted for many years, Hellman (Fonda) accedes to a request to cross Europe, protected only by her fame and fallibility, in order to bring funds to Julia's persecuted Austrian Communists. Though rarely on screen together, Fonda and Redgrave admirably capture the comparative levels of political conviction, and Hellman's reunion with a Julia crippled by violence and worn with care, coming so soon after a >Hitchcockian train journey, might leave us emotionally drained of all but admiration for the heroines, but certainly doesn't diminish our anger at what we have witnessed.

•The rise of the Nazis is witnessed by Kit-Kat Klub singer Liza Minnelli in *Cabaret* (Bob Fosse 1972) (☆ ♫), and profits Dirk Bogarde and Ingrid Thulin's munitions manufacturing family in *The Damned* (*Götterdämmerung*) (*La Caduta degli Dei*) (>Luchino Visconti 1969) (☞ ▓).

•>Orson Welles' Harry Lime is Western writer Holly Martens (Joseph Cotten)'s elusive old friend, in >*The Third Man* (>Carol Reed 1949) (☆ ☞ ♫ ✍ ▓).

•Michael Redgrave and Margaret Lockwood experience a tense train journey through Germany when Dame May Whitty is kidnapped by spies, in *The Lady Vanishes* (>Alfred Hitchcock 1938) (☞ ✍ ☆).

•Barbara Sukowa plays a post-World War I Polish socialist and agitator in Germany in a biopic of *Rosa Luxemburg* (>Margarethe Von Trotta 1986) (☞ ☆).

•The most famous example of the work of Lillian Hellman the playwright is *The Little Foxes* (>William Wyler 1941) (☆ ☞ ✍), in which Herbert Marshall does his best to prevent his family, including >Bette Davis and Dan Duryea, inheriting his fortune.

Kagemusha ☞ ■ ✍ ☆

Japan • Toho/Kurosawa • 1980 • 181 mins • col

d >Akira Kurosawa   w Akira Kurosawa/
Masato Ide   ph Kazuo Miyagawa/Asaichi
Nakai/Takao Sato/Masaharu Ueda
m Shinichiro Ikebe

Tatsuya Nakadai, Tsutomu Yamazaki,
Kenichi Hagiwara, Kota Yui, Hideji Otaki,
Hideo Murata

In moviespeak, the word 'epic' suggests sprawling stories set in bygone days played in vulgarly
brilliant colours by casts of thousands. Akira
Kurosawa, much against the current vogue in
Japanese and world cinema, gave the genre a
new vitality and respectability with this magnificent study of leadership and loyalty. As in
Europe, 16th-century Japan was prone to civil
conflict. Shingen, the ruling warlord, whose
strong rule alone has subjugated rival clans,
bequeaths power to the lookalike thief he
spared from crucifixion, to prevent strife for
three years after the warlord's death. Gradually, the 'shadow warrior' displays Shingen's
ability for assured, respected rule, convincing
even those privy to the plot that he is a reincarnation. Despite the stunning pageantry of feudal chivalry and war and the ruthless ambition
of high politics, the most memorable moments
concern the duplicate's ingratiation with 'his'
grandson.

•A samurai's daughter is equally
bound by her duty, but after bearing a warlord his required son, Kinuyo Tanaka prefers prostitution to watching
the boy grow, in *The Life of O-Haru* (*Saikaku
Ichidai Onna*) (>Kenji Mizoguchi 1952) (☞ ✍
☆ ■).
•More puppets out of control are the warriors
hired to terrorize a village only to join the
villagers, in *The Seven Samurai* (*Shichinin No
Samurai*) (>Akira Kurosawa 1954) (☞ ■).
•Seven warriors had been granted immortality, but Clancy Brown has been killing them
off with an enchanted sword and only Christopher Lambert remains, in *Highlander* (Russell Mulcahy 1986) (☆ ✷).
•Italian families are feuding for hegemony of
Glasgow's ice cream trade, in *Comfort and Joy*
(Bill Forsyth 1984) (☞).

Karloff, Boris
(William Pratt) British-born Canadian actor (1887–1969)

Public-school educated Karloff spent 15 unproductive years as a heavy before 1931's *The Criminal Code* (>Howard Hawks)(☞ ✍)(an innocent man is provoked into committing murder in prison), *Five Star Final* (>Mervyn Le Roy) (✩ ✍ ☞) (an editor is ordered to resurrect and sensationalize an old murder to boost circulation) and the real clincher, *>Frankenstein* (James Whale 1931) (✩ ☞ ✍ ✳ ■) turned this dignified gentleman into the most sinister screen presence of all. Monster again in *The Mummy* (Karl Freund 1932) (✩ ✍) (resurrected by an archaeologist, Boris assumes modern garb to seek the wife for whom he was buried alive for trying to revive 3000 years before), *The Bride of Frankenstein* (James Whale 1935) (✩ ✍ ☞ ✳) (persuaded by Ernest Thesiger that the Monster needs a mate, Colin Clive produces Elsa Lanchester, but Boris is not to her taste) and *Son of Frankenstein* (Rowland V. Lee 1939) (✩ ✍) (>Bela Lugosi's Ygor uses Boris to kill off the jurors who condemned him, but the Baron's son >Basil Rathbone is at hand), Karloff also happily accepted typecasting as villain or grotesque in: *Scarface* (>Howard Hawks 1932) (☞ ✩) (Karloff as one of Paul Muni's bootlegging rivals in the gangster classic); *The Mask of Fu Manchu* (Charles Brabin 1932) (✩ ✍ ☞) (hypnotic Boris and his evil daughter >Myrna Loy capture pursuer Lewis Stone, but he lives to fight another day); *The Black Cat* (UK: *House of Doom*) (Edgar C. Ulmer 1934) (✩ ■) (Boris embalms >Bela Lugosi's wife and marries his daughter, so Lugosi skins him alive); *The Black Room* (Roy William Neill 1935) (✩ ✍) (bad twin Boris walls up benign Boris in said room and assumes the baronetcy; *The Raven* (Louis Friedlander 1935) (✩ ✍) (Boris as a mutant made by mad surgeon >Bela Lugosi who prevents him torturing those who blocked his marriage plans); and *Tower of London* (Rowland V. Lee 1939) (✩ ✍) (Boris as the keeper of the Tower for >Basil Rathbone's Richard III kills princes and drowns Vincent Price in malmsey). Producer Val Lewton provided *The Body Snatcher* (Robert Wise 1945) (Boris robs graves for Edinburgh doctor Henry Daniell and bumps off blackmailer >Bela Lugosi in this Robert Louis Stevenson tale) and *Bedlam* (Mark Robson 1946) (✩) (a blend of Edgar Allan Poe and William Hogarth sets the tone as Karloff asserts that the critic of his asylum is insane). Karloff later settled for pulp, with the exception of the parody *The Raven* (Roger Corman 1963) (✩) (>Peter Lorre is caught up in a war of spells between magicians Boris and Vincent Price) and the poignant *Targets* (Peter Bogdanovich 1968) (✩) (Boris as a fading horror star getting the better of a drive-in killer).

• *The Old Dark House* (James Whale 1934) (✩ ✍ ☞ ■): this J. B. Priestley chiller (adapted from his novel *Benighted*) has >Charles Laughton among those seeking shelter in the Welsh mansion that has Karloff as the butler and a secret.

• *The Lost Patrol* (>John Ford 1934) (☞ ■ ✩): Karloff and Victor McLaglen are among the British troops ambushed in the Mesopotamian desert.

• *The Walking Dead* (>Michael Curtiz 1936) (✩ ☞): Boris survives the electric chair and picks off his accusers, including Edmund Gwenn.

• *Mr Wong, Detective* (William Nigh 1938): Boris as the Oriental investigator in the first of a series produced at a time when everywhere you looked there was an Oriental investigator.

• *Isle of the Dead* (Mark Robson 1945) (✩ ☞): Boris is suspected of vampirism as plague hits an island during the 1912 Balkan War.

• *Comedy of Terrors* (Jacques Tourneur 1964) (✩ ✍): undertaking rivals Boris and Vincent Price view and >Basil Rathbone as custom.

Kazan, Elia
(Elia Kazanjoglou) Turkish-born American writer/director (b 1909)

Victimized in his own childhood, Kazan translated his pain and neglect into hard-hitting American Neo-Realist studies. PREJUDICE: *Gentleman's Agreement* (AA: 1947) (✩ ☞ ✍) (writer Gregory Peck assumes a Jewish identity to better understand anti-Semitism) and *Pinky* (1949) (☞) (half-caste Jeanne Crain is victimized by both white and black neighbours); FAMILY CONFLICT: *A Tree Grows in Brooklyn* (1945) (☆ ☞) (a father trying to improve the lot of his family is frustrated by his drinking bouts), *East of Eden* (AAN: 1955) (☞ ☆ ✍) (James Dean feuds with his father Raymond Massey and discovers his mother Jo Van Fleet [AA] in John Steinbeck's farming drama), and *Splendor in the Grass* (1961) (☞ ☆ ✍) (Natalie Wood goes insane when her family disapprove of her romance with Warren Beatty); and FICTIONAL DOCUMENTARY: *Boomerang* (1947) (☞ ■ ☆) (Dana Andrews clears an innocent man of a priest killing, but the culprit remains free) and *Panic in the Streets* (1950) (☞ ☆) (Richard Widmark is after hood Jack Palance - not for a crime but because he has the plague). Cofounding Lee Strasberg's Actors' Studio, Kazan introduced 'Method Acting' into cinema: >*On the Waterfront* (AA: 1954) (☞ ☆ ■ ✍); *A Face in the Crowd* (1957) (☞ ✍ ☆) (a country boy is transformed into an opinionated monster by TV); and *Wild River* (1960) (☞ ☆) (Jo Van Fleet refuses to leave her land even though Montgomery Clift and the Tennessee Valley Water Authority demand it). However, the quality of Kazan's work has been overshadowed by his testimony to the House UnAmerican Activities Committee: among those he 'named' was Arthur Miller, whose plays had presented Kazan with theatrical acclaim and reward.

VIEW ON ▶ •*A Streetcar Named Desire* (AAN: 1952) (✍ ☞ ☆): >Marlon Brando physically and mentally assaults sister-in-law >Vivien Leigh.
•*Viva Zapata!* (1952) (☞ ☆): fantasy on the life of Mexican revolutionary Emiliano Zapata (>Marlon Brando), geared towards anti-Communist propaganda.
•*Baby Doll* (1956) (☞ ☆): Karl Malden's child bride Carroll Baker is corrupted by his cotton trade rival Eli Wallach.
•*America, America* (UK: *The Anatolian Smile*) (1964) (☞): a Greek's dreams of leaving repressive Turkey come true and he lands in the USA.
•*The Last Tycoon* (1976) (☞ ☆): a movie mogul akin to Irving Thalberg (>Robert De

Niro) has problems with rival studio boss Robert Mitchum and union leader >Jack Nicholson, in this adaptation of F.Scott Fitzgerald's novel.

Keaton, Buster

(Joseph Francis Keaton) American actor/writer/director (1895–1966)

Vaudeville child star Keaton made a series of two-reelers for Joseph M. Schenck, co-directed with Eddie Cline, which were dependent on mechanized sight gags - *One Week* (1920) (☞) (Buster suffers one of those weeks when everything he touches goes wrong), *The Playhouse* (1921) (■) (this split-screen comedy has Buster playing both the entertainers and the audience during a show) and *The Electric House* (1921) (☞ ☆) (Buster finds modern gadgets difficult to understand) - and dazzling stunts: *Daydreams* (1922) (☆) (Buster is just at the head of a frantic chase) and *The Balloonatic* (1923) (☆ ☞) (Buster just about survives a disaster-fraught voyage). He then progressed to his self-directed parodic features, beginning with *The Three Ages* (1923) (☆ ✍), which spoofed >D. W. Griffith's >*Intolerance* (1916) (☞ ■ ☆). Straight-faced, athletic and unconcerned with social comment, Keaton played underdogs who, through courage and chase, save the day - *Sherlock Junior* (1924) (☆ ✍) (a cinema projectionist dreams of solving baffling crimes), >*The General* (1926) (☆ ✍ ☞ ■) and *College* (1927) (academic wimp Buster stuns all by becoming an all-round sports star) - and/or got the girl: *Our Hospitality* (1923) (☆ ✍) (Buster's marriage to Natalie Talmadge is opposed by her family and nearly prevented by a waterfall); *The Navigator* (1924) (millionaire Buster and Kathryn McGuire cope with being adrift and alone on a liner); and *Seven Chances* (1925) (✍ ☆) (Buster has to marry to inherit seven million). Poor business judgement and alcoholism sidetracked his career, his reputation only being enhanced by roles in *Limelight* (>Charles Chaplin 1952) (☆ ☞ ✍ ♪) (Buster and Charlie in a hilarious vaudeville act as part of a fading clown's comeback) and *A Funny Thing Happened on the Way to the Forum* (Richard Lester 1966) (☞ ■ ♪) (Buster as Erronius in Stephen Sondheim's musical story of a scheming slave in ancient Rome).

•*The Saphead* (Herbert Blach 1920) (☆): in his first full feature, Buster plays a family dolt who makes it big on the stock market.

CO-DIRECTED WITH EDDIE CLINE:

•*The Boat* (1921) (☆): Buster's boating trip ends in a sinking.

•*The Paleface* (1922) (☆): Buster survives the natural and human dangers of the west.

•*Cops* (1922) (☆): Buster once more is the subject of a frantic chase.

•*Battling Butler* (Buster Keaton 1926) (☆): Buster takes to the boxing ring to make money.

•*Steamboat Bill, Jr* (Charles Reisner 1928) (☆): Buster competes for business on the Mississippi and wins his rival's daughter.

•*The Cameraman* (Edward Sedgwick 1928) (☆): a behind-the-lens look at the trials and tribulations of filming a movie.

•*Spite Marriage* (Edward Sedgwick 1929) (☆): an actress marries Buster to torment her reluctant beau.

Keaton, Diane
(Diane Hall) American actress/director (b 1946)

Co-starring with >Woody Allen in the 1969 Broadway production and 1972 film version of *Play It Again, Sam* (🎭 ☆) (>Humphrey Bogart's >*Casablanca* character helps Allen woo Keaton), Keaton was his favourite leading lady until >*Manhattan* (1979) (🎭 ☆ ■ ☞ 🎵), returning to play a cameo role as a singer in *Radio Days* (1987) (🎭☞) (nostalgic look at the life and loves of a 1940s New York family). She has since found it difficult to shake off the zany lady image that won her an Oscar in >*Annie Hall* (1976) (🎭 ☆ ☞). However, her performances as Kay in >*The Godfather* (Part I & II) (>Frances Ford Coppola 1972 and 1974) (🎭☞ ■🎵 ☆) and as Louise Bryant in *Reds* (AAN: Warren Beatty 1981) (☆) (a political and personal biopic of American Communists John Reed (Beatty) and his wife (Keaton)) have demonstrated considerable dramatic credibility. However, her directorial debut with *Heaven* (1986) (☞) (various interviewees give their

impressions of what to expect in the next world) and her performance in *Baby Boom* (Charles Shyer 1987) (yuppy mother Keaton cooks up a market-stealing baby food) have leaned back towards the offbeat.

•*Sleeper* (1973) (☆): frozen specimen Woody Allen wakes in the future and falls for bored trendy Keaton.

•*Looking for Mr Goodbar* (Richard Brooks 1977) (☆): special needs teacher Keaton has peculiar requirements in bed.

•*Shoot the Moon* (Alan Parker 1982) (🎭 ☆): Keaton brings up the kids and finds a new man, despite still loving ex-husband Albert Finney.

•*The Little Drummer Girl* (George Roy Hill 1984) (☆): this John Le Carré tale has pro-Arab actress Keaton agreeing to spy for the Israelis.

•*Mrs Soffel* (Gillian Armstrong 1985) (☆): warder's wife Keaton abets Mel Gibson's jailbreak.

•*Crimes of the Heart* (Bruce Beresford 1986) (☆): episodes from the lives of Keaton and her sisters Jessica Lange and Sissy Spacek.

Kelly, Gene
American actor/director (b 1912)

Sportsman-turned-dancer, Kelly followed up his Broadway success with *For Me and My Gal* (Busby Berkeley 1942) (☆ ☞) (Gene competes for Judy Garland with fellow music-hall star George Murphy). Choreographing his own films with >Stanley Donen, he danced with himself in *Cover Girl* (Charles Vidor 1944) (☆ 🎵) (Kelly picks Rita Hayworth as the new face for his magazine) and with Tom of Tom and Jerry fame in *Anchors Aweigh* (George Sidney 1945) (☆ 🎵) (Gene and Frank Sinatra fall for the sister of a small boy who wants to join the navy). After spoofing swashbuckling in *The Pirate* (>Vincente Minnelli 1948) (☆ ☞) (Judy Garland takes strolling player Kelly for a high seas hero) and *The Three Musketeers* (George Sidney 1948) (☆ ☞ 🎭) (Kelly as D'Artagnan defending June Allyson from scheming Lana Turner in 17th-century France), he starred in and co-directed the classics >*On the Town* (1949) (🎵 ☆ ☞ 🎭) and >*Singin' in the Rain* (1952) (🎵 ☆ 🎭 ☞ ■) and headed the cast of the Best Film Oscar-winning *An American in*

Paris (>Vincente Minnelli 1951) (☆ ☞ ♫ ✍) (artist Gene resists wealthy seductress Nina Foch in favour of waif Leslie Caron). Directing himself in *Invitation to the Dance* (>Berlin Golden Bear Winner: 1956) (☆) (Kelly shows his modern and ballet genius in a trilogy of dance scenarios), he showcased his unique talent, but audiences preferred him in traditional musicals: *Brigadoon* (>Vincente Minnelli 1954) (Gene and Van Johnson want to remain in a Scottish ghost village which only reappears each century) and *It's Always Fair Weather* (>Stanley Donen 1955) (☞ ✍) (a sentimental TV show arranges a reunion for three army buddies who now dislike each other). They certainly gave a wide berth to his solely directorial projects – *Gigot* (1960) (mawkish life in a Parisian boarding house) and *A Guide for the Married Man* (1967) (☆) (Walter Matthau takes a husband on a distasteful course on 'how to commit adultery and get away with it').

•*The Ziegfeld Follies* (>Vincente Minnelli 1946) (☆ ☞ ✍): impresario >William Powell, now in heaven, sets up a show with Kelly and >Fred Astaire in the cast.
•*Take Me Out to the Ball Game* (UK: *Everybody's Cheering*) (Busby Berkeley 1948) (✍ ☞): Gene takes umbrage at the appointment of Esther Williams as his new baseball coach.
•*Summer Stock* (UK: *If You Feel Like Singing*) (Charles Walters 1950) (☆): Judy Garland's farm is used to rehearse Kelly's show and she soon wants a part.
•*Marjorie Morningstar* (Irving Rapper 1958) (☞): Natalie Wood dreams of stardom after attending Kelly's summer drama school.
•*Hello Dolly* (Gene Kelly 1969) (♫ ☆ ☞): widow Barbra Streisand attempts to matchmake herself with wealthy Walter Matthau.
•*Xanadu* (Robert Greenwald 1980): Olivia Newton John as the Muse of Music helps Kelly open a roller disco.

KIDNAP

The Bitter Tea of General Yen (>Frank Capra 1932) ☆
Missionary >Barbara Stanwyck is abducted by Chinese warlord Nils Asther.

The Bride Came C. O. D. (William Keighley 1941) ☆ ✍
Pilot >James Cagney kidnaps tetchy heiress >Bette Davis who drives him to distraction when they crash in the desert.

Crisis (Richard Brooks 1950) ☆
Surgeon >Cary Grant operates on hated dictator Jose Ferrer who has abducted his wife to assure secrecy.

Cry Terror (Andrew Stone 1958) ☆ ✍
Pilot James Mason thwarts Rod Steiger's bomb plot by hi-jacking his own plane.

High and Low (*Tengoku to Jigoku*) (>Akira Kurosawa 1963) ☞ ✍,
The son of Toshiro Mifune's chauffeur is kidnapped instead of his own, but he can't afford the ransom.

Nada (>Claude Chabrol 1974) ☞ ✍
An American ambassador is kidnapped from a Parisian brothel.

A Question of Rape (US: *The Rape*) (*Le Viol*) (aka *Overgreppet*) (Jacques Doniol-Valcroze 1967) ✍ ☆ ☞
The man who held Bibi Andersson hostage turns up that night at a dinner party for her husband.

Raising Arizona (Joel Coen 1987) ☆ ✍
Crook Nicholas Cage and cop Holly Hunter, desperate for children, kidnap one of a rich man's quadruplets.

Un Soir, Un Train (André Delvaux 1968) ☆
Free-loving >Yves Montand realizes the depth of his feelings for Anouk Aimée when she disappears.

State of Siege (*État de Siège*) (Constantin Costa-Gavras 1973) ☆ ✍ ☞
CIA agent >Yves Montand is held in return for political prisoners by Marxist terrorists.

Tiger Bay (J. Lee-Thompson 1959) ☆ ☞
A murderous Polish seaman regrets abducting John Mills' talkative child Hayley Mills.

KILLED ONE BY ONE

The Abominable Dr Phibes **(Robert Fuest 1971)** ☆
Vincent Price exacts revenge on the doctors who disfigured him, proceeding according to the ten curses of Pharaoh.

And Then There Were None **(>René Clair 1945)** ✍ ☆ ☞
Guests with hidden pasts gather together on a remote island.

Blood from the Mummy's Tomb **(Seth Holt 1971)** ✍
The spirit of an Egyptian princess gets her own back on the archaeologists who disturb her rest.

Bluebeard **(Edgar G. Ulmer 1944)** ☆
John Carradine as the artist who kills models who no longer inspire him, in a film that predates *The Two Mrs Carrolls*.

Dr Phibes Rises Again **(Robert Fuest 1972)** ☆
Vincent Price is at it again, this time to eliminate rivals for an elixir.

Fists in the Pocket **(US:** *Fist in His Pocket***)** **(***I Pugni In Tasca***)** **(Marco Bellocchio 1965)** ✍
An epileptic decides to kill himself and his infirm family to allow his healthy brother to have a normal life.

House of Fear **(Roy William Neill 1945)** ✍ ☆
>Basil Rathbone and Nigel Bruce's Holmes and Watson investigate secret society serial killings.

>***Kind Hearts and Coronets*** **(Robert Hamer 1949)** ✍ ☆ ☞

My Learned Friend **(Basil Dearden/Will Hay 1943)**
Will Hay and Claude Hulbert as inept lawyers on the chopping list of escapee Mervyn Johns.

>***Theatre of Blood*** **(Douglas Hickox 1973)** ✍ ☆ ☞

Kind Hearts and Coronets
✍ ☆ ☞ ▓

GB • Ealing • 1949 • 106 mins • b/w
d Robert Hamer   w Robert Hamer/John Dighton   ph Douglas Slocombe

Dennis Price, >Alec Guinness, Joan Greenwood, Valerie Hobson

On the eve of his execution, Louis Mazzini (Price) completes the chronicle of his crimes. Bent on avenging the ostracizing of his mother and his own exclusion from the family fortune, he murders the eight ghastly relations that stand between him and the D'Ascoyne dukedom. As much a snob as his prey, Louis is also a charming bounder, commanding such loyalty from both childhood sweetheart Sibella (Greenwood) and Edith (Hobson), the widow of one of his less detestable victims, that they strain to secure his eleventh hour reprieve. Price's suave villainy and erudite narrative are excellent, causing us to receive with certain ambiguity, the news he has left his incriminating memoir on the cell table (in the US version, he fails to retrieve it), but Alec Guinness' portrayals of the eight doomed D'Ascoynes, male, and female, are peerless.

•Alec Guinness plays a seaman disowned by his ghostly ancestors (also Guinness) because of his seasickness, in *Barnacle Bill* (US: *All at Sea*) (Charles Crichton 1957) (☆ ☞).
•Turri Ferro plays six different hitmen in a story of a man's wavering between Mafia and Communism, in *The Seduction of Mimi* (*Mimi Metallurgico Ferito Nell'Onore*) (Lina Wertmuller 1972) (☞ ☆).
•>Alastair Sim is a successful assassin until it comes to liquidating pompous cabinet minister Raymond Huntley, in *The Green Man* (Robert Day 1956) (☆ ✍).
•In order to inherit their cut of an eccentric's will, a family led by >Alastair Sim and George Cole have to commit crimes, in *Laughter in Paradise* (Mario Zampa 1951) (☆ ✍).
•A man about to commit suicide tells how he implicated his hearer in his crimes, in *Lovers and Thieves* (*Assassins et Voleurs*) (Sacha Guitry 1956) (✍).
•Sacha Guitry has a further touch of the memoirs, in *The Story of a Cheat* (*Le Roman d'un Tricheur*)(Sacha Guitry 1936) (☞ ☆ ✍).

KING, STEPHEN

Carrie (Brian De Palma 1976) ✍ ☞
Timid teenager Sissy Spacek uses her paranormal powers to pay back the classmates who humiliated her.

Cat's Eye (Lewis Teague 1981) ☆
A cat is caught up in two sinister tales, including James Woods' brutal smoking cure, before killing a vicious troll.

Children of the Corn (Fritz Kiersch 1984)
A couple journeying through the Bible Belt had better start saying their prayers.

Christine (John Carpenter 1984) ☞
A restored car with a gruesome past exacts revenge on those who try to destroy it.

Creepshow (George A. Romero 1982) ✍
A small boy revels in the spooky spoofs he reads in his comic.

Cujo (Lewis Teague 1983) ✳
A St Bernard dog becomes a rabid monster.

The Dead Zone (David Cronenberg 1983) ☞ ✍
Christopher Walken stalks a popular politician whom he knows, through his unusual insight, will cause another holocaust.

Firestarter (Mark L. Lester 1983) ✍
George C. Scott wants to harness Drew Barrymore's pyrotechnic powers for government use.

Pet Sematary (Mary Lambert 1989)
King's own adaptation of his tale about bones that won't stay buried.

Salem's Lot (Tobe Hooper 1979) ✍
David Soul investigates why people in his home town keep disappearing at James Mason's house.

The Shining (>Stanley Kubrick 1980) ☆ ☞
A hotel's supernatural past crazes writer >Jack Nicholson into attacking his wife Shelley Duvall and their son.

King Kong ✍ ✳ ☞ ■
USA · RKO · 1933 · 100 mins · b/w
d Merian C. Cooper/Ernest Schoedsack
w James Creelman/Ruth Rose
ph Edward Linden/Verne Walker   m Max Steiner

Fay Wray, Robert Armstrong, Bruce Cabot, Frank Reicher

Abducted by a bestial entrepreneur from the island where he is revered as a god, the shamelessly exhibited and maltreated Kong escapes in order to find the blonde actress who showed him humanity. Kong atop the Empire State Building, Fay Wray in one fist and swatting at bi-planes with the other, is one of cinema's most enduring images. But it was only made possible by a revolution in special effects technology that transformed a mass of wire, rubber and rabbit fur into the curiously endearing monster that reduced Skull Island and New York to rubble and us to tears. Fairytale, morality fable, religious allegory, psychological study, exploitation movie or weepie? Never has a horror shocker merited such academic dispute.

•John Guillermin's 1976 remake with Jeff Bridges and Jessica Lange could only have turned out as badly as it did through a lot of effort.
•*Mighty Joe Young* (Ernest Schoedsack 1949) was perhaps the best of the Kong rip-offs, while the film inspired 1000 imitations, the fish monster tale of *The Creature from the Black Lagoon* (Jack Arnold 1954) (✍) being the most fun.
•Beauty Gina Lollobrigida proved irresistible to Beast Anthony Quinn, in *The Hunchback of Notre Dame* (*Notre Dame de Paris*) (Jean Delannoy 1956) (☞ ■).
•The monsters are cute until wet, in *Gremlins* (Joe Dante 1984) (✳).
•Disputing the hegemony of the jungle is Christopher Lambert, in *Greystoke, the Legend of Tarzan, Lord of the Apes* (Hugh Hudson 1984) (■ ☆).
•Kong is king on *The Planet of the Apes* (Franklin J. Schaffner 1968) (✳ ✍).

Kubrick, Stanley
American writer/director (b 1928)
Involved at every stage of his movies, the meticulous Kubrick now takes up to five years to complete a project compared with the 20 days he took for debut feature *Killer's Kiss* (1955)

KRAKATOA, EAST OF JAVA
(Bernard Kowalski 1968)

LAND DISASTERS

FRIDAY THE THIRTEENTH
(Victor Saville 1933) ☞ ⚅
(lives of victims prior to a bus crash)

THE LAST DAYS OF POMPEII
(Merion C. Cooper/Ernest Schoedsack 1935) ■
(decadent hours before Vesuvius erupts)

SAN FRANCISCO
(W. S. Van Dyke 1936) ✩ ☞ ✳
(club owner >Clark Gable and priest >Spencer Tracy
are heroes of 1906 San Francisco earthquake)

IN OLD CHICAGO
(Henry King 1937) ✩ ☞
(the lives of various folk prior to the great Chicago fire)

THE RAINS CAME
(Clarence Brown 1939) ☞ ⚅ ■
(Raj parasites prove their worth during severe flood-
ing)

THE TOWERING INFERNO
(John Guillermin/Irwin Allen 1974) ☞ ■ ✳
(skyscraper blaze engulfs all-star cast)

AIR DISASTERS

NO HIGHWAY IN THE SKY (UK: NO HIGHWAY)
(Henry Koster 1951) ✩
(>James Stewart warns of mid-flight metal fatigue)

THE HIGH AND THE MIGHTY
(>William Wellman 1954) ☞ ✩ ⚅
(passengers panic as >John Wayne prepares to crash-
land a plane)

THE NIGHT MY NUMBER CAME UP
(Leslie Norman 1954) ✩
(Michael Hordern's crash premonition becomes a
reality)

THE HINDENBURG
(Robert Wise 1975)
(pioneering passenger airship explodes)

AIRPLANE!
(Jim Abrahams/David & Jerry Zucker 1980) ⚅ ✩
(hilarious spoof of *Zero Hour!* [Hall Bartlett 1957])

Land, sky and sea disaster after an enormous volcanic eruption

DISASTER AT SEA

ATLANTIC
(E. A. Dupont 1929) ▣

TITANIC
(Jean Negulesco 1953) ☞
A NIGHT TO REMEMBER
(Roy Baker 1958) ☆
(the liner that could never sink, sinks)

THE UNSINKABLE MOLLY BROWN
(Charles Walters 1964) ♫ ▣
(Wild West orphan Debbie Reynolds [AAN] survives the Titanic tragedy)

THE MYSTERY OF THE MARIE CELESTE (US:
PHANTOM SHIP)
(Denison Clift 1935) ✍
(famous tale of disappearing crew)

THE POSEIDON ADVENTURE
(Ronald Neame 1972) ☆ ✍
(passengers in capsized liner struggle to freedom)

JUGGERNAUT
(Richard Lester 1974) ☞
(liner has a bomb planted on board)

(☞) (a boxer and a gangster feud over a girl). *The Killing* (1956) (☞) (Sterling Hayden robs a racetrack), a latter-day *film noir*, developed his fascination with the motives for killing, which he has subsequently examined through the ages in *Spartacus* (1960) (☞ ☆) (>Kirk Douglas as the Roman slave who leads a revolt against the Empire), *Paths of Glory* (1957) (☆ ☞ ✍)(>Kirk Douglas defends three court-martialees in Adolphe Menjou's First World War court), >*Dr Strangelove or How I Learned To Stop Worrying and Love the Bomb* (AAN: 1963) (✍ ☞ ☆ ■) (how the holocaust arises out of the Cold War), *Full Metal Jacket* (1987) (☞ ✍ ☆) (Matthew Modine lives through hell training for and fighting in Vietnam) and *A Clockwork Orange* (AAN: 1971)(☞ ■) (thug Malcolm McDowell is released into a future society that is excessively violent even for his tolerance). The potential for killing inherent in breakdown was examined in the grandiose *2001 – A Space Odyssey* (AAN: 1968) (☞ ✍ ♫) (spaceship computer Hal malfunctions and threatens the lives of the crew) and *The Shining* (1980) (☆ ☞) (the combination of writer's block and a sinister hotel derange >Jack Nicholson).

•*Lolita* (1962) (☆ ☞ ✍): academic James Mason marries his beloved 14-year-old Sue Lyon's mother (Shelley Winters) to be near her in the screen version of Vladimir Nabokov's novel.
•*Barry Lyndon* (1975) (☞ ■ ✍): Ryan O'Neal as William Makepeace Thackeray's roguish 18th-century Irish soldier of fortune.

Kurosawa, Akira
Japanese writer/director (b 1910)

The most popular Japanese director with Western audiences, Kurosawa, like >Orson Welles and >Woody Allen, has produced the majority of his work with a settled technical and acting crew, including Toshiro Mifune and Takashi Shimura, lending it a distinctive unity and fluency. His fame rests on his JIDAI-GEKI or costume epics: *Rashomon* (1950) (☞ ■ ☆ ✍) (Venice Best Film in which the murder of a samurai and the rape of his wife is told from different perspectives during Toshiro Mifune's

trial); *The Seven Samurai* (*Shichinin no Samurai*) (1954) (☞ ■) (warriors hired to terrorize a village switch allegiance), *The Hidden Fortress* (*Kakushi Toride No San-Akunin*) (1958) (☞ ✍) (Kurosawa won the Best Director award at Berlin for this tale of samurai Mifune escorting an heiress to sanctuary during a medieval civil war), *Yojimbo* (1961) (☞ ☆ ✍) (samurai Mifune tricks bandits into wiping themselves out), *Sanjuro* (*Tsubaki Sanjuro*) (1962) (☞ ☆ ✍) (itinerant samurai Mifune saves a kidnapped minister from the clutches of an evil warlord) and >*Kagemusha* (1980) (☞ ■ ✍ ☆); and GENDAI-GEKI, or contemporary dramas: *Drunken Angel* (*Yoidore Tenshi*) (1948) (☞ ☆) (gangster Mifune has a bullet removed by doctor Takashi Shimura who is then implicated in his crimes), *The Quiet Duel* (aka *A Silent Duel*) (*Shizuka Naru Ketto*) (1949) (☆ ☞) (a doctor abandons his fiancée out of honour when he contracts syphilis from a war-wounded patient), *Stray Dog* (*Nora Inu*) (1949) (☞ ☆) (cop Mifune is tempted by the trappings of crime as he searches for his stolen gun), and *Living* (aka *Doomed*) (US: *To Live*) (*Ikiru*) (1952) (☞ ✍) (a cancer-ridden civil servant rouses himself from lethargy to get a slum playground built). He has also given literary classics Japanese settings: >Dostoyevsky's *The Idiot* (*Hakuchi*) (1951) (☞) (a saintly prince and a dissolute man fall for the same fallen woman); Gogol's *The Lower Depths* (*Donzoko*) (1952) (☞ ☆) (hiding from the police Mifune becomes involved with the residents of a shabby hostel); and >Shakespeare's *Macbeth* as *Throne of Blood* (US: *Castle of the Spider's Web*) (aka *Cobweb Castle*) (*Kumonosu-Jo*) (1952) (☞ ■ ✍ ☆) (samurai Mifune is urged by his wife and a ghost to murder a warlord, but he fails to hold power), and *King Lear* as >*Ran* (1986) (☞ ■ ✍ ☆).

•*The Men Who Tread on the Tiger's Tail* (aka *Walkers on the Tiger's Tail*) (*Tora no O o Fumu Otokotachi*) (1945) (■): a fleeing noble asks a squire to beat him up to help him escape from his wicked brother.
•*Red Beard* (*Akahige*) (1965) (☞ ■): an ambitious doctor Yuzo Kayama is taught the joys of

treating the 19th-century poor by Toshiro Mifune.

•*Dodes'kaden* (1970) (✍ ☞): a boy and an old man shelter from extreme poverty in an imaginary house.

•*Dersu Uzala* (1975) (☞ ■): Best Foreign Film Oscar winner has a Russian scientist relying on the guide he previously despised while charting the Siberian wastes.

Lamb ☆ ✍ ☞
Ireland • Cannon/Flickers/Limehouse/
Channel Four • 1986 • 110 mins • col
d Colin Gregg   w Bernard MacLaverty
ph Mike Garforth   m Van Morrison
Liam Neeson, Ian Bannen, Hugh O'Connor

Angered by the Christian Brothers' appropriation of the money he inherits from his father and disillusioned with headmaster Brother Benedict (Bannen)'s callous disciplining of Owen Kane (O'Connor), a diminutive but unruly epileptic, Mick (Neeson) decides his vocation is fathering the boy. Arriving in London where they become the subject of a kidnap hunt, they eke out a penurious existence, Owen's sole release from which is the ecstasy he feels prior to a convulsion. Wishing to spare him the pain of a hopeless future, Mick drowns Owen during an epileptic attack at the seaside. The most moving exploration of 'fathers and sons' since >*Bicycle Thieves*, this adaptation of Bernard MacLaverty's novel, without ever mentioning celibacy, persuasively propounds the suitability of the religious for parenthood.

•>Spencer Tracy is the priest presiding over the reform school known as *Boys' Town* (Norman Taurog 1938) (☆ ✍ ☞).
•Three Brazilian delinquents escape a detention centre and become involved with prostitution and drugs on the streets of São Paolo, in *Pixote* (Hector Babenco 1981) (☞ ✍ ☆).
•A remarkable documentary of children surviving homelessness in Seattle is *Streetwise* (Martin Bell 1984) (☞).
•'Kid'-nap, in this case quadnap, provides Nicholas Cage and Holly Hunter with the babies they can't have (they steal one of the four), but they are the heirs to a fortune and hotly pursued, in *Raising Arizona* (Joel Coen 1987) (☆ ✍).
•Charlie Chaplin cares for slum kid Jackie Coogan and is rewarded by the grateful mother who abandoned him (Edna Purviance), in *The Kid* (>Charles Chaplin 1921) (✍ ☞).

Lang, Fritz
Austrian-born American writer/director
(1890–1976)

Prominent in the German Expressionist movement, Lang's architectural and artistic background brought a developed sense of set and scene to the social and political comment of his crime and science fiction films: *Dr Mabuse, the Gambler* (*Doktor Mabuse, der Spieler*) (1922) (☞ ■) (a hypnotist and master-of-disguise criminal plots world domination); *M* (1931) (☞ ☆ ■ ✍) (>Peter Lorre is a child killer pursued by an underworld united in abhorrence at his crimes); *The Spiders* (*Die Spinnen*) (1919–1920) (in two episodes the eponymous criminal gang search for Inca treasure in an underwater city and diamonds in the shape of the Buddha's head); *Destiny* (US: *Between Two Worlds*) (aka *Beyond The Wall*) (*Der Müde Tod*) (1921) (☞ ■) (a wife sees Death through the eyes of various cultures as she bargains for her husband's life); and >*Metropolis* (1927) (☞ ■ ✴ ✍ ☆). Banned by the Nazis and abandoned by his pro-Hitler screenwriter wife Thea Von Harbou, he fled to the USA where, despite transferring from studio to studio, he managed to maintain his high standards, in INJUSTICE DRAMAS: *Fury* (1936) (☞ ☆ ■) (>Spencer Tracy avenges his near-lynching by the menfolk of an insular and frightened small town); *You Only Live Once* (1940) (☞ ☆) (framed >Henry Fonda flees for the border with wife Sylvia Sidney to avoid recapture) and *The Woman in the Window* (1944) (☆ ☞ ✍) (>Edward G. Robinson covers his tracks when a strange girl embroils him in an accidental murder); WAR ADVENTURES: *Man Hunt* (1941) (☞ ☆ ✍) (hunter Walter Pidgeon fails to assassinate Hitler and is pursued by Nazi agent George Sanders), *Hangmen Also Die* (1943) (☞ ■) (Brian Donlevy is wanted for the assassination of Czech Gestapo chief Reinhold Heydrich), and *The Ministry of Fear* (1944) (☞ ✍ ☆) (Ray Milland becomes the target of Nazis hoping to retrieve a secret microfilm); WESTERNS: *The Return of Frank James* (1940) (☆ ☞ ■) (>Henry Fonda avenges the shooting of brother Jesse) and *Rancho Notorious* (1952) (☆) (cowboy Arthur Kennedy disguises himself as a badman at >Marlene Dietrich's hostel to seek out a rapist); and CRIME NOIR: *The Blue Gardenia* (1953) (☞) (Anne Baxter wakes to find a dead man in her bed, but doesn't recall killing him), *The Big Heat* (1953) (☞ ☆) (cop Glenn Ford finds it hard to be restrained while

investigating the murder of his wife), *Human Desire* (1954) (☞ ■) (Glenn Ford and Gloria Grahame plot the murder of railwayman Broderick Crawford), and *While the City Sleeps* (1956) (☞ ✍ ☆) (Vincent Price sets his journalists Dana Andrews, George Sanders and Ida Lupino to find a paper-saving scoop). Other than *The Thousand Eyes of Dr Mabuse* (*Die Tausend Augen des Dr Mabuse*) (1960) (cop Gert Frobe is convinced that a sequence of crimes are due to the long-dead master criminal), the work following his 1957 return to Germany was disappointing.

•*Die Nibelungen* (1924) (☞ ■): two-part telling of the German myth of the murder of the Icelander Siegfried at the behest of Burgundian beauty Brunhilde and her killing by his bride Kriemhild.

•*The Woman in the Moon* (US: *By Rocket to the Moon*) (*Die Frau im Mond*) (1929) (☞ ■): financiers, hoping to coin it by mining gold, fly to the moon.

•*The Testament of Dr Mabuse* (aka *The Last Will of Dr Mabuse*) (*Das Testament des Dr Mabuse*) (1933) (☞ ■): the scheming Rudolf Klein-Rogge hypnotizes his way out of an asylum and sets out to rule the world again.

•*Scarlet Street* (1945) (☞ ✍): timid artist >Edward G. Robinson murders Joan Bennett in a jealous rage, but her sponging lover Dan Duryea is blamed.

•*Cloak and Dagger* (1946) (☞ ☆): scientist >Gary Cooper is dropped into Germany to learn how close the Nazis are to developing an atomic bomb.

•*Clash by Night* (1952) (☆): >Barbara Stanwyck returns to her coastal home, replacing >Marilyn Monroe as the centre of attention.

•*Moonfleet* (1955) (☞ ■): J. Meade Faulkner tale of a small boy discovering that his guardian Stewart Granger is a daring smuggler.

•*Beyond a Reasonable Doubt* (1956) (☞ ✍): >Joan Fontaine pleads Dana Andrews' innocence when he stacks clues against himself to prove the dangers of circumstantial evidence.

•*The Tiger of Eschnapur* (*The Indian Tomb*)

(*Der Tiger von Eschnapur*) (*Das Indische Grabmal*) (1958) (☞ ✍): an architect causes problems at the court of an Indian maharajah.

The Last Wave
Australia • United Artists • 1977 • 106 mins • col
d Peter Weir   w Peter Weir/Tony Morphett/Petru Popescu   ph Russell Boyd   m Charles Wain
Richard Chamberlain, Olivia Hamnet, Frederick Parslow, David Gulpilil

David Burton (Chamberlain) is the premonition-prone lawyer defending Chris Lee (Gulpilil) and his fellow aborigines for the murder of a compatriot who was about to betray their underground activities and whereabouts of their catacomb headquarters in Sydney. Guilt at the whites' savagery towards the aborigines and a torrential downpour induce visions of a great flood submerging the city, which Burton's attempts to understand lead him to a ruined subterranean world. The closing action of Peter Weir's chiller is often mystifying and distorted, but we are left in no doubt of the implication of the breaker, lifted from the US surf movie *Crystal Voyager*.

•Gregory Peck is the lawyer defending a client in a racially prejudiced culture in the screen version of Harper Lee's novel *To Kill a Mockingbird* (Robert Mulligan 1962) (☆ ✍ ■).
•Aborigine David Gulpilil leads Jenny Agutter across the Outback to safety, in *Walkabout* (Nicolas Roeg 1970) (☞ ■ ☆), while the threat to the aborigines' homelands by big business is explored in *Where the Green Ants Dream* (*Wo die Grünen Ameisen Träumen*) (>Werner Herzog 1982) (■).
•Spirits in the graveyard beneath the Freeling family's home threaten their daughter Heather O'Rourke, in *Poltergeist II - The Other Side* (Brian Gibson 1986) (✳).
•Mickey Rourke investigates a syndicate operating from another inner city cultural quarter, New York's Chinatown, in *The Year of the Dragon* (Michael Cimino 1986) (☆).
•In the catacombs of >*Metropolis* (>Fritz Lang

1927) (☞ ■ ✳ ✍ ☆), a rebellion against a tyrant is being prepared.
•When the floods hit India, Raj lizards >Myrna Loy and George Brent fathom previously uncharted depths of humanity, in *The Rains Came* (Clarence Brown 1939) (☆ ☞).

Laughton, Charles
British-born actor/director (1899–1962)
If few people enjoyed working with Laughton, audiences invariably enjoyed the resultant films. RADA trained, his dominant presence was tempered with a sensitivity that prevented his work lapsing into vulgar star vehicles. His excellence is evident in COSTUME MELODRAMA: *The Sign of the Cross* (Cecil B. De Mille 1932) (☆ ☞ ■) (Laughton as Nero fighting the rise of Christianity), >*The Private Life of Henry VIII* (AA: Alexander Korda 1933) (☆ ✍ ☞ ■), *The Barretts of Wimpole Street* (Sidney Franklin 1934) (Laughton as Elizabeth Barrett (Norma Shearer)'s brutal father opposing her romance with >Fredric March's Robert Browning), *Les Misérables* (Richard Boleslawski 1935) (☆ ✍ ☞) (Laughton pursues framed escapee >Fredric March despite the latter's new-found respectability), *Mutiny on the Bounty* (AAN: Frank Lloyd 1935) (☆ ☞ ✍) (Laughton's Captain Bligh is set adrift for his martinet regime by >Clark Gable's Fletcher Christian), *Rembrandt* (Alexander Korda 1936) (☆ ■) (Laughton as the teased and lonely 17th-century Dutch artist); and *The Hunchback of Notre Dame* (>William Dieterle 1939) (☞ ■ ☆) (Laughton as Victor Hugo's bellringer abused by the crowds and devoted to Maureen O'Hara's Esmerelda); COMEDY: *The Old Dark House* (James Whale 1932) (☆ ✍ ☞ ■) (Laughton is among those sheltering in a remote Welsh mansion where the family have a sinister secret to hide), *Ruggles of Red Gap* (>Leo McCarey 1935) (☆ ☞ ✍) (butler Laughton serves a family of cowboys), *It Started with Eve* (Henry Koster 1941) (☆) (Deanna Durbin is roped into playing Robert Cummings' fiancée to please dying Laughton, but he recovers), *The Canterville Ghost* (>Jules Dassin 1944) (☆) (the Oscar Wilde tale of 17th-century ghost Laughton desirous to rest in peace), and *Hobson's Choice* (>David Lean

1954) (☆ ✍ ☞) (worm John Mills turns against drunken, tyrannical cobbler Laughton); and CONTEMPORARY DRAMA: *Vessel of Wrath* (US: *The Beachcomber*) (Erich Pommer 1937) (☆ ✍) (drunken beachcomber grows to love prudish missionary Elsa Lanchester), *The Suspect* (Robert Siodmak 1944) (☆) (no sooner is Laughton free of his shrewish wife than he is blackmailed for her murder), *The Paradine Case* (>Alfred Hitchcock 1948) (☞ ☆ ✍) (Laughton and Gregory Peck as the counsels in the trial of Alida Valli), *The Big Clock* (John Farrow 1948) (☆ ✍) (Laughton lays clues for a murder he committed to incriminate journalist Ray Milland), *Witness for the Prosecution* (AAN: >Billy Wilder 1957) (✍ ☆ ☞) (recuperating lawyer Laughton is convinced of Tyrone Power's innocence of murder because of his wife >Marlene Dietrich's testimony) and *Advise and Consent* (Otto Preminger 1962) (Laughton and Burgess Meredith accuse senator >Henry Fonda of Communist sympathies).

•*Island of Lost Souls* (Erle C. Kenton 1932): Laughton lands on the island where Dr Moreau (>Bela Lugosi) experiments on humans.

•*St Martin's Lane* (US: *Sidewalks of London*) (Tim Whelan 1939) (☆): street musician Laughton forlornly loves rising dance star >Vivien Leigh.

•*They Knew What They Wanted* (Garson Kanin 1940): >Carole Lombard marries by post, but Laughton sent his vineyard foreman William Gargan's photo rather than his own.

•*This Land is Mine* (>Jean Renoir 1943) (☞ ☆ ✍): timid teacher Laughton refuses to name a traitor killer or his lover Maureen O'Hara in a Nazi court and becomes the village hero.

•*Because of Him* (Richard Wallace 1946) (☆): famous actor Laughton assists waitress Deanna Durbin to stardom.

•*The Man on the Eiffel Tower* (Burgess Meredith 1949) (☆ ✍): Laughton is among the suspects defying the director's Maigret in Simenon's tale *A Battle of Nerves*.

AS DIRECTOR:

•*Night of the Hunter* (1955) (☞ ■): sinister preacher Robert Mitchum stalks two children who know the whereabouts of some buried loot, in this, Laughton's sole directorial venture.

Laurel, Stan and Hardy, Oliver

(Arthur Stanley Jefferson) British actor (1890–1965)
(Norvell Hardy) American actor (1892–1957)

Stan Laurel, >Charlie Chaplin's understudy in Fred Karno's company, and Oliver Hardy, the vaudeville minstrel, first worked together (but unpartnered) in Hal Roach's *Lucky Dog* (1917). They shared 39 more silent comedies, including: *Putting Pants on Philip* (Clyde Bruckman 1927) (☆) (respectable Ollie's Scottish nephew Stan has nothing beneath his kilt); *The Battle of the Century* (Clyde Bruckman 1927) (☆ ☞) (the battle in question being the greatest custard pie fight in movie history); *The Finishing Touch* (Clyde Bruckman 1928) (☆ ✍) (Stan and Ollie should be in demolition instead of construction if this house is anything to go by); *You're Darn Tootin'* (Edgar Kennedy 1928) (☆ ☞) (musicians Stan and Ollie love the sound of tearing pants); *Big Business* (James W. Horne 1929) (☆ ✍) (the Christmas spirit is lacking in >Leo McCarey and H. M. Walker's script as Stan and Ollie scrap over a tree); *Double Whoopee* (Lewis R. Foster 1929) (☆ ✍) (McCarey and Walker have the pair as hotel doormen hindering guests, including >Jean Harlow); *Berth Marks* (Lewis R. Foster 1929) (☆) (a McCarey and Walker script again as Stan and Ollie's clumsiness with a double bass leads to clothes tearing among train passengers, while the partners squeeze into one bunk). Out of these shorts developed the dignified, know-all Hardy and the dumb, vengeful Laurel, the naïve, bowler-hatted couple who, despite constant bickering, countless failed schemes, nightmare marriages, prison terms and interminable vagrancies, affectionately and inalienably clung together. The 35 two-reelers and 27 features exhibited a comic genius infinitely more accessible than even the lightest moments of >Charlie Chaplin, Harold Lloyd and >Buster Keaton, and include many of the funniest films ever made.

THE SHORTS:

•*Men O'War* (Lewis R. Foster 1929) (☆): sailors Stan and Ollie invite two girls for sodas, but can only afford three.

•*The Perfect Day* (James Parrott 1929) (☆ ✍): McCarey, Walker and Roach among the writers as, once the car starts, a picnic gets no further than a huge, wet pothole.

•*The Hoosegow* (James Parrott 1929) (☆): chain gang cooks Stan and Ollie put rice in the carburettor of the governor's car.

•*Night Owls* (James Parrott 1930) (☆ ✍): McCarey and Walker have the boys as cops bribing tramps into a burglary to keep them on the force.

•*Blotto* (James Parrott 1930) (☆): McCarey and Walker have Stan's wife punish him after an illicit night out.

•*Brats* (James Parrott 1930) (☆ ✍ ▣): McCarey, Roach and Walker have Stan and Ollie babysit themselves in miniature.

•*Hog Wild* (James Parrott 1930) (☆ ☞): McCarey and Walker turn putting an aerial on a roof into mission impossible.

•*Another Fine Mess* (James Parrott 1930) (☆): Walker, now writing alone, has Ollie disguised as a butler and Stan as a maid ruining James Finlayson's dinner party.

•*Be Big* (James Parrott 1930) (☆): Ollie wants to avoid a family holiday but Stan's intervention makes sure he goes.

•*Laughing Gravy* (James W. Horne 1931) (☆): a noisy dog has the boys thrown out of a boarding house into the snow.

•*Our Wife* (James W. Horne 1931) (☆ ✍): Stan brings a ladder to help Ollie elope.

•*Come Clean* (James W. Horne 1931) (☆ ✍): Stan and Ollie rescue Mae Busch from drowning while on an errand for ice cream.

•*One Good Turn* (James W. Horne 1931) (☆ ✍): the boys mistake James Finlayson's play rehearsal for a threat on a little old lady.

•*Beau Hunks* (UK: *Beau Chumps*) (James W. Horne 1931) (☆): Stan and Ollie get lost on a Foreign Legion route march.

•*Helpmates* (James Parrott 1931) (☆): as the wives return, Stan and Ollie try to repair some party damage.

•*The Music Box* (James Parrott 1932) (☆ ✍ ☞): this winner of the Short Film AA sees Stan and Ollie take a crated piano up a narrow flight of steps.

•*County Hospital* (James Parrott 1932) (☆): Ollie has broken his leg and Stan cheers him up with hardboiled eggs and nuts.

•*Scram!* (Ray McCarey 1932) (☆): Stan and Ollie stash liquor in a water jug and get judge's wife Vivien Oakland drunk.

•*Towed in a Hole* (George Marshall 1932) (☆ ✍): fishmongers Laurel and Hardy do up a boat to cut out the middleman.

•*Twice Two* (James Parrott 1933) (☆ ▣): Stan and Ollie are married to each other's sisters.

•*The Midnight Patrol* (Lloyd French 1933) (☆): cops Stan and Ollie arrest their chief in his own house.

•*Busy Bodies* (Lloyd French 1933) (☆ ✍): Stan as co-scriptwriter of this tale of plane shaving and buzz saws.

•*Them Thar Hills* (Charles Rogers 1934) (☆): campers Stan and Ollie get tipsy in a whisky well.

•*The Live Ghost* (Charles Rogers 1934) (☆): press-ganged Stan and Ollie sail on a supposed ghost ship.

•*Tit for Tat* (Charles Rogers 1935) (☆): Short AAN for tale of feuding shopkeepers.

THE FEATURES:

•*Pardon Us* (James Parrott 1931) (☆ ✍): prisoners Stan and Ollie unintentionally lead a jailbreak.

•*Pack Up Your Troubles* (George Marshall/Ray McCarey 1932) (☆): war vets Stan and Ollie search for the family of their trench pal's orphaned daughter.

•*Fra Diavolo* (Hal Roach/Charles Rogers 1933) (☆): in a tale based on Auber's operetta, Stan and Ollie are inept thieves helping a romantic bandit.

•*Sons of the Desert* (UK: *Fraternally Yours*) (William A. Seiter 1933) (☆ ✍ ☞): Stan and Ollie's presence at a convention is betrayed by a newsreel.

•*Babes in Toyland* (Gus Meins/Charles Rogers 1934) (☆): Santa's toymakers make soldiers to the wrong measurements, but they animate to save Toyland.

•*The Bohemian Girl* (James W. Horne/Charles Rogers 1936) (☆): Stan and Ollie are gypsies helping true love find a kidnapped noble's daughter.

•*Our Relations* (Harry Lachmann 1936) (☆ ✍ ▓): Stan and Ollie, as their own reprobate sailor twins, misplace a diamond ring.

•>*Way Out West* (James W. Horne 1937) (☆ ✍♪☞)

•*Swiss Miss* (John G. Blystone 1938) (☆): Stan and Ollie sell mousetraps in the Alps and serenade an opera singer with a tuba.

•*Blockheads* (John G. Blystone 1938) (☆ ✍): left in the trenches, Stan is brought home by Ollie and destroys his home life.

•*A Chump at Oxford* (Alfred Goulding 1940) (☆ ✍ ▓): Stan and Ollie get a scholarship to a fantasized Oxford where Stan proves to be a college hero.

•*Saps at Sea* (Gordon Douglas 1940) (☆): recuperating from horn factory insanity, Ollie and Stan catch an escapee on their launch.

•*Great Guns* (Monty Banks 1941) (☆): Stan and Ollie volunteer for the army to protect their millionaire charge.

•*Air Raid Wardens* (Edward Sedgewick 1943): Stan and Ollie catch Nazis in their usual blundering way.

•*The Bullfighters* (Mal St Clair 1945) (☆): the boys are looking tired as Stan is mistaken for a Mexican bullfighter.

LAWRENCE, D. H.

The Fox (Mark Rydell 1967) ✍♪
Lesbians Anne Heywood and Sandy Dennis shelter sailor Keir Dullea on their farm.

Kangaroo (Tim Burstall 1987) ☆
Judy Davis and Colin Friels in a tale of post-World War I fascism in Australia.

Priest of Love (Christopher Miles 1981) ☆
A biopic of the author's final years, with Ian McKellen and Janet Suzman as D. H. and Frieda.

Lady Chatterley's Lover (Marc Allégret 1955) ✍/**(Just Jaeckin 1981)** ✍
The wife of a crippled noble takes up with her gamekeeper.

The Rainbow (Ken Russell 1989) ☞ ☆
Paul McGann, Glenda Jackson and Amanda Donohoe in this prequel to *Women in Love*.

The Rocking Horse Winner (Anthony Pelissier 1949) ☆ ✍
A small boy tries to use his psychic gifts to help his parents John Mills and Valerie Hobson.

Sons and Lovers (Jack Cardiff 1960) ☆ ▓ ✍
Dean Stockwell quarrels with miner father Trevor Howard, but is reconciled with him when mother Wendy Hiller dies.

The Virgin and the Gypsy (Christopher Miles 1970) ☆ ▓
A strict vicar's daughter Joanna Shimkus falls for fortune teller Franco Nero.

Women in Love (Ken Russell 1969) ☆ ☞ ✍
Sisters Glenda Jackson and Jennie Linden are introduced to sex by Oliver Reed and Alan Bates.

LAWYERS

Bordertown (Archie Mayo 1935) ☆
Mexican lawyer Paul Muni makes a play for businessman's bored wife >Bette Davis.

Brothers in Law (John Boulting 1957) ☆
Ian Carmichael and >Richard Attenborough have their first experiences of life at the bar.

Crime without Passion (Ben Hecht/Charles MacArthur 1934) ☆ ✍
Convinced he knows every legal loophole, Claude Rains kills an unfaithful mistress.

The Divorce of Lady X (Tim Whelan 1937) ☆ ✍
Believing he is arranging her divorce, >Laurence Olivier falls in love with wealthy Merle Oberon.

The Enforcer (UK: *Murder Inc.*) (Bretaigne Windust 1950) ☆ ☞
D. A. >Humphrey Bogart crusades to destroy an assassination bureau.

The Inquisitor (*Garde à Vue*) (Claude Miller 1981) ✍ ☞
A lawyer is the prime suspect in a case of child rape.

Love is My Profession (*En Cas de Malheur*) (Claude Autant-Lara 1958) ☆
>Jean Gabin abandons a dull marriage to abscond with client Brigitte Bardot.

Star of Midnight (Stephen Roberts 1935) ☆
>Ginger Rogers helps fast-talking lawyer >William Powell clear his name of murder.

Le Roy, Mervyn
American director (1900–1987)

Vaudeville juvenile as 'The Singing Newsboy', Le Roy's first film position was wardrobe junior, progressing through minor roles to gag writer. His directorial debut with *Little Caesar* (1930) (☆ ☞) (the rise and fall of gangster >Edward G. Robinson) set the pattern for a series of biting social dramas: *Five Star Final* (1931) (☆ ✍ ☞) (>Edward G. Robinson is ordered to dig up dirt on an unsolved murder to boost his paper's circulation); >*I Am a Fugitive from a Chain Gang* (1932) (☞ ☆ ✍); *Hard to Handle* (1933) (✍ ☆) (>James Cagney as an indomitable publicity man who can make a buck out of anything); *Oil for the Lamps of China* (1935) (☞ ✍) (Pat O'Brien is torn between serving his company and being true to his own principles); and *They Won't Forget* (1937) (based on a true story, Claude Rains exploits the lynching of a child rapist to win votes away from the governor who commuted the sentence to imprisonment). He was equally happy with comedy – *Tugboat Annie* (1933) (☆ ☞) (waterfront tipplers Marie Dressler and Wallace Beery matchmake for their son Robert Young and Maureen O'Sullivan), *Page Miss Glory* (1935) (☞ ✍ ☆) (conman Dick Powell wins a postal beauty contest with a photofit from magazine pics and finds his non-existent beauty's double in hotel cleaner Marion Davies) – and musical: *Gold Diggers of 1933* (1933) (☞ ♫) (a trio of showgirls would rather find rich husbands than fame); *Rose Marie* (1954) (when Mountie Howard Keel calls, Ann Blyth answers true); and *Gypsy* (1962) (☞) (the Stephen Sondheim musical about the role that mother Rosalind Russell had in the early career of stripper Gypsy Rose Lee [Natalie Wood]). However, dramas remained Le Roy's forte: *Blossoms in the Dust* (1941) (☞ ✍ ☆) (Anita Loos script has Greer Garson founding an orphanage when her family are killed), *Random Harvest* (1942) (☞ ☆ ✍) (Ronald Colman is enjoying the simple life until he recalls he is an unhappy aristocrat) and *Madame Curie* (1943) (☞ ☆) (Greer Garson and Walter Pidgeon as the discoverers of radium), although after *Little Women* (1949) (June Allyson, Elizabeth Taylor, Margaret O'Brien and Janet Leigh as Louisa M. Alcott's March sisters), Le Roy's work went into decline.

- *Hi Nellie!* (1934) (☆ ☞ ✍): Paul Muni is demoted to agony aunt, but still scoops a gangster story.
- *Waterloo Bridge* (1940) (☆): >Vivien Leigh resorts to prostitution when lover Robert Taylor goes missing in action.
- *Escape* (1940) (☞ ☆): Robert Young enlists the help of Nazi Conrad Veidt's countess mistress Norma Shearer to rescue his mother from a PoW camp.
- *Unholy Partners* (1941) (☞ ☆): editor >Edward G. Robinson is bribed by gangster Edward Arnold, only to expose him in his paper.
- *Thirty Seconds over Tokyo* (1944) (☞ ☆): >Spencer Tracy prepares US pilots for their 1942 bombing raid on Tokyo.
- *Quo Vadis?* (1950) (☞ ■): Roman soldier Robert Taylor loves Christian Deborah Kerr and Peter Ustinov's Nero has no objection to them going to the lions.
- *The FBI Story* (1959) (☞ ☆): >James Stewart's career covers the USA's problems from gangsters and racism to Nazi and Communist infiltrators.

Lean, David
British writer/director (1908–1991)

Rising from teaboy in the silent years to editor for Paul Czinner, >Anthony Asquith and >Michael Powell, Lean's collaboration with Noël Coward on *In Which We Serve* (1942) (✍ ☆ ☞) (as they float in the sea, the survivors of a sunken destroyer recall their recent lives), *This Happy Breed* (1944) (✍ ☞) (John Mills is a member of the inter-war London family headed by Robert Newton), *Blithe Spirit* (1945) (✍ ☆) (eccentric medium Margaret Rutherford summons up Rex Harrison's dead wife Kay Hammond much to the upset of new bride Constance Cummings) and *Brief Encounter* (1945) (☞ ☆ ✍) (Trevor Howard and Celia Johnson are British about it and end their restrainedly passionate affair) established him as one of the most important figures in British cinema. These works were followed by his >Dickens adaptations *Great Expectations* (1946) (☞ ■ ✍ ☆) (John Mills is repaid for his kindness to an escaped convict who turns out to be a rich man) and *Oliver Twist* (1948) (✍ ☞ ☆) (an orphan is involved in a tug-of-war between a wealthy guardian and London underworld pickpockets) and the Venetian romance *Summertime* (UK: *Summer Madness*) (AAN: 1955) (☆ ☞) (spinster >Katharine Hepburn is charmed by suave Italian lover Rossano Brazzi). Subsequently, Lean has exclusively handled big-budget epics with mixed results: *The Bridge on the River Kwai* (AA: 1957) (✍ ☆ ☞) (>Alec Guinness commands a British contingent of PoWs building the Burma railroad); *Lawrence of Arabia* (AA: 1962) (■ ☞ ♫) (Peter O'Toole in a biopic of Arab revolt hero T. E. Lawrence); *Dr Zhivago* (AAN: 1965) (☞ ☆ ♫) (Boris Pasternak's Russian revolutionary epic romance of Julie Christie and Omar Sharif); *Ryan's Daughter* (1970) (☞ ✍ ☆ ■) (Sarah Miles has an affair with a British soldier in a fiercely Republican Irish coastal town); and *A Passage to India* (1983) (☞ ☆ ■) (an Indian doctor is tried for the attempted rape of a British girl on a visit to the Marabar Caves in the screen version of E. M. Forster's novel).

 •*Madeleine* (1950) (☞ ✍): 19th-century Glaswegian maid Ann Todd is accused of killing her lover.
•*The Sound Barrier*) (US: *Breaking the Sound Barrier*) (1952) (☞): Ralph Richardson sacrifices lives to get one of his planes to go faster than the speed of sound.
•*Hobson's Choice* (1954) (☆ ✍ ☞): timid cobbler assistant John Mills is persuaded by Brenda De Banzie to turn against his father-in-law employer >Charles Laughton.

Leigh, Vivien
(Vivian Hartley) British actress (1913–1967)
Lending spirited beauty to *Fire over England* (William K. Howard 1937) (☆ ✍) (>Laurence Olivier fights in the defeat of the Armada and wins heart of Vivien, a lady-in-waiting to Flora Robson's Elizabeth I) and *A Yank at Oxford* (Jack Conway 1938) (☆ ✍) (Vivien is the townie who wins the heart of brash American student Robert Taylor), Leigh's options were transformed by her romance with >Laurence Olivier and the Oscar-winning role of Scarlett

O'Hara in >*Gone with the Wind* (Victor Fleming 1939) (☆ ■ ✍ ☞ ♫). Working with her new husband in *Lady Hamilton* (US: *That Hamilton Woman*) (Alexander Korda 1941) (☆) (factional account of the romance between Emma Hamilton and Horatio Nelson) predated a period of stage work, interrupted only by dullish literary adaptations: *Caesar and Cleopatra* (Gabriel Pascal 1945) (☆ ✍) (Claude Rains played the ageing Roman emperor to Vivien's Egyptian queen in this >G. B. Shaw comedy) and *Anna Karenina* (Julien Duvivier 1947) (☆) (Vivien abandons husband Ralph Richardson for army officer Kieron Moore in Leo Tolstoy's epic). Her second Oscar role, Blanche Dubois in *A Streetcar Named Desire* (Elia Kazan 1952) (✍ ☞ ☆) (Vivien is the victim of brother-in-law >Marlon Brando's cruel words and brutal lust in this Tennessee Williams script), echoed her own incipient illness, which contributed to the breakdown of her marriage and her career.

 •*Dark Journey* (Victor Saville 1937) (☆ ☞): double agent Leigh falls for her German spy master Conrad Veidt.
•*Storm in a Teacup* (Ian Dalrymple/Victor Saville 1937) (☆ ✍): Vivien gets nationwide support for an old lady who refuses to buy a dog licence.
•*St Martin's Lane* (US: *Sidewalks of London*) (Tim Whelan 1939) (☆): London street entertainer >Charles Laughton falls for aspiring dance star Vivien.
•*Waterloo Bridge* (>Mervyn Le Roy 1940) (☆): when Robert Taylor fails to come marching home Vivien is driven to prostitution to survive.
•*Ship of Fools* (Stanley Kramer 1965) (☆ ☞ ■): Vivien is one of an all-star passenger list considered in pen picture episodes.
•*The Roman Spring of Mrs Stone* (Jose Quintero 1961) (☆): this adaptation of the Tennessee Williams novella has Vivien as the declining actress exploited by ambitious gigolo Warren Beatty.

Lemmon, Jack
American actor (b 1925)
Although films such as *The China Syndrome*

(James Bridges 1979) (☆ ✍) (Lemmon's nuclear power plant is filmed by >Jane Fonda and >Michael Douglas during a threatened meltdown) and *Missing* (AAN: Constantin Costa-Gavras 1982) (☆ ✍) (Lemmon searches for his *disparu* son in Chile with the boy's wife Sissy Spacek) have demonstrated Lemmon's talents as a straight actor, he is best known for his comic portrayal of innocents driven to experience, initially by Tony Curtis and Joe E.Brown in >*Some Like It Hot* (AAN: >Billy Wilder 1959) (☆ ✍ ☞ ▓ ♫) and subsequently by Walter Matthau's inconsideration or corruption: *The Fortune Cookie* (UK: *Meet Whiplash Willie*) (>Billy Wilder 1966) (✍ ☆ ☞) (shyster lawyer Matthau persuades sports cameraman Lemmon to sue for damages when a footballer barges into him); *The Odd Couple* (Gene Saks 1968) (✍ ☞ ☆) (would-be sophisticate Lemmon shares a home with slob sportswriter Matthau); *Kotch* (Jack Lemmon 1971) (☆ ☞) (elderly eccentric Matthau walks out on his family and takes pity on a pregnant waif); *The Front Page* (>Billy Wilder 1974) (☞ ☆ ✍) (Matthau uses a variety of low tricks to keep ace reporter Lemmon from leaving for his wedding); and *Buddy Buddy* (>Billy Wilder 1981) (☆) (assassin Matthau's hard exterior is pierced by Lemmon's potential suicide and he fouls up the contract). Shirley MacLaine's energetic charm also had a hand in the undoing of Lemmon's innocents in *The Apartment* (AAN: >Billy Wilder 1960) (☞ ☆ ✍) (timid Lemmon finally discloses his love for MacLaine when boss Fred MacMurray hires his apartment for clandestine meetings) and >*Irma La Douce* (>Billy Wilder 1963) (✍ ☞ ☆). Unfortunately, his Oscar-winning study of mid-life crisis *Save the Tiger* (John G. Avildsen 1973) (☆) (moralist Lemmon is depressed at having to cook his books, pimp for a client and burn his factory for insurance) is in danger of typecasting him as a menopausal male: *The Prisoner of Second Avenue* (Melvin Frank 1975) (☆) (middle class mediocrity Lemmon loses his job and his frustration grows as his wife Anne Bancroft finds work, his neighbours irritate him and his house is burgled) and *That's Life* (Blake Edwards 1986) (hypochon-

driac Lemmon comes to value his health when his wife Julie Andrews falls ill).

•*Mister Roberts* (AA: >Mervyn Le Roy 1955) (☆): Lemmon as a cocky ensign alongside >Henry Fonda, >James Cagney and >William Powell lamenting the lack of naval action.

•*Days of Wine and Roses* (Blake Edwards 1962) (☆): Lemmon and his wife Lee Remick are driven to the bottle by the pressures and disappointments of their small lives.

•*How to Murder Your Wife* (Richard Quine 1965) (☆ ✍): cartoonist Lemmon's strip suggests he has murdered his own wife when she goes missing.

•*The Out-Of-Towners* (Arthur Hiller 1970) (☆ ✍): Sandy Dennis accompanies Lemmon for an interview, but as disasters pile upon each other they begin to hate New York.

•*Avanti!* (>Billy Wilder 1972) (☆ ☞ ✍ ♫ ▓): Lemmon falls for Juliet Mills, and discovers that her mother was his lately-dead father's mistress.

•*Mass Appeal* (Glenn Jordan 1985) (☆): Lemmon's priest struggles to answer the penetrating question of faith and morality posed by a doubting student.

LESBIANISM

Another Way (Egymásra Nézve) (Károly Makk 1982) ☆ ☞
Jadwiga Jankowska-Cieslak won Cannes Best Actress as the journalist who kills her husband to be with her lover during the Hungarian uprising.

The Children's Hour (UK: The Loudest Whisper) (>William Wyler 1961) ☞
A schoolgirl accuses Audrey Hepburn and teacher Shirley MacLaine of lesbianism, in Lillian Hellman's script from her play.

Club de Femme (Jacques Deval 1936) ✍
Lesbianism, transvestism and prostitution in a Parisian women's hostel.

Desert Hearts (Donna Deitch 1986) ☆ ▓
Staid academic Helen Shaver goes to Reno for a divorce and is seduced by Patricia Charbonneau.

Desperate Living (John Walters 1977) ☞
A lunatic kills her husband and heads for a town populated by lesbians and eccentrics.

The Killing of Sister George (Robert Aldrich 1969) ☆ ✍
Susannah York deserts TV actress Beryl Reid when her fame begins to fade.

Lianna (John Sayles 1984) ☆
Linda Griffiths leaves her family when she falls in love and causes a neighbourhood scandal.

Pandora's Box (aka *Lulu*) (*Die Büchse der Pandora*) (>G. W. Pabst 1929) ☆ ☞ ■
Femme fatale Louise Brooks' lovers include a countess (Alice Roberts).

Personal Best (Robert Towne 1982) ☆
Olympic athlete Mariel Hemingway's training is sidetracked by romance.

The Vampire Lovers (Roy Ward Baker 1970) ✍
Peter Cushing fatally cures Ingrid Pitt of her addiction to young girls' blood.

LETTERS

Address Unknown (William Cameron Menzies 1944) ✍
Paul Lukas is a Nazi but he is innocent of the crimes detailed in forged letters.

Dangerous Liaisons (Stephen Frears 1988) ☆ ☞ ■ ✍
Glenn Close bets John Malkovich he can't seduce virginal Michelle Pfeiffer in this screen version of the 18th-century epistolary classic *Les Liaisons Dangereuses*.

84 Charing Cross Road (David Jones 1987) ☆
Anne Bancroft loves bookseller Anthony Hopkins by mail.

The Letter (>William Wyler 1940) ☞ ☆ ✍
>Bette Davis claims that the death of her lover was self-defence, but a letter betrays her to her husband Herbert Marshall.

Letter from an Unknown Woman (>Max Ophüls 1948) ☞ ☆ ■
>Joan Fontaine tolerates Louis Jourdan's philandering in 19th-century Vienna.

A Letter to Three Wives (>Joseph L. Mankiewicz 1949) ✍ ☞ ☆
Three women imagine their husbands' adultery when a local spitfire writes that one of them is her lover.

Letters from a Dead Man (*Pisma Myortvovo Chelovyeka*) (Konstantin Lopushansky 1987) ■ ☞
An academic describes post-holocaust life in letters to his missing son.

Lonelyhearts (Vincent J. Donehue 1958) ☆
Robert Ryan makes life hell for drunken wife >Myrna Loy and over-involved agony columnist Montgomery Clift.

The Lost Moment (Martin Gabel 1947) ✍
A publisher seeks the *billets doux* of a famous poet in Venice.

Love Letters (>William Dieterle 1945) ☞ ♫
Jennifer Jones discovers that the letters she treasures were not written by her lover.

Macaroni (*Maccheroni*) (Ettore Scola 1985) ☞ ☆ ✍
For forty years, >Marcello Mastroianni has been sending letters to his sister pretending they are from her GI lover, >Jack Lemmon.

Poison Pen (Paul Stein 1939) ☆ ✍
Flora Robson spreads scandal around her village with vitriolic missives.

LIARS

The Adventures of Baron Munchhausen (Terry Gilliam 1988) ☞ ✳
John Neville as the tall-tale-telling noble who fights the Turks and flies to the moon.

Autumn Leaves (Robert Aldrich 1956) ✍
>Joan Crawford marries toyboy Cliff Robertson, but she cannot believe a word he says.

The Bad Seed (>Mervyn Le Roy 1956) ☆ ☞ ✍
A mother discovers that her small daughter is a lying murderess.

Baron Munchhausen (*Baron Prasil*) (Karel Zeman 1962) ✳ ■
An astronaut accompanies Milos Kopecky on his adventures against beautiful cartoon backdrops.

Billy Liar (>John Schlesinger 1963) ☞ ☆ ✍ ■
Tom Courtenay as Keith Waterhouse and Willis Hall's fibber who dreams of everything but the realities of life.

Real Life (Francis Megahy 1983) ☆
Rupert Everett's lies embroil him in a series of thefts.
The Supergrass (Peter Richardson 1985) ☆
The police believe Adrian Edmondson's invented drug smuggling story.
The Window (Ted Tetzlaff 1949) ☞ ☆
Slum boy Bobby Driscoll cries wolf once too often over a New York murder.

LIGHTHOUSES

Back Room Boy (Herbert Mason 1942) ☆
Arthur Askey captures Nazis off the Scottish coast.
Captain January (David Butler 1936) ☆
Shirley Temple helps Guy Kibbee and Buddy Ebsen keep their lighthouse.
The Phantom Light (>Michael Powell 1934) ☞ ☆
Gordon Harker refuses to be scared away by a gang of shipwreckers.
The Seventh Survivor (Leslie Hiscott 1941) ✍
One of seven survivors collected at a lighthouse is a Nazi spy.
Thunder Rock (Roy Boulting 1942) ☆ ☞ ✍ ▇
Michael Redgrave is haunted by ghosts of drowned 19th-century immigrants James Mason and Lilli Palmer.
Tower of Evil (Jim O'Connolly 1972)
A lighthouse is affected by malevolent spirits.
The Tower of Terror (Lawrence Huntington 1941) ☆
World War II spies feud on a rock tended by an eccentric keeper.

LINERS AND OTHER CRAFT

And the Ship Sails On (E le Nave Va) (>Federico Fellini 1983) ▇ ☞
Celebrities accompany a singer's ashes en route to an island burial in the summer of 1914.
Anything Goes (Lewis Milestone 1936) ✍
Cast of a floating review sort out their romantic problems in this P. G. Wodehouse/Guy Bolton/Cole Porter musical.

The Captain's Table (Jack Lee 1958) ☆ ✍
Rough seaman John Gregson is put in charge of a luxury liner.
Carry On Cruising (Gerald Thomas 1961) ☆ ✍
The passengers and crew band together to celebrate Sid James' last cruise as captain.
China Seas (Tay Garnett 1935) ☆
>Clark Gable and >Jean Harlow have enough problems with Wallace Beery without pirates too.
The Great Lover (Alexander Hall 1949) ☆ ✍
Bob Hope's unprepared scoutmaster catches killer Roland Young on an ocean-going liner with the help of Rhonda Fleming.
Lifeboat (>Alfred Hitchcock 1944) ☞ ✍ ☆
Survivors dispute the trustworthiness of a Nazi U-boat skipper in their ranks.
Love Affair (>Leo McCarey 1939) ☞ ☆ ✍
Irene Dunne's accident prevents her renewing contact with shipboard lover Charles Boyer.
A Night to Remember (Roy Baker 1958) ☆ ✍
Kenneth More mans the lifeboats as the *Titanic* sinks in 1912.
Outward Bound (Robert Milton 1930) ☆ ✍
>Leslie Howard is among the passengers on a one-way trip to purgatory.
A Ship Bound for India (aka The Land of Desire) (US: Frustration) (Skepp Till Indialand) (>Ingmar Bergman 1947) ☞
A salvage skipper and his hunchback son squabble over a dancer.

Little Dorrit ✍ ☞ ☆ ▇
GB • Curzon • 1987 • 357 mins • col
wd Christine Edzard **ph** Bruno De Keyzer **m** Giuseppe Verdi
>Alec Guinness, Derek Jacobi, Sarah Pickering, Miriam Margolyes, Joan Greenwood, Max Wall, Eleanor Bron

Dividing >Charles Dickens' mammoth novel into two films – *Nobody's Fault* and *Little Dorrit's Story* – Christine Edzard traces the romance of bankrupted engineer Arthur Clennam (Jacobi) and the eponymous heroine (Pickering) through the eyes of each, neatly uniting the threads in a whodunnit-like finale.

While perhaps guilty of missing the opportunity to contrast current worldwide economic theories with the evils of Victorian self-help and occasionally of interpreting 'Dickensian' as shabby grandeur rather than miserable deprivation, particularly in the case of William Dorrit (Guinness), the film never allows the story of the lovers' contrasting fortunes to sprawl out of control, remaining throughout a visual and dramatic delight.

 •>Boris Karloff consigns Anna Lee to a cell for daring to criticize his Victorian institution, in *Bedlam* (Mark Robson 1946) (☆).

•Carpenter Serge Reggiani loses his respectability when he falls for moll Simone Signoret, in *Casque d'Or* (US: *Golden Marie*) (Jacques Becker 1952) (☆ ☞ ■).

•>Michael Redgrave has the interests of the workers at heart as he rises to political prominence, in *Fame is the Spur* (Roy Boulting 1947) (☆).

•John Hurt is subjected to the miseries and exploitation of London lowlife, in *The Elephant Man* (David Lynch 1980) (■ ☆ ✍ ☞ ✳).

•19th-century travelling medicine man Edward Arnold is accompanied from rags to riches by >Cary Grant in the biopic of financier Jim Fisk *The Toast of New York* (Rowland V. Lee 1937) (☆).

LIVING DEAD

City of the Dead (US: *Horror Hotel*) (John Moxey 1960) ☆
A burned witch lures victims to her hotel 250 years later.

The Ghost Breakers (George Marshall 1940) ☆ ✍ ☞
Bob Hope and Paulette Goddard survive zombies and live happily ever after in her Caribbean castle.

The Ghoul (T. Hayes Hunter 1933) ☆
>An Egyptian jewel theft is foiled by the resurrected professor Boris Karloff.

The House of Usher (UK: *The Fall of the House of Usher*) (Roger Corman 1960) ☆ ■
Vincent Price is haunted by his buried-alive sister in this Edgar Allan Poe tale.

I Walked with a Zombie (Jacques Tourneur 1943) ☞ ■
A nurse tends to a planter's voodoo-cursed wife and nearly succumbs herself.

Night of the Living Dead (George A. Romero 1968) ✍
Radioactive zombies hunt human flesh in a once peaceful small town.

The Plague of the Zombies (John Gilling 1965) ✍
Cornish squire André Morell uses corpse labour in his tin mine.

The Return of the Living Dead (Dan O'Bannon 1986) ✍ ✳
Leaked gas unleashes a graveyard full of brain-hungry zombies.

White Zombie (Victor Halperin 1932) ☆
>Bela Lugosi uses Haitian zombies in his sugar mill.

LOLITAS

A Nos Amours (UK: *To Our Loves*) (Maurice Pialat 1983) ☆ ☞
Neglected Sandrine Bonnaire is free with her favours in the hope of finding real affection.

Baby Doll (>Elia Kazan 1956) ☞ ☆
Karl Malden's child bride Carroll Baker is seduced by his business rival Eli Wallach.

Lolita (>Stanley Kubrick 1962) ☞ ☆ ✍
Academic James Mason marries Sue Lyon's mother Shelley Winters to be closer to her, in the screen version of Vladimir Nabokov's notorious novel.

Middle of the Night (Delbert Mann 1959) ☆
Ageing businessman >Fredric March falls for Kim Novak.

The Miracle of Morgan's Creek (>Preston Sturges 1943) ☞ ✍ ☆
A do-gooder's attempts to help a pregnant young girl disrupt a prejudiced country town.

Pretty Baby (>Louis Malle 1978) ☞ ☆
Brooke Shields' virginity is sold to the highest bidder in Susan Sarandon's brothel.

A Summer Affair (US: *One Wild Moment*) (*Un Moment d'Égarement*) (Claude Berri 1977) ✍ ☞
The last person a father suspects of sleeping with his teenage daughter is his best friend.

Sundays and Cybèle (Cybèle ou les Dimanches de Ville d'Avray) **(Serge Bourgignon 1962)** ✍ ☞ ■

Best Foreign Film Oscar-winning tale of an amnesiac pilot spending Christmas in the forest with a 12-year-old orphan.

That Certain Age **(Edward Ludwig 1938)** ☆

Deanna Durbin falls for Melvyn Douglas, a reporter on her father's newspaper.

Lombard, Carole

(Jane Alice Peters) American actress (1908–1942)

Originally cast because of her teen tomboyish involvement in a street baseball game, Lombard's comic gift and glamour enabled her to effortlessly progress from slapstick shorts to screwball: *Fast and Loose* (Fred Newmeyer 1930) (☆ ✍) (while rich Miriam Hopkins loves a mechanic, her brother loves chorus girl Carole, in a script with added >Preston Sturges dialogue); *It Pays To Advertise* (Frank Tuttle 1931) (☆) (Carole boosts mild-mannered Norman Foster to success), *Twentieth Century* (>Howard Hawks 1934) (☆ ☞ ✍) (Lombard's actress rebels against her Svengali, Lionel Barrymore); *My Man Godfrey* (Gregory La Cava 1936) (☆) (millionaire >William Powell acts as butler to Carole's eccentric family); *Nothing Sacred* (>William Wellman 1937) (☆ ☞ ✍) (dying Carole is turned into a brave heroine by >Fredric March's newspaper, but she isn't really ill); *Mr and Mrs Smith* (>Alfred Hitchcock 1941) (☞ ☆ ✍) (Carole discovers her marriage to Robert Montgomery is not legal and plays hard to get before retying the knot); and *To Be or Not to Be* (>Ernst Lubitsch 1942) (☞ ✍ ☆) (Polish acting troupe led by Jack Benny and Carole impersonate Hitler's retinue in an underground plot). Married to >William Powell before >Clark Gable, she was killed in a plane crash on a bond-selling tour in 1942.

VIEW ON ▶ •*Man of the World* (Richard Wallace 1931) (☆): >William Powell falls for Carole while conning tycoons in Paris.

•*I Take This Woman* (Marion Gering 1931)

(☆): socialite Carole goes to live on >Gary Cooper's ranch.

•*No Man of Her Own* (Wesley Ruggles 1932) (☆ ☞): >Clark Gable tries to prevent Carole finding out he married her for a wager.

•*White Woman* (Stuart Walker 1933) (☆): singer Carole endures the hardship of jungle life as >Charles Laughton's wife in Malaysia.

•*Supernatural* (Victor Halperin 1933) (☆ ■): widowed Lombard is possessed by a murderess seeking revenge on a clairvoyant who has cheated them both.

•*Bolero* (Wesley Ruggles 1934) (☆ ☞): Carole is powerless as dancer George Raft is lured away by the bright lights.

•*Fools for Scandal* (>Mervyn Le Roy 1938) (☆): French noble Fernand Gravet acts as butler to film star Carole.

•*Made for Each Other* (John Cromwell 1939) (☆): >James Stewart and Lombard's marriage is saved by their son's illness.

•*In Name Only* (John Cromwell 1939) (☆ ✍ ☞): >Cary Grant wants to marry Carole but Kay Francis won't divorce him.

•*Vigil in the Night* (>George Stevens 1940) (☆): Carole as a selfless nurse sacrificing her life helping Brian Aherne in this screen version of A. J. Cronin's novel.

•*They Knew What They Wanted* (Garson Kanin 1940) (☆ ☞): Carole marries >Charles Laughton by post under the impression he is handsome vineyard foreman William Gargan.

London

Brannigan **(Douglas Hickox 1975)** ☆

>John Wayne and >Richard Attenborough employ different tactics to get their man.

Frenzy **(>Alfred Hitchcock 1972)** ☞

Barry Foster is a necktie killer in Covent Garden.

The Long Good Friday **(John Mackenzie 1980)** ☆ ✍ ♫

Gangster Bob Hoskins has trouble with rival gangs and the IRA.

Otley **(Dick Clement 1968)** ☆

Dreamer Tom Courtenay finds himself involved with a spy ring.

Passport to Pimlico **(Henry Cornelius 1949)**
✍ ☆

An ancient treaty shows that part of the capital is owned by the Dukes of Burgundy.

Piccadilly Jim **(Robert Z. Leonard 1936)** ✍

P. G. Wodehouse tale has cartoonist Robert Montgomery lampooning his father's would-be in-laws.

A Run for Your Money **(Charles Frend 1949)** ☆ ✍

>Alec Guinness leads some Welsh rugby fans on a merry dance around the city.

Sammy and Rosie Get Laid **(Stephen Frears 1987)** ☞

Inter-racial romance and social deprivation in Thatcher's London.

Up for the Cup **(Jack Raymond 1931)** ✍

Yorkshireman Sydney Howard experiences the North/South divide when he heads for Wembley for the Cup Final.

LONELINESS

The Enchanted Cottage **(John Cromwell 1945)** ☆

Dorothy McGuire and Robert Young fall in love as the cottage refuses to allow them to see each other's physical deficiencies.

Life Upside Down **(La Vie à l'Envers) (Alain Jessua 1964)** ☞

A contented man suddenly withdraws from life and is placed in solitary confinement.

Lonelyhearts **(Vincent J. Donehue 1958)** ☆

Montgomery Clift is affected by the human tragedies he discovers as a newspaper's agony aunt.

Man Friday **(Jack Gold 1975)**

Peter O'Toole discovers that Richard Roundtree's Friday wasn't born yesterday.

Miss Mary **(Maria Luisa Bemberg 1986)** ☞ ☆

Governess Julie Christie seeks solace in her Argentinian teenage charge.

A New Leaf **(Elaine May 1970)** ☆ ✍

Playboy Walter Matthau needs a rich wife to replenish his dwindling wealth.

Rachel, Rachel **(>Paul Newman 1968)** ☆ ☞

Dowdy teacher Joanne Woodward scandalizes her small town with her first affair.

This Sweet Sickness **(Dîtes-lui Que Je l'Aime) (Claude Miller 1977)** ☆ ✍

>Gérard Depardieu spends his weekends at the mountain retreat he built for a woman who has married someone else.

Lorre, Peter

(Laszlo Löwenstein) Hungarian-born actor (1904–1964)

Lorre's role as the child killer hunted by both police and underworld in >Fritz Lang's *M* (1931) (☞ ☆ ■) moulded the actor's screen image of mournful murderer, reinforced by his work in >Alfred Hitchcock's *The Man Who Knew Too Much* (1934) (☞ ✍) (dentist Leslie Banks's child is abducted by Lorre's spies to prevent him exposing their activities) and *The Secret Agent* (1936) (Lorre is the target of unwilling spy John Gielgud) – an image that both sustained and stifled Lorre's Hollywood career. *Mr Moto Takes a Chance* (Norman Foster 1938) (☆) (Lorre and aviatrix Rochelle Hudson uncover a revolt in a Cambodian prince's household), the best of the eight 'B'-movies he made portraying the Japanese detective, preceded his fabled partnership with Sydney Greenstreet: *The Maltese Falcon* (>John Huston 1941) (☞ ☆ ■ ✍) (>Humphrey Bogart beats the evil duo to the eponymous statue); *Background to Danger* (>Raoul Walsh 1943) (☆) (the pair as Nazi nasties pursued by George Brent in this screen version of the Eric Ambler novel *Uncommon Danger*); *The Mask of Dimitrios* (Jean Negulesco 1944) (the bad lads are on the tail of Zachary Scott as he follows the clues leading to a fortune); *Passage to Marseilles* (>Michael Curtiz 1944) (☆) (Lorre and Greenstreet join >Humphrey Bogart in escaping from Devil's Island); and *The Verdict* (Don Siegel 1946) (☆) (nosey Lorre hinders Scotland Yard man Greenstreet, who having been sacked for incompetence, commits a murder of his own to show up his successor). Little of note followed his performance in *The Beast with Five Fingers* (Robert Florey 1946) (☆) (only Lorre can see the severed hand of a dead pianist committing crimes).

•*Mad Love* (UK: *The Hands of Orlac*) (Karl Freund 1935) (☆ ☞): Lorre as a mad surgeon transplanting killers' hands on to pianist Colin Clive.

•*Crime and Punishment* (>Josef Von Sternberg 1935) (☞ ☆): Lorre as an impoverished student racked by guilt after a murder.

•*The Face Behind the Mask* (Robert Florey 1941) (☆ ■): disfigured Lorre takes to crime in bitterness.

•*All Through the Night* (Vincent Sherman 1942) (☆): gangsters >Humphrey Bogart and Lorre smoke out Conrad Veidt's Nazi infiltrators.

•*The Cross of Lorraine* (Tay Garnett 1944) (✍): German guard Lorre is powerless as >Gene Kelly leads a rising in an occupied French village.

•*The Raven* (Roger Corman 1963) (☆ ☞): 15th-century wizards Vincent Price and >Boris Karloff embroil Lorre in their battle of spells.

Losey, Joseph
American director (1909–1984)

Harvard undergraduate and student of >Eisenstein, Losey's theatre successes led to *The Boy with Green Hair* (1948) (☞) (Dean Stockwell's hair discolours at the loss of his parents in the Blitz) and *The Prowler* (1951) (☞) (cop Van Heflin commits murder with Evelyn Keyes after her emergency call). Blacklisted in 1951, he came to Britain, struggling to adapt until *Blind Date* (US: *Chance Meeting*) (1959) (☞) (artist Hardy Kruger is falsely accused of the murder of his mistress). His best work came in collaboration with Harold Pinter – *The Servant* (1963) (☞ ✍ ☆) (Dirk Bogarde takes over the life of his employer James Fox), *Accident* (1967) (☆ ■ ☞) (Dirk Bogarde's life is turned upside down during one Oxford summer by Michael York and Stanley Baker), and *The Go-Between* (1971) (✍ ☞ ☆) (a young boy conveys messages between Alan Bates and Julie Christie in Pinter's adaptation of L. P. Hartley's novel) – although Losey's favourite 'dangerous liaisons' theme was also prominent in *Boom!* (1968) (☞ ☆) (Elizabeth Taylor's last lover >Richard Burton proves to be the Angel of Death), *Secret Ceremony* (1968) (☞ ☆) (Mia Farrow moulds prostitute Elizabeth Taylor

into a replica of her mother), *Figures in a Landscape* (1970) (☞) (Robert Shaw and Malcolm McDowell in a race for sanctuary beyond the border) and *Mr Klein* (1977) (☞) (Alain Delon assumes the identity of a mysterious Jewish namesake in occupied Paris).

 •*The Sleeping Tiger* (1954) (☞ ☆): gunman Dirk Bogarde moves in with his psychoanalyst and attracts his wife.

•*The Intimate Stranger* (aka *Finger of Guilt*) (directed as Joseph Walton 1956): studio boss Richard Basehart has to prevent his wife finding out about a blackmailing ex-mistress and a flirtatious actress.

•*Time without Pity* (1957) (☆): drunken father Michael Redgrave mounts an eleventh hour attempt to prove his son's innocence of murder.

•*The Criminal* (US: *The Concrete Jungle*) (1960) (✍): accomplices watch Stanley Baker's every move as he knows where the loot is stashed.

•*Eva* (1962) (✍): novelist Stanley Baker is manipulated by gold-digging Jeanne Moreau on a Venetian holiday.

•*Modesty Blaise* (1966) (☞): comic strip heroine Monica Vitti foils diamond smuggling operation.

•*A Doll's House* (1973) (☞ ✍): >Jane Fonda rebels against husband David Warner, in Henrik Ibsen's play.

•*Galileo* (1975) (☞ ■): Topol as the astrologer persecuted for his ideas by the Inquisition.

•*Don Giovanni* (1979) (♫ ■): Mozart's opera of the adventures of the great lover.

•*Steaming* (1984): Vanessa Redgrave and Sarah Miles amongst those with problems at a London sauna.

LOVE TRIANGLES

Adieu Philippine (Jacques Rozier 1962) ☞
Having a final fling before military service, Jean-Claude Amini has two holiday romances.
Alexander's Ragtime Band (Henry King 1938) ☞ ♫
Songwriters Tyrone Power and Don Ameche feud over star Alice Faye.

King, Queen, Knave (Herzube) **(Jerzy Skolimowski 1972)** ☆ ☞

This adaptation of Vladimir Nabokov's novel has an orphan coming between David Niven and Gina Lollobrigida.

Max, My Love (Max, Mon Amour) **(Nagisa Oshima 1986)** ☞ ✍

Diplomat Anthony Higgins shares his home with Charlotte Rampling and her chimpanzee lover.

The Mother and the Whore (La Maman et la Putain) **(Jean Eustache 1973)** ✍ ☞

Cannes Special Jury winner shows the good times and the demise of a *ménage à trois*.

My Best Friend's Girl (La Femme de mon Pote) **(Bertrand Blier 1983)** ☞

Isabelle Huppert comes between a ski instructor and his slobbish businessman friend.

The Return of the Soldier **(Alan Bridges 1983)** ☆ ■

Shellshocked Alan Bates remembers his mistress but not his wife.

Rita, Sue and Bob Too **(Alan Clarke 1987)** ✍

A Bradford Lothario seduces two babysitters.

These Three **(>William Wyler 1936)** ☞ ☆

A schoolgirl accuses teachers Merle Oberon and Miriam Hopkins of a *ménage* with Joel McCrea.

The Unbearable Lightness of Being **(Philip Kaufman 1988)** ☆ ☞ ■ ✍

Milan Kundera novel sees Daniel Day Lewis marry Juliette Binoche and sleep with Lena Olin during the 1968 Czech uprising.

Wife Versus Secretary **(Clarence Brown 1936)** ☆ ✍ ☞

Wife >Myrna Loy is sure >Clark Gable is having an affair with secretary >Jean Harlow.

Loy, Myrna

(Myrna Williams) American actress (b 1905)

Proclaimed 'Queen of Hollywood', ruling alongside King >Gable, Myrna Loy progressed to the role of 'perfect wife' through a series of villainous Orientals – *Across the Pacific* (Roy Del Ruth 1925) (☆) (island girl Myrna lures Monte Blue before he returns to his true love Jane Winton) – spies (black too) – *Ham and Eggs at the Front* (Roy Del Ruth 1927) (regrettable spoof on coloured troops in the trenches)

– gypsies – *The Squall* (Alexander Korda 1929) (☆) (Myrna breaks the hearts of farmers Carroll Nye and Richard Tucker) – schemers – *A Connecticut Yankee* (David Butler 1931) (☆ ✍) (Myrna plots to prevent time travelling Will Rogers living happily with Maureen O'Sullivan) – and 'sadistic nymphomaniac' – *The Mask of Fu Manchu* (Charles Brabin 1932) (☆) (Loy as >Boris Karloff's daughter waylaying Lewis Stone's Nayland Smith). Her performance as Nora Charles in >*The Thin Man* (W. S. Van Dyke 1934) (☆ ☞ ✍) – and the subsequent series – transformed Loy's career, the beautiful, unflappable wife with an answer for everything becoming the trademark stamped on to: *Wife versus Secretary* (Clarence Brown 1936) (☆ ✍ ☞) (Myrna believes >Clark Gable is having an affair with >Jean Harlow); *Libeled Lady* (Jack Conway 1936) (☆ ✍ ☞) (>Spencer Tracy dispatches >William Powell to marry Myrna out of suing their paper, but >Jean Harlow claims she is already Mrs Powell); *Double Wedding* (Richard Thorpe 1937) (☆ ✍) (artist >William Powell prevents meddlesome Myrna running everyone's lives, then marries her); *I Love You Again* (W. S. Van Dyke 1940) (☆ ✍) (Myrna marries dullard >William Powell, but he proves to be an amnesiac con man); >*The Best Years of Our Lives* (>William Wyler 1946) (☆ ☞ ✍ ■); and *Bachelor Knight* (US: *The Bachelor and the Bobbysoxer*) (Irving Reis 1947) (☆ ✍) (Shirley Temple tries to steal judge sister Myrna's man >Cary Grant); *Mr Blandings Builds His Dream House* (H. C. Potter 1948) (☆ ✍) (Myrna gets sympathy from Melvyn Douglas as pompous >Cary Grant fusses over the construction of a new home); and *Cheaper by the Dozen* (Walter Lang 1950) (the whimsical adventures of Myrna and Clifton Webb and their 12 children). In the 1950s and 1960s she concentrated on political and charity work, making rare cameo appearances such as playing Burt Reynolds' mother, in *The End* (Burt Reynolds 1978).

 •*The Black Watch* (>John Ford 1929) (☆ ☞): Myrna as a descendant of Alexander the Great worshipped as an Indian goddess and by Victor McLaglen.

•*Love Me Tonight* (Rouben Mamoulian 1932): Loy tries to woo tailor Maurice Chevalier away from princess Jeanette MacDonald.

•*Thirteen Women* (George Archainbaud 1932) (☆): Irene Dunne is next on the list as Myrna murders her old classmates.

•*The Animal Kingdom* (UK: *The Woman in His House*) (Edward H. Griffith 1932) (☆): artist >Leslie Howard leaves restrictive Myrna for old love Ann Harding.

•*When Ladies Meet* (Harry Beaumont 1933): novelist Myrna falls for her publisher Robert Montgomery but he is already married to Ann Harding.

•*Men in White* (Richard Boleslawski 1934) (☆): Loy as a spoiled socialite who insists that doctor >Clark Gable puts her before his career.

•*Stamboul Quest* (Sam Wood 1934) (☆): spy Myrna, sent by Lionel Atwill to check on a secrets leak in Constantinople, falls for George Brent.

•*Evelyn Prentice* (William K. Howard 1934) (☆ ✍): Loy believes her husband >William Powell is seeing Rosalind Russell, so she has an affair herself.

•*Broadway Bill* (UK: *Strictly Confidential*) (>Frank Capra 1934): Myrna helps rebellious rich boy Warner Baxter train a winning race-horse.

•*Wings in the Dark* (James Flood 1935) (☆ ■): stunt pilot Myrna finds true love with safe-flying equipment pioneer >Cary Grant.

•*Whipsaw* (Sam Wood 1935) (☆): Myrna loses the jewels she has stolen and searches for them in competition with >Spencer Tracy's FBI agent.

•*Parnell* (John M. Stahl 1937) (☆): >Clark Gable as the 19th-century Irish political leader Charles Stewart Parnell ruined in a scandalous affair with Myrna's Katherine O'Shea.

•*The Red Pony* (Lewis Milestone 1949) (☆ ✍): this John Steinbeck story has Myrna's son blame hired hand Robert Mitchum for the death of his beloved pet.

•*Belles on Their Toes* (Henry Levin 1952) (☆ ✍): now widowed, Myrna raises the *Cheaper by the Dozen* brood and confounds chauvinists to succeed as an engineer.

Lubitsch, Ernst
German-born American director
(1892–1947)

Graduate of the Max Reinhardt theatre company, Lubitsch acted in comic shorts before turning to directing in 1914. The subtle sight gags and gestures that characterized the 'Lubitsch Touch' were early evident in *Madame Dubarry* (1919) (☞ ☆) (Pola Negri as the mistress who came to rule the court of >Emil Jannings' Louis XV) which, renamed *Passion* in the USA, became the single biggest foreign box-office hit of the silent era. Mary Pickford brought him to Hollywood, where his reputation for 'intimate detail' was enhanced by his technically immaculate costume dramas: *Forbidden Paradise* (1924) (☞ ■ ☆) (Pola Negri as Catherine the Great, toys with lover Adolphe Menjou); *Lady Windermere's Fan* (1925) (☞ ☆ ✍) (Ronald Colman's affair causes a society scandal, in this adaptation of Oscar Wilde's play); and *The Student Prince in Old Heidelberg* (1927) (☞) (Ramon Novarro falls for barmaid Norma Shearer). After refining the Talkie musical – *The Love Parade* (1929) (☞ ☆ ■) (Jeanette MacDonald as Queen of Sylvania marries her suave ambassador Maurice Chevalier), *One Hour with You* (co-directed with >George Cukor 1932) (☞ ✍ ☆) (doctor Maurice Chevalier's bedside manner with Genevieve Tobin lands him in trouble with his wife Jeanette MacDonald) and *The Merry Widow* (1934) (☞ ✍ ☆) (bankrupt king Edward Everett Horton sends Maurice Chevalier to charm Jeanette MacDonald into bolstering the economy) – Lubitsch embarked on his celebrated sophisticated comedies: >*Trouble in Paradise* (1932) (☞ ✍ ☆ ■); *Design for Living* (1933) (☞ ✍ ☆) (>Gary Cooper and >Fredric March both love Miriam Hopkins so they share a house in Ben Hecht's version of the Noël Coward play); and *Angel* (1937) (☞ ☆ ✍) (diplomat Herbert Marshall neglects >Marlene Dietrich into the arms of friend Melvyn Douglas). The humour sharpened in his later films: >*Ninotchka* (1939) (✍ ☞ ☆ ■); *To Be or Not to Be* (1942) (☞ ✍ ☆) (Warsaw actors Jack Benny and >Carole Lombard impersonate Hitler and his retinue in a Resistance plot) and *Heaven Can Wait* (AAN: 1943) (☞ ✍ ☆) (Satan

Laird Cregar is disappointed with playboy Don Ameche's notorious antics).

 •*The Eyes of the Mummy* (*Die Augen der Mummie Ma*) (1918) (☞ ☆): >Emil Jannings keeps Pola Negri in a tomb until Harry Liedtke comes along.

•*The Oyster Princess* (*Die Austernprinzessin*) (1919): an American Quaker's daughter hopes to marry a Prussian prince.

•*The Mountain Cat* (US: *The Wildcat*) (*Die Bergkatze*) (1921) (☞ ☆): Pola Negri prefers an officer to the rogue her father intends for her.

•*The Marriage Circle* (1924) (☞): Monte Blanc commits bigamy with Florence Vidor and Marie Prevost.

•*The Patriot* (AAN: 1928) (☞ ☆): government minister Lewis Stone assassinates >Emil Jannings' Tsar Paul.

•*Monte Carlo* (1930) (☞ ✍): Jeanette MacDonald is torn between a a rich count pretending to be poor and an impoverished prince affecting wealth.

•*Broken Lullaby* (UK: *The Man I Killed*) (1932) (☞ ☆ ✍): Lionel Barrymore goes to Germany to apologise to the family of the man he killed in the trenches.

•*The Shop Around the Corner* (1940) (☞ ✍ ☆): rival shop assistants >James Stewart and Margaret Sullavan prove to be pen pals.

•*Cluny Brown* (1946) (☞ ✍ ☆): émigré academic Charles Boyer prevents clumsy maid Jennifer Jones marrying boring chemist Richard Haydn.

Lugosi, Bela
(Béla Blasko) Hungarian actor (1882–1956)

A Broadway Dracula in 1927, Lugosi was similarly employed throughout his career, ultimately to the point of humiliation, as though studios actually believed he would perish without regular ventures into veins, from >*Dracula* (Tod Browning 1931) (☞ ☆ ■ ✍) through *The Mark of the Vampire* (Tod Browning 1935) (Lugosi is caught up in Lionel Atwill's plot to smoke out a killer by hiring Lionel Barrymore's actors to pose as vampires) to *Old Mother Riley Meets the Vampire* (Maclean Ro-

gers 1952) (Arthur Lucan's pantomime dame puts one over on Bela's Count). Despite refusing >*Frankenstein* in 1931, sinister villains and freaks abounded: *The Black Cat* (Edgar G. Ulmer 1934) (☆) (Lugosi as a satanist who betrayed >Boris Karloff during the First World War); *Son of Frankenstein* (Rowland V. Lee 1939) (☆ ✍) (>Basil Rathbone rebuilds >Boris Karloff aided by Lugosi's Igor); and *The Wolf Man* (George Waggner 1941) (✳ ☆) (Lon Chaney, Jr is bitten by gypsy Lugosi and becomes a werewolf). >*Ninotchka* (>Ernst Lubitsch 1939) (✍ ☞ ☆ ■) suggested better things, but Lugosi's career closed in the pay of the 'turkey' maestro Edward D. Wood Jr, whose seminal *Plan Nine from Outer Space* (1959) (zombie flesh eaters invade earth) was constructed around the seconds of footage filmed before Lugosi's death.

 •*The Murders in the Rue Morgue* (Robert Florey 1931) (✍ ☆ ☞): Lugosi trains an ape to commit a series of Parisian murders.

•*White Zombie* (Victor Halperin 1932) (☆): Lugosi uses zombie labour in his sugar mill.

•*The Raven* (Lew Landers 1935) (☆): Poe-obsessed Lugosi tortures gangster >Boris Karloff to insanity.

•*The Invisible Ray* (Lambert Hillyer 1936) (☆): Lugosi is among the scientists on whom >Boris Karloff wreaks revenge with his radioactive ray.

•*Dark Eyes of London* (aka *The Human Monster*) (Walter Summers 1939) (☆ ✍): Lugosi's insurance salesman disposes of his new clients in a home for the blind.

•*The Return of the Vampire* (Lew Landers 1944) (☆): as if the Nazis weren't enough, Londoners have to put up with Lugosi's Count.

•*Abbott and Costello Meet Frankenstein* (UK: *Abbott and Costello Meet the Ghosts*) (Charles Barton 1948) (☆ ✍): the boys deliver Lugosi's Count, Glenn Strange's Monster and Lon Chaney, Jr's Wolf Man to a waxworks.

•*Bride of the Monster* (Edward D. Wood, Jr 1955) (☆): looking every inch the dying drug addict he was, Lugosi still turns in a superb performance as a scientist whose strength-giving ray does more for an octopus than himself.

Lumet, Sidney
American director (b 1924)

Gaining his directorial experience in television, Lumet's cinema concentrates on the reaction of a group to crime – >*Twelve Angry Men* (1957) (☆ ☞ ✍), *The Hill* (1965) (☞) (>Sean Connery mutinies against the military police during the North Africa campaign), *Child's Play* (1972) (☞) (teacher James Mason is either the victim of fellow masters or of supernatural phenomena), *Murder on the Orient Express* (1974) (✍ ☆) (the >Agatha Christie tale of murder on a snowed-in train) and *Dog Day Afternoon* (AAN: 1975) (☞ ☆) (Al Pacino and accomplice get to know their hostages in a bank siege) – or individuals whose actions are dictated by their emotions rather than reason: *The Fugitive Kind* (1960) (☞) (>Marlon Brando steps off his horse and into trouble with Anna Magnani and Joanne Woodward); *The Appointment* (1969) (Omar Sharif reacts with violence when he jealously suspects his wife Anouk Aimée of whoring); *Serpico* (1974) (☞) (Al Pacino as cop finding corruption has powerful adherents); *Network* (1976) (☆ ☞) (William Holden tries to silence TV celebrity Peter Finch when he begins to speak his mind on air); and *The Verdict* (AAN: 1983) (☆ ☞) (lawyer >Paul Newman makes a court comeback against the arrogant James Mason). Lumet has also successfully adapted a string of stage dramas: *A View from the Bridge* (1961) (✍) (Arthur Miller's drama has a longshoreman breaking down when his niece resists his advances); *Long Day's Journey into Night* (1962) (☆ ✍ ☞) (this Eugene O'Neill play sees Ralph Richardson coping with drug-addicted wife >Katharine Hepburn and his worthless sons); *The Sea Gull* (1968) (✍) (Anton Chekhov's story of family rivalries and loves embroils James Mason, Simone Signoret and Vanessa Redgrave); and *Equus* (1977) (☆ ☞) (>Richard Burton attempts to fathom Peter Firth's fascination with horses).

• *Fail Safe* (1964) (✍ ☞ ☆): President >Henry Fonda prepares to blast New York as a rogue US bomb heads for Moscow.

• *The Pawnbroker* (1965) (☆): Rod Steiger is unable to forget his experiences in a Nazi death camp.

• *The Deadly Affair* (1967) (☞ ☆): James Mason investigates a Foreign Office colleague's suicide, in this adaptation of John Le Carré's novel *Call for the Dead*.

• *Bye Bye Braverman* (1968) (☞): menopause men drink in self-pity after a contemporary's funeral.

• *The Anderson Tapes* (1971) (☆): >Sean Connery plans a robbery, unaware that the police have taped his briefings.

• *The Offence* (1972) (☆ ☞): >Sean Connery is the cop and Ian Bannen the child-molester – at least that's how it seems.

• *Lovin' Molly* (1973) (☆): the lives and disappointments of three brothers, all of whom at one time love Blythe Danner.

• *Just Tell Me What You Want* (1979): Ali McGraw seeks >Myrna Loy's help in loosening a tycoon's possessive grip on her life and career.

• *Running on Empty* (1989) (✍): pianist River Phoenix's talent threatens to expose his parents Christine Lahti and Judd Hirsch who are on the run.

• *Family Business* (1989) (☆ ☞): >Dustin Hoffman, >Sean Connery and Matthew Broderick keep their next robbery in the family.

McCarey, Leo
American writer/director (1898–1969)

Director of slapstick silents for, among others, Charley Chase (*Bad Boy* [1925]), McCarey teamed >Laurel & Hardy in 1926, supervising many of their classic two-reelers and directing *Liberty* (1929) (☆ ✍ ☞) (escapees Stan and Ollie wish they'd stayed put as they end up atop some scaffolding with a crab in Ollie's trousers) and *Wrong Again* (1929) (☆) (Stan and Ollie deliver a horse instead of a painting to irate Del Henderson's house). McCarey's early Talkies involved other prominent comic acts: >the Marx Brothers, (>*Duck Soup* [1933] [☆ ☞ ✍]); >W.C. Fields, (*Six of a Kind* [1934] [☆ ☞] [Fields as a grouchy sheriff joining the chase for buried loot]); and Mae West (*Belle of the Nineties* [1934] [☆ ☞ ✍] [singer Mae is loved by a boxer and a millionaire and pestered by her boss]). Preventing gentle comedy descending into sentiment, McCarey often capped >Capra: *Ruggles of Red Gap* (1935) (☆ ☞ ✍) (>Charles Laughton acts as butler to a Wild West family); *The Awful Truth* (AA: 1937) (☆ ☞ ✍) (>Cary Grant and Irene Dunne decide against divorce at the last moment); *Going My Way* (AA: Direction & Story: 1943) (☞ ✍ ☆)

(priest Barry Fitzgerald is the salt to Bing Crosby's sugar in this tale of parish life) and its sequel *The Bells of St Mary's* (AAN: 1945) (☆ ✍) (Bing Crosby has schoolroom squabbles with >Ingrid Bergman's nun in RKO's biggest earner). *An Affair to Remember* (1957) (☞ ☆) (Deborah Kerr fails to make her reunion with shipboard lover >Cary Grant), a remake of his 1939 *Love Affair* (☞ ☆ ✍) with Irene Dunne and Charles Boyer in the leads, was the best of an indifferent twilight.

 •*The Kid from Spain* (1932) (☞ ☆): Eddie Cantor is a cowardly buffoon, but he looks like a bullfighter.
•*The Milky Way* (1935) (☞ ☆): milkman Harold Lloyd foils Adolphe Menjou's criminal activities.
•*Make Way for Tomorrow* (1937) (☞ ☆): elderly and impoverished Victor Moore and Beulah Bondi have to separate as their children have abandoned them.
•*My Favorite Wife* (1940) (☆ ☞ ✍): Irene Dunne returns from shipwreck to find >Cary Grant has married again.
•*Once Upon a Honeymoon* (1942) (☞ ☆): radio reporter >Cary Grant saves >Ginger Ro-

gers from her Viennese Nazi husband.

•*Good Sam* (1948) (☞ ☆): >Gary Cooper is so benevolent that he bankrupts himself, but he is bailed out by those he has helped.

THE MAFIA

Black Hand (Richard Thorpe 1949) ☆
>Gene Kelly avenges the death of his father.
The Brotherhood (Martin Ritt 1968) ☆
>Kirk Douglas is killed by the brother he loves (Alex Cord).
The Captive City (Robert Wise 1951) ☞
Journalist John Forsythe exposes Mafia corruption in a small town.
Charley Varrick (Don Siegel 1973) ☆
Walter Matthau's crook has been foolish enough to steal Mafia money.
Gloria (John Cassavetes 1980) ☆
A small boy survives his family's slaughter and neighbour Gena Rowlands helps him escape his pursuers.
>*The Godfather Parts I & II* (>Francis Ford Coppola 1972 & 1974) ♫ ☞ ■ ♫ ☆
Prizzi's Honor (>John Huston 1986) ☞ ☆ ♫
Assassins >Kathleen Turner and >Jack Nicholson prove you always kill the one you love.
Rocco and his Brothers (*Rocco e I Suoi Fratelli*) (>Luchino Visconti 1960) ☞
Alain Delon and his family find poverty just as uncompromising in Milan as in southern Italy.
Salvatore Giuliano (Francesco Rosi 1961) ☞ ■
The life and times of a Sicilian gangster.
The Sicilian (Michael Cimino 1986) ☆
Christopher Lambert is a ruthless Mafioso in this film treatment of Mario Puzo's novel.
Things Change (David Mamet 1988) ♫ ☆
Don Ameche is mistaken for the head of a family at a Mafia convention.

MAGICIANS

Eternally Yours (Tay Garnett 1939) ☆
Loretta Young believes David Niven no longer has anything up his sleeve and flirts with Broderick Crawford.
The Face (US: *The Magician*) (*Ansiktet*) (>Ingmar Bergman 1958) ☆ ☞
Max Von Sydow is barred from 19th-century

Stockholm as he uses hypnotism to extort money.
Houdini (George Marshall 1953) ☆
Tony Curtis as the famous escapologist.
The Mad Magician (John Brahm 1954) ☆
Vincent Price butchers those who are preventing his name appearing in lights.
The Magus (Guy Green 1968)
>Michael Caine, Candice Bergen and Anna Karina are among those held on an island by Anthony Quinn.
Mr North (Danny Huston 1988) ☞
An eccentric brings chaos to a small town: watch for hands in a tree catching Anthony Edwards as he swings from a flag pole!...
The Sword in the Stone (Wolfgang Reitherman 1963) ☞
A Disney tale of Merlin educating the young King Arthur.
Yeelen (aka *Brightness*) (Souleymane Cissé 1987) ☞
A village magician in Mali competes with his father for supremacy.

The Magnificent Ambersons ☞ ♫ ☆ ■

USA • RKO • 1942 • 88 mins • b/w
wd >Orson Welles ph Stanley Cortez
m Bernard Herrmann
Joseph Cotten, Dolores Costello, Agnes Moorehead, Tim Holt, Anne Baxter, Ray Collins, Richard Bennett

Welles' flawed masterpiece. Demanding dollars, RKO entrusted Welles with an adaptation of Booth Tarkington's 1919 Pulitzer Prize-winning novel of turn-of-the-century small-town life, hoping for a reproduction of his worthy 1939 radio version. The portrayal of this transient and transitional period, brilliantly evoked by a parade of changing styles and the joyous novelty of a motor-car ride, proved acceptable, but the depiction of the Amberson-Minafers as bigoted, mentally unstable reactionaries, willing to destroy individuals to preserve the whole, was hardly the apple pie, all-American family that the studio aimed to promote. Consequently, Welles was sent to Brazil on an abortive project, and in his absence 43 minutes were cut and a jarring ending, complete with syrupy score, was tacked on. Bloodied, but unbowed.

 •The family snobbery that caused Dennis Price's mother to be exiled explains the comic carnage in >*Kind Hearts and Coronets* (Robert Hamer 1949) (✍ ☆ ☞ ■).

•>William Powell and Irene Dunne have an almost ideal family, providing he can keep his temper, in *Life with Father* (>Michael Curtiz 1947) (☆ ☞ ✍).

•Separated from his mother Theresa Russell at birth, Gary Oldman finds her again to display his disturbed mind, in *Track 29* (Nic Roeg 1988) (☆).

•Sting finds the disturbed atmosphere in Denholm Elliott's household very much to his liking, in *Brimstone and Treacle* (Richard Loncraine 1982) (♫ ☆).

•A different use was found for the *Ambersons'* set when producer Val Lewton hired it for the spooky backgrounds of *Cat People* (Jacques Tourneur 1942) (■ ✍ ☞).

Malle, Louis
French writer/director (b 1932)

Assistant to diver/film-maker Jacques Cousteau, cameraman on Jacques Tati's *Mon Oncle* (1957) (☞ ☆ ✍ ■) (Monsieur Hulot is confronted with a house of the future and its snobbish neighbours) and TV reporter in Algeria and Vietnam, Malle, a member of the 'Left Bank' faction of the New Wave, has demonstrated a similar diversity in his films. He has made absorbing thrillers – *Lift to the Scaffold* (US: *Frantic*) (*Ascenseur pour l'Échafaud*) (1958) (☞ ☆) (Maurice Ronet helps Jeanne Moreau kill her husband only to be nearly convicted for another crime altogether) and *The Thief of Paris* (*Le Voleur*) (1967) (☆ ✍ ☞) (>Jean-Paul Belmondo is taught crime by a priest after being cheated out of his inheritance) – and sordid romances: *The Lovers* (*Les Amants*) (1958) (☞♫ ☆) (Malle won the Venice Special Jury Prize for this tale of housewife Jeanne Moreau's sexual adventures) and *Viva Maria* (1965) (vaudeville stars Jeanne Moreau and Brigitte Bardot encourage George Hamil-

ton to lead a revolution). However, Malle excels in the direction of youth: *Zazie* (*Zazie dans le Métro*) (1960) (☞ ☆ ✍) (female impersonator >Philippe Noiret's promise that his niece can ride the Metro is unfulfilled, but she has plenty of other hilarious adventures), *Dearest Love* (US: *Murmur of the Heart*) (*Le Souffle au Coeur*) (1971) (☞) (a sick boy and his mother turn to incest for consolation at a health spa), *Lacombe, Lucien* (1973) (✍ ☞ ☆) (a teenager who collaborated with the Nazis pays for victimizing one particular family), *Pretty Baby* (1978) (☞ ☆) (Susan Sarandon sells Brooke Shields' virginity to stranger Keith Carradine) and *Au Revoir Les Enfants* (1988) (☞ ✍ ☆ ■) (autobiographical tale of a boy's friendship with a Jew hiding at his boarding school).

 •*A Very Private Affair* (*Vie Privée*) (1962) (☞ ☆): film star Brigitte Bardot has a long-awaited affair with her best friend's husband >Marcello Mastroianni.

•*Le Feu Follet* (aka *Will o'the Wisp*) (US: *The Fire Within*) (aka *A Time to Live, a Time to Die*) (1963) (☞ ✍ ☆): Maurice Ronet gives his friends a chance to talk him out of suicide, but they don't.

•*Spirits of the Dead* (*Histoires Extraordinaires*) (Roger Vadim/>Louis Malle/>Federico Fellini) (1968) (☞ ■): three Poe tales of violent death.

•*Calcutta* (*L'Inde Fantôme*) (1969) (☞ ■): stark view of the vibrance, despair and beauty of this bustling Indian city.

•*Black Moon* (1975) (☞ ■): a kind of *Alice in Wonderland* in which the battle of the sexes is mortal.

•*Atlantic City, USA* (1980) (☞): Malle won the BAFTA Best Director award for this tale of petty thieves planning a gambling con.

•*My Dinner with André* (1981) (☞): André Gregory cures his writer's block at a meal with Wallace Shawn.

•*Alamo Bay* (1985) (☞ ☆): a Vietnamese immigrant is victimized by racist Texan fishermen.

MAN MADE MONSTER (UK: THE ELECTRIC MAN)
(George Waggner 1940) ☆

CLASSIC HORROR

>*DRACULA*
(Tod Browning 1931) ☞ ☆ ■ ✍
(vampire >Bela Lugosi comes to terrorize Whitby)

>*FRANKENSTEIN*
(James Whale 1931) ☆ ☞ ✍ ✳ ■
(scientist loses control of freak creation >Boris Karloff)

THE MUMMY
(Karl Freund 1932) ☆ ✍
(archaeologist's find >Boris Karloff resurrects to terrify London)

THE WOLF MAN
(George Waggner 1940) ✳ ☆
(aristocrat Lon Chaney, Jr becomes a werewolf)

THE PHANTOM OF THE OPERA
(Rupert Julian 1925)/(Arthur Lubin 1943)/(Terence Fisher 1962) ☆
(Lon Chaney, Claude Rains and Herbert Lom respectively as disfigured musician who kidnaps opera singer)

SINISTER HOUSES

THE UNINVITED
(Lewis Allen 1944) ✍ ☞ ☆
(Gail Russell's ghost moves into Ray Milland and her daughter Ruth Hussey's home)

THE HOUSE OF WAX
(André De Toth 1953) ☆ ✍ ■
(sculptor Vincent Price makes wax models from his victims)

THE HOUSE THAT DRIPPED BLOOD (Peter John Duffell)
(1970) ✍
(four stories of a doom-laden domicile)

SUSPIRIA
(Dario Argento 1976) ☞
(hidden secrets of a girls' dance school)

THE AMITYVILLE HORROR
(Stuart Rosenberg 1979)
(James Brolin and Margot Kidder driven from home by cast of brutal murder)

VAMPIRES

THE VAMPIRE LOVERS
(Roy Ward Baker 1970) ✍
(lesbian vampire preys on the privileged)

BLACULA
(William Crane 1972)
(African prince stalks victims in Los Angeles)

ZOLTAN, HOUND OF DRACULA
(US: *DRACULA'S DOG*)
(Albert Bland 1977) ✍
(a canine not afraid to use his incisors)

THE LOST BOYS
(Joel Schumacher 1987) ■
(brutal teenage vampires in modern West Coast America)

NEAR DARK
(Kathryn Bigelow 1987) ✍
(farm boy saved from vampire curse by love)

Lon Chaney, Jr in
man-with-electricity-in-veins shocker

MODERN NASTIES

THE TEXAS CHAINSAW MASSACRE
(Tobe Hooper 1974)
(maniac slices through young weekenders)

HALLOWEEN
(John Carpenter 1978)
(small town threatened by escapee from Donald Pleasance's asylum)

FRIDAY THE 13TH
(Sean S. Cunningham 1980)
(summer camp terrorized by gruesome killer Jason)

POLTERGEIST
(Tobe Hooper 1982)
(psychic girl, TV set and old cemetery spell trouble)

A NIGHTMARE ON ELM STREET
(Wes Craven 1984)
(Freddie Kruger and a cursed house scares wits out of decent family)

SPOOF HORROR

THE GHOST TRAIN
(Walter Forde 1931) ✍
(stranded passengers expose smugglers' fake ghosts)

THE OLD DARK HOUSE
(James Whale 1932) ☆ ✍ ☞ ▉
(travellers endure butler >Charles Laughton and a house full of eccentrics)

AN AMERICAN WEREWOLF IN LONDON
(John Landis 1981) ✳ ☆ ✍ ☞
(US tourist savaged by monster on the Yorkshire moors stalks the capital)

GHOSTBUSTERS
(Ivan Reitman 1984) ♫
(incompetent exorcists fight powers of darkness)

FRIGHT NIGHT
(Tom Holland 1985) ✍
(cowardly TV star Roddy McDowall conquers fears and a vampire)

Manhattan 🖉 ☞ ▤ ♫ ☆

USA • United Artists • 1979 • 96 mins • b/w
d >Woody Allen w >Woody
Allen/Marshall Brickman ph Gordon
Willis m George Gershwin & others
>Woody Allen, >Diane Keaton, Mariel
Hemingway, >Meryl Streep, Michael
Murphy

Another homage to a hero (not >Bogart this
time, but New York), a further lament on the
seeming impossibility of lasting love and a
fresh assault on the pretensions of pseudo-in-
tellectuals. There is little wonder that Woody
Allen plays restless neurotics, for the adulterous, pompous highbrows who populate his
world are unbearable. Isaac Davies (Allen) is
similarly cursed, suffering from a shallow best
friend (Murphy) and an ex-wife (Streep) who is
about to publish a book dissecting their marriage, but he *is* loved by the bright, genuine
Tracy (Hemingway), is a creative success and
should have the sense to recognize Keaton's
artificial intellectualism. Only when his affair
with her fails and, in the familiar role of victim,
he recognizes Tracy's worth, does he regain
our sympathy. Harder work than >*Annie Hall*
(1977) (🖉 ☆ ☞), but more rewarding.

•New York is shown to good effect
as scatty call girl Audrey Hepburn
leads writer George Peppard on a
merry dance, in *Breakfast at Tiffany's* (Blake
Edwards 1961) (☞ ☆).
•Another hometown homage is *Berlin: Symphony of a Great City* (*Berlin, die Symphonie
einer Großstadt*) (Walter Ruttman 1927) (▤
☞).
•Jill Clayburgh received an AAN for her performance as a New York sophisticate who survives
the break-up of her marriage to see a new side
of life, in *An Unmarried Woman* (Paul Mazursky 1977) (☆ 🖉).
•American hang-ups are satirized in the story
of Carrie Snodgress (AAN) and Richard Benjamin's search for answers in group therapy, in
Diary of a Mad Housewife (Frank Perry 1970)
(☆ 🖉).
•A decade on Woody revisited Manhattan in
one of a trio of stories under the umbrella title

of *New York Stories* (1989) (☞ 🖉), with the
other, lesser, episodes being directed by >Mar-
tin Scorsese and >Francis Ford Coppola.
•Just as Woody Allen is blind to his love for
Mariel Hemingway, Billy Crystal and Meg Ryan
know each other for over a decade before they
find their New York love in *When Harry Met
Sally ...* (Rob Reiner 1989) (☆ 🖉 ☞).

Mankiewicz, Joseph L.

*(Joseph Leo Mankiewicz) American
writer/director (b 1909)*
A foreign correspondent in Berlin, he returned
to the US to screenwrite for his brother, producer Herman J. Mankiewicz: *Skippy* (AAN
with Norman McLeod) (Norman Taurog 1931)
(☆ 🖉) (health inspector's son Jackie Cooper
makes friends with slum children) and *Manhattan Melodrama* (with Oliver Garrett) (W. S.
Van Dyke 1934) (>William Powell has to pros-
ecute his childhood friend gangster >Clark
Gable). He turned producer himself for among
others, >*The Philadelphia Story* (>George
Cukor 1940) (☆ ☞ 🖉) and *Woman of the Year*
(>George Stevens 1942) (☆ ☞ 🖉) (sportswriter >Spencer Tracy tires of wife >Ka-
tharine Hepburn's national importance),
before a directing debut with *Dragonwyck*
(1946) (☆ ☞) (Gene Tierney marries Vincent
Price who has already poisoned one wife). Mankiewicz became the master of voice-over narrative and flashback – with the notable
exceptions of *A Letter to Three Wives* (AA Director & Screenplay: 1949) (🖉 ☞ ☆) (a local
spitfire informs three women she is having an
affair with one of their husbands) and >*Sleuth*
(1972) (🖉 ☆ ☞) – Mankiewicz's best work was
done in the 1950s: >*All About Eve* (AA Director
& Screenplay: 1950) (☆ 🖉 ☞); *Five Fingers*
(AAN: 1952) (🖉 ☆ ☞) (valet James Mason
steals secrets from his diplomat employer);
Julius Caesar (1953) (🖉 ☆ ☞) (James Mason
and John Gielgud's handiwork gets >Marlon
Brando's Mark Antony asking his countrymen
for a loan of their ears), *The Barefoot Contessa*
(AAN Screenplay: 1954) (🖉) (>Humphrey Bogart turns dancer Ava Gardner into a star, but
she fails to find love); and *Suddenly Last Summer* (1959) (☆ ☞ 🖉) (>Katharine Hepburn
tries to keep the nature of her homosexual

son's death a secret). Mankiewicz's career never quite recovered from the mauling meted out to *Cleopatra* (1963) (Elizabeth Taylor in the title role, >Richard Burton as Antony and Rex Harrison as Caesar).

•*Somewhere in the Night* (1946) (☞ ☆ ✍): war amnesiac John Hodiak returns home with the sole clue to his identity being a letter from a girl who seems to detest him.
•*The Late George Apley* (1947): Ronald Colman lives and dies without achieving anything, and it bothers him.
•*The Ghost and Mrs Muir* (1947): Gene Tierney allows herself to die to be with beloved sea captain Rex Harrison.
•*House of Strangers* (1949) (☞): >Edward G. Robinson has trouble with his four sons.
•*No Way Out* (1950) (☆ ☞): racist crook Richard Widmark blames coloured doctor Sidney Poitier for the death of his friend.
•*Guys and Dolls* (1955) (♫ ☆): Frank Sinatra bets >Marlon Brando he can't seduce Salvation Army girl Jean Simmons.
•*The Quiet American* (1958) (✍ ☞): Michael Redgrave betrays Audie Murphy to the Communists in 1950s Vietnam.
•*The Honey Pot* (1967): >Maggie Smith discovers that Rex Harrison is faking illness to con his mistresses.
•*There Was a Crooked Man* (1970) (☆ ☞): kindly >Henry Fonda runs a happy prison of ageing outlaws, until >Kirk Douglas arrives.

Manon des Sources ☆ ■ ✍ ☞
France • Renn Productions/A2/RAI 2/DD • 1986 • 114 mins • col
d Claude Berri   w Claude Berri/Gérard Brach   ph Bruno Nuytten   m Jean-Claude Petit
>Yves Montand, Daniel Auteuil, Emmanuelle Béart, Hippolyte Girardot

A remake of the 1952 *Manon Des Sources* (✍ ☞) that Marcel Pagnol novelized and extended, Claude Berri's beautiful film continues the action of >*Jean de Florette*. Since her father's destruction, Manon (Béart) has tended goats, while the Soubeyrans' ill-gained carnation empire flourishes. Manon exacts her vengeance by diverting the stream away from Les Bastides Blanches, inciting rumours of divine retribution and accusations against César and Ugolin among the villagers. When Manon marries a schoolmaster, the spurned Ugolin hangs himself, and the only intrusion into César's lonely old age is the discovery that Jean, the man he drove to death, was his own son. Impeccable cinema.

•Superstitious peasants are gently mocked in four stories in *Kaos* (Paolo & Vittorio Taviani 1984) (☞ ■ ✍).
•Shirley Temple is one girl and her goats in *Heidi* (Allan Dwan 1937) (✍).
•A man's doomed love for a wilderness girl is the subject of both *The Sin of Father Mouret* (*La Faute de l'Abbé Mouret*) (Georges Franju 1970) (☞ ✍ ■) (>Emile Zola's tale of priest Francis Huster, whose devotion to Mary is abandoned in favour of adoration of Gillian Hills) and *Susana* (US: *The Devil and the Flesh*) (*Demonio y Carne*) (>Luis Buñuel 1951) (✍ ☞) (a rich boy's obsession with a promiscuous girl splits his family).
•The sins of a girl's mother lead her to be persecuted on the Greek island of Hydra, in *The Girl in Black* (*To Koritsi me ta Mavra*) (Michael Cacoyannis 1955) (☆ ■).
•When the villagers refuse to help Bernadette Lafont with her mother's funeral expenses, she exacts revenge, in *Dirty Mary* (*La Fiancée du Pirate*) (Nelly Kaplan 1969) (☆ ♫).

March, Fredric
(Ernest Bickel) American actor (1897–1975)
Subtly authoritative, March was one of the most intelligent Hollywood actors of the Golden Age. Oscar-nominated for his John Barrymore impersonation in *The Royal Family of Broadway* (UK: *Theatre Royal*) (>George Cukor 1930) (☆ ☞), he went one better with his exceptional *Dr Jekyll and Mr Hyde* (Rouben Mamoulian 1931) (☆ ☞ ■) (March swallows potion and brutalizes prostitute Miriam Hopkins) in 1932. Costume melodrama saw out the decade: *The Barretts of Wimpole Street* (Sidney Franklin 1934) (☆ ✍) (March's Robert

MARIE ANTOINETTE
(W. S. Van Dyke 1938) ☆ ☞

TRUE-LIFE ROMANCE

CLEOPATRA
(Cecil B. De Mille 1934) ■ ☆
(Antony fails to conquer queen Claudette Colbert or ancient Egypt)

THE PRIVATE LIVES OF ELIZABETH AND ESSEX
(>Michael Curtiz 1939) ☞ ☆
(Virgin Queen >Bette Davis resists the charms of swashbuckler Errol Flynn)

LADY HAMILTON (US: THAT HAMILTON WOMAN)
(Alexander Korda 1941) ☆ ✍
(>Vivien Leigh loves the parts Laurence Olivier's got left)

SAMSON AND DELILAH
(Cecil B. De Mille 1949) ☞
(biblical epic of betrayal and unwanted haircuts)

CLASSIC COSTUME ROMANCE

ANNA KARENINA
(Clarence Brown 1935) ☆ ☞
(>Basil Rathbone's wife >Greta Garbo is disgraced by affair with >Fredric March)

>CAMILLE
(>George Cukor 1936) ☆ ☞ ✍ ■
(courtesan >Greta Garbo loved to death by rich younger man)

WUTHERING HEIGHTS
(>William Wyler 1939) ☆ ☞ ■ ✍ ♫
(>Laurence Olivier and Merle Oberon share tempestuous passions on Yorkshire Moors)

>GONE WITH THE WIND
(Victor Fleming 1939) ☆ ■ ✍ ☞ ♫
(Civil War belle fights for plantation and love)

VALMONT
(>Miloš Forman 1989) ☞ ■ ☆ ✍
(18th-century Lothario Colin Firth seeks to seduce Meg Tilly)

French queen Norma Shearer prefers diplomat
Tyrone Power to Robert Morley[AAN]'s Louis XVI

MAD LOVE

>*SOME LIKE IT HOT*
(>Billy Wilder 1959) ☆ ✍ ☞ ■ ♫
(millionaire Joe E. Brown falls for drag-disguised >Jack
Lemmon)

WHAT'S UP, DOC?
(Peter Bogdanovich 1972) ✍ ☆
(Barbra Streisand and Ryan O'Neal comedy of ca-
lamities results in love)

>*ANNIE HALL*
(>Woody Allen 1977) ✍ ☆ ☞ ■
(unconventional couple Allen and >Diane Keaton have
fun fling)

WE THINK THE WORLD OF YOU
(Colin Gregg 1989) ☆
(Alan Bates and Gary Oldman's gay relationship is
hindered by a dog)

MODERN LOVE

LOVERS AND OTHER STRANGERS
(Cy Howard 1969) ☆
(marriage proves more problematic than cohabitation)

DESERT HEARTS
(Donna Deitch 1985) ☆ ☞
(young lesbian seduces staid, bourgeois woman)

CROSSING DELANCEY
(Joan Micklin Silver 1988) ☆
(bookseller Amy Irving loves author and pickle salesman)

SEX, LIES AND VIDEOTAPE
(Steven Sonderbergh 1989) ☞ ☆
(impotent man gets his kicks watching films of women
talking about sex)

THE TALL GUY
(Mel Smith 1989) ☞ ☆ ✍
(Jeff Goldblum is exploited by comic Rowan Atkinson
and consoled by nurse Emma Thompson)

Browning skirts >Charles Laughton's disapproval to court Norma Shearer's Elizabeth Barrett); *Anna Karenina* (Clarence Brown 1935) (March lures >Greta Garbo away from staid government minister husband >Basil Rathbone only to abandon her for war); *Les Misérables* (Richard Boleslawski 1935) (☆ ☞ ✍) (March as Jean Valjean unable to rebuild his life after false imprisonment because of >Charles Laughton's persistence); *Anthony Adverse* (>Mervyn Le Roy 1936) (☆ ✍) (on his picaresque adventures, March loves >Olivia De Havilland and encounters a villainous Claude Rains). March was also an adept comedian: *Design for Living* (>Ernst Lubitsch 1933) (☞ ✍ ☆) (March and >Gary Cooper both love Miriam Hopkins so they set up house together) and *Nothing Sacred* (>William Wellman 1937) (☆ ☞ ✍) (journalist March turns a dying >Carole Lombard into a heroine, only she isn't ill). However, he particularly excelled at social realism in such films as *The Road to Glory* (>Howard Hawks 1936) (☞ ☆) (March, Warner Baxter and Lionel Barrymore as French trench soldiers), *A Star Is Born* (AAN: >William Wellman 1937) (☆ ☞ ✍) (as Janet Gaynor's fame grows, Hollywood turns its back on fading husband March), >*The Best Years of Our Lives* (AA: >William Wyler 1946) (☆ ☞ ✍ ■), *Death of a Salesman* (AAN: Laslo Benedek 1951) (☆) (March as Arthur Miller's mediocrity who commits suicide after quarrelling with his son Kevin McCarthy) and *The Desperate Hours* (>William Wyler 1955) (☆) (March keeps calm when >Humphrey Bogart and his gang hide out in his home).

VIEW ON ▶ •*Laughter* (Harry D'Abbadie D'Arrast 1930) (☆): Nancy Carroll isn't content with millionaire husband Frank Morgan; she wants ex-love March as well.
•*Merrily We Go To Hell* (Dorothy Arzner 1932) (☆): the ups-and-downs of playwright March's marriage to Sylvia Sidney.
•*The Affairs of Cellini* (Gregory La Cava 1934) (☆): March as the 16th-century Italian artist and lover.
•*Dark Angel* (Sidney Franklin 1935) (■ ☆): war-blinded March urges fiancée Merle Oberon to marry Herbert Marshall.
•*Mary of Scotland* (>John Ford 1936) (☆ ☞): March as the loyal Earl of Bothwell to >Katharine Hepburn's Mary, Queen of Scots.
•*Victory* (John Cromwell 1940) (☆): March as the recluse hero of Joseph Conrad's novel threatened by Cedric Hardwicke for money he doesn't have.
•*I Married a Witch* (>René Clair 1942) (☞ ☆): March is persecuted because his ancestors burned Cecil Kellaway and his now wife Veronica Lake.
•*The Adventures of Mark Twain* (Irving Rapper 1944) (☆ ✍): March as the man who brought wit and a love of the Mississippi to literature.
•*Hombre* (Martin Ritt 1966): March as an Indian agent despised by his fellow coach travellers for hold-up cowardice.

The Marx Brothers
American actors:
Chico (Leonard 1886–1961);
Harpo (Arthur 1888–1964);
Groucho (Julius Henry 1890–1977);
Zeppo (Herbert 1901–1979)

Dropping Gummo (Milton) during their vaudeville days, the Marx Brothers continued the anarchy of their stage shows in *The Cocoanuts* (Robert Florey/Joseph Santley 1929) (☆ ✍) (hotelier Groucho wheels and deals to make more money than his business brings in), *Animal Crackers* (Victor Heerman 1930) (☆ ✍) (the Brothers steal a painting from Margaret Dumont who is trying to get Groucho to the altar), *Horse Feathers* (Norman Z. McLeod 1932) (☆ ✍) (the writers alone knew the plot as Groucho's university president is bothered by dog catcher Harpo and racketeer Chico) and >*Duck Soup* (>Leo McCarey 1933) (☆ ☞ ✍), after which straight man Zeppo departed. Italianate 'anti-straight man' Chico conned, mute Harpo chased girls and tooted a horn, and wise-cracking Groucho stoop-walked and waggled his cigar as they skitted their way through the more structured, but equally exhausting *A Night at the Opera* (Sam Wood 1935) (☆ ✍) (the Phantom was preferable to the Brothers until they change their tune), *A Day at the Races* (Sam Wood 1937) (Harpo the jockey,

Chico the tipster and Groucho the horse doctor help Maureen O'Sullivan win a race), *Go West* (Edward Buzzell 1940) (☆) (the Brothers round up baddy John Carroll) and *A Night in Casablanca* (Archie Mayo 1946) (☆) (the Brothers spoof the famous film and capture Nazis in the process). Drifting apart and into assorted radio, TV and theatre shows, they individually failed to match their collective achievements.

 •*Monkey Business* (Norman Z. McLeod 1931) (☆): villains are captured on board ship.

•*Room Service* (William A. Seiter 1938) (☆): the Brothers wait for the money to put on a show.

•*At the Circus* (Edward Buzzell 1939): Groucho's fascination switches from Margaret Dumont to 'Lydia, the Tattooed Lady'.

•*The Big Store* (Charles Reisner 1941) (☆): eccentric detective Groucho swoops on crooks planning a major shoplift.

Mastroianni, Marcello
Italian actor (b 1923)

Interned by the Nazis in 1943, after the war Mastroianni joined >Luchino Visconti's theatre group, playing small roles through the 1950s, until *White Nights* (*Le Notti Bianche*) (>Luchino Visconti 1957) (☞ ☆) (Marcello dreams of chivalry towards a girl who is obsessed by her distant lover, in this >Dostoyevsky story), *Persons Unknown* (US: *Big Deal on Madonna Street*) (aka *The Usual Unidentified Thieves*) (*I Soliti Ignoti*) (Mario Monicelli 1958) (☆) (crooks break into the building next door to the targeted pawn shop) and >*La Dolce Vita* (US: *The Sweet Life*) (>Federico Fellini 1960) (☞ ☆ ■ ♫♪), since when he has been the most popular and prolific of Italian actors. His partnership with Sophia Loren echoed Hollywood romantic teams of the Golden Age: *Yesterday, Today and Tomorrow* (*Ieri, Oggi, Domani*) (AAN: >Vittorio De Sica 1963) (Marcello keeps Sophia out of prison by helping her get repeatedly pregnant!); *Marriage, Italian Style* (*Matrimonio all'Italiana*) (>Vittorio De Sica 1964) (☞) (Sophia feigns illness to keep Marcello from marrying a younger girl); and *A Special Day* (*Una Giornata Particolare*) (AAN:

Ettore Scola 1977) (☆ ♫) (Sophia as a hassled mother and Marcello as a gay radio announcer, who become friends on the day Hitler comes to Rome). His character performances prove that his talent exceeds standard romantic leads: *Handsome Antonio* (*Il Bell'Antonio*) (☆ ■) (Mauro Bolognini 1960) (womanizer Marcello is publicly humiliated by his annulment for impotence); *The Organizer* (*I Compagni*) (☆ ☞) (Mario Monicelli 1967) (noble academic Marcello supports a factory strike in Turin); and *The Night of Varennes* (*La Nuit de Varennes*) (Ettore Scola 1981) (■ ☆) (Marcello as Casanova in a coach travelling behind the fleeing French Royal family in 1791). However, his forte is satire: >*8½* (*Otto e Mezzo*) (>Federico Fellini 1963) (☞ ☆ ♫ ■); *The Tenth Victim* (*La Decima Vittima*) (Elio Petri 1965) (♫) (murder replaces birth control in a future society and Marcello aims for a productivity bonus); *Allonsanfan* (Paolo & Vittorio Taviani 1974) (■ ☆) (noble Marcello despises Louis XVIII's Restoration, but betrays a revolutionary to protect his own comfort); *City of Women* (*La Città delle Donne*) (>Federico Fellini 1979) (☞ ☆) (Marcello experiences all his phobias about women when he lands in a place where they rule) and *Ginger and Fred* (*Ginger e Fred*) (>Federico Fellini 1986) (☞ ☆) (>Astaire and >Rogers impersonators Marcello and Giulietta Masina reunite for a TV show).

 •*The Night* (*La Notte*) (>Michelangelo Antonioni 1961) (■ ☞): a day in the life of novelist Marcello and his wife Jeanne Moreau.

•*Divorce Italian Style* (*Divorzio all'Italiana*) (Pietro Germi 1961): Marcello arranges for his wife's adultery so he can commit a *crime passionnel* and remarry.

•*The Assassin* (US: *The Ladykiller of Rome*) (*L'Assassino*) (Elio Petri 1961) (☆): crooked cops try to pin a murder on antique dealer Marcello.

•*The Stranger* (*Lo Straniero*) (>Luchino Visconti 1967) (■): Marcello as Albert Camus' condemned man contemplating his life in Algeria prior to his crime.

•*Sunflower* (*Il Girasole*) (>Vittorio De Sica 1969): Sophia and Marcello are reunited long after he is reported missing at the Russian front.

•*Jealousy, Italian Style* (US: *Drama of Jealousy*) (aka *The Pizza Triangle*) (*Dramma della Gelosia -Tutti I Particolare in Cronaca*) (Ettore Scola 1970) (☆ ☞): Marcello was voted Best Actor at Cannes as a man who sees green when Monica Vitti falls for waiter Giancarlo Giannini.

•*La Grande Bouffe* (US: *Blow-Out*) (Marco Ferreri 1973) (☆): bored Marcello, >Philippe Noiret, Ugo Tognazzi and Michel Piccoli eat themselves senseless.

•*Wifemistress* (*Mogliamante*) (Marco Vicario 1977) (☆): Marcello witnesses the blossoming into independence of Laura Antonelli in turn-of-the-century Italy.

•*The Bee Keeper* (*O Melissokomos*) (Theo Angelopolous 1986): Marcello drives his bees on a tour of Greek beehives and meets a hitch-hiker who assuages his morbidity.

•*Splendor* (Ettore Scola 1989) (☆ ✍♫ ☞ ■): business at Marcello's cinema reflects the fortunes and recalls the classics of cinema from silents to sci-fi.

A Matter of Life and Death (US: Stairway to Heaven) ✍ ☞ ■ ☆ ✳

GB • GFD/Archers • 1946 • 104 mins • b/w & col

wd >Michael Powell/Emeric Pressburger ph Jack Cardiff m Allan Gray

David Niven, Roger Livesey, Raymond Massey, Marius Goring, Kim Hunter, Abraham Sofaer

At a time when film-makers of the calibre of >Marcel Carné, >Frank Capra and Leni Riefenstahl were making national glorification movies, Michael Powell and Emeric Pressburger seemed to delight in defying the wishes of authority. Churchill wanted to suppress their 1943 *The Life and Death of Colonel Blimp* (☞ ✍ ☆) (Roger Livesey serves queen, two kings and country in three campaigns) for depicting the German military in a sympathetic light, while this 1946 film, made at the behest of Prime Minister Clement Attlee's Ministry of Information to demonstrate the Allies' close

ties, is the story of an American revolutionary (Massey) and a French aristocrat (Goring) feuding over whether an RAF pilot (Niven) involved in a crash should live or die. With its superb blending of monochrome and colour and that majestic moving staircase, this tense, touching celestial courtroom drama further embarrassed the Establishment by being selected as the first Royal Command Performance film.

 •The more clear an idea he has of his family's shortcomings means Barry Otto will not be so malleable when he returns to life, in *Bliss* (Ray Lawrence 1987) (☆ ✍) the screen adaptation of Peter Carey's novel.

•Whether portrayed by human beings – *Alice in Wonderland* (Norman Z. McLeod 1933) (☆) – or in Disney cartoon form *Alice in Wonderland* (Clyde Geronomi/Hamilton Luske/Wilfred Jackson 1951) (☞) – or by puppets *Alice* (Jan Svankmajer 1987) (✳ ☞), Lewis Carroll's classic is all in the mind, albeit a sleeping one.

•Another celestial courtroom has Eddie 'Rochester' Anderson on trial, in *Cabin in the Sky* (>Vincente Minnelli 1943) (☞♫).

•A Communist and a woman poisoned by a Fascist fall in afterlife love, in *Les Jeux Sonts Faits* (Jean Delannoy 1947) (☆), while Simone Berriau explains to her three admirers why she had ruined their lives, in *The Tender Enemy* (*La Tendre Ennemie*) (>Max Ophüls 1936) (☞ ■).

Metropolis ☞ ■ ✳ ✍ ☆

Germany • UFA • 1926 • 120 mins • b/w

d >Fritz Lang w Thea Von Harbou/Fritz Lang ph Karl Freund/Gunther Rittau m (1984) Giorgio Moroder

Brigette Helm, Alfred Abel, Gustav Frohlich, Rudolf Klein-Rogge

Recently restored to something akin to Fritz Lang's original three hour-plus vision, this tale of class warfare in a future society would make a splendid promo for the UN or similar arbitration body. Evil magician Rotwang advises John Frederson that his towering city would be spared dissension if the labouring masses which created it were replaced by robots. Popular agitator Maria (Helm) is switched with a mechanical replica, whose mission is to lead the workers to their deaths. But Frederson counts without his son Freder, whose love for Maria inspires her rescue and ultimately, an amicable accord. Although religious reference abounds – the opposite levels of society couched in heaven and hell, the followers of the parable-preaching rebel leader hiding in catacombs and the manner of Maria's execution recalling Joan of Arc - *Metropolis*'s Expressionism was the inspiration for countless horror and sci-fi 'B' pictures.

 •The robot workforce are butlers in *Sleeper* (>Woody Allen 1973) (☆).
•Books are made illegal in a mass act of brainwashing in some future society, in *Fahrenheit 451* (>François Truffaut 1966) (☞ ✍).
•The cast of silent movies were the anonymous labourers in *The Life and Death of 9413 – A Hollywood Extra* (Robert Florey/Slavko Vorkapich 1927) (✍).
•Jonathan Pryce is caught up in >Robert De Niro's attempts to overthrow a repressive government, in *Brazil* (Terry Gilliam 1985) (☞ ✳).

MEXICO

The Bullfighters **(Mal St Clair 1945)** ☆
Detective >Stan Laurel is mistaken for a famous matador, while he and >Oliver Hardy are on a case.

A Fistful of Dynamite **(Sergio Leone 1971)** ☞
Bandit Rod Steiger and IRA explosives expert James Coburn rob a bank.

Juarez **(>William Dieterle 1939)** ☆
>Bette Davis' Hapsburg empress becomes deranged by Paul Muni's overthrow of her husband, Brian Aherne.

The Leopard Man **(Jacques Tourneur 1943)** ■
Dennis O'Keefe questions a leopard's role in the maulings plaguing a border town.

The Night of the Iguana **(>John Huston 1964)** ☞ ☆
Sordid goings on at Ava Gardner's hotel revolve around defrocked priest >Richard Burton and a party of schoolgirls.

The Old Gringo **(Luis Puenzo 1989)** ☆ ✍
During the 1910 revolution, journalist Gregory Peck disappears and teacher >Jane Fonda is the last to see him alive.

Touch of Evil **(>Orson Welles 1958)** ☆ ✍ ☞
Welles and Charlton Heston feud over a murder case in >Marlene Dietrich's brothel.

Vera Cruz **(Robert Aldrich 1953)** ☆ ☞ ✍
>Gary Cooper and Burt Lancaster are caught up in Juarez's plot against the 19th-century emperor Maximilian.

Viva Villa **(Jack Conway 1934)** ✍ ☞
Wallace Beery leads the 1910 revolution.

Viva Zapata **(>Elia Kazan 1952)** ☞ ☆
Anthony Quinn betrays revolutionary >Marlon Brando in 1919.

MID-LIFE CRISIS

Another Woman **(>Woody Allen 1989)** ☞ ☆ ✍
Academic Gena Rowlands' life is jolted by a series of bizarre events and uncomfortable memories.

Bob and Carol and Ted and Alice **(Paul Mazursky 1969)** ☞
The folks go to group therapy sessions to improve their inhibited little lives.

The Return of the Musketeers **(Richard Lester 1989)** ☞ ✍ ☆
Michael York, Richard Chamberlain, Oliver Reed and Frank Finlay find heroism requires muscles they haven't used in years.

10 **(Blake Edwards 1979)** ☆
Dudley Moore's sense of inadequacy finds an outlet in an obsession with Bo Derek.

That's Life **(Blake Edwards 1986)** ☆
>Jack Lemmon displays his menopause malaise through hypochondria.

Twice in a Lifetime **(Bud Yorkin 1985)** ☆
Gene Hackman hits 50 and decides to abandon his life and start again.

Vincent, François, Paul and Others **(*Vincent, François, Paul...et les Autres*) (Claude Sautet 1971)** ■ ☆
Menopausal professional men watch their friends' marital failures with curiosity and despair.

Wilt (Michael Tuchner 1989) ✍ ☆

Bored further education teacher Griff Rhys Jones is suspected by inspector Mel Smith of murdering wife Alison Steadman.

MIDDLE AGES

Becket (Peter Glenville 1964) ☆ ■

Peter O'Toole's Henry II feuds with >Richard Burton's Archbishop of Canterbury.

The Black Rose (Henry Hathaway 1950) ☆

Tyrone Power visits >Orson Welles' Mongols and studies their country.

Blanche (Walerian Borowczyk 1971) ☞

A page, a king and a son breach a man's elaborate defence of his young wife.

Cinderella – Italian Style (US: *More Than a Miracle*) (*C'Era una Volta*) (Francesco Rosi 1967) ■

Omar Sharif's noble is continually thwarted in his attempts to marry peasant Sophia Loren.

The Crusades (Cecil B. De Mille 1935) ☞

Loretta Young's Berengaria suggests that a trip to the Holy Land would do Henry Wilcoxson's Richard I a power of good.

The Decameron (*Il Decamerone*) (>Pier Paolo Pasolini 1971) ■ ☞

This collection of eight of Boccaccio's tales studying dubious human nature won the Berlin Special Jury Prize.

Jabberwocky (Terry Gilliam 1977) ✍

Michael Palin fights Lewis Carroll's nonsense monster.

Monty Python and the Holy Grail (Terry Gilliam/Terry Jones 1975) ✍ ☆

King Arthur is hampered by a giant rabbit, Marxist peasants and eccentric French soldiers.

The Navigator (Vincent Ward 1988) ✍ ■ ☞

A spire must be placed on a cathedral in 1348 Cumbria if the Black Death is to be driven away.

MILLIONAIRES

Annie (>John Huston 1982) ☞ ♫

Albert Finney comes to love the orphan who has brightened the life of his household.

Brewster's Millions (Thornton Freeland 1935)/(Allan Dwan 1945) ✍

Jack Buchanan and Dennis O'Keefe, respectively, have two months to spend a million and inherit a fortune.

Brewster's Millions (Walter Hill 1985)

Baseball amateur Richard Pryor has to spend a million a day for a month to inherit his fortune.

Dames (Ray Enright 1935) ☆

Puritan Hugh Herbert tries to stop a show, despite its Busby Berkeley choreography.

The Devil and Miss Jones (Sam Wood 1941) ☆ ✍

Disguised Charles Coburn investigates Jean Arthur's complaints about the running of his store.

Gentlemen Prefer Blondes (>Howard Hawks 1953) ☞ ☆ ♫

Charles Coburn is one of the men fished for by Jane Russell and >Marilyn Monroe.

Has Anybody Seen My Girl? (Douglas Sirk 1952) ☆ ✍

Charles Coburn pretends to be poor to test relatives before making his will.

How to Marry a Millionaire (Jean Negulesco 1953) ☆ ✍

>William Powell is among those lured into >Marilyn Monroe, Lauren Bacall and Betty Grable's luxury apartment.

Le Million (>René Clair 1931) ☞ ✍

Artist René Lefèvre searches Paris for a lost lottery ticket.

>*Some Like It Hot* (>Billy Wilder 1959) ☆ ✍ ☞ ■ ♫

> Gold diggers

MINIATURIZATION

Alice's Adventures in Wonderland (William Sterling 1972) ☆ ■

Fiona Fullerton learns to be more discriminating in what she eats and drinks when it comes to getting through doors.

Attack of the Puppet People (UK: *Six Inches Tall*) (Bert I. Gordon 1957) ✍

Toymaker John Hoyt learns how to shrink people and misuses his power.

The Devil-Doll (Tod Browning 1936) ☆ ✍

Lionel Barrymore, disguised as an old lady, uses mini-killers to avenge his imprisonment.

Dr Cyclops (Ernest Schoedsack 1940) ☆

Jungle crackpot Albert Dekker puts his learned

shrunken head techniques into practice on whole bodies.

Fantastic Voyage (Richard Fleischer 1966) ☆ ✳

Stephen Boyd's craft is injected into the bloodstream to cure a patient.

The Incredible Shrinking Man (Jack Arnold 1957) ✳

A radioactive fog turns Grant Williams into an interesting toy for the cat.

The Incredible Shrinking Woman (Joel Schumacher 1981) ☆

Lily Tomlin spoofs the above thanks to a perfume.

Innerspace (Joe Dante 1987) ☆ ✳

Dennis Quaid is injected into Martin Short and guides him away from crooks who could kill them both.

Tom Thumb (George Pal 1958) ☆

Russ Tamblin is exploited by comic baddies Peter Sellers and Terry-Thomas.

Minnelli, Vincente
American director (1910–1986)

A set and costume designer before assuming directorial responsibility, Minnelli is regarded as cinema's greatest decorative stylist, justly famous for his musicals: *Cabin in the Sky* (1942) (☞♫) (the soul of a ne'er-do-well is the target of angels from both camps); *Meet Me in St Louis* (1944) (☞ ☆) (Judy Garland and Margaret O'Brien prepare for the 1904 Fair); *The Pirate* (1948) (☞ ☆) (>Gene Kelly allows Judy Garland to believe he is the famous pirate who is really her hated suitor); *An American in Paris* (AAN: 1951) (☆ ☞) (artist >Gene Kelly prefers waif Leslie Caron to patroness Nina Foch); *The Band Wagon* (1953) (✍☞♫) (faded dancer >Fred Astaire teams with Jack Buchanan to put on a show); *Brigadoon* (1954) (☆ ☞ ✍) (>Gene Kelly and Van Johnson decide to stay in a Scottish ghost town); and *Gigi* (AA: 1958) (☞■) (trainee courtesan Leslie Caron is reformed by suave aristo Louis Jourdan). He not only ensured that songs developed narrative, but also used dream sequences – often 'ballets' – to explore central themes and symbols. His melodramas, on the other hand, suffer from sacrificing crux for chic: *The Bad and the Beautiful* (1952) (☆ ☞) (producer >Kirk Douglas needs a favour of people he's maltreated); *The Cobweb* (1955) (>Lillian Gish, Charles Boyer and Lauren Bacall are among personnel of a smart mental clinic); *Lust for Life* (1956) (☆ ☞) (>Kirk Douglas as disturbed artist Vincent Van Gogh); *Some Came Running* (1959)(☆) (writer Frank Sinatra draws inspiration from gambler Dean Martin and whore Shirley MacLaine); *Home from the Hill* (1960) (☞) (father Robert Mitchum has problems with sons George Peppard and George Hamilton); and *The Four Horsemen of the Apocalypse* (1962) (☞) (father Charles Boyer is reconciled with son Glenn Ford when the latter proves himself in war).

●*The Clock* (UK: *Under the Clock*) (1945) (☞ ✍): Judy Garland meets Robert Walker at Pennsylvania Station and in the course of the day they decide to marry.

●*Yolanda and the Thief* (1945): >Fred Astaire has designs on heiress Lucille Bremer's fortune.

●*The Ziegfeld Follies* (1946) (☆ ☞ ✍): >Fred Astaire interprets dead impresario >William Powell's ideas for a show.

●*Undercurrent* (1946) (☆ ☞): when Robert Taylor begins to act strangely, >Katharine Hepburn turns to brother-in-law Robert Mitchum.

●*Madame Bovary* (1949) (✍ ☆): Jennifer Jones defies doctor husband Van Heflin for an affair with Louis Jourdan as narrated by James Mason's Gustave Flaubert.

●*Father of the Bride* (1951) (☆ ☞): >Spencer Tracy is unable to whip up enthusiasm for Elizabeth Taylor's wedding.

●*Tea and Sympathy* (1956) (☆): housemaster's wife Deborah Kerr takes pity on unhappy schoolboy John Kerr.

●*The Reluctant Debutante* (1958) (✍): Rex Harrison and Kay Kendall introduce daughter Sandra Dee into London society.

●*Bells Are Ringing* (1960) (☆ ✍): Judy Holliday as a telephonist whose ear for a conversation leads to a romance with Dean Martin.

●*Two Weeks in Another Town* (1962): alcoholic

director >Kirk Douglas' comeback is haunted by his past.

MIRACLES

The First Legion (Douglas Sirk 1951) ☆
Priest Charles Boyer is treated with suspicion by peers when he claims a miracle.

Gabriel over the White House (Gregory La Cava 1933) ☆
Villainous Walter Huston is transformed once he becomes president.

Heavenly Pursuits (*The Gospel According to Vic*)(Charles Gormley 1987) ☆
Glasgow teacher Tom Conti saves a boy and believes he has special powers.

A Kid for Two Farthings (>Carol Reed 1955) ☞ ✍
Life improves around a London boy who believes his goat is a unicorn.

The Miracle of Our Lady of Fatima (UK: *The Miracle of Fatima*) (John Brahm 1952) ✍♫
The story of the Marian appearances to some Portuguese children in 1917.

Resurrection (Daniel Petrie 1981) ☆
Ellen Burstyn survives a car crash and begins to cure the sick.

> Saints

MIRRORS

Coming Apart (Milton Moses Ginsberg 1969) ■
A psychiatrist's mental breakdown is shown through mirror images.

The Lady from Shanghai (>Orson Welles 1948) ☞ ☆ ✍
Having been dragged into a murder mystery by Rita Hayworth, Orson Welles shoots it out to a conclusion in a hall of mirrors with her husband Everett Sloane.

The Man in the Mirror (Maurice Elvey 1936) ☆
Cowardly Edward Everett Horton's reflection turns him into a man.

The Man with the Golden Gun (Guy Hamilton 1974) ✳
Roger Moore's 007 shoots it out in Christopher Lee's sinister hall of mirrors.

Orphée (aka *Orpheus*) (Jean Cocteau 1949) ☞ ✍ ■
Jean Marais gets into the underworld through a looking glass to pursue the Princess of Death Maria Casarès.

>*Snow White and the Seven Dwarfs* (David Hand 1937) ☞ ■ ✍♫

Up Tight (Jules Dassin 1968) ☞ ■
An informer is hunted down by those he betrayed, a chase that leads to a fairground hall of mirrors.

The Mission ✍ ■ ☆ ☞ ♫

GB • Goldcrest/Kingsmere/Enigma/Fernando Ghia • 1986 • 128 mins • col
d Roland Joffé w Robert Bolt
ph Norman Dorme/Franceso Broznik/George Richardson/John King
m Ennio Morricone
Jeremy Irons, >Robert De Niro, Ray McAnally, Liam Neeson, Cheri Lunghi

While Spain and Portugal squabble for South American supremacy, Jesuit missionaries strive to save the souls of the Gurani Indians. Father Gabriel (a devout, determined Irons) and rugged novice Rodrigo (De Niro) establish a sanctuary above a waterfall, but with Papal connivance, the Iberian imperialists suppress the mission to supply slaves to an Enlightened Europe. Provocatively played against a background of terrifying natural beauty, the rather bookish subjects of high politics, simple faith and desperate trust give rise to some exhilarating action, notably the spectacular crucifixion opening and the anguished battle finale.

•Hispano-Portuguese imperialism pervades as Klaus Kinski searches for El Dorado in *Aguirre, Wrath of God* (*Aguirre, der Zorn Gottes*) (>Werner Herzog 1972) (■ ☞) and as >Marlon Brando aids revolutionaries on a Caribbean island in *Quiemada!* (aka *Burn!*) (Gillo Pontecorvo 1970) (☆).
•Klaus Kinski is the brutal slave trader in *Cobra Verde* (>Werner Herzog 1988) (☞ ■).
•A small serving boy is initiated into a Mau-Mau sect, but only aids the anti-imperialist

cause for fear of reprisal, in *The Kitchen Toto* (Harry Hook 1988) (☞ ☆ ✍).

•>Alec Guinness is the troubled cardinal tortured by Jack Hawkins for opposing a Fascist regime, in *The Prisoner* (Peter Glenville 1955) (☆).

•Claude Rains and Glenn Ford lead the epic Alpine climb in *The White Tower* (Ted Tetzlaff 1950) (☆).

MISSIONARIES

Chariots of Fire (Hugh Hudson 1981) ☆ ✍ ♫

Ian Charleson's sprinter Eric Liddell is torn between athletics and his missionary ambitions – he fulfils both.

The Inn of the Sixth Happiness (Mark Robson 1958) ☆ ☞

Mandarin >Robert Donat helps >Ingrid Bergman lead the children in her care away from the Sino-Japanese war zone.

The Keys of the Kingdom (John M. Stahl 1944) ☆

Gregory Peck meets resistance from 19th-century Chinese mandarin Vincent Price.

The Missionary (Richard Loncraine 1983) ☆ ✍

Sent by bishop Denholm Elliott to minister to fallen women, Michael Palin becomes a pimp.

Mosquito Coast (Peter Weir 1986) ☆

A sinister evangelist poses more threat to >Harrison Ford's family than do the natural dangers of the jungle.

Rain (Lewis Milestone 1932) ■

Ambitious whore >Joan Crawford is lectured by lecherous missionary Walter Huston.

Seven Women (>John Ford 1966) ☞ ☆

Anne Bancroft and Flora Robson lead the staff of a besieged Chinese mission.

Stanley and Livingstone (Henry King 1939) ☆ ☞

>Spencer Tracy's H. M. Stanley finds Cedric Hardwicke's dedicated David Livingstone.

MISTRESSES

Back Street (John M. Stahl 1932)/(Robert Stevenson 1941)/(David Miller 1961) ☆

Irene Dunne, Margaret Sullavan, Susan Hay-

ward are respectively the long-suffering mistresses of the banker, played in each case by John Boles, Charles Boyer and John Gavin.

Black on White (Mustaa Valkoisella) (Jorn Donner 1967) ■

The Finnish director leaves his stable home for a chancey affair with his secretary.

Bonjour Tristesse (Otto Preminger 1957) ☆ ✍

Jean Seberg causes the death of father David Niven's lover Deborah Kerr, in a screen adaptation of Françoise Sagan's novel.

East Side West Side (>Mervyn Le Roy 1949) ☞ ☆

James Mason is torn between worthy wife >Barbara Stanwyck and tantalizing lover Ava Gardner.

Fallen Angel (Otto Preminger 1945) ☆ ✍

Dana Andrews' plans to murder his wife go wrong when his mistress is killed instead.

Nell Gwyn (Herbert Wilcox 1934) ☆

Anna Neagle as the orange-selling favourite of Charles II (Cedric Hardwicke).

A Touch of Class (Melvin Frank 1973) ☆ ✍

George Segal and Glenda Jackson's wisecracking affair is unable to stand external demands.

MIXED BLESSINGS

Duty Free Marriage (Vámmentes Házasság) (aka Tullivapaa Avioliitor) (János Zsombolyai 1980) ✍ ☞

A Hungarian arranges a marriage of convenience with a Finn so she can join her exiled boyfriend in Finland.

>Fear Eats the Soul (US: Ali: Fear Eats the Soul) (Angst Essen Seele Auf) (>Rainer Werner Fassbinder 1973) ☞ ☆ ✍

The Great White Hope (Martin Ritt 1970) ☆

In a *film à clef* of Jack Johnson, a black heavyweight boxing champion (James Earl Jones) causes a scandal by living with a white girl.

Hiroshima Mon Amour (>Alain Resnais 1959) ✍ ☞

A French actress falls for a Japanese architect in this Marguerite Duras script.

A Letter to Brezhnev (Chris Barnard 1985) ✍ ☆

Liverpudlian Alexandra Pigg battles to emigrate to the Soviet Union to join her sailor lover Peter Firth.

90 Days (Giles Walker 1985) ✍ ☆
A Canadian and the Korean girl he has selected from a mail-order catalogue get to know each other in this charming comedy.

Sayonara (Joshua Logan 1957) ■
US major >Marlon Brando falls for Japanese actress Miyoshi Umeki.

Mizoguchi, Kenji
Japanese director (1898–1956)

Funded through art school by his geisha sister, Mizoguchi was a champion of women's liberation. Indeed his 1956 film *Street of Shame* (*Akasen Chitai*) (☞) (the working life of prostitutes in Tokyo's red light district) was instrumental in securing the prohibition of prostitution in Japan in 1957. The bulk of his silent output has perished, but in collaboration with scriptwriter Yoshikata Yoda, who tolerated his professional and personal petulance, he produced a series of technically conservative, but textually radical studies of women: *The Story of the Late Chrysanthemums* (*Zangiku Monogatari*) (1939) (☞ ■) (ham Shotaro Hanayagi is transformed into a brilliant actor through marriage to housemaid Kakuko Mori); *Osaka Elegy* (*Naniwa Hika*) (1940) (✍ ☞) (a secretary sleeps with her boss before resorting to whoring to pay her father's debts and brother's schooling); *Five Women Around Utamaro* (US: *Utamaro and His Five Women*) (*Utamaro O Meguru Gonin no Onna*) (1946) (☞ ■) (18th-century artist is inspired by the bickering courtesans he seduces); *The Life of O-Haru* (*Saikaku Ichidai Onna*) (1951) (☞ ✍) (having abandoned an arranged marriage to be with lover Toshiro Mifune, Kinuyo Tanaka drifts into degradation when he is beheaded); and *Ugetsu Monogatari* (*Ugetsu*) (1953) (☞ ✍ ☆) (by the time potter Masayuki Mori returns from pursuing a woman who proves to be a ghost, he discovers that his wife Kinuyo Tanaka is now a ghost too). Ultimately more popular in the West, Mizoguchi was a profound influence on French New Wave cinema.

 •*The Sisters of the Gion* (*Gion no Shimai*) (1936): geisha sisters Yoko Umemura and Isuzu Yamada are betrayed by their lovers.

•*My Love Has Been Burning* (US: *Flame Of My Love*) (*Waga Koi Wa Moenu*) (1949) (☞): a feminist teacher's resolve to teach women the realities of life is undeterred by misfortune.

•*Sansho the Bailiff* (*Sansho Dayu*) (1954) (☞ ■ ✍): noble children are sold to a cruel slaver, but the son escapes and finds his way home.

•*Gion Festival Music* (US: *Geisha*) (*Gion Bayashi*) (1953) (☞): shocked at the sordidness of the 'art', a trainee geisha rebels.

•*The Tale of the Crucified Lovers* (US: *The Crucified Lovers*) (*Chikamatsu Monogatari*) (1954) (☞ ☆): doomed lovers fall victim to the prejudices of Japanese 17th-century society.

•*The Empress Yang Kwei Fei* (*Yokihi*) (1955) (☞ ✍): the affair of the 8th-century Huan Tsung and his mistress is set against the factions of the court.

•*New Tales of the Taira Clan* (*Shin Heike Monogatari*) (1955) (☞ ✍): a class drama examining the feudal feuds between the monarchy, the priests and the samurai.

MOBSTERS

Odds against Tomorrow (Robert Wise 1959) ☆ ✍
Robert Ryan and Ed Begley botch a raid through their racial hatred of partner Harry Belafonte.

Portrait of a Mobster (Joseph Pevney 1961)
Vic Morrow as racketeer Dutch Schultz.

The Public Enemy (UK: Enemies of the Public) (>William Wellman 1931) ☞ ☆ ✍
The life of bootlegger >James Cagney from childhood to door-to-door delivery death.

Racket Busters (Lloyd Bacon 1938) ☆
Government man George Brent thwarts >Humphrey Bogart's crooked trucking deal.

The Roaring Twenties (>Raoul Walsh/Anatole Litvak 1939) ☞ ☆
War vet >James Cagney is forced to turn to crime to survive.

St Valentine's Day Massacre (Roger Corman 1967) ■
Jason Robards, Jr's Al Capone and George

Segal's Bugs Moran shoot it out and about in Chicago.

Scarface (>Howard Hawks 1932) ☞ ☆
Paul Muni is more than a brother to Ann Dvorak, but hardly best friends with George Raft.

White Heat (>Raoul Walsh 1949) ☞ ☆ ✍
Edmond O'Brien is the traitor in >James Cagney's gang.

Modern Times ☆ ✍ ☞ ■

USA • Charles Chaplin • 1936 • 87 mins • b/w
wdm >Charles Chaplin ph Rollie Totheroh/Ira Morgan
Charlie Chaplin, Paulette Goddard, Chester Conklin

A brilliant stroke of Chaplin, *Modern Times*, a silent film in the Golden Age of Talkies, condemns the destruction of individuality and humanity by the advance of industry. Before settling for love on the dole, Charlie endures work as a shipbuilder, nightwatchman and singing waiter in between spells in prison. The factory episode, in which Charlie falls prey (in every sense) to 'industrial disease', owes much to >René Clair's *A Nous La Liberté* (US: *Freedom for Us*) (1931) (☞ ♫) (a gramophone factory goes bankrupt and its owner becomes a drifter) and the flag-waving scene evokes *Mother* (*Mat*) (>V. I. Pudovkin 1926) (☞ ■) (a mother takes up the cause when her revolutionary son is killed), but the rest is pure, if recycled, Chaplin – skating in the toy department hails from *The Rink* (1916) (☆); the meal he can't afford but plays with hails from >*The Gold Rush* (1925), devotion to a penniless gamine recalls *The Immigrant* (1917) (✍ ☞ ☆) and the slum poverty echoes *Easy Street* (☆ ☞) (1917). But here familiarity breeds content.

 •A clerk imprisoned by work has a fling on the annual outing, but his wife finds out, in *Early Spring* (*Soshun*) (Yasujiro Ozu 1956) (☞ ✍).

•Surviving poverty becomes easier when baby transforms the lives of a couple and their neighbours in the *shomin-geki* (everyday life) melodrama *Where Chimneys Are Seen* (aka

Four Chimneys) (*Entotsu no Mieru Basho*) (Heinosuke Gosho 1953) (☆ ☞).

•A slapstick director, Joel McCrea is determined to make serious films and takes off to see how the poor live, in *Sullivan's Travels* (>Preston Sturges 1941) (☞ ✍ ☆).

•Maid Greer Garson causes ructions when she marries mill owner Lionel Barrymore's son Gregory Peck, in the industrial soap opera *Valley of Decision* (Tay Garnett 1945) (☆ ✍).

•The bosses are the butt of the jokes in Jirí Menzel's study of a Czechoslovakian brewery – *Cutting it Short* (*Postrinzi*) (1980) (☞).

MONARCHY

Alfred the Great (Clive Donner 1965) ✍
David Hemmings usurps the throne from timid brother Michael York.

Anna and the King of Siam (John Cromwell 1946) ☆ ☞ ✍
Irene Dunne acts as governess to Rex Harrison's multitude of offspring.

Beau Brummel (Curtis Bernhardt 1954) ■
Stewart Granger rubs shoulders with Robert Morley's George III and Peter Ustinov's Prince Regent before falling from favour.

Jubilee (Derek Jarman 1978) ■
Queen Elizabeth I travels through time to the new Elizabethan age and despairs at what she sees.

The King and I (Walter Lang 1956) ☆ ♫ ✍
Deborah Kerr and Yul Brynner in the musical version of *Anna and the King of Siam*.

The Mudlark (Jean Negulesco 1950) ☆ ✍
A small boy breaks into Windsor Castle and meets Queen Victoria.

Nicholas and Alexandra (Franklin Schaffner 1971) ☆ ■ ✍
Michael Jayston and Janet Suzman as the tragic end of the Romanov dynasty, overthrown in 1917.

The Prince and the Pauper (William Keighley 1937) ✍ ☆
The Mauch Brothers as Edward VI and his peasant lookalike, in Mark Twain's story.

Sixty Glorious Years (US: *Queen of Destiny*) (Herbert Wilcox 1938) ☆ ✍
Anna Neagle as Queen Victoria and Anton Walbrook as Prince Albert.

Victoria the Great **(Herbert Wilcox 1937)** ☆
The romance of Victoria and Albert with the principals as above.
The Wedding March **(>Erich Von Stroheim 1928)** ☞ ✍
The director as a Hapsburg prince who is murdered by the guardian of the peasant he loves.

MONKS

Brother Orchid **(Lloyd Bacon 1940)** ☆
Having been fleeced by fellow gangster >Humphrey Bogart, >Edward G. Robinson becomes a monk.
Crooks in Cloisters **(Jeremy Summers 1963)** ✍
Villains, including Barbara Windsor, lay low in an island monastery and enjoy the lifestyle.
El **(US: *This Strange Passion*) (>Luis Buñuel 1952)** ☞ ☆
A middle-aged man enters a monastery after attempting to murder his young bride.
The Garden of Allah **(Richard Boleslawski 1936)** ☆ ☞
>Marlene Dietrich is loved by lapsed desert monk Charles Boyer.
Gate of Hell **(*Jigokumon*) (Teinosuke Kinugasa 1953)** ☆ ■
A warlord does penance in a monastery for his sexual excesses.
Letters from My Windmill **(*Lettres de Mon Moulin*) (Marcel Pagnol 1954)** ☞ ✍
Three tales: monks brew a new liqueur; the Devil tempts a gluttonous priest and a miller sells off a broken-down windmill.
The Monk **(*Le Moine*) (Ado Kyrou 1972)** ✍
This >Luis Buñuel co-scripted version of Matthew Lewis's Gothic novel has Franco Nero as the monk tormented by his sexual desires.
The Name of the Rose **(Jean-Jacques Annaud 1986)** ☆ ■ ✍
>Sean Connery investigates the deaths of monks in a medieval whodunnit.

Monroe, Marilyn
(Norma Jean Mortenson) American actress (1926–62)
>John Huston directed Monroe at both the start and the close of her career, in *The Asphalt*

Jungle (1950) (☞ ✍) (Marilyn as the mistress of crook Louis Calhern who is planning to double-cross his fellow thieves) and *The Misfits* (1961) (☞ ☆) (Marilyn despairs of cowboys >Clark Gable and Montgomery Clift's views on life). In the intervening 11 years, she passed through international stardom, stormy marriages to Joe DiMaggio and Arthur Miller, professional capriciousness that not even the Actors Studio could assuage, and increasing alcohol and drug dependency. Fame proved as difficult to handle as her unhappy childhood, but by the time of her suspicious death, the voluptuous, vivacious Marilyn had also passed from dumb blonde to accomplished comedienne: *Monkey Business* (>Howard Hawks 1952) (☆) (Marilyn as secretary to >Cary Grant's boss Charles Coburn, taking Grant's and >Ginger Rogers' regression into youth with equanimity); *Gentlemen Prefer Blondes* (>Howard Hawks 1953) (☞ ☆♫) (Jane Russell and Marilyn go to Europe to find millionaires); *The Seven Year Itch* (>Billy Wilder 1955) (☆ ☞ ✍) (Marilyn uses the subway breeze to cool her, but conscience alone can take the heat out of Tom Ewell's lust); *Bus Stop* (Joshua Logan 1956) (☆ ✍) (Marilyn steps off the bus and into a romance with an unstable cowboy); and >*Some Like It Hot* (>Billy Wilder 1959) (☆ ✍ ☞ ■♫).

 •>*All About Eve* (>Joseph L. Mankiewicz 1950) (☆ ✍ ☞).
•*Clash by Night* (>Fritz Lang 1952) (☞ ☆): Marilyn's allure is diminished by city slicker >Barbara Stanwyck's return to her fishing port home.
•*We're Not Married* (Edmund Goulding 1952) (✍): Marilyn is one of the many discovering their marriages were invalid.
•*Niagara* (Henry Hathaway 1953): unfaithful wife Marilyn plans to murder husband Joseph Cotten, but he is ready for her.
•*How to Marry a Millionaire* (Jean Negulesco 1953) (☆ ✍): Marilyn, Lauren Bacall and Betty Grable put all they have into renting an apartment to lure millionaires.
•*River of No Return* (Otto Preminger 1954) (☆): Robert Mitchum tries to cheat singer Marilyn of her gold claim.

•*The Prince and the Showgirl* (>Laurence Olivier 1957) (■): Marilyn proudly defends her lifestyle when she is picked up by Ruritanian prince Olivier.

•*Let's Make Love* (>George Cukor 1960): stuffy millionaire >Yves Montand falls for Marilyn who is in the cast of a show lampooning him.

Monsieur Hulot's Holiday (Les Vacances de Monsieur Hulot) ☆
⚐ ☞ ■ ♫

France • Cady/Discina • 1953 • 91 mins • b/w
d Jacques Tati w Jacques Tati/Henri Marquet p Jacques Mercanton/Jean Mouselle m Alain Romans
Jacques Tati, Nathalie Pascaud, Michèle Rolla, Valentine Camax

One of the funniest-ever films, firmly rooted in the tradition of the pre-Hollywood sketch comedies of Georges Méliès and Edwin S. Porter, Jacques Tati's masterpiece almost single-handedly ended the tyranny of narrative over 20th-century cinema. Hulot the walking catastrophe would be hilarious alone, but pitched into the seaside *ennui*, with holidaymakers so normal they are eccentric, he is chokingly funny. There are riotous set-pieces such as the picnic, the funeral and the evening's home entertainment and such slick sight slapsticks as the station platform, the rumble seat and the wife collecting shells only for her husband to toss them away instantly. Only >Laurel & Hardy and occasionally Clouseau can compete with the tennis game for inducing tears of laughter.

 More Tati – *Jour de Fête* (1949) (☆ ⚐ ☞): Tati as a postman inspired to speed up his round by an American postal film; *Playtime* (1968) (☞): the middle classes at play are ridiculed at the opening of a new club in Tativille; *Traffic* (*Trafic*) (1971) (☆ ☞): Hulot is confounded by a car of the future en route to an exhibition; *Parade* (1974) (☆): Tati puts some of his famous music hall sketches on film, including his hapless goalkeeper and incompetent cyclist.

•Pierre Etaix was Tati's nearest mime rival, witness *As Long As You're Healthy* (*Tant qu'on a la Santé*) (1965) (Etaix finds modern life more than he can stand).

•The chaos at a Miami hotel is all the fault of *The Bellboy* (Jerry Lewis 1960) (☆).

•Gordon Harker and >Alastair Sim's rain-ruined seaside holiday is brightened by a murder, in *Inspector Hornleigh on Holiday* (Walter Forde 1939) (☆ ⚐).

•Nathalie Baye despairs of teaching, but after *A Week's Holiday* (*Une Semaine de Vacances*) (Bertrand Tavernier 1980) (☆), she is more than happy to return to Lyons.

Montand, Yves
(Ivo Livi) Italian-born French actor (b 1921)

A singer, introduced into films by Edith Piaf, Montand had to wait for eight years before *The Wages of Fear* (*Le Salaire de la Peur*) (Henri-Georges Clouzot 1953) (⚐ ☞ ■ ☆) (poverty-stricken truckers transport explosives across pot-holed roads) brought cinema fame to match his cabaret celebrity. Disappointing romantic leads followed – for example, *Let's Make Love* (>George Cukor 1960) (☆) (stuffy millionaire Yves falls for member of the show that is lampooning him, >Marilyn Monroe) and *Goodbye Again* (Anatole Litvak 1962) (☆) (in an adaptation of Françoise Sagan's novel *Aimez-Vous Brahms?* >Ingrid Bergman dumps Yves for Anthony Perkins). *The Sleeping Car Murders* (*Compartiment Tueurs*) (1965) (⚐ ☆ ☞) (Yves solves a whodunnit on the Marseilles-Paris overnight train) commenced his collaboration with Constantin Costa-Gavras, and he starred in many of the Greek director's thrillers, radicalizing his own political views in the process: *Z* (1969) (☆ ⚐ ☞) (pacifist politician Montand is a hit-and-run victim in a Fascist state in this Best Foreign Film Oscar winner); *The Confession* (*L'Aveu*) (1970) (☆ ⚐) (Montand as Czech minister Artur London, tortured after the 1951 purge); and *State of Siege* (*État de Siège*) (1973) (☆ ☞) (Montand as a CIA agent held hostage by Marxist guerrillas in exchange for political prisoners). Improving with age, Montand was superb as the rascally César in >*Jean de Florette* (Claude Berri 1986) (☆ ⚐ ☞ ■) and

>*Manon des Sources* (Claude Berri 1987) (☆ ■ ✍ ☞).

 •*The Witches of Salem* (aka *The Crucible*) (*Les Sorcières de Salem*) (Raymond Rouleau 1957) (✍ ☆): Arthur Miller's play about religious hysteria in 17th-century Massachusetts.

•*The War is Over* (*La Guerre est Finie*) (>Alain Resnais 1966) (☆ ☞): Montand realizes that the Spanish Civil War achieved nothing as Franco is still in power.

•*Live for Life* (*Vivre pour Vivre*) (Claude Lelouch 1967) (☆): this AAN film has Montand's TV reporter having affairs and adventures in Kenya, Vietnam and the Congo.

•*The Red Circle* (*Le Cercle Rouge*) (Jean-Pierre Melville 1970) (☞ ☆): there is little honour among jewel thieves Montand, Alain Delon and André Bourvil.

•*Tout Va Bien* (>Jean-Luc Godard/Jean-Pierre Gorin 1972) (☞ ☆): TV ad director Montand and journalist >Jane Fonda grow to understand the striking workers who kidnap them.

•*César and Rosalie* (Claude Sautet 1972): Yves, Romy Schneider and Sami Frey are caught in a love triangle.

•*Vincent, Paul, François and the Others* (*Vincent, Paul, François…Et les Autres*) (Claude Sautet 1974): tool-hire owner Montand and his middle-aged friends mourn their wasted lives.

•*The Savage* (US: *Lovers Like Us*) (*Le Sauvage*) (Jean-Paul Rappeneau 1978) (☆): Yves is washed up on a desert island with heiress >Catherine Deneuve.

Monty Python's Life of Brian
✍ ☆ ♫ ☞

GB • Hand Made • 1979 • 93 mins • col
d Terry Jones   w Cast   ph Peter Bizou
m Various
Graham Chapman, John Cleese, Terry Gilliam, Eric Idle, Michael Palin, Terry Jones

>François Truffaut claimed that he simply made films that he would have liked to see himself. Ex-Beatle and now film producer George Harrison's adherence to the same principle not only rescued Monty Python's foundering project, but also bought him what has been called the most expensive cinema ticket ever. Money well spent though, as this controversial lampoon of religious fanaticism, imperialism, Middle East politics and everything else that happened to be passing is quite brilliant. Mistaken for Christ at birth, Brian Cohen (Chapman), a member of the People's Front of Judea is sought by the Romans as a terrorist and the Jews as the Messiah. The highlights are legion, the best being the Sermon on the Mount heard from the back of the crowd; the PFJ's recognition that Roman rule is beneficial; the prophet and hermit scenes and the interrogations before Palin's lisping Pilate.

 •>Jean Gabin plays Pilate in a more serious, but sympathetic way in *Golgotha* (Julien Duvivier 1935) (☆ ☞ ■).

•Nikos Kazantzakis's novel spawned another Christ controversy when Barbara Hershey subjected Willem Dafoe to *The Last Temptation of Christ* (>Martin Scorsese 1988) (☞ ✍).

•Jeffery Hunter's mournful-eyed Messiah was a more commendable Christ in *King of Kings* (>Nicholas Ray 1961) (☞ ☆).

•A series of sketches provided the format for *Kentucky Fried Movie* (John Landis 1977) (✍).

•There is more spoof history in *The History of the World Part One* (Mel Brooks 1981) (✍).

•Peter Sellers' retarded gardener is mistaken as a genius by Melvyn Douglas and Shirley MacLaine, in *Being There* (Hal Ashby 1979) (☆).

Moonlighting ☆ ✍ ☞
GB • Michael White/Channel Four • 1982 • 97 mins • col
wd Jerzy Skolimowski   ph Tony Pierce Roberts   m Stanley Myers
Jeremy Irons, Eugene Lipinski, Jiri Stanislaw, Eugeniusz Haczkiewicz

Made at a time when the name of Lech Walesa was on everyone's lips in one pronunciation or another, Jerzy Skolimowski's black comedy sets in a Thatcherite London microcosm the rise and repression of Solidarity. Arriving in

Britain from Poland with three colleagues handpicked for their ignorance and subservience, Jeremy Irons (who dominates the teasing plot with consummate skill) has detailed orders but insufficient money to turn a suburban house into a love nest for his boss. Driven to shoplifting to feed them and imposing curfews and altering watches to keep them working, Irons hides the news of the events in Poland to prevent mutiny, but succeeds only in precipitating it. Enthralling.

 •Brian Donlevy is an Eastern European labourer made good, in *An American Romance* (>King Vidor 1944) (☞ ☆).

•>Carole Lombard and Jack Benny are the Poles mutinying against Hitler, in *To Be or Not to Be* (>Ernst Lubitsch 1942) (☞ ✍ ☆).

•Solidarity's effects on Poland are explored in *Man Of Iron* (*Czlowiek z Zelaza*) (>Andrej Wajda 1981) (a radio reporter goes to Gdansk to report on events at the Lenin Shipyard) (☞ ▓) and *To Kill a Priest* (Agnieszka Holland 1988) (✍) (Christopher Lambert in a *film à clef* on the assassination of Father Jerzy Popieluszko).

•Anthony Quinn refuses to disclose the facts, when Nazi Hardy Kruger demands the whereabouts of a village's wine, in *The Secret of Santa Vittoria* (Stanley Kramer 1969) (✍ ☆).

•The perils of shoplifting come home to Richard Berry when he lands in prison in *L'Addition* (aka *The Patsy*) (Denis Amar 1983) (✍).

MOTHER LOVE

Bellissima (>Luchino Visconti 1951) ☞ ✍
An ambitious mother tries all she knows to make her daughter a film star.

Bloody Mama (Roger Corman 1969) ☞ ☆
This biopic of Kate 'Ma' Barker has Shelley Winters leading her four boys on the rampage in Depression America.

The Divided Heart (Charles Crichton 1954) ☞ ✍
A Blitz orphan's long-lost mother returns to break the hearts of his foster parents.

Evergreen (Victor Saville 1934) ✍
Jessie Matthews replaces her mother in a vaudeville act and is pestered by her mum's lovers.

The Good Mother (Leonard Nimoy 1988) ☆
>Diane Keaton's affair with Liam Neeson threatens the custody of her daughter.

I Remember Mama (>George Stevens 1948) ☆ ☞
Irene Dunne is the Norwegian immigrant mother struggling to raise her family in San Francisco.

Oedipus Rex (>Pier Paolo Pasolini 1967) ☞ ▓
Franco Citti kills his father and marries his mother in the Greek myth.

The Silver Cord (John Cromwell 1933) ☆
Irene Dunne threatens to leave mummy's boy Joel McCrea.

Stella Dallas (Henry King 1925) ☞/(>King Vidor 1937) ☆ ☞ ✍
Belle Bennett and >Barbara Stanwyck respectively alienate their daughters Lois Moran and Anne Shirley through their slovenliness.

To Each His Own (Mitchell Leisen 1946) ☆ ✍
>Olivia De Havilland accidentally gives away her son, but follows his life from a distance until reconciliation.

The World According to Garp (George Roy Hill 1982) ☆ ✍
Robin Williams' literary career is watched with pride by his prominent feminist mother Glenn Close.

MOTORCYCLES

Easy Rider (Dennis Hopper 1969) ☆
Hopper and Peter Fonda bike their way across the USA.

Eat the Peach (Peter Ormrod 1986) ✍
Unemployed Irishmen set up a 'wall of death'.

Electra Glide in Blue (James William Guercio 1973) ✍
Motorcycle cop Robert Blake grows to hate the methods employed to fight crime.

The Leather Boys (Sidney J. Furie 1963) ☞
A teenage newlywed's gay past is revealed when he shares a room with a biker friend.

Little Fauss and Big Halsy **(Sidney J. Furie 1970)** ♫
Robert Redford and Michael J. Pollard roar around the US to the accompaniment of country-and-western music.

The Loveless **(Kathryn Bigelow/Monty Montgomery 1982)** ✍
Bikers experience the bigotry of a small Georgia town while their machines are repaired.

Once a Jolly Swagman **(US: *Maniac on Wheels*) (Jack Lee 1948)** ☆
Factory worker Dirk Bogarde joins a speedway club.

Rumble Fish **(>Francis Ford Coppola 1983)** ☞
Mickey Rourke and Matt Dillon defend their gang's honour against their rivals.

Silver Dream Racer **(David Wickes 1980)** ♫
David Essex as a grand prix bike-rider heading for a crash.

The Wild One **(Laslo Benedek 1954)** ☞
Bikers >Marlon Brando and Lee Marvin rev engines and terrorize a small town.

MURDERERS

Badlands **(Terence Malick 1974)** ☆ ■ ✍
This *film à clef* of Charles Starkweather has Martin Sheen and his girlfriend (Sissy Spacek) on a deadly rampage in the 1950s.

The Boston Strangler **(Richard Fleischer 1968)** ☆
Tony Curtis as the sex killer who stalked 1960s Boston.

Compulsion **(Richard Fleischer 1959)** ✍
>Orson Welles prosecutes joy-killers Leopold and Loeb, played by Dean Stockwell and Bradford Dillman.

Dance with a Stranger **(Mike Newell 1985)** ☆ ✍ ♫
Miranda Richardson's Ruth Ellis murders racing driver lover Rupert Everett.

Dr Crippen **(Robert Lynn 1962)** ✍
Donald Pleasence as the Edwardian killer who eloped with his mistress (Samantha Eggar) having murdered his wife Coral Browne.

I Want to Live **(Robert Wise 1958)** ☆ ✍
Susan Hayward as Barbara Graham who was executed despite guilt doubts.

In Cold Blood **(Richard Brooks 1967)** ✍
Based on Truman Capote's book, the film tells of the murder of a family by two mentally-unstable strangers.

The Life of Charles Peace **(William Haggar 1905)** ✍
Silent telling of the crimes of the notorious gentleman thief and killer.

>*Ten Rillington Place* **(Richard Fleischer 1971)** ☆ ✍ ☞

Murnau, F. W.
(Friedrich Wilhelm Plumpe) German director (1888–1931)

Scholar and air corps hero, Murnau was another product of Max Reinhardt's company. Much of his German canon perished, although fortunately his horror classic *Nosferatu* (*Nosferatu, Eine Symphonie des Grauens*) (1922) (☞ ■ ☆) (Max Schreck as the screen's first Dracula) and his collaborations with >Emil Jannings – *The Last Laugh* (*Der Letzte Mann*) (1924) (☆ ☞) (the decline and humiliation of a pompous hotel doorman), *Tartuffe* (*Tartüff*) (1926) (☞ ☆) (schemer Jannings takes over the life and lover of his patron in Molière's play) and *Faust* (1926) (☞ ■) (Jannings as the Devil purchasing Gösta Ekman's soul in return for youth) – survived. He introduced the moving camera to Expressionist chiaroscuro, and it is best illustrated in his 1927 Hollywood masterpiece *Sunrise* (☞) (George O'Brien plans to kill wife Janet Gaynor but can't go through with it). Murnau had just completed *Tabu* (■ ☞) (a study of a Tahitian pearl diver in the South Seas) with documentary specialist Robert Flaherty (and for which cameraman Floyd Crosby was to win an AA), in 1931 when he was killed in a car crash.

•*The Haunted Castle* (aka *Castle Vogelod* (*Schloss Vogelöd*) (1921) (☞ ■): the atmosphere at a hunting party extracts a confession from a guest.
•*Four Devils* (1928) (☞): the interaction between four trapeze artists.
•*City Girl* (aka *Our Daily Bread*) (1930) (☞ ■): Mary Duncan is the town mouse frightened by the countryside.

MUSICIANS

Autumn Sonata (>Ingmar Bergman 1978) ☆
Pianist >Ingrid Bergman visits her daughter Liv Ullmann to get over the loss of her lover.

Dangerous Moonlight (US: *Suicide Squadron*) (Brian Desmond Hurst 1941) ♫
Polish pilot pianist Anton Walbrook has a bout of amnesia after being shot down. This was the film that introduced Richard Addinsell's *Warsaw Concerto*.

Deception (Irving Rapper 1946) ☆ ✍
Cellist Paul Henreid returns from war to find >Bette Davis in the arms of composer Claude Rains.

It's Great to Be Young (Cyril Frankel 1956) ☆
Headmaster Cecil Parker orders John Mills to disband the school orchestra.

Intermezzo: A Love Story (US: *Escape to Happiness*) (Gregory Ratoff 1939) ☆
Violinist >Leslie Howard falls for piano teacher >Ingrid Bergman.

Mélo (Paul Czinner 1932)/(>Alain Resnais 1986) ✍
A violinist's wife falls for his pianist best friend.

The Seventh Veil (Compton Bennett 1945) ☆ ✍
Pianist Ann Todd comes to love guardian James Mason with the help of psychiatrist Herbert Lom, in Muriel and Sydney Box's AA-winning script.

Swing High Swing Low (Mitchell Leisen 1937) ☆
>Carole Lombard rescues trumpeter Fred MacMurray from ruining his career through drink.

That Uncertain Feeling (>Ernst Lubitsch 1941) ☞ ✍
Merle Oberon has an affair with Burgess Meredith, who is convinced he is a great pianist, but Melvyn Douglas determines to save his marriage.

MYTHS AND LEGENDS

The Adventures of Robin Hood (>Michael Curtiz/William Keighley 1938) ☞ ☆ ■
Errol Flynn as the Lincoln Green outlaw hiding out in Sherwood Forest.

Camelot (Joshua Logan 1967) ☆
King Arthur (Richard Harris) fights Franco Nero's Lancelot for Vanessa Redgrave's Guinevere in the Lerner & Loewe musical.

Clash of the Titans (Desmond Davis 1981) ☆
>Laurence Olivier's Zeus and Claire Bloom's Hera thwart >Maggie Smith's Thetis's toying with mortals.

Excalibur (John Boorman 1981)
Arthur and the Knights of the Round Table go in search of the Holy Grail.

Gawain and the Green Knight (Stephen Weeks 1973) ■
Murray Head meets the challenge of the supernatural knight.

Jason and the Argonauts (Don Chaffey 1963) ✳
Todd Armstrong beats man, monsters and divinities to retrieve the Golden Fleece.

Medea (>Pier Paolo Pasolini 1969) ☞ ■
Jason (Giuseppe Gentile) wishes to rid himself of bride Maria Callas so she puts her contingency plans into operation.

MY DARLING CLEMENTINE
(>John Ford 1946) ☞ ☆ ♫

LAWMEN

DODGE CITY
(>Michael Curtiz 1939)
(bang bang and railroad town is cleaned up by Errol Flynn)

>HIGH NOON
(>Fred Zinnemann 1952) ☆ ☞
✍♫
(marshal >Gary Cooper forced to go it alone in cowardly town)

CARRY ON COWBOY
(Gerald Thomas 1963) ☆ ✍
(Sid James and Kenneth Williams confronted by idealistic marshall Jim Dale)

SILVERADO
(Laurence Kasdan 1985) ☆ ☞
(pioneers are hampered by designs of corrupt sheriff Brian Dennehy)

GREAT OUTDOORS

THE LUSTY MEN
(>Nicholas Ray 1952) ☞
(rivalries brew on rodeo tour)

THE FAR COUNTRY
(Anthony Mann 1955) ☆
(prospectors outsmarted by ruthless con men)

THE SEARCHERS
(>John Ford 1956) ☞ ■ ☆
(war hero >John Wayne seeks kidnapped niece among Indians)

THE HALLELUJAH TRAIL
(John Sturges 1965) ☆
(hostile forces try to waylay cargo of whisky)

JEREMIAH JOHNSON
(Sydney Pollack 1972) ■ ☆
(lone trapper Robert Redford survives the changing seasons)

INDIANS

BROKEN ARROW
(Delmer Daves 1950) ☆
(army scout >James Stewart arbitrates between warring factions)

THE BIG SKY
(>Howard Hawks 1952) ☞
(>Kirk Douglas's expedition troubled by unimpressed local tribes)

MAJOR DUNDEE
(Sam Peckinpah 1965) ☆
(brutal army squad massacre raiding Indians)

DULE AT DIABOLO
(Ralph Nelson 1965) ■
(racial tension appeased by slaughtering Indians)

THE SCALPHUNTERS
(Sydney Pollack 1968) ☆
(Burt Lancaster leads light-hearted crusade against primitive killers)

A MAN CALLED HORSE
(Elliot Silverstein 1970) ☆
(captive nobleman Richard Harris learns Indian ways)

> >Henry Fonda as Wyatt Earp
> restoring law to Tombstone

GUNFIGHTERS

THE GUNFIGHTER
(Henry King 1950) ☞ ☆
(Gregory Peck tries to live down a violent past)

SHANE
(>George Stevens 1953) ☞ ☆
(Alan Ladd defends family against jealous ranchers)

GUNFIGHT AT THE OK CORRAL
(John Sturges 1957) ☆
(Burt Lancaster and >Kirk Douglas team up to clean up)

THE WONDERFUL COUNTRY
(Robert Parrish 1959) ☆
(gunman Robert Mitchum offered respectable job with the Texas Rangers)

CAT BALLOU
(Elliot Silverstein 1965) ☆ ✍♫
(drunkard gunman Lee Martin rescues outlaw >Jane Fonda)

OUTLAWS

JESSE JAMES
(Henry King 1939) ☞ ☆
(Frank [>Henry Fonda] and Jesse [Tyrone Power] have some hold-up fun)

BEND OF THE RIVER (US:WHERE THE RIVER BENDS)
(Anthony Mann 1952) ☆
(outlaw gives settlers a cold welcome)

THE LEFT-HANDED GUN
(Arthur Penn 1958) ☆
(Billy the Kid [>Paul Newman] avenges friend's murder)

RIO BRAVO
(>Howard Hawks 1959) ☞ ☆
(stranger >John Wayne and drunken sheriff Dean Martin combat small-town baddies)

LONELY ARE THE BRAVE
(David Miller 1962) ☆
(modern transport makes life tough for >Kirk Douglas's latter day cowboy)

Napoléon ☆ ■ ✍

France • WESTI/Société Générale De Films •
1927 • 270 mins • b/w

wd Abel Gance   ph Jules Kruger

**Albert Dieudonné, Wladimir Roudenko,
Gina Manès, Nicolas Koline**

Intended to be the first of six instalments, Gance's 1927 factitious tracing of Bonaparte's progress to his destiny from *École Militaire* through the Revolution to the Italian campaign of 1796 was initially a 378-minute silent. A much shorter sound version appeared in 1934 (and another, with some material restored, in 1971), but thanks to Kevin Brownlow's restoration, it is now available in something approaching the original. The snowball battle, the ball and the Revolutionary rabble-rousing are unforgettable but regrettably, encumbered as they are with a single screen, TV audiences will be deprived of the triptych finale. Prone to idolatry, Gance's clumsy symbolism and suspenseless narrative show that he was more a daring technical innovator than a natural storyteller, but this is still a riveting work.

VIEW ON ▶
•>Alec Guinness's Charles I is opposed by Richard Harris's soldier-ruler in *Cromwell* (Ken Hughes 1970) (☆ ✍).

•George C. Scott is the master tactician of the Second World War in *Patton* (Franklin Schaffner 1969) (☆ ✍ ☞).

•The early career of another national hero has >Henry Fonda as *Young Mr Lincoln* (>John Ford 1939) (☆ ☞ ■).

•At the other end of Napoleon's career was his *Waterloo* (Sergei Bondarchuk 1970) (☞ ■) with Rod Steiger as the Emperor and Christopher Plummer as Wellington.

NAPOLEONIC WARS

Adieu Bonaparte (*Al-Wedaa Ya Bonaparte*) (Youssef Chahine 1984) ■

A family's experiences during the 1798 Egyptian campaign.

The Adventures of Gerard (Jerzy Skolimowski 1970) ✍

Peter McEnery as Sir Arthur Conan Doyle's Grand Army hussar cracking a spy ring.

The Duellists (Ridley Scott 1977) ■
Joseph Conrad's story 'The Point of Honour' pits Keith Carradine against Harvey Keitel.
Eagle in a Cage (Fielder Cook 1970) ☆
John Gielgud and Ralph Richardson guard Kenneth Haigh on St Helena.
The Iron Duke (Victor Saville 1934) ☆
George Arliss as Wellington in the days after Waterloo.
Lady Hamilton (US:*That Hamilton Woman*) (Alexander Korda 1941) ☆
>Laurence Olivier's Nelson takes shore leave to woo >Vivien Leigh.
Marie Walewska (US:*Conquest*) (Clarence Brown 1937) ☆ ☞ ✍
>Greta Garbo as the Polish countess who gave Charles Boyer a son.
The Marquise of O (*Die Marquise von O*) (>Erich Rohmer 1976) ☞ ✍ ■
In this Cannes Special Jury winner, an Italian countess forces the Russian officer who raped her to marry her when she becomes pregnant.
The Pride and the Passion (Stanley Kramer 1957) ✍
>Cary Grant, Sophia Loren and Frank Sinatra lead the resistance to the puppet monarchy of Spain.
War and Peace (*Voina i Mir*) (Sergei Bondarchuk 1966 –1967) ☞ ✍ ■
Best Foreign Film Oscar-winning version of Leo Tolstoy's epic of family life in the Russia of 1812.

NAVY LIFE

The Bedford Incident (James B. Harris 1965) ✍ ☆
Pursuing a Soviet sub, Richard Widmark gives the command to launch an atomic missile.
The Caine Mutiny (Edward Dmytryk 1954) ☆
>Humphrey Bogart accuses his crew of mutiny, but his incompetence emerges at the court-martial.
Captain Horatio Hornblower RN (>Raoul Walsh 1951) ✍ ☞
Gregory Peck as C. S. Forester's hero battling through the Napoleonic Wars.
Carry On Jack (Gerald Thomas 1962) ☆ ✍
Kenneth Williams loses his ship to mutiny, but

Charles Hawtrey, Bernard Cribbins and Juliet Mills are at hand.
The Cruel Sea (Charles Frend 1952) ✍ ☞
Jack Hawkins commands a corvette in Nicholas Monsarrat's war classic.
In Which We Serve (Noël Coward/>David Lean 1942) ✍ ☆ ☞
Clingers to the wreckage recall their private and battle lives.
>*On the Town* (>Gene Kelly/>Stanley Donen 1949) ♫ ☆ ☞ ✍
Orion's Belt (*Orions Belte*) (Ola Solum 1985) ✍ ■
The Soviet navy proves too powerful for three roguish Norwegian sailors.
The Sand Pebbles (Robert Wise 1966) ✍
Steve McQueen (AAN) and >Richard Attenborough and their old tub take on Chinese warlords and win an AAN for Best Picture.

NEW TESTAMENT

The Gospel According to St Matthew (*Il Vangelo Secondo Matteo*) (>Pier Paolo Pasolini 1964) ☞ ■
Enrique Irazoqui's Christ preaches equality and charity in this Venice Special Jury Prize winner.
The Greatest Story Ever Told (>George Stevens 1965) ☞ ☆
Max Von Sydow as an authoritative Christ getting the message across.
King of Kings (>Nicholas Ray 1961) ☞ ☆
Jeffrey Hunter as a compassionate Christ preaching and curing with twinkling blue eyes.
The Last Temptation of Christ (>Martin Scorsese 1988) ☞ ✍
Willem Dafoe is subjected to Barbara Hershey's over-converted Mary Magdalen.
>*Monty Python's Life of Brian* (Terry Jones 1979) ✍ ☆ ♫ ☞
The Robe (Henry Koster 1953) ☆ ■
>Richard Burton, Jean Simmons and Victor Mature are among those hoping to retrieve Christ's Crucifixion garment.
Salome's Last Dance (Ken Russell 1988)
Glenda Jackson and Stratford Johns are among those recreating Oscar Wilde's telling of the death of John the Baptist.

NEW YORK

The Clock (UK:*Under the Clock*) (>Vincente Minnelli 1945) ☞ ☆
Soldier Robert Walker meets Judy Garland at Pennsylvania Station and spends his leave with her.

Crocodile Dundee (Peter Faiman 1986) ✍ ☆
Outbacker Paul Hogan experiences the Big Apple with reporter Linda Kozlowski.

Dead End (>William Wyler 1937) ☆ ☞ ■
Gangster >Humphrey Bogart extorts from the slum tenements of the East Side.

From This Day Forward (John Berry 1946) ☆
>Joan Fontaine and Mark Stevens are poor but happy in the Depression slums.

>Manhattan (>Woody Allen 1979) ✍ ☞ ■ ♫ ☆

New York, New York (>Martin Scorsese 1977) ☞ ☆
Saxophonist >Robert De Niro leaves Liza Minnelli in the slums, but she is the one to find fame.

The Out of Towners (Arthur Hiller 1970) ☆ ✍
>Jack Lemmon and Sandy Dennis as the provincials finding life is very different in the big city.

Slaves of New York (James Ivory 1989) ☞ ☆
Tama Janowitz's stories of young bohemian life in the Greenwich Village of the 1980s.

Stars and Bars (Pat O'Connor 1988) ☆
Daniel Day Lewis is the gauche Englishman in the city to win a painting at auction, in this William Boyd tale.

A Thousand Clowns (Fred Coe 1965) ☆
Inspectors try to force drifter Jason Robards, Jr's nephew back to school.

Two for the Seesaw (Robert Wise 1962)
Dance teacher Shirley MacLaine has an affair with out-of-town lawyer Robert Mitchum.

West Side Story (Robert Wise/Jerome Robbins 1961) ♫ ☞ ■
The Sharks and the Jets are the rival dockland gangs in this updating of *Romeo and Juliet*.

Newman, Paul
American actor/director (b 1925)

For a pin-up superstar, Newman has played a lot of unpleasant characters: *Somebody Up There Likes Me* (Robert Wise 1956) (■) (Newman as a tough kid who turns his aggression from crime to boxing); *The Hustler* (AAN: Robert Rossen 1961) (☆ ✍) (Newman as Eddie Felson making a fast buck in the pool halls); *Hud* (AAN: Martin Ritt 1963) (☆ ☞ ✍) (Newman unnerves housekeeper Patricia Neal and refuses to play cowboy for father Melvyn Douglas); *WUSA* (Stuart Rosenberg 1970) (☆) (Newman's hobo goes against the party line as announcer on a right-wing radio station); and *The Colour of Money* (AA: >Martin Scorsese 1986) (Eddie Felson trains Tom Cruise in the tricks of the hustle). Newman looks distinctly uneasy in romances: *A New Kind of Love* (Melville Shavelson 1963) (☆) (journalist Newman changes careerist Joanne Woodward's mind about romance) and *What a Way To Go* (J. Lee-Thompson 1963) (☆) (Newman as one of the many husbands discarded by Shirley MacLaine). He is more comfortable as an anti-hero: *Cat on a Hot Tin Roof* (Richard Brooks 1958) (☆) (stern father Burl Ives is disgusted that Newman is unable to have sex with his wife Elizabeth Taylor); *From the Terrace* (Mark Robson 1960) (Newman has problems with alcoholic, adulterous mother >Myrna Loy); *Cool Hand Luke* (AAN: Stuart Rosenberg 1967) (☆ ✍) (tough jailbird Newman scorns George Kennedy's bullying and they plan an escape together); and *Slap Shot* (George Roy Hill 1977) (☆) (ice hockey coach Newman resorts to win-at-all-costs tactics to keep his team afloat). However, his box-office hits have come in the comedy melodramas *Butch Cassidy and the Sundance Kid* (George Roy Hill 1969) (☆ ✍ ☞ ♫ ■) (Newman and Robert Redford as happy-go-lucky Wild West outlaws cleaning up any stray banks or trains they might find) and *The Sting* (George Roy Hill 1973) (✍ ☆) (Newman and Robert Redford fleece Robert Shaw with a bookmaking con). His better directing efforts have been with the participation of his wife, Joanne Woodward: *Rachel, Rachel* (1968) (☆ ☞) (a dowdy teacher scandalizes her small town with a passionate affair) and *The Glass*

Menagerie (1987) (John Malkovich refuses to help either his clutching, self-deceiving mother (Woodward) or his naïve sister Karen Allen come to terms with themselves).

 •*The Long Hot Summer* (Martin Ritt 1958) (☆): farmer Newman feuds with local bigwig >Orson Welles.

•*The Left-Handed Gun* (Arthur Penn 1958) (☆): Newman as Billy the Kid out to avenge the shooting of his buddy.

• *The Prize* (Mark Robson 1963) (☆ ✍ ☞): Nobel laureate-to-be Newman is helped by Elke Sommer to confound a Soviet plot to replace >Edward G. Robinson with a double.

•*Torn Curtain* (>Alfred Hitchcock 1966) (☞ ☆): Newman's fake defection is blown by Julie Andrews' hysterics and they have to flee for their lives.

•*Absence of Malice* (Sydney Pollack 1981) (✍): journalist Sally Field tries to blame a political killing on Newman.

•*The Verdict* (>Sidney Lumet 1982) (☆ ☞): Newman's washed-up lawyer is given another chance, but his opponent is ruthless James Mason.

Nichols, Mike
American director (b 1931)

A satirist in partnership with Elaine May and a four-time Tony winner, Nichols has devastatingly dissected modern America: sexually, in *Who's Afraid of Virginia Woolf?* (AAN: 1966) (☆ ☞) (academic >Richard Burton and his wife Elizabeth Taylor blaze away regardless in front of their dinner guests George Segal and Sandy Dennis), >*The Graduate* (1967) (☆ ☞ ♫ ✍) and *Carnal Knowledge* (1971) (☞ ☆) (>Jack Nicholson seduces his way through Candice Bergen and Ann-Margret but gets bored with sex); and politically in *Catch-22* (1970) (✍ ☞) (Alan Arkin as Yossarian trying to survive the ever-increasing number of flying missions required before leave can be taken, in an adaptation of Joseph Heller's novel), *The Day of the Dolphin* (1973) (George C. Scott uncovers a plot to use dolphins as kamikazes on to the president's yacht) and *Silkwood* (1983) (☆ ☞ ✍) (nuclear processor >Meryl Streep discovers safety is being compromised, but is killed en route to testify against the plant).

 •*The Fortune* (1975) (☆): Warren Beatty asks >Jack Nicholson to help him kill his heiress fiancée.

•*Heartburn* (1986) (☆ ☞): >Meryl Streep accepts >Jack Nicholson's first infidelities, then strikes out alone.

•*Working Girl* (1988) (☆ ☞): Melanie Griffith exploits Sigourney Weaver's incapacity to succeed in business and seduce >Harrison Ford.

Nicholson, Jack
American actor (b 1937)

Ex-office junior in the MGM cartoon department, Nicholson endured 'B' biker movies and Corman horrors before arriving at the dislocated character, at odds with life and himself, that served him in: *Easy Rider* (AAN: Dennis Hopper 1969) (☆) (Nicholson as a seedy lawyer introduced to dope by bikers Hopper and Peter Fonda); *Five Easy Pieces* (AAN: Bob Rafelson 1970) (☆) (Jack leaves girlfriend Karen Black for future sister-in-law Susan Anspach, but when this falls through, he hits the road); *Carnal Knowledge* (>Mike Nichols 1971)(☞ ☆) (Jack and Art Garfunkel lead wild sex lives, but have done it all by their late 30s); *The Last Detail* (AAN: Hal Ashby 1973) (☆ ☞ ✍) (sailors Nicholson and Otis Young take heading-for-jail Randy Quaid on a last binge); and *Chinatown* (AAN: >Roman Polanski 1974) (☆ ☞ ✍) (Nicholson as a private eye investigating the interest being shown in local reservoirs). >*One Flew over the Cuckoo's Nest* (AA: >Miloš Forman 1975) (☆ ✍ ☞) presented him with a new persona, the cynical, wild-eyed rogue, harmless in *Goin' South* (Jack Nicholson 1978) (☆) (Nicholson survives hanging and works as Mary Steenburgen's hired hand), *Terms of Endearment* (AA: James L. Brooks 1983) (☆) (Jack as a wacky astronaut who loves then leaves then loves Shirley MacLaine) and *Heartburn* (>Mike Nichols 1986) (☆ ☞) (Jack and >Meryl Streep try and overcome their marital problems, but fail), but lethal in *The Shining* (>Stanley Kubrick 1980) (☆ ☞) (Jack as a blocked writer losing his control in a spooked hotel), *The Postman Always Rings Twice* (Bob Rafelson 1981) (✫) (Jack and Jessica Lange murder her garage-owner husband, but fail to keep their eyes on the road) and *The Witches Of Eastwick* (George Miller 1987) (✫ ✍) (this John Updike tale pits chauvinistic wizard Jack against the women he has seduced – Cher, Susan Sarandon and Michelle Pfeiffer). Rarely a dull moment.

 •*The King of Marvin Gardens* (Bob Rafelson 1972) (✫): Nicholson as a radio announcer caught up with brother Bruce Dern's gangster friends.

•*The Fortune* (>Mike Nichols 1975) (✫): Jack helps Warren Beatty elope with an heiress so they can kill her.

•*Reds* (Warren Beatty 1981) (✫): Jack as Eugene O'Neill trying to patch up things between Beatty's Jack Reid and >Diane Keaton's Louise Bryant.

•*Prizzi's Honor* (>John Huston 1986) (✫ ☞ ✍): Jack and >Kathleen Turner are Mafia assassins in love, but out to kill each other.

•*Ironweed* (Hector Babenco 1987) (✫ ☞): Nicholson and >Meryl Streep as hobos who enjoy life and love, despite Depression poverty.

•*Batman* (Tim Burton 1989) (✫ ✍ ■): although Jack's Joker's face has been reconstructed into a smile, his voice is still familiar to Michael Keaton's Caped Crusader.

Nights of Cabiria (Le Notti di Cabiria) ✫ ☞ ✍ ■

Italy • Dino De Laurentiis/Les Films Marceau • 1956 • 110 mins • b/w

d >Federico Fellini w Federico Fellini/ Ennio Flaiano/Tullio Pinelli/Pier Paolo Pasolini ph Otello Martelli m Nino Rota

Giulietta Masina, Amadeo Nazzari, François Perier, Dorian Gray

Desperate to love, Fellini's unwanted, child-like prostitute Cabiria is the ultimate screen victim of heartlessness. Her inability to treat even business relationships dispassionately enables clients to steal her purse, toss her into a river or use her to arouse jealousy in inattentive lovers. At the music hall, a hypnotist hu-

miliates her before a derisive audience by instructing her to enact her romantic fantasies for an imaginary lover called Oscar. Playing on her susceptibilities, a man claims he is the Oscar she seeks, inducing her to sell her belongings and begin afresh with him. Fleeced and drenched again, shedding tears as much of determination as desperation, she returns to town surrounded by singing children – the hope for a better future. *Nights of Cabiria* won the Best Foreign Film Oscar.

•The story was given the musical treatment in *Sweet Charity* (Bob Fosse 1969) (✫): Shirley MacLaine is a New York taxi-dancer who is let down by every man she trusts.

•Another *Cabiria* (Giovanni Pastrone 1914) (☞) is a slave girl in ancient Rome accompanied on adventures by a faithful strongman and her soldier lover.

•>Ginger Rogers is hired by Walter Connolly to arouse emotions in his awful family by impersonating his mistress, in *Fifth Avenue Girl* (Gregory La Cava 1939) (✫ ✍ ☞).

•Whereas Giulietta Masina feels deeply all that happens to her, Peter Sellers' Inspector Clouseau remains oblivious to the assassination attempts being made on him by Commissioner Dreyfus (Herbert Lom), in *The Pink Panther Strikes Again* (Blake Edwards 1976) (✫ ✍).

1900 (Novecento) ✍ ✫ ■ ☞

Italy/France/West Germany • Twentieth Century Fox/Artistes Associés/Artemis • 1976 • 320 mins • col

d >Bernardo Bertolucci w Bernardo Bertolucci/Franco Arcalli/Giuseppe Bertolucci ph Vittorio Storaro m Ennio Morricone

>Robert De Niro, >Gérard Depardieu, Burt Lancaster, Donald Sutherland, Sterling Hayden, Dominique Sanda

On the day Giuseppe Verdi dies, sons are born into both an aristocratic and a peasant family. Alfredo (De Niro) and Olmo (Depardieu) defy class barriers to become David and Jonathan companions, but the First World War leads to divergence. Olmo returns a Marxist and challenges Alfredo's tepid liberalism and his tolerance of the brutal management of the Parmesan estate of Fascist Party member foreman Attila (Sutherland). Bertolucci's panoramic view of family and friendship, war and peace in the first half of the *novocento* provides a powerful warning that political extremism emanates from indolence, not conviction.

 •Elsewhere in 1900: *Casque D'Or* (US: *Golden Marie*) (France: Jacques Becker 1952) (☆ ☞ ■): a carpenter falls for a gangster's moll and is drawn into the world of crime.
•*Picnic at Hanging Rock* (Australia: Peter Weir 1975): (☞ ■) on St Valentine's Day, three girls and their teacher go missing during a school outing).
•*The Time Machine* (Britain: George Pal 1960) (☆ ✳): Rod Taylor leaves Victorian London and lands in 802701, in this adaptation of H. G. Wells' novel.
•>Clark Gable's gangster and >William Powell's lawyer are the diverging friends, in *Manhattan Melodrama* (W. S. Van Dyke 1934) (☆ ☞).
•Reprisals in postwar Italy are examined in the Neo-Realist *Vivere in Pace* (Luigi Zampa 1947) (☞ ■).

Ninotchka ✍ ☞ ☆ ■
USA • MGM • 1939 • 110 mins • b/w
d >Ernst Lubitsch w Charles Brackett/
>Billy Wilder/Walter Reisch ph William
Daniels m Werner Heymann
>Greta Garbo, Melvyn Douglas, Sig
Rumann, Alexander Granach, Felix
Bressart, >Bela Lugosi

It seems remarkable that *Ninotchka* – which, through the massive 'Garbo Laughs!' publicity (not that she hadn't laughed before) and a highly sophisticated comic performance, brought one of the greatest successes of her career – should have been Greta Garbo's penultimate movie. Equally surprising is the script, which presents Communism (then marginally trailing Nazism in the world's Feared Ideology League) as a minor infection afflicting blundering buffoons and intense in-

tellectuals, which could be cured by the love of a good capitalist (Douglas's French aristo) under an exotic sky. If politically naïve, it was classic Lubitsch comedy-of-manners material and, as such, is infinitely preferable to the paranoid propaganda of subsequent Cold War atrocities.

 •Commie comedy is tempered with thrills as emigrés posing as servants Charles Boyer and Claudette Colbert are traced to Paris by >Basil Rathbone, in *Tovarich* (Anatole Litvak 1937) (☆ ☞ ✍), and as slob cop James Belushi teams with Soviet counterpart Arnold Schwarzenegger in *Red Heat* (Walter Hill 1988) (✍).
•A series of sketches showing the iniquities of capitalism and the benefits of Communism make up *La Vie est à Nous* (US: *The People of France*) (>Jean Renoir/Jean-Paul Le Chanois/Jacques Becker/Andre Zwoboda/Pierre Unik/Henri Cartier-Bresson 1936) (✍ ■).
•Just as Melvyn Douglas made Garbo laugh, Anne Shirley brings smiles to all around her, in this adaptation of L. M. Montgomery's children's classic *Anne of Green Gables* (George Nicholls, Jr 1934) (☆ ✍).
•Melvyn Douglas is the Communist discovering the 'joys' of capitalism from Loretta Young, in *He Stayed for Breakfast* (Alexander Hill 1940) (☆).
•The musical version of *Ninotchka*, *Silk Stockings* (Rouben Mamoulian 1957) (☆ ☞) has >Fred Astaire and Cyd Charisse in the leads and >Peter Lorre heading the attendant Communists.

Noiret, Philippe
French actor (b 1931)
A late developer, Noiret has demonstrated an admirable range in both French- and English-language films. Cold and calculating in *The Judge and the Assassin* (*Le Juge et l'Assassin*) (Bertrand Tavernier 1976) (☆ ✍) (Noiret's judge has to decide whether child killer Michel Galabru acted wilfully or is insane) and *Clean Slate* (*Coup de Torchon*) (Bertrand Tavernier 1981) (☆ ☞ ✍) (bored colonial cop Noiret shoots his way through the people who make his life a trial, including wife >Stéphane Au-

dran and mistress Isabelle Huppert); sharp and eccentric in *Zazie* (*Zazie dans le Métro*) (>Louis Malle 1960) (☞ ☆ ✍) (female impersonator Noiret is forced by unforeseen circumstances to break a promise to take his niece on the Métro) and *La Grande Bouffe* (US: *Blow-Out*) (Marco Ferreri 1973) (☆ ✍) (Noiret is joined in eating himself to death by >Marcello Mastroianni, Ugo Tognazzi and Michel Piccoli); dignified in historical dramas *Cyrano et D'Artagnan* (Abel Gance 1964) (☞ ■) (Noiret as Louis XIII protected by poet Jose Ferrer and musketeer Jean-Pierre Cassel) and *Let Joy Reign Supreme* (*Que la Fête Commence*) (Bertrand Tavernier 1975) (☆ ☞ ■) (Noiret as the Duc d'Orléans, regent to Louis XV, aided by scheming priest Jean Rochefort); and archetypically French in *The Night of the Generals* (Anatole Litvak 1967) (☞ ✍) (Noiret is on the trail of a Nazi general who is the >Jack the Ripper of Warsaw), *The Assassination Bureau* (Basil Dearden 1969) (✍ ☆) (Noiret as one of Oliver Reed's gang of killers, before Diana Rigg crusades to disband it) and *Topaz* (>Alfred Hitchcock 1969) (☞) (Noiret is called in to help out flailing US intelligence).

•*All the Gold in the World* (*Tout l'Or du Monde*) (>René Clair 1961) (☞ ☆ ✍): scheming Noiret tries to buy up land from a family of farmers to open a health spa.
•*Thérèse Desqueyroux* (Georges Franju 1962) (☆): mild Noiret bores wife Emmanuele Riva to the point of poisoning.
•*La Vie de Château* (Jean-Paul Rappeneau 1965) (☆): Noiret and >Catherine Deneuve's marriage rivals World War II for action.
•*Alexandre* (US: *Very Happy Alexandre*) (Yves Robert 1968) (☆ ✍): Noiret hides away with his dog when his wife dies, then suddenly sets out to enjoy himself.
•*The Tender Age* (aka *Adolphe*) (aka *The Awkward Age*) (*Adolphe ou l'Âge Tendre*) (Bernard T. Michel 1968) (☆): a film-maker falls for noble Noiret's mistress.
•*La Vieille Fille* (aka *The Old Maid*) (Jean-Pierre Blanc 1972) (☆): Noiret enjoys a quaint hotel affair with Anne Girardot.
•*Dear Inspector* (US: *Dear Detective*) (*Tendre*

Poulet) (Philippe De Broca 1977): cop Anne Girardot and academic Noiret fall in love and solve a murder case.
•*The Northern Star* (*L'Étoile du Nord*) (Pierre Granier-Deferre 1982) (☆): between Egypt and Simone Signoret's Belgian boarding house, absent-minded killer Noiret leaves a trail of destruction.
•*Le Cop* (Claude Zidi 1986) (☆): idle cop Noiret prefers corruption to crime fighting, but new partner Thierry Lhermitte still has much to learn.

Notorious ☞ ☆ ✍ ■
USA • RKO • 1946 • 101 mins • b/w
d >Alfred Hitchcock **w** Ben Hecht
ph Ted Tetzlaff   **m** Roy Webb
>Cary Grant, >Ingrid Bergman, Claude Rains, Louis Calhern, Leopoldine Konstantin

Having seen Claude Rains help Ingrid Bergman escape from the baddies in >*Casablanca* (>Michael Curtiz 1943) (☆ ☞ ✍♫■), we can't help feeling sorry for him in Hitchcock's wonderfully tense story of a Nazi atomic conspiracy, because although he is 'the enemy' and is, at his mother's suggestion, slowly poisoning wife Ingrid, we know he really loves her. Which is more than can be said for Cary Grant, her FBI controller, whose chauvinistic refusal to disclose his affections – which he was to repeat in *Indiscreet* (>Stanley Donen 1958) (☆ ☞) – has landed her in this mess, extracting her from which is the very least he could do. The scene in the wine cellar and the tip-toe escape from the old dark house are amongst Hitch's most nail-biting.

•Composer Claude Rains puts up more of a fight after losing >Bette Davis to cellist Paul Henreid, in *Deception* (Irving Rapper 1946) (☆ ✍).
•Newly discharged from an asylum Jean Simmons is the victim of sinister goings-on, in *Home Before Dark* (>Mervyn Le Roy 1958) (☞ ☆).
•>Basil Rathbone and Nigel Bruce trace a Nazi radio propagandist to the British cabinet, in

Sherlock Holmes and the Voice of Terror (John Rawlins 1942) (✫ ✍).
•Ingrid Bergman is subjected to more marital danger, this time from husband Charles Boyer, in *Gaslight* (UK: *The Murder in Thornton Square*) (>George Cukor 1944) (☞ ✫ ✍).
•>Katharine Hepburn marries Robert Taylor and has her life endangered by brother-in-law Robert Mitchum, in *Undercurrent* (>Vincente Minnelli 1949) (✫ ☞ ✍).
•Julie Andrews and Christopher Plummer and his singing children have to flee the Nazis, in *The Sound of Music* (Robert Wise 1965) (♫ ✫ ✍).

Nuns

Agnes of God (**Norman Jewison 1985**) ✫ ✍
Superior Anne Bancroft endeavours to keep Meg Tilly's secret from journalist >Jane Fonda.

Les Anges du Péché (**US: Angels of the Streets**) (>**Robert Bresson 1943**) ✍ ☞ ✫
Novice Renée Fauré risks her own safety to befriend murderer Jany Holt.

Appointment with Danger (**Lewis Allen 1949**) ✫
Alan Ladd protects nun Phyllis Calvert as the star witness in a murder case.

The Bells of St Mary's (>**Leo McCarey 1945**) ✫ ✍
>Ingrid Bergman has staffroom squabbles with priest Bing Crosby.

Black Narcissus (>**Michael Powell/Emeric Pressburger 1946**) ☞ ■
Somewhere in the Himalayas, Judith Furse's jealousy over Deborah Kerr's friendship with David Farrar leads to a bell tower struggle.

Come to the Stable (**Henry Koster 1949**) ✫
Nursing nuns Loretta Young and Celeste Holm get local male support in the building of their hospital.

Conspiracy of Hearts (**Ralph Thomas 1960**) ✫
Lilli Palmer and Sylvia Syms shelter Jewish escapees and then smuggle them to safety.

Nurses

The Blue Veil (**Curtis Bernhardt 1951**) ✍
Becoming a children's nurse on the death of her own baby, Jane Wyman is rescued from poverty by a former charge.

Carry On Matron (**Gerald Thomas 1958**) ✫ ✍
Hattie Jacques has equal trouble from nurses, patients and philandering doctors.

A Farewell to Arms (**Frank Borzage 1932**) ✫ ☞
Wounded >Gary Cooper falls for war nurse Helen Hayes.

The Girl in the News (>**Carol Reed 1940**) ☞
Margaret Lockwood is suspect number one when her patient dies suddenly.

The Lady with a Lamp (**Herbert Wilcox 1951**) ✫
Anna Neagle as Florence Nightingale ministering to the troops during the Crimean War.

Nurse Edith Cavell (**Herbert Wilcox 1939**) ✫
Anna Neagle is rounded up for spying by First World War German officer George Sanders.

Sister Kenny (**Dudley Nichols 1946**) ✫
Rosalind Russell received an AAN as the Australian nurse who developed treatment for polio victims.

So Proudly We Hail (**Mark Sandrich 1943**) ✫
Claudette Colbert, Veronica Lake and Paulette Goddard tend the wounded in the Pacific War.

Vigil in the Night (>**George Stevens 1940**) ✫
>Carole Lombard takes the blame for Anne Shirley's fatal mistake and helps Brian Aherne establish a plague clinic.

OBSESSIONS

>*The Belly of an Architect* (Peter Greenaway 1987) ▓ ☞ ☆ ✍♫

Clockwise (Christopher Morahan 1986) ☆ ✍
Fanatically punctual headmaster John Cleese is late for a conference thanks to a series of bizarre incidents.

Cluny Brown (>Ernst Lubitsch 1946)
Housemaid Jennifer Jones is obsessed with plumbing; professor Charles Boyer is obsessed with her.

Kes (Ken Loach 1969) ✍ ☆
Neglected schoolboy David Bradley's hopeless life is improved by his training of a kestrel.

Man of Flowers (Paul Cox 1984) ☆ ✍
A quiet, lonely artist Norman Kaye finds love with the girl he hires weekly to come and strip for him.

Moby Dick (>John Huston 1956) ☞ ☆ ✍
Gregory Peck as Captain Ahab, obsessed with the capture of the great white whale.

The Mystery of the Wax Museum (>Michael Curtiz 1933) ☞ ☆ ✍
Lionel Atwill replaces the models lost in a fire with real people.

September 30, 1955 (James Bridges 1978) ✍
Richard Thomas devotes his life to the memory of James Dean.

The Illustrated Man (Jack Smight 1969) ☆
Rod Steiger tells stories based on the tattoos all over his body.

That Obscure Object of Desire (*Cet Obscur Objet du Désir*) (>Luis Buñuel 1978) ☞ ☆
Fernando Ray ruins his life in the hope of sleeping with his maid.

OCCUPIED EUROPE

Battle of the Rails (*La Bataille du Rail*) (René Clément 1946) ☞ ▓
Semi-documentary tale of the debt owed to saboteurs of the French rail system under the Vichy government.

The Four Days of Naples (*Le Quattro Giornate di Napoli*) (Nanni Loy 1962) ☞ ✍
The population of Naples rises against the deportation of men between the ages of 5 and 50.

General della Rovere (>Roberto Rossellini 1959) ☞ ☆ ✍
>Vittorio De Sica as the Nazi puppet designed

to smoke out partisans, who instead joins their cause.

A Generation (Pokolenie) (>Andrej Wajda 1954) ☞ ☆
Love turns a Warsaw Resistance fighter into a heroic leader.

Ivan's Childhood (Ivanovo Detstvo) (>Andrei Tarkovsky 1962) ☞ ☆
Such is Kolya Burlyaev's fury at his parents' murder that he insists on increasingly dangerous Resistance missions.

Kanal (aka *They Loved Life*) (aka *Sewer*) (>Andrej Wajda 1957) ☞ ☆
Warsaw partisans are driven into the sewers, in this telling of a true incident.

La Ligne de Démarcation (US: *The Line of Demarcation*) (>Claude Chabrol 1966) ☞ ☆ ✍
A small town risks sheltering Allied agents and airmen prior to a border escape.

Le Silence de la Mer (Jean-Pierre Melville 1947) ✍
A peasant and his niece vow non-communication with the Nazis billeted on them, but one is a Francophile.

ODD ACADEMIES

Against the Wind (Charles Crichton 1946) ✍ ☞
A saboteurs training school is infiltrated by a Nazi agent.

Back to School (Alan Metter 1986) ☆
Rodney Dangerfield as a millionaire who pays the famous to do his homework when he returns to school.

Brother Rat (William Keighley 1938) ☆
Ronald Reagan, Edward Albert and Wayne Morris lightheartedly learn about things military.

Les Chiens (Alain Jessua 1978) ☆
>Gérard Depardieu's guard dog school booms during a rape crisis, but earns him the hatred of an ambitious politician.

Fame (Alan Parker 1980) ☞
Aspiring stars learn to sing, dance and act as well as how to cope with disappointment.

National Lampoon's Animal House (John Landis 1978) ✍
John Belushi leads the high jinx expected of students in films about early 1960s college life.

Police Academy (Hugh Wilson 1984) ✍
Criminals of the world rejoiced when they got a sneak preview of these incompetents going through basic training.

School for Scoundrels (Robert Hamer 1960) ☆ ✍
>Alastair Sim teaches Ian Carmichael 'one-up-manship' so he can pay back arrogant Terry-Thomas.

School for Secrets (US: *Secret Flight*) (Peter Ustinov 1946) ✍
Radar inventor Ralph Richardson finds a traitor among his students.

13 Rue Madeleine (Henry Hathaway 1946) ☆
>James Cagney is among the agents trained to locate a missile base in occupied France.

ODD COUPLES

Ann Vickers (John Cromwell 1933) ☆
Feminist Irene Dunne sets up home with cantankerous, crooked judge Walter Huston.

The Assam Garden (Mary McMurray 1985) ■
Raj widow Deborah Kerr creates an exhibit garden with immigrant Madhur Jaffrey.

Bride of Frankenstein (James Whale 1935) ☆ ✍ ☞ ✳
>Boris Karloff's Monster is repellent to custom-built bride Elsa Lanchester.

Mad Max (George Miller 1979) ✍
Mel Gibson and Steve Bisley as cops Max and The Goose out to crush motorcycle gang The Glorys.

The Odd Couple (Gene Saks 1968) ✍ ☞ ☆
Walter Matthau as superslob Oscar sharing a flat with obsessively tidy Felix (>Jack Lemmon).

Trains, Planes and Automobiles (John Hughes 1987) ☆ ✍
Steve Martin's journey home is complicated by travelling companion John Candy.

Zorba the Greek (Michael Cacoyannis 1964) ☆ ✍ ♫
Writer Alan Bates is befriended by Greek

strongman Anthony Quinn in the screen version of Nikos Kazantzakis's novel.

The Official Version (US: The Official Story) (La Historia Official) ☆ ✍ ☞ ▪

Argentina • Historias Cinematograficas/ Progress Communications • 1985 • 115 mins • col

d Luis Puenzo   w Luis Puenzo/Aida Bortnik   ph Felix Monti   m Atilio Stampone

Norma Aleandro, Chela Ruiz, Héctor Alterio, Chunchuna Villafane

A compelling story of a history teacher (Aleandro) whose acceptance of the political situation in Argentina is challenged by her growing suspicion that her adopted daughter is the child of a *desaparecido*. In probing her daughter's background, she drifts apart from her acquiescent businessman husband, and the revision of her views from contact with the grief of the ever-vigilant mothers and grandmothers of Buenos Aires' Plaza de Mayo transforms her personally and professionally. An emotive study of human rights and motherhood, the film offers hope of redemption for the politically entrenched worldwide.

 •While Miguel Angel Sola has been imprisoned for political activities, his wife Susu Pecoraro has grown away from him and begun a new life, in *South (Sur)* (Fernando E. Solanas, Argentina 1988) (✍ ☞).

•The history of Argentina and its revolutionary heritage is examined in *The Hour of the Furnaces* (*La Hora de los Hornos*) (Fernando E. Solanas 1968) (☞).

•Irene Dunne (AAN) is the selfless mother recalled by Barbara Bel Geddes (AAN) in *I Remember Mama* (>George Stevens 1948) (☆ ☞).

•Powers Boothe searches for his son kidnapped by Brazilian Indians, in *The Emerald Forest* (John Boorman 1985) (☞).

Oil

Boom Town (Jack Conway 1940) ☆
>Clark Gable and >Spencer Tracy strike it rich with black gold and Claudette Colbert and Hedy Lamarr.

The Burning Earth (*Der Brennende Acker*) (>F. W. Murnau 1922) ☞ ▪
A farmer becomes caught up in a love triangle with a countess and her step-daughter in the hope of securing an oil-rich plot.

Campbell's Kingdom (Ralph Thomas 1957) ☆
Convinced he is fatally ill, Dirk Bogarde throws himself into running his well, in this adaptation of the Hammond Innes novel.

Giant (>George Stevens 1956) ☞ ☆ ▪
A strike brings nothing but misery to Rock Hudson, Elizabeth Taylor and James Dean.

Local Hero (Bill Forsyth 1983) ✍ ☞ ☆
Sent by Burt Lancaster to buy a Scottish bay for an oil company, Peter Riegert finds the residents want to haggle.

Louisiana Story (Robert Flaherty 1948) ▪ ☞
A small boy's attention switches from river wildlife to the sinking of an exploratory well.

Oil for the Lamps of China (>Mervyn Le Roy 1935) ☞ ✍
Pat O'Brien is torn between his own principles and company policy.

When Time Ran Out (James Goldstone 1980) ☆
>Paul Newman's drilling operation is threatened by a brooding volcano.

Old age

Batteries Not Included (Matthew Robbins 1987) ✳
Aliens help elderly tenants fight off the bailiffs.

Cocoon (Ron Howard 1985) ☆ ✍
Don Ameche, Wilford Brimley and Hume Cronyn rejuvenate in a pool containing pods occupied by Brian Dennehy's fellow aliens.

The End of the Road (Wolf Rilla 1954) ☆
After a full life Finlay Currie is loath to eke out his days in an old people's home.

I Never Sang for My Father (Gilbert Cates 1969) ☆
Gene Hackman (AAN) has to care for his bad-

tempered and recently widowed father Melvyn Douglas (AAN).

Make Way for Tomorrow (>Leo McCarey 1937) ☞ ☆
Beulah Bondi and Victor Moore are forced apart as their children refuse to provide for them.

Odd Obsession (aka The Key) (Kagi) (Kon Ichikawa 1959) ✍ ☞
This Cannes Special Jury Prize-winner has Ganjiro Nakamura arranging to be cuckolded in the hope of curing his impotence.

The Pied Piper (Irving Pichel 1942) ☆
Child-hating Monty Woolley picks up an international brood as he leads friends' kids to the Channel.

Pocketful of Miracles (>Frank Capra 1961) ☆ ☞
>Bette Davis is helped by well-meaning gangster Glenn Ford to convince her daughter Ann-Margret that she is secure.

The Sunshine Boys (Herbert Ross 1975) ☆ ✍
Stand-up duo Walter Matthau and George Burns (AA) blow their TV comeback.

Umberto D (>Vittorio De Sica 1952) ☞ ☆ ■
Proud pensioner Carlo Battisti begs to support his dog and pregnant maid.

The Whisperers (Bryan Forbes 1966) ☆
Edith Evans (AAN) is persecuted by her malicious family.

Old Testament

The Bible (>John Huston 1966) ■
A retelling of Genesis complete with the director himself as Noah.

The Green Pastures (William Keighley/ Marc Connelly 1936) ☞ ☆ ✍
Bible stories retold by a devout black family.

King David (Bruce Beresford 1985)
Richard Gere leads Israel into battle and Cherie Lunghi into bed.

Noah's Ark (>Michael Curtiz 1929) ☞
Noah Beery and Dolores Costello lead in the animals two by two.

Samson and Delilah (Cecil B. De Mille 1949) ☞
Victor Mature's strength is sapped by Hedy Lamarr's scissors.

Solomon and Sheba (>King Vidor 1959) ☞
George Sanders is furious at Yul Brynner getting the succession over him and plots rebellion.

The Ten Commandments (Cecil B. De Mille 1923 & 1956) ☆ ☞
Theodore Roberts and Charlton Heston, respectively, keep the Israelites taking the tablets while leading them to the Promised Land.

Older Women

Autumn Leaves (Robert Aldrich 1956) ✍
>Joan Crawford's toyboy husband Cliff Robertson proves to be a killer.

Bombay Talkie (James Ivory 1970) ☆ ☞
Jennifer Kendal falls for young Indian film star Shashi Kapoor.

Forty Carats (Milton Katselas 1973) ☆
Liv Ullmann recovers from a messy divorce by sleeping with a young Greek.

>The Graduate (>Mike Nichols 1967) ☆ ☞ ♫ ✍
Harold and Maude (Hal Ashby 1971) ♫
Obsessed with death, Bud Cort pays court to octogenarian Ruth Gordon.

In Praise of Older Women (George Kaczender 1979) ☆
In postwar Vienna and 1956 Budapest, Tom Berenger learns the joy of books and sex from Karen Black.

King, Queen, Knave (Jerzy Skolomowski 1972) ☆
Gina Lollobrigida abandons David Niven for a younger man.

Miss Mary (Maria Luisa Bemberg 1986) ☞ ☆
Governess Julie Christie falls for her charge in inter-war Argentina.

Room at the Top (Jack Clayton 1958) ☆
Ambitious Laurence Harvey (AAN) abandons Simone Signoret (AA) as his star rises.

The Woo Woo Kid (US: In the Mood) (Phil Alden Robinson 1987) ☆ ✍
The true story of 15-year-old Patrick Dempsey's brace of under-age marriages in 1944 America.

OH WHAT A LOVELY WAR!
(>Richard Attenborough 1969) ♫ ☞ ■ ☆

THE FIRST WORLD WAR

WESTFRONT 1918 (aka COMRADES OF 1918)
(>G. W. Pabst 1930) ☞ ✍
(German view of trench monotony and horror)

MATA HARI
(George Fitzmaurice 1932) ☆
(exotic dancer >Greta Garbo spies against France)

THE EAGLE AND THE HAWK
(Stuart Walker 1933) ☆
(flyboys >Cary Grant and >Fredric March love >Carole Lombard and hate each other more than the enemy)

SERGEANT YORK
(>Howard Hawks 1941) ☆ ☞
(country boy >Gary Cooper [AA] performs heroic deeds in the trenches)

THE BLUE MAX
(John Guillermin 1966) ☆
(German air ace proves to be utter cad)

SECOND WORLD WAR (FACT)

THE DESERT FOX (UK: ROMMEL, THE DESERT FOX)
(Henry Hathaway 1951) ☆ ✍
(James Mason in biopic of Afrika Korps' commander Erwin Rommel)

THE BATTLE OF THE RIVER PLATE
(US: PURSUIT OF THE GRAF SPEE)
(>Michael Powell/Emeric Pressburger 1956) ☞ ■ ☆
(German battleship Graf Spee pursued into Argentinian waters)

THE LONGEST DAY
(Andrew Marton/Ken Annakin/Bernhard Wicki 1962) ☆
(tense telling of the D-Day landings)

THE BATTLE OF BRITAIN
(Guy Hamilton 1969) ☞ ■
(much owed by many to few)

TORA! TORA! TORA!
(Richard Fleischer/Ray Kellogg/Toshio Masuda/Kinji Fukasaku 1970) ☞ ✍
(Japanese surprise attack on Pearl Harbor)

A BRIDGE TOO FAR
(>Richard Attenborough/Sidney Hayers 1977) ☞
(allies fail to land in Low Countries in 1944)

SECOND WORLD WAR (FICTION)

THE HOUSE ON 92ND STREET
(Henry Hathaway 1945) ☆ ✍ ☞
(Nazi spies seek atomic formula in USA)

A WALK IN THE SUN
(Lewis Milestone 1946) ☞ ☆
(A US batallion lands in Italy in 1943)

ATTACK!
(Robert Aldrich 1956) ☆
(coward leads Americans to victory in Belgium)

ICE COLD IN ALEX (US: DESERT ATTACK)
(J. Lee-Thompson 1958) ☆ ■
(lost desert ambulance patrol reach a cold drink)

THE GUNS OF NAVARONE
(J. Lee-Thompson 1961) ☆
(crack saboteurs Gregory Peck and David Niven invade Turkish island)

THE EAGLE HAS LANDED
(John Sturges 1976) ☆
(Nazi >Michael Caine's attempt to assassinate Churchill is foiled)

Lunacy of war
emphasized by period songs

SECOND WORLD WAR
HOME FRONT

THIS LAND IS MINE
(>Jean Renoir 1943) ☞ ☆ ♿
(teacher >Charles Laughton defies Nazi court)

SINCE YOU WENT AWAY
(John Cromwell 1944) ☆ ☞ ■ ♫
(Claudette Colbert keeps US family's heads up in husband's war absence)

BALLAD OF A SOLDIER (BALLADA O SOLDATE)
(Grigori Chukrai 1959) ☆ ♿
(Russian on leave finds family have been killed)

THE TWO OF US (LE VIEIL HOMME ET L'ENFANT)
(Claude Berri 1966) ☞ ■
(Jewish boy evacuated to escape concentration camp)

HOPE AND GLORY
(John Boorman 1987) ☆ ♿
(schoolboy enjoys Blitz and evacuation)

THE ASSAULT (DE AANSLAG)
(Fons Rademakers 1987) ☆ ☞
(horrors of occupation continue to haunt Dutch man)

THE DRESSMAKER
(Jim O'Brien 1988) ☆
(young girl finds GI love in wartime Liverpool)

POW CAMPS

THE LAST STAGE (OSTATNI ETAP)
(Wanda Jakubowska 1948) ☆ ☞
(interpreter forced to witness Auschwitz horrors)

STALAG 17
(>Billy Wilder 1953) ☞ ☆ ♿
(William Holden is chief suspect in witty traitor-in-midst thriller)

KAPO
(Gillo Pontecorvo 1960) ☞ ♿
(Nazi doctor provides Jewish girl with false identity)

VERY IMPORTANT PERSON (US: A COMING-OUT PARTY)
(Ken Annakin 1961) ☆
(British boffin rescued from PoW camp)

ESCAPE TO VICTORY (US: VICTORY)
(>John Huston 1981) ☞ ♿
(soccer players escape during challenge match against the Nazis in Paris)

Olivier, Laurence (Lord Olivier)
British actor/director (1907–1989)

The greatest stage actor of his day, Olivier brought Shakespearian and literary classics to the screen with a masterful and acclaimed blend of fidelity and invention: *As You Like It* (Paul Czinner 1936) (☆ ■) (Orlando [Olivier] woos Rosalind [Elisabeth Bergner] in the Forest of Arden); *Wuthering Heights* (AAN; >William Wyler 1939) (☆ ☞ ■ ✍ ♫) (Emily Brontë's Yorkshire Moors novel of Cathy [Merle Oberon]'s love for Olivier's Heathcliff); *Pride and Prejudice* (Robert Z. Leonard 1940) (☆ ✍ ☞) (Jane Austen's haughty heroine Elizabeth Bennett [Greer Garson] sufficiently conquers her repugnance of rich Mr Darcy [Olivier] to marry him); *Henry V* (AAN and Special Oscar Award; Laurence Olivier 1944) (✍ ☆ ■ ☞) (the director as the English king rallying troops on eve of Agincourt); *>Hamlet* (AA; Laurence Olivier 1948) (☆ ☞ ■ ✍ ♫), *Richard III* (AAN: Laurence Olivier 1955) (☆ ☞ ✍ ■) (Olivier as the seminal hunchback opportunist murdering his way to the English throne); and *Othello* (AAN; Stuart Burge 1966) (☆ ✍) (Olivier as the Moor driven by jealous rage to murder his wife Desdemona [>Maggie Smith]). Although a stiff comedian, he had fine timing: *The Divorce of Lady X* (Tim Whelan 1938) (☆ ✍) (Olivier believes he is arranging Merle Oberon's divorce but is in fact paving the way for their marriage) and *The Demi-Paradise* (US: *Adventure for Two*) (>Anthony Asquith 1943) (☆) (Larry as a Russian inventor investigating what makes the British tick). However, his aptitude for character was best demonstrated in COSTUMERS: *Fire Over England* (William K. Howard 1937) (☆) (Olivier helps singe the King of Spain's beard for Flora Robson's Elizabeth I), *Lady Hamilton* (US: *That Hamilton Woman*) (Alexander Korda 1941) (☆ ✍) (syrupy telling of Horatio Nelson [Olivier]'s love for Emma Hamilton [>Vivien Leigh]) and *Khartoum* (Basil Dearden 1966) (■) (Olivier as the Mahdi besieging Charlton Heston's General Gordon in the Sudanese capital); and MELODRAMAS: *>Rebecca* (AAN; >Alfred Hitchcock 1940) (☞ ☆ ■ ✍ ♫), *Carrie* (>William Wyler 1952) (☆ ☞) (country actress Jennifer Jones' failing career ruins doting restaurateur Olivier), *The Entertainer* (AAN; Tony Richardson 1960) (☆ ✍) (fading comic [Olivier]'s affair with young admirer Shirley Anne Field is disapproved of by her parents and his daughter Joan Plowright), *Bunny Lake is Missing* (Otto Preminger 1965) (☆ ✍) (Olivier's hunt for a small girl is complicated by the fact that no one believes she exists), *>Sleuth* (AAN; >Joseph L. Mankiewicz 1972) (✍ ☆ ☞), *Marathon Man* (>John Schlesinger 1976) (☆ ☞) (runner >Dustin Hoffman becomes tangled up in diamond smuggling with ex-Nazi dentist Olivier) and *The Boys from Brazil* (Franklin Schaffner 1978) (☆ ✍) (Nazi-hunter Olivier tracks evil doctor Gregory Peck's Hitler Youth cloning operation to the Brazilian jungle). His talents were also effortlessly aired in a wealth of cameos: *The Battle of Britain* (Guy Hamilton 1969) (■ ☆) (Olivier as Air Minister Lord Dowding, one of many stars owing much to the few); *Lady Caroline Lamb* (Robert Bolt 1972) (■ ☆) (Olivier as the Duke of Wellington, Ralph Richardson as George III and John Mills as George Canning, disapproving of Sarah Miles' amorous adventures with the poet Byron [Richard Chamberlain]); *The Seven Per Cent Solution* (Herbert Ross 1976) (Olivier as Professor Moriarty fights to perpetuate Sherlock Holmes's cocaine addiction); and *The Jazz Singer* (Richard Fleischer 1980) (♫) (Jewish singer Neil Diamond reconciles himself and his career with cantor father Olivier).

●*Q Planes* (US: *Clouds over Europe*) (Tim Whelan 1939) (☆): spies Ralph Richardson and Olivier steal a revolutionary plane.
●*49th Parallel* (US: *The Invaders*) (>Michael Powell 1941) (☞ ✍ ☆): Olivier and >Leslie Howard unite to prevent Nazi U-boat men Anton Walbrook and Eric Portman crossing Canada for refuge in the USA.
●*The Prince and the Showgirl* (Laurence Olivier 1957) (■): cold-hearted Eastern European prince Olivier is rejected by >Marilyn Monroe.
●*Term of Trial* (Peter Glenville 1962) (☆): Olivier as the teacher accused of propositioning pupil Sarah Miles on a school trip to Paris.
●*Oh! What a Lovely War* (>Richard Attenborough 1969) (♫ ☞ ■ ☆): Olivier as Sir John

French refusing to acknowledge the seriousness and senselessness of the First World War.
•*Dracula* (John Badham 1979): Olivier as Professor Van Helsing to Frank Langella's Count.

Olympische Spiele 1936 (UK: Olympiad) (US: Olympia) ☞ ■ ♫
Part One – Festival Of The Nations
Part Two – Festival Of Beauty
Germany • Tobis • 1938 • 225 mins • b/w
wd Leni Riefenstahl ph Hans Ertl/Walter Franz & others m Herbert Windt

Refreshingly free of the facts and figures beloved of the avid sports bore, Leni Riefenstahl's film contains much to interest the fan and the viewer. Filmed only with International Olympic Committee approval, the film spends too little time on Hitler and too much on non-Aryan success to be pure propaganda (which explains her welcome at subsequent Olympiads). This beautifully photographed record of athletic bodies at the peak of performance remains true to the spirit of the Games for, with the deserving exception of Jesse Owens, competing overshadows winning. Along with Owens, the Opening Ceremony, floodlit pole vault, stumbling sprint start and the agonizing marathon dominate Part I; the Olympic Village, equestrian water jump, Finale and breathtaking diving sequences, comprise Part II. Interesting athletical technical details too, such as handmade starting ditches, scissor kick high-jumping and butterfly breaststroking.

 Nazi smugness emerges as journalist Hilmar Thate investigates the career of UFA Studios actress Rosel Zech in *Veronika Voss* (>Rainer Werner Fassbinder 1981) (■ ☞).
•Riefenstahl's acting as well as directing genius was evident in *The Blue Light* (*Das Blaue Licht*) (1932) (☞ ■) (the director is considered a witch as she can climb a treacherous peak, but in fact simply knows a secret route) and *Triumph of the Will* (*Triumph des Willens*) (1934) (☞ ■) (Hitler's charismatic character is captured in this compelling study).

•The triumphs and tragedies of the 1972 Munich Olympics are recalled in *Visions of Eight* (☞ ■) (>Miloš Forman/Kon Ichikawa/Claude Lelouch/Yuri Ozerov/Arthur Penn/Michael Pfleghar/>John Schlesinger/Mai Zetterling).

On the road

Dust Be My Destiny (Lewis Seiler 1939) ☆
John Garfield puts his criminal past behind him while tramping the countryside.
Elvira Madigan (Bo Widerberg 1967) ☆ ☞
A high-wire walker and an army officer incur 19th-century moral wrath and hit the road.
The Good Companions (Victor Saville 1932) ☆ ⌐
Edmund Gwenn and John Gielgud join a mime troupe, in the screen version of J. B. Priestley's novel.
Harry and Tonto (Paul Mazursky 1974) ☆ ⌐
Art Carney and his cat migrate to Chicago after being evicted from New York.
O Lucky Man (Lindsay Anderson 1973) ☆
Travelling salesman Malcolm McDowell comes off the road to perform charitable works.
Rain Man (Barry Levinson 1988) ☆ ☞ ⌐
>Dustin Hoffman's *idiot savant* and half-brother Tom Cruise's gambling adventures throughout the USA bring them closer together.
A Strange Place to Meet (*Drôle d'Endroit pour une Rencontre*) (François Dupeyron 1989) ☆
>Catherine Deneuve and >Gérard Depardieu settle their relationship on the motorway hard shoulder.

On the run

The Adventurer (>Charles Chaplin 1917) ☆
Escapee Charlie holes out in Eric Campbell's mansion.
Alive and Kicking (Cyril Frankel 1958) ☆ ⌐
Kathleen Harrison, Sybil Thorndike and Estelle Winwood escape from an old people's home and land on an Irish island.
Black Tuesday (Hugo Fregonese 1954) ☆
Escapee >Edward G. Robinson holds hostages in an abandoned warehouse.

City of Fear **(Irving Lerner 1958)** ☞ ✍

A convict tries to peddle a radioactive powder believing it to be heroin.

Down by Law **(Jim Jarmusch 1987)** ☞ ☆

Tom Waits, John Lurie and Roberto Benigni find a new life in a remote Italian restaurant.

It Always Rains on Sundays **(Robert Hamer 1947)** ☆ ☞

Jack Warner pursues John McCallum to the home of the latter's mistress Googie Withers.

Sugarland Express **(>Steven Spielberg 1974)** ☆ ☞

Goldie Hawn begs Ben Johnson to escape to prevent their child being taken into care.

They Drive by Night **(Arthur Woods 1938)** ✍ ☆

Truckers and a hitcher help Emlyn Williams clear his name of Ernest Thesiger's 'stocking murders'.

The Walls of Malapaga **(*Au-delà des Grilles*) (*Le Mura di Malapaga*) (René Clément 1949)** ☆ ☞

Murderous stowaway >Jean Gabin falls for waitress Isa Miranda in Genoa.

Young and Innocent **(US: *A Girl Was Young*) (>Alfred Hitchcock 1937)** ☞

Suspect Derrick De Marney flees the police with the chief inspector's daughter Nova Pilbeam after he finds a body.

On the Town ♫ ☆ ☞ ✍

USA • MGM • 1949 • 98 mins • col

d >Gene Kelly/>Stanley Donen w Betty Comden/Adolph Green ph Harold Rosson m Various; ballet Leonard Bernstein

Gene Kelly, Frank Sinatra, Jules Munshin, Vera-Ellen, Betty Garrett, Ann Miller, Alice Pearce

A film to delight and exhaust even the most dedicated hater of musicals. No Busby Berkeley production numbers; no songs that leave the plot kicking its heels until dewy eyes meet. Even the ballet is tolerable. Three sailors (Kelly, Sinatra and Munshin) on a 24-hour pass scour New York for romance, but apart from Kelly, who searches for Miss Turnstiles (Vera-Ellen) believing her to be a celebrity, love *finds*

them in the shape of feisty taxi driver Garrett and anthropologist Miller. Garrett's ensnaring of Sinatra on his taxi tour of the city with her rendition of *Come back to My Place* pips *New York, New York* for star song, and Kelly's blind date with adenoidal Alice Pearce is wonderful.

•>John Wayne and his fellow crew members get into trouble on their shore leave after a perilous transatlantic crossing, in *The Long Voyage Home* (>John Ford 1940) (■ ☞ ✍ ☆).

•Cover girl Sophia Loren persuades hack >Marcello Mastroianni and count Charles Boyer to turn her into a movie star in *How Lucky to Be a Woman* (*La Fortuna di Essere Donna*) (Alessandro Blasetti 1956) (☆ ✍).

•Taxi driver John Payne is caught up in a jewel theft in *99 River Street* (Phil Karlson 1953) (✍).

•>Cary Grant is the anthropologist pestered by heiress >Katharine Hepburn and bone-burying dog George (Asta), in *>Bringing Up Baby* (>Howard Hawks 1938) (✍ ☆ ☞).

On the Waterfront ☞ ☆ ■ ✍

USA • Columbia • 1954 • 108 mins • b/w

d >Elia Kazan w Budd Schulberg ph Boris Kaufman m Leonard Bernstein

>Marlon Brando, Eva Marie Saint, Lee J. Cobb, Karl Malden, Rod Steiger

Terry Malloy (Brando) 'coulda been a contender' but ended up a longshoreman who strongarms for gangster Johnny Friendly (Cobb). Remorseful at luring debtor Doyle to his death, Terry's conscience is easy prey for moralizing Father Barry (Malden) and Doyle's sister Edie (Saint) who persuade him to testify to the Waterfront Crimes Commission, a resolution only strengthened by the murder of his brother (Steiger). Based on Malcolm Johnson's Pulitzer Prize press articles, this powerful film is still tainted by accusations that it is a justification for Oscar-winning director Kazan and writer Schulberg's informing on alleged Hollywood Communists to the House Un-American Activities Committee.

•Elsewhere on the waterfront, Marie Dressler and Wallace Beery demonstrate the cheerful side of poverty as they matchmake for their daughter Maureen O'Sullivan, in *Tugboat Annie* (>Mervyn Le Roy 1933) (☆ ☞).
•Sylvester Stallone is the debt-collecting boxer in >*Rocky* (John G. Avildsen 1976) (🖉 ☞ ☆).
•Dockland corruption and racism engulf John Cassavetes and Sidney Poitier, in *Edge of the City* (UK: *A Man is Ten Feet Tall*) (Martin Ritt 1957) (☆).
•Bob Hoskins is Jack Higgins' worldly wise priest protecting IRA assassin Mickey Rourke from comrade Liam Neeson and gangster Alan Bates, in *A Prayer for the Dying* (Mike Hodges 1987) (🖉).

Once upon a Time in America
🖉 ☆ ☞ 🎵
USA • Warner/Embassy/Ladd/PSO • 1984 • 228 mins • col
d Sergio Leone w Leonardo Benvenuti/ Piero De Bernardi/Enrico Medioli/Franco Arcalli/Franco Ferrini/Sergio Leone
ph Tonino Delli Colli m Ennio Morricone
>Robert De Niro, >James Woods, Tuesday Weld, Elizabeth McGovern

A specialist in mingling wry humour with incessant violence, Sergio Leone here turned his attention from one distinctive aspect of American history – the winning of the West – to another: gangsters. Having learned their trade in the back streets of Depression New York (in the best *Public Enemy* (UK: *Enemies of the Public*) (>William Wellman 1931) (☞ ☆ 🖉) tradition), Noodles (De Niro) and Maxie (Woods) make a comfortable living from their 'respectable' protection racket. Anxious to emerge from Noodles' shadow, Maxie plans a raid so reckless that Noodles, gauging that prison is better than death, informs the police. But the gang are butchered beyond recognition and the loot disappears without trace, until 1968 . . . De Niro and Woods are superb together and the 228 minutes fly by.

•Child gangsters armed with splurge guns run the town in *Bugsy Malone* (Alan Parker 1976) (☞ ☆ 🖉).
•>Greta Garbo manages to survive slum life in Depression Vienna in *Joyless Street* (US: *The Street of Sorrow*) (aka *Sorrow Street*) (*Die Freudlose Gasse*) (>G. W. Pabst 1925) (☞ ☆).
•Naïve Alfonso Mejía is driven to crime in the streets of Mexico City, in *The Young and the Damned* (aka *The Forgotten*) (*Los Olvidados*) (>Luis Buñuel 1950) (☆ ☞).
•Jodie Foster keeps her head above water amid the violence and hopelessness of 1964 Bronx in *Five Corners* (Tony Bill 1988) (☆).
•Wallace Beery's Long John Silver and Jackie Cooper's Jim Hawkins are after the booty buried on *Treasure Island* (Victor Fleming 1934) (☆ 🖉).

One Flew over the Cuckoo's Nest
☆ 🖉 ☞
USA • United Artists/Fantasy Films • 1975 • 134 mins • col

d >Miloš Forman w Laurence Hauben/ Bo Goldman ph Haskell Wexler m Jack Nitzche

>Jack Nicholson, Louise Fletcher, William Redfield, Dean Brooks, Scatman Crowthers, Danny De Vito, William Duell, Christopher Lloyd

Miloš Forman's adaptation of Ken Kesey's novel is esteemed as a classic of hell-raising rebellion. Because Randal McMurphy, who feigns insanity to escape a sentence for underage sex, is played by everyone's favourite manic rebel Jack Nicholson, it has been largely forgotten that, although he leads the internees on a series of riotous escapades, he is not acting as a liberator from Nurse Ratched's despotism but is a pretender for it. The fact that he only champions their rebellion for his own amusement is also eclipsed because, as his usurpation is resisted only by straitjackets and drugs, he again appears to be repressed victim. Nicholson and Louise Fletcher are so good they deserved two Oscars each.

•Joanne Woodward won an Oscar for her portrayal of a woman with multiple personalities, in *The Three Faces of Eve* (Nunnally Johnson 1957)(☆).

•Matthew Modine is the traumatized patient encouraged towards recovery by Nicholas Cage, in *Birdy* (Alan Parker 1984) (☆ ✍ ☞).

•Riita Viiperi is a Finnish asylum nurse assigned to pyromaniac Eeva Eloranta, in *Burning Angel* (*Palava Enkeli*) (Lauri Torhonen 1984) (☆).

•Warren Beatty falls in love with his crazed patient Jean Seberg, in *Lilith* (Robert Rossen 1964) (☆).

Opera

Aïda (Clemente Fracassi 1953) ♫ ☆
Sophia Loren dubbed as Verdi's Ethiopian princess in love with an Egyptian army officer.

Aria (Nicolas Roeg/Charles Sturridge/ >Jean-Luc Godard/Julien Temple/ Bruce Beresford/>Robert Altman/ Franc Roddam/Ken Russell/ Derek Jarman/Bill Bryden 1987)
Ten directors interpret their favourite arias.

The Bartered Bride (*Die Verkaufte Braut*) (>Max Ophüls 1932) ☞ ♫ ■
A Bohemian mayor's daughter escapes marriage to a wealthy imbecile in Smetana's opera.

La Bohème (Luigi Comencini 1987) ☞ ♫
Puccini's tale of a poverty-stricken artist and his love for a poor seamstress who dies of consumption.

Don Giovanni (>Joseph Losey 1979) ♫ ☞
Mozart's tale of the legendary lover's descent into Hell.

Lady Macbeth of Mtsensk (*Katerina Ismailova*) (Mikhail Shapiro 1966) ☞ ☆ ♫
Shostakovich's opera of passion and murder among the Russian middle classes.

The Magic Flute (*Trollflötjen*) (>Ingmar Bergman 1975) ☞ ♫ ■
Mozart's tale of the priest Sarastro uniting lovers Tamino and the Queen of the Night's daughter Pamina, with the help of bird-catcher Papageno.

Otello (Franco Zeffirelli 1986) ☞ ♫ ■
Placido Domingo strangles his wife Katia Ric-

ciarelli out of jealousy, in Verdi's version of Shakespeare's play.

Parsifal (Hans Jürgen Syberberg 1982) ♫ ■
A daring version of Wagner's monumental work about the redemption of the leader of the Knights of the Round Table, by Parsifal.

La Tosca (Carl Koch 1940) ♫ ✍
>Jean Renoir's version of Sardou's play about a sister's sacrifice to keep her brother out of jail, best known in Puccini's opera, where brother becomes lover.

La Traviata (Franco Zeffirelli 1982) ♫ ☞ ■
Verdi's opera is based on Dumas's *The Lady of the Camellias*, with Teresa Stratas as Violetta and Placido Domingo as Alfredo.

Ophüls, Max

(Max Oppenheimer) German-born French writer/director (1902–1957)

In *The Tender Enemy* (*La Tendre Ennemie*) (1936) (☞ ✍) (three men meet in Hell to discuss the woman who has ruined their lives) and *Sarajevo* (US: *Mayerling to Sarajevo*) (*De Mayerling à Sarajevo*) (1940) (☞) (the uneventful marriage between Archduke Franz Ferdinand [John Lodge] and Countess Sophie [Edwige Feuillère] ends in assassination), Ophüls cultivated the technically adroit elegance that makes his pictures a pleasure to look at. However, his Hollywood films – *Letter from an Unknown Woman* (1948) (☞ ☆ ■) (>Joan Fontaine suffers in silence as pianist Louis Jourdan philanders in Vienna), *Caught* (1949) (☞ ☆) (pregnant Barbara Bel Geddes leaves millionaire Robert Ryan for James Mason, but he won't let his heir go), *The Reckless Moment* (1949) (☆ ✍) (James Mason blackmails Joan Bennett for accidentally killing her daughter's rakish lover) – and those of his second French period – *La Ronde* (1950) (☞ ✍ ☆) (a vicious circle of infidelity as consecutive characters are connected by lust in Arthur Schnitzler's play), *Le Plaisir* (US: *House of Pleasure*) (1952) (☞ ✍) (a trio of stories by Guy De Maupassant), *Madame De. . .* (US: *The Earrings of Madame De . . .*) (1953)(✍ ☞ ☆) (Charles Boyer gives his wife's earrings to his mistress, and they are later given back to his wife by her lover >Vittorio De Sica) and *Lola Montes* (1955) (✍ ☞) (a circus ringmaster tells the tale of courtesan Martine Carol's affair with mad King Ludwig of Bavaria [Anton Walbrook]) – comprised a dissection of chauvinism and female oppression amongst both the upper and middle classes which presaged much feminist cinema.

 •*The Bartered Bride* (*Die Verkaufte Braut*) (1932) (☞ ♫ ■): a Bohemian mayor's daughter escapes marriage to a wealthy imbecile, in Smetana's opera.
•*Liebelei* (1939) (☞): when an officer dies in a duel, his lover Magda Schneider plunges to her death.
•*Werther* (1938) (☞): based on Goethe's *Sorrows of Young Werther*, Pierre-Richard Willm loves, but leaves the fiancée of his best friend and declines into heartbreak.

ORPHANS

Blossoms in the Dust (>Mervyn Le Roy 1941) ☞ ✍ ☆
Greer Garson founds an orphanage when her own family is killed.

Bright Eyes (David Butler 1934) ☆
Shirley Temple has a fine old time with fellow tot Jane Withers until her foster parents split up.

Careful, He Might Hear You (Carl Schultz 1984) ✍
A boy is the subject of a bitter custody wrangle between his aunts.

Dark Waters (André De Toth 1944) ☞ ☆
A young girl has a harrowing time staying with her aunt Merle Oberon and uncle Franchot Tone.

The Divided Heart (Charles Crichton 1954) ☞
A Blitz boy is raised by foster parents until his believed-dead mother comes to claim him.

First Love (Henry Koster 1939) ☆
Deanna Durbin brings a little happiness to the home of her stuffy cousins.

The Good Fairy (>William Wyler 1935) ✍ ☞
>Preston Sturges's script has orphan usherette Margaret Sullavan pursued by beau trio.

Lili (Charles Walters 1952) ☆ ✍
The Paul Gallico tale has Leslie Caron (AAN) fall for a carnival puppet maker.

Oscars

No awards for supporting roles were made until 1936. The winners received plaques until 1943, when they too won statuettes.
Foreign film awards were made in the Special Award category from 1947–1949, then irregularly in the Honorary and Other Awards section until 1956, when the Foreign Language Film category was established.

1927/8

FILM: *Wings* (>William Wellman) ☞ ■
Fly-boy buddies shoot each other down accidentally.

DIRECTOR: Frank Borzage (*Seventh Heaven*) ☞ ☆
A sewer worker returns blind from the war and is cared for by a waif to whom he had once shown charity.

ACTOR: >Emil Jannings (*The Last Command*) (>Josef Von Sternberg) ☞ ☆

Tsarist officer Jannings becomes a Hollywood star and is persecuted by director >William Powell,
and for: *The Way of All Flesh* (Victor Fleming) ☆ ✍
Jannings is so ashamed of flirting with a blonde who robs him that he can't go home.

ACTRESS: Janet Gaynor (*Street Angel*) (Frank Borzage) ☆ ☞
Janet escapes prostitution by joining the circus,

and for *Sunrise* (>F. W. Murnau) ☞
Gaynor's husband plots to kill her but she
is too sweet and he doesn't,
and for: *Seventh Heaven*
as the street waif who comes to the aid of a
blinded war veteran.

1928/9

FILM: *Broadway Melody* (Harry
Beaumont)
Aspiring chorus girls make it big in the first
screen musical.

DIRECTOR: Frank Lloyd (*The Divine
Lady*) ☞
Corinne Griffith as Lady Hamilton.

ACTOR: Warner Baxter (*In Old
Arizona*) (>Raoul Walsh/Irving
Cummings) ☞ ☆
Baxter as the western hero, the Cisco Kid.

ACTRESS: Mary Pickford (*Coquette*)
(Sam Taylor) ☆
A flirtatious belle perjures herself at her
father's murder trial.

1929/30

FILM: >*All Quiet on the Western Front*
(Lewis Milestone) ☞ ✍ ☆ ♫

DIRECTOR: Lewis Milestone (>*All Quiet
on the Western Front*)

ACTOR: George Arliss (*Disraeli*) (Alfred
E. Green) ☆
The private and political life of the 19th-
century statesman.

ACTRESS: Norma Shearer (*The
Divorcee*) (Robert Z. Leonard)
Her own marriage shattered by adultery,
Norma resists breaking another with an
affair.

1930/1

FILM: *Cimarron* (Wesley Ruggles) ☞
Richard Dix and Irene Dunne at home on
the range.

DIRECTOR: Norman Taurog (*Skippy*)
✍ ☆
A health inspector's son befriends slum
children.

ACTOR: Lionel Barrymore (*A Free Soul*)
(Clarence Brown) ☆
Lionel wants Norma Shearer to court
>Leslie Howard, but she goes for gangster
>Clark Gable instead.

ACTRESS: Marie Dressler (*Min and Bill*)
(George Hill) ☆
Waterfront tipplers Dressler and Wallace
Beery risk losing their daughter because of
their lifestyle.

1931/2

FILM: *Grand Hotel* (Edmund Goulding)
✍
Adventures of the guests include romance,
murder and solitude.

DIRECTOR: Frank Borzage (*Bad Girl*) ☞
Also AAN for Best Picture, as two-too-
young-to-be-marrieds find life tough.

ACTOR: Wallace Beery (*The Champ*)
(>King Vidor) ☞ ☆
A washed up boxer is driven to success by
his son, Jackie Cooper.
shared with: >Fredric March (*Dr Jekyll
and Mr Hyde*) (Rouben Mamoulian) ☆
☞ ✍
March's respected doctor's alter ego menaces Miriam Hopkins.

ACTRESS: Helen Hayes (*The Sin of
Madelon Claudet*) (UK: *The Lullaby*)
(Edgar Selwyn)
Convention dictates that Helen must lose
her illegitimate child.

1932/3

FILM: *Cavalcade* (Frank Lloyd) ✍ ☞
Noël Coward's play details the lives of a
turn-of-the-century family.

DIRECTOR: Frank Lloyd (*Cavalcade*)

ACTOR: >Charles Laughton (>*The
Private Life of Henry VIII*) (Alexander
Korda) ☆ ✍ ☞

ACTRESS: >Katharine Hepburn
(*Morning Glory*) (Lowell Sherman) ☆
Aspiring actress Kate is helped in her
career by Adolphe Menjou and Douglas
Fairbanks, Jr.

1934

FILM: >*It Happened One Night* (>Frank Capra) ✍ ☆ ☞

DIRECTOR: >Frank Capra (>*It Happened One Night*)

ACTOR: >Clark Gable (>*It Happened One Night*)

ACTRESS: Claudette Colbert (>*It Happened One Night*)

1935

FILM: *Mutiny on the Bounty* (Frank Lloyd) ☆ ☞ ✍

>Charles Laughton's Captain Bligh is opposed by >Clark Gable's Fletcher Christian.

DIRECTOR: >John Ford (*The Informer*) ☆

An IRA supporter is pursued after betraying his leader.

ACTOR: Victor McLaglen (*The Informer*)

ACTRESS: >Bette Davis (*Dangerous*) (Alfred E. Green) ☆

Franchot Tone keeps Bette off the bottle during her actress's comeback.

1936

FILM: *The Great Ziegfeld* (>Vincente Minnelli) ☆ ☞ ✍

The career rise and complicated love life of impresario >William Powell.

DIRECTOR: >Frank Capra (*Mr Deeds Goes to Town*) ☞ ☆

>Gary Cooper retains his decency amid New York lowlifers.

ACTOR: Paul Muni (*The Story of Louis Pasteur*) (>William Dieterle) ☞ ✍

Biopic of the pioneering French scientist.

ACTRESS: Luise Rainer (*The Great Ziegfeld*)

As >William Powell's ex-wife Anna Held, she congratulates him on his marriage to >Myrna Loy's Billie Burke.

SUP ACT: Walter Brennan (*Come and Get It*) (>Harold Hawks/>William Wyler)

As the lumberjack who makes tycoon Edward Albert rich.

SUP ACTR: Gale Sondergaard (*Anthony Adverse*) (>Mervyn Le Roy) ☆ ☞

Gale tries to come between >Fredric March and >Olivia De Havilland in this costume drama.

1937

FILM: *The Life of Emile Zola* (>William Dieterle) ☞ ☆

Paul Muni as the crusading 19th-century French writer.

DIRECTOR: >Leo McCarey (*The Awful Truth*) ☆ ☞ ✍

>Cary Grant and Irene Dunne leave it until court to abandon their divorce.

ACTOR: >Spencer Tracy (*Captains Courageous*) (Victor Fleming) ☆ ✍

As the fisherman who tames brattish Freddie Bartholemew after the boy falls off a yacht.

ACTRESS: Luise Rainer (*The Good Earth*) (Sidney Franklin) ☆

Chinese peasant Paul Muni survives famine, storms and locusts, but loses wife Luise.

SUP ACT: Joseph Schildkraut (*The Life of Emile Zola*)

As Captain Alfred Dreyfus, the Jew falsely accused of treason in Third Republic France.

SUP ACTR: Alice Brady (*In Old Chicago*) (Henry King) ☞ ☆

As Tyrone Power and Don Ameche's mother on the eve of the Great Fire of 1871.

1938

FILM: *You Can't Take It with You* (>Frank Capra) ☞ ☆ ✍

The daughter of tax-dodging Lionel Barrymore Jean Arthur falls for Wall Street tycoon's boy >James Stewart.

DIRECTOR: >Frank Capra (*You Can't Take It with You*)

ACTOR: Spencer Tracy (*Boys' Town*) (Norman Taurog) ☆ ✍ ☞

As Father Flanagan who founded a reform school for tough kids.

ACTRESS: >Bette Davis (*Jezebel*) (>William Wyler) ☆ ☞ ✍ ■

Southern belle Bette scandalizes society with her red dress, but is rehabilitated by >Henry Fonda.

SUP ACT: Walter Brennan (*Kentucky*) (David Butler) ☞

As Loretta Young's father in a horse breeding *Romeo and Juliet*.

SUP ACTR: Fay Bainter (*Jezebel*)

As >Bette Davis's Aunt Belle, the one relative who does not abandon her during her disgrace.

1939

FILM: >*Gone with the Wind* (Victor Fleming) ☆ ■ ✍ ☞ ♫

DIRECTOR: Victor Fleming (>*Gone with the Wind*)

ACTOR: >Robert Donat (>*Goodbye Mr Chips*) (Sam Wood) ☆ ☞ ✍ ■

ACTRESS: >Vivien Leigh (>*Gone with the Wind*)

SUP ACT: Thomas Mitchell (>*Stagecoach*) (>John Ford) ☞ ☆ ✍

SUP ACTR: Hattie McDaniel (>*Gone with the Wind*)

1940

FILM: >*Rebecca* (>Alfred Hitchcock) ☞ ✍ ☆ ■ ♫

DIRECTOR: >John Ford (>*The Grapes of Wrath*) ☞ ■ ☆ ✍

ACTOR: >James Stewart (>*The Philadelphia Story*) (>George Cukor) ☆ ✍ ☞

ACTRESS: >Ginger Rogers (*Kitty Foyle*) (Sam Wood) ☆ ☞ ✍

Ginger has and loses the boss's baby son and sets out to make it alone in this classic 'Woman's Picture'.

SUP ACT: Walter Brennan (*The Westerner*) (>William Wyler) ☞ ☆

As Judge Roy Bean enamoured of Doris Davenport's Lily Langtry.

SUP ACTR: Jane Darwell (>*The Grapes of Wrath*)

1941

FILM: *How Green Was My Valley* (>John Ford) ☞

The Morgan family respond to strikes and disasters at the local coal mine.

DIRECTOR: >John Ford (*How Green Was My Valley*)

ACTOR: >Gary Cooper (*Sergeant York*) (>Howard Hawks) ☆ ☞

As a gentle giant country boy who becomes a World War I hero.

ACTRESS: >Joan Fontaine (*Suspicion*) (>Alfred Hitchcock) ☞ ☆ ✍ ■

Joan suspects that husband >Cary Grant is a killer.

SUP ACT: Donald Crisp (*How Green Was My Valley*)

SUP ACTR: Mary Astor (*The Great Lie*) (Edmund Goulding) ☆ ✍

Pianist Mary gives her baby away to >Bette Davis, wife of her former lover George Brent.

1942

FILM: *Mrs Miniver* (>William Wyler) ☞ ☆ ✍

Greer Garson and Walter Pidgeon survive the separations and bombs of the London Blitz in the film that Dr Goebbels wanted German propaganda to copy.

DIRECTOR: >William Wyler (*Mrs Miniver*)

ACTOR: >James Cagney (*Yankee Doodle Dandy*) (>Michael Curtiz) ♫ ☆

As patriotic songwriter and dance man George M. Cohan.

ACTRESS: Greer Garson (*Mrs Miniver*)

SUP ACT: Van Heflin (*Johnny Eager*) (>Mervyn Le Roy) ☞ ☆

As a drunken leech hindering gangster Robert Taylor's pursuit of Lana Turner.

SUP ACTR: Teresa Wright (*Mrs Miniver*)

As the rich girl married to the Minivers' son Richard Ney.

1943

FILM: >*Casablanca* (>Michael Curtiz)
☆ ☞ ✍ ♫ ■

DIRECTOR: >Michael Curtiz
(>*Casablanca*)

ACTOR: Paul Lukas (*Watch on the Rhine*) (Herman Shumlin) ☆ ✍
Engineer Lukas and wife >Bette Davis flee the Nazis to Washington.

ACTRESS: Jennifer Jones (*The Song of Bernadette*) (Henry King) ☆ ☞
As the peasant inspired by Marian visions to dig a well at Lourdes.

SUP ACT: Charles Coburn (*The More the Merrier*) (>George Stevens) ☆ ☞ ✍
Matchmaker Coburn shares Jean Arthur's flat with Joel McCrea.

SUP ACTR: Katina Paxinou (*For Whom the Bell Tolls*) (Sam Wood) ☞ ☆
As a member of the loyalist band helped by >Ingrid Bergman's lover >Gary Cooper.

1944

FILM: *Going My Way* (>Leo McCarey)
☞ ✍ ☆
Bing Crosby's gushing goodness is tempered by crusty parish priest Barry Fitzgerald.

DIRECTOR: >Leo McCarey (*Going My Way*)

ACTOR: Bing Crosby (*Going My Way*)

ACTRESS: >Ingrid Bergman (*Gaslight*) (UK:*The Murder in Thornton Square*) (>George Cukor) ☞ ☆ ✍
Ingrid is slowly driven insane for discovering husband Charles Boyer is a killer.

SUP ACT: Barry Fitzgerald (*Going My Way*)

SUP ACTR: Ethel Barrymore (*None but the Lonely Heart*) (Clifford Odets) ☆ ☞
As wastrel Londoner >Cary Grant's cancer-ridden mother.

1945

FILM: *The Lost Weekend* (>Billy Wilder)
☞ ✍ ☆
Blocked writer Ray Milland drowns his sorrows on an alcohol-filled bender.

DIRECTOR: >Billy Wilder (*The Lost Weekend*)

ACTOR: Ray Milland (*The Lost Weekend*)

ACTRESS: >Joan Crawford (*Mildred Pierce*) (>Michael Curtiz) ☆ ☞
Joan in a 'Woman's Picture' par excellence as a rebellious housewife who opens a restaurant and is accused of murder.

SUP ACT: James Dunn (*A Tree Grows in Brooklyn*) (>Elia Kazan) ☆ ☞
As the father whose attempts to provide for his family are frustrated by drink.

SUP ACTR: Anne Revere (*National Velvet*) (Clarence Brown) ✍
As Elizabeth Taylor's mother helping her train a Grand National winning horse.

1946

FILM: >*The Best Years of Our Lives* (>William Wyler) ☆ ☞ ✍ ■

DIRECTOR: >William Wyler (>*The Best Years of Our Lives*)

ACTOR: >Fredric March (>*The Best Years of Our Lives*)

ACTRESS: >Olivia De Havilland (*To Each His Own*) (Mitchell Leisen) ☆ ☞ ✍
Olivia's plans to adopt her illegitimate baby backfire and she has to watch him grow up at a distance.

SUP ACT: Harold Russell (>*The Best Years of Our Lives*)

SUP ACTR: Anne Baxter (*The Razor's Edge*) (Edmund Goulding) ☆ ✍
As a wife who becomes a dipsomaniac when her family are killed, in W. Somerset Maugham's story of wealthy young man Tyrone Power's search for truth.

1947

FILM: *Gentleman's Agreement* (>Elia Kazan) ☆ ☞ ✍
Writer Gregory Peck impersonates a Jew to better understand anti-Semitism.

DIRECTOR: >Elia Kazan (*Gentleman's Agreement*)

ACTOR: Ronald Colman (*A Double Life*) (>George Cukor) ✍ ☞ ☆

As an unhinged actor playing Othello on and off stage.

ACTRESS: Loretta Young (*The Farmer's Daughter*) (H.C. Potter) ☆

Homespun politics take Loretta to Congress and a showdown with lover and rival Joseph Cotten.

SUP ACT: Edmund Gwenn (*Miracle on 34th Street*) (UK: *The Big Heart*) (George Seaton) ☆ ✍

As a department store Santa who goes to court to prove he is the real thing.

SUP ACTR: Celeste Holm (*Gentleman's Agreement*)

As the fashion writer on Gregory Peck's magazine.

FOREIGN: *Shoeshine* (*Sciuscia*) (>Vittorio De Sica) ☞ ☆ ✍

Two young black marketeers' hopes of buying a horse are thwarted by arrest.

1948

FILM: >*Hamlet* (>Laurence Olivier) ☆ ☞ ✍ ■ ♫

DIRECTOR: >John Huston (*The Treasure of the Sierra Madre*) ☆ ☞ ♫

Gold prospectors are undone by their own greed as well as ruthless bandits.

ACTOR: >Laurence Olivier (>*Hamlet*)

ACTRESS: Jane Wyman (*Johnny Belinda*) (Jean Negulesco) ☆ ✍

Deaf-mute single mother Wyman has to cope with small town prejudice.

SUP ACT: Walter Huston (*The Treasure of the Sierra Madre*)

As a prospector along with Tim Holt and >Humphrey Bogart.

SUP ACTR: Clare Trevor (*Key Largo*) (>John Huston) ☆ ✍

As the drunken mistress of the gangster >Edward G. Robinson, who holds up Lionel Barrymore's hotel.

FOREIGN: *Monsieur Vincent* (Maurice Cloche) ☞ ☆ ✍

Pierre Fresnay (who won the 1947 Best Actor award at Venice) as the 17th-century saint of the Parisian poor.

1949

FILM: *All the King's Men* (Robert Rossen) ☞ ✍ ☆

A rising politician discovers that it is not just absolute power that corrupts.

DIRECTOR: >Joseph L. Mankiewicz (*A Letter to Three Wives*) ✍ ☞ ☆

A spitfire writes a confession saying she has had an affair with a local man, but doesn't say who he is.

ACTOR: Broderick Crawford (*All the King's Men*)

As the worthy small town lawyer who loses his principles upon becoming governor in this *film à clef* of the life of Huey Long.

ACTRESS: >Olivia De Havilland (*The Heiress*) (>William Wyler) ☞ ☆ ✍

Olivia takes revenge on Montgomery Clift when her father Ralph Richardson tells her that his love is of money, not her.

SUP ACT: Dean Jagger (*Twelve O'Clock High*) (Henry King) ☞ ☆

As an air force officer witnessing the mental stress Gregory Peck endures while turning his motley crew into a fighting force.

SUP ACTR: Mercedes McCambridge (*All the King's Men*)

As Broderick Crawford's aide, winning for her first screen role.

FOREIGN: >*Bicycle Thieves* (US: *The Bicycle Thief*) (*Ladri di Biciclette*) (>Vittorio De Sica) ☞ ☆ ✍ ■

1950

FILM: >*All about Eve* (>Joseph L. Mankiewicz) ☆ ✍ ☞

DIRECTOR: >Joseph L. Mankiewicz (>*All about Eve*)

ACTOR: Jose Ferrer (*Cyrano De Bergerac*) (Michael Gordon) ☆

As the 17th-century poet who writes *billets doux* to help his friend win the woman he loves himself.

ACTRESS: Judy Holliday (>*Born Yesterday*) (>George Cukor) ☆ ✍ ☞

SUP ACT: George Sanders (>*All about Eve*)

SUP ACTR: Josephine Hull (>*Harvey*) (Henry Koster) ☆ ✍ ☞

FOREIGN: *The Walls of Malapaga* (*Au delà des Grilles*) (*Le Mura di Malapaga*) (René Clément) ☆ ☞

Stowaway >Jean Gabin falls for Italian waitress Isa Miranda.

1951

FILM: *An American in Paris* (>Vincente Minnelli) ☆ ☞ ✍

Artist >Gene Kelly resists Nina Foch's wealth, but not Leslie Caron's simple charm.

DIRECTOR: >George Stevens (*A Place in the Sun*) ☞ ■

Ambitious worker Montgomery Clift's plan to marry Elizabeth Taylor is shattered when he is convicted of murdering Shelley Winters.

ACTOR: >Humphrey Bogart (>*The African Queen*) (>John Huston) ☆ ☞ ✍

ACTRESS: >Vivien Leigh (*A Streetcar Named Desire*) (>Elia Kazan) ✍ ☞ ☆

As Blanche Dubois, mentally and physically abused by brother-in-law Stanley Kowalski (>Marlon Brando).

SUP ACT: Karl Malden (*A Streetcar Named Desire*)

As Brando's friend Mitch who abandons Leigh, believing her to be evil.

SUP ACTR: Kim Hunter (*A Streetcar Named Desire*)

As Blanche's younger sister and Stanley's wife.

FOREIGN: *Rashomon* (>Akira Kurosawa) ☞ ■ ☆ ✍

A forest ambush is retold from four different perspectives.

1952

FILM: *The Greatest Show on Earth* (Cecil B. De Mille) ■

>James Stewart and Charlton Heston are among the artistes at a struggling circus.

DIRECTOR: >John Ford (>*The Quiet Man*) ✍ ☞ ☆ ■

ACTOR: >Gary Cooper (>*High Noon*) (>Fred Zinnemann) ☆ ☞ ✍ ♪

ACTRESS: Shirley Booth (*Come Back, Little Sheba*) (Daniel Mann) ☆ ☞

As the wife of alcoholic Burt Lancaster, and who is more interested in her missing dog than his weakening resolve.

SUP ACT: Anthony Quinn (*Viva Zapata*) (>Elia Kazan) ☞ ☆

As the man who betrays Mexican revolutionary leader >Marlon Brando.

SUP ACTR: Gloria Grahame (*The Bad and the Beautiful*) (>Vincente Minnelli) ☆ ☞

As an aspiring actress whose career was moulded and marred by movie producer >Kirk Douglas.

FOREIGN: *Forbidden Games* (*Jeux Interdits*) (René Clément) ✍ ☞ ☆

Two children build an animal cemetery during the Nazi occupation of France.

1953

FILM: *From Here to Eternity* (>Fred Zinnemann) ☞ ☆

Army life and love in Honolulu for Burt Lancaster, Montgomery Clift, Frank Sinatra, Deborah Kerr and Donna Reed.

DIRECTOR: >Fred Zinnemann (*From Here to Eternity*)

ACTOR: William Holden (*Stalag 17*) (>Billy Wilder) ✍ ☞ ☆

Holden is suspected of being the informer betraying escape plans in a PoW camp.

ACTRESS: Audrey Hepburn (*Roman Holiday*) (>William Wyler) ☞ ☆

Princess Audrey escapes protocol and during her adventure falls for journalist Gregory Peck.

SUP ACT: Frank Sinatra (*From Here to Eternity*)

As a *que sera* soldier who is victimized by sergeant Ernest Borgnine.

SUP ACTR: Donna Reed (*From Here to Eternity*)

As a night club singer who supplements her

income and eases her loneliness through prostitution.

1954

FILM: >*On the Waterfront* (>Elia Kazan) ☞ ☆ ✍ ◼

DIRECTOR: >Elia Kazan (>*On the Waterfront*)

ACTOR: >Marlon Brando (>*On the Waterfront*)

ACTRESS: Grace Kelly (*The Country Girl*) (George Seaton) ☆ ✍

As the dowdy wife of comeback-planning alcoholic singer Bing Crosby.

SUP ACT: Edmund O'Brien (*The Barefoot Contessa*) (>Joseph L. Mankiewicz) ✍

As the slimy press agent helping >Humphrey Bogart promote Spanish dancer Ava Gardner.

SUP ACTR: Eva Marie Saint (>*On the Waterfront*)

As the devoted girlfriend who sticks by Brando as things turn violent.

FOREIGN: *Gate of Hell* (*Jigokumon*) (Teinosuke Kinugasa) ☆ ☞

A medieval warlord does penance in a monastery for driving a woman to suicide.

1955

FILM: *Marty* (Delbert Mann) ☆ ☞ ✍

A dull New York butcher (Ernest Borgnine) decides the time has come to find a wife, to the distress of his clinging mother.

DIRECTOR: Delbert Mann (*Marty*)

ACTOR: Ernest Borgnine (*Marty*)

ACTRESS: Anna Magnani (*The Rose Tattoo*) (Daniel Mann) ◼ ☆

As the husband-obsessed widow whose affair with Burt Lancaster sets Jo Van Fleet and Virginia Grey gossiping.

SUP ACT: >Jack Lemmon (*Mister Roberts*) (>Mervyn Le Roy) ☆

As the laundry officer joining >Henry Fonda and >William Powell in despairing at the boredom on board >James Cagney's escort ship.

SUP ACTR: Jo Van Fleet (*East of Eden*) (>Elia Kazan) ☞ ☆ ✍

As the brothel madame mother of love-starved farm boy James Dean.

FOREIGN: *Samurai* (*Miyamoto Musashi*) (Hiroshi Inagki) ☞ ◼

Toshiro Mifune's chequered career includes imprisonment for being an outlaw before he becomes a warrior.

1956

FILM: *Around the World in 80 Days* (Michael Anderson/Kevan McClory) ☆ ✍ ☞

David Niven's Phileas Fogg and Cantinflas's Passepartout return from their trip with rescued Indian widow Shirley MacLaine.

DIRECTOR: >George Stevens (*Giant*) ☞ ☆ ◼

An oil strike brings nothing but misery to Rock Hudson, Elizabeth Taylor and James Dean.

ACTOR: Yul Brynner (*The King and I*) (Walter Lang) ☆ ♪ ✍

As the King of Siam, whose gaggle of children are educated by American governess Deborah Kerr.

ACTRESS: >Ingrid Bergman (*Anastasia*) (Anatole Litvak) ☆

Ingrid must convince exiles Yul Brynner and Helen Hayes that she is the surviving daughter of Tsar Nicholas II.

SUP ACT: Anthony Quinn (*Lust for Life*) (>Vincente Minnelli) ☆ ☞

As Paul Gauguin unable to take the excesses of >Kirk Douglas's Vincent Van Gogh.

SUP ACTR: Dorothy Malone (*Written on the Wind*) (Douglas Sirk) ☆

As Lauren Bacall and Robert Stack's sister aiming to win wealthy Rock Hudson.

FOREIGN: *La Strada* (>Federico Fellini) ☆ ✍ ☞ ◼

Giulietta Masina remains loyal to circus strongman Anthony Quinn despite his cruel indifference.

1957
FILM: *The Bridge on the River Kwai*
(>David Lean) ✍ ☆ ☞
The Japanese PoW movie that put the 'Colonel Bogey March' on the lips of the whistling world.
DIRECTOR: >David Lean (*The Bridge on the River Kwai*)
ACTOR: >Alec Guinness (*The Bridge on the River Kwai*)
ACTRESS: Joanne Woodward (*The Three Faces of Eve*) (Nunnally Johnson) ☆
As a woman with a triphasic personality: housewife, flirt and sophisticate.
SUP ACT: Red Buttons (*Sayonara*) (Joshua Logan) ■
As >Marlon Brando's air force buddy in occupied Tokyo.
SUP ACTR: Miyoshi Umeki (*Sayonara*) (Joshua Logan) ■
As the Japanese woman who captures the heart of >Marlon Brando.
FOREIGN: >*Nights of Cabiria* (*Le Notti di Cabiria*) (>Federico Fellini) ☆ ☞ ✍ ■

1958
FILM: *Gigi* (>Vincente Minnelli) ☞ ■
Trainee courtesan Leslie Caron is wooed by suave aristocrat Louis Jourdan.
DIRECTOR: >Vincente Minnelli (*Gigi*)
ACTOR: David Niven (*Separate Tables*) (Delbert Mann) ✍ ☆
As a war braggart who is still loved by Deborah Kerr when his exploits are exposed as fakes.
ACTRESS: Susan Hayward (*I Want to Live*) (Robert Wise) ☆ ✍
As a suspected murderess followed from arrest to trial, appeal to execution.
SUP ACT: Burl Ives (*The Big Country*) (>William Wyler) ♫ ☞ ☆
As a poor rancher caught in the dispute between Gregory Peck and Charlton Heston.
SUP ACTR: Wendy Hiller (*Separate Tables*)
As the owner of the seaside guest house and

bullying mother of Deborah Kerr in Terence Rattigan's play.
FOREIGN: *Mon Oncle* (Jacques Tati) ☞ ☆ ✍ ■

1959
FILM: >*Ben-Hur* (>William Wyler) ☆ ☞ ✍ ♫ ■
DIRECTOR: >William Wyler (>*Ben-Hur*)
ACTOR: Charlton Heston (>*Ben-Hur*)
ACTRESS: Simone Signoret (*Room at the Top*) (Jack Clayton) ☆
As the older woman exploited by ambitious social climber Laurence Harvey.
SUP ACT: Hugh Griffith (>*Ben-Hur*)
SUP ACTR: Shelley Winters (*The Diary of Anne Frank*) (>George Stevens) ☞ ☆ ■
As mother of the Van Daan family who shared the Frank hideout.
FOREIGN: *Black Orpheus* (*Orfeu Negro*) (Marcel Camus) ■
A Rio tram driver descends to Hell to trace the lover he accidentally killed.

1960
FILM: *The Apartment* (>Billy Wilder) ☞ ☆ ✍
>Jack Lemmon sees red when the woman Fred MacMurray brings to the apartment he has rented him is his beloved Shirley MacLaine.
DIRECTOR: >Billy Wilder (*The Apartment*)
ACTOR: Burt Lancaster (*Elmer Gantry*) (Richard Brooks) ☆
As a disreputable man who finds fame as an evangelist.
ACTRESS: Elizabeth Taylor (*Butterfield 8*) (Daniel Mann) ☆
As a disturbed call girl caught between Laurence Harvey and Eddie Fisher.
SUP ACT: Peter Ustinov (*Spartacus*) (>Stanley Kubrick) ☞ ☆
As slavemaster Batiatus making life unpleasant for >Kirk Douglas.
SUP ACTR: Shirley Jones (*Elmer Gantry*)
As a dishevelled whore in the film version

of Sinclair Lewis' novel of religious mania and fraud.

FOREIGN: *The Virgin Spring (Jungfrukällan)* (>Ingmar Bergman) ✍ ☆ ☞

Max Von Sydow's 14th-century Swedish peasant avenges the rape and murder of his daughter.

1961

FILM: *West Side Story* (Robert Wise/Jerome Robbins) ♫ ☞ ☆ ✍

A musical *Romeo and Juliet* set in New York and involving rival street gangs The Jets and The Sharks.

DIRECTOR: Robert Wise/Jerome Robbins (*West Side Story*)

ACTOR: Maximilian Schell (*Judgement at Nuremburg*) (Stanley Kramer) ✍ ☆

As an attorney defending Nazi supporters, including Burt Lancaster in >Spencer Tracy's court.

ACTRESS: Sophia Loren (*Two Women*) (*La Ciociara*) (>Vittorio De Sica) ☞ ☆

As a mother fleeing from Allies, Nazis and Italian partisans alike during the taking of Rome.

SUP ACT: George Chakiris (*West Side Story*)

As the tragic leader of The Sharks, brother of the film's Juliet, Natalie Wood's Maria.

SUP ACTR: Rita Moreno (*West Side Story*)

As Maria's dancer friend who delighted in being in 'America'.

FOREIGN: *Through a Glass Darkly (Såsom I en Spegel)* (>Ingmar Bergman) ☞ ☆

Writer Gunnar Björnstrand's daughter >Harriet Andersson goes insane on a remote island.

1962

FILM: *Lawrence of Arabia* (>David Lean) ☞ ♫

Peter O'Toole as the leader of an Arab revolt against the Turks in 1917.

DIRECTOR: >David Lean (*Lawrence of Arabia*)

ACTOR: Gregory Peck (*To Kill a Mockingbird*) (Robert Mulligan) ✍ ☆ ■

As Harper Lee's lawyer Atticus Finch defending a black man against a charge of rape.

ACTRESS: Anne Bancroft (*The Miracle Worker*) (Arthur Penn) ☆

As remarkable special-needs teacher Annie Sullivan.

SUP ACT: Ed Begley (*The Sweet Bird of Youth*) (Richard Brooks) ☆

As a brutal and corrupt politician aiming to avenge >Paul Newman's seduction of his daughter Shirley Knight.

SUP ACTR: Patty Duke (*The Miracle Worker*)

As deaf-dumb-blind girl Helen Keller.

FOREIGN: *Sundays and Cybèle (Cybèle ou les Dimanches de Ville D'Avray)* (Serge Bourgignon) ✍ ☆

Amnesiac pilot Hardy Kruger is accused of raping a pre-teenage girl during their Christmas in the woods.

1963

FILM: *Tom Jones* (Tony Richardson) ■ ☞ ✍ ☆

Albert Finney as the worthy hero of Henry Fielding's 18th-century satire of rural and urban English society.

DIRECTOR: Tony Richardson (*Tom Jones*)

ACTOR: Sidney Poitier (*Lilies of the Field*) (Ralph Nelson) ☆

Poitier teaches English to five European nuns and helps them build their chapel.

ACTRESS: Patricia Neal (*Hud*) (Martin Ritt) ☆ ☞ ✍

As the housekeeper whom >Paul Newman has designs upon.

SUP ACT: Melvyn Douglas (*Hud*)

As Newman's tough father who insists he learns the cattle business and succeed him.

SUP ACTR: **Margaret Rutherford (***The VIPs***) (>Anthony Asquith)**
Rutherford is fog-bound at the airport with >Richard Burton and Elizabeth Taylor.

FOREIGN: **>8½ (***Otto e Mezzo***) (>Federico Fellini)** ☞ ☆ ✍ ▓

1964

FILM: ***My Fair Lady* (>George Cukor)** ♫ ☞ ✍
Rex Harrison's Professor Higgins transforms Audrey Hepburn's flower girl Eliza Doolittle.

DIRECTOR: **>George Cukor (***My Fair Lady***)**

ACTOR: **Rex Harrison (***My Fair Lady***)**

ACTRESS: **Julie Andrews (***Mary Poppins***) (Robert Stevenson)** ☆ ☞ ♫ ✳
As the no-nonsense nanny joined on her adventures by two children and chimney sweep Dick Van Dyke.

SUP ACT: **Peter Ustinov (***Topkapi***) (>Jules Dassin)** ☆
As the snivelling snoop hired by the police to report on the plans of Melina Mercouri's jewel thieves.

SUP ACTR: **Lila Kedrova (***Zorba the Greek***) (Michael Cacoyannis)** ☆ ✍ ♫
As the ageing prostitute faced with destitution who turns to Anthony Quinn for assistance.

FOREIGN: ***Yesterday, Today and Tomorrow* (***Ieri, Oggi, Domani***) (>Vittorio De Sica)** ☞
A trio of stories: 'Adelina of Naples', 'Anna of Milan' and 'Mara of Rome'.

1965

FILM: ***The Sound of Music* (Robert Wise)** ♫ ☆ ✍
Julie Andrews and Christopher Plummer lead their singing family out of occupied Austria.

DIRECTOR: **Robert Wise (***The Sound of Music***)**

ACTOR: **Lee Marvin (***Cat Ballou***) (Eliot Silverstein)** ☆ ✍ ♫
As both a drunken gunfighter and the nose-

less villain hired by and threatening >Jane Fonda.

ACTRESS: **Julie Christie (***Darling***) (>John Schlesinger)** ☆ ☞
As an ambitious model exploiting the men in her life Dirk Bogarde and Laurence Harvey.

SUP ACT: **Martin Balsam (***A Thousand Clowns***) (Fred Coe)** ☆
As drifter Jason Robards, Jr's go-getting brother helping him avoid inspectors insisting their nephew goes to school.

SUP ACTR: **Shelley Winters (***A Patch of Blue***) (Guy Green)** ☆
As the mother of a blind girl who falls in love with Sidney Poitier unaware of his colour.

FOREIGN: **>***The Shop on the High Street* (US: *The Shop on Main Street*) (*Obchod od na Korze*) (Jan Kadar)** ✍ ☆ ☞

1966

FILM: ***A Man for All Seasons* (>Fred Zinnemann)** ☆ ☞ ✍ ▓
Paul Scofield as Sir Thomas More resisting the 1529 divorce of Robert Shaw's Henry VIII, in Robert Bolt's screen version of his own play.

DIRECTOR: **>Fred Zinnemann (***A Man for All Seasons***)**

ACTOR: **Paul Scofield (***A Man for All Seasons***)**

ACTRESS: **Elizabeth Taylor (***Who's Afraid of Virginia Woolf?***) (>Mike Nichols)** ☆ ☞
Arguing furiously with academic >Richard Burton at a drinks party, in the film version of Edward Albee's Pulitzer Prize-winning play.

SUP ACT: **Walter Matthau (***The Fortune Cookie***) (UK:***Meet Whiplash Willie***) (>Billy Wilder)** ☆ ☞ ✍
As a shyster lawyer milking brother >Jack Lemmon's supposed injuries obtained while reporting a football game.

SUP ACTR: **Sandy Dennis (***Who's Afraid of Virginia Woolf?***)**
As the phantomly pregnant wife of Bur-

ton's faculty colleague George Segal who are both dragged in to the blazing feud.

FOREIGN: *A Man and a Woman* (*Un Homme et une Femme*) (Claude Lelouch) ☞ ☆
Jean-Louis Trintignant and Anouk Aimée dither over committing themselves to an affair.

1967

FILM: *In the Heat of the Night* (Norman Jewison) ☆ ✍
Bigot Rod Steiger arrests Sidney Poitier out of habit only to discover he is also a cop, and together they solve a murder.

DIRECTOR: >Mike Nichols (>*The Graduate*) ☆ ☞ ♫ ✍

ACTOR: Rod Steiger (*In the Heat of the Night*)

ACTRESS: >Katharine Hepburn (*Guess Who's Coming to Dinner?*) (Stanley Kramer) ☆ ☞ ✍
Persuading >Spencer Tracy that their daughter is making a good match by marrying Sidney Poitier.

SUP ACT: George Kennedy (*Cool Hand Luke*) (Stuart Rosenberg) ☆ ✍
As the prison baron deposed by >Paul Newman, who joins him on his planned escape.

SUP ACTR: Estelle Parsons (*Bonnie and Clyde*) (Arthur Penn) ☆ ☞ ✍
As the sister-in-law of outlaw Clyde Barrow (Warren Beatty).

FOREIGN: *Closely Observed Trains* (US: *Closely Watched Trains*) (*Ostre Sledované Vlaky*) (Jiri Menzel) ☞ ✍
A train driver seeks to lose his virginity in Nazi occupied Czechoslovakia.

1968

FILM: *Oliver!* (>Carol Reed) ☞ ♫ ■
Lionel Bart's musical treatment of >Charles Dickens' tale of 19th-century London lowlife.

DIRECTOR: >Carol Reed (*Oliver!*)

ACTOR: Cliff Robertson (*Charly*) (Ralph Nelson) ☆
As a retarded man who is temporarily

transformed into a genius by wonder surgery.

ACTRESS: Barbra Streisand (*Funny Girl*) (>William Wyler) ☆ ☞
As Fanny Brice drifting apart from Omar Sharif in the process of hitting Broadway. shared with >**Katharine Hepburn** (*The Lion in Winter* (Anthony Harvey) ☆ ✍ ☞
As Eleanor of Aquitaine fighting with Peter O'Toole's Henry II over the succession of Anthony Hopkins' Richard I.

SUP ACT: Jack Albertson (*The Subject Was Roses*) (Ulu Grosbard) ☆
Vietnam vet Martin Sheen no longer has anything in common with parents Albertson and Patricia Neal.

SUP ACTR: Ruth Gordon (*Rosemary's Baby*) (>Roman Polanski) ✍ ☆ ☞
As the satanist neighbour who helps Mia Farrow deliver the Devil's son.

FOREIGN: *War and Peace* (*Voina i Mir*) (Sergei Bondarchuk) ☞ ✍ ☆
This epic version of Tolstoy's novel took over two years to make and 507 minutes to watch.

1969

FILM: *Midnight Cowboy* (>John Schlesinger) ♫ ☆
>Dustin Hoffman's sleazy Ratso Rizzo tries to pimp for gigolo Jon Voight.

DIRECTOR: >John Schlesinger (*Midnight Cowboy*)

ACTOR: >John Wayne (*True Grit*) (Henry Hathaway) ☆ ☞ ✍
The Duke as hard-drinking one-eyed Rooster Cogburn hired to avenge the death of Kim Darby's father.

ACTRESS: >Maggie Smith (*The Prime of Miss Jean Brodie*) (Ronald Neame) ☆ ✍
As the Edinburgh teacher attempting to make her girls the creme de la creme.

SUP ACT: Gig Young (*They Shoot Horses, Don't They?*) (Sydney Pollack) ✍ ☆

As the Master of Ceremonies at a dance marathon that ends in tragedy.

SUP ACTR: Goldie Hawn (*Cactus Flower*) (Gene Saks) ☆

Walter Matthau hires prudish secretary >Ingrid Bergman to prevent him having to marry mistress Goldie.

FOREIGN: *Z* (Constantin Costa-Gavras) ☆ ✍ ☞

Pacifist politician >Yves Montand is killed in a car accident in a Fascist state.

1970

FILM: *Patton* (>Franklin J. Schaffner) ☆ ✍ ☞

George C. Scott as the uncompromising leader of the Anzio landings in 1943.

DIRECTOR: Franklin J. >Schaffner (*Patton*)

ACTOR: George C. Scott (*Patton*)

ACTRESS: Glenda Jackson (*Women in Love*) (Ken Russell) ☆ ☞ ✍

The Brangwen sisters Gudrun (Jackson) and Ursula (Jennie Linden) have passionate affairs with respectively Oliver Reed and Alan Bates.

SUP ACT: John Mills (*Ryan's Daughter*) (>David Lean) ☞ ✍ ☆ ■

As the wordless idiot protected from the wrath of an Irish village by priest Trevor Howard.

SUP ACTR: Helen Hayes (*Airport*) (George Seaton) ☆ ☞

Hayes' stowaway old lady is the least of the problems facing the crew of a plane in a snow storm with a bomber on board.

FOREIGN: *Investigation of a Citizen above Suspicion* (*Indagine su un Cittadino al di Sopra di Ogni Sospetto*) (Elio Petri) ✍ ☆

A Rome cop kills his girlfriend and plants clues to see if his colleagues can catch him.

1971

FILM: *The French Connection* (William Friedkin) ☆ ✍

Gene Hackman as Popeye Doyle on to a drugs ring in Marseilles.

DIRECTOR: William Friedkin (*The French Connection*)

ACTOR: Gene Hackman (*The French Connection*)

ACTRESS: >Jane Fonda (*Klute*) (Alan J. Pakula) ☆ ✍

Donald Sutherland hunts down the deviant killer stalking a sexually disturbed hooker (Fonda).

SUP ACT: Ben Johnson (*The Last Picture Show*) (Peter Bogdanovich) ☞ ☆

As the owner of the cinema forced to close down through declining business.

SUP ACTR: Cloris Leachman (*The Last Picture Show*)

As the older woman, neglected by the town's football coach, who has an affair with Timothy Bottoms.

FOREIGN: *The Garden of the Finzi-Continis* (*Il Giardino dei Finzi-Continis*) (>Vittorio De Sica) ☞ ■ ☆ ✍

Wealthy Italian Jews shelter their coreligionists as the Fascist persecution intensifies.

1972

FILM: >*The Godfather* (>Francis Ford Coppola) ✍ ☞ ■ ♫ ☆

DIRECTOR: Bob Fosse (*Cabaret*) ♫ ✍

Political and night life in Berlin during the rise of Hitler.

ACTOR: >Marlon Brando (>*The Godfather*)

ACTRESS: Liza Minnelli (*Cabaret*)

As Sally Bowles, the star name at the famous Kit Kat Klub.

SUP ACT: Joel Grey (*Cabaret*)

As the untrustworthy, camp Master of Ceremonies at the Kit Kat Klub.

SUP ACTR: Eileen Heckart (*Butterflies Are Free*) (Milton Katselas) ☆
As the possessive mother opposing Goldie Hawn's relationship with blind songwriter son Edward Albert.

FOREIGN: >*The Discreet Charm of the Bourgeoisie (Le Charme Discret de la Bourgeoisie*) (>Luis Buñuel) ☞ ☆ ■ ✍

1973

FILM: *The Sting* (George Roy Hill) ✍ ☆ ♫ ☞
>Paul Newman and Robert Redford fleece Robert Shaw with a betting con.

DIRECTOR: George Roy Hill (*The Sting*)

ACTOR: >Jack Lemmon (*Save the Tiger*) (John G. Avildsen) ☆
Moralist Lemmon is depressed at having to cook his books, pimp for a client and burn his factory for the insurance money.

ACTRESS: Glenda Jackson (*A Touch of Class*) (Melvin Frank) ☆ ✍
Glenda's affair with George Segal is fun while it lasts.

SUP ACT: John Houseman (*The Paper Chase*) (James Bridges) ☆ ✍
Famed Broadway and Hollywood producer is seen here as a strict law professor bringing the best out of Timothy Bottoms.

SUP ACTR: Tatum O'Neal (*Paper Moon*) (Peter Bogdanovich) ☆ ■ ☞ ♫
As the cute girl Addie Pray whom Ryan O'Neal uses to help sell Bibles in Depression America.

FOREIGN: *Day for Night (La Nuit Americaine*) (>François Truffaut) ☞ ✍
Truffaut has problems with his cast during the making of a film on the Riviera.

1974

FILM: >*The Godfather Part II* (>Francis Ford Coppola) ✍ ☞ ■ ♫ ☆

DIRECTOR: >Francis Ford Coppola (>*The Godfather Part II*)

ACTOR: Art Carney (*Harry and Tonto*) (Paul Mazursky) ☆ ✍
Evicted New Yorker Carney walks to Chicago with his cat.

ACTRESS: Ellen Burstyn (*Alice Doesn't Live Here Anymore*) (>Martin Scorsese) ☞ ☆
Widow Burstyn hits the road with her son to pursue a singing career.

SUP ACT: >Robert De Niro (*The Godfather Part II*)

SUP ACTR: >Ingrid Bergman (*Murder on the Orient Express*) (>Sidney Lumet) ☆ ✍
As the nervous Swedish missionary Greta Ohlsson suspected by Albert Finney's Hercule Poirot.

FOREIGN: *Amarcord* (>Federico Fellini) ☞ ✍
A young man learns about life and love in Fascist Rimini.

1975

FILM: >*One Flew over the Cuckoo's Nest* (>Miloš Forman) ☆ ☞ ✍ ■

DIRECTOR: >Miloš Forman (>*One Flew over the Cuckoo's Nest*)

ACTOR: >Jack Nicholson (>*One Flew over the Cuckoo's Nest*)

ACTRESS: Louise Fletcher (>*One Flew over the Cuckoo's Nest*)

SUP ACT: George Burns (*The Sunshine Boys*) (Herbert Ross) ☆ ✍
As half of a comic duo with Walter Matthau whose feuding sabotages their TV comeback.

SUP ACTR: Lee Grant (*Shampoo*) (Hal Ashby) ☆
As a businessman's wife unable to wait for her sexual encounters with hairdresser Warren Beatty.

FOREIGN: *Derzu Uzala* (>Akira Kurosawa) ☞ ■
A Soviet scientist relies on a despised guide to help him through the Siberian wilderness.

1976

FILM: >*Rocky* (John G. Avildsen)
☆ ☞ ⚞

DIRECTOR: John G. Avildsen (>*Rocky*)

ACTOR: Peter Finch (*Network*)
(>Sidney Lumet) ☆ ☞
As a fired TV anchor man who speaks his mind on one of his last shows and threatens suicide.

ACTRESS: Faye Dunaway (*Network*)
As a ruthless channel executive who tries to raise Finch's falling ratings and falls for boss William Holden.

SUP ACT: Jason Robards, Jr (*All the President's Men*) (Alan J. Pakula) ☆ ⚞
As Ben Bradlee, editor of the *Washington Post*, encouraging Robert Redford and >Dustin Hoffman to investigate Watergate.

SUP ACTR: Beatrice Straight (*Network*)
Appearing in one scene only as William Holden's neglected wife.

FOREIGN: *Black and White in Colour* (*Le Victoire en Chantant*) (Jean-Jacques Annaud) ⚞ ☞ ☆
French colonials attempt to take a German fort in West Africa at the beginning of the First World War.

1977

FILM: >*Annie Hall* (>Woody Allen)
⚞ ☆ ☞

DIRECTOR: >Woody Allen (>*Annie Hall*)

ACTOR: Richard Dreyfuss (*The Goodbye Girl*) (Herbert Ross) ☆ ⚞
As an actor who excels as a camp Richard III and shares his living arrangements with Marsha Mason.

ACTRESS: >Diane Keaton (>*Annie Hall*)

SUP ACT: Jason Robards, Jr (>*Julia*)
(>Fred Zinnemann) ⚞ ☆ ☞ ■

SUP ACTR: Vanessa Redgrave (>*Julia*)

FOREIGN: *Madame Rosa* (*La Vie Devant Soi*) (Moshe Mizrahi) ☆ ⚞
Simone Signoret runs a home for the children of those who were murdered at Auschwitz.

1978

FILM: *The Deer Hunter* (Michael Cimino) ■ ♫ ☆
Three hunting friends are forced to play Russian roulette by the Vietcong.

DIRECTOR: Michael Cimino (*The Deer Hunter*)

ACTOR: Jon Voight (*Coming Home*)
(Hal Ashby) ⚞ ☆ ☞
As a crippled Vietnam vet who chains himself to the Marines recruiting centre when his buddy commits suicide.

ACTRESS: >Jane Fonda (*Coming Home*)
As a volunteer at a rehabilitation centre whose love for Voight survives the return of her own wounded husband.

SUP ACT: Christopher Walken (*The Deer Hunter*)
Who, along with >Robert De Niro and John Savage, finds his hunting experiences of little use in the Asian jungle.

SUP ACTR: >Maggie Smith (*California Suite*) (Herbert Ross) ☆ ⚞
As an actress fussing over her looks and bitching about her rivals as husband >Michael Caine helps her dress for the Oscar ceremony.

FOREIGN: *Get Out Your Handkerchiefs* (*Préparez vos Mouchoirs*) (Bertrand Blier) ⚞ ☆
>Gérard Depardieu hires men to help rekindle his marriage with Carole Laure.

1979

FILM: *Kramer versus Kramer* (Robert Benton) ☆
>Dustin Hoffman and >Meryl Streep in a courtroom custody battle.

DIRECTOR: Robert Benton (*Kramer versus Kramer*)

ACTOR: >Dustin Hoffman (*Kramer versus Kramer*)

ACTRESS: Sally Field (*Norma Rae*)
(Martin Ritt) ☆ ☞
As a worker receiving differing amounts of support from the men in her life for her campaign to unionize their mill.

Sup act: Melvyn Douglas (*Being There*) (Hal Ashby) ☆

As the dying financier who brings retarded Peter Sellers to the attention of US president Jack Warden.

Sup actr: >Meryl Streep (*Kramer versus Kramer*)

Foreign: *The Tin Drum* (*Die Blechtrommel*) (>Volker Schlöndorff) ☞ ☆

A young boy from Danzig stops growing through an act of will in this adaptation of Günter Grass's novel.

1980

Film: *Ordinary People* (Robert Redford) ☞

Timothy Hutton is helped and hindered by parents Mary Tyler Moore and Donald Sutherland and psychiatrist Judd Hirsch to get over the drowning of his brother.

Director: Robert Redford (*Ordinary People*)

An Oscar with his directorial debut.

Actor: >Robert De Niro (*Raging Bull*) (>Martin Scorsese) ☆ ☞ ■

As boxer Jake La Motta whose temper increased in direct proportion to his waistline.

Actress: Sissy Spacek (*Coal Miner's Daughter*) (Michael Apted) ☆

As country-and-western singer Loretta Lynn whose marriage collapsed in the wake of her fame.

Sup act: Timothy Hutton (*Ordinary People*)

Sup actr: Mary Steenburgen (*Melvyn and Howard*) (Jonathan Demme) ✑

As the realistic wife of Paul Le Mat who claims to be the man left a fortune in Howard Hughes (Jason Robards, Jr)'s will.

Foreign: *Moscow Distrusts Tears* (US:*Moscow Does Not Believe in Tears*) (*Moskava Slezam ne Verit*) (Vladimir Menshov) ✑

The lives and loves of three girls who share a workers' dormitory in 1958.

1981

Film: *Chariots of Fire* (Hugh Hudson) ☆ ✑ ♫

How Harold Abrahams (Ben Cross) and Eric Liddell (Ian Charleson) win their medals at the 1924 Olympics.

Director: Warren Beatty (*Reds*) ☆

Directing himself as Jack Reed facing stern resistance to the spread of Communism in the USA in the 1920s.

Actor: >Henry Fonda (*On Golden Pond*) (Mark Rydell) ☆ ■

The oldest recipient of an Oscar as an old man who enjoys showing the young son of his daughter's boyfriend the delights of life on the lake.

Actress: >Katharine Hepburn (*On Golden Pond*)

As Fonda's wife urging him to reconcile with their daughter >Jane Fonda.

Sup act: John Gielgud (*Arthur*) (Steve Gordon) ☆ ✑

As Hobson, the no-nonsense English valet to drunken playboy Dudley Moore, whose death brings Arthur to his senses.

Sup actr: Maureen Stapleton (*Reds*)

As disillusioned anarchist Emma Goldman despairing at the hopelessness of her cause in isolationist America.

Foreign: *Mephisto* (István Szabó) ☆ ☞ ✑ ■

Actor Klaus Maria Brandauer becomes a Nazi informer to further his career.

1982

Film: >*Gandhi* (>Richard Attenborough) ☞ ☆ ✑ ■

Director: >Richard Attenborough (>*Gandhi*)

Actor: Ben Kingsley (>*Gandhi*)

Actress: >Meryl Streep (*Sophie's Choice*) (Alan J. Pakula) ☆ ✑ ■

As a Polish refugee in New York tormented by her death camp experiences and the instability of her lover Kevin Kline.

Sup act: Louis Gossett, Jr (*An Officer and a Gentleman*) (Taylor Hackford)

As the tough drill sergeant who gives recruit Richard Gere a hard time when he isn't wooing and quarrelling with Debra Winger.

Sup Actr: >Jessica Lange (*Tootsie*) (Sydney Pollack) ☆

As the best friend of 'Dorothy' (>Dustin Hoffman) who does not know that the soap opera actress is a man in drag.

Foreign: *To Begin Again (Volver a Empezar)* (José Luis Garci) ✍

A fatally ill writer returns to the town where he fought in the Spanish Civil War.

1983

Film: *Terms of Endearment* (James L. Brooks) ☆

Shirley MacLaine's affair with >Jack Nicholson enlivens the story of her relationship with her daughter Debra Winger.

Director: James L. Brooks (*Terms of Endearment*)

Actor: Robert Duvall (*Tender Mercies*) (Bruce Beresford) ☆

As an alcoholic country-and-western singer who beats the booze and settles down on a farm with Tess Harpur and her son.

Actress: >Shirley MacLaine (*Terms of Endearment*)

Sup Act: >Jack Nicholson (*Terms of Endearment*)

Sup Actr: Linda Hunt (*The Year of Living Dangerously*) (Peter Weir) ☞ ☆ ✍

As male Chinese photographer Billy Kwan helping journalist Mel Gibson scoop stories in 1960s Indonesia.

Foreign: *Fanny and Alexander (Fanny och Alexander)* (>Ingmar Bergman) ☞ ■ ✍ ☆

1984

Film: >*Amadeus* (>Miloš Forman) ☆ ☞ ✍ ♫ ■

Director: >Miloš Forman (>*Amadeus*)

Actor: F. Murray Abraham (>*Amadeus*)

Actress: Sally Field (*Places in the Heart*) (Robert Benton) ☆

As the widow of a murdered policeman who farms her land despite the opposition of chauvinistic rivals.

Sup Act: Haing S. Ngor (*The Killing Fields*) (Roland Joffé) ☆ ♫

Himself a survivor of Cambodia, he plays Dith Pran, interpreter and adviser to photojournalist Sam Waterston.

Sup Actr: Peggy Ashcroft (*A Passage to India*) (>David Lean) ☞ ☆ ■

As Mrs Moore, a Raj matron whose health is unable to stand the attempted rape and trial in this film version of E. M. Forster's novel.

Foreign: *Dangerous Moves (La Diagonale du Fou)* (Richard Dembo) ☆ ✍

Official Soviet challenger Michel Piccoli meets defector Alexandre Arbatt for the World Chess Championship.

1985

Film: >*Out of Africa* (Sydney Pollack) ☆ ♫ ■ ✍ ☞

Director: Sydney Pollack (>*Out of Africa*)

Actor: >William Hurt (*The Kiss of the Spiderwoman*) (Hector Babenco) ☆ ☞ ■

As a homosexual prisoner planted by the authorities to glean revolutionary secrets from Raoul Julia.

Actress: Geraldine Page (*A Trip to Bountiful*) (Peter Masterson) ☆

As a woman returning to the scene of her childhood for a last visit before death.

Sup Act: Don Ameche (*Cocoon*) (Ron Howard) ☆ ✍

As one of a group of rejuvenated old people given the chance of immortality through emigration to another planet.

Sup Actr: Angelica Huston (*Prizzi's Honor*) (>John Huston) ☆ ☞ ✍

As Mafia assassin >Jack Nicholson's long-suffering girlfriend.

Foreign: >*The Official Version* (US: *The Official Story*) (*La Historia Oficial*) (Luis Puenzo) ☆ ✍ ☞ ■

1986

Film: *Platoon* (Oliver Stone)

Brutally candid account of the horror facing a foot soldier in Vietnam.

Director: Oliver Stone (*Platoon*)

Actor: >Paul Newman (*The Color of Money*) (>Martin Scorsese)

As pool hustler Fast Eddie Felson, passing tips to his heir apparent Tom Cruise.

Actress: Marlee Matlin (*Children of a Lesser God*) (Randa Raines) ☆ ✍

As the deaf-and-dumb cleaner who, as teacher >William Hurt's lover, demonstrates her intelligence and independence.

Sup Act: >Michael Caine (*Hannah and Her Sisters*) (>Woody Allen) ☆ ☞

As the husband of Mia Farrow's Hannah, obsessed with her bookish sister Barbara Hershey.

Sup Actr: Dianne Wiest (*Hannah and Her Sisters*)

As Farrow's third sister whose fear of never meeting the right men is allayed by marriage to hypochondriac >Woody Allen.

Foreign: *The Assault* (*De Aanslag*) (Fons Rademakers) ☆ ■

A Dutch boy witnesses the killing of his family by the Nazis.

1987

Film: *The Last Emperor* (>Bernardo Bertolucci) ☞ ■ ✍

John Lone as Pu Yi, the last Chinese emperor, used as the puppet ruler of Manchukuo by the Japanese.

Director: >Bernardo Bertolucci (*The Last Emperor*)

Actor: >Michael Douglas (*Wall Street*) (Oliver Stone) ☆

As ruthless financier Gordon Gekko who

uses Charlie Sheen to carry out his insider-dealing.

Actress: Cher (*Moonstruck*) (Norman Jewison) ☆ ✍ ♪

As a dowdy New York Italian who transforms her appearance and attracts Nicholas Cage, brother of her fiancé Danny Aiello.

Sup Act: >Sean Connery (*The Untouchables*) (Brian De Palma) ☆

As Irish cop Malone aiding Kevin Costner's Eliot Ness pin down >Robert De Niro's Al Capone.

Sup Actr: Olympia Dukakis (*Moonstruck*)

As Cher's long-suffering mother who tolerates the affairs of father Vincent Gardenia.

Foreign: >*Babette's Feast* (*Babettes Gaestebud*) (Gabriel Axel) ☆ ■ ☞ ✍

1988

Film: *Rain Man* (Barry Levinson) ☆ ☞ ✍

The half-brother of an autistic *savant* disputes their father's will, but comes to accept it as they become friends.

Director: Barry Levinson (*Rain Man*)

Actor: >Dustin Hoffman (*Rain Man*)

As Raymond, the television obsessed autistic kidnapped from his mental home by ambitious Tom Cruise.

Actress: Jodie Foster (*The Accused*) (Jonathan Kaplan) ☆ ✍

As a gang-rape victim accused of inviting her assault because of her dress and manner.

Sup Act: Kevin Kline (*A Fish Called Wanda*) (Charles Crichton) ☆ ✍ ☞

As the crazed boyfriend of Jamie Lee Curtis who is seducing lawyer John Cleese into getting a jewel thief bailed.

Sup Actr: Geena Davis (*The Accidental Tourist*) (Lawrence Kasdan) ☆ ☞ ✍

As the wacky but genuine dog walker who competes for travel writer >William Hurt with his wife >Kathleen Turner.

FOREIGN: >*Pelle the Conqueror* (*Pelle Erobreren*) (Bille August) ☆ ✍
Hating his life on a Danish island, a Swedish boy sets out to conquer the world.

1989

FILM: *Driving Miss Daisy* (Bruce Beresford 1989) ☆ ✍

DIRECTOR: Oliver Stone (*Born on the Fourth of July* 1989)

ACTOR: Daniel Day-Lewis (*My Left Foot*) (Jim Sheridan 1989) ☆ ✍

ACTRESS: Jessica Tandy (*Driving Miss Daisy*)

SUP ACT: Denzel Washington (*Glory*) (Edward Zwick 1989) ☆ ✍

SUP ACTR: Brenda Fricker (*My Left Foot*)

FOREIGN: *Cinema Paradiso* (*Nuovo Cinema Paradiso*) (Giuseppe Tornatore 1988) ☆ ■ ☞ ✍ ♫

Out of Africa ☆ ■ ✍ ☞ ♫

USA/GB • Universal • 1985 • 150 mins • col
d Sydney Pollack w Kurt Luedtke
ph David Watkin m John Barry
>Meryl Streep, Robert Redford, Klaus Maria Brandauer, Michael Gough

Meryl Streep's failure to win the Best Actress award for her outstanding performance as Karen Blixen must rate as one of the greatest injustices in Oscar history. Marrying a worthless Danish aristocrat (Brandauer), Karen – who always adapts to rather than manipulates her situation – and a workforce of Kikuyus develop his coffee plantation despite natural disasters and sabotage. The arrival of adventurer Denys Finch Hatton (Redford, with an accent as British as >Cary Grant's was French in *I Was a Male War Bride* (US: *You Can't Sleep Here*) [>Howard Hawks 1949] [☆ ☞ ✍]) provides a love interlude which director Sydney Pollack exploits to exhibit, through David Watkin's gorgeous photography, the continent's wondrous beauty. Stirring stuff, complete with lump-in-the-throat finale.

•Sissy Spacek makes the best of things as country-and-western star Loretta Lynn whose husband Tommy Lee Jones is jealous of her success, in *Coal Miner's Daughter* (Michael Apted 1980) (☆).

•Greta Scacchi and Charles Dance cause a colonial scandal with their affair and his murder by cuckolded Joss Ackland, in *White Mischief* (Michael Radford 1988) (■).

•Sally Field is faced with farming against the odds in *Places in the Heart* (Robert Benton 1984) (☆).

•Sigourney Weaver (AAN) is Dian Fossy, the woman at home in Africa in *Gorillas in the Mist* (Michael Apted 1988) (☆).

•Karen Blixen, writing as Isaac Dineson, was the author of >*Babette's Feast* (*Babettes Gaestebud*) (Gabriel Axel 1988) (☆ ✍ ☞ ■).

OUTER SPACE

Alien (Ridley Scott 1979) ✳
Sigourney Weaver is left to fight the monster that came on board the spaceship *Nostromo* attached to John Hurt's face.

Aliens (James Cameron 1986) ☆
Sigourney Weaver leads an expedition to the planet which first spawned the alien, to prevent their colonizing space.

Android (Aaron Lipstadt 1982) ☞
The hijack of a police spaceship affects the passengers in various ways, some dangerous.

Barbarella (Roger Vadim 1967) ■
>Jane Fonda has adventures in space while on the trail of a stolen death ray.

Close Encounters of the Third Kind (>Steven Spielberg 1977) ☆ ♫ ✳
Aliens select Richard Dreyfuss over >François Truffaut as the first human to visit another planet.

The Empire Strikes Back (Irvin Kershner 1980) ✳
Intergalactic war is engaged across the galaxy against the evil Empire, in script by Leigh Brackett and Lawrence Kasdan.

The Flight of the Navigator (Randall Kleiser 1986) ✳
Disney's space movie has a small boy (Joey Cramer) lending a hand to friendly aliens by piloting their craft.

Solaris (>Andrei Tarkovsky 1972) ☞
The personnel of a space station are gradually dwindling, but those remaining can transport people there merely by thinking of them.

Star Trek: The Motion Picture (Robert Wise 1979) ✍
Admiral Kirk (William Shatner) and Leonard Nimoy's Spock counter the galaxy-threatening force of V'ger.

OUTLAWS

Billy the Kid (>King Vidor 1930) ☞
Juvenile baddy Johnny Mack Brown is hunted down by Wallace Beery's Pat Garrett.

Bloody Mama (Roger Corman 1969) ✩ ☞
Shelley Winters as Ma Kate Barker having gangster gun fun with her four sons.

Catlow (Sam Wanamaker 1971) ✩
Baddy gunfighter Yul Brynner joins forces with goody counterpart Richard Crenna to recover his hidden gold.

The Eagle (Clarence Brown 1925) ✩
Rudolph Valentino as a man in a mask, who wins back his father's land and Vilma Banky.

The Flame and the Arrow (Jacques Tourneur 1950) ☞ ✩
Acrobatic Burt Lancaster wins Virginia Mayo as a medieval Italian Robin Hood.

Jesse James (Henry King 1939) ☞ ✩
Tyrone Power and >Henry Fonda protect Ma (Jane Darwell) by robbing her railroad persecutors.

Lorna Doone (Basil Dean 1934) ✍
Devon farmer John Loder skirts outlaw family threats to pay court to Victoria Hopper, in this screen version of R. D. Blackmore's novel.

Ned Kelly (Tony Richardson 1970)
Mick Jagger as the iron-clad Australian villain.

Robin Hood (Allan Dwan 1922) ✩
>Douglas Fairbanks steals from the rich while good king Wallace Beery is on crusade.

Three Godfathers (>John Ford 1948) ☞ ✩
On-the-run outlaws led by >John Wayne have to take care of an orphan.

Pabst, G. W.

(Georg Wilhelm Pabst) Austrian director
(1885–1967)

Interned by the French as an alien between 1914 And 1918, Pabst, the chronicler of early 20th-century Germany, later used Expressionism to depict the First World War – *Westfront 1918* (aka *Comrades of 1918*) (1930) (☞ ✍) (a striking comparison of home and trench views of the War) – and its aftermath: *Joyless Street* (US: *The Street of Sorrow*) (aka *Street of Sorrow*) (*Die Freudlose Gasse*) (1925) (☞ ✫) (>Greta Garbo is driven by Depression poverty into the employ of a Viennese brothel) and *Kameradschaft* (*La Tragédie de la Mine*) (1931) (☞ ✍ ■) (French and German miners are trapped when a shaft collapses). Following the making of *Secrets of a Soul* (*Geheimnisse einer Seele*) (1926) (☞) (academic Werner Krauss resorts to a psychiatrist to cure his knife nightmares) and *The Love of Jeanne Ney* (aka *Lusts of the Flesh*) (*Die Liebe der Jeanne Ney*) (1927) (a girl moves to Paris unaware that her lover is the man who killed her father in the Crimea during the Russian Revolution), he made the best of his studies of women with American siren Louise Brooks: *Pandora's Box*

(aka *Lulu*) (1929) (☞ ✫ ■) (Brooks taunts a doctor and his son and a lesbian countess before succumbing to >Jack the Ripper) and *Diary of a Lost Girl* (*Tagebuch einer Verloren*) (1929) (☞ ✫) (rich girl Brooks's pregnancy begins a downward spiral that ends in a brothel). Too unwell to flee Austria in 1939, he made historical melodramas for the Nazis, including *The Players* (aka *The Actors*) (*Komödianten*) (1941) (☞ ✍) (a girl runs away to join some struggling strolling players and persuades her aunt-in-law to build them a theatre) which was acclaimed at the then-Fascist-controlled Venice Festival. After the war, he attacked Hitler's anti-Semitism – *The Trial* (*Der Prozess*) (1947) (☞ ✫) (Pabst won Best Director at Venice and Ernst Deutsch won Best Actor as a Jewish defendant accused of a ritual killing in 1882 Hungary) – and his cowardice, *The Last Ten Days* (aka *The Last Ten Days of Adolf Hitler*) (*Der Letzte Akt*) (1955) (☞ ✍) (Albin Skoda as Hitler in Erich Maria Remarque's narrative of the Berlin bunker days).

•*The White Hell of Pitz-Palu* (*Die Weisse Hölle vom Piz Palü*) (1929) (co-directed with Arnold Franck)

(☞): a man returns each year to the mountain where his wife disappeared and meets her again in a storm.

•*The Threepenny Opera* (*Die Dreigroschenoper*) (1931) (☞ ✍): Bertolt Brecht and Kurt Weill's adaptation of John Gay's tale of London lowlife *The Beggar's Opera*.

•*L'Atlantide* (aka *Queen of Atlantis*) (*Die Herrin von Atlantis*) (1932) (☞): two soldiers fall for the Queen of Atlantis Brigitte Helm.

•*Don Quixote* (aka *Adventures of Don Quixote*) (*Don Quichotte*) (1954) (☞): a screen version of Cervantes' novel of an eccentric knight and his loyal squire.

•*Shanghai Drama* (*Le Drame de Shanghai*) (1938) (✍): white Russians sabotage the Chinese defences during the 1931 war with Japan.

•*The Jackboot Mutiny* (*Es Geschah am 20 Juli*) (1955): a dramatization of the 1944 briefcase bomb attempt on Hitler's life.

PACIFIC WAR

Across the Pacific (>John Huston 1942) ☆ ☞

Mary Astor and Sydney Greenstreet are among those whom >Humphrey Bogart suspects of being Japanese sympathizers.

The Burmese Harp (aka *Harp of Burma*) (*Biruma no Tategoto*) (Kon Ichikawa 1956) ☞ ■

As the Allies close in, a young soldier begins burying the war dead.

Destination Tokyo (Delmer Daves 1944) ☆
>Cary Grant steers his submarine into Tokyo harbour and prepares the way for James A. Doolittle's raid.

Empire of the Sun (>Steven Spielberg 1987) ■

A young English boy is befriended by black marketeers in a Japanese PoW camp.

Hell in the Pacific (John Boorman 1968) ☆
A Japanese (Toshiro Mifune) and an American (Lee Marvin) waive enmity to survive on a desert island.

King Rat (Bryan Forbes 1965) ☞ ☆
George Segal's collaboration with prison warders leads to a life of comparative luxury, in the film adaptation of James Clavell's novel.

The Long and the Short and the Tall (US: *Jungle Fighters*) (Leslie Norman 1960) ✍ ☆
Arguing British are soldiers caught behind the Japanese advance deep in the jungle, in the screen version of Willis Hall's play.

Sands of Iwo Jima (Allan Dwan 1949) ☆
>John Wayne's babes-in-arms kill every Japanese on the island, except the one who kills the Duke.

Tora! Tora! Tora! (Richard Fleischer/Ray Kellogg/Toshio Masuda/Kinji Fukasaku 1970) ✍ ☞

The hours before and during the attack on Pearl Harbor, seen through the eyes of the preparing Japanese and the unready Americans.

PARENTS AND CHILDREN

Deadly Run (*Mortelle Randonée*) (Claude Miller 1982) ☆ ✍
Cop Michel Serrault believes Isabelle Adjani, the murderess he is trailing, is his long-lost daughter.

Father and Son (*Fuzi Qing*) (Allen Fong (aka Fong Yuk-Ping) 1981) ✍
A strict father opposes his son's obsession with film-making.

Leave Her to Heaven (John M. Stahl 1945) ✍ ☆
Gene Tierney's father-fixation dictates her choice of husband and prompts her murderous behaviour.

The Marseilles Trilogy

Marius (Alexander Korda 1931) ☞ ☆ ✍
Marius (Pierre Fresnay) leaves his father César (Raimu)'s café and pregnant girlfriend Fanny (Orane Demazis) for a life at sea.

Fanny (Marc Allégret 1932) ☞ ☆ ✍
Fanny marries elderly Charpin and César persuades Marius to disown her and his son.

César (Marcel Pagnol 1936) ✍ ☆ ☞
Charpin dies and César now matchmakes between Fanny and his son, as he wants a grandchild.

Muddy River (*Doro no Kawa*) (Kohei Oguri, Japan 1981) ✍
A small boy makes friends with barge children, but their mother is a prostitute and his parents disapprove.

Taking Off (>Miloš Forman 1971) ☞
Parents seeking their daughter in a hippy commune have such a good time they forget what they came for.
> **Fathers and sons; Mother love**

PARIS

Cleo from Five to Seven (*Cleo de 5 à 7*) (Agnès Varda 1961) ☞ ☆
Corinne Marchand wanders around the city awaiting the results of her medical tests.
Frantic (>Roman Polanski 1988)☆
Doctor >Harrison Ford stumbles into a murder mystery after his wife is kidnapped on the eve of a conference.
>*The Frog Prince* (Brian Gilbert 1985) ☆ ⌂ ☞ ▧

The Legend of the Holy Drinker (*La Leggenda del Santo Bevitore*) (Ermanno Olmi 1989) ☞ ▧
An alcoholic tramp is the tragic toy of cruel fate.
The Moderns (Alan Rudolph 1988) ☆ ⌂
The lives and loves of a community of writers and artists in 1926 Paris.
A Pig Across Paris (US: *Four Bags Full*) (*La Traversée de Paris*) (Claude Autant-Lara 1956) ☆ ⌂ ☞
>Jean Gabin and Venice Best Actor winner Bourvil smuggle pork during the Nazi occupation.
So Long at the Fair (Terence Fisher/ Anthony Darnborough 1950) ☆
Visiting the 1889 Exposition, David Tomlinson goes missing and sister Jean Simmons goes to look for him.

PARODY

Airplane (Jim Abrahams/David & Jerry Zucker 1980) ⌂ ☆
Robert Hays and Julie Hegerty take control when the crew are food poisoned.
Airplane II: The Sequel (Jim Abrahams/ David & Jerry Zucker 1982) ⌂
Hays and Hegerty this time come to the rescue of a stricken passenger moon shot.

Blazing Saddles (Mel Brooks 1974) ⌂
Railroad barons are prevented from taking a town by black sheriff Cleavon Little.
The Cheap Detective (Robert Moore 1978) ⌂
The Neil Simon script has Peter Falk as >Humphrey Bogart solving a crime which boils down to a *Big Sleep* in *Casablanca*.
High Anxiety (Mel Brooks 1977)
Scenes from *Psycho*, *Vertigo* and *Spellbound* inform this affectionate lampoon of >Alfred Hitchcock.
Movie, Movie (>Stanley Donen 1978) ☞ ☆
George C. Scott in a double bill spoof of *film noir* boxing and MGM putting-on-a-show pictures.
Murder by Death (Robert Moore 1978) ☆
The Neil Simon script pokes fun at the cult of the detective and the red-herring, final twist whodunnit.
The Naked Gun (David Zucker 1988) ⌂
Leslie Nielsen and Priscilla Presley take a dig at TV cop shows.
Play It Again, Sam (Herbert Ross 1972) ☆
>Humphrey Bogart's spirit helps film buff >Woody Allen impress >Diane Keaton.
Top Secret! (Jim Abrahams/David & Jerry Zucker 1984) ⌂ ☆
Cold War exploits of agents and double agents are ridiculed as a 1950s rock singer cracks a spy ring.
Young Frankenstein (Mel Brooks 1974) ▧
Gene Wilder is helped to relive his grandfather's past by Marty Feldman.

Pasolini, Pier Paolo
Italian writer/director (1922–1975)
Escaped PoW, active Communist and author, Pasolini's artistic and political views influence all his films, particularly his studies of those living on the periphery of society: *Accatone* (1961) (☞ ♫ ⌂) (unable to live through honesty, a pimp turns to robbery); *Mamma Roma* (1962) (☆) (Anna Magnani is blackmailed back into prostitution to prevent a pimp revealing her past to her son); and *The Hawks and The Sparrows* (*Uccellacci e Uccellini*) (1966) (☞ ⌂) (father and son set out to convert the creatures of the air, with the help of a talking bird). Next

to be sumptuously interpreted was classical myth – *Oedipus Rex* (1967) (☞ ■) (Franco Citti fulfils the oracled prediction by murdering his father and marrying his mother) and *Medea* (1969) (☞ ■) (Giuseppe Gentile's Jason wishes to dismiss his wife Medea [Maria Callas], but she refuses to leave him) – and medieval literature: *The Decameron* (*Il Decamerone*) (1971) (■ ☞) (the peculiarities of human nature are revealed in eight of Boccaccio's tales); *The Canterbury Tales* (*I Racconti di Canterbury*) (1972) (■ ☞ ✍) (the director as Geoffrey Chaucer coaxes tales out of his fellow-pilgrims en route to St Thomas Becket's shrine); and *The Arabian Nights* (aka *A Thousand and One Nights*) (*Il Fiore delle Mille e una Notte*) (1974) (■ ☞) (ten tales told around a prince's search for a kidnapped servant girl). The idea, in the latter trilogy of equating sexual perversion with political tyranny and social lethargy was continued in Pasolini's final film before his murder *Salo, or The 120 Days of Sodom* (*Salo o le Centiventi Giornate di Sodoma*) (1975) (☞) (the Marquis De Sade's novel of sexual perversion updated to Mussolini's Italy).

 •*The Gospel According to St Matthew* (*Il Vangelo Secondo Matteo*) (1964) (☞ ■): Venice Special Jury winner has Enrique Irazoqui's Christ preaching equality and charity.
•*Theorem* (*Teorema*) (1968) (☞ ☆): gold-digging Terence Stamp beds an entire wealthy family from father Massimo Girotti to Venice Best Actress-winning maid Laura Betti.
•*Pigsty* (*Il Porcile*) (1969) (☞): a comparison of the lives of a medieval cannibal Pierre Clementi and the son of an ex-Nazi in modern Germany.

The Philadelphia Story ☆ ✍ ☞
USA • MGM • 1940 • 112 mins • b/w
d >George Cukor   w Donald Ogden Stewart   ph Joseph Ruttenberg   m Franz Waxman
>Katharine Hepburn, >Cary Grant, >James Stewart, Ruth Hussey, Roland Young, John Halliday, Mary Nash, Virginia Weidler, John Howard, Henry Daniell

Katharine Hepburn bought the rights to the Broadway play that Philip Barry wrote for her as it exemplified her popular image as a harsh, haughty unromantic, but neither she nor Grace Kelly in the musical remake *High Society* (Charles Walters 1956) (☆♫) (with Bing Crosby and Frank Sinatra in the Grant and Stewart roles) truly captures Tracy Lord's unforgiving snobbery, playing her instead as, respectively, a wisecracking screwball and a spoiled prig. Despite their blistering bust-up, C. Dexter Haven (Grant) schemes to win Tracy back by inducing *Spy Magazine* journalists Stewart and Hussey to thwart her prospective marriage to a boring nobody. A drunken wedding-eve, during which Stewart joins the Lord Appreciation Society, leaves Tracy with a headache and plenty to ponder. Great fun.

 •The rich and famous pass on the earrings that Danielle Darrieux sold, which are bought by her husband Charles Boyer for his mistress and which find their way back to his wife via her lover >Vittorio De Sica, in *Madame De...* (US: *The Earrings of Madame De...*) (>Max Ophüls 1953) (✍ ☞ ☆).
•Divorced socialite Shirley MacLaine finds herself fighting to keep her brother out of the clutches of Puerto Rican satanists, in *The Possession of Joel Delaney* (Waris Hussein 1971) (☆).
•Another divorce that didn't work out is Jean Arthur and >Cary Grant's, in *The Awful Truth* (>Leo McCarey 1937).
•>Bette Davis and Robert Montgomery are the reporters at the wedding of a *June Bride* (Bretaigne Windust 1948) (☆).
•Editor >Spencer Tracy risks the wrath of >Jean Harlow when he sends >William Powell to talk >Myrna Loy out of a law suit, in another 'press and the heiress' comedy *Libeled Lady* (Jack Conway 1936) (☆ ✍ ☞).

PICKING UP THE PIECES

All the Way Home (Alex Segal 1963) ☆
Jean Simmons raises her children through the pain of losing her husband Robert Preston.

>*The Best Years of Our Lives* (>**William Wyler 1946**) ☆ ☞ ✍ ▨
Dance Fools Dance (**Harry Beaumont 1931**) ☆
When her father's stocks crash, >Joan Crawford has to go out to work as a reporter and scoops a gangster killing.
Daughters Courageous (>**Michael Curtiz 1939**) ▨ ☆
Wandering Claude Rains returns home in time to prevent his ex-wife Fay Bainter marrying a businessman Donald Crisp.
The Devil to Pay (**George Fitzmaurice 1931**) ▨ ☆
Returning from East Africa, Ronald Colman renews his affair with >Myrna Loy; the fun begins when he meets Loretta Young.
For Queen and Country (**Martin Stellman 1988**)
Denzel Washington's Ulster and Falklands vet combats inner city racism and poverty.
The Great Santini (**Lewis John Carlino 1979**) ☆
Fighter pilot Robert Duvall compensates for there being no war by trying to make a man of son Michael O'Keefe.

PIRATES

The Black Pirate (**Albert Parker 1926**) ☆
Righting the wrongs done to his father, >Douglas Fairbanks brings fair raiding practices to the high seas.
The Buccaneer (**Cecil B. De Mille 1938**☆/ **Anthony Quinn 1958**)
Yul Brynner added the lustre but lacked the bravura that >Fredric March earlier showed as Jean Lafitte aiding the USA in the 1812 war with Britain.
Captain Blood (>**Michael Curtiz 1935**) ☞ ☆
Errol Flynn does his bit to resist James II by fencing with >Basil Rathbone's Judge Jeffreys.
Captain Clegg (**US: *Night Creatures***) (**Peter Graham Scott 1962**) ☆
Vicar Peter Cushing, a retired pirate, keeps his hand in by doing a little smuggling.
China Seas (**Tay Garnett 1935**) ☆
>Clark Gable and >Jean Harlow add a few pirates to the trouble they are having with crooked Wallace Beery.

A High Wind in Jamaica (**Alexander Mackendrick 1965**) ✍
Victorian children are captured by pirates on their way back to England from the West Indies.
The Pirate (>**Vincente Minnelli 1948**) ☞ ☆
>Gene Kelly allows Judy Garland to believe he is the daring hero, who is in fact her detested intended.
The Princess and the Pirate (**David Butler 1944**) ☆ ✍
The only consolation Bob Hope has when he impersonates a pirate is that Virginia Mayo gets him, not Victor McLaglen.
The Sea Hawk (>**Michael Curtiz 1940**) ☆ ☞
Errol Flynn rids the Spanish Main of Claude Rains for Flora Robson's Elizabeth I.

POETS

The Bad Lord Byron (**David MacDonald 1948**) ☆
Dennis Price looks back on his roguish amours with Mai Zetterling and Joan Greenwood.
Blood of the Poet (*Le Sang d'un Poète*) (**Jean Cocteau 1930**) ☞ ✍ ▨
Lee Miller's adventures through a looking glass include live statues, an execution and a fatal snowball fight.
The Colour of Pomegranates (*Tsvet Granata*) (aka *Sayat Nova*) (**Sergo Paradjanov 1969**) ▨
Factional life of 18th-century Armenian rags-to-vestments poet Sayat Nova.
A Fine Madness (**Irvin Kershner 1966**) ☆
>Sean Connery as a New York versifier subjecting Jean Seberg to his bursts of violence.
Gothic (**Ken Russell 1987**)
Natasha Richardson dreams up >*Frankenstein* while Gabriel Byrne's Byron talks Julian Sand's Shelley off the roof.
Orphée (*Orpheus*) (**Jean Cocteau 1949**) ☞ ✍ ▨ ☆
Leather jackets, motorcycles, mirrors and the Underworld as Jean Marais seeks the Princess of Death.
Reuben, Reuben (**Robert Ellis Miller 1984**) ☆
Tom Conti as a drunken poet leching and leeching his way through a USA lecture tour.

Polanski, Roman

French-born Polish actor/writer/director (b 1933)

An insignificant bit-player in some of the most significant postwar Polish pictures – *A Generation* (*Pokolenie*) (>Andrej Wajda 1954) (☞ ☆) (as a resistance fighter in occupied Warsaw) and *Kanal* (aka *They Wanted to Live*) (aka *Sewer*) (>Andrej Wajda 1957) (☞ ☆) (as one of a group of Warsaw partisans being driven into the sewers by the Nazis) – the state-trained Polanski was officially denounced in 1964 for presenting an unacceptable image of the nation in *Knife in the Water* (*Noz w Wodzie*) (1962) (☞ ☆) (a husband has to compete for his wife's affections with a freewheeler they invite on their sailing holiday). Forced to working in European and American exile, his subjects have a large range: CHILLERS: *Repulsion* (1965) (☞ ☆) (terrified of sex, >Catherine Deneuve kills men who come too close) and *Rosemary's Baby* (1968) (☞ ☜ ☆) (Mia Farrow gives birth to the anti-Christ); THRILLERS: *Cul-De-Sac* (1966) (☞) (gangsters hiding in a remote castle are tormented by its eccentric owners) and *Chinatown* (AAN: 1974) (☆ ☞ ☜) (>Jack Nicholson's private eye J. J. Gittes meets ruthless resistance and scared reluctance as he investigates a corrupt land deal); and LITERARY ADAPTATIONS: *Macbeth* (1971) (☜ ☞ ☆) (Jon Finch as the troubled Scottish thane and Francesca Annis his ambitious wife) and >*Tess* (AAN: 1979) (☞ ■ ☜ ☆). However, in each of his films he examines the plight of individuals powerless to escape the consequences of their claustrophobic circumstances.

VIEW ON ▶ •*Dance of the Vampires* (aka *The Fearless Vampire Killers, or Pardon Me, Your Teeth Are in My Neck*) (1967): Polanski sets out to save Sharon Tate from vampire Jack McGowran only to end up one himself.

• *The Tenant* (1976) (☞ ☆ ☜ ■): Isabelle Adjani is unable to allay Polanski's fears that boarding house hosts Melvyn Douglas and Shelley Winters are out to get him.

•*Pirates* (1986): castaway Walter Matthau rewards his rescuers with knavery.

•*Frantic* (1988) (☆): doctor >Harrison Ford seeks his kidnapped wife across Paris.

POLICE

The Big Heat (>Fritz Lang 1953) ☞ ☆
Glenn Ford throws restraint out of the window as he pursues the killers of his wife and a corrupt cop.

The Blue Lamp (Basil Dearden 1949) ☜ ☆
Dirk Bogarde's panic shooting of copper Jack Warner casts a gloom over the Dixon household, but the lodger is on his tracks.

Cops and Robbers (*Guardie e Ladri*) (Mario Monicelli 1951) ☆
Unless cop Aldo Fabrizi can find thief Toto, he will lose both his job and his pension.

Detective Story (>William Wyler 1951) ☆ ☞
As lowlife hums around a downtown police station, >Kirk Douglas discovers that his wife Eleanor Parker has a guilty secret.

Dragnet (Tom Mankiewicz 1987) ☆
Tom Hanks and Dan Aykroyd spoof the heroic cops of the long-running TV series, but still get their men.

Easy Street (>Charles Chaplin 1917) ☆ ☜
Charlie sends the villains scurrying after hefty Eric Campbell is laid out by a streetlight bowl.

Lethal Weapon (Richard Donner 1987)
Danny Glover teaches Mel Gibson there is more to life than being licensed to kill.

Midnight Patrol (Lloyd French 1933) ☆
>Laurel and Hardy arrest the chief of police for burglary in his own house.

POLICIERS or POLICE PROCEDURALS

Amsterdam Affair (Gerry O'Hara 1968) ☜
Dutch inspector Van Der Valk (Wolfgang Kieling) tracks down a writer accused of murder.

Angel Dust (*Poussière d'Ange*) (Edouard Niermans 1987) ☆ ☜
Bernard Giraudeau's curiosity about the man now living with his wife embroils him in a seedy murder case.

Le Cop (Claude Zidi 1985) ☆
Idle >Philippe Noiret prefers bribes to crime fighting, but new partner Thierry Lhermitte is still keen.

Cop au Vin (*Poulet au Vinaigre*) (>Claude Chabrol 1984) ☞ ☆

Jean Poiret's Inspecteur Lavardin investigates the death of a corrupt property developer.

Fourteen Hours (Henry Hathaway 1951) ☆ ☞

Richard Basehart puts his career on the ledge trying to talk Paul Douglas out of a suicide plunge.

Gideon of Scotland Yard (US: *Gideon's Day*) (>John Ford 1958) ☆

This adaptation of John Creasey's novel follows Jack Hawkins investigating a number of routine cases.

Inspecteur Lavardin (>Claude Chabrol 1986) ☞ ☆

Jean Poiret is troubled by a singularly baffling murder and his feelings for an old flame.

The Lineup (Don Siegel 1958) ☞

San Francisco police stalk a trigger-happy drug dealer.

The Long Arm (US: *The Third Key*) (Charles Frend 1956) ☆

Foiling a London safecracker is all in a day's work for Jack Hawkins.

>*Subway* (Luc Besson 1985) ✍ ☆ ♫ ■ ☞

The Glass Key (Frank Tuttle 1935) ☆ ✍/(Stuart Heisler 1942) ☆

George Raft and Alan Ladd keep respective political bosses Edward Albert and Brian Donlevy out of a murder scandal.

No Love For Johnnie (Ralph Thomas 1960) ☆

Labour MP Peter Finch's popularity wanes as his private life hits the tabloids.

Paris by Night (David Hare 1988) ✍ ☆

Charlotte Rampling as a Tory Euro MP prepared to go to any lengths to further her career and protect her reputation.

The Prime Minister (Thorold Dickinson 1941) ☆

Disraeli (John Gielgud)'s career is helped no end by his marriage to Diana Wynyard's Mary-Anne Wyndham Lewis.

Scandal (Michael Caton-Jones 1988) ☆

Joanne Whalley-Kilmer and Bridget Fonda's call girls Christine Keeler and Mandy Rice-Davies spark the Profumo Affair.

Wilson (Henry King 1944) ☆ ✍ ■

Alexander Knox as Woodrow Wilson who led the USA into the First World War, but couldn't get it to follow him into the peace treaty.

>Elections

POLITICS

Advise and Consent (Otto Preminger 1962) ☆ ✍

>Charles Laughton, Franchot Tone and Lew Ayres are among the senators scheming during a crisis in >Henry Fonda's presidency.

Alexander Hamilton (John G. Adolfi 1931) ☆

George Arliss as one of America's founding fathers having his career rocked by an adultery scandal.

The Best Man (Franklin Schaffner 1964) ☆ ✍

Convention candidates >Henry Fonda and Cliff Robertson compete for the backing of President Lee Tracy.

The Candidate (Michael Ritchie 1972) ☆

Robert Redford regrets allowing himself to be talked into running for senator as his life falls apart.

POLLYANNAS

Anne of Green Gables (George Nicholls, Jr 1934) ✍

Anne Shirley cheers up her elderly aunt and uncle during the Depression.

Annie (>John Huston 1982) ☞ ♫

An orphan transforms the life of a lonely millionaire.

The Blue Bird (Walter Lang 1940) ✍ ☞ ■

The Maeterlinck fairy tale has Shirley Temple and Johnny Russell searching the past and future for the blue bird of happiness.

Little Miss Marker (UK: *The Girl in Pawn*) (Alexander Hall 1934) ☆

Shirley Temple saves gambler Adolphe Menjou from himself and his enemies.

One Hundred Men and a Girl (Henry Koster 1937) ☆

Deanna Durbin persuades conductor Leopold Stokowski to form an orchestra to employ her father Adolphe Menjou.

Pollyanna (David Swift 1960) ☆ ✍
The Disney telling of Eleanor Porter's novel has Hayley Mills melting the hearts of crabby villagers.
The Secret Garden (Fred M. Wilcox 1949) ☆
The Frances Hodgson Burnett story of Margaret O'Brien spreading a little happiness in the household of uncle Herbert Marshall.

POP STARS

Catch Us If You Can (US: *Having a Wild Weekend*) (John Boorman 1965) ♫
Dave Clark abandons the other four and drives round London with model Barbara Ferris.
Ferry Cross the Mersey (Jeremy Summers 1964) ♫
Gerry and the Pacemakers and Cilla Black compete in a talent contest.
Head (Bob Rafelson 1968) ♫ ☆
The Monkees abandon their TV sit-com format for a series of psychedelic sketches.
Help! (Richard Lester 1965) ♫ ☆
The other three Beatles prevent Ringo Starr being sacrificed because of a ring wedged on his finger.
Jailhouse Rock (Richard Thorpe 1957) ♫
Jailbird Elvis Presley goes straight ... to the top of the charts.
Purple Rain (Albert Magnoli 1984) ♫
Prince's romantic problems inspire a passionate concert performance.
Rock around the Clock (Fred F. Sears 1956) ♫
Bill Haley and his Comets get them dancing in the aisles.
True Stories (David Byrne 1986) ✍ ♫
Satirical sketches are punctuated with what amount to Talking Heads' video promos.

POPES

The Agony and the Ecstasy (>Carol Reed 1965) ☆ ☞ ✍ ■
Rex Harrison's Julius II makes painting the Sistine ceiling difficult for Charlton Heston's Michelangelo.
Foul Play (Colin Higgins 1978) ☆
Goldie Hawn and Chevy Chase stumble on to a plot to assassinate the pope when he comes to San Francisco.
Never Take No for an Answer (Maurice Cloche/Ralph Smart 1951) ✍
A small boy and his sick donkey make a pilgrimage to find the pope in the hope of a miracle.
Pope Joan (Michael Anderson 1972) ■
Liv Ullmann as the 9th century German prostitute who was proclaimed pope.
Saving Grace (Robert M. Young 1986) ☆
Locked out of the Vatican, Tom Conti discovers the poor of Italy and vows to do something about them.
The Shoes of the Fisherman (Michael Anderson 1968) ☆ ✍
The screen version of Morris West's novel has Soviet cardinal Anthony Quinn elected to the Throne of St Peter.

POT-POURRI

And Now for Something Completely Different (Ian MacNaughton 1971) ✍ ☆
Collection of the best of the Monty Python team's early TV sketches.
Divine Madness (Michael Ritchie 1980) ☆
Bette Midler live on stage, combining song with inimitable humour.
Le Gai Savoir (>Jean-Luc Godard 1969)
Jean-Pierre Léaud and Juliette Berto sit in a studio and discuss education.
Heaven (>Diane Keaton 1987) ☞
Various interviewees give their impression of the afterlife.
Inauguration of the Pleasure Dome (Kenneth Anger 1954) ■
Avant-garde series of images drawn from Greek and Indian mythology.
Le Joli Mai (Chris Marker 1963) ☞
>Yves Montand's commentary links popular Parisian opinions on the topics of the day.
Jonathan Livingston Seagull (Hall Bartlett 1973) ■ ♫
Richard Bach's seagull holds a life-long ambition to be the fastest of birds.
Monty Python's Meaning of Life (Terry Jones 1983) ✍ ☆
A series of sketches tracing life from the cradle

to the grave without ever alluding to its meaning.

Swimming to Cambodia (Jonathan Demme 1987) ☆ ✍

In a brilliant monologue, Spalding Gray recalls his experiences during the making of *The Killing Fields*.

Tell Me Lies (Peter Brook 1967) ☞

This British protest at US involvement in Vietnam consists of satirical sketches and ironic stating of statistics.

Vincent – The Life and Death of Vincent Van Gogh (Paul Cox 1988) ☞ ■ ☆

Over photography evoking Van Gogh's individual view of Arles, John Hurt reads the artist's letters to his brother Theo.

Powell, Michael

British writer/director (1905–1990)

Working, usually co-directing, with Hungarian-born screenwriter Emeric Pressburger between 1942 and 1956, Powell excelled at fantasy and revelled in the controversial, although his earliest projects during the Second World War were morale-boosters: *The Lion Has Wings* (co-directed with Brian Desmond Hurst and Adrian Brunel 1939) (Merle Oberon and Ralph Richardson are among those helpless as war approaches), *The 49th Parallel* (US: *The Invaders*) (1941) (☞ ✍ ☆) (>Laurence Olivier and >Leslie Howard combine to prevent the safe passage of Nazi U-boat men through Canada) and *One of Our Aircraft Is Missing* (AAN [script]: 1942) (RAF pilots are sheltered from the Nazis by Dutch Resistance fighters). Churchill attempted to ban his exploration of military motivation – *The Life and Death of Colonel Blimp* (1943) (☞ ✍ ☆) (Roger Livesey serves the Empire against Kruger, Kaiser and Hitler) – and his *The Battle of the River Plate* (US: *Pursuit of the Graf Spee*) (1956) (☞ ■ ☆) (John Gregson sinks Peter Finch's *Graf Spee* in Montevideo harbour) suffered similar accusations of dishonouring the fallen. However, Technicolor fantasy was to fuel Powell's most popular films: *The Thief of Bagdad* (co-directed with Ludwig Berger and Tim Whelan 1940)(■ ☞ ✍) (Sabu is instrumental in bringing down wicked Conrad

Veidt); >*A Matter of Life and Death* (US: *Stairway to Heaven*) (1946) (✍ ☆ ☞ ■ ♫); *The Red Shoes* (1948) (■) (ballerina Moira Shearer commits suicide when asked to choose between her career and Anton Walbrook); *The Elusive Pimpernel* (1950) (David Niven's dandy rescues beleaguered nobles from the French Revolutionary guillotine); and *The Tales of Hoffman* (1951) (♫ ☞) (Offenbach's balletic opera tells of a poet's search for love). Recently reappraised as an original and visionary director, Powell's studio method occasionally failed to convince, notably, despite the award of a set decoration Oscar, the awful Himalayan scenery in *Black Narcissus* (1947) (☞ ■) (rivalries develop between nuns in a remote convent, in this screen version of Rumer Godden's novel) and just about everything in *Gone to Earth* (US: *The Wild Heart*) (1950) (■) (Jennifer Jones as Shropshire lass lusted after by squire David Farrar).

 •*The Spy in Black* (US: *U-Boat 29*) (1939) (☞ ☆): World War I German spies Conrad Veidt and Valerie Hobson fall in love in the Orkneys.

•*Contraband* (US: *Blackout*) (1940) (☞ ✍ ☆): waiters and rugby players help Valerie Hobson catch spy Conrad Veidt during the Blitz.

•*A Canterbury Tale* (1944) (☆): Charles Hawtrey and Dennis Price are among those showing how men, women and Americans can combine to win the war, even if that only means unmasking a doddering old judge.

•*I Know Where I'm Going* (1945) (■): Wendy Hiller is a castaway on Mull, where she meets and marries Roger Livesey.

•*The Small Back Room* (1948) (☞): a bomb-disposal expert regains the will to live when a new German device baffles him.

•*Ill Met by Moonlight* (US: *Night Ambush*) (1956): Dirk Bogarde leads partisans on Crete in a kidnap attempt on a Nazi general.

•*Peeping Tom* (1959) (☞ ■ ☆): film studio hand Carl Boehm murders women to photograph their fear and pain.

•*They're a Weird Mob* (1966) (☞): an Italian immigrant in Australia is given a hard time in Sydney.

•*Age of Consent* (1969) (☆): artist James

Mason seduces Helen Mirren on a Pacific island.

Powell, William
American actor (1892–1984)

Gaining his acting experience with provincial repertory companies and on Broadway, Powell began his film career typecast as a debonair villain in such silents as *The Sea Horses* (Gregory La Cava 1926) and *The Last Command* (>Josef Von Sternberg 1928) (☞ ☆) (Powell's sadistic film director victimizes >Emil Jannings) and in Paramount's first Talkie *Interference* (Lothar Mendes/Roy Pomeroy 1928) (☆ ♫) (Powell as a returned castaway suspected of murdering his bigamist wife). However, Powell possessed the looks, voice and charm to emerge as the most sophisticated upholder of the law in the movies, first as Philo Vance in *The Canary Murder Case* (Mal St Clair 1929) (☆ ♫) (Powell investigates the murder of blackmailing singer Louise Brooks) and *The Kennel Murder Case* (>Michael Curtiz 1933) (☞ ☆ ♫) (Powell reveals that Mary Astor's uncle did not take his own life), and then as Nick Charles, who along with >Myrna Loy's Nora, enjoyed the most idyllic of marriages and a series of adventures beginning with >*The Thin Man* (AAN: W. S. Van Dyke 1934) (☆ ☞ ♫). Such was the Powell/Loy chemistry that they shared a further dozen films, including: *Manhattan Melodrama* (W. S. Van Dyke 1934) (Loy switches allegiance from gangster >Clark Gable to his lawyer friend Powell); *I Love You Again* (W. S. Van Dyke 1940) (☆ ♫ ☞) (Loy loathes marriage to dull Powell until a blow on the head transforms him into a con man); and *Love Crazy* (Jack Conway 1941) (☆) (Powell impersonates his sister as he and Myrna engage in tit-for-tat infidelities). Recognized as a polished comedian, he oozed through *My Man Godfrey* (AAN: Gregory La Cava 1936) (☆) (millionaire Powell poses as butler to an eccentric family to pursue Carole Lombard), *Life with Father* (AAN: >Michael Curtiz 1947) (☆ ☞ ♫) (crotchety Powell's revelation that he is unbaptized distresses his wife Irene Dunne) and *Mister Roberts* (>Mervyn Le Roy/>John Ford 1955) (☆) (Powell as ship's doctor to the becalmed crew of >James Cagney's convoy escort vessel).

AS PHILO VANCE:

•*The Greene Murder Case* (Frank Tuttle 1929) (☆): as S. S. Van Dine's amateur sleuth suspecting Jean Arthur of a millionaire's murder.

•*The Benson Murder Case* (Frank Tuttle 1930) (☆): Paul Lukas is among those in the frame as Powell deduces the killer of a financier.

AS NICK CHARLES:

•*After the Thin Man* (W. S. Van Dyke 1936) (☆ ♫ ☞): >James Stewart is among those at the drawing-room denouement as Nick and Nora solve a murder and missing persons case.

•*Another Thin Man* (W. S. Van Dyke 1939) (☆ ☞ ♫): C. Aubrey Smith rightly suspects he is to be killed; Nick and Nora with baby Nickie and their dog Asta in tow find out whodunnit.

•*Shadow of the Thin Man* (W. S. Van Dyke 1941) (☆ ☞): journalists and jockeys go down like flies before the Charleses break up a gambling racket.

•*The Thin Man Goes Home* (Richard Thorpe 1944) (☆): an artist in Powell's home town is murdered for a microfilm in one of his canvases.

•*Song of the Thin Man* (Edward Buzzell 1947) (☆): in their last outing the pair become involved in a gambling mystery on a cruise.

OTHERS:

•*Charming Sinners* (Robert Milton 1929) (☆): Powell at his suave best in this W. Somerset Maugham comedy of infidelity.

•*For the Defense* (John Cromwell 1930) (☆ ☞ ♫): Powell as a society lawyer suspected of jury bribing to keep girlfriend Kay Francis out of jail.

•*Street of Chance* (John Cromwell 1930) (☆): Kay Francis and Jean Arthur stand by gambling brothers Powell and Regis Toomey during their card confrontation.

•*High Pressure* (>Mervyn Le Roy 1932) (☆ ♫): Powell's hopes of getting rich through rubber are hamstrung by the disappearance of an inventor.

•*Evelyn Prentice* (William K. Howard 1934) (☆ ♫): when neglected >Myrna Loy suspects

Powell of wooing client Rosalind Russell, she
has a fling herself with poet Harvey Stephens.
•*The Great Ziegfeld* (Robert Z. Leonard 1936)
(☆ ✍): Powell as theatre impresario Florenz
Ziegfeld torn between wives Luise Rainer (AA)
and >Myrna Loy.
•*The Ex-Mrs Bradford* (Stephen Roberts 1936)
(☆): doctor Powell and Jean Arthur patch up
their marriage by solving a race track mystery.
•*The Emperor's Candlesticks* (George Fitzmaurice 1937) (☆): this Baroness Orczy tale
has agents Powell and Luise Rainer searching
the palaces of Europe and falling in love.
•*The Ziegfeld Follies* (>Vincente Minnelli
1946) (☆ ☞ ■): Powell's late impresario puts
on a show from heaven courtesy of >Fred Astaire.
•*The Senator Was Indiscreet* (UK: *Mr Ashton
Was Indiscreet*) (George S. Kaufman 1947)
(☆): Powell is humoured by >Myrna Loy in his
attempt to rise from the ashes of political scandal to become president.
•*Mr Peabody and the Mermaid* (Irving Pichel
1948) (☆): bored husband Powell dreams of
amorous adventures with mermaid Ann Blyth.

THE PRESS

>*His Girl Friday* (>Howard Hawks 1940)
✍ ☞ ☆
It Happened Tomorrow (>René Clair 1944)
☞ ✍
A medium who has been predicting headlines
tells Dick Powell that he is going to die.
The Killing Fields (Roland Joffé 1984) ☆ ♫
Photojournalist Sam Waterston rescues his in-
terpreter Haing S. Ngor in Cambodia.
Libeled Lady (Jack Conway 1936) ☆ ☞ ✍
Editor >Spencer Tracy sends reporter >Wil-
liam Powell to woo >Myrna Loy out of a libel
suit against their paper.
The Salamander (Alain Tanner 1971) ✍
A journalist and a novelist interview a girl
suspected of killing her guardian.
Salvador (Oliver Stone 1986) ☆ ✍ ☞
Photographer James Woods tries to get his film
and his wife out of war-torn El Salvador.
Tell No Tales (Leslie Fenton 1938) ☆ ✍
Melvyn Douglas's run down paper is revived by
a juicy murder case.

The Year of Living Dangerously (Peter Weir
1982) ☞ ☆ ✍
Mel Gibson betrays the trust of contact Linda
Hunt by printing privileged information in
1960s Indonesia.

PRIESTS

The Devil's Playground (Fred Schepisi 1976)
Tempers flare in the class and staffrooms of an
Australian seminary.
The Diary of a Country Priest (*Journal d'un
Curé de Campagne*) (>Robert Bresson
1950) ☞ ☆
Claude Laydu dies of cancer in the knowledge
that he has done little to inspire faith in his
parishioners.
Fighting Father Dunne (Ted Tetzlaff 1948)
☆
Pat O'Brien fights to found a boy's home in St
Louis.
Full Confession (John Farrow 1939) ☆
Father Barry Fitzgerald talks killer Victor
McLaglen into turning himself in.
Going My Way (>Leo McCarey 1943)
☞ ✍ ☆
Bing Crosby bails out Barry Fitzgerald's
beloved but struggling St Dominic's.
I Confess (>Alfred Hitchcock 1953) ☞ ✍ ☆
Because of his confessional vow, Montgomery
Clift becomes Karl Malden's chief murder sus-
pect.
The Little World of Don Camillo (*Il Piccolo
Mondo di Don Camillo*) (Julien Duvivier
1952) ☆ ✍
Fernandel competes for the hearts and minds
of villagers with Communist mayor Gino
Cervi.
Mass Appeal (Glenn Jordan 1985) ☆
>Jack Lemmon is troubled by a battle of wits
with one of his students.
The Red and the Black (aka *Scarlet and
Black*) (*Le Rouge et le Noir*) (Claude
Autant-Lara 1954) ☞ ✍
Gérard Philipe as Stendhal's ambitious priest
who climbs the social ladder through seduc-
tion.

PRISON

Angi Vera (Pál Gábor 1978) ✍ ☆
Veronika Papp is sent to a prison hospital where she learns to toe the Communist Party line.

The Big House (George Hill 1930) ✍ ■
Robert Montgomery squeals on killer Wallace Beery in Frances Marion's AA-winning script.

Birdman of Alcatraz (John Frankenheimer 1961) ☆ ■
Burt Lancaster as lifer Robert Stroud who turned his cell into an aviary.

Brute Force (>Jules Dassin 1947) ☞
Burt Lancaster leads a revolt against brutal governor Hume Cronyn.

The Criminal Code (>Howard Hawks 1931) ☞ ✍
Self-defence killer Walter Huston finds himself suspected of a cell death.

Death by Hanging (*Koshikei*) (Nagisa Oshima 1968) ☞
Korean executee Yun-Do Yun is persecuted on death row, but he survives his hanging.

Each Dawn I Die (William Keighley 1939) ☆
Victim-of-injustice journalist >James Cagney is taught survival by cellmate George Raft.

Yield to the Night (J. Lee-Thompson 1956) ☆
Diana Dors relives her life and crime as she waits for her execution.

PRISONERS OF WAR

Albert RN (US: *Break to Freedom*) (Lewis Gilbert 1953) ✍
Jack Warner's chaps use a dummy to disguise absences at appel.

Camp Thiaroye (Ousmane Sembene 1989) ☞ ■
A brutal regime makes life miserable at a World War II repatriation camp in Senegal.

The Captive Heart (Basil Dearden 1946) ☞ ☆
PoWs protect a Czech impersonating a British officer.

The Colditz Story (Guy Hamilton 1954) ✍ ☆
Pat Reid (John Mills) leads a theatre tunnel escape from the impregnable Saxon castle.

The Cow and I (*La Vache et le Prisonnier*) (Henri Verneuil 1959) ☆ ✍
Fernandel takes a cow on his escape to make him less conspicuous.

Danger Within (US: *Breakout*) (Don Chaffey 1958) ☆
Home runs are thin on the ground as a traitor keeps the Nazis informed.

Eroica (US: *Heroism*) (Andrej Munk 1957) ☞ ✍
Two stories recall the 1944 Warsaw rising and the boosting of camp morale by teasing the Nazis about a man who has escaped.

The Great Escape (John Sturges 1963) ☆
The film version of Paul Brickhill's novel sees the escapes of Steve McQueen, >Richard Attenborough, James Garner and James Coburn.

The One that Got Away (Roy Baker 1957) ☆
Biopic of the Luftwaffe pilot Franz Von Werra (Hardy Kruger) that no British PoW camp could hold.

Slaughterhouse Five (George Roy Hill 1972) ♫ ✍
The screen version of Kurt Vonnegut's novel has Michael Sacks dividing his nightmares between PoW camps and a strange planet.

Stalag 17 (>Billy Wilder 1953) ☞ ☆ ✍
Cynical William Holden is suspected of being the Nazi plant who is betraying escape plans.

A Town Like Alice (US: *The Rape of Malaya*) (Jack Lee 1956) ✍
Nevil Shute tale of life among women prisoners in occupied Malaya.

The Wooden Horse (Jack Lee 1950) ✍
Eric Williams adaptation of his own novel about men using a vaulting horse to aid their digging of a tunnel.

PRIVATE EYES

>*The Big Sleep* (>Howard Hawks 1946) ☆ ☞ ✍ ■

Blood Simple (Joel Coen 1983) ✍ ☞
Emmet Walsh is hired to kill a wife and her lover, but the husband has bought more than he bargained for.

The Brasher Doubloon (UK: *The High Window*) (John Brahm 1946) ✍
A gold coin embroils George Montgomery's Marlowe in a deadly search.
Farewell, My Lovely (Edward Dmytryk 1944) (aka *Murder My Sweet*) ✍ ☆ ■/(Dick Richards 1975) ☆ ☞
Dick Powell and Robert Mitchum respectively search for an ex-con's missing lover.
Gumshoe (Stephen Frears 1971) ☆ ☞
Liverpool bingo-caller Albert Finney lives his dream of solving a murder mystery.
The Late Show (Robert Benton 1977) ☆
Lily Tomlin ensures that Art Carney survives murder suspects and the ravages of his ageing body.
Laura (Otto Preminger 1944) ✍ ☞ ☆
Dana Andrews probes Vincent Price and Clifton Webb (AAN) to discover whether Gene Tierney is really dead.
The Maltese Falcon (Roy Del Ruth 1931) ☆
Ricardo Cortez warms the shoes of Sam Spade for >Humphrey Bogart.
Marlowe (Paul Bogart 1969) ✍ ☆
In an adaptation of Raymond Chandler's *The Little Sister*, James Garner is hired to locate a missing brother.

The Private Life of Henry VIII
☆ ✍ ☞

GB • London Films • 1933 • 97 mins • b/w
d Alexander Korda w Lajos Biro/Arthur Wimperis ph Georges Périnal m Kurt Schroeder
>Charles Laughton, >Robert Donat, Elsa Lanchester, Merle Oberon

Fascinated by England's most notorious monarch, cinema has yet to present him accurately as a manipulated indolent. *A Man for All Seasons* (>Fred Zinnemann 1966) (☆ ✍ ■ ☞) (Robert Shaw's Henry reluctantly executes Paul Scofield's Thomas More) and *Anne of the Thousand Days* (Charles Jarrott 1969) (✍ ☆ ■) (>Richard Burton's Henry courts then condemns Genevieve Bujold's Anne Boleyn) come close with their portrayals of a hot-head who repents at leisure, but Alexander Korda's 1933

Henry, a Shakespearian tragi-comedian, prisoner of council and bedchamber, is the most original and interesting interpretation. Charles Laughton's Tudor *terrible* is dictated by the character of his current wife: amorous with Merle Oberon's Boleyn; caring with Jane Seymour; distraught at Howard's infidelity with Culpepper (Donat) and resigned to Parr's sobriety. The best scenes come with Laughton's real-life wife Elsa Lanchester as Anne of Cleves – a card game anticipating >*Born Yesterday* (>George Cukor 1950) (☆ ✍ ☞) and a heartfelt 'The things I do for England' that suggests Roger Moore's Bond in *Moonraker* (Lewis Gilbert 1979) (■). Crackly now, but masterly hokum.

•>Charlie Chaplin is another much-married wife killer as he seeks to provide a few luxuries for his crippled wife, in *Monsieur Verdoux* (Charles Chaplin 1947) (✍ ☆).
•George Sanders' Charles II woos Linda Darnell in Kathleen Winsor's dollar dreadful *Forever Amber* (Otto Preminger 1947) (■ ☆).
•>Emil Jannings's Henry sees Jane Seymour (Aud Egede Nissen) at court and plots to throw over Henny Porten in *Anna Boleyn* (US: *Deception*) (>Ernst Lubitsch 1920) (☞ ☆).
•Edward VI proves to be a chip off the old block in Mark Twain's *The Prince and the Pauper* (William Keighley 1937) (✍).

PROPAGANDA

The Big Blockade (Charles Frend 1941) ☞
John Mills, Michael Redgrave and Will Hay in fables about why it was important to starve Germany into submission.
The Fall of Berlin (M. Chiaureli 1949) ☞
Heroic soldier B. Andreyev gets to meet M. Gelovani's Stalin and V. Stanitsine's Churchill.
Happy Land (Irving Pichel 1943) ☆
Ghost Harry Carey assures Don Ameche and Frances Dee are doing the right thing in sending their grandson to a war death.
Lenin in 1918 (*Lenin v 1918*) (Mikhail Romm 1939) ☞
Boris Shchukin is helped to implement the

Revolution by Nikolai Cherkassov's Maxim Gorky and Mikhail Gelovani's Stalin.

Lenin in October (*Lenin v Oktiabrye*) (Mikhail Romm 1937) ☞

Life before and after Boris Shchukin descends the train at the Finland Station.

The Lion Has Wings (>Michael Powell/Brian Desmond Hurst/Adrian Brunel 1939)

Merle Oberon and Ralph Richardson are among those showing why war broke out on 3 September 1939.

Mission to Moscow (>Michael Curtiz 1943) ☆

Walter Huston as US Ambassador Joseph E. Davies who found it possible to do business with Oscar Homolka's Litvinov.

The Mortal Storm (Frank Borzage 1940) ☆

Robert Young, >James Stewart and Margaret Sullavan are members of a family divided by the rise of the Nazis.

Next of Kin (Thorold Dickinson 1942) ☆

Walls have ears, and so do members of a British commando raid.

Sherlock Holmes in Washington (Roy William Neill 1943) ☆

>Basil Rathbone ends his pursuit of fifth columnists with a nauseating speech on democracy.

The Three Caballeros (Various directors 1945) ✍

Disney persuades South America that, if it can laugh at Donald Duck, it can trust the USA.

The White Cliffs of Dover (Clarence Brown 1944) ☆

Irene Dunne urges women to lose their menfolk cheerfully as she has done in both world wars.

PROSTITUTION

>Belle De Jour (>Luis Buñuel 1967) ☞ ☆ ✍ ■

Crimes of Passion (Ken Russell 1984) ☆ ☞

Fashion executive >Kathleen Turner enjoys her nights as classy whore China Blue, until pestered by Anthony Perkins's crazed preacher.

Floating Clouds (*Ukigumo*) (Mikio Naruse, Japan 1955) ☆ ✍

A war nurse is forced into prostitution when her soldier lover remains with his wife.

It's My Life (US: *My Life to Live*) (*Vivre sa Vie*) (>Jean-Luc Godard 1962) ☞

Semi-documentary study of a girl's descent into prostitution.

Just a Gigolo (Paul Schraeder 1980)

>Marlene Dietrich as the elderly patron of struggling Berlin working boy David Bowie.

The Life of O-Haru (*Saikaku Ichidai Onna*) (>Kenji Mizoguchi 1952) ☞ ✍

A woman abandons an arranged marriage to a rich man, sees her lover executed and has to sell her body to survive.

Marked Woman (Lloyd Bacon 1937) ☆

Film à clef of Lucky Luciano in which DA >Humphrey Bogart uses the courtroom testimony of >Bette Davis to convict the gangster.

Midnight Cowboy (>John Schlesinger 1969) ♫ ☆

>Dustin Hoffman attempts to pimp for ambitious dishwasher Jon Voight.

>Brothels

PSYCHIATRISTS AND PSYCHOLOGY

The Astonished Heart (Terence Fisher/Anthony Darnborough 1949)

Celia Johnson allows psychiatrist husband Noël Coward to love Margaret Leighton in the hope of curing his obsession.

Bad Timing (Nicolas Roeg 1980) ☆

In Vienna to study Freud, Art Garfunkel takes advantage of Theresa Russell's instability.

Blind Alley (Charles Vidor 1939) ☞ ☆

Ralph Bellamy disarms killer Chester Morris by solving his psychological problems.

Equus (>Sidney Lumet 1977) ☆ ☞

>Richard Burton attempts to explain Peter Firth's obsession with horses.

Freud (>John Huston 1963) ☞

Montgomery Clift calls a boy's hatred for father Larry Parks and love for mother Susannah York the Oedipus complex.

Lady in the Dark (Mitchell Leisen 1944) ☆

>Ginger Rogers solves her love problems by living out her dreams.

Mine Own Executioner (Anthony Kimmins 1947) ☆
Disturbed war vet Kieron Moore repays Burgess Meredith's charity by murdering his wife Dulcie Gray.

Nineteen Nineteen (Hugh Brody 1984) ✍ ☆
Paul Scofield and Maria Schell meet in Vienna in the hope that reminiscing about Freud will help solve their present problems.

Secrets of a Soul (*Geheimnisse einer Seele*) (>G. W. Pabst 1926) ☆
Academic Warner Krauss seeks help from a psychoanalyst to end his knife nightmares.

Psycho ☞ ♫ ☆ ✍ ■

USA • Shamley • 1960 • 109 mins • b/w

d >Alfred Hitchcock/Saul Bass   w Joseph Stefano   ph John L. Russell   m Bernard Herrmann

Anthony Perkins, Janet Leigh, Vera Miles, John Gavin, Martin Balsam

Initially destined for the TV series *Alfred Hitchcock Presents*, probably the single most terrifying film in history was something of a departure from the good-natured suspensers that had sustained the director in postwar years. Marion Crane (Leigh)'s getaway with a stolen $40,000 is so hindered by driving rain that she is forced to seek shelter in a downbeat motel. Proprietor Norman Bates (Perkins)' timidity preys on her already frayed nerves, but a shower should prove therapeutic...Detective Arbogast (Balsam) seeks clues in the house on the hill behind the chalets, but gets no further than the staircase, and a nasty shock awaits Marion's sister Lila (Miles) in the fruit cellar. If Mother's voice and violence send shivers, wait until you see her face. Perkins expertly reprised the role in the solid *Psycho 2* (Richard Franklin 1983) (☆ ✍) (when Norman is released, the attempts by Leigh's relatives Vera Miles and Meg Tilly to unhinge him summon up Mother) and the admirable spoof *Psycho 3* (Anthony Perkins 1986) (☆) (novice Diana Scarwid accidentally kills a nun and holes up at the old Bates place).

 •Donald Pleasence is the shrink in pursuit of escaped small-town psycho lining up Jamie Lee Curtis, in *Halloween* (John Carpenter 1978), while George Brent terrorizes deformed Dorothy McGuire, in *The Spiral Staircase* (Robert Siodmak 1945) (✍ ☞ ☆) and timid Jean Yanne wields a handy cleaver, in *The Butcher* (*Le Boucher*) (>Claude Chabrol 1969) (☞ ☆).

•Hoteliers view stagecoach passengers as victims rather than clients, in *The Red Inn* (*L'Auberge Rouge*) (Claude Autant-Lara 1951) (✍).

•Inna Churikova is the dominant matriarch heading a shipping corporation in an adaptation of a Maxim Gorky play *Vassa Zhelenova*, in *Vassa* (Gleb Panfilov 1983) (☆ ✍), while lawyer George Segal is the mother's boy who allows Ruth Gordon to destroy his relationships, in *Where's Poppa?* (Carl Reiner 1970) (☞).

•Rod Steiger is obsessed with the memory of the actress mother who abandoned him as a child in the psychotic killer spoof *No Way to Treat a Lady* (Jack Smight 1967) (✍ ☆).

•Michael Sarrazin's plans to kill feline-fixated aunt Eleanor Parker are hamstrung by his hatred of cats in another Joseph Stefano thriller *Eye of the Cat* (David Rowell Rich 1969) (✍).

Pudovkin, Vsevolod I.
Soviet writer/director (1893–1953)

A physics and chemistry graduate of Moscow University, Pudovkin spent the First World War as a wounded PoW, escaping in 1918 and contributing to agit-prop productions during the Civil War. A student of Lev Kuleshov and assistant on his *Extraordinary Adventures of Mr West in the Land of the Bolsheviks* (*Neobychainye Priklucheniya Mistera Vesta v Stranye Bolshevikov*) (1924) (☞) (YMCA president Porfiry Podobed discards the myth that the only good Bolshevik is a dead Bolshevik), Pudovkin became one of Soviet cinema's greatest theorists, arguing for acting restraint, montage and *auteur* control for directors in his book *Film Director and Film Material*. Although he did not join the Communist Party until 1932, his *Mother* (*Mat*) (1926) (☞ ■)

(Maxim Gorky tale has Vera Baranovskaya atoning for her betrayal of her son Nikolai Batalov by embracing Communism) and *The End of St Petersburg* (*Konyets Sankt-Petersburga*) (1927) (☞ ☆) (young peasant Ivan Chuvelov witnesses the taking of the Winter Palace in Petrograd) celebrated the 1905 and 1917 Revolutions respectively.

•*The Death Ray* (*Luch Smerti*) (Lev Kuleshov 1925) (☞): Pudovkin was the writer and in the cast of this film, in which Fascists attempt to steal a secret weapon from scientist Porfiry Podobed.

•*Chess Fever* (*Shakhmatnaya Goryachka*) (co-directed 1925) (☞): Vladimir Fogel is so busy watching grand master Jose Raoul Capablanca play that he misses his wedding.

•*Storm over Asia* (aka *The Heir to Genghis Khan*) (*Potomok Chingis-khan*) (1928) (☞ ■): Mongolian patriots and the Red Army defeat a British volunteer force.

•*A Simple Case* (*Prostoi Sluchai*) (1932): joint survival of Civil War danger is not enough to keep a marriage together, but the Party disapproves of the adultery.

•*The Deserter* (*Dezertir*) (1933): a Red Army renegade finds that the city is no place to hide, in his hugely experimental first Talkie.

•>*Ivan the Terrible* (*Part One*) (*Ivan Grozny*) (>Sergei Eisenstein 1944) (☞ ■ ✍ ☆ ♫): Pudovkin as Nikolai the fanatic at the court of Nikolai Cherkassov's Ivan IV.

PUTTING ON A SHOW

The Band Wagon (>Vincente Minnelli 1953) ✍ ☞ ♫
Fading dancer >Fred Astaire and Jack Buchanan have heartaches before the hit, but then 'That's Entertainment'.

The Big Broadcast (Frank Tuttle 1932) ☆ ♫
Bing Crosby is among those rallying to the cause of an ailing radio station.

The Blues Brothers (John Landis 1980) ☆ ✍ ♫
John Belushi and Dan Aykroyd arrange a benefit for the orphanage in which they were raised.

The Boy Friend (Ken Russell 1971) ☞
Sandy Wilson's musical play sees Twiggy in the cast of an inept company's backstage performance.

Footlight Parade (Lloyd Bacon 1933) ☆ ☞
Busby Berkeley production numbers punctuate >James Cagney's attempt to save his company by performing prologues to picture shows.

42nd Street (Lloyd Bacon 1933) ☞
Warner Baxter has Busby Berkeley dance numbers up his sleeve to lure Ruby Keeler back into his show.

The Producers (Mel Brooks 1967) ✍ ♫ ☆ ☞
Zero Mostel and Gene Wilder bank on a play failing to make their fortune, but *Springtime for Hitler* is a runaway success.

Thank Your Lucky Stars (David Butler 1943) ☆
>Bette Davis sings and Errol Flynn and >Olivia De Havilland have cameos in Eddie Cantor's charity show.

The Young Ones (US: *Wonderful to be Young*) (Sidney J. Furie 1961) ♫
Cliff Richard defies father Robert Morley and gets the kids together for a fund-raising revue.

PYGMALION

>**Born Yesterday** (>George Cukor 1950) ☆ ✍ ☞

Educating Rita (Lewis Gilbert 1983) ☆ ✍ ♫
Drunken academic >Michael Caine kindles Julie Walters' hidden scholarly talents.

Kitty (Mitchell Leisen 1945) ☆ ■
18th-century noble Ray Milland transforms Paulette Goddard into a duchess in order to benefit financially from her marriage.

My Fair Lady (>George Cukor 1964) ♫ ☞ ✍
Rex Harrison's Professor Higgins grows accustomed to the face of Audrey Hepburn's Eliza Doolittle.

Never on Sunday (*Pote Tin Kyriaki*) (>Jules Dassin 1959) ☞
Dassin's American academic takes it upon himself to redeem Greek prostitute Melina Mercouri.

Night is My Future (aka *Music in the Dark*) (*Musik in mörker*) (>Ingmar Bergman 1948) ☞ ▪
A blind pianist tutors maid Mai Zetterling.

Now Voyager (Irving Rapper 1942) ☆ ◺
Psychiatrist Claude Rains guides plain >Bette Davis' transition into beauty, and she finds love, albeit doomed, with Paul Henreid.

Pygmalion (>Anthony Asquith 1938) ☆ ◺ ☞
>Leslie Howard makes a lady out of cockney flowergirl Wendy Hiller in >George Bernard Shaw's play.

A Taste of Water (*De Smaak van Water*) (Orlow Seunke 1982) ☆
Dutch social worker Gerard Thoolen wins the trust and affection of neglected waif Dorijn Curvers.

Trading Places (John Landis 1983) ☆
Ralph Bellamy and Don Ameche wager tramp Eddie Murphy can't make it in big business.

The Would Be Gentleman (*Le Bourgeois Gentilhomme*) (Jean Meyer 1960) ◺ ♫ ▪
Rich but not gentle, Louis Seigner yearns after manners in this screen adaptation of Molière's play.

The Quiet Man 🖉 ☞ ☆ ■ 🎵

USA • Republic/Argossy • 1952 • 129 mins • col

d >John Ford   w Frank Nugent
ph Winton C. Hoch/Archie Stout
m Victor Young
>John Wayne, Maureen O'Hara, Barry
Fitzgerald, Victor McLaglen, Ward Bond,
Mildred Natwick

John Ford and John Wayne, so at home with
dustbowl and danger that they were the Hollywood Western, saved their best for this collaboration amid the green and pleasantry of
Galway. Boxer Sean Thornton (Wayne) comes
to the land of his ancestors to forget killing a
man in the ring and falls for fiery Mary Kate
Danaher (O'Hara). However, believing him to
be a coward for refusing to wrestle her dowry
out of her bitter brother Will (McLaglen), she
refuses consummation. O'Hara is Wayne's
match in every department – indeed only >Wil-
liam Powell and >Myrna Loy in >*The Thin Man*
series enjoy such idyllic cut and thrust. Barry
Fitzgerald as Michaeleen Oge Flynn, Wayne's
trap driver, is Irish whimsy itself, and his ad-

monitory 'No patty fingers' when chaperoning
is delectable.

 •Robert Mitchum is the expatriate
Irishman attempting, with Debo-
rah Kerr, to learn the sheep busi-
ness in Australia, in *The Sundowners* (>Fred
Zinnemann 1960) (☞ ☆ ■), while Robert
Shaw's expectations of succeeding in Canadian
journalism are shaken in an adaptation of
Brian Moore's novel, *The Luck of Ginger Cof-
fey* (Irvin Kershner 1964) (🖉 ☆).
•Barry Fitzgerald leads the scheming villagers
planning to assassinate bounderish English
landlord David Niven, in *Happy Ever After* (US:
Tonight's the Night) (Mario Zampi 1954) (☆
🖉).
•Jean Simmons, Trevor Howard and Anthony
Hopkins are among those affected as the IRA's
1921 terrorist campaign shatters the rural
peace, in *The Dawning* (Robert Knights 1988)
(🖉 ■).
•Barbra Streisand spars with boxer Ryan
O'Neal before winning his love in the at-
tempted screwball *The Main Event* (Howard
Zieff 1979) (☆).

RACISM

Betrayed (Constantin Costa-Gavras 1988) ☞ ☆ ✍

Government agent Debra Winger falls for farmer Tom Berenger, the leader of a group suspected of killing a black DJ.

Black Legion (Archie Mayo 1937) ☆ ✍
>Humphrey Bogart joins a Ku Klux Klan equivalent after losing his job to a foreigner and lives to regret it.

Do the Right Thing (Spike Lee 1989) ☞ ✍
Tensions rise with the temperature during a hot New York summer.

Imitation of Life (John M. Stahl) 1934
The black cook behind Claudette Colbert's flapjack business, Louise Beavers dies, brokenhearted when her tormented daughter, trying to pass for white, runs away.

Imitation of Life (Douglas Sirk 1959) ✍ ☞ ☆
Actress Lana Turner's maid Juanita Moore dies of a broken heart when her daughter, ashamed of her colour, leaves home.

The Landlord (Hal Ashby 1970) ☞
Sickened by New York racism, Beau Bridges lets to black tenants, but his family object to his proposed marriage.

The Liberation of L. B. James (>William Wyler 1970) ☞ ✍
A whodunnit set amid racial tensions in a Tennessee town.

Putney Swope (Robert Downey 1969) ✍
Downey heads a smart advertising agency, and having sacked the white workforce, makes it big with ruthless practices.

Sapphire (Basil Dearden 1959) ☆
Nigel Patrick and Michael Craig of Scotland Yard investigate the death of a black musician.

Shadows (John Cassavetes 1959) ☞
A New York family struggle to find their niche in life and a hostile city.

Soul Man (Stephen Miner 1986) ☆
Thomas Howell adopts black face to gain a college scholarship and experiences racial abuse.

RADIO

The Big Broadcast of 1936 (Norman Taurog 1935) ☆
Singer Jack Oakie only just makes the big show

after being kidnapped by countess Lyda Roberti.

The Big Broadcast of 1937 (Mitchell Leisen 1936) ☆

Ray Milland falls in love while station manager Jack Benny seeks sponsorship for the big show.

The Big Broadcast of 1938 (Mitchell Leisen 1937) ☆

>W. C. Fields, Bob Hope and Dorothy Lamour jam the airwaves during a liner race.

Citizens Band (Jonathan Demme 1977) ☞ ☆

Giants of the airwaves prove tongue-tied when they meet in real life, unlike bigamist Paul Le Mat's wives.

The Couch Trip (Michael Ritchie 1988) ☆

Radio psychiatrist Dan Aykroyd offers the frankest sex therapy on the dial.

Death at Broadcasting House (Reginald Denham 1934) ✍

An actor is murdered during a play and the cast become suspects.

FM (John A. Alonzo 1978) ♫

The hits abound as Michael Brandon tries to save an ailing station from closure.

Good Morning, Vietnam (Barry Levinson 1987) ☆ ☞ ✍ ♫

Robin Williams as Adrian Cronaeur, the outspoken jock who delighted the GIs and distracted the authorities.

The King of Marvin Gardens (Bob Rafaelson 1972) ☆

>Jack Nicholson as the DJ caught up with brother Bruce Dern's gangster friends.

Short Cut (Postriziny) (Jirí Menzel 1981) ☞ ■

Radio transforms the lives of brewery workers in pre-1914 Czechoslovakia.

Talk Radio (Oliver Stone 1989) ☞ ☆

Eric Borgosian as a fast- and foul-talking phone-in host.

The Unsuspected (>Michael Curtiz 1947) ☞ ☆ ✍

Radio whodunnit star Claude Rains re-enacts for his fans the perfect murder he has himself committed.

RAGS TO RICHES

The Barefoot Contessa (>Joseph L. Mankiewicz 1954) ✍

Dancer Ava Gardner is turned into a star by >Humphrey Bogart and Edmond O'Brien.

Boudu Saved from Drowning (Boudu Sauvé des Eaux) (>Jean Renoir 1932) ☞ ☆

Tramp Michel Simon abuses his saviour Charles Grandval's hospitality by seducing the women in his life.

The Farmer's Daughter (H. C. Potter 1947) ☆

The heart-based politics of Swedish maid Loretta Young (AA) win her a seat in Congress.

The Good Earth (Sidney Franklin 1937) ☆

Luise Rainer (AA) dies before Chinese farmer Paul Muni reaps riches.

Little Lord Fauntleroy (John Cromwell 1936) ☆ ✍

The film version of Frances Hodgson Burnett's novel has Freddie Bartholomew going up in the world of grandfather C. Aubrey Smith.

Nothing but the Best (Clive Donner 1964) ☆

Alan Bates stabs workmate Denholm Eliott in the back during his meteoric and unscrupulous rise.

Possessed (Clarence Brown 1931) ☆

>Joan Crawford comes to New York in search of wealth and finds it in >Clark Gable.

RAILWAYS AND STATIONS

Anna Karenina (Clarence Brown 1935) ☆ ✍ ☞ /(Julien Duvivier 1947) ☆

Tolstoy's heroine – respectively >Greta Garbo and >Vivien Leigh – begins her love affair and ends her life on station platforms.

Brief Encounter (>David Lean 1945) ☞ ☆ ✍

Trevor Howard and Celia Johnson meet in a station buffet, but are too decent to continue their affair for long.

The Clock (UK: Under the Clock) (>Vincente Minnelli 1945) ☞ ✍

Judy Garland meets soldier Robert Walker at New York's Penn Station and marries him next day, in Paul and Pauline Gallico's story.

The Ghost Train **(Walter Forde 1931/1941)** ✍

Jack Hulbert and Arthur Askey respectively solve a spooky station smuggling mystery.

Grand Central Murder **(S. Sylvan Simon 1942)** ☆

Tom Conway and Virginia Grey are among the suspects under Van Heflin's eye in this New York station whodunnit.

Indiscretion of an American Wife **(>Vittorio De Sica 1954)** ☞

Montgomery Clift and Jennifer Jones talk through their separate marital problems during a night at Rome's train station.

Oh Mr Porter **(Marcel Varnel 1937)** ☆ ✍

Stationmaster Will Hay sees through Irish gun-runners' haunted station routine.

The Railway Children **(Lionel Jeffries 1970)** ✍ ■

In this E. Nesbit tale, three children's adventures are bound up with the people and engines of a Yorkshire railway line.

Union Pacific **(Cecil B. De Mille 1939)** ☞ ☆ ■

>Barbara Stanwyck encourages Joel McCrea to not let little things like train crashes and Indians hinder his rail building.

Union Station **(Rudolph Maté 1950)** ☞ ✍ ☆

William Holden rescues kidnapped blind girl Nancy Olson in tense station finale.

THE RAJ

Autobiography of a Princess **(James Ivory 1975)** ☞ ■

Now living in London, a maharajah's daughter (Madhur Jaffrey) relives Raj life with her former tutor James Mason.

Bhowani Junction **(>George Cukor 1956)** ☆

The screen version of John Master's novel has the Raj twilight lit up by Anglo-Indian Ava Gardner's romance with Stewart Granger.

The Chess Players (*Shatranj ke Khilari*) **(>Satyajit Ray 1977)** ☆ ☞

Sanjeev Kumar and Saeed Jaffrey prefer chess to contemplating >Richard Attenborough's oncoming troops.

The Deceivers **(Nicholas Meyer 1988)** ■

Pierce Brosnan infiltrates the murderous Thuggee cult to end its reign of terror.

>Gandhi **(>Richard Attenborough 1981)** ☞ ☆ ✍ ■

Heat and Dust **(James Ivory 1982)** ✍ ■ ☞ ☆

Greta Scacchi's romance with raja Shashi Kapoor ends in rebellious bloodshed.

King of the Khyber Rifles **(Henry King 1954)**

Half-caste Tyrone Power leads the resistance to an uprising in 1857.

Lives of a Bengal Lancer **(Henry Hathaway 1935)** ☞ ☆

>Gary Cooper and Franchot Tone keep the Afghans on their side of the Northwest Frontier.

Northwest Frontier **(US: *Flame over India*) (J. Lee-Thompson 1959)** ☆ ✍

Kenneth More, Lauren Bacall and Wilfrid Hyde White foil Herbert Lom's trainboard attempt to kidnap a prince.

A Passage to India **(>David Lean 1984)** ☆ ☞ ■

Victor Bannerjee goes on trial for the alleged rape of Judy Davis during an outing to the Marabar Caves.

The Rains Came **(Clarence Brown 1939)** ☞ ✍ ■

>Myrna Loy, George Brent and Tyrone Power rouse themselves from lethargy to aid flood victims.

Wee Willie Winkie **(>John Ford 1937)**

Shirley Temple as the mascot of Victor McLaglen and C. Aubrey Smith's regiment.

>British Empire

Ran (aka Chaos) ☞ ■ ✍ ☆

Japan • Herald Ace/Nippon Herald/ Greenwich Films • 1986 • 162 mins • col

d >Akira Kurosawa w Akira Kurosawa/ Hideo Oguni/Masato Ide

  ph Takao Saito/Masaharu Ueda

Tatsuya Nakadai, Satoshi Terao, Jinpachi Nezu, Daisuke Ryu, Mieko Harada, Yoshiko Miyazaki, Peter

Akira Kurosawa's texturally unparalleled adaptation of the life of 16th-century warlord Hi-

RAIDERS OF THE LOST ARK
(>Steven Spielberg 1981) ☆ ☞

ESCAPISM

JACK THE GIANT KILLER
(Nathan Juran 1961) ✳
(farmer rescues princess from a dragon)

THE ARABIAN NIGHTS (aka A THOUSAND AND ONE NIGHTS)
(IL FIORE DELLE MILLE E UNA NOTTE)
(>Pier Paolo Pasolini 1974) ■ ☞
(ten tales told around a prince's search for a missing slave girl)

INDIANA JONES AND THE TEMPLE OF DOOM
(>Steven Spielberg 1984)
(pre-*Raiders* search for Maharajah's jewel)

YOUNG SHERLOCK HOLMES AND THE PYRAMID OF FEAR (US: YOUNG SHERLOCK HOLMES)
(Barry Levinson 1985) ⚱
(schoolboy detective dashes designs of evil cult)

LICENCE TO KILL
(John Glen 1989) ☆
(Timothy Dalton's James Bond comes to the aid of CIA buddy Felix Leiter)

CLASSIC SWASHBUCKLING

THE EAGLE
(Clarence Brown 1925) ☆
(Russian Zorro Rudolph Valentino takes back stolen lands)

THE COUNT OF MONTE CRISTO
(Rowland V. Lee 1934) ☞ ☆
(framed noble >Robert Donat escapes from prison and seeks revenge)

THE PRISONER OF ZENDA
(John Cromwell 1937) ☆ ⚱ ■ ☞
(overthrow plot frustrated by English holidaymaker Ronald Colman)

THE BANDIT OF SHERWOOD FOREST
(George Sherman/Henry Levin 1946)
(Robin Hood keeps power from corrupt regent)

THE ELUSIVE PIMPERNEL
(>Michael Powell/Emeric Pressburger 1950) ☞ ☆
(powdered dandy David Niven preserves aristos from guillotine)

SCARAMOUCHE
(George Sidney 1952) ☆
(disguised actor pursues malevolent marquis)

IN OLDEN DAYS

THE MAN IN THE IRON MASK
(James Whale 1939) ☞
(Louis XIV is substituted for lookalike)

THE THREE MUSKETEERS
(George Sidney 1948) ☆ ☞ ⚱
(>Gene Kelly's swashbuckling dance version of Dumas)

THE EXILE
(>Max Ophüls 1948) ☞ ■
(Charles II's adventurous Dutch exile)

THE BLACK SHIELD OF FALWORTH
(Rudolph Maté 1954) ■
(medieval jousts of love and armed combat)

THE VIKINGS
(Richard Fleischer 1958) ☆ ☞ ■
(half-brothers >Kirk Douglas and Tony Curtis feud over lordship of Northumbria)

KNIGHTS OF THE TEUTONIC ORDER
(Aleksander Ford 1960) ☞
(Polish girl avenges the rape of her mother by over-zealous religious soldiers)

Unconventional archaeologist >Harrison Ford foils Nazi bounty hunters

FOREIGN LEGION

BEAU HUNKS
(James W. Horne 1931) ☆ ✍
(>Laurel & Hardy join Legion to forget >Jean Harlow)

LE GRAND JEU
(Jacques Feyder 1934) ☞ ■
(escaping from a woman, a legionnaire meets her singer double)

UNDER TWO FLAGS
(Frank Lloyd 1936) ☞ ☆
(café singer Claudette Colbert helps legionnaire Ronald Colman become a hero)

BEAU GESTE
(>William Wellman 1939) ☆ ☞
(P. C. Wren's classic of Legion brutality)

TEN TALL MEN
(Willis Goldbeck 1951) ✍
(lone patrol resists full-scale Arab attack)

THE LAST REMAKE OF BEAU GESTE
(Marty Feldman 1977) ✍
(the spoof desert exploits of the Brothers Geste)

JUNGLE

TARZAN, THE APE MAN
(W. S. Van Dyke 1932) ☞ ☆
(Edgar Rice Burroughs' hero lords it over the apes)

THE JUNGLE PRINCESS
(William Thiele 1936) ☆
(island girl Dorothy Lamour rescues hunter Ray Milland)

KING SOLOMON'S MINES
(Robert Stevenson 1937) ✍
(explorers search for jungle diamond mine)

WHITE CARGO
(Richard Thorpe 1942) ☆
(rubber planters feud over native girl Hedy Lamarr)

THE JUNGLE BOOK
(Zoltan Korda/André De Toth 1942) ■ ✍
(Rudyard Kipling's tale of animals rearing a boy, Sabu)

THE MACOMBER AFFAIR
(Zoltan Korda 1947) ☆ ✍
(Joan Bennett falls for jungle guide Gregory Peck in Ernest Hemingway story)

MOGAMBO
(>John Ford 1953) ☞ ☆
(archaeologist's wife Grace Kelly goes on >Clark Gable's gorilla hunt)

detora (Nakadai) is what would have happened had King Lear had Lady Macbeth for a daughter-in-law. Banishing his youngest son Saburo (Ryu) for warning him that his elder brothers Taro (Terao) and Jiro (Nezu) would misuse their inheritance, Hidetora divides his kingdom and lives to regret it, sharing the storms of nature and mind experienced by Lear. Taro's ambitious wife, Lady Kaede (Harada), who exploits the domestic discord to avenge her own family, victims of Hidetora's rise to power, is a wonderfully sadistic Cruella de Ville, and the last battle is stupefying.

 •Erland Josephson is the doting father of a recuperating son offering his life in return for world peace, in *The Sacrifice* (*Offret*) (>Andrei Tarkovsky 1987) (☞ ■ ☆).
•Yuri Yarvet is the fond, foolish old man dividing his kingdom in >Shakespeare's *King Lear* (*Korol Lir*) (Grigori Kozintsev 1970) (✍ ■).
•Machiko Kyo is a *femme fatale* in every sense of the phrase, being a ghost who lures Masayuki Mori away from his wife Kinuyo Tanaka, in *Ugetsu Monogatari* (*Ugestsu*) (>Kenji Mizoguchi 1953) (☞ ✍ ☆).
•Arlene Dahl is the ambitious wife out to win husband Van Heflin the top job in Clifton Webb's motor company over Lauren Bacall's Fred MacMurray and June Allyson's Cornel Wilde, in *Woman's World* (Jean Negulesco 1954) (✍ ☆).
•The making of *Ran* is documented in *A.K.* (Chris Marker 1985) (☞).
•Kurosawa spoofed the samurai genre in *Sanjuro* (>Akira Kurosawa 1962) (☞ ☆ ✍).

Rathbone, Basil
South African-born British actor
(1892–1967)
After winning a Military Cross in the First World War, Rathbone's West End and Broadway successes earned him romantic leads in early Talkies, such as *The Last of Mrs Cheyney* (Sidney Franklin 1929) (☆) (high-class con woman Norma Shearer falls in love with her victim Rathbone). However, he will be best remembered as a cold, pitiless villain – *David Copperfield* (>George Cukor 1935)(☞ ☆ ✍)

(Rathbone as David's evil stepfather Murdstone turning him out into the world), *Anna Karenina* (Clarence Brown 1935) (☆ ✍ ☞) (Rathbone's Karenin keeps >Greta Garbo from son Freddie Bartholomew during her affair with >Fredric March's Vronsky), *Captain Blood* (>Michael Curtiz 1935) (☞ ☆) (Errol Flynn flees to the seas from Rathbone's ruthless hanging Judge Jeffreys), *Romeo and Juliet* (AAN: >George Cukor 1936) (as Tybalt perpetuating the Montague/Capulet feud by duelling with >Leslie Howard's Romeo), *The Adventures of Robin Hood* (>Michael Curtiz 1938) (☞ ☆ ■) (Basil as Guy of Gisbourne scheming against Errol Flynn's hero outlaw) and *Tower of London* (Rowland V. Lee 1939) (☆ ✍) (as Richard III instructing >Boris Karloff's jailor to murder his princely nephews) – and as Sherlock Holmes to Nigel Bruce's Watson from >*The Hound of The Baskervilles* (Sidney Lanfield 1939) to *Dressed to Kill* (UK: *Sherlock Holmes and the Secret Code*) (Roy William Neill 1946) (☆ ✍) (musical box tunes lead to the Bank of England's stolen engraving plates). Although returning to villainy in *We're No Angels* (>Michael Curtiz 1955) (☞ ☆) (escapee >Humphrey Bogart prevents Rathbone from muscling in on Leo G. Carroll's shop) and *The Court Jester* (Norman Panama/Melvin Frank 1956) (☆) (bad king Basil is dethroned by his own fool, Danny Kaye), he was still capable of surprises – for example narrating the first section of *Ichabod and Mr Toad* (Jack Kinney/Clyde Geronimi/James Algar 1949) (☞) (Washington Irving's tale *The Legend of Sleepy Hollow* and Kenneth Grahame's *The Wind in the Willows* are given the Disney treatment). He reprised Holmes on radio and even hosted a TV game show *Your Lucky Clue* in 1952.

 •*The Last Days of Pompeii* (Merion C. Cooper/Ernest Schoedsack 1935) (■): as Pontius Pilate tormented by his deliverance of Christ to the Jews.
•*Dawn Patrol* (Edmund Goulding 1938): Rathbone, David Niven and Errol Flynn as fliers waiting for the command to scramble.
•*If I Were King* (AAN: Frank Lloyd 1938) (☆ ✍): Ronald Colman as rebel poet François Villon leads the peasants against Basil's Louis XI.

•*The Mark of Zorro* (Rouben Mamoulian 1940) (☞■ ☆ ✍): Basil as the Californian villain who appropriates Tyrone Power's father's land.

•*Frenchman's Creek* (Mitchell Leisen 1944) (✍ ☆): Rathbone's pompously respectable noble drives >Joan Fontaine to piracy.

•*The Last Hurrah* (>John Ford 1958) (☆ ☞): as one of a coterie of prominent men scheming to prevent >Spencer Tracy's re-election.

•*The Comedy of Terrors* (Jacques Tourneur 1963): as one of the victims measured up by >Boris Karloff and Vincent Price's rival down-on-luck undertakers.

AS HOLMES:

•*The Adventures of Sherlock Holmes* (Alfred Werker 1939) (☆ ✍): George Zucco's Moriarty seeks to steal the Crown jewels.

•*Sherlock Holmes and the Voice of Terror* (John Rawlins 1942) (☆ ✍): based on Arthur Conan Doyle's *His Last Bow*, it pits Basil against Nazis who give radio warnings of their sabotage.

•*Sherlock Holmes and the Secret Weapon* (Roy William Neill 1942) (✍ ☆): Lionel Atwill's Moriarty steals a precision bombsight and offers it to the Nazis.

•*Sherlock Holmes in Washington* (Roy William Neill 1943) (☆ ✍): a book of matches holds the key to a Nazi plot, but how can Basil get hold of it when everyone needs a light?

•*Sherlock Holmes Faces Death* (Roy William Neill 1943) (☆ ✍): an officers' hospital clock strikes 13 and a piece goes missing from a hall floor chessboard.

•*Sherlock Holmes and the Spider Woman* (Roy William Neill 1944) (✍ ☆): Dennis Hoey's Inspector Lestrade is baffled by apparent suicides, but by impersonating a raja Basil points the finger at Gale Sondergaard.

•*The Scarlet Claw* (Roy William Neill 1944) (☆ ✍ ☞): the Baker Street duo go to Canada on the trail of the murderer who haunts a misty marsh.

•*The Pearl of Death* (Roy William Neill 1944) (☆ ✍): Basil loses a pearl and has to get it back to restore his reputation.

•*The House of Fear* (Roy William Neill 1945) (✍ ☆): 'The Adventure of the Five Orange Pips' involves an insurance-inspired sequence of killings in a Scottish castle.

•*The Woman in Green* (Roy William Neill 1945) (☆ ✍): Hilary Brooke hypnotizes Basil to prevent him uncovering her murderous blackmail schemes.

•*Pursuit to Algiers* (Roy William Neill 1945) (☆ ✍): political opponents try to assassinate the young prince whom Holmes and Watson are escorting on his return home aboard a liner.

•*Terror by Night* (Roy William Neill 1946) (☆ ✍): a diamond theft and murder on the Edinburgh express.

Ray, Nicholas
(Raymond Nicholas Kienzle) American writer/director (1911–1979)

An interest in the diversity of American culture, developed by his experience of community theatre, informed much of Ray's work. His studies of doomed lives and loves are among the best examples of *film noir*: *They Live by Night* (1949) (prison turns accidental killer Farley Granger into a hardened criminal on the run), *Knock on Any Door* (1949) (☆) (lawyer >Humphrey Bogart pleads for a boy everyone is convinced is guilty), *In a Lonely Place* (1950) (☆) (screenwriter >Humphrey Bogart's temper lands him in the dock accused of murder and loses him Gloria Grahame), *On Dangerous Ground* (1952) (☞) (tough cop Robert Ryan falls for Ida Lupino, the blind sister of his chief murder suspect); and that anthem of disaffected youth *Rebel without a Cause* (AAN for Original Story: 1955) (☞ ☆) (James Dean kicks out against his comfortable upbringing and gets on the wrong side of the law). Ray played a leading role in the novelty war fought between cinema and TV, using wide screen VistaVision for *Run for Cover* (1955) (sheriff >James Cagney's deputy John Derek involves him in a train robbery), Trucolor for *Johnny Guitar* (1954) (☆) (gambling hostess >Joan Crawford and banker Mercedes McCambridge feud over a land deal), CinemaScope for *Bigger than Life* (1956) (☆) (the drugs James Mason is prescribed for his aches and pains turn him into a maniac) and SuperTechnirama for *The Savage Innocents* (co-directed with Baccio Bandini 1960) (☞) (Canada's frozen wastes prove more than a match for Eskimo

Anthony Quinn). Following the epics *King of Kings* (1961) (☞ ☆) (Jeffrey Hunter as Christ giving Robert Ryan's Peter the keys of the kingdom only for him to deny Him during His Passion) and *55 Days at Peking* (1962) (☞ ☆) (David Niven reluctantly allows Charlton Heston to defend the Chinese capital during an uprising demanded by Dowager Empress Flora Robson), he concentrated on lecturing and advising on projects such as >Wim Wenders' *Lightning over Water* (1981) (☞), a sad portrait of Ray coming to terms with the cancer that was to deny him a cherished comeback to directing.

 •*A Woman's Secret* (1948) (☞): Maureen O'Hara confesses to the murder of Gloria Grahame, the aspiring singer she had discovered.

•*The Flying Leathernecks* (1951) (☆): >John Wayne and Robert Ryan fight each other when the Japanese are otherwise occupied.

•*The Lusty Men* (1952) (☞ ☆): Robert Mitchum returns to the rodeo to save George Kennedy's marriage to Susan Hayward.

•*Hot Blood* (1956) (☞ ■): gypsies Jane Russell and Cornel Wilde have problems making their arranged marriage work.

•*Party Girl* (1958) (☞ ■): gangster's lawyer Robert Taylor and 'dancer' Cyd Charisse come to understand the sordidness of their worlds through their relationship.

•*Wind Across the Everglades* (1958) (☆ ☞): gamekeeper Christopher Plummer attempts to prevent Burl Ives's gang killing birds for their valuable feathers.

Ray, Satyajit
Indian writer/director/composer (b 1921)

Favouring French and Hollywood traditions over those of classical Indian cinema, Ray has concentrated on the inner and inter-reactions of his characters to examine contemporary social and political problems and their roots in the >Raj. The realism of the beautifully paced, visually striking >Apu Trilogy (*Pather Panchali*, 1955, *Aparajito* (*The Unvanquished*), 1956, *The World of Apu* (*Apur Sansar*), 1959) (☞ ⚐ ■ ☆), *The Music Room* (*Jalsaghar*) (1958) (☞ ■) (nobleman Chabi Biswas spends

the last of his dwindled fortune on a concert of classical Indian music) and *Charulata* (aka *The Lonely Wife*) (1964) (Ray won the Best Director at Berlin award for this story of an academic's bored wife who seeks excitement in an affair with her husband's poet cousin, but is disappointed) inspired his best work. While a more complex but equally textural style is demonstrated in *The Adversary* (*Pratiwandi*) (1970) (☞ ⚐) (student Dhritiman Chatterjee is forced to support his family when his father dies), *Distant Thunder* (*Asani Sanket*) (1973) (☞ ⚐) (Berlin Best Film shows the harrowing effects of famine on a Bengali village) and *The Chess Players* (*Shatranj ke Khilari*) (1977) (☆ ☞) (chess matters more to two Lucknow nobles than their subjection to the British East India Company), the bleaker political themes of these films render them more difficult for general audiences.

 •*Devi* (aka *The Goddess*) (1960) (☞ ■): Sharmila Tagore is persuaded by her father-in-law Chabi Biswas that she is the reincarnation of the goddess Kali.

•*Two Daughters* (*Teen Kanye*) (1961) (☞ ⚐): two tales by Rabindranath Tagore: an orphan housekeeps for a postmaster; and student Soumitra Chatterjee faces an arranged marriage.

•*Kanchenjungha* (1962) (☞): a bullying business tycoon's holiday meeting with a stranger transforms his character.

•*The Big City* (*Mahanagar*) (1963) (☞): Ray's direction of Madhabi Mukherjee as a housewife gaining her independence by door-to-door selling won him Best Director at Berlin.

•*The Adventures of Goopy and Bagha* (*Goopy Gyne Bagha Byne*) (1968) (☞ ■): the King of the Ghosts grants two itinerant musicians three wishes, helping them prevent a war.

•*Days and Nights in the Forest* (*Aranyer din Ratri*) (1970) (☞): the holiday adventures of four men at a country cottage.

•*Company Limited* (*Seemabaddha*) (1971) (☞): Barun Chanda's rise through his company causes him to lose touch with his roots.

•*The Home and the World* (*Ghare-Baire*) (1984) (☆ ☞): encouraged to live as a modern woman, a wife joins the fight against the Edwardian Raj.

Rear Window ☆ ☞ ✍ ■
USA • Alfred Hitchcock • 1954 • 112 mins • col

d >Alfred Hitchcock   w John Michael Hayes   ph Robert Burks   m Franz Waxman
>James Stewart, Grace Kelly, Raymond Burr, Wendell Corey, Thelma Ritter

Confined to his room with a broken leg, photographer Jeff Jeffries (Stewart) passes his time watching his neighbours: a sad Miss Lonelyhearts, a Casanova composer and the rowing Thurwalds. His fiancée, Lisa (Kelly at her coolest), joins the police in reviling him when he claims Thurwald (Burr) has murdered and dismembered his wife, but gradually she accedes and, with Jeff helplessly watching on, enters the apartment to obtain an incriminating handbag. Sharing Stewart's claustrophobia, fascination and dawning awareness that you can't really know anyone, we almost see this masterpiece through his zoom lens.

 •>Humphrey Bogart's gangsters, Claire Trevor's prostitute and the Dead End Kids inhabit the downbeat tenement neighbouring Joel McCrea and Sylvia Sidney's luxury apartments, in *Dead End* (>William Wyler 1937) (☆ ☞ ■).
•James Woods is the photojournalist in peril, in *Salvador* (Oliver Stone 1987) (☆ ✍).
•Camera fiend Carl Boehm is the danger to the women in his viewfinder, in *Peeping Tom* (>Michael Powell 1959) (☞ ■ ☆).
•Brooke Adams breaks her leg, and her husband (Griffin Dunne)'s affair with the nurse sets off a disturbing chain of events, in *Almost You* (Adam Brooks 1984) (☆ ✍).
•The murder of a photographer is witnessed by Kim Basinger as she attempts to recover some pornographic pictures, in *Nadine* (Robert Benton 1987) (☆ ✍).

Rebecca ☞ ☆ ■ ✍ ♫
USA • David O. Selznick • 1940 • 130 mins • b/w

d >Alfred Hitchcock   w Robert E. Sherwood/Joan Harrison   ph George Barnes   m Franz Waxman
>Laurence Olivier, >Joan Fontaine, George Sanders, Judith Anderson, Nigel Bruce, Gladys Cooper, Florence Bates, Reginald Denny, C. Aubrey Smith

Swept off her feet by widower Maxim De Winter (Olivier), a gauche girl (Fontaine) finds herself mistress of Manderley but victim of Maxim's insouciance and of housekeeper Mrs Danvers (Anderson)'s adverse comparisons with her predecessor, the beautiful, refined Rebecca. Only when the new Mrs De Winter suspects the nature of Rebecca's death and Maxim stands trial for murder does she regain the trust and affection of their honeymoon. Hitchcock had tendered for the film rights to >Daphne Du Maurier's novel even prior to publication and turned superior melodrama into riveting viewing. Fontaine's jitters are more infectious than the more skittish screen-tested >Vivien Leigh's would have been, and Olivier (in a role for which Ronald Colman, >William Powell and >Leslie Howard were considered) simply *is* Maxim de Winter, while Anderson is unforgettable as the steely-eyed 'Danny'.

 •*25 Fireman's Street* (*Tuzolto Utca 25*) (István Szabó 1973) (☞ ✍) is another house with a past, a past that includes the Nazi occupation of Hungary and the Communist suppression of the 1956 uprising.
•Joan Bennett is saved from Charles Bickford's cruelty-by-the-sea by coastguard Robert Ryan, in *The Woman on the Beach* (>Jean Renoir 1947) (☞).
•Dowdy wife Yvonne Mitchell loses husband Anthony Quayle's love in Ted Willis' play *Woman in a Dressing Gown* (J. Lee-Thompson 1957) (☆).
•Florinda Bolkan is better away from her difficult husband, *A Brief Vacation* (*Une Breve Vacanza*) (>Vittorio De Sica 1973) (☞ ■), help-

ing her recover both her health and self-esteem.

•Tierno Leye's marriage to his third wife is fraught with problems ranging from impotence to bankruptcy, in >*Xala* (aka *The Curse*) (Ousmane Sembene 1974) (☆ ✍ ☞ ■).

REBELS

Antigone (George Tzavellas 1960)
Irene Papas buries her brothers against the wishes of Manos Katrakis's King Creon in Sophocles' telling of the Greek myth.
>*Ashes and Diamonds* (*Popiol i Diament*) (>Andrej Wajda 1958) ☞ ☆ ■ ✍
Diner (Barry Levinson 1982) ☆ ☞
1950s nostalgia as college boys consider whether to rebel or conform in their adulthood.
One Night of Love (Victor Schertzinger 1934) ♫ ☆
AA-winning songs punctuate the story of an opera singer Grace Moore turning on tutor Tullio Carminati.
Rebel without a Cause (>Nicholas Ray 1955) ☞ ☆
James Dean becomes the hero of disaffected youth striking out against his comfortable but restrictive upbringing.
Rumble Fish (>Francis Ford Coppola 1983) ■
Motorcycle Boy Mickey Rourke comes to the aid of Matt Dillon when he is attacked by middle-class bullies.
Wild Game (*Wildwechsel*) (>Rainer Werner Fassbinder 1972) ☞ ♫ ✍
Jailed for under-age sex, a teenage boy kills his girlfriend's tyrannical father.
The Young and the Damned (aka *The Forgotten*) (*Los Olvidados*) (>Luis Buñuel 1950) ☆ ☞
Alfonso Mejía is taught to live on his wits and by crime on the streets of Mexico City.

RED INDIANS

Broken Arrow (Delmer Daves 1950) ☆
>James Stewart learns enough of the language to talk Jeff Chandler's Cochise into peace and to marry his sister Debra Paget.

Cheyenne Autumn (>John Ford 1964) ☞
Having been settled on a reservation, a tribe migrate back to their homelands.
Little Big Man (Arthur Penn 1970) ✳ ☆
>Dustin Hoffman is the last surviving eye witness to Custer's Last Stand.
A Man Called Horse (Eliot Silverstein 1970) ■
English noble Richard Harris embraces the ways of the Indians that capture him.
Naughty Marietta (W. S. Van Dyke 1935) ☞ ☆
French princess Jeanette MacDonald, part of a 'consignment' of wives for Canadian pioneers falls for Indian scout Nelson Eddy.
Ramona (>D. W. Griffith 1910)/(Henry King 1936) ☆
Mary Pickford and Henry B. Walthall and Loretta Young and Don Ameche respectively as the half-breed and Indian who resist land-greedy whites.
Tell Them Willie Boy is Here (Abraham Polonsky 1969) ☞ ☆
Robert Redford's sheriff is among those pursuing Indian Robert Blake into the desert after an accidental death.

Reed, Sir Carol
British director (1906–1976)
Gaining his directorial experience by adapting Edgar Wallace thrillers for the stage, Reed specialized in inherently British thrillers, usually depicting underdogs triumphing over evil or adversity and their own inadequacies: *Night Train to Munich* (1940) (☞ ✍) (Rex Harrison impersonates a Nazi agent to smuggle inventor out of Germany); *Odd Man Out* (US: *Gang War*) (1947) (☞ ☆ ■) (James Mason as an IRA assassin finding nowhere to hide when he is wounded); and the >Graham Greene trio *The Fallen Idol* (US: *The Lost Illusion*) (AAN: 1948) (✍ ☆) (a small boy's hero-worship of butler Ralph Richardson is dented when he witnesses the accidental death of Richardson's wife), >*The Third Man* (AAN: 1950) and *Our Man in Havana* (1959) (✍ ☆) (Foreign Office mandarin Noël Coward accepts >Alec Guinness' claim that vacuum cleaner diagrams are plans for Soviet missiles). His other favourite theme

– the fish out of water – formed the basis of *The Stars Look Down* (1939) (Michael Redgrave rises from pit to Parliament), *Kipps* (US: *The Remarkable Mr Kipps*) (1941) (✍ ☞ ☆) (draper's assistant Michael Redgrave's snubbing in high society teaches him not to get ideas above his station); *An Outcast of the Islands* (1951) (✍ ☆ ☞) (Trevor Howard is alienated by the rat race, but then alienates the Asians who befriend him, in this film version of Joseph Conrad's novel); and *The Running Man* (1963) (John Mortimer's screenplay has pilot Laurence Harvey faking his death to claim the insurance). The colourful and out-of-character musical *Oliver!* (1968) (☞ ✍ ■) (Ron Moody is Fagin in >Charles Dickens' story of Victorian London lowlife) won him his only Oscar.

•*Midshipman Easy* (US: *Men of the Sea*) (1933) (☞): Margaret Lockwood is rescued from Spanish pirates during the French Revolutionary wars.
•*Bank Holiday* (US: *Three on a Weekend*) (1938): events ranging from a beauty contest to nurse Margaret Lockwood consoling the husband of a dying woman occupy the day in Brighton.
•*Young Mr Pitt* (1942) (☆ ☞ ✍): >Robert Donat hits the port wine to get him through his Parliamentary and Napoleonic War difficulties.
•*The Way Ahead* (US: *Immortal Battalion*) (1944) (☞ ✍ ☆): commander David Niven and sergeant major William Hartnell alternately coax and bully recruits into shape.
•*A Kid for Two Farthings* (1955) (☞ ✍): life improves for poor Londoners after a small boy adopts a one-horned goat he believes is a unicorn.
•*Trapeze* (1956) (☆ ☞): Burt Lancaster and Tony Curtis feud over Gina Lollobrigida without a safety net.
•*The Key* (1958) (☆): prior to a dangerous wartime salvage mission, William Holden is given the key to the flat where Trevor Howard meets mistress Sophia Loren.
•*The Agony and the Ecstasy* (1965) (☆ ✍ ☞ ■): Charlton Heston's Michelangelo and Rex Harrison's Pope Julius II feud over the Sistine

Chapel ceiling, in the screen adaptation of Irving Stone's novel.

La Règle du Jeu (The Rules of the Game) ☞ ☆ ✍ ■
France • La Nouvelle Edition Française • 1939 • 113 mins • b/w

d >Jean Renoir w Jean Renoir/Carl Koch ph Jean Bachelet m Various
Marcel Dalio, Nora Gregor, Jean Renoir, Julien Carette, Gaston Modot, Roland Toutain, Paulette Dubost, Mila Parély

Jean Renoir's analysis of social alienation and a divided nation on the verge of betraying itself into submission. Octave (Renoir) gets intrepid aviator André Jurieu (Toutain) invited to the country estate of the Marquis La Chesnaye (Dalio) to enable him to press his suit with the marquise, Christine (Gregor). Following a barbarous rabbit hunt, the visit deteriorates into a series of 'upstairs downstairs' romances, resulting in gamekeeper Schumacher (Modot) mistakenly shooting Jurieu, taking him for ex-poacher Marceau (Carette) who is flirting with his wife Lisette (Dubost). So accurately exposing French fears and foibles that it provoked riots on release, the original was lost in an RAF bombing raid. Reconstructed in 1956, it is now an accepted masterpiece.

•A gentlemanly shoot at James Mason's country house results in tragedy when Edward Fox takes it too seriously, in the screen version of Isobel Colgate's *The Shooting Party* (Alan Bridges 1984) (☆ ✍ ■ ☞).
•James Wilby falls in love with gardener Rupert Graves, in the film adaptation of E. M. Forster's posthumously published novel *Maurice* (James Ivory 1987) (☞ ■ ☆).
•On film, Henry Fielding's 18th-century picaresque novel *Joseph Andrews* (Tony Richardson 1977) (✍ ■ ☆) sees Peter Firth's honour under threat from Beryl Reid and Ann-Margret in a 'musical' bedroom sequence.
•Downstairs moves up as valet Dirk Bogarde imposes his will on master James Fox, in *The Servant* (>Joseph Losey 1963) (☞ ✍ ☆).

RELIGIOUS CONVICTION

Ceddo (Ousmane Sembene 1976) ☞ ✍
The kidnapped daughter of a king leads a Senegalese group resisting conversion to Islam.

Elmer Gantry (Richard Brooks 1960) ☆
Con man Burt Lancaster makes it big as an uncompromising preacher.

Fanatic (US: *Die! Die! My Darling*) (Silvio Narizzano 1965) ☆
Stefanie Powers is tormented by the Biblebashing crackpot in Tallulah Bankhead's house.

God Told Me (UK: *Demon*) (Larry Cohen 1976) ✍
A Catholic cop tormented by his adultery discovers that Christ is urging his followers to commit murder.

Inherit the Wind (Stanley Kramer 1960) ☆
>Gene Kelly reports as >Spencer Tracy (AAN) and >Fredric March as Clarence Darrow fight courtroom case brought against a man for teaching Darwinism.

Life for Ruth (US: *Condemned to Life*) (Basil Dearden 1962) ✍
A small girl is denied a life-saving blood transfusion because of her parents' beliefs.

The Milky Way (*La Voie Lactée*) (>Luis Buñuel 1968) ☞
Tramps argue the Catholic faith with pilgrims travelling to a Spanish shrine.

The Miracle Woman (>Frank Capra 1932) ☆
Preacher >Barbara Stanwyck can't wait for heaven to enjoy a few rewards and begins to serve mammon.

Susan and God (UK: *The Gay Mrs Trexel*) (>George Cukor 1940) ✍ ☞
>Joan Crawford's Christianity is only skin deep, hence >Fredric March's resort to the bottle.

REMINISCENCE

Un Carnet De Bal (aka *Life Dances On*) (aka *The Dance Programme*) (Julien Duvivier 1937) ☞ ☆ ✍
Marie Bell discovers that her partners from a fondly recalled night of dancing have not stood the test of time.

Dreamchild (Gavin Millar 1985) ✳
Coral Browne relives her Oxford childhood when Ian Holm's Lewis Carroll wrote *Alice in Wonderland* for her.

The End of the Day (*La Fin du Jour*) (Julien Duvivier 1939) ☆ ☞ ■
Louis Jouvet and Michel Simon are among the actors and actresses reliving their triumphs, failures and rivalries in a retirement home.

Falling in Love Again (Stephen Paul 1980)
Elliott Gould escapes from present problems by indulging in a remembrance of loves past.

Loving Couples (*Älskande Pär*) (Mai Zetterling 1964) ✍ ☆
Expectant mothers >Harriet Andersson, Gunnel Lindblom and Glo Petre discuss the men who got them pregnant.

Margie (Henry King 1946) ☞ ☆
Jeanne Crain recalls her college days which revolved around compromising moments and teacher Alan Young.

The Snows of Kilimanjaro (Henry King 1952) ☞ ☆
Wounded hunter Gregory Peck looks back in nostalgia on his affairs with Ava Gardner and Susan Hayward.

The Testament of Orpheus (*Le Testament D'Orphée*) (Jean Cocteau 1959) ☞ ☆
Cocteau as The Poet remeeting characters from his previous works.

The Trip to Bountiful (Peter Masterson 1985) ☆
Geraldine Page returns to the small town where she grew up.

>*Wild Strawberries* (*Smultronstället*) (>Ingmar Bergman 1957) ☞ ☆ ■ ✍♫

Renoir, Jean
French and American writer/director/ actor (1894–1979)
Son of Impressionist artist Auguste Renoir and heavily Hollywood influenced, Jean Renoir – who claimed to be 'a citizen of the world of films' and who spent a career 'making one film' – is one of the most important figures in cinema history. He developed camera, location and narrative techniques that constituted a canon of such unrivalled excellence that even those sternest of critics, the New Wavers of the *Ca-*

hiers du Cinéma were forced to applaud and assimilate. In the 1930s, virtually every film he produced proved a classic, exploring class conflict in >*La Grande Illusion* (aka *Grand Illusion*) (1937) (☆ ☞ ✍ ■), >*La Règle du Jeu* (*The Rules of the Game*) (1939) (☞ ☆ ✍ ■) and proletariat potential in *Toni* (1935) (☞ ■) (an Italian immigrant and his ex-lover kill their way out of unsatisfactory marriages), *La Vie Est à Nous* (US: *The People of France*) (1936) (☞) (Renoir supervises the fables of young disciple directors in a French Communist Party election broadcast) and *Le Marseillaise* (1938) (☞ ♫) (how the anthem of the French Revolution reached Paris in 1792). In the US, he studied rural life in *Swamp Water* (UK: *The Man Who Came Back*) (1941) (☞ ■) (unjustly accused of murder, Walter Huston lays low in the Okefenokee Swamp in Georgia) and *The Southerner* (AAN: 1945) (Zachary Scott and his mother Beulah Bondi have it tough on their unresponsive farm). He returned to Europe and directed the glossy costumers *The Golden Coach* (*La Carrozza d'Oro*) (aka *Le Carrosse d'Or*) (1952) (☞ ☆ ♫) (Anna Magnani spurns rich lovers and luxurious gifts) and *French Cancan* (US: *Only the French Can*) (1954) (☆ ☞) (Moulin Rouge owner >Jean Gabin caught between dancer Françoise Arnoul and mistress Maria Felix) and *The Testament of Dr Cordelier* (US: *Experiment in Evil*) (*Le Testament du Dr Cordelier*) (1959) (☆ ☞) (>Jean-Louis Barrault's respectable doctor is discovered by his lawyer friend to be an alter-ego killer). In one of his last films, *The Vanishing Corporal* (*Le Caporal Épinglé*) (1962) (☞ ■) (Jean-Pierre Cassal is third time lucky in his attempt to escape from a PoW camp), he pursued his interest in *film noir* evident in *The Woman on the Beach* (1947) (☞) (Joan Bennett's closely guarded secret emerges during her fling with shell-shocked coastguard Robert Ryan).

VIEW ON ▶ •*The Little Matchgirl* (*La Petite Marchande d'Allumettes*) (1928) (☞ ✍): Catherine Hessling sees the delights of the luxury denied her in the flames of her matches, in the silent film version of Hans Christian Andersen's tale.
•*Tire-au-Flanc* (1928) (☆ ✍): Georges

Pomiés's timid noble poet is guided through his national service by valet Michel Simon.
•*La Chienne* (1931) (☞ ✍): Michel Simon ruins his respectable life out of love for prostitute Janie Marèze.
•*Boudu Saved from Drowning* (*Boudu Sauvé des Eaux*) (1932) (☞ ☆): tramp Michel Simon abuses his saviour Charles Grandval's hospitality by seducing the women in his life.
•*Madame Bovary* (1934) (☞ ✍): Valentine Tessier as Gustave Flaubert's bored country doctor's wife seeking sexual fulfilment in the town.
•*The Crime of Monsieur Lange* (*Le Crime de Monsieur Lange*) (1936) (☞ ☆): author René Lefèvre kills Jules Berry when he returns to the rejuvenated publishing house he abandoned when it was going downhill.
•*La Bête Humaine* (US: *The Human Beast*) (1938) (☞ ☆ ■ ✍): on film Émile Zola's novel sees train driver >Jean Gabin plotting with Simone Simon to kill her husband.
•*A Day in the Country* (*Une Partie de Campagne*) (1936) (☞ ✍): in this Guy De Maupassant story, a girl abandons her fiancé for another man while picnicking on an idyllic summer's day.
•*The Diary of a Chambermaid* (1946) (✍ ☞ ☆): Octave Mirbeau's 19th-century maid Paulette Goddard spends more time upstairs than downstairs.
•*Eléna et les Hommes* (US: *Paris Does Strange Things*) (1956) (☆ ☞): >Ingrid Bergman's Polish princess has to chose a suitor from a trio of dull worthies.

RESISTANCE FIGHTERS

The Battle of the Rails (*La Bataille du Rail*) **(René Clément 1946)** ☞ ■
A semi-documentary tale of the debt owed to saboteurs of the French rail system under the Vichy government.
The Four Days of Naples (*Le Quattro Giornate di Napoli*) **(Nanni Loy 1962)** ☞ ✍
The population of Naples unites against the deportation of men aged between 5 and 50.
General Della Rovere **(>Roberto Rossellini 1959)** ☞ ☆ ✍
>Vittorio De Sica as a Nazi puppet who dis-

obeys orders to smoke out partisans and joins their number.

A Generation (Pokolenie) (>Andrej Wajda 1954) ☞ ☆

Love turns a Warsaw coward into an heroic leader.

Ivan's Childhood (Ivanovo Detstvo) (>Andrei Tarkovsky 1962) ☞ ☆

Such is Kolya Burlyaev's fury at his parents' murder that he insists on increasingly danger-ous missions.

Kanal (aka They Wanted to Live) (aka Sewer) (>Andrej Wajda 1957) ☞ ☆

The true story of Warsaw partisans being driven into the sewers.

La Ligne de Démarcation (aka The Line of Demarcation) (>Claude Chabrol 1966) ☞ ☆ ✍

A small town risks sheltering Allied agents and airmen prior to their border escape.

Le Silence de la Mer (Jean-Pierre Melville 1947) ✍

A peasant and his niece vow non-communica-tion with billeted Nazis, but one is on their side.

Resnais, Alain
French writer/director (b 1922)

A leading figure in the Left Bank group of writers – which included Marguerite Duras, the novelist and screenwriter of his 1959 *Hiro-shima, Mon Amour* (✍ ☞) (French actress Emmanuele Riva finds love with Japanese architect Eiji Okada) – Resnais coasted into prominence on the New Wave swell created by >Jean-Luc Godard and >François Truffaut. Subsequently, through his use of flashback and fantasy, he has established himself as an inno-vative film-maker in his own right: *The War is Over* (*La Guerre est Finie*) (1966) (☆ ☞) (>Yves Montand laments the failure of Spanish Civil War to resist Fascism); *Je T'Aime, Je T'Aime* (1968) (Claude Rich's participation in time travel experiments jolts his past out of sequence and it begins to haunt him) and *Stavisky* (1974) (corrupt financier >Jean-Paul Belmondo threatens to take Establishment names down with him, but he doesn't live to testify). However, Resnais' perhaps most fa-mous film – *Last Year at Marienbad* (*L'Année*

Dernière à Marienbad) (1961) (☞ ☆ ■) (Gior-gio Albertazzi insists Delphine Seyrig should renew the affair they had enjoyed the year before) – did not meet with universal approval, finding its way into a Medved brothers' 'turkey' compendium.

 •*Night and Fog* (*Nuit et Brouil-lard*) (1955) (☞ ■): a disturbing documentary study of Auschwitz through footage of its workings and ruins.
•*Muriel* (1963): Delphine Seyrig won Venice Best Actress as a woman trying to conjure up the emotions of a past love through an ill-ad-vised reunion.
•*Providence* (1977) (☞ ☆): dying writer John Gielgud's adverse views of his sons Dirk Bo-garde and David Warner are not borne out when they visit him for lunch.
•*My American Uncle* (*Mon Oncle d'Amérique*) (1978) (☞): this film about an animal beha-viourist's study of the humdrum lives of three men won the Cannes Special Jury Prize.
•*Life is a Bed of Roses* (*La Vie est un Roman*) (1983) (☞): three stories on the possibility of finding beauty and happiness in life.
•*L'Amour à Mort* (1984) (☞): a man is pro-nounced clinically dead, but recovers con-sciousness and is better for his preview of death.
•*Mélo* (1986) (✍): a violinist's wife falls for her husband's pianist best friend.

RESTAURANTS

Alice's Restaurant (Arthur Penn 1969) ☞

Penn won an AAN for this tale of Arlo Guthrie's campaign to avoid the Vietnam draft.

La Belle Équipe (They Were Five) (Julien Duvivier 1936) ☆ ✍

>Jean Gabin and friends' country inn project flounders when they feud over the same woman.

Baghdad Café (Percy Adlon 1988) ☆ ☞

Fat German woman Marianne Sägebrecht transforms the fortunes of a run-down desert eatery.

The Cook, the Thief, His Wife and Her Lover (Peter Greenaway 1989) ☞ ☆ ✍ ■ ♫

Lust and revenge are high on the menu for staff and diners at a high-class establishment.

The Last of the Red Hot Lovers (Gene Saks 1972) ☆

Menopausal restaurateur Alan Arkin decides that adultery would be good for his confidence.

'68 (Steven Kovacs 1988) ☆

Hungarian restaurant-owning immigrant family laments the assassination of Martin Luther King.

Who is Killing the Great Chefs of Europe? (US: *Too Many Chefs*) (Ted Kotcheff 1978) ✍

Junk food tycoon George Segal is suspected of killing chefs to give people no option but to eat at his place.

The Return of Martin Guerre (Le Retour de Martin Guerre)

☆ ✍ ☞ ■

France • SFP/France Region 3/Marcel Dassault/Roissi Films • 1982 • 123 mins • col

d Daniel Vigne   w Jean-Claude Carrière/ Daniel Vigne   ph André Neau   m Michel Portal

>Gérard Depardieu, Nathalie Baye, Stéphane Peau, Bernard-Pierre Donnadieu

Initially welcomed as a returning prodigal, Martin Guerre (Depardieu) has altered so noticeably during his eight-year absence that only his young wife (Baye), whom he left as a pregnant teenager, has faith in his authenticity. The villagers suspect he is an imposter and put him on trial to prove his identity. Stylishly re-creating the rude hurly-burly of late medieval rural life, reminiscent of the historian Emmanuel Le Roy Ladurie's *Montaillou*, Vigne's suspenseful film is an intelligent study of blind faith, ignorance and prejudice as well as a teasing 'who he?' mystery. Try to avoid the disappointingly dubbed video version.

 •Student Assaf Dayan and noble Anjelica Huston seek solitude away from the ravages of the Hundred Years' War, in *A Walk with Love and Death* (>John Huston 1969) (☞ ■).

•Glenn Close attempts to prove Jeff Bridges innocent in the tense courtroom thriller *Jagged Edge* (Richard Marquand 1985) (✍ ☞ ☆).

•>Sean Connery's William of Baskerville discovers laughter is the key to Umberto Eco's medieval whodunnit *The Name of the Rose* (Jean-Jacques Annaud 1986) (✍ ■ ☆).

•Parochialism and prejudice are rife, in *The Stranger* (>Orson Welles 1946) (✍ ☞).

•Midwife Dagmar Bláhová becomes pregnant by clinic doctor Jirí Menzel in the Czechoslovakian rural comedy *The Apple Game* (*Hra O Jablko*) (Véra Chytilová 1976) (☞).

•A man returns from his imprisonment for a gunfight killing to find himself target of his victim's vengeful sons, in the Colombian novelist Gabriel García Márquez script *A Time to Die* (*Tiempo de Morir*) (Jorge Ali Triana 1985) (✍ ■).

•Ex-Nazi Christopher Plummer's guilty past is bound up in the ruins of a French village, in *Souvenir* (Geoffrey Reeve 1988).

•Franchot Tone returns from the Napoleonic Wars and fails to recognize lover >Katharine Hepburn, in *Quality Street* (>George Stevens 1937) (☆ ☞).

REUNIONS

Always (Henry Jaglom 1985) ☞

Jaglom shows how a reunion leads to the patching up of his marriage, but it is only in his imagination.

Beaches (Garry Marshall 1988)

Bette Midler and Barbara Hershey's girlhood friendship turns into adult rivalry; but then Barbara falls fatally ill.

The Big Chill (Lawrence Kasdan 1983) ☆ ☞ ✍

>William Hurt, Glenn Close (AAN), Kevin Kline, Jeff Goldblum and Meg Tilly are among those at a college friend's funeral.

The Four Seasons (Alan Alda 1981) ♫

Bourgeois American couples holiday four times a year, and enjoy making up after rows.

It's Always Fair Weather (>Gene Kelly/ >Stanley Donen 1955) ☞ ✍

Boxing trainer Kelly exposes a fight fix during a surprise TV meeting with old army buddies.

A Man and a Woman: Twenty Years Later (Un Homme et une Femme: Vingt Ans Déjà) (Claude Lelouch 1986) ☆

Anouk Aimée and Jean-Louis Trintignant make a film about their affair shown in *A Man and a Woman* and history repeats itself.

Same Time Next Year (Robert Mulligan 1978) ☆

Once a year Alan Alda and Ellen Burstyn meet to continue their affair.

Unfinished Piece for Mechanical Piano (US: *Unfinished Piece for Piano Player*) *(Neokonchennaya Pyesa Dlya Mekhanicheskogo Pianin)* (Nikita Mikhalkov 1977) ■

Two academics meet again on a country weekend and discover they have both married beneath themselves intellectually.

The Woman Next Door (La Femme d'à Côtê) (>François Truffaut 1981) ☆

>Gérard Depardieu renews his affair with Fanny Ardant when she becomes a neighbour in a snobbish village.

The Young Ladies of Wilko (Panny z Wilka) (>Andrej Wajda 1979) ☞ ✍

A bachelor's recuperation reawakens the romantic hopes of the sisters he knew as a young man.

REVENGE

An Actor's Revenge (Yukinojo Henge) (Kon Ichikawa 1963) ☞

A female impersonator sets the three nobles who were responsible for the death of his parents against each other.

Assault on Precinct 13 (John Carpenter 1976) ☞

Violent villains besiege the police station where they were charged in the past.

The Big Night (>Joseph Losey 1951) ☞

John Barrymore, Jr tracks down the gangster Howard St John who beat up his father Preston Foster.

Cape Fear (J. Lee-Thompson 1962) ☆

Robert Mitchum pays back lawyer Gregory

Peck for sending him to prison by kidnapping wife Polly Bergen.

Child's Play (Tom Holland 1988) ✍ ☞

A doll contains the spirit of the killer shot by cop Chris Sarandon.

Chronicle of a Death Foretold (Cronaca Di Una Morte Annunciata) (Francesco Rosi 1987) ■ ✍ ☆

Ornella Muti's brothers stalk the man whose taking of her virginity leads to her wedding night abandonment by Rupert Everett.

The Man from Laramie (Anthony Mann 1955) ☞ ☆

Itinerant cowboy >James Stewart follows the clues leading to the man who killed his brother.

The Pied Piper (Krysar) (Jirí Barta 1985)

An animated version of the tale of a piper taking revenge on the citizens of Hamlin's refusal to pay him for ridding the town of rats.

Time of Destiny (Gregory Nava 1988) ☆

Army 'buddy' >William Hurt aims to get Timothy Hutton before the Nazis do for causing his father to die in an accident.

Underworld USA (Samuel Fuller 1960) ☞ ✍

Gangster Cliff Robertson takes the killing of his father pretty badly.

Young Guns (Chris Cain 1988) ☆

Emilio Estevez, Kiefer Sutherland and Charlie Sheen pursue the killers of kindly rancher Terence Stamp.

REVOLUTION

Bananas (>Woody Allen 1971)

Woody becomes the leader of a South American guerrilla band planning a coup.

A Funny Dirty Little War (No Habra Mas Penas ni Olvido) (Hector Olivera 1983) ✍

This Berlin Special Jury winner tells of Argentinian village politicos shooting it out despite all supporting Juan Peron.

The Guns (Os Fuzis) (Ruy Guerra 1963) ☞

This Berlin Special Jury winner tells of Brazilian peasants revolting against oppressors and a potential saviour during a famine.

Guns of Darkness (>Anthony Asquith 1962) ☞ ☆

David Niven and Leslie Caron escape in time as

John Mortimer's script sends rebels on to their Central American plantation.

October (aka *Ten Days That Shook the World*) (*Oktyabr*) (>Sergei Eisenstein 1928) ☞ ▪

Lenin returns to Petrograd to overthrow Alexander Kerensky's provisional government.

Red Psalm (*Még Kér a Nép*) (Miklós Jancsó 1971) ☞ ▪

19th-century Hungarian farmers' revolt against a tyrannical noble is repressed by reluctant troops.

Revolution (Hugh Hudson 1985)

Al Pacino finds defeating the English so easy that he has time to fall in love with Nastassja Kinski.

RIVALS IN LOVE

Coney Island (Walter Lang 1943) ☆

New York fairground men Cesar Romero and George Montgomery squabble over Betty Grable.

End of the Game (Maximilian Schell 1976) ☆

Thirty years on, cop Jon Voight is still on the heels of tycoon Robert Shaw for killing their mutual love Jacqueline Bisset.

No Minor Vices (Lewis Milestone 1948) ☆

Artist Louis Jourdan tries to steal Lilli Palmer from doctor friend Dana Andrews.

Queen of Hearts (Jon Amiel 1989) ▪ ✍

A girl flees an arranged engagement in postwar Italy to be with her true love in London, but the jilted fiancé will not be denied.

Rachel and the Stranger (Norman Foster 1948) ☆

Robert Mitchum moves in on Loretta Young because farmer William Holden neglects her.

Reap the Wild Wind (Cecil B. De Mille 1942) ☆

19th-century divers >John Wayne and Ray Milland consider Paulette Goddard a pearl of great price.

The Talk of the Town (>George Stevens 1942) ✍ ☆ ☞

Jean Arthur is in love with both murder suspect >Cary Grant and the lawyer she hires to defend him Ronald Colman.

Tin Pan Alley (Walter Lang 1940) ♫

Dancers Betty Grable and Alice Faye both hold a candle for composer John Payne.

Today We Live (>Howard Hawks 1933) ☆ ☞

>Joan Crawford and rival lovers >Gary Cooper, Franchot Tone and Robert Young whittle down their numbers in the trenches.

Two Girls and a Sailor (Richard Thorpe 1944) ☆

With Van Johnson in the sights of June Allyson and Gloria De Haven.

What Price Glory? (>John Ford 1952) ☆ ☞ ✍

First World War captain >James Cagney and sergeant Dan Dailey hope to marry the same French girl Corinne Calvet.

ROBBERY

Bob the Gambler (*Bob le Flambeur*) (Jean-Pierre Melville 1955) ☆

Believing his luck is in, a retired crook attempts to rob a casino.

La Bonne Année (US: *Happy New Year*) (Claude Lelouch 1973) ☆ ☞

Reunited with his lover Françoise Fabian, paroled jewel thief Lino Ventura sets out to find the man who accompanied him on his last job.

Buster (David Green 1988)

Phil Collins' Buster Edwards participates in the Great Train Robbery because he loves his wife Julie Walters so much.

Experiment in Terror (UK: *The Grip of Fear*) (Blake Edwards 1962) ✍

An asthmatic threatens to kill bank teller Lee Remick's sister unless she helps with his robbery.

The First Great Train Robbery (Michael Crichton 1978) ☆

>Sean Connery holds up a steam train with a handpicked gang including Donald Sutherland.

The Lavender Hill Mob (Charles Crichton 1951) ✍ ☆ ☞

Meek bank clerk >Alec Guinness masterminds a security van heist and smuggles the bullion as Eiffel Towers.

The League of Gentlemen (**Basil Dearden 1960**) ✍ ☆ ☞

Jack Hawkins selects his gang, including >Richard Attenborough, Roger Livesey and Nigel Patrick, as they all have pasts to hide.

Second Breath (*Le Deuxième Souffle*) (**Jean-Pierre Melville 1966**) ☆

Gangster Lino Ventura is tricked into betraying his Marseilles robbery accomplices.

Straight Time (**Ulu Grosbard 1978**) ☆

>Dustin Hoffman lacks the willpower to keep his nose clean and participates in an armed robbery.

The Thomas Crown Affair (**Norman Jewison 1968**) ☆ ☞ ✍

After a daring bank raid, Steve McQueen is tracked down by insurance investigator Faye Dunaway.

Robinson, Edward G.

(Emmanuel Goldenberg) Rumanian-born American actor (1893–1973)

Multi-lingual sophisticate and fine art collector is not the impression we get of Robinson through gangster pictures such as *Little Caesar* (>Mervyn Le Roy 1930) (☆ ☞) (the life and times of an Al Capone style mobster) and *Outside the Law* (Tod Browning 1930) (☆) (Robinson has woman troubles as he plans to rob a bank). Often the worthy hard man – *Five Star Final* (>Mervyn Le Roy 1931) (☆ ✍ ☞) (editor Edward G. is ordered to delve into an old murder to boost circulation) and *A Slight Case of Murder* (Lloyd Bacon 1938) (☆ ✍) (Edward G. becomes rich during Prohibition because only his disgusting beer was available) – he was also a deft comedian: *The Whole Town's Talking* (UK: *Passport to Fame*) (>John Ford 1935) (☆ ☞) (Jean Arthur discovers that gangster Robinson lays low by impersonating a meek lookalike) and *Brother Orchid* (Lloyd Bacon 1940) (☆) (gangster Robinson is fleeced by rival >Humphrey Bogart and becomes a monk). An intelligent protagonist, threatened by insanity in *Scarlet Street* (>Fritz Lang 1945) (☞ ✍) (artist Robinson kills prostitute Joan Bennett in a frenzy and lets pimp Dan Duryea take the rap) and *Night Has a Thousand Eyes* (John Farrow 1948) (☆) (music-hall fortune-teller Edward G. accurately predicts a forthcoming tragedy) and circumstance in *Manpower* (>Raoul Walsh 1941) (☞ ☆) (Robinson's love for ex-con >Marlene Dietrich earns him the enmity of George Raft) and *The Woman in the Window* (>Fritz Lang 1944) (☆ ☞ ✍) (Edward G. covers his tracks when a mysterious girl implicates him in an accidental killing), he was also a restrained biographer: *Dr Ehrlich's Magic Bullet* (>William Dieterle 1940) (☞ ☆ ✍) (Edward G. discovers the cure for syphilis) and *A Dispatch from Reuters* (UK: *That Man Reuter*) (>William Dieterle 1940) (☞ ☆) (Robinson endures doubters and disasters to establish the international news agency). He died before the award of a long overdue Oscar, albeit honorary.

 •*The Hatchet Man* (UK: *The Honourable Mr Wong*) (>William Wellman 1932) (☞ ☆): during a gang war in San Francisco's Chinatown, Robinson has to kill his best friend, whose daughter (Loretta Young) he is already caring for.

•*The Little Giant* (Roy Del Ruth 1933) (☆ ✍): prohibition tycoon Robinson *faux pas* his way to love with society girl Mary Astor.

•*Barbary Coast* (>Howard Hawks 1935) (☞ ☆): Edward G. turns Miriam Hopkins into a star, but not into his wife.

•*The Sea Wolf* (>Michael Curtiz 1941) (✍ ☆ ☞): Jack London's story has Robinson's insane sea captain kidnapping wreck survivor Alexander Knox only to suffer a mutiny.

•*Tales of Manhattan* (Julien Duvivier 1942) (☞ ☆ ✍): Edward G. is one of many hiring a tailcoat; as a failure attending a reunion of college highflyers.

•*Flesh and Fantasy* (Julien Duvivier 1943) (✍ ☞ ☆): Robinson's tale from a trio has a palmist predict that he will commit murder, in this adaptation of Oscar Wilde's *Lord Arthur Savile's Crime*.

•*Double Indemnity* (>Billy Wilder 1944) (☞ ☆ ✍): insurance salesman Fred MacMurray is talked into murdering >Barbara Stanwyck's husband so that she can inherit the insurance money; Edward G. investigates.

•*Our Vines Have Tender Grapes* (Roy Rowland 1945) (☆): Edward G. and his Norwegian immigrant farming family lead a cute, but watchable life.

•*The Red House* (Delmer Daves 1947) (☆): one-legged farmer Robinson hides the evidence of his guilty past in the depths of the woods.

•*Key Largo* (>John Huston 1948) (☆ ✍): gangster Robinson shelters from the storm in Lionel Barrymore's hotel with lush moll Claire Trevor.

•*A Hole in the Head* (>Frank Capra 1959) (☆ ☞): Edward G. loans his worthless hotelier brother Frank Sinatra the money to survive and keep his young child.

•*Two Weeks in Another Town* (>Vincente Minnelli 1962): Robinson gives drunk director >Kirk Douglas another chance, but he is still uncontrollable.

ROBOTS AND ANDROIDS

Blade Runner (Ridley Scott 1982) ✳ ☆
Space cop >Harrison Ford pursues murderous rogue android Rutger Hauer.

Demon Seed (Donald Cammell 1977) ☆
Julie Christie is raped by her husband's computer and they have a child.

Dr Who and the Daleks (Gordon Flemyng 1965)
Time Lord Peter Cushing's confrontation with the Daleks is rarely made easier by the presence of his grandchildren.

Friendship's Death (Peter Wollen 1987) ■
Alien robot Tilda Swinton joins the Palestine Liberation Organization to the disgust of journalist Bill Paterson.

Making Mr Right (Susan Seidelman 1987) ✍ ☆
John Malkovich both as a scientist and his creation who inherits the capacity to love that he lacks.

>*Metropolis* (>Fritz Lang 1927) ☞ ■ ✳ ✍ ☆
Robocop (Paul Verhoven 1987) ✳ ✍
Keeping law is privatized and a company turn their asset cop into a man-tank when he is mutilated in Detroit.

Short Circuit II (Kenneth Johnson 1988) ✳
Robot Johnny Five is bewildered by the big city as he helps Fisher Stevens defeat baddies hampering his toy robot business.

The Stepford Wives (Bryan Forbes 1974) ✍
Katharine Ross is the only small-town wife with personality as the rest are all robots programmed by their husbands.

Westworld (Michael Crichton 1973) ✳ ☆ ✍
Yul Brynner leads a rebellion of ancient Roman, medieval and Western robots at a futuristic holiday resort.

ROCK CONCERTS

The Concert for Bangladesh (Saul Swimmer 1972) ♫
George Harrison's charity concert with guests Ravi Shankar, Ringo Starr and Bob Dylan.

Elvis – That's the Way It Is (Denis Sanders 1972) ♫
Overweight, and little more than a housewife-thrill cabaret performer, but Elvis Presley still shows glimmers of his 1950s style.

Eric Clapton and His Rolling Hotel (Rex Pyke 1980) ♫
Old 'Slowhand' is joined on his tour train by George Harrison, Elton John and Muddy Waters.

Gimme Shelter (David & Albert Maysles/ Charlotte Zwerin 1970) ♫ ☞
The Rolling Stones's 1970 tour that resulted in an on-camera killing as the Hell's Angels stewarded the Altamont concert.

Jimi Plays Berkeley (Peter Pilafian 1971) ♫
Jimi Hendrix shows how a few bitten strings and a touch of shrieking feedback can add up to some superb guitar playing.

The Last Waltz (>Martin Scorsese 1978) ♫
The farewell performance by The Band.

Monterey Pop (D.A. Pennebaker 1968) ♫
The Who, Jimi Hendrix, Janis Joplin, and Otis Redding headline at the 1967 International Pop Festival.

Pink Floyd Live at Pompeii (*Pink Floyd à Pompeii*) (Adrian Maben 1971)
A bold attempt to capture the place and the atmosphere by using split screens and editing to the beat of the songs.

Rattle and Hum (Phil Joannou 1988) ♫
U2's *Joshua Tree* tour of the USA.

Rock Show (no director credited 1976) ♫
Paul McCartney and Wings captured on their

mammoth tour of the USA in its bicentenary year.

The Song Remains the Same (Peter Clifton/ Joe Massott 1976) ♫
Led Zeppelin live at Madison Square Garden.

Stop Making Sense (Jonathan Demme 1984) ☞ ♫
Talking Heads in three performances put on specifically for the film.

Woodstock (Michael Wadleigh 1970) ♫
Legendary 1969 concert with Jimi Hendrix, The Who, Joan Baez, Jefferson Airplane and Crosby, Stills, Nash & Young on the bill.

Ziggy Stardust and the Spiders from Mars (D. A. Pennebaker 1982) ♫
David Bowie's band pose and pout their way through some glam-rock classics.

Rocky ✍ ☞ ☆

USA • United Artists • 1976 • 119 mins • col

d John G. Avildsen w Sylvester Stallone
ph James Crabe m Bill Conti

Sylvester Stallone, Burgess Meredith, Talia Shire, Burt Young, Carl Weathers

World heavyweight boxing champion Apollo Creed (Weathers)'s Independence Day title fight is postponed, and to embody the spirit of America, he selects a no-hoper to take a shot. Rocky Balboa (Stallone [AAN]) is coming towards the end of an inauspicious career and divides his time between debt-collecting on the waterfront and wooing Adrian (Shire [AAN]), gawky sister of meatpacker Paulie (Young), but under Mickey (Meredith [AAN])'s expert eye, he is honed to fighting fitness. Avildsen (AA) never allows the underdog formula to lapse into corniness and Rocky's touching relationships outside the ring are fascinating – indeed they are even more to the fore in *Rocky II* (Sylvester Stallone 1979) (✍), although machismo rears its head in *Rocky III* (Sylvester Stallone 1982) and jingoism tarnishes *Rocky IV* (Sylvester Stallone 1985). The fight scene choreography lacks realism, but is none the less exciting and the film thoroughly merited its Best Picture Oscar award.

 •>Robert De Niro is boxing legend Jake La Motta in the biopic *Raging Bull* (>Martin Scorsese 1980) (☆ ☞ ■).

•A horse that survived a shipwreck is given the chance to enter the big race, in *The Black Stallion* (Carroll Ballard 1979) (✍).

•One-armed Nicholas Cage is the aimless American-Italian whose love transforms dowdy Cher, in *Moonstruck* (Norman Jewison 1987) (☆ ✍ ♫).

•Film buff Fernandel is the no-hoper who comes good as a screen comedian, in *Le Schpountz* (US: *Heartbeat*) (Marcel Pagnol 1938) (☞ ✍ ☆).

•Escapee robber Keith Carradine is tended by ugly duckling Shelley Duvall, in *Thieves Like Us* (>Robert Altman 1974) (☞).

Rogers, Ginger

(Virginia McMath) American actress (b 1911)
Between her 1930 feature debut in *Young Man of Manhattan* (Monta Bell) and *Gold Diggers of 1933* (>Mervyn Le Roy 1933) (☞ ♫) there were only hints at the star quality she would reveal in the >Astaire/Rogers vehicles. Her performance in the all-girl-star *Stage Door* (Gregory La Cava 1937) (☆ ✍ ■) (Ginger and >Katharine Hepburn are among the aspiring stars at a theatrical bed-and-breakfast) clearly showed there was life after Fred, but the road to the 'legitimate' was strewn with worthy comedies such as: *Fifth Avenue Girl* (Gregory La Cava 1939) (☆ ✍ ☞) (Ginger is hired to impersonate a millionaire's mistress to shake up his awful family); *The Major and the Minor* (>Billy Wilder 1942) (☞ ☆ ✍) (army officer Ray Milland takes Ginger back to camp believing she is an abandoned 12-year-old); *Roxie Hart* (>William Wellman 1942) (☞ ☆ ✍) (Adolphe Menjou defends Ginger in courtroom comedy after she confesses to murder to boost show ratings); *The Lady in the Dark* (Mitchell Leisen 1944) (☆) (Ginger sorts out her three-way men troubles by reliving her dreams in a psychiatrist's office); and *Monkey Business* (>Howard Hawks 1952) (☆ ☞) (a chimp invents a youth potion that miniaturizes Ginger and >Cary Grant). However, she was able to excel in such serious dramas as *Kitty Foyle*

(AA: Sam Wood 1940) (☆ ☞ ✍) (Rogers has the boss's illegitimate baby and, when it dies, vows to make a success of herself in business); *I'll Be Seeing You* (>William Dieterle 1945) (☞ ☆) (self-defence killer Rogers is paroled for Christmas and saves shell-shocked Joseph Cotten from prying neighbours); and *Black Widow* (Nunnally Johnson 1954) (Van Heflin is suspected of murdering his wife Gene Tierney, but upstairs neighbour and fading star Rogers can't be ruled out either).

 •*Bachelor Mother* (Garson Kanin 1939) (☆ ☞ ✍): Ginger finds a baby and department store boss Charles Coburn's son David Niven is presumed the father.
•*Once Upon a Honeymoon* (>Leo McCarey 1942) (☞ ☆): Ginger unknowingly marries a Nazi informer Walter Slezak, but she is rescued by radio journalist >Cary Grant.
•*We're Not Married* (Edmund Goulding 1952) (✍): Ginger as half of one of the six couples discovering their marriages are invalid.
>Astaire, Fred

Rohmer, Erich
(Jean-Marie Scherer) French writer/director (b 1920)

A former teacher, Rohmer became editor-in-chief of the prestigious *Cahiers du Cinéma* in 1957. He then made his mark as a director with the first of his six Moral Tales, *La Boulangerie de Monceau* (1963) (☞). In each of the series a fiancé is tempted away from his commitment by another woman (or women, in the case of No. 5 *Claire's Knee* (*Le Genou de Claire*) [1970] [☞ ✍]) (a diplomat's pre-marriage holiday is enlivened by two sisters and his obsession to touch the elder's knee, his doubts and ultimate acceptance of his situation reflected in the physical world about him). The quiet humour of these superbly observed films, given added credibility by the non-actors in key roles, was developed in a second batch of six – Comedies and Proverbs – which considered individuals within relationships rather than in the previously preferred isolation. Beginning with *The Aviator's Wife* (*La Femme de l'Aviateur*) (1980) (☞ ■) (a man abandons spying on his

mistress in a Paris park when he meets another girl, but she deserts him too), the sequence ended in 1987 with the engaging *My Girlfriend's Boyfriend* (*L'Ami de mon Amie*) (☞ ✍) (while her friend is on holiday, Sophie Renoir steals her boyfriend).

 'SIX MORAL TALES': •*Suzanne's Profession* (*La Carrière de Suzanne*) (No. 2, 1963) (☞ ✍): a man's pre-wedding doubts are confirmed and then assuaged during his obsession with a beautiful, but unobtainable girl.
•*My Night with Maud* (US: *My Night at Maud's*) (*Ma Nuit chez Maud*) (No. 3, 1969) (☞ ☆): Jean-Louis Trintignant spends a night with Françoise Fabian, but still loves the girl who caught his eye in church, Marie-Christine Barrault.
•*La Collectioneuse* (No. 4, 1967) (☞ ☆ ✍): in this Berlin Special Jury winner, Patrick Bachau and Daniel Pommereulle try to resist the lure of a St Tropez Lolita, Haydée Politiff.
•*Love in the Afternoon* (US: *Chloe in the Afternoon*) (*L'Amour l'Après-midi*) (No. 6, 1972) (☞ ✍): a businessman rekindles a relationship with an old flame, but refuses her offer of sex.
COMEDIES AND PROVERBS: •*A Good Marriage* (*Le Beau Mariage*) (1981) (☞ ☆): Béatrice Romand was Venice Best Actress as the student who, searching for a husband, alights on a wealthy lawyer André Dussollier, who proves to be engaged elsewhere.
•*Pauline at the Beach* (*Pauline à la Plage*) (1983) (☞ ✍): a divorcee and a teenager mix up two cousins in this holiday comedy of errors.
•*The Green Ray* (US: *Summer*) (*Le Rayon Vert*) (1986) (☞ ☆): in this Venice Best Film, secretary Marie Rivière's holiday is a series of letdowns and boring visits, until she meets her ideal man in Biarritz.
•*Four Adventures of Reinette and Mirabelle* (*Quatre Aventures de Reinette et Mirabelle*) (1986) (☞ ✍): Sorbonne students Joëlle Miquel and Jessica Forde share a Paris flat and resist a trio of appalling men.

ROLE REVERSAL

Beauty and the Devil (*La Beauté du Diable*) (>René Clair 1949) ☞
Plain >Faust (Michel Simon) exchanges looks with the Devil (Gérard Philipe) in return for his soul; the actors exchange roles accordingly.

Big (Penny Marshall 1988) ☆ ✍
Tom Hanks makes the best of the adulthood thrust upon him (a 12-year-old) by a fairground machine and makes it big as a toy tycoon.

Freaky Friday (Gary Nelson 1976) ☆
Jodie Foster and her mother Barbara Harris change places through wishing, in this Disney comedy.

I Was a Male War Bride (US: *You Can't Sleep Here*) (>Howard Hawks 1949) ☆ ☞ ✍
French officer >Cary Grant is smuggled out of postwar France as a WAC by wife Ann Sheridan.

The Last Woman (*L'Ultima Donna*) (aka *La Dernière Femme*) (Marco Ferreri 1976) ☆
Ornella Muti follows >Gérard Depardieu's wife Zouzou's example by abandoning him so that he has to become a house husband.

Persona (>Ingmar Bergman 1966) ☆ ☞
Actress Liv Ullmann and nurse Bibi Andersson exchange personalities during the former's illness.

Trading Places (John Landis 1983) ☆
Ralph Bellamy and Don Ameche wager that con man Eddie Murphy can do executive Dan Aykroyd's job.

Vice Versa (Peter Ustinov 1947) ☞ ✍
A magic touchstone turns a 19th-century boy (Anthony Newley) into his stuffy father Roger Livesey.

Vice Versa (Brian Gilbert 1988) ☆
Yuppie Judge Reinhold learns what it's like to be son Fred Savage and vice. . .

ROME

A Man in Love (Diane Kurys 1987) ☆ ✍
Greta Scacchi has an affair with actor Peter Coyote while he is filming a life of Cesare Pavese.

The Pigeon that Took Rome (Melville Shavelson 1962)
Charlton Heston infiltrates occupied Rome to thwart the Nazis.

Roman Holiday (>William Wyler 1953) ☞ ☆
Princess Audrey Hepburn (AA) slips away from her entourage and falls for journalist Gregory Peck after a day's sightseeing.

The Roman Spring of Mrs Stone (Jose Quintero 1961) ☆
Fading actress and widow >Vivien Leigh is abused by Roman Romeo, Warren Beatty.

Rome, Open City (US: *Open City*) (*Roma, Città Aperta*) (>Roberto Rossellini 1945) ☞ ■
A wanted Resistance fighter brings tragedy to all who shelter him, including a pregnant woman and a priest.

Three Coins in the Fountain (Jean Negulesco 1954) ☆ ☞
This AAN Best Picture matchmakes Dorothy McGuire with Clifton Webb, Jean Peters with Louis Jourdan and Rossano Brazzi with Maggie McNamara.

A Room with a View ☆ ■ ☞ ✍
GB • Merchant Ivory/Goldcrest • 1985 • 115 mins • col
d James Ivory   w Ruth Prawer Jhabvala
ph Tony Pierce-Roberts   m Richard Robbins
>Maggie Smith, Denholm Elliott, Helena Bonham-Carter, Julian Sands, Daniel Day-Lewis, Simon Callow, Judi Dench, Rosemary Leach, Rupert Graves

Suffocated by the propriety of the Pensione Bertolini and her cousin Charlotte's cosseting, Lucy Honeychurch (an excellently truculent Bonham-Carter) slips out of Santa Croce and is caught in dead faint by humble George Emerson (Sands). Despite a romantic interlude on a picnic overlooking Florence, Lucy returns to her fastidious fiancé Cecil Vyse (Day-Lewis). As the Pensione dramatis personae begin to concentrate at Windy Corner in Surrey like suspects in a whodunnit drawing-room, Lucy is faced with a choice between the dictates of her heart or upbringing. Maggie Smith's flustered Charlotte is superb, epitomizing Merchant Ivory's immaculate production of E. M. Forster's novel.

 •>Katharine Hepburn finds late love in Italy with Rossano Brazzi in *Summertime* (UK: *Summer Madness*) (>David Lean (1955) (☆ ☞), while >Jack Lemmon and Juliet Mills parallel the illicit affair their parents enjoyed on their annual visits to an Italian island, in *Avanti!* (>Billy Wilder 1972) (☆ ☞ ✍ ■ ♫).
•Walter Huston and Ruth Chatterton go unhappily on the Grand Tour, in the screen version of Sinclair Lewis' novel *Dodsworth* (>William Wyler 1936) (☞ ☆ ✍), a trip also taken by Scottish heiress Barbara Mullen in *Jeannie* (US: *Girl in Distress*) (Harold French 1941) (☆).
•Susannah York grows up as her mother falls ill and she has a hotel romance with Kenneth More, in Rumer Godden's *The Greengage Summer* (US: *Loss of Innocence*) (Lewis Gilbert 1961) (☆).
•Student Liza Minnelli has her first taste of love, in *The Sterile Cuckoo* (US: *Pookie*) (Alan J. Pakula 1969) (☆).
•>Marcello Mastroianni is the Italian in England in *Leo the Last* (John Boorman 1969) (☆).

Rossellini, Roberto
Italian writer/director (1906–1977)
Entering the industry as a sound and film editor, Rossellini spent the war exploiting official Fascist facilities to film the activities of the Italian Resistance, footage he used in the influential Neo-Realist *Rome, Open City* (US: *Open City*) (*Roma, Città Aperta*) (1945) (☞ ■) (a resistance fighter brings tragedy to all who shelter him from the Nazis) and *Paisà* (US: *Paisan*) (1946) (☞) (a semi-documentary study of how the Italians responded to the liberating Allies). In the face of international disapproval of their liaison, the pictures Rossellini made with wife >Ingrid Bergman were disappointing, too often compromising their individual strengths: *Stromboli* (*Stromboli, Terra di Dio*) (1951) (☞ ☆) (Bergman as a refugee marrying a fisherman to remain in Italy, but attempts to

desert him before the birth of their child), *Europa '51* (US: *The Greatest Love*) (1952) (☆) (wealthy Ingrid's act of atonement for causing the death of her son is interpreted as insanity), *Journey to Italy* (aka *The Lonely Woman*) (US: *Strangers*) (*Viaggio in Italia*) (1953) (☆) (Ingrid and George Sanders patch up their marriage at an inherited villa) and *Fear* (*Die Angst*) (aka *Le Paura*) (1954) (Ingrid is blackmailed to keep her wartime affair from her PoW husband). The collaboration caused greater damage to his career, and only *General Della Rovere* (1959) (☞ ☆ ✍) (the Nazis order >Vittorio De Sica to impersonate a general to weed out partisans, but he joins their cause) and *The Rise of Louis XIV* (aka *The Rise to Power of Louis XIV*) (*La Prise de Pouvoir par Louis XIV*) (1964) (Louis rebels against the revolts and factions of his youth by building Versailles) rose above mediocrity.

 •*Germany, Year Zero* (*Germania, Anno Zero*) (1947) (☞ ☆ ■): unable to feed his family in the ruins of Berlin, a young boy poisons his father.
•*The Machine that Kills Bad People* (*La Macchina Ammazzacattivi*) (1948) (✍): an old man's camera can kill people and expose greed.
•*L'Amore* (US: *Woman*) (aka *Ways of Love*) (1948) (☞ ✍): two stories: a Cocteau tale shows a woman's telephoned bid to save her affair, and a >Fellini fable has a woman convinced her seducer is St Joseph.
•*India* (1959) (☞): a controversial view of the subcontinent, which précised his 10-episode 1958 documentary *L'India vista da Rossellini*.
•*Vanina Vanini* (US: *The Betrayer*) (1961) (☞ ✍): a 19th-century Carbonari revolutionary's mission to assassinate a traitor is betrayed by his princess lover.
•*The Age of Cosimo De Medici* (*L'Età de Cosimo De' Medici*) (1973) (☞ ■): a visually superb biopic of the ruthless oligarch who established the government machinery of Renaissance Florence.
•*Blaise Pascal* (1975) (■): biopic of the 17th-century French mathematician and religious controversialist.

RUSSIA

Agony (*Agonia*) (**Elem Klimov 1975**) ☞ ☆
Alexei Petrenko as Rasputin gains dangerous power at the Romanov court through his alleged ability to heal the heir's haemophilia.

Doctor Zhivago (>**David Lean 1965**) ☞ ☆ ♫
Omar Sharif and Julie Christie in Boris Pasternak's epic romance spanning the revolutionary years.

The Eagle (**Clarence Brown 1926**) ☆
Rudolph Valentino wins Vilma Banky as a Tsarist Zorro.

The Fall of the Romanov Dynasty (*Padenye Dinastii Romanovykh*) (**Esfir Shub 1927**) ☞ ▣
Newsreel footage and Romanov home movies study the Tsarist monarchy and why it fell.

Gorky Park (**Michael Apted 1983**) ☆ ✍
>William Hurt as a Moscow cop on the trail of Lee Marvin's sable smuggling operation.

The Inspector General (**Henry Koster 1949**) ✍
Danny Kaye is the potion seller mistaken for a government official by corrupt mayor Gene Lockhart, in this screen version of Nikolai Gogol's play.

Knight without Armour (**Jacques Feyder 1937**) ☆
>Robert Donat gets countess >Marlene Dietrich past the watchful eyes of the Red Army.

Nicholas and Alexandra (**Franklin Schaffner 1971**) ☆ ▣ ✍
Janet Suzman's Tsarina urges her Tsar husband Michael Jayston to rule his revolutionary realm with a firmer hand.

A Slave of Love (*Raba Lubvi*) (**Nikita Mikhalkov 1976**) ☞ ✍
Moviemakers in Odessa in 1917 film events around them, unaware there is a revolution going on.

War and Peace (*Voina i Mir*) (**Sergei Bondarchuk 1966–7**) ☞ ✍ ☆
Foreign Oscar winner portrays Leo Tolstoy's epic of three noble families' response to the 1812 Napoleonic invasion

SAINTS

Augustine of Hippo (Agostino di Ippone) (>Roberto Rossellini 1972) ☞
With the patience of a saint, Dary Berkani convinces the declining Roman Empire it is better off without pagan gods.

Brother Sun, Sister Moon (Franco Zeffirelli 1972) ☞ ■
>Alec Guinness's Pope Innocent III sanctions Francis of Assisi's order of monks.

Joan of Arc (Victor Fleming 1948) ■
>Ingrid Bergman as the 15th-century military maid burned for her claim to hear heavenly voices.

Monsieur Vincent (Maurice Cloche 1947) ☞ ☆ ✍
Foreign Oscar-winning biopic of Vincent De Paul who worked tirelessly among the poor of Paris.

Simon of the Desert (Simon del Desierto) (>Luis Buñuel 1965) ☞ ■
Claudio Brook imitates Simon Stylites by sitting atop a pillar in the Mexican desert.

The Song of Bernadette (Henry King 1943) ☆ ☞
Jennifer Jones as the French peasant girl ordered by the Virgin Mary to dig for a spring in the mud of Lourdes.

Thérèse (Alain Cavalier 1986) ■ ☞ ☆
Catherine Mouchet as the devout, consumptive nun, Thérèse of Lisieux.
>Miracles

SCARY MONSTERS AND SUPER CREEPS

The Abominable Snowman (Val Guest 1957) ☆
Peter Cushing's Himalayan expedition runs into a little yeti trouble.

The Dark Crystal (Jim Henson/Frank Oz 1982) ✳
Villainous creatures steal a fragment of the crystal and rule the world until our young heroes arrive.

Friday the 13th (Sean S. Cunningham 1980) ✍
A boy, Jason, exacts his revenge on successive summer camp officials for allowing him to 'drown'.

Gremlins (Joe Dante 1984) ✳
Cute cuddly mogwais prove to be little terrors when wet.

Hellraiser (Clive Barker 1987) ✳

A householder's brother's remains rejuvenate with blood and a variety of nasties emerge from the woodwork.

The Invisible Man (James Whale 1933) ☞

A bandaged Claude Rains perfects invisibility in the English village of Ipping but suffers from the side-effect of megalomania.

Jaws (>Steven Spielberg 1975) ✍ ☞

Roy Scheider, Robert Shaw and Richard Dreyfuss go fishing for the shark who has terrorized a seaside resort.

Man Made Monster (UK: The Electric Man) (George Waggner 1940) ☆

Lionel Atwill's electricity bills are enormous, but a lab accident allows him to run household gadgets off Lon Chaney Jr.

The Mummy (Karl Freund 1932) ☆ ✍/ **(Terence Fisher 1959)** ☆

>Boris Karloff and Christopher Lee don the binding clothes to search for their stolen treasure.

A Nightmare on Elm Street (Wes Craven 1984) ✳

Clad in a Dennis-the Menace sweater, Freddie Krueger (Robert Englund) threatens teenagers who have always dreaded meeting someone just like him.

The Phantom of the Opera (Rupert Julian 1926) ☆ ✳/**(Arthur Lubin 1943)** ☆

Lon Chaney and Claude Rains as the deformed composers kidnaping a diva and hiding her beneath Paris opera house.

Scanners (David Cronenberg 1981) ✳

A birth-easing drug creates a band of mind-readers who can explode the heads of anyone they take against.

The Sorcerers (Michael Reeves 1967) ☆

>Boris Karloff perfects a device to turn a man into a criminal daredevil and then watches his exploits for amusement.

Them! (Gordon Douglas 1954) ✳

Edmund Gwenn is faced with mutant ants in the New Mexico desert.

The Wolf Man (George Waggner 1940) ✳ ☆

>Bela Lugosi's gypsy bites Claude Rains's son Lon Chaney, Jr and doors are locked each full moon.

Schlesinger, John
British actor/writer/director (b 1926)

Uppingham and Oxford educated, Schlesinger made his directorial debut at just 22 with a short, *Black Legend* (1948), but postponed earning reputation and the luxury of selectivity for 15 years in favour of acting with Ngaio Marsh's theatre group and making TV magazine programme shorts and documentaries. Much of his best work has come from examining human relationships in social realist contexts: *A Kind of Loving* (1962) (☞ ✍ ☆) (Alan Bates and June Ritchie's marriage is not helped by having to live with her mother, Thora Hird); *Billy Liar* (1963) (☞ ☆ ✍ ■) (Keith Waterhouse's screen adaptation of his novel has dreamer Tom Courtenay wavering between his dual engagements and clerking job at an undertakers and a new life in London with Julie Christie); *Midnight Cowboy* (AA: 1969) (♫ ☆ ☞) (>Dustin Hoffman tries to pimp for socially ambitious stud Jon Voight); and *Sunday, Bloody Sunday* (AAN: 1971) (☞ ☆) (designer Murray Head has affairs with both businesswoman Glenda Jackson [AAN] and doctor Peter Finch [AAN]). He has also successfully undertaken a number of projects of varying difficulty and diversity: *Darling* (AAN: 1965) (☆ ☞) (Julie Christie exploits Dirk Bogarde and Laurence Harvey to further her modelling career); *Marathon Man* (1976) (☆ ☞) (ex-Nazi >Laurence Olivier tortures runner >Dustin Hoffman, convinced he knows the whereabouts of a stash of diamonds); and *Yanks* (1979) (☞ ✍) (Vanessa Redgrave and Lisa Eichhorn romance with Second World War GIs William Devane and Richard Gere).

 •*Terminus* (1961) (☞ ■): this short, capturing a day's bustle at Waterloo Station, won the documentary category at Venice.

•*Far from the Madding Crowd* (1967) (■ ✍ ☞ ☆): farmers Alan Bates and Peter Finch and soldier Terence Stamp compete for the love of Julie Christie in the screen version of Thomas Hardy's novel.

•*The Day of the Locust* (1975) (☞ ✍ ☆): 1930s film actress Karen Black rejects director William Atherton and introverted Donald Sutherland, whose frenzied response leads to a riot outside Grauman's Chinese Theatre.

•*Honky Tonk Freeway* (1981) (🖉): William Devane paints the town pink in an attempt to attract tourists, but regrets it when they are all eccentrics.

•*The Falcon and the Snowman* (1984): disillusioned Timothy Hutton sells military secrets on principle, drug dealer Sean Penn for cash.

•*The Believers* (1987) (☞): New York cop Martin Sheen investigates a number of stabbings.

•*Madame Sousatzka* (1989): a teenage boy is taught the piano by Shirley MacLaine in a boarding house full of eccentrics and lonely-hearts.

Schlöndorff, Volker
German writer/director (b 1939)

French educated, trained and inspired, Schlöndorff is the most texturally stylish and least personal of the New German directors. His films can be divided into two categories: LITERARY ADAPTATIONS: *Young Törless* (*Der Junge Törless*) (1966) (☞) (winner of the Cannes International Critics Prize tells of a boy standing idly by while boarding school bullies kill a timid student), *Michael Kohlhaas* (1969) (☞) (this screen version of Kleist's novel has a 16th-century horse-dealer locking horns with a corrupt, cruel landowner), *The Lost Honour of Katharina Blum* (*Die Verlorene Ehre der Katharina Blum*) (co-directed with >Margarethe Von Trotta 1975) (🖉 ☞) (this screen version of Heinrich Böll's novel has Angela Winkler subjected to police and press pressure after sleeping with a stranger), *The Tin Drum* (*Die Blechtrommel*) (1979) (☞ ☆) (Foreign Film Oscar and Cannes Best Film winner has David Bennent as the wilful boy whose refusal to grow or conform contrasts with the citizens of Danzig's capitulation to the Nazis), and *Swann in Love* (*Un Amour de Swann*) (1983) (☞ ■ ☆) (the screen version of Marcel Proust's novel *Remembrance of Things Past* has Jeremy Irons confiding the intensity of his jealous love for Ornella Muti to noble Alain Delon); and COLLABORATIONS WITH WIFE >MARGARETHE VON TROTTA which warn of the dangers of social and political apathy: *The Sudden Fortune of the Poor People of Kombach* (*Der*

Plötzliche Reichtum der Armen Leute von Kombach) (1971) (☞ 🖉) (19th-century peasants hijack a tax collector and spend excessively until they are executed), *Summer Lightning* (*Strohfeuer*) (1972) (☞ ☆) (Von Trotta is discriminated against both in her career and the custody case over her son after her divorce), and *Circle of Deceit* (*Die Fälschung*) (1981) (☞) (journalist Bruno Ganz has an affair with >Hanna Schygulla and stabs a man in a riot while covering events in the Lebanon).

•*A Degree of Murder* (*Mord und Totschlag*) (1967) (☞ 🖉): Anita Pallenberg dumps the body of her accidentally killed boyfriend in a building site, but it is discovered.

•*Coup de Grâce* (*Der Fangschuss*) (1976) (☞): when soldier Matthias Habich, commander of a unit detailed to resist the advances of Bolshevism, also resists those of >Margarethe Von Trotta, she sides with the Communists.

•*Germany in Autumn* (*Deutschland im Herbst*) (co-directed with Heinrich Böll/Alf Brustellin/Bernhard Sinkel/Peter Cloos/Katja Rupé/>Rainer Werner Fassbinder/Alexander Kluge/Beate Mainka/Peter Schubert/Edgar Reitz 1978) (☞): a complex study of West German socialist attitudes towards terrorism.

•*The Handmaid's Tale* (1989) (☞ 🖉): this adaptation of Margaret Attwood's novel tells of a future society where women are repressed as in ancient times.

Schygulla, Hanna
Polish-born German actress (b 1943)

Co-founding the Munich anti-theatre group linked Schygulla with >Rainer Werner Fassbinder, for whom she appeared in 17 films, usually as a devoted woman who arrives at sexual and feminist awareness through maltreatment or deprivation: *Katzelmacher* (1969) (☞ ☆) (Fassbinder's arrival attracts the interest of Schygulla and the violence of the teenagers of a rundown urban district); *The Bitter Tears of Petra Von Kant* (*Die Bitteren Tränen der Petra Von Kant*) (1972) (☞ ☆) (in this lesbian love triangle, fashion designer Margit Carstensen leaves Irm Hermann for Schygulla); and *Effi Briest* (*Fontane: Effi*

Briest) (1974) (✍ ☞ ☆) (Hanna's older aristocrat husband Wolfgang Schenck challenges her soldier lover Ulli Lommel to a duel); and following her return from hitch-hiking across America and an involvement in German children's theatre, *The Marriage of Maria Braun* (*Die Ehe der Maria Braun*) (1978) (☆ ☞) (Hanna leaves husband after he kills her black GI lover, and she makes her fortune as the mistress of an industrialist) and *Lili Marleen* (1981) (forced apart by war, singer Schygulla and Jewish composer Giancarlo Giannini remain in each other's thoughts through the song he wrote for her). Although Schygulla worked with other directors – >Wim Wenders on *Wrong Movement* (*Falsche Bewegung*) (1974) (☞ ☆) (Hanna is one of the people who writer Rüdiger Vogler meets on his travels around Germany, in an adaptation of Goethe's *Wilhelm Meister's Apprenticeship*) and >Volker Schlöndorff on *Circle of Deceit* (*Die Fälschung*) (1981) (☞) (journalist Bruno Ganz has an affair with Schygulla while covering events in the Lebanon) – since Fassbinder's death in 1982, she has further spread her wings: *Passion* (aka *Godard's Passion*) (>Jean-Luc Godard 1982) (☞ ☆) (Michel Piccoli has woman troubles: his wife Schygulla is sleeping with a film director and union boss Isabelle Huppert is leading a strike at his factory) and *A Love in Germany* (*Eine Liebe in Deutschland*) (>Andrej Wajda 1983) (☞ ☆) (shopkeeper Schygulla has an affair with Polish PoW Piotr Lysak and pays heavy penalty).

VIEW ON ▶ •*Gods of the Plague* (*Götter der Pest*) (>Rainer Werner Fassbinder 1969) (☞): Harry Baer's supermarket heist is betrayed by Schygulla and >Margarethe Von Trotta.

•*Why Does Herr R Run Amok?* (*Warum Läuft Herr R Amok?*) (>Rainer Werner Fassbinder/Michael Fengler 1969) (☞ ☆): Schygulla is part of the tedious bourgeois normality against which Kurt Raab rebels in his moment of violence.

•*Beware of a Holy Whore* (*Warnung vor einer Heiligen Nutte*) (>Rainer Werner Fassbinder 1970): as part of a film cast waiting to hear if there is enough money to complete their picture.

•*The Night of Varennes* (*La Nuit de Varennes*) (Ettore Scola 1981) (■ ☆): Hanna's noblewoman argues the merits of the French Revolution with Harvey Keitel's Tom Paine and >Jean-Louis Barrault's Restif De Bretonne.

Scorsese, Martin
American writer/director (b 1942)

Following a childhood marred by frequent illness and having a vocation to the priesthood frustrated by stringent entry requirements, Scorsese made the short *The Big Shave* (1967) and acted as editor on the rock concert documentary *Woodstock* (Michael Wadleigh 1971) (♫) before Roger Corman offered him *Boxcar Bertha* (1972) (☞ ☆ ✍) (Barbara Hershey and David Carradine act as Depression Robin Hoods to aid victims of anti-union legislation). He delights in pitching neurotics into downtown New York: *Mean Streets* (1973) (☞ ☆ ♫) (>Robert De Niro has gang trouble and family duty prevents brother Harvey Keitel escaping the crime and poverty of Little Italy); *Taxi Driver* (1976) (☆) (disturbed by war and rejection by Cybill Shepherd, >Robert De Niro attempts a political assassination), *New York, New York* (1977) (☞ ☆) (musician >Robert De Niro abandons Liza Minnelli to concentrate on his career, but she is the one to become the star), and *After Hours* (1986) (☞ ☆ ✍) (yuppie Griffin Dunne gets caught downtown late at night and becomes the victim of a hate pursuit after Rosanna Arquette commits suicide). One can but speculate on the consequences of a Scorsese New York neurotic meeting a >Woody Allen counterpart, although they are getting closer, each having directed episodes in *New York Stories* (1989) (the third section was directed by >Francis Ford Coppola) (☞ ✍). Despite the controversy, Scorsese's *Last Temptation of Christ* (AAN: 1988) (☞ ✍) (the preaching career of Willem Dafoe's Christ is punctuated with imaginings of life as an ordinary man) failed to capture the power or penetration of Nikos Kazantzakis's novel.

 •*Alice Doesn't Live Here Anymore* (1974) (☞ ☆): widow Ellen Burstyn takes her son on the road in search of singing stardom.

•*The Last Waltz* (1978) (♫): the farewell concert of The Band.

•*Raging Bull* (1979) (☆ ☞ ✍): >Robert De Niro won the Best Actor Oscar in this biopic of boxer turned stand-up comedian Jake La Motta.

•*The King of Comedy* (1982) (☆ ☞ ✍): >Robert De Niro kidnaps comic Jerry Lewis and demands his own TV chat show in return for his release.

•*The Color of Money* (AAN: 1986): >Paul Newman passes on pool room hustling tips to flash novice Tom Cruise in the 20-years-on sequel to Robert Rossen's *The Hustler*.

SCOTLAND

The Bridal Path (Frank Launder 1959) ☞
Hebridean Bill Travers comes to the Highlands to find a wife.

Brigadoon (>Vincente Minnelli 1954)
>Gene Kelly and Van Johnson find love in a ghostly village that only materializes once a century.

The Edge of the World (>Michael Powell 1937) ☞
Semi-documentary study of everyday life on the remote island of Foula.

Kidnapped (Alfred L. Werker 1938)/ (Robert Stevenson 1959)/(Delbert Mann 1971) ✍
Warner Baxter, Peter Finch and >Michael Caine are the respective Jacobite outlaws in R. L. Stevenson's classic adventure.

Local Hero (Bill Forsyth 1983) ✍ ☞ ☆
Oil boss Burt Lancaster abandons plans for a refinery when he discovers that the Highland location has an unrivalled view of the Northern Lights.

Macbeth (>Orson Welles 1948) ☞ ✍ ☆/(>Roman Polanski 1971) ✍ ☞ ☆
>Shakespeare's notoriously unlucky Scottish play, with Welles and Jon Finch as the victim of the witches' predictions.

The Maggie (US: *High and Dry*) (Alexander Mackendrick 1953) ☆
A battered ship attempts to bring its valuable cargo into a Scottish port.

On Approval (Clive Brook 1943) ☆ ✍
Roland Culver and Beatrice Lillie chaperone Brook and Googie Withers on their castle trial marriage.

Whisky Galore (US: *Tight Little Island*) (Alexander Mackendrick 1948) ✍ ☆
Whisky is smuggled ashore from a shipwreck under the noses of goverment inspectors, in the Ealing treatment of Compton Mackenzie's novel.

THE SEASIDE

Barnacle Bill (Richard Thorpe 1941) ☆
Wallace Beery courts Marjorie Main in the hope of getting her to keep his fishing business afloat.

Mr Hobbs Takes a Vacation (Henry Koster 1962) ☆
>James Stewart and Maureen O'Hara's worries are divided between their daughter's holiday romance and their awful accommodation.

>*Monsieur Hulot's Holiday* (*Les Vacances de Monsieur Hulot*) (Jacques Tati 1953) ☆ ✍ ☞ ♫ ▦

Pauline at the Beach (*Pauline à la Plage*) (>Eric Rohmer 1983) ☞ ✍
The romantic entanglements of two cousins – one a divorcee – with three men (one a teenager) won Rohmer Best Director at Berlin.

Such a Pretty Little Beach (US: *Riptide*) (*Une si Jolie Petite Plage*) (Yves Allégret 1949) ✍ ☆
Gérard Philipe is suspected of murdering the singer with whom he shared a holiday romance.

Sunday in August (*Domenica d'Agosto*) (Luciano Emmer 1950) ☞
>Marcello Mastroianni is among those on a trip from Rome to Ostia.

10 (Blake Edwards 1979) ☆
Dudley Moore rescues Bo Derek's newlywed husband from drowning and is rewarded with an offer of sex accompanied by Ravel's 'Bolero'.

La Vieille Fille (Jean-Pierre Blanc 1972) ☆ ☞
This Berlin Best Director winner tells of >Philippe Noiret's gentle hotel friendship with shy Annie Girardot.

Wish You Were Here (David Leland 1987) ☆
Emily Lloyd in a *film à clef* of Cynthia Payne's sexually punctuated seaside teenagehood.

SECRETARIES

Accent on Youth (Wesley Ruggles 1935) ☆ ☞
Sylvia Sidney falls for mature playwright Herbert Marshall during their dictation sessions.

Easy Living (Mitchell Leisen 1937) ☆ ⌁ ☞
Jean Arthur is mistaken for a millionaire's mistress when a fur coat lands on her as she rides an open-top bus.

The Gilded Lily (Wesley Ruggles 1935) ☞ ☆
Typist Claudette Colbert prefers poor but honest journalist Fred MacMurray to idle rich Ray Milland.

My Name is Julia Ross (Joseph H. Lewis 1945) ⌁ ☞
When Nina Foch awakes after her first day's employment with Dame May Whitty, she finds her identity has been changed and her life is in danger.

Nine to Five (Colin Higgins 1980) ☆
>Jane Fonda, Lily Tomlin and Dolly Parton teach their chauvinist boss a lesson or three.

Standing Room Only (Sidney Lanfield 1944) ☆
Paulette Goddard and boss Fred MacMurray impersonate domestics to avoid Washington hotel shortage.

Take a Letter, Darling (UK: *Green-Eyed Woman*) (Mitchell Leisen 1942) ☆ ⌁
Advertising executive Rosalind Russell hires a male secretary, Fred MacMurray, in this role reversal comedy.

That Touch of Mink (Delbert Mann 1962) ☆
Doris Day refuses to play swooning, devoted secretary to smooth-talking boss >Cary Grant.

Wife versus Secretary (Clarence Brown 1936) ☆ ⌁ ☞
>Myrna Loy is convinced her publisher husband >Clark Gable sees >Jean Harlow as more than just a treasure at the office.

The Seventh Seal (Det Sjunde Inseglet) ■ ☞ ☆ ⌁
Sweden • Svensk Filmindustri • 1957 • 90 mins • b/w
wd >Ingmar Bergman   ph Gunnar Fischer   m Max von Sydow, Erik Nordgren, Gunnar Björnstrand, Bengt Ekerot, Nils Poppe, Bibi Andersson

Antonius Blok (Von Sydow) has survived the Crusades, but on returning to his plague-ridden home, he is accosted on a bleak beach by Death and challenged to a game of chess, with his life forfeit if he loses. His skilful play allows the unsuspecting Mia (Andersson) and Joi (Poppe) to save themselves and their child. Employing the centrality of religion to Middle Ages life, Bergman's sombre allegory, based on his own play *Sculpture in Wood*, questions why a loving God would allow misery into his world in any era. Equating the Church with darkness and death throughout, Bergman still uses the feast of wild strawberries and the actors' simple pleasures to acknowledge the possibility of consolation through faith.

•Medieval superstition, society and government are all lampooned, in *Monty Python and the Holy Grail* (Terry Gilliam/Terry Jones 1975) (⌁ ☆).
•Feodor Chaliapin and Dorville are the knight and his squire in Miguel De Cervantes' *Don Quixote* (aka *Adventures of Don Quixote*) (*Don Quichotte*) (>G. W. Pabst 1933) (☞ ☆).
•Dudley Moore does a deal to sample the seven deadly sins with Devil Peter Cook, in *Bedazzled* (>Stanley Donen 1967) (☆).
•The bawdy nature of the Middle Ages informs the tales told by Geoffrey Chaucer's fellow pilgrims, in *The Canterbury Tales* (*I Racconti di Canterbury*) (>Pier Paolo Pasolini 1971) (■ ☞ ⌁).
•A 20th-century Holy Family parallel is drawn in *Hail Mary* (*Je Vous Salue, Marie*) (>Jean-Luc Godard 1984).
•The medieval view of death is captured in the fresco Colin Firth restores in the screen version of J. L. Carr's novella *A Month in the Country* (Pat O'Connor 1987) (■ ☆ ⌁).

•The Grim Reaper comes for Woody Allen in the *Seventh Seal* spoof *Love and Death* (>Woody Allen 1975) (☆ ✍).

SHAKESPEARE

The Angelic Conversation (Derek Jarman 1985) ■
A series of dramatic landscapes accompany Judi Dench's reading of a dozen of the Sonnets.

Antony and Cleopatra (Charlton Heston 1972) ☆
High politics come between Heston and Hildegarde Neil and they die of broken heart and asp.

As You Like It (Paul Czinner 1936) ☆ ■
>Laurence Olivier's exiled Orlando woos Elisabeth Bergner's Rosalind in the Forest of Arden.

>Hamlet (>Laurence Olivier 1948) ☆ ☞ ✍ ■ ♫

Henry V (>Laurence Olivier 1944) ✍ ☆ ■ ☞/**(Kenneth Branagh 1989)** ✍ ☆ ■
The respective directors inspire their troops on the eve of Agincourt and love in the heart of the princess Katherine.

Julius Caesar (>Joseph L. Mankiewicz 1952) ✍ ☆ ☞
James Mason and John Gielgud's assassination of Louis Calhern provokes >Marlon Brando into military vengeance.

King Lear (Korol Lir) (Grigori Kozintsev 1970) ✍ ■
Yuri Yarvet as the ruler who in his dotage loses his kingdom and the respect of his daughters in one fell swoop.

Macbeth (>Orson Welles 1948) ☞ ✍ ☆/**(>Roman Polanski 1971)** ✍ ☞ ☆
Welles and Jon Finch pay the price for murdering the king of Scotland.

A Midsummer Night's Dream (Max Reinhardt/>William Dieterle 1935) ✍ ☆ ☞ ■
The Fairy Royal Family feud and their potions affect two pairs of lovers and a troup of craftsmen rehearsing a play.

Othello (>Orson Welles 1951) ✍ ☆/**(Stuart Burge 1965)** ☆ ✍
Welles and >Laurence Olivier (AAN) as the Moor manipulated into murder by Micheal MacLiammoir and Frank Finley (AAN).

Richard III (>Laurence Olivier 1955) ☆ ☞ ✍ ■
Olivier (AAN) envisages the hunchback as a melodrama villain murdering his way to the throne.

Romeo and Juliet (>George Cukor 1936) ■ ☞/**(Franco Zeffirelli 1968)** ■ ✍
>Leslie Howard and Norma Shearer and Leonard Whiting and Olivia Hussey as the star-crossed lovers.

The Taming of the Shrew (Sam Taylor 1929) ☆/**(Franco Zeffirelli 1967)** ✍ ☆ ☞
>Douglas Fairbanks and Mary Pickford and >Richard Burton and Elizabeth Taylor as the squabbling lovers.

The Tempest (Derek Jarman 1980) ■
Tale of slavery, magic and power among the castaways on a remote island.

SHAW, GEORGE BERNARD

Androcles and the Lion (Chester Erskine 1953) ☆ ✍
Ancient Roman slave Alan Young's act of kindness to a lion leads to him and Jean Simmons being spared in the arena.

Caesar and Cleopatra (Gabriel Pascal 1945) ☆ ✍
>Vivien Leigh plays a capricious Egyptian queen to Claude Rains's worldly wise Julius.

The Devil's Disciple (Guy Hamilton 1959) ✍ ☆
Vicar Burt Lancaster saves rebel >Kirk Douglas from >Laurence Olivier's hanging order during the War of Independence.

The Doctor's Dilemma (>Anthony Asquith 1959) ✍
>Alastair Sim, Robert Morely and Felix Aylmer are among the doctors Leslie Caron and Dirk Bogarde consult about his TB.

Major Barbara (Gabriel Pascal/Harold French/>David Lean 1941) ☆ ✍ ♫
Heiress Wendy Hiller rejects Rex Harrison and the Salvation Army as she believes they only wanted her for her money.

The Millionairess (>Anthony Asquith 1960) ☆
Sophia Loren falls for Indian doctor Peter Sellers.

SHE DONE HIM WRONG
(Lowell Sherman 1933) ☞ ☆

SCREWBALL COMEDY

THE AWFUL TRUTH
(>Leo McCarey 1937) ☆ ☞ ✍
(>Cary Grant and Irene Dunne can't quite get round to divorce)

YOU CAN'T TAKE IT WITH YOU
(>Frank Capra 1938) ☆ ☞ ✍
(wealthy >James Stewart's parents disapprove of common Jean Arthur)

>NINOTCHKA
(>Ernst Lubitsch 1939) ✍ ☞ ☆ ■
(Communist >Greta Garbo seduced by charms of French noble)

ON APPROVAL
(Clive Brook 1943) ☆ ✍
(trial marriage in Scottish castle proves real trial)

A TOUCH OF CLASS
(Melvin Frank 1973) ☆ ✍
(opposites attract but adultery is too much strain)

COMEDY OF ERRORS

THE GAY DIVORCEE (UK: *THE GAY DIVORCE*)
(Mark Sandrich 1934) ☆ ☞
(>Ginger Rogers mistakes author >Fred Astaire for co-respondent)

IT STARTED WITH EVE
(Henry Koster 1941) ☆ ✍
(waitress Deanna Durbin fulfils millionaire >Charles Laughton's dying wish)

TWO-FACED WOMAN
(>George Cukor 1941) ☆
(wife >Greta Garbo poses as sister and seduces own husband)

THAT NIGHT IN RIO
(Irving Cummings 1941) ☆ ✍
(Don Ameche confuses countess by impersonating the count)

AFTER HOURS
(>Martin Scorsese 1987) ☞ ☆ ✍
(yuppie gets trapped in weird New York late at night)

Saloon hostess Mae West falls for undercover vice cop >Cary Grant

COMEDY ADVENTURE

NIGHT TRAIN TO MUNICH
(>Carol Reed 1940) ☞ ⏧
(agent infiltrates Nazis to rescue inventor)

MY FAVORITE BLONDE
(Sidney Lanfield 1942) ☆ ⏧
(Bob Hope's chivalry involves him in train intrigue)

MY LEARNED FRIEND
(Basil Dearden/Will Hay 1943) ☆
(convict picks off those who sent him to prison)

I SEE A DARK STRANGER (US: *THE ADVENTURESS*)
(Frank Launder 1945) ☆ ⏧
(Irish girl spies for Nazis but loves a British soldier)

NORTH BY NORTHWEST
(>Alfred Hitchcock 1959) ☞ ☆ ⏧ ■ ♫
(businessman >Cary Grant in peril when mistaken for spy)

THE LEAGUE OF GENTLEMEN
(Basil Dearden 1960) ☞ ☆
(high-class crooks plan a bank heist)

BLACK COMEDY

A SLIGHT CASE OF MURDER
(Lloyd Bacon 1938) ☆ ⏧
(hoping to kill brewer >Edward G. Robinson, assassins kill each other)

DAYS OF WINE AND ROSES
(Blake Edwards 1962) ☆
(executive >Jack Lemmon and wife Lee Remick slide into alcoholism)

THE LOVED ONE
(Tony Richardson 1965) ⏧ ☆
(poet works in a California pet cemetery in an adaptation of Evelyn Waugh's novel)

THE STEPFATHER
(Joseph Ruben 1987) ⏧ ■
(daughter fears her mother's new husband)

THROW MOMMA FROM THE TRAIN
(Danny De Vito 1987) ☆ ⏧
(unsuspecting author finds himself in murder pact)

Pygmalion (>Anthony Asquith/>Leslie Howard 1938) ☆ ✍ ☞
Howard's professor makes a lady out of cockney flower girl Wendy Hiller.

Shoah ✍ ☞

France • Les Films Aleph/Historia Films • 1985 • 583 mins • col

d Claude Lanzmann   ph Dominique Chapuis/Jimmy Glasberg/William Lubtchansky

Claude Lanzmann spent over a decade filming these nine hours (reduced from 350) of interview and footage that stand as an enduring monument to those who died in and survived the horrors of the ghettoes and death camps. Even now, the desolate ruins of Auschwitz and Chelmno induce revulsion, as do the remorseless recollections of Polish peasants, still tainted with bitter hatred for the wealthier Jews who perished in the gas ovens and chambers. Viewing the atrocities through the eyes of Polish railwaymen, SS sentries and Blue Guard survivors, the relentless camera chronicles every agonized breakdown, moment of gleeful defiance (including the origami model of four pigs whose backsides form Hitler's face) and satisfied assertion of unrepentence, such as the Treblinka guard who boasts that no *Figuren* left alive knows the words of the marching song that prisoners chanted as they were herded into the 'washrooms of death'.

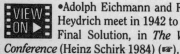 •Adolph Eichmann and Reinhard Heydrich meet in 1942 to plan the Final Solution, in *The Wannsee Conference* (Heinz Schirk 1984) (☞).
•Using the same techniques as employed on *Shoah*, Marcel Ophüls examines French collaboration with the Nazis, in *The Sorrow and the Pity* (*Le Chagrin et la Pitie*) (1971) (☞) and the crimes of the 'Butcher of Lyons' in *Hotel Terminus: The Life and Times of Klaus Barbie* (1988) (☞).
•The reasons why Bulgaria's Jews were the only ones to escape the Holocaust are considered in *The Transports of Death* (Borislav Pouncher 1986) (☞).
•Barbara Drapinska is an Auschwitz gas chamber interpreter witnessing the horrors of *The Last Stage* (*Ostatni Etap*) (Wanda Jakubowska, Poland 1948) (☆ ☞).
•>Meryl Streep won an Oscar playing a fictional survivor tormented by her father's role in the war in *Sophie's Choice* (Alan J. Pakula 1982) (☆ ✍ ■).
•Lanzmann looks at how the Jewish race have recovered from the Holocaust and are facing a new war against the Arabs, in *Israel, Why?* (Claude Lanzmann 1973) (☞).
•*Best Boy* (Ira Wohl 1979) (☞), a moving study of a handicapped man's growing independence and the sadness this brings to his less leaned-on parents won the Best Documentary (AA).
•Contemporary footage formed the basis of political protest documentaries *The Battle of Chile* (*La Batalla de Chile*) (Patricio Guzman 1977) (☞) (General Pinochet and his CIA allies overthrow Salvador Allende) and *Hearts and Minds* (Peter Davis 1974) (not only was the USA's involvement in Vietnam iniquitous, but so was the way it conducted the war).

SHOESTRING: LOW-BUDGET LOVE

Barefoot in the Park (Gene Saks 1967) ✍ ☆
>Jane Fonda and Robert Redford, forced to live in a cold-water walk-up, marry her mother (Mildred Natwick) to neighbour Charles Boyer.

The Big City (Mahanagar) (>Satyajit Ray 1963) ☞
A wife sells door-to-door because her bank clerk husband makes so little, but so enjoys her independence that she leaves him.

The Family Way (Roy Boulting 1966) ♫ ☆
This Bill Naughton script has Hywel Bennett and Hayley Mills concerned about his impotence and their poverty.

From This Day Forward (John Berry 1946) ☆
>Joan Fontaine and Mark Stevens were poor but happy in the New York slums of the Depression.

Ironweed (Hector Babenco 1988) ☆ ☞
>Jack Nicholson and >Meryl Streep are the

faithful hobos in the film adaptation of William Kennedy's Pulitzer Prize-winning novel.

Love on the Dole (John Baxter 1941) ✍ ☆

In this screen version of Walter Greenwood's novel, Deborah Kerr and Clifford Evans survive inter-war poverty in a Lancashire cotton-mill town.

The Shop on the High Street (US: The Shop on Main Street) (Obehod od na Korze) ☆ ✍ ☞

Czechoslovakia • Barrandov • 1965 • 128 mins • b/w

d Jan Kadar   w Jan Kadar/Elmar Klos
ph Vladimir Novotny
  m Zdenek Liška
Jozef Kroner, Ida Kaminská, Hana Slivková, František Zvarik

Tono (Kroner) and his dog enjoy an idyllic idleness until his brother-in-law, a petty Nazi official, makes him the 'Aryan Controller' of the button business of a selectively deaf elderly Jewish woman. Conscience prevents him exploiting the privilege of his position to cream off profit, and so Tono works as her assistant, ironically sponsored by the remainder of the Czech town's retailers. However, when the Gestapo deport the Jewish population, Tono must betray the widow (an extraordinary performance by Ida Kaminska) or shield her and face the fatal recrimination meted out to his friend Kuchar. Often very funny, Kadar and Klos's tragic tale expounds the need for a purpose in life and forcibly illustrates the dangers of sitting on the fence.

•Parallels between the Nazi occupation and the Franco-Prussian War of 1870–71 are drawn in the telling of Guy De Maupassant's tale of too-trusting prostitute Micheline Presle, in *Boule de Suif* (Christian-Jaque 1945) (✍ ☞).

•A concentration camp guard tries to protect the Jewish woman he has fallen for, in *Stars* (*Sterne*) (Konrad Wolf 1959) (✍ ☆).

•Judy Garland and Van Johnson's music store love begins as detestation, in *In the Good Old Summertime* (Robert Z. Leonard 1949) (☆ ✍).

•There is comedy in store as >The Marx Brothers prevent a major shoplift, in *The Big Store* (Charles Reisner 1941) (☆).

•A wounded partisan wonders whether his sacrifice has been worthwhile, in another Kadar and Klos occupation study *Death is Called Engelchen* (*Smrt si rika Engelchen*) (Jan Kadar 1963) (☞).

SHOPS

Business as Usual (Lezli-An Barrett 1987) ☆ ✍

Cathy Tyson is sexually harassed and Glenda Jackson is sacked from her post as manager of their Liverpudlian clothes shop for protesting.

The Devil and Miss Jones (Sam Wood 1941) ☆ ✍ ☞

Owner Charles Coburn impersonates a clerk and is persuaded by Jean Arthur to sympathize with Robert Cummings' union.

Fire Sale (Alan Arkin 1977) ✍

Arkin is the determined to run his chaotic family's store on more conventional and profitable lines.

The Little Shop of Horrors (Roger Corman 1960) ☞ ☆

The shop contains a man-eating plant with an appetite for flesh matched only by dental patient >Jack Nicholson's yen for pain.

Little Shop of Horrors (Frank Oz 1986) ✍ ✳ ☆

A puny shop boy loves an effervescent shop girl in this musical remake of the above, complete with Steve Martin as the mad dentist.

Look Up and Laugh (Basil Dean 1935) ☆

Gracie Fields rallies her fellow street-traders against the advent of a department store.

One Touch of Venus (William A. Seiter 1948) ✍

Mannequin Ava Gardner becomes enamoured of window dresser Robert Walker in S. J. Perelman and Ogden Nash's screenplay.

The Shop around the Corner (>Ernst Lubitsch 1940) ☞ ✍ ☆

Mutually repelled shop assistants >James Stewart and Margaret Sullavan are also unknowingly beloved pen pals.

>*The Shop on the High Street* (US: *The Shop on Main Street*) (*Obehod od na Korze*) (Jan Kadar 1965) ☆ ✍ ☞
Trouble in Store (John Paddy Carstairs 1953) ☆
Odd-job man Norman Wisdom's chaos arouses management fury, but such customer amusement that he is promoted.

SHORT STORIES

The Arabian Nights (aka *A Thousand and One Nights*) (*Il Fiore delle Mille e una Notte*) (>Pier Paolo Pasolini 1974) ■ ☞
Ten tales told around a prince's search for his kidnapped serving girl.
Boccaccio 70 (>Federico Fellini/>Luchino Visconti/>Vittorio De Sica 1962) ☞ ☆
Anita Ekberg, Romy Schneider and Sophia Loren respectively as a billboard model that comes to life, a wife who charges for sex and a beautiful raffle prize.
Dead of Night (Alberto Cavalcanti/Charles Crichton/Robert Hamer/Basil Dearden 1945) ☞ ☆ ✍
A troubled man's nightmares are described to a psychiatrist.
Enchantment (Irving Reis 1943) ☞ ☆ ■
In this screen version of the Rumer Godden novel *A Fugue in Time*, a house reminisces about three generations of the family that lived in it.
Encore (Pat Jackson/Anthony Pelissier/Harold French 1951) ✍
A trio of W. Somerset Maugham short stories: 'The Ant and the Grasshopper', 'Winter Cruise' and 'Gigolo and Gigolette'.
If I Had a Million (>Ernst Lubitsch/Norman Taurog/ Stephen Roberts/Norman Z. McLeod/James Cruze/William A. Seiter/H. Bruce Humberstone 1932) ☞ ☆
>W.C. Fields, >Gary Cooper and >Charles Laughton are among those inheriting when a millionaire makes his will from a phone book.
Immoral Tales (*Contes Immoraux*) (Walerian Borowczyk 1974) ☞
These tales of sexual awakening include Baroness Bathory's lesbian vampirism and Lucretia Borgia's papal incest.

Sim, Alastair
British actor (1900–1976)

A modest academic with mournful eyes and a gentle Scottish accent, Alastair Sim, who worked exclusively in Britain, was one of the greatest of screen comic actors. Increasing in competence, he rose through the ranks of Scotland Yard from sergeant in *Inspector Hornleigh* (Eugene Forde 1930) (☆) (Sim's Bingham and Gordon Harker's inspector recover the Chancellor of the Exchequer's dispatch case) to inspector in *Green for Danger* (Sidney Gilliat 1946) (☆ ✍) (Cockrill of the Yard tracks the perpetrators of hospital operating-table killings) and *An Inspector Calls* (Guy Hamilton 1954) (☆ ✍) (J. B. Priestley's play has Sim proving that members of a 1912 Yorkshire family were indirectly responsible for a murder). However, his most popular authority figures were school heads: a master in *The Happiest Days of Your Life* (Frank Launder 1950) (☆ ✍) (Margaret Rutherford's girls' school is forced upon Sim's boy's school by a mistaken evacuation order) and a mistress, *The Belles of St Trinian's* (Frank Launder 1954) (✳ ☆ ✍) (Sim's Miss Fritton shelters her crooked bookie brother Clarence [also Sim], while her girls conceal a prize race horse). The seminal miser in *Scrooge* (Brian Desmond Hurst 1951) (☆ ✍ ☞) (the ghosts of Christmas Past, Present and Future mellow Sim into the seasonal mood in >Charles Dickens's *A Christmas Carol*), he also portrayed a gallery of bumbling or rascally eccentrics: *Laughter in Paradise* (Mario Zampi 1951) (☆ ✍) (Sim is a member of a family who must commit crimes to come into a share of an inheritance); *Innocents in Paris* (Gordon Parry 1953) (☆ ✍) (Sim and Margaret Rutherford as naïve English tourists having cultural problems on a weekend trip); *The Green Man* (Robert Day 1956) (☆ ✍) (vacuum cleaner salesman George Cole frustrates Sim's attempts to assassinate politician Raymond Huntley); *School for Scoundrels* (Robert Hamer 1960) (☆ ✍) (Sim as Stephen Potter showing Ian Carmichael how to be one-up on bounderish Terry-Thomas); and *The Ruling Class* (Peter Medak 1971) (☆) (Sim is the bishop called in by a noble family when son Peter O'Toole [AAN] becomes convinced he is God).

 •*A Fire Has Been Arranged* (Leslie Hiscott 1935) (☆): Sim and fellow crooks Bud Flanagan and Chesney Allen find a building over their loot stash.

•*This Man is News* (David MacDonald 1938) (☆ ✍): Sim as a newspaper editor losing a jewel theft scoop to journalists Barry K. Barnes and Valerie Hobson.

•*Inspector Hornleigh Goes to It* (US: *Mail Train*) (Walter Forde 1941) (☆ ✍): Sim and Gordon Harker follow the clues to unlikely Nazi traitor Phyllis Calvert.

•*Cottage to Let* (US: *Bombsight Stolen*) (>Anthony Asquith 1941) (☞ ☆): Nazi agent John Mills is prevented from kidnapping inventor Sim by evacuee Leslie Banks.

•*Hue and Cry* (Charles Crichton 1946) (☆ ✍): Sim writes adventure stories for London boy Harry Fowler's newspaper which is used as a grapevine by a gang of villains.

•*Stage Fright* (>Alfred Hitchcock 1950) (☞ ✍): Sim investigates the theatre murder that Richard Todd tries to pin on actress >Marlene Dietrich.

•*Folly to be Wise* (Frank Launder 1952) (☆): Sim is exceptional as an incompetent entertainments officer, who arranges a brains' trust to enlighten National Service squaddies.

•*Blue Murder at St Trinian's* (Frank Launder 1957) (☆ ✍): Sim leads the ghoulish girls in the pursuit of jewel thieves after they win a cultural holiday to Rome.

•*The Doctor's Dilemma* (>Anthony Asquith 1959) (✍): the >George Bernard Shaw play has Sim as one of the Harley Street doctors consulted over artist Dirk Bogarde's TB.

•*Left, Right and Centre* (Sidney Gilliat 1959) (✍ ☆): Sim plays the ennobled uncle of Ian Carmichael, whose Tory election candidate is in love with his socialist opponent, Patricia Bredin.

Singin' in the Rain ♫ ☆ ✍ ☞ ■
USA • MGM • 1952 • 102 mins • col
d >Gene Kelly/>Stanley Donen w Adoph Green/Betty Comden
ph Harold Rossen m/ly Nacio Herb Brown/Arthur Freed
Gene Kelly, Donald O'Connor, Debbie Reynolds, Millard Mitchell, Jean Hagen, Rita Moreno, Cyd Charisse, Douglas Fowley

Vaudeville songster Don Lockwood (Kelly) has become a matinee idol co-starring in a series of silent romances with vain Lina Lamont (Hagen). However, the Talkies threaten their careers, as Lina's voice – the moll-squeak speak Judy Holiday used in >*Born Yesterday* (>George Cukor 1950) (☆ ✍ ☞) – contradicts her sophisticated screen image. Lockwood's suggestion that his girlfriend Kathy Selden (Reynolds) should dub Lamont's lines proves a successful but unsatisfactory solution. Kelly and Donen's dual direction puts real zest into this marvellous entertainment, particularly the legendary *Singin' in the Rain* sequence and O'Connor's phenomenal *Make 'em Laugh* routine. The film's funniest aspect, however, is the fact that Reynolds' songs were actually performed by Betty Noyes and that Lina's dubbed lines weren't Reynolds either, but Hagen herself.

 •Red Skelton's hilarious failures as a melodrama extra turn him into a silent slapstick star in *Merton of the Movies* (Robert Alton 1947) (✍ ☆), while Bourvil ruins ham actor Louis Jouvet's show, in *Miquette* (Henri-Georges Clouzot 1950) (☞ ☆).

•Rudolph Nureyev plays the legendary matinee idol in *Valentino* (Ken Russell 1977) (☞ ☆).

•>James Cagney believes the coming of the silents will harm his theatre company, so he moves with the times and pioneers cine-variety, in *Footlight Parade* (Lloyd Bacon 1933) (☆ ■ ♫).

•Vaudeville comics Ole Olsen and Chic Johnson turn their hit show into a movie, in *Hellzapoppin'* (H. C. Potter 1942) (✍).

•Don Ameche finds it difficult to adapt to Talkies after successfully producing silent slapsticks, in *Hollywood Cavalcade* (Irving Cummings 1939) (☆).

•Making modern movies proves no easier as >*Marcello Mastroianni* discovers in >*8½ (Otto e Mezzo)* (>Federico Fellini 1963) (☞ ☆ ✍ ☞).

SINGLE PARENTS

Alice Doesn't Live Here Anymore (>Martin Scorsese 1974) ☞ ☆
Ellen Burstyn takes her 12-year-old son Alfred Lutter with her as she heads to Monterey to become a singing star.

Bachelor Mother (Garson Kanin 1939) ☆ ☞ ✍
>Ginger Rogers finds a baby and shop boss Charles Coburn's son David Niven is presumed to be the father.

Dear John (*Kare John*) (Lars Magnus Lindgren, Sweden 1964) ☆
Waitress Christina Schollin and sailor Jarl Kulle skirt around commitment as they've been hurt before.

Johnny Belinda (Jean Negulesco 1948) ☆ ✍
Deaf-mute Jane Wyman is raped and has to suffer small town accusations when she has a son.

Kramer versus Kramer (Robert Benton 1979) ☆
>Dustin Hoffman and >Meryl Streep fight a court battle for the right to be the single parent of Justin Henry.

The Miracle of Morgan's Creek (>Preston Sturges 1943) ☞ ✍ ☆
Betty Hutton has quadruplets, convinces gormless suitor Eddie Bracken that he is the father and the events become national news.

Shenandoah (Andrew V. McLaglen 1965) ☆
Widowed farmer >James Stewart, father of six, is forced to abandon his neutrality in the US Civil War when his eldest son is kidnapped.

An Unmarried Woman (Paul Mazursky 1977) ☆ ☞
This AAN Best Picture has Jill Clayburgh feud with her daughter over her affairs with Alan Bates and Michael Murphy.

SISTERS

The Dolly Sisters (Irving Cummings 1945) ✍
Betty Grable and June Haver as a Hungarian immigrant vaudeville act.

Hannah and Her Sisters (>Woody Allen 1986) ☆ ☞
The complex lives and loves of Mia Farrow, Barbara Hershey and Dianne Wiest.

Music for Millions (Henry Koster 1944) ☆
Margaret O'Brien helps pregnant June Allyson's career by becoming the darling of a symphony orchestra.

Orphans of the Storm (>D. W. Griffith 1921) ☞ ☆ ■
The sisters Gish, Lillian and Dorothy, are in danger in French Revolutionary Paris.

Sisters or The Balance of Happiness (*Schwestern oder die Balance des Glücks*) (>Margarethe Von Trotta 1979) ☞ ☆
When fragile, introspective Gudrun Gabriel can no longer bear her dependency on her sister Jutta Lampe, she kills herself.

The Sisters (Anatole Litvak 1938) ☆ ✍
The troubles of >Bette Davis, Anita Louise and Jane Bryan culminate in the 1906 San Francisco earthquake.

The Strange Affair of Uncle Harry (aka *Uncle Harry*) (Robert Siodmak 1945) ☞ ☆ ✍
George Sanders' sisters Sara Allgood and Geraldine Fitzgerald use their wiles to thwart his romance with small town newcomer Ella Raines.

Storm Warning (Stuart Heisler 1951) ☆ ✍
>Ginger Rogers consoles Doris Day as the latter's husband Steve Cochran is a Deep South Ku Klux Klan racist.

The Three Sisters (>Laurence Olivier 1970) ☞ ☆ ■
Anton Chekhov play has Olivier's doctor bewildered by his sisters' desire to abandon the country for city life.

Three Smart Girls (Henry Koster 1936) ☆
Deanna Durbin, Barbara Read and Nan Grey patch up their parents' marriage.

Three Smart Girls Grow Up (Henry Koster 1939) ☆
Deanna Durbin matchmakes for sisters Nan Grey and, this time, Helen Parrish.

Toys in the Attic (**George Roy Hill 1963**) ☆

In Lillian Hellman's play, Geraldine Page and Wendy Hiller's love for brother Dean Martin borders on the incestuous.

SKELETONS IN THE CLOSET

Ada (**Daniel Mann 1961**) ✍

As election time approaches, it emerges that candidate Dean Martin's wife Susan Hayward is a former prostitute.

Among the Living (**Stuart Heisler 1941**) ☆ ✍

Albert Dekker is unjustly accused of murder because he is ashamed of his insane twin brother.

The Assassin (**US:** *The Ladykiller of Rome*) (*L'Assassino*) (**Elio Petri 1961**) ☆

Suave >Marcello Mastroianni's true nature emerges as he suffers the pressures of a false murder accusation.

Bad Day at Black Rock (**John Sturges 1954**) ☆ ✍ ☞

One-armed >Spencer Tracy (AAN) uncovers a small town's persecution of an immigrant Japanese farmer.

Confidential Report (**aka** *Mr Arkadin*) (**>Orson Welles 1955**) ☆ ☞

Welles feigns amnesia while bumping off the people who know how he came into his ill-gotten fortune.

The House of the Angel (**US:** *End of Innocence*) (*La Casa del Angel*) (**Leopoldo Torre-Nilsson 1957**) ☆

Elsa Daniel's strict Argentinian Catholic family victimize her for the tragic failure of her first love affair.

Laburnum Grove (**>Carol Reed 1936**) ☞ ✍

This J. B. Priestley play has respectable father Cedric Hardwicke announcing he is a forger.

The Red House (**Delmer Daves 1947**) ☆

Farmer >Edward G. Robinson is obsessed with the cottage where he murdered his parents.

>Ten Rillington Place (**Richard Fleischer 1970**) ☆ ☞ ✍

SLAVERY

Cobra Verde (**>Werner Herzog 1988**) ☞ ▦

Klaus Kinski as a slaver having to face up to the abolition of the trade.

The King and I (**Walter Lang 1956**) ☆ ♫ ✍

A performance of Harriet Beecher Stowe's *Uncle Tom's Cabin* is used to persuade Yul Brynner to free his prospective bride.

The Last Supper (*La Ultima Cena*) (**Tomás Gutiérrez Alea 1976**) ✍

A Cuban slave owner executes 11 of the dozen he selects to play the apostles to his Christ in a Maundy Thursday play.

Mandingo (**Richard Fleischer 1975**) ✍

Slave breeder James Mason's daughter Susan George is obsessed with Perry King.

>The Mission (**Roland Joffé 1986**) ✍ ▦ ☆ ☞ ♫

Sansho the Bailiff (*Sansho Dayu*) (**>Kenji Mizoguchi 1954**) ☞ ▦ ✍

Noble children are kidnapped and sold to a slaver, but years later, the son escapes his brutality and returns to his mother, now crippled and blind.

Seven Angry Men (**Charles Marquis Warren 1954**) ☆

Raymond Massey as the 19th-century outlaw and slave liberator John Brown.

Slave Ship (**Tay Garnett 1937**) ☆

Wallace Beery leads a mutiny against Warner Baxter when the latter refuses to continue slave trading.

Sleuth ✍ ☆ ☞

GB • Palomar • 1972 • 139 mins • col
d >Joseph L. Mankiewicz w Anthony Shaffer ph Oswald Morris m John Addison
>Laurence Olivier, >Michael Caine

Thriller writer Andrew Wyke (Olivier) invites Milo Tindle (Caine) to his elaborate home to exact revenge for his cuckolding. Humiliated and terrorized by a string of sinister and bizarre hoaxes, Milo pleads for mercy only to be shot. Wyke is glorying in his execution of the perfect murder, when an inspector calls. The tense screen adaptation of Anthony Shaffer's play might lack the technical excitement of a theatre production, but the sets, like those in >*The Cabinet of Dr Caligari* (Robert Wiene 1919) (☞ ■ ✍ ☆), are mesmerizing, and Olivier and Caine turn in splendidly flamboyant performances, gaining *Sleuth* the distinction of being the only film in Oscar history to have the entire cast nominated for the Best Actor award.

•Playwright Jean-Pierre Kalfon has Jane Birkin and Geraldine Chaplin put on a private performance of his play, in *Love on the Ground* (*L'Amour par Terre*)(Jacques Rivette 1984) (☆).
•Two's company for Japanese and American Pacific War castaways Lee Marvin and Toshiro Mifune in *Hell in the Pacific* (John Boorman 1968) (☆), cursing captain >Humphrey Bogart and crusty missionary >Katharine Hepburn, in >*The African Queen* (>John Huston 1951) (☆ ☞ ✍) and >Marilyn Monroe and lustful neighbour Tom Ewell in *The Seven Year Itch* (>Billy Wilder 1955) (☆ ☞ ✍).

SMALL TOWN

Ah, Wilderness **(Clarence Brown 1935)** ☆
Uncle Wallace Beery and father Lionel Barrymore help Eric Linden through adolescence, in this screen version of the Eugene O'Neill play.

All My Good Countrymen **(US: *All Good Citizens*) (*Všichni Dobrí Radací*) (Vojtech Jasny 1968)** ☞
Cannes Best Director-winning study of the effects that the deaths of three prominent inhabitants have on a Moldavian town.

Harvest **(*Regain*) (Marcel Pagnol 1937)** ☞ ■ ✍
Poacher Gabriel Gabrio and waif Orane Demazis rejuvenate the ghost town where they live together.

The Human Comedy **(Clarence Brown 1943)** ☞
Telegram boy Mickey Rooney (AAN) has to deliver news from the front to anxious GI families.

King's Row **(Sam Wood 1941)** ☆ ☞ ✍
Mysterious deaths and insanity forge the friendship between Robert Cummings, Ronald Reagan and Ann Sheridan.

The Long Hot Summer **(Martin Ritt 1958)** ☆
Farmer >Paul Newman feuds with Mississippi town bigwig >Orson Welles.

The Music Man **(Morton Da Costa 1962)** ♫ ☆
Con man Robert Preston impersonates a music professor, but still manages to transform the town's brass band, in this AAN picture.

Near Dark **(Kathryn Bigelow 1937)** ☞
A farmhand is caught up with a vanload of vampires, one of whom is a US Civil War veteran.

Our Town **(Sam Wood 1940)** ✍
AAN Best Picture tells of the everyday life of honest New Hampshire folks, from Thornton Wilder's classic play.

Peyton Place **(Mark Robson 1957)** ✍
Lana Turner, Arthur Kennedy, Hope Lange, Russ Tamblyn, Diane Varsi,the director and the film itself were all AAN for this simmering look at life in New England.

Picnic **(Joshua Logan 1956)** ✍ ☞
AAN Best Picture has drifter William Holden breaking down a town's conventionalism, but still insisting that Kim Novak marries him.

Promised Land **(Michael Hoffman 1988)** ☆
Sports star Jason Gedrick is now a no-hope cop faced with arresting the college-bullying butt Keifer Sutherland and his girlfriend Meg Ryan.

Sweet Hearts Dance **(Robert Greenwald 1988)** ☆
Bored Vermont builder Don Johnson abandons Susan Sarandon and old friend Jeff Daniels mediates.

Smith, Maggie
British actress (b 1934)
Although restricted by National Theatre commitments, Maggie Smith's screen appearances in the 1960s demonstrated considerable talent for dramatic roles: *The Pumpkin Eater* (Jack Clayton 1964) (✍ ☆) (as Philpot repaying mother of eight Anne Bancroft's kindness by sleeping with her husband Peter Finch, in the screen version of Penelope Mortimer's novel); *Othello* (AAN: Stuart Burge 1966) (☆ ✍) (as Desdemona, victim of Frank Finlay's Iago

vengeance on >Laurence Olivier's jealous Moor); and *The Prime of Miss Jean Brodie* (AA: Ronald Neame 1969) (☆ ✍) (as the Edinburgh girls' school teacher pursued by masters Robert Stephens and Gordon Jackson). Her appearances in *The VIPs* (>Anthony Asquith 1963) (☆) (as the prudish secretary Miss Mead loyally supporting troubled businessman Rod Taylor) and *Hot Millions* (Eric Till 1968) (☆ ✍) (con man Peter Ustinov and secretary Maggie confuse Karl Malden and his computer and make a fortune from fake companies) testified to her capacity for comedy. This has since been channelled into her characteristic snobbish woman whose dignity is underminded by anxiety: *Love and Pain and the Whole Damn Thing* (Alan J. Pakula 1972) (☆) (recuperating Timothy Bottoms falls for fatally ill older woman Smith); *California Suite* (AA: Herbert Ross 1978) (☆ ✍) (>Michael Caine puts up with actress Maggie's fussing as she prepares for the Oscar ceremony); *A Private Function* (Malcolm Mowbray 1985) (✍ ☆) (BAFTA Best Actress winner as chiropodist Michael Palin's wife helping him hide a stolen pig that was destined for a 1947 royal wedding dinner); >*A Room with a View* (James Ivory 1986); and *The Lonely Passion of Judith Hearne* (Jack Clayton 1988) (☆ ✍) (this film adaptation of Brian Moore's novel has dowdy music teacher Smith drinking to excess, having interpreted Bob Hoskins's friendship as love).

VIEW ON ▶ •*Young Cassidy* (Jack Cardiff/ >John Ford 1965) (☆ ✍ ☞): as playwright Rod Taylor's devoted girlfriend in a *film à clef* of Sean O'Casey's early life.

•*The Honey Pot* (>Joseph L. Mankiewicz 1967) (☆): secretary Smith discovers that Rex Harrison is defrauding his lovers by pretending to be fatally ill.

•*Oh! What a Lovely War* (>Richard Attenborough 1969) (♫ ☞ ■ ☆): as a music hall star talking men into showing their manhood by volunteering to fight in the First World War.

•*Travels with My Aunt* (AAN: >George Cukor 1972) (✍ ☞): as >Graham Greene's eccentric Aunt Augusta enlivening accountant Alec McCowen's European holiday.

•*Death on the Nile* (John Guillermin 1978) (✍ ■ ☆): as one of the passengers under suspicion in the all-star >Agatha Christie whodunnit.

•*Evil under the Sun* (Guy Hamilton 1982) (☆ ✍): Peter Ustinov's Hercule Poirot investigates the murder of a film star at Smith's hotel, in this Agatha Christie mystery.

•*The Missionary* (Richard Loncraine 1982) (☆ ✍): Smith's Lady Ames despairs of Michael Palin, the worthy vicar she loves who becomes a pimp in the East End.

SMUGGLERS

Ask a Policeman (Marcel Varnel 1938) ☆ ✍
Incompetent cops Will Hay, Moore Marriott and Graham Moffatt see through a ghostly horseman routine.

Brandy for the Parson (John Eldridge 1951) ✍
Sailing holidaymakers Kenneth More and Jean Lodge are unaware they are running liquor.

Calcutta (John Farrow 1946) ☆
Alan Ladd and William Bendix track down Casbah jewel smugglers.

Dr Syn (Roy William Neill 1937) ☆ ☞
George Arliss as the 18th-century vicar who divides his time between pulpit and beach caves.

Frenchman's Creek (Mitchell Leisen 1944) ✍ ☆
>Daphne Du Maurier tale of 17th-century Cornwall has >Joan Fontaine leaving bullying husband >Basil Rathbone for a smuggler.

I Walk Alone (Byron Haskin 1948) ☆
Burt Lancaster wants revenge on >Kirk Douglas for betraying his smuggling ring and stealing Lizabeth Scott.

Jamaica Inn (>Alfred Hitchcock 1939) ✍ ☆ ☞
Orphan Maureen O'Hara is adopted by Regency Cornish smuggler >Charles Laughton, in this screen version of >Daphne Du Maurier's novel.

The Man Within (US: The Smugglers) (Bernard Knowles 1947) ✍ ☆
>Richard Attenborough discovers that his guardian, Michael Redgrave is a smuggler, in the film adaptation of >Graham Greene's novel.

Mollenard (US: *Hatred*) (Robert Slodmak 1937) ☞
An arms smuggler finds his comfort in the arms of prostitutes in Shanghai.
Moonfleet (>Fritz Lang 1955) ☞ ■
An orphan finds that his guardian Stewart Granger is a smuggler off the coast of 18th-century Dorset.
No Man's Land (Alain Tanner 1987) ☞
Four strangers grow closer while smuggling merchandise from France into Switzerland.

Snow White and the Seven Dwarfs ☞ ■ ✍♫
USA • Walt Disney • 1937 • 82 mins • col
d David Hand   w Ted Sears/Otto
Englander/Earl Hurd/Dorothy Ann
Blank/Richard Creedon/Dick
Richard/Merrill De Maris/Webb Smith
m Frank Churchill/Leigh Harline/Paul
Smith songs Larry Morey/Frank Churchill

The Brothers Grimm story that revolutionized animation and nearly bankrupted Walt Disney in the making has delighted audiences ever since. Snow White, a servant at the castle of the Wicked Queen, has her life put in jeopardy by the Mirror on the Wall's persistent assertion that she is the fairest of them all. Finding the Seven Dwarfs' cottage deep in the forest, she gains their affection and protection, but they are working their mine when the Queen, disguised as a frighteningly hideous hag, discovers her whereabouts. Forget the biblical significance of the magic apple and the Freudian implications of Snow White's relationship with the Dwarfs. Just sit back and enjoy the fabulous fairytale world and some of the best songs Disney ever produced.

•A small boy is taken on a journey through the holes in time by six roguish dwarfs in *Time Bandits* (Terry Gilliam 1981) (✍ ✳ ☆).
•David Bennent stopped growing through an act of will, in the screen adaptation of Günter Grass' novel *The Tin Drum* (*Die Blechtrommel*) (>Volker Schlöndorff 1979) (☞ ☆).
•The Snow White story was twice made by

director >Howard Hawks and cinematographer Gregg Toland in *Ball of Fire* (1942) (☞ ☆ ■) (striptease >Barbara Stanwyck is sheltered by >Gary Cooper's household of lexicographers) and *A Song is Born* (1948) (■ ☞) (gangster's moll Virginia Mayo transforms the lives of musicologist Danny Kaye and his colleagues).
•Governess Julie Andrews arrives to bring love back to David Tomlinson's family, in *Mary Poppins* (Robert Stevenson 1964) (☆ ☞♫ ✳), while aunt Christine Lahti's eccentricities meet with a mixed reception, in *Housekeeping* (Bill Forsyth 1987) (☆ ☞).

Some Like It Hot ☆ ✍ ☞ ■♫
USA • United Artists/Mirisch • 1959 • 122 mins • b/w
d >Billy Wilder   w Billy Wilder/I. A. L.
Diamond   ph Charles Lang   m Adolphe
Deutsch
>Jack Lemmon, Tony Curtis, >Marilyn
Monroe, Joe E. Brown, George Raft, Pat
O'Brien

Unemployed musicians Jerry (Lemmon) and Joe (Curtis), forced to leave town after witnessing the St Valentine's Day Massacre, join an all-girl band. By the time the now Daphne and Josephine arrive for a season at a seaside hotel, Joe is in love with Sugar Kane (an utterly bewitching Monroe), the band's singer, while Daphne soon becomes the target of millionaire Osgood Fielding III (Brown). Jerry agrees to keep Osgood occupied while Joe, posing as a frigid millionaire, complete with >Cary Grant accent ('Nobody talks like that!') seduces or rather is, seduced by Sugar on board Osgood's yacht. It's then that Spats Columbo (Raft), the boss behind the garage murder, arrives at the hotel for a mobster's conference. This dynamic comedy of sexual duplicity and tolerance somehow entirely skirts tastelessness and cliché and is Wilder and Diamond's undoubted masterpiece.

•>Dustin Hoffman and Anthony Sher, respectively, turn to transvestism, one for a career move, the other through sexual preference, in *Tootsie*

(Sydney Pollack 1982) (☆) and *Shadey* (Philip Savile 1985) (☆).

•Drag queen Harvey Fierstein and gay lover Matthew Broderick adopt a son, much to the disgust of Jewish mother Anne Bancroft, in *Torch Song Trilogy* (Paul Bogart 1988) (✍ ☆ ♫).

•>Katharine Hepburn is a woman masquerading as a man, in *Sylvia Scarlett* (>George Cukor 1935) (☞ ☆), while >Greta Garbo dressed androgynously as Sweden's 17th-century monarch, in *Queen Christina* (Rouben Mamoulian 1933) (☆ ☞).

•Helen Slater and Melanie Mayron are the poor musicians handed a package containing a million dollars, in *Sticky Fingers* (Caitlin Adams 1988) (☆ ☞).

•Manicurist >Carole Lombard has set her heart on a millionaire and gets Fred MacMurray, in *Hands across the Table* (Mitchell Leisen 1935) (☆ ✍ ☞).

SONGWRITERS

Alexander's Ragtime Band (Henry King 1938) ♫ ✍

This AAN Best Picture has Don Ameche and Tyrone Power both inspired by Alice Faye.

The Buddy Holly Story (Steve Rash 1978) ♫ ☆

Gary Busey (AAN) as the hugely influential rock 'n' roll singer from Lubbock, Texas.

Deep in My Heart (>Stanley Donen 1954) ☆

Jose Ferrer's Sigmund Romberg is guided to fame by Paul Henreid and Merle Oberon.

Dixie (A. Edward Sutherland 1943) ☆

Bing Crosby as the 19th-century minstrel and songster Dan Emmett.

The Great Victor Herbert (Andrew L. Stone 1939) ☆

Biofic of composer who guards over the marriage of his two feuding stars.

Irish Eyes are Smiling (Gregory Ratoff 1944) ♫

Dick Haymes as *belle époque* tunesmith Ernest B. Ball.

Night and Day (>Michael Curtiz 1946) ☆ ☞ ♫

>Cary Grant in a factional biopic of Cole Porter.

Rhapsody in Blue (Irving Rapper 1945) ♫

Robert Alda as George Gershwin, with Herbert Rudley as his lyricist brother Ira.

St Louis Blues (Allen Reisner 1958) ♫

Nat King Cole as preacher's son and blues maestro W. C. Handy.

Swannee River (Sidney Lanfield 1939) ♫ ☆

Don Ameche as Deep South songsmith Stephen Foster.

Till Clouds Roll By (Richard Whorf 1946) ♫

Robert Walker as Jerome Kern with all-star cast singing his songs; Judy Garland's number was directed by her husband, >Vincente Minnelli.

Words and Music (Norman Taurog 1948) ☞ ☆ ♫

Tom Drake as Richard Rodgers and Mickey Rooney as Lorenz Hart.

SPANISH CIVIL WAR

The Angel Wore Red (Nunnally Johnson 1960) ☆

Prostitute Ava Gardner is driven into the arms of priest Dirk Bogarde.

Blockade (>William Dieterle 1938) ☆ ☞ ✍

Farmer >Henry Fonda's pacifism goes to the wall as his land is threatened.

The Confidential Agent (Herman Shumlin 1945) ✍ ☆

On a munitions mission to England, Charles Boyer falls for arms dealer's daughter Lauren Bacall, in this >Graham Greene tale.

Cousin Angelica (La Prima Angelica) (Carlos Saura 1978) ☞

A man returns to Segovia to discover childhood sweetheart has married a Fascist they mutually detested during the war.

The Fallen Sparrow (Richard Wallace 1943) ☆

John Garfield survives the war only to be pursued to New York by the Nazis for the secret he has kept through two years in jail.

For Whom the Bell Tolls (Sam Wood 1943) ☞ ☆

>Gary Cooper helps >Ingrid Bergman's parti-

sans blow up a bridge, but is fatally wounded in the attempt.

Man's Hope (US: *Days of Hope*) (*Espoir*) (aka *Sierra de Teruel*) (André Malraux 1939) ✍

Partisans overcome all odds to detonate a bridge.

Spielberg, Steven

American writer/producer/director (b 1947)

If not a *Wunderkind*, then certainly a creator of wonder in kids (of all ages). If not artistically acclaimed (witness no Oscars – yet!), unprecedentally commercially vindicated. If directing standards have declined from *Jaws* (1975) (✍ ☞) (a killer shark terrorizes a seaside resort) and >*E.T. – The Extra Terrestrial* (1982) (✳ ✍ ■ ☆ ☞) to *Indiana Jones and the Temple of Doom* (1984) (☆) (>Harrison Ford and Kate Capshaw go in search of a sacred stone, in a prequel to *Raiders*) and *The Color Purple* (1986) (✍) (Whoopi Goldberg makes the best of her hard life in this screen adaptation of Alice Walker's novel), his habit of executive producing others' films (notably those of Joe Dante and Robert Zemeckis) in the manner of an itinerant rock star guesting on albums has linked him with some of the biggest-ever grossers (in both senses of the word), including *Gremlins* (Joe Dante 1984) (✳) (cute little creatures go berserk when wet) and *Back to the Future* (Robert Zemeckis 1986) (✍ ☆) (Michael J. Fox goes back in time and transforms his parents' lives by making his father Crispin Glover stand up to a school bully). If he can convince the public that what he makes is what they want to see, whether it is special-effects remakes – *Raiders of the Lost Ark* (1981) (☆ ☞) (>Harrison Ford prevents the Nazis getting hold of the Ark that contained the Ten Commandments) closely resembles *Pimpernel Smith* (US: *Mr V*; *The Fighting Pimpernel*) (>Leslie Howard 1941) (✍ ☆) (archaeologist Howard rescues refugees from the Nazis) and *Innerspace* (Joe Dante 1988) (☆ ✳) (Dennis Quaid is injected into the bloodstream of supermarket assistant Martin Short vividly recalls *Fantastic Voyage* (Richard Fleischer 1966) (☆ ✳) (a minisub containing Stephen Boyd and Raquel Welch is injected into a man's body to perform intricate surgery) – or action adventures such as *Empire of the Sun* (1988) (■) (a boy is befriended by black marketeers in a Japanese PoW camp), then the one-idea man will continue to rule the kingdom of the bland.

•*Duel* (1974) (☞): travelling salesman Dennis Weaver looks in his mirror and sees that a petrol tanker is still following him.

•*Sugarland Express* (1974) (☆ ☞): Goldie Hawn and Ben Johnson cause untold chaos while trying to prevent their child being taken from them.

•*Close Encounters of the Third Kind* (1977) (☆♫✳): Richard Dreyfuss locates aliens' landing site and they offer to take him with them; a 'special edition' was released in 1980.

•*1941* (1979): Dan Aykroyd and John Belushi respond to Pearl Harbour by smashing up their air base.

•*The Blues Brothers* (John Landis 1980) (☆ ♫): Spielberg as the tax clerk who receives the money that Dan Aykroyd and John Belushi have raised to save an orphanage.

•*Indiana Jones and the Last Crusade* (1989) (☆): >Harrison Ford and father >Sean Connery succeed where the Knights of the Round Table failed, by locating the Holy Grail.

Stagecoach ☞ ☆ ■ ✍

USA • United Artists • 1939 • 99 mins • b/w
d >John Ford w Dudley Nichols ph Bert Glennon/Ray Binger m Richard Hageman & others
>John Wayne, Claire Trevor, Thomas Mitchell, George Bancroft, John Carradine, Berton Churchill, Donald Meek, Andy Devine

The Western that set the standards others couldn't reach, John Ford's first venture in Monument Valley, Utah established a genre tradition with virtually every scene (including, regrettably, the racism and sexism). The lowlifers – the outlaw (Wayne), tart with a heart (Trevor), gambler (Carradine) and whisky doctor (Mitchell) – redeem themselves through various degrees of heroism, while the respectable banker, salesman, and society woman prove indolent or corrupt. There is an Indian raid (with Indian Yakima Canutt chasing himself, as he was also Wayne's stunt double), a shootout, a romance and a domestic crisis in the shape of a birth in the wilderness. The clashes of personality within the confines of the coach are fascinating, suggesting an amendment to the conclusion of Jean-Paul Sartre's *Huis Clos* – hell is only *certain* other people.

 •Another stagecoach sees halfcaste >Paul Newman despised by fellow-travellers until he foils a hold-up, in *Hombre* (Martin Ritt 1967) (☆).

•John Mills keeps up his submarine crew's spirits in another claustrophobic crisis *Morning Departure* (US: *Operation Disaster*) (Roy Baker 1950) (☆).

•>James Cagney is the bad guy who has a decent streak, in *Angels with Dirty Faces* (>Michael Curtiz 1938) (☆ ☞ ✍).

•>Marlene Dietrich is the heart-of-gold whore helping >James Stewart clean up the town in *Destry Rides Again* (George Marshall 1939) (☆ ✍).

•A prostitute, a priest, a beautiful mute, a trader and a man of fortune are forced to rely on one another on a trek through the South American jungle, in *Evil Eden* (*La Mort en ce Jardin*) (>Luis Buñuel 1956) (☞ ✍).

Stanwyck, Barbara
(Ruby Stevens) American actress (b 1907)
Orphaned at five, Stanwyck took the succession of menial and chorus jobs that undoubtedly developed the feisty, throaty determination that characterized her dramatic and comic performances alike. Her versatility was almost boundless: WIFE in *The Locked Door* (George Fitzmaurice 1929) (☆) (Stanwyck and her husband each believe the other guilty of murder and try to prove their innocence) and *Illicit* (Archie Mayo 1931) (☆) (Stanwyck leaves her husband because she's neglected); BAD GIRL REDEEMED in *Ladies of Leisure* (>Frank Capra 1930) (☞) (gold-digger Barbara's conscience attack causes her to free a reluctant lover) and *Remember the Night* (Mitchell Leisen 1940)

(☆ ✍) (>Preston Sturges' script has lawyer Fred MacMurray offering Barbara a family Christmas); and WESTERN HEROINE (which she reprised in TV's *The Big Valley*) in *Annie Oakley* (>George Stevens 1935) (☆ ☞) (circus sharpshooter Preston Foster is matched by country girl Barbara) and *Union Pacific* (Cecil B. De Mille 1939) (☞ ☆ ✍) (Stanwyck urges Joel McCrea to ignore threats and disasters and build his railroad). However, she had three specialities: SCREWBALL COMEDIENNE: *Breakfast for Two* (Alfred Santell 1937) (☆) (Barbara rids playboy Herbert Marshall of gold-digging Glenda Farrell and teaches him responsibility),*The Lady Eve* (>Preston Sturges 1941) (✍ ☞ ☆) (Barbara determines to take revenge against >Henry Fonda for seeing through her cardsharping con) and *Ball of Fire* (AAN: >Howard Hawks 1942) (☞ ☆ ■) (stripteaser Barbara transforms lexicographer >Gary Cooper); WOMEN'S PICTURE VICTIM: *The Bitter Tea of General Yen* (>Frank Capra 1932) (☆) (missionary's fiancée Stanwyck falls for Chinese kidnapper Nils Asther), *Stella Dallas* (AAN: >King Vidor 1937) (☆ ☞ ✍) (Stanwyck's slovenliness loses her her husband John Boles and sparks a feud with daughter Anne Shirley) and *The Great Man's Lady* (>William Wellman 1942) (☞ ☆) (Stanwyck instils her ambition to strike oil into husband Joel McCrea) and FILM NOIR: *Double Indemnity* (>Billy Wilder 1944) (☞ ☆ ✍) (Stanwyck persuades lover Fred MacMurray to murder her husband with promises of insurance-funded happy-ever-afters) and *Sorry Wrong Number* (AAN: Anatole Litvak 1948) (☆ ✍ ☞) (bed-ridden Stanwyck overhears husband Burt Lancaster's plot to kill her and phones desperately for help).

 •*Night Nurse* (>William Wellman 1931) (☆ ☞): Stanwyck prevents sadistic chauffeur >Clark Gable starving her patient's children.

•*So Big* (>William Wellman 1932) (☞ ☆): widowed Stanwyck is helped to maintain her farm by her long-time sculptor lover George Brent.

•*Ladies They Talk About* (Howard Bretherton 1933) (☆): Barbara evolves from tough

STAR WARS
(George Lucas 1977) ☆ ✳

SPACESHIPS

A TRIP TO THE MOON (LE VOYAGE DANS LA LUNE)
(Georges Méliès 1902)
(early French film of pioneer moonshot)

THUNDERBIRD SIX
(David Lane 1968) ✳ ✍
(International Rescue puppets save the world again)

2001: A SPACE ODYSSEY
(>Stanley Kubrick 1968) ☞ ✍ ♫
(history of the world culminates in space travel)

ALIEN
(Ridley Scott 1979) ✳
(survivor from dead planet wipes out craft crew)

STAR TREK IV – THE VOYAGE HOME
(Leonard Nimoy 1986) ✍
(USS Enterprise crew come to 1980s America)

THE FLIGHT OF THE NAVIGATOR
(Randal Kleiser 1986) ✳
(small boy finds himself at controls of spaceship)

SPACE INVADERS

THE DAY THE EARTH STOOD STILL
(Robert Wise 1951) ✍
(world is warned that war must stop or else)

IT CAME FROM OUTER SPACE
(Jack Arnold 1953) ✍
(astronomer warns of invaders who adopt human form)

THE QUATERMASS EXPERIMENT (US: THE CREEPING UNKNOWN)
(Val Guest 1955) ✍
(astronaut brings back vampire-like fungus)

INVASION OF THE BODY SNATCHERS
(Don Siegel 1956) ✍ ■
(alien doubles arrive in giant pods)

VILLAGE OF THE DAMNED
(Wolf Rilla 1960) ✍ ■
(children of sleepy village prove to be aliens)

THE MAN WHO FELL TO EARTH
(Nicolas Roeg 1976) ■
(invading alien David Bowie falls prey to the evils of celebrity)

Galactic Boudicca and robot army
resist evil Empire

IS THIS PLANET EARTH?

20,000 LEAGUES UNDER THE SEA
(Richard Fleischer 1954) ☆ ✍
(Jules Verne's classic Victorian submarine voyage)

JOURNEY TO THE CENTER OF THE EARTH
(Henry Levin 1959) ✍ ✳
(more Verne, this time an expedition to the planet's core)

THE TIME MACHINE
(George Pal 1960) ✳ ☆
(Rod Taylor travels to year 802701 and notices things have changed)

PLANET OF THE APES
(Franklin Schaffner 1968) ✳ ✍
(evolution reversed on distant-future Earth)

THE LAND THAT TIME FORGOT
(Kevin Connor 1974) ■
(First World War sub survivors land on prehistoric polar island)

LATE NIGHT IN THE LAB

DR JEKYLL AND MR HYDE
(Rouben Mamoulian 1931) ☆ ☞ ■
(>Fredric March in R. L. Stevenson's classic of dual personality)

THE MAN IN THE WHITE SUIT
(Alexander Mackendrick 1951) ✍ ☆
(chemist >Alec Guinness discovers indestructible textile)

THE DAY THE EARTH CAUGHT FIRE
(Val Guest 1961) ✍
(nuclear scientists detach earth from its axis)

UNEARTHLY POWERS
(John Krish 1963) ✍
(wife of one of a group of scientists is an alien, but which one?)

ALTERED STATES
(Ken Russell 1980) ☆ ☞ ✳
(>William Hurt arrives at Mr Hyde by sensory deprivation experiments)

THE MAN WITH TWO BRAINS
(Rob Reiner 1983)
(spoof of the mad scientist genre with Steve Martin and >Kathleen Turner)

THE FLY
(David Cronenberg 1986) ☆ ✍ ✳
(scientist Jeff Goldblum's crazy scheme turns him into insect)

prisoner to the wife of the preacher who had condemned her.

•*Baby Face* (Alfred E. Green 1933) (☆): Stanwyck flutters her eyelashes to get herself out of the slums, but fails to find happiness in wealth.

•*The Mad Miss Manton* (Leigh Jason 1938) (☆): cop >Henry Fonda falls for society girl Barbara during a murder case.

•*Meet John Doe* (>Frank Capra 1941) (✍ ☆ ☞): tramp >Gary Cooper is exploited for a political stunt and Stanwyck alone can talk him out of suicide.

•*The Bride Wore Boots* (Irving Pichel 1946) (☆): Stanwyck's marriage to Robert Cummings is threatened as his hatred matches her love of horses.

•*The Strange Love of Martha Ivers* (Lewis Milestone 1946) (✍ ☆): >Kirk Douglas threatens to reveal Stanwyck's childhood murder to husband Van Heflin.

•*The Two Mrs Carrolls* (Peter Godfrey 1947) (☆): when he is no longer inspired by Barbara, >Humphrey Bogart begins to poison her milk.

•*The File on Thelma Jordan* (Robert Siodmak 1950) (☆): prosecution lawyer Wendell Corey proves his love for Stanwyck by deliberately losing her murder trial.

•*Clash by Night* (>Fritz Lang 1952) (☞ ☆): city slicker Barbara returns to her seaside home and rouses amorous and bitter passions.

•*All I Desire* (Douglas Sirk 1953) (☞ ☆): failed actress Stanwyck returns to the small-town she left under a cloud following a steamy love affair.

•*Executive Suite* (Robert Wise 1954) (☆ ✍): >Fredric March and William Holden compete for boardroom control and Stanwyck has the casting vote.

•*Cattle Queen of Montana* (Allan Dwan 1954) (☆): government agent Ronald Reagan helps rancher Stanwyck defend her cattle against rustlers.

•*There's Always Tomorrow* (Douglas Sirk 1956) (☆): successful toymaker Fred MacMurray's comfortable life is disturbed by the return of Stanwyck, a love from his past.

•*Forty Guns* (Samuel Fuller 1957) (☆ ☞): rancher Stanwyck hires world-weary gun-fighter Barry Sullivan to defend her shifty brother from his pursuers.

Stevens, George
American director/producer (1904–1975)

>Laurel and Hardy's cameraman on *The Battle of the Century* (Clyde Bruckman 1927) (☆ ☞) (the funniest custard pie fight in movie history) and *Big Business* (James W. Horne 1929) (☆ ✍) (the Christmas spirit is lacking as Stan and Ollie fight over the last tree), Stevens made comic shorts until >Katharine Hepburn personally asked for him to direct *Alice Adams* (1935) (☆) (humble Hepburn wins wealthy Fred MacMurray despite the prejudices of both families), a gesture she repeated in 1941 with *Woman of the Year* (☆ ☞) (sports journalist >Spencer Tracy is hurt by campaigning wife Hepburn's national popularity). He displayed a flair for the debonair with >Fred Astaire and >Ginger Rogers' *Swing Time* (1936) (☞ ☆) (Fred can't marry partner Ginger as he is committed to childhood sweetheart Helen Broderick), Astaire's *A Damsel in Distress* (1937) (✍ ☆) (dancer Fred woos aristocratic >Joan Fontaine in this P. G. Wodehouse script) and Rogers' *Vivacious Lady* (1938) (☆ ✍) (Ginger is disapproved of by academic >James Stewart's parents). His comic touch was intact with *Gunga Din* (1939) (☞ ☆) (just as he is about to retire Douglas Fairbanks, Jr has to join Victor McLaglen in rescuing >Cary Grant from an Indian sect), *The Talk of the Town* (1942) (☆ ☞ ✍) (Jean Arthur loves both >Cary Grant and Ronald Colman, the latter being lawyer defending the former on arson charges) and *The More the Merrier* (1943) (☆ ☞ ✍) (Jean Arthur shares her apartment with Charles Coburn who matchmakes her with Joel McCrea; while he kindled a kindred with kitsch in *Penny Serenade* (1941) (☆ ✍) (>Cary Grant and Irene Dunne's ideal courtship declines into troubled marriage, ended by the death of their child) and *I Remember Mama* (1948) (☆ ☞) (Barbara Bel Geddes recalls the devotion of her Norwegian immigrant mother Irene Dunne). Decorated for covering D-Day and the liberation of Dachau, Stevens indulged his penchant for big budgets and extended shoots with *A Place in the Sun* (AA: 1951) (☞ ■) (ambitious

worker Montgomery Clift's marriage to rich girl Elizabeth Taylor is shattered when he is convicted of killing Shelley Winters); *Shane* (1953) (☞ ☆) (gunfighter Alan Ladd rids Van Heflin and Jean Arthur of villains, but alienates them from their hero-worshipping son); and *Giant* (AA: 1956) (☞ ☆ ✍) (an oil strike brings nothing but misery to Rock Hudson, Elizabeth Taylor and James Dean).

 •*Quality Street* (1937) (☞ ☆): J. M. Barrie play has >Katharine Hepburn impersonating her own niece to win back Napoleonic war veteran Franchot Tone.
•*Something to Live For* (1952) (☆ ☞): drunk Ray Milland dries out with actress >Joan Fontaine but their love is doomed.
•*The Diary of Anne Frank* (1959) (☞ ☆ ■): biopic of the Jewish Dutch family who hid in a secret room to avoid the Nazis.
•*The Greatest Story Ever Told* (1965) (☞ ☆): Max Von Sydow as Christ intent on getting across the message of his teaching.

Stewart, James
American actor (b 1908)

A much-imitated drawl and an unimpeachable amiability have contributed to Princeton architecture graduate Stewart's popularity, while his relaxed, authoritative screen presence does much to explain his professional longevity. His understated comedy style made him an ideal screwball foil – >*The Philadelphia Story* (AA: >George Cukor 1940) (☆ ✍ ☞) – or light lead: *The Shop around the Corner* (>Ernst Lubitsch 1940) (☞ ✍ ☆) (Jimmy hates fellow assistant Margaret Sullavan, unaware she is the pen pal he has long loved) and >*Harvey* (AAN: Henry Koster 1950) (☆ ✍ ☞). His versatility permitted effortlessly effective excursions into: the musical, *Born to Dance* (Roy Del Ruth 1936) (☆) (sailor Stewart meets Eleanor Powell on shoreleave and sings and dances too!); Westerns: *Destry Rides Again* (George Marshall 1939) (☆ ✍) (saloon singer >Marlene Dietrich is among those disbelieving that mild-mannered Jimmy can tame a rowdy town); melodramas: *Call Northside 777* (Henry Hathaway 1948) (☆ ✍) (journalist Stewart

helps a poor Chicago mother prove her son has been unjustly accused of murder); and biopics, *The Glenn Miller Story* (Anthony Mann 1954) (♫ ☆ ☞ ✍) (as the trombonist bandleader, inspired by wife June Allyson into giving the world his inimitable brand of swing). >Frank Capra capitalized on his essential decency in *You Can't Take It with You* (1938) (☆ ✍ ☞) (rich eccentric Stewart's love for Jean Arthur is opposed by their respective fathers Lionel Barrymore and Edward Arnold), *Mr Smith Goes to Washington* (AAN: 1939) (☆ ☞ ✍) (senator Stewart is supported by secretary Jean Arthur in his campaign against corrupt Claude Rains) and >*It's a Wonderful Life* (AAN: 1946) (✍ ☆ ☞). It was this characteristic of his that Anthony Mann transferred to the West: *Winchester 73* (1950) (☞ ☆) (after it is stolen, Stewart tries to regain the prized rifle he won in Dodge City); *Where the River Bends* (US: *Bend of the River*) (1952) (☆) (ex-border raiders escort a wagon train, but unlike Stewart, Arthur Kennedy is still a criminal at heart); *The Far Country* (1955) (☆) (gold prospectors Stewart and Walter Brennan resist Alaskan con man John McIntire); and *The Man from Laramie* (1955) (☞ ☆) (itinerant cowboy Stewart tracks down his brother's killer). >Alfred Hitchcock inverted it in *Rope* (1948) (☞ ☆ ✍ ■) (academic Stewart suspects two ex-students of knowing more than they are telling of their friend's disappearance); >*Rear Window* (1954) (☆ ☞ ✍ ■); *The Man Who Knew Too Much* (1956) (☞ ☆) (agents, believing Stewart and Doris Day have uncovered their operation, kidnap their son); and *Vertigo* (1958) (☞ ☆ ✍) (Stewart witnesses Kim Novak's plunge from a bell tower, and becomes obsessed with grooming her lookalike into an exact replica).

 •*After the Thin Man* (W. S. Van Dyke 1936) (☆ ✍ ☞): >William Powell and >Myrna Loy suspect that Stewart is a murderous kidnapper.
•*Vivacious Lady* (>George Stevens 1938) (☆ ☞): academic Jimmy's parents disapprove of singer >Ginger Rogers.
•*The Mortal Storm* (Frank Borzage 1940) (☆): Stewart, Robert Young and Margaret Sullavan

are part of German family torn by the rise of the Nazis.

•*Broken Arrow* (Delmer Daves 1950) (☆): scout Stewart learns the language and customs of Jeff Chandler's Red Indian tribe.

•*No Highway in the Sky* (UK: *No Highway*) (Henry Koster 1951): this screen version of the Nevil Shute novel has Stewart warning of a plane design fault but only passenger >Marlene Dietrich and stewardess Glynis Johns believe him.

•*The Greatest Show on Earth* (Cecil B. De Mille 1952): Stewart and Charlton Heston are among the artistes at a struggling circus.

•*The Spirit of St Louis* (>Billy Wilder 1957) (☞ ☆): biopic of the pioneer aviator Charles Lindbergh, who flew the Atlantic in 1927.

•*Anatomy of a Murder* (AAN: Otto Preminger 1959) (☆): lawyer Stewart's main motive for defending Ben Gazzara is an interest in his wife Lee Remick.

•*Two Rode Together* (>John Ford 1961) (☞ ☆): riding to negotiate with the Comanches for the release of some prisoners, Stewart and Richard Widmark realize they dislike each other.

•*The Man who Shot Liberty Valance* (>John Ford 1962) (☞ ☆ ✍): was Stewart or >John Wayne responsible for gunning down baddy Lee Marvin?

•*Mr Hobbs Takes a Vacation* (Henry Koster 1962) (☆): Jimmy and Maureen O'Hara's holiday is spoiled by a dive of a hotel and their daughter's unsuitable romance.

•*The Flight of the Phoenix* (Robert Aldrich 1965) (☆): Stewart pressgangs dispirited crew into repairing their desert-marooned plane.

•*The Shootist* (Don Siegel 1976) (☆): fatally ill gunfighter >John Wayne makes his farewells to comrade Stewart and old flame Lauren Bacall.

Stories

>*Intolerance* (>D. W. Griffith 1916) ☞ ■ ☆

Kaos (Paolo & Vittorio Taviani 1984) ☞ ■ ✍

A quartet of stories studying Sicilian superstitions, hopes and disappointments.

Kwaidan **(Masaki Kobayashi 1964)** ☞ ■

Ghost stories by Lafcadio Hearn are given Japanese interpretations.

The Little Theatre of Jean Renoir (*Le Petit Théâtre de Jean Renoir*) (>**Jean Renoir 1969**) ☞

Dreaming tramps, a floor polisher obsessed housewife, an act of adultery and a costume song star turn make up this quartet.

Love and the Frenchwoman (*La Française et l'Amour*) **(Henri Decoin/Jean Delannoy/ Michel Boisrond/>René Clair/Henri Verneuil/Christian-Jaque/Jean-Paul Le Chanois 1960)** ☞

The seven ages, or at least stages, passed through by modern French women.

Love at Twenty (*L'Amour à Vingt Ans*) (>**François Truffaut/Renzo Rossellini/ Shintaro Ishihara/Marcel Ophüls/>Andrej Wajda 1962**) ☞

Frustrated and fulfilled love, violent passion and personal humiliation inform these five tales.

Love in the City (*Amore in Città*) **(Dino Risi/ >Michelangelo Antonioni/>Federico Fellini/Francesco Maselli/Cesare Zavattini/Alberto Lattuada/Carlo Lizzani 1953)** ☞

A sextet of newspaper scoops demonstrate press objectivity, or the lack of it.

Streep, Meryl

(Mary Louise Streep) American actress (b 1951)

A graduate of the Yale School of Drama, who progressed surprisingly slowly from support to leading roles, Meryl Streep is undoubtedly the greatest actress of her generation, able to define character with the simplest gesture, wistful glance, accurate accent or tightened lip. Although her tantalizing beauty suggests vulnerability – *The Deer Hunter* (AAN: Michael Cimino 1978) (■ ♫ ☆) (as Christopher Walken's girlfriend worrying about his departure for and non-return from Vietnam), *The French Lieutenant's Woman* (Karel Reisz 1981) (Jeremy Irons is broken by his love for Meryl, both in 1867 Lyme Regis and while making a costume drama based on that story) and *Sophie's*

Choice (AA: Alan J. Pakula 1982) (Polish refugee Streep's New York happiness is disrupted by lover Kevin Kline's insanity and memories of her decision to sacrifice her daughter in an effort to save her son from the Nazis) – her repertoire contains numerous strong, even ruthless women: *The Seduction of Joe Tynan* (Jerry Schatzberg 1979) (☆) (Alan Alda's political career is ruined by his affair with researcher Streep); *Silkwood* (AAN: >Mike Nichols 1983) (☆ ☞ ✍) (Streep detects a safety shortfall at a nuclear processing plant, but is murdered before she can reveal it); *Plenty* (Fred Schepisi 1985) (☆) (Streep is troubled by her unhappy experiences of fighting with the Resistance in occupied France); and >*Out of Africa* (AAN: Sydney Pollack 1985) (☆ ■ ♫ ☞). If the material is occasionally prosaic, Streep is always compelling: *Falling in Love* (Ulu Grosbard 1984) (☆) (Meryl bumps into >Robert De Niro in a bookshop at Christmas and they begin an affair); *Heartburn* (>Mike Nichols 1986) (☆ ☞) (Streep struggles to carry on a career and cope with >Jack Nicholson's infidelities); and *Ironweed* (Hector Babenco 1988) (☆ ☞) (tramps Streep and >Jack Nicholson struggle to find the bright side of life during the Depression).

 •>*Julia* (>Fred Zinnemann 1977) (☆ ✍ ☞ ■); her film debut as Anne Marie, a snobby socialite disapproving of Vanessa Redgrave's political convictions.

•>*Manhattan* (>Woody Allen 1979).

•*Kramer versus Kramer* (AA: Robert Benton 1979) (☆): Streep walks out on >Dustin Hoffman who considers her an unfit mother and fights for custody.

•*Still of the Night* (Robert Benton 1982) (☆): psychiatrist Roy Scheider is stalked by a patient and we all think it's Meryl: but is it?

•*A Cry in the Dark* (AAN: Fred Schepisi 1988) (☆): as Australian mother Lindy Chamberlain who was persecuted by press and public during the court case following the killing of her baby by a dingo.

STUDENTS AND CAMPUS LIFE

Bachelor of Hearts (**Wolf Rilla 1958**) ☆
German student Hardy Kruger wins fellow Cambridge undergraduate Sylvia Syms after clichéd scrapes.

Charley's Aunt (**Archie Mayo 1941**) ✍ ☆
Brandon Thomas's play has Jack Benny forced to impersonate a long-lost aunt from Brazil.

A Chump at Oxford (**Alfred Goulding 1939**) ☆ ✍
Much to >Oliver Hardy's surprise, >Stan Laurel's bang on the head turns him into the ennobled college hero.

The Freshman (**Fred Newmeyer/Sam Taylor 1925**) ☆ ✍
Timid Harold Lloyd single-handedly wins a vital football game.

Lucky Jim (**John Boulting 1957**) ☆
Ian Carmichael as the blundering lecturer at a provincial university, in this film version of the Kinglsey Amis novel.

Oxford Blues (**Robert Boris 1984**) ☆
Supersnob Julian Sands inflicts on Rob Lowe pranks that were old hat when Hardy Kruger and Robert Taylor were students.

The Paper Chase (**James Bridges 1973**) ☆ ✍
John Houseman (AA) drives law student Timothy Bottoms to his limits as he recognizes that he has talent.

Privileged (**Michael Hoffman 1982**) ✍
The cast of an Oxford undergraduate production of *The Duchess of Malfi* squabble while the leads fall in love.

The Wind (*Finyê*) (**Souleymane Cissé 1982**) ☞ ✍
A poor male and a privileged female student fall in love and protest against prejudice in Mali's universities.

A Yank at Oxford (**Jack Conway 1938**) ☆ ✍
Robert Taylor learns to control his arrogance and falls for townie >Vivien Leigh.

STUDIO PROMOS

Elstree Calling (**Adrian Brunel/>Alfred Hitchcock/Jack Hulbert/André Charlot/Paul Murray 1930**) ☞
Tommy Trinder, Hulbert and Cicely Courtneidge top the bill.

Follow the Boys (A. Edward Sutherland 1944)
>Orson Welles, >Marlene Dietrich and >W. C. Fields are among the Universal stars entertaining the troops via celluloid.

Hollywood Canteen (Delmer Daves 1944)
>Joan Crawford, >Bette Davis, >Peter Lorre and >Barbara Stanwyck in another morale booster, this one from Warners.

Hollywood Revue of 1929 (Charles F. Reisner 1929) ☆
This MGM showcase for >Buster Keaton, >Joan Crawford, >Laurel & Hardy, Lionel Barrymore and Norma Shearer received a Best Picture AAN.

It's a Great Feeling (David Butler 1949) ☆
Warner stars >Gary Cooper, >Edward G. Robinson and >Joan Crawford refuse to appear in a film in which Jack Carson is planning to showcase his protégé, Doris Day.

The Oscar (Russel Rouse 1966)
Merle Oberon, Bob Hope, Frank Sinatra and Joseph Cotten are among those putting in an appearance.

Paramount on Parade (Dorothy Arzner/ Otto Brower/Edmund Goulding/Victor Heerman/Edwin H. Knopf/Rowland V. Lee/>Ernst Lubitsch/Lothar Mendes/ Victor Schertzinger/Edward A. Sutherland/Frank Tuttle 1930) ☞ ☆
>William Powell, >Gary Cooper, Jean Arthur and >Fredric March are among the many who smile for the camera.

Star Spangled Rhythm (George Marshall 1942) ☆
The highlight of this Paramount promo is Ray Milland, Fred MacMurray and Franchot Tone's card game.

That's Entertainment (Jack Haley, Jr 1974) ☆ ☞ ♫
MGM highlights introduced by backslapping stars.

That's Entertainment II (>Gene Kelly 1976) ☆
More of the same with Kelly and >Fred Astaire acting as masters of ceremonies.

Thousands Cheer (George Sidney 1943) ☆
MGM flagwaver with >Gene Kelly, Judy Garland, June Allyson and Lionel Barrymore performing for the troops.

Variety Girl (George Marshall 1947) ☆
On the Paramount lot at the time were >Gary Cooper, >Barbara Stanwyck, Bob Hope, and Bing Crosby.

Sturges, Preston
(Edmond P. Binden) American writer/director (1898–1959)

Privately educated around Europe and the inventor of kissproof lipstick for his mother's cosmetics firm, Sturges first wrote during a hospital stay in 1927, devising his distinctive film directorial style while observing the filming of *The Power and the Glory* (William K. Howard 1933) (☆ ✍) (>Spencer Tracy seeks glory, but is corrupted by power), *Easy Living* (Mitchell Leisen 1937) (☆ ✍ ☞) (secretary Jean Arthur's life is transformed when a fur coat lands on her) and *Remember the Night* (Mitchell Leisen 1940) (☆ ✍) (Fred MacMurray takes shoplifter >Barbara Stanwyck home for Christmas). Cultivated dialogue, stinging one-liners and pioneering the use of flashback and inverted reality in his narrative characterized the brilliant sequence of satires he wrote and directed in the early '40s: *The Great McGinty* (UK: *Down Went McGinty*) (AA for Script: 1940) (☞ ✍ ☆) (crook Akim Tamiroff makes tramp Brian Donlevy governor to manipulate him); *The Lady Eve* (1941) (>Barbara Stanwyck and >Henry Fonda find love through their mutual con tricking); *Sullivan's Travels* (1941) (☞ ✍ ☆) (director Joel McCrea hits the road to research real life in order to break from filming slapstick); *The Palm Beach Story* (1942) (☞ ☆ ✍) (Claudette Colbert seeks to seduce a millionaire to help finance her husband Joel McCrea's business); and *Hail the Conquering Hero* (1944) (☞ ✍ ☆) (Eddie Bracken fails the army medical, but hasn't the heart to disillusion the small town that believes he has been decorated for valour). The additional responsibilities of producing tainted his later projects, with only two meriting recollection: *Mad Wednesday* (aka *The Sin of Harold Diddlebock*) (1947) (☞ ☆) (after the heroics of *The Freshman* Harold Lloyd settles for a clerking job until he buys a circus while under the influence of a potent cocktail) and *Unfaithfully*

Yours (1948) (☞) (conductor Rex Harrison is convinced Linda Darnell is unfaithful and dreams of various ways of bumping her off).

 •*Christmas in July* (1940) (☞ ✍): believing he has won a coffee slogan contest, Dick Powell takes Ellen Drew on a spending spree.

•*The Miracle of Morgan's Creek* (AAN Script: 1944) (☞ ✍ ☆): single mother Betty Hutton's quadruplets become national news.

•*The Great Moment* (1944) (☞): Joel McCrea as Dr W. T. G. Morgan pioneers the first anaesthetics.

•*The Beautiful Blonde from Bashful Bend* (1949) (☞): Betty Grable accidentally kills a sheriff in a bar room and lays low by impersonating a teacher.

SUBMARINES

Above Us the Waves (Ralph Thomas 1955) ☆

John Mills stalks John Gregson's battleship in Norwegian fiords.

The Bedford Incident (James B. Harris 1965) ☆ ✍

Richard Widmark accidentally fires a nuclear weapon while pursuing a Soviet sub.

The Boat (Das Boot) (Wolfgang Petersen 1981) ☞

A U-boat has to sail through depth-charged waters during World War II.

The Damned (Les Maudits) (René Clément 1947) ☞ ✍

Nazis fleeing a defeated Germany in a U-boat have to kidnap a French doctor when one of their number is injured in a blast.

The Enemy Below (Dick Powell 1957) ☞

Robert Mitchum in his destroyer and Curt Jurgens in his sub jockey for position to get in the telling shot.

Morning Departure (US: Operation Disaster) (Roy Baker 1950) ☆

A diving bell has four too few places as far as a trapped submarine crew of 12 are concerned.

On the Beach (Stanley Kramer 1959) ☆

Guilty scientist >Fred Astaire and whore Ava Gardner await the nuclear cloud in Australia, while sub captain Gregory Peck and his crew search for signs of life.

Operation Petticoat (Blake Edwards 1960) ✍ ☆

>Cary Grant will stop at nothing to keep his ramshackle sub going, while Tony Curtis is equally determined to seduce a passenger nurse.

Run Silent, Run Deep (Robert Wise 1958) ☆

Burt Lancaster tries to dampen >Clark Gable's obsession with sinking any Japanese shipping available while endangering the crew.

20,000 Leagues under the Sea (Richard Fleischer 1954) ☆ ✍

>Kirk Douglas, James Mason and >Peter Lorre crew Jules Verne's 19th-century sub in this Disney adventure.

We Dive at Dawn (>Anthony Asquith 1943) ☞

John Mills risks his crew's lives in the reckless pursuit of a Nazi sub.

Subway ☆ ♫ ✍ ☞ ■

France • Films Du Loup/TSF/TF1 • 1985 • 102 mins • col

d Luc Besson w Luc Besson/Alain Le Henry/Pierre Jolivet/Sophie Schmit/Marc Perrier ph Carlo Varini m Eric Serra

Christopher Lambert, Isabelle Adjani, Richard Bohringer, Jean-Hugues Anglade, Michel Galabru

Fred (Lambert) is a safe-cracking punk fleeing the henchmen of the Parisian businessman from whom he has stolen incriminating papers. Following a car chase in the best traditions of *The Italian Job* (Peter Collinson 1969) (☆ ✍ ■), Fred ducks down into the Paris Métro where he finds refuge among the small-time crooks who operate the subway stations and trains. Helena (Adjani) is more romantically interested in the man who can expose her spouse's corruption and enlists cynical cop (Galabru), weary of petty crime and small fry such as the roller-skating pickpocket (Anglade), in her quest to find Fred before her husband does. Luc Besson's frantic thriller is packed with many stunning moments, notably the spark shower during the track repair, and Eric Serra's soundtrack is scintillating.

 •Walter Matthau is the cop down in the tube station seeking to end a siege bloodlessly, in *The Taking of Pelham 123* (Joseph Sargent 1974) (☞).
•Colin Friels is the eccentric crook who carries out his crimes by remote control model, in *Malcolm* (Nadia Tass 1986) (✳ ☆), while Vincent Friell and Joe Mullaney are the motorbike highwaymen disguised as a clown and a wolfman, in *Restless Natives* (Michael Hoffman 1985) (✍ ☆♪).
•Marianne Sägebrecht searches the subway for the train driver she is obsessed with, in *Sugarbaby* (*Zuckerbaby*) (Percy Adlon 1984) (☞ ☆).

Sunset Boulevard ☞ ☆ ✍ ■
USA • Paramount • 1950 • 110 mins • b/w
d >Billy Wilder w Billy Wilder/Charles Brackett/D. M. Marshman, Jr ph John F. Seitz m Franz Waxman
Gloria Swanson, >Erich Von Stroheim, William Holden, Fred Clark, Nancy Olson, Cecil B. De Mille, >Buster Keaton, Hedda Hopper, W. B. Warner

A savage attack on every creative and administrative aspect of Hollywood, Wilder's film is also a sad acknowledgment that the Golden Age of the Movies has passed. Hounded by creditors, writer Joe Gillis (Holden) accepts the offer of silent star Norma Desmond to refine her comeback screenplay, *Salome* and moves into her mansion as her lover. However, when his attentions stray elsewhere, Desmond guns him into the swimming pool. De Mille, Keaton, Hopper and Warner appear as themselves, but so in effect do Swanson as Norma and Von Stroheim as Max, her ex-husband/director now her butler, even to the point of reminiscing over their unfinished real-life 1928 silent *Queen Kelly*. Ever the star, Norma claims she is still big: 'it was the pictures that got small'. True in 1950 and even more so today.

 •Geraldine Page is the embittered actress obsessed with >Paul Newman, in *Sweet Bird of Youth* (Richard Brooks 1962) (☆ ✍).
•Wilder and Holden revisit similar territory to that explored in *Sunset*, in *Fedora* (>Billy Wilder 1978) (☞ ■).
•Anne Bancroft's dying wish is to meet movie legend >Greta Garbo, in *Garbo Talks* (>Sidney Lumet 1984) (☆ ✍ ☞).
•Journalist Hilmar Thate investigates the career of fading star Rosel Zech, in *Veronika Voss* (>Rainer Werner Fassbinder 1981) (☞ ■).
•Franchot Tone boosts actress >Bette Davis' comeback by keeping her off the bottle, in *Dangerous* (Alfred E. Green 1935) (☆).

SUPERHEROES

Batman (Leslie Martinson 1966) ✍ ☆
Adam West and Burt Ward as the Dynamic Duo ridding Gotham City of the combined might of the Joker, the Riddler, Catwoman and the Penguin.

Batman (Tim Burton 1989) ☆
Robinless and fighting crime without so much spoof, Michael Keaton is on the trail of Joker >Jack Nicholson.

Condorman (Charles Jarrott 1981) ■
Cartoonist Michael Crawford adopts the character of his strip hero and brings Oliver Reed to book.

Flash Gordon (Michael Hodges 1980) ♪
Max Von Sydow is the villain up to no good on 25th-century Mongo.

The Return of Captain Invincible (Philippe Mora 1982) ☆
With little crime to fight, Alan Arkin has become a drunk, but then Christopher Lee arrives on the scene.

Superman (Richard Donner 1978) ✳ ☆ ✍
Christopher Reeve as mild-mannered journalist Clark Kent, who always has his blue tights and red cape handy to thwart Gene Hackman.

Superman II (Richard Lester 1980) ✳ ☆
Reeve's night of love with Margot Kidder's Lois Lane saps the strength required to crush a trio of Kryptonian rebels.

Tarzan and His Mate (Cedric Gibbons 1934) ✍ ☆
Johnny Weissmuller embarrasses Maureen O'Sullivan when her high society friends visit them in the jungle.

Tarzan the Ape Man **(W. S. Van Dyke 1932)** ☞ ☆

Olympic swimmer Weissmuller kidnaps rich girl O'Sullivan and convinces her to adopt his way of life.

Thunderbird Six **(David Lane 1966)** ✳ ✍

Puppet brothers Scott, Virgil, Alan, Gordon and John at the wheels of Brains' International Rescue craft aiding a nuclear-powered plane.

SURREALISM AND SYMBOLISM

>*L'Âge D'Or* **(US:** *The Golden Age***) (>Luis Buñuel 1930)** ☞ ■ ✍

Anaemic Cinema **(Marcel Duchamp 1926)** ☞

Swirling spirals and nonsense words ballet across the screen in an exercise in shape and form.

Beauty and the Beast **(***La Belle et la Bête***) (Jean Cocteau 1946)** ☆ ☞ ✳

Beauty (Josette Day) takes her father's place in Beast's (Jean Marais) castle and falls in love with him.

The Blood of the Poet **(***Le Sang d'un Poète***) (Jean Cocteau 1930)** ☞ ✍ ■

Lee Miller wipes the mouth of a painting on to his hands, it kisses him all over, transfers to a statue and directs him through a mirror.

Un Chien Andalou **(aka** *The Andalusian Dog***) (>Luis Buñuel 1928)** ☞ ■

Sliced eyeballs, ants crawling from hands, fondled breasts and puritans being hauled along with pianos are among the images thought up by Buñuel and his co-writer Salvador Dali.

Emak Bakia **(Man Ray 1927)** ☞

Tumbling dice become lights, sticks and eventually legs in an exploration of shape.

L'Etoile de Mer **(***Star of the Sea***) (Man Ray 1928)** ☞

A man's relationship with a female newspaper seller goes from the platonic to the surrealistic.

The Fall of the House of Usher **(***La Chute de la Maison Usher***) (Jean Epstein 1928)** ☞ ■

Slow motion, distortion, multiple exposure and mysterious sets help tell Edgar Allan Poe's tale.

The Falls **(Peter Greenaway 1980)** ☞ ■

How 92 people whose names begin with 'fall' survive something akin to a holocaust.

Return to Reason **(***Le Rétour à la Raison***) (Man Ray 1923)** ☞ ■

Nails, drawing pins, paint and scraps of paper form darting shadows when pasted on to film and exposed to light.

The Tomb of Ligeia **(Roger Corman 1964)** ☞ ■

Vincent Price turns wife Elizabeth Shepherd into a cat and then into a beautiful woman, in another of Edgar Allan Poe's tales.

SVENGALIS

Barbary Coast **(>Howard Hawks 1935)** ☞ ☆

>Edward G. Robinson turns Miriam Hopkins into a star, but not into his wife.

Expresso Bongo **(Val Guest 1959)** ♫ ☆

Laurence Harvey shoots Soho cafe singer Cliff Richard to fame.

The Great Ziegfeld **(Robert Z. Leonard 1936)** ☆ ✍

>William Powell as Florenz Ziegfeld torn between Luise Rainer (as Anna Held) and >Myrna Loy (as Billie Burke).

The King of Burlesque **(Sidney Lanfield 1936)** ☆

Warner Baxter puts on the show that makes Alice Faye a star.

Love Me or Leave Me **(Charles Vidor 1955)** ☆ ♫

>James Cagney drives Doris Day's Ruth Etting so hard she is almost destroyed by drink.

Maytime **(Robert Z. Leonard 1937)** ☆

John Barrymore shoots Nelson Eddy when the latter threatens to take opera star Jeanette MacDonald away from him.

Once Upon a Time **(Alexander Hall 1944)** ☆

Producer >Cary Grant takes showbiz by storm with a boy's dancing caterpillar act.

Svengali **(Archie Mayo 1931)** ☆

Belle époque hypnotist John Barrymore hopes that making Marian Marsh an opera star will win her love, in this screen version of George Du Maurier's novel *Trilby*.

Twentieth Century (>Howard Hawks 1934)
☆ ☞ ✍

Actress >Carole Lombard rebels against John Barrymore.

What Price Hollywood? (>George Cukor 1932) ☞ ✍

Film director Lowell Sherman drinks to suicide, having made Constance Bennett a star.

SWASHBUCKLING

Aan (aka *Savage Princess*) (Mehboob 1952) ☞ ■

A peasant ends the tyrannical rule of a savage brother and sister.

Anne of the Indies (Jacques Tourneur 1951) ☆

Louis Jourdan's pirate Blackbeard is jealous of Anne Bonney's (Jean Peters) success on the high seas.

The Black Swan (Henry King 1942) ■ ♫ ✍

Captain Morgan (Tyrone Power), now a governor in the West Indies, turns on his old pirate buddies.

The Elusive Pimpernel (>Michael Powell/ Emeric Pressburger 1950) ☆ ☞

David Niven as the English dandy who fearlessly rescues aristocrats during the French Revolution.

The Princess Bride (Rob Reiner 1988) ■ ✍

Cary Elwes overcomes giants, dwarfs ad magicians to rescue Robin Wright, in this film adaptation of William Goldman's novel.

The Prisoner of Zenda (John Cromwell 1937) ☆ ✍ ■ ☞

Ronald Colman saves Ruritania by impersonating its kidnapped king.

Scaramouche (George Sidney 1952) ☆

Stewart Granger impersonates an actor to have the longest sword fight in cinema history with tyrant Mel Ferrer.

SWINDLERS

Mado (Claude Sautet 1976) ✍ ☞

Cross-class partners in a property deal share a red-headed whore Ottavia Piccolo.

The Miracle Woman (>Frank Capra 1932) ☆

>Barbara Stanwyck's preacher, realising she can't serve God and mammon, opts for mammon.

Paper Moon (Peter Bogdanovich 1973) ✍ ☆ ■ ☞ ♫

Tatum O'Neal plays mother and partner to her shady Bible-selling father Ryan.

The Sting (George Roy Hill 1973) ✍ ☆

>Paul Newman and Robert Redford rifle Robert Shaw in a rigged betting con.

The Swindlers (US: *The Swindle*) (Il Bidone) (>Federico Fellini 1955) ☆

A trio of small-time villains pose as priests to sponge off the poor, but they fall out over the share out.

Volpone (Maurice Tourneur 1940) ✍ ☞

Ben Jonson's play about a miser who feigns fatal illness to swindle gifts out of the sycophants who would be his heirs.

Young in Heart (Richard Wallace 1938) ☆ ☞ ✍

Douglas Fairbanks, Jr and Janet Gaynor's plot to cheat an old lady meets with her determination to reform them.

TALES

***Quartet* (Ray Smart/Harold French/Arthur Crabtree/Ken Annakin 1948)** 🎞
W. Somerset Maugham stories: 'The Facts of Life', 'The Alien Corn', 'The Kite' and 'The Colonel's Lady'.

***RoGoPaG* (>Roberto Rossellini/>Jean-Luc Godard/>Pier Paolo Pasolini/Ugo Gregoretti 1962)** ☞
Four tales on modern world topics: sex, the bomb, cinema (with >Orson Welles) and consumerism.

***Three Cases of Murder* (Wendy Toye/David Eady/George More O'Farrall 1954)** 🎞 ☆
The best two being about a painting that draws in its viewers and >Orson Welles's portrayal of a murderously ambitious politician Lord Mountdrago.

***Trio* (Ken Annakin/Harold French 1950)** 🎞
Maugham of the same: 'The Verger', 'Mr Knowall' (an excellently brash Nigel Patrick) and 'Sanitorium'.

***The Witches* (*Le Streghe*) (>Luchino Visconti/Mauro Bolognini/Franco Rossi/>Pier Paolo Pasolini/>Vittorio De Sica 1966)** ☞
Tales about a holidaying film star, a mercy

dash, literally a gunshot wedding, two dreaming tramps and a husband competing with superheroes.

***The Yellow Rolls Royce* (>Anthony Asquith 1964)**
>Ingrid Bergman, Rex Harrison and gangster George C. Scott variously own the luxury car in Terence Rattigan's screenplay.

Tarkovsky, Andrei
Soviet director (1932–1986)
Son of poet Arsenii Tarkovsky, Andrei Tarkovsky's short career established him at the forefront of modern Soviet and world cinema. Full of personal and political imagery, his visually splendid, but sometimes rather leaden films were often hindered by his own perfectionism as well as official restrictions. Although *Ivan's Childhood* (*Ivanovo detstvo*) (1962) (☞ ☆) (a boy's respone to his parents' murder is to undertake increasingly dangerous anti-Nazi missions) and *Andrei Rublev* (1966) (☞ ■) (factional episodes from the life of the 15th-century icon artist) celebrated Russian courage and culture, they offended the Establishment. Following what amounts to a Soviet *2001*, *Solaris* (1972) (☞) (spaceship

crew are able to transport people they think of on to their beleaguered craft) and the autobiographical *Mirror* (aka *A White White Boy*) (*Zerkalo*) (1975) (☞ ■) (an artist ruminates on his relationships with his parents and his wife and child), he tended to work in the West. He died shortly after the completion of his masterpiece *The Sacrifice* (*Offret*) (1986) (☞ ■ ☆), a Faust for the nuclear age, which won the Special Jury prize at Cannes.

 •*Stalker* (1979) (☞ ■): in a bleak future society, the Truth is locked away in a room and a man is guided to it.

•*Nostalgia* (*Nostalghia*) (1983) (☞ ■): while a poet and a musicologist research the life of a composer, the former is required to carry a candle across a sulphur pit.

A Taste of Honey ✍ ☞ ☆

GB • British Lion/Bryanston/Woodfall • 1961 • 100 mins • b/w

d Tony Richardson   w Shelagh Delaney/ Tony Richardson   ph Walter Lassally m John Addison

Rita Tushingham, Dora Bryan, Murray Melvin, Robert Stephens, Paul Danquah

At a time of angry young men, Jo (Tushingham) is a naïve young woman living in a permanent state of conflict with Helen (Bryan), her sluttish mother. Friendship with a homosexual already lowering Jo's standing with the neighbours in their working-class Salford street, her pregnancy and inter-racial love affair only intensifies her isolation and misery. Shelagh Delaney's adaptation of her own stage hit completed Tony Richardson's trilogy of social-realist plays, the other two being John Osborne's *Look Back in Anger* (1959) (✍ ☆) (>Richard Burton as the original Angry Young Man) and *The Entertainer* (1960) (☆ ✍) (>Laurence Olivier as fading comedian Archie Rice). Marginally avoiding the 'satanic mills' view of the industrial North, the film's discussion of racial and sexual discrimination remains relevant: little has changed.

 •James Mason's stern father feuds with rebellious daughter Susan George, in Bill Naughton's *Spring and Port Wine* (Peter Hammond 1970) (☆ ✍ ☞).

•Molly Ringwald has to endure life as a teenage single mother when she quarrels with husband Randall Batinkoff, in *Maybe Baby* (US: *For Keeps*) (John G. Avildsen 1988) (☆).

•>Bette Davis is the dominant mother, in *The Anniversary* (Roy Ward Baker 1968) (☆).

•The French view of 'kitchen sink' Britain is seen in *Knave of Hearts* (US: *Lover Boy*) (aka *Happy Lovers*) (*Monsieur Ripois*) (René Clément 1954) (☞ ■ ☆) (Gérard Philipe seduces a number of self-obsessed girls including Valerie Hobson and Joan Greenwood).

•Modern British realism is explored in *Knights and Emeralds* (Ian Emes 1988) (✍ ☞) (an anti-Establishment couple object to her working-class royalist mother's new yuppie lodger and *Looks and Smiles* (Kenneth Loach 1981) (✍) (one youth joins the army and goes to Northern Ireland, his friend remains on the dole in Sheffield).

TEACHERS

The Blackboard Jungle (Richard Brooks 1955) ♫

While Glenn Ford tries to drum facts into his pupils' heads, Bill Haley and his Comets *Rock around the Clock*.

A Day in the Death of Joe Egg (Peter Medak 1971) ☆ ✍

Teacher Alan Bates and Janet Suzman's determination to raise their handicapped daughter at home gradually wanes.

The Dead Poets Society (Peter Weir 1989) ☆ ✍

Robin Williams' teaching methods inspire the boys in his class and irritate their parents.

Frenzy (US: *Torment*) (*Hets*) (Alf Sjöberg 1944) ✍ ☞

This >Ingmar Bergman script has a Latin master bully a boy into the arms of prostitute Mai Zetterling.

The Ghost of St Michael's (**Marcel Varnel 1941**) ☆
Will Hay discovers that an Isle of Skye ghost is a Nazi agent.

Good Morning Boys (**Marcel Varnel 1937**) ☆
Will Hay's students expose an international art smuggling ring.

Good Morning Miss Dove (**Henry Koster 1955**)
Jennifer Jones surveys her career at a small town school.

>*Goodbye Mr Chips* (**Sam Wood 1939**) ☆ ☞ ✍ ■

King of the Children (*Hai zi Wang*) (**Chen Kalge, 1988**) ■
Though unqualified, a Chinese farm labourer rises to the task of teaching peasant children.

To Sir with Love (**James Clavell 1967**) ☆
Sidney Poitier tames the lads and charms the lasses in a London school.

Topaze (**Harry D'Abbabie D'Arrast 1933**) ☆ ✍
This Marcel Pagnol play has schoolmaster John Barrymore lured into becoming a fizzy drinks tycoon by a baron's mistress >Myrna Loy.

Up the Down Staircase (**Robert Mulligan 1967**) ☆
Quiet Sandy Dennis has a rough time in a tough New York school.

TEAR-JERKERS

An Affair to Remember (>**Leo McCarey 1957**) ☆ ☞
>Cary Grant waits in vain for Deborah Kerr to renew their shipboard romance.

Applause (**Rouben Mamoulian 1929**) ☞ ☆
Drunken singer Helen Morgan hides her lifestyle from her snooty student daughter.

Blossoms in the Dust (>**Mervyn Le Roy 1941**) ☞ ✍ ☆
Greer Garson founds an orphanage when her own family is killed.

Brief Encounter (>**David Lean 1945**) ☞ ☆ ✍
Trevor Howard and Celia Johnson's doomed love begins and ends at a railway station.

The Good Mother (**Leonard Nimoy 1988**) ☆
>Diane Keaton's affair with Liam Neeson jeopardizes her case during a custody trial.

My Foolish Heart (**Mark Robson 1949**) ☆
Dana Andrews leaves Susan Hayward when he discovers he is not the father of her baby.

Now Voyager (**Irving Rapper 1942**) ☆ ✍
Psychiatrist Claude Rains encourages >Bette Davis to lead a full life, but disapproves of her affair with Paul Henreid.

Stella Dallas (>**King Vidor 1937**) ☆ ☞ ✍
>Barbara Stanwyck's lack of airs and graces drives away her husband and daughter.

Tender Comrade (**Edward Dmytryk 1943**) ☆
War welder >Ginger Rogers' missing her man keeps the audience welded to their tissues.

TEENAGERS

Babes in Arms (**Busby Berkeley 1939**) ☞
Judy Garland and Mickey Rooney put on a show, as all teenagers seemed to do in 1939.

Dreszcze (US: *Creeps*) (aka *Shivers*) (**Wojciech Marczewski 1981**) ☞ ✍
In postwar Poland, a boy is sent to a camp to be trained to be a good Stalinist.

Good Morning (*Ohayu*) (**Yashujiro Ozu 1959**) ☞ ✍
When they are refused a TV set by their strict father, two boys take a vow of silence.

The Happy Time (**Richard Fleischer 1952**) ☆
Charles Boyer and Louis Jourdan demonstrate how young Canadians should woo.

The Job (US: *The Sound of Trumpets*) (*Il Posto*) (**Ermanno Olmi 1961**) ☞ ☆
Nervous Sandro Panzeri starts on the bottom rung at a busy Milan office.

The Last Picture Show (**Peter Bogdanovich 1971**) ☞ ☆
Jeff Bridges has problems with teen bitch Cybill Shepherd, while older woman Cloris Leachman brings Timothy Bottoms out of his shell.

One Crazy Summer (**Savage Steve Holland 1986**) ☆ ✍
John Cusack is an artist in a family of sportsmen who needs to illustrate a love story to gain his scholarship.

Pretty in Pink (**Howard Deutch 1986**) ☆
Harry Dean Stanton advises Molly Ringwald to ignore social snobbery and pursue Andrew McCarthy.

Risky Business (Paul Brickman 1983) ☆
While his parents are away, Tom Cruise makes a fortune pimping for prostitute Rebecca De Mornay.

Sixteen Candles (John Hughes 1984) ☆
No one remembers Molly Ringwald's birthday, but in the midst of her sulk, she grows up.

Square Dance (Daniel Petrie 1987) ☆
Jane Alexander detests life on the farm with grumpy grandpa Jason Robards, Jr so she joins her mother in the city.

TELEVISION

The Barefoot Executive (Robert Butler 1970) ✍
Kurt Russell conducts a viewing poll and discovers that the most reliable opinions are those of a chimp.

Broadcast News (James L. Brooks 1987) ☆ ☞ ✍
News editor Holly Hunter is loved and lost by front man >William Hurt and ace reporter Albert Brooks.

Comic Magazine (*Komikku zasshi nanka iranai!*) (Yojiro Takita 1987) ✍ ☆
Japanese news interviewer Yuya Uchida seeks a serious scoop after years of covering end-of-bulletin funnies.

A Face in the Crowd (>Elia Kazan 1957) ☞ ✍ ☆
A country boy is transformed into a megalomaniac through the popularity of his show.

Ginger and Fred (*Ginger e Fred*) (>Federico Fellini 1986) ☞ ☆
>Astaire and >Rogers impersonators >Marcello Mastroianni and Giulietta Masina reunite for TV special.

The Great Man (Jose Ferrer 1956) ✍ ☆
A TV tribute to Ferrer deteriorates into an exposé of his faults and failures.

Kamikaze (Didier Grousset 1989) ☞ ✍
Angered by the poor quality of TV programmes, Michel Galabru invents a device with which he can kill people on the screen at will.

Medium Cool (Haskell Wexler 1969) ☆
Cameraman Robert Forster despairs of the corruption and hatred he witnesses covering the 1968 Democratic convention.

Meet Mr Lucifer (Anthony Pelissier 1953) ☆
As attendances at his pantomime plunge, Stanley Holloway dreams he is the Devil with the power to prevent people watching TV.

My Favorite Year (Richard Benjamin 1982) ☆
Notorious drunken film star Peter O'Toole's antics drive a comedy TV series' producer to despair.

Network (>Sidney Lumet 1976) ☆ ☞
William Holden tries to silence Peter Finch when he begins to air his opinions.

Switching Channels (Ted Kotcheff 1988) ☆ ✍
News editor Burt Reynolds persuades ace-reporter ex-wife >Kathleen Turner to abandon marriage to Christopher Reeve.

TELEVISION SPIN-OFFS

Dad's Army (Norman Cohen 1971) ☆
Arthur Lowe as the pompous Home Guard captain leading his aged and ailing troops in a war game against rival platoons.

Dragnet (Tom Mankiewicz 1987) ☆
Dan Aykroyd, the nephew of the TV hero, is joined in cracking a drugs ring by partner Tom Hanks.

The Likely Lads (Michael Tuchner 1976) ☆ ✍
A disastrous camping holiday disrupts James Bolam and Rodney Bewes' domestic arrangements.

Please Sir (Mark Stuart 1971) ☆
John Alderton as the teacher dealing with disruptive students and a discontented staffroom at Fenn Street School: from the series that was itself inspired by the 1967 film *To Sir with Love*.

Porridge (Dick Clement 1979) ☆
Cellmates Ronnie Barker and Richard Beckinsale seek to improve prison life under the beady eye of Fulton Mackay.

Steptoe and Son (Cliff Owen 1972) ☆ ✍
Harry H. Corbett is consoled in the breakdown of his marriage by rag-and-bone man father Wilfrid Brambell.

Up Pompeii (Bob Kellett 1971) ☆
Frankie Howerd as Michael Hordern's slave

commenting on the goings-on prior to the eruption of Vesuvius.

Ten Rillington Place ☆ ✍ ☞
GB • Columbia/Filmways • 1970 • 111 mins • col
d **Richard Fleischer** w **Clive Exton**
ph **Denys Coop** m **Johnny Dankworth**
>**Richard Attenborough, John Hurt, Judy Geeson, Pat Heywood**

Timothy Evans was executed for the murder of his wife Beryl and daughter at No. 10 Rillington Place in 1949, in spite of his continued assertion that 'Christie done it.' John Reginald Christie, the Evans' landlord and a wartime special constable who boasted of his ability to perform minor operations was finally convicted in 1953 for these and six other murders, including that of his wife Ethel, the bodies having been secreted about the house and garden. Based on the Ludovic Kennedy book that helped win Evans his posthumous pardon in 1966, Fleischer's film, with its authentic depiction of postwar London, summons up a brilliant performance of sinister timidity from Attenborough as the seedy killer.

 •Bellboy Robert Montgomery is the unassuming murderer stalking May Whitty, in *Night Must Fall* (Richard Thorpe 1937) (☆ ✍).
•Sadistic Scottish husband Robert Newton makes life miserable for wife Beatrice Varley and daughter Deborah Kerr, in A. J. Cronin's *Hatter's Castle* (Lance Comfort 1941).
•>Joan Fontaine poisons her impoverished artist husband to marry into money, in *Ivy* (Sam Wood 1947) (☞ ■).
•Drunken escorts Rik Mayall and Adrian Edmondson share their premises with habitual killer Peter Cook, in the murder spoof *Mr Jolly Lives Next Door* (Stephen Frears 1988) (☆ ✍ ☞ ♫).

TERRORISM

Airport **(George Seaton 1970)** ☆ ☞
Van Heflin has a bomb in his hand luggage on the disaster struck flight.
Angel **(Neil Jordan 1982)** ☞
Saxophonist Stephen Rea encounters terrorist and gangster violence as he traces the killers of a mute girl he had befriended.
Beyond the Walls **(*Me'Achorei Hasoragim*) (Uri Barbash 1984)** ✍
Arab and Israeli political prisoners are held in the same cell block.
Black Sunday **(John Frankenheimer 1977)** ✍
The Black September gang intend to detonate an airship over a football stadium before Robert Shaw can prevent them.
Cal **(Pat O'Connor 1984)** ✍ ♫
IRA member John Lynch falls for Helen Mirren, the widow of a man at whose killing he acted as getaway driver.
Die Hard **(John McTiernan 1988)** ✍
It may be Christmas Eve, but Bruce Willis's rooftop deliveries are some terrorist hostages.
The Long Good Friday **(John Mackenzie 1980)** ☆ ✍ ♫
London gangster Bob Hoskins' operation is under threat from rivals and the IRA.
Not Quite Jerusalem **(Lewis Gilbert 1985)** ✍
Cross-section of volunteers at a kibbutz have their enjoyable stay disrupted by a terrorist attack.
A Prayer for the Dying **(Mike Hodges 1987)** ✍ ☆
IRA man Mickey Rourke is sheltered from comrade Liam Neeson and gangster Alan Bates by priest Bob Hoskins.
Shake Hands with the Devil **(Michael Anderson 1959)** ☆
Dublin doctor >James Cagney is an IRA leader who comes to relish violence.

Tess ■ ☞ ✍ ☆

France/GB • Renn-Burrill • 1979 • 180 mins • col
d >Roman Polanski w Roman Polanski/
Gerard Brach/John Brownjohn
ph Geoffrey Unsworth/Ghislain Cloquet
m Philippe Sarde
Nastassja Kinski, Leigh Lawson, Peter
Firth, John Collin

Despite the fact that Thomas Hardy's Wessex melodramas have a huge literary following, they have been curiously neglected by film-makers. Sumptuously photographed by Unsworth and Cloquet, Polanski's feminist interpretation of *Tess of the d'Urbervilles* should have heralded a Hardy stampede to match the pre-occupation with E. M. Forster that followed the inferior *A Passage to India* (>David Lean 1983) (☞ ☆ ■). Discovering her kinship with the landowning D'Urberville family proves the ruination, rather than the making of Tess Durbeyfield (Kinski), as the secret of her seduction by cousin Alec (Lawson) surfaces years later to wreck her marriage to jealous farmer Angel Clare (Firth). A latter-day 'woman's picture'.

■**VIEW ON** ▶ •Julie Christie is Bathsheba Everdene, beloved of Alan Bates' itinerant shepherd Gabriel Oak, in another Hardy classic *Far from the Madding Crowd* (>John Schlesinger 1967) (■ ✍ ☞ ☆).
•Jennifer Jones causes country hearts to flutter, in *Gone to Earth* (US: *The Wild Heart*) (>Michael Powell/Emeric Pressburger 1948) (■).
•In Thomas Keneally's story of Australia in 1900, an aborigine cracks under the strain of going up in society, in *The Chant of Jimmie Blacksmith* (Fred Schepisi 1978) (☞ ✍).
•Alan Bates is L. P. Hartley's farmer expressing his love for Julie Christie by letter, in *The Go-Between* (>Joseph Losey 1970) (✍ ☞ ☆).
•The complex implications of a love triangle are examined, in *Early Spring* (*Soshun*) (Yashujiro Ozu 1956) (☞ ■ ✍).

Theatre of Blood ✍ ☆ ☞

GB • United Artists/Cineman • 1973 • 102 mins • col
d Douglas Hickox w Anthony
Greville-Bell ph Wolfgang Suschitsky
m Michael J. Lewis
Vincent Price, Diana Rigg, Ian Hendry,
Harry Andrews, Coral Browne, Jack
Hawkins, Michael Hordern, Arthur Lowe,
Robert Morley, Dennis Price, Diana Dors,
Joan Hickson, Milo O'Shea, Eric Sykes

Passed over for a major stage award, ham actor Edward Lionheart (Vincent Price) is presumed dead after plummeting into the Thames. However, he survives to wreak his vengeance on those who panned his performances. Supported by daughter Edwina (Rigg) and a repertory company of winos, he murders the critics in wickedly tailored adaptations of the particular Shakespearian plays he had starred in and about which they had been most scathing. Vincent Price revels in the lead devising the devilish deaths, the best being Dennis Price's reprise of Hector's spearing and drawing from *Troilus and Cressida* and Robert Morley's poodle pie, recalling Tamora's feast of her children in *Titus Andronicus*, but the rest are also entertainingly ingenious.

•Female impersonator Kazuo Hasegawa is the bitter thespian, in *An Actor's Revenge* (*Yukinojo Henge*) (Kon Ichikawa 1963) (☆ ☞).
•Vincent Price is the perpetrator of another series of theme killings, in *The Abominable Dr Phibes* (Robert Fuest 1971) (☆).
•Jeanne Moreau exacts revenge when she is made a widow on her wedding day, in *The Bride Wore Black* (*La Mariée Était en Noir*) (>François Truffaut 1967) (☞ ☆).
•Eccentric millionaire Peter Sellers and his ward Ringo Starr inflict just deserts on the greedy, in *The Magic Christian* (Joseph McGrath 1970) (☆).

The Thin Man ☆ ✍ ☞
USA • MGM • 1934 • 93 mins • b/w
d W. S. Van Dyke   w Frances
Goodrich/Albert Hackett   ph James
Wong Howe   m William Axt
>William Powell, >Myrna Loy, Maureen
O'Sullivan, Nat Pendleton, Cesar Romero

Although the evidence of >*Julia* (>Fred Zinnemann 1977) (✍ ☆ ☞ ■) would suggest otherwise, Dashiell Hammett based Nick and Nora Charles, the most enviable married couple in screen history, on himself and Lillian Hellman. Retired from the Trans-American Detective Agency, Nick is drinking, loafing and loving his way through sophisticated Nora's wealth until a murder at a laboratory and the disappearance of a thin inventor entice him back into circulation. Made in just 12 days by 'One-Take Woody' Van Dyke, this screwball mystery is supreme entertainment, with the silent svelte villain William Powell and glamorous vamp Myrna Loy of silent films now exquisitely funny in the roles they were to reprise with Asta the Airedale in *After the, Another, Shadow of the Thin Man, The Thin Man Goes Home* and *The Song of the Thin Man* (for details see entry for >William Powell).

 •>William Powell played another suave detective – S. S. Van Dine's Philo Vance, in *The Kennel Murder Case* (>Michael Curtiz 1933) (☞ ☆ ✍).
•George Segal and lover Glenda Jackson exchange machine-gun wit, charm and repartee, in *A Touch of Class* (Melvin Frank 1973) (☆ ✍).
•Albert Finney and Audrey Hepburn are the model couple reliving their first dozen years of marriage, in *Two for the Road* (>Stanley Donen 1966) (☆ ☞).
•>Philippe Noiret is the man and his dog locking themselves away from the world, in *Alexandre* (US: *Very Happy Alexandre*) (Yves Robert 1967) (☆ ✍).
•>Jane Fonda and George Segal are the bantering couple who turn to commiting rather than solving crime for amusement, in *Fun with Dick and Jane* (Ted Kotcheff 1976) (☞ ☆).
•>Carole Lombard and Robert Montgomery

discover they aren't really married, in the comedy of marriage *Mr & Mrs Smith* (>Alfred Hitchcock 1941) (☞ ☆ ✍).
•Jane Russell and Vincent Price's unhappy marriage is not helped by a case of murder and her reunion with old flame Victor Mature, in *The Las Vegas Story* (Robert Stevenson 1952) (✍ ☞ ☆).

The Third Man ☆ ☞ ♫ ✍ ■
GB • British Lion/London Films • 1949 • 100 mins • b/w

d >Carol Reed   w >Graham Greene
ph Robert Krasker   m Anton Karas

>Orson Welles, Joseph Cotten, Trevor
Howard, Alida Valli, Wilfrid Hyde White

Graham Greene's screenplay (from a story he wrote at director Carol Reed's instigation) is a study of treachery and tension within relationships. In a postwar Vienna controlled by Soviet, French, British and American forces, Western writer Holly Martins (Cotten) fiercely disputes with the British major Calloway (Howard) 'murdered' friend Harry Lime's involvement in an adulterated penicillin racket and betrays Lime's girlfriend Anna (Valli) despite falling in love with her, before gunning down Lime in a sewer shootout, after Harry boasts of his guilt atop a ferris wheel in the Prater. Anton Karas's omnipresent zither music and Orson Welles' fleeting cameo dominate a gripping picture.

 •Rosanna Arquette goes missing in pursuit of Madonna, in *Desperately Seeking Susan* (Susan Seidelman 1985) (☆ ♫ ☞).
•>Lillian Gish believes David Janssen is innocent of murder, but he needs proof, in *Warning Shot* (Buzz Kulik 1966) (☆).
•Robert Ryan and Merle Oberon protect anti-Nazi Paul Lukas in four nation policed Berlin, in *Berlin Express* (Jacques Tourneur 1948) (✍ ☆).
•A musical adaptation of >Ingmar Bergman's *Smiles of a Summer's Night* is set in the Vienna of another age, in *A Little Night Music* (Harold Prince 1977) (♫ ☆).

This Is Spinal Tap ♫ ☆ ✍
USA • 1984 • 122 mins • col
d Rob Reiner w Rob Reiner/Michael McKean/Christopher Guest/Harry Shearer ph Peter Smokler m Michael McKean/Christopher Guest/Harry Shearer/Rob Reiner

Michael McKean, Christopher Guest, Harry Shearer, Tony Hendra, June Chadwick, Patrick MacNee, Fran Drescher, Angelica Huston

Superbly parodying >Martin Scorsese's enjoyable, but pompous 'rockumentary' of The Band's farewell concert *The Last Waltz* (1978) (♫), this staggeringly funny film follows the disastrous American tour of declining heavy metal band, Spinal Tap. Discussing their '60s incarnations, exploding drummers and musical direction, David St Hubbins (McKean), Nigel Tufnel (Guest) and Roy Smalls (Shearer) perfectly capture the fortune cookie philosophy and *macho* vacuousness of the rock star in a series of hilarious interview extracts. The songs are brilliant pastiche, particularly *Big Bottom* and the strutting stage routines for *In The Beginning* and *Stonehenge* are brilliant and, in the case of the latter, one might say, inch perfect.

•Neil Innes provided The Beatles pastiches for Eric Idle's exceptional rock spoof *The Rutles – All You Need Is Cash* (Gary Weiss 1978) (♫ ✍ ☆).
•>Dustin Hoffman is a rock singer resorting to a psychiatrist to cope with the problems of fame, in *Who is Harry Kellerman and Why is He Saying Those Terrible Things about Me?* (Ulu Grosbard 1971) (☆).
•Jimmy Nail and Paul Brown are among the aliens exploited as rock stars by Griff Rhys Jones, in *Morons from Outer Space* (Michael Hodges 1985) (☆).
•Bob Dylan directed the study of his own concert tour *Renaldo and Clara* (1978) (♫).
•Artist Pablo Picasso is the real genius caught at work, in *The Picasso Mystery* (Henri-Georges Clouzot 1956) (☞).
•Harry Shearer eventually escapes the perspex shell that clams up during a stage show; not so the luckless Jose Luis Lopez Vasquez, in *The Telephone Box* (*La Cabina*) (Antonio Mercero 1974) (✍).

THOSE MAGNIFICENT MEN IN THEIR FLYING MACHINES

***Aces High* (Jack Gold 1976)** ☞
First World War novice Peter Firth worships Malcom McDowell, unaware he cannot fly unless he is drunk.

***Air Force* (>Howard Hawks 1943)** ☞ ■
The crew of the Mary Ann win their wings in battles over the Philippines and the Coral Sea before repairing to Australia.

***The Blue Max* (John Guillermin 1966)** ☆
German First World War flier George Peppard entices Ursula Andress away from James Mason.

***The Dam Busters* (Michael Anderson 1954)** ☆ ♫ ✍
Michael Redgrave's Barnes Wallis perfects the bouncing bomb used on the mission to destroy the Ruhr dams led by Richard Todd's Guy Gibson.

***The Dawn Patrol* (>Howard Hawks 1930) ☞ ■/(Edmund Goulding 1938)** ☆ ☞
Richard Barthelmess and Douglas Fairbanks Jr, then Errol Flynn, >Basil Rathbone and David Niven wait for a crack at the Kaiser.

***The Great Waldo Pepper* (George Roy Hill 1975)** ■ ☞
Robert Redford puts his World War I experience into putting on an aerial stunt flying show.

***Hell's Angels* (Howard Hughes 1930)** ☞ ☆
Brothers Ben Lyon and James Hall spend non-flying time feuding over >Jean Harlow.

***Only Angels Have Wings* (>Howard Hawks 1939)** ☆ ☞
>Cary Grant and Richard Barthelmess fly over the jungles of South America and are rivals for the love of Jean Arthur.

***Reach for the Sky* (Lewis Gilbert 1955)** ☆
Kenneth More as Douglas Bader, the pilot who overcame losing his legs to fly again.

***The Sound Barrier* (US: *Breaking the Sound Barrier*) (>David Lean 1952)** ☞
Ralph Richardson is unconcerned who suffers

provided his plane flies faster than the speed of sound.

Those Magnificent Men in Their Flying Machines or How I Flew from London to Paris in 25 Hours and 11 Minutes (Ken Annakin 1965) ☆ ■
Assorted pioneer aviators compete comically in the first cross-Channel air race.

Twelve O'Clock High (Henry King 1949) ☞ ☆
Gregory Peck has a nervous breakdown while commander of a US bomber unit in Britain during World War II.

The Way to the Stars (US: Johnny in the Clouds) (>Anthony Asquith 1945) ☞ ☆ ✍
Local residents and families worry about their boys at a neighbouring RAF airfield.

Wings (>William Wellman 1927) ☞ ■
Flyboys Charles Buddy Rogers and Richard Arlen both love Clara Bow, and after an accidental killing, one has a free hand.

TIME TRAVEL

Back to the Future (Robert Zemeckis 1985) ✍ ☆
Michael J. Fox goes back in time and makes a man of his wimpish father and warns a professor of an assassination.

Berkeley Square (Frank Lloyd 1933) ☆ ✍
>Leslie Howard finds himself the 18th-century owner of his family home.

Biggles (John Hough 1986)
Far removed from the W. E. Johns original as a yuppie goes back to the First World War to help the daring air ace defeat German spies.

A Connecticut Yankee in King Arthur's Court (UK: A Yankee in King Arthur's Court) (Tay Garnnett 1948) ✍ ☆ ♫
Bing Crosby is busy doin' nothin' until he is called on to rid Cedric Hardwicke of ambitious Mervyn Vye.

Maxie (Paul Aaron 1985)
Kevin Kline looks bemused as Glenn Close shuttles between being a yuppie and a 1920s society girl.

Peggy Sue Got Married (>Francis Ford Coppola 1986) ☆ ✍
>Kathleen Turner goes from class reunion to prom night, putting her life to rights as she goes.

Somewhere in Time (Jeannot Szwarc 1980) ☆
Christopher Reeve failed to win Jane Seymour's heart in a past life, but gets another chance.

Things to Come (William Cameron 1936) ☞
Raymond Massey samples the tragedies destined to overtake London, in this film based on H. G. Wells's *The Shape of Things to Come*.

Time Bandits (Terry Gilliam 1981) ✍ ✳ ☆
While searching for a time map, a young boy meets >Sean Connery's Agamemnon, John Cleese's Robin Hood and Ian Holm's Napoleon.

Time Flies (Walter Forde 1944) ☆
Eccentric inventor Tommy Handley fetches up at the court of Evelyn Dall's Elizabeth I.

The Time Machine (George Pal 1960) ☆ ✳
Rod Taylor leaves Victorian London for the dangers of the future in this adaptation of H. G. Wells's novel.

Where Do We Go from Here? (Gregory Ratoff 1945) ☆
Genie June Haver takes Fred MacMurray on a whistle-stop tour of US history.

Top Hat ☆ ♫ ☞ ✍

USA • RKO • 1935 • 100 mins • b/w
d Mark Sandrich w Dwight Taylor/Allan Scott ph David Abel/Vernon Walker m Irving Berlin
>Fred Astaire, >Ginger Rogers, Edward Everett Horton, Helen Broderick, Eric Blore, Erik Rhodes

Having danced *Cheek to Cheek*, cinema's most serene piece of choreography, Jerry Travers (Astaire) wants Dale Tremont (Rogers) as a life, not just a dancing, partner, but she resists, believing him to be already hitched to her best friend, Madge Hardwick (Broderick). Astaire and Rogers transformed such mundane plots throughout their partnership, this film becoming RKO's biggest grosser of the 1930s. Their dance routines are so thrilling and transcendent that we urge the soundtrack to hurry on to such classics as *Top Hat, White Tie and Tails* and *Isn't It a Lovely Day (To Be Caught in the*

TOM JONES
(Tony Richardson 1962) ■ ☞ ✍ ☆

HISTORICAL ADVENTURE

HUDSON'S BAY
(Irving Pichel 1940) ☆
(Canada won for Charles II of England)

THE BLACK SWAN
(Henry King 1942) ✍
(Captain Morgan routs Caribbean pirates)

BRIDE OF VENGEANCE
(Mitchell Leisen 1948) ☆
(the Borgias scheme to dominate medieval Italy)

IVANHOE
(Richard Thorpe 1952) ✍
(Sir Walter Scott's tale of medieval chivalry and romance)

VERA CRUZ
(Robert Aldrich 1953) ☆ ☞ ✍
(>Gary Cooper caught up in plot to overthrow Emperor Maximilian of Mexico)

LET JOY REIGN SUPREME (QUE LA FÊTE COMMENCE)
(Bertrand Tavernier 1975) ☞ ■
(Louis XV's Regent fights masses and upper classes)

HISTORICAL 'FACTION'

>NAPOLEON
(Abel Gance 1927) ☞ ☆ ■ ✍
(Bonaparte rises through military academy and French Revolutionary ranks)

THE HITLER GANG
(John Farrow 1944) ✍
(the rise of the Nazi party)

ANASTASIA
(Anatole Litvak 1956) ☆
(>Ingrid Bergman claims to be Tsar's escaped daughter)

KHARTOUM
(Basil Dearden 1966) ■
(General Gordon's last stand against Mahdi >Laurence Olivier)

THE RISE OF LOUIS XIV (aka THE RISE TO POWER OF LOUIS XIV) (LA PRISE DE POUVOIR PAR LOUIS XIV)
(>Roberto Rossellini 1966)
(the Sun King establishes his power)

CROMWELL
(Ken Hughes 1970) ☆ ✍
(A chronicle of the English Civil War)

Adventures of Henry Fielding's foundling
who marries into squirearchy

HISTORICAL ROMANCE

MADAME DUBARRY (US: PASSION)
(>Ernst Lubitsch 1919) ☞ ☆
(career of Louis XV [>Emil Jannings]'s famous mistress)

CATHERINE THE GREAT
(Paul Czinner 1934) ☆
(love affairs of Russia's Scarlet Empress)

THE BARRETTS OF WIMPOLE STREET
(Sidney Franklin 1934) ☆ ✍
(Norma Shearer's Elizabeth is wooed by >Fredric March's poet Robert Browning)

ALL THIS AND HEAVEN TOO
(Anatole Litvak 1940) ☆ ✍
(nobleman Charles Boyer has affair with governess >Bette Davis)

KITTY
(Mitchell Leisen 1945) ☆ ■
(18th-century London noble/waif Pygmalion)

JOSEPH ANDREWS
(Tony Richardson 1977) ■ ✍
(Henry Fielding's footman fights to preserve his innocence)

Rain)? Ginger's famous feathered dress is eyecatching, but watch the turn-ups of Fred's trousers, they are hypnotic.

 •>Gene Kelly and Judy Garland eventually find showbiz love, in *For Me and My Gal* (Busby Berkeley 1942) (☆ ☞).

•>Marcello Mastroianni and Giulietta Masina have made their living impersonating Fred and Ginger, in *Ginger and Fred* (*Ginger e Fred*) (>Federico Fellini 1986) (☞ ☆).

•>Ingrid Bergman believes >Cary Grant to be already married, in *Indiscreet* (>Stanley Donen 1958) (☆ ♫).

•>Gene Kelly is so delighted with the inclement weather he begins >*Singin' in the Rain* (Gene Kelly/>Stanley Donen 1952) (♫ ☆ ♫ ☞ ■).

Town and Country Mice

The Boys from Fengkuei (aka *All the Youthful Day*) (*Feng-Kuei-Lai-Tejen*) (Hou Hsiao-hsien 1983) ☞
A Taiwanese teenage trio are so thrilled by the big city that they are unaware they are being exploited.

City Girl (aka *Our Daily Bread*) (>F. W. Murnau 1930) ☞ ■
Mary Duncan finds the country full of hidden terrors.

Coogan's Bluff (Don Siegel 1968) ☆
Arizona Sheriff >Clint Eastwood's prisoner escapes in New York, so he recaptures him using cowboy methods.

Les Cousins (*The Cousins*) (>Claude Chabrol 1958) ☞ ■
Jean-Claude Brialy enjoys the Sorbonne success deserved by country cousin Gerard Blain.

Days and Nights in the Forest (*Aranyer din Ratri*) (>Satyajit Ray 1969) ☞
Four city men spend their holiday at a country cottage and fare very differently in their unfamiliar surroundings.

The Egg and I (Chester Erskine 1947) ☆ ♫
City slickers Claudette Colbert and Fred MacMurray learn the country code when they buy a farm.

A Girl from Lorraine (*La Provinciale*) (Claude Goretta 1980) ☆
All that leaving the country brings to Nathalie Baye is an unsatisfactory fling with Bruno Ganz.

The Lacemaker (*La Dentellière*) (Claude Goretta 1977) ☆ ☞
Isabelle Huppert's romance with Yves Beneyton flourishes in the Normandy countryside, but perishes in Paris.

Mr Deeds Goes to Town (>Frank Capra 1936) ☞ ☆
Poet >Gary Cooper retains his innocence amid the temptations of New York.

My Sister Eileen (Alexander Hall 1942) ☆
Rosalind Russell (AAN) and Janet Blair find their basement apartment is open house to a host of New York eccentrics.

Tracy, Spencer
American actor (1900–1967)

Although his later irascibility made him difficult to work with, Tracy was always a most reliable performer. His instinctive faculty for screen acting is demonstrated by his nine Academy Award credits (a record equalled only by >Laurence Olivier): *San Francisco* (AAN: W. S. Van Dyke 1936) (☆ ☞ ✳) (Tracy smoothes the path of >Clark Gable and Jeanette MacDonald's saloon romance); *Captains Courageous* (AA: Victor Fleming 1937) (☆ ♫) (when spoiled Freddie Bartholemew falls from a liner, fisherman Tracy adds a few rough edges); *Boys' Town* (AA: Norman Taurog 1938) (☆ ♫ ☞) (priest Tracy grants reform school inmates the autonomy to learn how to go straight); *Father of the Bride* (AAN: >Vincente Minnelli 1950) (☆ ☞) (Tracy is too concerned with the cost to whip up any excitement for Elizabeth Taylor's wedding); *Bad Day at Black Rock* (AAN: John Sturges 1955) (☆ ♫ ☞) (the citizens of a small town resent one-armed Tracy's prying into their treatment of a Japanese immigrant farmer); *The Old Man and the Sea* (AAN: John Sturges 1958) (☆ ☞ ■) (fisherman Tracy endures the worst that nature can inflict to land a prize catch, in this screen version of the Ernest Hemingway novel); *Inherit the Wind* (AAN: Stanley Kramer 1960) (☆) (Tracy and

>Fredric March as counsels in the 1925 'monkey trial' of Darwinist teacher Dick York); *Judgement at Nuremberg* (AAN: Stanley Kramer 1961) (✍ ☆) (Tracy as the judge hearing the prosecution of Nazi war criminals, including Burt Lancaster); and *Guess Who's Coming to Dinner?* (AAN: Stanley Kramer 1967) (☆ ☞ ✍) (>Katharine Hepburn talks worried Tracy into accepting their daughter's black fiancé, Sidney Poitier). The last film also concluded his inspired partnership with Katharine Hepburn, the most Oscar nominated female actress (13): *Woman of the Year* (>George Stevens 1942) (☆ ☞) (sportswriter Spencer is unable to live with Kate's nationwide celebrity, thus putting their marriage at risk); *Keeper of the Flame* (>George Cukor 1943) (☞ ☆) (journalist Tracy investigates the death of Hepburn's youth hero husband); *Without Love* (Harold S. Bucquet 1945) (☆) (in wartime Washington, widow Hepburn slowly comes to understand scientist lodger Tracy); *The Sea of Grass* (>Elia Kazan 1947) (☆) (Hepburn demands that Tracy make a choice between his ranch and his family); *State of the Union* (UK: *The World and His Wife*) (>Frank Capra 1948) (☆ ☞) (Tracy is up for election and Hepburn postpones their divorce to campaign at his side); *>Adam's Rib* (>George Cukor 1949) (✍ ☆ ☞ ♫); *Pat and Mike* (>George Cukor 1952) (☆ ☞) (sports entrepreneur Tracy's passion for games is not shared by wife Hepburn).

•*Up the River* (>John Ford 1930) (☆ ☞): >Humphrey Bogart helps ex-jailbird Tracy keep his secret safe.
•*20,000 Years in Sing Sing* (>Michael Curtiz 1933) (☞ ☆): Tracy takes the blame when >Bette Davis kills a man while helping him escape from prison.
•*The Power and the Glory* (William K. Howard 1933) (☆): Tracy rises from rags to riches but finds that power corrupts.
•*Dante's Inferno* (Harry Lachman 1935) (☆ ■): Claire Trevor despairs as Tracy's ambitions for his carnival sideshow become dangerously grandiose.
•*Broken Lance* (Edward Dmytryk 1954) (☆):

rancher Tracy has trouble with his sons Richard Widmark and Robert Wagner.
•*The Last Hurrah* (>John Ford 1958) (☆ ☞): >Basil Rathbone is among the town elders campaigning against Tracy's re-election.
•*It's a Mad, Mad, Mad, Mad World* (Stanley Kramer 1963) (☆): Tracy and >Buster Keaton are among those seeking the fortune buried beneath San Franciscan palm trees.

TRAINS

La Bête Humaine (US: *The Human Beast*) (>Jean Renoir 1938) ☞ ☆ ✍ ■ ♫
Driver >Jean Gabin can't bring himself to kill lover Simone Simon's stationmaster husband.

The Cassandra Crossing (George Pan Cosmatos 1976) ☆
Sophia Loren, Richard Harris, Burt Lancaster and Ava Gardner are threatened by a killer virus carried by a fellow passenger.

>The General (>Buster Keaton/Clyde Bruckman 1926) ☆ ☞ ✍ ■

The Lady Vanishes (>Alfred Hitchcock 1938) ☞ ✍ ☆
Dame May Whitty disappears from her compartment and Michael Redgrave and Margaret Lockwood trap the agents who have kidnapped her.

Murder on the Orient Express (>Sidney Lumet 1974) ✍ ☆
>Agatha Christie whodunnit on board a train caught in a snowdrift.

My Favorite Blonde (Sidney Lanfield 1942) ☆ ✍
Gale Sondergaard's espionage keeps Bob Hope and Madeleine Carroll occupied on their journey.

The Narrow Margin (Richard Fleischer 1952) ✍
Gangsters think they have killed a protected witness, but the victim was a police decoy and the hunt for the real woman begins again.

Northwest Frontier (US: *Flame over India*) (J. Lee-Thompson 1959) ☆ ✍
Kenneth More drives a train through northern India to bring a Raj prince to safety.

Shanghai Express (>Josef Von Sternberg 1932) ☆ ☞
Clive Brook protects >Marlene Dietrich from Warner Oland's Chinese bandit.

3.10 to Yuma (Delmer Daves 1957) ☞ ☆
Van Heflin escorts Glenn Ford to jail, even though the latter's band of outlaws are in hot pursuit.

The Titfield Thunderbolt (Charles Crichton 1952) ☞ ■
Enthusiasts keep a steam train going in the face of competition from a local bus company.

The Train (John Frankenheimer 1964) ☆ ☞
Resistance driver Burt Lancaster thwarts Paul Scofield's attempts to smuggle art treasures back to Germany.
> See Railways and Stations

TRAMPS AND DRIFTERS

Boudu Saved from Drowning (*Boudu Sauvé des Eaux*) (>Jean Renoir 1932) ☞ ☆
Michel Simon repays Charles Grandval by seducing his wife and his mistress.

Down and Out in Beverly Hills (Paul Mazursky 1985) ✍
Con man Nick Nolte takes over Richard Dreyfuss and Bette Midler's luxury home.

Five Easy Pieces (Bob Rafelson 1970) ☆
When >Jack Nicholson tries to dump uneducated Karen Black for his brother's fiancée Susan Ansbach and it falls through, he hits the road.

Meet John Doe (>Frank Capra 1941) ✍ ☆ ☞
When hobo >Gary Cooper is exploited by an ambitious politician to help him win an election, only >Barbara Stanwyck prevents his suicide.

The Sign of Leo (*Le Signe de Lion*) (>Eric Rohmer 1959) ☞ ✍
Jess Hahn thinks he has inherited a fortune, hasn't and sleeps rough in Paris, but salvation is at hand.

Sullivan's Travels (>Preston Sturges 1941) ☞ ✍ ☆
Director Joel McCrea impersonates a tramp to see life as it is, but loses proof of his real identity.

The Tramp (>Charles Chaplin 1915) ✍
Charlie takes care of abandoned Edna Purviance, only to be abandoned in his turn when her errant lover returns.

Vagabonde (*Sans Toit Ni Loi*) (Agnès Varda 1985) ☞ ✍
Witnesses tell what they know of the life of a woman discovered frozen in a ditch.

Vessel of Wrath (US: *The Beachcomber*) (Erich Pommer 1938) ☆ ✍
Drunken beachcomber >Charles Laughton comes to love missionary Robert Newton's prudish sister Elsa Lanchester.

TRANSVESTITES

Angelos (US: *Angel*) (George Katakouzinos, Greece 1982) ☆
Gay Michael Maniatis is persuaded to work as a drag prostitute by idle sailor lover.

Aren't Men Beasts? (Graham Cutts 1937) ☆
Robertson Hare impersonates inheritance-toting aunt to stop his son's undesirable marriage.

Dressed to Kill (Brian De Palma 1980) ☞
>Michael Caine stalks Nancy Allen after she witnesses his mental home murder.

Glen or Glenda (Edward D. Wood, Jr 1952) ✍
The turkey maestro was himself a transvestite and here in two tales tells of a man's love for an angora sweater and of another's sex change.

Love Crazy (Jack Conway 1941) ☆
>William Powell impersonates his own sister as he and >Myrna Loy exchange tit-for-tat infidelities.

Performance (Nicolas Roeg/Donald Cammell 1970) ☆
Gangster James Fox plays role reversal games while holing out with retired pop star Mick Jagger.

Shadey (Philip Savile 1985) ☆
Anthony Sher considers all offers of dubious employment to finance his sex-change operation.

The Tenant (>Roman Polanski 1976) ☞ ☆ ✍ ■
Polanski as a boarding-house tenant driven to obsession with the previous suicidal occupant of his room.

Tootsie (Sydney Pollack 1982) ☆
>Dustin Hoffman dons drag to win a role in a TV soap and becomes a nationwide star.

Viktor und Viktoria (Reinhold Schunzel 1933) ☆ ✍
Drag queen Hermann Thimig and singer Renate Müller become a hit music-hall act, but the 'sex' changes affect their relationship.

Yentl (Barbra Streisand 1983) ☆
This Isaac Bashevis Singer story has Polish Streisand impersonating a boy to pursue her career ambitions.

TREASURE TROVE

Boy on a Dolphin (Jean Negulesco 1957) ☆
Alan Ladd and Clifton Webb compete for the statue discovered by diver Sophia Loren.

It's a Mad, Mad, Mad, Mad World (Stanley Kramer 1963) ☆
>Spencer Tracy and >Buster Keaton are among those seeking a stash buried somewhere in San Francisco.

The Maltese Falcon (>John Huston 1941) ☞ ☆ ✍ ■
>Humphrey Bogart aims to get at a statue before >Peter Lorre and Sydney Greenstreet.

Le Million (>René Clair 1931) ☞ ✍
Artist René Lefèvre searches Paris for his lost lottery ticket.

>*Once upon a Time in America* (Sergio Leone 1984) ✍ ☆ ☞ ♫

Treasure Island (Victor Fleming 1934) ☆ ✍
Wallace Beery as Long John Silver, peg-legged pirate hero of Robert Louis Stevenson's classic adventure.

Wait until Dark (Terence Young 1967) ☆ ✍ ☞
Alan Arkin, Richard Crenna and Jack Weston terrorize blind Audrey Hepburn while searching for a drug-filled doll.

The Wake of the Red Witch (Edward Ludwig 1948) ☆ ✍
Skipper >John Wayne and the craft's owner Luther Adler scour the Indian Ocean for buried loot.

TROUBLE AT MILL

Baara (Souleymane Cissé 1978) ☞
A murder inquiry at a factory in Mali reveals corruption as well as a killer.

Bayan Ko: My Own Country (*Bayan Ko – Kapit sa Patalim*) (Lino Brocka 1984) ✍
Filipino worker breaks into a factory having been dismissed during a strike he had promised not to join.

Blue Collar (Paul Schrader 1978) ☞
Car workers turn to crime when unionization doesn't improve pay fast enough.

Comrades (Bill Douglas 1987) ☞ ■
In 1834 Dorset, labourers form a union and are transported to Australia, in this study of the Tolpuddle Martyrs.

The Molly Maguires (Martin Ritt 1970) ☆
Richard Harris is sent to Pennsylvania to infiltrate >Sean Connery's mine union.

Norma Rae (Martin Ritt 1979) ☆ ☞
Sally Field shocks husband Ron Liebman by organizing a strike at the Deep South mill where she works.

The Pajama Game (>Stanley Donen 1957) ☞ ☆
Doris Day gets a fair day's wage for her members by falling in love with the boss's rep.

Salt of the Earth (Herbert Biberman 1954) ☞
Documentary recalling a New Mexico zinc strike during which wives lined the picket when it was illegal for their husbands to do so.

Strike (Peter Richardson 1988) ✍ ☆
Richardson as Al Pacino and Jennifer Saunders as Meryl Streep as Alexei Sayle's 1986 miners' strike script is filmed by Hollywood.

They Don't Wear Black Tie (*Eles Nao Usam Black Tie*) (Leon Hirszman 1981) ☞
A Brazilian family feud over the rights and wrongs of crossing a picket line.

Trouble in Paradise ☞ ✍ ☆ ■
USA • Paramount • 1932 • 86 mins • b/w
d >Ernst Lubitsch w Samson
Raphaelson/Grover Jones ph Victor
Milner m W. Franke Harling
Herbert Marshall, Miriam Hopkins, Kay
Francis, Edward Everett Horton, Charles
Ruggles, C. Aubrey Smith

Beginning in Venice, Ernst Lubitsch's daring
comedy of criminal and sexual manners is the
story of jewel thief Gaston Monescu (Marshall),
who charms his and accomplice Lily's (Hopkins) way into the Paris household of wealthy
Mariette Colet (Francis), only to find himself
in love with them both. In addition to an audacious shadow sex scene between the thief and
the heiress, the sophisticated plot, reminiscent
of a P. G. Wodehouse novel, plays host to some
wonderful gags, particularly the garbage gon-
dola, the pickpocketing dinner for two and a
minimalist ridiculing of opera. A mischievous
fingerprint on the sheen of romance.

 •Mafia assassins >Kathleen Turner
and >Jack Nicholson are the lovers
in crime in *Prizzi's Honor* (>John
Huston 1985) (☆ ☞ ✍).
•David Niven is E. W. Hornung's urbane jewel
thief in *Raffles* (Sam Wood 1940) (☆ ✍).
•Joan Greenwood is the wicked and Valerie
Hobson the worthy woman waiting for Dennis
Price when he is released from prison, in >*Kind
Hearts and Coronets* (Robert Hamer 1949) (✍
☆ ☞ ■).
•Donald Sutherland and Julie Christie go to
Venice to forget the death of their toddler
daughter, in *Don't Look Now* (Nicolas Roeg
1973) (☞ ☆ ■), while composer Dirk Bogarde
is there to recharge his creative batteries, in
Death in Venice (*Morte a Venezia*) (>Luchino
Visconti 1971) (☞ ☆ ■).

The Trouble with Harry ■ ☞ ☆ ✍
USA • Paramount • 1955 • 99 mins • col
d >Alfred Hitchcock w John Michael
Hayes ph Robert Burks m Bernard
Herrmann
Edmund Gwenn, Mildred Natwick, John
Forsythe, Shirley MacLaine

Hitchcock's thrillers always contained more
than a dash of wit, but in 1955, with *To Catch
a Thief* and this adaptation of Jack Trevor
Story's novel, he demonstrated a genuine flair
for comedy. Set in an autumnal New England
wood so magical it might be the Forest of
Arden, the film deals with the repeated burial
and exhumation of Harry, a man whom three
people believe they have murdered: Edmund
Gwenn with his rabbit gun, Mildred Natwick
with her shoe and Shirley MacLaine (quite
stunning in her film debut) with a milk bottle.
John Forsythe is cynically calm as the artist
who helps them unravel the mystery. Hitchcock had a soft spot for this one and it's easy to
see why.

 •A corpse, by a railway line and on
a river bank respectively, is the
starting point for the action in
Stand by Me (Rob Reiner 1986) (☆) and
River's Edge (Tim Hunter 1986) (☆), while
>James Stewart suspects there is a body on the
premises during a drinks party, in *Rope* (>Al-
fred Hitchcock 1948) (☞ ☆ ✍ ■).
•Alan Bates is the cheerful cynic making his
way up the company ladder, in *Nothing but
the Best* (Clive Donner 1964) (☆).
•Shakespeare's woods are beautifully captured
by cinematographer Harold Rosson in *As You
Like It* (Paul Czinner 1936) (☆ ■).
•Cartoonist Tom Hulce is the cynical artist
caught up in a murder mystery, in *Slam Dance*
(Wayne Wang 1987) (☆ ✍).

TRUCKERS

The Big Gamble (Richard Fleischer/Elmo
Williams 1960) ✍
Stephen Boyd hopes to set up an African haul-
age business from the starting point of one
battered truck.

Coast to Coast (Joseph Sargent 1980) ☆
Dyan Cannon hitches a ride after she storms
out on her husband, but he is soon on her trail.

Convoy (Sam Peckinpah 1978) ☞
Kris Kristofferson rounds up a major traffic
jam to annoy the police.

Hell Drivers (C. Raker Endfield 1957) ☆
>Sean Connery, Stanley Baker, Herbert Lom
and Sidney James are among the truckers competing for an important contract.

Quick Millions (Rowland Brown 1931) ☆
>Spencer Tracy finds there is more money in
being behind a successful gang than a wheel.

Racket Busters (Lloyd Bacon 1938) ☆
George Brent steps in to prevent >Humphrey
Bogart from making a major trucking take-
over.

Road Games (Richard Franklin 1981) ☆
Jamie Lee Curtis helps Stacey Keach escape the
murderous hitch-hiker he has picked up.

They Drive by Night (Arthur Woods 1938)
🖋 ☆

Truckers help Emlyn Williams prove he is not
a killer.

The Wages of Fear (*La Salaire de la Peur*)
(Henri-Georges Clouzot 1953) 🖋 ☞ ■ ☆
>Yves Montand transports explosives across
pot-holed roads to a South American oil field.

Truffaut, François
French actor/writer/director (1932–84)

Jailed for the indebtedness of his Paris ciné-
club and pardoned for army desertion on account of character instability, Truffaut, as a
Cahiers du Cinéma critic, was responsible for
the auteur theory that celebrated film-making
and attacked script-filming, while his *The 400
Blows* (*Les Quatre Cents Coups*) (1959) (☞ ☆
🖋) (Jean-Pierre Léaud as Antoine Doinel sentenced to and escaping from a reform school)
helped define the New Wave movement in
French cinema. He continued the Doinel
chronicle (played by protege Léaud) in *Love at
Twenty* (*L'Amour à Vingt Ans*) (1962) (☞)
(Antoine spends the evening with a girl's parents after she rejects him), *Stolen Kisses* (*Bai-
sers Volés*) (1968) (☞ ☆ 🖋) (Doinel returns to
civvy street from national service, but can't
hold down a steady job), *Bed and Board* (*Do-*

micile Conjugale) (1970) (☞ ☆) (marriage to
Claude Jade spawns a novel, an affair with a
Japanese girl and a child) and *Love on the Run*
(*L'Amour en Fuite*) (1979) (☞ ☆) (separated
from Jade, Doinel is encouraged to write by
ex-girlfriend Marie-France Pisier). Doinel
agonized over an autobiographical novel and
the creative process informs much of Truf-
faut's other work: LITERARY, *The Man Who
Loved Women* (*L'Homme qui Aimait les Fem-
mes*) (1977) (☞ ☆) (Charles Denner is ob-
sessed with women, but his passion leads to his
fatal downfall) and *The Green Room* (*La
Chambre Verte*) (1978) (☆ ☞ 🖋) (Nathalie
Baye sees death as the route to death-obsessed
obituary writer Truffaut's heart): CINEMATIC,
Day for Night (*La Nuit Americaine*) (1973) (☞
🖋) (Foreign Film Oscar winner has Jean-
Pierre Léaud's falling for actress Jacqueline
Bisset being the least of the problems facing a
location film crew), and THEATRICAL: *The Last
Metro* (*Le Dernier Métro*) (1980) (☞ ☆ 🖋)
(>Catherine Deneuve keeps her Jewish husband's theatre open during the Nazi occupa-
tion of Paris). Like his heroes >Jean Renoir and
>Alfred Hitchcock, Truffaut frequently ap-
peared in his own films and guested in *Close
Encounters of the Third Kind* (>Steven Spielberg 1977) (☆ ♫ ✳) (Truffaut's scientist is
pipped by Richard Dreyfuss for selection as the
first human to fly in an alien spacecraft).

•*Shoot the Pianist* (US: *Shoot the
Piano Player*) (*Tirez sur le Pianiste*) (1960) (☞ ☆): reduced to
playing seedy bars, Charles Aznavour gets his
brother out of gangster trouble at the cost of
his girlfriend's death.

•>*Jules et Jim* (1961) (☞ ☆ 🖋 ■).

•*Silken Skin* (US: *The Soft Skin*) (*La Peau
Douce*) (1964) (🖋 ☞): when academic Jean
Desailly's affair fails his wife's response to his
pleas for reconciliation is fatal.

•*Fahrenheit 451* (1966) (☞ 🖋): Julie Christie
smuggles books when they are outlawed in a
future society.

•*The Bride Wore Black* (*La Mariée Était en
Noir*) (1967) (☞ ☆): Jeanne Moreau picks off
the men who made her a wedding day widow.

•*The Wild Child* (*L'Enfant Sauvage*) (1970) (☆

☞ ✍): an 18th-century boy proves deaf not wild under the tutelage of doctor Truffaut.

•*Anne and Muriel* (US: *Two English Girls*) (*Les Deux Anglaises et le Continent*) (1971) (☞): >*Jules et Jim* is reworked in Wales with Kika Markham and Sylvia Marriott beloved by Jean-Pierre Léaud.

•*The Story of Adèle H.* (*L'Histoire d'Adèle H*) (1975) (☆ ☞ ■): Isabelle Adjani as Victor Hugo's daughter whose obsessive love of an English soldier resulted in destitution in the West Indies.

•*Small Change* (*L'Argent de Poche*) (1976): (☞): pre-adolescents find out about life and love at school and in a tenement block.

•*La Petite Voleuse* (Claude Miller 1989) (☞ ☆ ✍ ■): Truffaut's long-cherished project post-humously completed has Charlotte Gainsbourg treading the path Doinel went down in *The 400 Blows*.

TURKIES

The Attack of the Fifty-Foot Women (Nathan Hertz 1958)
Turned giantess by aliens, Allison Hayes makes her husband's mistress feel small.

The Attack of the Killer Tomatoes (John De Bello 1980)
Tomatoes avenge themselves on the eaters and politicians of San Diego.

It Came from beneath the Sea (Robert Gordon 1953)
A giant octopus that is quite at home on land takes a dislike to San Francisco.

The Night of the Ghouls (Edward D. Wood Jr 1960) ☞
Clairvoyant Dr Acula fakes resurrections and cleans up on relatives who pay him to make them rest in peace.

Percy (Ralph Thomas 1971)
Hywel Bennett has a penis transplant.

Plan Nine from Outer Space (Edward D. Wood, Jr 1959) ☞ ✍
Aliens land on earth and turn the undead into vampires, but rest assured the police are on to them.

Tarzan and the Valley of Gold (Robert Day 1966)
Edgar Rice Burroughs is sent spinning in his grave as Mike Henry cavorts around in the modern-day South American jungle.

Tenue du Soirée (Evening Dress) (Bertrand Blier 1986) ☆
Gay crook >Gérard Depardieu seduces Michel Blanc into becoming his partner in bed and crime.

They Saved Hitler's Brain (David Bradley 1963) ✳
Hitler's brain survives the bunker and is taken to South America from where it can have another crack at world domination.

Wild Women of Wongo (James L. Wolcott 1958)
The women of Wongo care for the handsome but hopeless men of Goona.

Turner, Kathleen
American actress (b 1954)
Strikingly beautiful, Turner used her sexuality to exploit hypnotized males in >*Body Heat* (Laurence Kasdan 1981) (☆ ✍ ☞ ■), *The Man with Two Brains* (Carl Reiner 1983) (Turner would be the ideal wife without her temper, so scientist Steve Martin gives her a brain transplant) and *Prizzi's Honor* (>John Huston 1985) (☆ ☞ ✍) (Mafia assassin Turner falls for her opposite number >Jack Nicholson), although it ensnared her in *Crimes of Passion* (Ken Russell 1984) (☆ ☞) (fashion designer Turner's alter ego – prostitute China Blue – is stalked by religious maniac Anthony Perkins) and as the voice characterization for Jessica Rabbit in >*Who Framed Roger Rabbit?* (Robert Zemeckis 1988) (✳ ☞ ✍ ☆). A more reticent side emerged in *Romancing the Stone* (Robert Zemeckis 1984) (☆ ✍) (Turner's romantic novelist Joan Wilder is rescued from a South American fate worse than death by adventurer >Michael Douglas), its sequel *Jewel of the Nile* (Lewis Teague 1985) (☆) (Turner and Douglas prevent the Middle Eastern *coup* planned by a sheik whose biography she has been commissioned to write) and *Peggy Sue Got Married* (>Francis Ford Coppola 1986) (☆ ✍) (Turner returns to her teens and has a one night stand with a rebel poet before settling for eventual husband Nicholas Cage).

•*A Breed Apart* (Phillipe Mora 1984) (☆): Turner loves Rutger Hauer who aims to prevent Powers Boothe stealing eagles' eggs.

•*Julia & Julia* (Peter De Monte 1988) (☆): Sting complicates Turner's between life and death search for husband Gabriel Byrne.

•*Switching Channels* (Ted Kotcheff 1988) (☆ ✍): TV news editor Burt Reynolds persuades ace-reporter ex-wife Turner to delay her wedding to Christopher Reeve and cover an escaped-criminal story.

•*The Accidental Tourist* (Laurence Kasdan 1988) (☆ ☞ ✍): Turner competes for guidebook-writer husband >William Hurt with dog-trainer Geena Davis (AA).

Turtle Diary ☆ ✍ ■ ☞
GB • CBS/United British Artists/Britannic •
1985 • 97 mins • col
d John Irvin   w Harold Pinter   ph Peter
Hannan   m Geoffrey Burgon
Ben Kingsley, Glenda Jackson, Michael
Gambon, Richard Johnson, Rosemary
Leach, Eleanor Bron, Harriet Walter, Nigel
Hawthorne

William (Kingsley) and Neaera (Jackson)'s visits to the aquarium at London Zoo convince them it's their duty to free the three sea turtles from the confines of their 'little bedsitter of ocean'. Everyone is isolated in their own small space in Pinter's adaptation of Russell Hoban's splendid novel. William works in a cramped bookshop and lives in a boarding house where he feuds over kitchen hygiene with one resident and pays scant attention to another until her suicide. Keeper George (Gambon) buries himself in his tiny office, and Neaera hides away in her apartment writing children's stories inspired by a water beetle, which, despite playing her part in the turtles' kidnap and journey to the coast, she imprisons in a tiny tank.

•Bookshop assistant George Segal has fellow boarding-house tenant Barbra Streisand evicted for prostitution, in *The Owl and the Pussycat* (Herbert Ross 1970) (✍ ☆).

•In a lonely bedsit, >Jean Gabin reminisces about his doomed affair with Arletty, in >*Le Jour se Lève* (US: *Daybreak*) (Marcel Carné 1939) (☆ ☞ ✍ ■).

•>Robert De Niro and >Meryl Streep begin their romance in a bookshop in *Falling in Love* (Ulu Grosbard 1984) (☆), while antiquarian bookseller Anthony Hopkins carries on a romance by post with customer Anne Bancroft, in *84 Charing Cross Road* (David Jones 1987) (☆).

•A gay Liverpudlian and a Scottish socialist free the dolphins from Brighton Oceanland, in *The Fruit Machine* (Philip Savile 1988) (✍ ☆).

•Southport cinema projectionist Barry Jackson is the quiet man belying a passionate nature, in *Mr Love* (Roy Battersby 1986) (☆).

•A pig destined for a royal wedding dinner is the kidnapped animal, in *A Private Function* (Malcolm Mowbray 1984) (✍ ☆).

•Orphan Loretta Young comes to live with a zookeeper, in *Zoo in Budapest* (Rowland V. Lee 1933) (☆), while zoological imagery informs *A Zed and Two Noughts* (Peter Greenaway 1985) (☞ ■ ♫).

Twelve Angry Men ☆ ☞ ✍
USA • United Artists • 1957 • 95 mins • b/w
d >Sidney Lumet   w Reginald Rose
ph Boris Kaufman   m Kenyon Hopkins
>Henry Fonda, Lee J. Cobb, E. G.
Marshall, Jack Warden, Ed Begley, Martin
Balsam, Jack Klugman, John Fiedler,
George Voskovec, Robert Webber,
Edward Binns, Joseph Sweeney

A young Puerto Rican has the evidence stacked against him, and the jury's retiring to consider its verdict appears a formality, especially as the trial has been tedious and it is swelteringly hot. However, Henry Fonda isn't convinced, and through a recreation of events, discussion of the boy's motives and the prejudices of his fellow jurymen, he persuades the other 11 to vote 'not guilty'. The jurors' gradual capitulation recalls the relentless dwindling of numbers in *And Then There Were None* (>René Clair 1945) (✍ ☆ ☞), while each man states his position like a Chaucerian pilgrim telling a tale. Lumet, in his film debut, expertly turns

Fonda's almost quixotic commitment and Lee J. Cobb's recalcitrance into engrossing entertainment.

 •An old woman and a young boy are the unlikely saviours of a racially victimized black man, in *Intruder in the Dust* (Clarence Brown 1951) (☞ ✍ ☆).

•The private lives of the jury have a bearing on the verdict, in *Justice est Faite* (aka *Let Justice Be Done*) (US: *Justice Is Done*) (André Cayatte 1950) (☞ ✍).

•>Michael Douglas joins a coterie of judges who execute those exonerated by juries, in *The Star Chamber* (Peter Hyams 1983).

•A question of doubt arises in court, in *The Paradine Case* (>Alfred Hitchcock 1947) (☞ ☆ ✍) (lawyer Gregory Peck falls in love with murder suspect Alida Valli) and *Boomerang* (>Elia Kazan 1947) (☞ ■ ☆) (DA Dana Andrews pleads for an unjustly accused man after a priest is killed).

•Jill Clayburgh is the woman Supreme Court judge proving her competence to chauvinist Justice Walter Matthau, in *First Monday in October* (Ronald Neame 1981) (☆).

•Alan Bates (AAN) is a Jew accused of crimes he did not commit in Tsarist Russia, in *The Fixer* (John Frankenheimer 1968) (☆ ✍ ☞).

TWINS

***Among the Living* (Stuart Heisler 1941)** ☆
One Albert Dekker is a killer and Susan Hayward doesn't know which.

***The Black Room* (Roy William Neill 1935)** ☆ ✍
Bad >Boris Karloff kills off benign Boris and abuses his position as a petty German ruler.

***The Dark Mirror* (Robert Siodmak 1946)** ☆ ☞
Cop Lew Ayres has to guess which >Olivia De Havilland to trust.

***Dead Ringers* (David Cronenberg 1988)** ☆
Gynaecologists Jeremy Irons begin mutually to deteriorate as they grow more successful.

***Keep 'Em Flying* (Arthur Lubin 1941)** ☆
Bumbling airmen Bud Abbott and Lou Costello mix up identical twin girls.

***The Man in the Iron Mask* (James Whale 1939)** ☞
This Alexandre Dumas tale has Louis Hayward's Louis XIV keeping his twin in prison until D'Artagnan Warren William strikes.

***Nicky and Gino* (US: *Dominick and Eugene*) (Robert M. Young 1988)** ☆
Ray Liotta reckons that his mentally retarded twin Tom Hulce is holding back his life.

***Twin Sisters of Kyoto* (aka *The Old Capital*) (*Koto*) (Noboru Nakamura 1963)** ■
As twins are considered bad luck, girls are separated at birth.

***Twins* (Ivan Reitman 1988)** ☆
Danny De Vito and Arnold Schwarzenegger scour Texas for their lost mother.

Upstairs downstairs

The Amorous Adventures of Moll Flanders (Terence Young 1965) ✍

Kim Novak as Daniel Defoe's ambitious serving maid.

Blighty (Adrian Brunel 1926) ✍

World War I veteran chauffeur heads the household from below stairs when the master is killed.

Cavalcade (Frank Lloyd 1933) ✍ ☞

The Noël Coward script traces the life of a London house in the first third of the 20th-century.

The Courtneys of Curzon Street (US: *The Courtenay Affair*) (Herbert Wilcox 1947) ☆

As his father married a maid, Michael Wilding sees nothing wrong in marrying factory girl Anna Neagle.

Emma (Clarence Brown 1932) ☆

>Myrna Loy is the daughter opposing her father Jean Hersholt's marriage to nanny Marie Dressler.

Everybody Sing (Edwin L. Marin 1937) ✍

A snobbish family's servants put on a Broadway show.

Forever and a Day (>René Clair/Edmund Goulding/Cedric Hardwicke/Frank Lloyd/Victor Saville/Robert Stevenson/ Herbert Wilcox 1943) ☞ ☆ ✍

>Charles Laughton, Merle Oberon, Claude Rains and Ray Milland are among those living in a London house between 1804 and 1940.

La Régle du Jeu (*The Rules of the Game*) (>Jean Renoir 1939) ☞ ☆ ✍ ■

Spring in Park Lane (Herbert Wilcox 1948) ☆

Noble Michael Wilding impersonates a foot-man and falls for the daughter of the house, Anna Neagle.

That Obscure Object of Desire (*Cet Obscur Objet du Désir*) (>Luis Buñuel 1978) ☞ ☆

Businessman Fernando Rey ruins himself through his obsession with a maid.

The Valley of Decision (Tay Garnett 1945) ☆

Lionel Barrymore's Pittsburgh household is upset by son Gregory Peck's marriage to maid Greer Garson.

UMBERTO D
(>Vittorio De Sica 1952) ☞ ☆ ▦ ▣

ITALIAN NEO-REALISM

SHOESHINE (SCIUSCIA)
(>Vittorio De Sica 1946) ☞ ☆ ✍
(black marketeers covet horse but end in reform school)

PAISÀ (US: PAISAN)
(>Roberto Rossellini 1946) ☞
(interaction of Italians and liberating GIs)

LA TERRA TREMA
(>Luchino Visconti 1948) ☞ ▣
(hardships of exploited Sicilian fishermen)

STROMBOLI (STROMBOLI, TERRA DI DIO)
(>Roberto Rossellini 1950) ☞ ♫
(prejudice and isolation inflicted on stranger >Ingrid Bergman)

THE LADY WITHOUT CAMELLIAS (US: CAMILLE WITHOUT CAMELLIAS) (LA SIGNORA SENZA CAMELIE)
(>Michelangelo Antonioni 1953) ☞ ☆
(starlet's brief fame culminates in bit parts)

THE JOB (US: THE SOUND OF TRUMPETS) (IL POSTO)
(Ermanno Olmi 1961) ☞ ☆
(shy boy's first job in Milan office)

GERMAN EXPRESSIONISM

DESTINY (US: BETWEEN TWO WORLDS) (aka BEYOND THE WALL) (DER MÜDE TOD)
(>Fritz Lang 1921) ☞ ▣
(wife bargains with death to save husband's life)

DIE NIBELUNGEN
(>Fritz Lang 1924) ☞ ▣
(classic epic of Siegfried's trials)

WAXWORKS (DAS WACHSFIGURENKABINETT)
(Paul Leni 1924) ☆ ☞
(poet tells of excesses of three malevolent personages portrayed in wax exhibit)

NOSFERATU (NOSFERATU, EINE SYMPHONIE DES GRAUENS)
(>F. W. Murnau 1924) ☆ ☞
(vampire leaves Transylvania for Bremen to pursue beautiful woman)

VARIETY (aka VAUDEVILLE) (VARIÉTÉ)
(E. A. Dupont 1925) ☆
(jealous trapeze artist >Emil Jannings kills his lover)

SECRETS OF A SOUL (GEHEIMNISSE EINER SEELE)
(G. W. Pabst 1926) ☞
(a man seeks cure for his knife phobia through the analysis of his dreams)

Old man and dog face
destitution and death

FRENCH NEW WAVE

>À BOUT DE SOUFFLE (BREATHLESS)
(>Jean-Luc Godard 1959) ☞ ☆ ■
(thief >Jean-Paul Belmondo and girlfriend on run after accidental killing)

SHOOT THE PIANIST (US: SHOOT THE PIANO PLAYER) (TIREZ SUR LE PIANISTE)
(>François Truffaut 1960) ☞ ☆
(concert pianist down on luck dragged into gangland)

ADIEU PHILIPPINE
(Jacques Rozier 1962) ☞
(TV technician torn between two holiday lovers)

BAY OF ANGELS (BAIE DES ANGES)
(Jacques Demy 1962) ☞ ☆
(bankteller's lucky streak exploited by gambler)

LIFT TO THE SCAFFOLD (US: FRANTIC) (ASCENSEUR POUR L'ECHAFAUD)
(>Louis Malle 1957) ☞ ☆
(having got away with killing his lover's husband, a man is convicted of a crime he didn't commit)

LE BONHEUR (aka HAPPINESS)
(Agnès Varda 1965) ✍
(adulterer marries mistress when wife dies)

BRITISH SOCIAL REALISM

WOMAN IN A DRESSING GOWN
(J. Lee-Thompson 1957) ☆
(husband finally walks out on dowdy housewife)

SPARE THE ROD
(Leslie Norman 1961) ☆
(teacher gets through to tough school kids)

THE LONELINESS OF THE LONG DISTANCE RUNNER
(Tony Richardson 1962) ☆ ☞
(Tom Courtenay has the chance to improve his lot at reform school through his running)

THE LEATHER BOYS
(Sidney J. Furie 1963) ☞
(teenagers marry from lust but drift apart)

THIS SPORTING LIFE
(Lindsay Anderson 1963) ☆ ✍
(miner finds Rugby League can't bring happiness)

NOTHING BUT THE BEST
(Clive Donner 1964) ☆ ✍
(careerist clerk Alan Bates stoops at nothing to progress)

US CIVIL WAR

***Bad Company* (Robert Benton 1972)** ✍
Jeff Bridges and Barry Brown take advantage of the war and roam the countryside as outlaws.

***The Beguiled* (Don Siegel 1971)** ☆
Injured Union soldier >Clint Eastwood lays low at a Confederate girls' school and finds it more dangerous than battle.

***Escape from Fort Bravo* (John Sturges 1953)** ☆
Yankee commander William Holden forgets sides to help Eleanor Parker save Confederate escapee John Forsythe from the Indians.

***Friendly Persuasion* (>William Wyler 1956)** ☞ ✍
Quaker >Gary Cooper is forced to reject his pacifist beliefs when his own family is threatened.

***>Gone with the Wind* (Victor Fleming 1939)** ☆ ■ ✍ ☞ ♫

***The Horse Soldiers* (>John Ford 1959)** ☞
>John Wayne and William Holden blow up a Confederate railway line.

***Major Dundee* (Sam Peckinpah 1965)** ☆
Charlton Heston and Richard Harris take a break from the war to butcher Indians.

***The Red Badge of Courage* (>John Huston 1951)** ☞ ✍
Audie Murphy and Bill Mauldin are innocents terrified at the front.

***Shenandoah* (Andrew V. McLaglen 1965)** ☆
Virginia farmer >James Stewart abandons his neutrality when one of his family of six is kidnapped.

***So Red the Rose* (>King Vidor 1935)** ☞ ■
Belle Margaret Sullavan keeps the home fires burning while Randolph Scott fights on the losing side.

***Virginia City* (>Michael Curtiz 1940)** ☞
Southern dancer Miriam Hopkins tries to steal Union gold from Errol Flynn.

VAUDEVILLE AND BURLESQUE

Lights of Variety (US: *Variety Lights*) (*Luci del Varietà*) (Alberto Lattuada/>Federico Fellini 1950) ✍ ☆
A stand-up comic falls for a new recruit, but she nurses higher ambitions.

The Night They Raided Minsky's (UK: *The Night They Invented Striptease*) (William Friedkin 1968) ☆
Britt Ekland is hired to dance scenes from the Bible to silence puritan Denholm Elliott, but her act has nothing to do with religion.

On the Avenue (Roy Del Ruth 1937) ☆ ✍
Dick Powell lampoons Madeleine Carroll in a revue, and she threatens to sue, but settles romantically out of court.

The Seven Little Foys (Melville Shavelson 1955) ☆ ✍
Bob Hope as Eddie Foy, father of the celebrated family entertainers, jousting with >James Cagney's George M. Cohan.

Show Business (Edwin L. Marin 1944) ☆
Eddie Cantor marries Joan Davis, George Murphy weds Constance Moore and all four make it to the top.

Stormy Weather (Andrew Stone 1943) ☆
Bill Robinson in a *film à clef* of his own rise to fame.

There's No Business Like Show Business (Walter Lang 1954) ☆
One of the Five Donahues, Donald O'Connor, falls for Broadway star >Marilyn Monroe and threatens the act.

When My Baby Smiles at Me (Walter Lang 1948) ☆
Fading star Dan Dailey (AAN) is persuaded by his wife Betty Grable that the show must go on.

Venice Film Festival
The Golden Lion of St Mark is awarded to the Best Foreign Film

1934
Man of Aran (Robert Flaherty) ☞ ■
Documentary on the lives of the fishermen and crofters of the Irish Sea island.
1935
Anna Karenina (Clarence Brown) ☆ ✍ ☞
>Greta Garbo leaves government minister >Basil Rathbone for cavalry officer >Fredric March in this film adaptation of Leo Tolstoy's novel.
1936
The Emperor of California (*Der Kaiser von Kalifornien*) (Luis Trenker) ✍
A Swiss rebel wins the immigrant vote, but is corrupted by power.
1937
Un Carnet de Bal (aka *Life Dances On*) (aka *The Dance Programme*) (Julien Duvivier) ☞ ☆ ✍
Marie Bell reminisces about the men she danced with at a ball.
1938
>*Olympische Spiele 1936* (UK: *Olympiad*) (US: *Olympia*) (Leni Riefenstahl) ☞ ■ ♫
1939
No Award
1940
Der Postmeister (Gustav Vciclay) ✍ ☞
Based on a Pushkin short story, this tale tells of a postmaster's drunken decline after his daughter runs away to St Petersburg with a soldier.
1941
Ohm Krüger (Hans Steinhoff) ☆
>Emil Jannings as Paul Kruger inspiring the South African farmers against the British during the Boer War.
1942
Der Grosse König (The Great King) (Veit Harlan) ✍
A biopic of Frederick the Great, the Enlightened Despot who recovered from his unhappy youth to rule Prussia from 1740 to 1786.
1943–45
No Festival
1946
The Southerner (>Jean Renoir) ☞ ■
Zachary Scott and Ma (Beulah Bondi) have it tough on their unresponsive farm.
1947
Sirena (*The Strike*) (Karel Stekly) ✍
A Czech family is punished for its role in an 1889 factory strike.
1948
>*Hamlet* (>Laurence Olivier) ☆ ☞ ■ ✍ ♫
1949
Manon (Henri-Georges Clouzot) ☞ ✍
Abbé Prevost's novel is here updated to postwar France with Manon, a Nazi collaborator remaining loyal to her Resistance hero lover, despite tribulations.
1950
Justice est Faite (aka *Let Justice Be Done*) (US: *Justice Is Done*) (André Cayatte) ☞ ✍
The private lives of jury members prejudice their verdict.
1951
Rashomon (>Akira Kurosawa) ☞ ■ ☆ ✍
The rape and murder of a samurai's wife is retold by various witnesses during Toshio Mifune's trial.
1952
Forbidden Games (US: *The Secret Game*) (*Jeux Interdits*) (René Clément) ✍ ☞ ☆
A small girl and a peasant boy create an animal cemetery during the Nazi occupation of France.
1953
No Award
1954
Romeo and Juliet (Renato Castellani)
Laurence Harvey and Susan Shentall as the star-crossed lovers.

1955
Ordet (The Word) (Carl Dreyer) ☞ ☆ ✍
A religious bigot has three sons, one of whom prays for the resurrection of his sister-in-law, who died in childbirth.
1956
No Award
1957
>Aparajito (The Unvanquished)
(>Satyajit Ray) ☞ ✍ ■ ☆
1958
Muhomatsu No Issho (Muhomatsu the Rickshaw Man) (Hiroshi Inagaki) ✍
Rickshaw man Toshiro Mifune makes a fool of himself out of love for wealthy widow Hidcko Takamine.
1959
General della Rovere (>Roberto Rossellini) ☞ ☆ ✍
>Vittorio De Sica is forced by the Nazis to impersonate an Italian officer to smoke out partisans, but he joins their cause.
1960
The Crossing of the Rhine (US: Tomorrow Is My Turn) (Le Passage du Rhin) (André Cayatte) ☞
PoWs Charles Aznavour and Georges Rivière meet again in Paris after making a successful escape.
1961
Last Year at Marienbad (L'Année Dernière à Marienbad) (>Alain Resnais) ☞ ☆ ✍
A man insists he had an affair with a woman the year before, but she does not recall him.
1962
Ivan's Childhood (Ivanovo Detstvo) (>Andrei Tarkovsky) ☞ ☆
When the Nazis murder his parents, a boy embarks on a series of dangerous missions to exact his revenge.
1963
Hands over the City (aka Hands on the City) (Le Mani sulla Città) (Francesco Rosi) ☞
The collapse of a slum is exploited by candidates during an election in Naples.

1964
The Red Desert (Il Deserto Rosso)
(>Michelangelo Antonioni) ☞
Monica Vitti's affair fails to alleviate her depression caused by her drab industrial surroundings.
1965
Of a Thousand Delights (US: Sandra) (Vaghe Stelle dell'Orsa) (>Luchino Visconti) ☆ ☞
Claudia Cardinale holds her mother responsible for the death of her Jewish father and is held in lustful esteem by her brother.
1966
The Battle of Algiers (La Battaglia di Algeria) (Gillo Pontecorvo) ☞ ■
Semi-documentary study of how ordinary people saw the Algerian War.
1967
>Belle de Jour (>Luis Buñuel) ☞ ☆ ✍ ■
1968
Artists at the Top of the Big Top: Disorientated (Die Artisten in der Zirkuskuppel: Ratlos) (Alexander Kluge) ☞
When his father accidentally dies on a trapeze, his son vows to set up the world's greatest circus.
1969–79
No Awards
1980
Gloria (John Cassavetes) ☆
Gena Rowlands (AAN) protects a small boy from New York gangsters.
Shared with *Atlantic City, USA* (>Louis Malle) ☞
Con man Burt Lancaster plans to fleece a gambling joint.
1981
The German Sisters (Die Bleierne Zeit) (>Margarethe Von Trotta) ☞ ☆
Journalist Jutta Lampe gets to know her terrorist sister Barbara Sukowa during her prison hunger strike.
1982
The State of Things (>Wim Wenders) ☞
A film producer steals the budget of a sci-fi

picture being made in Portugal, but runs into the Los Angeles Mafia.

1983

First Name Carmen (Prénom Carmen) (>Jean-Luc Godard) ☞

A woman exploits the fact that her uncle is making a film to execute a kidnapping.

1984

A Year of the Quiet Sun (Rok Spokojnego Słońca) (Krzysztof Zanussi) ▓ ☞

An American soldier falls for a woman during the liberation of Poland, but she is prevented from leaving Europe with him.

1985

Vagabonde (Sans Toit Ni Loi) (Agnès Varda) ☞ ⚏

Witnesses tell what they know of the last hours of a girl found frozen to death in a ditch.

1986

The Green Ray (US: Summer) (*Le Rayon Vert*) (>Eric Rohmer) ☞ ☆

Moody Marie Rivière's holidays are a disaster, until she meets her ideal man in Biarritz.

1987

Au Revoir les Enfants (>Louis Malle) ☞ ⚏ ☆ ▓

A Jewish boy is hidden from the Nazis at a boarding school in occupied France.

1988

The Legend of the Holy Drinker (La Leggenda del Santo Bevitore) (Ermanno Olmi) ☞

Rutger Hauer, sleeping rough and drinking for survival, must pay back a debt of money to St Thérèse of Lisieux, but can he?

1989

City of Sadness (Beiqing Chengschi) (Hou Hsiao-hsien) ▓

As the Japanese evacuate Taiwan in 1945, thousands of refugees pour in from the Chinese mainland.

Ventriloquists

The Dummy Talks (Oswald Mitchell 1943) ☆

Blackmailing ventriloquist Jack Warner is murdered, but whodunnit?

The Great Gabbo (James Cruze 1929) ☆

Voice-thrower >Erich Von Stroheim assumes the character of his evil dummy.

Knock on Wood (Norman Panama/Melvin Frank 1954) ☆

This AAN script has Mai Zetterling leading the chase for the secret papers stashed in Danny Kaye's dummy.

Letter of Introduction (John M. Stahl 1938) ☆

Edgar Bergen and his dummy Charlie McCarthy are on the bill as Adolphe Menjou makes a star of his daughter.

Magic (>Richard Attenborough 1978) ☆

Anthony Hopkins is driven to kill by his manic dummy.

Unholy Three (Tod Browning 1925) ☆ ☞/ (Jack Conway 1930) ☆

In both films, a circus dwarf, a strongman and a ventriloquist (Lon Chaney) commit crimes wherever they appear.

Vicars

>The Bishop's Wife (Henry Koster 1947) ☆ ⚏ ▓ ☞

Day of Wrath (Vredens Dag) (Carl Dreyer 1943) ☞ ⚏ ▓

Danish pastor Thorkild Roose is cursed by a witch; his wife commits adultery, the shock of which kills him, and she is burned as a witch.

Heavens Above (John Boulting 1963) ☆

Socialist vicar Peter Sellers is appointed to a snobbish country parish.

The Holly and the Ivy (George More O'Ferrall 1952) ☆

Ralph Richardson's Christmas is disrupted by wife Celia Johnson's confession of a fling.

The Little Minister (Richard Wallace 1934)
☆ ■

Squire's daughter >Katharine Hepburn impersonates a gypsy to fool Scottish minister John Beal.

A Man Called Peter (Henry Koster 1955) ■
Richard Todd as Peter Marshall, the Scotsman who became Chaplain to the US Senate.

One Foot in Heaven (Irving Rapper 1941) ☆
Itinerant Methodist preacher >Fredric March dreams of a church of his own.

Romance (Clarence Brown 1930) ☆ ☞
Opera singer >Greta Garbo is torn between industrialist Gavin Gordon and vicar Lewis Stone.

Stars in My Crown (Jacques Tourneur 1950) ☆ ✍
Gun-toting clergyman Joel McCrea keeps a town's morals and law and order on the straight and narrow.

Winter Light (aka The Communicants) (Nattvardsgasterna) (>Ingmar Bergman 1962) ☞ ☆
Pastor Gunnar Björnstrand's crisis of faith disturbs his mistress and a couple fearing the end of the world.

Vidor, King
American director (1894–1982)

Vidor's road to success reads like an exaggeration of *Merton of the Movies* (Robert Alton 1947) (✍ ☆), littered as it was with home movies, rejected scripts (52 before he sold one), dismissals, gofering and the bankruptcy of his studio, Vidor Village. However, by 1925 his persistence landed him the anti-war epic *The Big Parade* (☞ ☆ ✍) (John Gilbert volunteers in 1917, but is relieved to be wounded out of action), which he followed with *The Crowd* (AAN: 1928) (☞ ☆ ✍) (James Murray finds that the USA is not a land for heroes and struggles through the Depression; cinemas could choose to show a happy or a sad ending – seven were filmed), whose images of urban decay fostered many imitations. His first Talkie, *Hallelujah* (1929) (☞) (remorse at the accidental death he has caused, drives a black cotton worker to religion) is now obviously racist; *Our Daily Bread* (1934) (☞ ✍) (the couple from *The Crowd* inherit a farm and slave to make it pay) delivers patronizing socialism; and *Northwest Passage* (1940) (☆ ☞) (>Spencer Tracy and Robert Young endure the harshness of the wilds to clear it of Canadian Indians to allow settlement) is a Christian Scientist sermon on the power of nature. However, his control of >Capra-corn subjects had improved by the time he directed *Stella Dallas* (1937) (☆ ☞ ✍) (>Barbara Stanwyck's lack of airs and graces lose her the love of her husband and daughter), *The Citadel* (1938) (☆ ☞) (doctor >Robert Donat leaves a Welsh mining town for Harley Street) and *An American Romance* (1944) (☆ ☞) (immigrant Brian Donlevy rises from labourer to business tycoon). Vidor bowed out with a worthy adaptation of *War And Peace* (co-directed with Mario Soldati 1956) (☞ ✍ ■ ☆) (>Henry Fonda heads one of three families enduring crises other than Napoleon's 1812 invasion of Russia) and the unworthy *Solomon and Sheba* (1959) (☞) (Yul Brynner and Gina Lollobrigida are the Old Testament lovers resisting George Sanders's bid for the throne of Israel).

•*Peg o' My Heart* (1923): an English nobleman is cut off from his family for loving an Irish peasant.
•*La Bohème* (1926): silent version of Puccini's opera with >Lillian Gish as the woman torn between artists.
•*The Champ* (1931) (☞): Jackie Cooper believes in his has-been boxer father Wallace Beery.
•*Bird of Paradise* (1932) (☞): Joel McCrea's marriage to South Sea islander Dolores Del Rio is disapproved of by her folks.
•*A Duel in the Sun* (1946) (☆ ☞): brothers Gregory Peck and Joseph Cotten fall for and feud over half-caste Indian Jennifer Jones.
•*Beyond the Forest* (1949) (☆ ☞ ✍): doctor's wife >Bette Davis murders a witness to her adultery.
•*Ruby Gentry* (1952) (☞): Jennifer Jones as a tomboy having sexual, tragic and swashbuckling adventures.

Vietnam

>Apocalypse Now (>Francis Ford Coppola 1979) ☆ ☞ ■ ✍ ♫

Birdy (Alan Parker 1985) ☆ ✍ ☞
Nicholas Cage tries to coax Matthew Modine out of his 'Nam-heightened belief that he can fly.

Coming Home (Hal Ashby 1978) ✍ ☆ ☞
>Jane Fonda (AA) falls for wheelchair bound veteran Jon Voight (AA).

Full Metal Jacket (>Stanley Kubrick 1987) ☞ ✍ ■
Having endured boot camp hell, Matthew Modine is still unprepared for the horrors of combat.

Gardens of Stone (>Francis Ford Coppola 1988) ☞ ☆ ✍
James Caan sees the slaughter in Vietnam from the point of view of an officer at Arlington Cemetery.

Go Tell the Spartans (Ted Post 1978)
Burt Lancaster leads his raw recruits out of a tight corner.

The Green Berets (>John Wayne/Ray Kellogg/>Mervyn Le Roy 1968)
Journalist David Janssen joins John Wayne's army unit in routing the Vietcong.

Hamburger Hill (John Irvin 1987) ☞
Semi-documentary reconstruction of an assault on an impregnable Vietcong stronghold.

Hanoi Hilton (Lionel Chetwynd 1987) ☞
Semi-documentary telling of life in a Vietcong PoW camp.

Platoon (Oliver Stone 1987)
Charlie Sheen hero-worships commander Tom Berenger.

The Quiet American (>Joseph L. Mankiewicz 1957) ✍ ☞
Journalist Michael Redgrave betrays Audie Murphy to the Communists in 1950s Vietnam.

Saigon (Christopher Crowe 1988) ✍
An army officer accused of rape is hunted down by cops Willem Dafoe and Gregory Hines.

Visconti, Luchino
(Count Don Luchino Visconti Di Modrone)
Italian writer/director (1906–1976)
Following an aristocratic, Catholic upbringing, complete with service in the cavalry, Visconti entered films in the late 1930s as >Jean Renoir's assistant during the latter's scripting and short-lived directorial involvement in *La Tosca* (Carl Koch – who completed the film after Renoir left Italy on the declaration of war – 1940) (♫ ✍) (in the story based on Puccini's opera, a sister sacrifices herself to keep her brother out of jail). Visconti's carefully crafted films can be divided into three genres: MARXIST NEO-REALISM: *Ossessione* (1942) (☞) (murdering her brutal husband proves the beginning of the end for a handsome couple), *La Terra Trema* (1948) (☞ ■) (Sicilian fishermen are buffeted but unbowed by nature and businessmen) and *Rocco and His Brothers* (*Rocco e I Suoi Fratelli*) (1960) (☞) (Venice Best Director winner has Alain Delon and his brothers finding life just as tough in Milan as it is in the south), the latter two using Sicilian non-actors; luxuriant HISTORICAL DRAMAS with modern overtones: *Senso* (aka *The Wanton Contessa*) (1954) (☞ ■ ✍) (an Austrian soldier is betrayed as a deserter by the Venetian woman he has jilted), *The Leopard* (*Il Gattopardo*) (1963) (■ ☞ ✍) (as Italy approaches Risorgimento, petty prince Burt Lancaster despairs of his state and his family) and *The Damned* (aka *Götterdämmerung*) (*La Caduta degli Dei*) (1969) (☞ ☆ ■) (a munitions-manufacturing family are split over supplying the Nazis); and overstaged, LITERARY ADAPTATIONS: *White Nights* (*Le Notti Bianche*) (1957) (☞ ☆) (>Marcello Mastroianni as the chivalry-obsessed anti-heroic dreamer in >Dostoyevsky's story), *The Stranger* (*Lo Straniero*) (1967) (this film version of Albert Camus' novel has >Marcello Mastroianni as the prisoner on death row reminiscing about his ordinary life) and *Death in Venice* (*Morte a Venezia*) (1971) (☞ ☆ ■) (composer Dirk Bogarde goes to Venice for inspiration and becomes obsessed with a young Polish boy in a screen adaptation of Thomas Mann's novel).

•*Bellissima* (1951) (☞ ✍): an ambitious mother does everything she can to get her daughter into pictures.

•*Of a Thousand Delights* (US: *Sandra*) (*Vaghe*

Stelle dell'Orsa) (1965) (☆ ☞): Venice Best Film has Claudia Cardinale being blamed by her mother for her Jewish father's wartime death.

•*Ludwig* (1973) (☆): Bavaria's mad king (Helmut Berger) becomes obsessed with Richard Wagner (Trevor Howard)'s music.

•*Conversation Piece* (*Gruppo di Famiglia in un Interno*) (1974) (☞): a group of high society parasites transform the life of a staid academic when they take the apartment below him.

•*The Innocent* (aka *The Intruder*) (*L'Innocente*) (1976) (☞): a woman's revenge adultery backfires and results in tragedy.

Von Sternberg, Josef
(Jonas Sternberg) Austrian writer/director (1894–1969)
Cinema's greatest illusionist spent his career putting noses out of joint, notably those of >Charles Chaplin, >Ernst Lubitsch and Alexander Korda, and his vision of people and places on to the screen. Although unproven, the German UFA studio entrusted him with their first sound film in 1930 at >Emil Jannings' suggestion. >*The Blue Angel* (*Der Blaue Engel*) (☆ ☞ ✍ ■ ♫) introduced him to >Marlene Dietrich, and he spent much of the ensuing half-decade in Hollywood iconizing her beauty in haloes of light: *Morocco* (AAN: 1930) (☆ ☞) (cabaret singer Marlene teases >Gary Cooper and Adolphe Menjou); *Shanghai Express* (AAN: 1932) (☆ ☞) (Clive Brook protects Dietrich from Warner Oland's Chinese bandits); *Blonde Venus* (1932) (☞) (>Cary Grant tempts Marlene away from marriage to dependable Herbert Marshall); *The Scarlet Empress* (1934) (☞ ☆) (Dietrich in a historical romance based on the loves of Catherine the Great); and *The Devil Is a Woman* (1935) (☞) (Lionel Atwill and Cesar Romero are among those in the thrall of Spanish singer Marlene). Von Sternberg's creative instability and personal intransigence frustrated his later career, with only *The Saga Of Anatahan* (1953) (Japanese marines continue to man their posts on a Pacific island for seven years after the war's end) worthy of consideration.

•*The Salvation Hunters* (1925) (☞ ■): Georgia Hale abandons her weak-kneed boyfriend for a city slicker, but he sends her to a brothel.

•*Underworld* (UK: *Paying the Penalty*) (1928) (✍ ☞): scriptwriter Ben Hecht won an AA for this tale of a gangster accepting the loss of his moll to his second-in-command.

•*The Last Command* (1928) (☞ ☆): >Emil Jannings comes to Hollywood after the war, but suffers under martinet director >William Powell.

•*Dishonored* (1931) (☞ ☆): prostitute >Marlene Dietrich is recruited as an agent by Victor McLaglen.

•*An American Tragedy* (1931) (☞ ✍): a man attempts to save his chances of marrying into money by murdering the factory girl whom he has got pregnant.

•*Crime and Punishment* (1935) (☞ ☆): >Peter Lorre as >Dostoyevsky's murderous student repenting his crime.

•*The Shanghai Gesture* (1941) (☞): a gambling den hostess and her ex-husband use their daughter's antics to torment each other.

•*Jet Pilot* (1957) (☞): Soviet pilot Janet Leigh lands in Alaska and falls in love with >John Wayne while awaiting political asylum.

Von Stroheim, Erich
Austrian-born American actor/writer/director (1885–1957)
In a life shrouded in self-invention, Von Stroheim's silent film directing career was transparently sabotaged by both his own erratic genius and dollar-conscious studio executives. Assistant director on >D. W. Griffith's >*Intolerance* (1916) (☞ ■ ☆), he made the audacious comedies *Blind Husbands* (1919) (☞ ☆) (Von Stroheim's Austrian army officer brightens up his mountain holiday by having an affair) and *Foolish Wives* (1921) (☞ ☆) (Mae Busch is blackmailed in Monte Carlo by nobleman impersonator Von Stroheim) prior to his mutilated masterpiece >*Greed* (1923) (☞ ■ ☆). After co-writing the script for *The Devil-Doll* (Tod Browning 1936) (☆ ✍) (Lionel Barrymore impersonates an old woman avenging his imprisonment with killer dolls), his later career largely consisted of acting, and he

was invariably but effectively typecast as 'The Hun' in such films as *Crimson Romance* (David Howard 1934) (☆) (Von Stroheim trains two Americans volunteering to fight in the First World War on the German side), >*La Grande Illusion* (aka *Grand Illusion*) (>Jean Renoir 1937) (☆ ☞ ✍ ■) and *Five Graves to Cairo* (>Billy Wilder 1943) (Franchot Tone cuts off Rommel (Von Stroheim)'s North African supply lines). He was reunited with Gloria Swanson, the star of the aborted *Queen Kelly* (1928) (which he had directed and she had produced) as her ex-husband-director now butler in what was almost his *film à clef*, >*Sunset Boulevard* (>Billy Wilder 1950) (☆ ☞ ✍).

 •*The Merry Widow* (1925) (☞): John Gilbert is sent to boost the finances of an impoverished kingdom by seducing a millionairess.
•*The Wedding March* (1928) (☆): Hapsburg prince Von Stroheim loves peasant Fay Wray but is forced to marry crippled princess Zasu Pitts.
•*Snares* (aka *Personal Column*) (Robert Siodmak 1929) (☆ ☞): women answering an advert in newspaper columns disappear.
•*The Great Gabbo* (James Cruze 1929) (☆): ventriloquist Von Stroheim assumes the character of his dummy.
•*As You Desire Me* (George Fitzmaurice 1932) (☆): amnesiac >Greta Garbo has a fling with writer Von Stroheim unaware she is married to Melvyn Douglas.
•*The Lost Squadron* (George Archainbaud 1932) (☆): World War I veteran pilot performs the stunts for sadistic director Von Stroheim's film.
•*Les Disparus de Saint-Agil* (Christian-Jaque 1938) (☆ ☞): schoolboys who discover that their headmaster is a murderous forger begin to mysteriously disappear.
•*Napoleon* (Sacha Guitry 1954) (☞ ☆): Von Stroheim appears as Ludwig Van Beethoven as Guitry's Talleyrand reminisces about Napoleonic France.

Von Trotta, Margarethe
German actress/director (b 1942)

A graduate in romance languages and literature, Von Trotta moved from provincial theatre to cinema in the late 1960s, with roles in >Rainer Werner Fassbinder's *Gods of the Plague* (*Götter der Pest*) (1969) (☆ ☞) (Von Trotta and >Hanna Schygulla betray their mutual lover to prevent him robbing a supermarket) and *The American Soldier* (*Der Amerikanische Soldat*) (1970) (☞) (a Vietnam veteran becomes an assassin in Munich), and in two of her husband >Volker Schlöndorff's films – *The Sudden Fortune of the Poor People of Kombach* (*Der Plötzliche Reichtum der Armen Leute von Kombach*) (1971) (☞ ✍) (19th-century peasants rob a tax cart and enjoy a wild spending spree before they are apprehended) and *Summer Lightning* (*Strohfeuer*) (1972) (☞ ☆) (Von Trotta is descriminated against both in her career and in a custody trial) – both of which she co-scripted. Since co-directing (with Schlöndorff) *The Lost Honour of Katharina Blum* (*Die Verlorene Ehre der Katharina Blum*) (1975) (✍ ☞) (a woman is subjected to press and public pressure after she sleeps with a stranger who is under police surveillance), she has written and directed powerful combinations of socialism and feminism. She concentrated primarily on women's struggle for political acceptance in *The Second Awakening of Christa Klages* (*Das Zweite Erwachen der Christa Klages*) (1977) (☞ ✍) (Tina Engel is so committed to her nursery school that she robs a bank and ruins her life to raise funds for it), *The German Sisters* (*Die Bleierne Zeit*) (1981) (☞ ☆) (journalist Jutta Lampe grows closer to terrorist sister Barbara Sukowa during the latter's prison hunger strike) and *Rosa Luxemburg* (1986) (☆) (Barbara Sukowa won Best Actress at Cannes as the Jewish Polish socialist who was assassinated in the early days of the Weimar Republic), and examined inter-female relationships in *Sisters or The Balance of Happiness*) (*Schwestern oder die Balance des Glücks*) (1979) (☞ ☆) (her dependency on sister Jutta Lampe drives immature Gudrun Gabriel to suicide, and when Lampe takes up with a friend at work, the pattern repeats itself) and *Friends and Husbands* (*Heller Wahn*) (1982) (☆ ☞) (academic >Hanna Schygulla and repressed artist Angela Winkler become so dependent on their friendship it destroys them).

•*Coup de Grâce* (>Volker Schlöndorff 1976): when a soldier in an anti-Bolshevik detachment rebuts Von Trotta's advances, she embraces the Communist cause.

WAGERS AND RACES

Around the World in Eighty Days (Michael Anderson/Kevin McClory (1956) ☆ ✍ ☞
David Niven accepts the challenge thrown down by members of his club, and returns to find them clock-watching.

The Cannonball Run (Hal Needham 1980)
Burt Reynolds and Roger Moore are among those participating in and gambling on a madcap car race across the USA.

>Genevieve (Henry Cornelius 1954) ✍ ☆ ♫ ☞

The Great Race (Blake Edwards 1965) ☆ ✍
>Jack Lemmon and Tony Curtis employ more foul means than fair in the first New York-to-Paris car race.

Those Daring Young Men in Their Jaunty Jalopies (UK: Monte Carlo or Bust) (Ken Annakin 1969) ☆
Terry-Thomas, Tony Curtis, Peter Cook and Dudley Moore compete in the Monte Carlo Rally.

Those Magnificent Men in Their Flying Machines or How I Flew from London to Paris in 25 Hours and 11 Minutes (Ken Annakin 1965) ☆ ■
International aviators in comic competition to be the first to cross the Channel.

The Wrong Box (Bryan Forbes 1966) ✍ ☆
Brothers Ralph Richardson and John Mills aim to kill each other to win a tontine.

WAGON TRAINS AND STAGECOACHES

The Big Trail (>Raoul Walsh 1930) ☞
>John Wayne refuses to be defeated by the vicissitudes of nature or by human hindrances on the Oregon trail.

Brigham Young (Henry Hathaway 1940) ☆
Tyrone Power, Linda Darnell, Vincent Price, Mary Astor, John Carradine and Jane Darwell are among the Mormons following Dean Jagger to Utah.

The Paleface (Norman Z. McLeod 1948) ☆ ✍
Cowardly dentist Bob Hope bumbles into heroics as he and Jane Russell's Calamity Jane save the day.

Rawhide (Henry Hathaway 1950) ☆
Susan Hayward puts on a brave face as Tyrone Power gets the better of escapees.

The Red Inn (*L'Auberge Rouge*) (Claude Autant-Lara 1951) ✍

Travelling monk Fernandel catches on to the fact that a hotelier and his wife view stagecoach passengers as victims, not guests.

>*Stagecoach* (>John Ford 1939) ☞ ☆ ■ ✍

Stand Up and Fight (W. S. Van Dyke 1939) ☞

Robert Taylor breaks the slave ring that Wallace Beery runs behind the cover of a coaching service.

A Ticket to Tomahawk (Richard Sale 1950) ☆

Anne Baxter and Dan Dailey fight a losing battle when the railroad poaches their custom.

Wagonmaster (>John Ford 1950) ☞

Mormons face a variety of perils on the trek to Utah.

The War Wagon (Burt Kennedy 1967) ☆ ✍

Bruce Cabot put >John Wayne in jail, but Duke gets his revenge when he and >Kirk Douglas attack Cabot's armoured gold wagon.

Westward Ho the Wagons (William Beaudine 1956)

Fess Parker defends his wagon train against Indian attack in this Disney adventure.

WAITERS AND WAITRESSES

Because of Him (Richard Wallace 1945) ☆

Actor >Charles Laughton guides waitress Deanna Durbin to stardom.

The Big Street (Irving Reis 1942) ☆

Crippled singer Lucille Ball exploits the friendship of waiter >Henry Fonda.

Bread and Chocolate (*Pane e Cioccolata*) (Franco Brusati 1973) ☆

A Neapolitan working in a Swiss hotel is victimized because he is an illegal immigrant.

Long Live the Lady (*Lunga Vita alla Signora!*) (Ermanno Olmi 1987) ☞

Six teenagers from a catering college are hired to wait at a dinner party given by a frosty hostess at a country chateau.

Of Human Bondage (John Cromwell 1934) ☆ ✍

Waitress >Bette Davis ruins the life of well-to-do >Leslie Howard.

Our Relations (Harry Lachman 1936) ☆ ✍ ☞

>Laurel & Hardy and their sailor twins confuse the waiter who is holding a diamond ring as security for their meal.

What Price Hollywood? (>George Cukor 1932) ☞ ✍

Former waitress Constance Bennett watches the man who made her a star become a drunk.

When Tomorrow Comes (John M. Stahl 1939) ☆

This *Jane Eyre*-like story has waitress Irene Dunne kept from pianist Charles Boyer by his insane wife Barbara O'Neil.

Wajda, Andrej
Polish writer/director (b 1927)

Picture restorer and Resistance fighter during the Nazi occupation, the formally trained Wajda directly examined his and Poland's sufferings in wartime: *A Generation* (*Pokolenie*) (1954) (☞ ☆) (love turns a Warsaw Resistance fighter into a hero); *Kanal* (*They Loved Life*) (aka *Sewer*) (1957) (☞ ☆) (freedom fighters are driven into the sewers beneath Warsaw by the Nazis); *Lotna* (1959) (☞ ■) (a white horse is ridden by various soldiers during a cavalry charge against Nazi tanks); and *Samson* (1961) (☞ ✍) (a Jewish pacifist is driven to resistance by Nazi atrocities). He also turned his attention to the repression that followed Poland's 'liberation': >*Ashes and Diamonds* (*Popiól i Diament*) (1958) (☞ ☆ ✍) and *Landscape after Battle* (*Krajobraz po Bitwie*) (1970) (✍ ☞) (a Jewish girl survives a concentration camp only to be accidentally killed by an American soldier while awaiting repatriation). Subsequently he has used both historical and contemporary drama to demonstrate the immemorial external and internal exploitation of the nation: *Ashes* (aka *The Lost Army*) (*Popióly*) (1965) (■) (Poles fighting with Napoleon are punished by partition at the Congress of Vienna); *Promised Land* (*Ziemia Obiecama*) (1974) (☞ ■) (peasants find they are worse off than before after the collapse of serfdom); *Man of Marble* (*Czlowiek z Marmuru*) (1978) (☞) (student Krystyna Janda's film project into a working hero is hampered by the authorities); *The Con-*

ductor (aka *The Orchestra Conductor*) (*Dyrygent*) (1979) (☆ ☞) (John Gielgud's exiled conductor returns to breathe life into a provincial orchestra); *Man of Iron* (*Czlowiek z zelaza*) (1981) (☞) (a journalist compares the birth of Solidarity with a worker's rising of the 1950s) to demonstrate the immemorial external and internal exploitation of the nation; and *Danton* (1982) (☆ ☞ ■) (>Gérard Depardieu's popularity with the people is resented by Wojciech Pszoniak's Robespierre). More personal works – including *Innocent Sorcerors* (*Niewinni Czarodzieje*) (1960) (☞) (a jazz-loving doctor shies away from marriage) and *Everything for Sale* (*Wszystko na Sprzedaz*) (1968) (☞) (*film à clef* of the hero of >*Ashes and Diamonds*, Zbigniew Cybulski, who was also killed while trying to jump onto a moving train) – have been less interesting.

•*Siberian Lady Macbeth* (*Sibirska Ledi Magbet*) (1961) (☞): having murdered her husband and his father to take over a mill with her lover, Olivera Markovic begins to suffer from conscience.
•*Hunting Flies* (*Polowanie na Muchy*) (1969) (☞ ✍): a socialite tries to make a celebrity out of a dullard in this *Pygmalion* comedy.
•*Rough Treatment* (aka *Without Anaesthesia*) (*Bez Znieczulenia*)(1978) (☞ ■): a TV journalist's wife feels neglected and leaves him for a younger, poorer man.

WALES

Boy Soldier (Karl Francis 1987) ✍ ☞
A Welsh soldier is put on trial for a civilian shooting in Northern Ireland.

Coming Up Roses (Rhosyn a Rhith) (Stephen Bayly 1987) ✍
In this Welsh-language film, a cinema projectionist turns the building into a community centre to prevent its demolition.

The Corn Is Green (Irving Rapper 1945) ☆ ✍
Teacher >Bette Davis adopts miner John Dall (AAN)'s illegitimate child so that he can take up a scholarship to Oxford.

Dangerous Exile (Brian Desmond Hurst 1957) ✍
Louis Jourdan smuggles Louis XVII away from the French Revolution to Pembrokeshire.

The Foreman Went to France (US: Somewhere in France) (Charles Frend 1941) ☆
Clifford Evans leaves Wales to recover vital machinery from France before the Nazis get it.

How Green Was My Valley (>John Ford 1941) ☞
Roddy McDowall's childhood is affected by the fortunes of the local coal mine.

The Last Days of Dolwyn (US: The Women of Dolwyn) (Emlyn Williams 1949) ☞
True story of the 19th-century transformation of a valley into a reservoir.

On the Black Hill (Andrew Grieve 1988) ✍
The film adaptation of Bruce Chatwin's novel about the effects of the 20th-century on sheep-farming twins.

Only Two Can Play (Sidney Gilliat 1962) ☆
Peter Sellers as the Lothario librarian of Kinglsey Amis's novel, *That Uncertain Feeling*.

Perceval (Perceval le Gallois) (>Eric Rohmer 1978) ☞ ■
Welsh Round Table knight Fabrice Luchini, fleetingly sees the Holy Grail, but can't find it again.

A Run for Your Money (Charles Frend 1949) ☆
Welsh Rugby supporters led by >Alec Guinness find London a weird and wonderful place.

The Three Weird Sisters (Dan Birt 1948) ✍
Co-scripted by Dylan Thomas, this story has three wicked old dears planning to murder their brother.

Walsh, Raoul
American writer/director (1887–1980)
Raoul Walsh was a cowboy, surgeon's assistant, undertaker and member of >D. W. Griffith's Biograph production team (appearing as John Wilkes Booth in *The Birth of a Nation* [1915] [☞ ☆ ■]), before directing silents including *The Thief Of Bagdad* (1924) (☆ ☞ ■) (>Douglas Fairbanks fights a magic Casbah duel with a wicked caliph), *What Price Glory?* (1926) (☞ ✍) (in the First World War American soldiers

fall for the same French girl) and *Sadie Thompson* (1928) (religious maniac Lionel Barrymore becomes obsessed with prostitute Gloria Swanson in the film version of the Somerset Maugham novel). The remarkable Walsh lost an eye when a rabbit crashed through his windscreen during the making of his first Talkie, *In Old Arizona* (AAN: co-directed with Irving Cummings 1929) (☞ ☆) (Warner Baxter won an AA playing the Cisco Kid in this now crackly western). Only *The Roaring Twenties* (co-directed with Anatole Litvak 1939) (☞ ☆) (bootlegger >James Cagney fights a gang war with >Humphrey Bogart) illuminated his relatively dormant 1930s, but it set the pattern for the action *film noir*s of the vigorous '40s: *They Drive by Night* (UK: *The Road to Frisco*) (1940) (☞ ■) (truckers >Humphrey Bogart and George Raft are implicated in Ann Sheridan's ambitious plans); *High Sierra* (1941) (☞ ☆) (>Humphrey Bogart can't concentrate on his swansong robbery as he is obsessed with Ida Lupino); and *They Died with Their Boots On* (1941) (☞ ☆) (Errol Flynn's General Custer kisses >Olivia De Havilland goodbye and gets slaughtered by Sitting Bull); *Desperate Journey* (1942) (☞ ☆) (escaped PoWs Errol Flynn, Ronald Reagan and Alan Hale cross occupied Europe); and *White Heat* (1949) (☞ ☆ ☒) (>James Cagney as a gangster who prefers mother Margaret Wycherly to Virginia Mayo). Quality failed to keep pace with vitality in his later career, and only barely did himself justice with *Battle Cry* (1955) (☞) (this screen adaptation of the Leon Uris novel has every soldier's favourite officer Van Heflin killed in the Pacific war) and *The Naked and the Dead* (1958) (Walsh's film of Norman Mailer's novel has Raymond Massey telling Cliff Robertson that the more he hates sadistic officer Aldo Ray, the more Japanese he will kill).

• *The Cockeyed World* (1929) (☆ ☞): having rowed over the same girl in *What Price Glory?*, Victor McLaglen and Edmund Lowe fight at the front, too.
• *Me and My Gal* (UK: *Pier 13*) (1932): cop >Spencer Tracy and cook Joan Bennett wisecrack their way to catching a thief.

• *The Bowery* (1933) (☞ ☆): gangsters Wallace Beery and George Raft exchange more banter than blows in 1890s New York.
• *Klondike Annie* (1936) (☞ ☆): Salvation Army missionary Mae West turns heads rather than saves souls in the frozen north.
• *The Strawberry Blonde* (1941) (☆ ☒): dentist >James Cagney can't decide between >Olivia De Havilland and Rita Hayworth.
• *Gentleman Jim* (1942) (☞ ☆): Errol Flynn in a biopic of boxer Jim Corbett.
• *Pursued* (1947) (☆): cowboy Robert Mitchum looks for the answers to his disturbed childhood at the home of his father's mistress Judith Anderson.
• *Silver River* (1948): Wild West gambler Errol Flynn is destroyed by his own temper and his love for Ann Sheridan.
• *Colorado Territory* (1949) (☞ ☆): Virginia Mayo has reservations about outlaw Joel McCrea going on one last raid.
• *Distant Drums* (1951): >Gary Cooper rescues Indian kidnap victims.
• *The Sheriff of Fractured Jaw* (1958) (☆): this amiable comedy sees English inventor Kenneth More mistaken for a gunfighter in a no-good town.

WAR CRIMINALS

The Boys from Brazil (Franklin Schaffner 1978) ☆ ☒
Concentration camp doctor Gregory Peck is pursued by Nazi hunter >Laurence Olivier.
Hotel Terminus: The Life and Times of Klaus Barbie (Marcel Ophüls 1988) ☞
The atrocities of the 'Butcher of Lyons' are recalled in this harrowing documentary.
Judgment at Nuremberg (Stanley Kramer 1961) ☒ ☆
Nazi judge Burt Lancaster is defended by Maximilian Schell (AA) in >Spencer Tracy's court.
The Lion Has Seven Heads (Der Leone Have Sept Cabecas) (Glauber Rocha, Congo 1970) ☞
A Nazi, a missionary, and a mercenary are among those taking refuge in the Congo.
Marathon Man (>John Schlesinger 1976) ☆ ☞
Concentration camp dentist >Laurence Olivier

believes that >Dustin Hoffman knows the whereabouts of his diamonds.

The Memory of Justice (Marcel Ophüls 1975) ☞

A documentary study of what makes a war crime, with evidence drawn from wars since 1939.

The Night of the Generals (Anatole Litvak 1967) 🔍 ☆

One among a coterie of Nazi generals has been committing Jack the Ripper murders since the First World War.

None Shall Escape (André De Toth 1944) ☞

Alexander Knox's career is recalled during his trial.

>Shoah (Claude Lanzmann 1985) ☞ ■

Way Out West ☆ 🔍 🎵 ■

USA • Hal Roach • 1937 • 66 mins • b/w

d James Horne w Jack Jevne/Charles Rogers/James Parrott/Felix Adler ph Art Lloyd/Walter Lundin m Marvin Hatley >Stan Laurel, >Oliver Hardy, James Finlayson, Sharon Lynne, Rosina Lawrence, The Avalon Boys

Stan and Ollie, at their brilliant best in this gentle Western parody, are duped by James Finlayson into believing that his wife (Lynne) is entitled to the gold mine deed they have been entrusted to deliver. Can anyone resist the bedroom chase scene, when Lynne tickles Laurel into surrendering the deed and he stands in the doorway hooting with laughter at the ensuing melee. Ever popular with audiences, Laurel & Hardy's rendition of *The Trail of the Lonesome Pine* was released as a single following a TV showing in Britain in 1975 and reached No. 2 in the charts, but the musical highlight is the Avalon Boys' number *Commencin' Dancin'*, as Stan and Ollie's charmingly inept dance sums up their screen personae.

VIEW ON ▶ •Milkman Harold Lloyd is the unlikely hero fooling Adolphe Menjou's criminal plans, in *The Milky Way* (>Leo McCarey 1936) (☞ ☆).

•Jesse Birdsall is the innocent relying on Helena Bonham Carter and Lynn Redgrave to help him discover sex, in *Getting It Right* (Randall Kleiser 1989) (☆).

•Dick Van Dyke and Mickey Rooney re-live the era of the slapstick clowns, in *The Comic* (Carl Reiner 1969) (☆).

•The Western was also parodied in *Go West* (>Buster Keaton 1925) (taking the genre literally, Keaton's cowboy befriends a cow), while >The Marx Brothers' identically titled but very different version (Edward Buzzell 1940) (☆) has the three brothers rounding up bad guy John Carroll.

Wayne, John

(Marion Michael Morrison) American actor (1907–1979)

A University of Southern California graduate (via a football scholarship), Wayne touted his cynical charm and rugged honesty in 1930s' 'B' movies and serials until >John Ford's >*Stagecoach* (1939) (☞ ☆ ■ 🔍) made him a star. World War II led to more contemporary bravado: *The Fighting Seebees* (Edward Ludwig 1944) (☆) (Wayne's building engineer is dragged into the Pacific war to the chagrin of Susan Hayward), *They Were Expendable* (>John Ford 1945) (☞) (Wayne and Robert Montgomery feud over using their torpedo boats to fight the Japanese); and *Sands of Iwo Jima* (AAN: Allan Dwan 1949) (☆) (Wayne leads raw recruits on an impossible mission in the Pacific). After the war came the flourishing of 'the Duke' as the Western hero: *Red River* (>Howard Hawks 1948) (☞ ☆) (Wayne and Montgomery Clift pioneer a cattle trail); *Fort Apache* (>John Ford 1948) (☞ ☆ ■) (Wayne and commander >Henry Fonda have different ideas about repelling an Indian attack); *She Wore a Yellow Ribbon* (>John Ford 1949) (☆ ☞) (Victor McLaglen is the sergeant major at the cavalry camp from which Wayne is about to retire); *Rio Grande* (>John Ford 1950) (☞) (Wayne has Indian problems on the Mexican border); *The Searchers* (>John Ford 1956) (☞ ■ ☆) (Wayne's brother and sister-in-law are murdered and his niece is kidnapped by Indians and Wayne sets out to find her); and *Rio Bravo* (>Howard Hawks 1959) (☞ ☆) (Wayne helps drunken lawman Dean Martin clean up the town). Touting his patriotism in *The Alamo* (1960) (☆) (AAN Best Picture recalls Davy Crockett [Wayne]'s last stand against Mexican rebels) and *The Green Berets* (co-directed with Ray Kellogg and with technical assitance from >Mervyn Le Roy 1968) (Wayne enjoys every minute of training for his mission in Vietnam), which was attacked for its fiercely pro-war stance, Wayne reinforced his national institution status in: *El Dorado* (>Howard Hawks 1966) (gunfighter Wayne and drunken sheriff Robert Mitchum tame rogue cattle baron James Caan); *True Grit* (AA: Henry Hathaway 1969) (☆ ☞ ✍) (eye-patched Rooster Cogburn exacts revenge for the death of Kim Darby's father); *Rio Lobo* (>Howard Hawks 1970) (☞) (US Civil War colonel Wayne foils a Confederate gold robbery); *Rooster Cogburn* (Stuart Millar 1975) (☆) (crotchety Bible-basher >Katharine Hepburn helps the one-eyed Wayne outwit outlaws); and *The Shootist* (Don Siegel 1976) (☆) (dying gunfighter Wayne takes his leave of old friends >James Stewart and Lauren Bacall).

•*The Big Trail* (>Raoul Walsh 1930) (☞), Wayne guides a wagon train across Indian country and to safety.

•*The Dark Command* (>Raoul Walsh 1940) (☞ ☆): respectable teacher Wayne is also an outlaw.

•*The Long Voyage Home* (>John Ford 1940) (■ ☞ ✍ ☆): Wayne is a member of a crew smuggling weapons into Scandinavia past the Nazi Atlantic blockade.

•*Without Reservations* (>Mervyn Le Roy 1946) (☞ ☆): Wayne's marine would make the perfect hero for the film of writer Claudette Colbert's bestseller.

•*The Fighting Kentuckian* (George Waggner 1949) (☆): Wayne is helped to keep his farm baddy-free by >Oliver Hardy.

•>*The Quiet Man* (>John Ford 1952) (✍ ☞ ☆ ■ ♪).

•*The Horse Soldiers* (>John Ford 1959) (☞): Wayne and William Holden blow up a Confederate train.

•*The Man Who Shot Liberty Valance* (>John Ford 1962) (☞ ☆ ✍): >James Stewart gets the credit when Wayne shoots baddy Lee Marvin.

•*McLintock* (Andrew V. McLaglen 1963) (☆): rancher Wayne's rule of iron does not impress his wife Maureen O'Hara – Wayne's partner in many a classic screen squabble.

•*Donovan's Reef* (>John Ford 1963) (☆ ☞ ✍): Lee Marvin helps Wayne persuade his daughter that he is a South Sea island success.

•*Chisum* (Andrew V. McLaglen 1970) (☆): rancher Wayne resists a tycoon's take-over bid.

•*The Cowboys* (Mark Rydell 1972) (☆ ✍): young boys help Wayne drive his cattle and turn mean when Bruce Dern shoots him.

•*Cahill, US Marshal* (Andrew V. McLaglen 1973) (☆): Wayne puts duty before family when he finds out his sons are bank robbers.

•*McQ* (John Sturges 1974) (☆): Seattle cop Wayne avenges the killing of his buddy.

•*Brannigan* (Douglas Hickox 1975) (☆ ✍): Wayne tracks down a gangster in London with the help of >Richard Attenborough of Scotland Yard.

WEDDINGS AND MARRIAGE

Banjo on My Knee **(John Cromwell 1936)** ☆ ☞

Joel McCrea spends his first night married to >Barbara Stanwyck in jail.

Father of the Bride **(>Vincente Minnelli 1950)** ☆ ☞

>Spencer Tracy fails to share his wife Joan Bennett and daughter Elizabeth Taylor's enthusiasm for the latter's approaching wedding.

Forsaking All Others **(W. S. Van Dyke 1934)** ☞ ☆ ✍

The >Joseph L. Mankiewicz script has >Joan Crawford jilted at the altar by Robert Montgomery; then she meets >Clark Gable.

In Name Only **(John Cromwell 1939)** ☆ ✍ ☞

>Cary Grant loves widow >Carole Lombard, but wife Kay Francis won't let him go.

>*The Italian Straw Hat* (*Un Chapeau de Paille d'Italie*) **(>René Clair 1927)** ☞ ✍ ☆ ■

Petulia **(Richard Lester 1968)** ☆ ☞ ✍

George C. Scott wants Julie Christie to leave her brutal husband Richard Chamberlain.

Sweet Smell of Success (**Alexander Mackendrick 1957**) ☞ ■ ☆
PR man Tony Curtis helps journalist Burt Lancaster smash his sister's marriage to a man he detests.

A Wedding (>**Robert Altman 1978**) ☆ ☞
A society wedding involves one disaster after another.

The Wedding (*Wesele*) (>**Andrej Wajda 1972**) ☞
The intellectuals at a wedding reception panic at the news that their country is about to be invaded.

When We Are Married (**Lance Comfort 1942**) ⚼ ☆
J. B. Priestley's play has a trio of silver wedding couples coming to terms with the fact their marriages are illegal.

Welles, Orson
American actor/writer/director (1915–1985)

Having appeared in prestigious Dublin Gate Theatre and Broadway productions and directed a black cast in *Macbeth*, Welles attracted worldwide attention with his terrifyingly authentic 1938 radio adaptation of H. G. Wells' *The War of the Worlds*. His reputation persuaded RKO to offer him both generous budgets and unprecedented artistic freedom, although studio executives were disappointed with the 'one-and-a-half masterpieces' of 1941 and 1942 – respectively >*Citizen Kane* (☞ ☆ ■ ⚼♫) and >*The Magnificent Ambersons* (☞ ⚼ ☆ ■). Such perfection proved impossible to recapture, the only testaments to his undoubted, but wayward cinematic genius being a few FILM NOIR THRILLERS: *Journey into Fear* (co-directed with Norman Foster 1943) (☞ ☆) (Joseph Cotten makes a stand against pursuing Nazi agents in Istanbul where Welles is police chief), *The Lady from Shanghai* (1948) (☞ ☆ ⚼) (Welles rescues Rita Hayworth from rape but when framed for murder, is defended by her crippled lawyer husband Everett Sloane) and the widely acclaimed *Touch of Evil* (1958) (☆ ⚼ ☞) (brothel keeper >Marlene Dietrich spectates with cynical amusement as cops Welles and Charlton Heston feud over the solving of Janet Leigh's kidnapping) and SHAKESPEARIAN ADAPTA-TIONS: *Macbeth* (1948)(☞ ⚼ ☆) (Welles as the Scottish thane who has to cover his tracks having murdered his way to the throne), *Othello* (1952) (⚼ ☆) (Micheal MacLiammoir's Iago avenges himself on Welles' Moor by driving him to murder his wife Fay Compton) and *Chimes at Midnight* (1966) (John Gielgud's Henry IV disapproves of Prince Hal's association with Welles' Falstaff, Margaret Rutherford's Mistress Quickly and Jeanne Moreau's Doll Tearsheet). Despite a compelling screen presence, he largely confined his acting assignments to sinister, unsympathetic cameos: >*The Third Man* (>Carol Reed 1949) (☆ ☞ ♫ ⚼ ■); *The Long Hot Summer* (Martin Ritt 1958) (☆) (farmer >Paul Newman feuds with Welles, the mayor of the neighbouring town); and *A Man for All Seasons* (>Fred Zinnemann 1966) (☆ ⚼ ■ ☞) (Welles's Cardinal Wolsey is overthrown by Leo McKern's Thomas Cromwell when Robert Shaw's Henry VIII demands a divorce from Katherine of Aragon).

•*Jane Eyre* (Robert Stevenson 1943) (☆ ☞ ⚼ ■ ♫): Welles's Mr Rochester is beloved by governess >Joan Fontaine in this screen version of Charlotte Brontë's novel.

•*The Stranger* (>Orson Welles 1946) (☞ ☆): Nazi Welles marries Loretta Young, but war crimes investigator >Edward G. Robinson is not far behind him.

•*Prince of Foxes* (Henry King 1949) (☆ ⚼ ■): Welles's Cesare Borgia is outwitted by opportunist soldier and diplomat Tyrone Power.

•*Confidential Report* (aka *Mr Arkadin*) (>Orson Welles 1955) (☆ ☞): Welles feigns amnesia to cover his murdering of those aware of his guilty past.

•*The Trial* (*Le Procès*) (>Orson Welles 1962) (⚼ ☞): Welles as Franz Kafka's anti-hero Joseph K who is imprisoned and tried for an unknown crime.

•*Waterloo* (Sergei Bondarchuk 1970) (☞ ■): Welles' Louis XVIII has his reign interrupted by Napoleon (Rod Steiger)'s One Hundred Days.

•*Malpertuis* (Harry Kumel 1971) (☆): a sailor is kidnapped and taken to Welles's Gothic mansion, which houses a sinister collection of characters.

•*Ten Days' Wonder* (*La Décade Prodigieuse*) (>Claude Chabrol 1971) (☞ ☆): Anthony Perkins's nightmares can only be explained through an examination of his relationship with his father, (Welles).

•*F for Fake* (*Vérités et Mensonges*) (>Orson Welles 1973) (☞): Welles discusses art, authorship and film-making.

•*The Muppet Movie* (James Frawley 1979) (☆): Welles is one of the guests as the Muppets take Hollywood by chaos.

•*Someone to Love* (Henry Jaglom 1988) (☞ ☆): Welles' last film has him passing judgement on Jaglom's making of a film about his friends' loneliness.

Wellman, William
American director (1896–1975)

Ex-professional ice hockey player and Foreign Legionnaire – he recalled his experiences in *Beau Geste* (1939) (☆ ☞) (>Gary Cooper, Ray Milland and Robert Preston are bullied by sergeant Brian Donlevy [AAN]) – Wellman's claimed experiences in the Lafayette Escadrille flying Corps lent thrilling authenticity to: *Wings* (☞ ■) (heroic pilots are involved in a dog-fight accident), the first-ever Best Picture Oscar winner, in 1927; *Men with Wings* (1938) (☞) (Fred MacMurray and Ray Milland try to get an affair with Louise Campbell into the air); *Gallant Journey* (1946) (☞) (Glenn Ford proves the cynics wrong and gets his plane off the ground) and *The High and the Mighty* (AAN: 1954) (>John Wayne brings a crippled plane down safely). Brawny cameraderie remained a common theme in such WAR ADVENTURES as: *The Story of G.I. Joe* (1945) (☞ ✍ ☆) (Burgess Meredith as journalist Ernie Pyle irritates Robert Mitchum as he covers the Anzio landings) and *Battleground* (AAN: 1949) (this AAN Best Picture has Van Johnson leading men through wind, rain and snow to participate the the Battle of the Bulge). However, Wellman was equally comfortable with MELODRAMA: *A Star Is Born* (Best Director AAN and Best Original Screenplay AA: 1937) (☆ ☞ ✍) (as Janet Gaynor becomes a star of the silver screen, >Fredric March becomes a has-been) and

Magic Town (1947) (☆ ☞ ✍) (>James Stewart's opinion poll man discovers the most average small town in the country); COMEDY, *Nothing Sacred* (1937) (☆ ☞ ✍) (journalist >Fredric March turns dying >Carole Lombard into a celebrity, but she isn't really ill); and WESTERNS, *The Ox-Bow Incident* (UK: *Strange Incident*) (1943) (☆ ✍ ☞) (>Henry Fonda argues in vain for clemency towards three accused outlaws) and *Buffalo Bill* (1944) (☞ ☆) (factional life story with Joel McCrea as William Cody).

•*Beggars of Life* (1928) (☆): Louise Brooks is sheltered from the pursuing police by Wallace Beery's band of tramps.

•*The Public Enemy* (UK: *Enemies of the People*) (1931) (☞ ☆ ✍): streetkid >James Cagney rises to Prohibition breaker only to die in a gang war.

•*Night Nurse* (1931) (☆ ☞): >Barbara Stanwyck prevents sadistic chauffeur >Clark Gable starving the children in her care.

•*Call of the Wild* (1935) (☆ ☞): this screen version of the Jack London novel has widow Loretta Young attracted by gold prospector >Clark Gable.

•*The Light that Failed* (1939) (☆): Rudyard Kipling tale has artist Ronald Colman's career ruined by blindness.

•*Roxie Hart* (1942) (☞ ☆ ✍): Adolphe Menjou defends >Ginger Rogers in court after she confesses to a murder to boost her failing show's ratings.

•*The Great Man's Lady* (1942) (☞ ☆): >Barbara Stanwyck instils her ambition to strike oil into her reluctant husband Joel McCrea.

•*Across the Wide Missouri* (1951) (☞ ☆): fur trappers >Clark Gable and Adolphe Menjou fight off the Indians.

Wenders, Wim
German director/writer (b 1945)

Wenders is very much a contemporary director, drawing on the immediate and the familiar for his narrative and imagery, and in the modern West, little is more familiar than his twin obsessions, AMERICA: *Alice in the Cities* (*Alice in den Städten*) (1973) (☞ ■) (a photo-journalist helps a small girl find her grandmother), *Kings of the Road* (*Im Lauf der Zeit*) (1976) (☞ ♫) (a constant diet of American pop music accompany a trucker and his hitch-hiker as they repair cinema projectors on the East/West German border) and *Paris, Texas* (1984) (☞ ■) (Harry Dean Stanton is reunited with his son and they hit the road to find wife Nastassja Kinski) and CINEMA: *The American Friend* (*Der Amerikanische Freund*) (1977) (dying Bruno Ganz becomes an assassin to leave his wife money to live on in this adaptation of Patricia Highsmith's thriller *Ripley's Game*), starring directors Samuel Fuller and >Nicholas Ray, whose work Wenders' most resembles) and *Lightning over Water* (1981) (☞) a documentary of the last weeks of Ray's life.

•*The Anxiety of the Goalie at the Penalty Kick* (aka *The Goalkeeper's Fear of the Penalty Kick*) (US: *The Goalie's Anxiety at the Penalty Kick*) (*Die Angst des Tormanns Beim Elfmeter*) (1971) (☞): Arthur Brauss is so traumatized by letting in a vital goal he kills a girl after a one-night stand.

•*The Scarlet Letter* (*Der Scharlachrote Buchstabe*) (1972) (✍ ☞ ■): a screen version Nathaniel Hawthorne's powerful novel of adultery, religious mania and revenge set in 18th-century New England.

•*Wrong Movement* (*Falsche Bewegung*) (1975) (☞ ☆): writer Rüdiger Vogler's travels bring him into contact with an actress, a poet and a suicide.

•*Hammett* (1982) (☞): crime writer Dashiell Hammett helps a Chinese girl get home and is inspired to write another novel.

•*Wings of Desire* (*Der Himmel über Berlin*) (1987) (■ ☞): angel Bruno Ganz, sent to watch over Berlin, falls in love with a circus artiste.

Who Framed Roger Rabbit?

☞ ■ ✍ ☆

USA • Touchstone • 1988 • 103 mins • col
d Robert Zemeckis   w Jeffrey Price/Peter S. Seaman   ph Dean Cundey   m Alan Silvestri
Bob Hoskins, Christopher Lloyd, Joanna Cassidy, Stubby Kaye
Voices: Charles Fleischer, >Kathleen Turner, Amy Irving, Lou Hirsch, Mel Blanc

Private eye Eddie Valiant (Hoskins) loathes Toons because his brother was killed by one, but his involvement with cartoon star Roger Rabbit (Fleischer) and his glamorous wife Jessica (Turner) embroils him in a sinister scheme to rub out Toontown. An astounding blend of reality and animation, director Robert Zemeckis' and animator Richard Williams' homage to detective *film noir* and veiled condemnation of apartheid is full of party pieces from a host of cartoon celebrities – Betty Boop as a waitress, Mickey Mouse and Bugs Bunny parachuting, and a duck piano duet that becomes a duel between Daffy and Donald – although the funniest sequence is the opening archetype of short-feature 'socko' slapstick. Plenty of clever rabbit references, too, including one to invisible rabbit >*Harvey* (Henry Koster 1950) (☆ ✍ ☞).

•Laughter is regarded as an evil in *The Name of the Rose* (Jean-Jacques Annaud 1986) (☆ ■ ✍).

•Another bunny, Brer Rabbit was the hero of an early real-animation film *Song of the South* (Harve Foster 1947) (☞ ■).

•Dwarfs populate another unusual town in *The Terror of Tiny Town* (Sam Newfield 1938) (✍).

•Another cartoon place which is viewed with suspicion and fear, this time by the ancient Romans is the village inhabited by some indomitable Gauls, in *Asterix and the Big Fight* (Philippe Grimond 1989) (✍).

WIDOWS

***Carve Her Name with Pride* (Lewis Gilbert 1958)** ☆ ✍

Virginia McKenna as Violette Szabo, the war widow-turned-agent who is executed by the Nazis.

***Dishonoured* (>Josef Von Sternberg 1931)** ☞ ☆

Officer's widow >Marlene Dietrich is rescued from prostitution and sent spying by Victor McLaglen.

***So Evil My Love* (Lewis Allen 1948)** ☆

19th-century con man artist Ray Milland gets missionary's widow Ann Todd to steal paintings.

***The Tamarind Seed* (Blake Edwards 1974)** ☆

British widow Julie Andrews goes on a West Indian holiday and falls in love with Soviet officer Omar Sharif.

***Whatever Happened to Aunt Alice?* (Lee H. Katzin 1969)** ✍

A dotty old widow kills her housekeepers after having got them to leave her their money.

***Without Love* (Harold S. Bucquet 1945)** ☆

Widow >Katharine Hepburn opens her Washington home to scientist >Spencer Tracy during the wartime housing shortage.

Wild Strawberries (Smultronstället) ☞ ☆ ■ ✍ ♫

Sweden • Svensk Filmindustri • 1957 • 93 mins • b/w

wd >Ingmar Bergman   ph Gunnar Fischer   m Erik Nordgren

Victor Sjöström, Ingrid Thulin, Gunnar Björnstrand, Bibi Andersson, Max Von Sydow

Viktor Sjöström and Ingmar Bergman, Sweden's greatest silent and sound directors, come together in this study of regret and atonement, based on *King Lear* and Strindberg's *A Dream Play*. Isak Borg (Sjöström), an academic en route to an awards ceremony, realizes through a series of dreams and chance meetings that his life of achievement has been devoid of happiness and love and that the blame lies as much with himself as with his mercenary family. Condemning the trappings of middle age and class more gently than, say, a >Buñuel, Bergman puts his faith in the optimistic vigour of youth, typified by the trio of hitch-hikers, and we leave Borg hopeful that he will enjoy, through grandfatherhood, his newly discovered youth at heart.

• >Alastair Sim is the misery redeemed by the ghosts of Christmas, in *Scrooge* (Brian Desmond Hurst 1951) (☆ ✍ ☞).
• Geraldine Page relives the past, in *The Trip to Bountiful* (Peter Masterson 1985) (☆).
• >Paul Newman is caught up in espionage when he goes to collect his academic awards, in *The Prize* (Mark Robson 1963) (☆ ✍ ☞).
• Old men Don Ameche, Wilford Brimley and Hume Cronyn are rejuvenated by an alien pod in a swimming pool, in *Cocoon* (Ron Howard 1985) (☆ ✍), and find life on earth something of a challenge when they pay a flying visit, in *Cocoon: The Return* (Daniel Petrie 1989) (☆).

Wilder, Billy
(Samuel Wilder) Austrian-born American writer/director (b 1906)

A *film noir*-type tough crime reporter and then a UFA studio screenwriter in Berlin, Wilder quit Nazi Germany and, via Paris, reached Hollywood in 1934. In partnership with Charles Brackett, he wrote the classic comedies: *Bluebeard's Eighth Wife* (>Ernst Lubitsch 1938) (☞ ✍) (impoverished Claudette Colbert cures playboy >Gary Cooper of marriage mania); *Midnight* (Mitchell Leisen 1939) (✍ ☆ ☞) (John Barrymore hires Claudette Colbert to stop Don Ameche chasing his wife Mary Astor); >*Ninotchka* (AAN: >Ernst Lubitsch 1939) (✍ ☞ ☆ ■); and *Ball Of Fire* (Original Story AAN: >Howard Hawks 1942) (☞ ☆ ■) (lexicographer >Gary Cooper is roused from his bookishness by stripper >Barbara Stanwyck). Satirically edged comedy remained his forte as a director: *The Seven Year Itch* (1955) (☆ ☞ ✍) (>Marilyn Monroe cools down on a hot night in Tom Ewell's apartment), >*Some Like It Hot* (1959) (☆ ✍ ☞ ■ ♫); >*Irma La Douce* (1963) (✍ ☞ ☆); and *The*

THE WICKED LADY
(Leslie Arliss 1945) ☆ ■

FEMMES FATALES

DEAD RECKONING
(John Cromwell 1947) ☆
(soldier's girlfriend Lizabeth Scott threatens buddy >Humphrey Bogart)

ANGEL FACE
(Otto Preminger 1952) ☆
(chauffeur Robert Mitchum is talked into Jean Simmons' murder scheme)

PIERROT LE FOU
(>Jean-Luc Godard 1965)
(bored Parisian >Jean-Paul Belmondo caught up in girl's crimes)

ONE DEADLY SUMMER (L'ÉTÉ MEURTRIER)
(Jean Becker) ☆
(disturbed girl Isabelle Adjani schemes to avenge her mother's rape)

BLACK WIDOW
(Bob Rafelson 1987) ☆
(gold-digger Theresa Russell kills her way through rich husbands)

'WOMEN'S PICTURES'

THE WIND
(Victor Sjöström 1927) ☆ ☞ ■
(>Lillian Gish survives isolation, molestation and sandstorm)

REMEMBER THE NIGHT
(Mitchell Leisen 1940) ☆ ✍
(shoplifter >Barbara Stanwyck transforms staid lawyer)

MILDRED PIERCE
(>Michael Curtiz 1945) ☆ ☞
(hard work and trials transform dowdy housewife >Joan Crawford)

NORA PRENTISS
(Vincent Sherman 1946) ☆ ✍
(>Blue Angelesque tale of love ruining life)

FLAMINGO ROAD
(>Michael Curtiz 1949) ☆
(dancer >Joan Crawford begins to influence small-town politics)

MY FOOLISH HEART
(Mark Robson 1949) ✍ ☆
(J. D. Salinger tale has pregnant wife convincing husband her child is his)

Gentlewoman Margaret Lockwood becomes highwayman James Mason's partner

FEMINISM

GERTRUD
(Carl Dreyer 1964) ☞ ■ ✍
(woman enjoys love without marriage)

MY BRILLIANT CAREER
(Gillian Armstrong 1979) ☆ ☞
(outback bluestocking writes literary memoir)

THE WORLD ACCORDING TO GARP
(George Roy Hill 1982) ☆ ✍
(nurse Glenn Close becomes a prominent feminist activist)

90 DAYS
(Giles Walker 1985) ☞
(the problems facing men trying to respect feminism)

THE BOSTONIANS
(James Ivory 1985) ✍ ■
(>Henry James story of early feminist campaigners)

FEMALE FILM-MAKERS

CHRISTOPHER STRONG
(Dorothy Arzner 1933) ☆ ☞
(pregnancy drives aviator >Katharine Hepburn to suicide)

LOWLAND (TIEFLAND)
(Leni Riefenstahl 1935-1954) ☞
(version of Eugene D'Albert's opera, the finishing of which was hindered by war and propaganda duties)

THE HITCH-HIKER
(Ida Lupino 1953) ☞
(hiker murders his way around USA)

CLEO FROM FIVE TO SEVEN (CLÉO DE 5 À 7)
(Agnès Varda 1965) ☞ ☆
(singer awaits the results of her medical tests)

INDIA SONG
(Marguerite Duras 1975) ✍
(diplomat's wife pursues a number of affairs)

MEN (MÄNNER)
(Doris Dorrie 1985) ☞
(husband falls in love with his wife's lover)

DESPERATELY SEEKING SUSAN
(Susan Siedelman 1985) ☆ ☞ ♫
(eccentric's jacket sparks comedy of errors)

HIGH TIDE
(Gillian Armstrong 1988) ☞
(mother finds lost daughter but wants it kept secret)

Front Page (1974) (☞ ☆ ✍) (ruthless editor Walter Matthau persuades ace reporter >Jack Lemmon to cover one last story). The Wilder-Brackett AAN script for *Hold Back the Dawn* (Mitchell Leisen 1941) (☆ ☞) (Best Picture AAN has Charles Boyer marrying >Olivia De Havilland to skirt immigration rules) showed an incisive understanding of contemporary America, as did other films he directed: *The Lost Weekend* (AA Direction and [with Brackett Script]: 1945) (☞ ✍ ☆) (blocked writer Ray Milland [AA] drinks to find inspiration); >*Sunset Boulevard* (AA [with Brackett] Script and AAN Direction: 1950) (☆ ☞ ✍); *Ace in the Hole* (aka *The Big Carnival*) (1951) (☞ ✍ ☆) (journalist >Kirk Douglas exploits a caving accident to boost paper sales); and *The Apartment* (Script AA [with I. A. L. Diamond] and AA Direction: 1960) (☞ ☆ ✍) (timid >Jack Lemmon discloses his love for Shirley MacLaine when Fred MacMurray seduces her in his apartment). Wilder's fascination with Americans in Europe was explored in: *The Emperor Waltz* (1947) (☞ ☆) (gramophone salesman Bing Crosby strikes the right note with Austrian emperor's niece >Joan Fontaine); *A Foreign Affair* (1948) (☆ ✍) (soldier John Lund is torn between congresswoman Joan Arthur and Nazi moll >Marlene Dietrich); *One, Two, Three* (1961) (☆ ☞ ✍) (>James Cagney aims to sell Coca Cola to East Berlin); and *Avanti!* (1972) (☆ ☞ ✍ ■ ♫) (>Jack Lemmon discovers Juliet Mills' mother was his father's mistress).

■VIEW ON ▶ •*The Major and the Minor* (1942) (☞ ☆ ✍): army officer Ray Milland takes >Ginger Rogers back to camp believing she is 12 years old.
•*Five Graves to Cairo* (1943) (☞ ☆): Franchot Tone cuts off Rommel (>Erich Von Stroheim)'s supply lines.
•*Stalag 17* (AAN: 1953) (☞ ☆ ✍): William Holden proves he is not the informer in a PoW camp.
•*The Spirit of St Louis* (1957) (☞ ☆): >James Stewart as Charles Lindbergh flying the Atlantic in 1927.
•*Love in the Afternoon* (1957) (☆): >Gary Cooper is informed of jealous Maurice Chevalier's intentions by lover Audrey Hepburn.
•*The Fortune Cookie* (UK: *Meet Whiplash Willie*) (1966) (✍ ☆ ☞): shyster lawyer Walter Matthau gets TV cameraman >Jack Lemmon to sue for damages after a trivial collision on an American football field.
•*The Private Life of Sherlock Holmes* (1970) (☞): Christopher Lee's Mycroft involves Robert Stephens in a Scottish Highlands submarine mystery.
•*Portrait of a 60% Perfect Man: Billy Wilder* (*Portrait d'un Homme à 60% Parfait: Billy Wilder*) (Annie Tresgot 1980) (✍): interviews with the man himself and with, among others, >Jack Lemmon and Walter Matthau add up to a fascinating tribute.

WITCHCRAFT

The Dunwich Horror (Daniel Haller 1970) ✍
H. P. Lovecraft story has Dean Stockwell dragging Sandra Dee to a fertility ceremony.

I Married a Witch (>René Clair 1942) ☞ ☆
>Fredric March's wife Veronica Lake was burned by his ancestor after the Salem witch trials.

Night of the Eagle (US: *Burn, Witch, Burn*) (Sidney Hayers 1961) ✍
Witches trade spells in a medical school.

Witchcraft through the Ages (*Häxan*) (Benjamin Christiansen 1922) ☞ ■ ✍
Dramatic reconstructions and art evidence tell the story.

The Witches of Eastwick (George Miller 1987) ☆ ✍
>Jack Nicholson's devil is paid back by Michelle Pfeiffer, Susan Sarandon and Cher, the women he has seduced.

The Witches of Salem (aka *The Crucible*) (*Les Sorcières de Salem*) (Raymond Rouleau 1957) ✍ ☆
Jean-Paul Sartre's adaptation of Arthur Miller's play *The Crucible* has >Yves Montand and Simone Signoret as John and Elizabeth Proctor, who are tried for witchcraft.

Witchfinder General (US: *The Conqueror Worm*) (Michael Reeves 1968) ☆
17th-century lawyer Vincent Price roams the countryside in search of victims.

WITNESSES

The Accused (Jonathan Kaplan 1988) ☆ ✍
Bar-room customers, having urged on Jodie Foster's rapist, are taken to task in court.
Lady on a Train (Charles David 1945) ☆
This adaptation of Leslie Charteris' novel has Deanna Durbin failing to persuade New York cops that she saw a murder.
Moving Violation (Charles S. Dubin 1976) ✍
Small town sheriff seeks to silence the teenagers who saw him kill.
The Narrow Margin (Richard Fleischer 1952) ✍
Gangsters kill a decoy and then have to try again to get the real witness before a train reaches its destination.
Phantom Lady (Robert Siodmak 1944) ☞ ✍
When witnesses deny the very existence of the woman who is an accused man's only alibi, his secretary and a suspicious cop investigate.
She Loves Me Not (Elliott Nugent 1934) ☆ ✍
Miriam Hopkins lays low in Bing Crosby's college after seeing the murder of a fellow chorus girl.
Someone to Watch Over Me (Ridley Scott 1987) ✍
Cop Tom Berenger falls in love with the babysitter he is detailed to protect.
The Star Witness (William Wellman 1931) ☞ ✍
Gangsters try to silence murder witness Walter Huston.
The Window (Ted Tetzlaff 1949) ✍ ☞
Bobby Driscoll is always crying wolf, and so no one believes him when he sees a murder from the window of his New York slum.
Witness (Peter Weir 1985) ✍ ☞ ☆
>Harrison Ford joins an Amish community to protect Kelly McGillis's son from killer cop Danny Glover.

The Wizard of Oz ☆ ✍ ♫ ■ ☞
USA • MGM • 1939 • 102 mins • b/w & col
d Victor Fleming　w Noël Langley/
Florence Ryerson/Edgar Allan Wolfe
ph Harold Rosson　m E. Y. Harburg/
Harold Arlen
Judy Garland, Frank Morgan, Ray Bolger, Jack Haley, Bert Lahr, Margaret Hamilton

Miserable on her aunt and uncle's Kansas farm, Dorothy (Garland) is dreaming of better things *Somewhere over the Rainbow* when she and dog Toto are deposited in a land somewhere over a tornado. The natives of Oz, the Munchkins, suggest she follows the Yellow Brick Road to the Emerald City and the palace of the Wizard who can send her home, but accompanied by a scarecrow without a brain (Bolger), a tin man without a heart (Haley) and a cowardly lion (Lahr), her journey is hampered by the Wicked Witch of the West (Hamilton). Judy Garland, only selected because Deanna Durbin and Shirley Temple were unavailable, is adorably spirited in the lead, and as with >*Gone with the Wind*, Victor Fleming's direction was aided and abetted, this time by >King Vidor and Richard Thorpe.

•Michael Jackson and Diana Ross star in the soul music remake of the *Wizard of Oz – The Wiz* (>Sidney Lumet 1978), while Rosanna Arquette's lover was so obsessed with the film that he called out to Dorothy during love-making, in *After Hours* (>Martin Scorsese 1986) (☞ ☆ ✍).
•Tragic ballerina Moira Shearer also has ruby slippers in *The Red Shoes* (>Michael Powell/Emeric Pressburger 1948) (■).
•Veronica Lake is the good witch married to >Fredric March in *I Married a Witch* (>René Clair 1942) (☞ ☆).
•A witch predicts ill-fortune for Danish pastor Thorkild Roose in *Day of Wrath* (*Vredens Dag*) (Carl Dreyer 1943) (☞ ✍ ■).
•Shirley Temple's adventure to a fantasy world, the Land of Luxury, is told in an adaptation of the Grimm Brothers' fairy tale, *The Blue Bird* (Walter Lang 1940) (☆ ■).
•While Judy Garland is keen to escape despite the friends she has made in Munchkinland, a

mad woman resists her husband's efforts to free her from an asylum, in *A Page of Madness* (*Kurutta Ippeji*) (Teinosuke Kinugasa 1926) (☞).

WRITERS

***Author Author!* (Arthur Hiller 1982)** ☆
Al Pacino frets that Dyan Cannon is being unfaithful while he is writing a play.

***Beloved Infidel* (Henry King 1959)** ☆
Dancer Deborah Kerr tries to wean Gregory Peck's Scott Fitzgerald off the bottle.

***Benvenuta* (Andrée Delvaux 1983)** ☞ ☆
Screenwriter Matthieu Carrière meets Françoise Fabian, author of a scandalous novel to, discuss its adaptation.

***Charlie Bubbles* (Albert Finney 1968)** ☆ ✍
Bestselling author Finney returns to his working-class roots and receives a mixed reception.

***Devotion* (Curtis Bernhardt 1943)** ☆
>Olivia De Havilland, Ida Lupino and Nancy Coleman as the Brontë sisters, Charlotte, Emily and Anne.

***Theodora Goes Wild* (Richard Boleslawski 1936)** ☆ ✍
A small-town girl writes a penny dreadful revealing the secrets of her parents' (Irene Dunne and Melvyn Douglas) marriage.

***Throw Momma from a Train* (Danny De Vito 1988)** ✍ ☞ ☆
Writing student De Vito suggests he and teacher Billy Crystal commit each other's murders for alibi purposes.

***The World According to Garp* (George Roy Hill 1982)** ☆ ✍
As Robin Williams achieves writing fame, his mother Glenn Close becomes a leading women's rights activist.

Wyler, William

(Willy Wyler) German-born American director (1902–1981)

Invited to Hollywood by his cousin and Universal chief Carl Laemmle, Wyler directed unremarkable silent Westerns before beginning his association with Sam Goldwyn, working for whom he developed the fondness for depth of focus within claustrophobic confines which would characterize his films, particularly those involving cinematographer Gregg Toland: *These Three* (1936) (☞ ☆) (lying student accuses girls' school teachers Miriam Hopkins and Merle Oberon of a menage with Joel McCrea); *Wuthering Heights* (1939) (☆ ☞ ■ ✍ ♫) (>Laurence Olivier and Merle Oberon as Heathcliff and Cathy in the film version of the Emily Brontë novel); *The Little Foxes* (1941) (☆ ☞ ✍) (>Bette Davis manipulates and bitches to get what she wants from her Deep South family); and >*The Best Years of Our Lives* (AA: 1946) (☆ ☞ ✍ ■). Versatility combined with his visual expertise contributed to his record nine Oscar nominations. He was equally successful with STAGE AND LITERARY ADAPTATIONS: *Dodsworth* (AAN: 1936) (☞ ✍ ☆) (Best Picture AAN version of Sinclair Lewis's novel has a holiday to Europe transforming the lives of Walter Huston and Mary Astor); *Dead End* (1937) (☞ ☆ ■) (in the Lillian Hellman adaptation of Sidney Kingsley's play, >Humphrey Bogart's gangster lives in the slums adjoining a luxury apartment block); *The Heiress* (1949) (☞ ☆ ✍) (>Henry James's tale of how >Olivia De Havilland takes revenge on gold-digging lover Montgomery Clift); >*Ben-Hur* (AA: 1959) (☆ ☞ ✍ ♫ ■); and *The Collector* (AAN: 1965) (John Fowles' butterfly chaser Terence Stamp kidnaps Samantha Eggar (AAN); WESTERNS: *The Westerner* (1940) (☆) (>Gary Cooper tries to keep outlaw judge Walter Brennan from falling for Lily Langtry) and *The Big Country* (1958) (♫ ☞ ☆) (ranchers Gregory Peck and Charlton Heston quarrell over water rights); and CONTEMPORARY DRAMA: *Mrs Miniver* (AA: 1942) (☞ ☆ ✍) (Greer Garson and Walter Pidgeon survive separations and the Blitz) and *The Desperate Hours* (1955) (☆) (>Fredric March's family show great fortitude when they are taken hostage by escapee >Humphrey Bogart).

•*Counsellor at Law* (1933): a day in the life of Jewish lawyer John Barrymore.
•*The Good Fairy* (1934) (✍): >Preston Sturges's script has men falling over themselves to meet usherette Margaret Sullavan.
•*Come and Get It* (co-directed with >Howard

Hawks 1936): lumberjack Walter Brennan (AA) works to make Edward Albert rich.

•*Jezebel* (1938) (☆ ☞ ✍ ■): >Bette Davis (AA) becomes an outcast in Deep South high society because of her red dress.

•*The Letter* (1940) (☞ ☆ ✍): >Bette Davis claims a killing was self-defence, but husband Herbert Marshall finds evidence to the contrary.

•*Detective Story* (1951) (☞ ☆ ✍): >Kirk Douglas is so disgusted with Eleanor Parker for having fooled round with a gangster that he can hardly concentrate on a murder case.

•*Friendly Persuasion* (AAN: 1956) (☞ ✍): Quaker >Gary Cooper tries to remain neutral in US Civil War.

•*How to Steal a Million* (1966) (☞ ☆): Charles Boyer's daughter Audrey Hepburn involves private eye Peter O'Toole in an art theft.

Xala (The Curse) ☆ ✍ ☞ ■

Senegal • Filmi Domireew/Société National De Cinematographie • 1974 • 123 mins • col

wd Ousmane Sembène   ph Georges Caristan   m Samba Diabara Samb

Tierno Leye, Seune Samb, Miriam Niang, Younouss Seye, Dieynaba Niang, Fatim Diagne

Tying together the themes of his previous studies of past and present Senegal – *Black Girl from...* (*La Noire de...*) (1966) (☞) (the first sub-Saharan film to gain critical acclaim studies life after the end of French rule) and *The Money Order* (*Le Mandat*) (*Mandabi*) (1968) (☞ ✍ ☆) (a nephew in Paris sends Makouredia Gueye some money and everyone wants a share) – Ousmane Sembene pinpoints the internal and international problems facing most modern Third World countries. Following a coup, a businessman celebrates his inclusion in the commerce cabinet by taking a new wife, his third, only to immediately lose his potency and gradually his position and dignity. Bitingly satirical, *Xala* (a curse bestowing temporary impotence) depicts men of all colours as monochrome stereotypes, ruthless in the pursuit of supremacy but powerless in equality, while women of all ages are brightly coloured, indicating their mastery of diverse historical and contemporary influences. The political content is vital, but not suffocating.

•>Philippe Noiret is a bored French colonial policeman wiping out those who have made his life troublesome, in *Clean Slate* (*Coup de Torchon*) (Bertrand Tavernier 1981) (☆ ☞ ✍).

•Hayley Mills tells Hywel Bennett not to worry about his impotence, in *The Family Way* (Roy Boulting 1966) (♫).

•A corrupt mayor is continually exhumed by one of his victims, in *Repentance* (*Pokjaniyeaka, Monanieba*) (Tengiz Abuladze 1987) (✍ ☆).

•Shareholder Judy Holliday is invited to join a company to prevent her exposing the corruption of the board, in *The Solid Gold Cadillac* (Richard Quine 1956) (☆ ✍).

•Euro MP Charlotte Rampling is the politician whose ability to control her life diminishes as her career star rises, in *Paris by Night* (David Hare 1989) (✍ ☆).

YUPPIES

Almost You (Adam Brooks 1987) ✍
Griffin Dunne finds himself down among the graspers and pseuds of New York.

Big (Penny Marshall 1988) ☆ ✍
Grown up over night, Tom Hanks makes it big in the toy business.

Bright Lights, Big City (James Bridges 1988) ✍
Kiefer Sutherland's guide to decadent night life destroys Michael J. Fox's promising career.

How to Get Ahead in Advertising (Bruce Robinson 1989) ☆
Richard E. Grant has to come up with an ad campaign to make everyone want spots and boils.

The Marriage of a Young Stockbroker (Laurence Turman 1971) ✍ ☆
All work and no play for Richard Benjamin, so he takes to voyeurism and kinky sex to liven things up.

The Money Pit (Richard Benjamin 1986) ☆ ✍
Tom Hanks and Shelley Long beat rising house prices by buying a house that is about to fall down.

The Ploughman's Lunch (Richard Eyre 1981) ✍
Ian McEwan's script has radio journalist Jonathan Pryce and businessman Tim Curry questioning but sticking with Thatcherism.

The Secret of My Success (Herbert Ross 1987) ☆ ✍
Michael J. Fox rises from the mailroom and wins the heart of whizz kid Helen Slater.

Something Wild (Jonathan Demme 1986) ☆ ✍
Financier Jeff Daniels is taught how to be a rebel by Melanie Griffith as they escape from her crazed lover Ray Liotta.

Wall Street (Oliver Stone 1987) ☆
Charlie Sheen is ruined when he is caught insider-dealing for tycoon >Michael Douglas.

Working Girl (>Mike Nichols 1988) ☆ ☞
Secretary Melanie Griffith takes advantage of boss Sigourney Weaver's broken leg to deal with >Harrison Ford.

YANKEE DOODLE DANDY
(>Michael Curtiz 1942) ♫ ☆

SHOWBIZ BIOPICS

THE JOLSON STORY
(Alfred E. Green/Joseph H. Lewis 1946) ♫ ☆

JOLSON SINGS AGAIN
(Henry Levin 1949) ♫
(minstrel-to-movie-star life with Larry Parks)

THE GLENN MILLER STORY
(Anthony Mann 1954) ♫ ☆ ☞ ⚖
(life and mysterious death of bandleader >James Stewart)

LADY SINGS THE BLUES
(Sidney J. Furie 1972) ♫
(blues singer Billie Holiday's tragic decline)

LENNY
(Bob Fosse 1974)
(>Dustin Hoffman as hounded comedian Lenny Bruce)

VALENTINO
(Ken Russell 1977) ☞ ☆
(life and loves of silent screen idol)

ARTISTIC LIVES

THE LIFE OF EMILE ZOLA
(>William Dieterle 1937) ☞ ☆
(writer Paul Muni campaigns against injustice in Dreyfus Case)

DEVOTION
(Curtis Bernhardt 1944) ☆ ⚖
(the Brontë sisters' life at Haworth Parsonage)

THE MAGIC BOW
(Bernard Knowles 1946) ♫ ■
(Stewart Granger as violin virtuoso Paganini)

ISADORA (US: THE LOVES OF ISADORA)
(Karel Reisz 1968) ☆ ■
(decline and demise of dancer Isadora Duncan)

ALOÏSE
(Liliane De Kermadec 1975) ☆
(female painter who worked in Swiss asylum)

EDITH AND MARCEL (EDITH ET MARCEL)
(Claude Lelouch 1983) ☞ ♫
(Edith Piaf's romance with boxer Marcel Cerdan)

SCIENTISTS

THE STORY OF ALEXANDER GRAHAM BELL (UK: THE MODERN MIRACLE)
(Irving Cummings 1939) ☆
(the telephone is invented)

DR ERLICH'S MAGIC BULLET
(>William Dieterle 1940) ☞ ☆ ⚖
(more a biopox as >Edward G. Robinson discovers cure for syphilis)

MADAME CURIE
(>Mervyn Le Roy 1944) ☞ ☆
(Greer Garson discovers radium)

THE DAM BUSTERS
(Michael Anderson 1954) ⚖ ☆ ♫
(Michael Redgrave's Barnes Wallis perfects the bouncing bomb)

FREUD
(>John Huston 1963) ☞
(Montgomery Clift comes to know the true meaning of the term 'mummy's boy')

>James Cagney (AA) as vaudeville star George M. Cohan

SAINTS AND SINNERS

RASPUTIN THE MAD MONK
(Richard Boleslawski 1932) ☆
(evil monk bewitches Tsarina Alexandra)

THE TOAST OF NEW YORK
(Rowland V. Lee 1937) ☆
(Jim Fisk rises from barker to Wall Street banker)

NURSE EDITH CAVELL
(Herbert Wilcox 1939) ☆
(British nurse executed as spy in First World War)

BABY FACE NELSON
(Don Siegel 1957) ☆
(childish visage hides gangster heart of solid pitch)

THE INN OF THE SIXTH HAPPINESS
(Mark Robson 1958) ☆ ■
(>Ingrid Bergman's Gladys Aylward spends life as missionary in China)

THE MIRACLE WORKER
(Arthur Penn 1962) ☆
(Helen Keller's afflictions eased by Annie Sullivan)

HISTORICAL HOMAGE

THE IRON DUKE
(Victor Saville 1934) ☆
(Wellington fights post-Napoleonic War smear campaign)

JUAREZ
(>William Dieterle 1939) ☆
(Mexican leader resists European imperialism)

WILSON
(Henry King 1944) ☆ ✍ ■
(pacifist president takes the USA into the First World War)

BECKET
(Peter Glenville 1964) ☆ ■
(Henry II's friendship with Archbishop becomes a feud)

HENRY VIII AND HIS SIX WIVES
(Waris Hussein 1972)
(Keith Michell as the Tudor king obsessed with getting a male heir)

CHE!
(Richard Fleischer 1969) ☞
(portrait of Bolivian guerilla leader)

Zelig

USA • Orion/Rollins-Joffe • 1983 • 79 mins • b/w
wd >Woody Allen   ph Gordon Willis
m Dick Hyman
Woody Allen, Mia Farrow

Leonard Zelig's (Allen) yearning for approbation and acceptance cause him to adopt the mental and physical characteristics of those around him. Briefly a celebrated darling of the novelty-seeking Jazz Age, the Human Chameleon is implicated in a series of scandals which reinforce his insecurities. Behavioural scientist Eudora Fletcher (Farrow) becomes his last hope of salvation. Returning to the documentary style of *Take the Money and Run* (1969) (✍ ☆), Allen further indulges his passion for nostalgia, and with perfect understanding of an era and its people and masterly use of newsreel and special effect (that allows Zelig to appear, for example, on the Vatican balcony, behind Hitler at a Nazi rally, and with celebrities ranging from golfer Bobby Jones to playwright Eugene O'Neill), creates a brilliant period piece with a cutting contemporary edge.

• Intercut footage film brings >Humphrey Bogart, >Barbara Stanwyck and Lauren Bacall (among others) into private eye Steve Martin's investigation, in *Dead Men Don't Wear Plaid* (Carl Reiner 1982) (☞ ■).
• Newsreel footage tells the story to the music of The Beatles in *All This and World War Two* (Susan Winslow 1977) (☞ ♫).
• The excitement and danger of the Roaring Twenties is captured in *The Cotton Club* (>Francis Ford Coppola 1982) (♫).
• Psychiatrists Tom Conti and Glenda Jackson are crazier than patients Jeff Goldblum and Julie Haggerty, in *Beyond Therapy* (>Robert Altman 1987) (☆).

Zinnemann, Fred
Austrian-born American director (b 1907)
People on Sunday (*Menschen am Sonntag*) (1928), a semi-documentary silent about a day trip from Berlin to the countryside, boasted the latent talents of future Hollywood directors

Robert Siodmak, >Billy Wilder and law graduate Zinnemann. Heavily influenced by contemporary documentary techniques, particularly those of tutor Robert Flaherty, Zinnemann's earliest films were shorts; *That Mothers Might Live* (1938) and, much later, *Benjy* (1951) (☞) both winning Oscars. The Second World War and its aftermath furnished him with excellent material: *The Seventh Cross* (1944) (☆ ☞) (>Spencer Tracy is one of the Germans sought by the Nazis after breaking out of a concentration camp), *From Here to Eternity* (AA: 1953) (☞ ☆) (the screen version of James Jones' novel of army life and love before Pearl Harbor); >*Julia* (AAN: 1977) (☆ ✍ ☞ ■); *The Search* (AAN: 1947) (☞) (semi-documentary telling of soldier Montgomery Clift [AAN] caring for a German orphan); and *The Men* (1950) (☆ ☞) (Teresa Wright helps >Marlon Brando come to terms with his war injuries). However, Zinnemann, who has made but 15 films in 39 years, has also demonstrated great versatility: the classic anti-hero Western, >*High Noon* (AAN: 1952) (☆ ✍ ☞ ♫), the Rogers & Hammerstein musical *Oklahoma!* (1955) ♫ (Rod Steiger tries to prevent true love between Gordon Macrae and Shirley Jones); the historical drama *A Man for All Seasons* (AA: 1966) (☆ ✍ ☞ ■) (Robert Bolt's adaptation of his own play has Robert Shaw's Henry VIII reluctantly executing Thomas More [Paul Scofield] [AA] for refusing to accept his 1529 divorce); and the political thriller *The Day of the Jackal* (1973) (☆ ✍ ☞) (the screen version of the Frederick Forsyth novel has Edward Fox preparing to assassinate Charles De Gaulle).

•*The Kid Glove Killer* (1942) (✍): forensic scientist Van Heflin discovers the killer of a small-town mayor is his best friend.
•*The Member of the Wedding* (1952) (☞ ✍): brought up by the cook, 12-year-old Julie Harris (AAN) (the actress was actually 27) returns to loneliness when her playmate dies at her sister's wedding.
•*A Hatful of Rain* (1957) (☞): disturbed by the war, Don Murray becomes a drug addict.

•*The Nun's Story* (AAN: 1958) (☞ ☆ ✍): doctor Peter Finch guides Audrey Hepburn through her novitiate.
•*The Sundowners* (AAN: 1960) (☞ ☆): Deborah Kerr (AAN) follows itinerant sheep drover Robert Mitchum around Australia.
•*Behold a Pale Horse* (1964) (☞ ✍ ☆): this adaptation of Emeric Pressburger's novel *Killing a Mouse on Sunday* has Spanish Civil War veteran Gregory Peck out to assassinate Anthony Quinn.

ZOLA, ÉMILE

La Bête Humaine (US: *The Human Beast*) (>Jean Renoir 1938) ☞ ☆ ✍ ■ ♫
Train driver >Jean Gabin plots with Simone Simon to kill her railwayman husband.

Germinal (Yves Allégret 1963) ✍ ☆
The appalling conditions of the coal mines in the 1860s provoke Jean Sorel into leading a strike.

Gervaise (René Clément 1956) ☞ ☆
Maria Schell won Best Actress at Venice for her portrayal of the impoverished Parisian washerwoman driven to drink in the screen version of the novel *L'Assommoir*.

House of Lovers (*Pot Bouille*) (Julien Duvivier 1957) ✍ ☆
Gérard Philipe is pursued by the owner of the draper's shop where he works and by two girls at the boarding house where he lives.

Human Desire (>Fritz Lang 1954) ☞ ■
Glenn Ford and Gloria Grahame plan to murder train driver Broderick Crawford in a remake of *La Bête Humaine*.

The Life of Emile Zola (>William Dieterle 1937) ☞ ☆
Paul Muni (AAN) fights the anti-Semitism aimed at army officer Alfred Dreyfus (Joseph Schildkraut) (AA).

Nana (>Jean Renoir 1926) ☞
Actress-turned-prostitute Catherine Hessling enjoys a brief break from poverty before her death.

Nana (UK: *Lady of the Boulevards*) (Dorothy Arzner 1934) ■ ✍
Anna Sten in the lead, with Lionel Atwill as her

ZÉRO DE CONDUITE
(Jean Vigo 1933) ☞ ☆ ✍

PUBLIC SCHOOL

YOUNG WOODLEY
(Thomas Bentley 1929) ☆
(a pupil falls in love with a teacher's wife)

>GOODBYE MR CHIPS
(Sam Wood 1939) ☆ ☞ ✍ ■
(young master >Robert Donat becomes a school institution)

THE HAPPIEST DAYS OF YOUR LIFE
(Frank Launder 1950) ☆ ✍
(boys' and girls' schools have to share premises)

DECLINE AND FALL
(John Krish 1968) ✍
(Evelyn Waugh tale of trials of a master at a second rate prep school)

IF...
(Lindsay Anderson 1968) ☞ ☆ ✍
(Malcolm McDowell leads revolt against headmaster Peter Jeffrey)

UNMAN, WITTERING AND ZIGO
(John Mackenzie 1971) ✍ ☞
(murderous class terrorize master to keep a secret)

UNPLEASANT SCHOOLS

THE GOOSE STEPS OUT
(Will Hay/Basil Dearden 1942) ☆ ✍
(eccentric English master teaches at Nazi academy)

LES DIABOLIQUES
(Henri-Georges Clouzot 1954) ✍ ☞ ☆
(headmaster's corpse returns to torment his killers)

THE 400 BLOWS (LES QUATRE CENTS COUPS)
(>François Truffaut 1959) ☞ ☆ ✍
(Jean-Pierre Léaud endures life in a brutal reform school)

FEAR IN THE NIGHT
(Jimmy Sangster 1972) ✍ ☆ ☞
(Judy Geeson and headmaster Peter Cushing are the victims of their spouses' [Ralph Bates and Joan Collins] evil scheme)

SUNDAY DAUGHTERS
(VASÁRNAPI SZÜLOK)
(János Rósza 1979) ☞ ✍
(girls plot escape from a Hungarian reformatory)

THE BREAKFAST CLUB
(John Hughes 1985) ☆ ☞
(the awakening of a Saturday morning detention group)

TEENAGE

GREASE
(Randal Kleiser 1978) ♫
(tough guy John Travolta loses face falling for soppy Olivia Newton-John)

AN IMPUDENT GIRL
(L'EFFRONTÉE)
(Claude Miller 1985) ☞ ☆
(lonely Charlotte Gainsbourg pursues her pianist heroine)

PRETTY IN PINK
(John Hughes 1986) ☆
(Molly Ringwald and Andrew McCarthy romance across class barriers)

ALOHA SUMMER
(Tommy Lee Wallace 1988) ✍
(beach love and laughs on a Hawaiian holiday)

LA PETIT VOLEUSE
(Claude Miller 1989) ☞ ☆ ✍ ■
(Charlotte Gainsbourg pays for her kleptomania, but lives to steal another day)

Boys rebel against oppressive school regime

CHILDHOOD

THE ROAD TO LIFE (PUTYOVKA V ZHIZN)
(Nikolai Ekk 1931) ☞ ■
(children taught life skills at Soviet revolutionary commune)

PAPER MOON
(Peter Bogdanovich 1973) ✍ ☆ ■ ☞ ♫
(a girl helps a con man sell Bibles)

FROG DREAMING
(Brian Trenchard-Smith 1985) ■ ✍
(boy discovers the Aboriginal secret of a creepy lake)

PAPERHOUSE
(Bernard Rose 1988) ☞
(a girl's drawing of a house effects her dreams)

LE GRAND CHEMIN
(Jean Loup Hubert 1988) ☞ ☆
(town boy shown life by a ten-year-old country girl)

CHILDREN'S LITERATURE

SHE
(Irving Pichel/Lansing G. Holden 1935) ☆
(Randolph Scott and Nigel Bruce in H. Rider Haggard's tale of an immortal goddess dying through love)

TOM BROWN'S SCHOOLDAYS
(Gordon Parry 1951) ✍ ☆
(Robert Newton as Dr Thomas Arnold in Thomas Hughes's classic)

HUCKLEBERRY FINN
(>Michael Curtiz 1960) ☞ ✍
(Mark Twain's classic adventures on the Mississippi)

IN SEARCH OF THE CASTAWAYS
(Robert Stevenson 1961) ✍
(professor Maurice Chevalier helps children find missing father in Jules Verne tale)

THE RAILWAY CHILDREN
(Lionel Jeffries 1970) ✍ ■
(three children win friends on Yorkshire railway line)

chief admirer.

The Sin of Father Mouret (La Faute de l'Abbé Mouret) (Georges Franju 1970) ☞ ✍ ▨

A priest's devotion to the Virgin wanes when he falls for an unruly local girl.

Thérèse Raquin (The Adulteress) (>Marcel Carné 1953) ✍ ☆

Murder and blackmail follow housewife Simone Signoret's affair with Italian trucker Raf Vallone.

INDEX OF FILM TITLES

A

Aan 354
Abbott and Costello in Hollywood 122
Abbott and Costello Meet Frankenstein 213
Abbott and Costello Meet the Ghosts 213
Abominable Dr Phibes, The 190, 360
Abominable Snowman, The 323
À Bout de Souffle 1, 2, 32, 137, 377
Above Suspicion 1, 78
Above Us the Waves 351
Abraham Lincoln 146
Absence of Malice 182, 245
Abuse 16
Accatone 38, 283
Accent on Youth 328
Accident 210
Accidental Tourist, The 165, 279, 373
Accused, The (William Dieterle) 77
Accused, The (Jonathan Kaplan) 278, 401
Ace in the Hole 101, 159, 400
Aces High 362
Across the Bridge 144
Across the Pacific 49, 211, 282
Across the Wide Missouri 395
Actors, The 281
Actor's Revenge, An 314, 360
Actress, The 80, 122
Ada 337
Adalen 31 119
Adalen Riots, The 119
Adam Had Four Sons 35
Adam's Rib 3, 6, 80, 156, 367
Addition, L' 237
Address Unknown 205
Adieu Bonaparte 242
Adieu Philippine 210, 377
Admirable Crichton, The 55
Adolphe 248
Adulteress, The 63, 412
Adventure for Two 21, 256
Adventurer, The 66, 257
Adventures of Arsène Lupin, The 182
Adventures of Baron Munchausen, The 205
Adventures of Don Juan, The 143

Adventures of Don Quixote 109, 282, 328
Adventures of Gerard, The 242
Adventures of Goopy and Bagha, The 306
Adventures of Marco Polo, The 112
Adventures of Mark Twain, The 224
Adventures of Robin Hood, The 81, 86, 239, 304
Adventures of Robinson Crusoe, The 54, 176
Adventures of Sherlock Holmes, The 90, 305
Adventures of Tom Sawyer, The 67
Adventuress, The 331
Adventure Starts Here 14
Adversary, The 306
Advise and Consent 199, 287
Aerograd 102
Affair of the Heart, An 108
Affairs of Cellini, The 224
Affairs of Susan, The 124
Affair to Remember, An 100, 143, 215, 357
African Queen, The 4, 17, 49, 156, 157, 166, 267
After Hours 326, 330, 401
After Office Hours 183
After the Thin Man 290, 347, 361
Against the Wind 5, 39, 251
Agatha 161, 177
Âge d'Or, L' 5, 53, 353
Age of Consent 289
Age of Cosimo De Medici, The 321
Age of Infidelity 2
Agnes of God 124, 249
Agony 30, 322
Agony and the Ecstasy, The 309
Aguirre, Wrath of God 16, 157, 230
Ah, Wilderness 338
Aïda 260
Ai No Corrida 6
Air Force 362
Airplane! 77, 192, 283
Airplane II: the Sequel 283
Airport 273, 359
Air Raid Wardens 201
A.K. 304
Alamo Bay 217
Alamo, The 393

Albert RN 292
Al Capone 133
Alexander Hamilton 287
Alexander Nevsky 6, 110
Alexander's Ragtime Band 210, 341
Alexander the Great 11, 54
Alexandre 248, 361
Alex and the Gypsy 148
Alex in Wonderland 121
Alfie 58, 143
Alfred the Great 233
Algiers 18, 182
Alias Nick Beal 91
Ali Baba and the Forty Thieves 18
Alibi 45, 68
Alice 226
Alice Adams 156, 346
Alice Doesn't Live Here Anymore 28, 274, 326, 336
Alice in the Cities 395
Alice in Wonderland 116, 121, 142, 217, 226, 310
Alice's Adventures in Wonderland 228
Alice's Restaurant 312
Alien 279, 317, 344
Aliens 279
Ali: Fear Eats the Soul 118, 120, 231
Alive and Kicking 257
All About Eve 7, 84, 220, 234, 266, 267
All at Sea 190
All Good Citizens 338
All I Desire 346
All My Good Countrymen 338
All My Sons 119
All Night Long 103, 180
All of Me 181
Allonsanfan 76, 225
All Quiet on the Western Front 8, 79, 262
All That Heaven Allows 120
All That Jazz 61
All That Money Can Buy 91, 93
All the Gold in the World 181, 248
All the King's Men 42, 76, 266
All the President's Men 77, 160, 183, 275
All These Women 14, 34
All the Way Home 284
All the Youthful Day 366

All This and Heaven Too 3, 85, 365
All This and World War Two 408
All Through the Night 210
Almost You 307, 405
Aloha Summer 410
Aloïse 19, 406
Along the Great Divide 101
Alphaville 36, 130, 137
Alpine Fire 170
Alsino and the Condor 173
Altered States 165, 181, 345
Always 313
Always a Bride 73
Amadeus 10, 72, 126, 277
Amarcord 120, 274
Amazing Dr Clitterhouse, The 133
Amazing Mr Beecham, The 55
Amazing Mr Blunden, The 135
America 146
America, America 169, 187
American Friend, The 21, 119, 396
American Graffiti 75
American in Paris, An 12, 188, 229, 267
Americanization of Emily, The 11
American Madness 29, 62
American Romance, An 237, 383
American Soldier, The 119, 386
American Tail, An 116
American Tragedy, An 385
American Werewolf in London, An 219
Amityville Horror, The 154, 218
Among the Living 337, 374
Amore, L' 109, 321
Amorous Adventures of Moll Flanders, The 375
Amour à Mort, L' 312
Amsterdam Affair 286
Anaemic Cinema 353
Anastasia 34, 268, 364
Anatolian Smile, The 169, 187
Anatomy of a Murder 77, 348
Anchors Aweigh 99, 188
Andalusian Dog, The 53, 353
Anderson Tapes, The 214
And God Created Woman 53
And Now for Something Completely Different 288
Andrei Rublev 355
Androcles and the Lion 329
Android 279
And Then There Were None 24, 68, 71, 190, 373

And the Ship Sails On 121, 206
And Woman Was Created 53
Angel (Neil Jordan) 368
Angel (George Katakouzinos) 368
Angel (Ernst Lubitsch) 93, 212
Angel Dust 286
Angel Face 49, 398
Angel Heart 87, 91
Angelic Conversation, The 329
Angel On My Shoulder 91
Angelos 368
Angels 14
Angels of the Streets 51
Angels Over Broadway 164
Angels with Dirty Faces 49, 57, 81, 343
Angel who Pawned her Harp, The 14
Angel Wore Red, The 341
Anges du Péché, Les 51
Angi Vera 292
Angry Silence, The 23, 169
Animal Crackers 224
Animal Farm 117
Animal Kingdom, The 212
Animals Film, The 96
Anna and the King of Siam 233
Anna Boleyn 180, 293
Anna Christie 134
Anna Karenina 134, 203, 222, 224, 300, 304, 380
Anne and Muriel 184, 372
Anne of Green Gables 247, 287
Anne of the Indies 354
Anne of the Thousand Days 55, 293
Annie 13, 166, 228, 287
Annie Get Your Gun 13, 69
Annie Hall 9, 15, 29, 40, 188, 220, 223, 275
Annie Oakley 343
Anniversary, The 356
Ann Vickers 251
À Nos Amours 5, 207
Another Country 16
Another Fine Mess 200
Another Part of the Forest 76
Another Thin Man 290, 361
Another Way 204
Another Woman 9, 227
À Nous La Liberté 70, 233
Anthony Adverse 76, 224, 263
Antigone 308
Antoine and Antoinette 59
Antonio das Mortes 147
Antony and Cleopatra 329

Anxiety of the Goalie at the Penalty Kick, The 396
Any Number Can Play 119
Any Number Can Win 132
Anything Goes 12, 206
Anzio 120
Aparajito 18, 306, 381
Apartment, The 176, 204, 269, 400
Apocalypse Now 17, 51, 61, 75, 384
Applause 7, 357
Apple Game, The 313
Appointment, The 214
Appointment with Danger 249
Appointment with Death 90
Apprenticeship of Duddy Kravitz, The 37, 183
À Propos de Nice 97
Apur Sansar 18
Apu Trilogy, The 18, 306
Arabesque 99
Arabian Nights, The 18, 284, 302, 334
Archimède the Tramp 132
Arch of Triumph 35
Aren't Men Beasts? 368
Aria 260
Arise My Love 183
Aristocats, The 117
Around the World in Eighty Days 268, 388
Arrowsmith 126
Arsenal 30
Arsenal Stadium Mystery, The 153
Arsenic and Old Lace 62, 142
Arthur 276
Artists and Models 4
Artists at the Top of the Big Top: Disorientated 381
Ascendancy 38
Ascenseur 37
Ascent, The 37
Ascent to Heaven 54
Ashes 389
Ashes and Diamonds 20, 308, 389, 390
Ash Wednesday 127
Ask Any Girl 69
Ask a Policeman 339
As Long As You're Healthy 235
Aspern 179
Asphalt Jungle, The 166, 234
Assam Garden, The 251
Assassination Bureau, The 248
Assassination of Trotsky, The 55

Assassination of the Duke of Guise, The 46
Assassin for Hire 21
Assassin, The 225, 337
Assault on Precinct 13 314
Assault, The 255, 278
Astaire, Fred 22
Asterix and the Big Fight 396
Asterix in Britain 116
Astonished Heart, The 294
Asylum 154
As You Desire Me 134, 386
As You Like It 256, 329, 370
As Young as You Feel 41
Atalante, L' 4, 70
Atlantic 193
Atlantic City, USA 133, 217, 381
Atlantide, L' 282
Atonement of Gösta Berling, The 134
Attack 78, 254
Attack of the Fifty-Foot Women, The 372
Attack of the Giant Leeches 85
Attack of the Killer Tomatoes, The 372
Attack of the Puppet People 228
At the Circus 225
Augustine of Hippo 323
Au Revoir les Enfants 141, 217, 382
Austerlitz 72
Author Author! 402
Autobiography of a Princess 301
Autumn Leaves 78, 205, 253
Autumn Sonata 33, 34, 239
Avanti! 204, 321, 400
Aviator's Wife, The 319
Avventura, L' 17, 24
Awful Truth, The 94, 142, 215, 263, 284, 330
Awkward Age, The 248

B

Baara 369
Babe Ruth Story, The 152
Babes in Arms 357
Babes in Toyland 200
Babette's Feast 24, 26, 278, 279
Baby Boom 26, 188
Baby Doll 187, 207
Baby Face 346
Baby Face Nelson 133, 407
Bachelor and the Bobbysoxer, The 5, 143, 211
Bachelor Girls 8
Bachelor Knight 5, 143, 211
Bachelor Mother 27, 319, 336

Bachelor of Hearts 349
Bachelor Party, The 7
Bachelor's Daughters, The 8
Background 94
Background to Danger 209
Backlash 147
Back of Beyond, The 97
Back Room Boy 206
Back Street 231
Back to School 251
Back to the Future 342, 363
Bad and the Beautiful, The 101, 229, 267
Bad Boy 215
Bad Company 378
Bad Day at Black Rock 337, 366
Bad Girl 262
Badlands 238
Bad Lord Byron, The 285
Bad News Bears, The 152
Bad Seed, The 205
Bad Timing 294
Bagdad Café 11, 312
Baker's Wife, The 3
Balance, La 176
Balance of Happiness, The 336, 386
Ballad of a Soldier 255
Ballad of Narayama, The 61
Ball of Fire 48, 155, 340, 343, 397
Balloonatic, The 187
Balthazar 15, 51
Bambi 116
Bananas 9, 314
Bandit of Sherwood Forest, The 302
Bandits at Orgosolo, The 157
Band of Outsiders 137
Band Wagon, The 22, 229, 296
Bang the Drum Slowly 87
Banjo on My Knee 393
Bank Detective, The 16, 29, 122
Bank Dick, The 16, 29, 122
Bank Holiday 309
Barbarella 124, 280
Barbarian and the Geisha, The 166
Barbary Coast 155, 316, 353
Barefoot Contessa, The 220, 268, 300
Barefoot Executive, The 358
Barefoot in the Park 123, 332
Barfly 105
Barkleys of Broadway, The 22
Barnacle Bill 190, 327
Baron Munchausen 205

Barretts of Wimpole Street, The 198, 221, 365
Barry Lyndon 194
Bar Sinister, The 97
Bartered Bride, The 260, 261
Bartleby 103
Basil, the Great Mouse Detective 117, 163
Batman (Tim Burton) 246
Batman (Leslie Martinson) 352
Batteries Not Included 252
Battle Cry 391
Battleground 395
Battle of Algiers, The 381
Battle of Austerlitz, The 72
Battle of Britain, The 254, 256
Battle of Chile, The 332
Battle of Elderbush Gulch, The 146
Battle of Gallipolli, The 21
Battle of the Century, The 199, 346
Battle of the Rails, The 59, 250, 311
Battle of the River Plate, The 254, 289
Battleship Potemkin, The 47, 110
Battling Butler 188
Bayan Ko: My Own Country 369
Bay of Angels 133, 377
Beachcomber, The 4, 199, 368
Beaches 313
Bears and I, The 15
Beast of the City, The 42
Beast with Five Fingers, The 209
Beat the Devil 49, 166
Beau Brummell 115, 233
Beau Chumps 200
Beau Geste 74, 303, 395
Beau Hunks 200, 303
Beau Serge, Le 65
Beauties of the Night 71, 103
Beautiful Blonde from Bashful Bend, The 351
Beauty and the Beast 353
Beauty and the Devil 71, 120, 320
Be Big 200
Because of Him 20, 199, 389
Becket 55, 228, 407
Bedazzled 91, 100, 328
Bedford Incident, The 111, 243, 351
Bedknobs and Broomsticks 117
Bedlam 186, 207
Bed-Sitting Room, The 30, 111
Bedtime for Bonzo 52

Bedtime Story, A 27
Beehive, The 38
Bee Keeper, The 226
Beetlejuice 154
Before the Revolution 38
Beggars of Life 395
Begone Dull Care 180
Beguiled, The 378
Behind the Mask 162
Behold a Pale Horse 409
Being There 16, 236, 276
Believers, The 325
Bellboy, The 235
Belle de Jour 31, 54, 86, 294, 381
Belle Équipe, La 131, 312
Belle of New York, The 22
Belle of the Nineties 215
Belles of St Trinian's, The 136, 334
Belles on Their Toes 212
Bellissima 178, 237, 384
Bellman and True 119
Bells are Ringing 229
Bells Go Down, The 45
Bells of St. Mary's, The 34, 215
Beloved Infidel 402
Ben-Hur (Fred Niblo) 46
Ben-Hur (William Wyler) 32, 269, 402
Bend of the River 241, 347
Benjamin or the Diary of an Innocent Young Man 87
Benji 97
Benjy 409
Benny Goodman Story, The 180
Benson Murder Case, The 290
Benvenuta 402
Berkeley Square 165, 363
Berlin-Alexanderplatz 118
Berlin Express 361
Berlin: Symphony of a Great City 35
Berth Marks 199
Bespoke Overcoat, The 136
Best Boy 332
Best House in London, The 53
Best Man, The 110, 287
Best Things in Life are Free, The 82
Best Years of Our Lives, The 211, 224, 265, 285, 402
Bête Humaine, La 49, 131, 311, 367, 409
Betrayal 3
Betrayed 299
Betrayer, The 76, 321
Betty Blue 1, 40
Between the Lines 159, 183

Between Two Worlds 197, 376
Beware of a Holy Whore 7, 119, 326
Beyond a Reasonable Doubt 124, 197
Beyond the Forest 383
Beyond the Limit 145
Beyond Therapy 10, 408
Beyond the Wall 197, 376
Beyond the Walls 359
Bezhin Meadow 110
Bhowani Junction 301
Bible, The 253
Biches, Les 24, 65
Bicycle Thief, The 89, 266
Bicycle Thieves 40, 89, 115, 196, 266
Biddy 115
Big 320, 405
Bigamist, The 44
Big Blockade, The 293
Big Broadcast, The 296
Big Broadcast of 1938, The 300
Big Broadcast of 1936, The 299
Big Broadcast of 1937, The 300
Big Business 199, 346
Big Carnival, The 101, 159, 400
Big Chill, The 165, 313
Big Circus, The 69
Big City, The 306, 332
Big Clock, The 199
Big Combo, The 133
Big Country, The 269, 402
Big Deal on Madonna Street 142, 225
Big Easy, The 76
Big Foot and the Hendersons 127
Big Gamble, The 370
Bigger than Life 305
Biggles 363
Big Heart, The 69, 266
Big Heat, The 42, 197, 286
Big House, The 292
Big Knife, The 45
Big Lift, The 71
Big Moments from Little Pictures 129
Big Night, The 314
Big Parade of Comedy, The 16
Big Parade, The 8, 67, 383
Big Shave, The 326
Big Sky, The 101, 155, 240
Big Sleep, The 41, 49, 155, 283, 292
Big Snatch, The 132
Big Store, The 225, 333
Big Street, The 389

Big Trail, The 388, 393
Billion Dollar Brain 57
Bill of Divorcement, A 80, 157
Billy Liar 103, 205, 324
Billy the Kid 280
Biloxi Blues 19
Birch Wood, The 53
Bird 109, 180
Birdman of Alcatraz 292
Bird of Paradise 383
Birds, The 106, 160
Birds, the Bees and the Italians, The 60
Birdy 260, 384
Birth of a Nation, The 46, 136, 146, 174, 390
Bishop's Wife, The 14, 44, 143, 382
Bit Part, The 2
Bitter Reunion 65
Bitter Tea of General Yen, The 63, 189, 343
Bitter Tears of Petra Von Kant, The 118, 325
Bizarre, Bizarre 30, 63
Black and White in Colour 275
Black Beauty 161
Blackboard Jungle, The 356
Black Cannon Incident, The 67
Black Cat, The 186, 213
Black Fox 94
Black Friday 96
Black Fury 81
Black Girl from … 404
Black Hand 216
Black Joy 170
Black Legend 324
Black Legion 299
Blackmail 45, 159
Blackmailed 45
Black Moon 217
Black Narcissus 249, 289
Black on White 231
Black Orpheus 2, 60, 269
Blackout 289
Black Peter 126
Black Pirate, The 114, 285
Black Rain 102
Black Room, The 163, 186, 374
Black Rose, The 228
Black Shield of Falworth, The 302
Black Stallion, The 161, 318
Black Sunday 103, 359
Black Swan, The 354, 364
Black Tuesday 257
Black Tulip, The 59
Black Watch, The 211

Black Widow 49, 139, 319, 398
Black Windmill 58
Blacula 103, 218
Blade Runner 125, 130, 317
Blaise Pascal 321
Blame it on Rio 58, 100
Blanche 5, 228
Blazing Saddles 283
Blessed Event 183
Blighty 375
Blind Alley 294
Blind Date 210
Blind Husbands 385
Bliss 226
Blithe Spirit 71, 202
Blitz on Britain 45
Blockade 118, 341
Blockheads 154, 201
Blonde Bombshell 122, 151
Blonde Crazy 73
Blonde in Love, A 126
Blonde Venus 93, 142, 385
Blood from the Mummy's Tomb 190
Blood of the Condor 173
Blood of the Poet, The 285, 353
Blood Simple 292
Blood Wedding 24, 65
Bloody Mama 237, 280
Blossoms in the Dust 202, 261, 357
Blotto 200
Blowing Wild 75
Blow-Out 226, 248
Blow Up 17, 60
Blue Angel, The 48, 93, 180, 385, 398
Bluebeard 190
Bluebeard's Eighth Wife 75, 397
Blue Bird, The 287, 401
Blue Collar 169, 369
Blue Dahlia, The 11
Blue Gardenia, The 197
Blue Lagoon, The 176
Blue Lamp, The 27, 286
Blue Light, The 257
Blue Max, The 254, 362
Blue Murder at St Trinian's 136, 335
Blues Brothers, The 296, 342
Blues in the Night 180
Blue Skies 13, 22
Blue Velvet 104
Boat, The 188, 351
Bob and Carol and Ted and Alice 227
Bob the Gambler 315
Boccaccio 70 109, 334

Body and Soul 152
Body Heat 48, 165, 372
Body Snatcher, The 186
Bohème, La 260, 383
Bohemian Girl, The 200
Bolero 83, 208
Bombay Talkie 253
Bombshell 122, 151
Bombsight Stolen 21
Bonheur, Le 4, 377
Bonjour Tristesse 231
Bonne Année, La 315
Bonnes Femmes, Les 24
Bonnie and Clyde 272
Bon Voyage, Charlie Brown 116
Boom! 210
Boomerang 187, 374
Boom Town 252
Bordertown 84, 201
Born Free 15
Born on the Fourth of July 279
Born to Be Bad 124
Born to Dance 20, 347
Born Yesterday 50, 80, 267, 293, 296, 335
Borsalino 32
Bostonians, The 179, 399
Boston Strangler, The 238
Boudu Saved from Drowning 10, 300, 311, 368
Boulangerie de Monceau, La 319
Boule de Suif 333
Boulevard, Sunset 386
Bound for Glory 143
Bowery, The 391
Boxcar Bertha 326
Boyars' Plot, The 178
Boy Friend, The 296
Boy Meets Girl 27, 57
Boy on a Dolphin 369
Boys from Brazil, The 256, 391
Boys from Fengkuei, The 366
Boys in the Band, The 7, 161
Boy Soldier 390
Boys' Town 110, 196, 263, 366
Boy with Green Hair, The 210
Brandy for the Parson 339
Brannigan 208, 393
Brasher Doubloon, The 293
Brats 200
Brave One, The 15
Brazil 87, 130, 227
Bread and Chocolate 389
Bread, Love and Dreams 89
Bread, Love and Jealousy 89
Breakfast at Tiffany's 139, 220
Breakfast Club, The 410
Breakfast for Two 343

Breaking the Sound Barrier 27, 203, 362
Breakout 292
Break the News 83
Break to Freedom 292
Breakup, The 24, 65
Breathless 1, 2, 32, 137, 377
Breed Apart, A 373
Brewster McCloud 10
Brewster's Millions 228
Bridal Path, The 327
Bride Came C. O. D., The 189
Bride of Frankenstein 186, 251
Bride of the Monster 213
Bride of Vengeance 364
Brides of Dracula 136
Brides of Fu Manchu, The 45
Bride Wore Black, The 360, 371
Bride Wore Boots, The 161, 346
Bride Wore Red, The 69
Bridge on the River Kwai, The 28, 147, 168, 203, 269
Bridge Too Far, A 23, 254
Brief Encounter 202, 300, 357
Brief Encounters 76
Brief Vacation, A 307
Brigadoon 189, 229, 327
Brigham Young 388
Bright Eyes 261
Bright Lights, Big City 4, 405
Brightness 216
Brighton Beach Memoirs 15
Brighton Rock 23, 144
Brimstone and Treacle 217
Bringing Up Baby 52, 142, 155, 156, 258
Brink of Life 33
Britannia Hospital 162
British Agent 165
Broadcast News 165, 358
Broadway Bill 162, 212
Broadway Danny Rose 9
Broadway Melody 262
Broadway Melody of 1940 22
Broken Arrow 240, 308, 348
Broken Blossoms 46, 136, 146
Broken Lance 367
Broken Lullaby 213
Brother from Another Planet 112
Brotherhood, The 216
Brotherly Love 170
Brother Orchid 234, 316
Brother Rat 251
Brothers 53
Brothers, The 53
Brothers in Law 201
Brothers Karamazov, The 100

Brother Sun, Sister Moon 323
Browning Version, The 21
Brute Force 84, 292
Buccaneer, The 285
Buddy Buddy 204
Buddy Holly Story, The 341
Buffalo Bill 395
Buffalo Bill and the Indians 10, 37
Buffet Froid 88
Bugsy Malone 259
Build My Gallows High 43
Bull Durham 152
Bullets or Ballots 1, 49
Bullfighters, The 201, 227
Bunny Lake is Missing 256
Burkino Faso 173
Burmese Harp, The 282
Burn! 51, 230
Burning Angel 260
Burning Earth, The 252
Burn, Witch, Burn 400
Burton, Richard 54
Bushido 36
Business as Usual 333
Bus Number Three 67
Bus Stop 177, 234
Buster 315
Busy Bodies 200
Butch Cassidy and the Sundance Kid 28, 244
Butcher, The 24, 65, 295
Butterfield 8 269
Butterflies are Free 45, 274
By Candlelight 55
Bye Bye Braverman 214
By Rocket to the Moon 197

C

Cabaret 13, 28, 35, 184, 273
Cabinet of Dr Caligari, The 47, 56, 338
Cabin in the Sky 14, 226, 229
Cabiria 46, 246
Cactus Flower 273
Caesar and Cleopatra 203, 329
Cage aux Folles, La 161
Caged 8
Cahill, US Marshal 393
Caine Mutiny, The 30, 49, 243
Cal 175, 359
Calcutta 217, 339
California Split 10
California Suite 58, 162, 275, 339
Call Me Bwana 112
Call Me Madam 13
Call Northside 777 171, 347

Call of the Cuckoo 129
Call of the Wild 395
Camelot 239
Cameraman, The 122
Camila 173
Camille 58, 79, 119, 134, 222
Camille Claudel 88
Camille Without Camellias 17, 376
Campbell's Kingdom 252
Camp Thiaroye 292
Canary Murder Case, The 290
Can Can 12
Candidate, The 110, 287
Candleshoe 55
Cannonball Run, The 388
Canon City 42
Canterbury Tale, A 289
Canterbury Tales, The 37, 284, 328
Canterville Ghost, The 84, 198
Can't Help Singing 13, 155
Cape Fear 314
Captain Blood 81, 86, 285, 304
Captain Boycott 175
Captain Clegg 285
Captain Horatio Hornblower RN 243
Captain January 206
Captains Courageous 263, 366
Captains of the Clouds 57, 81
Captain's Paradise, The 44
Captain's Table, The 206
Captive City, The 216
Captive Heart, The 292
Carabiniers, Les 9, 137
Caravaggio 19
Card, The 147
Carefree 22
Careful, He Might Hear You 261
Carmen 83
Carnal Knowledge 245
Carnet De Bal, Un 310, 380
Carnival in Flanders 76
Carousel 12
Carpetbaggers, The 122
Carrie 191, 256
Carrington VC 77
Carry On Cleo 11
Carry On Cowboy 240
Carry On Cruising 206
Carry On Don't Lose Your Head 127
Carry On Jack 243
Carry On Matron 249
Carry on Nurses 162
Carry On Up the Khyber 19
Cars that Ate Paris, The 63

Carve Her Name with Pride 397
Car Wash 135
Casablanca 34, 49, 64, 81, 188, 248, 265, 283
Casanova 121, 144
Casanova's Big Night 124, 141, 144
Case of the Missing Switchboard Operator, The 108
Cash on Demand 29
Casino Royale 9, 95
Casque d'Or 207, 247
Cassandra Crossing, The 367
Cast a Giant Shadow 101
Castaway 176
Castle of the Spider's Web 194
Castle Vogelod 238
Cat and the Canary, The 154
Cat and Two Women, A 44
Cat Ballou 123, 147, 241, 271
Catch-22 245
Catch Us If You Can 288
Catherine the Great 365
Catlow 280
Cat on a Hot Tin Roof 244
Cat People 80, 217
Cat's Eye 191
Cattle Queen of Montana 346
Caught 260
Caught in the Draft 78
Cavalcade 149, 262, 375
Ceddo 310
Ceiling Zero 57
Cela S'Appelle L'Aurore 54
Celine and Julie Go Boating 154
Centennial Summer 13, 150
Ceremony, The 172
César and Rosalie 236
Chained 19, 132
Champ, The 262, 383
Champagne 98
Champagne for Caesar 11, 109
Champagne Murders, The 24, 65
Champion 101
Champions 153
Chance Meeting 210
Chan is Missing 11
Chant of Jimmie Blacksmith, The 360
Chaos 301
Chapayev 72
Chapman Report, The 80, 124
Charade 99, 142
Charge of the Light Brigade, The 86
Chariots of Fire 29, 152, 231, 276

Charles, Dead or Alive 103
Charley's Aunt 349
Charley Varrick 138, 216
Charlie Bubbles 402
Charlie Chan at the Opera 90
Charly 112, 272
Charming Sinners 290
Charulata 306
Chase a Crooked Shadow 155
Chaser, The 128
Chase, The 158
Che! 407
Cheap Detective, The 283
Cheaper by the Dozen 211, 212
Chess Fever 296
Chess Players, The 23, 301, 306
Cheyenne Autumn 126, 308
Cheyenne Social Club, The 53
Chien Andalou, Un 5, 53, 353
Chienne, La 311
Chiens, Les 88, 251
Children are Watching Us, The 104
Children of a Lesser God 165, 278
Children of Hiroshima 39
Children of Paradise 30, 63
Children of the Corn 191
Children's Hour, The 204
Child's Play 214, 314
Chiltern Hundreds, The 55
Chimes at Midnight 394
China Seas 151, 206
China Syndrome, The 102, 123, 203
Chinatown 166, 170, 245, 286
Chinese Girl, The 94, 137
Chinese Roulette 118
Chinoise, La 94, 137
Chips are Down, The 100
Chisum 393
Chitty Chitty Bang Bang 63, 135
Chloe in the Afternoon 319
Chorus Line, A 13, 20, 23, 102
Christiane F. 105
Christine 191
Christmas Eve 68
Christmas Holiday 64
Christmas in Connecticut 68
Christmas in July 351
Christopher Columbus 113
Christopher Strong 156, 399
Chronicle of a Death Foretold 174, 314
Chronicle of a Love 17
Chronicle of Anna Magdalena Bach, The 72

Chronicle of the Burning Years 61
Chronicle of the Years of the Brazier 61
Chronicle of the Years of Embers 61
Chump at Oxford, A 201, 349
Churning, The 172
Cia 302
Cimarron 262
Cincinnati Kid, The 133
Cinderella 36, 46, 69
Cinderella – Italian Style 228
Cinema Paradiso 279
Circle of Deceit 325, 326
Circle of Two 84
Circus, The 69
Citadel, The 96, 98, 383
Citizen Kane 70, 122, 394
Citizens Band 300
City for Conquest 45
City Girl 238, 366
City Lights 66, 105, 151
City of Fear 258
City of the Dead 207
City of Women 121, 225
City Streets 171
Civilization 174
Claire's Knee 319
Clairvoyant, The 71
Clash by Night 197, 234, 346
Clash of the Titans 239
Claudia 5
Claudine 136
Clay Pigeon, The 11
Clean Slate 23, 247, 404
Cleo from Five to Seven 119, 283, 399
Cleopatra 11, 221, 222
Climax, The 166
Cloak and Dagger 197
Clock, The 229, 244, 300
Clockwise 250
Clockwork Orange, A 130, 144, 194
Close Encounters of the Third Kind 280, 342, 371
Closely Observed Trains 107, 272
Closely Watched Trains 107, 272
Clouds over Europe 256
Clowns, The 69, 121
Club, The 153
Club de Femmes 8, 204
Cluny Brown 213, 250
Coal Miner's Daughter 276, 279
Coast to Coast 371
Cobra Verde 157, 230, 337

Cobweb, The 229
Cobweb Castle 194
Cockeyed World, The 391
Cocoanuts, The 224
Cocoon 252, 278, 397
Cocoon: the Return 397
Cold Cuts 88
Colditz Story, The 292
Cold Wind in August, A 172
Collectioneuse, La 319
Collector, The 402
College 187
Colonel Redl 72
Colorado Territory 391
Color of Money, The 153, 244, 278, 327
Color Purple, The 342
Colossus of New York, The 127
Colour of Pomegranates, The 285
Coma 102
Come and Get It 155, 263, 402
Come Back, Little Sheba 105, 267
Come Back to the Five and Dime, Jimmy Dean, Jimmy Dean 10
Come Clean 200
Comedians, The 137, 144
Comedy of Terrors, The 186, 305
Come Fill the Cup 105
Come Next Spring 118
Come On George 162
Come to the Stable 249
Comfort and Joy 185
Comic Magazine 358
Comic, The 122, 392
Coming Apart 230
Coming Home 123, 275, 384
Coming-Out Party, A 255
Coming Up Roses 390
Communicants, The 33, 383
Company Limited 306
Company of Wolves, The 5
Compulsion 238
Comrades 369
Comrades of 1918 9, 254, 281
Concert for Bangladesh, The 317
Concrete Jungle, The 210
Condemned of Altona, The 90
Condemned to Death 166
Condemned to Life 310
Condorman 352
Conductor, The 389
Conduct Unbecoming 23
Coney Island 315
Confessions of Felix Krull, The 73

Confession, The 171, 235
Confidential Agent, The 145, 341
Confidential Report 337, 394
Conformist, The 21, 38
Connecticut Yankee in King
   Arthur's Court, A 363
Connecticut Yankee, A 211
Connection, The 105
Conqueror Worm, The 400
Conquest 134, 243
Conquest of the Pole, The 107
Conspiracy of Hearts 249
Constant Husband, The 44
Constant Nymph, The 124
Contact Man, The 91
Contempt 32
Contraband 289
Conversation, The 61, 75, 125
Conversation Piece 385
Convicted 42
Convoy 371
Coogan's Bluff 109, 366
Cook, the Thief, His Wife and
   Her Lover, The 313
Cool Hand Luke 244, 272
Cop, Le 248, 286
Cop au Vin 24, 65, 287
Cops 188
Coquette 262
Corn is Green, The 390
Corridors of Blood 96
Cottage On Dartmoor 21
Cottage to Let 21, 335
Cotton Club, The 75, 408
Couch Trip, The 300
Counsellor at Law 402
Count Dracula 102
Countess from Hong Kong, The
   51, 66
Count of Monte Cristo, The 99,
   302
Country 118
Country Dance 170
Country Girl, The 48, 105, 268
County Hospital 200
Coup de Grâce 325, 387
Courier, The 105
Courtenay Affair, The 375
Court Jester, The 78, 304
Court Martial 78
Court-Martial of Billy Mitchell,
   The 75
Courtneys of Curzon Street, The
   375
Cousin Angelica 341
Cousins, Les 130, 366
Cousins, The 36, 65
Covered Wagon, The 46

Cover Girl 12, 188
Cow and I, The 292
Cowboys, The 393
Crack Up 11
Cranes are Flying, The 60
Crazy Ray 70
Crazy World of Laurel and
   Hardy, The 16
Creature from the Black
   Lagoon, The 190
Creeping Unknown, The 344
Creeps 357
Creepshow 191
Cries and Whispers 14, 33
Crime and Punishment 51, 100,
   210, 385
Crime of Monsieur Lange, The
   311
Crimes of Passion 294, 372
Crimes of the Heart 188
Crime without Passion 201
Criminal Code, The 155, 186,
   292
Criminal Life of Archibaldo de
   la Cruz, The 54
Criminal, The 210
Crimson Romance 386
Crisis 189
Crocodile Dundee 130, 244
Cromwell 147, 242, 364
Crooks in Cloisters 234
Crossfire 39
Crossing Delancey 223
Crossing of the Rhine, The 381
Cross of Lorraine, The 210
Crossroads 45
Crowd Roars, The 53, 154
Crowd, The 383
Crows and Sparrows 67
Crucible, The 236, 400
Crucified Lovers, The 232
Cruel Sea, The 173, 243
Cruel Tales of Bushido 36
Crusades, The 228
Cry, The 17
Cry Freedom 23, 79
Cry in the Dark, A 3, 349
Cry of the City 39, 42
Crystal Ball, The 71
Crystal Voyager 198
Cry Terror 189
Cuba Si! 97
Cujo 191
Cul-de-Sac 37, 286
Cure, The 66, 105
Curse, The 404
Curse of the Cat People, The 80
Curse of the Demon 71

Cutting it Short 233
Cycle, The 173
Cyclops, Dr 228
Cynara 4
Cyrano de Bergerac 139, 266
Cyrano et D'Artagnan 248

D

Da 175
Dad's Army 358
Daisy Miller 179
Dam Busters, The 362, 406
Dames 228
Dames du Bois de Boulogne, Les
   51
Damned Don't Cry, The 78
Damned, The (René Clément)
   351
Damned, The (Luchino
   Visconti) 184, 384
Damn Yankees 100
Damsel in Distress, A 12, 22,
   124, 346
Dance, Fools, Dance 78, 285
Dance Girl Dance 20
Dance of the Vampires 286
Dance Programme, The 310,
   380
Dance with a Stranger 238
Dancing Lady 22, 78
Dangerous 84, 263, 352
Dangerous Exile 390
Dangerous Liaisons 205
Dangerous Moonlight 239
Dangerous Moves 277
Danger Within 292
Daniel Webster and the Devil
   91, 93
Danish Blue 97
Dante's Inferno 367
Danton 88, 127, 390
Dark Angel 45, 224
Dark City 164
Dark Command, The 393
Dark Crystal, The 323
Dark Eyes of London 213
Dark Journey 203
Dark Mirror, The 86, 374
Dark Passage 50, 171
Dark Victory 49, 84
Dark Waters 261
Darling 144, 271, 324
Daughters Courageous 285
David 37
David and Lisa 171
David Copperfield 79, 92, 121,
   304
Dawning, The 298

Dawn Patrol, The 154, 304, 362
Day at the Races, A 140, 224
Daybreak 63, 131, 158, 182, 373
Daydreams 187
Day for Night 28, 110, 122, 145, 274, 371
Day in the Country, A 311
Day in the Death of Joe Egg, A 356
Day of the Dolphin, The 95, 245
Day of the Jackal, The 20, 21, 409
Day of the Locust, The 324
Day of Wrath 115, 382, 401
Days and Nights in the Forest 306, 366
Days of Heaven 170
Days of Hope 342
Days of Thrills and Laughter 16
Days of Wine and Roses 105, 204, 331
Day's Pleasure, A 66
Day the Earth Caught Fire, The 111, 345
Day the Earth Stood Still, The 71, 112, 344
Dead, The 26, 166, 175
Dead End 49, 244, 307, 402
Deadlier Than the Male 43
Deadly Affair, The 95, 214
Deadly Run 282
Dead Men Don't Wear Plaid 408
Dead of Night 32, 103, 334
Dead on Arrival 119
Dead Pigeon on Beethoven Street 24
Dead Poets Society, The 356
Dead Pool, The 108
Dead Reckoning 50, 398
Dead Ringers 374
Dead Zone, The 191
Dear Detective 248
Dearest Love 171, 217
Dear Inspector 248
Dear John 336
Dear Mr Prohack 154
Dear Octopus 150
Death at Broadcasting House 300
Death by Hanging 292
Death in Venice 370, 384
Death is Called Engelchen 333
Death of a Bureaucrat, The 173
Death of a Cyclist 2
Death of a Salesman 160, 224
Death on the Nile 68, 339
Death Ray, The 296
Deathtrap 58

Decameron, The 228, 284
Deceivers, The 301
Deception 85, 180, 239, 248, 293
Decline and Fall 410
Decline of the American Empire, The 1
Deep in My Heart 99, 341
Deer Hunter, The 87, 275, 348
Defence of the Realm 77
Defiant Ones, The 168
Degree of Murder, A 325
Delicate Balance, A 157
Delicious 12
Deliverance 85
Dementia 13 75
Demetrius and the Gladiators 11, 33
Demi-Paradise, The 21, 256
Demon 310
Demon Seed 317
Dentist, The 121
Départ, Le 37
Deprisa, Deprisa 38
Derzu Uzala 195, 274
Desert Attack 89, 254
Desert Bloom 96
Deserter, The 296
Desert Fox, The 254
Desert Hearts 204, 223
Design for Living 184, 212, 224
Desire 75, 93
Desirée 50
Desk Set, The 157
Despatch from Reuters, A 92
Desperate Hours, The 50, 224, 402
Desperate Journey 391
Desperate Living 205
Desperately Seeking Susan 361, 399
Destination Tokyo 282
Destiny 197, 376
Destry Rides Again 93, 343, 347
Detective 138
Detective Story 101, 286, 403
Detective, The 90, 147
Deux Timides, Les 71
Devi 306
Devil, The 36
Devil and Daniel Webster, The 91, 93
Devil and Miss Jones, The 228, 333
Devil and the Flesh, The 54, 221
Devil Doll, The 228, 385
Devil in the Flesh 182
Devil is a Woman, The 93, 385
Devils, The 91

Devil's Bride, The 91
Devil's Disciple, The 329
Devil's Envoys, The 63, 91
Devil's Eye, The 34, 91
Devil's Playground, The 291
Devil's Wanton, The 34
Devil to Pay, The 285
Devotion 86, 402, 406
Diaboliques, Les 141, 410
Dial M for Murder 10, 160
Diary for Timothy, A 97
Diary of a Chambermaid (Luis Buñuel) 54
Diary of a Chambermaid, The (Jean Renoir) 311
Diary of a Country Priest, The 51, 291
Diary of a Lost Girl 281
Diary of a Mad Housewife 220
Diary of Anne Frank, The 269, 347
Didn't You Kill My Brother? 40
Die! Die! My Darling 92, 310
Die Hard 359
Digby: the Biggest Dog in the World 97, 154
Dim Sum 11, 26
Diner 7, 308
Dinner at Eight 80, 151
Directed by Andrei Tarkovsky 110
Dirigible 62
Dirty Dancing 83
Dirty Harry 108
Dirty Mary 221
Dirty Money 87
Dirty Rotten Scoundrels 58
Discreet Charm of the Bourgeoisie, The 23, 54, 94, 274
Dishonored 93, 385, 397
Disparus de Saint-Agil, Les 386
Dispatch from Reuters, A 175, 316
Disraeli 262
Distant Drums 391
Distant Thunder 37, 306
Distant Voices, Still Lives 115, 174
Divided Heart, The 237, 261
Divine Lady, The 262
Divine Madness 288
Divorce American Style 94
Divorcee, The 262
Divorce Italian Style 95, 225
Divorce of Lady X, The 201, 256
Dixie 341
DOA 119

Dock Brief, The 23, 77
Docteur Popaul 32
Doctor Dolittle 15, 23
Doctor in the House 96
Doctor's Dilemma, The 21, 329, 335
Doctor Strangelove; or How I Learned to Stop Worrying and Love the Bomb 28, 95, 194
Doctor Takes a Wife, The 170
Doctor Zhivago 147, 322
Dodes'kaden 5, 195
Dodge City 81, 86, 240
Dodsworth 321, 402
Does, The 24, 65
Dog Day Afternoon 29, 214
Dog's Life, A 66
Dog Soldiers 105
Dolce Vita, La 60, 98, 121, 225
Doll's House, A 210
Dolly Sisters, The 170, 336
Dominick and Eugene 374
Dona Flor and Her Two Husbands 136
Don Camillo's Last Round 110
Don Giovanni 210, 260
Donkey Skin 87
Donovan's Reef 393
Don Q, Son of Zorro 114
Don Quixote 109, 282, 328
Don't Bother to Knock 27
Don't Look Back 97
Don't Look Now 106, 370
Don't Take It to Heart 136
Doomed 119, 194
Do the Right Thing 299
Double, The 39
Double Indemnity 48, 316, 343
Double Life, A 79, 266
Double Wedding 211
Double Whoopee 151, 199
Down and Out in Beverly Hills 368
Down by Law 258
Downhill Racer 152
Down Went McGinty 76, 350
Dracula 102, 157, 213, 218, 257
Dracula's Dog 218
Dragnet 286, 358
Dragonwyck 220
Drama of Jealousy 226
Draughtsman's Contract, The 32
Dr Crippen 238
Dreamchild 310
Dream of a Rarebit Fiend, The 107

Dreams 14
Dream Street 146
Dr Ehrlich's Magic Bullet 92, 165, 175, 316
Dressed to Kill (Brian de Palma) 58, 368
Dressed to Kill (Roy William Neill) 304
Dresser, The 2
Dressmaker, The 255
Dreszcze 357
Drifters 97
Driving Miss Daisy 279
Dr Jekyll and Mr Hyde 30, 34, 181, 221, 262, 345
Dr Jekyll and Sister Hyde 181
Dr Kildare's Wedding Day 96
Dr Mabuse, the Gambler 47, 56, 166, 197
Dr No 73, 95
Drôle de Drame 30, 63
Drowning by Numbers 5, 104
Dr Phibes Rises Again 190
Dr Socrates 93
Dr Syn 339
Drums Along the Mowhawk 123, 125
Drunken Angel 194
Dr Who and the Daleks 317
Dr X 96, 127
Dry Summer 36
Dr Zhivago 203
Duck Soup 105, 169, 215, 224
Duel 342
Duel in the Sun, A 53, 93, 137, 383
Duellists, The 243
Dulcimer Street 31
Dule At Diabolo 240
Dumbo 116
Dumb Waiter, The 10
Dummy Talks, The 382
Dunwich Horror, The 400
Dust Be My Destiny 257
Duty Free Marriage 231

E

E.T. – the Extra Terrestrial 81, 112, 342
Each Dawn I Die 292
Eagle and the Hawk, The 254
Eagle Has Landed, The 254
Eagle Has Two Heads, The 17, 169
Eagle in a Cage 243
Eagle, The 280, 302, 322
Eagle with Two Heads 169
Early Spring 233, 360

Early Works 37
Early Years 37
Earrings of Madame De ..., The 260, 284
Earth 118
Easter Parade 13, 22
East of Eden 187, 268
East of Shanghai 160
East Side West Side 231
Easy Living 52, 328, 350
Easy Rider 103, 104, 237, 245
Easy Street 66, 233, 286
Easy Virtue 160
Eating Raoul 31
Eat the Peach 175, 237
Ebb Tide 176
Eclipse, The 17
Ecstasy 31
Edge of Divorce 94
Edge of the City 259
Edge of the World, The 327
Edison the Man 175
Edith and Marcel 406
Educating Rita 2, 29, 58, 296
Edvard Munch 19
Eeny Meeny Miny Moe 37
Effi Briest 118, 325
Egg and I, The 143, 366
Egyptian Story, An 173
Eiger Sanction, The 108
8½ 109, 110, 120, 122, 225, 271, 336
84 Charing Cross Road 205, 373
Eighty Thousand Suspects 119
El 5, 54, 234
El Dorado 18, 155, 393
Electra Glide in Blue 237
Electric House, The 187
Electric Man, The 127, 218, 324
Eléna et les Hommes 35, 112, 311
Elephant God, The 163
Elephant Man, The 29, 112, 207
11 Harrowhouse 182
Elmer Gantry 269, 310
Elstree Calling 349
Elusive Pimpernel, The 289, 302, 354
Elvira Madigan 100, 257
Elvis – That's the Way It Is 317
Emak Bakia 353
Emerald Forest, The 252
Emigrants, The 170
Emil and the Detectives 67
Emma 375
Emperor of California, The 380
Emperor's Candlesticks, The 291
Emperor Waltz, The 124, 400

Empire of Passion 6
Empire of the Senses, The 6
Empire of the Sun 282, 342
Empire Strikes Back, The 125, 280
Empress Yang Kwei Fei, The 232
Enchanted Cottage, The 209
Enchantment 334
Encore 334
End, The 211
Endless Night 68
End of Innocence 337
End of St Petersburg, The 296
End of the Affair, The 145
End of the Day, The 310
End of the Game 315
End of the Road, The 252
End of the World in Our Usual Bed in a Night Full of Rain, The 130
Enemies of the People 395
Enemies of the Public 56, 132, 232, 259
Enemy Below, The 351
Enfants Du Paradis, Les 30, 63
Enfants Terrible, Les 41, 184
Enforcer, The (James Fargo) 108
Enforcer, The (Bretaigne Windust) 50, 201
England Made Me 145
Enigma of Kaspar Hauser, The 112, 157
Entertainer, The 7, 256, 356
Entr'acte 70, 177
Equus 55, 214, 294
Eric Clapton and His Rolling Hotel 317
Erlich's Magic Bullet, Dr 406
Eroica 107, 292
Erotikon 47
Escape 202
Escaped from Dartmoor 21
Escape from Fort Bravo 378
Escape from New York 79
Escape Me Never 100
Escape to Happiness 164, 239
Escape to Nowhere 6
Escape to Victory 58, 146, 166, 255
Eternal Husband, The 100, 140
Eternally Yours 216
Etoile de Mer, L' 353
Europa '51 321
Europeans, The 179
Eva 210
Evelyn Prentice 212, 290
Even Dwarfs Started Small 157
Evening Dress 88, 372

Evergreen 12, 237
Everybody's Cheering 99, 189
Everybody Sing 375
Every Day Except Sunday 97
Every Day's a Holiday 73
Every Man for Himself and God Against All 112, 157
Everything for Sale 390
Every Which Way But Loose 109
Evil Eden 343
Evil Under the Sun 339
Ex-Mrs Bradford, The 96, 291
Excalibur 239
Executive Suite 41, 346
Exile, The 302
Experiment in Evil 30, 311
Experiment in Terror 315
Expresso Bongo 353
Exterminating Angel, The 54
Extra Girl, The 129
Extraordinary Adventures of Mr West in the Land of the Bolsheviks 295
Eye of the Cat 295
Eyes of the Mummy, The 180, 213
Eyes Without a Face 127
Eyewitness 165

F

F.T.A. 123
Face Behind the Mask, The 210
Face in the Crowd, A 127, 187, 358
Face of Another, The 4
Face of Dr Fu Manchu, The 166
Faces 95
Face, The 33, 216
Face to Face 33
Fahrenheit 451 227, 371
Fail Safe 96, 214
Falcon and the Snowman, The 325
Falcon Strikes Back, The 90
Fallen Angel 231
Fallen Idol, The 27, 115, 145, 308
Fallen Sparrow, The 341
Falling in Love 87, 349, 373
Falling in Love Again 310
Fall of Berlin, The 293
Fall of the House of Usher, The 353
Fall of the Roman Empire, The 11
Fall of the Romanov Dynasty, The 97, 322
Falls, The 353

Fame 83, 251
Fame is the Spur 122, 207
Family, The 115
Family Business (Constantin Costa-Gavras) 119
Family Business (Sidney Lumet) 161, 214
Family Plot 71
Family Way, The 332, 404
Fanatic 92, 310
Fancy Pants 55
Fanny 282
Fanny and Alexander 14, 33, 115, 277
Fanny by Gaslight 21
Fantasia 116
Fantastic Voyage 229, 342
Fantômas 182
Fantôme du Moulin Rouge, Le 70
Far Country, The 240, 347
Farewell 169
Farewell, My Lovely 44, 293
Farewell to Arms, A 74, 162, 249
Far from the Madding Crowd 324, 360
Far Horizons, The 113
Farmer's Daughter, The 69, 266, 300
Farrebique 97, 118
Fashions of 1934 73
Fast and Loose 208
Fast, Fast 38
Fast Lady, The 63
Fatal Attraction 102, 141
Fatal Glass of Beer, The 121
Fata Morgana 157
Fat City 152, 166
Father 119
Father Brown 90, 147
Father Goose 17, 143
Father, Master 61
Father of the Bride 229, 366, 393
Father's Little Dividend 27
Fatty and Mabel Adrift 129
Faust 120, 180, 238
FBI Story, The 202
Fear 321
Fear Eats the Soul 118, 120, 231
Fear in the Night 166, 410
Fearless Vampire Killers, or Pardon Me, Your Teeth are in My Neck 286
Fedora 352
Fellini Satyricon 98, 121
Fellini's Casanova 121
Fellini's Roma 121
Female on the Beach, The 79

Ferris Bueller's Day Off 104
Ferry Cross the Mersey 288
Feu Follet, Le 105, 217
F for Fake 395
Fiddler On the Roof 13, 140
Fiddlers Three 14
Field of Dreams 118
Fifth Avenue Girl 246, 318
55 Days at Peking 306
Fighting 69th, The 57
Fighting Father Dunne 291
Fighting Kentuckian, The 393
Fighting Pimpernel, The 342
Fighting Seebees, The 392
Figures in a Landscape 210
File on Thelma Jordan, The 346
Final Test, The 21, 153
Fine Madness, A 74, 285
Finger of Guilt 210
Finian's Rainbow 75
Finishing Touch, The 129, 199
Firebird 93
Firefox 108
Fire Has Been Arranged, A 335
Firemen's Ball, The 94, 126
Fire over England 203, 256
Fire Sale 333
Fires on the Plain 158
Firestarter 191
Fires Were Started 45, 97
Fire Within, The 105, 217
First Great Train Robbery, The 315
First Legion, The 230
First Love 261
First Monday in October 374
First Name Carmen 138, 382
First of the Few, The 165, 175
Fish Called Wanda, A 3, 278
Fistful of Dollars, A 108
Fistful of Dynamite, A 227
Fist in His Pocket 190
Fists in the Pocket 190
Fitzcarraldo 4, 109, 157
Five 96, 111
Five Corners 259
Five Day Lover, The 4
Five Days One Summer 74
Five Easy Pieces 245, 368
Five Fingers 55, 220
Five Graves to Cairo 386, 400
Five Star Final 183, 186, 202, 316
Five Women Around Utamaro 232
Fixer, The 374
Flame and the Arrow, The 280
Flame of My Love 232

Flame of New Orleans, The 71, 94, 139
Flame over India 301, 367
Flamingo Road 81, 398
Flash Gordon 352
Flesh and Fantasy 316
Flesh and the Devil 46, 134
Flight of the Navigator, The 280, 344
Flight of the Phoenix, The 89, 348
Flight of the White Stallions, The 162
Flirting with Fate 114
Floating Clouds 172, 294
Floorwalker, The 66
Flying Doctors of East Africa, The 157
Flying Down to Rio 22
Flying Leathernecks, The 306
Fly, The 181, 345
FM 300
Fog over Frisco 92
Folies Bergère 170
Follow the Boys 350
Follow the Fleet 13, 22
Folly to Be Wise 94, 335
Fool for Love 10
Foolish Wives 385
Fools for Scandal 208
Footlight Parade 57, 296, 335
For a Few Dollars More 108
Forbidden Games 66, 104, 267, 380
Forbidden Paradise 212
Forbidden Planet 130
Force of Evil 134
Force Ten from Navarone 125
Foreign Affair, A 35, 94, 400
Foreign Correspondent 159, 160
Foreman Went to France, The 390
Forest, The 172
Forest of Hanged Men 108
Forest of the Hanged, The 108
Forever Amber 293
Forever and a Day 375
Forgotten, The 53, 259, 308
For Heaven's Sake 14, 128
For Keeps 356
For Me and My Gal 188, 366
For Queen and Country 285
Forsaking All Others 393
Fort Apache 123, 125, 392
For the Defense 290
Fortune, The 245, 246
Fortune Cookie, The 204, 271, 400

Forty Carats 253
48 Hrs 96, 145
Forty First, The 100
Forty Guns 346
49th Parallel, The 165, 256, 289
42nd Street 20, 296
For Whom the Bell Tolls 34, 74, 140, 265, 341
Foul Play 288
Fountainhead, The 41
Four Adventures of Reinette and Mirabelle 319
Four Bags Full 283
Four Chimneys 233
Four Daughters 81
Four Days of Naples, The 311
Four Devils 238
Four Feathers, The 6, 78
Four Friends 11
Four Horsemen of the Apocalypse, The 46, 229
400 Blows, The 371, 372, 410
Four Nights of a Dreamer 51, 100
Four's a Crowd 86
Four Seasons, The 313
Fourteen Hours 287
Fourteenth of July, The 71
Fourth Man, The 161
Fox 118
Fox, The 201
Fox and His Friends 118
Fox and the Hound, The 97, 117
Fra Diavolo 200
Frances 171
Francis 162
Frankenstein 10, 81, 126, 186, 213, 218, 285
Frantic 125, 217, 283, 286, 377
Fraternally Yours 200
Freaky Friday 320
Freedom for Us 70, 233
Free Soul, A 132, 262
Free the Army 123
•*Free to Live* 80
French Cancan 132, 311
French Connection, The 105, 273
French Lieutenant's Woman, The 348
Frenchman's Creek 106, 124, 305, 339
French They are a Funny Race, The 130
French without Tears 21, 127
Frenzy (Alfred Hitchcock) 159, 208
Frenzy (Alf Sjöberg) 146, 356

Freshman, The 128, 349, 350
Freud 166, 294, 406
Friday the 13th 219, 323
Friday the Thirteenth 192
Friendly Persuasion 60, 378, 403
Friends and Husbands 2, 387
Friends for Life 16
Friendship's Death 317
Fright Night 154, 219
Fritz the Cat 117
Frog Dreaming 411
Frog Prince, The 127, 283
From Here to Eternity 19, 267, 409
From Russia with Love 16, 73
From the Terrace 244
From This Day Forward 244, 332
Frontier 102
Front Page Story 139
Front Page, The (Lewis Milestone) 183
Front Page, The (Billy Wilder) 183, 204, 400
Front Page Woman 85
Front, The 9, 139
Fruit Machine, The 158, 373
Frustration 206
Fuck the Army 123
Fugitive Kind, The 214
Fugitive, The 123, 145
Full Confession 291
Full Metal Jacket 194, 384
Funeral in Berlin 6, 57
Funny Dirty Little War, A 314
Funny Face 99
Funny Girl 139, 272
Funny Thing Happened on the Way to the Forum, A 14, 187
Fun with Dick and Jane 124, 361
Fury 42, 168, 197
Fury, The 101
Future is Woman, The 8

G

Gabriel over the White House 230
Gai Savoir, Le 138, 288
Galileo 210
Gallant Journey 395
Galloping Major, The 162
Gambler, The 100
Gambling Lady 133
Games, The 152
Gandhi 23, 29, 133, 276, 301
Gang War 27, 308
Garbo Talks 352
Garden of Allah, The 93, 234

Garden of the Finzi-Continis, The 37, 89, 273
Gardens of Stone 75, 384
Gaslight 34, 80, 249, 265
Gate of Hell 59, 234, 268
Gate of Lilacs 71, 158
Gates of Paris 71, 158
Gates of the Night 63
Gaucho, The 114
Gawain and the Green Knight 239
Gay Deception, The 69
Gay Desperado, The 155
Gay Divorce, The 330
Gay Divorcee, The 22, 330
Gay Mrs Trexel, The 80, 310
Geisha 232
General, The 187, 367
General della Rovere 89, 250, 312, 321, 381
General Died at Dawn, The 75
General Line, The 47, 110
Generation, A 286, 312, 389
Genevieve 27, 63, 135, 388
Gentle Creature, A 51
Gentleman Jim 152, 391
Gentleman's Agreement 183, 186, 265, 266
Gentlemen Prefer Blondes 155, 228, 234
Gentle Sex, The 165
Geordie 152
Georgia's Friends 11
German Sisters, The 79, 381, 386
Germany in Autumn 325
Germany, Year Zero 35, 321
Germinal 409
Gertrud 95, 399
Gervaise 409
Get Out Your Handkerchiefs 88, 275
Getting Gertie's Garter 177
Getting It Right 392
Ghost and Mrs Muir, The 154
Ghost Breakers, The 91, 207
Ghostbusters 219
Ghost Goes West, The 70, 98
Ghost of St Michael's, The 357
Ghost That Never Returns, The 98
Ghost, The 221
Ghost Train, The 219, 301
Ghoul, The 207
Giant 10, 252, 268, 347
Gideon of Scotland Yard 287
Gideon's Day 287
Gigi 12, 229, 269

Gigot 189
Gilda 133
Gilded Lily, The 328
Gimme Shelter 317
Ginger and Fred 121, 225, 358, 366
Gion Festival Music 232
Girl Friends, The 17
Girl from Lorraine, A 366
Girl from Missouri, The 151
Girl in Black, The 221
Girl in Distress 321
Girl in Every Port, A 155
Girl in Pawn, The 287
Girl in the News, The 249
Girl Must Live, A 8
Girl Shy 128
Girls in Uniform 136
Girls, Les 80
Girls, The 14, 24
Girl was Young, A 160, 258
Girl with Green Eyes 5
Give a Girl a Break 99
Give My Regards to Broad Street 103
Given Word, The 60
Glass Key, The 42, 76, 287
Glass Menagerie, The 245
Glass Slipper, The 69
Glenn Miller Story, The 180, 347, 406
Glen or Glenda 368
Gloria 216, 381
Glory 279
G Men 57, 134
Go-Between, The 61, 210, 360
Goalie's Anxiety at the Penalty Kick, The 396
Goalkeeper's Fear of the Penalty Kick, The 396
Godard's Passion 326
Goddess, The 7, 115, 306
Godfather Part II, The 87, 274
Godfather Parts I & II, The 51, 75, 188, 216, 273
Gods of the Plague 326, 386
God Told Me 310
Going My Way 34, 215, 265, 291
Going Places 88
Goin' South 245
Goin' to Town 156
Gold 118
Gold Diggers of 1935 139
Gold Diggers of 1933 139, 202, 318
Golden Age, The 5, 53, 353
Golden Age of Buster Keaton, The 16

Golden Age of Comedy, The 16
Golden Coach, The 311
Golden Earrings 94, 148
Golden Marie 207, 247
Goldfinger 73
Gold of Naples 89
Gold Rush, The 66, 233
Golem, The 127
Golgotha 236
Gone to Earth 289, 360
Gone with the Wind 86, 132, 140, 164, 203, 222, 264, 378, 401
Goodbye Again 235
Goodbye Columbus 141
Goodbye Girl, The 2, 275
Goodbye Mr Chips 99, 140, 264, 357, 410
Goodbye My Lady 97
Good Companions, The 257
Good Earth, The 263, 300
Good Fairy, The 261, 402
Good Marriage, A 319
Good Morning 357
Good Morning Babylon 174
Good Morning Boys 357
Good Morning Miss Dove 357
Good Morning, Vietnam 300
Good Mother, The 237, 357
Good Sam 216
Good, the Bad and the Ugly, The 108
Goose Steps Out, The 48, 410
Gorillas in the Mist 279
Gorky Park 165, 322
Gospel According to St Matthew, The 243, 284
Gospel According to Vic 44
Go Tell the Spartans 384
Gothic 126, 285
Go West (Edward Buzzell) 135, 225
Go West (Buster Keaton) 392
Graduate, The 28, 160, 245, 253, 272
Graf Spee 289
Grail, The 51
Grand Central Murder 301
Grand Chemin, Le 411
Grande Bouffe, La 26, 226, 248
Grande Illusion, La 131, 311, 386
Grandes Familles, Les 131, 138
Grand Hotel 20, 134, 162, 262
Grand Illusion 131, 311, 386
Grand Jeu, Le 303
Grand Maneuver, The 71
Grandma's Boy 128

Grand Prix 33, 153
Grapes of Wrath, The 123, 125, 264
Grass is Greener, The 99, 143
Grease 410
Great Adventure, The 15
Great Dictator, The 66, 106
Great Ecstasy of Woodcarver Steiner, The 157
Great Escape, The 292
Greatest Love, The 321
Greatest Show on Earth, The 69, 267, 348
Greatest Story Ever Told, The 243, 347
Great Expectations 92, 146, 202
Great Gabbo, The 382, 386
Great Garrick, The 2
Great Gatsby, The 75, 98
Great Gilbert and Sullivan, The 10
Great Guns 201
Great Impersonation, The 170
Great Imposter, The 170
Great King, The 380
Great Lie, The 27, 84, 264
Great Locomotive Chase, The 135
Great Lover, The 206
Great Man's Lady, The 343, 395
Great Man, The 70, 358
Great Man Votes, The 110
Great McGinty, The 76, 350
Great Moment, The 175, 351
Great Mouse Detective, The 117, 163
Great Mr Handel, The 72
Great Race, The 63, 388
Great Santini, The 285
Great Sinner, The 100
Great Train Robbery, The 107
Great Victor Herbert, The 341
Great Waldo Pepper, The 135, 362
Great Wall, A 67
Great Waltz, The 72
Great White Hope, The 231
Great Ziegfeld, The 263, 291, 353
Greed 139, 144, 385
Green Berets, The 109, 384, 393
Green-Eyed Woman 3, 328
Greene Murder Case, The 290
Green for Danger 162, 334
Greengage Summer, The 321
Green Man, The 190, 334
Green Ray, The 319, 382

Green Room, The 371
Gregory's Girl 145
Gremlins 190, 323, 342
Greyfriars Bobby 97
Greystoke, the Legend of Tarzan, Lord of the Apes 1, 8, 190
Grim Reaper, The 38
Grip of Fear, The 315
Grisbi 132
Grosse König, Der 380
Group, The 8
Guess Who's Coming to Dinner? 120, 156, 272, 367
Guide for the Married Man, A 189
Guinea Pig, The 23
Gumshoe 293
Gun Crazy 1
Gunfight at the OK Corral 101, 241
Gunfighter, The 147, 241
Gunga Din 124, 142, 346
Guns, The 173, 314
Guns at Batasi 23, 52
Guns of Darkness 314
Guns of Navarone, The 254
Guys and Dolls 51, 134, 221
Gypsy 202

H

Hail Mary 138, 328
Hail the Conquering Hero 17, 350
Hair 126
Half-truth 172
Half-a-Sixpence 98
Half Moon Street 2, 58
Hallelujah! 2, 383
Hallelujah Trail, The 240
Halloween 219, 295
Ham and Eggs at the Front 211
Hamburger Hill 384
Hamlet 58, 149, 256, 266, 329, 380
Hammett 396
Handful of Dust, A 17, 147
Hands across the Table 341
Hands of Orlac, The 210
Hands of the Ripper 179
Handsome Antonio 225
Hands on the City 381
Hands over the City 381
Hang 'Em High 109
Hangmen Also Die 197
Hangover Square 11
Hannah and Her Sisters 9, 58, 278, 336

Hanoi Hilton 384
Hanover Street 45, 125
Hanussen 71
Happiest Days of Your Life, The 141, 334, 410
Happiness 4, 377
Happy Ever After 175, 298
Happy Gypsies 148
Happy Land 293
Happy Lovers 356
Happy New Year 315
Happy Time, The 357
Harakiri 76
Harder They Fall, The 50, 152
Hard, Fast and Beautiful 153
Hard Times 92
Hard to Handle 4, 57, 202
Harold and Maude 120, 253
Harold Lloyd's Funny Side of Life 16
Harp of Burma 282
Harry and the Hendersons 127
Harry and Tonto 257, 274
Harvest 338
Harvest: 3000 Years 173
Harvey 347, 396
Has Anybody Seen My Girl? 228
Hatari! 155
Hatchet Man, The 316
Hatful of Rain, A 409
Hatred 340
Hats Off 129
Hatter's Castle 359
Hatter's Ghosts 65
Haunted and the Hunted, The 75
Haunted Castle, The 238
Haunting, The 81, 154
Having a Wild Weekend 288
Hawks and the Sparrows, The 283
Head 5, 288
Health 10
Heartbeat 318
Heartbreak Kid, The 183
Heartbreak Ridge 109
Heartburn 122, 245, 349
Heart is a Lonely Hunter, The 85
Heartland 37
Heartless 104
Heart of Darkness 17
Heart of Glass 157
Heart of the Matter, The 52, 145
Hearts and Minds 332
Hearts of the West 20
Hearts of the World 137, 146
Heat and Dust 133, 301

Heaven 188, 288
Heaven Can Wait (Warren Beatty) 15
Heaven Can Wait (Ernst Lubitsch) 212
Heaven Knows Mr Allison 4, 166
Heavenly Pursuits 44, 230
Heavens Above 382
Heavy Traffic 117
Heidi 67, 221
Heimat 18
Heiress, The 52, 86, 156, 179, 266, 402
Heir to Genghis Khan, The 47, 178, 296
Hell Drivers 371
Hell in the Pacific 282, 338
Hello Dolly 189
Hellraiser 324
Hell's Angels 151
Hellzapoppin' 122, 335
Help! 150, 288
Helpmates 200
Henry V (Kenneth Branagh) 329
Henry V (Laurence Olivier) 7, 256, 329
Henry VIII and His Six Wives 407
Her Cardboard Lover 80
Here Comes Mr Jordan 15
Here Comes the Groom 63
Here Comes the Navy 57
Here Come the Huggetts 150
Here is a Man 91, 93
Her Majesty, Love 121
Heroism 107, 292
Herr Puntilia and His Servant Matti 105
He Stayed for Breakfast 247
Hester Street 183
Hidden Fortress, The 194
Hideout 158
High and Dizzy 128
High and Dry 327
High and Low 189
High and the Mighty, The 192, 395
High Anxiety 283
High Heels 32
Highlander 73, 185
High Noon 74, 158, 240, 267, 409
High Plains Drifter 108
High Pressure 290
High Sierra 42, 49, 165, 391
High Society 12, 284
High Spirits 154
High Tide 399

High Wind in Jamaica, A 285
High Window, The 293
Hill, The 74, 214
Hindenburg, The 192
Hi Nellie! 202
Hireling, The 61
Hiroshima, Mon Amour 231, 312
His First Flame 128
His Girl Friday 142, 155, 158, 291
His Other Woman 157
History of Mr Polly, The 17, 104
History of the World Part One, The 236
Hitcher, The 177
Hitch-hiker, The 399
Hitler 296
Hitler Gang, The 364
Hitler – the Last Ten Days 147
Hobson's Choice 27, 36, 198, 203
Hog Wild 200
Hold Back the Dawn 86, 170, 400
Hold That Co-Ed 111
Hold That Girl 111
Hold Your Man 151
Hole in the Head, A 53, 317
Holiday 14, 80, 142
Holiday Inn 23, 68
Holly and the Ivy, The 382
Hollywood Canteen 350
Hollywood Cavalcade 336
Hollywood Cowboy 20
Hollywood on Trial 166
Hollywood Revue of 1929 350
Hollywood Shuffle 20
Holy Matrimony 19
Hombre 224, 343
Home and the World, The 306
Home Before Dark 248
Homeboy 152
Home from the Hill 229
Homeland 18
Honey Pot, The 119, 221, 339
Honky Tonk 132
Honky Tonk Freeway 325
Honorary Consul, The 145
Honourable Mr Wong, The 316
Honour Among Thieves 132
Hoosegow, The 200
Hope and Glory 45, 255
Horn Blows at Midnight, The 15
Horror Hotel 207
Horror of Dracula 103
Horse Feathers 224
Horse's Mouth, The 147

Horse Soldiers, The 125, 378, 393
Horse Thief, The 67
Horse Without a Head, The 66
Hospital, The 162
Hot Blood 306
Hôtel du Nord 63
Hotel Paradiso 163
Hotel Reserve 163
Hotel Sahara 163
Hotel Terminus: the Life and Times of Klaus Barbie 332, 391
Hot Millions 339
Hot Rock, The 182
Houdini 216
Hound of the Baskervilles, The 90, 304
Hour of the Furnaces, The 97, 252
Hour of the Wolf 34, 103
Houseboat 142
House Calls 96
Housekeeping 109, 340
House of Bamboo 102
House of Doom 186
House of Fear 190, 305
House of Games 164
House of Lovers 409
House of Pleasure 260
House of Rothschild, The 76
House of Strangers, A 119, 221
House of the Angel, The 337
House of Usher, The 207
House of Wax, The 218
House On 92nd Street, The 254
House That Dripped Blood, The 218
Housing Problems 97
How Green Was My Valley 54, 126, 264, 390
How Lucky to Be a Woman 258
How to Get Ahead in Advertising 4, 405
How to Marry a Millionaire 139, 228, 234
How to Murder Your Wife 204
How to Steal a Diamond in Four Uneasy Lessons 182
How to Steal a Million 403
How to Succeed in Business without Really Trying 41
Huckleberry Finn 67, 411
Hucksters, The 4
Hud 244, 270
Hudson's Bay 113, 364
Hue and Cry 66, 335

Human Beast, The 49, 131, 311, 367, 409
Human Comedy, The 338
Human Desire 197, 409
Human Factor, The 145
Human Monster, The 213
Humoresque 78
Hunchback of Notre Dame, The 92, 148, 181, 190, 198
Hunger, The 86, 103
Hungry Hill 106
Hunting Flies 390
Hurricane, The 176
Husbands 8
Hush, Hush, Sweet Charlotte 86
Hustler, The 133, 244, 327

I

I Accuse 77
I am a Fugitive from a Chain Gang 42, 168, 202
I Am Curious – Yellow 6
Ice Cold in Alex 89, 254
Ichabod and Mr Toad 304
I Confess 44, 160, 291
Identification of a Woman 17
Idiot, The 101, 194
Idle Class, The 66
I Even Met a Happy Gypsy 148
If ... 16, 60, 410
If I Had a Million 334
If I Were King 76, 304
If You Could Only Cook 55
If You Feel Like Singing 189
I Had My Brother's Wife 36
I Know Where I'm Going 289
I'll Be Seeing You 319
I'll Cry Tomorrow 105
Illicit 343
Illicit Interlude 33
Ill Met by Moonlight 289
I Love You Again 211, 290
I Love You, Alice B. Toklas 104
I'm All Right, Jack 23, 169
I Married an Angel 15
I Married a Witch 70, 224, 400, 401
Imitation of Life 299
Immigrant, The 66, 170, 233
Immoral Tales 334
Immortal Battalion 8, 19, 309
Immortal Sergeant, The 89
I'm No Angel 142, 144, 164
Importance of Being Earnest, The 21
Impudent Girl, An 410
Inadmissable Evidence 171

In a Lonely Place 50, 115, 182, 305
Inauguration of the Pleasure Dome 288
In Cold Blood 238
Incredible Sarah, The 3
Incredible Shrinking Woman, The 229
Incredible Shrinking Man, The 229
India 321
Indiana Jones and the Temple of Doom 125, 302, 342
Indiana Jones and the Last Crusade 74, 125, 342
Indian Tomb, The 197
India Song 399
India vista da Rossellini, L' 321
Indiscreet 34, 64, 99, 143, 248, 366
Indiscretion 68
Indiscretion of an American Wife, The 89, 301
I Never Promised You a Rose Garden 171
I Never Sang for My Father 252
Infidelity 4
Informer, The 39, 126, 263
Inherit the Wind 310, 366
In Name Only 208, 393
Innerspace 229, 342
Innocent, The 385
Innocents, The 179
Innocents in Paris 130, 334
Innocent Sorcerors 390
Inn of the Sixth Happiness, The 35, 99, 231, 407
In Old Arizona 262, 391
In Old Chicago 192, 263
In Praise of Older Women 141, 253
Inquisitor, The 201
In Search of the Castaways 411
Inspecteur Lavardin 65, 287
Inspector Calls, An 334
Inspector General, The 322
Inspector Hornleigh 334
Inspector Hornleigh Goes to It 335
Inspector Hornleigh on Holiday 235
Inspector Maigret 131
Interference 290
Interiors 9, 115
Intermezzo 164, 239
Intermezzo: a Love Story 34
Interns, The 162
Intervista 121

In the Good Old Summertime 333

In the Heat of the Night 85, 272

In the Mood 253

In the Realm of the Senses 6

In the Wild Mountains 68

In This Our Life 171

Intimate Lighting 174

Intimate Stranger, The 210

Intolerance 146, 174, 187, 348, 385

Intruder, The 385

Intruder in the Dust 374

Invaders, The 165, 256, 289

Invasion of the Body Snatchers 344

Investigation of a Citizen Above Suspicion 79, 273

Invisible Man, The 324

Invisible Ray, The 213

Invitation to the Dance 36, 83, 189

In Which We Serve 23, 202, 243

Ipcress File, The 28, 57

I Remember Mama 237, 252, 346

Irish Eyes are Smiling 341

Irma La Douce 175, 204, 397

Iron Curtain 71

Iron Duke, The 243, 407

Iron Mask, The 114

Ironweed 246, 332, 349

Isadora 406

I See a Dark Stranger 331

Ishtar 161

Island, The 176

Island in the Sky 176

Island in the Sun 176

Island of Lost Souls 199

Isle of the Dead 186

Is Paris Burning? 32, 101

Israel, Why? 332

I Take This Woman 208

Italian Job, The 58, 351

Italian Straw Hat, An 393

Italian Straw Hat, The 70

It Always Rains on Sundays 158, 258

It Came from beneath the Sea 372

It Came from Outer Space 344

It Happened One Night 62, 132, 156, 176, 263

It Happened Somewhere in Europe 66

It Happened Tomorrow 70, 291

It Pays to Advertise 208

It's a Dog's Life 97

It's a Gift 121, 129, 181

It's a Great Feeling 350

It's Always Fair Weather 99, 189, 314

It's a Mad, Mad, Mad, Mad World 177, 367, 369

It's a Wonderful Life 15, 44, 177, 347

It's Great to Be Young 239

It Should Happen to You 80

It's Love I'm After 85, 86

It's My Life 137, 294

It Started with Eve 198, 330

It's Wonderful Life 62

Ivan 102

Ivanhoe 124, 364

Ivan's Childhood 251, 312, 355, 381

Ivan the Terrible 110, 144, 178

Ivan the Terrible (Part One) 296

I've Heard the Mermaids Singing 103

I Vitelloni 121

Ivy 124, 359

I Walk Alone 39, 339

I Walked with a Zombie 207

I Wanna Hold Your Hand 150

I Want to Live 238, 269

I Was a Fireman 45, 97

I Was a Male War Bride 143, 155, 279, 320

J

Jabberwocky 228

J'Accuse 77

Jackal of Nahueltoro, The 98

Jackboot Mutiny, The 282

Jacknife 88

Jack the Giant Killer 302

Jack the Ripper 179

Jagged Edge 77, 313

Jaguar 173

Jailbirds 98

Jailhouse Rock 288

Jamaica Inn 106, 339

James Dean Story, The 10

Jane Eyre 124, 394

Janitor, The 165

Jason and the Argonauts 239

Jaws 324, 342

Jazz on a Summer's Day 180

Jazz Singer, The 183, 256

Jealousy, Italian Style 226

Jean de Florette 29, 88, 118, 181, 221, 235

Jeanne Eagels 105, 115

Jeannie 321

Jennie 93, 136

Jenny 63

Jeremiah Johnson 240

Jerk, The 109

Jesse James 123, 241

Jesus Christ Superstar 13

Je T'Aime, Je T'Aime 312

Jet Pilot 385

Jeux Sont Faits, Les 100, 226

Jewel of the Nile 102, 372

Jew Suss 183

Jezebel 84, 165, 264, 403

Jimi Plays Berkeley 317

Jimmy the Gent 57, 81

Joan of Arc 7, 34, 323

Job, The 357, 376

John and Mary 15, 161

Johnny Belinda 266, 336

Johnny Come Lately 57

Johnny Eager 264

Johnny Got His Gun 39

Johnny Guitar 78, 305

Johnny in the Clouds 21, 363

Johnny Vagabond 57

Jokers, The 150

Jolson Sings Again 406

Jolson Story, The 406

Jonah Who Will Be 25 in the Year 2000 94

Jonathan Livingston Seagull 288

Joseph Andrews 309, 365

Jour de Fête 235

Journey for Margaret 48

Journey into Autumn 14

Journey into Fear 394

Journey's End 9

Journey to Italy 321

Journey to the Center of the Earth 345

Jour se Lève, Le 63, 131, 158, 182, 373

Joyless Street 134, 259, 281

Juarez 85, 92, 227, 407

Jubilee 233

Judex 46

Judge and the Assassin, The 247

Judgement at Nuremburg 270

Judgement at Nuremberg 367

Judge Priest 126

Judgment at Nuremberg 391

Judo Saga 172

Juggernaut 193

Jules Et Jim 144, 183, 184, 371, 372

Julia 29, 123, 184, 275, 349, 361, 409

Julia & Julia 373

Juliet of the Spirits 71, 120

Julius Caesar 50, 133, 220, 329
July 14 71
June Bride 284
June Night 35
Jungle Book, The 116, 303
Jungle Fighters 282
Jungle Princess, The 303
Juno and the Paycock 175
Jury of One 132
Just a Gigolo 94, 294
Just Before Nightfall 24, 65
Justice est Faite 374, 380
Justice is Done 374, 380
Just Tell Me What You Want 41, 214

K

Kagemusha 61, 185, 194
Kameradschaft 141, 281
Kamikaze 358
Kanal 20, 251, 286, 312, 389
Kanchenjungha 306
Kangaroo 201
Kansas City Confidential 43
Kaos 221, 348
Kapo 255
Katzelmacher 325
Keep 'Em Flying 374
Keeper of the Flame 32, 80, 157, 367
Keep Your Seats Please 139
Kennel Murder Case, The 290, 361
Kentucky 153, 264
Kentucky Fried Movie 236
Kes 250
Key, The 253, 309
Key Largo 20, 49, 166, 266, 317
Keys of the Kingdom, The 231
Khartoum 52, 256, 364
Kid, The 66, 196
Kid Auto Races at Venice 65
Kid Brother, The 128
Kid for Two Farthings, A 230, 309
Kid from Spain, The 215
Kid Galahad 81
Kid Glove Killer, The 409
Kidnapped 67, 327
Killer! 65
Killer's Kiss 191
Killers, The 42
Killing, The 194
Killing Fields, The 29, 277, 291
Killing of Sister George, The 205
Kind Hearts and Coronets 147, 190, 217, 370
Kind Lady 73

Kind of Loving, A 36, 324
King and I, The 12, 233, 268, 337
King David 253
King in New York, A 66
King Kong 190
King Lear 138, 194, 304, 329, 397
King of Burlesque, The 353
King of Comedy, The 87, 327
King of Kings 236, 243, 306
King of Marvin Gardens, The 246, 300
King of the Children 357
King of the Khyber Rifles 301
King of the Underworld 49
King, Queen, Knave 211, 253
King Rat 282
Kings of the Road 396
King Solomon's Mines 67, 303
King's Row 140, 171, 338
King's Vacation, The 169
Kipps 164, 309
Kismet 92
Kiss Me Deadly 96
Kiss Me Kate 12
Kiss Me Stupid 12
Kiss of Death 39, 42
Kiss of the Spiderwoman, The 1, 165, 277
Kiss, The 134
Kiss Tomorrow Goodbye 57
Kitchen Toto, The 52, 231
Kitty 296, 365
Kitty Foyle 140, 264, 318
Klondike Annie 391
Klute 124, 273
Knack ... And How to Get it, The 60, 144
Knave of Hearts 356
Knife in the Water 107, 286
Knights and Emeralds 356
Knights of the Teutonic Order 302
Knight without Armour 99, 322
Knock on any Door 50, 305
Knock on Wood 382
Knute Rockne, All American 152
Kotch 204
Krakatoa, East of Java 192
Kramer versus Kramer 77, 160, 275, 276, 336, 349
Kremlin Letter, The 71, 166
Kreutzer Sonata, The 59
Kwaidan 136, 348

L

Laburnum Grove 337

Lacemaker, The 100, 366
Lacombe, Lucien 28, 217
Ladies of Leisure 164, 343
Ladies of the Park 51
Ladies They Talk About 343
Lady and the Tramp 116
Lady Be Good 12
Lady Caroline Lamb 256
Lady Chatterley's Lover 201
Lady Eve, The 123, 133, 343, 350
Lady for a Day 63
Lady from Shanghai, The 43, 230, 394
Lady Hamilton 203, 222, 243, 256
Lady in the Dark 294, 318
Lady Jane 100, 178
Lady Killer 122
Ladykiller of Rome, The 225, 337
Ladykillers, The 147
Lady Macbeth of Mtsensk 260
Lady of the Boulevards 409
Lady of the Camelias, The 59
Lady on a Train 401
Lady Sings the Blues 406
Lady Vanishes, The 184, 367
Lady Windermere's Fan 212
Lady with a Lamp, The 249
Lady without a Passport, A 170
Lady Without Camellias, The 17, 376
Lafayette 127
Lamb 196
Lancelot of the Lake 51
Lancer Spy 170
Landlord, The 299
Land of Silence and Darkness 157
Land of the Pharoahs 14
Landru 24
Landscape after Battle 389
Land That Time Forgot, The 345
Land without Bread 53
Larceny Lane 73
Lásky Jedné Plavovlásky 126
Lassie Come Home 97
Last American Hero, The 153
Last Command, The 180, 261, 290, 385
Last Day of Winter, The 142
Last Days of Dolwyn, The 390
Last Days of Pompeii, The 14, 192, 304
Last Detail, The 8, 245
Last Emperor, The 6, 29, 39, 278
Last Flight, The 92
Last Holiday 178

Last Hurrah, The 111, 305, 367
Last Laugh, The 47, 180, 238
Last Metro, The 86, 88, 371
Last Millionaire, The 71, 106
Last of Mrs Cheyney, The 78, 304
Last of the Red Hot Lovers, The 313
Last Picture Show, The 273, 357
Last Remake of Beau Geste, The 303
Last Stage, The 255, 332
Last Supper, The 337
Last Tango in Paris 6, 38, 51
Last Temptation of Christ, The 236, 243, 326
Last Ten Days of Adolf Hitler, The 281
Last Ten Days, The 281
Last Tycoon, The 87, 187
Last Waltz, The 317, 327, 362
Last Wave, The 198
Last Will of Dr Mabuse, The 197
Last Woman, The 88, 320
Last Year at Marienbad 312, 381
Las Vegas Story, The 361
Late George Apley, The 221
Late Mathias Pascal, The 46
Late Show, The 293
Laughing Gravy 200
Laughter 139, 224
Laughter in Paradise 190, 334
Laura 43, 293
Laurel and Hardy 16
Lavender Hill Mob, The 27, 147, 315
Lawrence of Arabia 28, 89, 147, 203, 270
Lazarillo 36
League of Gentlemen, The 316, 331
Lease of Life 99
Leather Boys, The 237, 377
Leave Her to Heaven 282
Leda 32, 65
Left-handed Gun, The 241, 245
Left, Right and Centre 111, 335
Legal Eagles 3
Legend of Gösta Berling, The 134
Legend of the Holy Drinker, The 283, 382
Le Mans 63
Lenin in 1918 293
Lenin in October 294
Lenny 160, 406
Leopard, The 60, 76, 384
Leopard Man, The 227

Leo the Last 321
Lesson in Love, A 14
Lethal Weapon 286
Let It Be 150
Let Joy Reign Supreme 248, 364
Let Justice Be Done 374, 380
Let's Hope It's a Girl 87
Let's Make Love 80, 235
Letter, The 43, 84, 205, 403
Letter from an Unknown Woman 124, 205, 260
Letter of Introduction 382
Letters from a Dead Man 111, 205
Letters from My Windmill 234
Letter to Brezhnev 130, 231
Letter to Three Wives, A 101, 205, 220, 266
Let the People Sing 174
Lianna 205
Libel 86
Libeled Lady 151, 211, 284, 291
Liberation of L. B. James, The 299
Liberty 215
Licence to Kill 95, 302
Liebelei 261
Life and Death of 9413 – a Hollywood Extra, The 227
Life and Death of Colonel Blimp, The 19, 226, 289
Life and Times of Judge Roy Bean, The 166
Lifeboat 160, 206
Life Dances On 310, 380
Life for Ruth 310
Life is a Bed of Roses 312
Life of an American Fireman, The 107
Life of Charles Peace, The 238
Life of Émile Zola, The 92, 263, 406, 409
Life of O-Haru, The 185, 232, 294
Life Upside Down 209
Life with Father 81, 150, 217, 290
Lift, The 37
Lift to the Scaffold 217, 377
Lightning over Water 306, 396
Lights of Variety 379
Light that Failed, The 19, 395
Ligne de Demarcation, La 24, 65, 312
Like Father, Like Son 89
Likely Lads, The 358
Lili 69, 261
Lilies of the Field 270

Lili Marleen 326
Lilith 260
Limelight 7, 66, 187
Line of Demarcation, The 65, 251, 312
Lineup, The 105, 287
Lion Has Seven Heads, The 173, 391
Lion Has Wings, The 289, 294
Lion in Winter, The 143, 156, 272
Lion is in the Streets, The 76
List of Adrian Messinger, The 101, 166
Little Big Man 161, 308
Little Caesar 122, 134, 202, 316
Little Dorrit 92, 147, 206
Little Drummer Girl, The 188
Little Fauss and Big Halsy 238
Little Foxes, The 84, 184, 402
Little Giant, The 316
Little Lord Fauntleroy 67, 300
Little Matchgirl, The 311
Little Minister, The 148, 157, 383
Little Miss Marker 287
Little Night Music, A 361
Little Shop of Horrors, The 333
Little Shop of Horrors 333
Little Soldier, The 138
Little Song of the Road 18
Little Theatre of Jean Renoir, The 348
Little Women 67, 79, 156, 202
Little World of Don Camillo, The 40, 291
Live for Life 236
Live Ghost, The 200
Lives of a Bengal Lancer, The 74, 301
Living 119, 194
Lizards, The 141
Lloyd's of London 175
Local Hero 252, 327
Locked Door, The 343
Lodger, The 30, 159, 179
Logan's Run 130
Lola 48
Lola Montes 69, 260
Lolita 60, 194, 207
London Belongs to Me 31
London Can Take It 48
Lonedale Operator, The 146
Loneliness of the Long Distance Runner, The 377
Lonely are the Brave 101, 241
Lonelyhearts 209

Lonely Passion of Judith Hearne, The 11, 339
Lonely Wife, The 306
Lonely Woman, The 321
Long Absence, The 60
Long and the Short and the Tall, The 282
Long Arm, The 287
Long Day's Journey into Night 156, 214
Longest Day, The 30, 254
Long Goodbye, The 9, 44
Long Good Friday, The 208, 359
Long Hot Summer, The 245, 338, 394
Long Live the Lady 389
Long Night, The 182
Long Pants 62, 128
Long Voyage Home, The 8, 126, 258, 393
Look Back in Anger 54, 356
Looking for Mr Goodbar 188
Looks and Smiles 356
Look Up and Laugh 333
Lord of the Flies 25
Lord of the Rings, The 116
Lorna Doone 280
Loser Takes All 145
Loss of Innocence 321
Lost Army, The 389
Lost Boys, The 218
Lost Forest, The 108
Lost Honour of Katharina Blum, The 325, 386
Lost Horizon 63, 169
Lost Illusion, The 27, 115, 145, 308
Lost in a Harem 19
Lost in America 104
Lost Moment, The 180, 205
Lost Patrol, The 89, 126, 186
Lost Squadron, The 386
Lost Weekend, The 105, 144, 265, 400
Lotna 70, 389
Louisiana Story 252
Loulou 88
Love 134
Love Affair 108, 206, 215
Love and Anarchy 53
Love and Death 9, 329
Love and Pain and the Whole Damn Thing 339
Love and the Frenchwoman 348
Love at First Bite 103
Love at Twenty 348, 371
Love Bug, The 63
Love Crazy 95, 290, 368

Loved One, The 331
Love from a Stranger 68
Love Goddesses, The 16
Love in Germany, A 326
Love in the Afternoon 75, 319, 400
Love in the City 348
Love is My Profession 131, 201
Love is News 156
Loveless, The 238
Love Letters 11, 93, 205
Love Match 65, 95
Love Me or Leave Me 57, 353
Love Me Tonight 212
Love of Jeanne Ney, The 2, 281
Love on the Dole 333
Love on the Ground 338
Love on the Run 156, 371
Love Parade, The 212
Lover Boy 356
Lover Come Back 4
Lovers and Other Strangers 5, 223
Lovers and Thieves 190
Lovers Like Us 236
Lovers, The 6, 31, 217
Loves of a Blonde 126
Loves of Isadora, The 406
Loves of Pharaoh, The 180
Loves of Queen Elizabeth, The 46
Love Story 59
Love Streams 38
Love with the Proper Stranger 15
Loving 178
Loving Couples 14, 310
Lovin' Molly 214
Lower Depths, The 131, 194
Lowland 399
Loyal 47 Ronin, The 172
L-Shaped Room, The 23, 30
Lucia 104
Luck of Ginger Coffey, The 298
Lucky Dog 199
Lucky Jim 349
Ludwig 385
Ludwig II: King of Bavaria 92
Lullaby, The 262
Lulu 47, 48, 179, 205, 281
Lulu the Tool 61
Luna, La 38, 149, 171
Lust for Life 101, 229, 268
Lusts of the Flesh 2, 281
Lusty Men, The 240, 306

M

*M*A*S*H* 9, 60, 162
M 197, 209

Macaroni 205
Macbeth (Roman Polanski) 286, 327, 329
Macbeth (Orson Welles) 327, 329, 394
Machine that Kills Bad People, The 321
Mackintosh Man, The 166
Macomber Affair, The 303
Mad about Music 170
Madame Bovary 229, 311
Madame Curie 175, 202, 406
Madame De … 260, 284
Madame Dubarry 180, 212, 365
Madame Rosa 275
Madame Sin 85
Madame Sousatzka 325
Madame X 2
Mädchen in Uniform 136
Made for Each Other 208
Madeleine 203
Mademoiselle France 84
Mad Love 210
Mad Magician, The 216
Mad Max 251
Mad Miss Manton, The 346
Mado 354
Mad Wednesday 350
Madwoman of Chaillot, The 109, 157
Maggie, The 327
Magic 23, 382
Magic Box, The 99, 175, 406
Magic Christian, The 360
Magic Donkey, The 87
Magic Flute, The 260
Magician, The 33, 216
Magic Town 395
Magnificent Ambersons, The 394
Magnificent Obsession 45, 120
Magnificent Rebel, The 72
Magnificent Seven, The 147
Magnificent Tramp, The 132
Magnum Force 108
Magus, The 216
Mahler 73
Maigret et L'Affaire Saint-Fiacre 132
Maigret Sees Red 131
Maigret Sets a Trap 90, 131
Mail Train 335
Main Event, The 298
Major and the Minor, The 318, 400
Major Barbara 329
Major Dundee 240, 378
Major League 152
Make Me an Offer 183

Make Way for Tomorrow 215,
253
Making It 88
Making Mr Right 317
Malcolm 17, 352
Male Animal, The 2
Malpertuis 394
Maltese Falcon, The 41, 49, 166,
209, 293, 369
Mamma Roma 283
Man about Town 71
Man and a Woman, A 15, 60,
272, 314
Man and a Woman: Twenty
Years Later, A 314
Man Between, The 35
Man Called Horse, A 240, 308
Man Called Peter, A 383
Manchurian Candidate, The 21
Mandala 173
Mandingo 337
Man Escaped, A 51
Man for All Seasons, A 28, 271,
293, 394, 409
Man Friday 209
Man from Laramie, The 314,
347
Man from the Folies Bergère,
The 170
Manhattan 9, 29, 188, 220, 244,
349
Manhattan Melodrama 220,
247, 290
Man Hunt 197
Manhunter 164
Maniac on Wheels 238
Man I Killed, The 213
Man in Grey, The 76
Man in Love, A 320
Man in the Attic, The 179
Man in the Iron Mask, The 302,
374
Man in the Mirror, The 230
Man in the White Suit, The 127,
147, 345
Man is Ten Feet Tall, A 259
Man Made Monster 127, 218,
324
Man of Aran 380
Man of a Thousand Faces 57
Man of Evil 21
Man of Flowers 250
Man of Iron 61, 237, 390
Man of Marble 61, 110, 389
Man of the West 75, 158
Man of the World 208
Manon 380

Man on America's Conscience,
The 93
Manon des Sources 181, 221,
236
Man on the Eiffel Tower, The
199
Man On the Flying Trapeze 121
Manpower 94, 316
Mans, Le 153
Man's Favourite Sport 155
Man's Hope 342
Man Upstairs, The 182
Man Who Came Back, The 311
Man Who Came to Dinner, The
85
Man Who Cheated Himself, The
43
Man Who Could Work Miracles,
The 178
Man Who Fell to Earth, The
112, 344
Man Who Knew Too Much, The
144, 159, 209, 347
Man Who Loved Women, The
371
Man Who Shot Liberty Valance,
The 126, 348, 393
Man Who Would Be King, The
7, 58, 74, 166
Man Within, The 339
Man with the Golden Arm, The
105
Man with the Golden Gun, The
230
Man with the Green Carnation,
The 77
Man with Two Brains, The 56,
345, 372
Mapantsula 79, 112
Marathon Man 144, 160, 256,
324, 391
Margie 310
Marie Antoinette 222
Marie Walewska 134, 243
Marius 282
Marjorie Morningstar 189
Marked Woman 294
Mark of the Vampire, The 213
Mark of Zorro, The 114, 305
Marlowe 293
Marnie 74, 159
Marquise of O, The 76, 243
Marriage Circle, The 213
Marriage, Italian Style 90, 225
Marriage of a Young
Stockbroker, The 405
Marriage of Maria Braun, The
118, 326

Married Woman, A 137
Married Woman, The 137
Marrying Kind, The 80
Marseillaise, La 127, 311
Marseilles Trilogy, The 282
Martha 119
Martin Roumagnac 94
Marty 59, 172, 268
Mary Names the Day 96
Mary of Scotland 156, 224
Mary Poppins 117, 271, 340
Masculine-Feminine 104, 137
Maskerade 77
Mask of Dijon, The 167
Mask of Dimitrios, The 19, 209
Mask of Fu Manchu, The 186,
211
Masque of the Red Death, The
91
Masquerade 40
Masquerade in Vienna 77
Masquerader, The 129, 170
Mass Appeal 204, 291
Master of the House, The 47
Mata Hari 134, 254
Mattei Affair, The 61
Matter of Life and Death, A 226,
289
Maurice 161, 309
Maxie 363
Maxim Trilogy, The 18
Max, My Love 211
Max's Words 37
Maybe Baby 356
Mayerling 72, 86
Mayerling to Sarajevo 72, 260
Maytime 353
McCabe and Mrs Miller 9
McLintock 393
McQ 393
Me and My Gal 391
Mean Streets 87, 326
Medea 239, 284
Medium Cool 358
Meet John Doe 62, 346, 368
Meet Me in St Louis 150, 229
Meet Mr Lucifer 358
Meet Whiplash Willie 204, 271,
400
Mélo 239, 312
Melvyn and Howard 276
Member of the Wedding, The
409
Memoirs of a Survivor 130
Memory Expert, The 121
Memory of Justice, The 392
Men 399
Men, The 51, 409

Men in White 212
Men of the Sea 309
Men O'War 200
Menschen am Sonntag 408
Men Who Tread on the Tiger's Tail, The 194
Men with Wings 395
Mephisto 3, 72, 276
Merchant of the Four Seasons, The 118
Merrily We Go to Hell 224
Merry Christmas, Mr Lawrence 141
Merry Widow, The 169, 212, 386
Merton of the Movies 122, 335, 383
Metropolis 197, 198, 226, 317
Meurte est un Meurte, Un 24
Mexican Bus Ride, A 54
MGM's Big Parade of Comedy 16
Michael Kohlhass 325
Michurin 102
Mickey 129
Middle of the Night 207
Midnight 164, 397
Midnight Cowboy 28, 272, 294, 324
Midnight Express 98
Midnight Patrol 200, 286
Midnight Run 87
Midshipman Easy 309
Midsummer Night's Dream, A 57, 92, 329
Midsummer Night's Sex Comedy, A 9, 33
Mighty Joe Young 190
Mikael 19
Milagro Beanfield War, The 149, 181
Mildred Pierce 78, 81, 140, 265, 398
Milky Way, The 54, 215, 310, 392
Million, Le 70, 228, 369
Millionairess, The 21, 329
Million Dollar Mermaid 104, 152
Millions Like Us 48
Min and Bill 262
Mine Own Executioner 171, 295
Ministry of Fear, The 145, 197
Miquette 335
Miracle in Milan 59, 89
Miracle in the Rain 136
Miracle of Fatima, The 230
Miracle of Morgan's Creek, The 207, 336, 351
Miracle of Our Lady of Fatima, The 230

Miracle of the White Stallions, The 162
Miracle on 34th Street 69, 266
Miracle Woman, The 62, 310, 354
Miracle Worker, The 45, 270, 407
Mirror 356
Mirror Crack'd, The 68
Misérables, Les 132, 171, 198, 224
Misfits, The 132, 166, 234
Missing 41, 61, 204
Missing Rembrandt, The 163
Missionary, The 231, 339
Mission, The (Roland Joffé) 62, 88, 230, 337
Mission, The (Paruiz Sayyad) 22
Mission to Moscow 294
Mississippi 87
Mississippi Gambler 133
Mississippi Mermaid, The 32, 87
Miss Julie 59
Miss Mary 209, 253
Missouri Breaks, The 51
Mister Roberts 57, 204, 268, 290
Mister V; the Fighting Pimpernel 165
Moby Dick 166, 250
Moderato Cantabile 32
Modern Dubarry, A 93
Modern Miracle, The 123, 175, 406
Moderns, The 283
Modern Times 66, 233
Modesty Blaise 210
Mogambo 126, 132, 303
Molière 10
Mollenard 340
Mollycoddle, The 114
Molly Maguires, The 369
Moment of Truth, The 153
Mommie Dearest 78
Mona Lisa 58, 143, 176
Money 52
Money Order, The 404
Money Pit, The 405
Monika 33, 100
Monkey Business (Howard Hawks) 142, 155, 234, 318
Monkey Business (Norman Z McLeod) 225
Monkey in Winter, A 132
Monk, The 234
Mon Oncle 109, 217, 269
Monsieur Hulot's Holiday 235, 327
Monsieur Verdoux 44, 66, 293

Monsieur Vincent 266, 323
Monte Carlo 213
Monte Carlo or Bust 388
Monterey Pop 317
Montevideo 289
Month in the Country, A 19, 184, 328
Monty Python and the Holy Grail 228, 328
Monty Python's Life of Brian 236, 243
Monty Python's Meaning of Life 288
Moon and Sixpence, The 20, 122
Moonfleet 197, 340
Moon in the Gutter, The 40, 88
Moonlighting 236
Moonraker 293
Moonstruck 11, 138, 278, 318
Moonwalker 117
More Than a Miracle 228
More the Merrier, The 265, 346
Morgan – a Suitable Case for Treatment 154
Morning After, The 11, 124
Morning Departure 23, 343, 351
Morning Glory 7, 156, 262
Morocco 74, 93, 385
Morons from Outer Space 150, 362
Mortal Storm, The 294, 347
Moscow Distrusts Tears 8, 276
Moscow Does Not Believe in Tears 8, 276
Moscow Nights 21
Mosquito Coast, The 125, 231
Mother 47, 233, 295
Mother and the Whore, The 211
Mother Kusters Goes to Heaven 118
Mouchette 51
Moulin Rouge 20, 166
Mountain Cat, The 213
Mourning Becomes Electra 171
Mouse That Roared, The 106, 169
Movie, Movie 283
Moving Violation 401
Mr and Mrs Smith 208, 361
Mr Arkadin 337, 394
Mr Ashton Was Indiscreet 291
Mr Blandings Builds His Dream House 143, 211
Mr Deeds Goes to Town 62, 74, 154, 263, 366
Mr Denning Drives North 2
Mr Hobbs Takes a Vacation 327, 348

Mr Jolly Lives Next Door 359
Mr Klein 210
Mr Love 373
Mr Lucky 142
Mr Moto's Gamble 90
Mr Moto Takes a Chance 209
Mr North 216
Mr Peabody and the Mermaid 291
Mr Skeffington 45, 85
Mrs Miniver 264, 402
Mr Smith Goes to Washington 62, 76, 347
Mrs Soffel 188
Mr V 342
Mr Wong, Detective 186
Muddy River 282
Mudlark, The 147, 233
Muhomatsu No Issho 381
Muhomatsu the Rickshaw Man 381
Mummy, The 186, 218, 324
Muppet Movie, The 395
Murder 159
Murder Ahoy 68
Murder at the Gallop 68
Murder by Death 283
Murder by Decree 163, 179
Murderers Among Us 35
Murderers are Among Us, The 35
Murder Inc. 50, 201
Murder in Thornton Square, The 34, 249, 265
Murder is a Murder…Is a Murder, A 24
Murder Most Foul 68
Murder My Sweet 44, 293
Murder of Dmitri Karamazov, The 100
Murder of Thornton Square, The 80
Murder on the Orient Express 34, 68, 214, 274, 367
Murder She Said 68
Murders in the Rue Morgue, The 56, 213
Muriel 312
Murmur of the Heart 171, 217
Music Box, The 129, 200
Music for Millions 336
Music in the Dark 297
Music Lovers, The 11, 73
Music Man, The 338
Music Room, The 174, 306
Musketeers of Pig Alley, The 146
Mutiny on the Bounty 50, 132, 198, 263

My American Uncle 88, 312
My Beautiful Laundrette 161
My Best Friend's Girl 211
My Brilliant Career 399
My Cousin Rachel 54, 86, 106
My Darling Clementine 123, 125, 158, 240
My Dinner with Andre 110, 217
My Fair Lady 50, 80, 271, 296
My Favorite Blonde 331, 367
My Favorite Wife 44, 142, 215
My Favourite Year 122, 358
My Foolish Heart 357, 398
My Girlfriend's Boyfriend 319
My Learned Friend 190, 331
My Left Foot 279
My Life as a Dog 66
My Life to Live 137, 294
My Little Chickadee 121
My Love Has Been Burning 232
My Man Godfrey 55, 208, 290, 366
My Name is Julia Ross 156, 328
My Name is Nobody 123
My Night at Maud's 319
My Night with Maud 319
My Sister Eileen 366
Mystery of Edwin Drood, The 92
Mystery of Kaspar Hauser, The 112, 157
Mystery of the Marie Celeste, The 193
Mystery of the Wax Museum, The 81
My Two Husbands 44
My Way Home 100

N

Nada 65, 189
Nadine 307
Naked and the Dead, The 391
Naked City, The 84
Naked Edge, The 75
Naked Hearts 40
Naked Night, The 14, 33
Naked Truth, The 45
Name of the Rose, The 73, 234, 313, 396
Nana 409
Nanou 130
Napoléon 242, 364, 386
Napoleon and Samantha 102
Narrow Margin, The 367, 401
Nashville 10
Nasty Habits 111
National Health, The 162
National Lampoon's Animal House 251

National Velvet 153, 162, 265
Native Land 169
Natural, The 152
Naughty Marietta 308
Navigator, The 187, 228
Nazarin 54, 168
Near Dark 218, 338
Ned Kelly 280
Nell Gwyn 231
Nest of Gentlefolk, A 164
Network 115, 214, 275, 358
Never Give a Sucker an Even Break 122
Never on Sunday 84, 296
Never Say Never Again 74
Never Take No for an Answer 15, 288
New Adventures of Don Juan, The 143
New Babylon, The 47
New Kind of Love, A 244
New Land, The 170
New Leaf, A 209
New Tales of the Taira Clan 232
New York, New York 87, 244, 326
New York Stories 220, 326
Next of Kin 294
Next Stop, Greenwich Village 20, 183
Niagara 234
Nibelungen, Die 197, 376
Nicholas and Alexandra 233, 322
Nicholas Nickleby 92
Nicky and Gino 374
Night Ambush 289
Night and Day 81, 142, 341
Night and Fog 312
Night and the City 42, 84
Night at the Opera, A 105, 140, 224
Night Beauties 71, 103
Night Creatures 285
Night Has a Thousand Eyes 316
Night in Casablanca, A 64, 225
Night in June, A 35
Night is My Future 297
Nightmare 167
Nightmare Alley 112
Nightmare On Elm Street, A 219, 324
Night Must Fall 359
Night My Number Came Up, The 192
Night Nurse 343, 395
Night of the Demon 71
Night of the Eagle 400

Night of the Generals, The 248, 392
Night of the Ghouls, The 372
Night of the Hunter 137, 199
Night of the Iguana, The 55, 166, 227
Night of the Living Dead 207
Night of Varennes, The 30, 127, 225, 326
Night Owls 200
Nights of Cabiria 120, 246, 269
Night, The 17, 36, 225
Night They Invented Striptease, The 379
Night They Raided Minsky's, The 379
Night to Remember, A 193, 206
Night Train to Munich 308, 331
Nineteen Nineteen 295
Nine to Five 123, 328
Ninotchka 134, 169, 212, 213, 247, 330, 397
Noah's Ark 81, 253
Nobody's Fool 3
No Highway 94, 192, 348
No Highway in the Sky 94, 192, 348
No Love for Johnnie 287
No Man of Her Own 170, 208
No Man's Land 340
No Minor Vices 315
None but the Lonely Heart 142, 265
None Shall Escape 392
Nora Prentiss 398
Norma Rae 140, 275, 369
North by Northwest 142, 159, 331
North Dallas Forty 152
Northern Star, The 248
Northwest Frontier 301, 367
Northwest Passage 383
Nosferatu 103, 238, 376
Nosferatu the Vampire 157
Nostalgia 111, 356
No Surrender 64, 150
Not as a Stranger 96
Nothing but the Best 300, 370, 377
Nothing in Common 119
Nothing Sacred 208, 224, 395
Notorious 34, 142, 159, 248
Not Quite Jerusalem 359
Notte, La 17, 36
Now About These Women 14, 34
No Way Out 77, 221
No Way to Treat a Lady 295
Now Voyager 84, 297, 357

Number 17 159
Numéro Deux 137, 150
Nun's Story, The 74
Nun, The 74, 409
Nurse Edith Cavell 407
Nuts 49
Nutty Professor, The 181

O

Oath of Obedience 36
Oberwald Mystery, The 17, 169
Oblomov 59
October 110, 315
October Man, The 64
Odd Couple, The 204, 251
Odd Man Out 27, 308
Odd Obsession 253
Odds against Tomorrow 232
Oedipus Rex 237, 284
Of a Thousand Delights 171, 381, 384
Offence, The 214
Officer and a Gentleman, An 19, 276
Official Story, The 278
Official Version, The 278
Of Human Bondage 85, 139, 164, 389
Of Mice and Men 127, 144
Ohm Krüger 52, 380
Oh Mr Porter 301
Oh, Sun 173
Oh! What a Lovely War 9, 256, 339
Oh What a Lovely War! 23, 254
Oil for the Lamps of China 252
Oklahoma! 12, 409
Old Acquaintance 84
Old and the New, The 47, 110
Old Capital, The 374
Old Curiosity Shop, The 92
Old Dark House, The 186, 198, 219
Old Fashioned Way, The 121
Old Gringo, The 227
Old Maid, The 85, 248
Old Man and the Sea, The 366
Old Mother Riley Meets the Vampire 213
Old Yeller 97
Oliver! 13, 272, 309
Oliver and Company 117
Oliver Twist 92, 147, 203
Olivia 136
O Lucky Man 257
Olympia 152, 257, 380
Olympiad 152, 257, 380

Olympische Spiele 1936 152, 257, 380
Omen, The 91
On Approval 327, 330
Once a Jolly Swagman 238
Once Upon a Honeymoon 215, 319
Once Upon a Time 353
Once Upon a Time in America 87, 259, 369
Once Upon a Time in the West 39, 123
On Dangerous Ground 43, 305
One-Piece Bathing Suit, The 104
One Crazy Summer 357
One Deadly Summer 49, 398
One Exciting Night 146
One Flew Over the Cuckoo's Nest 29, 102, 126, 245, 259, 274
One Foot in Heaven 383
One from the Heart 75
One Good Turn 200
One Hour with You 3, 31, 212
One Hundred Men and a Girl 287
One Magic Christmas 69, 81
One Man Mutiny 75
One Night of Love 308
One of Our Aircraft is Missing 289
One Piece Bathing Suit, The 152
One Summer of Happiness 36
One that Got Away, The 292
One Touch of Venus 333
One, Two, Three 35, 57, 400
One Week 187
One Wild Moment 207
On Golden Pond 123, 124, 156, 276
Only Angels Have Wings 142, 155, 362
Only the French Can 132, 311
Only Two Can Play 23, 390
On the Avenue 13, 379
On the Beach 111, 351
On the Black Hill 390
On the Town 12, 99, 188, 243, 258
On the Waterfront 50, 152, 187, 258, 268
Open City 120, 320, 321
Operation Disaster 23, 343, 351
Operation Petticoat 351
Ophelia 149
Orchestra Conductor, The 390
Orchestra Wives 180
Ordet 381

Ordinary People 276
Organizer, The 225
Orion's Belt 243
Orphans of the Storm 137, 146, 336
Orphée 230, 285
Orpheus 230, 285
Osaka Elegy 232
Oscar, The 350
Ossessione 384
Otello 260
Othello 59, 79, 180, 256, 266, 329, 338, 394
Otley 208
Otto e Mezzo 225
Our Betters 164
Our Daily Bread 238, 366, 383
Our Hospitality 135, 187
Our Man in Havana 145, 147, 308
Our Relations 201, 389
Our Town 338
Our Vines Have Tender Grapes 316
Our Wife 177, 200
Outback 135
Outcast of the Islands, An 309
Outcry, The 17
Outlaw Josey Wales, The 108
Out of Africa 118, 277, 279, 349
Out of the Past 43
Out of Towners, The 204, 244
Outsiders, The 137, 172
Outsider, The 23
Outside the Law 316
Outward Bound 206
Owd Bob 97
Owl and the Pussycat, The 373
Ox-Bow Incident, The 123, 395
Oxford Blues 349
Oyster Princess, The 213

P

Pack Up Your Troubles 200
Padre Padrone 61
Page Miss Glory 202
Page of Madness, A 120
Paid 78
Pain in the A**, A 22
Painted Veil, The 31, 134
Paint Your Wagon 53, 109
Paisà 120, 321, 376
Paisan 120, 321, 376
Pajama Game, The 99, 369
Paleface, The (Buster Keaton/Eddie Cline) 188
Paleface, The (Norman Z McLeod) 144, 388

Pale Rider 108
Palermo or Wolfsburg 38
Pal Joey 12
Palm Beach Story, The 350
Palmy Days 71
Pandemonium 172
Pandora's Box 47, 48, 179, 205, 281
Panic in the Streets 187
Paper Chase, The 274, 349
Paperhouse 411
Paper Moon 5, 274, 354, 411
Papillon 161
Parade 235
Paradine Case, The 64, 160, 199, 374
Paradise Lagoon 55
Parallax View, The 22
Paramount on Parade 350
Pardon Us 98, 168, 200
Parents Terrible, Les 120
Paris 190
Paris Blues 180
Paris by Night 287, 404
Paris Does Strange Things 35, 112, 311
Paris, Texas 62, 177, 396
Parnell 212
Parsifal 260
Partie de Plaisir, Une 65, 95
Parting Glances 161
Partner 39
Party and the Guests, The 108
Party Girl 306
Party, The 133
Pa Solsidan 34
Passage to India, A 147, 203, 277, 301, 360
Passage to Marseilles 49, 81, 209
Passenger, The 17
Passing of the Third Floor Back, The 31
Passion 180, 212, 326, 365
Passion of Joan of Arc, The 47
Passport to Fame 170, 316
Passport to Pimlico 209
Pat and Mike 80, 367
Patch of Blue, A 45, 271
Pather Panchali 18, 306
Paths of Glory 78, 101, 141, 194
Patriot, The 180, 213
Patsy, The 237
Patterns 41
Patterns of Power 41
Patton 75, 242, 273
Patton – Lust for Glory 75
Pauline at the Beach 319, 327
Pawnbroker, The 214

Pawnshop, The 66
Pay Day 66
Paying the Penalty 385
Pearl of Death, The 305
Pearls of the Crown, The 30, 77
Peeping Tom 289, 307
Pee Wee's Big Adventure 40
Peggy Sue Got Married 75, 178, 363, 372
Peg o' My Heart 383
Pelle the Conqueror 62, 279
Penny Serenade 142, 346
People of France, The 247, 311
People on Sunday 408
People Will Talk 162
Pépé le Moko 19, 131
Perceval 390
Percy 372
Perfect Couple, A 10
Perfect Day, The 200
Perfect Friday 29
Perfect Strangers 99
Performance 368
Persona 15, 33, 320
Personal Best 146, 205
Personal Column 386
Personal Services 31, 122
Persons Unknown 142, 225
Peter and Pavla 126
Peter Pan 116
Peter Rabbit and the Tales of Beatrix Potter 83
Petite Voleuse, La 372, 410
Petrified Forest, The 42, 49, 85, 165
Pet Semetary 191
Petulia 393
Peyton Place 338
Phantom Carriage, The 47
Phantom Fiend, The 30, 179
Phantom Lady 401
Phantom Light, The 206
Phantom Love 6
Phantom of Liberty, The 54
Phantom of the Opera, The 218, 324
Phantom President, The 111
Phantom Ship 193
Phar Lap 162
Philadelphia Story, The 12, 80, 142, 156, 220, 264, 347
Picasso Mystery, The 362
Piccadilly Jim 209
Pickpocket 51
Pick Up Artist, The 164
Pickwick Papers, The 92
Picnic 44, 338
Picnic at Hanging Rock 25, 247

Picture of Dorian Grey, The 181
Pied Piper, The (Jirí Barta) 314
Pied Piper, The (Irving Pichel) 116, 253
Pier 13 391
Pierrot Le Fou 32, 137, 398
Pig Across Paris, A 283
Pigeon that Took Rome, The 320
Pigsty 284
Pilgrimage 125
Pilgrim, The 66
Pimpernel Smith 165, 342
Pink Floyd Live at Pompeii 317
Pink Panther Strikes Again, The 246
Pinky 186
Pinocchio 116
Pirates 286
Pirate, The 188, 229, 285
Pixote 196
Pizza Triangle, The 226
Place in the Sun, A 171, 267, 346
Place of Weeping, A 171
Places in the Heart 118, 277, 279
Plague of the Zombies, The 207
Plaisir, Le 260
Planet of the Apes 30, 190, 345
Plan Nine from Outer Space 213, 372
Platinum Blonde 62, 151
Platoon 18, 278, 384
Players, The 281
Playhouse, The 187
Play it Again, Sam 64, 188, 283
Play Misty for Me 109
Playtime 235
Plaza Suite 163
Please Sir 358
Pleasure Party 65, 95
Plenty 349
Plough and Stars, The 175
Ploughman's Lunch, The 405
Pocketful of Miracles 253
Poison Pen 205
Police 88
Police Academy 251
Pollyanna 288
Poltergeist 219
Poltergeist II – the Other Side 198
Pookie 321
Pope Joan 288
Popeye 10
Popi 11
Poppy 121
Porgy and Bess 12

Porridge 358
Port of Shadows 63, 131
Portrait of a 60% Perfect Man: Billy Wilder 400
Portrait of a Mobster 232
Portrait of Jennie 93, 136
Poseidon Adventure, The 193
Possessed 78, 300
Possession of Joel Delaney, The 284
Possessors, The 131, 138
Postman Always Rings Twice, The 246
Postmeister, Der 380
Potemkin 47, 110
Power 183
Power and the Glory, The 70, 350, 367
Prayer for the Dying, A 259, 359
Presidio, The 74
Pretty Baby 53, 207, 217
Pretty in Pink 357, 410
Prick Up Your Ears 161
Pride and Prejudice 256
Pride and the Passion, The 143, 243
Pride of the Yankees, The 74
Priest of Love 201
Prime Minister, The 287
Prime of Miss Jean Brodie, The 136, 272, 339
Prince and the Pauper, The 233, 293
Prince and the Showgirl, The 25, 235, 256
Prince of Foxes 394
Princess and the Pirate, The 285
Princess Bride, The 354
Prison 34
Prisoner of Second Avenue, The 204
Prisoner of Zenda, The 169, 302, 354
Prisoner, The 147, 231
Private Benjamin 19
Private Function, A 339, 373
Private Life of Don Juan, The 114
Private Life of Henry VIII, The 98, 198, 262
Private Life of Sherlock Holmes, The 163, 400
Private Lives of Elizabeth and Essex, The 81, 85, 222
Private's Progress 19, 23, 169
Privileged 349
Prize, The 6, 245, 397

Prizzi's Honor 138, 166, 216, 246, 278, 370, 372
Producers, The 296
Promised Land 338, 389
Promoter, The 147
Proud Ones, The 65
Providence 312
Prowler, The 64, 210
Psycho 159, 163, 283, 295
Psycho 2 295
Psycho 3 295
Public Enemy, The 56, 132, 151, 232, 259, 395
Pulp 58
Pumpkin Eater, The 338
Puritan, The 30
Purple Rain 288
Purple Rose of Cairo, The 9, 15, 29
Pursued 391
Pursuit of the Graf Spee 254, 289
Pursuit to Algiers 305
Putney Swope 299
Putting Pants On Philip 129, 199
Pygmalion 21, 165, 297, 332, 390

Q

Q Planes 256
Quai des Brumes 63, 131
Quality Street 313, 347
Quartet 174, 355
Quatermass Experiment, The 344
Queen Christina 134, 341
Queen Kelly 352, 386
Queen of Atlantis 282
Queen of Destiny 233
Queen of Hearts 315
Queen of Spades, The 120
Queimada! 51, 230
Querelle 161
Question of Rape, A 189
Quick Millions 371
Quiet American, The 145, 221, 384
Quiet Duel, The 96, 194
Quiet Man, The 109, 126, 175, 267, 393
Quiet Place in the Country, A 154
Quiet Wedding 21
Quo Vadis? 33, 46, 202

R

Rachel and the Stranger 315

Rachel, Rachel 209, 244
Racket Busters 49, 232, 371
Racket, The 43
Radio Days 9, 15, 188
Raffles 182, 370
Raggedy Rawney, The 148
Raging Bull 87, 152, 276, 318, 327
Ragtime 57, 126
Raiders 342
Raiders of the Lost Ark 125, 342
Railroad 283
Railway Children, The 301, 411
Rain 78, 231
Rainbow, The 201
Rainmaker, The 156
Rain Man 38, 161, 257, 278
Rain People, The 75, 104
Rains Came, The 192, 198, 301
Raising Arizona 189, 196
Rambo II 18
Ramona 308
Ran 194, 301, 304
Rancho Notorious 94, 197
Randolph Family, The 150
Random Harvest 11, 202
Rape of Malaya, The 292
Rape, The 189
Rashomon 194, 267, 380
Rasputin the Mad Monk 407
Rats, The 36
Rattle and Hum 317
Raven, The 186, 210, 213
Rawhide 388
Razor's Edge, The 265
Reach for the Sky 27, 362
Real Glory, The 18
Real Life 206
Reap the Wild Wind 85, 315
Rear Window 159, 307, 347
Rebecca 2, 106, 124, 159, 256, 264, 307
Rebel 20
Rebel Without a Cause 305, 308
Reckless 151
Reckless Moment, The 2, 77, 260
Red and the Black, The 291
Red and the White, The 108
Red Badge of Courage, The 166, 378
Red Balloon, The 66
Red Beard 194
Red Circle, The 236
Red Desert, The 17, 381
Red Dust 132, 151
Red Headed Woman 151
Red Heat 247
Red House, The 317, 337

Red Inn, The 295, 389
Red Pony, The 162, 212
Red Psalm 118, 315
Red River 155, 392
Reds 188, 246, 276
Red Shoes, The 83, 289, 401
Red Sorghum 38, 68
Red Wedding 65
Reed, Carol 59
Reed Dolls 173
Reflections in a Golden Eye 51
Règle du Jeu, La 311, 375
Rehearsal for a Crime 54
Reivers, The 85
Religieuse, La 74
Reluctant Debutante, The 229
Remarkable Mr Kipps, The 164, 309
Rembrandt 20, 198
Remember Last Night? 164
Remember the Night 343, 350, 398
Renaldo and Clara 362
Rendez-Vous 40
Repentance 76, 404
Repo Man 135
Report on the Party and the Guests, A 108
Republic of Sin 98
Repulsion 86, 286
Rescued from an Eagle's Nest 107, 146
Rescuers, The 117
Restless Natives 352
Resurrection 230
Return of Captain Invincible, The 352
Return of Frank James, The 123, 197
Return of Martin Guerre, The 88
Return of Maxim, The 18
Return of the Jedi, The 125
Return of the Living Dead, The 207
Return of the Musketeers, The 227
Return of the Pink Panther, The 182
Return of the Soldier, The 211
Return of the Vampire, The 213
Return to Glennascaul 154
Return to Reason 353
Reuben, Reuben 40, 285
Reunion in France 84
Revolution 315
Rhapsody in Blue 12, 341
Rich and Famous 79
Rich and Strange 160

Richard III 27, 256, 304, 329
Richardson, Tony 280
Rich Man's Folly 92
Riff Raff 151
Rififi 84
Riflemen, The 9, 137
Right Stuff, The 158
Rink, The 66, 233
Rio Bravo 155, 241, 392
Rio Grande 125, 392
Rio Lobo 155, 393
Riptide 158, 327
Rise and Rise of Michael Rimmer, The 4
Rise of Helga, The 134
Rise of Louis XIV, The 321, 364
Rise to Power of Louis XIV, The 321, 364
Rising Damp 31
Risky Business 358
Rita, Sue and Bob Too 211
Rite, The 3
River of No Return 234
River's Edge 370
Road Games 371
Road, The 120
Road to Frisco, The 49, 391
Road to Glory, The 155, 224
Road to Life, The 411
Road to Morocco 19
Road to Rio 167
Roaring Twenties, The 50, 57, 232, 391
Roberta 13, 22
Robe, The 54, 243
Robin and Marian 73
Robin Hood 114, 117, 148, 280
Robocop 317
Rocco and His Brothers 53, 216, 384
Rock around the Clock 288
Rocking Horse Winner, The 201
Rock Show 317
Rocky 152, 259, 275, 318
Rocky Horror Picture Show 13
Rocky II 318
Rocky III 318
Rocky IV 318
RoGoPaG 355
Rogue Cop 42
Romance 134, 383
Romance Sentimentale 110
Romancing the Stone 4, 102, 372
Roman Holiday 267, 320
Roman Scandals 14
Roman Spring of Mrs Stone, The 203, 320

Romeo and Juliet 79, 130, 164, 244, 264, 270, 304, 329, 380
Rome, Open City 120, 320, 321
Rommel, the Desert Fox 254
Ronde, La 30, 260
Roof, The 89
Room at the Top 28, 253, 269
Room Service 225
Room Upstairs, The 94
Room with a View, A 29, 339
Rooster Cogburn 157, 393
Rope 159, 347, 370
Rosalie 12
Rosa Luxemburg 184, 386
Rose Marie 202
Rosemary's Baby 27, 91, 272, 286
Rose Tattoo, The 268
Rouge Baiser 130
Rough Treatment 390
Round Midnight 174, 181
Roxanne 17, 139
Roxie Hart 318, 395
Royal Family of Broadway, The 3, 221
Royal Hunt of the Sun, The 113
Royal Hunt, The 172
Royal Wedding 23, 99
Ruby Gentry 383
Ruggles of Red Gap 55, 198, 215
Rules of the Game, The 311, 375
Ruling Class, The 334
Rumble Fish 75, 238, 308
Run for Cover 305
Run for Your Money, A 209, 390
Running Man, The 309
Running on Empty 214
Run Silent, Run Deep 351
Rupture, La 24, 65
Russians are Coming, the Russians are Coming, The 71
Rutles – All You Need is Cash, The 362
Ryan's Daughter 203, 273

S

Sabotage 106
Saboteur 159
Saboteur – Code Name Morituri, The 51
Sabrina 146
Sabrina Fair 146
Sacrifice, The 110, 120, 304, 356
Sadie Thompson 391
Safety Last 128, 135
Saga of Anatahan, The 385
Sahara 89
Saigon 384

Saint Takes Over, The 90
Salaam Bombay! 18
Salamander, The 291
Salem's Lot 191
Sally of the Sawdust 69
Salome's Last Dance 243
Salo: the 120 Days of Sodom 5, 284
Salt of the Earth 172, 369
Salut l'Artiste 3
Salvador 291, 307
Salvation Hunters, The 385
Salvatore Giuliano 139, 216
Same Time Next Year 314
Sammy and Rosie Get Laid 209
Samson 389
Samson and Delilah 222, 253
Samurai (Hiroshi Inagki) 268
Samurai, The (Jean-Pierre Melville) 40
Sandakan-8 53
Sand Pebbles, The 243
Sandra 381, 384
Sands of Iwo Jima 282, 392
San Francisco 132, 192, 366
Sanjuro 194, 304
San Quentin 49
Sansho the Bailiff 33, 232, 337
Sans Toit Ni Loi 70
Santa Claus – the Movie 69
Santa Fe Trail 81
Saphead, The 188
Sapphire 28, 299
Saps at Sea 201
Sarajevo 72, 260
Saratoga 132, 151
Saratoga Trunk 35
Sarraounia 173
Satan's Brew 118
Satchmo the Great 181
Saturday Night and Sunday Morning 28
Saturday Night Fever 83
Savage Innocents, The 305
Savage Messiah 20
Savage Princess 354
Savage, The 236
Save the Tiger 204, 274
Saving Grace 288
Sawdust and Tinsel 14, 33
Sayonara 232, 269
Scalphunters, The 240
Scandal 287
Scanners 324
Scapegoat, The 106
Scaramouche 302, 354
Scarecrow 61
Scarface 155, 168, 186, 233

Scarlet and Black 291
Scarlet Claw, The 305
Scarlet Empress, The 93, 178, 385
Scarlet Letter, The 137, 396
Scarlet Pimpernel, The 127
Scarlet Street 197, 316
Scenes from a Marriage 34
School for Scoundrels 251, 334
School for Secrets 251
Schpountz, Le 318
Scott of the Antarctic 113
Scoundrels in White 32
Scoundrel, The (Ben Hecht/Charles MacArthur) 136
Scoundrel, The (Jean-Paul Rappeneau) 32
Scram! 200
Scrooge 69, 334, 397
Sea Gull, The 214
Sea Hawk, The 81, 285
Sea Horses, The 290
Séance on a Wet Afternoon 23, 71
Sea of Grass, The 367
Searchers, The 25, 125, 240, 392
Searching Wind, The 93
Search, The 409
Seashell and the Clergyman, The 5
Sea Wolf, The 316
Second Awakening of Christa Klages, The 386
Second Breath 316
Secret Agent, The 160, 209
Secret Ceremony 210
Secret Flight 251
Secret Four, The 43
Secret Game, The 66, 104, 380
Secret Garden, The 67, 288
Secret Honor 10
Secret Life of Walter Mitty, The 31, 103
Secret of My Success, The 405
Secret of Santa Vittoria, The 237
Secrets of a Soul 281, 295, 376
Secrets of Women 34
Secret, The 64
Seduction of Joe Tynan, The 6, 349
Seduction of Mimi, The 190
Seedling, The 172
See Here My Love 87
Senator Was Indiscreet, The 291
Senso 72, 384
Separate Tables 31, 269
September 9, 115

September 30, 1955 250
Serenade 124
Sergeant Rutledge 125
Sergeant York 74, 155, 165, 254, 264
Serpent's Egg, The 34
Serpico 214
Servant, The 210, 309
Set-up, The 152
Seven Angry Men 337
Seven Brides for Seven Brothers 12, 99
Seven Chances 187
Seven Days in May 96, 101
Seven Little Foys, The 379
Seven Per Cent Solution, The 163, 256
Seven Samurai, The 148, 185, 194
Seventh Cross, The 409
Seventh Heaven 261, 262
Seventh Seal, The 33, 120, 329
Seventh Survivor, The 206
Seventh Veil, The 239
Seven Women 8, 231
Seven Year Itch, The 49, 234, 338, 397
Several Days in the Life of I.I.Oblomov 59
Sewer 20, 251, 286, 312, 389
sex, lies and videotape 62, 223
Sexton Blake and the Hooded Terror 90, 164
Shadey 341, 368
Shadow of a Doubt 64, 159
Shadow of the Thin Man 290, 361
Shadows 299
Shake Hands with the Devil 359
Shakespeare Wallah 3
Shall We Dance? 22
Shame, The 34
Shampoo 144, 274
Shane 41, 148, 241, 347
Shanghai 282
Shanghai Drama 282
Shanghai Express 93, 368, 385
Shanghai Gesture, The 385
She 411
She Danced for the Summer 36
She Done Him Wrong 142, 330
Sheik, The 46, 129, 144
She Loves Me Not 401
Shenandoah 336, 378
Sheriff of Fractured Jaw, The 391
Sherlock Holmes 90, 163

Sherlock Holmes and the Secret Weapon 305
Sherlock Holmes and the Spider Woman 305
Sherlock Holmes and the Voice of Terror 249, 305
Sherlock Holmes and the Secret Code 304
Sherlock Holmes and the Deadly Necklace 163
Sherlock Holmes Faces Death 305
Sherlock Holmes in Washington 294, 305
Sherlock Junior 163, 187
She's Gotta Have It 144
She Wore a Yellow Ribbon 125, 392
Shining, The 163, 191, 194, 245
Ship Bound for India, A 206
Ship of Fools 203
Shivers 357
Shoah 183, 332, 392
Shocking Accident, A 145
Shoeshine 89, 266, 376
Shooting Party, The 309
Shootist, The 119, 348, 393
Shoot the Moon 95, 188
Shoot the Pianist 115, 371, 377
Shoot the Piano Player 115, 371, 377
Shop 347
Shop Around the Corner, The 213, 333, 347
Shop on Main Street, The 271, 334
Shop on the High Street, The 271, 334
Shors 102
Short Circuit II 317
Short Cut 300
Short Encounters 76
Short Film About Killing, A 49
Short Meetings 76
Shoulder Arms 66
Showboat 13
Show Business 379
Shriek of Araby, The 129
Siberia 102
Siberian Lady Macbeth 390
Sicilian, The 216
Sid and Nancy 100
Sidewalks of London 83, 199, 203
Sidewalks of New York, The 31
Sign of Leo, The 368
Sign of the Cross, The 14, 198
Signs of Life 157, 171

Silence de la Mer, Le 312
Silence is Golden 71
Silence, The 26, 33
Silent Duel, A 96, 194
Silent One, The 6
Silent World, The 60
Silken Skin 371
Silk Stockings 247
Silkwood 245, 349
Silverado 240
Silver Cord, The 237
Silver Dream Racer 238
Silver River 391
Simon and Laura 3
Simon of the Desert 54, 323
Simple Case, A 296
Since You Went Away 255
Singing Nun, The 74
Singin' in the Rain 12, 99, 122, 188, 335
Sing You Sinners 162
Sin of Father Mouret, The 221, 412
Sin of Harold Diddlebock, The 350
Sin of Madelon Claudet, The 262
Sir Arne's Treasure 26, 47
Sirena 380
Sister Kenny 249
Sisters 336
Sisters of the Gion, The 232
Sisters or the Balance of Happiness 386
Sisters, The 85, 336
Sitting Bull's History Lesson 37
Sitting Pretty 109
Six Inches Tall 228
Six of a Kind 121, 215
Sixteen Candles 358
Sixth of July, The 22
Sixty Glorious Years 233
Skater's Debut, A 107
Skippy 220, 262
Slam Dance 370
Slap in the Face, A 154
Slap Shot 152, 244
Slaughterhouse Five 292
Slave of Love, A 322
Slave Ship 337
Slaves of New York 172, 244
Sleeper 9, 188, 227
Sleeping Car Murders, The 235
Sleeping Tiger, The 210
Sleuth 58, 164, 220, 256, 337
Slight Case of Murder, A 316, 331
Slipper and the Rose, The 69
Small Back Room, The 289

Small Change 146, 372
Small Voice, The 158
Smiles of a Summer's Night 14, 33, 361
Smilin' Through 2
Smugglers, The 339
Snake Pit, The 86, 171
Snares 386
Snows of Kilimanjaro, The 310
Snow White and the Seven Dwarfs 48, 116, 230, 340
So Big 343
So Close to Life 33
So Dark the Night 43
So Evil My Love 397
Soft Skin, The 371
Soir, Un Train, Un 189
Solaris 280, 355
Soldiers, The 9, 137
Soleil O 173
Solid Gold Cadillac, The 76, 404
Solomon and Sheba 253, 383
So Long at the Fair 11, 283
Somebody Up There Likes Me 244
Some Came Running 229
Some Like It Hot 204, 223, 228, 234, 340, 397
Someone Behind the Door 11
Someone to Love 395
Someone to Watch Over Me 401
Something to Live For 347
Something to Shout About 12
Something Wild 405
Somewhere in Europe 66
Somewhere in France 390
Somewhere in the Night 221
Somewhere in Time 363
Song for Europe, A 77
Song is Born, A 48, 155, 340
Song of Bernadette, The 265, 323
Song of Love 73
Song of the South 117, 396
Song of the Thin Man 290
Song Remains the Same, The 318
Song to Remember, A 73
Son of Frankenstein 186, 213
Sons and Lovers 201
Sons of the Desert 200
Sophie's Choice 276, 332, 348
So Proudly We Hail 249
Sorcerers, The 324
So Red the Rose 378
Sorrow and the Pity, The 332
Sorrow Street 259
Sorry Wrong Number 343

Soufrière, La 157
Soul Man 299
Sound and the Fury, The 86
Sound Barrier, The 27, 203, 362
Sound of Music, The 4, 74, 249, 271
Sound of Trumpets, The 357, 376
Soursweet 170
Sous Les Toits de Paris 63, 70, 112
South 252
Southerner, The 311, 380
South Pacific 12
Souvenir 313
Spare the Rod 377
Spartacus 33, 101, 194, 269
Special Day, A 225
Spellbound 35, 159, 283
Spiders, The 197
Spiral Staircase, The 154, 295
Spirit of St Louis, The 175, 348, 400
Spirit of the Beehives, The 81
Spirits of the Dead 217
Spite Marriage 188
Spitfire 165, 175
Splendor 226
Splendor in the Grass 171, 187
Spring and Port Wine 356
Spring in Park Lane 375
Spring Parade 69
Spring River Flows East 68
Spy in Black, The 289
Spy, The 95
Spy Who Came in from the Cold, The 6, 28, 54
Squall, The 148, 211
Square Dance 358
Stacking 140
Stagecoach 125, 264, 342, 389, 392
Stage Door 8, 157, 318
Stage Fright 93, 160, 335
Staircase 100
Stairway to Heaven 289
Stakeout 41
Stalag 17 142, 255, 267, 292, 400
Stalker 356
Stamboul Quest 212
Stammheim 38
Stand-In 165
Stand by Me 370
Standing Room Only 328
Stand Up and Fight 389
Stanley and Livingstone 113, 231

Star Chamber, The 102, 374
Stardust Memories 7, 9, 139
Star is Born, A 79, 224, 395
Star of Midnight 201
Star of the Sea 353
Stars 108, 333
Stars and Bars 244
Stars in My Crown 383
Stars Look Down, The 169, 309
Star Spangled Rhythm 350
Star, The 85
Star Trek IV – the Voyage Home 344
Star Trek: the Motion Picture 280
Star Wars 125, 147, 344
Star Witness, The 401
State Fair 12, 150
State of Siege 189, 235
State of the Union 62, 111, 156, 367
State of Things, The 381
Stavisky 32, 312
Steamboat Bill, Jr 188
Steaming 210
Steel Trap, The 29
Stekly 380
Stella Dallas 237, 343, 357, 383
Stepfather, The 331
Stepford Wives, The 317
Steptoe and Son 358
Sterile Cuckoo, The 321
Sticky Fingers 341
Still of the Night 349
Sting, The 50, 164, 244, 274, 354
St Louis Blues 341
St Martin's Lane 83, 199, 203
Stolen Kisses 371
Stolen Life, A 85
Stone Wedding 108
Stop Making Sense 318
Storm in a Teacup 98, 203
Storm Over Asia 47, 178, 296
Storm Warning 336
Storm Within, The 120
Stormy Monday 64
Stormy Weather 379
Story of a Cheat, The 190
Story of Adèle H, The 372
Story of Alexander Graham Bell, The 123, 175, 406
Story of a Love Affair 17
Story of G.I. Joe, The 395
Story of Gilbert and Sullivan, The 10
Story of Louis Pasteur, The 92, 175, 263

Story of the Late
  Crysanthemums, The 3, 232
Story of Vernon and Irene
  Castle, The 22
Strada, La 120, 268
Straight Time 161
Strange Affair of Uncle Harry,
  The 336
Strange Boarders 31
Strange Cargo 78, 132
Strange Incident 123, 395
Strange Love of Martha Ivers,
  The 101, 346
Strange Ones, The 184
Strange One, The 41
Strange Place to Meet, A 257
Strangers 321
Stranger's Hand, The 145
Strangers on a Train 159
Strangers When We Meet 101
Stranger, The 225, 313, 384, 394
Strawberry Blonde, The 57, 86,
  391
Straw Dogs 160
Stray Dog 194
Streamers 10
Street Angel 69, 261
Streetcar Named Desire, A 50,
  187, 203, 267
Street of Chance 290
Street of Shame 232
Street of Sorrow 134, 281
Street of Sorrow, The 134, 259,
  281
Streetwise 196
Strictly Confidential 162, 212
Strike (Sergei Eisenstein) 110, 369
Strike, The (Karel Stekly) 380
Stroke of Midnight, The 47
Stromboli 321, 376
Stronger Than the Night 108
Strong Man, The 62, 128
Stroszek 157
Struggle, The 146
Student of Prague, The 120
Student Prince, The 212
Study in Terror, A 179
St Valentine's Day Massacre 232
Subject Was Roses, The 272
Subway 287, 351
Such a Pretty Little Beach 158,
  327
Sudden Fear 78
Sudden Fortune of the Poor
  People of Kombach, The
  325, 386
Sudden Impact 108
Suddenly Last Summer 156, 220

Sugarbaby 352
Sugarland Express 258, 342
Suicide Squadron 239
Suitor, The 177
Sullivan's Travels 104, 233, 350,
  368
Summer 319, 382
Summer Affair, A 207
Summer at Grandpa's, A 115
Summer Interlude 33
Summer Lightning 325, 386
Summer Madness 156, 203, 321
Summer Manoeuvres 71
Summer Stock 189
Summertime 156, 203, 321
Summertree 102
Summer with Monika 14, 33,
  100
Sunday, Bloody Sunday 28,
  161, 324
Sunday Daughters 410
Sunday in September, A 14
Sundays and Cybèle 208, 270
Sundowners, The 298, 409
Sunflower 225
Sunrise 238, 262
Sunset 352
Sunset Boulevard 7, 38, 352, 400
Sunshine Boys, The 253, 274
Sun Shines Bright, The 126
Supergrass, The 206
Superman 51, 95, 352
Superman II 352
Supernatural 208
Surrender 58
Susana 54, 221
Susan and God 80, 310
Susan Lenox: Her Fall and Rise
  134
Suspect (Peter Yates) 3
Suspect, The (Robert Siodmak)
  45, 199
Suspicion 64, 124, 142, 264
Suspiria 136, 218
Suzanne's Profession 319
Suzy 44
Svengali 353
Swallows and Amazons 67
Swamp Water 311
Swanee River 341
Swann in Love 325
Sweet Bird of Youth 7, 270, 352
Sweet Charity 13, 246
Sweet Hearts Dance 338
Sweet Liberty 2
Sweet Life, The 60, 98, 121, 225
Sweet Lorraine 163
Sweet Smell of Success 42, 394

Swimmer, The 104, 164
Swindlers, The 121, 354
Swindle, The 121, 354
Swing High Swing Low 239
Swing Shift 39
Swing Time 13, 22, 346
Swiss Family Robinson, The 176
Swissmakers, The 170
Swiss Miss 201
Switchboard Operator, The 108
Switching Channels 159, 358,
  373
Sword in the Stone, The 116,
  216
Sylvia and the Ghost 136
Sylvia and the Phantom 136
Sylvia Scarlett 79, 142, 156, 341
Symphonie Fantastique 30, 73

T

Tabu 238
Tailor's Son, The 89
Take a Letter, Darling 3, 328
Take Me Out to the Ball Game
  99, 189
Take the Money and Run 9, 29,
  168, 408
Taking Off 126, 283
Taking of Pelham 123, The 352
Tale of the Crucified Lovers, The
  232
Tale of Two Cities, A 92, 127
Tales of Beatrix Potter 83
Tales of Hoffman, The 289
Tales of Manhattan 316
Talk of the Town, The 142, 315,
  346
Talk Radio 300
Tall Guy, The 223
Tamarind Seed, The 397
Taming of the Shrew, The 55,
  114, 329
Tampopo 26
Targets 186
Tartuffe 180, 238
Tarzan and His Mate 352
Tarzan and the Valley of Gold
  372
Tarzan, the Ape Man 303, 353
Taste of Honey, A 28, 356
Taste of Water, A 297
Taxi Driver 61, 87, 326
Taxing Woman II, A 158
Tchaikovsky 73
Tea and Sympathy 16, 229
Teacher's Pet 132
Teahouse of the August Moon,
  The 50

Telephone Box, The 362
Tell England 21
Tell Me Lies 289
Tell No Tales 291
Tell Them Willie Boy is Here 308
Tempest, The 329
Temptress, The 134
Tenant, The 286, 368
Ten Commandments, The 253
Ten Days That Shook the World 110, 315
Ten Days' Wonder 395
Tender Age, The 248
Tender Comrade 357
Tender Enemy, The 226, 260
Tenderloin 81
Tender Mercies 48, 115, 277
Ten Little Niggers 68, 71
Tennessee Johnson 93
Ten Rillington Place 23, 238, 337, 359
Ten Tall Men 303
Tenth Victim, The 225
Tenue de Soirée 88, 372
Terminus 324
Term of Trial 50, 256
Terms of Endearment 119, 245, 277
Terra Trema, La 376, 384
Terror by Night 305
Terror of Tiny Town, The 396
Tess 286, 360
Testament of Dr Cordelier, The 30, 311
Testament of Dr Mabuse, The 197
Testament of Orpheus, The 310
Testimony 73
Test Pilot 132
Texas Chainsaw Massacre, The 219
Thank You, Jeeves 55
Thank Your Lucky Stars 296
Thark 154
That Certain Age 208
That Cold Day in the Park 10
That Hamilton Woman 203, 222, 243, 256
That Man from Rio 32
That Man Reuter 175, 316
That Mothers Might Live 409
That Night in Rio 330
That Obscure Object of Desire 54, 250, 375
That's Entertainment 16, 350
That's Entertainment II 16, 350
That's Life 204, 227

That Touch of Mink 143, 328
That Uncertain Feeling 239, 390
The Amityville Horror 218
Theatre of Blood 190, 360
Theatre Royal 221
Them! 324
Theme, The 38
Them Thar Hills 200
Theodora Goes Wild 402
Theorem 284
There's Always Tomorrow 346
Thérèse 63, 74, 323
Thérèse Desqueyroux 248
Thérèse Raquin 63, 412
There's No Business Like Show Business 13, 379
There Was a Crooked Man 101, 221
There Was a Father 119
These Three 211, 402
They All Kissed the Bride 78
They Died with Their Boots On 86, 391
They Don't Wear Black Tie 369
They Drive by Night (Raoul Walsh) 49, 391
They Drive by Night (Arthur Woods) 258, 371
They Got Me Covered 6
They Knew What They Wanted 199, 208
They Live by Night 305
They Loved Life 20, 251, 389
They're a Weird Mob 289
They Saved Hitler's Brain 372
They Shoot Horses, Don't They? 83, 124, 273
They Wanted to Live 286, 312
They Were Expendable 125, 392
They Were Five 131, 312
They Won't Forget 202
Thief of Bagdad, The 19, 114, 289, 390
Thief of Paris, The 32, 217
Thieves' Highway 84
Thieves Like Us 10, 318
Thing from Another World, The 155
Things Change 216
Things to Come 130, 363
Thing, The 155
Thin Man Goes Home, The 290, 361
Thin Man, The 52, 211, 290, 298, 361
Third Key, The 287
Third Lover, The 24, 65

Third Man, The 27, 59, 145, 184, 308, 361, 394
Thirst 34
Thirteen Days in France 152
Thirteen Women 212
Thirty-Nine Steps, The 6, 56, 98, 159
Thirty Seconds over Tokyo 202
This Gun for Hire 145, 148
This Happy Breed 150, 202
This is Korea 125
This is Spinal Tap 362
This is the Army 13
This Land is Mine 64, 199, 255
This Man is News 335
This Man Must Die 65
This Man Reuter 92
This Sporting Life 377
This Strange Passion 5, 54, 234
This Sweet Sickness 88, 209
Thistles of Baragan, The 108
Thomas Crown Affair, The 316
Thomas, Gerald 249
Thomas Graal's Best Film 47
Those Daring Young Men in Their Jaunty Jalopies 388
Those Magnificent Men in Their Flying Machines or How I Flew from London to Paris in 25 Hours and 11 Minutes 363, 388
Thousand and One Nights, A 18, 284, 302, 334
Thousand Clowns, A 244, 271
Thousand Eyes of Dr Mabuse, The 197
Thousands Cheer 350
Thou Shalt Honour Thy Wife 47
Three Ages, The 174, 187
Three Caballeros, The 294
Three Cases of Murder 355
Three Coins in the Fountain 320
Three Comrades 8
Three Days of the Condor 22
Three Faces of Eve, The 260, 269
Three Godfathers 280
Three Little Words 23
Three Men and a Baby 27
Three Men and a Cradle 27
Three Musketeers, The 114, 188, 302
Three on a Weekend 309
Threepenny Opera, The 182, 282
Three Sisters, The 336
Three Smart Girls 336
Three Smart Girls Grow Up 336
Three Strange Loves 34
Three Weird Sisters, The 390

Three who Were Doomed, The 26, 47
Three Women 10
Throne of Blood 194
Through a Glass Darkly 14, 33, 270
Throw Momma from the Train 331, 402
Thunderball 6, 73
Thunderbird Six 344, 353
Thunderbolt 50
Thunderbolt and Lightfoot 109
Thunder Over Mexico 110
Thunder Rock 206
THX 1138 75
Thy Soul Shall Bear Witness 47
Ticket to Tomahawk, A 389
Tiger Bay 189
Tiger of Eschnapur, The 197
Tiger Shark 155
Tight Little Island 327
Till Clouds Roll By 13, 341
Tille and Gus 121
Time Bandits 73, 340, 363
Time Flies 363
Time for Revenge, A 41
Time Machine, The 247, 345, 363
Time of Destiny 314
Time of Your Life, The 8, 57
Time to Die, A 313
Time to Live and a Time to Die, A (Louis Malle) 105, 217
Time to Live and the Time to Die, The (Hou Hsaiohsien) 18
Time without Pity 210
Tin Drum, The 61, 276, 325, 340
Tin Pan Alley 315
Tire-au-Flanc 19, 311
Titanic 193
Titfield Thunderbolt, The 135, 368
Tit for Tat 200
Toast of New York, The 41, 207, 407
Tobacco Road 126, 143
To Bed … or Not to Bed 36
To Begin Again 277
To Be or Not to Be 208, 212, 237
To Catch a Thief 142, 160, 182, 370
Today We Live 155, 315
To Each His Own 48, 86, 237, 265
To Have and Have Not 41, 49, 64, 155
To Joy 4

To Kill a Mockingbird 198, 270
To Kill a Priest 237
Tokyo Story 5
To Live 119, 194
Tomb of Ligeia, The 353
Tom Brown's Schooldays 16, 411
Tom Jones 10, 28, 270, 364
Tommy 45
Tomorrow is My Turn 381
Tom Thumb 229
Toni 311
Tonight's the Night 175, 298
Too Hot to Handle 132
Too Many Chefs 313
Too Many Husbands 44
Tootsie 160, 277, 340, 369
To Our Loves 5, 207
To Paris with Love 147
Topaz 71, 248
Topaze 357
Top Hat 22, 363
Topkapi 84, 182, 271
Topper 136, 142
Topper Returns 136
Top Secret! 72, 283
Tora! Tora! Tora! 254, 282
Torch Song 78
Torch Song Trilogy 161, 341
Torment 146, 356
Torn Curtain 72, 160, 245
Tosca, La 260, 384
To Sir with Love 357, 358
To the Devil a Daughter 91
To the Victor 97
Touch of Class, A 231, 274, 330, 361
Touch of Evil 93, 227, 394
Touch of Zen, A 173
Touch, The 33
Tout Va Bien 137, 236
Tovarich 247
Towed in a Hole 200
Towering Inferno, The 22, 192
Tower of Evil 206
Tower of London 186, 304
Tower of Terror, The 206
Town Like Alice, A 292
Toys in the Attic 337
Track 29 217
Trading Places 297, 320
Traffic 235
Tragedy of a Ridiculous Man, The 39
Tragedy of a Switchboard Operator, The 108
Trail of the Lonesome Pine, The 123

Trains, Planes and Automobiles 251
Train, The 368
Tramp, The 65, 368
Tramp, Tramp, Tramp 62, 78, 128
Transports of Death, The 332
Trapeze 69, 309
Travelling North 104
Travels with My Aunt 79, 145, 339
Traviata, La 260
Treasure Island 67, 259, 369
Treasure of the Sierra Madre, The 49, 139, 166, 266
Tree Grows in Brooklyn, A 150, 187, 265
Tree of Wooden Clogs, The 61, 118
Trial and Error 23
Trial of Joan of Arc, The 51
Trials of Oscar Wilde, The 77
Trial, The (G W Pabst) 281
Trial, The (Orson Wells) 394
Trio 355
Trip to Bountiful, The 277, 310, 397
Trip to the Moon, A 107, 344
Tristana 54, 87
Triumph of the Will 133, 257
Trouble in Paradise 182, 212, 370
Trouble in Store 334
Trouble with Harry, The 160, 176, 370
Trouts, The 37
True Confessions 44, 53, 88
True Grit 272, 393
True Heart Susie 137
True Stories 288
Tucker: the Man and His Dreams 76
Tugboat Annie 202, 259
Tunes of Glory 19, 147
Turning Point, The 83, 93
Turtle Diary 31, 373
TV 219, 377
Twelve Angry Men 36, 123, 214, 373
Twelve O'Clock High 266, 363
Twentieth Century 50, 155, 208, 354
Twenty-One Days 2
20,000 Leagues Under the Sea 345, 351
20,000 Years in Sing Sing 81, 84, 367

Twenty-Three Paces to Baker Street 45
25 Fireman's Street 307
Twice in a Lifetime 227
Twice Two 200
Twins 374
Twin Sisters of Kyoto 374
Two-Faced Woman 80, 134, 330
Two Cents Worth of Hope 39, 59
Two Daughters 306
Two English Girls 184, 372
Two for the Road 99, 361
Two for the Seesaw 244
Two Girls and a Sailor 315
Two Lane Black Top 64
Two Minds for Murder 11
Two Mrs Carrolls, The 50, 190, 346
Two Mules for Sister Sara 109
Two of Us, The 255
Two or Three Things I Know About Her 137
Two Pennyworth of Hope 39
Two Pennyworth Worth of Hope 59
Two Rode Together 126, 348
Two Smart People 84
2001: a Space Odyssey 174, 194, 344, 355
Two Way Stretch 98
Two Weeks in Another Town 101, 229, 317
Two Women 89, 270

U

U-Boat 29 289
Ugetsu 232, 304
Ugetsu Monogatari 232, 304
Ulysses 158, 175
Umberto D 89, 253, 376
Umbrellas of Cherbourg, The 60, 87, 174
Unbearable Lightness of Being, The 6, 211
Uncle Harry 336
Uncle Tom's Cabin 107
Unconventional Linda 80
Under Capricorn 35, 52
Undercurrent 229, 249
Under Milk Wood 55
Under Satan's Sun 62, 88
Under the Clock 229, 244, 300
Under the Roofs of Paris 63, 70
Under Two Flags 303
Underworld 385
Underworld USA 314
Unearthly Powers 345
Unfaithfully Yours 64, 350

Unfaithful Wife, The 24, 65
Unfinished Dance, The 83
Unfinished Piece for Mechanical Piano 314
Unfinished Piece for Piano Player 314
Unholy Partners 202
Unholy Three 382
Uninvited, The 154, 218
Union Pacific 301, 343
Union Station 301
Unman, Wittering and Zigo 410
Unmarried Woman, An 220, 336
Unsinkable Molly Brown, The 12
Unsuspected, The 300
Untouchables, The 30, 73, 87, 278
Unvanquished, The 18, 306, 381
Up for the Cup 209
Up in Mabel's Room 177
Up Pompeii 358
Up the Down Staircase 357
Up the River 367
Up Tight 230
Usual Unidentified Thieves, The 142, 225
Utamaro and His Five Women 232

V

Vacation from Marriage 99
Vagabonde 70, 368, 382
Valentino 335, 406
Valley of Decision, The 233, 375
Valmont 222
Vampire, The 205
Vampire Lovers, The 103, 218
Vanina Vanini 321
Vanishing Corporal, The 311
Variety 180, 376
Variety Girl 350
Variety Lights 379
Vassa 295
Vaudeville 180, 376
Vera Cruz 227, 364
Verdict (André Cayatte) 132
Verdict, The (Sidney Lumet) 77, 214, 245
Verdict, The (Don Siegel) 209
Veronika Voss 38, 257, 352
Vertigo 160, 283, 347
Very Curious Girl, A 87
Very Happy Alexandre 248, 361
Very Important Person 255
Very Private Affair, A 217
Vessel of Wrath 4, 199, 368
Vice Versa 320
Victim 161

Victoria the Great 234
Victory 58, 166, 224, 255
Victory in Right-Bank Ukraine and the Expulsion of the Germans 102
Victory Through Air Power 117
Vie de Chateau, La 248
Vie est à Nous, La 247, 311
Vieille Fille, La 248, 327
Vietnam, Vietnam 125
Vieux de la Veille, Le 131
View from the Bridge, A 214
Vigil in the Night 208, 249
Vikings, The 101, 302
Viktor und Viktoria 369
Village of the Damned 67, 344
Vincent, François, Paul and the Others 24, 227, 236
Vincent – the Life and Death of Vincent Van Gogh 289
Violette 24
Violette et François 40
Violette Noziere 24, 65
VIPs, The 21, 271, 339
Virgin and the Gypsy, The 148, 201
Virginia City 81, 378
Virgin Soldiers, The 19
Virgin Spring, The 33, 270
Viridiana 54, 60, 74
Visions of Eight 257
Visiteurs du Soir, Les 63, 91
Vivacious Lady 52, 346, 347
Viva Maria 217
Viva Villa 227
Viva Zapata! 50, 187, 227, 267
Vivere in Pace 247
Vivre Sa Vie 137
Volpone 354
Von Ryan's Express 135
Voyage Surprise 177
Vyborg Side, The 18

W

Wages of Fear, The 36, 59, 235, 371
Wagonmaster 125, 389
Waiting Women 34
Wait until Dark 45, 369
Wake of the Red Witch, The 369
Walkabout 198
Walkers on the Tiger's Tail 194
Walking Dead, The 186
Walk in the Sun, A 9, 254
Walk on the Wild Side 53, 124
Walk with Love and Death, A 313

Walls of Malapaga, The 132, 258, 267

Wall Street 102, 139, 278, 405, 407

Walpurgis Night 34

Wannsee Conference, The 332

Wanton Contessa, The 72, 384

War and Peace 123, 243, 272, 322, 383

War is Over, The 236, 312

Warning Shadows 47

Warning Shot 361

War Requiem 162

War Wagon, The 389

Watchmaker of St Paul, The 119

Watch on the Rhine 85, 265

Water 58

Waterless Summer 36

Waterloo 242, 394

Waterloo Bridge 202, 203

Watership Down 116

Waxworks 178, 180, 376

Way Ahead, The 8, 19, 309

Way Down East 136, 146

Way of All Flesh, The 180, 261

Way of Love 109

Way Out West 201, 392

Ways of Love 321

Way to the Stars, The 21, 363

Way We Were, The 100

Web of Passion 32, 65

Wedding, A (Robert Altman) 10, 137, 177, 394

Wedding, The (Andrej Wajda) 394

Wedding Bells 23, 99

Wedding in Blood 24, 65

Wedding March, The 72, 234, 386

We Dive at Dawn 21, 351

Weekend, Le 137

Week's Holiday, A 235

Wee Willie Winkie 126, 301

Well Groomed Bride, The 86

Went the Day Well? 145

We're No Angels 82, 304

We're Not Married 234, 319

Werther 261

Westerner, The 74, 264, 402

Westfront 1918 9, 254, 281

West Side Story 244, 270

Westward Ho the Wagons 389

Westworld 317

Wetherby 26, 38

We Think the World of You 223

Whales of August, The 85, 137

What a Man 122

What a Way to Go 244

Whatever Happened to Aunt Alice? 397

Whatever Happened to Baby Jane? 78, 84

What Lola Wants 100

What Price Glory? 315, 390, 391

What Price Hollywood? 79, 354, 389

What's New Pussycat? 9

What's Up, Doc? 52, 223

What's Up, Tiger Lily? 9

When Comedy Was King 16

When Father Was Away on Business 62, 120

When Harry Met Sally … 220

When Ladies Meet 212

When My Baby Smiles at Me 379

When the Wind Blows 111, 117

When Time Ran Out 252

When Tomorrow Comes 389

When We are Married 394

When Willie Comes Marching Home 39

When Worlds Collide 111

Where Chimneys are Seen 233

Where Do We Go from Here? 363

Where Eagles Dare 55, 108

Where's Poppa? 295

Where the Green Ants Dream 198

Where the River Bends 241, 347

While the City Sleeps 159, 197

While the Sun Shines 21

Whipsaw 212

Whirlpool 167

Whisky Galore 327

Whisperers, The 253

Whistle Blower, The 77

Whistle Down the Wind 23, 67

White Cargo 303

White Christmas 69, 81

White Cliffs of Dover, The 294

White Heat 57, 233, 391

White Hell of Pitz-Palu, The 281

White Mischief 52, 279

White Nights 100, 101, 103, 225, 384

White Sheik, The 121

White Tower, The 231

White White Boy, A 356

White Woman 208

White Zombie 207, 213

Who Framed Roger Rabbit? 117, 372, 396

Who is Harry Kellerman and Why is He Saying Those Terrible Things about Me? 362

Who is Killing the Great Chefs of Europe? 313

Whole Town's Talking, The 170, 316

Who'll Stop the Rain? 105

Whoops Apocalypse 111

Who's Afraid of Virginia Woolf? 54, 245, 271

Who Saw Him Die? 37

Why Does Herr R Run Amok? 118, 326

Why We Fight 62

Why Worry? 128

Wicked Lady, The 398

Wifemistress 226

Wife of Pharaoh, The 180

Wife Versus Secretary 151, 211, 328

Wildcat, The 213

Wild Child, The 371

Wild Game 308

Wild Heart, The 289, 360

Wild One, The 51, 238

Wild Orchids 134

Wild River 187

Wild Strawberries 2, 33, 36, 110, 178, 310, 397

Wild Women of Wongo 372

Will o' the Wisp 105, 217

Willy Wonka and the Chocolate Factory 140

Wilson 287, 407

Wilt 228

Winchester 73 347

Wind, The 349, 398

Wind Across the Everglades 306

Wind Bloweth Where It Listeth, The 51

Window, The 206, 401

Wings 46, 261, 363, 395

Wings in the Dark 212

Wings of Desire 15, 35, 396

Wings of the Morning 123, 148

Winner Take All 57

Winnie the Pooh and the Honey Tree 116

Winning 64

Winslow Boy, The 21, 99

Winter Light 33, 383

Wish You Were Here 5, 328

Witchcraft Through the Ages 47, 400

Witches, The 355

Witches of Eastwick, The 246, 400
Witches of Salem, The 236, 400
Witchfinder General 400
Withnail & I 109
Without a Clue 58, 163
Without Anaesthesia 390
Without Love 367, 397
Without Reservations 393
Witness 125, 401
Witness for the Prosecution 68, 77, 93, 199
Wiz, The 401
Wizard of Oz, The 112, 401
Wolf at the Door, The 20
Wolf Man, The 213, 218, 324
Woman 109, 321
Woman Alone, A 106
Woman and the Stranger, The 38
Woman in a Dressing Gown 307, 377
Woman in Green, The 305
Woman in His House, The 212
Woman in the Dunes 89
Woman in the Moon, The 197
Woman in the Window, The 2, 197, 316
Woman is a Woman, A 32, 138
Woman Next Door, The 88, 314
Woman of Paris, A 66
Woman of the Dunes 89
Woman of the Year 156, 220, 346, 367
Woman on the Beach, The 43, 307, 311
Woman or Two, A 52
Woman Rebels, A 156
Woman's Face, A 78, 80
Woman's Secret, A 306
Woman's World 41, 304
Women in Love 201, 273
Women of Dolwyn, The 390
Women, The 8, 80, 124
Wonderful Country, The 241
Wonderful to be Young 296
Wooden Horse, The 292
Woodstock 318, 326
Woo Woo Kid, The 253
Words and Music 341
Words of Max, The 37
Word, The 381
Working Class Goes to Heaven, The 61
Working Girl (Mike Nichols) 125, 245, 405

Working Girls (Lizzie Borden) 31, 53
World According to Garp, The 237, 399, 402
World and his Wife, The 62, 111, 156, 367
World Apart, A 79
World of Apu, The 18, 306
World of Henry Orient, The 115
Would Be Gentlemen, The 297
Woyzeck 157
Written on the Wind 268
WR – Mysteries of the Organism 108
Wrong Again 215
Wrong Box, The 56, 388
Wrong Man, The 123, 159
Wrong Movement 326, 396
WUSA 244
Wuthering Heights 54, 222, 256, 402

X

Xala 81, 308, 404
Xanadu 189

Y

Yank at Oxford, A 203, 349
Yankee Doodle Dandy 57, 81, 264, 406
Yankee in King Arthur's Court, A 363
Yanks 324
Yearling, The 15
Year of Living Dangerously, The 277, 291
Year of the Dragon, The 198
Year of the Quiet Sun, A 382
Years Between, The 106
Yeelen 216
Yellow Earth 68
Yellow Rolls Royce, The 21, 355
Yellow Submarine 117
Yentl 183, 369
Yesterday Girl 72
Yesterday, Today and Tomorrow 89, 176, 225, 271
Yield to the Night 292
Yojimbo 148, 194
Yol 61
Yolanda and the Thief 23, 229
You Can't Cheat an Honest Man 121
You Can't Sleep Here 143, 155, 279, 320
You Can't Take it with You 62, 263, 330, 347

You'll Never Get Rich 22
Young and Innocent 160, 258
Young and the Damned, The 53, 259, 308
Young and the Passionate, The 121
Young Cassidy 122, 339
Young Dr Kildare 162
Young Frankenstein 283
Young Guns 314
Young in Heart 354
Young Ladies of Wilko, The 314
Young Lions, The 51
Young Man of Manhattan 318
Young Man of Music 101
Young Man with a Horn 101
Young Mr Lincoln 123, 125, 242
Young Mr Pitt 7, 99, 309
Young Ones, The 296
Young Scarface 23, 144
Young Sherlock Holmes 163, 302
Young Sherlock Holmes and the Pyramid of Fear 163, 302
Young Stranger, The 172
Young Tom Edison 175
Young Törless 325
Young Winston 23
Young Wolves, The 63
Young Woodley 410
You Only Live Once 123, 197
You're a Big Boy Now 75
You're Darn Tootin' 129, 199
Your Past is Showing 45
You Were Never Lovelier 22
Yoyo 112

Z

Z 235, 273
Zabriskie Point 17
Zazie 217, 248
Zed and Two Noughts, A 373
Zelig 9, 408
Zéro de Conduite 410
Zero Hour 192
Ziegfeld Follies, The 12, 23, 189, 229, 291
Ziggy Stardust and the Spiders from Mars 318
Zoltan, Hound of Dracula 218
Zoo in Budapest 373
Zorba the Greek 251, 271
Zouzou 131
Zulu 52
Zvenigora 102

INDEX OF PEOPLE AND THEMES

A

Abbott, Bud 19, 374
Academics 21, 47, 48, 55, 58, 70, 77, 78, 84, 96, 99, 102, 110, 120, 111, 132, 155, 160, 165, 173, 178, 187, 194, 204, 205, 207, 213, 224, 225, 227, 245, 248, 250, 271, 281, 295, 296, 306, 314, 332, 338, 346, 347, 371, 385, 387, 397, 411
Actors and actresses 2, 7, 14, 22, 33, 38, 40, 55, 58, 68, 71, 72, 78, 80, 84, 85, 92, 93, 111, 122, 129, 155, 156, 157, 160, 163, 165, 171, 188, 199, 203, 205, 208, 210, 212, 213, 231, 232, 251, 256, 257, 262, 263, 266, 267, 275, 276, 277, 295, 299, 300, 302, 310, 312, 320, 324, 328, 335, 339, 346, 347, 352, 354, 371, 360, 389, 396, 409
Adjani, Isabelle 40, 49, 88, 157, 161, 282, 286, 351, 372, 398
Adultery 2, 3, 24, 31, 33, 45, 52, 54, 60, 72, 86, 87, 100, 115, 122, 137, 156, 157, 183, 189, 205, 220, 225, 244, 245, 260, 262, 287, 290, 296, 310, 313, 330, 348, 349, 368, 377, 382, 383, 385, 396
Agents and double agents 1, 3, 5, 9, 16, 21, 24, 28, 31, 48, 49, 54, 56, 57, 65, 67, 71, 72, 73, 77, 78, 95, 102, 108, 122, 134, 138, 142, 145, 156, 159, 160, 163, 165, 166, 170, 184, 188, 189, 197, 203, 206, 208, 209, 211, 212, 235, 242, 248, 251, 254, 256, 283, 289, 291, 299, 308, 312, 331, 332, 335, 346, 347, 357, 367, 385, 394, 397
Aimée, Anouk 48, 60, 98, 109, 189, 214, 272, 314
Albert, Edward 287, 403
Aldrich, Robert 45, 78, 85, 86, 89, 96, 205, 227, 253, 254, 348, 364
Aliens 71, 81, 112, 252, 280, 342, 344, 345, 362, 371, 372, 397
Allégret, Marc 45, 131, 201, 282
Allégret, Yves 158, 327, 409
Allen, Woody 7, 9, 15, 29, 33, 40, 58, 64, 110, 115, 139, 168, 188, 194, 220, 223, 227, 244, 275, 278, 283, 314, 326, 329, 336, 349, 408
Allyson, June 13, 180, 188, 202, 304, 315, 336, 347, 350
Altman, Robert 9, 37, 44, 60, 137, 162, 177, 260, 318, 394, 408
Ambler, Eric 19, 64, 84, 209
Ameche, Don 12, 123, 164, 170, 175, 210, 213, 216, 252, 263, 278, 293, 297, 308, 320, 330, 336, 341, 397
Anderson, Judith 391
Anderson, Lindsay 16, 60, 85, 97, 137, 162, 257, 377, 410
Anderson, Michael 23, 155, 268, 288, 362, 388
Andersson, Bibi 14, 15, 26, 33, 34, 91, 189, 320, 328, 397
Andersson, Harriet 14, 33, 115, 270, 310
Andrews, Dana 39, 71, 124, 159, 187, 197, 231, 293, 315, 357, 374
Andrews, Julie 11, 72, 74, 117, 160, 204, 245, 249, 271, 340, 397
Animals 5, 15, 23, 44, 51, 60, 66, 67, 68, 71, 83, 87, 102, 116, 117, 126, 137, 151, 154, 158, 162, 191, 228, 229, 230, 257, 267, 274, 288, 292, 295, 298, 303, 309, 339, 353, 373, 380, 392
Annakin, Ken 30, 63, 144, 145, 150, 163, 174, 176, 254, 255, 355, 363, 388
Annaud, Jean-Jacques 73, 275, 313
Antonioni, Michelangelo 17, 24, 36, 60, 169, 225, 348, 376, 381
Aristocrats and nobles 11, 12, 17, 19, 22, 24, 32, 35, 48, 59, 76, 77, 78, 80, 86, 87, 91, 92, 94, 98, 99, 101, 104, 106, 118, 121, 127, 131, 134, 141, 143, 148, 156, 161, 164, 165, 170, 176, 179, 183, 194, 201, 202, 205, 208, 212, 218, 225, 226, 228, 229, 232, 240, 243, 246, 247, 248, 252, 258, 260, 269, 279, 281, 284, 289, 296, 300, 302, 305, 306, 308, 309, 311, 313, 314, 316, 322, 325, 326, 328, 330, 334, 337, 343, 346, 354, 363, 365, 375, 383, 390, 394
Arletty 63, 111, 182, 373
Arliss, George 76, 169, 243, 262, 287, 339
Armstrong, Louis 181
Army life 13, 14, 17, 18, 19, 21, 26, 35, 48, 51, 54, 57, 58, 67, 69, 71-74, 72, 75, 76, 77, 78, 82, 89, 94, 96, 99, 100, 101, 102, 108, 109, 120, 134, 136, 137, 141, 147, 148, 155, 157, 166, 171, 172, 173, 189, 194, 200, 201, 202, 203, 224, 228, 240, 242, 243, 246, 257, 260, 261, 267, 282, 293, 294, 300, 301, 302, 314, 318, 324-326, 329, 331, 344, 350, 356, 358, 372, 378, 382, 384, 385, 387, 389, 390, 392, 397, 398, 400, 409
Arthur, Jean 35, 41, 44, 52, 55, 62, 94, 96, 142, 148, 154, 155, 170, 228, 263, 265, 284, 290, 291, 315, 316, 328, 330, 333, 346, 347, 350, 362, 400
Artists 12, 19, 20, 34, 38, 47, 50, 51, 66, 70, 81, 88, 93, 100, 101, 103, 122, 136, 139, 147, 154, 160, 163, 166, 178, 189, 190, 196, 197, 198, 210–212, 218, 224, 228, 229, 232, 250, 260, 267, 268, 283, 288, 289, 290, 309, 315, 316, 335, 355–357, 359, 362, 369, 370, 383, 387, 395, 397, 403, 406
Arzner, Dorothy 20, 69, 156, 224, 350, 399, 409
Ashby, Hal 8, 16, 120, 123, 143, 144, 236, 245, 253, 274–276, 299, 384
Asquith, Anthony 21, 77, 86, 99, 130, 153, 165, 202, 256, 271, 297, 314, 329, 332, 335, 339, 351, 355, 363
Assassination 20, 27, 38, 39, 40, 42, 50, 53, 72, 87, 95, 108, 119, 138, 145, 146, 166, 169, 197, 201, 204, 213, 216, 237, 246, 254, 259, 260, 278, 288, 298, 305, 308, 313, 321, 326, 329, 331, 334, 363, 370, 372, 386, 396, 409
Astaire, Fred 12, 13, 16, 22, 68, 75, 78, 83, 99, 111, 121, 124,

189, 225, 229, 247, 291, 296, 318, 330, 346, 350, 351, 358, 363

Astor, Mary 27, 49, 84, 114, 132, 151, 164, 264, 282, 290, 316, 388, 397, 402

Attenborough, Richard 9, 13, 19, 20, 23, 29, 31, 52, 77, 79, 89, 102, 133, 144, 145, 169, 180, 182, 201, 208, 243, 254, 256, 276, 292, 301, 316, 339, 359, 382, 393

Atwill, Lionel 81, 93, 163, 212, 213, 250

Audran, Stéphane 23, 26, 65, 94, 247

Australia 2, 25, 35, 52, 97, 104, 135, 152, 162, 198, 201, 247, 249, 280, 289, 291, 298, 349, 351, 360, 362, 369, 409

Autant-Lara, Claude 131, 136, 182, 201, 283, 291, 295, 389

Avildsen, John G. 204, 274, 275, 318, 356

Ayres, Lew 8, 86, 96, 134, 162, 287, 374

B

Bacall, Lauren 41, 50, 119, 139, 145, 155, 171, 228, 229, 234, 268, 301, 304, 341, 348, 393, 408

Bacon, Lloyd 20, 27, 49, 57, 152, 232, 234, 294, 296, 316, 331, 335, 371

BAFTA 27, 217

Baker, Roy 23, 27, 64, 103, 140, 181, 193, 206, 292, 343, 351

Baker, Stanley 52, 210, 371

Bancroft, Anne 45, 83, 124, 141, 161, 204, 205, 231, 249, 270, 338, 341, 352, 373

Banks 29, 32, 46, 63, 76, 78, 118, 122, 132, 136, 142, 145, 170, 177, 180, 197, 207, 214, 227, 231, 244, 276, 278, 290, 304, 305, 315, 316, 331, 332, 377, 386, 393, 405, 407

Barrault, Jean-Louis 29, 63, 73, 77, 111, 127, 311, 326

Barrymore, John 50, 80, 110, 157, 162, 164, 221, 353, 354, 357, 397, 402

Barrymore, Lionel 20, 53, 58, 62, 96, 132, 134, 137, 146, 151, 155, 162, 166, 177, 208, 213, 224, 228, 233, 262, 263,

266, 317, 338, 347, 350, 375, 385, 391

Bartholomew, Freddie 67, 263, 300, 304, 366

Basinger, Kim 74, 307

Bates, Alan 23, 36, 61, 67, 201, 210, 211, 223, 251, 259, 273, 300, 324, 336, 356, 359, 360, 370, 374, 377

Baxter, Anne 7, 155, 197, 216, 265, 389

Baxter, Warner 35, 126, 162, 212, 224, 262, 296, 327, 337, 353, 391

Baye, Nathalie 138, 176, 235, 313, 366, 371

Beatles, The 117, 150, 236, 288, 362, 408

Beatty, Warren 9, 15, 22, 144, 161, 171, 187, 188, 203, 245, 246, 260, 272, 274, 276, 320

Becker, Jacques 59, 132, 182, 207, 247

Bed and board 4, 8, 21, 23, 30, 157, 178, 179, 189, 200, 248, 269, 286, 318, 325, 356, 363, 367, 371, 373, 409

Beery, Wallace 67, 114, 151, 202, 206, 227, 259, 262, 280, 285, 292, 327, 337, 338, 369, 383, 389, 391, 395

Beineix, Jean-Jacques 40, 88

Belmondo, Jean-Paul 1, 32, 87, 132, 137, 138, 217, 312, 377, 398

Bennett, Constance 79, 136, 142, 164, 183, 354, 389

Bennett, Joan 2, 77, 197, 260, 303, 307, 311, 316, 391, 393

Benton, Robert 77, 118, 160, 279, 307, 378

Bergman, Ingmar 2–4, 9, 14, 15, 26, 33, 34, 36, 91, 100, 103, 110, 115, 120, 146, 178, 206, 216, 239, 260, 270, 277, 297, 310, 320, 328, 356, 361, 383, 397

Bergman, Ingrid 7, 21, 33, 34, 52, 64, 75, 80, 99, 112, 140, 143, 159, 164, 181, 215, 231, 235, 239, 248, 249, 265, 268, 273, 274, 311, 321, 323, 341, 355, 364, 366, 376, 407

Berkeley, Busby 57, 71, 99, 139, 188, 189, 228, 258, 296, 357, 366

Berlin Film Festival 6, 10, 13, 15, 24, 28, 35, 36, 53, 57, 67,

71, 88, 89, 94, 105, 132, 137, 139, 152, 154, 157, 189, 194, 220, 228, 273, 281, 294, 306, 314, 319, 321, 327, 361, 396, 400, 408

Berlin, Irving 13, 22, 363

Berri, Claude 29, 88, 118, 181, 207, 221, 235, 236

Bertolucci, Bernardo 6, 21, 29, 38, 51, 87, 88, 149, 171, 246, 278

Betrayal 1, 39, 47, 48, 50, 57, 62, 72, 80, 137, 142, 147, 168, 200, 205, 213, 221, 222, 225, 227, 230, 232, 263, 267, 292, 296, 316, 321, 326, 339, 384

Big business 32, 35, 41, 75, 122, 145, 178, 197, 207, 208, 214, 263, 274, 276, 278, 290, 297, 313, 315, 316, 320, 357, 383, 393, 405,

Biopics 12, 22, 23, 27, 28, 35, 41, 57, 71, 74, 81, 82, 87, 92, 93, 99, 102, 104, 105, 109, 113, 115, 142, 146, 152, 160, 165, 168, 184, 188, 201, 203, 207, 237, 254, 263, 292, 318, 321, 323, 327, 341, 347, 348, 380, 391, 406

Bitzer, Billy 146, 174

Björnstrand, Gunnar 14, 270

Blier, Bertrand 88, 211, 275, 372

Blondell, Joan 136, 157, 165

Bogarde, Dirk 11, 21, 27, 86, 92, 96, 127, 161, 184, 210, 238, 252, 271, 283, 286, 289, 309, 312, 324, 329, 335, 341, 370, 384

Bogart, Humphrey 1, 4, 20, 30, 41, 42, 49, 50, 64, 81, 82, 85, 89, 115, 133, 139, 146, 152, 155, 165, 166, 171, 182, 188, 201, 209, 210, 220, 224, 232, 234, 243, 244, 266–268, 282, 283, 293, 294, 299, 300, 304, 305, 307, 316, 346, 367, 369, 371, 391, 398, 402, 408

Bogdanovich, Peter 5, 52, 179, 186, 223, 273, 274, 354, 357, 411

Boleslawski, Richard 31, 78, 93, 134, 171, 198, 212, 224, 234, 402, 407

Boorman, John 45, 85, 239, 252, 255, 282, 288, 321, 338

Borowczyk, Walerian 5, 228

Borzage, Frank 8, 69, 74, 75, 78, 93, 132, 162, 249, 261, 262, 294, 347

Boulting, John 19, 23, 99, 144, 169, 175, 201, 349, 382

Boulting, Roy 23, 122, 206, 207, 332, 404

Boyer, Charles 3, 18, 32, 34, 35, 72, 80, 85, 86, 94, 123, 124, 134, 145, 170, 182, 206, 213, 229–231, 234, 243, 247, 249, 250, 258, 260, 265, 284, 332, 341, 357, 365, 389, 400, 403

Brahm, John 11, 30, 216, 230, 293

Brandauer, Klaus Maria 3, 71, 72, 74, 276, 279

Brando, Marlon 17, 33, 38, 50, 51, 66, 133, 134, 138, 158, 187, 203, 214, 220, 221, 227, 230, 232, 238, 258, 267–269, 273, 329, 409

Brennan, Walter 101, 263, 264, 347, 402, 403

Brent, George 31, 49, 84, 85, 118, 134, 171, 198, 209, 212, 232, 264, 295, 301, 343

Bresson, Robert 15, 51, 100, 249, 291

Bridges, James 4, 102, 123, 204, 250, 274, 349

Bridges, Jeff 20, 76, 77, 153, 190, 313, 357, 378

Britain 18, 21, 23, 30, 40, 74, 111, 130, 142, 145, 166, 175, 178, 202, 203, 210, 247, 255, 256, 282, 285, 289, 292, 296, 302, 321, 324, 331, 334, 354, 356, 361, 363, 364, 372, 377, 380, 383, 407

Broadway 13, 23, 57, 90, 102, 105, 115, 139, 151, 165, 188, 213, 272, 274, 284, 304, 375, 379, 394

Brooks, James L. 119, 165, 245, 277, 358

Brooks, Louise 47, 48, 155, 179, 205, 281, 290, 395

Brooks, Mel 296

Brooks, Richard 7, 100, 188, 189, 238, 244, 269, 270, 310, 352, 356

Brothers 2, 11, 23, 36, 38, 40, 43, 44, 54, 56, 68, 74, 75, 88, 93, 99, 100, 128, 132, 134, 138, 146, 155, 156, 161, 162, 163, 164, 167, 174, 190, 194, 197, 208, 214, 216, 232, 233,

246, 257, 258, 260, 270, 271, 276, 278, 284, 289, 290, 293, 298, 300, 302-304, 308, 314, 317, 324, 326, 337, 341, 346, 347, 353, 354, 362, 368, 371, 383, 384, 388, 390, 392, 396

Brown, Clarence 15, 46, 73, 132, 134, 151, 153, 162, 175, 192, 198, 211, 222, 224, 243, 262, 265, 280, 294, 300–302, 304, 322, 328, 338, 374, 375, 380, 383

Browning, Tod 218, 316, 382

Bruce, Nigel 64, 90, 142, 163, 190, 248, 304, 307, 411

Bruckman, Clyde 121, 129, 135, 199, 346, 367

Brynner, Yul 12, 34, 51, 86, 147, 233, 253, 268, 280, 285, 317, 337, 383

Buñuel, Luis 5, 23, 31, 53, 60, 74, 86, 87, 94, 98, 104, 168, 176, 221, 234, 250, 259, 274, 294, 308, 310, 323, 343, 353, 375, 381, 397

Burton, Richard 6, 11, 21, 28, 55, 84, 86, 100, 106, 108, 137, 144, 166, 210, 214, 221, 227, 228, 243, 245, 271, 293, 294, 329, 339, 356

Butler, David 6, 12, 19, 78, 153, 206, 211, 261, 264, 285, 296, 350

Butlers 27, 55, 59, 115, 145, 186, 198, 200, 208, 215, 219, 220, 227, 276, 290, 308, 309, 311, 352

C

Cage, Nicholas 11, 75, 189, 196, 260, 278, 318, 372, 384

Cagney, James 4, 8, 27, 35, 45, 49, 50, 53, 56, 57, 73, 76, 81, 86, 105, 122, 132, 134, 151, 155, 189, 202, 204, 232, 233, 251, 264, 268, 290, 292, 296, 305, 315, 335, 343, 353, 359, 379, 391, 395, 400, 406

Cahiers du Cinéma 1, 63, 65, 137, 311, 319, 371

Caine, Michael 2, 6, 7, 28, 29, 52, 57, 74, 77, 100, 143, 145, 146, 163, 166, 176, 216, 254, 275, 278, 296, 327, 337, 339, 368

Campbell, Eric 257, 286

Canada 10, 81, 113, 165, 256, 289, 305, 308, 357, 364, 383

Cannes Film Festival 32, 40, 59, 72, 89, 108, 119, 132, 136, 138, 147, 204, 211, 226, 243, 253, 312, 325, 338, 356, 386

Capone, Al 30, 73, 87, 122, 134, 155, 168, 232, 278, 316

Capra, Frank 15, 29, 44, 50, 53, 62, 74, 76, 111, 128, 132, 142, 151, 154, 156, 162, 164, 169, 176, 177, 189, 212, 215, 226, 253, 263, 310, 317, 330, 343, 346, 347, 354, 366–368, 383

Cardinale, Claudia 109, 123

Carmichael, Ian 19, 111, 169, 201, 251, 334, 335, 349

Carné, Marcel 30, 63, 91, 111, 131, 158, 182, 226, 373, 412

Caron, Leslie 12, 17, 23, 30, 69, 189, 229, 261, 267, 269, 314, 329

Carpenter, John 191, 219, 295, 314

Carradine, John 190, 342

Cassavetes, John 8, 38, 91, 95, 102, 216, 259, 299, 381

Castro, Fidel 97

Cavalcanti, Alberto 32, 92, 103, 105, 145, 334

Chabrol, Claude 1, 24, 32, 36, 65, 95, 130, 149, 189, 251, 287, 295, 312, 366, 395

Chaffey, Don 66, 97, 182, 239, 292

Chandler, Raymond 11, 41

Chaney, Jr, Lon 127, 144, 158, 213, 218, 324, 382

Chaney, Sr, Lon 57, 148

Chaplin, Charles 7, 44, 51, 65, 66, 69, 105, 106, 129, 139, 151, 170, 187, 196, 199, 200, 233, 257, 286, 293, 368, 385

Charisse, Cyd 22, 83, 247, 306, 335

Chevalier, Maurice 3, 27, 31, 71, 75, 83, 169, 170, 212, 400, 411

Childhood 11, 15, 33, 66, 92, 115, 134, 155, 186, 310, 390, 391, 411

China 8, 11, 18, 29, 31, 39, 63, 67, 75, 93, 99, 112, 136, 146, 151, 189, 231, 243, 263, 277, 278, 282, 285, 300, 306, 343, 357, 368, 385, 396, 407

Christian-Jaque 30, 77, 333, 348, 386

Christie, Agatha 24, 68, 77, 90, 161, 177, 214, 339, 367

Christie, Julie 9, 15, 61, 63, 96, 103, 106, 130, 133, 144, 147, 203, 209, 210, 253, 271, 317, 322, 324, 360, 370, 371, 393

Christmas 68, 81, 115, 166, 175, 199, 208, 266, 270, 319, 334, 343, 346, 349, 350, 359, 382, 397

Churchill, Winston 7, 23, 165, 254, 289, 293

Cimino, Michael 87, 109, 198, 216, 275, 348

Clair, René 63, 68, 70, 83, 94, 98, 103, 106, 112, 120, 139, 158, 177, 181, 190, 224, 228, 233, 248, 291, 320, 348, 369, 373, 375, 393, 400, 401

Clayton, Jack 11, 28, 75, 98, 136, 179, 253, 269, 338, 339

Cleese, John 3, 236, 250, 278, 363

Clément, René 32, 59, 66, 101, 104, 132, 250, 258, 267, 311, 351, 356, 380, 409

Clift, Montgomery 44, 51, 52, 71, 86, 89, 155, 156, 160, 166, 171, 187, 205, 209, 234, 266, 267, 291, 294, 301, 347, 392, 402, 406, 409

Cline, Eddie 16, 29, 121, 122, 187

Close, Glenn 77, 102, 141, 165, 205, 237, 313, 363, 399, 402

Clouzot, Henri-Georges 36, 59, 141, 235, 335, 362, 371, 380, 410

Coburn, Charles 133, 228, 234, 265, 319, 333, 336, 346

Cocteau, Jean 17, 41, 120, 169, 184, 230, 285, 310, 321, 353

Colbert, Claudette 11, 62, 75, 123, 125, 143, 164, 176, 183, 222, 247, 249, 252, 255, 263, 299, 303, 328, 350, 366, 393, 397

Colman, Ronald 4, 10, 11, 19, 63, 76, 79, 92, 109, 126, 127, 142, 169, 170, 202, 212, 221, 266, 285, 302–304, 307, 315, 346, 354, 395

Comencini, Luigi 260

Communism 20, 22, 37, 40, 53, 108, 110, 117, 118, 130, 137, 145, 169, 184, 187, 188, 189, 190, 199, 202, 221, 226, 228, 235, 246, 247, 258, 276, 283,

291, 295, 296, 307, 311, 315, 325, 330, 384, 387

Composers 10, 11, 18, 30, 67, 72, 73, 83, 85, 100, 102, 210, 239, 246, 248, 315, 324, 326, 370, 384, 406

Con man 33, 50, 57, 58, 73, 76, 78, 121, 132, 133, 142, 151, 156, 164, 202, 208, 211, 217, 221, 224, 240, 244, 274, 290, 304, 310, 320, 338, 339, 343, 347, 350, 368, 381, 397, 411

Concentration camps 35, 108, 214, 255, 275, 276, 312, 332, 333, 389, 391, 409

Connery, Sean 6, 7, 30, 58, 73, 87, 95, 159, 161, 166, 214, 234, 278, 285, 313, 315, 342, 363, 369, 371

Conrad, Joseph 17, 224, 243, 309

Conway, Jack 4, 45, 92, 127, 132, 151, 203, 211, 227, 252, 284, 290, 291, 349, 368, 382

Cooper, Gary 18, 34, 35, 41, 48, 60, 62, 74, 93, 112, 140, 154, 155, 158, 162, 165, 171, 184, 197, 208, 212, 216, 224, 227, 240, 249, 254, 263–265, 267, 301, 315, 334, 340, 341, 343, 346, 350, 364, 366, 368, 378, 385, 391, 395, 397, 400, 402, 403

Cooper, Merion C. 14, 190, 192, 304

Coppola, Francis Ford 17, 32, 51, 61, 75, 87, 104, 125, 138, 178, 188, 216, 220, 238, 273, 274, 308, 326, 363, 372, 384, 408

Corman, Roger 75, 91, 186, 207, 210, 232, 237, 245, 280, 326, 333, 353

Cornelius, Henry 162, 209, 388

Costa-Gavras, Constantin 41, 61, 119, 171, 189, 204, 235, 273, 299

Costello, Lou 19, 374

Costner, Kevin 73, 77, 87, 118, 152

Cotten, Joseph 11, 29, 35, 53, 64, 69, 70, 86, 93, 136, 137, 157, 159, 184, 216, 234, 266, 319, 350, 361, 383, 394

Court cases 3, 11, 38, 44, 47, 49, 51, 64, 68, 69, 70, 71, 76, 77, 91, 99, 101, 141, 160, 194, 199, 203, 214, 226, 243, 255, 262, 263, 266, 269, 270, 275,

277, 294, 301, 307, 310, 313, 318, 325, 336, 346, 349, 357, 373, 380, 386, 390, 392, 394, 395, 401

Coward, Noël 23, 58, 71, 136, 137, 145, 146, 149, 150, 202, 212, 243, 262, 294, 308, 375

Crawford, Broderick 18, 42, 50, 76, 121, 197, 216, 266, 409

Crawford, Joan 1, 22, 62, 69, 78, 80, 81, 85, 124, 128, 132, 140, 155, 156, 162, 205, 231, 253, 265, 285, 300, 305, 310, 315, 350, 393, 398

Crichton, Charles 3, 5, 27, 32, 39, 66, 103, 135, 147, 190, 237, 251, 261, 278, 315, 334, 335, 368

Crichton, Michael 315, 317

Cromwell, John 7, 8, 18, 43, 50, 67, 85, 92, 115, 139, 164, 169, 182, 208, 209, 224, 233, 237, 251, 255, 290, 300, 302, 354, 389, 393, 398

Cronenberg, David 345, 374

Cronin, A. J. 96, 169, 208, 359

Crosby, Bing 13, 19, 22, 23, 34, 48, 63, 68, 69, 81, 105, 124, 162, 167, 215, 249, 265, 268, 284, 291, 296, 341, 350, 363, 400, 401

Cukor, George 3, 8, 12, 31, 32, 34, 50, 58, 67, 78, 79, 92, 119, 121, 122, 124, 134, 140, 142, 145, 151, 156, 157, 164, 212, 220–222, 235, 249, 264–267, 271, 284, 293, 296, 301, 304, 310, 329, 330, 335, 339, 341, 347, 354, 367, 389

Cummings, Constance 164, 202

Cummings, Irving 123, 170, 175, 262, 330, 336, 391, 406

Cummings, Robert 69, 77, 159, 161, 180, 198, 333, 338, 346

Curtis, Tony 63, 69, 101, 168, 170, 204, 216, 238, 302, 309, 340, 351, 388, 394

Curtiz, Michael 13, 34, 49, 57, 64, 67, 69, 78, 81, 84–86, 96, 101, 118, 127, 140, 142, 150, 165, 186, 209, 217, 222, 239, 240, 248, 250, 253, 264, 265, 285, 290, 294, 300, 304, 316, 341, 343, 361, 367, 378, 398, 406, 411

Cushing, Peter 29, 75, 103, 136, 145, 205, 285, 317, 323

Czinner, Paul 100, 202, 239, 256, 329, 365, 370

D

Dahlbeck, Eva 14, 33

Dance 7, 12, 13, 20, 22, 33, 36, 45, 56, 57, 69, 75, 78, 80, 81, 83, 93, 105, 109, 115, 117, 132, 134, 136, 146, 151, 170, 188, 199, 203, 206, 208, 218, 220, 229, 244, 251, 254, 262, 264, 268, 270, 273, 289, 296, 310, 300, 302, 306, 311, 315, 346, 353, 363, 378, 379, 392, 398, 401, 402, 406

Dante, Joe 190, 229, 323, 342

Dassin, Jules 42, 84, 182, 198, 230, 271, 292, 296

Daves, Delmer 11, 33, 50, 171, 240, 282, 308, 317, 337, 348, 350, 368

Davis, Bette 3, 7, 27, 42, 43, 45, 49, 57, 73, 78, 81, 84, 86, 92, 137, 139, 164, 165, 171, 184, 189, 201, 205, 222, 227, 239, 248, 253, 263, 264, 265, 284, 294, 296, 297, 336, 350, 352, 356, 357, 365, 367, 383, 389, 390, 402, 403

Day Lewis, Daniel 244, 279

Day, Doris 4, 57, 99, 132, 143, 328, 336, 347, 350, 353, 369

Dean, Basil 2, 280, 333

Dean, James 10, 20, 187, 250, 252, 268, 305, 308, 347

Dearden, Basil 27, 28, 32, 40, 45, 48, 52, 103, 161, 180, 190, 248, 256, 286, 292, 299, 310, 316, 331, 334, 364, 410

De Havilland, Olivia 2, 48, 52, 54, 57, 76, 81, 85, 86, 96, 106, 118, 140, 156, 170, 171, 179, 182, 224, 237, 263, 265, 266, 296, 374, 391, 400, 402

Delannoy, Jean 100, 131, 132, 190, 226, 348

Delon, Alain 17, 32, 40, 53, 55, 59, 60, 87, 132, 210, 216, 236, 325, 384

Del Ruth, Roy 13, 20, 57, 73, 122, 136, 152, 170, 183, 211, 293, 316, 347, 379

De Mille, Cecil B. 11, 14, 69, 85, 198, 222, 228, 253, 285, 301, 315, 343, 348, 352

Demy, Jacques 60, 87, 133, 174

Deneuve, Catherine 31, 32, 54, 60, 86, 88, 103, 174, 236, 248, 257, 286, 371

De Niro, Robert 30, 44, 53, 61, 73, 87, 91, 130, 138, 152, 187, 227, 230, 244, 246, 259, 274–276, 278, 318, 326, 327, 349, 373

Dennis, Sandy 10, 357

De Palma, Brian 30, 58, 73, 87, 101, 191, 278, 368

Depardieu, Gérard 40, 52, 62, 86, 88, 127, 181, 209, 246, 251, 257, 275, 313, 314, 320, 372, 390

De Sica, Vittorio 37, 40, 44, 59, 89, 104, 109, 115, 157, 176, 225, 250, 253, 260, 266, 270, 271, 273, 284, 301, 307, 312, 321, 334, 376, 381

Detectives 16, 24, 31, 43, 65, 90, 91, 117, 126, 131, 147, 166, 170, 186, 199, 209, 225, 227, 283, 290, 295, 302, 361, 394

De Toth, André 261, 303

Devil 27, 34, 63, 71, 91, 93, 120, 180, 212, 234, 238, 272, 320, 328, 358

Dickens, Charles 13, 69, 77, 79, 92, 117, 127, 146, 147, 202, 206, 272, 309, 334

Dieterle, William 11, 57, 73, 77, 85, 91, 92, 118, 121, 136, 164, 165, 175, 178, 181, 198, 205, 227, 263, 316, 319, 329, 341, 406, 407, 409

Dietrich, Marlene 24, 35, 48, 68, 71, 74, 75, 77, 93, 99, 139, 142, 148, 160, 178, 197, 199, 212, 227, 234, 294, 316, 322, 335, 343, 347, 348, 350, 368, 385, 394, 397, 400

Disney, Walt 36, 55, 63, 69, 72, 97, 102, 112, 116, 117, 135, 148, 154, 162, 163, 176, 216, 226, 280, 288, 294, 304, 320, 340, 351, 389

Divorce 8, 22, 28, 80, 94, 128, 142, 160, 201, 204, 208, 215, 253, 256, 263, 271, 284, 319, 325, 327, 330, 367, 394, 409

Dmytryk, Edward 30, 39, 44, 49, 51, 53, 84, 90, 122, 124, 145, 243, 293, 357, 367

Doctors 3, 21, 24, 31, 33, 35, 47–49, 54, 56, 74, 80, 93, 96, 99, 120, 125, 127, 145, 147, 159, 161, 162, 163, 166, 170,

179, 186, 189, 190, 194, 203, 210, 212, 221, 229, 249, 255, 256, 262, 281, 283, 286, 290, 291, 311, 313, 315, 324, 329, 335, 336, 342, 351, 359, 372, 374, 383, 390, 391

Documentaries 9, 16, 35, 42, 45, 48, 53, 59, 61, 62, 84, 89, 94, 96, 102, 105, 108, 121, 137, 157, 169, 187, 238, 250, 294, 311, 312, 321, 324, 326, 327, 332, 369, 380, 381, 384, 392, 408, 409

Dogs 52, 88, 89, 97, 105, 116, 154, 165, 191, 200, 203, 218, 223, 224, 248, 251, 253, 258, 267, 279, 333, 361, 373, 376, 401

Donat, Robert 6, 21, 35, 56, 70, 96, 98, 140, 159, 175, 231, 264, 293, 302, 309, 322, 383, 410

Donen, Stanley 12, 23, 34, 58, 64, 91, 99, 122, 142, 143, 188, 189, 243, 248, 258, 283, 314, 328, 335, 341, 361, 366, 369

Donlevy, Brian 39, 42, 76, 93, 197, 237, 287, 350, 383, 395

Donner, Jörn 14, 231

Donner, Richard 51, 91, 95, 286

Dostoevsky, Fyodor 39, 51, 100, 140, 194, 225, 384, 385

Douglas, Kirk 33, 39, 43, 78, 101, 141, 155, 158, 159, 194, 216, 221, 229, 230, 240, 241, 267–269, 286, 302, 317, 329, 339, 346, 351, 389, 400, 403

Douglas, Melvyn 44, 78, 80, 93, 134, 208, 211, 212, 236, 239, 244, 247, 253, 270, 276, 286, 291, 386, 402

Douglas, Michael 4, 13, 20, 23, 102, 123, 139, 141, 204, 278, 372, 374, 405

Dovzhenko, Alexander 30, 102, 118

Dreams 2, 5, 31, 32, 34, 46, 47, 94, 101, 103, 107, 116, 121, 183, 208, 225, 229, 291, 293, 294, 318, 324, 348, 351, 355, 358, 384

Dreyer, Carl 19, 47, 95, 115, 381, 382, 399, 401

Dreyfuss, Richard 2, 41, 37, 49, 75, 183, 275, 280, 324, 342, 368, 371

Drink 48, 52, 55, 57, 65, 79, 80, 118, 144, 174, 187, 204, 214, 234, 239, 263, 265, 272, 310, 339, 352, 353, 354, 400, 409

Drugs 38, 88, 92, 98, 100, 104, 115, 156, 161, 163, 170, 196, 206, 214, 234, 256, 259, 273, 287, 305, 324, 325, 358, 369, 409

Drunks 2, 4, 11, 29, 35, 47, 58, 66, 85, 101, 105, 110, 115, 122, 128, 134, 145, 146, 150, 151, 155, 160, 165, 187, 199, 200, 202, 205, 210, 229, 241, 244, 262, 265, 266, 267, 268, 271, 276, 277, 283–285, 296, 317, 331, 347, 352, 357–359, 362, 368, 389, 392, 393, 402

Dumas *fils*, Alexandre 58, 59

Dumas *père*, Alexandre 99, 114, 302, 374

Du Maurier, Daphne 54, 86, 106, 307, 339

Dunaway, Faye 78, 105, 171, 275, 316

Dunne, Irene 13, 22, 44, 45, 81, 94, 120, 142, 147, 150, 206, 212, 215, 217, 231, 233, 237, 251, 252, 262, 263, 290, 294, 330, 346, 389, 402

Durbin, Deanna 13, 20, 64, 69, 155, 170, 198, 199, 208, 261, 287, 330, 336, 389, 401

Duvall, Robert 17, 44, 48, 53, 75, 88, 115, 138, 163, 277, 285

Duvivier, Julien 19, 40, 72, 127, 131, 203, 236, 291, 300, 310, 312, 316, 380, 409

Dwan, Allan 67, 114, 177, 221, 228, 282, 346, 392

E

Eagels, Jeanne 105

Ealing 135, 147, 190, 327

Eastwood, Clint 53, 55, 108, 180, 366, 378

Eccentrics 2, 4, 10, 14, 30, 62, 63, 92, 109, 121, 140, 154, 157, 164, 190, 202, 204, 205, 206, 208, 216, 219, 225, 228, 235, 248, 282, 286, 290, 325, 334, 339, 340, 347, 352, 360, 363, 366, 399, 410

Edwards, Blake 63, 105, 133, 139, 182, 204, 220, 227, 246, 315, 327, 331, 351, 388, 397

Eisenstein, Sergei 6, 30, 47, 110, 135, 144, 174, 178, 210, 296, 315

Elections 55, 88, 110, 305, 311, 335, 337, 367, 368, 381

Explorers 67, 107, 112

Expressionism 19, 56, 118, 127, 159, 196, 227, 238, 281, 376

F

Fairbanks, Douglas 21, 66, 114, 129, 280, 285, 329, 390

Farmers 15, 59–61, 91, 93, 118, 127, 140, 143, 146, 148, 149, 155, 160, 170, 171, 172, 173, 181, 187, 189, 211, 218, 245, 248, 252, 268, 277, 279, 280, 299, 300, 302, 311, 315, 317, 324, 336–338, 341, 343, 357, 358, 366, 378, 380, 383, 390, 393, 394, 401

Farrow, Mia 9, 15, 27, 29, 32, 58, 75, 91, 98, 115, 161, 210, 272, 278, 286, 336, 408

Fascism 21, 37, 38, 40, 87, 89, 98, 106, 117, 121, 130, 147, 226, 231, 235, 247, 273, 274, 296, 312, 341

Fassbinder, Rainer Werner 7, 38, 118, 120, 161, 231, 257, 308, 325, 326, 352, 386

Fatal illness 59, 90, 119, 252, 277, 313, 339, 348, 354

Fathers and Sons 18, 21, 27, 38, 61, 62, 65, 110, 119, 138, 144, 145, 173, 181, 196, 201, 204, 209, 216, 229, 232, 244, 253, 256, 258, 265, 270, 280, 282, 283, 294, 319, 321, 324, 338, 342, 357, 381

Faust 71, 120, 138, 320, 356

Faye, Alice 210, 315, 341, 353

Fellini, Federico 9, 60, 69, 71, 98, 109, 120, 122, 144, 206, 217, 225, 246, 268, 269, 271, 274, 321, 334, 336, 348, 354, 358, 366, 379

Feminism 5, 10, 88, 111, 144, 156, 159, 183, 232, 237, 251, 261, 325, 360, 386, 399, 402

femmes fatales 49, 86, 205, 304

Ferrer, Jose 20, 70, 99, 166, 167, 189, 248, 266, 341, 358

Ferreri, Marco 8, 26, 88, 226, 248, 320

Feyder, Jacques 76, 99, 134, 322

Field, Sally 58, 118, 140, 182, 245, 275, 277, 279, 369

Fielding, Henry 364, 365

Fields, W.C. 16, 29, 69, 79, 121, 122, 181, 215, 300, 334, 350

film à clef 122, 231, 237, 238, 266, 294, 328, 339, 379, 386, 390

film noir 9, 42, 48, 78, 84, 118, 137, 149, 182, 194, 197, 283, 305, 311, 343, 391, 394, 396, 397

Film-making 2, 9, 12, 17, 27, 28, 45, 47, 57, 80, 88, 98, 99, 101, 104, 109, 119, 121, 122, 138, 165, 151, 172, 173, 180, 187, 188, 208, 217, 229, 230, 233, 237, 248, 253, 258, 267, 282, 290, 314, 320, 322, 324, 326, 339, 350, 352, 354, 358, 368, 376, 382, 389, 395 406

Finch, Peter 3, 5, 28, 74, 77, 90, 115, 145, 161, 183, 214, 275, 287, 289, 324, 327, 338, 358, 409

Finlayson, James 98, 200

Finney, Albert 2, 13, 28, 34, 68, 95, 99, 166, 188, 228, 270, 274, 293, 361, 402

Fisher, Terence 11, 136, 163, 218, 283, 294, 324

Fitzgerald, Barry 52, 84, 176, 215, 265, 291, 298

Fitzgerald, F. Scott 8, 75, 87, 98

Fitzmaurice, George 44, 254, 285, 291, 343, 386

Flaherty, Robert 238, 252, 380, 409

Fleischer, Richard 3, 11, 15, 23, 101, 183, 229, 238, 254, 256, 282, 302, 337, 342, 345, 351, 357, 359, 367, 370, 401, 407

Fleming, Victor 7, 34, 67, 86, 112, 114, 122, 132, 140, 151, 164, 180, 181, 203, 222, 259, 261, 263, 264, 323, 366, 369, 378, 401

Florey, Robert 56, 210, 213, 224, 227

Flying and fliers 21, 22, 24, 27, 31, 46, 57, 65, 71, 75, 77, 81, 89, 92, 94, 102, 109, 122, 132, 135, 141, 142, 151, 154, 155, 156, 158, 175, 183, 189, 190, 192, 203, 208, 209, 212, 226, 239, 245, 251, 254, 256, 261, 266, 269, 270, 273, 285, 289, 292, 304, 309, 312, 342, 348, 353, 362, 363, 374, 386, 388, 395, 399

Flynn, Errol 81, 85, 86, 122, 143, 152, 222, 239, 240, 285, 296, 304, 362, 378, 391

Fonda, Henry 2, 39, 53, 57, 84, 89, 96, 101, 110, 118, 122, 125, 127, 133, 143, 145, 148, 156, 158, 159, 165, 182, 197, 199, 204, 214, 221, 240–242, 264, 268, 276, 280, 287, 341, 343, 346, 350, 373, 383, 389, 392, 395

Fonda, Jane 11, 53, 80, 83, 102, 123, 124, 137, 147, 158, 162, 184, 204, 210, 227, 236, 241, 249, 271, 273, 275, 276, 280, 328, 332, 361, 384

Fontaine, Joan 12, 22, 44, 64, 106, 124, 141, 142, 144, 159, 176, 197, 205, 244, 260, 264, 305, 307, 332, 339, 346, 347, 359, 394, 400

Forbes, Bryan 23, 30, 56, 67, 69, 71, 109, 157, 253, 282, 317, 388

Ford, Glenn 42, 51, 85, 133, 197, 229, 231, 253, 286, 356, 368, 395, 409

Ford, Harrison 45, 74, 125, 130, 231, 245, 283, 286, 302, 317, 342, 401, 405

Ford, John 8, 25, 39, 57, 89, 111, 122, 123, 125, 132, 143, 145, 156, 158, 170, 175, 186, 211, 224, 231, 240, 242, 258, 263, 264, 267, 280, 287, 290, 298, 301, 303, 305, 308, 315, 316, 339, 342, 348, 367, 378, 389, 390, 392, 393

Forman, Miloš 10, 29, 57, 72, 94, 102, 126, 222, 245, 257, 259, 274, 277, 283

Formby, George 139, 162

Forster, E. M. 161, 203, 277, 309, 321, 360

Forsyth, Bill 109, 145, 185, 252, 327, 340

Forsyth, Frederick 20

Fosse, Bob 13, 28

France 3, 26, 30, 32, 41, 43, 46, 58, 59, 61, 63, 65, 72, 73, 86, 97, 99, 104, 106, 118, 130, 131, 136, 137, 138, 141, 146, 155, 163, 173, 184, 188, 208, 210, 222, 226, 228, 231, 232, 247, 250, 251, 254, 263, 267, 281, 311, 312, 313, 135, 320, 321, 323, 330, 340, 344, 348,

349, 351, 356, 361, 377, 380, 382, 386, 391, 404

Frankenheimer, John 21, 33, 96, 101, 153, 172, 292, 359, 368, 374

Frankenstein 10, 213

Franklin, Sidney 2, 45, 134, 198, 221, 224, 263, 300, 304, 365

Frears, Stephen 161, 205, 209, 293, 359

French, Harold 150

French, Lloyd 200, 286

Frend, Charles 99, 113, 209, 243, 287, 293, 390

Freud, Sigmund 31, 163, 294

Freund, Karl 186, 210, 218, 226, 324

Friedkin, William 7, 105, 161, 273, 379

Fuller, Samuel 24, 102, 314, 346, 396

Furie, Sidney J. 296, 377, 406

G

Gabin, Jean 19, 49, 63, 90, 94, 131, 138, 141, 182, 201, 236, 258, 267, 283, 311, 312, 367, 373, 409

Gable, Clark 4, 22, 62, 78, 119, 126, 132, 134, 140, 151, 156, 166, 176, 183, 192, 198, 206, 208, 211, 212, 220, 234, 247, 252, 262, 263, 285, 290, 300, 303, 328, 343, 351, 366, 393, 395

Gallico, Paul 15, 69, 74, 261, 300

Gambling 10, 50, 78, 89, 100, 119, 133, 162, 164, 217, 229, 257, 287, 290, 305, 342, 377, 381, 385, 388, 391

Gance, Abel 72, 77, 242, 248, 364

Gangsters 19, 23, 24, 37, 39, 42, 43, 48–51, 57, 58, 63, 64, 71, 73, 78, 79, 81, 87, 91, 93, 94, 101, 105, 112, 115, 122, 131, 132, 133, 151, 155, 158, 163, 170, 173, 186, 194, 202, 208, 210, 213, 216, 220, 234, 244, 246, 247, 253, 258, 259, 262, 264, 266, 280, 285, 286, 290, 294, 300, 306, 307, 314, 316, 317, 326, 340, 355, 359, 367, 368, 371, 377, 381, 385, 391, 393, 395, 401, 402, 403, 407

Ganz, Bruno 35, 325, 326, 366, 396

Garbo, Greta 20, 31, 46, 58, 80, 134, 162, 169, 222, 224, 243,

247, 254, 259, 281, 300, 304, 330, 341, 352, 380, 383, 386

Gardner, Ava 55, 111, 126, 132, 166, 220, 227, 231, 268, 300, 301, 310, 333, 341, 351, 367

Garfield, John 78, 134, 257, 341

Garland, Judy 13, 22, 79, 112, 188, 189, 229, 244, 285, 300, 333, 341, 350, 357, 366, 401

Garnett, Tay 151, 156, 165, 206, 210, 216, 233, 285, 337, 363, 375

Garson, Greer 140, 175, 202, 233, 256, 261, 264, 357, 375, 402, 406

Gaynor, Janet 69, 224, 238, 261, 354, 395

Germany 2, 6, 8, 11, 14, 22, 24, 38, 47, 48, 51, 93, 94, 102, 108, 118, 119, 127, 141, 145, 148, 151, 157, 163, 170, 182, 184, 197, 203, 210, 213, 238, 254, 275, 281, 284, 288, 289, 293, 308, 312, 326, 349, 351, 362, 363, 368, 374, 376, 385, 396, 397, 409

Germi, Pietro 95, 225

Gershwin, George 12, 22, 220, 341

Ghosts 69, 70, 71, 84, 93, 98, 135, 142, 149, 154, 189, 194, 198, 200, 206, 213, 218, 219, 229, 232, 293, 306, 327, 334, 339, 348, 357, 394

Gielgud, John 50, 133, 146, 160, 182, 209, 220, 243, 276, 287, 312, 329, 390, 394

Gilbert, Lewis 2, 27, 29, 55, 58, 95, 143, 292, 296, 321, 359, 362, 397

Gilliam, Terry 87, 130, 205, 227, 228, 236, 328, 340, 363

Gilliat, Sidney 10, 23, 31, 44, 48, 68, 111, 162, 334, 335, 390

Gish, Dorothy 137, 336

Gish, Lillian 46, 53, 85, 127, 136, 146, 174, 229, 336, 361, 383, 398

Godard, Jean-Luc 1, 2, 9, 32, 36, 94, 104, 130, 137, 150, 236, 260, 288, 294, 312, 326, 328, 355, 377, 382, 398

Goddard, Paulette 71, 85, 91, 154, 207, 233, 249, 296, 311, 315, 328

Gogol, Nikolai 136, 194, 322

Goldblum, Jeff 223, 345

Goldcrest 127, 133, 230, 320

Gordon, Ruth 3, 80, 91, 122, 253, 272, 295

Goulding, Edmund 5, 20, 27, 49, 84, 85, 112, 124, 134, 162, 234, 262, 264, 265, 304, 319, 350, 362, 375

Grable, Betty 139, 170, 228, 234, 315, 336, 351, 379

Grahame, Gloria 50, 115, 177, 182, 197, 267, 305, 306, 409

Granger, Stewart 21, 76, 115, 175, 197, 301, 340, 354, 406

Grant, Cary 5, 17, 34, 41, 44, 52, 62, 64, 79–81, 93, 94, 99, 100, 124, 136, 142, 144, 155, 156, 158–160, 162, 164, 182, 189, 207, 208, 211, 212, 215, 234, 243, 248, 254, 258, 263–265, 279, 282, 284, 315, 318–320, 328, 330, 331, 340, 341, 346, 351, 353, 357, 362, 366, 385, 393

Green, Alfred E. 346, 352

Greenaway, Peter 5, 31, 104, 250, 313, 353, 373

Greene, Graham 2, 23, 27, 52, 79, 115, 123, 137, 144, 145, 148, 308, 339, 341, 361

Greenstreet, Sydney 19, 41, 49, 64, 81, 166, 209, 282, 369

Greenwood, Joan 206, 285, 356

Gregson, John 135, 206, 289, 351

Griffith, D. W. 46, 66, 69, 107, 127, 136, 137, 146, 174, 187, 308, 336, 348, 385, 390

Grosbard, Ulu 87, 88, 272, 316, 349, 362, 373

Guillermin, John 22, 23, 52, 68, 190, 192, 254, 362

Guinness, Alec 19, 27, 28, 44, 90, 92, 106, 127, 137, 145, 146, 163, 178, 190, 203, 206, 209, 231, 242, 269, 308, 315, 323, 345, 390

Guitry, Sacha 30, 77, 386

Gwenn, Edmund 14, 69, 186, 257, 266, 324, 370

H

Hackman, Gene 61, 75, 77, 95, 105, 125, 227, 252, 273, 352

Hall, Alexander 15, 78, 156, 170, 206, 287, 353, 366

Hamer, Robert 32, 90, 103, 106, 147, 158, 190, 217, 251, 258, 334, 370

Hamilton, Guy 6, 57, 68, 73, 125, 230, 254, 256, 292, 329, 334, 339

Hammer 91, 103

Hammett, Dashiell 41, 75, 76, 85, 171, 361, 396

Hanks, Tom 112, 119, 286, 320, 358, 405

Happy families 68, 76, 116, 138, 143, 149, 172, 290, 334, 348

Hardwicke, Cedric 21, 99, 113, 224, 231

Hardy, Oliver 7, 16, 98, 129, 146, 151, 154, 168, 177, 199, 215, 227, 235, 286, 303, 346, 349, 350, 389, 392, 393

Hardy, Thomas 324, 360

Harlow, Jean 42, 44, 62, 122, 132, 151, 199, 206, 211, 284, 285, 303, 328, 362

Harris, Richard 308, 367

Harrison, George 150, 236, 317

Harrison, Rex 23, 44, 50, 54, 64, 71, 100, 119, 154, 202, 221, 229, 233, 271, 288, 296, 308, 309, 329, 339, 351, 355

Harvey, Laurence 21, 28, 53, 151, 253, 267, 269, 271, 309, 324, 353, 380

Hathaway, Henry 18, 39, 42, 45, 74, 171, 228, 234, 251, 254, 272, 287, 301, 347, 388, 393

Haunted houses 81, 146, 154, 248

Hawkins, Jack 32, 139, 147, 231, 243, 287, 316, 360

Hawks, Howard 1, 14, 41, 48–50, 52, 53, 57, 64, 74, 101, 142, 143, 154, 155, 156, 158, 165, 168, 186, 208, 224, 228, 233, 234, 240, 241, 254, 258, 263, 264, 279, 291, 292, 315, 316, 318, 320, 340, 343, 353, 354, 362, 392, 393, 397, 402

Hawn, Goldie 19, 39, 45, 258, 273, 274, 288, 342

Hawtrey, Charles 48, 127, 243, 289

Hay, Will 48, 190, 293, 301, 331, 339, 357, 410

Hayes, Helen 74, 162, 249, 262, 268, 273

Hayward, Susan 105, 119, 231, 238, 269, 306, 310, 337, 357, 374, 388, 392

Hayworth, Rita 12, 22, 23, 43, 57, 86, 133, 188, 230, 391, 394

Hecht, Ben 136, 154, 158, 164, 201, 212, 248, 385

Heflin, Van 13, 41, 64, 78, 93, 101, 148, 210, 229, 264, 301, 304, 319, 346, 347, 359, 368, 391, 409

Heisler, Stuart 22, 42, 76, 85, 337, 374

Hellman, Lillian 76, 85, 93, 184, 204, 337, 361, 402

Hemingway, Ernest 41, 74, 303, 366

Henreid, Paul 64, 73, 84, 85, 99, 140, 239, 248, 297, 341, 357

Hepburn, Audrey 45, 50, 73–75, 99, 139, 142, 146, 156, 204, 220, 267, 271, 296, 320, 346, 361, 369, 400, 403, 409

Hepburn, Katharine 3, 4, 7, 8, 32, 52, 62, 67, 73, 79, 80, 109, 111, 120, 123, 142, 143, 148, 156, 203, 214, 220, 224, 229, 249, 258, 262, 272, 276, 284, 313, 318, 321, 338, 341, 346, 347, 367, 383, 393, 397, 399

Herrmann, Bernard 70, 216, 295, 370

Herzog, Werner 4, 16, 109, 112, 157, 171, 198, 230, 337

Heston, Charlton 30, 32, 52, 69, 93, 113, 164, 227, 253, 256, 267, 269, 288, 306, 309, 320, 329, 348, 378, 394, 402

Hill, George Roy 28, 50, 115, 135, 152, 164, 188, 237, 244, 274, 292, 337, 354, 362, 399, 402

Hiller, Arthur 11, 162, 163, 204, 244, 402

Hiller, Wendy 21, 31, 165, 201, 269, 289, 297, 329, 332, 337

Hitchcock, Alfred 1, 2, 6, 10, 34, 35, 44, 45, 52, 56, 64, 65, 71, 72, 74, 93, 98, 99, 106, 123, 124, 142, 144, 159, 163, 175, 176, 179, 182, 184, 199, 206, 208, 209, 245, 248, 256, 258, 264, 283, 291, 295, 307, 331, 335, 339, 347, 349, 361, 367, 370, 371, 374

Hobson, Valerie 94, 106, 201, 356

Hoffman, Dustin 15, 28, 38, 77, 141, 144, 160, 183, 214, 256,

257, 272, 275, 277, 278, 294, 308, 316, 324, 336, 340, 349, 362, 369, 392, 406

Holden, William 41, 44, 50, 93, 105, 115, 125, 142, 146, 214, 255, 267, 275, 292, 301, 309, 315, 338, 346, 352, 358, 378, 393, 400

Holidays 43, 54, 74, 83, 85, 100, 107, 156, 178, 200, 210, 235, 286, 302, 306, 313, 317, 319, 327, 335, 339, 348, 358, 366, 377, 382, 385, 397, 402, 410

Holliday, Judy 3, 50, 76, 80, 229, 267, 335, 404

Hollywood 1, 7, 27, 33, 34, 39, 53, 79, 90, 115, 118, 122, 140, 142, 158, 177, 180, 209, 211, 212, 221, 225, 235, 238, 258, 260, 261, 274, 298, 306, 310, 352, 354, 369, 385, 395, 397, 402, 408

Holmes, Sherlock 41, 58, 90, 179, 190, 256, 304

Homosexuality 1, 16, 35, 77, 86, 88, 100, 118, 141, 156, 158, 161, 165, 220, 223, 225, 237, 277, 341, 356, 368, 372, 373

Hope, Bob 6, 19, 55, 78, 91, 112, 124, 141, 144, 154, 167, 206, 207, 285, 300, 331, 350, 367, 379, 388

Hopkins, Anthony 23, 149, 205, 272, 298, 373, 382

Hopkins, Miriam 84, 85, 155, 181, 184, 208, 211, 212, 221, 224, 262, 316, 353, 370, 378, 401, 402

Hordern, Michael 192

Hoskins, Bob 2, 11, 58, 117, 143, 148, 176, 208, 259, 339, 359, 396

Hospitals 9, 60, 77, 86, 96, 127, 162, 173, 200, 249, 292, 305, 334

Hotels 20, 22, 23, 43, 47, 53, 69, 73, 105, 132, 134, 138, 158, 162, 166, 180, 191, 194, 199, 202, 207, 224, 227, 235, 238, 246, 248, 262, 266, 295, 317, 321, 327, 328, 339, 340, 348, 389

Howard, Leslie 2, 21, 34, 42, 49, 79, 85, 86, 127, 139, 140, 164, 175, 206, 212, 239, 256, 262, 289, 297, 304, 307, 329, 332, 342, 363, 389

Howard, Trevor 50, 52, 133, 145, 201, 202, 273, 298, 300, 309, 357, 361, 385

Howard, William K. 57, 70, 163, 203, 212, 256, 290, 350

Hudson, Hugh 29, 152, 231

Hudson, Rock 4, 33, 45, 120, 155, 268, 347

Hugo, Victor 92, 132, 168, 171, 181, 198

Huppert, Isabelle 19, 24, 59, 65, 88, 100, 211, 248, 326, 366

Hurt, John 29, 55, 98, 112, 153, 207, 279, 289, 359

Hurt, William 48, 165, 181, 277–279, 313, 314, 322, 345, 358, 373

Huston, John 4, 7, 9, 13, 20, 26, 41, 49, 51, 55, 58, 71, 74, 85, 101, 132, 138, 139, 146, 152, 156, 165, 171, 175, 209, 216, 227, 228, 234, 246, 250, 253, 255, 266, 267, 278, 282, 287, 294, 313, 317, 338, 369, 370, 372, 378, 406

Huston, Walter 42, 49, 62, 91, 93, 139, 146, 166, 230, 231, 251, 266, 292, 294, 311, 321, 401, 402

Ichikawa, Kon 158, 253, 257, 282, 314, 360

Idle, Eric 236, 362

Impersonation 35, 41, 51, 56, 66, 80, 86, 89, 94, 98, 106, 111, 121, 122, 159, 169, 170, 185, 202, 208, 212, 215, 217, 221, 225, 233, 245, 246, 248, 265, 285, 290, 292, 302, 303, 305, 308, 313, 316, 318, 321, 328, 330, 333, 338, 340, 341, 344, 347, 349, 351, 354, 358, 360, 366, 368, 369, 375, 381, 383, 385

India 3, 18, 21, 25, 101, 133, 147, 155, 163, 198, 203, 211, 217, 240, 253, 268, 288, 301, 329, 343, 346, 367, 378, 383, 389, 391–393, 395

Insanity 47, 95, 147, 149, 171, 186, 187, 201, 213, 247, 259, 261, 265, 270, 316, 321, 337, 338, 349, 389

Ireland 11, 12, 38, 64, 75, 77, 106, 148, 150, 151, 154, 166, 170, 175, 194, 203, 212, 237,

257, 273, 278, 285, 298, 301, 331, 356, 383, 390

Irons, Jeremy 3, 230, 236, 325, 348, 374

Islands 14, 24, 25, 33, 37, 51, 54, 55, 58, 68, 95, 98, 121, 143, 166, 176, 186, 190, 199, 206, 211, 216, 221, 230, 236, 254, 257, 270, 279, 282, 290, 303, 321, 327, 329, 380, 383, 385, 393

Italy 5, 11, 24, 35, 37, 59, 60, 63, 76, 88, 89, 95, 109, 112, 115, 120, 134, 136, 138, 144, 170, 174, 185, 203, 216, 224, 225, 242, 243, 254, 258, 267, 270, 273, 278, 280, 283, 284, 288, 289, 311, 315, 321, 357, 363, 364, 376, 381, 384, 412

Ivory, James 3, 29, 133, 161, 172, 179, 244, 253, 301, 309, 320, 339, 399

J

Jack the Ripper 30, 48, 54, 159, 163, 178, 179, 248, 281, 392

Jackson, Glenda 3, 28, 96, 111, 161, 201, 231, 243, 273, 274, 324, 333, 361, 373, 408

James, Henry 52, 86, 179, 399, 402

James, Sid 19, 27, 127, 206, 240, 371

Jancsó, Miklós 100, 108, 118, 315

Jannings, Emil 47, 48, 52, 120, 178, 180, 212, 213, 238, 261, 290, 293, 365, 376, 380, 385

Japan 17, 29, 36, 38, 39, 49, 50, 53, 68, 76, 102, 110, 136, 141, 143, 148, 158, 166, 172, 185, 202, 231, 232, 254, 269, 278, 282, 306, 312, 338, 342, 348, 351, 358, 371, 385, 391, 392

Jarman, Derek 19, 162, 233, 329

Jennings, Humphrey 45, 97

Jewison, Norman 11, 13, 71, 85, 124, 133, 138, 140, 172, 249, 272, 278, 316, 318

Johnson, Celia 44, 150, 202, 294, 357, 382

Johnson, Nunnally 143, 260, 269, 319, 341

Johnson, Van 13, 45, 136, 145, 189, 229, 315, 327, 333, 395

Jones, Jennifer 11, 49, 53, 89, 93, 136, 205, 213, 229, 250,

256, 265, 289, 301, 323, 357, 360, 383

Jones, Terry 31, 122, 228, 236, 243, 288, 328

Jourdan, Louis 12, 205, 229, 260, 269, 315, 320, 354, 357, 390

Journalism 6, 29, 38, 48–50, 57, 61, 62, 65, 66, 70, 77, 78–80, 85, 92, 96, 98, 101, 105, 113, 122, 124, 132, 139, 145, 151, 152, 156, 157, 159–161, 165, 170, 171, 175, 176, 182, 197, 199, 202, 204, 208, 209, 211, 216, 224, 227, 236, 244, 245, 249, 257, 267, 277, 284, 285, 290, 292, 298, 317, 319, 320, 325, 326, 328, 335, 346, 347, 348, 352, 358, 367, 373, 381, 384, 386, 390, 394, 395, 400, 405

Judaism   13, 32, 37, 39, 46, 72, 73, 76, 86, 88, 89, 92, 119, 127, 141, 161, 171, 175, 183, 186, 210, 217, 236, 249, 255, 256, 263, 265, 273, 281, 304, 326, 332, 333, 341, 347, 371, 374, 381, 382, 385, 386, 389, 402

K

Kadar, Jan 271, 333, 334

Kanin, Garson 3, 27, 44, 110, 142, 199, 208, 319, 336

Karina, Anna 32, 137, 138, 216

Karloff, Boris 81, 89, 90, 96, 103, 126, 163, 166, 186, 207, 210, 211, 213, 218, 251, 304, 305, 324, 374

Kasdan, Lawrence 48, 165, 240, 279, 280, 313, 372, 373

Kaye, Danny 31, 48, 69, 78, 82, 103, 155, 304, 322, 340, 382

Kazan, Elia 50, 87, 127, 150, 169, 171, 180, 183, 186, 203, 207, 227, 258, 265–268, 358, 367, 374

Keaton, Buster 16, 31, 122, 135, 163, 174, 187, 200, 350, 352, 367, 369, 392

Keaton, Diane 9, 15, 26, 40, 95, 138, 188, 220, 223, 237, 246, 275, 283, 288, 357

Keighley, William 1, 49, 57, 81, 85, 86, 134, 189, 233, 239, 251, 253, 292, 293

Kelly, Gene 12, 16, 36, 53, 64, 83, 99, 122, 188, 210, 216,

229, 243, 258, 267, 285, 302, 310, 314, 327, 335, 350, 366

Kelly, Grace 10, 48, 105, 126, 132, 142, 158, 160, 182, 268, 284, 303, 307

Kendall, Kay 3, 44, 80, 135, 229

Kern, Jerome 12, 13, 22, 341

Kerr, Deborah 4, 12, 16, 19, 55, 75, 99, 100, 143, 145, 166, 179, 202, 215, 229, 231, 233, 249, 251, 267–269, 298, 333, 357, 359, 402, 409

Kershner, Irvin 178, 280, 285

Kidnap 6, 18, 21, 23, 38, 39, 40, 45, 56, 57, 58, 63, 65, 71, 81, 85, 87, 97, 111, 117, 119, 132, 138, 144, 145, 155, 156, 159, 165, 169, 182, 184, 189, 196, 201, 218, 236, 240, 252, 257, 283, 284, 286, 289, 300, 301, 310, 314, 316, 324, 327, 334, 335, 336, 337, 343, 347, 351, 353, 354, 367, 373, 378, 382, 391, 392, 394, 402

Kimmins, Anthony 2, 44, 162, 171, 295

King, Henry 12, 113, 123, 147, 150, 175, 192, 210, 231, 237, 241, 263, 265, 266, 280, 287, 301, 308, 310, 323, 341, 354, 363, 364, 394, 402, 407

King, Stephen 191

Kingsley, Ben 4, 58, 73, 133, 163, 276, 373

Kinski, Klaus 16, 109, 157, 230, 337

Kinski, Nastassja 40, 62, 88, 91, 177

Kipling, Rudyard 7, 19, 116, 126, 303, 395

Kline, Kevin 79, 165, 276, 278, 313, 349, 363

Korda, Alexander 20, 21, 93, 98, 99, 114, 148, 198, 203, 211, 222, 243, 256, 262, 282, 293, 385

Koster, Henry 14, 44, 50, 54, 69, 74, 83, 86, 94, 106, 143, 151, 192, 198, 243, 249, 261, 267, 287, 322, 327, 330, 336, 347, 348, 357, 382, 383, 396

Kotcheff, Ted 37, 124, 135, 152, 159, 183, 313, 358, 361, 373

Kramer, Stanley 96, 111, 120, 143, 156, 168, 177, 203, 237, 243, 270, 272, 310, 351, 366, 367, 369, 391

Kubrick, Stanley 28, 33, 78, 95, 101, 130, 141, 144, 163, 174, 191, 207, 245, 269, 344, 384

Kurosawa, Akira 5, 61, 96, 119, 148, 172, 185, 189, 194, 267, 274, 301, 304, 380

L

La Cava, Gregory 8, 55, 157, 208, 224, 230, 246, 290, 318, 366

Ladd, Alan 41, 42, 76, 98, 145, 148, 241, 249, 287, 339, 347, 369

Lahti, Christine 109, 140, 214, 340

Lake, Veronica 70, 145, 148, 224, 249, 400, 401

Lamarr, Hedy 18, 31, 170, 182, 252, 253, 303

Lambert, Christopher 18, 73, 185, 190, 216, 237, 351

Lamour, Dorothy 19, 78, 167, 300, 303

Lancaster, Burt 19, 39, 60, 69, 76, 84, 96, 101, 104, 105, 119, 133, 156, 164, 227, 240, 241, 246, 252, 267–270, 280, 292, 309, 310, 327, 329, 339, 343, 351, 367, 368, 381, 384, 391, 394

Lanchester, Elsa 44, 186, 199, 251, 293, 368

Landis, John 219, 236, 251, 296, 297, 320, 342

Lanfield, Sidney 22, 86, 163, 304, 328, 331, 341, 353, 367

Lang, Charles 340

Lang, Fritz 2, 32, 42, 47, 56, 94, 123, 124, 145, 159, 166, 168, 182, 196, 198, 209, 226, 234, 286, 316, 317, 340, 346, 376, 409

Lang, Walter 12, 13, 109, 150, 157, 211, 233, 268, 287, 315, 337, 379, 401

Langdon, Harry 62, 78

Lange, Jessica 160, 171, 188, 190, 246, 277

Laughton, Charles 14, 20, 27, 35, 36, 45, 55, 64, 68, 77, 83, 84, 90, 92, 93, 106, 132, 137, 160, 181, 186, 198, 203, 208, 215, 219, 224, 255, 262, 263, 287, 293, 330, 334, 339, 368, 375, 389

Launder, Frank 48, 94, 136, 141, 152, 175, 176, 327, 331, 334, 335, 410

Laurel, Stan 7, 16, 98, 129, 146, 151, 154, 168, 177, 199, 215, 227, 235, 286, 303, 346, 349, 392

Lawrence, D. H. 201

Lawyers 2, 3, 14, 48–50, 68, 71, 77, 92, 93, 103, 127, 131–134, 142, 161, 171, 183, 190, 198, 199, 201, 204, 214, 244, 245, 247, 266, 270, 271, 278, 290, 295, 305, 306, 311, 314, 315, 319, 343, 346, 348, 374, 394, 398, 400, 402

Lean, David 23, 27, 28, 36, 71, 89, 92, 146, 147, 150, 156, 168, 198, 202, 243, 269, 270, 273, 277, 300, 301, 321, 322, 329, 357, 360, 362

Léaud, Jean-Pierre 104, 137, 138, 288, 371, 372, 410

Le Carré, John 28, 95, 188, 214

Lee, Christopher 45, 91, 96, 103, 163, 166, 230, 324, 352, 400

Lee, Rowland V. 41, 68, 99, 186, 207, 213, 302, 304, 350, 373, 407

Lee-Thompson, J. 89, 189, 254, 292, 301, 307, 314, 367, 377

Leigh, Vivien 50, 83, 98, 140, 187, 199, 202, 203, 222, 243, 256, 264, 267, 300, 307, 320, 329, 349

Leisen, Mitchell 3, 48, 52, 86, 94, 106, 124, 148, 164, 170, 183, 237, 239, 265, 294, 296, 300, 305, 318, 328, 339, 341, 343, 350, 364, 365, 397, 398, 400

Lelouch, Claude 15, 60, 152, 236, 257, 272, 314, 315, 406

Lemmon, Jack 41, 57, 61, 63, 80, 102, 105, 123, 148, 175, 183, 203, 204, 223, 227, 244, 251, 268, 269, 271, 274, 291, 321, 331, 340, 388, 400

Lennon, John 104, 150

Leonard, Robert Z. 22, 78, 134, 151, 183, 209, 256, 262, 291, 333, 353

Leone, Sergio 39, 87, 108, 123, 227, 259, 369

Le Roy, Mervyn 4, 11, 33, 42, 57, 76, 104, 119, 122, 134, 139, 152, 168, 175, 183, 186, 202–205, 208, 224, 231, 248, 252, 259, 261, 263, 264, 268, 290, 316, 318, 357, 384, 393, 406

Lesbians 24, 48, 65, 179, 201, 204, 218, 223, 281, 325, 334

Lester, Richard 14, 30, 60, 73, 111, 144, 150, 187, 193, 227, 288, 352, 393

Levinson, Barry 7, 38, 152, 161, 163, 257, 278, 300, 302, 308

Lewis, Joseph H. 156, 170, 328

Lewis, Sinclair 126, 270, 321

Lewton, Val 186, 217

Lindblom, Gunnel 26, 33

Litvak, Anatole 3, 34, 45, 50, 57, 72, 85, 86, 133, 171, 180, 182, 232, 235, 247, 248, 268, 336, 343, 364, 365, 391, 392

Livesey, Roger 19, 226, 289, 316, 320

Lloyd, Frank 76, 132, 149, 165, 198, 262, 263, 303, 304, 375

Lloyd, Harold 16, 128, 135, 215, 349, 350, 392

Lockwood, Margaret 8, 106, 160, 184, 249, 309, 367, 398

Logan, Joshua 12, 44, 53, 109, 177, 232, 234, 239, 269, 338

Lom, Herbert 218, 371

Lombard, Carole 50, 55, 61, 83, 132, 155, 199, 208, 212, 224, 237, 239, 249, 254, 290, 341, 354, 361, 366, 393, 395

London 11, 13, 23, 28, 45, 53, 63, 90, 97, 99, 106, 112, 117, 130, 135, 143, 150, 159, 161, 163, 164, 170, 180, 182, 196, 202, 203, 204, 207–210, 213, 218, 219, 229, 230, 236, 247, 264, 265, 272, 282, 287, 288, 301, 309, 315, 324, 335, 357, 359, 363, 365, 375, 388, 390, 393

Loos, Anita 15, 80, 114, 132, 146, 202

Loren, Sophia 21, 51, 66, 89, 90, 132, 142, 143, 176, 225, 228, 243, 258, 260, 270, 309, 329, 334, 367, 369

Lorre, Peter 19, 41, 49, 64, 69, 90, 100, 132, 142, 160, 166, 186, 197, 209, 247, 350, 351, 369, 385

Losey, Joseph 55, 61, 64, 210, 260, 309, 314, 360

Love triangles 8, 17, 24, 62, 65, 112, 134, 144, 184, 210, 236, 252, 325, 360, 362, 377

Loy, Myrna 5, 39, 41, 81, 95, 132, 143, 148, 151, 162, 186, 198, 205, 211, 214, 244, 263, 284, 285, 290, 291, 298, 301, 328, 347, 353, 357, 361, 368, 375

Lubitsch, Ernst 3, 31, 75, 93, 134, 169, 180, 182, 184, 208, 212, 213, 224, 237, 239, 247, 250, 293, 330, 333, 334, 347, 350, 365, 370, 385, 397

Lucas, George 75, 125, 147, 344

Lugosi, Bela 56, 96, 102, 186, 199, 207, 213, 218, 247, 324

Lukas, Paul 55, 85, 156, 205, 265, 290, 361

Lumet, Sidney 8, 11, 29, 34, 36, 41, 55, 58, 68, 74, 77, 95, 96, 115, 123, 124, 156, 161, 214, 245, 274, 275, 294, 352, 358, 367, 373, 401

Lupino, Ida 4, 44, 49, 86, 153, 155, 159, 197, 305, 391, 399, 402

M

MacDonald, Jeanette 15, 132, 169, 212, 213, 308, 353, 366

Mackendrick, Alexander 42, 127, 147, 285, 327, 345, 394

MacLaine, Shirley 12, 13, 69, 83, 109, 119, 175, 204, 229, 236, 244–246, 268, 269, 277, 284, 325, 370, 400

MacMurray, Fred 1, 3, 44, 78, 113, 123, 143, 156, 162, 176, 204, 239, 269, 304, 316, 328, 341, 343, 346, 350, 363, 366, 395, 400

Magnani, Anna 178, 214, 268, 283, 311

Malle, Louis 6, 28, 31, 32, 53, 60, 105, 110, 133, 141, 171, 207, 217, 248, 377, 381, 382

Malone, Dorothy 268

Mamoulian, Rouben 7, 134, 155, 171, 181, 212, 221, 247, 262, 305, 341, 345, 357

Mankiewicz, Joseph L. 7, 11, 50, 51, 54, 55, 58, 84, 101, 119, 133, 134, 145, 154, 156, 162, 164, 205, 220, 234, 256, 266, 268, 300, 329, 337, 339, 384, 393

Mann, Anthony 11, 75, 124, 158, 180, 240, 241, 314, 347, 406

Mann, Daniel 51, 105, 269

Mann, Delbert 4, 7, 31, 59, 67, 143, 172, 207, 268, 269, 327, 328

Marais, Jean 87, 169, 230, 285, 353

March, Fredric 2, 3, 14, 39, 41, 45, 50, 70, 76, 80, 90, 101, 113, 134, 139, 155, 156, 181, 184, 198, 207, 208, 212, 221, 222, 254, 262, 263, 265, 285, 304, 310, 343, 345, 346, 350, 365, 367, 380, 383, 395, 400–402

Marshall, George 11, 55, 91, 93, 111, 121, 200, 207, 216, 343, 347, 350

Marshall, Herbert 45, 55, 67, 84, 93, 134, 142, 156, 159, 170, 184, 205, 212, 224, 288, 328, 343, 370, 385, 403

Martin, Steve 17, 56, 58, 109, 139, 181, 251, 333, 345, 372, 408

Marvin, Lee 51, 53, 109, 123, 126, 147, 165, 241, 238, 271, 282, 322, 338, 348, 393

Marx Brothers 64, 105, 135, 140, 215, 224, 333, 392

Masina, Giulietta 71, 120, 121, 225, 246, 268, 358, 366

Mason, James 15, 21, 27, 35, 45, 50, 55, 76, 77, 79, 95, 133, 142, 163, 176, 182, 189, 194, 206, 207, 214, 220, 229, 231, 239, 245, 254, 260, 289, 301, 305, 308, 309, 329, 337, 351, 356, 362, 398

Massey, Raymond 41, 62, 78, 81, 105, 187, 226, 337

Mastroianni, Marcello 3, 17, 36, 44, 76, 89, 90, 95, 98, 101, 109, 121, 127, 141, 205, 217, 225, 248, 258, 321, 327, 336, 337, 358, 366, 384

Maté, Rudolph 14, 111, 133, 136, 301, 302

Matthau, Walter 96, 99, 138, 142, 152, 163, 183, 189, 204, 209, 216, 251, 253, 271, 273, 274, 286, 352, 374, 400

Mature, Victor 11, 39, 42, 54, 69, 123, 125, 152, 199, 243, 253, 361

Maugham, Somerset 20, 78, 85, 134, 160, 164, 174, 265, 290, 334, 355, 391

Mayo, Archie 42, 49, 64, 84–86, 91, 112, 133, 165, 180, 201, 225, 299, 343, 349, 353

Mayo, Virginia 39, 48, 155, 280, 285, 340, 391

Mazursky, Paul 20, 183, 220, 227, 257, 274, 336, 368

McCarey, Leo 34, 55, 94, 100, 105, 121, 129, 142, 143, 151, 169, 198, 199, 206, 215, 224, 249, 253, 263, 265, 284, 291, 319, 330, 357, 392

McCartney, Paul 103, 150, 317

McCloud, Norman Z. 121

McCrea, Joel 104, 159, 160, 175, 211, 233, 237, 265, 301, 307, 343, 346, 350, 351, 368, 383, 391, 393, 395, 402

McGuire, Dorothy 5, 154, 209, 295

McLaglen, Andrew V. 336, 378, 393

McLaglen, Victor 39, 89, 93, 126, 142, 155, 186, 211, 263, 285, 291, 298, 301, 346, 385, 391, 392, 397

McLeod, Norman Z. 12, 31, 103, 121, 124, 136, 141, 142, 144, 167, 181, 220, 224–226, 334, 388

McQueen, Steve 15, 63, 133, 243, 316

Medieval 5, 6, 33, 59, 63, 73, 88, 91, 143, 178, 194, 210, 228, 234, 268, 270, 280, 284, 302, 313, 317, 323, 328, 355, 364

Méliès, Georges 107, 235, 344

Melville, Jean-Pierre 40, 41, 87, 236, 315, 316

Menjou, Adolphe 7, 8, 23, 66, 74, 78, 93, 101, 139, 141, 156, 183, 194, 215, 262, 287, 318, 382, 385, 392, 395

Menzel, Jiri 107, 233, 272, 300, 313

MGM 3, 16, 32, 58, 84, 122, 134, 140, 176, 245, 247, 258, 283, 284, 335, 350, 361, 401

Mid-life crisis 5, 8, 24, 37, 54, 58, 78, 92, 100, 151, 172, 204, 214, 227, 236, 397

Mifune, Toshiro 148, 189, 194, 232, 268, 282, 338, 380, 381

Milestone, Lewis 8, 12, 35, 50, 75, 78, 79, 101, 127, 128,

144, 162, 171, 183, 206, 212, 231, 254, 262, 315, 346

Milland, Ray 10, 21, 52, 71, 85, 86, 91, 94, 105, 144, 145, 148, 154, 160, 170, 176, 183, 197, 199, 218, 265, 296, 300, 303, 315, 318, 328, 347, 350, 375, 395, 397, 400

Miller, Arthur 119, 132, 160, 187, 214, 224, 234, 236, 400

Miller, Claude 209, 282, 372

Millionaires 13, 21, 22, 24, 55, 71, 75, 78, 80, 86, 90, 105, 106, 112, 128, 139, 142, 151, 154, 155, 158, 164, 166, 176, 187, 201, 208, 209, 213, 215, 223, 224, 228, 234, 235, 251, 260, 276, 287, 290, 318, 328, 330, 334, 340, 341, 343, 350, 360, 386

Mills, John 2, 17, 19, 21, 27, 36, 56, 64, 89, 92, 104, 113, 133, 140, 146, 147, 176, 189, 199, 201–203, 239, 256, 273, 292, 293, 335, 343, 351, 388

Minnelli, Vincente 12, 14, 16, 22, 23, 27, 101, 150, 188, 189, 226, 229, 244, 249, 263, 267–269, 285, 291, 296, 300, 317, 327, 341, 366, 393

Missionaries 4, 8, 35, 63, 99, 113, 152, 189, 199, 230, 231, 274, 338, 343, 368, 391, 397, 407

Mistresses 4, 14, 21, 24, 32, 34, 62, 65, 93, 119, 120, 132, 154, 157, 158, 170, 180, 201, 202, 204, 210–212, 221, 231, 232, 234, 238, 246, 248, 258, 260, 266, 273, 284, 309, 311, 318, 319, 326, 328, 357, 365, 368, 372, 377, 383, 391, 400

Mitchum, Robert 4, 39, 41, 43, 44, 49, 96, 99, 101, 137, 143, 155, 162, 166, 187, 199, 212, 229, 234, 241, 244, 249, 293, 298, 306, 314, 315, 351, 391, 393, 395, 398, 409

Mizoguchi, Kenji 3, 33, 172, 185, 232, 294, 304, 337

Monarchy 10, 12, 19, 22, 28, 30, 46, 54, 55, 69, 72, 76, 77, 78, 86, 87, 93, 100, 108, 111, 114, 116, 117, 134, 143, 147, 151, 156, 169, 173, 178, 180, 194, 203, 209, 212, 213, 218, 222, 224, 225, 228, 227, 232, 233, 234, 243, 248, 256, 260,

261, 267, 268, 271, 272, 280, 282, 285, 289, 293, 301, 302, 304, 308, 310, 311, 320, 321, 322, 329, 334, 340, 341, 354, 362, 363, 364, 365, 374, 385, 386, 390, 394, 407, 409
Monicelli, Mario 87, 89, 142, 225
Monroe, Marilyn 7, 13, 25, 27, 49, 80, 132, 139, 151, 155, 166, 177, 197, 228, 234, 235, 256, 338, 340, 379, 397
Montand, Yves 24, 32, 33, 36, 63, 80, 138, 153, 171, 181, 189, 221, 235, 273, 288, 312, 371, 400
Montgomery, Robert 15, 78, 125, 208, 209, 212, 284, 292, 359, 361, 392, 393
More, Kenneth 27, 55, 96, 135, 206, 301, 321, 339, 362, 367, 391
Moreau, Jeanne 6, 17, 31, 32, 36, 54, 133, 161, 183, 210, 217, 225, 360, 371, 394
Morgan, Michèle 63, 71, 131
Mother love 9, 12, 18, 24, 26, 45, 47, 54, 68, 79, 90, 120, 128, 140, 161, 178, 179, 188, 202, 204, 205, 211, 217, 221, 233, 237, 245, 248, 252, 263, 265, 268–271, 274, 278, 282, 294, 295, 302, 324, 331, 332, 337, 341, 346, 347, 374, 381, 384, 391, 398, 399, 402
Muni, Paul 81, 84, 91–93, 113, 155, 168, 175, 186, 201, 202, 227, 233, 263, 300, 406, 409
Munich 325, 331, 386
Murderers 166, 238
Murnau, F. W. 47, 103, 120, 180, 238, 252, 262, 366, 376
Musicals 22, 41, 51, 80, 126, 140, 188, 189, 202, 206, 212, 229, 233, 239, 246, 247, 258, 262, 272, 284, 309, 347, 361, 409
Musicians 4, 11, 14, 34, 52, 64, 78, 85, 87, 103, 108, 110, 115, 123, 126, 164, 167, 174, 180, 181, 199, 209, 214, 218, 239, 248, 260, 264, 287, 299, 306, 312, 325, 326, 336, 340, 347, 359, 377, 389, 406, 410

N

Napoleon 9, 30, 32, 50, 54, 72, 76, 77, 123, 134, 143, 322, 363, 383, 386, 389, 394

Navy life 8, 10, 11, 13, 19, 21, 22, 99, 130, 134, 154, 155, 161, 189, 190, 200, 201, 204, 221, 232, 243, 245, 258, 336, 347, 389, 394
Nazis 3, 8, 13, 20, 21, 24, 28, 34, 35, 37, 39, 41, 48, 49, 51, 52, 55, 58, 60, 61, 64, 65, 66, 70, 71, 72, 74, 81, 84, 85, 89, 94, 106, 107, 108, 111, 133, 144–146, 148, 152, 155, 157, 160, 162, 165, 166, 171, 180, 183, 184, 197, 199, 201, 202, 205, 206, 208, 209, 210, 212, 213, 214, 216, 217, 225, 237, 247, 248, 250, 251, 254–257, 265, 267, 270, 272, 273, 276, 278, 281, 283, 284, 286, 289, 292, 294, 302, 305, 307, 308, 312, 313, 314, 319, 320, 321, 324, 325, 331, 332, 333, 335, 341, 342, 347–349, 351, 355, 357, 361, 364, 367, 371, 372, 380, 381, 382, 384, 389, 390, 391–394, 397, 400, 408, 409, 410
Neagle, Anna 231, 233, 249, 375
Neame, Ronald 19, 136, 147, 193, 272, 339, 374
Neeson, Liam 108, 196, 230, 237, 259, 357, 359
Negri, Pola 180, 212, 213
Negulesco, Jean 19, 41, 78, 139, 147, 193, 209, 228, 233, 234, 266, 304, 320, 336, 369
Neill, Roy William 163, 186, 190, 294, 304, 305, 339, 374
Nelson, Ralph 17, 143
Neo-Realism 24, 89, 120, 186, 247, 321, 376, 384
New Wave 1, 32, 70, 217, 232, 311, 312, 371, 377
New York 7, 9, 11, 12, 15, 46, 60, 62, 63, 74, 83, 84, 96, 97, 115, 117, 150, 161, 170, 172, 182, 183, 188, 198, 204, 206, 214, 220, 244, 246, 257–259, 263, 268, 270, 274, 276, 278, 285, 299–301, 315, 325, 326, 330, 332, 341, 349, 357, 366, 381, 388, 391, 401, 405
Newman, Paul 6, 7, 28, 50, 64, 72, 77, 133, 152, 153, 160, 164, 166, 180, 182, 209, 214, 241, 244, 252, 270, 272, 274, 278, 327, 338, 352, 354, 394, 397

Newton, Robert 67, 150, 202, 359, 411
Niblo, Fred 114, 134
Nichols, Dudley 249, 342
Nichols, Mike 19, 28, 54, 95, 122, 125, 141, 160, 245, 246, 253, 271, 272, 349, 405
Nicholson, Jack 5, 8, 17, 51, 103, 122, 138, 163, 166, 170, 187, 191, 194, 216, 245, 259, 274, 277, 278, 286, 300, 332, 333, 349, 352, 368, 370, 372, 400
Niven, David 8, 9, 18, 27, 31, 44, 55, 69, 75, 77, 175, 182, 211, 216, 226, 231, 253, 254, 268, 269, 289, 298, 302, 304, 306, 309, 314, 319, 336, 354, 362, 370, 388
Noiret, Philippe 24, 64, 87, 119, 181, 217, 226, 247, 286, 327, 361, 404
Nouvelle Vague see New Wave
Novak, Kim 12, 44, 101, 105, 115, 160, 207, 338, 347, 375
Nuns 4, 51, 54, 60, 74, 91, 109, 111, 124, 166, 215, 249, 270, 289, 295, 323, 409
Nurses 15, 33, 74, 78, 84, 89, 172, 207, 208, 223, 249, 260, 294, 307, 309, 320, 351, 395, 399, 407

O

Oberon, Merle 45, 73, 99, 114, 127, 170, 201, 211, 222, 224, 239, 256, 261, 289, 293, 294, 341, 350, 361, 375, 402
O'Brien, Edmond 44, 233, 268, 300
O'Brien, Margaret 48, 83, 202, 229, 288, 336
O'Brien, Pat 27, 49, 57, 62, 152, 183, 202, 252, 291, 340
Obsession 10, 17, 38, 70, 76, 79, 81, 104, 120, 135, 154, 157, 213, 214, 221, 225, 227, 250, 251, 253, 268, 278, 282, 294, 295, 319, 337, 347, 348, 351, 352, 356, 368, 371, 372, 375, 384, 385, 391, 395, 401, 407
Occupied Europe 4, 64, 65, 66, 88, 104, 111, 210, 250, 251, 255, 267, 269, 271, 272, 283, 286, 292, 307, 320, 333, 349, 371, 380, 382, 389, 391

O'Hara, Maureen 92, 106, 109, 198, 199, 298, 306, 327, 339, 348, 393

Old age 95, 11, 117, 131, 137, 221, 228, 252, 253, 257, 278, 321, 333, 376

Olivier, Laurence 2, 7, 21, 25, 27, 50, 52, 144, 149, 160, 162, 165, 183, 201, 203, 222, 235, 239, 243, 256, 266, 289, 307, 324, 329, 336, 337, 339, 356, 364, 366, 380, 391, 402

Olmi, Ermanno 61, 118, 283, 357, 376, 382, 389

O'Neill, Eugene 134, 214, 246, 338

Opera and operetta 4, 10, 38, 76, 83, 90, 105, 109, 134, 149, 157, 166, 171, 178, 200, 201, 210, 218, 224, 260, 261, 289, 308, 324, 353, 383, 384, 399

Ophüls, Max 2, 30, 69, 72, 77, 118, 124, 205, 226, 260, 284, 302

Orphans 12, 13, 48, 53, 63, 66, 67, 87, 92, 117, 200, 202, 203, 211, 228, 237, 261, 280, 287, 296, 306, 339, 340, 342, 357, 373, 409

Oscars 2, 69, 89, 94, 126, 138, 149, 158, 188, 195, 208, 235, 243, 261, 289, 323, 327, 332

Oshima, Nagisa 6, 73, 141, 172, 211, 292

O'Sullivan, Maureen 202, 211, 225, 259, 352, 361

O'Toole, Peter 28, 55, 89, 122, 140, 143, 154, 156, 170, 203, 209, 228, 270, 272, 335, 358, 403

Outlaws 47, 59, 67, 74, 86, 94, 114, 117, 157, 158, 166, 221, 239, 241, 244, 268, 272, 280, 304, 327, 337, 342, 368, 378, 391, 393, 395, 402

Ozu, Yasujiro 5, 119, 233, 357

P

Pabst, G. W. 2, 9, 47, 48, 109, 134, 141, 179, 182, 205, 254, 259, 281, 295, 328, 376

Pacino, Al 29, 61, 138

Pagnol, Marcel 3, 181, 221, 234, 282, 318, 338, 357

Pakula, Alan J. 22, 77, 160, 183, 273, 275, 276, 321, 332, 339, 349

Palin, Michael 228, 231, 236, 339

Paramount 105, 138, 290, 350, 352, 370

Paris 1, 3, 11, 13, 19, 22, 29–32, 40, 47, 51, 54, 58, 63, 64, 66, 70, 75, 86, 88, 90, 92, 101, 109, 111, 112, 125, 130, 131, 146, 155, 157, 163, 164, 177, 182, 183, 189, 204, 208, 210, 213, 217, 228, 235, 247, 255, 256, 266, 267, 281, 283, 286–288, 311, 319, 323, 324, 336, 351, 366, 368–371, 381, 388, 397, 398, 404, 409

Parker, Alan 83, 87, 91, 95, 98, 188, 251, 259, 260, 384

Parker, Eleanor 20, 101, 286, 295, 378, 403

Pasolini, Pier Paolo 5, 18, 37, 38, 228, 237, 239, 243, 283, 302, 328, 334, 355

Peck, Gregory 15, 35, 53, 64, 91, 93, 99, 100, 111, 137, 147, 159, 160, 166, 183, 186, 198, 199, 227, 231, 233, 241, 243, 250, 254, 256, 265–267, 269, 270, 303, 310, 314, 320, 351, 363, 374, 375, 383, 391, 402, 409

Pelissier, Anthony 201

Penn, Arthur 11, 45, 51, 158, 161, 241, 245, 257, 270, 272, 308, 312, 407

Perkins, Anthony 11, 235, 294, 295, 372, 395

Perry, Frank 104, 171

Petri, Elio 61, 79, 154, 225, 273, 337

Philipe, Gerard 98, 291, 320, 327, 356, 409

Pialat, Maurice 5, 62, 88, 207

Piccoli, Michel 31, 32, 65, 226, 248

Pichel, Irving 113, 161, 253, 291, 293, 346, 364

Pickford, Mary 21, 66, 114, 136, 212, 262, 308, 329

Pinter, Harold 4, 10, 87, 210, 373

Pitts, Zasu 72, 144, 148, 386

Plummer, Christoper 125

Poe, Edgar Allan 56, 186, 207, 213, 217, 353

Poets 19, 40, 58, 62, 63, 74, 76, 105, 118, 154, 162, 175, 180, 198, 205, 248, 256, 266, 285, 289, 291, 304, 306, 310, 311, 331, 356, 365, 366, 372, 376, 396

Poirot, Hercule 34, 68, 90, 274, 339

Poitier, Sidney 12, 45, 85, 120, 156, 168, 172, 180, 221, 259, 270–272, 357, 367

Polanski, Roman 27, 37, 86, 91, 107, 125, 166, 170, 245, 272, 283, 286, 327, 329, 360, 368

Police 1, 16, 21, 24, 28, 38, 39, 42, 43, 45, 52, 64, 65, 66, 74, 79, 84, 85, 88, 89, 90, 93, 101, 105, 112, 119, 145, 159, 160, 172, 176, 189, 194, 197, 209, 210, 214, 228, 237, 247, 259, 271, 272, 273, 278, 279, 282, 283, 286, 305, 307, 310, 314, 315, 317, 322, 325, 338, 346, 351, 352, 371, 372, 374, 391, 393, 394, 395, 401, 404

Politicians 2, 21, 42, 58, 69, 76, 81, 88, 91, 106, 131, 147, 156, 170, 191, 251, 266, 270, 273, 287, 334, 355, 368, 372

Politics 42, 76, 266, 287, 291, 329, 349, 398

Pollack, Sydney 22, 83, 100, 104, 118, 124, 160, 164, 182, 240, 245, 273, 277, 279, 341, 349, 369

Porter, Cole 12, 81, 142, 206, 341

Porter, Edwin S. 107, 146, 235

Potter, H. C. 22, 57, 69, 117, 122, 142, 211, 266, 300, 335

Powell, Dick 13, 70, 202, 291, 293, 351, 379

Powell, Eleanor 12, 22, 347

Powell, Michael 19, 83, 165, 202, 206, 226, 249, 254, 256, 289, 294, 302, 307, 327, 354, 360, 401

Powell, William 12, 23, 45, 55, 57, 73, 78, 81, 95, 96, 139, 150, 151, 180, 189, 201, 204, 208, 211, 212, 217, 220, 228, 229, 247, 261, 263, 268, 284, 290, 291, 298, 307, 347, 350, 353, 361, 366, 368, 385

Power, Tyrone 68, 93, 112, 123, 133, 156, 175, 210, 222, 228, 241, 263, 265, 280, 301, 305, 341, 354, 388, 394

Pregnancy 14, 33, 60, 65, 75, 76, 87, 89, 156, 170, 171, 176, 204, 207, 225, 243, 253, 260, 281, 282, 310, 313, 320, 336, 356, 398, 399

Preminger, Otto 12, 13, 43, 49, 75, 77, 105, 145, 150, 167, 199, 231, 234, 256, 287, 293, 348, 398

Pressburger, Emeric 19, 83, 226, 249, 254, 289, 302, 354, 360, 401, 409

Prévert, Jacques 30, 63, 111, 177, 182

Price, Dennis 19, 23, 106, 190, 217, 285, 289, 360, 370

Price, Vincent 69, 91, 109, 137, 159, 182, 186, 190, 197, 207, 210, 216, 218, 220, 231, 293, 305, 353, 360, 361, 388

Priestley, J. B. 186, 394

Priests 32, 44, 51, 53–55, 60, 74, 88, 90, 91, 110, 121, 132, 134, 145, 147, 160, 166, 168, 173, 175, 192, 196, 204, 215, 217, 221, 227, 230, 232, 234, 237, 248, 249, 259, 260, 265, 273, 291, 320, 326, 341, 343, 354, 359, 366, 374, 409, 412

Prison 8, 39, 40, 42, 49, 60, 64, 70, 78, 84, 98, 126, 132, 155, 161, 165, 166, 168, 171, 177, 186, 200, 221, 233, 237, 244, 252, 272, 277, 282, 288, 290, 292, 305, 308, 314, 331, 341, 346, 358, 359, 367, 370, 374, 381, 384, 385, 386, 389, 393, 394

Prisoners of war 28, 38, 55, 58, 107, 141, 142, 146, 147, 166, 168, 202, 203, 255, 267, 269, 282, 283, 292, 311, 321, 326, 342, 381, 384, 391, 400

Private eyes 24, 36, 41, 43, 65, 87, 96, 130, 137, 166, 245, 286, 292, 396, 403, 408

Prostitutes 30, 31, 34, 38, 51, 53, 54, 58, 69, 77, 78, 87, 93, 94, 105, 119, 132, 134, 137, 143, 146, 151, 154, 161, 172, 176, 179, 181, 185, 196, 202–204, 210, 214, 220, 221, 229, 231, 232, 246, 261, 268, 269, 271, 273, 282, 283, 287, 288, 294, 296, 307, 311, 316, 333, 337, 340, 341, 343, 351, 354, 356, 358, 368, 372, 373, 385, 391, 397, 409

Psychiatrists and Psychology 22, 33, 35, 55, 56, 80, 84, 86, 103, 115, 159, 160, 164, 171, 190, 210, 230, 239, 276, 281,

294, 297, 300, 318, 334, 349, 357, 362, 408

Pudovkin, Vsevolod I. 47, 174, 178, 233, 295

Purviance, Edna 65, 66, 170, 196, 368

Pygmalion 50, 80, 84, 296, 365

Q

Quinn, Anthony 19, 75, 120, 190, 216, 227, 237, 252, 267, 268, 271, 285, 288, 306, 409

R

Racism 11, 20, 28, 45, 111, 112, 172, 173, 176, 198, 202, 217, 221, 232, 240, 259, 285, 299, 336, 342, 374, 383

Radford, Michael 52, 55

Rafelson, Bob 5, 49, 139, 245, 246, 288, 300, 368, 398

Raft, George 49, 83, 94, 208, 233, 287, 292, 316, 340, 391

Railways and stations 28, 49, 59, 81, 86, 89, 146, 147, 135, 168, 197, 203, 229, 240, 244, 250, 280, 311, 332, 343, 351, 357, 370, 378, 389, 411

Rainer, Luise 263, 291, 300, 353

Rains, Claude 45, 49, 62, 64, 71, 81, 84, 85, 91, 92, 118, 201–203, 218, 224, 231, 239, 248, 285, 297, 300, 324, 329, 357, 375

Raj 18, 23, 126, 133, 192, 198, 251, 277, 301, 306, 307, 367

Rape 40, 49, 76, 88, 108, 132, 137, 189, 197, 201, 202, 203, 251, 277, 278, 302, 317, 336, 380, 394, 398, 401

Rapper, Irving 12, 15, 84, 85, 189, 224, 239, 248, 297, 341, 357, 383, 390

Rathbone, Basil 45, 68, 73, 76, 78, 79, 81, 82, 86, 90, 106, 112, 121, 124, 134, 144, 163, 164, 186, 190, 213, 222, 224, 247, 248, 285, 294, 304, 339, 362, 367, 380

Ratoff, Gregory 12, 35, 164, 170, 239, 341, 363

Rattigan, Terence 21, 31, 269, 355

Ray, Nicholas 20, 43, 50, 78, 115, 124, 182, 236, 240, 243, 305, 308, 396

Ray, Satyajit 18, 23, 37, 163, 174, 301, 306, 332, 366, 381

Reagan, Ronald 13, 52, 84, 152, 251, 346

Redford, Robert 3, 22, 28, 50, 75, 77, 98, 100, 110, 123, 135, 149, 152, 158, 160, 164, 181–183, 238, 240, 244, 274, 276, 279, 287, 308, 332, 354, 362

Redgrave, Michael 21, 106, 122, 130, 145, 160, 162, 164, 169, 171, 184, 206, 207, 210, 221, 293, 309, 339, 362, 367, 384, 406

Redgrave, Vanessa 26, 38, 91, 154, 161, 177, 179, 184, 210, 214, 239, 275, 324

Reed, Carol 7, 8, 13, 19, 27, 35, 59, 69, 99, 115, 145, 147, 158, 164, 169, 184, 230, 249, 272, 288, 308, 331, 337, 361, 394

Reiner, Carl 56, 109, 122, 181, 392, 408

Reis, Irving 5, 11, 119, 143, 211, 389

Reisner, Charles 19, 225, 333

Reisz, Karel 28, 100, 105, 154, 348, 406

Religious conviction 33, 91, 161, 176, 236, 270, 302, 310, 372, 381, 391, 393, 396

Remick, Lee 91, 157, 204, 331

Renoir, Jean 1, 19, 30, 35, 43, 49, 64, 112, 127, 131, 132, 141, 199, 247, 255, 260, 300, 307, 309, 310, 348, 367, 368, 371, 375, 380, 384, 386, 409

Resnais, Alain 1, 32, 88, 231, 236, 239, 312, 381

Revenge 39, 49, 50, 57, 59, 65, 70, 71, 75, 84, 85, 86, 78, 95, 108, 114, 131, 136, 146, 149, 158, 164, 168, 172, 174, 181, 182, 190, 191, 197, 201, 208, 213, 216, 221, 228, 241, 245, 266, 270, 272, 283, 291, 295, 302, 313, 314, 323, 329, 337, 339, 343, 360, 372, 381, 385, 389, 393, 394, 396, 398, 402

Revolution 1, 30, 47, 50, 51, 60, 74, 76, 85, 92, 97, 101, 109, 127, 146, 165, 173, 175, 187, 194, 203, 209, 217, 225–227, 230, 242, 233, 252, 267, 270, 277, 292, 294, 314, 321, 322, 410, 411

Richardson, Ralph 27, 56, 115, 145, 156, 203, 214, 243, 251,

256, 266, 289, 294, 308, 362, 382, 388

Richardson, Tony 7, 10, 28, 54, 149, 157, 256, 270, 280, 309, 331, 356, 364, 365, 377

Riefenstahl, Leni 133, 152, 226, 257, 380, 399

Ritt, Martin 6, 9, 28, 49, 54, 86, 139, 140, 180, 216, 224, 231, 244, 259, 270, 275, 338, 343, 369, 394

RKO 52, 70, 80, 177, 190, 215, 216, 248, 363, 394

Robards, Jr, Jason 184, 232, 244, 271, 275, 276, 358

Robbery 17, 27, 43, 49, 57, 103, 132, 155, 157, 165, 166, 214, 305, 315, 318, 326, 331, 391, 393

Robertson, Cliff 110, 205, 253, 287, 314

Robin Hood 73, 302, 326

Robinson, Bruce 4, 109

Robinson, Edward G. 1, 2, 20, 49, 53, 92, 94, 101, 119, 122, 133, 134, 155, 166, 167, 170, 175, 183, 197, 202, 221, 234, 245, 257, 266, 316, 331, 337, 350, 353, 394, 406

Robson, Flora 81, 231, 256, 306

Robson, Mark 6, 35, 50, 99, 101, 135, 152, 186, 207, 231, 244, 245, 338, 357, 397, 398, 407

Rodgers, Richard 12, 341

Roeg, Nicolas 106, 112, 176, 198, 217, 260, 294, 344, 368, 370

Rogers, Ginger 8, 13, 22, 27, 52, 83, 121, 140, 142, 155, 201, 215, 225, 234, 246, 264, 294, 318, 330, 336, 346, 347, 357, 358, 363, 395, 400, 409

Rohmer, Eric 65, 76, 243, 319, 327, 368, 382, 390

Rooney, Mickey 67, 133, 161, 162, 175, 338, 341, 357

Rosi, Francesco 61, 139, 153, 174, 216, 228, 314, 381

Ross, Herbert 2, 58, 64, 83, 140, 162, 163, 253, 256, 274, 275, 283, 339, 373, 405

Rossellini, Roberto 34, 35, 76, 89, 109, 120, 250, 312, 320, 321, 323, 355, 364, 376, 381

Rossen, Robert 11, 42, 54, 76, 133, 152, 176, 244, 260, 266, 327

Rota, Nino 109, 246

Rourke, Mickey 7, 75, 87, 91, 105, 198, 238, 259, 308, 359

Rowlands, Gena 9, 216

Ruggles, Wesley 44, 83, 142, 144, 162, 164, 208, 262, 328

Russell, Jane 155, 228, 234, 306, 361, 388

Russell, Ken 11, 20, 45, 57, 73, 91, 165, 181, 201, 243, 260, 273, 285, 294, 296, 335, 345, 372, 406

Russell, Rosalind 3, 158, 202, 212, 249, 291, 328, 366

Russell, Theresa 49, 139, 217, 294, 398

Russia 7, 9, 13, 20, 34, 37, 47, 51, 55, 59, 71, 73, 76, 77, 95, 99, 100, 102, 110, 111, 116, 120, 122, 126, 130, 145, 154, 159, 169, 174, 178, 195, 232, 233, 243, 245, 247, 255, 256, 260, 277, 282, 288, 293, 294, 302, 308, 322, 351, 355, 357, 361, 365, 374, 383, 385, 397, 411

Rutherford, Margaret 21, 68, 71, 130, 140, 202, 271, 334, 394

Ryan, Robert 39, 43, 152, 205, 232, 260, 305–307, 311, 361

Rydell, Mark 85, 123, 124, 156, 201, 393

S

Saks, Gene 15, 123, 204, 251, 273, 313, 332

Sanders, George 7, 53, 80, 90, 122, 159, 170, 181, 197, 249, 253, 267, 293, 307, 321, 336, 383

Sandrich, Mark 13, 22, 23, 68, 156, 249, 330, 363

Sarandon, Susan 13, 53, 86, 103, 133, 152, 207, 217, 246, 338, 400

Saura, Carlos 18, 38, 83, 341

Sautet, Claude 227, 236

Saville, Victor 12, 98, 192, 203, 237, 243, 257, 375, 407

Schaffner, Franklin 75, 110, 273

Schepisi, Fred 3, 17, 139, 291, 349, 360

Schlesinger, John 28, 36, 103, 144, 160, 161, 205, 256, 257, 271, 272, 294, 324, 360, 391

Schlöndorff, Volker 61, 160, 325, 326, 340, 386, 387

Schoedsack, Ernest 14, 144, 192, 228, 304

Schools 16, 39, 48, 65, 66, 88, 96, 110, 140, 171, 174, 178, 189, 215, 239, 247, 256, 263, 271, 302, 334, 342, 366, 371, 372, 377, 400, 410

Schraeder, Paul 169, 294, 369

Schygulla, Hanna 2, 8, 118, 127, 325, 386, 387

Scofield, Paul 157, 295

Scola, Ettore 30, 115, 127, 205, 225, 226, 326

Scorsese, Martin 28, 61, 87, 152, 153, 220, 236, 243, 244, 274, 276, 278, 317, 318, 326, 330, 336, 362, 401

Scott, George C. 75, 95, 101, 191, 242, 245, 273, 283, 355, 393

Scott, Lizabeth 50, 164, 339, 398

Scott, Ridley 102, 125, 279

Screwball comedy 3, 16, 52, 94, 135, 146, 176, 208, 284, 298, 330, 343, 347, 361

Seaton, George 14, 48, 69, 71, 105, 132, 266, 268, 273, 359

Seberg, Jean 1, 4, 74, 109, 231, 260, 285

Segal, George 55, 182, 231, 232, 245, 271, 274, 282, 295, 313, 361, 373

Seiter, William A. 13, 22, 55, 200, 225, 333, 334

Sellers, Peter 9, 16, 21, 23, 45, 77, 95, 98, 104, 106, 133, 169, 182, 229, 236, 246, 276, 329, 360, 382, 390

Sembène, Ousmane 81, 292, 308, 310, 404

Shakespeare, William 3, 27, 50, 55, 79, 114, 133, 138, 149, 194, 256, 260, 293, 304, 327, 329, 360, 370, 394

Sharif, Omar 86, 203, 214, 228, 272, 322, 397

Shaw, George Bernard 21, 80, 203, 297, 329, 335

Shaw, Robert 61, 73, 113, 125, 164, 210, 244, 271, 274, 293, 298, 315, 324, 354, 359, 394, 409

Shearer, Norma 2, 8, 79, 80, 124, 132, 164, 198, 202, 212, 222, 224, 262, 304, 329, 350, 365

Sheridan, Ann 49, 143, 320, 338, 391

Sherman, Vincent 45, 84, 143, 210

Sidney, George 12, 13, 69, 98, 99, 115, 188, 350, 354

Sidney, Sylvia 93, 123, 171, 197, 224, 307, 328

Siegel, Don 58, 105, 108, 109, 119, 133, 138, 216, 287, 344, 348, 366, 378, 393, 407

Signoret, Simone 28, 63, 141, 207, 214, 248, 253, 269, 275, 400, 412

Sim, Alastair 21, 31, 66, 69, 94, 111, 130, 136, 140, 152, 162, 174, 175, 190, 235, 251, 329, 334, 397

Simenon, Georges 65, 90, 131, 199

Simmons, Jean 11, 49–51, 54, 80, 92, 106, 122, 134, 149, 176, 221, 243, 248, 283, 284, 298, 329, 398

Simon, Michel 63, 71, 300, 310, 311, 320, 368

Simon, Neil 15, 19, 283

Simon, Simone 49, 80, 131, 311, 367, 409

Sinatra, Frank 12, 13, 21, 51, 53, 99, 101, 105, 134, 135, 143, 188, 221, 229, 243, 258, 267, 284, 317, 350

Singers 10, 12, 13, 22, 28, 35, 38, 48, 52, 79, 91, 93, 104, 109, 112, 121, 134, 142, 149, 156, 158, 166, 183, 184, 188, 201, 206, 208, 215, 218, 234, 249, 251, 256, 267, 268, 271, 274, 276, 277, 290, 303, 306, 326, 327, 340, 347, 353, 357, 336, 362, 369, 383, 385, 389, 399, 406

Single parents 2, 100, 266, 351, 336, 356

Siodmak, Robert 36, 39, 42, 45, 64, 86, 100, 154, 199, 295, 336, 340, 346, 374, 386, 401, 409

Sirk, Douglas 45, 118, 120, 228, 230, 268, 299, 346

Sisters 5, 9, 10, 14, 21, 26, 33, 40, 49, 58, 67, 78–80, 85, 86, 88, 115, 134, 137, 143, 151, 156, 170, 179, 188, 200-202, 207, 211, 232, 245, 258, 260, 267, 268, 273, 278, 283, 290, 295, 314, 318, 319, 330, 336, 354, 368, 381, 384, 386, 390, 394, 406

Sjöström, Victor 2, 4, 47, 110, 137, 178, 397, 398

Skeletons in the closet 35, 80, 86, 101, 171, 198, 230, 237, 283, 286, 311, 313, 317, 337, 394

Skolimowski, Jerzy 37, 211, 236, 242, 253

Slavery 32, 46, 67, 81, 101, 107, 157, 188, 194, 230, 232, 246, 269, 302, 329, 337, 358, 389

Small town 12, 24, 51, 65, 81, 85, 94, 106, 126, 160, 168, 171, 174, 177, 197, 207, 209, 216, 219, 238, 241, 244, 251, 266, 295, 310, 312, 317, 336–338, 346, 350, 357, 366, 395, 398, 401, 402, 409

Smith, Maggie 11, 58, 79, 119, 136, 145, 221, 239, 256, 272, 275, 320, 321, 338

Smuggling 8, 90, 94, 98, 105, 106, 122, 143, 148, 161, 165, 197, 206, 210, 219, 249, 256, 283, 285, 301, 308, 320, 322, 327, 339, 357, 368, 317, 390

Soldati, Mario 123

Sondergaard, Gale 167, 263, 305, 367

South Africa 52, 79, 112, 133, 171, 380

South America 9, 41, 50, 59, 61, 95, 98, 102, 128, 132, 133, 158, 173, 176, 204, 230, 258, 294, 314, 332, 359, 362, 371, 372

Spacek, Sissy 188, 191, 204, 238, 276, 279

Spain 18, 53, 54, 75, 76, 83, 114, 134, 143, 145, 162, 230, 243, 268, 285, 309, 310, 385

Spanish Civil War 34, 38, 75, 118, 140, 236, 277, 312, 341, 409

Spielberg, Steven 74, 81, 112, 125, 258, 280, 282, 302, 324, 342, 371

Spoofs 9, 13, 44, 64, 66, 72, 77, 103, 106, 129, 135, 168, 169, 174, 186, 187, 192, 209, 211, 219, 235, 236, 225, 229, 236, 283, 286, 295, 303, 304, 328, 329, 345, 352, 359, 362, 379, 392

Sport 58, 66, 74, 87, 99, 100, 118, 152, 153, 159, 166, 189, 208, 209, 228, 377

Stahl, John M. 19, 45, 89, 120, 212, 231, 282, 299, 382, 389

Stallone, Sylvester 18, 125, 146, 259, 318

Stanwyck, Barbara 41, 48, 50, 53, 62, 63, 68, 75, 101, 123, 124, 133, 155, 161, 164, 170, 175, 189, 197, 231, 234, 237, 301, 310, 316, 340, 343, 350, 354, 357, 368, 383, 393, 395, 397, 398, 408

Starr, Ringo 150, 288, 317, 360

Steiger, Rod 12, 50, 85, 133, 144, 172, 189, 214, 227, 242, 250, 258, 272, 295

Steinbeck, John 50, 143, 187, 212

Steiner, Max 41, 64, 140, 190

Stevens, George 12, 13, 22, 41, 52, 124, 142, 148, 156, 171, 177, 208, 220, 237, 241, 243, 249, 252, 265, 267–269, 313, 315, 343, 346, 347, 367

Stevenson, Robert 16, 63, 67, 97, 117, 124, 231, 271, 303, 327, 340, 361, 375, 394, 411

Stevenson, Robert Louis 67, 80, 186, 327, 345, 369

Stewart, James 20, 44, 52, 53, 62, 69, 76, 77, 89, 93, 94, 119, 126, 144, 151, 159, 160, 171, 175, 177, 180, 192, 202, 208, 213, 240, 263, 264, 267, 284, 290, 294, 307, 308, 314, 327, 330, 333, 336, 343, 346, 347, 348, 370, 378, 393, 395, 400, 406

Stiller, Mauritz 26, 47, 134

Stone, Andrew 8, 29, 189, 379

Stone, Oliver 18, 102, 139, 278

Stories 34, 36, 89, 107, 108, 175, 178, 217, 218, 220, 221, 228, 234, 260, 271, 284, 292, 302, 306, 312, 321, 328, 334, 348, 355, 368

Streep, Meryl 3, 6, 77, 87, 122, 160, 220, 245, 246, 275, 276, 279, 332, 336, 348, 373

Streisand, Barbra 49, 52, 100, 139, 183, 189, 223, 272, 298, 369, 373

Students 8, 13, 16, 17, 21, 58, 65, 83, 84, 88, 100, 102, 110, 130, 141, 149, 183, 203, 251, 291, 306, 313, 319, 321, 325, 357, 366, 385, 389, 401, 402

Sturges, John 101, 147, 240, 241, 254, 292, 337, 366, 378, 393

Sturges, Preston 17, 52, 64, 70, 76, 104, 123, 130, 133, 175, 207, 208, 233, 261, 336, 343, 350, 368, 402

Suicide 38, 51, 59, 62, 63, 68, 72, 79, 86, 95, 100, 103, 105, 110, 133, 151, 156, 160, 171, 177, 190, 204, 214, 217, 224, 268, 275, 287, 289, 305, 326, 346, 354, 368, 373, 386, 396, 399

Sullavan, Margaret 213, 231, 261, 294, 333, 347, 378, 402

Surrealism and Symbolism 5, 53, 63, 70, 353

Sutherland, Donald 20, 106, 121, 123, 124, 144, 162, 246, 273, 276, 315, 324, 370

Swanson, Gloria 352, 386, 391

Szabó, István 3, 71, 72, 119, 307

T

Tarkovsky, Andrei 111, 120, 251, 280, 304, 312, 355, 381

Tati, Jacques 109, 112, 217, 235, 269, 327

Taurog, Norman 22, 27, 67, 110, 111, 170, 175, 196, 220, 262, 263, 299, 334, 341, 366

Tavernier, Bertrand 24, 119, 174, 181, 235, 247, 248, 364, 404

Taviani, Paolo & Vittorio 61, 76, 174, 221, 225, 348

Taylor, Elizabeth 11, 21, 51, 54, 55, 68, 97, 127, 153, 156, 162, 171, 202, 210, 221, 229, 244, 245, 252, 265, 267–269, 271, 329, 347, 366, 393

Taylor, Robert 45, 58, 80, 120, 162, 202, 203, 229, 249, 264, 306, 349, 389

Taylor, Rod 122, 247, 339, 345, 363

Teachers 2, 24, 26, 29, 34, 44, 48, 60, 64, 68, 84, 92, 98, 100, 136, 144, 146, 159, 164, 165, 175, 204, 209, 214, 211, 221, 227, 228, 230, 232, 235, 239, 244, 247, 250, 252, 255, 256, 270, 272, 278, 301, 310, 339, 351, 356, 358, 367, 377, 390, 393, 402

Teenagers 5, 8, 14, 18, 20, 24, 28, 33, 37, 39, 51, 58, 67, 69, 72, 75, 100, 105, 115, 121, 136, 140, 145, 158, 170-173, 191, 207, 209, 217, 218, 237,

308, 313, 319, 324, 325, 327, 328, 338, 356, 357, 366, 372, 377, 389, 401, 410

Television 3, 31, 38, 45, 70, 80, 87, 99, 102, 111, 115, 121, 137, 138, 154, 159, 160, 165, 187, 205, 214, 225, 236, 253, 274, 275, 283, 288, 314, 327, 357, 358, 369, 373, 400

Temple, Shirley 5, 67, 123, 125, 126, 143, 206, 211, 221, 261, 287, 301, 401

Terrorism 18, 27, 38, 39, 65, 87, 118, 126, 130, 175, 189, 208, 227, 236, 259, 263, 298, 308, 325, 359, 381, 386

Terry-Thomas 19, 45, 169, 229, 251, 334, 388

Tetzlaff, Ted 206, 248, 291, 401

Thalberg, Irving 58, 137, 140, 144, 187

Thomas, Gerald 11, 19, 127, 162, 206, 240, 243

Thomas, Ralph 92, 252, 287, 351

Thorpe, Richard 23, 78, 124, 211, 216, 290, 303, 315, 327, 364

Thulin, Ingrid 26, 33, 397

Tierney, Gene 154, 167, 220, 221, 282, 293, 319

Toland, Gregg 39, 44, 49, 70, 71, 143, 155, 340, 402

Tolstoy, Leo 9, 52, 59, 134, 203, 243, 272, 300, 322, 380

Tone, Franchot 20, 44, 63, 69, 74, 84, 122, 151, 155, 261, 263, 287, 301, 313, 315, 347, 350, 352, 386, 400

Totheroh, Rollie 66, 139, 233

Toulouse-Lautrec, Henri 20, 166

Tourneur, Jacques 43, 71, 80, 186, 207, 217, 227, 280, 305, 354, 361, 383

Tracy, Spencer 3, 27, 32, 34, 42, 62, 70, 80, 81, 84, 110, 111, 113, 120, 122, 132, 151, 156, 157, 168, 175, 177, 181, 192, 196, 197, 202, 211, 212, 220, 229, 231, 252, 263, 270, 272, 284, 291, 305, 310, 337, 346, 350, 366, 369, 371, 383, 391, 393, 397, 409

Trains 68, 93, 107, 131, 135, 170, 180, 184, 199, 214, 272, 301, 305, 311, 315, 317, 331, 351, 352, 367, 390, 393, 401, 409

Tramps 36, 54, 55, 60, 61, 62, 76, 104, 132, 139, 180, 200, 244, 246, 283, 297, 300, 310, 311, 333, 346, 348, 349, 350, 355, 368, 395

Transvestites 13, 58, 148, 158, 160, 161, 204, 213, 217, 248, 277, 314, 340, 368

Trevor, Claire 41, 266, 307, 317, 342, 367

Trintignant, Jean-Louis 21, 24, 38, 53, 60, 64, 65, 272, 314, 319

Trouble at mill 41, 61, 81, 92, 98, 99, 110, 119, 126, 138, 162, 169, 182, 187, 201, 233, 236, 225, 264, 275, 326, 333, 369, 378, 409

Truckers 26, 36, 49, 59, 63, 84, 109, 232, 235, 258, 370, 391, 396, 412

Truffaut, François 1, 28, 32, 86–88, 110, 115, 122, 144–146, 183, 184, 227, 236, 274, 280, 312, 314, 348, 360, 371, 377, 410

Turner, Kathleen 4, 48, 56, 75, 102, 138, 159, 165, 166, 178, 216, 246, 279, 294, 345, 358, 363, 370, 372, 396

Turner, Lana 133, 188, 264, 299, 338

Tuttle, Frank 14, 208, 290, 296, 350

Twain, Mark 67, 293

Twentieth Century Fox 7, 16, 65, 143, 163, 184, 246

Twins 59, 80, 85, 86, 134, 201, 337, 374, 389, 390

U

UFA 38, 48, 226, 257, 385, 397

Ullmann, Liv 15, 33, 34, 87, 103, 170, 239, 253, 288, 320

United Artists 15, 66, 95, 114, 135, 139, 141, 150, 158, 175, 198, 220, 259, 318, 340, 342, 360, 373

Universal 8, 79, 102, 112, 126, 279, 350, 402

US Civil War 34, 60, 72, 76, 81, 84, 85, 135, 136, 140, 146, 155, 166, 171, 174, 222, 296, 336, 338, 364, 378, 393, 403

US War of Independence 13, 123, 329

USA 11, 57, 61, 70-72, 87, 98, 150, 157, 165, 168, 169, 176,

179, 182, 186, 187, 202, 203, 226, 237, 238, 253, 254, 256, 257, 274, 276, 282, 285, 287, 289, 290, 294, 296, 313, 338, 344, 361, 363, 382, 383, 388, 389, 390, 395, 407
Ustinov, Peter 19, 33, 48, 68, 69, 82, 90, 115, 163, 202, 233, 251, 269, 271, 320, 339

V

Valentino, Rudolph 46, 280, 302, 322
Valli, Alida 179, 199, 361, 374
Vampires 13, 86, 103, 154, 186, 213, 218, 286, 334, 338, 344, 372, 376
Van Dyke, W. S. 12, 15, 48, 132, 156, 192, 211, 220, 222, 247, 290, 303, 308, 347, 353, 361, 366, 389, 393
Van Gogh, Vincent 101, 229, 268, 289
Varda, Agnès 4, 70, 377, 399
Vaudeville and burlesque 13, 22, 48, 56, 121, 122, 170, 187, 188, 199, 202, 217, 224, 235, 237, 246, 316, 335, 336, 339, 369, 379, 406
Veidt, Conrad 19, 31, 56, 78, 120, 178, 202, 203, 210, 289
Venice Film Festival 72, 100, 106, 132, 145, 156, 194, 203, 205, 210, 217, 243, 266, 281, 283, 284, 312, 319, 324, 370, 380, 384, 385, 409
Vera-Ellen 22, 258
Vicars and preachers 26, 33, 34, 44, 47, 66, 98, 99, 109, 115, 137, 146, 148, 157, 199, 201, 285, 294, 310, 329, 339, 341, 346, 354, 382, 401
Vidor, Charles 12, 57, 73, 133, 188, 294, 353
Vidor, King 2, 4, 41, 53, 93, 96, 98, 123, 137, 237, 253, 262, 280, 343, 357, 378, 383, 401
Vietnam 8, 17, 61, 75, 77, 87, 102, 105, 108, 119, 123, 126, 145, 194, 217, 221, 236, 272, 275, 278, 289, 300, 312, 332, 348, 384, 386, 393
Vigo, Jean 1, 4, 70, 97, 410
Visconti, Luchino 53, 60, 72, 76, 101, 103, 109, 171, 178, 184, 216, 225, 237, 334, 355, 370, 376, 381, 384

Vitti, Monica 17, 24, 210, 226, 381
Voight, Jon 28, 96, 123, 160, 272, 275, 294, 315, 324, 384
Von Sternberg, Josef 48, 50, 74, 93, 100, 142, 178, 180, 210, 261, 290, 368, 385, 397
Von Stroheim, Erich 45, 72, 134, 137, 139, 141, 144, 146, 167, 234, 352, 382, 385, 400
Von Sydow, Max 33, 34, 62, 74, 103, 170, 216, 243, 270, 328, 347, 352, 397
Von Trotta, Margarethe 2, 79, 184, 325, 326, 336, 381, 386

W

Wajda, Andrej 20, 53, 61, 70, 88, 110, 127, 237, 251, 286, 308, 312, 314, 326, 348, 389, 394
Walbrook, Anton 77, 83, 120, 233, 239, 256, 261, 289
Walker, Robert 13, 159, 333
Wallace, Richard 20, 354, 383, 389
Walsh, Raoul 4, 15, 42, 49, 50, 57, 76, 86, 101, 114, 152, 165, 209, 232, 233, 243, 262, 316, 388, 390, 393
Walters, Charles 12, 13, 22, 69, 78, 189, 261, 284
Ward Baker, Roy 154, 205, 218
Warner Brothers 7, 13, 41, 48, 64, 81, 84, 168, 259, 350
Warner, Jack 21, 27, 150, 153, 158, 258, 286, 292, 382
Waugh, Evelyn 17, 24, 331, 410
Wayne, John 25, 84, 85, 108, 119, 123, 125, 126, 155, 157, 166, 176, 192, 208, 240, 241, 258, 272, 280, 282, 298, 306, 315, 342, 348, 369, 378, 384, 385, 388, 389, 392, 395
Weaver, Sigourney 2, 52, 58, 125, 165, 245, 279
Webb, Clifton 14, 109, 211, 293, 304, 320, 369
Weddings 2, 63, 118, 138, 144, 158, 177, 229, 284, 296, 314, 355, 360, 366, 371, 393, 409
Weir, Peter 25, 63, 125, 198, 231, 247, 277, 291, 356, 401
Welles, Orson 32, 43, 59, 70, 93, 122, 124, 154, 155, 184, 194, 216, 227, 228, 230, 238, 245, 313, 327, 329, 337, 338, 350, 355, 361, 394, 395

Wellman, William 19, 46, 56, 71, 74, 97, 123, 151, 192, 208, 224, 232, 259, 261, 303, 316, 318, 343, 363, 395, 401
Wells, H. G. 17, 98, 130, 164, 178, 247, 363, 394
Wenders, Wim 15, 21, 35, 62, 75, 119, 177, 306, 326, 381, 395
Wertmüller, Lina 53, 130, 141, 190
West, Mae 73, 121, 142, 144, 156, 164, 215, 330, 391
Westerns 9, 12, 28, 37, 53, 55, 81, 69, 94, 101, 108, 109, 121, 125, 148, 155, 158, 177, 197, 198, 215, 234, 244, 262, 298, 314, 317, 342, 343, 347, 366, 391, 392, 395, 402, 409
Whale, James 2, 9, 13, 55, 126, 164, 186, 198, 218, 219, 251, 302, 324, 374
Whelan, Tim 19, 83, 201, 203, 256, 289
Widmark, Richard 39, 42, 84, 96, 102, 111, 126, 147, 187, 221, 367
Widows and widowers 21, 28, 37, 44, 54, 64, 92, 93, 100, 118, 119, 120, 142, 159, 160, 161, 169, 173, 175, 189, 190, 208, 212, 251, 253, 268, 274, 277, 307, 320, 326, 333, 336, 343, 359, 360, 367, 371, 393, 395, 397
Wilcox, Herbert 231, 233, 234, 249, 375, 407
Wilde, Oscar 21, 84, 181, 198, 212, 243, 316
Wilder, Billy 7, 12, 35, 48, 49, 57, 67, 68, 75, 77, 93, 94, 101, 105, 124, 142, 144, 146, 159, 163, 170, 175, 176, 183, 199, 204, 223, 228, 234, 247, 255, 265, 267, 269, 271, 292, 316, 318, 321, 338, 340, 343, 348, 352, 386, 397, 409
Wilder, Gene 140, 296
Wilding, Michael 79, 150, 375
Williams, Kenneth 11, 19, 127, 240, 243
Williams, Tennessee 7, 50, 55, 203
Willis, Gordon 15, 138, 220, 408
Winger, Debra 3, 19, 49, 119, 139, 277, 299

Winters, Shelley 79, 171, 194, 207, 267, 269, 271, 280, 286, 347

Wise, Robert 4, 41, 71, 74, 80, 81, 112, 152, 154, 186, 192, 216, 232, 238, 243, 244, 249, 269–271, 280, 344, 346, 351

Witchcraft 71, 103, 115, 207, 210, 224, 246, 257, 327, 382, 400, 401

Wood, Jr, Edward D. 213, 368, 372

Wood, Sam 2, 34, 35, 74, 78, 99, 105, 124, 140, 151, 171, 182, 212, 224, 228, 264, 265, 319, 333, 338, 341, 357, 359, 370, 410

Woods, James 148, 191, 259, 291, 307

Woodward, Joanne 181, 244, 269

Woolley, Monty 19, 41, 44, 85, 253

World War I 9, 22, 23, 38, 46, 57, 72, 74, 78, 81, 89, 101, 121, 134, 137, 141, 146, 149, 154, 162, 170, 183, 184, 194, 201, 213, 246, 254, 257, 264, 275, 287, 289, 304, 315, 339, 345, 362, 363, 375, 386, 390, 392, 407

World War II 8, 20, 36, 75, 135, 163, 172, 242, 254, 255, 289, 324, 409, 20, 101, 117, 206, 248, 292, 351, 363, 392

Writers 5, 14, 17, 24, 27, 30, 32, 33, 36, 38, 47, 50, 57, 58, 63, 65, 73, 75, 77, 79, 80, 84, 86, 92, 101, 105, 110, 111, 134, 136, 139, 154, 155, 156, 161, 163, 165, 177, 179, 182–184, 186, 180, 191, 194, 197, 204, 210, 212, 217, 220, 223, 224, 225, 229, 245, 251, 256, 260, 263, 265, 266, 270, 277, 279, 283, 286, 291, 305, 311, 312, 326, 328, 330, 331, 337, 338, 339, 352, 361, 371, 372, 373, 386, 393, 396, 400, 402, 406

Wyler, William 32, 39, 43, 49, 50, 52, 60, 69, 74, 84, 86, 101, 139, 155, 156, 165, 177, 179, 184, 204, 205, 211, 222, 224, 244, 256, 261, 263–267, 269, 272, 285, 286, 299, 307, 320, 321, 378, 402

Wyman, Jane 45, 63, 120, 136, 249, 266, 336

Y

Yates, Peter 2, 3, 15, 161, 165, 182

York, Michael 210, 227

York, Susannah 23, 51, 83, 170, 205, 294, 321

Young, Loretta 44, 62, 69, 77, 123, 148, 151, 156, 170, 216, 228, 247, 249, 264, 266, 285, 300, 308, 315, 316, 373, 394, 395

Young, Robert 5, 39, 48, 69, 93, 109, 155, 164, 202, 209, 294, 315, 347, 383

Young, Roland 136, 139, 142, 178, 206, 284

Young, Terence 6, 16, 45, 73, 95

Yuppies 4, 26, 172, 320, 326, 330, 356, 363, 405

Z

Zampi, Mario 45, 175, 190, 298, 334

Zeffirelli, Franco 55, 260, 323, 329

Zemeckis, Robert 4, 102, 117, 150, 342, 363, 372, 396

Zetterling, Mai 14, 146, 257, 285, 297, 310, 356, 382

Zinnemann, Fred 12, 19–21, 28, 29, 51, 74, 123, 158, 184, 240, 267, 271, 275, 293, 298, 361, 394, 408

Zola, Émile 49, 63, 146, 221, 263, 311, 409